TWENTIETH CENTURY ENCYCLOPEDIA

OF

RELIGIOUS KNOWLEDGE

An Extension of
THE NEW SCHAFF-HERZOG
ENCYCLOPEDIA OF RELIGIOUS KNOWLEDGE

Editor-in-Chief
LEFFERTS A. LOETSCHER, Ph.D., D.D.
PROFESSOR OF AMERICAN CHURCH HISTORY
PRINCETON THEOLOGICAL SEMINARY

*
AACHEN
to
KODESH

BAKER BOOK HOUSE
GRAND RAPIDS, MICHIGAN
1955

Printed in the United States of America
American Book–Stratford Press, Inc., New York

TWENTIETH CENTURY ENCYCLOPEDIA

OF

RELIGIOUS KNOWLEDGE

EDITORIAL STAFF

TWENTIETH CENTURY ENCYCLOPEDIA

OF

RELIGIOUS KNOWLEDGE

EDITORIAL STAFF

Editor-in-Chief

Lefferts A. Loetscher, Ph.D., D.D.,
Professor of American Church History,
Princeton Theological Seminary

Old Testament

Elmer E. Flack, Th.D., D.D., Dean and Professor of Exegetical Theology,
Hamma Divinity School

New Testament

Bruce M. Metzger, Ph.D., D.D., Professor of New Testament Language and
Literature, Princeton Theological Seminary

Ancient Church History

William A. Mueller, S.T.M., Ph.D., Professor of Philosophy of Religion,
Southern Baptist Theological Seminary

Medieval and Reformation Church History

Albert Hyma, Ph.D., Professor of History, University of Michigan

Post-Reformation Church History

Theodore G. Tappert, A.M., D.D., Litt.D., Professor of Church History,
Lutheran Theological Seminary, Philadelphia

Contemporary Biography

Raymond W. Albright, Th.D., Litt.D., Professor of Church History, Episcopal
Theological School, Cambridge, Massachusetts

Comparative Religion

Edwin E. Calverley, Ph.D., Visiting Professor, School of Oriental Studies,
American University, Cairo, Egypt

Systematic Theology

Andrew K. Rule, Ph.D., D.D., Professor of Church History and Apologetics,
Louisville Presbyterian Seminary

Practical Theology

Andrew W. Blackwood, A.B., B.D., Professor of Preaching and Bible, School
of Theology, Temple University

Ecclesiastical Terminology

Georges A. Barrois, S.T.D., Th.D., Associate Professor of Biblical Literature
and Theology, Princeton Theological Seminary

EDITORIAL STAFF

Editor-in-Chief
Lefferts A. Loetscher, Ph.D., D.D.
Professor of American Church History,
Princeton Theological Seminary

Old Testament
Elmer E. Flack, Th.D., D.D.
Dean and Professor of Exegetical Theology, Hamma Divinity School

New Testament
Bruce M. Metzger, Ph.D., D.D.
Professor of New Testament Language and Literature, Princeton Theological Seminary

Ancient Church
William A. Mueller, S.T.M., Ph.D.
Professor of Philosophy of Religion, The Southern Baptist Theological Seminary

Medieval and Reformation Church
Albert Hyma, Ph.D.
Professor of History, University of Michigan

Post-Reformation Church
Theodore G. Tappert, A.M., D.D., Litt.D.
Professor of Church History, Lutheran Theological Seminary, Philadelphia

Contemporary Biography
Raymond W. Albright, Th.D., Litt.D.
Professor of Church History, Episcopal Theological School, Cambridge, Massachusetts

Comparative Religion
Edwin E. Calverley, Ph.D.
Visiting Professor, School of Oriental Studies, American University, Cairo, Egypt

Systematic Theology
Andrew K. Rule, Ph.D., D.D.
Professor of Church History and Apologetics, Louisville Presbyterian Seminary

Practical Theology
Andrew W. Blackwood, A.B., B.D.
Professor of Preaching and Bible, School of Theology, Temple University

Ecclesiastical Terminology
Georges A. Barrois, S.T.D., Th.D.
Associate Professor of Biblical Literature and Theology, Princeton Theological Seminary

CONTRIBUTORS

Adam, Alfred, Th.D.
Professor der Theologie, Bethel, Germany

Albaugh, Gaylord, A.B., B.D.
Associate Professor of Christian History, McMaster University, Hamilton, Ontario, Canada

Albright, Raymond W., Th.D., Litt.D.
Professor of Church History, Episcopal Theological School, Cambridge, Massachusetts

Albright, William Foxwell, Ph.D., Th.D., Litt.D., D.H.L.
W. W. Spence Professor of Semitic Languages, Johns Hopkins University

Allbeck, Willard D., S.T.M., Ph.D., D.D.
Professor of Historical Theology, Hamma Divinity School

Allen, Devere, A.B.
Editor and Director, Worldover Press, Wilton, Connecticut

Almand, Claude, M.M., Ph.D.
Dean, Stetson University School of Music

Allwardt, Paul, D.S.M.
Professor of Music, Gustavus Adolphus College

Alt, Albrecht, Th.D., Ph.D., J.D.
Professor, University of Leipzig, Germany

Ammundsen, Peter
Manager, the Danish Parole and Probation Service

Anderson, Stuart LeRoy
President, Pacific School of Religion

Andren, Carl-Gustaf, Th.D.
Clergyman in Lund, Sweden

Ansted, Harry B., LL.D.
Administrative Director, United Temperance Movement of Minnesota

Archer, John Clark, B.D., Ph.D.
Hoober Professor Emeritus of Comparative Religion, Yale University

Archer, Raymond L.
Bishop, Methodist Center, Singapore, Malaya

Arden, G. Everett, B.D., Ph.D.
Professor of Church History and Liturgics, Augustana Theological Seminary

Armstrong, Maurice W., S.T.M., Ph.D.
Professor of History and Head of Department of History, Ursinus College

Atkinson, Henry A., D.D.
General Secretary of Church Peace Union and the World Alliance for International Friendship through Religion

Aubrey, Edwin E., Ph.D., D.D.
Professor of Religious Thought, University of Pennsylvania

Baab, Otto J., B.D., Ph.D.
Professor of Old Testament Interpretation, Garrett Biblical Institute

Bach, Marcus, Ph.D., D.D.
Professor, School of Religion, University of Iowa

Bachmann, E. Theodore, S.T.M., Ph.D.
Professor of Church History and Missions, Pacific Lutheran Theological Seminary

Bailey, Moses, S.T.M., Ph.D.
Nettleton Professor of Old Testament, Hartford Seminary Foundation

Bainton, Roland H., Ph.D., Dr.Theol., D.D.
Professor of Ecclesiastical History, Yale University

Barnes, Roswell P., D.D.
Associate General Secretary, National Council of Churches of Christ in the U.S.A.

Barrois, Georges A., S.T.D., Th.D.
Associate Professor of Biblical Literature and Theology, Princeton Theological Seminary

Bartels, Theophil
Deutscher Verband fuer Gemeinschaftspflege, Goettingen, Germany

Bates, Miner Searle, Ph.D.
Professor of Missions, Union Theological Seminary

Batten, Joseph Minton, B.D., Ph.D.
Late Professor of Church History, Scarritt College

Baughman, Harry F., D.D., L.H.D.
President, Gettysburg Lutheran Theological Seminary

Baxter, Edna M., B.R.E., B.D., A.M.
Professor of Religious Education, Hartford Seminary Foundation

Baynes, Norman H., D.D., Litt.D.
Professor Emeritus of Byzantine History, University of London

Beahm, William M., Ph.D., D.D.
Dean and Professor of Christian Theology and Missions, Bethany Biblical Seminary, Chicago

Beckmann, Joachim, Ph.D., Lic.Theol., Th.D.
Oberkirchenrat in Duesseldorf; Professor in the Kirchlichen Hochschule, Wuppertal, Germany

Belvin, B. Frank, D.R.E.
General Missionary to Creek and Seminole Indians, Baptist Home Mission Board

Bender, Harold S., Th.D.
Dean and Professor of Church History, Goshen College Biblical Seminary

Benton, John Keith, Ph.D., D.D.
Dean, Vanderbilt School of Religion, Vanderbilt University

Bergendoff, Conrad, Ph.D., Th.D., LL.D.
President, Augustana College, Rock Island, Illinois

Bernard, Robert J.
Managing Director, Claremont College

Bernhardt, William H., B.D., Ph.D., Litt.D.
Professor of Philosophy of Religion, The Iliff School of Theology

Beste, Niklot, Ph.D., Th.D.
Landesbischof, Mecklenburg, Germany

Bilheimer, Robert S., D.D.
Associate General Secretary, World Council of Churches

Birge, John Kingsley, B.D., Ph.D.
Formerly, Publications Department, American Board of Commissioners for Foreign Missions, Istanbul, Turkey

Bixler, Julius Seelye, Ph.D.
President, Colby College

Blackwood, Andrew W., A.B., B.D.
Professor of Preaching and Bible, School of Theology, Temple University

Blakemore, W. Barnette, B.Sc., B.D., Ph.D.
Dean, Disciples Divinity House of the University of Chicago

Blanton, Sankey L., Th.M., D.D.
President, Crozer Theological Seminary

Bornkamm, Heinrich, Ph.D., Th.D.
Professor of Church History, Heidelberg University, Germany

Bouvier, Andre
Clergyman of the Reformed Church, Geneva, Switzerland

Bower, William Clayton, D.D., LL.D.
Professor Emeritus, Divinity School, University of Chicago

Bowlby, Harry L., D.D.
General Secretary Emeritus, Lord's Day Alliance of the United States

Bowman, John Wick, Ph.D., D.D.
Robert Dollar Professor of New Testament Interpretation, San Francisco Theological Seminary

Braden, Charles S., Ph.D., D.D.
Professor Emeritus of History and Literature of Religion, Northwestern University; Visiting Professor of Religion, Scripps College, 1954–56

Bradley, William L., B.D., Ph.D.
Associate Professor of the Philosophy of Religion, Hartford Theological Seminary

Brenner, Scott Francis, Th.D.
Pastor of United Presbyterian Church, Carnegie, Pennsylvania

Bright, John, Th.M., Ph.D., D.D.
Professor of Hebrew and Interpretation of Old Testament, Union Theological Seminary in Virginia

Brightman, Edgar Sheffield, S.T.B., Ph.D., LL.D.
Late Borden Parker Bowne Professor of Philosophy, Boston University

Brilioth, Yngve, Ph.D., Th.D., D.D.
Archbishop, Stockholm, Sweden

Brinton, Howard H., Ph.D., Litt.D.
Director Emeritus and Lecturer, Pendle Hill School for Religious and Social Study

Brown, James Davis, M.A., D.D.
President of the Faculty, Gujranwala Theological Seminary, Gujranwala, Punjab, West Pakistan

Brown, Sterling W., B.D., Ph.D.
Executive Vice President, National Conference of Christians and Jews, Inc.

Bruce, Frederick Fyvie, A.M.
Head of the Department of Biblical History and Literature, University of Sheffield, England

Bruder, Ernest E., A.B., B.D.
Chief, Chaplain Services Branch, St. Elizabeths Hospital, Washington, D. C. and Editor-in-Chief, *The Journal of Pastoral Care*

Brunotte, Heinz, Th.D.
Praesident der Kirchenkanzlei und des Luth. Kirchenamtes, Hannover, Germany

Brush, John Woolman, B.D., Ph.D.
Professor of Church History, Andover-Newton Theological School

Bryan, Dawson C., D.D.
Director, Institute of Religion, Texas Medical Center, Houston, Texas

Buehring, Paul, A.M., D.D.
Professor of Historical Theology, Lutheran Seminary, Columbus, Ohio

Bulman, James M., Th.D.
Minister, East Spencer Baptist Church, East Spencer, North Carolina

Burch, George Bosworth, Ph.D.
Fletcher Professor of Philosophy, Tufts College

Burrows, Millar, B.D., Ph.D.
Winkley Professor of Biblical Theology, Yale University

Butler, J. Donald, M.R.E., Ph.D.
Professor of the History and Philosophy of Education, Princeton Theological Seminary

Byerly, Robert Crane, A.B.
Retired Missionary of the Presbyterian Church U.S.A., to Syria and Lebanon

Cadbury, Henry J., Ph.D., D.D., LL.D.
Lecturer, Harvard College; Professor Emeritus of Divinity, Harvard University

Cahill, Edward A., A.B., S.T.B.
Director, Department of World Churches; Minister, Unitarian Church, Charlotte, North Carolina

Caldwell, Frank, B.D., Ph.D.
President and Professor of Homiletics, Louisville Presbyterian Theological Seminary

Calverley, Edwin E., Ph.D.
Visiting Professor, School of Oriental Studies, American University, Cairo, Egypt

Campbell, E. Fay, D.D., LL.D.
Secretary, Division of Higher Education, Board of Christian Education, Presbyterian Church U. S. A.

Campbell, Thomas H., B.D., A.M.
Dean of Cumberland Presbyterian Theological Seminary

Carlson, Donald T.
Assistant Director of Information, Stanford University

Cashman, Robert, LL.D.
Retired, Springfield, Missouri

Cavert, Inez M., A.B.
Research Associate, National Council of the Churches of Christ in the U.S.A.

Cavert, Samuel McCrea, Th.D., D.D., LL.D.
Executive Secretary in the U.S.A., World Council of Churches

Chadwick, Anthony S.
Occupant of Studentship, Oxford University, England

Chakerian, Charles Garabed, B.D., Ph.D.
Graham Taylor Professor of Social Ethics, and Director of the Institute of Church Social Service, Hartford Seminary Foundation

Chamberlain, William Douglas, Ph.D., D.D.
Professor of New Testament Language and Literature, Louisville Presbyterian Theological Seminary

Chisholm, Roderick M., Ph.D.
Professor of Philosophy and Chairman of Philosophy Department, Brown University

Christian, William A., B.D., Ph.D.
Associate Professor of Religion, Yale University

Clark, Elmer T., S.T.D., LL.D., Litt.D.
Secretary, World Methodist Council; Executive
Secretary, Association of Methodist Historical
Societies

Clark, George Alfred, B.S., Ph.D.
Associate Professor of Philosophy and Chairman of Department of Philosophy, Lafayette
College

Clebsch, William Anthony, S.T.M.
Assistant Professor of Church History, The
Protestant Episcopal Theological Seminary in
Virginia

Clymer, R. Swinburne, M.D.
Founder of the Church of the Illumination,
Quakertown, Pennsylvania

Cohen, Mortimer J., Ph.D., D.D.
Rabbi, Beth Sholom Congregation, Philadelphia,
Pennsylvania

Cohon, Samuel S., D.D.
Professor of Jewish Theology, Hebrew Union
College, Cincinnati, Ohio

Collier, W. Edwin, A.M.
Leader, Philadelphia Ethical Society, Philadelphia, Pennsylvania

Colvin, Mrs. D. Leigh
President, National Woman's Christian Temperance Union

Come, Arnold B., Th.D.
Stuart Professor of Systematic Theology, San
Francisco Theological Seminary

Conn, Charles W.
Editor in Chief, Publications, Church of God,
Cleveland, Tennessee

Cooper, Charles M., Ph.D., D.D.
President of the Evangelical Lutheran Ministerium of Pennsylvania

Cope, Thomas Pym
Unitarian Service Committee, Inc., Boston

Correll, Sidney
Pastor, Christian Tabernacle Church, Dayton,
Ohio

Count, Earl W., B.D., Ph.D.
Professor of Anthropology, Hamilton College

Courvoisier, Jacques, Th.D.
Professor of Church History, University of
Geneva, Switzerland

Craig, Clarence T., Ph.D., D.D.
Late Dean of Drew Divinity School, Drew University

Creager, Harold L., D.D.
Professor of Old Testament, Lutheran Theological Southern Seminary

Cressy, Earl Herbert, B.D., LL.D.
Professor Emeritus of Chinese Studies, Hartford Seminary Foundation

Cross, Frank M., Jr., B.D., Ph.D.
Associate Professor of Old Testament, McCormick Theological Seminary

Cross, Rowland McLean, S.T.M., L.H.D.
Associate Secretary, United Board for Christian
Colleges in China

Crum, Terrelle, A.M.
Dean of the Faculty, Providence-Barrington
Bible College

Cummins, Robert, D.D.
General Superintendent, Universalist Church of
America

Dahl, George, Ph.D.
Holmes Professor Emeritus of the Hebrew Language and Literature, Yale University

Dahlgruen, Erich
Dean of the Lutheran Clergy in Italy

Daniel, John, B.D., Ph.D.
Pastor, St. John Lutheran Church; Instructor,
Department of History, Lehigh University

Daugherty, Donald H., Ph.D.
Assistant to the Director, American Council of
Learned Societies, Washington, D. C.

Davies, William David
Professor of New Testament, Princeton University

Davis, Natalie Zemon, A.M.
Graduate Student, University of Michigan

DeGroot, A. T., B.D., Ph.D.
Dean, Graduate School, Texas Christian University

DeKruyter, John G., B.D.
Minister, First Presbyterian Church, Jeffersonville, Indiana

Dentan, Robert Claude, Ph.D., S.T.D.
Professor of Old Testament, General Theological Seminary

Devreesse, Robert, Litt.D.
Vice-Prefect Emeritus of the Vatican Library

Dickie, Edgar Primrose, D.D.
Professor of Divinity, University of St. Andrews,
Scotland

Dicks, Russell L., D.D., Litt.D.
Associate Professor of Pastoral Care, Duke Divinity School

Dillistone, F. W., D.D.
Chancellor, Liverpool Cathedral, Liverpool,
England

Diringer, David, Litt.D.
University Lecturer in Semitic Epigraphy, University of Cambridge, England

Doberstein, John W., B.D., Litt.D.
Professor of Pastoral Theology, Lutheran Theological Seminary, Philadelphia

Donahue, Francis M., D.D.
Coadjutor to the Primate, Lansing, Michigan

Donaldson, Dwight M., Ph.D., D.D.
Retired Missionary of the Presbyterian Church
U.S.A., in Iran and India; Presbyterian Minister in Birmingham, Alabama

Dunn, David, A.M., D.D.
Dean, Evangelical and Reformed Theological Seminary, Lancaster, Pennsylvania

Dunstan, J. Leslie
Board of the Hawaiian Evangelical Association

Ebersole, Luke, Ph.D.
Professor of Sociology, University of Maryland

Eister, Allan W., Ph.D.
Associate Professor of Sociology, Wellesley College

Elfenbein, Elsie
Executive Director, National Council of Jewish Women, Inc.

Eller, Paul H., B.D., Ph.D.
President, Evangelical Theological Seminary, Naperville, Illinois

Ellis, John Tracy, Ph.D., L.H.D.
Professor of Church History, The Catholic University of America

Evans, C. Hans, Th.B., Ph.D.
Pastor, Presbyterian Church, Coatesville, Pennsylvania

Evjen, Victor H., B.A.S., A.M.
Assistant Chief, United States Probation System; and Editor, *Federal Probation Quarterly*

Fairbanks, Rollin Jonathan, A.B., B.D.
Professor of Pastoral Theology, Episcopal Theological School, Cambridge, Massachusetts

Farrer, Austin, D.D.
Fellow of Trinity College, University of Oxford, England

Fehl, Noah Edward, B.D., Ph.D.
Assistant Professor of the History and Philosophy of Religion, Seabury-Western Theological Seminary

Feldman, Abraham J., S.T.D., D.D., LL.D.
Rabbi of Temple Beth Israel, Hartford, Connecticut

Ferm, Vergilius, B.D., Ph.D.
Compton Professor and Head of the Department of Philosophy, The College of Wooster

Field, Jay Carleton, Ph.D.
Retired Missionary; Y.M.C.A. Secretary; Professor Emeritus of Latin America Studies, Hartford Seminary Foundation

Filson, Floyd V., Th.D., D.D.
Dean and Professor of New Testament Literature and History, McCormick Theological Seminary

Fine, Morris, M.S.
Editor, *American Jewish Year Book*

Finegan, Jack, Th.M., LL.D.
Professor of New Testament Literature and Interpretation, Pacific School of Religion

Finkelstein, Louis, Ph.D., S.T.D., Litt.D.
Chancellor and President of the Faculties, Jewish Theological Seminary of America

Fisch, Max H., Ph.D.
Professor of Philosophy, University of Illinois

Flack, Elmer E., Th.D., D.D., LL.D.
Dean and Professor of Exegetical Theology, Hamma Divinity School

Flemming, Arthur S., A.M., LL.D.
President, Ohio Wesleyan University

Fletcher, Joseph, S.T.D.
Robert Treat Paine Professor of Social Ethics, Episcopal Theological School, Cambridge, Massachusetts

Fliedner, George, A.B.
Clergyman in Madrid, Spain

Floreen, Harold, A.B., B.D.
Executive Director, American Committee on the Christian Approach to the Jews, The National Council of the Churches of Christ in the U. S. A.

Florovsky, Georges, S.T.D., D.D.
Dean and Professor of Divinity, St. Vladimir's Theological Seminary; Adjunct Professor of Religion, Columbia University; Adjunct Professor, Union Theological Seminary

Flower, J. Roswell
General Council, Assemblies of God

Foreman, Kenneth J., D.D.
Professor of Doctrinal Theology, Louisville Presbyterian Theological Seminary

Forrester, William Roxburgh, D.D.
Professor of Christian Ethics and Practical Theology, St. Mary's College, University of St. Andrews, Scotland

Foster, Hazel E., B.D., Ph.D.
Professor of New Testament, School of Religion, Morehouse College

Fraenkel, Peter, Th.B., A.M.
Pastor of the Evangelical Lutheran Church of France; Staff of the Lutheran World Federation, Geneva, Switzerland

Freedman, David Noel, Th.B., Ph.D.
Professor of Hebrew and Old Testament Literature, Western Theological Seminary, Pittsburgh

Freeman, E. G. D., D.D.
Dean, Faculty of Theology, United College, Winnipeg, Canada

Friedrich, Otto, D.Jur., Th.D.
Oberkirchenrat i. R. in Heidelberg, Germany; Lehrauftrag fuer Kirchenrecht

Fritsch, Charles T., Th.B., Ph.D.
Associate Professor of Old Testament, Princeton Theological Seminary

Froom, LeRoy Edwin, D.D.
Department of Church History, Seventh-day Adventist Theological Seminary

Fusco, Lucy V.
Staff of the National Headquarters of the Salvation Army

Gaer, Joseph
Author of books on Folklore

Gaillard, Andre, Ph.D.
Professor and Music Director, Lausanne, Switzerland

Gallagher, W. J., B.D., D.D.
General Secretary of the Canadian Council of Churches

Gapp, Kenneth S., Ph.D.
Librarian, Princeton Theological Seminary

Garvin, Lucius, Ph.D.
Professor and Head of Department of Philosophy, University of Maryland

Gehman, Henry S., Ph.D., S.T.D., Litt.D.
Professor of Old Testament Literature and Chairman of Department of Biblical Studies, Princeton Theological Seminary; Lecturer in Semitic Languages, Princeton University

Gezork, Herbert, Ph.D., D.D.
President, Andover-Newton Theological School

Gibson, George Miles, D.D.
Professor of Preaching, McCormick Theological Seminary

Gifford, Frank D., S.T.D., Ph.D.
Dean, Philadelphia Divinity School

Gingerich, Melvin, Ph.D.
Director of Research, Mennonite Research Foundation

Gingrich, F. W., Ph.D.
Professor of Greek, Albright College

Ginsberg, H. Louis, Ph.D.
Sabato Morais Professor of Bible, Jewish Theological Seminary of America

Glueck, Nelson, Ph.D., LL.D., D.H.L.
President, Hebrew Union College

Goodpasture, B. C., A.B.
Editor, *Gospel Advocate;* President, Gospel Advocate Company; Editor, Bible School Literature for Churches of Christ; President, Freedom Press

Goodykoontz, Harry Gordon, Th.D.
Professor of Christian Education, Louisville Presbyterian Theological Seminary

Goossens, H., Hist.D.
Friar, O.F.M., The Netherlands

Goossens, Mathias, S.T.D.
Friar, O.F.M., The Netherlands

Gordis, Robert, Ph.D., M.H.L., D.D.
Associate Professor of Bible, Jewish Theological Seminary; Adjunct Professor of Religion, Columbia University

Goulooze, William, Th.D., D.D.
Professor of Pastoral Theology and Christian Education, Western Theological Seminary, Holland, Michigan

Graf, Hermann
Pastor in Lindau/Anhalt, Germany

Grant, Frederick C., Th.D., D.D., D.S.Litt., D.C.L., S.T.D., L.H.D.
Professor of Biblical Theology, Union Theological Seminary

Grant, Robert M., Th.D., Ph.D.
Associate Professor of New Testament, Federated Theological Faculties, University of Chicago

Greenslade, William Gaius, D.D.
Retired Missionary, Minister of Presbyterian Church, Glenwood, Florida

Grimm, Harold, Ph.D.
Professor of History and Chairman of Department, Indiana University

Gueterbock, Hans Gustav, Ph.D.
Associate Professor of Hittitology, Oriental Institute, University of Chicago

Hairston, H. H.
Clergyman in Columbus, Ohio

Halleen, E. A.
President, Evangelical Free Church of America

Hamilton, Kenneth G., Ph.D., D.D.
Bishop of the Moravian Church; Vice President of Executive Board, Northern Province; Executive Officer, Board of Foreign Missions

Handy, Robert T., B.D., Ph.D.
Associate Professor of Church History, Union Theological Seminary

Hardy, Edward Rochie, S.T.M., Ph.D.
Professor of Church History, Berkeley Divinity School

Harris, D. H.
Bishop, Triumph the Church and Kingdom of God in Christ

Harrison, Max Hunter, S.T.M., Ph.D.
Principal, United Theological College of South India and Ceylon, Bangalore, South India

Hartman, Grover L., Ph.D.
Executive Secretary, Council of Churches of St. Joseph County, South Bend, Indiana

Harwood, Harry J., B.D., A.M.
Minister, Methodist Church, Marseilles, Illinois

Hatch, William H. P., Ph.D., Th.D., D.D.
Professor Emeritus of the Literature and Interpretation of the New Testament, Episcopal Theological School, Cambridge, Massachusetts

Hawk, Eugene B., D.D., LL.D.
Dean Emeritus of Perkins School of Theology, Southern Methodist University

Head, E. D., Th.D., D.D., LL.D.
President Emeritus, Southwestern Baptist Theological Seminary

Healey, James Christopher, B.D., Ph.D.
Senior Chaplain, Seamen's Church Institute, New York

Hebart, Siegfried, Th.D.
Professor of Systematic Theology and Principal, Immanuel Theological Seminary, North Adelaide, Australia

Heinecken, Martin J., B.D., Ph.D.
Professor of Systematic Theology, Lutheran Theological Seminary, Philadelphia

Henderson, Ian, D.D.
Professor of Systematic Theology, University of Glasgow, Scotland

Hendry, George S., D.D.
Charles Hodge Professor of Systematic Theology, Princeton Theological Seminary

Henke, Wilhelm, Th.D.
Bishop of the Evangelical Lutheran Church, Schaumburg-Lippe, Germany

Hetle, Erik, M.S.
Professor Emeritus, St. Olaf College, Northfield, Minnesota

Higgins, Howard D., Th.M., A.M.
Bishop, New York and Philadelphia Synod of the Reformed Episcopal Church

Hiltz, Robert Arthur, D.C.L., D.D.
Retired, Canon of St. James Cathedral, Toronto

Hitti, Philip K., Ph.D.
Professor Emeritus of Semitic Literature, Princeton University

Hoffman, Milton J., D.D., Litt.D.
Professor of Church History, New Brunswick Theological Seminary

Hoffmann, Jean G. H., Lic.D., Th.D.
Professor of Church History, Faculté Libre de Théologie Protestante, Paris, France

Holloway, Fred G., D.D., LL.D., L.H.D.
President, Drew University

Hollweg, Walter, Th.D.
Landessuperintendent i. R., Northwestern Germany

Holm, Bernard, Ph.D.
President, Wartburg Theological Seminary

Homrighausen, Elmer G., Th.D., D.D.
Dean and Professor of Pastoral Theology, Princeton Theological Seminary

Honigmann, John J., Ph.D.
Associate Professor of Anthropology, University of North Carolina

Hope, Norman V., Ph.D.
Professor of Church History and Chairman of History Department, Princeton Theological Seminary

Hopkins, Jeannette, M.S.
Special Projects Editor, Beacon Press; News Editor, American Unitarian Association

Hopkins, Robert M., D.D., LL.D.
President, The Golden Rule Foundation

Hornig, Ernst
Bischof von Schlesien in Goerlitz, Germany

Horton, Walter Marshall, S.T.M., Ph.D.
Fairchild Professor of Theology, Graduate School of Theology, Oberlin College

Hough, Lynn Harold, Th.D., D.D., LL.D., Litt.D.
Dean Emeritus, Drew Theological Seminary

House, R. Burton, A.M.
Chancellor, University of North Carolina

Howe, J. Ruskin, Ph.D., D.D.
Pastor, Emmanuel Church, Ashland, Ohio

Howe, Laurence Lee, Ph.D.
Associate Professor of History, University of Louisville

Hudson, Winthrop S., B.D., Ph.D.
James B. Colgate Professor of the History of Christianity, Colgate-Rochester Divinity School

Huelin, Gordon, Th.M., Ph.D.
Chaplain of London House and Deputy Minor Canon of St. Paul's Cathedral

Hume, Wilson M., Ph.D.
Associate General Secretary of the National Council of YMCA's in Egypt

Hung, Frederick (Hung Fu), A.B., Dr. del' Université
Associate Professor, Western College, Oxford, Ohio

Hutchinson, Paul, Ph.B., S.T.B.
Editor, *The Christian Century*

Hyatt, James Philip, B.D., Ph.D.
Professor of Old Testament and Head of Graduate Department of Religion, Vanderbilt University

Hyma, Albert, Ph.D.
Professor of History, University of Michigan

Iglehart, Charles, Th.D., D.D.
Professor Emeritus of Missions, Union Theological Seminary

Iversen, Iver, Ph.D.
Professor of Church History, Luther Theological Seminary

James, Edwin Oliver, Ph.D., Litt.D., D.D.
Professor of the History and Philosophy of Religion, University of London, England

Janssen, P. Canisius
Librarian of the Carmelite Monastery, Nijmegen, The Netherlands

Jeffery, Arthur, B.D., Ph.D., Litt.D.
Professor of Semitic Languages and Head of Department of Near and Middle East Languages, Columbia University

Johnson, E. H., B.S., Th.B.
Secretary for Overseas Missions, Presbyterian Church in Canada

Johnson, Sherman E., Ph.D., S.T.D.
Dean, Church Divinity School of the Pacific

Johnston, George, B.D., Ph.D.
Professor of New Testament Literature and Exegesis, Emmanuel College, University of Toronto

Jorgensen, K. E. Jordt, Th.D.
Second Pastor of Cathedral of Roskilde, Denmark

Jourdan, George V., D.D., Litt.D.
Beresford Professor of Ecclesiastical History, University of Dublin, Ireland

Kamlah, Theodor
Praeses des Bundes reformische Kirchen in Goettingen, Germany

Katz, Peter, Ph.D.
Lecturer on Septuagintal Studies, Faculty of Divinity, Cambridge University, England

Keller, Adolphe, Th.D., D.D., LL.D.
Professor Emeritus of Theology, Zurich, Switzerland

Kellersberger, Eugene R., M.D.
Retired from General Secretaryship of American Leprosy Missions, Inc.

Kelley, Alden Drew, S.T.D., D.D.
President and Professor of the Philosophy of Religion, Seabury-Western Theological Seminary

Kelsey, George D., B.D., Ph.D.
Associate Professor of Christian Ethics, Drew University

Kelso, James L., Th.D., D.D., LL.D.
Professor of Semitic Languages and Biblical Archaeology, Pittsburgh-Xenia Theological Seminary

Kerr, Hugh Thomson, Jr., S.T.B., Ph.D.
B. B. Warfield Professor of Systematic Theology and Chairman of the Department of Theology, Princeton Theological Seminary; Editor, *Theology Today*

Kieckbusch, Wilhelm, Th.D.
Landespropst of the Evangelical Church, Eutin, Germany

Kievits, A. P. M., Ph.D.
Conservator, University Library, Nijmegen, The Netherlands

Kimber, Harry, Ph.D.
Director of the Division of Social Science, School of Science and Arts, Michigan State College

Kingdon, Robert M., Ph.D.
Instructor in History, University of Massachusetts

Kloppenburg, Heinrich
Pastor in Dortmund, Germany

Knudsen, Johannes, S.T.M., Ph.D.
Dean of the Graduate School and Professor of Church History, Chicago Lutheran Seminary

Konvitz, Milton R., Ph.D., Jur.Dr., Litt.D.
Professor of Industrial and Labor Relations at Cornell University; Director, Liberian Codification Project

Kooiman, Willem Jan, Th.D.
Professor of Church History, University of Amsterdam, The Netherlands

Krabbes, Winfried, Ph.D.
Kirchenrat beim Evang. Konsistorium in Magdeburg, Germany

Kraeling, Emil G., Ph.D.
Formerly Professor of Old Testament in Union Theological Seminary

Krahn, Cornelius, Th.D.
Professor of Church History, Bethel College; Editor, *Mennonite Life*

Kromminga, John H., Th.D.
Professor of Historical Theology, Calvin Seminary

Kuecklich, Reinhold, Ph.D.
Praesident, Evangelische Theologische Schule, Reutlingen, Germany

Kuist, Howard Tillman, Ph.D.
Charles T. Haley Professor of Biblical Theology, Princeton Theological Seminary

Kundzins, Karlis, Th.D.
Professor, Pacific Lutheran College

Kunz, Alfred A.
Executive Secretary, Pocket Testament League

Kurland, Norman D., Ph.D.
Assistant Professor of History, Hobart and William Smith Colleges

Kuyper, E.
Friar, O.F.M., The Netherlands

Lacy, Ben R., Jr., D.D., LL.D., L.H.D.
President, Union Theological Seminary in Virginia

Lampen, Willibrord, Ph.D., D.D.
Professor Emeritus, University of Utrecht, The Netherlands

Landeen, William Martin, Ph.D.
Professor of History, State College of Washington

Landis, Benson Y., L.H.D., LL.D.
Editor of Research Publications, Bureau of Research and Survey, National Council of Churches of Christ in the U.S.A.

Larson, Grace
Librarian, University of Michigan

Lehmann, Paul L., Th.D., D.D.
Stephen Colwell Professor of Applied Christianity, Princeton Theological Seminary

Leiper, Henry Smith, D.D.
Executive Secretary, Congregational Missions Council; and Secretary, Friends of the World Council of Churches

Leslie, Elmer Archibald, S.T.B., Ph.D.
Head of Department of Old Testament and Biblical Literature, Boston University

Leslie, W. R., LL.B., Ph.D.
Associate Professor of History, University of Michigan

Letts, Harold C., D.D.
Secretary for Social Action, Board of Social Missions, United Lutheran Church in America

Liggitt, Eugene, D.D.
Professor Bible and Social Philosophy, Grove City College

Lindbeck, John M. H., B.D., Ph.D.
Assistant Professor of Far Eastern Studies, Yale University

Littmann, Enno, Ph.D., D.D.
Professor Emeritus of Arabic, University of Tuebingen, Germany

Loetscher, Frederick William, Ph.D., D.D., LL.D.
Archibald Alexander Professor Emeritus of Church History, Princeton Theological Seminary

Loetscher, Lefferts A., Ph.D., D.D.
Professor of American Church History, Princeton Theological Seminary

Lopez, Amy M. (Mrs. Frank G.)
Executive Secretary, International Order of the King's Daughters and Sons, Inc.

Louden, R. Stuart, A.M., B.D.
Minister of the Kirk of the Greyfriar, Edinburgh

Love, Julian Price, Ph.D., D.D.
Professor of Biblical Theology, Louisville Presbyterian Theological Seminary

Ludwig, Sylvester Theodore, D.D.
General Secretary, International Headquarters, Church of the Nazarene

Lund, Henrietta
Division of Welfare, National Lutheran Council

Lund-Quist, Carl E., D.D.
Executive Secretary, Lutheran World Federation, Geneva, Switzerland

Lyman, Mary Ely, B.D., Ph.D., Litt.D.
Jesup Professor of English Bible and Dean of Women Students, Union Theological Seminary

Lyon, E. Wilson, Litt.B., Ph.D.
President, Pomona College

Mackay, John A., Litt.D., D.D., LL.D., L.H.D.
President, Princeton Theological Seminary

Mackie, Alexander, D.D.
President, Presbyterian Ministers' Fund

Macleod, Donald, Th.D.
Associate Professor of Homiletics, Princeton Theological Seminary

Mangum, John M., B.D., M.S.
Associate Executive Secretary, The Luther League of America

Manross, William Wilson, S.T.B., Ph.D.
Librarian, The Church Historical Society, Philadelphia, Pennsylvania

Marcus, Ralph, Ph.D.
Professor of Hellenistic Culture, University of Chicago

Maring, Norman H., Th.B., Ph.D.
Professor of Church History, Eastern Baptist Theological Seminary

Marxsen, Willi, Th.D.
Studieninspektor Predigerseminar, Preetz, Germany; and Privatdozent, University of Kiel, Germany

Marquis, J. Gilmore, B.E., M.S.W.
Director of Field Service, Pacific Area, American National Red Cross

Mascall, Eric Lionel, D.D.
Oxford Lecturer in Philosophy of Religion, Oxford University, England

Masterson, W. H., Ph.D.
Associate Professor of History and Assistant to the President, Rice Institute

Matsunami, S.
Tokyo University, Tokyo, Japan

Maurer, Wilhelm, Th.D.
Professor of Theology, Erlangen, Germany

May, Herbert G., Ph.D., D.D.
Finney Professor of Old Testament Language and Literature, Graduate School of Theology, Oberlin College

Mayer, Frederick E., D.D.
Professor of Systematic Theology, Concordia Seminary

McCarrell, William, D.D.
Pastor of the Cicero Bible Church, Cicero, Illinois

McCarthy, John W., Ph.D.
Associate Professor of Philosophy, University of Louisville

McCarthy, Thomas J.
National Catholic Welfare Conference

McCracken, George E., Ph.D.
Professor of Classics, Drake University

McCutchan, Robert G., Mus.D., Sac.Mus.D., Litt.D.
Visiting Lecturer, Southern Methodist University; Lecturer Church Music, Claremont Graduate School

McGiffert, Arthur Cushman, Jr., Ph.D., D.D., Litt.D., LL.D.
President, Chicago Theological Seminary

McMahon, John F.
National Field Secretary, Volunteers of America

McNeill, John T., B.D., Ph.D., LL.D.
Professor Emeritus of Church History, Union Theological Seminary

Meacham, Paul L., Th.D.
Religious Book Editor, The Westminster Press

Meek, Theophile J., Ph.D., D.D.
Professor Emeritus of Oriental Languages, University College, University of Toronto, Canada

Meland, Bernard Eugene, B.D., Ph.D.
Professor of Constructive Theology, Chairman Theological Field, Federated Theological Faculty, University of Chicago

Mendenhall, George E., B.D., Ph.D.
Associate Professor of Near Eastern Languages and Literature, University of Michigan

Merrill, John Ernest, B.D., Ph.D.
President Emeritus, Aleppo College, Turkey

Merz, Georg, Ph.D.
Hochschulprofessor und Rektor der Augustana-Hochschule in Neuendettelsau, Germany

Metzger, Bruce M., Ph.D., D.D.
Professor of New Testament Language and Literature, Princeton Theological Seminary

Meyer, Erich
Member of Parliament, West German Republic

Meyer, Erwin
General Secretary, Martin Luther Bund, Erlangen, Germany

Meyer, Jacob
Elder, Apostolic Christian Church (Nazarean)

Meyer, Philipp, Th.D.
Oberlandeskirchenrat i. R. in Goettingen, Germany

Michalson, Carl, B.D., Ph.D.
Professor of Systematic Theology and the Philosophy of Religion, Drew University

Millard, Richard Marion, Ph.D.
Associate Professor and Chairman of the Department of Philosophy, Boston University

Minden, Mabel
Public Information Division, Girl Scouts of the U.S.A.

Mixon, John L., M.A., B.D.
Former Professor of Church Social Work, McCormick Theological Seminary

Moomaw, Ira W., M.S.C., Ph.D.
Executive Secretary, Agricultural Missions, Inc.

Morgan, Carl Hamilton, Ph.D., Th.D., D.D.
Dean and Professor of New Testament, Eastern Baptist Theological Seminary

Morgenstern, Julian, Ph.D., D.H.L., LL.D., D.D.
President Emeritus, Hebrew Union College-Jewish Institute of Religion

Morgenstern, W. V., Ph.B., J.D.
Director of Public Relations, The University of Chicago

Morrison, Charles Clayton, D.D., Litt.D.
Editor, The Pulpit; Former Editor, The Christian Century

Mosse, George L., Ph.D.
Associate Professor of History, University of Iowa

Muenchmeyer, Friedrich M., Th.D.
Hauptdirektor, Innere Mission, Evangelical Church in Germany

Mueller, William A., Th.D.
Professor of Philosophy of Religion, Southern Baptist Theological Seminary

Muilenburg, James, Ph.D., D.D., L.H.D.
Davenport Professor of Hebrew and Cognate Languages, Union Theological Seminary

Muller, Hugo A., A.M.
Retired Missionary to Iran

Mulligan, William E., Ph.B.
Senior Research Analyst, Arabian Research Division of the Arabian American Oil Company

Murray, John, Th.M.
Professor of Systematic Theology, Westminster Theological Seminary

Muste, A. J., A.M., B.D.
Secretary Emeritus, Fellowship of Reconciliation

Myers, Harry S., B.D., Ped.B., D.C.S.
Executive Director Emeritus, Joint Department of Stewardship and Benevolence, National Council of Churches of Christ in the U. S. A.

Myers, Jacob M., S.T.D., Ph.D.
Professor of Old Testament, Lutheran Theological Seminary, Gettysburg, Pennsylvania

Nace, I. George, D.D.
Executive Secretary, Division of Home Missions, National Council of the Churches of Christ in the U.S.A.

Nauta, D., D.D.
Professor of Church History and Ecclesiastical Law, Free University, Amsterdam, The Netherlands

Nelson, John Oliver, B.D., Ph.D., Litt.D.
Professor of Christian Vocation, Yale University

Neuser, Wilhelm, Lic.Theol.
Landessuperintendent of the Evangelical Church, Lippe, Germany

Nichols, Robert Hastings, Ph.D., D.D.
Late Professor of Church History, Union Theological Seminary

Nida, Eugene A., Ph.D.
Secretary of Translations, American Bible Society

Niebuhr, Hulda, A.M., Litt.D.
Professor of Religious Education, McCormick Theological Seminary

Nieting, Lorenz, B.D.
Professor, Lutheran Seminary, Manila, Philippine Islands

North, Eric M., Ph.D., D.D.
Secretary, American Bible Society

Noth, Martin, Th.D.
Professor, Bonn University, Germany

Oates, Wayne E., Th.D.
Assistant Professor of Psychology of Religion, Southern Baptist Theological Seminary

Oddo, Gilbert L., Ph.D.
Assistant Professor of History, St. Mary's College, Emmitsburg, Maryland

Parker, Francis Howard, Ph.D.
Associate Professor of Philosophy, Haverford College

Payne, Joan Gay
United Service Organizations, New York City

Pelikan, Jaroslav, B.D., Ph.D.
Assistant Professor of Historical Theology, Federated Theological Faculties, University of Chicago

Percy, J. O.
Administrative Vice President, Interdenominational Foreign Mission Association of North America

Peterson, John, Ph.D.
Editor, *Covenant Weekly,* of the Evangelical Mission Covenant Church of America

Pfeiffer, Robert H., Ph.D., S.T.M., LL.D.
Hancock Professor of Hebrew and other Oriental Languages; Curator of the Semitic Museum, Harvard University; Professor, Boston University

Pickens, Claude L., Jr., B.D., A.M.
Assistant Secretary, Overseas Department, National Council of the Protestant Episcopal Church

Pierce, Richard D., S.T.M., Ph.D.
Chairman of Faculty and Professor of History, Emerson College

Pinomaa, Lennart, Th.D.
Professor of Systematic Theology, Helsinki University, Finland

Piper, Otto A., Th.D., D.D., LL.D.
Professor of New Testament Literature and Exegesis, Princeton Theological Seminary

Pitt, Malcolm S., M.A., D.D.
Professor, Department of Indian Studies, Hartford Seminary Foundation

Porada, Edith, Ph.D.
Instructor, Art Department, Queens College

Pyatt, Charles Lynn, B.D., Th.D.
Dean Emeritus, Assistant to the President, The College of the Bible

Quasten, Johannes, D.D.
Professor of Ancient Church History and Christian Archaeology, Catholic University of America

Rahe, Wilhelm, Lic.Theol.
Landeskirchenrat, Westphalia, Germany

Rasmussen, Carl Christian, D.D.
Professor of Systematic Theology, Lutheran Theological Seminary, Gettysburg, Pennsylvania

Read, Osceola J.
Pastor General of the Congregational Councils of the Christian Congregation

Reichardt, Erich, D.Jur.
Kirchenverwaltungsrat, Eisenach, Germany

Reid, J. K. S., B.D., A.M.
Professor of Systematic Theology, University of Leeds, England

Reinartz, F. Eppling, D.D.
Secretary, The United Lutheran Church in America

Rentz, George, Ph.D.
Adviser on Arab Affairs, Arabian American Oil Company, Dhahran, Saudi Arabia

Rhodes, Arnold Black, Th.D., Ph.D.
Professor of Old Testament, Louisville Presbyterian Theological Seminary

Richardson, Harry V., S.T.B., Ph.D.
President, Gammon Theological Seminary

Rightmyer, Nelson, Th.B., Ed.D.
Rector, St. John's Church, Worthington Valley, Maryland; formerly Professor of Church History, Philadelphia Divinity School

Ringenberg, Jonas A.
Clergyman in Fort Wayne, Indiana

Ritter, Gerhard, Ph.D., Th.D., Dr.Jur.
Professor of Modern History, University of Freiburg i. Breisgau, Germany

Rockwell, William Walker, Ph.D., Th.D.
Librarian Emeritus, Union Theological Seminary

Roeger, William Coley, S.T.M.
Pastor, St. James' Evangelical Lutheran Church, Chalfont, Pennsylvania

Rogers, William L.
Executive Secretary, The Religious Film Association, Inc.

Rolston, Holmes, Th.D., D.D.
Editor-in-Chief, Board of Christian Education, Presbyterian Church in the U.S.

Rose, Lawrence, S.T.D.
Dean, General Theological Seminary

Rosenthal, Franz, Ph.D.
Professor of Arabic, University of Pennsylvania

Rowley, H. H., Th.D., D.D., Litt.D.
Professor of Hebrew, University of Manchester, England

Rudolph, LaVere Christian, A.B., B.D.
Instructor in Church History, Louisville Presbyterian Theological Seminary

Ruff, G. Elson, Litt.D.
Editor, *The Lutheran*

Rule, Andrew K., Ph.D., D.D.
Professor of Apologetics and Church History, Louisville Presbyterian Theological Seminary

Ryberg, James A., A.B.
Assistant Public Relations Director, Evangelical Lutheran Church; formerly with the World Council of Churches, Geneva, Switzerland

Rycroft, W. Stanley, Ph.D.
Secretary for Latin America, Board of Foreign Missions, Presbyterian Church in U.S.A.

Saarnivaara, Uuras, Ph.D., S.T.D.
Editor of Church Paper, Helsinki, Finland

Sailer, T. H. P., Ph.D.
Honorary Secretary of Commission on Missionary Education

Salley, Claudia Louise, Ph.D.
Assistant Professor of History, Florida State University

Saulpaugh, Ivane
Secretary of Information, Church World Service

Saunders, Wilbour Eddy, D.Ed., D.D., LL.D., L.H.D.
President, Colgate-Rochester Divinity School

Schade Rudolf G., S.T.M., Th.D.
Associate Professor of Greek and Philosophy, Elmhurst College

Schaller, Theodor, Th.D.
Oberkirchenrat in Speyer, Germany

Scherzer, Carl J., D.D.
Chaplain of the Protestant Deaconess Hospital, Evansville, Indiana

Schiotz, Fredrik A., D.D.
President, The Evangelical Lutheran Church

Schmidt, Johann
Oberkonsistorialrat in Kiel, Germany

Schmidt, Wilhelm-Ferdinand
Oberkirchenrat in Munich, Germany

Schneider, Carl E., Ph.D.
Professor of Church History, Eden Theological Seminary

Schorger, William, Ph.D.
Assistant Professor of Anthropology (and of Near Eastern Studies), University of Michigan

Schuck, Arthur A., LL.D., L.H.D.
Chief Scout Executive, Boy Scouts of America

Schulz, Kurd, Ph.D.
Bibliotheksrat in Bremen, Germany

Schwiebert, Ernest G., Ph.D.
Professor of History, Air Research and Development Command, Baltimore, Maryland

Scott, R. B. Y., Ph.D., D.D.
Professor of Old Testament, Princeton University

Seele, Keith C., Ph.D., L.H.D.
Oriental Institute Professor of Egyptology, University of Chicago

Sellers, Ovid R., B.D., Ph.D.
Dean Emeritus and Professor Emeritus of Old Testament Language and Literature, McCormick Theological Seminary

Seltzer, George R., S.T.M., Ph.D.
Professor of Liturgics and Church Art, Lutheran Theological Seminary, Philadelphia

Shedd, Clarence P., B.D., Ph.D., L.H.D.
Professor of Christian Methods, Director of Studies, Religion in Higher Education, Yale University

Shepherd, Massey H., Jr., Ph.D., S.T.D.
Professor of Liturgics, Church Divinity School of the Pacific

Short, David William, D.D.
Archbishop and Chief Primate of the Orthodox Christian Spiritual Faith and Universal Church

Simsar, Mehmed A., D.C.S., Ph.D.
Information Specialist, United States Information Agency

Slawson, John, Ph.D.
Executive Vice President, The American Jewish Committee

Smalley, William F., Th.B.
General Secretary, The Christian and Missionary Alliance

Smith, Horace G., D.D.
President Emeritus, Garrett Biblical Institute

Smith, Wilford Cantwell, Ph.D.
Professor of Comparative Religion and Director, Institute of Islamic Studies, McGill University, Montreal

Smith, W. E. L., Ph.D.
Professor of Church History, Queens Theological College; Kingston Associate Professor of History, Queens University, Kingston, Ontario, Canada

Smits, Karel
Librarian, Catholic University, Nijmegen, The Netherlands

Snead, A. C.
Secretary, Foreign Department of the Christian and Missionary Alliance

Soe, Niels, Th.D.
Professor of Systematic Theology, University of Copenhagen, Denmark

Speiser, Ephraim Avigdor, Ph.D., D.H.L.
Ellis Professor of Hebrew and Semitic Languages and Literature; Chairman, Oriental Studies, University of Pennsylvania

Spinka, Matthew, Th.D., D.D.
Waldo Professor of Church History, Hartford Theological Seminary

Staack, Hagen, S.T.M., Ph.D.
Head of Department of Religion, Muhlenberg College

Stauffer, Milton T., D.D.
Editor, Braille Publications of John Milton Society

Steere, Douglass V., Ph.D., L.H.D.
Professor of Philosophy, Haverford College

Steiner, Robert
Pastor in Barmen, Germany

Stensvaag, John, S.T.M., Ph.D.
Dean of the Theological Seminary and Professor of Old Testament, Augsburg Theological Seminary

Stephens, Ferris J., B.D., Ph.D.
Associate Professor of Assyriology and Curator of the Babylonian Collection, Yale University

Stitt, David L., LL.D., D.D.
President, Austin Presbyterian Theological Seminary

Stokman, E.
Friar, O.F.M., The Netherlands

Stone, Gene, D.D.
General Secretary, International Society of Christian Endeavor

Stoudt, John J., B.D., Ph.D.
Minister, Evangelical and Reformed Church, Norristown, Pennsylvania

Strodach, George K., Ph.D.
Associate Professor of Philosophy, Lafayette College

Stupperich, Robert, Th.D., Ph.D.
Professor of Church History, Evangelical Theological Faculty, University of Munster, Germany

Sweet, William W., Ph.D., D.D., Litt.D.
Professor Emeritus, History of American Christianity, University of Chicago

Tappert, Theodore, D.D., Litt.D.
Professor of Church History, Lutheran Theological Seminary, Philadelphia

Taylor, Charles L., Th.D., D.D.
Dean, Episcopal Theological School, Cambridge, Massachusetts

Theron, Daniel Johannes, Th.D.
Assistant Professor of New Testament, Princeton Theological Seminary

Thiele, Edwin R., Ph.D.
Head, Department of Religion, Emmanuel Missionary College

Thomas, Edith Lovell, B.R.E., M.Ed., M.S.M.
Consultant, Teacher, Writer on Music and Children of the Church

Thomas, John Newton, Ph.D., D.D.
Robert L. Dabney Professor of Systematic Theology, Union Theological Seminary in Virginia

Thompson, William Taliaferro, A.B., B.D.
Professor of Christian Education, Union Theological Seminary in Virginia

Thomson, S. Harrison, Ph.D., Litt.D.
Professor of Medieval History, University of Colorado

Thomson, William, B.D., Ph.D.
James Richard Jewett Professor Emeritus of Arabic, Harvard University

Tomas, Vincent, Ph.D.
Associate Professor of Philosophy, Brown University

Tomkins, Oliver S., D.D.
Warden of the Theological College, Lincoln, England

Torbet, Robert G., B.D., Ph.D.
Editor, Board of Education and Publication of American Baptist Convention

Troeger, Walther, Dr.J.
Late Konsistorialpraesident in Berlin, Germany

Trueblood, D. Elton, S.T.B., Ph.D.
Chief of Religious Information, United States Information Agency

Urwin, Evelyn Clifford, B.D., A.M.
Honorary Secretary, Department of Christian Citizenship, Methodist Church of Great Britain

van Dyke, Tertius, D.D.
Dean Emeritus, Hartford Seminary Foundation

Van Til, Cornelius, Th.M., Ph.D.
Professor of Apologetics, Westminster Theological Seminary

Verduin, Leonard, Th.B., A.M.
Director, Campus Chapel at the University of Michigan

Vinay, Valdo
Professor of Church History, Theological Faculty of the Waldensian Church in Italy, Rome, Italy

Vincze, Charles, Th.M., S.T.D.
Late Pastor of the Magyar Reformed Church, Perth Amboy, New Jersey

Visser 't Hooft, W. A., Th.D., D.D.
General Secretary, World Council of Churches

Von Hase, Hans Christoph, Th.D.
Pastor, Muenster Church, Herford, Westphalia, Germany

Von Scheven, Karl, Th.D.
Late Bishop of Pomerania, Greifswald, Germany

Vööbus, Arthur, Th.D.
Professor of New Testament, Chicago Lutheran Theological Seminary

Waesberghe, M. M. J. Smits van, Ph.D., Th.D.
Lecturer at the Catholic University of Nijmegen, The Netherlands

Wagner, Ernst, Th.D.
Pastor in Baden, Germany

Wahlstrom, Eric H., D.D.
Professor of New Testament Language and Literature, Augustana Theological Seminary

Walker, Sheafe, A.M.
Rector of Christ Church, Portsmouth, New Hampshire

Walther, Daniel, Litt.D.
Professor of Church History and Chairman of the Department, Seventh-day Adventist Theological Seminary

Warwick, Herbert Sherwood, Ph.D.
Professor of History, University of Louisville

Watson, Philip Saville, A.M., B.D.
Principal and Tutor in Systematic Theology and Philosophy of Religion, Handsworth College, Birmingham, England

Weddell, Sue
Executive Secretary, Division of Foreign Missions, National Council of the Churches of Christ, U.S.A.

Weeber, Rudolf, Th.D., Dr.Jur.
Direktor im Evangelisches Oberkirchenrat in Stuttgart, Germany

Weinlick, John R., B.D., Ph.D.
Professor of Historical Theology, Moravian Theological Seminary, Bethlehem, Pennsylvania

Welch, Claude, Ph.D.
Associate Professor of Theology, Yale University

Wentz, Abdel Ross, Ph.D., Th.D., Litt.D., LL.D.
Professor of Church History, Lutheran Theological Seminary, Gettysburg, Pennsylvania

Wickey, Gould, Ph.D., D.D., LL.D., Litt.D., L.H.D.
Executive Secretary, Board of Higher Education, United Lutheran Church in America

Wikgren, Allen, Ph.D.
Associate Professor of New Testament Language and Literature, Federated Theological Faculty; Chairman, Department New Testament and Early Christian Literature, University of Chicago

Wilder, Amos N., Th.D., D.D.
Professor of New Testament Interpretation, Harvard Divinity School

Will, Robert, Th.D., D.D.
Honorary Professor, Strasbourg University, France

Willaert, Leopold, Ph.D., D.D., Litt.D.
Professor in the Faculty of Notre-Dame de la Paix, Namur, Belgium

Williams, Daniel D., Ph.D., Th.D.
Professor of Systematic Theology, Union Theological Seminary

Williams, George H., Th.D., D.D.
Associate Professor of Church History, Divinity School, Harvard University

Wilson, J. Christy, D.D.
Dean of Field Service, Princeton Theological Seminary

Wingate, Rachel Orde, A.B.
Late Secretary of the Royal Central Asian Society and of the Palestine Exploration Fund, London

Winnet, Frederick Victor, Ph.D.
Professor, Department of Oriental Language, University College, University of Toronto

Wolf, C. Umhau, S.T.M., Ph.D.
Pastor, St. Paul's Lutheran Church, Toledo, Ohio

Wolf, William J., Th.D.
Howard Robbins Professor of Theology, Episcopal Theological School, Cambridge, Massachusetts

Wolseley, Roland E., M.S.
Professor of Journalism and Chairman, Magazine Department, School of Journalism, Syracuse University

Wolters, Ernst-Georg, Ph.D.
Propst in Wolfenbuettel, Germany

Woolley, Paul, Th.M.
Professor of Church History, Westminster Theological Seminary

Wright, G. Ernest, Ph.D., D.D.
Professor of Old Testament History and Theology, McCormick Theological Seminary

Wuensch, Georg, Th.D.
Professor of Systematic Theology and Social Ethics, University of Marburg, Germany

Wunsch, William Frederic, A.B., LL.B.
Minister, The Church of the Holy City (National Church of the Swedenborgians), Washington, D. C.

Young, Herrick Black, A.M.
President, Western College

Zabriskie, Alexander C., S.T.D., D.D.
Professor of Church History, the Protestant Episcopal Theological Seminary in Virginia

Zahn, Leon N., A.B., B.D.
Pastor, St. Michael's Lutheran Church, Germantown, Philadelphia; formerly consultant of the Division of Welfare, National Lutheran Council

Zimmermann, Bernhard, Th.D.
Pastor of the Kreuzkirche in Graz, Styria, Austria

PREFACE

The New Schaff-Herzog Encyclopedia of Religious Knowledge has long been recognized by scholars and librarians to be what Constance M. Winchell's authoritative *Guide to Reference Books* calls it, "one of the most important reference books in its subject in English." A brief history of this classic reference work was given in the Preface of the *New Schaff-Herzog*, Volume I.

Recent decades have made the supplementation of the encyclopedia highly desirable. Far-reaching social and cultural changes which have altered in important ways both the contents and the structure of the theological disciplines; the discovery of new source materials, both manuscript and archaeological; the rise of new presuppositions and techniques, both in scholarly research and in the practical strategies of ecclesiastical administration and parish work; and a plethora of new events, institutions, and personalities—such factors as these have made necessary supplementary volumes.

The supplementary volumes presented herewith, which contain more than a million words, parallel the original volumes in scope, and deal with all principal areas of theological scholarship. Biblical archaeology, text and versions, languages, criticism, history, exegesis, and theology are treated in the light of most recent scholarship. Church history was a principal forte of the original Schaff-Herzog, and the new volumes present the results of the most important recent scholarship in the patristic, medieval, Reformation, and post-Reformation periods, offering articles which supplement articles of the same titles in the original volumes, and articles on new subjects where needed. The new and complex church history of the twentieth century has been a major concern of the present publication, and careful coverage has been given to the religious history not only of the English-speaking world but also of the European Continent, where the Schaff-Herzog has had notable strength, and of other areas of world Christianity. Articles on individual nations summarize leading religious developments within those nations during the twentieth century. A vast number of denominations, sects, and cults are treated in individual articles, as are many other organizations, institutions, and movements, including various organs of contemporary ecumenicity. Numerous lectureships are identified by name.

Following the example of the original volumes, considerable attention has been given to biographies of contemporaries, some of whom are not elsewhere listed. Because of the theological nature of this encyclopedia, the selective process has in general favored those connected with theological scholarship and teaching as compared, for example, with pastors and church executives, though some representatives of the latter groups have been included. While the chief concern of this encyclopedia of religious knowledge continues to be with the Christian religion, the supplementary volumes, like the earlier ones, provide important material on Judaism, Islam and other non-Christian religions. Numerous entries deal with theology and ethics as well as with broader cultural and social backgrounds that are of importance for religion.

Two new features have been introduced in the present volumes. Primarily for the benefit of pastors, the Department of Practical Theology deals in a very practical and advisory way with concrete problems of the pulpit, the parish, and church administration. It is believed that this will prove helpful to many. The Department of Ecclesiastical Terminology offers numerous brief definitions and occasional longer discussions of ecclesiastical terms, some of which are quite technical. An important proportion, though not all, of these lie in the area of recent or contemporary Roman Catholicism. In a day when these terms appear in secular as well as in religious journals and other literature, ready and authentic definition or discussion of them will be found useful.

For an introduction to some of the principal developments in the religious thought and life of the twentieth century, the reader will find helpful the following key articles, which open up the fields of the respective departments by a brief summary of leading developments and by numerous cross references to other leading articles: OLD TESTAMENT STUDIES, TWENTIETH CENTURY TRENDS IN; NEW TESTAMENT STUDIES, TWENTIETH CENTURY TRENDS IN; PATRISTICS, TWENTIETH CENTURY TRENDS IN THE STUDY OF; MEDIEVAL CHURCH HISTORY, TWENTIETH CENTURY TRENDS IN THE STUDY OF; REFORMATION CHURCH HISTORY, TWENTIETH CENTURY TRENDS IN THE STUDY OF; EUROPE IN THE TWENTIETH CENTURY, CHRISTIANITY IN; UNITED STATES IN THE TWENTIETH CENTURY, CHRISTIANITY IN THE; COMPARATIVE RELIGION, TWENTIETH CENTURY TRENDS IN THE STUDY OF; THEOLOGY, TWENTIETH CENTURY TRENDS IN; PRACTICAL THEOLOGY, TWENTIETH CENTURY TRENDS IN; ROMAN CATHOLIC CHURCH.

The effort has been made to maintain a proper proportion between longer, more comprehensive articles and shorter, more specific ones. Copious cross references, both within articles and as main entries, have been supplied for co-ordinating similar topics and as a guide to further treatment of related themes. Cross references always refer to articles in the new volumes except where the volume number of one of the original volumes is given. All of the articles for the two supplementary volumes are new, written expressly for these volumes. All articles of fifty words or more are signed by their authors, except articles on contemporary biography. Most, though not all, of the unsigned contemporary biographies are autobiographical.

A list of contributors in the front of the first supplementary volume identifies all who contributed signed articles to either or both volumes. The list is not repeated in the second volume. Whenever an article in the new volumes bears the same title as an article in the original volumes, it is marked supplementary "[Sup.]," whether it corrects details of the earlier article or supplants it entirely. In case the new article is supplementing an earlier article which had a different title, that fact is indicated. Thus, the new article, ACTS OF THE APOSTLES, because it supplements material found in the original volumes under LUKE, Section II, is marked "[Sup. to LUKE, II.]" Where an article in the new volumes is not marked as supplementary, it deals with a subject not specifically treated in the original volumes. These supplementary volumes, with their numerous and full bibliographies, are intended both for the specialized scholar and the more general reader.

The editors are deeply grateful to the more than five hundred contributors of the Protestant, Roman Catholic, Eastern Orthodox, and Jewish faiths, not only from the English-speaking world but also from the European Continent and other lands, whose scholarship and whose co-operation have made possible the appearance of these supplementary volumes.

THE EDITORS.

LIST OF ABBREVIATIONS

In most articles the bibliographical references are not abbreviated, or else use abbreviations which are only partial and whose meaning is self-evident. In other articles abbreviations are used with the meanings here listed.

ABC	Abingdon Bible Commentary
AJA	American Journal of Archaeology
AJP	American Journal of Philology
AJSL	American Journal of Semitic Languages
AJT	American Journal of Theology
ANF	Ante-Nicene Fathers, ed. by A. C. Coxe, 8 vols., 1887; Vol. IX ed. by A. Menzies, 1897
ARG	Archiv fuer Reformationsgeschichte
ASB	Acta sanctorum, ed. by J. Bolland and others, Antwerp, 1643 ff.
ASOR	American Schools of Oriental Research
ATR	Anglican Theological Review
BA	Biblical Archaeologist
BASOR	Bulletin of the American Schools of Oriental Research
BJRL	Bulletin of the John Rylands Library, Manchester
BR	Biblical Review
BZAW	Beiheft, Zeitschrift fuer die alttestamentliche Wissenschaft
CAH	Cambridge Ancient History
CB	Cambridge Bible
CHQ	Church Quarterly Review
CHR	Catholic Historical Review
CQ	Crozer Quarterly
CSEL	Corpus scriptorum ecclesiasticorum Latinorum, Vienna, 1867 ff.
CW	Classical Weekly
DACL	Dictionnaire d'archéologie chrétienne et de liturgie
DNB	Dictionary of National Biography, ed. by L. Stephen and S. Lee, 63 vols. and supplementary vols., 1885 ff.
EB	Estudios Bíblicos
EQ	Evangelical Quarterly
ERE	Hastings' Encyclopaedia of Religion and Ethics
ET	Expository Times
Exp	Expositor
HAT	Handbuch zum alten Testament
HE	Historia ecclesiastica
HERE	Hastings' Encyclopaedia of Religion and Ethics
HKAT	Handkommentar zum alten Testament, ed. by Nowack
HSAT	Die heilige Schrift des alten Testaments, 4th ed., ed. by A. Bertholet
HTR	Harvard Theological Review
HUCA	Hebrew Union College Annual
HV	Historische Vierteljahrschrift
HZAT	Handbuch zum alten Testament
ICC	International Critical Commentary
IJA	International Journal of the Apocrypha
JAOS	Journal of the American Oriental Society
JBL	Journal of Biblical Literature
JBR	Journal of Bible and Religion
JNES	Journal of Near Eastern Studies
JourAs	Journal asiatique
JQR	Jewish Quarterly Review
JR	Journal of Religion
JRAS	Journal of the Royal Asiatic Society
JRS	Journal of Roman Studies
JTS	Journal of Theological Studies
KAT	Kommentar zum alten Testament, ed. by Sellin
KlT	Kleine Texte, ed. by H. Lietzmann
LXX	The Septuagint
MBVP	Maxima bibliotheca veterum patrum, et antiquorum scriptorum ecclesiasticorum, ed. by Marguerin de la Bigne, 27 vols., Lugduni, 1677
MGEp	Monumenta Germaniae historica, Epistolae
MGH	Monumenta Germaniae historica, ed. by G. H. Pertz and others, Hanover and Berlin, 1826 ff.
MPG	J. P. Migne, Patrologiae cursus completus, series Graeca, 162 vols., Paris, 1857–66
MPL	J. P. Migne, Patrologiae cursus completus, series Latina, 221 vols., Paris, 1844–64
NKZ	Neue kirchliche Zeitschrift
NTT	Norsk Teologisk Tidsskrift
OC	Oriens Christianus
PG	J. P. Migne, Patrologiae cursus completus, series Graeca, 162 vols., Paris, 1857–66
PL	J. P. Migne, Patrologiae cursus completus, series Latina, 221 vols., Paris, 1844–64
PRE	Protestantische Realencyclopaedie, Hauck-Herzog, 3rd ed.
PS	Patrologia syriaca
RB	Revue biblique
RBen	Revue bénédictine
RE	Pauly-Wissowa Realencyclopaedie der klassischen Altertumswissenschaft
RGG	Die Religion in Geschichte und Gegenwart
RHE	Revue d'histoire ecclésiastique
RHPR	Revue d'histoire et de philosophie religieuses
RHR	Revue d'histoire des religions
ROC	Revue de l'Orient chrétien
RSR	Recherches de science religieuse
SBA	Sitzungsberichte der Berliner Akademie
SNTS	Studiorum Novi Testamenti Societas
SVRG	Schriften des Vereins fuer Reformationsgeschichte
ThLZ	Theologische Literaturzeitung
ThSt	Theological Studies
ThZts	Theologische Zeitschrift
TLZ	Theologische Literaturzeitung
TQ	Theologische Quartalschrift
TR, NF	Theologische Rundschau, Neue Folge
TT	Theology Today
TU	Texte und Untersuchungen zur Geschichte der altchristlichen Literatur, ed. by O. von Gebhardt and A. Harnack, 1882 ff.
TZ	Theologische Zeitschrift
VC	Vigiliae Christianae
WDB	Westminster Dictionary of the Bible
ZATW	Zeitschrift fuer die alttestamentliche Wissenschaft
ZAW	Zeitschrift fuer die alttestamentliche Wissenschaft
ZDAL	Zeitschrift fuer deutsches Altertum und deutsche Literatur
ZDMG	Zeitschrift der deutschen morgenlaendischen Gesellschaft
ZKG	Zeitschrift fuer Kirchengeschichte
ZMRW	Zeitschrift fuer Missionskunde und Religionswissenschaft
ZNTW	Zeitschrift fuer die neutestamentliche Wissenschaft
ZNW	Zeitschrift fuer die neutestamentliche Wissenschaft
ZST	Zeitschrift fuer systematische Theologie

THE NEW SCHAFF-HERZOG
ENCYCLOPEDIA OF RELIGIOUS KNOWLEDGE

A

AACHEN, SYNODS OF:

BIBLIOGRAPHY: A. Werminghoff, "Die Beschluesse des Aachener Konzils im Jahre 816," in *Neues Archiv*, Vol. 27 (1902), pp. 605–625; E. Seckel, "Die Aachener Synoden von Januar 819," in *Neues Archiv*, Vol. 44 (1922), pp. 11–42.
[Sup.]

ABANDONMENT AND EXPOSURE: A

form of criminal negligence or malicious destruction of life. It may be infanticide, which is the murder of a child by its parents or with their consent. Child murder by others is simply murder. It is an ancient practice due to various motives—birth control, economic scarcity, jealousy, disease and debility, parental indifference, inheritance complications, ritual sacrifice, illegitimacy, malformation. Infanticide has more commonly taken the form of drowning, suffocating, or choking, but exposure to starve, freeze, or be eaten by animals is found in some cultures. Exposure may also be a form of "geronticide," or the destruction of the aged and infirm. In Europe and America, in the Christian era, the most frequent motive in exposing a child has been abandonment rather than infanticide; i.e., the hope has been that the child would be found and reared by others. Both abandonment (when surreptitious) and infanticide are prohibited by law in modern Oriental and Western lands. In law, infanticide is directly killing a child after it has become a "human being"; i.e., after it has left the womb. This conflicts with the Roman Catholic moral theology, in which "infanticide" is a blanket category including contraception and abortion as well as murder of a *post partum* baby, thus denying the distinctions between germicide (contraception), foeticide (abortion, *q.v.*) and infanticide (child murder). At present, the law holds abandonment to be "cruelty to children"—a criminal offense which also includes assault, ill-treatment, neglect, and exposure. Doubtless its most common cause now is illegitimacy. The usual social stigma and moral condemnation of illegitimacy in parentage has always encouraged abandonment. The early Christian Fathers condemned abandonment, out of respect for life and personality. Abandonment was a common practice among the Greeks: Spartan law required it; Aristotle and Plato approved it (though only for eugenic reasons, not because of selfishness or shame). The Koran condemns it (17:38), but there is no mention of the practice as an ethical question in the Bible (which is an extremely fragmentary commentary on sex ethics, *q.v.*). The Hebrews put too high a value on progeny to permit abandonment or exposure, and the isolated cases mentioned in the Old Testament are due to special circumstances (e.g., Hagar and Ishmael, Gen. 21:15 ff.; and Moses' exposure in the bulrushes, Ex. 2:1–10). The idea that children dying unbaptized go to hell or limbo helped to restrain infanticide and abandonment, but abandonment revived once foundling asylums were started. The church in Italy opened the first one in the sixth century, and by the early middle ages they were equipped with a *tour* or turning box whereby the child could be received directly from the mother anonymously. Today in urban communities abandonment (chiefly of "illegitimate" children) is carried out through such confinement homes as those of the Florence Crittenton and Salvation Army programs. Child welfare agencies (with state licenses and public authority) find foster homes and adoptive parents for babies, thus largely eliminating the old evils of malicious neglect and murder. There is danger, in such a system of semi-approved abandonment, of profit-making exploitation through baby farming, but the civil authorities suppress such enterprises. Increasing sterility among married couples tends to increase the demand for "abandoned" babies.

BIBLIOGRAPHY: E. Westermarck, *The Origin and Development of Moral Ideas*, 2 vols., 1912–17; Robert Briffault, *The Mothers*, 3 vols., 1927; W. E. H. Lecky, *The History of European Morals*, 2 vols., 1927; publications of the United States Childrens' Bureau.

JOSEPH FLETCHER.

ABBO OF FLEURY: B. *ca.* 945. His most

important work is *Collectio Canonum*, which often has been incorrectly associated with the Pseudo-Isidorian Decretals.

BIBLIOGRAPHY: U. Berlière gives in *Dict. d'Histoire et de géographie ecclésiastique*, Vol. I (1912), a complete list of his works with extensive bibliography. See also G. Chessenau, *L'Abbaye de Fleury à St. Benoit-sur-Loire*, 1931.

[Sup.] MATHIAS GOOSSENS.

ABBOT, BENJAMIN: Educator; b. Andover,

Mass., Sept. 17, 1762, son of Capt. John and

Abigail (Abbot) Abbot; d. Exeter, Oct. 25, 1849. Fitted for college at Phillips Academy, Andover, and graduated from Harvard in 1788, receiving the degree of A.M. Appointed the following October as principal of Phillips Academy, Exeter, N. H. He continued in this capacity for fifty years, teaching at the same time Latin, Greek, and mathematics, setting high standards of scholarship and moral conduct. He was averse to corporal punishment and succeeded in enforcing strict discipline without its use. Among his pupils were Edward Everett and Jared Sparks, both subsequently presidents of Harvard College, Lewis Cass, and Daniel Webster.

BIBLIOGRAPHY: F. G. Cunningham, *Familiar Sketches of Phillips Academy*, 1883.

RICHARD D. PIERCE.

ABBOTT, LYMAN: Congregational clergyman and editor; d. Oct. 22, 1922. Among his later books are: *Problems of Life* (1900); *The Rights of Man* (1901); *Henry Ward Beecher* (1903); *The Other Room* (1904); *The Great Companion* (1904, 1905); *Christian Ministry* (1905); *Personality and God* (1905); *Industrial Problems* (1905); *The Home Builder* (1908); *The Temple* (1909); *The Spirit of Democracy* (1910); *My Four Anchors* (1911); *America in the Making* (1911); *Letters to Unknown Friends* (1913); *Reminiscences* (1915); *The Twentieth Century Crusade* (1918); and *What Christianity Means to Me* (1921).

[Sup.] RAYMOND W. ALBRIGHT.

ABDICATION: Canon law uses preferably the term renunciation, that is, resignation from an ecclesiastical dignity. No resignation, even for legitimate motives, becomes effective until it is formally accepted by the proper authority. Thus bishops and archbishops may abdicate in the hands of the pope with the latter's consent. A decree of Pope Boniface VIII, confirming the abdication of his predecessor Celestine V, states that a pope may freely resign. It should normally belong to the Sacred College to acknowledge such a resignation, as it pertains to that body to elect a successor to the pope. According to the Code of Canon Law, however, the acquiescence of the cardinals, or of anyone else, is not necessary for making the pope's resignation effective. Church history records a few clear instances of papal abdications, such as those of Benedict IX, 1044; Gregory VI, 1046; Celestine V, 1294; Gregory XII, 1415. Pope Pius VII, 1800–1823, is said to have prepared an act of abdication, to take effect in case he would have been forcibly deprived of his liberty by Napoleon I. GEORGES A. BARROIS.

ABGAR: Syriac manuscripts are extant. There exist also Armenian and Coptic translations and two independent Greek versions which are shorter than the Syriac. This supports the suspicion that the original contains long interpolations.

The time of Uchama's reign is not certain. Lawlor and Oulton, e.g., date it A.D. 13–50 (Eusebius, *Ecclesiastical History*, II, 57).

Portraits which are now exhibited in Rome and Genoa are claimed to be the original "Holy Face of Eddessa."

BIBLIOGRAPHY: A. Buffa, *La légende d'Abgar et les origines de l'église*, 1893; E. von Dobschuetz, *Christusbilder* (1899), pp. 102 ff., 158 ff.; J. B. Aufhauser, *Antike Jesuszeugnisse* (1913), pp. 17 ff.; I. O. de Urbina, *Le origini del cristianesimo in Edessa* (*Gregorianum*, 14, 1934), pp. 82 ff.

[Sup.] DANIEL JOHANNES THERON.

ABJURATION: A public renunciation of unlawful allegiance and erroneous belief, which canon law demands for the admission into the Roman Catholic Church of persons over fourteen years of age, who have been baptized in schismatic churches, Protestantism, or sects, and prior to the reconciliation of such Roman Catholics as have become apostates from the faith, heretics, schismatics, or members of secret societies such as Free Masonry. The abjuration is to be made in presence of the bishop having jurisdiction or of his delegate, and of at least two witnesses. [Sup.] GEORGES A. BARROIS.

ABOMINATION OF DESOLATION: An enigmatic phrase in Christ's discourse regarding his Parousia (Matt. 24:15; Mark 13:14; compare the Greek version of Dan. 9:27, 11:31, 12:11, and I Maccabees 1:54). Of many suggested interpretations the most likely finds the reference to the desecrating invasion by Roman armies in Jerusalem and even in the temple area (A.D. 70). This warning of the "desolating abomination" is frequently held to look forward also to the final conflict between Christ and Antichrist prior to the triumphant establishment of the kingdom of God.

BIBLIOGRAPHY: For the meaning of the phrase in Daniel, see *Encycl. Biblica*, Vol. II, pp. 2148–2150; G. F. Moore, *Judaism*, I, 367, note 6; and, for the New Testament usage, especially Strack-Billerbeck, *Kommentar*, Vol. I, pp. 945, 951, and Adolf Schlatter, *Der Evangelist Matthaeus*, pp. 702 ff.

BRUCE M. METZGER.

ABORTION: The premature delivery of a foetus before the twenty-six weeks of gestation needed to give it viability. Plato and Aristotle approved this ancient practice; Hippocrates forbade it; and the Stoics generally condemned it on ethical grounds. It is not mentioned in the Bible. From the beginning, the Christian church has denounced it, usually on the premise that after conception there is an intra-uterine "life" and "person" at stake with all human rights and integrity. Roman Catholic moralists still hold this view; Protestants have no uniform opinion on the matter. Modern civil law usually attributes "human being" only after the child has left the womb. Medical science has somewhat abated the dangers to health in abortion, but the ethical objections still remain and must be decided upon the basis of validated presuppositions as to when both life and personality come into being. Abortion is commonly practised in over-populated lands such as Japan, as a method of birth control, even by Christians (except Roman Catholics). "Therapeutic" abortion is generally accepted (except by Roman Catholics); but, as a birth control or eugenical device, it is, in most nations, a statutory crime.

BIBLIOGRAPHY: E. Westermarck, *The Origin and Development of Moral Ideas*, 2 vols., 1912–17; A. A. Tardieu, *Étude medico-legal sur l'avortement*, 1904; A. O'Malley, *The Ethics of Medical Homicide and Mutilation*, 1919.

JOSEPH FLETCHER.

ABRAHAM. See PATRIARCHS, OLD TESTAMENT.

ABRAHAM'S BOSOM: The picturesque designation of the future state of bliss of the righteous (Luke 16:22, 23). The expression (which occurs also, although quite infrequently, in the Talmud) is taken from the ancient custom of reclining at table, so that the head of the guest leaned back upon the bosom and lap of his neighbor (cf. John 13:23). To recline upon Abraham's bosom, therefore, signified enjoying the highest honor in paradise.

BIBLIOGRAPHY: Paul Haupt, "Abraham's Bosom," *American Journal of Philology*, Vol. 42 (1921), pp. 162–167; Israel Abrahams, *Studies in Pharisaism and the Gospels*, 2nd series (1924), pp. 202–203.

BRUCE M. METZGER.

ABSALON (AXEL):
BIBLIOGRAPHY: Hans T. Olrik, *Absalon*, 2 vols., 1908–9.
[Sup.]

ABSOLUTE: The Absolute was the supreme metaphysical conception in post-Kantian idealism. Hegel gave it its classical expression and subsequent absolutists were essentially his disciples. The school flourished in England and America in the last third of the nineteenth century and the first quarter of the twentieth, F. H. Bradley being its greatest English-speaking representative.

A clue to the conception may be found in the idea of spatial position. We define the position of one object by its relation to another; but that defines only its *relative* position. If we could give an exhaustive organized account of the universe and of this thing in it, we should have assigned it its *absolute* position, but only in the course of assigning everything else its absolute position too. The absolute position of anything is a function of the whole system of positions, and this obviously cannot be stated.

The philosophy of the Absolute may be said to generalize this discussion of position. Everything we say about anything is said relatively and locates it in a system. Only the statement of the whole system could be an absolute statement. Moreover, all systems, whether of positions, causes, quantities, or anything else are relative to one another. For example, no system of positions is a system of bare positions: a position is the position of an event, determined in respect of quantity, quality, and so forth. So there is no absolute statement except the statement of the system of all systems, and that cannot be stated in its infinite detail. But philosophy can examine its general structure, determine how many overlapping mutually relative universal systems go to make it up, and show in what order they fit together. The structure of structures in the universal system was called by Hegel the Absolute Idea.

A pluralistic realist might assent to much of this and still decry its metaphysical importance. For him distinct things, such as our bodily selves, are known by direct acquaintance as having distinct existence. The question what it would be like to be able to give absolute descriptions of them is of secondary concern. But the absolutist thinks differently. As an idealist he knows no substance more solid than truth. If nothing but the whole of truth is wholly true, then nothing but the whole of substance is wholly substantial. The stuff of absolute statement *is* reality. So the metaphysical issue for him is the place of partial facts or truths in the Absolute of fact or truth, not the relation of finite beings to the infinite being.

The absolute unity of fact or truth is not, as such, the God of Christians. Theology is, according to Hegel, a mythical presentation of the Absolute Idea. Would-be Christian Hegelians had several courses open to them. They could argue that the mythical view of the Absolute was humanly necessary, and no less adequate than the philosophical. They could argue that, on grounds of strict philosophical reason, it was necessary to personify the Absolute. They could abandon the equation between God and the Absolute and equate God-and-his-creatures with the Absolute. None of these positions, however, promised solid comfort.

AUSTIN FARRER.

ABSOLUTENESS OF CHRISTIANITY: The affirmation of the Christian faith is that God has given full and final revelation of himself in Jesus Christ. This is implicit in the doctrine of the deity of Christ. "God, who at sundry times and in divers manners spake in time past unto the fathers by the prophets, hath in these last days spoken unto us by his Son" (Heb. 1:1–2a). The eternal Son, who is the Second Person of the Trinity, has become man and is the Revealer of God in the context of our earthly life. If Christ be fully God, it follows that there cannot be a revelation which goes beyond him. Paul writes to the Galatian converts that the gospel which he had received was not man-made but God-given and that its terms cannot be altered (Gal. 1:1–12).

But the belief in the absoluteness of Christianity does not mean that Christians attribute finality to any of the human systems in which men have sought to express for themselves the meaning of the light of the knowledge of the glory of God which they have seen in Jesus Christ. These systems partake of the frailty and the error which is characteristic of all things human. And the full meaning of Christian truth is seen only as that truth is related to the contemporary questions which agitate the church and the world. Christian thinkers must constantly seek to understand more perfectly the revelation which they have received and to state in each generation the relevancy of divine truth to the actual human situation which men confront in their time.

Acceptance of the absoluteness of Christianity inevitably affects the attitudes of Christians towards the non-Christian faiths. We do not need to brand as false all that is taught by other religions because we believe that Christianity gives us the full and final revelation of the character of God and of his will for man. Christianity may come as the fulfilment of truth that has already been disclosed in part in other religions. But Christian thinkers cannot be content with the statement that Jesus Christ is one of many roads that lead to God. They cannot agree that the various ways of approaching God are all equally valid. Christians must continue to hold that "there is one God, and one mediator between God and men, the man Christ Jesus; who gave himself a ransom for all" (I Tim. 2:5–6). For this reason there must be at the heart of Christianity a certain intolerance of other religions as these faiths seek to prevent men from coming to the acknowledgment of God in Christ.

BIBLIOGRAPHY: Robert E. Speer, *The Finality of Jesus Christ;* Emil Brunner, *The Mediator.*

HOLMES ROLSTON.

ABYSSINIA. See AFRICA.

ABYSSINIA AND THE ABYSSINIAN CHURCH. See ETHIOPIA, CHURCH OF.

ACADEMIES, EVANGELICAL: Paralleling comparable developments in other countries (see ECUMENICAL INSTITUTES; IONA COMMUNITY; KIRKRIDGE; SIGTUNA; PENDLE HILL), the academies in German Protestantism seek to help laymen and women recover the power of religion in life and the relevance of the church to community needs. Week-end or week-long conferences, away from distractions and led by pastors and specialists, annually reach over 12,-000 people. Teachers, lawyers, physicians, officials, newsmen, workers, employers, farmers, social workers, housewives, unemployed, artists, and other groups participate. A typical session includes informal Bible study, presentation of

professional or vocational problems peculiar to the group in attendance, transition to questions of faith, examination of Christianity in life situations.

Academies at Bad Boll (near Stuttgart) and Hermannsburg (near Hanover) pioneered in the work since 1945. Others, near Kassel, Frankfurt, Munich, and in Hamburg, Eisenach, and elsewhere, have joined in the common cause of relating the Christian faith to everyday work.

Co-operating in a common association, the academies maintain a "Study Fellowship" in which over 200 members of university faculties participate, investigating basic questions of theology in relation to natural law, the sciences, anthropology, and social problems. Church leaders support the academies as a means of overcoming lay passivity and spiritual illiteracy, and of restoring wholeness to the Christian life.

BIBLIOGRAPHY: Eberhard Mueller, "The Evangelical Academies in Germany," in *The Lutheran World Review,* Vol. II (1949), pp. 18–26; "Professional Life as a Christian Vocation," in *Papers of the Ecumenical Institute,* Vol. III (1948).

E. THEODORE BACHMANN.

ACARIE, SISTER MARIA OF THE HOLY INCARNATION: Known generally under the name of Madame Acarie; b. 1566 in Paris; d. 1618 at Pontoise. Her original name was Barbara Avrillot, being the daughter of the Lord of Avrillot, chancellor of Queen Margaret of Navarre. In 1572 she married the nobleman Pierre Acarie, and became one of the great figures in Parisian society. After her husband's death she became a Carmelite nun in Amiens, following the example of her three daughters. With the aid of Bérulle she introduced the Theresian Reformation, and in 1603 she founded the first convent in Paris. Brémond gives her credit for having exerted a powerful influence on the mystical movement of which Francis of Sales became the chief leader. In 1791 she was declared blessed. Her letters were published in two volumes by Richadeau, 1876.

BIBLIOGRAPHY: H. Brémond, *Hist. Litt. du sentiment relig. en France,* Vol. II, 1923; P. Bruno de Jésus Marie, *Madame Acarie, Épouse et mystique,* n.d.

MATHIAS GOOSSENS.

ACCESS: The privilege of admittance to, and of speech with, one of higher station. If the seeker must stand silent in an august presence, then, even though freely admitted, he does not have real access. In Eastern courts it was the custom to appoint an officer who should vouch for a new suppliant to the throne. This custom evidently affected several situations recounted in the Bible, as the introduction of David by a "young man" at the court of King Saul (I Sam. 16:14–21) and of Paul to the Jerusalem church by Barnabas (Acts 9:26–29).

Paul three times uses the word "access" (*prosagogē*). He applies the figure to the right of the Christian to approach God and enjoy fellowship with him because Christ has "introduced" him (Rom. 5:2; Eph. 2:18; 3:12). In the first passage, the access is to the grace that follows "justification." In the second, there is assurance that the same access to the Father has been provided for both Jew and Greek through Christ in the Spirit. In the third, the stress is on the bold confidence in which we may make use of our access to God, since Christ has opened the way. Here the note of fellowship with him in prayer is in the writer's thought. Thus "access" is delivered from any merely formal judicial right obtained through great effort, and is made to suggest warmth and welcome before the throne of grace. This may have been what moved Tyndale to translate *prosagogē* as "an open way in."

In the background of Paul's thought is the memory of the temple and the symbolism of the priest's entrance into the presence of God. The elaborate ritual of atonement that is developed in the book of Leviticus culminates in the high priest only being admitted to the "holy place" once a year (Lev., Chap. 16). It is this restriction that fires the imagination of the author of Hebrews to contrast the free access of Christ (Heb. 10:19–23). Because Jesus has entered, not a temple made with hands, but heaven itself; because he comes, not with the blood of beasts, but with his own blood; he is able to bring with him all whom he has redeemed, and bring them, not into a mere symbol of God's existence, but into his living presence. Here again the high notes of joy and fellowship are sounded. Similarly, the author of I Peter writes of Christ's purpose, "that he might bring us to God" (I Pet. 3·18), and the Fourth Gospel recalls that Jesus had admonished his inner circle, "I am the way . . . no one comes to the Father, but by me" (John 14:6). The New Testament makes it clear that we can never enter God's presence in our own right, but that we always need Christ to present us.

In the Roman Catholic and Anglican churches the term has attained a technical meaning. "Prayers of access" are offered in connection with the serving of the Eucharist, the Anglican custom being to make these prayers just before the prayer of consecration of the elements.

See also SOTERIOLOGY.   JULIAN PRICE LOVE.

ACCREDITING ASSOCIATION OF BIBLE INSTITUTES AND BIBLE COLLEGES. See BIBLE INSTITUTES AND COLLEGES.

ACKERMANN AUS BOEHMEN, DER (The Farmer of Bohemia): An anonymous German piece of poetry intended to teach proper religious values to young people, composed about the year 1400 in an early humanistic style. It consists largely in a colloquy in which God, death,

and the farmer participate, and it is generally ascribed to John of Saaz. The farmer has recently lost his wife through death, for which reason he is greatly concerned about the question as to what caused her demise. This work is of a high literary quality, which is reflected in the fact that fourteen manuscript copies are extant, besides seventeen printed editions dating from the fifteenth and sixteenth centuries.

BIBLIOGRAPHY: A. Bernt and K. Burdach in 1917 issued a critical edition with commentary. There is also a modern version in the *Inselbuecherei*, No. 198, n.d. See also K. Burdach, *Vom Mittelalter zur Reformation*, III, 2, 1. Haelfte: *Der Ackermann aus Boehmen und seine Zeit*, 1926.

         MATHIAS GOOSSENS.

ACOLYTE. See ORDERS, MINOR.

ACOSMISM: A term applied to metaphysical theories which assert (1) that the world known by ordinary experience or science is not real, but is illusory; or (2) that there is no world distinct from God. In sense (2), acosmism is virtually synonymous with pantheism, and, indeed, the two terms are equated by some authorities.

The term is derived from the Greek *a* ("not") and *kosmos* ("order" or "world"). However, although an acosmic theory denies that there is an order or world, this denial is not to be understood as implying that, despite the appearance of order, there is chaos instead. Rather, it is to be understood as implying that the experienced world, however orderly or well organized it is, has, relative to "ultimate reality" or "true Being," the status of an illusion, appearance, or manifestation merely.

W. Windelband (*A History of Philosophy* [1926], p. 38) asserts that the theory of Parmenides is an acosmism in sense (1). Parmenides maintained that the individuality, heterogeneity, and change characteristic of things in the perceived world "are deception and seeming"; strictly speaking, all there "is" is unitary, homogeneous, and unchangeable Being. It would seem that any theory that distinguishes between appearance and reality, and then ascribes a superior status ontologically and as an object of knowledge to the latter, would be an instance of acosmism in sense (1). The theories of Plato and Plotinus would be two examples.

Spinoza's theory as expounded in his *Ethics* has been described as an acosmism in sense (2). According to Spinoza, the idea of God is the idea of substance; there can be but one substance; and God and the world (Nature) are identical. Of the infinite attributes of Substance, Nature, or God, we know only two, thought and extension.

See also PHILOSOPHY.   VINCENT TOMAS.

ACOSTA, JOSÉ DE: His *Historia natural y moral de las Indias,* which in 1940 was published anew in Mexico City, has become a model of Spanish didactic prose, because of its elegant style. The book was often published, and was translated into many European languages. For Peru it is an important ethnological and historical source. His *De procuranda Indorum salute libri sex* (1588) is of great value as being the first theoretical work about missions.

BIBLIOGRAPHY: Sommervogel, *Bibliothèque de la Compagnie de Jesus*, Vol. I, 31–38; Vol. VIII, 1568–69; the latest and excellent biography is L. Lopetegui, *El Padre José de Acosta S.J. y las Misones*, 1942.

[Sup.] MATHIAS GOOSSENS.

ACTA APOSTOLICAE SEDIS, ACTA SANCTAE SEDIS: Collections of papal enactments, issued in Rome periodically. The first collection, under the title *Acta Sanctae Sedis,* was due to the initiative of a secular priest, Pietro Avanzini, who edited the first volume in 1865. The *Acta* became an official publication of the Holy See by decision of Pope Pius X, May 23, 1904. The title was changed into *Acta Apostolicae Sedis,* beginning January, 1909. The new collection lists the pontifical documents in the following order: personal acts of the pope; acts of the Roman Congregations, of the Pontifical Biblical Commission and of the Tribunals; appointments of persons to ecclesiastical charges and honors.   GEORGES A. BARROIS.

ACTA MARTYRUM, ACTA SANCTORUM: Delehaye has classified the acts of martyrs in three groups. The earliest consists of historical acts which simply give facts about the martyrdoms; later we find panegyric passions which honor the martyrs on their festal days and edify believers, and epic passions, in which there is an added element of romance. The earliest group was transmitted in three ways: (1) encyclical letters (Gallican martyrs, Polycarp); (2) trial reports (Justin, Scillitans); and (3) little treatises (Perpetua). All these were historical records, but they were also intended to have teaching value (Eusebius, *H. E.* v. praef. 1).

The most significant factor in the creation of these acts was the fact of martyrdom; the martyrs were the greatest of witnesses (*martyres*), and their example could inspire endurance in others. They do not seem to be closely related to the passion narrative in the gospels (Polycarp is a partial exception) or to stories of martyrs for philosophy (but cf. Benz). The non-Christian martyrs under Nero, about whom stories were told by opponents of the emperor (cf. Pliny, *Ep.* v. 5. 3), provide a partial parallel, as do the "heathen martyr-acts" of Alexandrians in the first and second centuries (cf. H. A. Musurillo, *The Acts of the Pagan Martyrs,* 1954). The fourth book of Maccabees, a rhetorical encomium of the seven Jewish martyrs, may not have been written before the second century, and it is more philosophical than most

of the martyr-acts. We must conclude that the literary form was essentially the creation of the circumstances (cf. Musurillo, p. 262).

Grégoire's arguments for dating Polycarp's martyrdom in 177 have been rejected by most scholars, and his acts remain the earliest complete narrative we possess.

If we include among Acta Sanctorum all biographies of Christian saints, we shall have to begin with the apocryphal acts of the apostles and the *Life of Cyprian* composed not long after his death, as well as the *Life of Antony* by Athanasius. In general, the hagiographical literature includes a strong emphasis on the miraculous, closely related to folk lore (cf. Loomis). It is also inextricably mixed with the history of the cultus of saints, as W. Telfer has shown in his study of Gregory Thaumaturgus. On the other hand, H. Usener wrongly identified the Christian Pelagia with Aphrodite Pelagia. The legends of the saints usually, though not invariably, deal with what the ancients called "divine men," not with gods.

BIBLIOGRAPHY: H. Usener, *Legenden der Pelagia,* 1879; H. Delehaye, *Les légendes hagiographiques,* 3d ed., 1927; *Les passions des martyrs et les genres littéraires,* 1921; W. Telfer in *Harvard Theological Review,* XXIX (1936), 225–344; C. G. Loomis, *White Magic,* 1948; H. Grégoire in *Analecta Bollandiana,* LXIX (1951), 1–38 (this journal is invaluable); E. Benz, *Der gekreuzigte Gerechte bei Plato, im Neuen Testament und in der alten Kirche,* 1950; further bibliography in B. Altaner, *Patrologie* (2d ed., 1950), 182–93.

[Sup.] ROBERT M. GRANT.

ACTS OF PAUL. See APOCRYPHA, NEW TESTAMENT.

ACTS OF THE APOSTLES: The Book of Acts is our one independent history of the apostolic age. Apart from possible written sources, much briefer in scope, it was the first such history; all later accounts obviously use it as their basic source.

I. Author and Date: With rare exceptions (e.g., Clark), scholars agree that Luke and Acts come from the same author; indeed, as the prefaces to the two books show, they form two parts of one account of the origins of Christianity. The literary preface shows definite literary consciousness, and suggests that from publication the author's name was attached to his work. This gives strong support to the unvarying tradition that Luke wrote Luke-Acts. The high probability that Luke wrote the travel diary used in the "we" passages (16:10–17; 20:5–15; 21:1–18; 27:1–28:16), and the linguistic evidence that the author of this diary also wrote the complete work, confirm Lucan authorship.

The main objection to this conclusion is the contention that though Luke was a companion of Paul, Acts does not reflect Paul's thought nor state correctly Paul's relations with the church at Jerusalem. The Gentile Luke may not have grasped the depths of Paul's thought, but he did not write as a partisan of Paul; he was a spokesman for the church. The alleged differences concerning Paul's relations with Jerusalem are more serious. They come to a head in the comparison of Gal. 2 with Acts 11 and 15. In particular, why does not Paul mention the decree of Acts 15:29 in Galatians (and in I Cor. 8–10)? One may identify the conference of Gal. 2:1–10 with the visit of Acts 11:30, but more likely it is the one in Acts 15. In the latter case, the decree of Acts 15:29 may be considered a later decision of the Jerusalem church, wrongly connected with the conference by Luke; or if passed by the council of Acts 15, Paul may have considered it a voluntary working arrangement that was no longer binding on him once the Judaizers had broken it by demanding that all Gentile Christians must be circumcised. The difficulty does not exclude Lucan authorship.

To date Acts about A.D. 60 and consider it a defense document for use in Paul's trial at Rome involves too early a date for Luke and Mark. A date A.D. 80 to 90 seems most likely. It is improbable that Luke used Josephus and so wrote after A.D. 95. To date Luke-Acts A.D. 150, and regard it as an answer to Marcion (J. Knox), seems impossible.

II. Written Sources? Did Luke use written sources, apart from his travel diary? Such sources, had they existed, would have given him needed help in describing the earliest years of the church. That one Aramaic document covering chs. 1:1–15:35 (Torrey, Sahlin, *et al.*) lies behind Acts is highly improbable; the parts of this section vary greatly in the degree to which they reflect Semitic language. That chs. 2–5 contain two parallel accounts of the same events (Harnack) is unlikely. Possibly a document telling how Hellenistic Christianity developed and spread (6:1–8:4; 11:19–30; 12:25 ff.) was at Luke's disposal. However, it seems more likely that chs. 1–15 rest not on written sources but on various units and lines of tradition, some bearing clear marks of original Aramaic setting. Thus study of the process and form of oral tradition is needed. The "speeches," which bear the marks of Luke's style and are only brief summaries of what was said on important occasions, probably come mainly from tradition which Luke gave its present form. They are not literal reports nor mere inventions but summaries of typical apostolic preaching. Ch. 10:34–43 represents well the common pattern. Chs. 14:15–17 and 17:22–31, which diverge most from it, may show how Paul sought a point of contact, but do not show what he regularly preached as the Gospel.

III. The Original Text: Clark contends that the "Western" text of Acts is the original form, which the Alexandrian text has shortened. Most scholars, however, agree that the Alexandrian or neutral text, though not invariably preferable, more nearly approaches the original work of Luke. Blass's theory that Luke made both of these versions of Acts no longer appears plausible.

IV. The Value of Acts: Luke writes the story of the apostolic age after the bitterness of early conflicts has passed. He writes to inform Christians, to answer questions of officials (Theophilus?) and inquirers, and to show that his faith is true Judaism and is politically nonrevolutionary. His work is essentially trustworthy. From personal experience and from acquaintance with Paul and his companions he knows the latter part of his story. From good sources of tradition he has learned, not the complete details, but the important stages of the development of the earliest church. The opening chapters of Acts, it is increasingly recognized, reflect very early Christian thinking. As Dodd has shown, the speeches are a trustworthy source of the basic message of the apostolic leaders. The book contains historical difficulties and does not answer all questions, but it gives the valuable basic information necessary to understand the apostolic age and the epistles it produced.

BIBLIOGRAPHY: A. Harnack, *The Date of the Acts and of the Synoptic Gospels*, 1911; E. Norden, *Agnostos Theos*, 1913; C. C. Torrey, *The Composition and Date of Acts*, 1916; A. Loisy, *Les Actes des Apotres*, 1920; F. J. Foakes Jackson and K. Lake, *The Beginnings of Christianity; Part I: The Acts of the Apostles*, 5 vols., 1920–33; M. Goguel, *Introduction au Nouveau Testament; Tome III: Le Livre des Actes*, 1922; M. Dibelius, "Stilkritisches zur Apostelgeschichte," in *EUCHARISTERION*, 1923; H. J. Cadbury, *The Making of Luke-Acts*, 1927; E. J. Goodspeed, *New Solutions of New Testament Problems*, 1927; A. C. Clark, *The Acts of the Apostles*, 1933; C. H. Dodd, *The Apostolic Preaching and its Developments*, 1937; H. Sahlin, *Der Messias und das Gottesvolk*, 1945; W. L. Knox, *The Acts of the Apostles*, 1948; F. F. Bruce, *The Acts of the Apostles*, 1951.

[Sup. to LUKE, II.] FLOYD V. FILSON.

ADALBERT: Dutch saint, d. 741. Feast day is June 25. He was a companion of St. Willibrord and preached especially in the region around Haarlem known as Kennemerland. About the year 1000 Ekbert, the archbishop of Trier, ordered to have the *Vita et miracula Sancti Adalberti* properly composed. Above his grave about the middle of the tenth century the abbey of Egmond was built, which in 1572 was destroyed by the Geux. Since 1935 there has been once more a monastic settlement at Egmond, which in 1950 was made an abbey.

BIBLIOGRAPHY: ASB Iun. VII (1867), 82–95; A. Beekman, *Tien eeuwen Egmond*, 1950.

[Sup.] MATHIAS GOOSSENS.

ADALBOLD: Introduced the monastic reform of Poppo of Stavelot in the Low Countries, from the Abbey of St. Paul. He became bishop of Utrecht while remaining a Benedictine monk.

BIBLIOGRAPHY: *Nederl. Biographisch Woordenboek*, Vol. 4; Manitius, *Gesch. des lateinischen Literatur des Mittelalters*, Vol. 2 (1923), pp. 743 ff.

[Sup.]

ADAM. See Patriarchs, Old Testament.

ADAM, KARL: Roman Catholic, b. at Purs-ruck, Bavaria (the Upper Palatinate), Oct. 22, 1876. He studied at the Philosophical and Theological Seminary in Regensburg and at the University of Munich, from which he received his doctorate in 1904. In 1900 he was ordained to the priesthood. From 1908 he was a privat-docent and from 1915 a professor at the University of Munich. In 1917 he moved to the chair of moral theology at the University of Strasbourg. In 1919 he went to the University of Tuebingen, where he was lecturing till 1950. Now he is emeritus professor of dogmatic the-ology at Tuebingen. He is most widely known as the author of *The Spirit of Catholicism; Christ Our Brother;* and *The Son of God,* trans-lated into two dozen languages, from the original German, *Das Wesen des Katholizismus* (11th ed., 1948); *Christus unser Bruder* (8th ed., 1950); *Jesus Christus* (8th ed., 1949). Two of the earlier works are: *Tertullian's Conception of the Church* (1907), and *The Eucharistic Teaching of St. Augustine* (1908). In January, 1934, he had difficulties with the Nazi government for his opposition to the so-called "German re-ligion." In 1947 he gave three lectures on the problem of a union between Catholics and Protestants, published under the title *Una Sancta* (1948) with several translations (*One and Holy,* 1951).

ADAM OF BREMEN: The fourth book of his *Gesta* is entitled, *Descriptio insularum aquilonis.* It gives a description of the land and peoples of Denmark, Sweden, Norway, and Russia, besides voyages of the Northmen (Vi-kings) to Greenland and North America.

Bibliography: New ed. of the *Gesta* by B. Schmeidler, 1926; P. Kohlmann, *Untersuchungen zur Hamburger Kirchengeschichte Adams,* 1908; B. Schmeidler, *Kritische Untersuchungen zur Hamb. Kirchengeschichte des Adams,* 1918.

[Sup.] Mathias Goossens.

ADAM OF MARSH (DE MARISCO): B. at the end of the twelfth century, in the bishopric of Bath; d. 1258. After having served as pastor at Wearmouth for three years, he became one of the first Franciscans in England; was a pupil and friend of Robert Grosseteste. According to Roger Bacon he was one of the most learned men of his time. Posterity named him Doctor Illustratus. After 1247 he became magister regens at Oxford University, and became in-volved in all important affairs of his order and his country. This can be seen in his 247 letters published by J. S. Brewers in *Monumenta Fran-ciscana,* Vol. 1, pp. 77–489 (*Rerum Britanicorum Mediaevi Scriptores*) (1858). With Count Simon of Montfort and Robert Grossesteste he formed a triumvirate to defend the rights of the people against their king, introducing demo-cratic principles in England. He wrote several exegetical works which have not yet been pub-lished.

Bibliography: *Dict. of Writers of the XIIIth Cent.,* 1936; A. G. Little, *The Franciscan School at Oxford in the XIIIth Cent.,* in *Archivum Franc. Historicum,* Vol. 19 (1926), 831–837.

Mathias Goossens.

ADAM OF SAINT VICTOR: His date of birth and of death are unknown. But it is re-garded certain that he was a canon regular at St. Victor in Paris, where he died in 1177 or 1192. About his writings little is known. If Misset and Auby have correctly ascribed to him the Graduale of St. Victor as it appeared at the end of the thirteenth century, he must be con-sidered one of the greatest poets of the Middle Ages.

Bibliography: Migne, *P.L.,* Vol. 196; E. Misset and P. Auby, *Mélanges de musicologie critique: Les proses d'Adam de Saint Victor,* text and music, preceded by a critical study, 1900; *Analecta hymnica,* Vol. 54 (1915) and Vol. 55 (1922).

[Sup.] Mathias Goossens.

ADAM THE SCOTCHMAN: B. *ca.* 1130 on the border of England and Scotland, hence was called also Adamus Anglicus, or Adam the Englishman, while the names Premonstratensian and Carthusian were added because he was first a monk in one order and then in the other. The name Adam of Dryburgh was given him because in 1180 he became abbot of the Norbert Abbey of Dryburgh, where he had previously been a canon. But he must not be confused with Adam of Whithorn, as has been done by the followers of M. du Pré (in his *Annales breves Ordinis Praemonstratensis,* Amiens, 1645) and of G. Ghiselbertus (in his *Eximii D. Magistri Adami Praemonstratensis opera,* Antwerp, 1659). At the age of twenty-five he was consecrated Premonstratensian priest, and in 1188 he joined the Carthusian monastery at Witham, whose abbot was also called Adam, hence the confu-sion mentioned above. He remained at Witham until his death in 1212.

His writings are of considerable value for our understanding of twelfth century monasticism, especially the conception of prayer. From his earlier period date *De ordine et habitu atque professione canonicorum ordinis praemonstraten-sis,* which deals with the superior qualities of his order, the clothes worn, and the formula of pro-fession; *De tripartito tabernaculo,* which dis-cusses the tabernacle of Moses and the biblical texts that refer to it, besides a practical appli-cation for daily lives among Christians; and *De triplici genere contemplationis,* which dis-tinguishes three kinds of meditation, in accord-ance with the three aspects of God which hu-man beings may view: God as the incompre-hensible source of all power and good things, far surpassing any creatures, and as the judge of evil men, and as the kind father of those who repent of their sins and accept redemption.

His most important work, which is also one of the most valuable of all medieval writings, *De quatripartito exercitio cellae*, dates from his Carthusian period, *ca.* 1190. It was often ascribed to Guigo II, as by Migne, *P.L.*, Vol. 153. A. Wilmart has proved that Adam wrote it. The first part deals with the religious life of the Carthusians: humility, mortification, imitation of Christ, peaceful seclusion, and renunciation of worldly things. The second part treats of the four exercises which like the four streams of Paradise fructify life: religious literature, meditation, prayer and manual labor.

BIBLIOGRAPHY: The four works named above are in Migne, *P.L.*, Vols. 153 and 198; E. M. Thomson, *A History of the Somerset Carthusians*, 1895; idem, *The Carthusian Order in England*, 1930; idem, "A Fragment of a Witham Charterhouse Chronicle and Adam of Dryburgh, Premonstratesian and Carthusian of Witham," in *Bulletin of the John Rylands Library*, Vol. 16 (1932), pp. 482–506; W. de Gray-Birch, *Sermones Fratris Adae Ordinis Praemonstratenis: Twenty-eight Discourses of Adam Scotus of Withorn Hitherto Unpublished*, 1901; F. Petit, *Ad viros religiosos: Quatorze sermons d'Adam Scot*, 1934; F. Petit, *La spiritualité des Prémontrés aux XIIe siècle*, 1947.

[Sup.] MATHIAS GOOSSENS.

ADDAMS, JANE: Settlement worker; b. Sept. 6, 1860, at Cedarville, Ill.; d. May 21, 1935. She studied at Rockford (Ill.) College (A.B., 1881) and spent the following two years in Europe. With Ellen Gates Starr she opened the social settlement of Hull House in Chicago in 1889. She later became head resident and is best remembered for her unselfish social work in the streets and alleys in this neighborhood. For three years she was president of the National Conference on Charities and Corrections; president of the Woman's International League for Peace. In 1931 she was awarded the $5,000 Bryn Mawr Achievement Award and in the same year shared with Nicholas Murray Butler the Nobel Peace Prize. She was the author of: *Democracy and Social Ethics* (1902); *Newer Ideals of Peace* (1907); *The Spirit of Youth and the City Streets* (1909); *Twenty Years at Hull House* (1910); *A New Conscience and an Ancient Evil* (1911); *The Long Road of Women's Memory* (1916); *Peace and Bread in Time of War* (1922); *The Second Twenty Years at Hull House* (1930); and *The Excellent Becomes the Permanent* (1932).

BIBLIOGRAPHY: J. W. Linn, *Jane Addams*, 1935; W. E. Wise, *Jane Addams of Hull House*, 1935; L. H. de K. Bowen, *Open Windows*, 1946.

RAYMOND W. ALBRIGHT.

ADDISON, JAMES THAYER: Episcopalian; b. at Fitchburg, Mass., March 21, 1887; d. Feb. 13, 1953. He studied at Groton, Harvard (A.B., 1909; S.T.M., 1917) and the Episcopal Theological School (B.D., 1913). Ordained in 1913, he was minister in charge at St. Mark's, Nowata, and St. Paul's, Claremore, Okla. (1913–15). He taught history of religion and missions in the Episcopal Theological School, Cambridge, Mass. (1915–40) and was acting master at Kirkland House, Harvard (1932–33). He taught in St. John's University, Shanghai, China (1909–10). During his incumbency at the Episcopal Theological School he taught at intervals in Japan, China, Egypt and Lebanon. He was a chaplain in World War I. He was vice-president of the National Council of the Protestant Episcopal Church and director of the Overseas Department (1940–47). He was a trustee of the American University, Cairo, Egypt. He wrote: *The Story of the First Gas Regiment* (1919); *Chinese Ancestor Worship* (1925); *Our Father's Business* (1927); *Francis Xavier* (1929); *François Coillard* (1929); *Our Expanding Church* (1930; 1951); *Religion in India* (1930); *Life Beyond Death in the Beliefs of Mankind* (1932; in French, 1936; in Hungarian, 1936); *The Way of Christ* (1934; in Chinese, 1939; reissued 1949); *The Medieval Missionary* (1936); *The Lord's Prayer* (1938; also in Chinese); *World of Islam* (1938); *Variety in the Devotional Life* (1939); *Parables of Our Lord* (1940); *Why Missions* (1940); *The Christian Approach to the Moslem* (1940); *The Episcopal Church in the United States* (1951); *War, Peace and the Christian Mind* (1953); and contributed to *The Church's Teaching*, Vol. VI.   RAYMOND W. ALBRIGHT.

ADELBERT OF HAMBURG-BREMEN: His biographer was Adam of Bremen.

BIBLIOGRAPHY: J. Beinlich, *Die Persoenlichkeit Erzbisch. Adelb. v. Bremen in der Darstellung seiner Biogr. Adam*, 1918.   [Sup.]

ADELBERT OF PRAGUE: He was a Benedictine monk in the monastery of St. Alexis in Rome. In 993, after his return to Prague, he founded in its vicinity the Benedictine monastery of Brewnow. Adelbert was martyred at Tenkitten. In the Roman Catholic Church he is revered as a saint.

BIBLIOGRAPHY: B. Bretholz, *Gesch. Boehmens und Maehrens*, 1912.

[SUP.] MATHIAS GOOSSENS.

ADELHEID OF VILICH: B. *ca.* 970; d. 1017. daughter of St. Megengos, count of Gelre and Zutphen, and St. Gerberga. Educated at the convent of St. Ursula in Cologne. Her parents founded the convent at Vilich for canons regular, of which Adelheid became abbess. She changed the convent into a Benedictine convent, with approval of Pope Gregory V (bull of May 24, 996). Gerberga was buried there in 995, Megengos in 998. She was revered as a saint, beloved by the many poor and outcasts who were aided by her. It was reported that she had been responsible for the miraculous flowing of a well named Adelheids-Quelle at Puetzchen, which is still a source of attraction for pilgrims. She also founded a hospital that is still in existence, as well as schools. Emperor Henry II appointed her abbess of St. Maria in Capitolis in Cologne (Feb. 26, 1003). She died there (Feb. 3, 1017). St. Neribert, archbishop of Cologne, declared her a saint. She was buried at Vilich.

BIBLIOGRAPHY: "Vita Adelheidis, auct. Bertha," in *Mon. Germ. Scriptores*, XV, 755–63; *Acta SS.* Febr. I, 714–721, 3rd ed. 721–727; Albert Groeseken, *Die hl. Adelheid von Vilich und ihre Familie*, 1937.

WILLIBRORD LAMPEN.

ADLER, ALFRED: Jewish convert to Christianity; b. Vienna, Feb. 7, 1870; d. Aberdeen, Scotland, May 28, 1937. Because of his own ill health he studied medicine, at Vienna University (M.D., 1895), specializing first in internal medicine, later turning to neurology and psychiatry. A study of children with congenital somatic difficulties, *Studie ueber Minderwertigkeit von Organen* (1907), indicated that inferiority feelings are compensated for by achieving superiority at some point. Adult personality, therefore, is to be explained in terms of early inferiority. In 1907, he joined Sigmund Freud (*q.v.*) and adopted, disseminated, and contributed to the latter's views. Adler was a loyal and ardent admirer of Freud, defending him vigorously. Whereas Jung (*q.v.*) finally broke with Freud in 1911, Adler continued for another year before the relationship was severed because of disagreement over Freud's theory that the libido is the force behind neurosis. Adler held instead that a sort of will to power or "guiding fiction," when excessive and unreal, precipitates neurosis. He rejected Freud's theory that infantile wishes affect behavior. Whereas Freud emphasized the influence of the past, Adler stressed that an individual's future (i.e., potentialities and expectations) was the determining factor. He believed that man is restrained by organic inferiorities, but compensations are encountered in his community life. Man's personality is the product of his relationship to society, work, and love. By co-operating, the *ego* can meet basic needs (*id*) within communal activity. The meaning given to experiences is self-determined. Behavior patterns are acquired through identification and not by inheritance. Prestige and superiority are purely compensatory and do not solve real problems. Serving the community is the healthy and mature way out.

After World War I, Adler's views spread rapidly to England and the United States. His concept of the "inferiority complex" was widely, if not always accurately, known and used. He founded the International Society for Individual Psychology; was made an Honorary Citizen of Vienna (1930); lectured at Vienna University and at Columbia University, and became a professor at Long Island College of Medicine (1934). Like Freud he was a prolific writer.

His publications include: *The Practice and Theory of Individual Psychology; The Neurotic Constitution; Understanding Human Nature; The Science of Living; Problems of Neurosis* (1930); *The Case of Miss R; The Case of Mrs. A; The Education of Children; The Patterns of Life;* and *What Life Should Mean to You* (1931).   ROLLIN JONATHAN FAIRBANKS.

ADLER, FELIX: D. April 24, 1933. He was professor of political and social ethics at Columbia University (1902–21). He gave regular Sunday discourses to the New York Society for Ethical Culture which he founded in 1876. During 1908–9 he was Roosevelt Exchange Professor in the University of Berlin. His additional publications include: *The World Crisis and Its Meaning* (1915); *An Ethical Philosophy of Life* (1918); and *The Reconstruction of the Spiritual Ideal* (Hibbert Lectures, 1923).

[Sup.] RAYMOND W. ALBRIGHT.

ADLER, MORTIMER: B. in New York, N. Y., Dec. 28, 1902. He studied at Columbia University (Ph.D., 1928) and was an instructor in psychology there (1923–29). After two years as assistant director of the People's Institute of New York City (1927–29) he taught philosophy of law at the University of Chicago (1930–45). From 1945 he has been associate editor of "Great Books of the Western World" and headed the staff which produced the *Syntopicon*, a cross-reference index to the great ideas of the Western world. He was editor of *The Great Ideas*. Among his books are: *Dialectic* (1927); *Crime Law and Social Science* (with Jerome Michael, 1933); *Diagrammatics* (with Maude Phelps Hutchins, 1935); *Art and Prudence* (1937); *What Man Has Made of Man* (1938); *St. Thomas and the Gentiles* (1938); *How to Read a Book* (1940); *Problems for Thomists; The Problems of Species* (1940); *A Dialectic of Morals* (1941); and *How to Think about War and Peace* (1944).   RAYMOND W. ALBRIGHT.

AD LIMINA APOSTOLORUM: Roman Catholic bishops are under obligation of visiting the pope every five years "at the threshold of the Apostles," i.e., in the Vatican, in order to report on the state of their respective dioceses.

ADOPTION. See SOTERIOLOGY.

ADRIAN VI: His name originally was Adrianus Florisze. In the German-Dutch church in Rome (Santa Maria dell'Anima) his sorrowful figure is depicted, his tired head resting upon his arm, and the following words are inscribed to express his sentiments of regret for having failed to reform the papacy: "Alas, how important is it in which time the activities of the best are deployed!"

BIBLIOGRAPHY: G. Pasolini, *Adriano VI*, 1913; E. Hocks, *Der letzte deutsche Papst Adrian VI*, 1939, Dutch translation, 1942.

[Sup.] ALBERT HYMA.

ADULT WORK: This program is a comparatively recent development. In the past the conventional form has been that of adult Bible classes, but a program of adult education comparable with that for children and young people has not been achieved. As director of adult work for the International Council of Religious Education (1930–48), Harry C. Munro laid the necessary foundations. Recent developments include the formation of programs for young adults, the organization of laymen among various communions, and a renewed emphasis upon the place of the family in Christian education. Some communities have witnessed a similar movement in secular education.

J. DONALD BUTLER.

ADVENTISTS: Nearly all Adventists are premillenarians; that is, they believe that Christ will return before the millennial reign of Rev. 20:1-6. The creed involves much more than belief in the second advent, however. It is bound up with a total cosmology or world view based upon more or less literal interpretations of apocalyptic literature, especially Daniel and Revelation. It involves the principle of struggle between demonic and divine cosmic powers, the ultimate triumph of the latter, and the inauguration of an eternal state of bliss for the faithful. There is distrust of the ameliorative influence of social process and a belief that human ills are to be corrected by direct divine intervention and cosmic cataclysm.

These general principles are almost universal among Adventists. They are elaborated in considerable detail by various groups, and there are differences of opinion on these details. Among them are the "rapture" or resurrection of the saints to meet the returning Lord in the "upper air," the appearance and depredations of Antichrist, the millennial reign of Christ, the wars of Armageddon, the destruction of the present order, and the final consummation of all things.

Adventism in one form or another dates from the earliest Christian times and by no means originated in the Millerite movement near the middle of the nineteenth century. Neither is it confined to, or even most influential in, the religious bodies which sprang from that movement and bear the Adventist name. It is a leading tenet of so-called fundamentalism (q.v.), is widespread in all the groups which incline to the conservative position in theology, and is found in some of the largest denominations.

Many, perhaps most, of the small sects believe that the return of the Lord is imminent. This is prominent in the Mormons (q.v.), the International Church of the Foursquare Gospel (q.v.), and the Jehovah's Witnesses (q.v.). In fact, the last named body is more aggressive in its promulgation than any of the churches which carry the Adventist title.

The preaching of William Miller (q.v., Vol. VII) produced numerous Adventist bodies, among which considerable reshifting, splits, and consolidations have occurred. The disagreements concerned the inspiration of Mrs. Ellen G. White, the state of the dead, the observance of the seventh day as the Sabbath, the scriptural name of the church, and similar matters. The original Millerite group adopted the name of American Millennial Association in 1858 and subsequently became the Evangelical Adventists; it disappeared from the scene around 1920.

The Adventist denominations in the United States, with the approximate number of members and congregations in 1951, are as follows:

Church	Members	Congregations
Seventh-Day Adventists ...	210,000	2,500
Advent Christian Church...	30,000	400
Church of God (Adventist)	5,000	45
Church of God (Oregon, Ill.)	5,000	80
Church of God (Seventh Day)	1,200	40
Primitive Advent Christian Church	500	12
Life and Advent Union....	300	6

Only the Seventh-Day Adventists (q.v.) have experienced much growth.

The Church of God (Seventh Day) represents a schism from the Church of God (Adventist), or Advent Christians, led by Elder A. N. Dugger in 1933 over matters of church government. Its headquarters are at Salem, W. Va. Its twelve apostles, seventy evangelists, and seven elders are selected by lot. It is pentecostal in nature, observes the seventh day as the Sabbath, practices foot washing, and prohibits the eating of pork.

The Church of God (Oregon, Ill.) is one of several groups that regard "Church of God" as the only scriptural name, and it is census practice to identify them by adding the name of the founder or the location of the headquarters. It was organized as the Church of God in Jesus Christ at Philadelphia in 1888 and represented an amalgamation of the Church of the Blessed Hope, Brethren of the Abrahamic Faith, Restitution Church, Church of God, Age-to-Come Adventists, and other scattered congregations. It observes Sunday and adheres to the customary premillenarian doctrine. (See CHURCH [CHURCHES] OF GOD.

The Primitive Advent Christian Church was formed by a merger of several congregations of the Advent Christians in West Virginia. Its headquarters are at Sissonville, W. Va.

BIBLIOGRAPHY: Basic documents are the writings of William Miller and Mrs. Ellen G. White. See also M. Ellsworth Olsen, *A History of the Origin and Progress of the Seventh-Day Adventists*, 1926; Elmer T. Clark, *The Small Sects in America*, rev. ed., 1949.

[Sup.] ELMER T. CLARK.

ADVENTISTS, SEVENTH-DAY. See SEVENTH-DAY ADVENTISTS.

ADVOCATE: One who assists, and often pleads, the cause of another; an intercessor. This is a judicial term. Its only occurrence in the English Bible is in I John 2:1, where it is the translation of *parakletos*. Christ is here called our "paraclete," our advocate. Since the believer is accused of having sinned, Christ pleads for him before the Father. His pleading is acceptable, both because he is righteous and has made expiation for sins. It is at this point that John's soteriology (*q.v.*) comes closest to that of Paul. (Cf. Rom. 3:25, and see C. H. Dodd, in *The Moffatt Commentary* or the Epistles of John, p. 24 f.)

The word *parakletos* occurs also in the Gospel of John (14:16, 26; 15:26; 16:7), where its reference is obviously to the Holy Spirit (*q.v.*). In these passages the legal term "advocate" hardly does justice to the richness of the thought. In most English versions the term "comforter" is used, but in the Revised Standard Version the more general word, "counselor"; for the Spirit not only consoles, but encourages to action. In addition to any pleading that may be necessary for disciples, he gives them needed guidance (14:16), he testifies in their hearts to the truth (14:26), he brings Jesus back to their memories (15:26), and he convinces the world that it is sinful, that the righteousness of God is possible, and that judgment is real (16:7-11).

But although the use of this term is limited, the idea of the timely advocate is common in the Bible. The Synoptics recall Jesus' promise that when his disciples are brought before councils for his sake, they are not to worry, since they will be directed in what they ought to say (Mark 13:11, and parallels). Throughout the Bible the intercessor is a frequent figure. Jonathan intercedes for David before his father (I Sam. 19:1-7); David himself intercedes with God for his child (II Sam. 12:15-17). The Psalms are full of intercessory prayers. Paul urges intercession on his readers (I Thess. 5:25; I Tim. 2:1). Christ is said to be our intercessor, the one who "happens in on our behalf" (Rom. 8:27, 34; 11:2; Heb. 7:25). And the Holy Spirit is said to intercede with God in prayer for believers who do not know how to pray (Rom. 8:26).

In the Latin church the term "advocate" became associated with ecclesiastical rights. The eleventh Council of Carthage (407) appointed certain officers as "advocati ecclesiae," one of their duties being to defend the rights of the church before the state. During the Middle Ages, the office tended to become hereditary, although always the nomination of the church had to be approved by the civil power. It is easy to understand how the office readily lent itself to abuse and even to extortion. In the Roman Catholic Church, whenever there is a move to canonize a new saint, there is always appointed an "advocatus diaboli," a devil's advocate, who is to list all possible objections to the proposed beatification. He is answered in turn by an "advocatus dei."

JULIAN PRICE LOVE.

AEQUIPROBABILISM. See PROBABILISM, in Vol. IX.

AESTHETIC, THE, AND RELIGION: The connection between aesthetic and religious experience has been variously conceived. There have been times when religious tradition has treated the cultivation of art and devotion to beauty as alien, if not antithetical, to the spirit and practice of religion. Contrariwise, worship, especially as culminating in the vision of God, has been presented as being pre-eminently an aesthetic experience.

There has probably been no time at which either of these attitudes toward the aesthetic has had its whole way. It is true that writers of the early Christian church—and to some extent medievalism in general—tended to show a kind of "moral resistance" to art. Sculpture, as suggesting idolatry, the theater as representing sensuality, poetry and music as appealing to the passions—all of these were distrusted and condemned. When sculpture and music were enlisted in the service of spiritual ends, they were in large measure treated frankly as instruments or symbols rather than for their own sakes as fine arts. Even mysticism (*q.v.*), which often described experiencing God as an experiencing of beauty, invested beauty with a non-sensuous, other-worldly meaning.

On the other hand, doctrines of beauty were developed, on an essentially philosophical basis, by such writers as Augustine, Thomas Aquinas, and Bonaventura. Beauty was defined generally by these writers as a pleasing quality, arising from proportion of parts and agreeableness of color, which could be found not only in architecture and painting, but in man and in the whole spectacle of the universe. The order and harmony found in physical and human nature reflect God's love of order and of beauty and hence may be used as starting points or stepping stones to the understanding of divine nature. So Francis of Assisi, though he eschewed natural beauty as such, yet found in nature, in animals and all growing things, the symbols and materials which vivified his religious teaching.

Speaking broadly, there is a clear, indeed a striking resemblance between the common characterizations of aesthetic experience on the one hand and of religious experience on the other. Each is described, for example, in terms of self-surrender. The spectator of art loses himself in, abandons himself to the quality and movement of the aesthetic object. In the same way the religious person seeks to merge his will with the object of his devotion. So, too, each experience is described in terms of joyousness, contentment, the sense of desires consummated and brought to rest. The object of worship, like the object of beauty, is judged perfect, giving unity and completion to the scattered demands of our natures.

Finally, and more broadly still, the aesthetic attitude may be said to confront life as a whole in a way that is akin to the religious attitude. Each tends to transform existence as found, either by taking it up into the imagination or by constructively altering it in terms of a vision of things possible. In either case there is involved an emotional participation in the world which gives to life fresh significance and dramatic import.

See also AESTHETICS; ART, ECCLESIASTICAL.

LUCIUS GARVIN.

AESTHETICS: The systematic study of art and beauty, with particular emphasis on questions concerning the creation, experience, and criticism of works of art. Aesthetic investigations may be (1) technical or scientific—analyzing the structure and composition of art objects or the psychology of creation and appreciation. Or they may be (2) philosophical—inquiring into the nature and function of art and examining the meaning of such concepts as beauty, ugliness, sublimity, and so on.

Since the development of experimental aesthetics hardly lends itself to brief summary, the present discussion will be limited to a survey of some of the basic questions in the philosophy (*q.v.*) of art. What is the nature of the activity that makes a man an artist? How do we judge whether his activity has been successful? The first question has to do with the definition of art; the second, with the standards by which we criticize art.

I. The Nature of Art: In general most of the prevailing theories of artistic activity deny that the artist seeks only to imitate nature. Artists, it is held, are creative in a way that goes beyond mere faithful reproduction. Though they may work from "original" models, they put something of themselves—their sense of values, their feelings, moods, or aspirations—into the created object. Works of art, therefore, may be said to express or objectify the insights

and reactions of their composers—to reflect their ways of seeing things. John Dewey in particular has emphasized the relation of the experience of the artist (and of the spectator) to the art work. Art, he says, *is* experience, but experience organized, according to the artist's perspective, so as to be more meaningfully coherent, more vividly expressive than it is under the conditions of practical life.

But if it is agreed that art expresses something of the artist's inner self, the question *what* inner self is expressed remains a point of major dispute among opposing schools. Some theorists have related art activity to the unconscious needs of the ego. Art is explained as objectifying volitions, as a mode of relief from the tensions of life. Art becomes a world of illusion (in "play" theories of art) or of fantasy (in "psychoanalytic" theories of art) in which the artist is enabled imaginatively to express and fulfill his underlying desires.

Others deny that the demands of our natures which get expressed in art need be basically unconscious. We may not wholly comprehend our specific impulses to create, but they can be brought to the surface and clarified by the art-creative activity. Whether what is thus clarified is *emotion* or *vision* is a question on which aestheticians have been sharply divided. Writers of the "emotionalist" school, like Leo Tolstoy, interpret art as the language of the emotions. That the emotions conveyed should be pleasing rather than displeasing is usually held to be unimportant, the sincerity of the artist's self-revelation being all that is required to define artistic purpose. On the other hand, emotionalist theories do ordinarily define beauty in terms of the pleasantness of the feeling response aroused.

Opposed to the emotivist interpretation of art are those writers who regard their creative process as being the rendering of a vision—an apprehension of pattern, order, relationship, or whatever may be the specific qualities of the individual artistic intuition. The Italian philosopher Croce (*q.v.*) has been particularly influential in promoting the view that artistic experience is intuitive knowledge, imaginative vision, the physical art object being only a kind of "memorandum" of an expressive activity that has taken place wholly in the mind. The tendency to regard the artist as concerned only with the individual qualities of things has given rise to "formal" and "abstractionist" conceptions of art. These emphasize formal values— the values that lie in design or pattern, in rhythm and contrast, in unity and balance, quite apart from any subject matter which the art work may represent. What count are the features given directly to aesthetic vision, treated without reference to their social meaning or their practical or scientific connections.

Beauty is characteristically interpreted, on such views, not so much in terms of pleasure given in contemplation, as in terms of vividness, evocativeness, felt unity or harmony, or—in Clive Bell's terms—"significant form."

The treatment of art as separated from life and society provoked a strong reaction on the part of those, like Dewey, who saw this in the guise of an esoteric escape movement. Out of this protest came the formulation of the "contextualist" position, with its contention that the work of art cannot be separated, in the experience either of creator or contemplator, from the social context.

II. The Criticism of Art: Such differences of opinion as to the nature and purpose of artistic creation imply, of course, correspondingly different positions as to proper standards for judging the products created. Obviously it is possible to judge art works from the standpoint of the social or religious values they express or engender. It is commonly contended, however, that such judgments cannot correctly be considered *aesthetic* criticism. Theories of aesthetic criticism fall into two groups, those that may be called "objective," and those that may be called "subjective" or "relative." Objective theories of criticism describe beauty or aesthetic excellence as an inherent quality of the art work, as belonging to the object quite independently of the experience of the contemplator. Such theories, while they give a basis for standards that are not merely relative to the taste or preferences of the individual critic, have been widely regarded as untenable on the ground that they tend to treat beauty as ineffable and, therefore, a mystery. More generally accepted are the relativist theories which define beauty in terms of the kind of response evoked in the spectator by the object contemplated. Theories of this sort deny that there is such a thing as "good taste" in any absolute sense and hold that critical judgment is relative to the cultural inheritance and the psychological peculiarities of the individual. This leaves for criticism the task of analyzing the particular features of works of art which experience indicates may most fully satisfy the aesthetic capacities of a given audience.

See also AESTHETIC, THE, AND RELIGION.

BIBLIOGRAPHY: J. Dewey, *Art as Experience*, 1934; L. W. Flaccus, *The Spirit and Substance of Art*, 1941; K. E. Gilbert, and H. Kuhn, *A History of Esthetics*, 1939; T. M. Greene, *The Arts and the Art of Criticism*, 1940; E. J. Mather, *Concerning Beauty*, 1935; D. H. Parker, *The Principles of Aesthetics*, 1946; M. M. Rader, *A Modern Book of Aesthetics*, 1952 (an anthology of recent writings, with an excellent bibliography).

LUCIUS GARVIN.

AETERNI PATRIS: 1. Apostolic letters issued by Pope Pius IX on June 29, 1868, to summon the Vatican Council.

2. An encyclical of Pope Leo XIII, issued on August 4, 1879, for promoting the philosophy of Thomas Aquinas. While rejecting those systems which oppose reason to faith, it states that true philosophy ought to promote the acceptance of Christian revelation, to help in building up theology as a science, and to defend the doctrine of the church against rationalism and subjectivism. It advocates the revival of Thomistic philosophy, as the best suited to achieve this threefold aim. The notable development of so-called Neo-Thomism (*q.v.*) in modern Roman Catholic institutions of learning can be traced back to this encyclical.

Original text in *Leonis XIII Pontificis Maximi Acta,* Rome, 1881–1905, I, pp. 255–284. English translation in J. J. Wynne, *The Great Encyclical Letters of Pope Leo XIII* (1903), pp. 34–57.   GEORGES A. BARROIS.

AFFIRMATION, AN: Often called the "Auburn Affirmation," was published in January, 1924, with 150, and republished in May, 1924, with 1,274 signatures of Presbyterian ministers. The General Assembly of the Presbyterian Church in the U.S.A. in 1923, following similar action by the Assemblies of 1910 and 1916, had declared each of five designated doctrines to be "an essential doctrine." The Affirmation stated that each of these five Christian truths might, in accordance with historic Presbyterian liberties, be legitimately stated in other ways also. The Affirmation also declared the General Assembly's action to be unconstitutional because it in effect amended the church's Constitution without the required concurrent action by the church's presbyteries; and the General Assembly of 1927 later affirmed this principle. See also LIBERALISM.

BIBLIOGRAPHY: L. A. Loetscher, *The Broadening Church; A Study of Theological Issues in the Presbyterian Church Since 1869,* 1954; R. H. Nichols, "Fundamentalism in the Presbyterian Church," *Journal of Religion,* V (1925), 14–36.

LEFFERTS A. LOETSCHER.

AFGHANISTAN: A country of Central Asia bordering the USSR on the north, Pakistan on the east and south and Iran on the west. The area is about 250,000 square miles; the country is about 600 miles from east to west and beyond this a narrow strip running to the northeast between Soviet Russian territory and Pakistan. The distance diagonally across the country from the northeastern frontier of the USSR on the Oxus River to the southwestern extremity is about 700 miles. The population is estimated at about 12,000,000. The land is a high plateau crossed by mountain ranges and the climate something like that of the Southwest in New Mexico or Arizona.

There are no railroads; passable motor roads connect the capital city of Kabul (elevation about 6,000 feet, population 200,000) with the Khyber Pass and run to the various provincial capitals.

The Morrison-Knudson Construction Company was engaged by the government to construct dams and hydroelectric plants which bring irrigation to about half a million acres of land.

The government is a constitutional monarchy. The king bears the title of *Shah;* there is a parliament or *Mejlis* with a senate of 50 members appointed by the king and 171 elected members in the lower house.

The government university founded in 1932 in Kabul embraces a number of schools including law, medicine, dentistry, engineering, normal training, arts and sciences. New buildings on a fine campus outside the city will unite the rather loosely connected schools in a more unified institution of higher learning. There are secondary schools in the provincial capitals, and in Kabul for both boys and girls. Nearly four hundred primary schools are operated by the Department of Education.

The religion of the country is Islam (*q.v.*), predominantly Sunni, though there may be about 1,000,000 Shi'a Moslems in the country. The women are tightly veiled in public. Afghanistan is the one nation which has consistently refused to allow Christian missions to operate in the country, consequently it is practically the only land without a Christian church. Many American construction workers have been in the country of late years and the government employs a number of American and European teachers in the higher schools. There are in Kabul large embassy staffs representing the various nations.

BIBLIOGRAPHY: Akram, *Bibliographie Analytique de l'Afghanis..an*, 1947; Sykes, . *History of Afghanistan*, 1940; Byron, *The Road to Oxiana*, 193'. ; Fraser-Tytler, *Afghanistan*, 1950.

                                        J. CHRISTY WILSON.

AFRICA: I. Political Changes: Africa was brought into the consideration of the rest of the world as a result of its strategic importance, both geographic and economic, during two world wars.

African soldiers during World War II fought under the flags of European nations outside of Africa. These men returned to their villages with a very different outlook. The old certainty of tribal life and of a fixed status in society was gone. Fear and superstition were not so easy to be rid of. European overlords coldly ignored or savagely hit back, according to the degree of insecurity and apprehension felt.

Western civilization has disrupted the agricultural pattern of life in Africa. Leisure time is more plentiful in an industrial day. Instead of being filled by ritual and ceremony, leisure time hangs heavily on youthful minds and spirits. The domination of the African people by Europeans is fast reaching a conclusion.

Communist agents have played up the ad-vantage of racial equality offered by the Kremlin as compared with the discriminatory practices of the Western nations, which are thought of as Christian nations. An increased interest in Islam (*q.v.*) is evident throughout West Africa as a result of the activities of the Hausa traders from North Africa. In the Gold Coast Legislative Assembly, as a result of the elections in 1951, 75 seats out of 84 were in 1952 held by Africans, while 8 Africans served on an Executive Council of 11 members. In Nigeria the first House of Representatives met in 1951.

North Africa has been in political turmoil, with Islam as a common bond among the Arab states, particularly since the establishment of Israel (*q.v.*) as an independent country. This recrudescence of Islam has had its effect on religious freedom throughout the area. Libya is already "free." Italian Somaliland will be in 1961. Tunisia is struggling for independence, as is Morocco.

The report of the Conference for Closer Association in Central Africa, published in 1951, has had far-reaching results. Widespread recognition of the economic value of the plan put forward for the federation of Northern and Southern Rhodesia and Nyasaland has been voiced. Generally speaking, European opinion favors federation, while Africans, nervous for their rights, stand with oppressive solidarity against it.

In South Africa, race relations (*q.v.*) deteriorated to a dangerous degree after World War II. The attitude of the churches in this connection is watched with great care by the African population. On the racial issue there was a wide gulf dividing the Dutch Reformed Churches from those represented in the Christian Council of South Africa.

II. Religion and Missions: In the development of missions in Africa one finds the usual three stages, childhood, adolescence, adulthood. The child is completely dependent. The adolescent begins to sense his own strength, questioning his parents and all society. In adulthood the negative attitude is outgrown and responsibility is demonstrated.

In many parts of Africa the church is still in the childhood stage, with dependence on missionary societies from abroad for funds and leadership. However, an increasingly large section of the church is to be found in the adolescent stage, wanting more to say about the direction of its own affairs. Fortunately, some of the churches in Africa have arrived at the adult stage, fully responsible for their own government and financial support. This does not mean that missionaries are no longer desired. They serve as friends and counselors, as aids in the training of national leaders, and in higher schools of various kinds.

The constant pressure for autonomy and independence and the demand for educational opportunities at every level brought home to the churches and missions in Africa their responsibility for reaching the best and most constructive use, in terms of Christian life, of new freedoms as they were won.

The support of Christian Councils (which now exist in nearly every country of Africa) was given priority by the Protestant mission boards of the West as part of the co-operative approach that was being made.

The great increase in literacy resulted in attention to the preparation of Christian literature for Africa. A significant conference composed of theological leaders from the area resulted in the drawing up of lists covering not only the more familiar fields of doctrine, biblical commentary, and devotional work, but material taken from African church history and Christian classics, which will strengthen the African consciousness of historical ties with a world church.

As a result of the swift advance of Islam throughout Central and Western Africa, emphasis was placed on a more adequate preparation for the study of Islam, both for purposes of evangelism and in recognition of the fact that over large areas of Africa it is no longer solely a matter of winning men and women from a pagan background to the Christian faith but of competing with the Moslem missions from North Africa. The fact that these Hausa traders are not professional missionaries, but give their witness while carrying on business, was at last recognized.

African nationalism was reflected in the criticism of white missionaries. In Nigeria the Anglican Church created new dioceses in Ibadan and the Niger delta, both with native African bishops.

The centralizing of training facilities, with three main colleges for East Africa, Nigeria, and the Gold Coast respectively, is being sought.

Roman Catholic missions were increasingly active throughout Africa. In Nigeria alone there are five Roman Catholic high schools and teacher training colleges as against five similar institutions operated by the Anglican Mission. At the primary level the great bulk of education remained in Protestant hands, but this was not the case at the higher levels of education.

III. **North Africa:** The Arab countries in North Africa are members of the Near East Christian Council, since the predominant religion in Egypt, Algiers, Morocco, Tunis, and the Sudan is Islam. Egypt provided the most nationalistic setting within the Arab League countries. The recent literacy campaign in Egypt resulted in an increased interest in Bible reading. Progress was made in co-operation with the Coptic Church, which as a national indige-

nous church of the country is in a position to provide a more familiar environment for converts than has generally been the case.

The problem of the industrialized proletariat was a disturbing one throughout North Africa. The breaking up of tribal life through the settling of individuals and families in towns accentuated the need for social centers with adequate youth programs.

IV. **West Africa:** Co-operative planning is the pattern that is followed by the missions in West Africa. In eastern Nigeria the Anglican, Methodist, and Presbyterian churches built a United Mission Training Hospital with the assistance of a generous government grant. Though staffed at first by missionary doctors, the hospital follows a long-range plan for more advanced medical training, which will qualify an increasing number of Nigerians to take over responsibility.

At Dakar the Foyer Missionaire Protestante was inaugurated in 1951, providing a valuable means for maintaining contact with African Christians away from their tribal environment. In the Cameroons the reorganization of the Fédération des Missions Évangéliques provided for the representation of African churches. In the Congo five missionary societies joined forces in setting up a medical institute, which also provided a hospital and leprosy colony. The world-wide publicity given to the work of Albert Schweitzer (q.v.) resulted in greater interest in the work of all mission boards throughout Africa.

In the Portuguese African territories, both East and West, Portuguese missions were encouraged by the terms of Article 46 of the revised constitution of Portugal (q.v.), which permits the establishment of missions other than Roman Catholic and promises them equal legal recognition.

V. **East and Central Africa:** The increasing pressure on Christian educational institutions and the constant demand for their further extension are more clearly felt each year. Emphasis has been laid on the need for African Christian parents to encourage their children to become teachers. In Uganda the Church Missionary Society was asked and felt obliged to take over the supervision of primary schools and assigned a full-time worker to that purpose. In the field of technical and vocational training plans were made for a technical college in Tanganyika to serve East Africa as a whole. A domestic science course for girls was included. The institution will be fully interracial.

Evangelism continues to be the major emphasis, and the response is a gratifying evidence of the spiritual vitality of the African church. Christian literature contributed largely to evangelism in East Africa, and the Scriptures were distributed widely, thanks to the United Society for Christian Literature operating in Northern Rhodesia.

VI. South Africa: The church in South Africa is faced with one of the most complicated problems to be found anywhere in the world. Racial tension, accentuated by the problems of the industrial revolution, made the difference in point of view between the Dutch Reformed Churches and the Christian Council of South Africa a matter of deep regret. The Christian Council of South Africa in 1951 officially repudiated the Dutch Reformed statement that the African is incapable of voting "with responsibility to God."

The gold mine developments in the Orange Free State offered a challenge which was accepted by the Methodist, Paris, S.P.G., and Mission Suisse groups. The extension of Y.M.C.A.'s in the urban centers of Natal was encouraging. The Baptist Union of South Africa opened a theological college. New Anglican dioceses were formed in Basutoland. Above all is the problem of African delinquency in towns and cities without adequate housing or educational and recreational facilities. Human rights are a missionary as well as a political responsibility.

BIBLIOGRAPHY: On exploration and politics see L. Van der Post, *Venture to the Interior,* 1951; V. McKay, *Nationalism in British West Africa,* 1948; A. Paton, *South Africa Today,* 1951; N. Chukwumeka, *African Dependencies,* 1950; N. Tarsey, *Last Chance in Africa,* 1950. On missions see R. K. Orchard, *Africa Steps Out,* 1952; G. Sadler, *A Century in Nigeria,* 1950; B. Miller, *Twenty Stories from Africa,* 1951; E. W. Grant, *South Africa— What of the Church?* 1952; J. B. McCord and J Scott Douglas, *My Patients Were Zulus,* 1951; E. Ross. *African Heritage,* 1952; E. Horner, *Jungles Ahead,* 1952; L. C. Sayre, *African Safari,* 1952.

[Sup.] HERRICK BLACK YOUNG.

AFRICAN METHODIST EPISCOPAL CHURCH. See METHODISTS.

AFRICAN METHODIST EPISCOPAL ZION CHURCH. See METHODISTS.

AFRICAN ORTHODOX CHURCH: Organized in 1921 by George Alexander McGuire, until 1919 a clergyman of the Protestant Episcopal Church who believed that Negro Episcopalians should have a religious body of their own. Congregations, at first called Independent Episcopal, were organized. On Sept. 2, 1921, the first General Synod was convened in New York, the name African Orthodox Church was adopted, and McGuire was elected the first bishop. In doctrine, worship, and polity the body reflects the position of Anglo-Catholicism (q.v.) with some influence from Eastern Orthodoxy. It is sometimes classified as a body of Old Catholics (q.v.). There are congregations in the United States, Canada, Latin America, and the Union of South Africa, with 30 congregations and 6,021 members in the United States in 1951.

THEODORE G. TAPPERT.

AGAPE (LOVE): The verb *agapan,* "to love," occurs in the Greek language since the time of Homer. The noun, *agape,* "love" (q.v.), does not appear until the Septuagint (q.v.). In the Septuagint it has not yet acquired its distinctive Christian sense of a spontaneous, uncaused, self-giving love. It retains its older and more general usage of love of a man for a woman (Gen. 29:20), man for his neighbor (Lev. 19:18), man for God (Deut. 6:5), God for his people (cf. Isa. 63:9, where God's love is coupled with his pity).

In contrast to *eros* (q.v.), acquisitive love, *agape* "seeketh not her own things" (I Cor. 13:5). The Crucifixion of Christ is regarded as the supreme manifestation of God's love in that Christ died for helpless, sinful, unworthy man (Rom. 5:5–8). The *agape* concept of love is a new creation of the Christian faith.

While *agape* does not, in every instance, acquire its full New Testament meaning, its spontaneous uncaused character underlies most New Testament usage. *Agape* is due to the character of the lover, not to the merits of the beloved. In the New Testament, as in the Old, husbands still should love their wives, but to a new degree, as Christ loved the church and gave himself for it (Eph. 5:25 f.). A Christian should even love his enemies, for this is a requisite to being a son of God (Matt. 5:44).

In the Synoptic Gospels love is still a requirement made by the law: we are to love God with all our being and our neighbor as ourselves (Matt. 22:37, 39). But in Paul, love is a gift of the Holy Spirit (I Cor. 12:31–13:13). The New Testament emphasis is on love for our fellowman, with God supplying the gift, enabling the Christian to love. God's *agape* works through the Christian to others. In I John, only those who have been begotten of God have *agape*-love (I John 4:7–12). We are able to love because he first loved us (I John 4:19). The correct text for this verse is not "We love him" but "We love, because he first loved us." *Agape*-love is not native to man's soul; self-seeking, rather than self-giving, is characteristic of human nature until made new by a work of God.

The New Testament emphasis is not placed upon the first great command, but on the second (Matt. 22:37, 39 and parallels). The first command is quoted only here, but great emphasis is placed upon loving one's neighbor (Rom. 13:8, 9; Gal. 5:14; Jas. 2:8; etc.). This was apparently due to the fact that some "pious people" claimed to love God, but hated their brothers. This is morally impossible (I John 4:20). *Agape*-love is an essential part of Christian character; God bestows the capacity for this love.

In late ecclesiastical Greek, *agape* refers to the love feast, observed among Christians.

There is one example of this usage in the New Testament (Jude 12). It is unfortunate that this late meaning is still the one in general use today.

See also ETHICS.

BIBLIOGRAPHY: Walter Bauer, *Woerterbuch zum Neuen Testament*, 1937; Gerhard Kittel, *Theologisches Woerterbuch zum Neuen Testament*, 1933; Moulton and Geden, *Concordance to Greek Testament*, 1897; Anders Nygren, *Agape and Eros*, 1932; Paul Tillich, *Systematic Theology*, Vol. I, 1951.

WILLIAM DOUGLAS CHAMBERLAIN.

AGAPE (LOVE FEAST): Additional source material can be summarized as follows: The New Testament refers to a common meal in several places: Acts 2:42, 46; 6:1 f.; I Cor. 10:16 ff. The early writings: *Didache*, 9 and 11; *Didascalia Apostolorum* VIII; Ignatius; Ephesians 20; Romans 7; Smyrnaeans 8; Pliny, *Epistola* xcvi; *Martyrium Polycarpi* 18; Justin Martyr, *Apologia* 65-67; Celsus in Origen, *Contra Celsum* I.1; Minucius Felix, *Octavius* XXI.5; Lucian, *De morte Peregrini* 12; *Epistola ad Diognetum* 5; *Acta Pauli et Theclae* 25(?); Clement of Alexandria, *Paedagogos* II.1; *Stromateis* III.2; Tertullian, *Apologia* 39; *De jejuniis* 17; *De corona militis* 3; *Canones Hippolyti* 164–177; *Passio Jacobi et Mariana* (Ruinart, second edition, p. 228); Cyprian, *Epistola* LXII (LXIII), 16; *Didascalia* in *Verona Fragments* XXVI (Hauler, p. 38); Council of Laodicea in Phrygia, canon 28; Third Council of Carthage, canon 29 (30); Council of Gangra in Paphlagnia, canon 11; Chrysostom, *Homilia* 27 and 31; Augustine, *Contra Faustum manichaeum* XX.20; Socrates, *Historia ecclesiastica* 5.22; Sozomen, *Historia ecclesiastica* 7.19; Trullan Council, canon 74.

The traditional view combines a meal with the Eucharist, modeled after the Last Supper. This view was challenged long ago, e.g., by Anton Joseph Binterim (*Denkwuertigkeiten*, II,2, 1828). Adolf Juelicher (*Zur Geschichte der Abendmahlsfeier*, 1892) and Friedrich Spitta (*Die urchristlichen Traditionen ueber Ursprung und Sinn des Abendmahles*, 1893) launched the theory that the Eucharist grew out of the common meal called agape. John Fritzstephen Keating (*The Agape*, 1901) defended the traditional viewpoint and contended that abuses in the time of Paul were the earliest known reasons for the eventual separation of the agape and the Eucharist. He found the origin of the name agape in John 13:34. Johannes Hoffmann (*Das Abendmahl im Urchristentum*, 1903) thought that the Eucharist formed the sacramental part of a meal which was later separated from the common meal. Pierre Batiffol (*Etudes*, 1907) opposed Keating with the theory that the agape did not come into existence until the third century as an ecclesiastical assembly. Before that time it was not connected with the Eucharist except by way of abuse. In apostolic

and subapostolic times the word "agape" refers commonly to the Eucharist. Ephrem Baumgartner (*Eucharistic und Agape im Urchristentum*, 1909) concluded that the Eucharist was celebrated at midnight or early on Sunday mornings and that the agape was a separate meeting on Sunday evenings. Its origin is to be found in Jewish practices. R. Lee Cole (*Love-Feasts*, 1916) follows Arthur John Maclean (*Encyclopaedia of Religion and Ethics*, 1908) and regards both Jewish and pagan practices as the origin of the agape. The name agape, he advocates, came from the lakeside meal described in John 21. Burkard Frischkopf (*Die neuesten Eroerterungen ueber die Abendmahlsfrage*, 1921) holds rather closely to his Catholic forerunner Baumgartner, with a definite distinction between the agape and Eucharist. Henri Leclercq (*Catholic Encyclopedia*, 1907) saw a close connection between the agape and the funeral banquet. William Oscar Emil Oesterley (*The Jewish Background of the Christian Liturgy*, 1925) sees a connection between the Eucharist and agape from the earliest times and found the origin of the latter in the Jewish *Chabûrah*, a fellowship of friends, and in their celebration of a weekly meal immediately preceding the *Kiddûsh*. Hans Lietzmann (*Messe und Herrenmahl*, 1926) questions the influence of the Sabbath meal and the *Kiddûsh* and thinks that the *Chabûrah* alone offers ample explanation for the origin of the agape. Karl Voelker (*Mysterium und Agape*, 1927) argues that real evidence of the agape as a meal is not extant until the patristic period. Its origin is to be sought in Gnosticism. *Ca.* A.D. 160–200 the church adopted the agape to counteract Gnosticism with its own practices. August Arnold (*Der Ursprung des christlichen Abendmahls*, 1937) regarded the Eucharist and agape as originally identical (I Cor. 11:17 ff.), but saw evidence of an incipient separation in the *Didache*.

BIBLIOGRAPHY: F. E. Warren, *The Liturgy and Ritual of the Antenicene Church*, 1897; V. Ermoni, *L'Agape*, 1904; F. X. Funk, *Kirchengeschichtliche Abhandlungen*, 3, 1907; G. Wetter, *Altchristliche Liturgien*, 1921; W. Goossens, *Les origines de l'Eucharistie Sacrament et Sacrifice*, 1931.

[Sup.] DANIEL JOHANNES THERON.

AGAPEMONITES. See MESSIAHS, FALSE.

AGATHO: His system of dogmatics was accepted with joy at the Sixth General Church Council, 680–81. He defended the thesis that the bishops of Rome were infallible. He sent the Roman archicantor Johannes to England in order to extend there the use of the liturgy.
[Sup.]

AGED, CARE OF THE: The increase, since 1900, in the population of aged people brought to the fore concern for their welfare and social planning as never before in the history of the church. With changing living conditions and expanding human knowledge, new problems and new opportunities for service have arisen. Research on the aging population is pointing the way to more effective methods of prevention and treatment of mental and physical disabilities, and people are helped to be well and useful in advancing years.

In the United States, as elsewhere, government responsibility has a major part in maintenance plans, freeing many from accepting relief (see SOCIAL SECURITY), thus changing the emphasis in the work of the church from custodial and protective care to preventive aspects. Two programs provide a regular income to people at the age of sixty-five years—old age and survivors' insurance (based on earnings in jobs covered by law) and old-age assistance (based on need)—with a recognition of the right of the individual to be self-directing. These grants may be used by aged persons to maintain themselves in their own homes, private boarding places, or church institutions which meet required standards of care set by the state. This is an important step forward.

Present-day planning of the church is facing more realistically the need to give protection within old-age homes to those requiring it most of all, the chronic sick and infirm aged; other kinds of services are developed for those who can successfully live outside an institution. This has involved the wider use and stimulation of community resources in the way of parish activities for older people, counseling, profitable use of leisure time, health clinics. Homes for the aged, which meet only a small part of the need, have been integrated into this broader program for the general good.

Other social services of the church include home care of the aged, supervised foster home care (with the aid of visiting nurse, housekeeper, and friendly visitor), medical care, and daytime centers for the companionship and edification of lonely old people in the community. For those who want to be independent, but require some measure of care, there is group living in apartments, colonies of cottages, or other co-operative housing projects designed to meet the needs of older people. Group living for the aged is no longer an experiment, although the architectural phase is still in its infancy. There was active participation by church social workers (see SOCIAL WORK, CHURCH) in the first National Conference on Aging (1950) and the second International Gerontological Congress (1951). A three-year study of religious ministry to older people was conducted by the former Federal Council of the Churches of Christ in America (*q.v.*). Other Protestant agencies, including Presbyterians, Episcopalians, Methodists, and Lutherans, have taken leading

parts in the development of standards of service in old-age homes, including an adequate program of spiritual development, health care, work and play therapies, social services, infirmaries for the chronically ill with modern plant and equipment, and an extension of service into the community.

Religion has joined with industry, medicine, the press, education, and civic, health, welfare, and recreational departments in gearing itself, through co-operative planning and social action, to increase the services of the church to meet the requirements of the older population.

BIBLIOGRAPHY: George Lawton, *Aging Successfully*, 1946; N. W. Schock. *Bibliography of Gerontology and Geriatrics*, 1951; P. B. M ves and J. L. Cedarleaf, *Older People and the Church*, 1949.

HENRIETTA LUND.

AGLIPAYAN CHURCH. See PHILIPPINE ISLANDS.

AGNELIUS OF PISA: B. 1194; d. March 13, 1235. In 1215 he joined the companions of St. Francis, and in 1223 he was sent to England, where he introduced the Franciscan rule. He built a monastic school at Oxford, where Grosseteste taught the brothers. This is the main reason why the Franciscans had such close relations with the University of Oxford, where several learned Franciscan professors taught, as is well known.

BIBLIOGRAPHY: Th. Eccleston, *De adventu Fratrum Minorum in Angliam*, ed. in *Analecta Franciscana*, Vol. I (1885), pp. 217 ff.; C. Mariotti, *Il B. Agnello da Pisa*, 1895; A. Gemelli, *Il Francescanesimo*, 1942.

MATHIAS GOOSSENS.

AGRICOLA, RUDOLPH (RODOLPHUS): Dutch humanist, widely known as the Petrarch of Germany; b. at Baflo in the province of Groningen, the Netherlands, ca. 1444; d. at Heidelberg, 1485. He was first educated in the school attached to St. Martin's in the city of Groningen. At the age of thirteen he matriculated in the University of Erfurt, where he received the degree of A.B. After a short stay at the University of Cologne he removed to Louvain. Here at the local university he won the A.M. with highest honors (1465). Now followed several years of traveling in Italy. At Ferrara he learned Greek, and here he distinguished himself by delivering a brilliant lecture in classical Latin, such as had never been delivered before by northern "barbarians" in Italy. On his way home through Germany in 1479 he finished his masterpiece, *De inventione dialectica*, which replaced Aristotle's textbook in rhetoric at the University of Paris. For five years he received numerous flattering offers of positions, all of which he, the wandering humanist, declined, until in 1484 he accepted an invitation from Bishop Johannes of Dalberg to become "court humanist" at the University of

Heidelberg. Here he gave some far-famed lectures and took up the study of Hebrew, in order to grasp more fully than before the literature of the Old Testament. It was his aim to prepare a Latin translation of the Old Testament, but this task he could not complete, since death claimed him the next year.

His religious poetry and his lecture delivered before the higher clergy at the University of Heidelberg indicate his interest in religion. Moreover, the lecture he prepared for the bishop of Worms, delivered in Rome before Pope Innocent VIII, proves his familiarity with the Bible and the Christian faith. It would not be fair to him, though this has been done on several occasions by noted writers, to claim that he was devoid of true religious feeling, and that form meant much more to him than content. The lecture which the good bishop delivered in Rome attracted a great deal of attention. Twice it was published in Rome, and ascribed to Agricola. In 1511 the works of Agricola were published, and here it was stated by the learned editor that he had composed and delivered the lecture. Erasmus, who despised the teachers employed by the Brethren of the Common Life, and who thought Alexander Hegius rather mediocre, cherished the highest respect for Agricola. Melanchthon also recognized his genius. Great indeed was the fame of Agricola's admirable work, *De formando studio*. In 1539 the learned Dutch humanist, Alardus of Amsterdam, published his *Opera omnia* in two handsome volumes. In 1911 another Dutch admirer stated in his doctoral dissertation: "We could fill pages after pages with eulogies penned by Agricola's contemporaries and the next generations of humanists." He quoted only one, however, written by Hermolaus Barbarus, who noted that Agricola had succeeded in his task to make the German lands equal Italy in the field of classical languages.

BIBLIOGRAPHY: Rodolphus Agricola, *Opera omnia*, ed. Alardus of Amsterdam, 1539; H. E. J. M. van der Velden, *Rodolphus Agricola (Roelof Huusman)*, 1911; J. Lindeboom, *Het Bijbelsch humanisme in Nederland*, 1913.

ALBERT HYMA.

AGRICULTURAL MISSIONS, INC: Incorporated in 1933, Agricultural Missions has for its purpose the strengthening of the Christian mission to rural people by all appropriate means. The founders believed that world agriculture must be guided by Christian ethics in order effectively to relieve poverty and famine among the vast numbers of distressed rural people in the world.

The services include: (1) Literature on the improvement of village life, especially in lands where foreign missionaries serve. (2) Specialized training courses for agricultural and other rural missionaries. (3) Counsel and guidance in training for college and university students in preparation for service in agricultural missions. One of the secretaries visits agricultural colleges at regular intervals to confer with students in regard to agricultural missions and related technical fields. (4) A clearinghouse of appropriate services for missionaries, board executives, and other voluntary agencies. (5) Current survey of experience and progress of agricultural missions.

While Agricultural Missions, Inc., is an independent, nondenominational organization, it is related directly to the National Council of Churches of Christ (*q.v.*) through the Rural Missions Co-operating Committee of the Division of Foreign Missions. The committee, consisting of representatives from various denominational mission boards, was formed in 1934 in order that the Foreign Missions Conference of North America (*q.v.*) and its constituent boards might co-operate more closely with Agricultural Missions, Inc., and make effective use of its services. The secretaries of Agricultural Missions, Inc., also serve by appointment as secretaries of the Rural Missions Co-operating Committee.

See also EXPANSION OF CHRISTIANITY, IV.

IRA W. MOOMAW.

AI. See ARCHAEOLOGY, BIBLICAL.

AILRED: Canonized 1191, feast day January 12. His most important work, *Speculum caritatis* (Migne, *P.L.*, 195, col. 505–620), treats the high value of love to God in its different grades. As a complement to this work may be regarded his best known composition, which is still used and translated in our time: *De spirituali amicitia*; see Migne, *P.L.*, Vol. 195, col. 659–702, which deals with love for mankind. The chief source of the latter is Cicero's *De amicitia*.

BIBLIOGRAPHY: F. M. Powicke, *Aelred of Rievau and His Biographer Walter Daniel*, 1922; J. Dubois, *Aelred de Rievau, L'Amitié spiruuelle*, 1948; most of his works are in Migne, *P.L.*, Vol. 195; the *Regula sive institutio incluso̠rum* is listed in Migne under the name of St. Augustine, vol. 32; the *De Jesu puero* under the name of St. Bernard, Vol. 184.

[Sup.] MATHIAS GOOSSENS.

AINSLIE, PETER: Disciples of Christ; pastor and editor; b. June 3, 1867, at Dunnsville, Va.; d. Feb. 23, 1934. He attended Transylvania College (1886–89). After two years as temporary supply pastor in Newport News, Va., he became pastor of the Disciples of Christ congregation in Baltimore, Md. (1891–1934), where he soon erected a new building called the Christian Temple and also developed nine branch churches. He was greatly interested in the world peace movement and in Christian unity, founding and editing the *Christian Union Quarterly* (1911–34). In addition to his successful pastoral service he attended most of the major world conferences on peace and Christian unity and wrote as well the following books: *Religion in Daily Doings* (1903); *Studies in the Old Testament* (1907); *Among the Gospels and the Acts* (1908); *God and Me* (1908); *Brother and I* (1911); *The Unfinished Task of the Reformation* (1910); *Introduction to the Study of the Bible* (1910); *The Message of the Disciples for the Union of the Church* (1913); *Christ or Napoleon—Which?* (1915); *Working with God* (1917); *If Not a United Church—What?* (1920); *Christian Worship* (with H. C. Armstrong, 1923); *The Way of Prayer* (1924); *The Scandal of Christianity* (1929); and *Some Experiments in Living* (1933).

RAYMOND W. ALBRIGHT.

AKKAD, AKKADIANS. See ASSYRIA; BABYLONIA; HITTITES; MESOPOTAMIA.

ALAND, KURT: Lutheran; b. in Berlin March 28, 1915. He studied at Berlin and has taught church history and New Testament in the theological faculties at Halle and Berlin. In addition to editing several theological journals he has been editor-in-chief of the Commission on the Church Fathers of the Berlin Academy. He has also brought out new editions of F. Loofs, *Dogmengeschichte* (1951) and P. Feine, *Theologie des Neuen Testaments* (1951).　　　　RAYMOND W. ALBRIGHT.

ALANEN, YRJö JAAKKO EDVIN: Lutheran; b. Raisio, Finland, on Sept. 20, 1890. He has been professor of theological ethics at the University of Helsinki. He has written (all in the Finnish language) *Studies on the Doctrine of Atonement* (2 vols., 1932); *Christianity and Culture* (1933); *Conscience in Luther* (1933); *Fighters and Winners* (1938); *Faith and Humanity* (1942); *The Individual and Society* (1942); *The Guides of Our Nation* (1944); *Gustaf Johansson, a biography* (1947); *Christianity and Science* (1950); *The Nature and Aim of Theology* (1950); and, in English, *Revolution or Reformation* (1946).

RAYMOND W. ALBRIGHT.

À LASCO, JOHN. See LASCO, JOHANNES À.

ALBANIA: Of Thracian and Illyrian origin, the Albanians emerged as an independent nation in 1912, and this independence was renewed after World War I (1920). Among the 1,100,000 inhabitants, about 70 per cent are Moslems, 20 per cent Eastern Orthodox, and 10 per cent Roman Catholics.

The Eastern Orthodox, hitherto subject to the patriarch of Constantinople, established an independent Albanian Orthodox Church. The Greek metropolitan and his clergy were expelled. Albanian liturgy was introduced. A native Holy Synod was organized. This signi-

fied a nationalistic revolt against the Greek cultural predominance, maintained by the Constantinopolitan patriarch. The latter energetically opposed the move. After fifteen years, with the aid of the Serbian Church, independence was won.

The revival of Roman Catholicism was initiated in 1891 by Jesuit and Franciscan, and later by Salesian, missionaries. The archdioceses of Durazzo and Scutari and three dioceses were organized. The work, particularly educational, was successful, especially after 1939, when Mussolini's troops occupied the country.

When German and Italian troops withdrew in 1944, Communist influences predominated and succeeded in incorporating the country into the Soviet bloc. Persecution of the clergy, both Orthodox and Catholic, became common: in 1945 eighty Catholic priests were put to death. Church property was alienated. Religious instruction was abolished. All schools were nationalized. By 1950 not a single Catholic bishop was left. The Orthodox archbishop of Tirana was deposed, and the church placed under the Moscow patriarchate.

BIBLIOGRAPHY: *Echoes d'Orient*; Gary MacEoin, *The Communist War on Religion*, 1951.

MATTHEW SPINKA.

ALBERONI, GIULIO: Cardinal and statesman; b. May 30, 1664, of humble parents at Firenzuola in the duchy of Parma. After his ordination the Duc de Vendome, who was in command of French troops in Italy, became his patron. Alberoni accompanied Vendome to the court of Spain and won considerable acclaim for his diplomatic skill. He established more favorable relations between the Roman Curia and Spain under Philip V. In 1717 Pope Clement XI elevated him to the post of cardinal deacon of San Adriano. Alberoni strove to make Spain a manufacturing nation. He reformed many abuses in the Spanish government, started a school of navigation for the sons of the Spanish nobility, and sought to recover Spain's lost foreign colonies in Italy. Alberoni is blamed for the unwarrantable invasion of Sardinia and Sicily by Spain. In 1719, in order to save himself from being treated as the common enemy of Europe, Philip V expelled Alberoni. He returned to Italy to face the indignation of Pope Clement XI. Under Innocent XIII he was cleared of any wrongdoing by a commission of cardinals. Alberoni died in 1752.

BIBLIOGRAPHY: Bersani, *Storia del Cardinale Giulio Alberoni*, 1861–72.

GILBERT L. ODDO.

ALBERT OF PRUSSIA:

BIBLIOGRAPHY: Martin Luther. *D. Martin Luthers Werke*, Weimar Edition, *Briefwechsel*, 8 vols. (1930–38); Johannes Rindfleisch, *Herzog Albrecht von Hohenzollern, der letzte Hochmeister und die Reformation in Preusser.*, 1880; Friedrich Spitta. "Die Bekenntnissschriften des Herzogs Albrecht von Preussen," *Archiv fuer Reformationsge-*

schichte, VI (1908–09), 1–15; Johannes Voigt, *Deutsches Hofleben zur Zeit der Reformation*, 1928; Erich Maschke, *Der deutsche Ordensstaat. Gestalten seiner grossen Meister*, 1935; Walther Hubatsch, ed., *Albrecht Herzog in Preussen (1490–1568); europaeische Briefe im Reformationszeitalter*, 1949; Kurt Forstreuter, *Vom Ordensstaat zum Fuerstentum. Geistige und politische Wandlungen im Deutschordensstaate Preussen unter den Hochmeistern Friedrich und Albrecht (1498–1525)*, 1951.

[Sup.] HAROLD J. GRIMM.

ALBIZZI, BARTOLOMEO: D. Dec. 10, 1361, at Pisa. He was confused with Bartholomeus de Rinonico of Pisa, usually called Bartholomew of Pisa, who wrote his *Liber de conformitate* between 1385 and 1390 at Pisa; it was printed in 1510, 1513, and 1590.

BIBLIOGRAPHY: Modern critical edition of the *Liber de conformitate* appeared in *Analecta Franciscana*, Vol. IV (1906) and Vol. V (1907), with extensive and scholarly introduction, indicating that this work ever since the sixteenth century has often been unjustly condemned.

[Sup.] MATHIAS GOOSSENS.

ALBRIGHT, RAYMOND WOLF: B. at Akron, Pa., on July 16, 1901. He studied at Albright College and at Franklin and Marshall College (A.B., 1923; A.M., 1924); the Theological Seminary of the Reformed Church in the United States, Lancaster, Pa. (B.D., 1924); the University of Pennsylvania (university scholar 1928–29) and the Divinity School of the Protestant Episcopal Church, Philadelphia, Pa. (Th.D., 1933). A great-great-grandson of Jacob (Albrecht) Albright (*q.v.*, Vol. I), founder of the Evangelical Church (*q.v.*), he was ordained in the Evangelical Church (*q.v.*, now the Evangelical United Brethren Church), in 1923 and in the Protestant Episcopal Church in 1953. He was a fellow on the Carl Schurz Memorial Foundation in Europe in 1937. After brief pastorates at Wyomissing, Lebanon, and Matamoras, Pa. he became professor of church history in the Evangelical School of Theology, Reading, Pa. (1926–52); concurrently served as professor of graduate church history in Temple University (1935–45); and is now professor of church history in the Episcopal Theological School, Cambridge, Mass. (1952–). He has been the secretary of the American Society of Church History (1944–) and is department editor for contemporary biography of the supplementary volumes of the *Schaff-Herzog Encyclopedia of Religious Knowledge*. He has written: *A History of Religious Education in the Evangelical Church* (with Roy B. Leedy, 1932); *The Peace Movement in Retrospect and Prospect* (1935); *A History of the Evangelical Church* (1942; 2nd rev. ed., 1945); *A Historical Map of Berks Co. (Pa.)* (1947); and *Two Centuries of Reading, Pa.* (1948).

ALBRIGHT, WILLIAM FOXWELL: Lay archaeologist and biblical scholar; b. at Coquimbo, Chile, May 24, 1891, son of American Methodist missionaries. He studied at Upper Iowa University (A.B., 1912) and Johns Hop-

kins University (Ph. D., 1916). In 1919 he went to Palestine as fellow in the American School of Oriental Research in Jerusalem, which he later directed (1920–29, 1933–36). From 1922 to 1934 he excavated at many biblical sites, including Gibeah of Saul, Kirjath-sepher (Tell Beit Mirsim), Beth-zur, Bethel, while devoting himself to recovery of the historical, geographical, and cultural background of the Bible. Since 1932 he has devoted most of his time to the elucidation of the Old Testament, having accepted the W. W. Spence professorship of Semitic languages at Johns Hopkins University in 1929. His critical position may be described as liberal with strong conservative orientation; his own publications and those of his students have been directed largely toward the restoration of confidence in the antiquity and reliability of the Old Testament in reaction against the so-called Wellhausen School. Among more than seven hundred books and other contributions are his: *The Archaeology of Palestine and the Bible* (1932–35); *The Excavation of Tell Beit Mirsim* (1932–43); *From the Stone Age to Christianity* (1940–46, German ed., 1949); *Archaeology and the Religion of Israel* (1942–46); *Archaeology of Palestine* (1949–51); *The Biblical Period* (reprinted from *The Jews*, ed. Louis Finkelstein, 1950).

BIBLIOGRAPHY: *An Indexed Bibliography of the Writings of William Foxwell Albright*, 1941; *American Spiritual Autobiographies* (ed. Louis Finkelstein), 1948, pp. 156–181.

ALCOHOL QUESTION. See TEMPERANCE MOVEMENT.

ALCOHOLICS ANONYMOUS: A fellowship of men and women who share their experience, strength, and hope with one another in order to solve their common problem and help others to recover from alcoholism. The only requirement for membership is an honest desire to stop drinking. AA has no dues or fees. It is not allied with any sect, denomination, politics, organization, or institution; does not wish to engage in any controversy; neither endorses nor opposes any causes. The primary purpose is to stay sober and help other alcoholics to achieve sobriety. The AA book of experience, *Alcoholics Anonymous*, and other literature, including *The Twelve Steps* and *The Twelve Points of Tradition*, are available through any group or the General Service Headquarters, P. O. Box 459, Grand Central Annex, New York 17, N. Y.

Alcoholics Anonymous has (1951) a membership of 120,000, divided into some 4,100 local groups in the United States and Canada and in other countries throughout the world. Of those who make a genuine effort to stop drinking through AA principles, 50 per cent achieve sobriety at once and stay sober. Another 25 per cent stay sober after some relapses. Of those who drop away, many come back later, and permanently, if they live.

BIBLIOGRAPHY: G. A. Taylor, *A Sober Faith: Religion and Alcoholics Anonymous*, 1953.

ANONYMITY REQUIRED.

ALCUIN AND OTHER EARLY ANGLO-SAXON SCHOLARS AND MISSIONARIES ON THE CONTINENT:

At one time numerous Irish and English missionaries went to the Continent to introduce there both religious and educational ideas and practices. Alcuin was the outstanding scholar at the court of Charlemagne, and far away in St. Gallen in Switzerland the ancient institutions of the men from the British Isles have left tokens of their labors. The articles on Willibrord and St. Boniface by Professor Willibrord Lampen indicate how much the Dutch people owe to the Irish and Anglo-Saxons. The Saxons on the Continent were slow to respond to the missionary efforts, and it was not until Charlemagne had subdued them by force of arms that they became acquainted with Christianity. The Frankish emperor used harsh methods, which impelled Alcuin to write one day: "Faith is a product of the will; it must not be inculcated through forceful actions. It is permitted to appeal to the conscience, but it is wrong to employ brute force: Mittantur praedicatores et non praedatores." New bishoprics were founded among the formerly wild Saxons: Bremen had its first bishop (Willehad) from 787 to 789, while the first bishop of Muenster was the missionary from the northern Low Countries: Ludgerus (804–809).

BIBLIOGRAPHY: S. Crawford, *Anglo-Saxon Influence on Western Christendom, 600–800*, 1933; W. Levison, *England and the Continent in the Eighth Century*, 1946; M. Laistner, *Thought and Letters in Western Europe*, A.D. *500–900* 1931; J. Jung-Diefenbach, *Die Friesenbekehrung bis zum Martertode des Heiligen Bonifacius*, 1931; E. Amann, *L'Époque carolienne*, 1937; A. Kleinclausz, *Charlemagne*, 1934; J. Calmette, *Charlemagne*, 1945; H. Wiedemann, *Die Sachsenbekehrung*, 1932; Fr. Flaskamp, *Die Anfaenge friesischen und saechsischen Christentums*, 1929; E. S. Duckett, *Alcuin*, 1951.

[Sup.] ALBERT HYMA.

ALCUIN CLUB:

The Alcuin Club is an association of Anglicans, chiefly English, interested in promoting the study of the history and use of the Book of Common Prayer. By publication of books and pamphlets it encourages the practical study of the English liturgical traditions as to ceremonial, arrangement of churches, and ornaments in strict accord with the rubrics of the English liturgy. Representative members have been Percy Dearmer, Athelstan Riley, Christopher Wordsworth, Charles Gore, Walter Howard Frere. The present headquarters is The Deanery, Chicester, Sussex, England. NELSON RIGHTMYER.

ALDEN-TUTHILL LECTURES:

Established at the Chicago Theological Seminary by the gifts of the Rev. Edmund K. Alden, of Boston, Mass., and Frank Hall Tuthill, of Chicago, to provide supplementary instruction in the field of home and foreign missions or for other purposes at the discretion of the seminary. Publication of lectures is not required, but those of John C. Bennett, Halford E. Luccock, Richard H. Niebuhr, Douglas V. Steere, and Henry A. Wallace have been published with additional materials in book form.

ARTHUR CUSHMAN MCGIFFERT, JR.

ALEXANDER, SAMUEL:

Jewish; b. at Sydney, Australia, Jan. 6, 1859; d. Sept. 13, 1938, at Manchester, England. Alexander's reconcilation of science and values is reminiscent of Spinoza's mechanical interpretation of nature, which Alexander modernizes by making time central. Nisus is the creativeness of time which evolves the successive levels of existents from Space-Time which is pervasive to Deity. God is conceived both immanently and transcendently, that is, as both process and as process directed toward Deity. His principal works are: *Moral Order and Progress*, 1906; *Space-Time and Deity*, 1920; *Beauty and Other Forms of Value*, 1933. JOHN W. MCCARTHY.

ALEXIANS:

Abbreviation C.F.A. An American province of this congregation was founded in 1866 with headquarters in Chicago. The brothers man hospitals and asylums, and conduct two schools of nursing for male students. Professed brothers: 171. [Sup.]

ALLEMAN, HERBERT CHRISTIAN:

Theologian; b. Bloomsburg, Pa., May 13, 1868; d. Feb. 8, 1953. He studied at Pennsylvania College, Gettysburg (A.B., 1887); Lutheran Theological Seminary, Gettysburg (graduated 1891); University of Pennsylvania (1908–11). Ordained to the Lutheran ministry in 1891, he served as pastor Trinity Church, Chambersburg, Pa. (1891–96); College Church, Gettysburg, Pa. (1896–1900); Messiah Church, Philadelphia (1900–11). He became professor of Old Testament literature and theology, Lutheran Theological Seminary (1911–). He is author of: *The Gist of the Sermon* (1905); *The Book—A Brief Introduction to the Bible* (1908); *Prayers for Boys* (1925); *The Old Testament—A Study* (1934); *The New Testament—A Study* (1934); *New Testament Commentary* (1936); coeditor (with Flack) *Old Testament Commentary* (1948).

ALLEN, ALEXANDER VIETS GRISWOLD:

D. 1908. He taught church history in the Episcopal Theological School, Cambridge, Mass., from 1867 until his death in 1908. His additional books are: *Phillips Brooks* (1907) and *Freedom in the Church* (1907). [Sup.]

ALLINE, HENRY: Nova Scotian New Light; b. Newport, R. I., June 14, 1748; d. North Hampton, N. H., Feb. 2, 1784; went to Falmouth, N. S., 1760. During the American Revolution his emotional and highly speculative preaching stimulated the growth of New Light Congregational and Baptist churches in the Maritime Provinces. He wrote *Two Mites* (1781) and *The Anti-Traditionist* (1783), which show the influence of William Law (*q.v.*, Vol. VI). His *Hymns and Spiritual Songs* (1786) were reprinted by the Free Will Baptists of New England.

BIBLIOGRAPHY: *Life and Journal of the Rev. Henry Alline*, 1806; M. W. Armstrong, *The Great Awakening in Nova Scotia*, 1948.

MAURICE W. ARMSTRONG.

ALL SOULS' DAY: The constitution *Incruentum altaris* of Pope Benedict XV, August 10, 1915, allows every priest to offer three Masses of Requiem on All Souls' Day. This extension of a custom of Spanish churches to the entire Roman Catholic Church was meant as a compensation for the loss or inadequacy of pious endowments in favor of the souls in purgatory.

[Sup.] GEORGES A. BARROIS.

ALOMBRADOS: Erred, no doubt, more in the field of practical application than in actual doctrines. Their ideas were concerned largely with the *oratio mentalis* and the *contemplatio*. The concepts of the illuminati (*q.v.*, Vol. V) reached their most pronounced expressions in the assertion that man can attain a degree of prayer and a state of perfection in which sin ceases to be sin. One of the most harmful aspects of their activities was the suspicion generated among high and low that even the great Spanish mystics shared their strange ways and thoughts. That is the reason why the Spanish Inquisition through Juan de Valdès, placed two works of Louis of Granada on the Index. Juan de Avila and Ignatius Loyola were imprisoned for a time. Franciscus Borgia and Theresa and John of the Cross were accused also of heresy.

BIBLIOGRAPHY: H. C. Lea, *A History of the Inquisition in Spain*, 1906–7; J. de Guibert, *Documenta ecclesiastica Christianae perfectionis studium spectantia*, Rome 1931. Nrs. 405 ff.; H. Bremond, *Hist. Littér. du sentiment religieux en France*, Vol. 8, 1929; P. Pourrat, *La spiritualité Chrétienne*, Vol. 3, 1944.

[Sup.] MATHIAS GOOSSENS.

ALOYSIUS, SAINT, OF GONZAGA:

BIBLIOGRAPHY: The 17th century *Vita* by V. Cepari was published with the latest data in German translation by E. Raitz von Frentz, 1929; G. Martindale, *The Vocation of Aloysius Gonzaga*, 1929; A. Koch, "Aloysius' Charakterbild aus seinen Briefen," in *Zeitschrift fuer Aszese und Mystik* (1928), pp. 42–60   [Sup.] MATHIAS GOOSSENS.

ALSACE AND LORRAINE: From 1871 to 1918 Alsace and Lorraine were incorporated in the German Empire and formed but one political administration, called "Reichsland Elsass-

Lothringen." Restored to France in 1918, the two provinces were divided (as before the war of 1870–71) into three departments, Bas-Rhin, Haut-Rhin, and Moselle. But the established order of the Lutheran Church of the Augsburg Confession and the Reformed Church is still maintained throughout the territory, which is limited on the north by Luxembourg (*q.v.*) and Saarland, on the east by the German province of Baden (*q.v.*), on the south by Switzerland (*q.v.*), and on the west by four French departments. Its area is 5,603 square miles with a population (1946) of 1,767,051.

The French state is neutral as to confessional matters and no longer conducts a religious census. In 1905 there were 1,375,900 Roman Catholics, 406,100 Protestants, 33,130 Jews. The preponderance of Catholics points back to the political conditions of the sixteenth century. The Reformation found entrance chiefly in the free city of Strasbourg, where Martin Bucer (*q.v.*) became the Protestant leader. The confessional proportions were first changed to the advantage of Catholicism by the work of the Jesuits during the reign of Louis XIV, and after the war of 1870–71 to the advantage of Protestantism by the immigration of German Protestants.

I. Lutherans: The Church of the Augsburg Confession is still constituted according to the law of the first French Republic (1802), as amended in 1852. A presbyteral council, chosen by the parish under the presidency of the pastor, has general oversight over the spiritual and temporal concerns of each congregation. Its acts and decisions must be confirmed by the next higher ecclesiastical board, the consistory. The parish is authorized to choose its own minister through the presbyteral council. The nomination and confirmation of the election are reserved to superior authorities.

The consistory sometimes represents a single congregation, sometimes several. Its functions are in general the same as those of the presbytery: to maintain discipline, care for the order of divine service, and manage church property. There are also seven inspection districts, each having one clerical and two lay inspectors. The members of the inspectorate name delegates to the superior consistory. At the head of the church is a directory (standing board) and the superior consistory. The directory consists of two laymen, one of the seven clerical inspectors appointed by the government, and two lay members chosen by the superior consistory. It has power to review all acts of presbyteries and consistories, manages all church property, serves as intermediary between church and government, and appoints all ministers after consultation with presbyteral councils and consistories. It executes the decrees of the superior consistory. The president of the directory presides over the superior consistory. The latter meets annually. The business to be brought before it must have the consent of the government, and its decisions require government confirmation.

The most important foundations are under the administration of the Chapter of St. Thomas in Strasbourg. The Gymnase Protestant receives large subventions from St. Thomas. This secondary school was formed in the year 1538 and is called after its first rector, Johannes Sturm (q.v.). It was the birthplace of the University of Strasbourg.

II. Reformed and Others: The Reformed Church of Alsace and Lorraine has substantially the same constitution. Its congregations are led and governed by similar presbyteral councils and four consistories; the latter are united in an administrative unit, the commission synodale. The synod meets annually. Three visitors are responsible for the observance of ecclesiastical discipline in the parishes. The Reformed have a numerical strength about one-fifth of that of the Lutherans. During his stay at Strasbourg John Calvin (q.v.) became one of the first ministers of the small French refugees' church there.

Among the Protestants of Alsace are also a few Methodists, Baptists, and Mennonites.

III. Roman Catholics: The Roman Catholic Church of Alsace and Lorraine comprises the two bishoprics of Strasbourg (Alsace) and Metz (Lorraine), independent of all archiepiscopal or metropolitan jurisdiction. The bishops are named by the government and receive canonical institution from Rome. They select all books to be used in church services and present priests for appointment to the civil authorities, but directly name the lower clergy as well as the directors and professors of the diocesan seminaries. Each bishop has two vicars-general and a chapter, which becomes influential only if a vacancy occurs.

A certain number of church buildings and rectories belong, legally, to the civil authorities, which are charged with their maintenance if the ordinary revenues do not suffice. Many churches are used by both Protestants and Roman Catholics (see UNION CHURCH). The cemeteries also are sometimes common property.

The University of Strasbourg has two faculties of theology: origins of the Protestant faculty go back to the Reformation when Martin Bucer, John Calvin, and Wolfgang Capito were teachers there. The Catholic faculty, an episcopal foundation, was created at the beginning of the twentieth century.

The Jews are divided into three consistories, each with a chief rabbi at Strasbourg, Colmar, and Metz. Rabbis receive salaries from the state.

BIBLIOGRAPHY: H. Strohl, *Le Protestantisme en Alsace,* 1950; *Protestantisme française,* 1945; C. H. Bishop, *France Alive,* 1947.

[Sup.] ROBERT WILL.

ALT, ALBRECHT: Lutheran; b. at Stuebach, Bavaria, Sept. 20, 1883. He studied at the universities of Erlangen and Leipzig and specialized in Old Testament and Oriental research. He was private lecturer (1909–12; Lic. Theol., 1909) and professor extraordinarius (1912–14; Dr. Theol., 1914) at the University of Greifswald, professor ordinarius at the universities of Basle (1914–21), Halle (1921–22), and Leipzig (since 1923). He worked sometimes at the German Evangelical Institute for the Antiquities of the Holy Land in Jerusalem, edited the yearbooks of this institution (1927–41), and was president of the German Palestine Exploration Society (1926–49). He is coeditor of the *Biblia Hebraica* founded by Rudolf Kittel, and wrote *inter alia: Israel und Aegypten* (1909); *Die griechischen Inschriften der Palaestina Tertia* (1921); *Die Landnahme der Israeliten in Palaestina* (1925); *Der Gott der Vaeter* (1929); *Die Staatenbildung der Israeliten in Palaestina* (1930); *Die Urspruenge des israelitischen Rechts* (1934).

ALTAR FELLOWSHIP. See INTERCOMMUNION.

ALTERNATE SERVICE WORK CAMPS. See CONSCIENTIOUS OBJECTORS.

ALTHAUS, A. W. H. PAUL: Lutheran: b. at Obershagen, Hannover, on April 2, 1888. He studied at Goettingen, Tuebingen, and in the theological seminary at Erichsburg, Hannover. He was *Privatdozent* at Goettingen in 1914; a chaplain in the German army (1915–18); taught at Rostock (1920–25) and has been professor of systematic and New Testament theology at Erlangen (1925–   ). He is a specialist in dogmatics and ethics and stands in opposition to the dialectical theology of Karl Barth. His chief works are: *Die letzten Dinge* (1922, 5th ed., 1949); *Der Roemerbrief* (1932, 6th ed., 1949); *Die Christliche Wahrheit* (1948); *Communio Sanctorum* (1929); *Paulus und Luther ueber den Menschen* (1938, 2nd ed., 1951); *Grundriss der Dogmatik* (I, 1929, 3rd ed., 1947; II, 1932, 3rd ed., 1949); and *Grundriss der Ethik* (1931).   RAYMOND W. ALBRIGHT.

ALTRUISM: Comte adopted this term to describe the disposition to further the welfare or happiness of others: "To live for others, with love as the principle, order as the foundation, and progress as the goal." It is similar in meaning to "benevolence" or "beneficence" except that it has the additional force of its antithesis to egoism, which is the contrary disposition to seek one's own interests, and Comte several times uses "abnegation" as its synonym. The term was popularized by Herbert Spencer who discussed at length in his *Data of Ethics* the problem of reconciling egoism and altruism.

In the seventeenth century Thomas Hobbes maintained that the individual is fundamentally egoistic. He reduced the motives which are usually regarded as altruistic to forms of self-interest. Pity is simply "imagination or fiction of future calamity to ourselves proceeding from the sense of another man's calamity," and benevolent action springs from the pleasure of exercising power over others. Men only act socially at all out of a desire either "for gain or glory."

British moralists of the next two centuries were concerned to assert, in opposition to Hobbes, that human nature is endowed with social affections and benevolent sympathies, which are as natural as the tendency to seek one's own interests, either in self-preservation or in the search for pleasure or for power. The real problem that must be faced is the right relationship of these two sets of impulses. Locke accepted psychological hedonism (*q.v.*), the theory that human behavior is always motivated by the desire for pleasure and aversion to pain, and rested the case for obedience to moral law on the supernatural sanctions attached to it. Shaftesbury, however, was concerned to demonstrate the existence of disinterested affections whose direct object is the welfare of others, and maintained that goodness consists in the proper balance of these benevolent impulses with those whose object is the preservation of the individual. The criterion of this due proportion is the public good, but its achievement is also conducive to the happiness of the individual in whom it exists. Although virtue must be pursued for its own sake under the direction of the "moral sense," yet it remains true that virtue is a source of happiness to the virtuous.

Joseph Butler followed Shaftesbury in exhibiting that the social affections are no less natural to man than the appetites and desires which aim at self-preservation. Pleasure is not the immediate objective of either group of impulses, but it is rather a result that follows their successful achievement of their natural ends. Nor can a man be consistently egoistic without exercising self-control, for the passions frequently come into conflict with a man's true interests. Butler believed that in practice there is seldom a clash between the impulses of self-love and those of benevolence, but when such conflict occurs they must be submitted to the regulative principle of conscience. He remains, however, so impressed with the strength of self-love that he can write: "Though virtue or moral rectitude does indeed consist in affection to and pursuit of what is right and good as such; yet when we sit down in a cool hour, we can neither justify to ourselves this or any other pursuit, till we are convinced that it will be for our happiness, or at least not contrary to it." (Sermon 11.)

Hutcheson agreed with Shaftesbury and Butler in believing in the ultimate coincidence of virtue with the happiness of the virtuous agent, but he is more careful to guard the necessity for disinterestedness in the social affections.

Utilitarianism sought to transcend the conflict between egoism and altruism in setting up the ethical goal of "the greatest happiness of the greatest number." Bentham maintained that every individual should count as one and nobody as more than one in assessing the potential results of any action contemplated, yet he admits in the end that "the only interests which a man is, at all times, sure to find adequate motives for consulting are his own." He believed, therefore, in the necessity of legal penalties in order to curb the impulses of self-interest. J. S. Mill advocated the subordination of the happiness of the individual to that of the whole. Between the claims of an agent's own interests and those of another he should act as impartially as a disinterested and benevolent spectator. The general assumption remained however that there was in fact no ultimate contradiction between the claims of the self and those of society, an optimistic view which has been challenged by F. H. Bradley (*q.v.*) and A. E. Taylor (*q.v.*), who believe that self-development and self-sacrifice are both good, that they sometimes clash, and their conflict constitutes an ultimate dualism in the nature of morality.

Although earlier evolutionists had stressed the elements of competition in nature, later discussion has found the germs of social life in the gregariousness of animals, and a basis for altruism in the relationships of mating and of parenthood. Westermarck has traced the development of altruism in mankind from the narrow family circle to the kinship group, the tribe, the nation, and finally to the whole human race.

In Christian theology it has generally been maintained that self-love is the essence of human sinfulness, and that an inordinate love of self is universal among men. Salvation consists in a reorientation of the self toward the love of God and of one's neighbor. Theologians have differed as to how far this transformation does in fact take place, some maintaining that self-love is never more than partially eradicated, while others have defended the possibility of "Christian perfection," and the achievement of a truly disinterested love for God and man.

True happiness is promised to those who follow the Christian life, but it is a reward that comes to those who serve without thought for reward. Both religious and philosophical ethics are agreed in accepting the paradox that "virtue" is the way to happiness, yet it must be pursued for its own sake or it will cease to be virtuous. See also BROTHERHOOD OF MAN; ETHICS.

BIBLIOGRAPHY: Discussions of this topic will be found in most textbooks on ethics. See, for instance: Henry Sidgewick, *Outlines of the History of Ethics*, 1939; Hastings Rashdall, *The Theory of Good and Evil*, 1907; C. D. Broad, *Five Types of Ethical Theory*, 1930; Edward Westermarck, *The Origin and Development of the Moral Ideas*, 1912.

ANTHONY S. CHADWICK.

ALVAREZ DE PAZ, DIEGO: B. in Toledo in 1578; d. at Potosi in Bolivia in 1620. He lived in Peru from 1584 to 1620, where he was professor of theology and provincial. He composed three important works: *De vita spirituali ejusque perfectione libri V* (Lyons, 1606), *De exterminatione mali et promotione boni libri V* (Lyons, 1613), and *De inquisitione pacis sive studio orationis* (Lyons, 1617). The best ed. of these works is *Opera Jacobi Alvarez de Paz Toletani e societate Jesu*, 1875–76; they were edited by Louis Vivès. These three very methodical treatises, written with great care and spiritual insight, form the first great synthesis of ascetic and mystical theology. Alvarez was the first to use the term *oratio affectiva*. He based his works largely on the church fathers and the medieval writers, with which he was thoroughly familiar.

BIBLIOGRAPHY: A. Poulain, in *Dict. de Théol. Cath.*, Vol. I, 1930; P. Pourat, *La spiritualité Chrétienne*, Vol. III, 1944.

MATHIAS GOOSSENS.

AMANDUS: Born near the end of the sixth century and died Feb. 6, 675 or 676. He not only preached numerous sermons but also devoted much energy to the dissemination of St. Columban's teachings. In the southern Netherlands he founded five abbeys.

BIBLIOGRAPHY: L. van der Essen, *Étude critique et littéraire sur les Vitae des Saints mérovingiens ae l'ancienne Belgique*, 1907; E. de Moreau, *Saint Amand*, 1927

[Sup.] MATHIAS GOOSSENS.

AMARNA TABLETS: Study of the Amarna letters in the past generation has resulted in a much more adequate understanding of their language and content. Especially in the work of J. A. Knudtzon, who published between 1907 and 1915 a transcription and translation of all the tablets then known, was great advance made. Additional tablets acquired largely from antiquities dealers were published by Thureau-Dangin in 1925, and others found in excavations in 1933 were published by C. H. Gordon in 1947 (see Bibliography).

Recent discussion of these letters has been largely concerned with the language in which they were written. Of the 377 Amarna tablets known, about 300 were written by Canaanite scribes who did not sufficiently know the Babylonian language to write it without using words, grammatical forms, and idioms derived from their own native language. Occasionally a letter is written in almost pure Canaanite with a few Babylonian words and phrases scattered here and there. Isolation and study of these Canaanite elements have been a very valuable source for the study of the prehistory of the later Hebrew-Canaanite language, though there is yet much work to be done in this field.

A second problem arising from the study of the Amarna letters has been that of the Habiru (*q.v.*), and their relationship to the Israelites. It has been argued that the references to the Habiru as an increasing danger to the Canaanite princes loyal to Egypt are actually references to the conquest by the Israelites seen from the Canaanite point of view. Against this is the lack of reference to any of the biblical personalities, and the naming of several Habiru whose names are foreign to the biblical onomastics; and also the fact that the destruction of the Canaanite cities mentioned in Joshua-Judges took place, according to archaeological investigation, in most cases, a century at least after the Amarna period which cannot be later than *ca.* 1360 B.C. It seems preferable to regard the conflict recorded in the Amarna letters as an otherwise unknown incident in the almost unceasing attempts of the nomadic peoples of the desert fringes to the east of Palestine to invade and settle down in the more fertile and fruitful lands west of the Jordan.

BIBLIOGRAPHY: J. A. Knudtzon, *Die El-Amarna-Tafeln*, 1907–15; F. Thureau-Dangin, "Nouvelles lettres d'el-Amarna," *Revue d'Assyriologie*, XIX (1925), 91–108; C. H. Gordon, "The New Amarna Tablets," *Orientalia*, XVI, 1–21. For a translation of selected letters with notes, see J. B. Pritchard (ed.) *Ancient Near Eastern Texts* . . . (1950), 483–490. For studies of the Canaanite elements see F. Boehl, *Die Sprache der Amarnabriefe*, 1909; E. Dhorme, "La langue de Canaan," *Revue Biblique*, X (1913), 369 ff; XI (1914), 37 ff., 344 ff. For their relationship to the Israelite conquest see especially H. H. Rowley, *From Joseph to Joshua* (1950), and the literature cited there.

[Sup.] GEORGE E. MENDENHALL.

AMBOINA. See MALAY ARCHIPELAGO.

AMBROSE (AMBROSIUS), SAINT, OF MILAN: Was born of a distinguished Roman family at Trier, where his father, Ambrosius, resided as Pretorian Prefect of the Gauls; probably A.D. 339. After his father's death he received a classical education at Rome, where among his early memories was his sister Marcellina's profession as a virgin by Pope Liberius. Studying law, he rose to distinction on the staff of the Prefect Probus. Though still a catechumen, he probably wrote at this time his *De Bello Judaico*, an adaptation of Josephus. About 370 he became consular of Aemilia-Liguria (northern Italy), dispatched by Probus with the words, "Go, and behave not like a governor but like a bishop" (Paulinus, *Vita,* 5). In the fall of 373 the see of Milan became vacant by the death of the Arian Auxentius. Ambrose went to the church to maintain order at the election. A child, perhaps misunderstanding his appearance on the ambo, cried out "Bishop Ambrose"—the crowd took this up as an inspiration and elected Ambrose by acclamation. His refusal was overcome, and at the beginning of December he was baptized, ordained, and consecrated in rapid succession.

Ambrose at once put his vigorous intellect and executive ability at the service of the Catholic cause. The external events of his episcopate revolve around the defense of Catholic orthodoxy and varied relations with successive emperors. Leading in the final overthrow of Latin Arianism, Ambrose dedicated his *De Fide ad Gratianum* to the young emperor, whose close friendship he soon won. In 381 followed his *De Spiritu Sancto,* largely based on the work of St. Basil on the Holy Spirit. In the same year Ambrose was the leader of the Council of Aquileia, which marked the general acceptance of the Nicene faith in the Western Church, though confusing relations with the East by its attempt to intervene in the disputes at Antioch and Constantinople. In 382 Ambrose joined the other leaders of the Western Church at a Roman council.

In 383 Gratian was murdered at Lyons. For the five most dramatic years of Ambrose's life the usurper Maximus ruled north of the Alps, while Gratian's young brother Valentinian II reigned at Milan under the guardianship of his mother, the Arian Justina. Ambrose represented Valentinian's interests in a mission to Maximus at Trier in 383 (in the position, apparently, of both bishop and ex-consular). In 384 he secured, as before under Gratian, the rejection of the petition of the pagan party at Rome for the restoration of the Altar of Victory in the Senate House, an issue of symbolic importance. In 385 Ambrose defended the Basilicas of Milan against Justina's demand that one be surrendered to the Arians. Twice the people kept vigil in the churches in protest, and the government yielded. To occupy the crowds on these occasions Ambrose first produced a new form of Christian literature, the simple metrical hymn later known as Ambrosian. The new basilica (the original Sant' Ambrogio) opened in 384, was adorned with the newly discovered relics of the martyrs Gervasius and Protasius, and the consecration and translation produced a great outburst of popular piety. But the chief trophy of the year was the conversion of the young professor Augustine. The impression made by Ambrose's firm yet kind personality, his preaching, and his satisfying exegesis of Scripture had a large part in leading to St. Augustine's con-

version in 386; he was baptized by Ambrose at Easter of 387.

A second mission of Ambrose to Maximus was less successful. The usurper invaded Italy in 388 and Valentinian fled until his colleague Theodosius defeated Maximus in July. Theodosius left Valentinian in power in Gaul, while he himself spent some time at Milan. To this period belong Ambrose's famous rebukes of the emperor in the name of Christian standards. He secured Theodosius' revocation of his order to the Christians of Callinicum in Syria to restore a synagogue destroyed in a riot, and (to modern concepts more honorably) in 390 subjected Theodosius to penance and exacted amends for the massacre at Thessalonica. In 391–2 Ambrose was the leading figure of a Western council at Capua, which somewhat advanced the solution of problems raised by the schism at Antioch. Meanwhile Valentinian had become like his brother a disciple of Ambrose; he was looking forward to baptism at the bishop's hands when he was killed (or driven to suicide) by the Frank Count Arbogast in May, 392. Ambrose's funeral oration is of some theological interest for the doctrine of the baptism of desire. Under Arbogast and his puppet Emperor Eugenius Ambrose withdrew to Florence. After Theodosius' last victory in September, 394 the two greatest Romans of the age were together for a few months. Theodosius died at Milan in January, 395. Ambrose was still active in church affairs, but soon followed his imperial friend, dying on Easter Eve, April 4, 397.

Most of Ambrose's writings were either delivered as sermons or addresses, or are written in that form. He was not a profound original theologian, but won his title of doctor of the church by his clear statement of classical Christian teaching. His formulation of the phraseology of the doctrines of the Trinity and the Incarnation became permanent in the Latin Church—no wonder that mediaeval tradition ascribed to him, with St. Augustine, the authorship of the *Te Deum,* and that some modern writers have claimed for him the so-called Athanasian Creed. His careful use of allegory to solve the difficulties of Scripture especially appealed to St. Augustine—his homiletic commentaries include the *Hexaemeron* (drawing largely on Basil), a series on the patriarchs, expositions of a number of Psalms, and of the Gospel according to Luke. In ethics Ambrose christianizes Roman Stoicism. *De Officiis Ministrorum* follows the order of Cicero's *De Officiis* —social ethics is dealt with in *De Elia* (against luxury), *De Tobia* (against usury), and *De Nabuthae* (on the abuse of private property)— and several addresses develop the duties of Christian virgins and widows. Sacramental doctrine appears in the addresses to the newly baptized, *De Mysteriis* and *De Sacramentis;* the recovery of the latter for Ambrose is an important recent development in Ambrosian studies (see R. Hugh Connolly, *The De Sacramentis a Work of St. Ambrose,* privately printed, 1942). *De Sacramentis* is important in liturgics for its quotations from the Canon of the Mass. Ambrose has probably merely an honorific connection with the Ambrosian rite of Milan, but he originated the use of hymns in the daily offices, and may be responsible for the Milanese cursus of bi- (originally perhaps tri-) weekly recitation of the Psalter (see W. C. Bishop, "The Breviary at Milan," in *The Mozarabic and Ambrosian Rites,* 1924).

BIBLIOGRAPHY: Materials for the life of Ambrose are abundant, beginning with his own writings, especially the *Epistolae* and his funeral orations on his brother Satyrus and the three Emperors, the *Vita* by Paulinus, written at the request of St. Augustine, and references in contemporary church historians. Works of St. Ambrose were first printed in 1485; the best early edition is that of Erasmus, 1527. The great Benedictine edition of 1686–90 was reprinted in Migne, *Patrologia Latina,* vols. XIV–XVII; considerable parts have appeared in the Vienna *Corpus* (CSEL vols. 32, 62, 64); a series of convenient editions, with translations, have appeared in the *Catholic University of America Patristic Studies* (nos. 9 *De Obitv Theodosii,* 1925; 15 *De Nabuthae,* 1927; *De Elia,* 1927; 33 *De Tobia,* 1935; 58 *De Consolatione Valentiniani,* 1940; and 16 the *Vita,* 1928). The *Letters* are translated in the *Oxford Library of the Fathers,* 1881, and a number of works in the *Nicene and Post-Nicene Fathers,* Second Series, Vol. X, 1896. T. Thompson and J. H. Srawley, *St. Ambrose "On the Mysteries" and the Treatise on the Sacraments,* 1919, was revised as *St. Ambrose "On the Sacraments" and "On the Mysteries,"* 1950. Valuable works, with bibliographies of previous studies, are F. Homes Dudden, *The Life and Times of St. Ambrose,* 2 vols., 1935, and J-R. Palanque, *Saint Ambroise et l'Empire Romain,* 1933. On Aquileia and Capua cf. S. L. Greenslade, "The Illyrian Churches and the Vicariate of Thessalonica," *Journal of Theological Studies,* Vol. 46 (1945), pp. 17–30.

[Sup.] EDWARD ROCHIE HARDY.

AMBROSIAN CHANT: General appellation for all music of the Milanese Liturgy, though none of it can be traced authoritatively to St. Ambrose himself. The four so-called "Ambrosian Modes" no longer have historical justification, for we now have evidence of Ambrosian usage of the plagal ("Gregorian") additions as well as the four authentic modes.

Three general forms of this chant are associated with the Milanese Liturgy. The Ambrosian Hymn was introduced by Ambrose (333–397), Bishop of Milan, when he and his faithful fled from the Arians; all consist of eight four-line stanzas of iambic dimeters in simple syllabic settings in triple meter, and were intended for public worship.

Ambrosian Psalm tones are much simpler than the Gregorian, do not identify modes, and consist only of the formula of a reciting-tone concluding with an embryonic cadence at the conclusion of each verse.

Ambrosian Chant is much more florid than the Gregorian, melismatic renderings of upward to two hundred notes being not uncommon.

BIBLIOGRAPHY: Willi Appel, *Harvard Dictionary of Music,* 1944; W. H. Frere, *Oxford History of Music,* 1929; Paul

Henry Lang, *Music in Western Civilization,* 1941; Hugo Leichtentritt, *Music, History, and Ideas,* 1938; Karl Nef, *An Outline of the History of Music,* 1935; Gustave Reese, *Music in the Middle Ages,* 1940.

[Sup.] CLAUDE ALMAND.

AMBROSIAN LITURGY: It is used in all the territory of the Roman Catholic archdiocese of Milan, except the bishoprics of Monza, Trezzo, and Trevi, and in a few churches located on the former estates of the Borromaeo family. It is not to be ascribed to Saint Ambrose, whose name became associated with it later because of his fame as Archbishop of Milan. In fact, it appears that, in the course of the fourth century, the church of Milan was already in possession of a well-defined liturgy similar to the early Roman liturgy, previous to its reformation by Gregory the Great, with a strong admixtion of Gallican and Eastern features. The Ambrosian Liturgy received its definitive shape in the sixteenth century. Its early characteristics were the celebration of solemn vigils in appointed churches, *vigiliae stationales,* and the introduction of alternate psalmody and of hymns into the divine office, which is now a standard practice of all Western liturgies. The Ambrosian Mass differs from the Roman by the following details: the *Kyrie* comes after the *Gloria in Excelsis,* and the Creed after the Offertory. On the Sundays in Lent, the litanies following the *Kyrie* resemble the litanies of the Greek, in which the deacon leads the people.

BIBLIOGRAPHY: P. Lejay, *Dictionnaire d'Archéologie Chrétienne et de Liturgie, s.v.* "Ambrosien"; *Atti del Congresso liturgico Ambrosiano,* 1948.

GEORGES A. BARROIS.

AMBROSIASTER: The unknown author of the *Commentaria in xiii epistolas beati Pauli,* so named by Erasmus, who in 1527 disproved the medieval assumption of Ambrosian authorship. In 1908 Souter demonstrated his authorship of the *Quaestiones veteris et novi testamenti,* ascribed to Augustine in the Middle Ages and until the Benedictine editors of 1679–1700 disproved the attribution. Attempts to attribute several lesser works to Ambrosiaster have not succeeded.

Latin-speaking by birth, and at some time resident in Spain, northern Italy, and Rome, Ambrosiaster flourished about A.D. 375 and was probably a high civil official. He had considerable knowledge of Jewish customs and was of a thoroughly Roman temperament, disdainful of Greek Christian learning. The efforts (especially 1880–1928) of notable scholars (Souter, Morin, Turner, *et al.*) to identify him (as, e.g., Isaac the converted Jew, Evagrius of Antioch, various "Hilarys") have been vain.

His works preserve a pre-Vulgate Latin version of the Pauline corpus (except Hebrews, presumably considered non-Pauline) and other passages. His exegesis—unusual for his day—is not allegorical but literal and practical. He was millenarian, and, like Jerome, held a "presbyterian" view of the ministry. Above all, he was the father of Latin Christian royalist thought— *Dei enim imaginem habet rex, sicut et episcopus Christi.* (*Quaestiones* XXXV; cf. *Com.* Rom. 13.)

BIBLIOGRAPHY: Editions: *Commentaria* MPL XVII, 45-507; *Quaestiones* MPL XXXV, 2213-2416; A. Souter (CSEL 50) 1908. Studies: C. Martini, *Ambrosiaster: de auctore, operibus, theologia,* 1944; G. Bardy, "Ambroiaster," *Dictionnaire de la Bible,* I (1928), 225-241; G. Morin, "La critique dans une impasse," *Revue benedictine,* XL (1928), 251-255; A. Souter, "A Study of Ambrosiaster," *Texts and Studies,* VII, No. 4, 1905.

[Sup.] N. F. LANG.

AMERICAN ASSOCIATION OF THEOLOGICAL SCHOOLS. See THEOLOGICAL SCHOOLS, AMERICAN ASSOCIATION OF.

AMERICAN CATHOLIC CHURCH. See OLD CATHOLICS.

AMERICAN CHRISTIANITY IN THE TWENTIETH CENTURY. See UNITED STATES IN THE TWENTIETH CENTURY, CHRISTIANITY IN THE.

AMERICAN CONFERENCE OF UNDENOMINATIONAL CHURCHES. See FUNDAMENTAL CHURCHES OF AMERICA, INDEPENDENT.

AMERICAN CONTRIBUTIONS TO THEOLOGICAL SCIENCE. See THEOLOGICAL SCIENCE, AMERICAN CONTRIBUTIONS TO.

AMERICAN COUNCIL OF CHRISTIAN CHURCHES: A North American organization to make common testimony to the historic faith of the church, including the inerrancy of the Bible, the deity of Christ, his virgin birth, atoning death, bodily resurrection, coming again, and salvation by grace.

Organized in 1941, it included in its membership in 1951 about fourteen denominations. Its membership also embraces some congregations and individuals in about twenty other denominations. The headquarters are in New York City, and its activities include representing its membership in Washington, D.C., in such matters as concern the chaplaincy, legislation, and governmental policy affecting foreign missions and radio.

Its position is one of vigorous opposition to the National Council of Churches of Christ in the U.S.A. (*q.v.*). No voting member of the American Council may sustain a connection with the National Council.

The public pronouncements of the American Council stress opposition to theological Modernism (see LIBERALISM) and defend the authority of the Bible, private property, the capitalistic system, democratic, representative government, and just wars. Such pronouncements are often issued in comment upon matters of current theological or political interest.

The Council provides radio stations with transcriptions of addresses on religious themes. It has encouraged the formation of local church councils in various cities in opposition to those councils which work in harmony with the National Council of Churches of Christ. Its primary organ of publicity is an independent paper, not controlled by the Council, the *Christian Beacon,* published weekly at Collingswood, N. J.

BIBLIOGRAPHY: Carl McIntire, *Twentieth Century Reformation,* 1941.

PAUL WOOLLEY.

AMERICAN FRIENDS' SERVICE COMMITTEE. See FRIENDS' SERVICE COMMITTEE, AMERICAN.

AMERICANISM: The name given to a group of beliefs concerning the exposition and propagation of Catholicism allegedly held in certain American Roman Catholic circles during the last decade of the nineteenth century. The fundamental point of view of Americanism was that, in order to spread Roman Catholicism most effectively, discipline and even doctrine should be accommodated to the modern mind in such matters as (1) emphasizing individual initiative rather than the supposed leading of the Holy Spirit through the official hierarchy; (2) stressing the active virtues rather than the passive virtues, traditionally inculcated by the church, of humility, charity, and obedience; (3) playing down the value of monastic and other religious vows as tending to restrict initiative.

The controversy over Americanism, which had been simmering for about a decade, came to a head with the appearance in 1897 of a French translation of Walter Elliot's life of Father Isaac Thomas Hecker (*q.v.,* Vol. V), American founder of the Paulist Fathers. This French translation had an introduction by Abbé Felix Klein. The book, particularly the introduction, was deemed heretical and attacked in certain high Roman Catholic quarters in France. So, in January, 1899, Pope Leo XIII addressed an apostolic letter, *Testem benevolentiae,* to Cardinal James Gibbons, of Baltimore, in which he strongly condemned the doctrines of Americanism since they violated the traditionally unchanging character of Roman Catholic doctrine as formulated by successive popes and councils.

On receipt of this papal letter the American hierarchy, led by Cardinal Gibbons, denied that the condemned doctrines were widespread in their midst and expressed their complete obedience to the pope's authority and their acquiescence in the viewpoint of his apostolic letter. Thereupon the ten year old controversy died a natural—or, as some might think, an unnatural —death.

BIBLIOGRAPHY: James MacCaffrey, *History of the Catholic Church in the Nineteenth Century*, Vol. II, 1910; William L. Sullivan, *Under Orders*, 1944; Walter Elliott, *Life of Father Hecker*, 1891.

NORMAN V. HOPE.

AMERICANIZATION: The process of assimilating immigrants to American life, customs, speech, and institutions. The process existed long before the term. Its history is difficult to trace both on this account and because what is American has itself undergone change and development. Understanding of the process is also obscured by the fairly common failure to recognize that immigrants from the British Isles have been subjects of Americanization as well as immigrants from other countries, and by the popular notion that to be an American means to be a Protestant.

Although the North American Civic League for Immigrants was formed in 1907, an organized campaign of Americanization did not begin until World War I, when a reawakened concern for national unity was accompanied by alarm over the tide of immigration from southern and eastern Europe. The first Americanization Day was observed in Cleveland, Ohio, in 1914, and the National Americanization Committee was organized in 1915. These were quickly followed by the establishment of Americanization schools for training immigrants (called "New Americans") in United States history, civics, language, and literature. Public schools, YMCA's (*q.v.*), boy scouts (*q.v.*), and settlement houses (see SETTLEMENT MOVEMENT), which had long been contributing to this end, now adopted more conscious Americanization programs. Denominational boards and societies of home missions (*q.v.*) published literature for and about New Americans. Other church agencies (see EMIGRANTS AND IMMIGRANTS) impressed upon immigrants, in ports of entry, their responsibilities in the New World. By 1921 enthusiasm for Americanization was waning.

A campaign in Canada for "New Canadians" paralleled efforts in the U.S.A. and continued longer.

Meanwhile foreign-language churches—especially Lutheran, Reformed, and Catholic—were contributing more quietly to Americanization by (1) ministering to immigrants in their own languages and thus preserving among them that Christian culture which is a part of "Americanism," (2) preparing for gradual language transition in bilingual services, (3) bridging the gap which often separated second from first generations in immigrant families, (4) holding immigrants, uprooted from Old World ties, to moral standards which might otherwise have been abandoned, (5) providing a congenial atmosphere for training in the democratic procedures of church and auxiliary organizations, (6) encouraging naturalization.

BIBLIOGRAPHY: Edward G. Hartmann, *The Movement to Americanize the Immigrant*, 1948; Hannibal G. Duncan, *Immigration and Assimilation*, 1933; David F. Bowers, ed., *Foreign Influences in American Life*, 1944; Charles A. Brooks, *Christian Americanization: A Task for the Churches*, 1919.

THEODORE G. TAPPERT.

AMERICAN JEWISH CONGRESS. See JEWISH CONGRESS, AMERICAN.

AMERICAN LECTURES ON THE HISTORY OF RELIGIONS: The American Committee for Lectures on the History of Religions in 1936 transferred its program and resources to the American Council of Learned Societies which, for the administration of the lectures, appointed a Committee on the History of Religions. The old series was published by G. P. Putnam's Sons; the new series, which bears the general title, "Lectures in the History of Religions," has been published by the Columbia University Press. Volumes which have been published (with dates in which delivery of the lectures was begun) in the two series, as corrected, are:

1894. T. W. Rhys-Davids, *Buddhism: Its History and Literature*, 1896.

1896. Daniel G. Brinton, *Religions of Primitive Peoples*, 1897.

1897. T. K. Cheyne, *Jewish Religious Life after the Exile*, 1898.

1898. Karl Budde, *Religion of Israel to the Exile*, 1899.

1904. Georg Steindorff, *The Religion of the Ancient Egyptians*, 1905.

1905. George W. Knox, *The Development of Religion in Japan*, 1907.

1906. Maurice Bloomfield, *The Religion of the Veda*, 1908.

1909. Morris Jastrow, *Aspects of Religious Belief and Practice in Babylonia and Assyria*, 1911.

1910. J. J. M. deGroot, *Religion in China*, 1912.

1911. Franz Cumont, *Astrology and Religion among the Greeks and Romans*, 1912.

1914. C. Snouck Hurgronje, *Mohammedanism*, 1916.

1916. J. E. Carpenter, *Phases of Early Christianity*, 1916.

1939. Martin P. Nilsson, *Greek Popular Religion*, 1940.

1948. H. Frankfort, *Ancient Egyptian Religion*, 1948.

1950. Wing-tsit Chan, *Religion in Modern China*, 1951.

[Sup.] DONALD H. DAUGHERTY.

AMERICAN PROTECTIVE ASSOCIATION. See INTERFAITH RELATIONS.

**AMERICAN SCHOOLS OF ORIENTAL RE-
SEARCH:** The establishment of the American
Schools of Oriental Research was the culmination of an interest in Bible lands on the
part of American scholars which goes back at
least to the explorations of Professor Edward
Robinson in 1838. A committee was organized
in 1895, on the initiative of Professor Joseph
Henry Thayer, to explore the possibility of setting up a permanent school for "Oriental Study
and Research in Palestine" and this was finally
accomplished in 1900 when the American School
in Jerusalem began its work with Professor
Charles Cutler Torrey as its first director. By
the articles of incorporation, adopted in 1921,
the title became the American Schools of Oriental Research in order to make provision for
the establishment of a second school in Bagdad.
This project came to fruition when activities in
the field were begun in 1933 with Professor
George Aaron Barton as director. At first the
Jerusalem School had no buildings of its own,
but in 1925, through the generosity of Dr. and
Mrs. James Nies, it was possible to begin work
on the attractive and commodious structure,
not far from Herod's gate, which the School
now occupies. The Bagdad School has no buildings and operates merely as a center for research. The Schools are supported by a small
endowment and by annual contributions from
the sixty-seven universities, theological seminaries, and other institutions (Protestant, Catholic, and Jewish) which are members of the
corporation, as well as by contributions from
some six hundred individual members.

During the winter the Jerusalem School conducts a regular academic program of classes and
conferences under the leadership of its director
and annual professor. More important, however, are the archaeological field trips which
are also part of the winter program, and the
important projects of excavation and exploration which are organized from time to time,
frequently in conjunction with other institutions. The most important of those which have
been conducted in whole or in part by the
Jerusalem School are as follows: 1901, excavation of a Phoenician necropolis at Sidon by
Torrey; 1922 and 1933, excavation of Tell el-
Ful, by Albright; 1926 and following, Tell Beit
Mirsim, also by Albright; 1930 and following,
Jerash, by Fisher, McCown, and Glueck; 1931,
Beth-zur, by Albright and Sellers; 1934, Bethel,
by Albright and Kelso; 1938–40, Ezion-geber,
by Glueck; and the surface explorations of
Trans-Jordan by Glueck beginning in 1933. The
Bagdad School has been in part responsible for
the following important excavations: 1925 and
following, Nusu in Assyria, by Chiera and
Starr; 1927 and following, Tepe Gawra in As-
syria, by Speiser and Bache; 1927, Ctesiphon-
Seleucia in Babylonia, by Waterman; 1930 and

following, Tell Billa in Assyria, by Speiser and
Bache; and, 1937 and following, Khafajeh, by
Speiser and Delougaz.

The headquarters of the Schools are maintained at Yale University. The presidency of
the corporation has been held successively by
James Alan Montgomery (1921–33), Millar
Burrows (1934–48), and Carl Hermann Kraeling
(since 1948). In addition to issuing quarterly
the popular *Biblical Archaeologist,* the more
technical *Bulletin* and the *Journal of Cuneiform Studies,* the Schools publish a series of
technical monographs in the form of an *Annual*
and briefer ones as *Supplementary Studies.*
Among the more important separate publications of the Schools, in addition to technical
studies and reports on particular excavations,
are: Nelson Glueck, *The Other Side of the
Jordan,* 1940; Millar Burrows, *What Mean These
Stones?* 1941; Albert Henry Detweiler, *Manual
of Archaeological Surveying,* 1948; and Millar
Burrows, ed., *Dead Sea Scrolls,* 1950.

ROBERT CLAUDE DENTAN.

**AMERICAN THEOLOGICAL LIBRARY AS-
SOCIATION.** See THEOLOGICAL LIBRARIES.

AMES, EDWARD SCRIBNER: Disciples of
Christ; b. Eau Claire, Wisc., April 21, 1870. He
studied at Drake University (A.B., 1889; A.M.,
1891); at Yale (1892–94) and the University of
Chicago (Ph.D., 1895). He taught philosophy
and pedagogy at Butler (1897–1900) and from
that time to his retirement taught philosophy
at the University of Chicago (1900–35). He
was also dean of the Disciples Divinity House
at Chicago (1927–45) and pastor of the University Church of the Disciples of Christ
(1900–40). He wrote: *Psychology of Religious
Experience* (1910); *Divinity of Christ* (1911);
The Higher Individualism (1915); *The New
Orthodoxy* (1918); *Religion* (1929); *Letters to
God and the Devil* (1933); and was coauthor
of *Varieties of American Religion* (1936);
American Philosophies of Religion (1936); and
he contributed to *Contemporary American Theology* (1933); and *The Church at Work in the
Modern World* (1935).

RAYMOND W. ALBRIGHT.

**AMES, WILLIAM (AMESIUS, GUILIEL-
MUS):** His father was a merchant, and his parents both died when he was still very young.
He was then placed in the care of his maternal
uncle, Robert Snelling. Parents and uncle were
determined Puritans. In 1594 he went to Cambridge, where he studied under William Perkins.
The latter exerted a powerful influence upon
his mind and career. In 1607 Ames got his
A.B. degree; in 1609 he was at Colchester, expecting a call to the pastorate. But his frank
admission that he was a Puritan and the fact

that he translated into Latin the work of William Bradshaw, *English Puritanism,* rendered his efforts fruitless. In 1610, he went with Robert Parker to Rotterdam. At Leiden he met John Robinson, with whom he disputed whether Puritans should leave the Church of England. Robinson favored separation to some extent, while Ames could not find sufficient grounds for leaving the church of his fathers. From 1611 to 1618 he served as chaplain in the English church in the same city. During this period he participated in the quarrels between Arminians and their opponents. He engaged in polemics with Grevinchoven, a Remonstrant preacher, defending the Counter Remonstrants.

While assisting President Bogerman at the Synod of Dort, he aided as much as possible the orthodox Calvinists. He and his friends made several attempts to obtain a chair at the University of Leiden for him, but unsuccessfully. He did, however, for some time serve as leader or chairman of the Amsterdam *bursales.* During that time he composed his magnum opus, *Medulla theologiae,* which went through numerous editions.

Notwithstanding strong opposition by the English authorities he was finally appointed professor of theology at the flourishing University of Franeker. Owing largely to the influence of Hugo Grotius, both King James I and his archbishop of Canterbury were siding with the Arminians, though opposing theologians like Vorstius whom they accused of fostering heresies. On May 7, 1622, he delivered his inaugural lecture at the Frisian University. A few days later followed his promotion as D.D. under the celebrated and very able Sibrandus Lubbertus. Here he taught till 1632, thinking all the time about emigrating to New England, where many other English Puritans had found homes and useful occupations. In 1632 he became associated pastor of the English church in Rotterdam, besides rector of the school intended for the education of young Englishmen. As he was about to leave for America, he suddenly died. His widow donated his library to English colonists in America.

Ames was a very important figure. His influence on early New England Puritanism was formative. It was important, too, in the Netherlands. He attacked, not only the Remonstrants, but also the Roman Catholics, as is indicated in his work, *Bellarminus enervatus.* He also carried on a controversy with Maccovius regarding the basis for worshiping Christ. His book on Christian ethics (*Conscience*) went through many editions, both in Latin and English; in the Dutch Reformed Church it was widely regarded as authoritative. In his views on ecclesiastical government he was a moderate, non-separating Congregationalist. In the field of theology he opposed the scholastic method

employed in shaping the Reformed confession of faith, emphasizing with Peter Ramus the importance of the will above that of reason. He attempted with some success to give suitable direction to the development of Calvinistic pietism. His aim was to follow the example of those practical mystics of the fifteenth century who wrote books and articles on spiritual exercises. Because of his work in this field, O. Ritschl and Reuter have designated him a precursor of Schleiermacher. Unfortunately for him his Dutch contemporaries did not pay sufficient attention to methodical organization of daily living and thought control. He must have felt rather lonesome among the Continental Calvinists. An excellent discussion of his compositions is to be found in the useful book by H. M. Dexter, *The Congregationalism of the Last Three Hundred Years, as Seen in Its Literature* (1879).

BIBLIOGRAPHY: Perry Miller, *Orthodoxy in Massachusetts, 1630–1650,* 1933; idem, *The New England Mind; The Seventeenth Century,* 1939; R. P. Stearns, *Congregationalism in the Dutch Netherlands,* 1940; H. Visscher, *Guilielmus Amesius: Zijn leven en werken,* 1894; K. Reuter, *Wilhelm Amesius der fuehrende Theologe des erwachenden reformierten Pietismus,* 1940; W. Goeters, *Die Vorbereitung des Pietismus in der Reformierten Kirche der Niederlande bis zur Labad. Krisis 1670,* 1911; O. Ritschl, *Dogmengeschichte des Protestantismus,* Vol. III (1926), pp. 381–392; D. Nauta, *Samuel Maresius,* 1935; P. C. Molhuysen, *Bronnen tot de geschiedenis der Leidsche universiteit,* Vol. II, 1916.

[Sup.] D. NAUTA.

AMILLENNIALISM. See MILLENNIUM.

AMMON, AMMONITES: The original Ammonite kingdom, contemporary with the kingdoms of Edom and Moab, was supported by agriculture and animal husbandry and particularly by trade. It produced an excellent early Iron Age pottery from the thirteenth to the sixth century B.C. Its appearance as a kingdom followed the disintegration of a strong Bronze Age civilization in the eighteenth century B.C., with a nomadic era extending in between. Prior to the Bronze Age, earlier inhabitants left massive dolmens to mark their stay in Ammon as elsewhere east of the Jordan. Biblical records retain a vague memory of the early predecessors of the Ammonites under the names of Refaim and Zamzummim (Deut. 2:20; 3:11). Of the same Semitic background and culture as the Moabites and others (Gen. 19:38), the Ammonites worshiped Milcom and Molech (I Kings 11:5, 7, 33) among other gods.

The Ammonite kingdom was long one of the smallest and weakest of the kingdoms east of the Jordan which had had approximately a century of existence before the Israelites appeared on the scene. The territory of Ammon consisted at first of a small, fairly fertile strip on the east side of the south-north stretch of the Jabbok River (Wadi Zerqa), which rises in Amman. Amman is the present capital of the

Hashemite kingdom of the Jordan, and as Rabbath Amman was the capital of the Ammonite kingdom.

Ammon's western boundary was formed thus by the south-north beginnings of the Jabbok River. Its eastern boundary was marked by the desert. Its northern and southern boundaries were not clear cut. In the area between the Jabbok and the desert, and for some distance to the north and south of Rabbath Amman, extending from the beginning of the east-west line of the Jabbok River almost south to the Arnon River, were some very strong towns and fortresses, the latter protected by distinctive round towers (Num. 21:24; Deut. 2:19, 37). Rabbath Amman was the strongest city of them all. Its strategic position has given it a more continuous historical pre-eminence than enjoyed by any other capital city in Trans-Jordan. It was called Philadelphia during Hellenistic-Roman times, when it became one of the most important cities of the Decapolis. The ruins of its great amphitheater still testify to its former glory.

From the time of the judges of Israel, when Jephthah smote them (Judg. 11:13, 22, 33), to and through the times of Ezra and Nehemiah, there was a constant struggle for power between Israel and then Judah on the one hand and the Ammonites on the other. There was one brief period of friendship between David and Nahash, king of the Ammonites. The enmity between Israel and Ammon is reflected in many passages of the Bible (cf. Amos 1:13–15; Jer. 49:1–6; Ezek. 25:1–7).

BIBLIOGRAPHY: Nelson Glueck, *Explorations in Eastern Palestine*, III, *ASOR*, XVIII–XIX, 1939; *The Other Side of the Jordan*, 1940; *The River Jordan*, 1946; G. Ernest Wright and Floyd V. Filson, *The Westminster Historical Atlas to the Bible*, 1946.

[Sup.] NELSON GLUECK.

AMMUNDSEN, OVE VALDEMAR: Lutheran; b. in Denmark, Aug. 19, 1875; d. in Haderslev (Denmark), Dec. 1, 1936. After graduating in divinity (1899), he studied in Germany (1900–1). He was professor of church history in Copenhagen (1901–23) and bishop of Haderslev (1923–36). At his death he was president of the World Alliance for International Friendship through the Churches and joint president of the Universal Christian Council for Life and Work. His most important works are: *The Young Luther* (1907); *English Labour Leaders on Christianity* (1911); *The Youth of S. Kierkegaard* (1912); *The Christian Church of XIX Century* (1925); *The Age of Enlightenment* (1930); *Social Christianity* (1932).

BIBLIOGRAPHY: H. L. Henriod, W. H. Drummond, *In Memoriam Bishop Valdemar Ammundsen*, 1937.

PETER AMMUNDSEN.

AMORITES: Recent discussion of the Amorite problem has resulted in serious doubt that the Accadian term *amurru* was ever used as an ethnic designation. This, together with the Sumerian equivalent *MAR.TU ki*, was originally a geographic designation for the "West," and was later used as a general term for "mercenary soldiers." The term Amorite, derived from the Babylonian through Hebrew, continues in use among scholars as a broad term to refer to the peoples who lived between Mesopotamia (*q.v.*) proper and the coastal plains of the East Mediterranean region, whose language was much more closely related to Canaanite than to the East Semitic Accadian, but who were differentiated from the Canaanites culturally. These peoples were in general nomads engaged in raising sheep or goats, using the ass instead of the camel for transportation, and characterized by a strong tendency to invade the fertile plains whenever possible to settle down to an agricultural way of life. Some scholars prefer the term East-Canaanite to distinguish these peoples from the Canaanites proper.

The Amorites are known from many personal names occurring in cuneiform texts from the close of the Third Dynasty of Ur (*ca.* 1960 B.C.) to the latter half of the second millennium B.C. After the fall of UR III, these West Semites poured into many parts of Mesopotamia, taking over in the process the government of a number of regions. During the course of the nineteenth century B.C. most of northern Mesopotamia was under the domination of Amorites, and it is commonly believed that the First Dynasty of Babylon was Amorite (*ca.* 1850 B.C.). In every case the Amorites took over the culture of the region, becoming assimilated so rapidly that very little evidence remains for the study of their original culture and religion other than their proper names. The original home of the Amorites is still questioned. Both central Arabia and the middle Euphrates region have been suggested as their place of origin, but it can hardly be doubted that West Semites have been located in the middle Euphrates territory since the time of Lugal-Anne-Mundu, before 2500 B.C. It is possible that they began migrating toward the west long before 2000 B.C., and we know with certainty that even in the Mari period (*ca.* 1700 B.C.) they were still oriented toward the west.

In this framework of migrations the Israelite patriarchs are now to be placed. It is very likely that the Hyksos domination of Egypt is also connected with these same movements of West Semites, since most of the Hyksos chieftains whose names have been preserved bear definite Amorite associations.

BIBLIOGRAPHY: Th. Bauer, *Die Ost-Kanaanaeer*, 1926. For a very useful discussion of the West-Semitic Arameans, see R. Bowman, "Arameans, Aramaic, and the Bible," *JNES*, VII (1948), 65–90; R. De Vaux, "Les Patriarches hébreux et les découvertes modernes," *Revue Bi-

blique (1946), 321-348; (1948), 321-347; (1949), 1 ff.; W. F. Albright, *From the Stone Age to Christianity* (1946), 109-112, 119-122, 179-189; T. J. Meek, *Hebrew Origins*, 1950.

[Sup.] GEORGE E. MENDENHALL.

AMOS, BOOK OF: Before his inaugural visions (7:1-9), Amos herded sheep and cultivated fruit near Tekoa (1:1; 7:14). He traveled to markets and shrines in the Northern Kingdom and observed society there (4:1, 4 ff.; 6:1-6). He knew Israel's and her neighbors' history well (1:3-2:10; 6:2; 9:7). He prophesied at Bethel sometime between 767 and 752 B.C. (1:1; 7:10 ff.). But who recorded his messages remains unknown. As the earliest prophet whose collected words we have, Amos is often contrasted with his younger contemporary Hosea as teaching only God's righteous rule and stern judgment. Yet he also looked for mercy (7:2 ff., 9:8 ff.). He revealed before the disasters of the Assyrian conquests that the covenant people with all their privileges must expect judgment for sin (2:9 ff., 3:3 ff., 5:1 ff., 7:8 f., 9:7). His message of social justice has abiding significance.

BIBLIOGRAPHY: R. S. Cripps, *The Book of Amos*, 1929; G. A. Smith, *The Book of the Twelve Prophets*, rev., 1929; T. H. Robinson, *Die zwoelf kleinen Propheten, Hosea bis Micha*, 1936; R. Gordis, "The Composition and Structure of Amos," *HTR*, XXXIII, 1940, pp. 239 ff., J. Morgenstern, *Amos Studies*, 1941; R. E. Wolfe, *Meet Amos and Hosea*, 1945; A. Cohen, *The Twelve Prophets (Soncino Bible)*, 1948.

[Sup.] CHARLES M. COOPER.

AMSDORF, NICHOLAS OF (NIKOLAUS VON): Was appointed professor at Wittenberg but preferred pastoral work to teaching and left for Magdeburg in 1524. In the disputes about the doctrine of the Eucharist and with the Roman Catholic scholars he rendered valuable service to the Lutheran cause. In January, 1542, he was personally introduced at Naumburg by Luther (*q.v.*) as the new bishop there. The unfortunate turn of events in the Schmalkaldic War forced him to leave Naumburg for Magdeburg, where he labored hard for the Lutherans against the Augsburg Interim. He lived at Eisenach from 1552 till his death, and was buried there in the Georgenkirche. Next to Flacius (*q.v.*) he was the most important figure in the right wing of Lutheranism. After Luther's death he fought valiantly against Melanchthon and his pupils (the Philippists), but also against other theologians. Although he tended to go to extremes, he did accomplish a great deal in helping maintain Luther's doctrines.

BIBLIOGRAPHY: K. Schottenloher, *Bibl. z. deutschen Gesch. im Zeitalter der Glaubensspaltung*, Vol. I (1933), Nr. 474-490, Vol. V (1939), Nr. 44799-44805; C. Eichhorn, *Amsdorfiana*, in *Zeitschr. fuer Kirchengesch.*, Vol. XXII (1901), pp. 605-645; O. Ritschl, *Dogmengesch. des Protestantismus*, Vol. II, 1912; O. Henning Nebe, *Reine Lehre: Zur Theologie des Niklas von Amsdorf*, 1935; O. Lerche, *Amsdorf und Melanchthon*, 1937.

[Sup.] HEINRICH BORNKAMM.

ANABAPTISTS: The name Anabaptist (meaning "Rebaptizer") is commonly used today in a broad sense to designate the entire "left wing" of the Protestant Reformation, without any derogatory sense, and including both peaceful and revolutionary groups, both evangelicals and spiritualistic elements. In the Reformation and later, however, it was a term of opprobrium and abuse, not used by any party or group for itself, but applied by both Catholics and Protestants apparently to all those elements separating themselves from the state churches. "Anabaptists" were heretics and criminals under the imperial law which, dating back to the code of Justinian (A.D. 529), had made rebaptism one of the two heresies punishable by death. The first imperial mandate of Reformation times against the Anabaptists (Jan. 4, 1528, at Speier) specifically grounds their required suppression on this ancient legislation. The "Anabaptists" of the earlier centuries were those who required rebaptism because they rejected the validity of the office of certain bishops (Novatians, Donatists, etc.). The sixteenth century Anabaptists, however, rebaptized because they considered true baptism to be possible only upon confession of faith and commitment to discipleship; hence, infant baptism was rejected and only adult baptism permitted. Certain medieval sects had, to be sure, rejected infant baptism but none practiced adult rebaptism. The 16th century Anabaptists therefore represented a new departure at this point, having no historical connection with earlier dissident groups. They had their origin in the Reformation and did not appear before 1525. It should be noted that in the early years of the Reformation, before 1525, most of the Reformers wavered on the question of infant baptism, particularly Zwinghi, Oecolampad, and the Strasbourg reformers, but even Luther and Melanchthon were uncertain for a time. The Zwickau prophets had already raised the cry against infant baptism in 1521 at Wittenberg, but did not advocate adult baptism, and are therefore not to be classed as Anabaptists. Neither did Thomas Muentzer advocate or practice adult baptism. The Zwickau prophets and Muentzer have erroneously been called the founders of Anabaptism, ever since the time of Luther.

Anabaptist scholars are now generally agreed that the Anabaptist movement had its origin in Zurich in 1524-25 among the followers of Zwingli (first adult baptism January 21, 1525), that it was definitely a religious movement, and that it was initially and throughout its history basically evangelical and peaceful, not heretical or revolutionary. Earlier theories of origin have been proved untenable: e.g., that they came from the Waldenses or other medieval sectaries (Keller, *et al.*), or from the Franciscan tertiarties (Ritschl), or from the Peasants' War of 1525, or in general the theory of socio-economic rather than religious origin (Kautsky, Anabaptists the first socialists).

The rapid spread of Anabaptism from Chur to Luebeck, from Strasbourg to Nikolsburg, from Ghent to Emden, from Cologne to Koenigsberg (by 1540 it had covered Middle Europe) indicates fertile soil in many places, produced both by the afterglow from certain medieval movements, such as the Brethren of the Common Life in Holland, and the stimulus of Lutheran and Reformed teaching. It was clearly a genuinely popular movement of considerable power, which was stopped only by severe persecution. Its rapid spread, without organization, largely without literary guidance, together with the harsh suppression which drove the movement in part underground, also accounts in part for the diversity which developed as well the inability of the sound leadership to prevent occasional individual and group aberrations and excesses. However, not all the left wing aspects of the Reformation can rightly be called Anabaptist, and certainly the spiritualistic, rationalistic and anti-Trinitarian elements should be classified as distinct groups, as Alfred Hegler, Walther Koehler, and others have done. Dewind has shown, for instance, that the Italian rationalist elements were not really Anabaptists but only called so by the state church leaders as a convenient way to condemn them.

One section of the Anabaptist movement, the Hutterites in Moravia (from 1528 on), did develop a remarkably effective and permanent Christian communistic brotherhood, but completely within the framework of evangelical faith and peaceful methods. Only once did fringe elements, with an initial impulse from Melchior Hoffmann's peaceful apocalypticism (1530–33), develop into a serious revolutionary movement (1534–35) which temporarily established a "kingdom" at Muenster in Westphalia. Although this briefly notorious affair, so shocking to the whole Christian world (the peaceful Anabaptists included), actually had very little significance, it created the typical "meaning" for the term "Anabaptist" for 300 years, and furnished the best of grounds for the harsh persecutions which lasted throughout the sixteenth century and resulted in the almost total extinction of the movement outside of the Hutterites in Moravia, a small remnant of Swiss Brethren, and the relatively large continuing Mennonite movement in Holland. All of these groups repudiated the Muensterites, and the Swiss Brethren repudiated Melchior Hoffmann specifically.

The large main line Anabaptist movement, which falls geographically and connectionally into three parts, Swiss-South German, Hutterite-Moravian, and Dutch (from Flanders to East Friesland, Holstein, the Vistula delta, and Koenigsberg), was completely peaceful, solidly evangelical in its central theological and ethical vision and commitments, and well-disciplined and organized. It conceived of itself as carrying through in a more complete and consistent fashion the original goals of the Reformation which had been abandoned by Luther and Zwingli; namely, the restoration of original, unadulterated New Testament Christianity.

I. Switzerland: The centers of the movement in Switzerland were Zurich, Bern, and Basel. Apart from the original leaders in Zurich, Conrad Grebel (d. 1526), Felix Manz (executed January, 1527, as the first martyr), and George Blaurock (exiled in January, 1527, and executed in Tirol in 1529), no outstanding personalities developed. The heavy and continuing persecution suppressed but did not wipe out the movement, and in the canton of Bern remnants have survived to this day. Forced emigration, 1650–1750, to Alsace and the Palatinate as well as to Pennsylvania is the source of the present large Mennonite population in eastern United States of America (see Mennonites) and Canada, as well as the smaller Mennonite groups in South Germany and Eastern France.

II. South Germany: As early as 1525–26 Augsburg and Strasbourg became vigorous centers, with a rapid spread across all South Germany. Outstanding leaders were Michael Sattler (executed May, 1527) and Pilgram Marpeck (d. 1556) whose writings are most important (*Vermahnung*, 1542; *Verantwortung*, 1544; *Testamentserlaeuterung*, 1544?). By 1600 the movement was completely eradicated here by persecution. All later Mennonites in this area are descendants of immigrant groups from Switzerland, coming after 1650.

III. Austria, Moravia: The strong movement in Tirol and Austria, deriving from Switzerland and South Germany, was wiped out by severe persecution by 1550. Nikolsburg, where Balthasar Hubmaier was the leader (executed at Vienna, May, 1528), was the strong early center in Moravia. Refugees fleeing from other regions to Moravia founded the Hutterite brotherhood (named after Jacob Hutter; also earlier called "Staebler" because they were nonresistant, using the staff, but not the sword) at Austerlitz and Auspitz in 1528 after a separation from the Hubmaier group (called "Schwertler" because they allowed the use of the sword to fight the Turks). Later they spread also into Hungary. The Hutterites enjoyed the favor of the nobles and flourished greatly until the Thirty Years' War, when they were all but wiped out by Jesuit action. At one time they had over 100 *Bruderhofs* (communal estates) and deserve credit for notable craft and medical achievements. Survivors fled to Transylvania and finally (1770) to over 100 Bruderhofs in the

Dakotas, Montana, Manitoba, and Alberta. The Hubmaier "Schwertler" early died out.

IV. Middle and North Germany: The movement developed early and strongly in Thuringia and Hesse (here there were no executions because of Philip of Hesse's more tolerant policy) where, it is now agreed, their pressure led to the introduction of confirmation and a stricter church discipline in the state church. However, by mid-century the movement was broken here also. In the Lower Rhine territory and North Sea region the movement derived largely from Holland. The Muensterite episode (1534–35) was a passing aberration. Permanent congregations were established in Juelich and Cleve, from Cologne and Aachen to Goch and Emmerich, with a large Mennonite congregation in Crefeld today as direct descendants. Emden, Norden, and Leer have had continuous congregations since about 1530. The Holstein group, now concentrated in Hamburg-Altona, was largely built up by later refugees from Holland (1580–1650), as was the Danzig and Vistula delta group (1540–1600). A large group of Mennonites persisted in this latter area until evacuated westward in 1945 because of the war; it was the mother of the large Mennonite settlements in the Ukraine and elsewhere in southern Russia and later in Siberia (1789–1945) now largely destroyed, which in turn were the mother of large settlements in the prairie states of the United States of America and in Manitoba, Canada, 1874–80.

V. Holland: Originated here by Melchior Hoffmann in 1530–32 and Obbe Philips in 1533–36, the movement came under the able leadership of Menno Simons (1496–1561) in 1536, aided by Dirk Philips (d. 1567 at Danzig), both of whom were influential writers (Menno's *Fundamentboek* 1539 and numerous other writings, Dirk's *Enchiridion* 1560). The Dutch movement became very vigorous and extensive, covering the Low Countries from Flanders to Groningen. From 1535 to 1555 it constituted the larger part of the Protestant movement in Holland, being only thereafter supplanted by the Reformed Church. As late as 1700 there were still 200,000 Mennonites in Holland (today 65,000), and throughout their history the Dutch *Doopsgezinden* (the name replaced Mennonite in the seventeenth century) have been influential in Dutch cultural life far beyond their numbers. Outstanding Dutch artists such as Carel van Mander, Jacob van Ruisdael, Lambert Jacobs, even Rembrandt as either a member or an adherent, and the greatest Dutch poet, Joost van den Vondel, were *Doopsgezinden*.

VI. England: The Dutch Anabaptist refugees certainly contributed to the rise of independent and separatist movements in England in the sixteenth century but no organized movement developed here. In the early seventeenth century English refugees in Holland affiliated with Dutch Mennonites at several places, notably Amsterdam, some of whom on their return to England shared in the founding of the Baptist Church.

Anabaptism, due to the nature of its origin and development as well as its strong emphasis on local responsibility, never developed an overall organization. However, each national or regional group developed a solidarity, which together with the weighty office of elder or bishop and the strong group discipline, and in spite of certain schisms (particularly in Holland —Frisians, Flemish, Waterlanders), gave stability and direction to the total movement, which remained remarkably united in spirit and in fundamental theological and ethical principles.

Several confessions, issued more as testimonies and bases for union than as binding creeds, were adopted, and had considerable importance. The chief ones were: (Swiss-South German) *Bruederlich Vereinigung* (by Michael Sattler at Schleitheim, 1527); (Hutterite) Peter Riedemann's *Rechenschaft unserer Religion, Lehr, und Glaubens* (1545); (Lower Rhine) *Concept of Cologne* (1591); Hans de Ries and Lubbert Gerritsz (Waterlander, 1610); *Eighteen Articles of Dordrecht* (1632), which has become the standard confession of the largest Mennonite branch (United States of America and Canada) and all Amish groups (Amish division in Switzerland and Alsace 1693–97, led by Elder Jacob Ammann).

The distinctive Anabaptist tenets were: a voluntary church of believers only, with baptism of adults on confession of faith and commitment to discipleship; separation of church and state; full liberty of conscience; holiness of life in full obedience to Christ; nonconformity to the world; a love-ethic including nonresistance and total rejection of warfare and the use of force; a brotherhood type of church with mutual aid; non-swearing of oaths; literal obedience to the Sermon on the Mount and the other teachings of Jesus; and simplicity of life and dress. The doctrines of the historic early Christian creeds, as well as the Protestant doctrines of justification by faith, the sole authority of Scripture, and the priesthood of all believers, were fully held, though not theologically developed. The Anabaptists emphasized an existential more than a theological Christianity. Their major break with Protestantism was on the central concept of the gathered church rather than the folk-church, and the nature of Christianity as discipleship or transformation of life rather than primarily as the enjoyment of forgiveness and salvation as status. Their rejection of war and insistence on religious liberty in an age when even the church (both Roman Catholic and Protestant) used war and force as an instrument of promotion and protection of the faith, is remarkable. They have been the almost forgotten forerunners of much that is today commonly accepted by Protestant Christendom, particularly in England and the United States.

BIBLIOGRAPHY: The distorted and negative interpretation of Anabaptism created by its enemies in the state churches, and perpetuated in historical and theological literature, has only recently been overcome and replaced by a more positive and historically valid understanding as the result of careful source research. The change began with the work of Max Goebel, C. A. Cornelius, Ludwig Keller, Gustav Bossert, and Johann Loserth, in the previous century. Ernst Troeltsch's treatment of the Anabaptists in his *Social Teaching of the Christian Churches* (German ed., 1912) was epoch-making and influential. Among the many notable recent publications are: F. H. Littell, *The Anabaptist View of the Church* (1952), which contains an excellent review of Anabaptist historiography; R. J. Smithson, *The Anabaptists*, 1935; C. Henry Smith, *The Story of the Mennonites*, rev. ed., 1952; John Horsch, *The Mennonites in Europe*, 1941; idem, *Menno Simons*, 1916; idem, *The Hutterian Brethren 1528-1931*, 1931; W. J. Kuehler, *De Geschiedenis der Nederlandsche Doopsgezinden in de zestiende Eeuwe*, 1940; H. E. Dosker, *The Dutch Anabaptists*, 1915; Rufus Jones, *Spiritual Reformers in the 16th and 17th Centuries*, 1914; A. H. Newman, *A History of Antipedobaptism to 1609*, 1897; H. S. Bender, *Conrad Grebel 1498-1526, The Founder of the Swiss Brethren*, 1950; Delbert Gratz, *Bernese Anabaptists and Their American Descendants*, 1953; W. Wiswedel, *Bilder und Fuehrergestalten aus dem Tauefertum*, 3 vols., 1928, 1930, 1953; T. J. Van Braught, *The Bloody Theatre or Martyrs' Mirror*, 1950, tr. of the Dutch original of 1685; E. A. Payne, *The Anabaptists of the 16th Century and Their Influence in the Modern World*, 1949; Roland H. Bainton, "The Left Wing of the Reformation," *The Journal of Religion*, 1941; H. S. Bender, "The Anabaptist Vision," *Church History*, 1944; Robert Friedmann, "Conception of the Anabaptists," *Church History*, 1940; idem "Recent Interpretations of Anabaptism," *Church History*, 1953; Ethelbert Stauffer, "The Anabaptist Theology of Martyrdom," *Mennonite Quarterly Review*, 1945. A vast amount of material is assembled in *Mennonitisches Lexikon*, I (1913); III incomplete. The *Mennonite Quarterly Review*, 1927 ff., has published a great amount of Anabaptist material. See also the article "Anabaptist Bibliographies" by H. S. Bender, *Mennonite Quarterly Review*, 1950. The *Verein fuer Reformationsgeschichte* is publishing a comprehensive series of volumes of Anabaptist source-documents, *Tauefer-Akten*, of which five volumes have now appeared: 1930, 1934, 1951, with others to follow. Similar source volumes have been published by others for Hesse, 1951, and Zurich, 1952; other volumes are in process. Other major source publications of recent date are: *Die aelteste Chronik der Hutterischen Brueder*, ed. by A. J. F. Zieglschmid, 1943: *Pilgram Marbecks Antwort auf Kaspar Schwenckfelds Beurteiling . . .* ed. by J. Loserth, 1929. A volume of Anabaptist and Spiritualist writings is included in the series, *The Library of Christian Classics*, now being published.

[Sup.] HAROLD S. BENDER.

ANALOGY: Analogy is the name both of a philosophical problem about the meaning of theological statements and of a particular solution offered for that problem.

I. The Problem of Analogy: It is obvious that much religious language is metaphorical, figurative or parabolical. It bases itself upon some sort of analogy between divine things and creaturely things, using the latter to set forth the former, as St. Paul uses the relation of members to head in an animal body to express the relation of Christians to Christ. When we use simile and metaphor outside theology, e.g. when, using music to illustrate painting, we talk of color-*tones*, the analogy is an aid, but one with which we can dispense. We can talk about colors in non-analogical terms—about

shades, not *tones*. To interpret an analogical statement is to substitute proper terms for analogical terms. But the special problem of theological analogy lies in the fact that theological truth cannot be stated in terms which are wholly "proper," and from which all analogical character has been eliminated.

Admittedly some theological terms appear to be more proper than others: it is more proper to speak of God as the eternal Spirit who wills the continuation of our existence than as the Rock of Ages on which we are founded; and, if called upon to interpret the second description, we should substitute the former for it. But the former description is not free from analogicality. God really is eternal Spirit, and really wills; but the positive meaning we assign to the words "eternal," "spirit," and "will" is borrowed from finite experiences of our own. Our type of the eternal is (say) a law of nature exemplified in all physical events throughout time; our type of spirit is our own rational consciousness; our type of will is our own act of will. When we apply such ideas to God, we throw in additions like "supreme," "absolute," or "perfect." Such additions express the belief that there is in God an eternity, spirituality, voluntariness we should find at that supreme height, if we could go so far. But we are left to judge the superlatives we cannot conceive from the positives that we can. Unless finite eternity, spirituality, and will bear some real analogy to aspects of God's being, what we say about him in such terms must be meaningless.

The problem of analogy is not avoided by claiming for the human spirit a direct contact with God. We are condemned to analogize in speaking of God not because God is inferred by us from other things but because, whether inferred or encountered, he transcends us. We cannot enter into God's way of being and acting: his touch upon us is wholly ineffable unless it moves us to stammer about it in creaturely terms. Nor can the problem be evaded by a pretended renunciation of the claim to objective truth. We cannot say, "It is unnecessary to claim that what we say of God is at all true of God. It suffices that it is true of our idea of God, so long as that idea guides us into a suitable attitude towards God." By attributing loving-kindness to God we are certainly determining the nature of our attitude to him as one of responsive love; but we cannot give responsive love to a being we do not actually believe to have loved us first.

The problem was formalized by St. Thomas Aquinas thus. If we are to use creaturely terms significantly for the Creator without degrading him to creaturely status, there must be terms applicable to creature and Creator neither *univocally* (in an identical sense) nor merely *equivocally* (in unrelated senses) but in some third way, viz. *analogically* (in senses not identical, but somehow related). *How* related, then? St. Thomas offers a solution.

II. The Doctrine of Analogy: St. Thomas finds his key in the metaphysics of being (see BEING). He claims to have demonstrated philosophically that being belongs to things in various degrees of fullness or of intensity, and that in God alone sheer or unqualified being is to be found. Such a way of thinking was greatly assisted by the physical theories of medieval science. He could quote the theory of heat. Things are hot in various degrees, through the direct or indirect influence of flame. But flame is hot of itself: it is elemental heat. In like manner God is elemental being, while other things *are* in various degrees, and in dependence on his influence. We do not know how hot flame is, for our sensory organs are destroyed by so great a heat and cannot register it. Similarly our intellectual faculty is incapable of appreciating how full, or intense, the being of God is. Nevertheless the mere notion of sheer or elemental being is intelligible: to say that while creatures possess being partially and derivatively, God is being elementally and absolutely, is to express an intelligible relation between created and uncreated being; a relation which, in scholastic language, can be called a simple proportion. And so between created and uncreated being there is an *analogy of proportion*.

According to St. Thomas's Aristotelianism, sentences which, when put into their most appropriate form, have the verb "to be" as their verb express in some way the being of their subjects. To say that God is wise is to place wisdom in the being of God. Now the sense in which a predicate is to be understood is always relative to the sort of being its subject has. I may say that a man is wise and that a project is wise. "To be wise" is a different thing for a man and for a project, because "to be" is a different thing for a man and for a project. A man has the being of a finite self-subsistent individual; a project has the being of a form taken by an interior act of a man's mind. To understand that difference is to understand the difference between "being wise" in the one case and in the other. If, then, it is right both to say that a man is wise and that God is wise, the difference between "being wise" for God and for man will be determined by the difference between what it is for God to be, and what it is for a man to be. We can therefore say, "As human wisdom is to man's being, so divine wisdom is to God's being," and this is called *analogy of proportionality*. When we are talking about God's wisdom we are talking about something which we do not directly or properly know, and of which we are

forced to judge from our knowledge of our own. So to say that God is wise is to say that something stands to God's being as our wisdom stands to our being. It would mean nothing to say this, unless we had some understanding (however formal) of the relation or "proportion" between our being and God's. But, according to St. Thomas, we have such an understanding. We have understanding of God's being by analogy of proportion with our own, and therefore we can have understanding of his attributes and acts by analogy of proportionality.

This lucid, coherent, and relatively simple doctrine of analogy appears to be part and parcel of St. Thomas's metaphysics. It is the effort of modern Thomists (see NEO-THOMISM) to extract from St. Thomas a formula which shall be independent of the purely medieval elements in his system, and tenable in conjunction with a more advanced physics and logic. The success of such efforts is very variously estimated. But the doctrine of analogy can be saved only as part of a more comprehensive pattern of metaphysical doctrine.

St. Thomas's doctrine was reformed and elaborated by Duns Scotus, and turned against itself by William of Occam. Occam's criticism is of more than historical interest. Accepting the doctrine that all theological conceptions are analogical, he called attention to the impossibility of reasoning validly from analogical premises. If we can at best know that there is in God's being something analogous to the excellences of our own, but differing from them by an infinite and indeterminable difference, can we ever say, "God is wise, and therefore . . ."? For the "therefore" must repose upon the confidence that God's wisdom is like our own in a certain respect; and how can we ever know that the difference between God's being and ours does not make his wisdom unlike ours precisely in that respect? Occam showed that rational or metaphysical theology employs analogical arguments throughout and is therefore inconclusive, and so he removed it to make way for a theology wholly dependent on divine revelation. But the Occamist cannot escape the analogical net so easily. For if all reasoning from analogical premises is utterly worthless, revealed theology itself is useless. Its statements are themselves analogical in form, and theological statements from which no inferences, practical or otherwise, can be drawn are sterile and virtually meaningless. Theological thinking, not theological statement only, must be possible; and it is possible, for we engage in it. If it is not governed by the strict rules of syllogistic form, it must be governed by other rules, or by some sort of intellectual tact; and this will be a proper subject for philosophical enquiry. Moreover it will have to be considered whether the sort of intellectual tact which makes thinking about revealed theology possible does not in like manner make thinking about natural or metaphysical theology possible.

Thomism underwent a revival in the Counter Reformation period, and the doctrine of analogy was systematized and defended by commentators, especially by Cajetan. But the rising tide of scientific rationalism in the seventeenth century confined the scholastic philosophy to the seminaries. The temper of Descartes and his successors was particularly unfavourable to the doctrine of analogy, as being a doctrine of half-knowledge. They aimed at building on clear knowledge only and neglected the twilight regions as unprofitable. Bishop Berkeley summarized Cajetan on analogy for the benefit of an objector: but not without an ironic apology for being so unfashionable. Kant shook the hard and bare dogmatism of eighteenth century deism and held a highly sophisticated view about our twilight knowledge of real being and especially of God; but he turned away from the mysteries and lacked that desire to contemplate divine being which is the motive for a serious consideration of analogy.

The latter part of the nineteenth century and the beginning of our own saw the spread of agnosticism about the nature of God. The contemporaneous revival of Thomism has appeared to its disciples to furnish the instrument required for dealing with the trouble of the times: analogy removes the confusions of agnosticism. But their attempts to modernize analogy have met with little acceptance outside Roman Catholicism and the circles most sympathetic to it. The doctrine has been opposed not only as logically and metaphysically obsolete but also as anti-Christian. Karl Barth and his school have denounced *analogy of being* for attributing too much to corrupted human reason, laying down a rational theology a priori, controlling the interpretation of revealed truth by it, and not allowing the self-revealing God to be his own interpreter. What is rejected by such a polemic is the Thomistic doctrine of analogy. But the problem of theological analogy remains, and the critique exercised by modern linguistic philosophy upon the very meaningfulness of theological statements forces it upon our attention. The inescapableness of the problem appears to a believer to be the shadow cast by the transcendent mysteriousness of God.

BIBLIOGRAPHY: For a select list of the Catholic literature see T. L. Penido, *La Rôle de l'Analogie en Théologie Dogmatique* (1931), 12, and the index on pp. 451 ff. for the principal texts in St. Thomas and his scholastic commentators. For modern Protestant rejection of the doctrine see Karl Barth, *The Doctrine of the Word of God* (Eng. transl., 1936), esp. 43–44, 192, 274, 279, 383–399. Recent English philosophical discussions in E. L. Mascall, *Existence and Analogy* (1949), and D. M. Emmet, *The Nature of Metaphysical Thinking*, 1945.

AUSTIN FARRER.

ANAMNESIS: Greek for "memorial," "commemoration." This term refers to a prayer in the early celebration of the Eucharist, already mentioned by Justin Martyr (*Dial. with Trypho*, 70), and Cyprian (*Epist.* LXIII, 16–17). In the Western liturgies, it is recited by the priest after the consecration of the elements. It recalls, with slight differences according to the various Latin rites, the passion, resurrection, and ascension of Jesus, and begs the Father to accept the eucharistic offering, as he once accepted the sacrifices of Abel, Abraham, and Melchizedek, which are its traditional types in the Old Testament. In the Eastern liturgies, the anamnesis is inserted between the narrative of the eucharistic institution and the *epiklesis*. It mentions the redeeming deeds of Jesus, his death, burial, resurrection, session at the right hand of God, and it ends with an announcement of his second coming.

BIBLIOGRAPHY: F. J. Moreau, *Les liturgies eucharistiques*, 1924.

GEORGES A. BARROIS.

ANARCHISM: The word is from the Greek privative, *an*, and *arche*, which, in this case, means an organizing principle or power. Thus, in the popular mind, anarchy is chaos in social relations, political disorder or lawlessness; and anarchists are people who advocate that as a good and who seek to bring it about by violence and terror. This is certainly a misconception, if it is thought to characterize the thinking and activity of those who have advocated Anarchism. It is not without some historical justification, if such an anarchist as Bakunin is regarded as typical or as the most consistent exponent of the spirit of anarchism; it is true that the basis of anarchism, negatively, is the conviction that organized government, the state, is an evil; and it is true that the first result of anarchist success would probably be chaos and violence. But anarchists have not typically been long-haired, wild-eyed, crack-brained products of the political slums. Proudhon was of humble birth; but he was a man of outstanding ability. Bakunin and Kropotkin were of high birth. Tolstoi needs no word of tribute, and he was a man of the greatest gentleness advocating nonviolent methods. The conviction that the state is an evil is quite old, and it has been shared by many who, because they were convinced that it was also a temporary or permanent necessity, did not become anarchists. The anarchists however denied that necessity, and actively advocated the abolition of political power.

Unlike the Nihilists (see NIHILISM), who shared these convictions and this destructive program, the anarchists had something positive to advocate. The evil of political government, so they believed, consisted in its essentially repressive character. Instead of that, they laid stress on the necessity of building upon those human impulses which, so they believed, made for harmony among men. Thus they advocated the ordering of society by good manners, or by means of such local economic organizations as naturally expressed a community of interests.

Thus Proudhon (1809–1865), the founder of French anarchism, insisted, as against Marx, that it was the political, not the bourgeois, character of the French Revolution that was responsible for its failure. What was required was simply that, all political power having been abolished, the economic interests of man should be adjusted through the exertions of private individuals. His was therefore an extreme application of the doctrine of *laissez faire*. Similarly the Russian anarchists, sometimes, as in the case of M. Bakunin (1814–1876), urging the destruction of the state by violent means, but sometimes, as in the case of L. Tolstoi (1828–1910), recommending and seeking to practise nonviolence instead, were, positively, advocates of extreme decentralization, a peaceful federation of small, self-governing, natural economic units, which already existed and which seemed to express the Russian character.

The anarchists were essentially individualists, hence their opposition to big, centrally strong government. They had a romantically high estimate of the value and dignity of the individual, and an intense sympathy for human suffering, which caused them to resent, sometimes in blind and impatient anger, all use of coercion among men.

BIBLIOGRAPHY: Among the more modern books bearing on this subject, the following may be suggested: Martin Buber, *Paths in Utopia*, 1950; E. H. Carr, *Bakunin*, 1937; C. P. Maximoff, comp. and ed., *The Political Philosophy of Bakunin: Scientific Anarchism*, 1953; T. G. Masaryk, *The Spirit of Russia*, 2 vols., 1919; E. Yaroslavsky, *History of Anarchism in Russia*, 1926; M. L. Berneri, *Neither East nor West*, 1952.

ANDREW K. RULE.

ANASTASIUS BIBLIOTHECARIUS: Is the same as the cardinal-priest of St. Marcellus who from August to September, 855, acted as the antipope of Benedict III. His works are in Migne, *P.L.*, Vol. 23, 33; 122, 127–129; *P. G.*, Vols. 29 and 108; his correspondence with Pope Adrian II in *M.G. Ep.*, VI, 2, 1912.

BIBLIOGRAPHY: E. Perels, *Papst Nikolaus I und Anastasius Bibliothecarius*, 1920.

[Sup.] MATHIAS GOOSSENS.

ANDERSON, CHARLES ALBERT: Presbyterian; b. at Orange, N. J., July 10, 1889. He studied at Williams College (A.B., 1912), at Auburn Theological Seminary (B.D., 1916), and at University of Pennsylvania (M.A., 1926); was assistant at First Presbyterian Church, Watertown, N. Y. (1916–17); minister of Prospect Presbyterian Church, Maplewood, N. J. (1917–21); Presbyterian minister to students, University of Pennsylvania (1921–31); president Tusculum College, Greeneville, Tenn. (1931–42);

president Coe College, Cedar Rapids, Ia. (1942–44); and has been manager, Presbyterian Historical Society, Philadelphia, Pa. since 1944 and editor of its quarterly *Journal*.

ANDORRA: A diminutive state on the border between France and Spain in the eastern Pyrenees Mountains with a population of 6,000. Officially named the Valleys and Suzerainties of Andorra, the state is under the influence of France, which controls the major public services. The population is Roman Catholic.

ANDOVER CONTROVERSY: In the last two decades of the nineteenth century the faculty of Andover Theological Seminary, which had been founded by New England Congregationalists in 1808, were involved in a debate with various ecclesiastical bodies over the doctrine which had become established at Andover that heathen who die without knowledge of the gospel will have an opportunity in the future life to have the gospel presented to them, and either to accept or reject it before being brought to final judgment. This was not the only controversy in which the Andover faculty engaged. Earlier disputes are sometimes referred to as "Andover controversies" but the discussion of "future probation," as the doctrine was called, is the most widely known of these theological engagements.

Newman Smyth, brother of Egbert Smyth, Andover professor, introduced the doctrine of future probation in America. German theologians such as Dorner and Martensen were teaching it. The faculty at Andover which published the new *Andover Review* from 1884 to 1893 defended the doctrine in articles later published in book form under the title *Progressive Orthodoxy*.

Future probation became an issue in the church at large when certain graduates of Andover were refused commissioning by the American Board of Commissioners for Foreign Missions because they accepted the new teaching.

Behind this controversy there lay the wider theological movement in which the Andover faculty was participating. They were working out of their inherited Calvinism in the spirit of the liberal emphasis upon the immanence of God, the doctrine of progress, the rights of biblical criticism, and the conception of human nature as progressively educable toward the good. It was the development of this theological standpoint with its implications for the theology of missions which concerned the Andover theologians, Egbert C. Smyth, William Jewett Tucker, and George Harris. Future probation was only one aspect of the larger issue in their minds.

Charges were finally brought against Egbert

C. Smyth by some of the ruling bodies of the seminary that his teaching departed from the creed required of professors. The controversy soon died with the general ascendancy of the point of view for which the Andover faculty was contending throughout the Congregational Churches.

BIBLIOGRAPHY: See Henry K. Rowe, *History of Andover Theological Seminary*, 1933; Daniel D. Williams, *The Andover Liberals*, 1941; Thomas P. Field, "The Andover Theory of Future Probation," *The Andover Review*, VII (1886), 461–475.

DANIEL D. WILLIAMS.

ANDRADA DIDACUS:

BIBLIOGRAPHY: A. de Backer and C. Sommervogel, *Bibliothèque des écrivains de la Compagnie de Jésus*, 1890–1909.   [Sup.]

ANDRAE, TOR JULIUS EFRAIM: (1885–1947) Swedish bishop.

He became professor of the history of comparative religion in Stockholm in 1927 and at Uppsala in 1929; minister of Ecclesiastical Affairs and Public Instruction in 1936; bishop of Linköping in 1936. He did research on comparative religion, especially Islam, and on the psychology of religion. Andrae was a low churchman. He was of a literary turn. In 1932 he was elected a member of the Swedish Academy.

BIBLIOGRAPHY: *Tor Andræ in memoriam*, 1947.

CARL-GUSTAF ANDRÉN.

ANDREWES, LANCELOT: John Hacket,

Bishop of Lichfield, was one of many contemporaries who paid well-deserved tribute to him. He wrote in part as follows: "This is that Bishop of Winton whose learning King James admired above all his chaplains." He was besides "full of alms and charity," in the pulpit he was a "Homer among preachers" and the "ointment of his name" was "sweeter than all spices." Hacket was one of the boys at Westminster School when Andrewes was dean there, and he always remembered how this learned scholar charged the masters to give "lessons out of none but the most classical authors." At the age of sixteen he had mastered more than the rudiments of Latin, Greek, and Hebrew. When he studied at Cambridge he never left the college precincts even on holidays. He was intimately concerned with the preparation of the so-called Authorised Version of the Bible, being chairman of a group appointed to translate the earlier books of the Old Testament. As dean of the Chapel Royal he wielded great influence upon King James and was his most favoured court preacher. Although his collected sermons went through five editions from 1629 to 1661, his fame among readers was derived from his admirable work, *Private Devotions* (*Preces privatae*), written in Greek, Hebrew, and Latin. His manuscript, so his friends tell us, was "slubbered with his pious hands and watered with penitential tears." He was one of the leaders of the High Church party, and his love of outward beauty and dignified ceremonial in worship was evident in his care of his chapel at Ely, where he was appointed bishop in 1609. From there nine years later he was translated to the bishopric of Winchester. Despised and derided by numerous Puritans and Independents, he was nevertheless a model of virtue, except in his subservience to the king. And in this respect his opponents were correct in condemning him. When the wife of Essex wished to marry the king's favourite, Robert Carr, Earl of Somerset, James did not want to refuse Somerset even this pleasure, but the archbishop of Canterbury and the bishop of London were critical of Andrewes' meekness in complying with the king's orders, though the bishop himself undoubtedly believed his decision to be an honest one.

BIBLIOGRAPHY: F. Higham, *Lancelot Andrewes*, 1952; C. H. McIlwain, *The Political Works of James I* (1918), Introduction; Charles Williams, *James I*, 1934; G. Davies, *The Earlier Stuarts*, 1937.

[Sup.] ALBERT HYMA.

ANDREWS, CHARLES FREER: B. February 12, 1871, at Newcastle-on-Tyne; d. April 5th, 1940.

He was educated at King Edward VII School, Birmingham, and Pembroke College, Cambridge. He was head of Pembroke College Mission (1896); Fellow of Pembroke College (1900); Vice-Principal of Westcott House (1900). He joined Cambridge Brotherhood, Delhi (1904), and after being a Fellow of Punjab University (1908), he joined Rabindranath Tagore's settlement at Santiniketan in 1913. He supported Gandhi on his advocacy of the claims of Indian laborers in South Africa; assisted in the Smuts-Gandhi agreement (1913–15). Afterwards he represented Indians of Fiji, Kenya and British Guiana. He wrote *Renaissance in India; Christ and Labour; Mahatma Gandhi's Ideas; Sadhu Sundar Singh; The Challenge of the North-West Frontier; Rise and Fall of the Congress in India*.

EDWIN OLIVER JAMES.

ANDREWS, E(LISHA) BENJAMIN: Baptist, d. Oct. 30, 1917.

He was chancellor of the University of Nebraska (1900–08, emeritus 1908–17). His additional books are: *Cosmology* (1900); *History of the United States in Our Own Times* (1904); and *The Call of the Land* (1913).   [Sup.]

ANGELA OF FOLIGNO: B. at Foligno in 1246,

she led a worldly life till she was forty, and then, after the death of her husband and her children, she joined the Third Order of St. Francis. In 1290–1291 she made her profession, followed by numerous contacts with the Spiritual Franciscans. Around her gathered a circle of devout sisters, until in 1309 she died at

Foligno. She dictated the account of her teaching and her visions to Arnaldus the Franciscan, completing the task in 1297. In addition she left twenty-five smaller works, letters, conversations, and notes. Her religious beliefs were strictly Franciscan, with a strongly individualistic love for God. Her writings were highly praised by Francis of Sales, Fénélon, Bousset, and Alphonsus de Liguori. A critical edition of these compositions was issued in 1926 by P. Doncoeur in Paris. Numerous editions of earlier dates, including that by the Bollandists and that by Ernest Hello, were based upon a poor compilation dating from the sixteenth century.

BIBLIOGRAPHY: Faloci-Pulignani, *La Beata Angela da Foligno*, 1926; M. J. Ferré, *La spiritualité de S. Angèle de Foligno*, 1927; L. Leclève, *Sainte Angèle de Foligno*, 1936.

MATHIAS GOOSSENS.

ANGELS, GUARDIAN: Roman Catholic theologians commonly teach that each individual soul is entrusted by God to the care and vigilance of a guardian angel. This, however, was never defined as an article of faith. Texts from the Old and New Testament are quoted as authorities in support of this doctrine, such as Ps. 91:11; Matt. 18:10. Communities also are said to enjoy the protection of guardian angels (cf. Ex. 32:34; Rev. 2, 3). The liturgical calendar of the Roman Church prescribes the celebration of a feast in honor of the guardian angels on October 2. GEORGES A. BARROIS.

ANGELUS CLARENUS (DE CINGOLI): B. in the Mark of Ancona, probably at Fossembrone. In *ca.* 1270 he entered the Order of the Franciscans at Cingoli. In 1274 he was imprisoned because of his ideas on poverty, but was released in 1289. In 1302 he founded the group of hermits known as the Fratres Clareni. After the death of Frater Liberatus (Petrus of Macerata) in 1307 he became the leader of the Spiritual Franciscans in Italy. His writings, in which he defended the teachings of the Spiritual Franciscans, are of considerable value in that they reflect the current ideas of their time. They are entitled: *Historia septem tribulationum ordinis minorum; Epistola responsitiva contra Fr. Alvarum Pelagium; Epistola excusatoria ad Papam de falsa impositis et fratrum calumniis;* and *Expositio regulae Ordinis Fratrum Minorum.* He also wrote two smaller ascetic treatises. He translated from Greek into Latin the following: *Regula S. Basilii; Scala Paradisi Johannis Climaci;* and *Dialogus S. Macarii.*

BIBLIOGRAPHY: P. Ehrle published several works and studies in the first four volumes of *Archiv fuer Litteratur und Kirchengeschichte des Mittelalters*, 1885–88; L. Oliger, *Expositio Regulae Fratrum Minorum*, Quarrachi 1912; V. Doucet, *Angelus Clarinus ad Alvarum Pelagium, Apologia pro vita sua*, in *Archivum Franciscanum historicum*, Vol. 39 (1946), pp. 63–200.

MATHIAS GOOSSENS.

ANGLO-CATHOLICISM: A movement in the Anglican communion (see ENGLAND, CHURCH OF) which emphasizes the Catholic as against the Protestant heritage of the Church of England and of other churches which originated in it. The term came into usage at the middle of the nineteenth century. Forerunners of the movement in England include the high church "Caroline Divines" of the seventeenth century, and William Law (*q.v.*, Vol. VI) and Alexander Knox; in America, the Rev. Samuel Johnson (*q.v.*), Bishop Samuel Seabury (*q.v.*, Vol. X), and Bishop John Henry Hobart (*q.v.*, Vol. V). The theological roots of the movement lie in the Oxford Movement, led mainly by John Henry Newman, Edward Bouverie Pusey (*q.v.*, Vol. IX), and John Keble (*q.v.*, Vol. VI). The theology of the Oxford Tracts, formed in reaction to the revolutionary measures of various liberal forces in England during the 1830's, is conservative, patristic, and emphatic in its claims regarding sacraments and the authority of episcopally ordained ministers. Newman's emphasis upon the Catholic nature of the Church of England led him, in Tract 90, to assert that the Thirty-nine Articles (*q.v.*, Vol. XI) agree with the Council of Trent (see TRENT, COUNCIL OF). Variously rebuked for Roman Catholic tendencies, he submitted to that communion in 1845. A number of adherents of the Oxford Movement, both in England and America, followed suit. But the main energy of the movement stimulated a theological and devotional revival in the Church of England which counteracted many moribund tendencies evidenced in the first quarter of the nineteenth century.

The liturgical roots of Anglo-Catholicism lie in the work of the Cambridge Camden Society (formed 1839 and led by John Mason Neale [*q.v.*, Vol. VIII] and Benjamin Webb) and of such Tractarians as John Jebb (*q.v.*, Vol. VI), and Walter Farquhar Hook (*q.v.*, Vol. V). This movement studied and worked toward the revival of medieval ceremonial, hymnody, and architecture as elements of the Catholicity of the Church of England.

Both the liturgical and theological movements were deeply informed by contemporary romanticism (*q.v.*, Vol. X). The two streams were combined by numerous clergy during the nineteenth century, especially in parishes of working people.

A liberal phase of Anglo-Catholicism came to life as various adherents rethought the meaning of Christianity under the criticism of such movements of modern thought as socialism, biblical criticism, scientific historical research, evolution, etc. The biblical and theological work of Charles Gore (*q.v.*) is representative of the contributions of a number of outstanding "liberal Catholics."

Modern leaders of Anglo-Catholicism, such as the theologian Kenneth Kirk and the liturgiologist Dom Gregory Dix, represent a reaction against the liberal phase and a reassertion of exclusive claims for episcopacy (q.v.), Catholic dogma and liturgy, and the Catholic nature of Anglicanism.

Since the time of the Tractarians, Anglo-Catholicism has had a large following within the Protestant Episcopal Church in the U.S.A. (see EPISCOPALIANS), although Americans have never seized the leadership in the thought of the movement. Early it evoked staunch opposition among Episcopalian Evangelicals (see EVANGELICALISM, ANGLICAN), and many controversies developed between these two factions, despite efforts by leading Episcopalians to combine the insights of both in church pronouncements and policies.

BIBLIOGRAPHY: George E. DeMille, *The Catholic Movement in the American Episcopal Church*, 1941; Wilfred L. Knox and Alec R. Vidler, *The Development of Modern Catholicism*, 1933; Y. Brilioth, *The Anglican Revival*, 1925; S. C. Carpenter, *Church and People*, 1933.

WILLIAM ANTHONY CLEBSCH.

ANGLO-ISRAEL: Known variously as Anglo-Israel, British-Israel, the Anglo-Saxon Federation, etc., this movement holds as its central article of faith that the Anglo-Saxon peoples are the true Israel and therefore heirs to all the promises made by God to Israel in the Bible. As a religious group it is fundamentalist (see FUNDAMENTALISM) in respect to its view of the Bible. All Scripture is true, given of God, and therefore must be fulfilled. God promised Abraham, and later others, that so long as the sun, moon, and stars endure, so long should Israel survive as a *nation* before him *forever*. Therefore Israel must exist somewhere as a *nation* today. But could this not be fulfilled in the creation of the new state of Israel? By no means, declare the Anglo-Israelites, for the present state of Israel is Jewish, and the Jews are not to be confused with Israel. The true Israel is the Anglo-Saxon peoples.

Support for this view is to be found in books dating from as early as 1694, but it was John Wilson's *Our Israelitish Origin* (1840) that first clearly stated the theory as held today by Anglo-Israelites. They succeed in proving to their own satisfaction that by three different routes ancient Israel was transplanted to British soil. First a migration reached Britain as early as 1000 B.C. Another came with Jeremiah and Baruch and the princess Tamar Tephi, who wed king Eochaid, ruler of Ireland, himself descended from the earlier Israelite migration. From this pair is descended, they believe, the present royal family of Britain, thus linked to the line of King David. With them the migrants brought from Israel the famous stone Jacob rested his head on at Bethel, which be-

came England's famous coronation "stone of Scone." The other migration was that of the ten lost tribes of Israel which after many centuries of wandering through the Near East and Europe entered Britain as the Anglo-Saxons, Celts, Jutes, Danes, etc. Elaborate arguments from secular history and geography are made to support the view.

The movement is widespread and active. In America a national magazine, *Destiny*, is published as well as many tracts and propaganda leaflets. Local groups are known as Kingdom Gospel Institutes. There is a British-Israel World Federation with branches in every part of the English-speaking world. As long ago as 1901 it was estimated that 2,000,000 people held the British-Israel view.

BIBLIOGRAPHY: John Wilson, *Our Israelitish Origin*, 1840; M. H. Gayer, *The Heritage of the Anglo-Saxon Race*, 3rd ed., 1941; Charles S. Braden, *These Also Believe*, 1949; H. G. May, in *Biblical Archaeologist*, VI (1943), 55–60.

CHARLES S. BRADEN.

ANGLO-SAXON FEDERATION: See ANGLO-ISRAEL.

ANGLO-SAXONS, CONVERSION OF THE:
BIBLIOGRAPHY: *Anglo-Saxon Chronicle*, ed. by B. Thorpe, in *Rolls Series*, No. 23, 2 vols., 1861; also ed. by C. Plummer, 1892; Bede, historical works, particularly *Hist. eccl.*, ed. by C. Plummer, 2 vols., 1896; Gildas, *De excidio et conquestu Britanniae*, ed. by T. Mommsen, in MGH, *Chronica minora*, III (1898), 1–85; also ed. by H. Williams, with transl., 1899; the letters of Gregory the Great, ed. P. Ewald and L. M. Hartmann, in MGH, *Epistolae*, I–II, 1887–93; those relating to the mission to England, with other material pertaining to St. Augustine, in *The Mission of St. Augustine*, ed. by A. J. Mason, 1897; Haddan and Stubbs, *Councils*, Vol. III; J. M. Lappenberg, *Geschichte von England*, I, 1834, Eng. transl., *A History of England, under the Anglo-Saxon Kings*, 2 vols., 1845; B. Thorpe, *Ancient Laws and Institutes of England*, 1840; R. Schmid, *Die Gesetze der Angelsachsen*, 1858; J. M. Kemble, *The Saxons in England*, II (1876), 342–496; J. R. Green, *History of the English People*, Vol. I, Book I, 1877; idem, *The Making of England*, 1882; W. Stubbs, *The Constitutional History of England*, I, chap. VIII, Oxford, 1883; E. Winkelmann, *Geschichte der Angelsachsen bis zum Tode Koenig Alfreds*, 1884; W. Bright, *Early English Church History*, 1897; G. F. Browne, *Augustine and His Companions*, 2nd ed., 1897; F. Liebermann, *Die Gesetze der Angelsachsen*, 3 vols., 1898–1916; W. Hunt, *The English Church from Its Foundation to the Norman Conquest*, 1899; W. Hunt, *The English Church in the Middle Ages* (n. d.), pp. 1–54; A. Plummer, *The Churches in Britain before A.D. 1000*, Vols. I–II, 1911–1912; H. H. Howorth, *The Golden Days of the Early English Church from the Arrival of Theodore to the Death of Bede*, 3 vols., 1917; T. A. Tidball, *The Making of the Church of England, A.D. 597–1087*, 1919; J. A. Robinson, *Times of Saint Dunstan*, 1923; A. J. Robertson, *Laws of the Kings of England from Edmund to Henry I*, 1925; G. Sheldon, *The Transition from Roman Britain to Christian England, A.D. 368–664*, 1932; R. H. Hodgkin, *A History of the Anglo-Saxons*, 2 vols., 2nd ed., 1939; F. M. Stenton, *Anglo-Saxon England*, 1943; R. G. Collingwood, *Roman Britain and the English Settlements*, Oxford History of England, Vol. I, 2nd ed., 1949; D. Jerrold, *An Introduction to the History of England: from the Earliest Times to 1204*, 2nd ed., 1952. [Sup.] HARRY KIMBER.

ANHALT: The Evangelical Church of Anhalt is an independent territorial church in the political districts of Magdeburg and Halle in the eastern zone of Germany (q.v.). Its territory embraces 906 square miles and includes (1952) 400,000 Evangelicals, 65,000 Roman Catholics (whose numbers were increased since 1945 by refugees, q.v.), and a few Jehovah's Witnesses (q.v.) and adherents of the New Apostolic Church (q.v.). The Evangelical Church was separated from the state in 1919, and the constitution adopted in 1920 has remained in force ever since. According to this constitution the members of congregational councils and of the synod are elected by members of the congregations. The synod in turn elects members of the superior church council (*Oberkirchenrat*) which, with its seat in Dessau, administers affairs of the Church. When, in 1946, religious education in public schools was forbidden, pastors, aided by specially trained catechists, supplied instruction in the churches. In 1952 there were 222 churches, 142 parishes, and 121 pastorates; pastors to fill all these posts were not available. The deaconess motherhouse (see DEACONESSES), founded in Dessau in 1893, and an Evangelical Academy are supported by offerings of the people. A union church (q.v.) since 1820, the Evangelical Church of Anhalt reintroduced Luther's Catechism in 1892 and adheres formally to the Augsburg Confession (q.v.).

[Sup.] HERMANN GRAF.

ANNIHILATIONISM: Theories which either imply or directly teach annihilationism, or conditional immortality, have continued to appear in the current century. In so far as they are simply restatements of views already dealt with in the article on this topic in Volume I of this encyclopedia, they perhaps call for no further notice. But a form of the doctrine, based on evolutionary points of view (see EVOLUTION), was enunciated by McConnell in his *Evolution of Immortality* and a similar view, that man is not immortal but "immortable," was independently reached by J. Y. Simpson, and elaborated in his *Man and the Attainment of Immortality.* The theory is, in brief, that when the evolutionary process, operating under the kind of law made familiar by Darwin, had produced man, a stage was reached when further evolution was dependent only or mainly on laws of the moral and spiritual type; and that immortality was achieved only when a certain stage in moral and spiritual evolution had been attained.

Since this view was presented in support of the Christian system, it was natural and inevitable that critics should raise the question of the immortality of those dying in infancy. Since they have had no opportunity to achieve such spiritual development through their own efforts, it would seem to follow that they must perish. Dr. Simpson noticed the objection in a footnote (page 233). "The case of those dying in infancy," he wrote, "presents no particular difficulty on this view: these innocents could not have willed themselves out of relationship with God." The reply, however, is not conclusive. It assumes that human individuals are in that relationship with God which guarantees their immortality until they will themselves out of it; but the theory is that human individuals are not in that relationship until they have reached a stage of spiritual development at which they may will themselves into it; and that presumably infants have not done.

The theory also, by its insistence on human achievement as a condition of immortality, seems at least to obscure the distinction between immortality and eternal life (q.v.) and to do less than justice to the doctrine of regeneration (q.v.) as a creative act of God alone.

[Sup.] ANDREW K. RULE.

ANNOTATED BIBLES. See BIBLES, ANNOTATED.

ANSGAR: Although his whole life was fired with the saintly ambition to do missionary work, he accomplished very little. His biographer mentions the building of only two churches by him, one among the Danes and one among the Swedes. He was sadly hampered by lack of assistants. Being of a contemplative nature, like St. Boniface, he differed from the latter in developing too little initiative. His honorary title of "Apostle of the North" should be seen in its proper light, as too great an honor.

BIBLIOGRAPHY: *Dict. d'Hist. et de Géogr. Eccl.*, Vol. III (1924), 435–441; E. de Moreau, *St. Anschaire, missionaire en Skandinavie au IXe siècle*, 1930; P. Oppenheim, *Der Heilige Ansgar und die Anfaenge des Christentums in den nordischen Laendern,* 1931.

[Sup.] MATHIAS GOOSSENS.

ANTES, HENRY: German Reformed lay preacher and ecumenical pioneer; b. at Freinsheim, Germany, 1701; d. on his farm in eastern Pennsylvania, 1755. Coming to America, 1721, he became a Reformed elder at Falkner Swamp (now New Hanover, Pa.). Visiting and preaching among the spiritually destitute German settlers, he deplored their religious divisions. Following the arrival of Nicolaus Zinzendorf (q.v., Vol. XII) and with his approval, Antes sent out a call to the various German-speaking religious groups to meet in conferences. From these issued a union proposal for a "Congregation of God in the Spirit." When the plan failed (1742), Antes became more closely associated with the Moravians, helping for a while to manage their economy at Bethlehem.

BIBLIOGRAPHY: McMinn, *On the Frontier with Colonel Antes,* 1900.

DAVID DUNN.

ANTHEM: A choral setting of a sacred text, permitted, but not prescribed by liturgical usage. Some denominations limit the selection of texts to excerpts from the Bible or official denominational publications; others allow the composer much more freedom in his choice. The anthem is peculiarly a British development, originating in Elizabethan times as the Protestant counterpart to the sixteenth century motet, from which it differed in the use of the vernacular, of solo voices, and of an obligato accompaniment. In general the musical setting reflects at least some of the musical trends of the period in which it was written.

PAUL ALLWARDT.

ANTHOLOGION: A liturgical book of the Greek Church, in which the various parts of the main offices of the liturgical year and of the saints, originally contained in separate books, were gathered together for reason of commodity. Thus it corresponds roughly to the Roman Breviary. GEORGES A. BARROIS.

ANTHONY (KHRAPOVITZKY): Eastern Orthodox; b. on the estate of his father, Novgorod district, in 1864; d. Aug. 11, 1936, at Sremski Karlovci, Yugoslavia. He studied at the St. Petersburg Theological Academy, and was there lecturer in the Old Testament. Later he became rector of the Moscow Theological Academy, rector of the Kazan Academy and suffragan bishop of the diocese of Kazan, bishop of Oufa, Volynia, Kharkov, and finally metropolitan of Kiev. He left Russia after the Revolution and settled finally in Yugoslavia, as the president of the Synod of the Russian Church abroad. He was widely known for his political ideas and activities, very conservative and even reactionary. But more important was his contribution to theology. He insisted on an ethical interpretation of dogmas. His programmatic essay "Concerning the Dogma of Redemption" has been published in English in *The Constructive Quarterly* (June, 1919).

GEORGES FLOROVSKY.

ANTHONY, SAINT, OF PADUA: His talents as preacher were made known during the consecration of a priest at Forli, where Anthony was called upon to deliver an oration, and not on the occasion of his own consecration. In 1946 he was finally elevated to the rank of doctor of the church. The sources on his life are not easy to evaluate, particularly those that refer to the miracles he was said to have performed. The oldest source is that called *Legenda Assidua*, composed about 1232 by an unknown writer, but ascribed by some to Thomas of Celano, published by L. de Kerval, *St. Antonii de Padua vitae duae* (Paris, 1904), and by R. Cessi, *Legende Antoniane* (Milan, 1936). Closely related to this source is that written between 1235 and 1240 by Julianus of Speier: *Vita Antonii*, ed. H. Dausens O.F.M.: *S. Francisci Assisiensis et S. Antonii Patavini Officia rythmica* (Muenster, 1934). Later accounts were largely based upon

the two just mentioned, but a third source appeared *ca.* 1367 called *Liber miraculorum*, and published in *Analecta Franciscana*, Vol. 3 (Quaracchi, 1897, pp. 121–158). The latter might be termed the Fioretti of Anthony.

He wrote at least two collections of sermons: *Sermones Dominicales* and *Sermones sanctorum*, edited by A. Locatelli and after his death by his colleagues I. Munaron, G. Perrin, and M. Scremin (Padua, 1895–1903). In dispute are the *Sermones in Psalmos*, which are probably authentic, and the *Concordantiae morales*, which are probably not his work.

He taught the traditional Augustinian-Franciscan dogma, with his own additions, such as that of the Virgin Mary's bodily ascension into heaven, the sharply defined doctrine of creation out of nothing: *facere ex nihilo*, his classic description of original sin (*spoliatum gratuitis, vulneratum in naturalibus*), his delineation of mystic powers, and the formulation of the term *transsubstantio*, probably his own creation.

BIBLIOGRAPHY: R. M. Huber, *St. Anthony of Padua; Doctor of the Church Universal*, 1948; L. F. Rohr, *The Use of Sacred Scripture in the Sermons of St. Anthony of Padua*, 1948; L. de Kerval, *L'evolution et le developpement du merveilleux dans les Légendes de S. Antoine de Padoue*, in *Opuscules de critique historique*, 1906; K. Wilk, *Antonius von Padua*, 1907; J. Pou y Martin, "De fontibus S. Antonii Patavini" in *Antonianum*, Vol. VI (1931), 225–252; B. Kleinschmidt, *Antonius von Padua, in Leben und Kunst, Kult und Volkstum*, 1931; *Die Antoniuswunder nach den aelteren Quellen untersucht*, 1933; Willibrord de Paris, *S. Antoine de Padoue. Docteur de l'Église. Sa vie et son oeuvre*, 1947.

[Sup.] MATHIAS GOOSSENS.

ANTHONY, SUSAN BROWNELL: B. Feb. 18, 1820; d. Mar. 13, 1900, she was the champion of women's suffrage whose celebrated trial in 1872 sought to test the legality of women's right to vote (United States vs. Susan B. Anthony, in Blatchford, *Report on Cases in the Circuit Court*, XI, 200-212). Born to a well-to-do New England Quaker father who encouraged his daughter's independence of mind, she grew through a precocious youth to restless maturity. Full of schemes of reform, her first public efforts were directed on behalf of temperance (*q.v.*), but when, in 1852, as delegate to a meeting of the Sons of Temperance in Albany, she was refused the privilege of speaking because of her sex, she began her fight against the prevailing prejudice against women in public affairs. She was an early advocate of Negro suffrage. Her endless tours and campaigns, her writing, and her association with others like Elizabeth Cody Stanton led to the founding in 1869 of the National Suffrage Association which sought a sixteenth amendment to the Federal Constitution enfranchizing women.

See WOMAN, EMANCIPATION OF.

BIBLIOGRAPHY: Ida H. Harper, *The Life and Work of Susan B. Anthony*, 1925.

JOHN JOSEPH STOUDT.

ANTHONY (VADKOVSKY): Eastern Orthodox; b. in Tambov district, 1864; d. Nov. 2,

1912. He studied at the Theological Academy of Kazan, and was there professor of homiletics; then transferred to the Academy of St. Petersburg, to become its rector; bishop of Vyborg, archbishop of Finland, finally metropolitan of St. Petersburg and the presiding member of the Holy Synod. He was a strong promoter of a reorganization of the church in Russia, which would restore more freedom and independence to the church. He was chairman of the Commission preparatory to the Council in 1906–07, but the Council was not convened at that time. His scholarly work was confined to the history of preaching in the Slavic East in the early Middle Ages. GEORGES FLOROVSKY.

ANTHONY, SAINT, ORDERS OF: The information presented by the historians of the period up to 1297 must be used with great caution. The accounts concerning the origin and development of the order contain numerous legends. The extensive practice of revering Abbot Anthony as a saint of the people in Western Europe was caused largely by the expanding knightly orders, especially that of the Hospital Brothers. Afterward the reverence for him was progessively reduced by that given to the later St. Anthony of Padua.

BIBLIOGRAPHY: Aymarus Falco, *Antonianae historiae compendium*, 1534; L. Maillet-Guy, *Les commanderies de l'ordre de St. Antoine en Dauphiné*, 1928; P. Noordeloos, *Enige gegevens over de broederschappen van S. Antonius*, in *Publications de la société historique et archéologique dans le Limburg* (1949), 477–497.

[Sup.] MATHIAS GOOSSENS.

ANTHROPOCENTRIC: A term applied to a doctrine which is "man-centered," as contrasted with one that is "God-centered" (theocentric). A doctrine is anthropocentric if, denying or ignoring the existence of God and non-human purpose, it grounds values in human nature and directs religious sentiments toward human ideals. Currently, the term seems to be applied most often to religious humanism (*q.v.*).

The classic expression of anthropocentrism is by Protagoras: "Man is the measure of all things." Auguste Comte's Religion of Humanity is anthropocentric in that it makes mankind, not God, the object of devotion. The philosophy of Friedrich Nietzsche is explicitly anthropocentric with respect to values, as is the "atheistic existentialism" (*q.v.*) of Jean-Paul Sartre.

BIBLIOGRAPHY: Auguste Comte, *The Catechism of Positive Religion*, trans. by R. Congreve, 1858; Oscar Levy, ed. *The Complete Works of Friedrich Nietzsche*, 1909 ff.; Jean-Paul Sartre, *Existentialism*, 1947; Corliss Lamont, *Humanism as a Philosophy*, 1949.

VINCENT TOMAS.

ANTHROPOSOPHY: A religious and philosophical system founded by Rudolf Steiner (1861–1925)), a former Roman Catholic, born in Kraljewic, Hungary, who had become the general secretary of the Theosophical Society in Germany. Steiner, a brilliant combination of occultist, clairvoyant, scientific thinker, and Goethe scholar, broke with Theosophy (*q.v.*) in 1913, proclaimed himself the herald of Anthroposophy, and drew with him most of the Theosophical Societies in Germany. Under the leadership of Friedrich Rittelmeyer (1872–1938), a former Evangelical pastor, the movement was organized into Christian Fellowships (*Christengemeinschaften*), the first in Stuttgart, 1922. The societies were banned under National Socialism, but grew rapidly again after the war, until now there are about 150 "priests" and "priestesses" in Germany and societies elsewhere in Europe, England, and one in New York.

Anthroposophy (the wisdom of humanity), despite the assertions of its founder to the contrary, shares the basic tenets of Theosophy (the wisdom of God) and cannot be understood without a knowledge of Theosophy's characteristics as a syncretistic system which amalgamates Vedantism, Neo-Platonism (*q.v.*, Vol. VIII), Gnosticism (*q.v.*), Sufism (*q.v.*), the sects of medieval mysticism (*q.v.*), and Jacob Boehme (*q.v.*). Theosophy emphasizes the twin beliefs, reincarnation and karma, which promise final escape from the wheel of life to chosen initiates who have learned the secrets of the esoteric teaching of the *arhats* or masters. Anthroposophy shifts the emphasis to humanity as the center of all perceptions of this "spiritual science," and is a method of attaining knowledge of higher worlds by occult powers resident in man. Through mental, physical, and spiritual exercises of meditation and concentration, based on *yoga*, the disciple becomes a *Hellseher*, a master of clear vision, gaining supersensuous means of perception.

Steiner's special contribution is the doctrine of the seven lotus flowers. The seer sees that man possesses, not merely body, soul, and spirit, but seven bodies, the physical, etheric, astral, the "I" proper, etc., which open out like seven lotus blooms. As the rainbow has seven colors, so the universe is constructed of seven planets: Saturn, Sun, Moon, Earth, Jupiter, Venus, Vulcan. But the seer not only pierces the universe by concentration and meditation directed to the depth of the human soul, he sees all history, human, sacred, and prehistoric, without the aid of books, Bible, or palaeontology. This is recorded in the so-called *Akasha Chronicle*, the details of which Steiner never fully revealed.

Steiner and his followers assign a central place to Christ, who is not merely one of a number of *arhats* or avatars, as in Theosophy, but the one avatar, the great solar being who appeared to rescue the world from ruin. The supersensual world is revealed fully in Christ, and the celebration of the sacrament is the central act in the worship of the Christian Fellowships. The bread and wine are transfused with the spirit and body of Christ so that the communicant is made truly "man," whereas before he was only an image distorted by hostile powers. The service is therefore called the "act of the consecration of man" (*Menschenweihehandlung*). The celebration is rich in symbolism and color, interpretative of Steiner's basic teachings. The movement, like similar cults, attracts mostly the rootless, disillusioned "intellectuals." See also THEOSOPHY.

BIBLIOGRAPHY: Most of Steiner's writings have been translated into English, published by the Anthroposophic Press in London and New York: *Knowledge of the Higher Worlds and its Attainment*, 6th ed., 1947; *World History in the Light of Anthroposophy*, 1951; *Christianity as Mystical Fact and the Mysteries of Antiquity*, rev. ed., 1947. The same press is publishing the works of Friedrich Rittelmeyer: *Reincarnation*, n.d.; *Meditation*, n.d. Critical: Articles, *"Anthroposophie"* and *"Christengemeinschaft,"* RGG, 2nd ed., 1927–31; Kurt Hutten, *Seher, Gruebler, Enthusiasten*, 1950; Paul Scheurlen, *Die Sekten der Gegenwart*, 3rd ed., 1923; Paul Althaus, *Evangelischer Glaube und Anthroposophie*, 1949; W. F. Lofthouse, "Anthroposophy," *Expository Times*, LIV, pp. 285–290.
JOHN W. DOBERSTEIN.

ANTI-CATHOLIC MOVEMENTS. See INTERFAITH RELATIONS.

ANTICLERICALISM. See CLERICALISM.

ANTI-DEFAMATION LEAGUE: Organized in 1913 to combat Anti-Semitism (*q.v.*), the League has counteracted the ridicule of Jews in the press and on the stage, exposed attacks on Jews on racial grounds, and co-operated with the National Conference of Christians and Jews (*q.v.*) to promote better understanding. The League is an agency of B'nai B'rith (Sons of the Covenant), a Jewish fraternal organization founded in New York City on Oct. 13, 1843, and given its present name in 1930.
THEODORE G. TAPPERT.

ANTIDORON: In Eastern liturgies, pieces of bread from the loaf from which the fragments to be consecrated for the Eucharist have been lifted. The antidoron is blessed and given to the people. Paralleled in the West by the distribution of the holy bread (*pain bénit*), a custom still observed in French churches at Sunday high mass.   GEORGES A. BARROIS.

ANTILLES, LESSER. See WEST INDIES.

ANTIMISSIONARY MOVEMENT: A nineteenth century American phenomenon which mushroomed into life in various parts of the country about 1820, flourished through 1840, then gradually lost ground. Only a token expression of its main spirit exists today.

Its rise must be viewed against the backdrop of constitutional separation of church and state in 1791. Faced with the necessity of autonomous organization, the American churches had turned to the neo-Calvinist principle of free "association" for attainment of religious ends and had taken to the founding of voluntary missionary societies on an unprecedented scale: to further home and foreign missions generally; then distribution of Bibles and tracts, establishment of Sunday Schools, and founding of theological seminaries; also a great variety of social movements of reform. Finally, toward 1820, a number of larger denominations pooled resources to found, in order, the American Tract, Education, Bible, Colonization, Sunday School, Temperance, Home Mission, and Peace Societies. To smaller groups this was carrying the missionary idea too far; if not a single denomination, a group of them might become sufficiently powerful to nullify separation of church and state, at the very minimum put an effective damper on democratic polity. It was imperative that all societies centralizing authority on the national level be opposed.

Thus, about 1820, certain groups turned antimissionary: "Primitive" and "Two-Seed-in-the-Spirit" Baptists and Disciples on the frontier; Christian Connection, Universalists, and "Free Thinkers," active both on the frontier and in the East; Unitarians, Hicksite Friends, and Protestant Methodists in the East only. To these should be added a sizable body of passive sympathizers whose inescapable connections with missionary denominations made silence the better part of valor.

These groups were polemicists *par excellence*. Turning to Scripture and church history they defied missionists to cite specific authority for their actions. What chapter or verse of Scripture commanded formation of Bible, Tract, Sunday School, or other missionary society? Where did these appear in history before modern times? They were inventions of man, the product of scheming doctors of divinity whose money-gathering propensities and zeal for organization threatened the future of the faith. Each group added its own particular brand of argument. Calvinistic "Primitive" Baptists ridiculed this attempt by man to secure his own salvation; completely corrupt since his fall, man could but sit and await the outcome of election. Universalists, believing in ultimate comprehension of all in the love of God, felt missionary effort a hindrance rather than a help to salvation; high pitch of excitement and centralization of authority were robbing man of the two things he needed most to right himself with God— reason and liberty. Most groups took a middle road between these positions. Whatever the argument, the frontiersman tended to carry it to the extreme. Himself a primary object of missionary endeavor, he deeply resented Eastern assumption that he had no religion of his own, did his best to harass the ministry of the salaried "priestly" graduates of theological seminaries who came west to tell him how to believe. He much preferred the unschooled farmer-preacher, "called" of God, not by salary, who witnessed but to the "primitive" faith.

Time proved this particular antimissionary movement to be a passing phase of American religious life. Lessening fear of a union of church and state and abatement of East-West rivalry in the face of an impending struggle over slavery gradually deprived it of vital *raison d'etre.* Only "Primitive" and "Two-Seed-in-the-Spirit" Baptists continued adamant in their stand, about 70,000 of the former and 200 of the latter existing in 1950, as opposed to missions as ever.

Antimissionism currently existing in Fundamentalism (*q.v.*), and in sects like the Jehovah's Witnesses (*q.v.*) bears resemblances to the movement here discussed but has different origins.

BIBLIOGRAPHY: B. H. Carroll, *The Genesis of American Anti-Missionism,* 1902; W. W. Sweet, *Religion on the American Frontier: the Baptists* (1931), Chap. IV; G. P. Albaugh, An Annotated Bibliography of Religious Periodicals and Newspapers Published in America, 1730–1830, with Library Locations (unpublished manuscript, Mills Memorial Library, McMaster University, Hamilton, Canada), which lists antimissionary periodicals of all descriptions.

GAYLORD ALBAUGH.

ANTIMODERNIST OATH: A profession of faith instituted by Pope Pius X, *motu proprio "Sacrorum Antistitum,"* September 1, 1910, in connection with the condemnation of modernism. The antimodernist oath is to be taken by clerics prior to their ordination to the subdeaconate; by priests admitted to the ministry of confession and preaching; by rectors and diocesan or papal dignitaries before entering office; by superiors of religious orders, and by doctors and teachers in ecclesiastical institutions of learning.

It supplements the "Profession of Catholic faith" prescribed by canon law, which is based on the Nicene Creed, on articles from the Council of Trent (profession of Pius IV) and from the Council of the Vatican.

The first part of the oath contains the following statements: The existence of God can be proved rationally. The divine nature of Christianity is manifested most certainly by external facts, namely by miracles and the fulfillment of prophecies. Christ personally founded the Roman Catholic Church, the papal system being an essential feature thereof. The traditional doctrine of the church was handed down unchanged from the time of the apostles and is not subject to evolution. Christian faith is a true and objective assent of the human intellect to revealed truth.

The second part of the oath bears on modernist principles condemned in the decree *Lamentabili sane exitu* and the encyclical *Pascendi dominici gregis* (*qq.v.*). It specifically repudiates any distinction between historical and dogmatic truth, and the interpretation of Scripture at variance with tradition, as well as the modernists' denial of supernatural elements in history, and their pantheistic view of the universe. Text (Latin) in *Acta Apostolicae Sedis,* II (1910), 669 ff. H. Denzinger, *Enchiridion Symbolorum* (1937), numbers 2145–2147.

GEORGES A. BARROIS.

ANTIOCH IN SYRIA. See ARCHAEOLOGY, BIBLICAL.

ANTIPHONARY: Latin *liber antiphonarius, antiphonarium, antiphonale.* In the medieval church, any book containing the text of the liturgy sung by the choir at mass and at the canonical hours. Today the name *antiphonary* applies specifically to a liturgical book containing the text and plain-chant notation of the sung portions of the breviary, whereas the *graduale* contains the portions of the mass sung by the choir.

GEORGES A. BARROIS.

ANTI-SALOON LEAGUE. See TEMPERANCE MOVEMENT.

ANTI-SEMITISM: Strictly speaking, the term anti-Semitism refers, not to dislike for Semitic peoples in general, but to a modern type of antagonism toward the Jews which emphasizes race rather than religion. The Jews are falsely regarded as a racial group in order that, by contrast, the myth of so-called Aryan superiority might gain support. In common usage, however, the expression is applied to any antagonism toward the Jews regardless of the motivation.

Living in a church-dominated society, the Jews of the Middle Ages had no standing as citizens and came to be barred from all desirable occupations. They were victims of superstitious mobs and were bled by greedy monarchs in return for a doubtful protection. Neither the Renaissance nor the Protestant Reformation brought the speedy emancipation they seemed to promise, but the principles they set forth were eventually to bear fruit. Foreshadowed by eighteenth-century liberalism, the French Revolution (1791) brought emancipation to the Jews in France and some neighboring countries. The revolutionary movements of the nineteenth century continued the process, but every intervening period of reaction saw a partial return of old restrictions. Hence some younger Jews joined the radicals, thus giving rulers occasion to suspect the Jews of inciting the revolts. Similarly, the success of Jewish financiers during the industrial revolution aroused jealousy and bitterness, especially in time of financial crisis. In Prussia modern racial anti-Semitism developed among reactionaries and the same spirit spread to Austria and France.

In 1881 the Russian Tzarist regime initiated a plan to divert from itself the resentment of the downtrodden peasants by inciting terrible pogroms against the Jews. A vast emigration resulted, directed principally to the United States. Liberation finally came to the Russian Jews in 1917. Persecution proved even more persistent in Rumania. Following World War I there was a rise of anti-Semitism in Germany, stimulated in part by an influx of eastern Jews. When Hitler came to power in 1933, he blamed all of Germany's ills upon the Jews. The Nuremberg racial laws of 1935 deprived Jewish people of citizenship rights; and a campaign of violence, initiated in 1938, continued until the defeat of Germany in 1945, resulting in the murder in Central Europe of about 6,000,000 Jews. The existence of anti-Semitism in the United States is clearly revealed by the presence of anti-Semitic organizations and of individual rabble-rousers, as well as by occasional local outbreaks of property destruction and violence. However, such activities have never been supported or sanctioned by the federal government. Jews from many countries are now finding a haven from anti-Semitism in the new State of Israel, which came into being in 1948.

BIBLIOGRAPHY: H. Valentine, *Antisemitism*, 1935; J. Parkes, *The Jewish Problem in the Modern World*, 1946; S. Grayzel, *A History of the Jews*, 1947; Graeber and Britt, *Jews in a Gentile World*, 1942; E. Simmel, *Anti-Semitism, A Social Disease*, 1946.

HAROLD FLOREEN.

ANTONIUS, SAINT, OF FLORENCE: A distinguished moralist who developed exceptionally profound and fresh theories on economic and sociological subjects. His views on the relation among the factors involved in the production of goods are a reflection of the atmosphere he found in Florence during the fifteenth century, when some 200 guilds operated there and most daring ideas were published concerning the inherent powers of the people as a whole, the rights of workmen, and the just price that should be charged for manufactured goods. The proper interaction of labor and capital which he envisaged sounds very up-to-date in the twentieth century. He ascribed to labor a high moral position and he also understood the fundamental principles involved in commerce and industry. In his opinion the value of articles of trade depended upon their usefulness and the actual cost of production. In this field the government had the right and the duty to supervise the relations between capital and labor, as well as between purchaser and seller. His concepts regarding the proper rates of interest charged on loans were more realistic than those of Luther and Calvin, who depended too much upon doctrines derived by clergymen from biblical passages.

BIBLIOGRAPHY: R. Morcay, *St. Antonin*, Paris 1914; A. Masseron, *St. Antonin* (Collection les Saints), 1926; C.

Ilgner, *Die volkswirtschaftlichen Anschauungen Antonius von Florenz*, 1904; A. Hyma, *Renaissance to Reformation* (1951), Chap. II; A. Doren, *Italienische Wirtschaftsgeschichte*, Vol. I, 1934.

[Sup.] MATHIAS GOOSSENS.

APOCALYPTIC LITERATURE. See PSEU-DEPIGRAPHA, OLD TESTAMENT.

APOCALYPTIC LITERATURE, MUSLIM. See MUSLIM ESCHATOLOGY.

APOCRYPHA: I. Old Testament: In Greek "apocrypha" means "hidden [things]" and eventually "spurious, noncanonical [books]." For Roman Catholics the term indicates the books which Protestants call Pseudepigrapha, while Protestants understand by Old Testament Apocrypha the books outside of the Hebrew Bible included in the Septuagint and in the Vulgate. When the canon of the Hebrew Bible was fixed at the Council of Jamnia (*ca.* A.D. 90) the Books of the Apocrypha were excluded for one of the following reasons: some books survived only in Greek after the Hebrew or Aramaic original was lost (Tob., Jth.); others were patently written later than Ezra, after whom prophecy, and consequently inspired writings, were believed to have ceased (I Macc., Ecclus.); others had been written in Greek (Wisd. of Sol., II Macc.). But in Alexandria this chronological limitation was unknown: all writings translated from Hebrew or Aramaic were included in the canonical scriptures in Greek, and even some Jewish books written in Greek were regarded as inspired. The Jewish Septuagint probably did not differ materially from the Christian copies, which include the Apocrypha. Allusions to the Apocrypha occur in the New Testament; some Apocrypha are quoted as Scripture by Tertullian, Clement of Alexandria, Origen, Cyprian, and later Fathers. Cyril of Jerusalem and Jerome denied the canonicity of the Apocrypha, but the Roman Catholic Church at the Council of Trent (1546) and at the Vatican Council (1870) declared these books "sacred and canonical," except I and II [III and IV] Esdras, and the Prayer of Manasses, printed after the New Testament in the Vulgate. The Protestants limit the Old Testament to the Hebrew Bible, although the Apocrypha were printed as an appendix in Luther's German Bible (1534) and were included in all English Bibles published before 1629. It is only since 1827 that Protestant English Bibles were generally issued without the Apocrypha.

A. I ESDRAS (*III Esdras* in the Vulgate) is a torso of the earliest and best Greek version of Chronicles-Ezra-Nehemiah. It begins with II Chron. 35:1–36:21, and continues with Ezra, ends with Neh. 7:73—8:13a (leaving the last sentence unfinished); Neh. 1:1–7:72 is omitted.

I Esd. 1:23–24 and 3:1—5:6 lack parallels in the Hebrew Bible. *The Story of the Three Youths at the Court of Darius* (3:1–5:6), which was popular among Christians, saved the book from oblivion. It was translated from the Aramaic, but was probably Persian in origin: moralized under Zoroastrian influence ("Great is Truth and mighty above all things"), it was finally inserted into Chronicles-Ezra-Nehemiah about 200 B.C. by Jewish editors, who identified the third youth with Zerubbabel (4:13) and linked the fictitious tale to the rebuilding of the Jerusalem Temple in 516.

B. II ESDRAS. This disconsolate apocalypse, (called *IV Esdras* in the Vulgate), was written in Aramaic *ca.* A.D. 90 and reflects Jewish despair and bewilderment following the destruction of Jerusalem in A.D. 70. It survives in a Latin version from the Greek, and in Syriac. The Jewish apocalypse (3–13), supplemented by an account of Ezra's restoration of the Scriptures (14), in Latin and translations from the Latin is enclosed within two Christian apocalypses (1–2 and 15–16) dated A.D. 150 and 250, respectively. The six visions of Salatiel (Shealtiel, in Ezra 3:2, etc.), explained by the angel Uriel, fail to solve the problem of Jewish suffering, although in this book eternal bliss is reserved for the righteous among the Jews exclusively.

C. TOBIT is a short story written in Aramaic soon after 200 B.C. God sent Raphael to help blind Tobit in Nineveh, and (in Ecbatana) Sara, the widow of seven husbands murdered on the wedding night by the demon Asmodeus (1–3). Tobit's son Tobias went to Media with Azarias, i.e., Raphael, and having married Sara drove Asmodeus to Egypt by burning the liver and heart of a fish caught in the Tigris (4–9); with its gall Tobit's sight was restored. (10–11). Raphael returned to heaven and Tobias went to Ecbatana with Sara (12–14). The author drew his material from folkloristic motifs (healing through the organs of a fish) and plots (the cycles of "the dangerous bride" and "the grateful dead").

D. JUDITH, written in Hebrew about 150 B.C., describes the deliverance of the Jews besieged in Bethulia through Judith's decapitation of Holophernes. The story is fiction, but reflects the patriotism and the religion of the Jews after the Maccabean rebellion.

E. THE REST OF THE CHAPTERS OF THE BOOK OF ESTHER. Six sections (107 verses) in the Greek Esther are added to the Hebrew text to supply the piety it lacks. According to the colophon, the Greek version, containing these additions, was made in 114 or in 78 B.C. The Hebrew Esther was probably written about 125 B.C.

F. THE WISDOM OF SOLOMON is a discourse attributed to Solomon, composed in Greek by an Alexandrian Jew during the period 100–50 B.C. Solomon warns apostate Jews about eternal damnation (1–5), reminds the pious Jews of Wisdom's deeds in behalf of Israel (10–12; 16–19), and strives to prove to the heathen both the nobility of Judaism (6–9) and the folly of idolatry (13–15). The notions about life after death combine Platonic and Stoic doctrines with Jewish teachings.

G. THE WISDOM OF JESUS THE SON OF SIRACH (ECCLESIASTICUS). Sirach, a scribe and teacher in Jerusalem, about 180 B.C. composed this work in two volumes (1–23 and 24–50); it was translated into Greek by his grandson soon after 132 B.C. Almost two thirds of the Hebrew text have been recovered through the decipherment of eleventh and twelfth century manuscripts excavated at Old Cairo. Without forgetting the Temple worship and alluding once to the synagogue (39:6), Sirach stresses personal religion, consisting of observance of the Law of Moses (especially its moral precepts) and kindness to the poor. His "Wisdom" includes, besides this religion, also shrewd common sense in business and social intercourse.

H. BARUCH is a composite work extant in a Greek version from the Hebrew. In 1:1–3:8 (*ca.* 150–100 B.C.) the Jews implore God's forgiveness. The poem in 3:9–4:4 (180–100 B.C.) praises Wisdom, which God gave to Israel exclusively. The poem in 4:5–5:9 (*ca.* 100 B.C.) promises, like Is. 40–66, salvation to Jerusalem and ruin to Babylon. The sixth chapter, in the Vulgate and the A.V., is *The Epistle of Jeremy,* a sarcastic denunciation of Babylonian idolatry written in Aramaic *ca.* 300–100 B.C.

I. THE SONG OF THE THREE HOLY CHILDREN, inserted *ca.* 100 B.C. after Dan. 3:23 into the Greek Bible, contains the prayer of Azarias in the fiery furnace, some details about the furnace, and the Song of the Three Children inviting all creation to bless the Lord.

J. SUSANNA. This detective tale was added to the Greek Daniel *ca.* 100 B.C., but in Aramaic may be three centuries earlier. Two Jewish elders in Babylon accused Susanna of adultery, but were cleverly convicted of false testimony by Daniel.

K. BEL AND THE DRAGON was translated from the Aramaic and added to the Greek Daniel *ca.* 100 B.C. Daniel proved to Cyrus that the priests, not Bel, consumed the food placed in his temple. Daniel slew the Babylonian dragon "without sword or staff" by feeding it with lumps of pitch, fat, and hair.

L. THE PRAYER OF MANASSES is a penitential psalm composed in Hebrew (first century B.C.) as a supplement to II Chron. 33:11–13. As often, sudden calamity produces repentance.

M. I MACCABEES is the best history of the Palestinian Jews from 175 to 135 B.C., from Judas Maccabeus to Simon. The Greek text was translated from a Hebrew original written about 100 B.C.

N. II MACCABEES is the epitome of a lost five-volume history of the Palestinian Jews from 175 to 161 B.C., written in Greek by Jason of Cyrene (see 2:19–32; 15:37–39). The rhetorical book describes divine interventions to save the Temple from heathen pollution. The two letters to the Jews in Egypt added at the beginning (1:1–10a and 1:10b–2:18), dated in 123 and 164, respectively, were translated from the Aramaic.

See CANON OF SCRIPTURE, II, B.

BIBLIOGRAPHY: R. H. Charles, *The Apocrypha and Pseudepigrapha of the Old Testament, in English*, 1913; W. O. E. Oesterley, *An Introduction to the Books of the Apocrypha*, 1935; E. J. Goodspeed, *The Apocrypha: An American Translation*, 1938; C. C. Torrey, *The Apocryphal Literature*, 1945; S. Zeitlin, "The Apocrypha," *JQR*, Vol. 37 (1947), pp. 219–248; cf. Vol. 40 (1950), pp. 223–250; Ralph Marcus, "Selected Bibliography (1920–45) of the Jews in the Hellenistic-Roman Period," *Proceedings of the American Academy for Jewish Research*, Vol. 16 (1946–47). pp. 97–181; R. H. Pfeiffer, *History of New Testament Times, with an Introduction to the Apocrypha*, 1949; A. Lods, *Histoire de la littérature hebraïque et juive depuis les origines jusqu'à la ruine de l'état juif*, 1950.

[SUP.] ROBERT H. PFEIFFER.

II. New Testament: Since the turn of the century, we have not only learned much more about the New Testament Apocrypha, but we have also attained to a far deeper appreciation of their worth. For a long time these writings had been treated merely as a detail in the development of the New Testament canon from which they were rejected, but we have now come to realize their vast importance as sources not only for the history of the early church, its customs, its outlook on life, its hopes and aspirations, but also for the art and literature of the Middle Ages. The reliefs of ancient sarcophagi, the mosaics of Christian basilicas, the miniatures of illuminated manuscripts, the stained glass windows of the cathedrals, the mystery plays—all owe their inspiration to the New Testament Apocrypha.

Moreover, a great number of discoveries have been made during the last decades. Of the *Acts of Paul*, C. Schmidt came upon major portions both of a Coptic translation in a papyrus of the University of Heidelberg and of the original Greek in a third-century papyrus at Hamburg. Of the *Apocalypse of Peter* a large section of the Greek text turned up at Akhmim and the entire work in Ethiopic. An apocryphal *Apocalypse of John* was edited by F. Nau from a manuscript at Paris. A. Vasiliev, M. Chaine, and M. R. James published several unknown *Apocalypses of the Virgin*. The *Epistle of the Apostles*, the most important and valuable of the apocryphal epistles, was first edited in 1919 from three versions, the complete Ethiopic and the mutilated Coptic and Latin. The main part of the letter consists of revelations made by the Saviour to his disciples after the Resurrection. The introduction contains a confession to Christ and a summary of his miracles. The conclusion describes the Ascension. The work shows definite anti-Gnostic tendency and does not reveal the least trace of chiliastic views. It contains a short creed of five articles. The Eucharist is called Pascha and regarded as a memorial of the death of Jesus. The Incarnation of the Logos is clearly stated, but Gabriel appears as a personification of the Logos. The beginning refers to Simon Magus and Cerinthus as "the false apostles." The epistle was probably written about A.D. 150. De Bruyne published in 1925 an apocryphal *Epistle of Titus, the Disciple of Paul*, which apparently originated in Priscillianist circles in Spain.

An entirely new period began for the history of the New Testament Apocrypha with the discovery in Egypt in 1946 of a great collection of Gnostic texts in a jar near Nag-Hammadi, close to ancient Chenoboskion and thirty miles north of Luxor. Their publication, already begun, will cast an altogether different light on the New Testament Apocrypha. The find appears to be the most impressive collection of books on papyrus that has ever been seen, whether from the point of view of quantity, of antiquity, or of state of preservation. It consists of thirteen documents, eleven complete volumes with their supple leather bindings and two other volumes preserved only in part. With the exception of one volume of the beginning of the fourth century A.D., they all belong to the third century of our era. Their content matches their archaeological value, for they contain on more than 1,000 pages 37 complete and five fragmentary works, of most of which we had nothing, of others only parts. Since a large number of apocryphal gospels and apocalypses occur among them, we have now the whole of the gospels according to Thomas, Philip, and the Egyptians, and besides, among those previously unknown, a *Second Apocalypse of James*, the *Secret Book of John*, the *Traditions of Matthias*, the *Dialogue of the Savior*, the *Apocalypse of Messos*, the *Apocalypse of Dositheos*, etc. These treatises are all in Coptic from Greek originals.

BIBLIOGRAPHY: M. R. James, *The Apocryphal New Testament*, 1924; E. Hennecke, *Neutestamentliche Apokryphen*, 2nd ed., 1924; idem, *Handbuch zu den neutestamentlichen Apokryphen*, 1914; B. Pick, *Paralipomena*, 1908; idem, *The Apocryphal Acts of Paul, Peter, John, Andrew and Thomas*, 1909; A. F. Findlay, *Byways in Early Christian Literature*, 1923; J. A. Robinson, *Excluded Books of the New Testament*, 1927; H. J. Bardsley, *Reconstructions of Early Christian Documents*, Vol. I, 1935; M. Dibelius, *A Fresh Approach to the New Testament and Early Christian Literature*, 1936; W. Schubart and C. Schmidt, *Praxeis Paulou*, 1936; H. Idris Bell and T. C. Skeat, *Fragments of an Unknown Gospel*, 1935; C. Schmidt, *Gespraeche Jesu mit seinen Juengern nach der Auferstehung*, 1919. For further editions, translations, and studies, see J. Quasten, *Patrology*, I (1950), 106–157. For the discovery of a Gnostic library, see Togo Mina, *Vigiliae Christianae*, 2 (1948). 129–136; 137–160; 3 (1949), 129–141. J. Doresse, "A Gnostic Library from Upper Egypt," *Archaeology* 3 (1950), 69–73. G. Quispel, *Gnosis als Weltreligion,* 1951.

[Sup.] JOHANNES QUASTEN.

APOLOGETICS: The first half of the twentieth century has been rich in polemics, but poor in apologetics. Professing Christians could, and did, argue freely among themselves, usually on specific doctrines or areas of thought; and their polemics often involved apologetic problems and procedures. But these were incidental to the polemics; and if we may, with Richardson (*Christian Apologetics,* p. 19) distinguish between apology and apologetics (cf. Warfield, this encyclopedia, Vol. I, p. 232 ff.) as the specific from the general, they were apology rather than apologetics.

A basic reason for this poverty in apologetics was the centrifugal character of our general culture. No philosophical system that could be used apologetically was widely accepted. The systems most in vogue were obstacles rather than aids to apologetics. Men gave their attention to specific problems, treated "factually," rather than to broader and deeper problems, treated "theoretically."

Divisiveness also characterized the theological culture of the period. Here the dominant tendency was liberalism (*q.v.*), but it was not a unifying tendency. For (1) though it was roughly unified by its employment of an empirical, inductive method, this still left room for emphatic methodological differences between the "social theologians" and the "new theists" (see D. S. Robinson, *The God of the Liberal Christian,* 1926). And (2) though the liberals did display a tendency to agree on a "liberal orthodoxy" in many areas of thought, they gloried in their freedom to differ widely in doctrinal conclusions.

Opposed to the liberals, in non-Catholic circles, were the fundamentalists and the Protestant conservatives. For the latter, see V. Ferm, ed., *Religion in the Twentieth Century* (1948), Chapter XIII. But their controversy with the liberals confined itself largely to specific problems, such as historical criticism, the virgin birth of Christ, the atonement, the doctrine of evolution, and the "social gospel." It produced polemics, not apologetics.

Thus the divisiveness of our general and theological culture was not conducive to work in apologetics. Two further influences, deriving from liberalism, worked to the same effect. (1) The theological liberals strove to replace methods and ideas which they regarded as outmoded by an up-to-date reconstruction based on wholehearted acceptance of the methods and discoveries of science. In order to overcome a tendency to face scientific discoveries and their own reconstruction in a spirit of grudging acknowledgment and final rejection, they characterized

that spirit and procedure as "apologetics," and poured scorn upon it. See W. L. Sperry, *"Yes, But"—the Bankruptcy of Apologetics,* 1931. (2) Their advocacy of a new construction, beginning empirically with the psychology of religion, checking the results by an appeal to the natural sciences, and taking up the whole into the philosophy of religion, together with their scornful attitude toward apologetics, caused that type of study largely to supplant apologetics, regarded as a systematic explication and defence of a system of Christian doctrine already exegetically set up.

But the problems of the present have moved to a deep level which calls more for apologetics than for polemics; and there are evidences that apologists are recovering their nerve and their freedom to operate, while the self-confidence of those who turned rather to the philosophy of religion is no longer so daunting. Such books as Alan Richardson's *Christian Apologetics* (1947), and E. J. Carnell's *Introduction to Christian Apologetics* (1948) and W. M. Smith's *Therefore Stand* (1945), may be harbingers of a vigorous apologetics.

[Sup.] ANDREW K. RULE.

APOLOGY OF THE AUGSBURG CONFESSION. See AUGSBURG CONFESSION, APOLOGY OF THE.

APOSTASY: The Code of Canon Law distinguishes between apostasy from religion, viz., the unlawful abandonment of religious life by a professed member of an order or congregation, and apostasy from the faith. The latter is defined as the obdurate rejection of Christian faith in its entirety, by a baptized person. The Roman Church cautions its members against marrying such persons. Apostates from the faith are denied church funerals, unless they give some mark of repentance before dying. A formal abjuration (*q.v.*) is required prior to the reconciliation of apostates from the faith.

[Sup.] GEORGES A. BARROIS.

A POSTERIORI. See A PRIORI.

APOSTLES' CREED: I. Method of Study: In order to clarify the history of the Apostles' Creed it is necessary to make clear distinctions among its various stages of development. The full creed is not identical with the Roman baptismal symbol, which in turn is not identical with earlier confessions of faith. Without such distinctions discussion is impossible. Moreover, the proper method for studying creedal history or any other kind of history is chronological. Such a method avoids the danger of reading later formulations into earlier documents. Since, however, Harnack's article is arranged in reverse order, we shall follow him, correcting his conclusions where correction seems necessary. The section numbers are derived from his article.

II. Revision of Harnack's Views: (1) The Apostolicum is first found in the tract *De singulis libris canonicis* (chapters 10 and 12) of Priminius, who apparently represents the usage of southwestern France and wrote between 710 and 724. This creed was probably made official by the theologians of Charlemagne in support of his ideal of uniformity, and along with Gallican liturgical forms probably reached Rome during the ninth century.

(2) The "details" which Harnack dismisses are fundamental for creedal history. Actually there is no reason to suppose that the Apostolicum *in its present form* originated earlier than the seventh century.

(3) Closely related to the Apostolicum are the Gallican creeds of Faustus of Riez, Caesarius of Arles (who wrote the sermon in the *Missale Gallicanum vetus*), and Cyprian of Toulon (a disciple of Caesarius). These creeds are undoubtedly descendants of the Roman symbol, though, as Harnack says, Rome was no longer using the symbol after the sixth century.

(4) No ancient Christian would have questioned the apostolic origin of the common faith, as we can see from the remarks of Irenaeus and Tertullian (see RULE OF FAITH). This consideration, however, cannot be used to determine matters of chronology or to test novelty.

(5) The text of the Roman symbol is set forth in Latin by Rufinus (*ca.* 404), whose text is confirmed by a sixth or seventh-century manuscript in the Bodleian Library and an eighth-century manuscript in the British Museum. A Greek version is represented in the *Psalter of Aethelstan* (ninth century). Something like it is quoted in Greek by Marcellus of Ancyra in the year 340 (text in Epiphanius, *Pan. haer.* lxxii. 3), with the omission of "Father" at the beginning and the addition of "eternal life" at the end. Marcellus, writing in Asia Minor, is giving the Roman church his own creed in the belief that it is theirs. He was fond of the expression "God Almighty" (not "Father"), and his omission may be personal. "Eternal life" is common, however, in various Eastern creeds at this time, and we must suppose that its inclusion reflects them rather than Roman usage. Whether the symbol was originally Latin or Greek cannot be determined. We may note that the creedal form underlying the writings of Augustine is not Roman but African. In any event, this Roman symbol of the fourth century must be distinguished from its predecessors.

(6) The direct ancestor of the Roman symbol, however, must come from the middle of the third century (as Harnack says), because all later local Western creeds are based on it.

(7) There is no reason to suppose that the ancestor of the Roman symbol was derived from Asia Minor. In the *Apostolic Tradition* of Hippolytus (*q.v.*), bishop of Rome early in the third century, we find a series of baptismal interrogations which correspond almost exactly to the affirmations of the symbol. The questions are (*Apost. Trad.* 21),

"Do you believe in God the Father Almighty?

"Do you believe in Christ Jesus, the Son of God, who was born of the Holy Spirit from the Virgin Mary and crucified under Pontius Pilate and died and was buried and was raised (rose) again on the third day, living from the dead, and ascended into the heavens and sat at the right hand of the Father, (and) will come to judge the living and the dead?

"Do you believe in the Holy Spirit, (in) the Holy Church and the resurrection of the flesh?"

About the same time, Tertullian (*Praescr.* xxxvi) shows some familiarity with something resembling this form, though he omits "Father" at the beginning and makes some relatively unimportant additions. It is probable that Hippolytus' interrogations represent only one of several formularies current not only in Christian churches generally but even in the Roman church. At this period creeds were in a fluid state. To say with P. Nautin (*Je crois à l'Esprit Saint,* 1947) that Hippolytus either introduces or reflects a symbol which speaks of the Holy Spirit as residing in the Holy Church and effecting the resurrection of the flesh is to go beyond the evidence.

What can be said is that the baptismal formula of Hippolytus presumably looks back to an earlier period in which a short trinitarian creed was combined with a longer Christological statement. Such a trinitarian formulation is represented in Justin (*Apol.* i. 61. 3), where we read of baptism "in the name of God the Father of the universe and sovereign, and of our Savior Jesus Christ, and of the Holy Spirit" (cf. Matt. 28:19). The antiquity of formulas at least implicitly trinitarian seems to be guaranteed by the New Testament, though it must be admitted with Oscar Cullmann that the earliest confessions of faith are either Christological or "binitarian" (cf. I Cor. 8:6). We can hardly look for a fully developed trinitarian doctrine in the New Testament.

It should be said that the attempts of various scholars in this century to explain the development of the creed as due to a desire for symmetry—each of the three articles of belief was to be provided with three subheadings—do not explain it at all. The creed is not symmetrical; the disproportionate length of the second article is due to the Christian gospel of Christ. There is little evidence to prove that any of it was written against heresies. Instead, it represents the common faith of the early church.

(8) The Apostles' Creed is the result of a long process characterized by accretions intended to make explicit what was formerly only implicit. Its sources were primarily baptismal confessions, which were based in part on the apostolic preaching about Christ and in part on more general considerations taken from the "rule of faith." Later additions such as the *descensus ad inferos* (first found in Rufinus) and the *communio sanctorum* (Nicetas of Remesiana, end of the fourth century) do not essentially modify its meaning.

BIBLIOGRAPHY: H. Lietzmann, *The Founding of the Church Universal* (1938), 136–60; F. J. Badcock, *The History of the Creeds*, 2d ed., 1938; J. de Ghellinck, *Patristique et Moyen Age*, I, 2d ed., 1949; O. Cullmann, *The Earliest Christian Confessions*, 1949; W. Bieder, *Die Vorstellung von der Hoellenfahrt Jesu Christi*, 1949; J. N. D. Kelly, *Early Christian Creeds* (1950), the best book on the subject.

[Sup.]   ROBERT M. GRANT.

APOSTLES' CREED IN WORSHIP: Bodies liturgical and non-liturgical use this Creed in public worship more often than any other "form of sound words." In length and in clarity they find it suitable as an expression of common faith. Many non-liturgical churches omit the obscure clause: "He descended into hades." Some say "Holy Spirit," not "Holy Ghost." Lutherans and others employ the word "Christian," instead of the "Holy Catholic Church." Customs vary concerning the place of this Creed in the service. Some have it early in the hour; others, at a climactic stage before the sermon. Some use the Creed after a hymn, and then have the Gloria in Excelsis. Others prefer the Creed after the main lesson from Holy Writ, thus letting the people voice their response to God's revelation of Himself. The Creed throughout stresses objective facts about the triune God. Toward the end it might also voice Christian beliefs about other aspects of revealed truth, such as the kingdom of God, interracial brotherhood, and world missions. Lovers of the Creed all agree that worshipers should stand during the recital, and few would object to the custom of bowing the head at each naming of a Person in the Holy Trinity.   ANDREW W. BLACKWOOD.

APOSTLESHIP OF THE SEA. See SEAMEN, MISSIONS TO.

APOSTOLIC CHRISTIAN CHURCH (NAZAREAN): Founded by the Swiss clergyman, S. H. Froelich, the Church has 31 congregations and 1,663 members in the United States. It emphasizes sanctification. Its members refuse to bear arms. Each congregation is served by elders who are authorized to baptize, lay on hands, administer the Lord's Supper, and exercise discipline. [Supplement to article in Vol. VII, p. 389.]   JACOB MEYER.

APOSTOLIC CHRISTIAN CHURCH OF AMERICA. See HOLINESS CHURCHES.

APOSTOLIC CHURCH OF NORTH AMERICA. See CATHOLIC APOSTOLIC CHURCH.

APOSTOLIC CONSTITUTIONS AND CANONS: I. Sources of the Liturgical Directory of the Eighth Book: Interest in the *Apostolic Constitutions and Canons* in the last half century has centered in the relation of the liturgical directory in Book Eight to Hippolytus' *Apostolic Tradition,* formerly known as the *Egyptian Church Directory.* Brightman's definitive study of the early Syrian rite here presented together with its sources and related documents has won almost unanimous acceptance for the thesis of the compiler's direct dependence upon Hippolytus. It is evident, however, from the comparison of the *Constitutions* with the *Tradition* that the compiler did not regard the latter as inviolable except in so far as it accorded with contemporary Antiochene liturgical practice. The elaborations and amendments of the litany reflect indeed just those usages current in the Syrian rite evidenced in quotations from Chrysostom and the Antiochene *diakonika.* Little weight can now be given to the attempts of Probst and Bickell to find in the *Constitutions* the liturgy of the ante-Nicene church. Their arguments, based on the length of the prayers, parallels with the language of Justin Martyr, and the affinities between this liturgy and the Jewish passover ritual have been convincingly answered by Brightman, Cabrol, and Srawley. These general considerations together with specific matters of language, dependence, and liturgical preference have led more recent commentators confidently to identify the "constitutor" with the author of the Larger Recension of the Ignatian Epistles, and to approve a date for the *Constitutions* around A.D. 375. Turner's suggestion that this Pseudo-Ignatius belonged to the Arian party has been rejected by all except Dix.

II. The Place of the Constitutions Among Early Church Orders: The place of the *Apostolic Constitutions* in relation to other similar and connected documents has been with fair certainty established in recent studies of the textual materials of *The Apostolic Tradition.* Behind the work of Hippolytus are the *Doctrina* and the *Didache.* The *Didascalia* (ca. A.D. 250) followed Hippolytus' *Tradition,* and its author may have known it. Next in chronological order is the revision of the *Didache,* with elaborations and additions derived from *Barnabas,* known variously as *The Apostolic Church Order,*

The Apostolic Church Directory, III Clement, The Apostolic Canons, and *The Roman Church Order.* Then came *The Apostolic Constitutions and Canons* followed by *The Epitome of the Eighth Book of the Apostolic Constitutions,* in reality simply a series of extracts which Achelis wrongly considered a first draft of the *Constitutions.* Three later documents belonging to this family are *The Testament of Our Lord* based largely on *The Apostolic Tradition,* the *Canons of Hippolytus,* a fifth century revision of *The Apostolic Tradition,* and *Sarapion's Prayers* which evidence the influence of both the *Didache* and *The Apostolic Tradition.*

BIBLIOGRAPHY: Editions: F. X. Funk, *Didascalia et Constitutiones Apostolorum,* 2 vols., 1905. For discussion of the liturgical directory in Book viii see F. E. Brightman, *Liturgies Eastern and Western,* 1896; Probst, *Liturgie der drei ersten christl. Jahrhunderte,* 1870; Bickell, *The Lord's Supper and the Passover Ritual,* 1891; Cabrol, *Les origines liturgiques,* 1906. On the relation of the *Constitutions* to the *Apostolic Tradition* see R. H. Connolly, *The So-Called Egyptian Church Order* (Cambridge Texts and Studies viii), 1916; B. S. Easton, *The Apostolic Tradition of Hippolytus,* 1934; G. Dix, *The Treatise on the Apostolic Tradition of Hippolytus of Rome,* 1937; J. H. Srawley, *The Early History of the Liturgy,* 1947. On the dating of Bk. VIII see H. Lietzmann, *Messe und Herrenmahl,* 1926. The theological orientation of the "constitutor" is discussed by C. H. Turner in *JTS,* Vols. XV and XVI.

[Sup.] NOAH EDWARD FEHL.

APOSTOLIC EPISCOPAL CHURCH. See OLD CATHOLICS.

APOSTOLIC FAITH MOVEMENT. See HOLINESS CHURCHES.

APOSTOLIC FATHERS: I. History of Texts and Studies: The collection and textual criticism of these early Christian writings began in 1628 with the publication by Patrick Young, royal librarian, of I and II Clement from the Codex Alexandrinus which had come to London as a gift to the English crown from the patriarch of Constantinople. Within the next quarter century Greek texts of Polycarp (Halloix in 1633), Barnabas (Menard d'Achey, 1645) and Ignatius (Voss, 1646) appeared. The first general edition of the documents under the present title was published by Cotelier in 1672 as the works of "the holy fathers who flourished in apostolic times." The last year of the seventeenth century witnessed Ittig's more finished work (*Library of the Apostolic Fathers*), and it was not until the editions of Dressel (1857) and Gebhardt, Harnack, and Zahn (1877) that any further substantial contributions were made to the study of these texts. Discoveries of papyrus fragments and oriental versions stimulated modern interest and facilitated the recent texts of Lightfoot-Harmer (1891), Lake (Loeb Series 1913), Bihlmeyer's revision in 1924 of Funk's 1881 edition, and Bonner's text of *Hermas* (1934) based on the Michigan papyrus.

II. Canon: No definite canon of these subapostolic documents has ever been promulgated.

To the universally included letters of *Barnabas, I and II Clement, Ignatius,* and *Polycarp,* and the *Shepherd of Hermas* which comprised Cotelier's collection, subsequent editions added the fragments of *Papias* and *Quadratus,* the *Didache,* the *Letter to Diognetus,* and the *Martyrdom of Polycarp.* Quasten (*Patrology,* 1950) has elected to include the Pseudo-Clementine literature together with *II Clement* within his discussion of the Apostolic Fathers, and Goodspeed's *American Translation* begins with the *Doctrina.*

III. Nature and Significance of These Documents: It would be difficult to overemphasize the importance of the Apostolic Fathers in the history of the thought and development of the Christian Church. Forming the most valuable supplement to the New Testament, they provide on the whole an artless witness to the life within the several vital church centers of the second century. Doctrinal, ecclesiastical, and devotional emphases reflect the diversity of perspective in the churches of Rome, Corinth, Alexandria, Smyrna, and Antioch. In the personalities behind the writings is exhibited a significant variety of representative types in the expression of Christian experience. From the common witness of the documents it is apparent that second century Christians regarded themselves as a separated people, a new Israel builded upon the new law revealed in Christ. Entrance into the True Israel was by repentance culminating in baptism. Life in the new community was characterized by liturgical observance, a general movement away from personal to official charisma in leadership, and an ascetic ideal. No longer do we find the full Pauline emphasis upon justification by faith; nor is Christian character understood to be, in the Pauline sense, the expression of a redeemed personality that has through the operation of divine grace been set in a new relationship before God. In the place of this given relationship, the basis in New Testament theology for moral progress, the subapostolic age holds up ascetic discipline and moral progress as the condition of the new relationship with the Father. With this misinterpretation of the Gospels and the Pauline Epistles the church is launched upon a development of asceticism as the ethics of a mystical and sacramental theology. Despite these general tendencies in doctrine, worship, and ecclesiastical organization characteristic of the Apostolic Fathers as a whole, we must, with Streeter (*The Primitive Church*) and Goodspeed (*Early Christian Literature*), recognize the greater richness of variety and diversity in the early church to which these fathers give abundant witness through their several media of apocalypse (*Hermas* and *Barnabas*), church orders (The *Doctrina* and the *Didache*), homily (*II Clement*), pastoral and episcopal epistles (*I Clement, Ignatius, Polycarp*), martyrology (*Polycarp*) and apologetic (*Quadratus* and the *Epistle to Diognetus*).

BIBLIOGRAPHY: Editions: K. Bihlmeyer, *Die apostolischen Vaeter*, 1924; K. Lake, *Apostolic Fathers* (Loeb Classical Lib.) 1913; H. Hemmer, Oger, Laurent, and Lelong, *Les Pères apostoliques*, 4 vols., 2nd ed., 1926. Translations: Lake, *Apostolic Fathers*, 1913; Glimm, Walsh, Marique, *Apostolic Fathers*, 1947; E. J. Goodspeed, *The Apostolic Fathers, An American Translation*, 1950. Studies: Goodspeed, *Early Christian Literature;* J. Quasten, *Patrology*, 1950; and see bibliographies on individual authors and writings.

[Sup.] NOAH EDWARD FEHL.

APOSTOLICITY. See MARKS OF THE CHURCH.

APOSTOLIC LUTHERANS. See LAESTADIUS.

APOSTOLIC OVERCOMING HOLY CHURCH OF GOD. See CHURCH (CHURCHES) OF GOD.

APOTHEOSIS: The attribution to a man of the status of a god. The attribution may be made unconsciously, as when, among the ancients, founders of cities, heroes, etc. were deified through the growth of legend; or by a formal act, as when the Roman senate conferred divine honors upon Julius Caesar and, subsequently, upon successive rulers of the empire. In either case, deification is associated with polytheistic religion. VINCENT TOMAS.

APPEALS TO THE POPE: The Code of Canon Law states that it is the privilege of all the faithful to introduce or to carry any litigation or criminal procedure before the jurisdiction of the pope, on account of his primacy over the Church Universal. It is understood, however, that such a recourse does not suspend or terminate the original procedure, until the Holy See actually declares its exclusive competence. This extraordinary power of the pope in judiciary matters must be distinguished from his appellate jurisdiction. The main stipulations of canon law concerning appeal in canonical procedure are as follows: There is no appealing from a decision of the pope, nor of the tribunal of the *Signatura,* nor from a sentence of a judge especially appointed by the Holy See with the clause "appeal excluded." Nor is it permissible to appeal from a ruling of a judge, as long as the definitive sentence has not yet been pronounced.

[Sup.] GEORGES A. BARROIS.

A PRIORI: A term used by Kant to refer to knowledge which is "absolutely independent of all experience"; also applied to the statements in which such knowledge is expressed. A priori knowledge is to be contrasted with a posteriori knowledge, which is "empirical," having its "sources in experience." For example, the statements, "No circles are rectangles," "All quadrupeds have feet," and "Either it is raining or it is not raining," can be known to be true independently of any examination of particular instances and are thus a priori; but the statements, "No lakes are rectangles," "All quadrupeds are vertebrates," and "It is raining," can be known only a posteriori. It is generally held that all a priori statements are necessary.

Many of the statements expressing a priori knowledge are analytic or tautologous and are therefore of such a form that it would be contradictory to deny them. The most important philosophical question concerning a priori knowledge is the question whether there are a priori statements which are synthetic, i.e., not analytic or tautologous. Most empiricists and positivists held that all a priori statements are analytic, but Kant and others have held that some a priori statements are synthetic.

BIBLIOGRAPHY: Immanuel Kant, *Kritik der reinen Vernunft*, Introduction, 1787. C. I. Lewis, *Mind and the World-order* (1929), Chaps. 7 and 8.

RODERICK M. CHISHOLM.

AQUARIANS: At no time did they constitute a sect, but were persons addicted to ascetic ideas and the practices which proceeded from them. Their chief characteristic was an antipathy to the use of wine, even at the Lord's Supper. Sometimes they were accounted orthodox Christians who, apart from the practices peculiar to them, lived conformably to the rules of the church. Sometimes, however, their ascetic tenets led them into undoubted heresies. Even in the Christian church, from the first, the eucharistic cup contained a wine greatly diluted with water, probably in accordance with traditional Jewish custom. The Latin name Aquarii was applied to them by Philastrius; the Greek name Hydroparastatae by Theodoretus and others.

How early their error manifested itself in the worship of the church cannot be exactly determined. Early writers refer to it, but not to its origin. Clement of Alexandria, for instance, cautioned his pupils and readers against the Encratites who consecrate bread and water for the Eucharist, in contravention of the church's rule and scriptural appointment. That Tatian held Encratite and other erroneous opinions seems very probable, but that he was an implacable opponent of the use of wine in the Eucharist is not so certain. The case of Pionius of Smyrna provides a doubtful instance of a water-Eucharist, according to Tillemont, but Batiffol's only comment thereon is: "At Smyrna, as well as in Africa, there were Aquarians among the Catholics." St. Cyprian's testimony would support this comment, for his epistle to Caecilius is wholly occupied with the Aquarian practice followed by certain Christians of his time and neighborhood. St. Augustine is brief, as if he had no direct experience of them: "the

Aquarians are so called because they offer water in the cup of the Sacrament, not that which the church offers."

The Aquarians were to be met with mostly in Asiatic districts and even in Africa, during the third and fourth centuries, and also in other quarters, though rarely, during the fifth century. After that time they gradually disappeared. When, in the seventh century, other eucharistic irregularities manifested themselves and were condemned (at the Councils of Braga, A.D. 675, canon 2, and of Trullo, A.D. 692, canon 32), the Aquarian heresy was merely a memory of the past.

Harnack's theory concerning water-Eucharists gave a new importance to the whole subject of aquarianism sixty years ago when he published his treatise, *Brod und Wasser*. The theory he set out to establish was the frequent use by the early Christians of water as the second element of the Lord's Supper. For this purpose he assumed that bread and water were the only eucharistic elements for Justin Martyr. In the following year (1892) appeared Theodor Zahn's reply, entitled: *Brot und Wein im Abendmahl der alten Kirche*. It may be stated at once that Harnack's theory had a mixed reception in scholarly circles at its issue. Undoubtedly, the Greek words *kai kramatos* which Justin used in *Apol*. I, 65, 3, are peculiar, since *krama* meant "a mixture (of water and wine)," so that what Justin wrote, strictly interpreted, was: "to the president there is brought bread and a cup of water and of water-and-wine." Several suggestions have been offered in explanation of Justin's curious phraseology, but the simplest and probably most correct is that the Martyr was using *krama* in the general sense of "wine." In its ordinary meaning of a mixed drink, it formed with the previous word "water" perhaps a hyperbole, but even as such it would constitute an expression appropriate to the usage of that epoch.

BIBLIOGRAPHY: Irenaeus, *Contra Haereses*, I, 28, V, 1 & 2; Clement of Alexandria, *Paedagogos*, II, 2, *Stromateis*, I, 19; Cyprian, *Epistola 63 (ad Caecilium)*; Augustine, *De Haeresibus*, I, 64; Philastrius, *Diversarum Hereseon Liber* (ed. Fridericus Marx, Lipsiae, 1898); Gregory of Nyssa, *Oratio Catech. Magna*, 37; Jerome, *Prologue to Commentary on Titus, Commentary on Amos, II:12*; Theodoret, *Compendium Haereticarum Fabularum*, I, 20; Leo I, *Sermo XLII*, 5; Theodoricus Ruinart, *Acta Primorum Martyrum*, Amstelaedami, 1713; Philippus Labbeus, et al., *Sacrorum Conciliorum Collectio*, Florentiae, 1765, t.XI, 155, 956–957; Adolf Harnack, *Brod und Wasser: die eucharistischen Elemente bei Justin (Texte und Untersuchungen, VII)*, 1891; Theodor Zahn, *Brot und Wein im Abendmahl der alten Kirche*, 1892; Arthur Lukyn Williams, *Dialogue with Trypho*, 1930; A. W. F. Blunt, *The Apologies of Justin Martyr*, 1911.

GEORGE V. JOURDAN.

ARAB LEAGUE. See ISLAM.

ARABIA, ANCIENT: Arabia proper, the southwestern and largest peninsula in Asia, is mostly a desert, habitable only along the coast, in the north central highlands, and in scattered oases in the interior. The entire population is no more than 8,000,000. The mountain range that skirts the western coast and rises to a height of over 9,000 feet in Midian and over 12,000 feet in Yemen intercepts the moisture from the westerlies and leaves the interior, especially of the south, exceedingly dry. There lies al-Rab'al-Kháli (the empty quarter), which was never crossed by a European before 1932. Hejaz, the birthplace of Islam, is rich in dates, Yemen in wheat, and Oman in rice. The coffee plant, for which Yemen today is famous, was not introduced from Abyssinia until the fourteenth century after Christ.

The population of North Arabia—Hejaz and Nejd—are mostly nomadic Bedouins; those of the south—Yemen and Hadramaut—sedentary. The southerners, whose land receives enough rain to make it cultivable, were the first to step on the threshold of history. They provided Pharaonic Egypt with frankincense for temple use and mummification. To the classical writers Arabia was a land of fabulous wealth and luxury. Herodotus calls it "the aromatic land" (Herodotus, Bk. XVI, ch. 4, par. 25). The Sumerians procured their copper, the earliest metal used in industry, presumably from Oman. A Sumerian patesi, Gudaea (*ca.* 2350 B.C.), reports an expedition to procure stone and wood from Magan and Melukhkha, evidently in east and central Arabia. The Assyrian Shalmeneser III encountered in the battle of Karkar (854 B.C.), among the allies of the Aramaean king of Damascus, an Arabian Sheikh Jundub, the first unmistakable reference by name to an Arabian. Another Assyrian, Tiglathpileser III (745–727 B.C.), exacted tribute from Zabibi, the queen of "Aribi." In a number of their records other Assyrian kings cite Arabian chiefs offering presents of gold, precious stones, camels, and donkeys. The first reference to the camel in literature relates to North Arabia (Judg. 6:5). The horse was a comparatively late importation from Syria. All these Arabians of the inscriptions must have belonged to the north. The Assyrians' concern was to ensure the safety of the trade routes of their vast empire.

As the probable original home of the Semites Arabia looms in importance in the early history of the Hebrews. Echoes of the Hebrew desert origin are reiterated in the Old Testament (Deut. 32:10; Hos. 9:10). Esau's sons (Gen. 36:10–14) had mostly Arabic names. The divine covenant was made on Arabian soil, and Moses married a North Arabian woman (Ex. 3:1; 18:10–12). Ophir, from which Hiram and Solomon's navy brought algum and precious stones (I Kings 9:27–8; 10:11), was evidently in South Arabia. The queen of Sheba (*Saba'*) must have had her headquarters in some northern post on the caravan route rather than in the south.

The form of the name of Job (Iyyōb) is Arabic. The Arabia to which Paul retired (Gal. 1:17) was supposedly Nabataea, and the Arabians of the Pentecost (Acts 2:11) must have been Nabataeans.

The Sabaeans, Minaeans, and the Himyarites of South Arabia established kingdoms that lasted from *ca.* 1200 B.C. to A.D. 525. The literature that has thus far reached us from these peoples is all epigraphic, with the earliest inscription dating from the eighth century B.C. Their religion was in its essence a planetary astral system centering on the moon-god.

BIBLIOGRAPHY: G. A. Cooke, *A Textbook of North Semitic Inscriptions*, 1903; D. S. Margoliouth, *The Relations between Arabs and Israelites*, 1924; Ditlef Nielsen, *Handbuch der altarabischen Altertumskunde*, Vol. I, 1927; James A. Montgomery, *Arabia and the Bible*, 1934; Philip K. Hitti, *History of the Arabs*, 5th ed., 1951.

[Sup.] PHILIP K. HITTI.

ARABIA IN RECENT DECADES: A new era began in Arabia with the expulsion of the Turks. The Ottoman Empire had sought to hold the western and eastern coasts, though the interior was beyond its reach. Often weak or wholly eclipsed in the Yemen and the Hasa, Turkish authority was more tenacious in the Hijaz, where the great prize was the holy cities of Mecca and Medina. In 1913 Ibn Saʿud expelled the Turks from the Hasa, leaving them only Qatar in the east, which they evacuated shortly afterwards. In 1916 Sharif Husain of Mecca joined the Allies, took the title King of the Arabs, and erected his own government in the Hijaz. Turkish power withered on the vine in the Yemen, where the Zaidite Imam Yahya became fully independent.

In 1920–22 Ibn Saʿud's forces moved westwards into ʿAsir and Najd. Husain assumed the title of Caliph in 1924 but failed to win general recognition from the Islamic community. Contention between Husain and Ibn Saʿud led to war, and by 1925 Husain and his son ʿAli had been driven out of the Hijaz, which was incorporated into Ibn Saʿud's state. Part of the Red Sea coast of Tihamah was added to this state, which in 1932 became the Kingdom of Saudi Arabia. In 1934 Saudi Arabia defeated the Yemen in a brief war; the Peace of al-Taʾif gave Najran to Saudi Arabia but in its other terms Ibn Saʿud treated the Imam generously.

The peninsula's states did not fight in World War II, though Saudi Arabia followed a policy sympathetic to the Allies and in 1945 declared war on Germany and Japan. A charter member of the United Nations, Saudi Arabia co-operates with various international organizations. The Yemen joined the United Nations in 1947. Founding members of the Arab League in 1945, Saudi Arabia and the Yemen were among the Arab states arrayed against Israel in 1948–49, Saudi Arabia sending troops that operated under the Egyptian command.

In 1950 Ibn Saʿud, establisher of peace and security within his realm, celebrated the golden jubilee of his first triumph, the capture of al-Riyad in 1902 (forty-eight Christian years equaling fifty Hegira years).

Imam Yahya of the Yemen, assassinated in 1948 after reigning over forty years, was succeeded by his son Ahmad under whom the country slowly emerged from its old isolation.

The only foreign possession on the Arabian mainland is Aden, a British crown colony, consisting of the seaport and its immediate surroundings. Recently the British have increased their influence in the Aden Protectorate stretching hundreds of miles along the southern coast and an undefined distance into the interior. Hadramaut, center of an old civilization, lies in the Eastern Aden Protectorate. Arab rulers, bound to Great Britain by treaties, administer the various states comprising the protectorate, often aided by British advisers.

The Sultan of Muscat, who has close ties with the British, holds the Batinah coast on the Gulf of Oman and the coast of Zafar on the Indian Ocean. In the interior of Oman the ancient Ibadite Imamate, re-established in 1913, rules on the model of the early Islamic Caliphate; this is the most withdrawn and least known of the Arabian states.

The eight chiefs of the Trucial Coast and the rulers of Qatar, Bahrain, and Kuwait are likewise by treaty under British protection. Within their domains, in large measure of undefined extent, fall those portions of the eastern coast not possessed by Saudi Arabia.

The Bahrein Petroleum Company, then owned solely by Standard Oil of California, discovered oil in Bahrain in 1932. After the Standard Oil Company of California secured a concession in Saudi Arabia in 1933, oil in commercial quantities was found at Dhahran in 1938. Three other American companies now share ownership of the Arabian American Oil Company with Standard of California. Since 1946 production has increased tremendously, stimulated by the completion of the Trans-Arabian pipeline to the Mediterranean in 1950; Saudi Arabia ranks fourth among the oil-producing countries of the world. As a result of the oil crisis in Iran, the production of the Kuwait Oil Company, owned in equal shares by British and American interests, is soaring. Petroleum Development (Qatar) of the Iraq Petroleum Company group has substantial production; Bahrain, though its production is small, remains an important refining center; and prospecting continues in other places.

Oil royalties are put to good use in Kuwait, Bahrain, and Qatar, while Saudi Arabia has built modern ports at Jiddah on the Red Sea and Dammam on the Persian Gulf, a railroad connecting Dammam with al-Riyad, and airports and motor roads. The completion of a transpeninsular railroad is planned. The remarkable improvement in communications is binding the different parts of the country together and opening the whole up to new ideas and devices. Funds are spent on education, public health, agriculture, and other enterprises in the general welfare.

The growth of Saudi Arabia has been accompanied by the spread of Wahhabism (see WAHHABIS) into all provinces of the kingdom. Wahhabite influence is felt elsewhere in the peninsula but is dominant nowhere outside of Saudi Arabia. Zaidite Islam flourishes in the Yemen and Ibadite Islam in Oman. In other parts non-Wahhabite Sunnism prevails, excepting Shi'ite centers in Bahrain and eastern Saudi Arabia and a few small groups representing less prevalent sects. Christian missionary activity is confined to the peninsula's fringes—Kuwait, Bahrain, Qatar, the Sultanate of Muscat, and Aden. American medical missionaries are occasionally allowed into the interior for the specific purpose of providing medical treatment. King Abdulaziz Ibn Sa'ud died in November 1953 and was succeeded by his oldest living son, Su'ud, with his next son, Faysal, as heir apparent.

BIBLIOGRAPHY: H. St. J. B. Philby, *Arabia* (1930) and *Arabian Jubilee*, 1952; K. S. Twitchell, *Saudi Arabia*, 1947; Max Steineke, George Rentz, Roy Lebkicher, *The Arabia of Ibn Saud*, 1952; Hugh Scott, *In the High Yemen*, 1942; W. H. Ingrams, *Arabia and the Isles*, 1942; D. van der Meulen, *Aden to the Hadhramaut*, 1947.

[Sup.] GEORGE RENTZ.

ARABIC PHILOSOPHY: Arabic philosophy is historically a development of the Platonic (Neo-Platonic) Aristotelian tradition of the schools of the Eastern Christian Churches influenced in some of its aspects by Muslim beliefs and persuasions. Its inspiration was essentially Greek, predominantly Neo-Platonic with al-Fārābī and Ibn Sīnā (Avicenna), Aristotelian with Ibn Rushd (Averroes); and it rejected, or evaded, fundamental Qur'anic and Muslim propositions, such as the temporal origin of the world and its creation ex nihilo, for example (cf. later on al-Ghazālī), to which an Islamic philosophy must have adjusted its thought. Arabic philosophy did not do so; and even Islamic theology did not altogether integrate its statements on the philosophical preliminaries and principles of religious thought, to which so large a part of its later treatises are devoted, with its articles of faith.

Arabic knowledge of Greek thought was derived ultimately from the two schools of Alexandria and Antioch, and it was transmitted to the Arabs chiefly by the schools of the two heretical sects, the Nestorians and Monophysites. The two Nestorian schools of Edessa and Nisibis inherited the Aristotelian traditions of Antioch and from the fifth century devoted

themselves to the study and translation into Syriac of Aristotle's works along with the commentaries of Theodore of Mopsuestia; and the two Jacobite (Monophysite) schools of Resh'aina and Qenneshrin were no less active in the promotion of Aristotelian learning. Sergius of Resh'aina (d. 536) translated into Syriac the *Categories* of Aristotle and the *Isagoge* of Porphyry and composed *The Causes of the Universe according to Aristotle;* Severus Sebokht (d. 666/7) wrote commentaries on the *Prior Analytics* and the *Perihermeneias;* and George the Arab (d. 724), bishop of the Christian Arab nomad tribes, translated the whole of the *Organon* with annotations. The commentaries of John Philiponos were celebrated and exerted a profound influence all over the Monophysite world and still later on the apologetic orientation of Muslim theology.

With the advent of the Arabs and the establishment of Arabic as the common language of the Muslim empire Nestorians and Monophysites also played a dominant role both in the awakening and in the satisfaction of the intellectual curiosity of their overlords. The Nestorian Patriarch, Timotheos I (d. 823), translated part of Aristotle's *Topics* directly from Greek into Arabic; and that brilliant coterie of Nestorian scholars, the physician Ḥunayn b. Isḥaq (d. 876), his son, Isḥaq (d. 911) and his nephew, Hubaysh, rendered into Arabic, sometimes directly from the Greek and again through the Syriac, the whole, or almost the whole of Galen, Hippocrates, Dioscorides, the *Republic, Laws* and *Timaeus* of Plato, and the *Categories, Physics, Magna Moralia, Metaphysics, De Anima, De Generatione et Corruptione* and *Hermeneutics* of Aristotle, or the Aristotelian tradition, along with the commentaries of Alexander of Aphrodisias and Themistius.

Jacobites, among them Qustā b. Lūqā (c. 950), undertook an Arabic translation of the commentaries on the *Physics*, as did also somewhat later the Nestorian, Abū Bishr Mattā. Another Jacobite, Ibn 'Adī, translated Plato's *Laws* and Aristotle's *Poetics* from the Greek and the fourth book of the *Topics*, the *Poetics*, the *Fallacies*, the *Meteorology*, and the *Physics* from Syriac; and his contemporary, Yaḥyā b. Biṭrīq, translated Plato's *Timaeus* and many Aristotelian texts.

But the Jacobite and Nestorian contribution to Arabic knowledge of Greek philosophy was not confined to the transmission of the thought of Aristotle and Plato. Many of the texts which the Jacobites translated into Syriac were borrowed either from the Alexandrian patristic, or Neo-Platonic, tradition; and to this category belong two books which exercised a pronounced and perhaps a perversive influence upon the development of Arabic philosophical thought,

The Theology of Aristotle and the *Liber de Causis.* The first, a compilation of books four to six of the *Enneads* of Plotinus, translated into Syriac in the sixth century and into Arabic a century later by the Jacobite, 'Abdu'l-Masīḥ of Emessa, was accepted by Arabic scholars as a genuine work of Aristotle, as was also the second, which was a summary with a running commentary of the *Stoicheiosis Theologike* of Proclus. The false attribution of these two works was the source of much confusion in Arabic philosophical circles respecting Aristotle's conceptions of God, man, and the world; and to them is largely due the marked Neo-Platonic bias in eastern Arabic philosophy with its emanation doctrine and its thesis of the soul as a pure intellectual substance. In both works the Neo-Platonic One, taken by Arabic scholars as an Aristotelian concept, was equated by their Christian translators with the Creator God of the Old Testament, facilitating its conciliation with the One God of the Qur'ān. But Neo-Platonic doctrines were also taught and disseminated by the Nestorian school of Gunishapūr, founded by the Sasanian Emperor Khosru Anusharwān, and by the Gnostic school of the Sabians of Harran. (See "Die Bedeutung der syrischen Theologen als Vermittler der griechischen Philosophie an den Islam" in *Zeitschrift fuer Kirchengeschichte* III [1939], pp. 346–386 and I. Madkour, *L'Organon d'Aristote dans le monde arabe*, 1944).

In this manner and mainly through these channels Greek thought reached the Muslim world—Euclid, Archimedes, Ptolemy, Hippocrates, Galen, Dioscorides and Plato, with some Stoic, Epicurean, and Sceptical ideas derived probably from the philosophical textbooks of the schools, but especially and notably Aristotle with the commentaries of Alexander and Aphrodisias and Themistius. The famous Muslim historian of religion and philosophy, al-Shahrastānī (d. 1253), writes that the Arabic philosophers followed Aristotle save in a few details, which they borrowed from Plato and earlier philosophers. But the Aristotle, whom they followed, appeared to them in the light cast by his Neo-Platonic interpreters, and his thought had been compounded for them with that of Plotinus, Proclus and Porphyry.

Arabic philosophers may conveniently be divided into two groups, separated from one another not only in time but in place, an eastern and a western group. The chief proponents of philosophy in the East were al-Kindī, al-Fārābī and Ibn Sīnā (Avicenna), and in the West Ibn Bājja (Avempace), Ibn Ṭufayl and Ibn Rushd (Averroes). To the eastern group should be added perhaps that renowned critic of philosophy, al-Ghazālī, and the encyclopedists known as the Sincere Brethren of Basra, and to the western Ibn Masarra (d. 931), who

first apparently introduced into the West the form of Neo-Platonism represented by the *Pseudo-Empedocles,* which postulated a prime matter, or element, as the first object of God's creation, symbolized by the throne of God, a doctrine adopted with other salient principles from the Pseudo-Empedocles by some later Jewish philosophers, among them Ibn Gabīrōl (Avicebron) (d. 1058).

Al-Kindī (d. 870), named the "Philosopher of the Arabs," translated various Greek works and was a zealous student of Aristotle; but his theory of the universe is Neo-Platonic. For him the cause of the world's existence is the divine intelligence, the activity of which is mediated to the terrestrial world through the heavenly spheres created by the World-soul, which is intermediary between God and the corporeal world. The human soul is an emanation of the World-soul, free and independent in so far as it acts in accordance with its spiritual origin, but subject to the influences of the spheres by virtue of its union with a corporeal body; and man rises to the intelligible world, where alone freedom and immortality reign, by acquiring a correct knowledge of God and the world. (Al-Kindī's *De Intellectu* was edited by Nagy in 1897, and the publication of his *Epistles* [Rasā'il] was begun in the *Revue al-Azhar* by Abū Riḍā in 1947).

Al-Kindī, the Arab, so far as we know, never achieved a coherent system of knowledge, as did al-Fārābī (d. 980), of Turkish origin, a century later, whom Ibn Khallikān declared to be the greatest of the earliest philosophers, and who was named the "Second Master," Aristotle being the first. The pupil of a Christian physician, he studied and taught in Baghdad and wrote commentaries on most of the works of Aristotle and the known books of Plato. He also composed treatises on *The Soul, The Faculties of the Soul,* and *The Intelligence,* and tried to establish a *Concordance between Plato and Aristotle;* and in a political romance, *The Ideal City* (*al-Madina al-Fāḍila*), he sketched a unique organization, which comprehends the whole of the habitable world and finally unites the immortal dead in celestial blessedness.

With al-Fārābī we already find a coherent doctrine of the emanation of the world from a First Cause beginning with the intellect and the corollary doctrines of the eternity of the world and matter, a first adumbration of the metaphysics of Avicenna; and in him we also meet those arguments for the existence of God, which constantly recur in Arabic philosophy and in Islamic and Christian theology—the necessary and the contingent, the impossibility of an infinite chain of causes and the postulate of a First Cause necessarily existent in and for itself, and the two methods of acquiring knowledge of God, the via remotionis and the via affirmationis (the processes of exclusion and of pre-eminence). His *Catalogue of the Sciences* (*Iḥsā' al-'ulūm*) was the first Arabic classification of the sciences and the basis of all succeeding classifications with its division into the five groups of (1) linguistic sciences, (2) logical, (3) mathematical, (4) physics and metaphysics and (5) political sciences (including the *Kalām*, or theology).

Nine of al-Fārābī's treatises have been edited by Dieterici in *Al-Fārābīs philosophische Abhandlungen,* the *Treatise on the Intelligence* by Bouyges, the *Catalogue of the Sciences* by Muḥammad Riḍā al-Shabībī (1921), Osman Amine (1949) and by Angel Gonzalez Palencia (1932) with a Spanish translation (a partial translation by E. Wiedemann in *Beitraege zur Geschichte der Naturwissenschaften,* XI, a pamphlet on the "Vacuum" with a Turkish and English translation by Necati Lugel and Aydin Sayili (1951). I. Madkour has published *La place d'al-Fārābī dans l'école philosophique musulmane* (1934).

But undoubtedly the most prolific and original of Arabic philosophers was Ibn Sīnā (Avicenna) (d. 1037), who tells us in his autobiography that at the age of sixteen he had acquired all the known sciences and was already practicing medicine. A problem in Aristotle's *Metaphysics* baffled him, however, until by chance he bought and read a treatise by al-Fārābī on the meaning of the *Metaphysics*.

Avicenna's debt to al-Fārābī is quite clear; but with him Arabic philosophy reached its zenith. It is stated on good authority that he composed an Oriental Philosophy, in which he identified God with the heavenly spheres and expounded a pantheistic system; but in his extant works and especially in his *al-Shifā'* (The Sufficiency) he devoted himself apparently to the interpretation of Aristotle rather than to an exposition of his own ideas, seeking to define and systematize the thought of the Greek philosopher. His Aristotelianism, however, is rounded off with a Neo-Platonic explication of the creation, according to which the world is the eternal effect of an eternal God, who is absolutely one and from whom can emanate only one being (at a time). From God comes forth the First Intelligence, which knows its essence and origin, and which is necessary, since it derives its being from the First Cause, but also contingent, since there is no necessity for the First Cause to cause it, whence arises a duality in the world, from which issues triplicity. From the First Intelligence comes forth the Second, which knows itself as the soul and body of the ninth sphere; and down through the spheres the series of emanations proceeds in this fashion to the sphere of the Moon, the Intelligence of which engenders a last pure Intelligence, the Active Intelligence, which produces human souls and the four elements.

At this point Avicenna has abandoned the principle, which hitherto he has observed, that "from one only one can proceed"; for although the elements might conceivably be one materially by virtue of a common substratum, there are four forms. But to preserve his principle and still allow for multiplicity in the world Avicenna advances the theory that matter is "prepared," or "disposed" to accept particular forms by the motions of the spheres, an ingenious attempt to resolve the ancient dilemma of the one and the many.

The spheres are thus in contact with and have knowledge and care of particulars. But God is an efficient cause with respect to the First Intelligence only and remains unaffected by the further course of emanation; and his knowledge, therefore, Avicenna concludes, extends to universals only, a much debated doctrine in medieval Christendom and rejected not only by Christian and Islamic theologians but also by Ibn Rushd (Averroes). Classic, however, is his doctrine of the soul with its division of the senses into five external and five internal senses and of the faculties into motor and intellectual.

There is a Latin translation of Avicenna's *Najāt* by Mgr. Carame, an edition and translation of his mystical treatises by Mehren (1889, 1894), a French translation of his *Risāla fī'l-ḥudūd* (*L'Épître des définitions*) by Mlle. Goichon (1937), who is also preparing a translation of the *Kitāb al-Ishārāt* (Book of Theorems, etc. Carra de Vaux has published *Avicenna* (1900), C. Sauter, *Avicennas Bearbeitung der aristotelischen Metaphysik* (1912), L. Gardet, "Quelques aspects de la philosophie avicennienne dans ses rapports avec l'orthodoxie musulmane" in *Revue thomiste* (1939), Mlle. Goichon, *La distinction de l'essence et de l'existence d'après Ibn Sina* and *Le Lexique* (1937).

Al-Ghazālī (d. 1111) belongs to the history of Islamic religious thought rather than to the history of Arabic philosophy; but he enters into the latter history, not only as the most pungent critic of Arabic philosophy, but also as the inaugurator of a new school of theology, which adopted and used Aristotle's logic and sought to incorporate into its system certain principles borrowed from philosophy, such as the ideas of contingency and necessity as proofs of the existence of God and the unity of God being implied in His perfection, and which abandoned the radical discontinuity of the ancient, orthodox, Ash'arite world-view by avoiding, or modifying, the early Baqillanian atomic doctrine.

But in his *Munqidh min al-ḍalāl* (Deliverance from Error) al-Ghazālī rejected the physical and metaphysical theories of the philosophers, and in his *Tahāfut al-falāsifa* (Refutation of the Philosophers) he refuted twenty of their theses, and especially four of them, namely, that the world is eternal and has no beginning, nor end, that God has no knowledge of particulars and that there is no bodily resurrection. His new school was continued by Shahrastānī (d. 1153), Rāzī (d. 1209), Bayḍāwī (d. 1286), Ijī (d. 1355), and Taftāzānī (d. 1389), and is represented today by the great universities of al-Azhar and Tunis.

The *Munqidh* has been translated into French by Barbier de Meynard in the *Journal Asiatique* (1877) and into English by Claud Field in *The Confessions of al-Ghazālī* (1909) and by W. Montgomery Watt in *The Faith and Practice of al-Ghazālī*, 1953, the *Iqtiṣād fī'l-iʿtiqād* into Spanish by Miguel Asín Palacios (1929), the *Mishkāt al-Anwār* by W. H. T. Gairdner (1924), *The Alchemy of Happiness* by Claud Field (1910) (cf. H. Ritter's *Al-Gazālī*), the *Mīzān al-ʿAmal* (Critère de l'Action) by Hikmat Hachem (1945), the *Book of the Iḥyā' on the Worship* by E. E. Calverley (1925). The *Tahāfut* has been published with a summary in French by Bouyges. J. Obermann has published *Der philosophische und religioese subjectivismus Ghazalis* (1921), Miguel Asín Palacios, *Algazel, dogmatica, moral, ascetica* (1901), *Le Espiritualidad de algazel y su sentido cristiana* (1934–41); A. J. Wensinck, *La pensèe de Ghazzālī* (1940); Carra de Vaux *Gazali*; Louis Gardet, "Raison et foi" in *Revue thomiste* (1937–38), S. de Beaurecuail, "Essai sur la preuve de l'existence de Dieu etc." in *Bulletin de l'Institut français d'archéologie orientale du Caire* (1947).

To the Sincere Brethren of Basra, a sort of secret society that flourished in the tenth century A.D., are attributed fifty-two treatises, which discuss in turn mathematics and logic, physics, metaphysics, religion, astrology and magic, an encyclopedia-like work of little, or no, originality, but which shows the eclectic doctrine that was in vogue with the informed of that period, dependent on Pythagorean and Platonic thought rather than on Aristotelian.

Of the western group Ibn Bājja (Avempace) (d. 1138) and Ibn Ṭufayl (Abubacer) (d. 1185) were mystics, or theosophists, like their more renowned successor, Ibnu'l-ʿArabī (d. 1240), rather than philosophers. The former wrote a sort of itinerary of the soul to God, and in a philosophical romance, named *Hayy ibn Yaqẓān*, the latter describes how man's natural reason can by its own power alone arrive at union with God without external help, human or divine, and also seeks to prove that Islamic Neo-Platonism, which he identifies with Islam, is the natural religion of the Qur'ān and the Traditions.

Hayy ibn Yaqẓān has been edited and translated into French by L. Gauthier (1900, 1937) and translated into English by J. Ockley (1708).

The importance of Ibn Rushd (Averroes)

(d. 1198) lies more in the influence which he exercised upon European thought, than on any contribution which he made to Arabic philosophy or to Islamic thought generally. He was "The Commentator" of Aristotle par excellence for over a century at least in the Christian West, where his influence as such endured until the sixteenth century. In the Averroist school, of which Siger of Brabant is the most typical representative, the doctrine of Aristotle as interpreted by Averroes was held to be the truth, and they renounced any attempt to reconcile their philosophy with their religion, setting up the so-called thesis of the double truth, a doctrine unjustly fathered on Averroes, who in his *Maqālatu'l-Faṣl* (Agreement of Religion and Philosophy) maintains with St. Thomas Aquinas the perfect harmony of faith and reason. Man's natural reason is, indeed, limited according to Averroes and cannot of itself attain to the knowledge of the mysteries delivered in revelation; but it can comprehend that supernatural knowledge, once it is given, and by virtue of that knowledge it is raised above its natural limitations, and its natural knowledge is perfected.

The aim of the Qur'ān, says Averroes, is to teach true knowledge and practice. Teaching is of two kinds, by conception and assent. The ways of assent are three: the demonstrative, the dialectical and the oratorical; and men are divided into three classes according to the manner of their assent: (1) the people of demonstration, or philosophers, who attain to an assured interpretation by rigorous proofs, advancing from the necessary to the necessary through the necessary, (2) the people of dialectical interpretation, or theologians, who are satisfied with probable arguments, and (3) the oratorical people, who are convinced by arguments which appeal to the imagination and passions, whose duty is faith in the literal sense of the Qur'ān, and in whose case interpretation is unbelief.

These three ways of assent should be kept separate and not confused together, as with al-Ghazālī and his fellow-theologians, to become the inexhaustible source of innovations and heresies; and the members of each class should abide by the method of their class and understand the Qur'ān according to their ability. Truth is one, but there are three ways of apprehending and accepting it.

As a critical commentator of Aristotle Averroes retains his significance, but he has been overrated as a systematic and original thinker. He does not depart essentially from the philosophy of Avicenna; and often when he attacks Avicenna, it is only to return in another place to the thought of his predecessor. The world is created by God, but eternally so, and, with Avicenna, by way of emanation, a multiplicity issuing from a unity by a series of emanations, where from one being only one being comes forth.

Matter also is eternal and with Aristotle the principle of individuation, so that no immaterial thing can conceivably be an individual thing. Only spiritual universals exist as substances, and consequently there is only one substance of the human spirit, in which all men participate. Belief in a personal immortality would seem to be a contradiction, and yet Averroes appears to be honestly convinced of an individual survival; and in opposition to Avicenna he holds that God knows individual things, since he is the cause of things, not in so far as he exists, or has some other determination, but in so far as he knows them.

BIBLIOGRAPHY: The *Tahāfut al-Tahāfut* (The Refutation of the Refutation [of al-Ghazālī]) has been translated and explained by M. Horten in *Die Hauptlehren des Averroes*, 1913; *The Epitome of the Metaphysic* by S. Van den Bergh, 1924. In general see M. Horten, *Die philosophischen Systeme der spekulativen Theologen im Islam*, 1912; T. G. De Boer, *The History of Philosophy in Islam*, trans. by E. R. Jones, 1903; S. Munk, *Mélanges de Philosophie juive et arabe*, 1857, 1927.

WILLIAM THOMSON.

ARAB LEAGUE. See ISLAM.

ARAM, ARAMAEANS, AND THE ARA-MAIC LANGUAGE: The oldest form of the name of Aram and the Aramaeans, as attested in Accadian sources, is *aramu* (*ªrumu, arimi, armªyª*). The later Hebrew form is *ªrâm* (*ªrammî*). The derivation of *aramu* is unknown. Its first occurrence dates from the time of Tiglath-pileser I (1100 B.C.). Any connection of the names of localities, such as *a-ra-am* (time of Naram-Sin, 22nd century B.C.) or *a-ra-mi* (near Eshnunna, ca. 2000 B.C.), with the later Aramaeans is hypothetical.

The history of the Aramaeans falls into four distinct periods which can be dated approximately from 1500 (?) to 700 B.C.; 700–1 B.C.; A.D. 1–700; and 700 to the present. The date at which Aramaic tribes from the Arabian desert made their first successful inroads into the fertile areas of Syria and Mesopotamia can as yet not be determined. According to the Old Testament, Aramaeans were politically prominent already in the world of the patriarchs. In the absence of direct attestation or linguistic evidence, it is difficult, however, at the present state of our knowledge to state whether any of the frequently-mentioned nomad groups, such as the Sutu or the earlier Akhlame, actually were Aramaeans. When the Aramaeans are first mentioned around 1100 B.C., they are already far advanced in the process of infiltration into Mesopotamia and Syria and of founding a number of Aramaic city-based states. Soon, the whole of northern Mesopotamia and northern Syria behind the Phoenician coastline was dominated by Aramaic states of changing

size and political influence. Their duration, however, was a rather brief one. The resurgence of Assyrian power made an end to their independence in the last quarter of the eighth century B.C.

The second period of Aramaic history extends from the seventh century to the beginning of our era. The Assyrian empire, which deprived the Aramaeans for all times of political independence, was ethnically almost completely, and linguistically to a very large degree aramaized. In addition, Aramaic had the advantage of being written in a script which was much simpler to use than cuneiform. Thus, some Mesopotamian form of Aramaic which we call "official Aramaic" became the successor of Accadian as the vehicle of international communication. With the exception of some inscriptions from Syrian city states, all the known pre-Christian Aramaic material was written in official Aramaic. The importance and extent of official Aramaic increased when it was adopted throughout the vast Achaemenid empire. The Elephantine papyri and other Aramaic documents from Egypt as well as documents from the farthest east of the Achaemenid empire were written in official Aramaic, which, however, was always tinged with the peculiarities of the native tongues of the writers. In the ethnically Aramaic region—i.e., the country between the Tigris and the Mediterranean, again with the exception of the Phoenician coastal cities and, possibly, some isolated areas of Palestine—Aramaic continued to be spoken in a form which, it seems, had become largely unified under the influence of official Aramaic. With the dissolution of the Achaemenid empire, the political importance of the Aramaic region decreased, and direct documentation for its cultural life is almost totally lacking. Official Aramaic was continued in the Nabataean and Palmyrenian inscriptions (ca. 100 B.C.–A.D. 300).

The third period of Aramaic history owes its world significance to the religious predominance which was held by the Aramaic region for several centuries. Aramaic was the language of early Christianity. The various Aramaic dialects which had developed locally came to be used for spreading Christianity, Judaism, and various gnostic religions, such as Manichaeism and Mandaism. The dialects of the western group have remained linguistically closer to the old official Aramaic. They are Samaritan, Jewish Palestinian, and Christian Palestinian. The dialects of the eastern group are Syriac, Mandaean, and Babylonian Talmudic.

The fourth period of Aramaic history was initiated by the Muslim conquest of the Aramaic region in the seventh century. It has continued to this day. Under the Muslims Aramaic became the language of minority religions, and suffered both from the numerical decrease of those religions and from the encroachment of the Arabic language upon them. The gradual process of attrition has resulted today in the existence of only very small remnants of native speakers of Aramaic.

BIBLIOGRAPHY: E. G. Kraeling, *Aram and Israel*, 1918; R. T. O'Callaghan, *Aram Naharaim*, 1948; F. Rosenthal, *Die aramaistische Forschung*, 1939.

[Sup.] FRANZ ROSENTHAL.

ARAMAIC ORIGINS OF THE GOSPELS. See GOSPELS.

ARCHAEOLOGY, BIBLICAL: Since the early years of the twentieth century this subject has been completely revolutionized by the tremendous progress of field archaeology. The use of stratigraphic method, chiefly responsible for this change, was initiated amateurishly by Schliemann at Troy (1870—) and inaugurated on a more scientific basis by Flinders Petrie at Tell el-Hesi in Palestine (1890). Two Americans, G. A. Reisner and his disciple, C. S. Fisher, developed its technique to its present level. Today, careful study of the successive strata or layers of human occupation in an ancient site is considered the first duty of an archaeologist. Hand in hand with stratigraphy goes typology, the study of types of objects made by the hand of man, which may be divided into classes, types, and varieties roughly parallel to biological families, genera, species, and varieties. In the case of archaeological objects the uniformity produced by imitation and standardization corresponds to the biological uniformity resulting from genetic relationship. While the methods of stratigraphers correspond to those of geologists, the methods of typologists parallel those of biologists. Excavators date archaeological deposits by their vertical relationship to one another; comparative archaeologists date them by comparing human artifacts from them with typologically identical artifacts found elsewhere under controlled observation. Archaeology has thus become just as scientific in its principles and techniques as any other similar science.

At the same time that biblical archaeology has been transformed by these new methods, the study of written remains has also been revolutionized. The progress achieved by philologians in interpreting the monuments of ancient writing has been accelerated in recent decades by the use of more scientific methods of decipherment, constructing grammars and dictionaries, and developing philological research in ways unimagined by early decipherers and interpreters of hieroglyphic and cuneiform. Since the Bible is a collection of ancient books, written in the midst of this archaeological world, it is obvious that the interpreter of ancient written documents from Bible lands will often have more material bearing directly on the Bible than the excavator of ancient mounds. Both must work together in order to obtain the fullest return from the investment in archaeology.

I. Excavations in Bible Lands: A. PALESTINE: Passing over the first excavations undertaken after 1890 by Bliss and Macalister, we come to R. A. S. Macalister's work at Gezer (1902–9), published in 1912. While representing almost incredible industry his results were very unsatisfactory from the standpoint of chronology and they were inadequately recorded, with poor photographs or none at all, and with sketchy plans and rough drawings. The early Austrian and German work at Taanach and Megiddo under Sellin and Schumacher (1901–5) was better in some ways (e.g., plans and photographs) than Macalister's, but paid much less attention to pottery and so did not provide enough material for future scholars to work with. It was not until the work of Sellin and Watzinger at Jericho (1907–9) and of Reisner and Fisher at Samaria (1908–10) that any Palestinian excavations were properly staffed and that modern archaeological technique was fully introduced. An unhappy blunder in dating at Jericho, influenced by Macalister's errors, threw the chronology of this excavation entirely off, and the otherwise excellent publication of the results in 1913 misled biblical scholars for a decade. The exceedingly well executed work of Reisner at Samaria, with its generally reliable chronology, was not published until 1924, though Fisher was able to employ the methods he had learned from Reisner in organizing the work at Beth-shan (1921–33) and Megiddo (1925–39), as well as in teaching younger men, who carried his principles to many other sites. Directly influenced by Fisher's methods were the American excavations at Tell Beit Mirsim (Kyle and Albright, 1926–33), Tell en-Nasbeh (Badè, 1926–35), Beth-shemesh (Grant, 1928–33), Beth-zur (Sellers and Albright, 1931), Bethel (Kelso and Albright, 1934). Among major excavations of this period the German excavation of Shechem (1913, 1926–34) should be mentioned, though its poor organization greatly reduced the significance of its results. In 1927 Petrie returned to Palestine, where he dug until 1934 at Tell Jemmeh (Gerar), Tell el-Far'ah (Sharuhen), and Tell el-Ajjul, all in the extreme south. Though he had introduced both stratigraphy and sequence dating into archaeology, he had by now sacrificed his leadership to a forty-year-old habit of disregarding the work of other scholars. As a result his methods were out of date and his chronology was almost invariably far out of line with the actual state of knowledge. However, first-class excavations were launched soon afterwards under British auspices at Samaria (Crowfoot, Sukenik, and others, 1931–35) and Lachish (Starkey, Harding, Inge, 1932–38).

Major work under Jewish auspices was under-taken at Ai near Bethel (Mme. Marquet-Krause, 1933–34), as well as at many synagogues and smaller sites. For lack of space we must pass over many other meritorious excavations carried out between the two World Wars.

Excavation was slowed down by the outbreak of the Arab rebellion in 1936 and was almost entirely halted by World War II in 1939. Fortunately, Nelson Glueck was able to con-tinue his archaeological survey of Trans-Jordan (1933–43), and to dig at Tell el-Kheleifeh (Ezion-geber) in 1937–40. Even during the war some Jewish work continued, and in 1944 Mais-ler and Stekelis began digging at the great Canaanite site of Khirbet Kerak (Beth-yerah); in 1947 Maisler commenced the excavation of Tell Qasileh at the mouth of the 'Auja. Mean-while R. de Vaux began excavating at Tell el-Far'ah northeast of Shechem (1946—). In 1950 and 1951 work at Herodian Jericho was under-taken by Kelso and Pritchard, while work was also started by Winnett at the old Moabite capital of Dibon. Future progress in Palestin-ian archaeology will probably come largely through the intense activity of the well-staffed Israeli department of antiquities, headed by Yeivin and Ben Dor, together with that of the archaeologists of the Hebrew University in Jerusalem, under Sukenik and Maisler. The chief curator of antiquities in Jordan, G. L. Harding, is a first-class man, but more men and money are imperatively needed.

B. SYRIA: Before World War I little had been done in Syrian archaeology. Ernest Renan's expedition to Phoenicia (1860–61) was mainly a surface reconnaisance. In 1887— the Germans dug at Zincirli (ancient Sham'al) in the extreme north, in 1908–11 Garstang dug at another Hit-tite site in the neighborhood (Sakcegözü), and in 1911–14 (also briefly in 1920) Woolley and Lawrence excavated at Carchemish on the Eu-phrates. When the French occupied Syria after the war and set up their mandate, excavation began in a number of important sites, especially at Byblos (Montet and Dunand, 1921—), Dura on the Euphrates (Cumont, Pillet, Hopkins, 1923—), Ugarit (Schaeffer, 1929—), at Hamath on the Orontes (Ingholt, 1931–38), at several mounds in the Plain of Antioch (McEwan and Braidwood, 1932–37), at Mari on the Euphrates (Parrot, 1933—), and at Alalakh (Woolley, 1936—). While much of the early work in Syria (before the late twenties) was inferior in scientific standards to the better work of the time in Palestine, much of the more recent work has been extremely good. In keeping with the far greater natural wealth of ancient Syria as compared to Palestine, the excavations there have been much more rewarding, especially in the discovery of written records and objects of art.

Because of the present political divisions we shall also include excavations in northwestern Mesopotamia, from the Upper Tigris westward to the Euphrates, under the head of "Syria." Baron Oppenheim carried on important exca-vations at Tell Halaf, biblical Gozan at the source of the Khabur, before World War I. We may also mention Thureau-Dangin's dig at Khadatu, modern Arslan Tash (1928), and Mal-lowan's work at Harran (1951). This region is rich in important ancient sites, whose contents are certain to throw much light on the Bible.

C. BABYLONIA AND ASSYRIA: Excavations were begun by Botta in Assyria in 1842 and by Layard in the same region in 1845. These in-trepid explorers, followed by others, exhumed the lost civilization of the great kings of Assyria be-tween 900 and 612 B.C. The finding of great numbers of cuneiform inscriptions at Nineveh led speedily to the completion of the task of deciphering cuneiform, which had begun half a century earlier but had made little progress. Work then shifted to Babylonia, where de Sarzec began digging at Lagash (Telloh) in 1877 and the University of Pennsylvania com-menced work at Nippur in 1889. These excava-tions recovered the lost Sumerian civilization of the third millennium, and expanded the horizon of the Assyriologist enormously.

The next great forward step was taken by the Germans, who introduced scientific archaeology into the Mesopotamian field at Babylon in 1899 and at Assur, earliest capital of Assyria, in 1903. Long-continued excavations at these cities un-folded the splendors of Chaldaean civilization under Nebuchadnezzar and the culture of As-syria in the second millennium. It was not, however, until after the end of World War I that scientific methods (including the use of pottery chronology, which the Germans had neglected) were extended to cover all the work in the field. Since 1919 prehistoric Mesopo-tamia has been recovered, from the first traces of early settlers through the successive stages of progress toward literate civilization. In 1922–34 Sir Leonard Woolley undertook a series of brilliant campaigns at Ur of the Chaldees; in 1928 the Germans began work at Erech (Warka), where they uncovered a remarkable civilization of the first literate ages. American excavations at the East-Tigris site of Nuzi (Nuzu) in 1925 and following years disclosed a Horite civilization of the late Patriarchal Age which has thrown important light on the tra-ditions of Genesis.

The high-water mark of scientific excavation in Mesopotamia is represented by the University of Chicago excavations in the Diyalah district east of Baghdad (1931—), under Frankfort's direction. The methods employed here have been copied elsewhere and are being applied in such sites as Nippur (where excavation was resumed after more than forty-five years of neglect) and Eridu (Abu Shahrein). Work was also resumed in Assyria where Frankfort dug at Khorsabad and Mallowan at Calah (Nimrud).

D. EGYPT: The discovery of the famous trilingual inscription of Ptolemy V (the Rosetta Stone) in 1798 led to the decipherment of Egyptian in 1802–22. This great achievement was followed by several major expeditions to explore and record Egyptian monuments, notably the Prussian mission headed by Richard Lepsius (1842–45). In 1850 Mariette's thirty-year monopoly of Egyptian excavation began, and though many important discoveries were made during this period, there was no scientific recording whatever and valuable data were irretrievably lost. The monopoly was broken by Mariette's death in 1881, and three years later Petrie began his remarkable career as an excavator. Since he was easily the most original archaeologist of modern times, it is scarcely surprising that he was able to revolutionize the science of archaeology by introducing stratigraphic excavation and sequence dating of pottery, two principles that are now generally taken for granted.

An important forward step was taken in 1901, when the Germans began digging at Abusir in Middle Egypt, under the direction of Ludwig Borchardt. From then on scientific methods were applied to the excavation and analysis of Egyptian architectural monuments. Moreover, the methods of Borchardt were combined with those of Petrie by an American archaeologist, G. A. Reisner (see above), who continued to work in Egypt until shortly before his death in 1942. Reisner contributed systematic recording and photography to the basic insights of his predecessors, and his methods have become standard in all well-organized excavations. Another first-class American excavator, who worked for many years at Medinet Habu in Upper Egypt, was Herbert Winlock.

Egypt is quite different from Mesopotamia in one outstanding respect: its monuments are largely accessible without excavation, and accurate recording of their reliefs and inscriptions is often more important than new excavation. The early expeditions were devoted largely to the recording of such monuments, but the introduction of photographic methods has made much of their work unsatisfactory in comparison with present possibilities. This was long ago recognized, and German Egyptologists performed a very valuable service by photographing reliefs of historical importance. No one saw the need as clearly as J. H. Breasted, who organized several expeditions for the purpose of recording the reliefs of temples and tombs, especially at Medinet Habu and Karnak (1924—). The method here developed for making repro-

ductions of such material is the most accurate ever devised.

Among the most striking series of discoveries made in Egypt since the introduction of more scientific methods of excavation have been the recovery of the Egyptian historic and prehistoric past before the Great Pyramids of the Fourth Dynasty (1895—), the discovery and study of the contents of the fabulous tomb of Pharaoh Tutankhamun (1922—), the discovery of the royal and noble tombs of the 21st and 22nd Dynasties (tenth-ninth centuries B.C.). Many other individual finds or bodies of material are mentioned below in connection with our survey of the contributions of archaeology to biblical studies.

E. ARABIA: The rediscovery of ancient Arabia began in the early nineteenth century and was spurred by the decipherment of the Sabaean inscriptions by Gesenius and Roediger in 1841. The explorations in Yemen of Arnaud, Halévy, and especially Eduard Glaser (between 1882 and 1894) yielded thousands of copies and squeezes of Sabaean, Minaean, and Qatabanian inscriptions. These documents were studied by Rhodokanakis, Hoefner, and Ryckmans, among others, and valuable results were obtained. Excavation was, however, essential to any reconstruction of the history and civilization of ancient Arabia. Aside from a few small digs, there were no excavations in Arabia until the campaigns of 1950–51 in ancient Qataban (modern Beihan at the southeastern corner of Yemen), under the auspices of the American Foundation for the Study of Man. These two seasons were exceedingly successful, establishing the evolution of ancient South Arabian culture and the chronology of its inscriptions on a solid basis. They were followed in 1951 by the beginning of systematic excavation in Maryab (modern Marib), the ancient capital of Saba (Sheba).

Meanwhile the work of collecting the accessible inscriptions of ancient North Arabia, mostly on the walls of rock scarps, has continued vigorously and it has become possible to correlate the development of the north with that of the south. The gain to our knowledge of the background of Israelite history and religion is greater than one might think, since Arabia played an important part in Old Testament history. Moreover, its thousands of inscriptions from about 1000 B.C. to A.D. 600 often reflect early Hebrew times, since the direction of migration as well as of cultural diffusion tended to be from north to south, and South Arabia may thus preserve exceedingly early elements of Israelite culture.

F. PERSIA: The archaeology of Iran has seldom been of direct significance for biblical archaeology. However, the excavation of Susa (biblical Shushan) has yielded the Code of

Hammurabi and other important monuments, and the work of the University of Chicago at Persepolis has resulted in the discovery of thousands of documents from the late sixth and fifth centuries B.C., illustrating the period from the rebuilding of the Temple under Darius Hystaspes to the time of Nehemiah. The great Behistun inscription of Darius is of the greatest value for our understanding of the Books of Haggai and Zechariah.

G. ASIA MINOR AND THE AEGEAN: Here, too, archaelogy abounds with material useful for the Bible student. Asia Minor has revealed the secrets of Hittite civilization, especially at the ancient capital of Khattusas (Boghazköy), excavated since 1907. Cyprus was so closely related in culture to Phoenicia that it has yielded many objects interesting to the student of Canaanite and Phoenician civilization, and hence instructive for our reconstruction of the material culture of Israel. For New Testament times we have in Asia Minor and Greece sites and individual finds which shed light on the travels and adventures of Paul. Particularly interesting has been the excavation of such sites as Ephesus, Sardis, Corinth, and above all, Athens. The American excavation of the Agora (market place and civic center) of Athens has yielded buildings and inscriptions of interest to the student of Acts.

II. Archaeology and the Bible: A. PREPA-TRIARCHAL TRADITIONS: The discoveries of the nineteenth century were too isolated to throw much light on the first eleven chapters of Genesis. Only in the twenties of this century did our information really begin to become coherent, and it was not until the forties that it became possible to see the picture of human beginnings and of the early traditions of the ancient East as a whole. We now know, thanks to the work of Dorothy Garrod and others, that the development of prehistoric man in the East followed the same general lines as in the West. The latest work of physical anthropologists, on the basis of finds in Western Europe, Eastern Asia, South Africa, and especially in the Near and Middle East, confirms previous results in large part, but also shows that the number of extinct races of man was much greater than used to be thought and that there is no real basis for assuming the existence of different human species. Just as Neanderthal man is now known to have interbred with *Homo sapiens* in the Mousterian Age of Palestine, so we may safely suppose that this was true of other so-called fossil types, which were races and varieties, not true species at all. Radiocarbon dating of archaeological material of organic origin by its carbon isotope 14 content proves that the end of the Old Stone Age (Palaeolithic) must be brought down to not over 10,000 years ago, but the chronology of the latter remains uncertain and extreme dates for the earliest flint tools (artifacts) of human manufacture vary from 500,000 to less than 200,000 years ago. It has frequently been thought by scientists that there was a catastrophic break in the continuity of Stone Age culture between the Old Stone and the Middle Stone (Mesolithic) Age which might be identified with the Deluge of Genesis. Certainly there was a relatively fast retreat of the icecaps which probably caused tremendous floods about 10,000 years ago, and their memory may be preserved in the traditions of a Great Flood which are diffused among primitive peoples over most of the world.

The stories of Gen. 1–11 are very ancient, and can in large part be traced eastward to the valleys of the Euphrates and Tigris. This is particularly true of the account of creation in Gen. 2:4 ff., of the story of Eden, of the lists of antediluvian patriarchs, of the story of the Flood, and of the Tower of Babel. Since these stories have nothing in common with Egyptian and Canaanite accounts of beginnings, and since the Hebrew Patriarchs came from Mesopotamia, there seems to be no escape from the conclusion that they belong to the oldest traditions of the Hebrew people. Where we have close contacts, as in the account of the Flood, it is clear that the biblical tradition does not depend upon the Babylonian, but that both go back to a common older source. Not all these narratives are of equal age: for instance, the Tower of Babel must reflect the temple tower of Babylon (Babel in Hebrew), built originally perhaps in the 24th century B.C. (under Sargon I of Accad). Here and there, scattered through the first chapters of Genesis, are details which come from early non-Babylonian sources, probably from the Northwestern Semites of Patriarchal times. The Table of Nations (Gen. 10) seems to reflect the tenth century B.C., since the Arabs and other peoples which emerged after that date do not appear in it at all, and famous peoples of earlier centuries are also missing.

B. THE PATRIARCHAL AND MOSAIC AGES: Archaelogical research has not disclosed any specific reference to any person named in Gen. -Deut., but it has completely transformed our knowledge of the background of these periods. We now know the archaeological and cultural history of Palestine and Syria through the entire second millennium. Egyptian political, cultural, and literary history is well known through this millennium with the exception of a gap in the Hyksos period (late eighteenth to early sixteenth century). Until recently there was no real history of Mesopotamia, though a great deal was known about several periods, such as the First Dynasty of Babylon, since it was impossible to fix Mesopotamian chronology before the fourteenth century. But the discovery of the Khorsabad List of the Assyrian kings and especially the finding of nearly 20,000 cuneiform tablets at Mari on the Middle Euphrates has made it possible to fix Mesopotamian dates within a century, and most scholars now date Hammurabi of Babylon about 1728–1686 B.C. Cross datings are established between Egypt, Syria-Palestine, and Mesopotamia, so a real history of the second millennium B.C. can be written.

It is practically certain that the Hebrew Patriarchs lived in the Middle Bronze Age, between 2000 and 1500 B.C., since historical background, personal and place names in Genesis, and many other details fit perfectly with this dating, whereas the only other possible date in the Late Bronze Age does not suit the picture in Genesis nearly so well. Personal names like "Abraham" and "Jacob," tribal names like "Benjamin" and "Zebulun," place names like "Nahor" (Gen. 24:10) are common in documents of the Middle Bronze. The Patriarchal customs are strikingly like the customs of northern Mesopotamia, as reflected in the Nuzi tablets of the fifteenth century B.C., which transmit practices inherited from earlier centuries. Unfortunately, the one most likely source of historical information, Gen. 14, has hitherto proved refractory, though individual names and details of this chapter have turned up in inscriptions from the early centuries of the second millennium.

The Late Bronze Age, during which the Oppression, the Exodus, and the Wilderness Wanderings must be placed, is best known in Egypt, next best in Palestine, Syria and Asia Minor, in some ways least in Mesopotamia. It was ushered in by the Egyptian conquest of Palestine immediately after the expulsion of the Hyksos from Egypt. The Egyptians ruled Palestine, Phoenicia and southern Syria about three hundred years. Monuments of Egyptian domination are scattered through this region. Among the most important finds from this period are several hundred cuneiform tablets discovered chiefly at Tell el-Amarna in Egypt; they throw much light on the language and culture of the Canaanites during the three centuries preceding the Conquest. Among the most interesting of these tablets are the letters of 'Abdu-Kheba, prince of Jerusalem about 1370 B.C. Two basalt stelae, covered with Egyptian hieroglyphs and dated in the reign of Sethos I (c. 1309–1290) give us details about local civil wars between settled and nomadic groups just before the probable date of the Exodus.

Since the Israelites were a very insignificant semi-nomadic tribe in Egyptian eyes, we must not expect to find direct references to them. The exploration of Serbit el-Khadim northwest of Mount Sinai by Petrie and others since 1905 has yielded about twenty-five short inscriptions

in the Canaanite alphabetic script dating from the fifteenth century B.C. Partly deciphered by Alan Gardiner and the present writer, these inscriptions and the accompanying drawings and sculptures reflect the life of partly Egyptianized Semitic laborers more than a century before the time of Moses; there are strong arguments in favor of including them among the Hebrews of the period "which knew not Joseph." Other interesting traces of the Hebrews in Egypt during this age have been found, and the names of Moses and other members of his family can be identified with Egyptian names popular at that time. There are also many indications of indirect Egyptian influence on Mosaic thought and life, especially in connection with the abortive religious revolution of the Amarna Age, which introduced a number of concepts later to become characteristic of the Mosaic movement, in spite of vital differences between the two forms of monotheism. For instance, the Egyptian solar disk was the "god beside whom there is none other" (cf. Ex. 20:3), the god "who creates what comes into existence," like Israelite Yahweh; his followers also emphasized the importance of the "teaching" (Heb. *torah*).

Of steadily increasing significance for our understanding of the biblical background is the discovery of three Babylonian collections of laws from the nineteenth to the seventeenth centuries B.C.: the Code of Hammurabi (1901), the fragmentary Sumerian Code of Lipit-Ishtar (published in 1948), and the shorter Code of Eshnunna (also published in 1948). Together with the remains of an Assyrian law code from about 1100 B.C. and of the Hittite code of the thirteenth century B.C., these documents furnish us extraordinary insight into the background of the Book of the Covenant (Ex. 21–23) and other Mosaic jurisprudence.

C. PERIOD OF THE JUDGES AND THE UNITED MONARCHY: While we have comparatively little direct light on this period from inscriptions, there is a rapidly increasing fund of indirect written illustration, while our knowledge of the material background is already very considerable. Direct information on the Israelite occupation of Canaan comes from the Israel Stele of Pharaoh Marniptah (*ca.* 1223–16), where the Israelites appear as nomads who menace Egyptian control of Palestine and are duly punished. Indirect evidence comes, e.g., from the ruins of such important Canaanite towns as Lachish, Bethel, and Tell Beit Mirsim (Debir?), all destroyed by fire in the thirteenth century B.C. and reoccupied by bearers of a different and much cruder material culture. From the results of excavations we see that most of these destroyed towns were rebuilt almost immediately, but that towns such as Jericho were not rebuilt for centuries (cf. Josh.

6:26). Many new towns and villages sprang up in Israelite territory; their existence was made possible by the rapid spread of the then recent art of lining cisterns with water-tight plaster made with baked lime.

Thanks to the monuments of Ramesses III at Medinet Habu in Upper Egypt, we know the date of the Philistine invasion of Palestine, several decades after the principal phase of the Israelite conquest, and we know something about their customs and dress, etc. The report of the Egyptian envoy Wen-Amun on his mission to Byblos for the purpose of procuring cedar beams from Lebanon (about 1060 B.C.) gives us extremely interesting information about the Philistines and their allied sea-peoples on the coast of Palestine not long before their conquest of Israel after the defeat of the latter at Ebenezer (I Sam. 4). The Danish soundings at Shiloh prove that the town never recovered from its destruction at the hands of the Philistines shortly after the middle of the eleventh century. The excavations at Bethel and Beth-shemesh, in particular, illustrate the life of typical Israelite patriarchal families during this age. The ivories of Megiddo from the first half of the twelfth century B.C. show how Canaanites and Israelites lived and dressed.

While no inscriptions throwing direct light on internal affairs in Israel under the United Monarchy have yet been discovered, much has been learned of their material culture. King Saul's citadel at Gibeah (Tell el-Ful) was still very simple, though solidly constructed, but there was nothing simple about the constructions of Solomon, known especially from Megiddo. The stables of this period at Megiddo held at least 450 chariot horses, and indications of similar stables have been found at several contemporary sites. Glueck's excavation of the Solomonic seaport at Ezion-geber has brought to light copper refineries of a degree of development not hitherto considered possible in such an early period. Though no remains of the Temple of Solomon have been found, its traditional plan appears in a Syrian temple from the ninth century B.C. excavated by the University of Chicago at Tainat in the Plain of Antioch. Moreover, many close parallels to its decorative elements and furnishings have been found in Palestine, Syria, and Cyprus, especially in contexts dated to the eleventh-ninth century B.C. It is now clear that Greek Doric temples of the sixth century B.C., which resemble the Temple of Solomon in a number of respects, also owe their architecture largely to Phoenician models.

Until the discovery at Ugarit and decipherment of the long-lost Canaanite religious literature in the thirties of this century, it was impossible to present an objective argument for dating much Hebrew poetry before the ninth century B.C., in accord with biblical tradition.

Now the situation has changed drastically. A great many Hebrew poems employ poetic forms and stylistic devices characteristic of Canaanite poems composed before the fourteenth century B.C. Among such common elements are climactic or repetitive parallelism, usually consisting of patterns of repeated words arranged in clusters of two or three poetic units (bicola or tricola), parallelism of pairs of given words which recur scores of times without variation in Canaanite and Hebrew literature, use of stock appellations and phrases, often coinciding exactly in the two literatures. We also have the common use of many archaic grammatical phenomena, unrecognized in the Bible until found in the Ugaritic tablets, and of many ancient words whose meaning had often been completely forgotten. That the Song of Deborah (Judg. 5) swarms with stylistic peculiarities also found in earlier Canaanite literature might be expected, since it is almost universally held to be an authentic document from the twelfth century B.C.; it is more surprising to find the same peculiarities in the Song of Miriam (Ex. 15) and elsewhere in poems attributed by tradition to the earliest history of Israel. Moreover, the Psalter includes many archaic psalms (29, 68, etc.) which contain much phraseology of Canaanite origin and which must therefore go back to before the ninth century B.C. In particular we have many psalms which date back to about the tenth century and may easily reflect the taste of King David for music and poetry, as recorded by tradition.

D. THE DIVIDED MONARCHY: The period from the death of Solomon to the destruction of Jerusalem by the Chaldaeans, covering over three centuries, is now very well illustrated by archaeology. Until systematic excavations began in Palestine in 1890, pertinent finds almost all came from outside the borders of Israel. Among them is the list of towns in Judah (including Edom) and North Israel which had been taken by Shishak, king of Egypt (I Kings 14:25), inscribed on the walls of Karnak in Upper Egypt. Another very important find is the Mesha Stone, which told of the victories of Mesha, king of Moab (II Kings 3), over the Israelites in the late ninth century B.C. During the excavations at Dibon in Moab in 1951 a fragment of a still earlier Moabite stele was discovered. The excavations carried out in the ancient capitals of Assyria yielded references to kings Ahab, Jehu, Menahem, Pekah and Hoshea of Israel, to Azaraiah (Uzziah), Ahaz, Hezekiah, and Manasseh of Judah, to events which preceded and accompanied the fall of Samaria, and especially to the campaign of Sennacherib against Judah (II Kings 18–19). In 1923 a portion of the Babylonian Chronicle was published, giving a detailed account of the events preceding and following the fall of Nineveh in

612 B.C.; it greatly increased our understanding of the course of Jewish history in the last decades before the fall of Jerusalem in 587 B.C. This was followed in 1939 by the publication of ration lists from the time of Nebuchadnezzar, mentioning Joniachin, king of Judah, and five of his sons, as well as many other captives from Palestine and Phoenicia.

The systematic excavation of ancient Israelite towns since 1890 has given us detailed information about the development of material civilization. The excavations at Samaria and Megiddo, Beth-shemesh and Tell en-Nasbeh, have thrown much light on life in Israel during the period between 900 and 750 B.C., while the following period, from 750 to 587 B.C., has been illuminated by the results of excavations at Tell Beit Mirsim and Lachish (Tell ed-Duweir), to mention only the most important sites. We know how the art of building houses and fortifications developed, how pottery changed, how the crafts expanded, what amulets the women employed, how writing evolved. Among written documents we may cite in particular the Ostraca of Samaria from the early eighth century B.C., the Siloam inscription from the end of the eighth century, and the Ostraca of Lachish from the last months before the Chaldaean invasion. A great many seal inscriptions have been recovered, and some of them mention the name of the reigning king: Jeroboam II, Uzziah, Jotham, Ahaz, Joniachin. Names of high officials mentioned in the Bible also occur. These documents are significant not only for the direct information they contain, but much more for the light they shed on the evolution of Hebrew spelling and language, as well as on dialectal differences between the speech of Judah and Northern Israel.

E. EXILE AND RESTORATION: Our knowledge of the period from the fall of Jerusalem to the Macedonian conquest in 330 B.C. owes even more than that of the preceding period to archaeology. Excavation and surface examination of scores of sites of pre-exilic towns of Judah have proved conclusively that the Chaldaean conquest was accompanied by a thoroughgoing devastation of the country, whose towns were not rebuilt for generations, if at all. There is no archaeological basis for the frequently expressed view that life continued in Judah during the Exile much as it had before—that there was no real break in Jewish life at this time. The traditional view is correct, though it must naturally be modified at points, where new information fills previous gaps in our knowledge.

The most valuable source of new evidence for the age of the Restoration comes from finds of Aramaic papyri of the fifth century B.C. in Egypt. The principal finds were made at Elephantine in Upper Egypt in 1904–07, but some papyri and ostraca had already been discovered previously and more have come to light in other sites since then. They are all in biblical Aramaic, and they give us a wealth of detail with regard to the life and culture of a Jewish colony at the southern boundary of Egypt in the age of Nehemiah and Ezra. Together with other data from contemporary Babylonian and Elamite tablets, they enable us to reconstruct the official life of the Persian Empire and to demonstrate the authenticity of the Aramaic documents in Ezra. It is no longer possible seriously to reject the historicity of the memoirs of Nehemiah and Ezra or to date them after the fifth century B.C.

Strata of this age excavated in Palestine have not yielded much material, but we gain some idea about the reoccupation of the country after the Exile, about the extent of Persian control, and about the spread of Greek civilization generations before Alexander the Great. Coins of the fourth century B.C. bearing the name "Judah" (*Yehud*) show that the little country had been granted a measure of autonomy, like several contemporary Phoenician and Syrian districts.

F. THE INTERTESTAMENTAL PERIOD: The three centuries of Macedonian control before the birth of Christ are much better known than they were at the beginning of this century, thanks to discoveries of papyri like the Zeno archives at Philadelphia (Gerza) in Egypt and of the leather scrolls from the Dead Sea cave (since 1947). The Zeno archives throw light on conditions in Palestine under Ptolemy Philadelphus (285–246 B.C.). The leather scrolls from the last two centuries B.C. have revolutionized our knowledge of the history of the Hebrew text of the Old Testament and of Jewish religion and literature in the period immediately before the rise of Christianity (see also Section "G" of this article).

Excavations in Palestine have uncovered the Hellenistic town of Marisa in Idumaea (Maresha of pre-exilic Judah), together with two extremely interesting painted tombs from the third and second century B.C. A campaign at Beth-zur north of Hebron (1931) disclosed remains of successive occupations and destructions in the Maccabaean age, when it was one of the most contested fortresses in Judah. Nearly 125 coins of Antiochus Epiphanes alone show the importance of the town at that time. The history of the Tobiad house of Ammon is illuminated by the discovery of a mausoleum and a neighboring tomb, inscribed with the name "Tobiah." The history of the princes of the Hasmonaean house who followed the early Maccabees has gained greatly from the discovery of their coins, while many of their constructions have been uncovered in Jerusalem, Gezer, Samaria, and elsewhere. Such Hasmonaean fortresses as Alexandrium, though identified, have not yet been dug.

G. THE NEW TESTAMENT AGE: The last century of the Second Temple, from the accession of Herod the Great (37 B.C.) to the capture of Jerusalem by Titus (A.D. 70), is now far better known than it was in the middle of the nineteenth century. Our knowledge of the background of the New Testament is immeasurably richer. Taking up different classes of material which have contributed to this state of affairs in their order of significance, as seen by the writer, we come first to one of the most recent discoveries, the Dead Sea Scrolls (see § "F"). These documents belonged in large part to a sect of Essene type which flourished in the last two centuries B.C.; they bridge the gap between such apocryphal and pseudepigraphic literature as Ecclesiasticus (Ben Sira), the Book of Jubilees, and the Testaments of the Twelve Patriarchs, on the one hand, and the New Testament on the other. John the Baptist was certainly influenced by them, and we find their language and style strikingly similar to corresponding features of the Gospel of John, with echoes in the Synoptic Gospels and the Pauline Epistles. It is no longer possible to attribute the Gospel of John to a Gnostic writer; we have in these scrolls part of the pre-Gnostic background of thought and language in which Jesus grew up.

After scattered earlier finds of Greek papyri in Egypt, discovery of such material began in earnest in 1897 and has continued ever since. A great mass of private documents in the vernacular Greek (*koiné*) of the Hellenistic-Roman period has made it certain that the authors of the Greek translations and original Greek books which we possess in the New Testament were writing the actual spoken language of their time, influenced only slightly by literary Attic Greek. Many details of life and speech have been clarified and illustrated by these extraordinary documents (see PAPYRUS). Since 1930 there have also been remarkable discoveries of New Testament papyri from the second century A.D., far earlier than anything previously known, and a whole library of lost early Gnostic literature from the third and fourth centuries A.D. has come to light since 1947 at Schoenoboskion in Upper Egypt. The importance of this last discovery lies particularly in the fact that the new picture of Gnostic beliefs in their formative period confirms and greatly expands the reports of the Church Fathers Hippolytus, Irenaeus, and Epiphanius. The Gnostics of the sub-apostolic age held even stranger and more pernicious doctrines than have been credited to them by modern scholars, and it becomes dangerous nonsense to fuse their ideas with those of Jesus and the Apostles, as has been popular in certain circles since the early twentieth century. See also APOCRYPHA, II.

Turning to Palestinian archaeology in the narrow sense, many buildings of this age have been excavated. The excavations in Jerusalem have brought to light extensive remains of Herodian and early Roman times in the Temple area, especially the exterior of the retaining wall of the Herodian temple enclosure and the substructure and pavement of the Praetorium at the Tower of Antonia. The line of the First and Second Walls of Herod has been traced in large part, and the long-lost line of Agrippa's wall is now known. Early Roman remains have been cleared in the southern part of the Western Hill (the traditional Mount Zion) and north of Herod's Palace near the present Jaffa Gate. A great many mausolea and tombs of the last century of the Second Temple have been cleared, with very important results (see below). Two excavations in New Testament Jericho (see above) have brought to light building remains from the time of Herod and his son, Archelaus, who was reigning in Jesus' boyhood. Herodian masonry and building plans have been uncovered elsewhere in the country, especially at Samaria, while Herodian buildings at Hebron and elsewhere have been carefully studied.

Clearance of the tombs of the New Testament period in and around Jerusalem has brought to light hundreds of short inscriptions in Aramaic, Hebrew, and Greek. For the first time these Aramaic inscriptions yield living evidence of the Aramaic used by Jesus, since all Aramaic literature from this age had perished. On the bone caskets (ossuaries) of the deceased often appear their names, which include all the common Jewish names of the New Testament, as well as many rarer ones; we find Miriam (Mary), Martha, Elizabeth, Salome, Sapphira, etc. Among the commonest male names are Joseph and Jeshua (Jesus); we also find Simon, John, Matthew, Ananias, Silas, and even such rare names as Alphaeus. A man is called "master, teacher" (*didáskalos*), like Jesus in the Gospel of John, though this appellation has been cited as a supposed indication of second century date. The most interesting of these inscriptions tells us of the removal and reburial of bones attributed to King Uzziah, who had died nearly eight centuries before.

One unexpected gap in our information about Palestine in the time of Christ is our failure to locate a single synagogue of this period in Palestine. Pre-Christian synagogues have been found outside of Palestine, and a Greek inscription found by Weill in Jerusalem probably refers to the Synagogue of the Libertines (Freedmen), mentioned in Acts 6:9, but all the synagogue remains found in considerable numbers throughout the land, especially in Galilee, belong to the late second century A.D. and sub-

sequent centuries (see SYNAGOGUE, EXCAVATIONS
OF). Earlier synagogues will undoubtedly be
discovered, either in hitherto untouched sites or
under the remains of Roman and Byzantine
synagogues. There was unquestionably a wholesale destruction of synagogues at the time of
the First Revolt (A.D. 66–70), in keeping with
other archaeological evidence for an almost
complete break in the continuity of Jewish and
early Christian life in Palestine. Without
archaeology it thus becomes impossible really
to understand New Testament history. See
also SYNAGOGUES, EXCAVATIONS OF; ROTAS-SATOR
SQUARE.

BIBLIOGRAPHY: W. F. Albright, *The Archaeology of Pal-
estine and the Bible,* 3rd ed., 1935; *idem, From the Stone
Age to Christianity,* 2nd ed., 1946; *idem, Archaeology and
the Religion of Israel,* 2nd ed., 1946; *idem, Archaeology of
Palestine,* 2nd ed., 1951; *idem,* in *Old Testament Com-
mentary,* 1948, pp. 134–170; *idem* in H. H. Rowley, ed.,
The Old Testament and Modern Study, 1951, pp. 1–47;
A. G. Barrois, *Manuel d'archéologie biblique,* 1939; M.
Burrows, *What Mean These Stones?* 1941; A. Deissmann,
Licht vom Osten, 4th ed., 1923 (translated in *Light from
the Ancient East,* 1927); R. Engelbach, *Introduction to
Egyptian Archaeology,* 1946; J. Finegan, *Light from the
Ancient Past,* 1946; H. Gressmann, *Altorientalische Texte
und Bilder zum Alten Testament,* 2nd ed., 1926–27;
S. Lloyd, *Foundations in the Dust,* 1947; C. C. McCown,
The Ladder of Progress in Palestine, 1943; A. Parrot,
Archéologie mésopotamienne, 1946; J. B. Pritchard, ed.,
*Ancient Near Eastern Texts Relating to the Old Testa-
ment,* 1950; R. W. Rogers, *History of Babylonia and
Assyria,* 5th ed., 1915; L. Speleers, *Les fouilles en Asie
Antérieure à partir de 1843,* 1928; C. Watzinger, *Denk-
maeler Palaestinas,* 1933–35.

[Sup.] WILLIAM FOXWELL ALBRIGHT.

ARCHAEOLOGY, CHRISTIAN: Christian
archaeology is concerned with the discovery and
interpretation of objects connected with the
history of early Christianity.

I. The Life of Jesus: Specific objects indubitably and directly connected with the life of
Jesus have not been found. The Chalice of
Antioch, discovered in 1910, a silver cup in an
openwork holder ornamented with figures probably of Christ and his followers, has been held
to be the cup of the Last Supper but is more
probably a piece of early Christian silver from
the fourth or fifth century. The Jerusalem
Ossuaries, found in 1945 in a Jewish tomb from
the middle of the first century, have inscriptions
mentioning Simeon Barsaba and Jesus. After
the name Jesus in one case is the Greek *iou,*
an interjection of grief in classical Greek, but
the spelling of the name Jehu in the Septuagint; and in the other case the word *alôth,*
perhaps derived from an Aramaic root meaning to lament, or perhaps a name or nickname
derived from the aloes plant. On the sides of
one ossuary are rough cross marks. While it
has been held that we have here lamentations
for the crucifixion of Jesus by some of his
disciples, it is more probable that there is no
connection with the founder of Christianity:
Jesus the son of Jehu and Jesus Aloes were
totally different persons; the cross marks were
only made to indicate that a receptacle was in

use. See also JESUS CHRIST, PICTURES AND IM-
AGES OF.

II. New Testament Sites in Palestine: Many
New Testament sites are known, but relatively
few have been excavated. At Capernaum on
the Sea of Galilee the Jewish synagogue has
been excavated and partially restored. Although
the remains date probably from around A.D.
200, they may represent a reconstruction of the
synagogue of the first century. At Samaria,
excavation has laid bare the strong fortifications
built by Herod the Great. Gerasa (Jerash) in
Trans-Jordan has revealed colonnaded streets,
temples and theaters, mostly later than the
first century. Excavations were begun at New
Testament Jericho in 1950, and brought to light
the civic center of the Roman city, with a
grand façade facing the Wadi Qelt. In Jerusalem an inscription was found recording the
building of a synagogue by Theodotus, doubtless before A.D. 70. Another inscription contained the warning which forbade foreigners to
go within the inner enclosures of the Temple.
Beyond the present northern wall of Jerusalem,
portions of a wall have been found which must
have been the "third wall" described by
Josephus as built by Herod Agrippa I. See also
SYNAGOGUES, EXCAVATIONS OF.

III. The World of Paul: Most of the finds in
the cities visited by Paul belong properly to
the realm of classical archaeology but occasional
discoveries may be connected directly with the
work of the apostle. In Ephesus the temple
of Artemis, mentioned in Acts 19:27, was found
after long search. The theater (Acts 19:29) also
was excavated, but the existing remains are
probably from a reconstruction of date later
than the time of Paul. At Philippi the forum
has been revealed. West of the city are the
ruins of a colonial archway which rose over the
Via Egnatia before it reached the banks of
the River Gangites. This may have been the
"gate" of Acts 16:13. In Thessalonica, a Roman
arch carried an inscription with the word
"politarchs," used in Acts 17:6 but otherwise
previously unknown in Greek sources. In
Athens not only the Acropolis, but also the
agora or market place (Acts 17:17), and the
Areopagus or Hill of Ares (Acts 17:19, 22), are
well known. Reminiscent of the address at
Athens reported in Acts 17:23 is an altar inscription found at Pergamum beginning, "To
unknown gods." At Corinth an agora inscription uses the Latin word for "market" which
corresponds to the Greek in I Corinthians
10:25; another inscription reads, "Synagogue
of the Hebrews"; and yet another mentions
an aedile Erastus who may perhaps be identified
with the city treasurer of the same name in
Romans 16:23. An inscription found at Delphi
makes it possible to date the arrival of the
proconsul Gallio in Corinth in the summer of

A.D. 51, and to conclude that the arrival of Paul in that city took place at the beginning of A.D. 50. At Herculaneum, destroyed by the eruption of Vesuvius in A.D. 79, there is the impression of a Latin cross on the wall of a small upper room. This may have been a private Christian chapel, and may reflect the preaching of the cross by Paul, who stopped at nearby Puteoli (Acts 28:13) on his way to Rome. In Rome much of the city of Paul's time has been revealed, including forum, aqueducts, temples, theaters, and basilicas.

IV. Manuscripts: The oldest known manuscripts of the New Testament were written on papyrus, the common writing material of the ancient world. A tiny fragment of the Gospel according to John dates probably in the first half of the second century A.D. An extensive codex of the Pauline letters comes from around A.D. 200. From the middle of the fourth century on, we have manuscripts on parchment and vellum. Among the oldest and most important are Codex Vaticanus, preserved in the Vatican Library at Rome; Codex Sinaiticus, found in the Monastery of Saint Catherine at Mount Sinai and now in the British Museum; Codex Alexandrinus, also in the British Museum; Codex Ephraemi rescriptus, in the Bibliothèque Nationale in Paris; and the Freer Gospels in Washington, D. C. Variant readings in the different manuscripts must be taken into account in the attempt to determine the original text of the New Testament. See also BIBLE TEXT, NEW TESTAMENT.

V. Catacombs: Catacombs were employed as burial places by the early Christians at numerous places in Italy, North Africa, Egypt, and elsewhere. Those at Rome are the best known and most extensive. The oldest Roman catacombs, according to the researches of Styger, date from the middle of the second century A.D., although some scholars would put them as early as the first century. The Crypts of Lucina contain the oldest paintings. In the Catacomb of Callistus is the Crypt of the Popes where a number of the popes of the third and fourth centuries were buried. The Catacomb of Domitilla is probably named after the Domitilla who was banished by the Emperor Domitian. The Catacomb of Priscilla contains in the Cappella Greca the greatest series of early Christian paintings preserved in any single room of the catacombs. In a painting of the resurrection of Lazarus is the earliest known picture of Christ, about the middle of the second century. At the Catacomb of Sebastian is a room where numerous graffiti contain appeals to Paul and Peter, whose remains appear to have been temporarily interred there on the occasion of the persecution of Valerian (A.D. 258). The art of the catacombs borrowed familiar pagan themes such as the orant, the good shepherd, and the fish, but infused these symbols with Christian meaning; adopted pictures from Jewish art such as Noah in the ark, and Daniel in the lions' den; and produced its own representations of New Testament subjects such as the healing of the paralytic and the resurrection of Lazarus. The dominant theme was that of deliverance or salvation.

VI. Sarcophagi: Sculptured stone coffins were employed occasionally in the catacombs and frequently in and around the churches which were built above ground after the conversion of Constantine. The oldest Christian sarcophagi are dated by Gerke in the middle of the third century. In the sculptures the orant and the good shepherd appear first, then biblical compositions with scenes from the Old Testament and the New Testament. In the fourth century the Latin frieze style, with a large number of subjects crowded side by side, and the Asiatic columnar style, where the figures are placed in a framework of columns and arches, are differentiated. Latin and Asiatic styles mingled to produce the magnificent sarcophagus of Junius Bassus, dated in A.D. 359, and found in the Church of St. Peter at Rome in 1595.

VII. Churches: The meeting places of the early Christians were in homes, as is made plain by numerous references in the New Testament (I Corinthians 16:19, etc.). A house church has been excavated at Dura-Europos on the middle Euphrates, a city which was abandoned soon after A.D. 256. The Christian chapel in this house was adorned with wall paintings showing both Old Testament and New Testament subjects. The figure of Jesus in a picture of the healing of the paralytic is the second oldest known painting of Christ. In Palestine the most famous churches were the Church of the Holy Sepulcher, erected by Constantine over the traditional site of the tomb of Christ; and the Church of the Nativity, built by Helena at Bethlehem where the grotto was shown in which Christ was supposed to have been born. In Rome the Churches of St. Peter and of St. Paul outside the walls, founded by Constantine, commemorated the traditional last resting places of the two apostles. In 1940 new excavations were begun under St. Peter's and in 1950 Pope Pius XII declared: "The tomb of the Prince of Apostles has been found. Such is the final conclusion after all the labor and study of these years." See also PETER THE APOSTLE.

BIBLIOGRAPHY: General: Jack Finegan, *Light from the Ancient Past, The Archeological Background of the Hebrew-Christian Religion*, 1946; Carl M. Kaufmann, *Handbuch der christlichen Archaeologie*, 3d ed., 1922; F. Cabrol and H. Leclercq, *Dictionnaire d'archéologie chrétienne et de liturgie*, 1924 ff.; Walter Lowrie, *Art in the Early Church*, 1947; Charles R. Morey, *Early Christian Art*, 1942; G. E. Wright and F. V. Filson, *The Westminster Historical Atlas to the Bible*, 1945. Life of Jesus: G. A. Eisen, *The Great Chalice of Antioch*, 1923; E. L.

Sukenik, *The Earliest Records of Christianity*, 1947. New Testament Sites in Palestine: Gustaf Dalman, *Sacred Sites and Ways*, 1935; G. Orfali, *Capharnaüm et ses ruines*, 1922. World of Paul: W. M. Ramsay, *The Cities of St. Paul*, 1908; A. G. Mackinnon, *The Rome of Saint Paul*, 1931. Manuscripts: W. H. P. Hatch, *The Principal Uncial Manuscripts of the New Testament*, 1939; Frederic Kenyon, *Our Bible and the Ancient Manuscripts*, 1940. Catacombs: Paul Styger, *Die roemischen Katakomben*, 1933; Joseph Wilpert, *Die Malereien der Katakomben Roms*, 1903. Sarcophagi: Friedrich Gerke, *Die christlichen Sarkophage der vorkonstantinischen Zeit*, 1940; J. Wilpert, *I Sarcofagi cristiani antichi*, 1929–36. Churches: M. I. Rostovtzeff, ed., *The Excavations at Dura-Europos*, Vol. 5, 1934. J. W. Crowfoot, *Early Churches in Palestine*, 1941; Hans Lietzmann, *Petrus und Paulus in Rom*, 1927. J. Wilpert, *Die roemischen Mosaiken und Malereien der kirchlichen Bauten vom IV bis XIII Jahrhundert*, 1916. In addition to the works cited above see various periodicals including the *American Journal of Archaeology* (Cambridge), *The Biblical Archaeologist* (New Haven), and the *Rivista di Archeologia Cristiana* (Rome).

[Sup.] JACK FINEGAN.

ARCHER, JOHN CLARK: Disciples of Christ; b. at Wilna, Md., Dec. 23, 1881. He studied at Hiram College (B.A., 1905), Yale University (B.D., M.A., 1914, Ph.D., 1922) and Harvard Divinity School. He was minister, Christian Church, Newton Falls, O. (1905–07), Congregational Church, Avon, Conn. (1912–14); assistant minister, South Congregational Church, Brockton, Mass. (1914–15); and ad interim minister, First Baptist Church, New Haven, Conn. (winter, 1918–19); has been lecturer at Christian College, Jabalpur, India (1907–11); Khalsa College, Amritsar, India (1937, 1946); Hartford Institute (1926); and an officer of the American Oriental Society (1923–36). His chief service has been at Yale as professor of comparative religion (1915–50), in the Hoober Chair (1932–50). In theology he is a liberal evangelical. Among his published works are: *Mystical Elements in Mohammed* (1940); *A New Approach in Missionary Education* (1926); *Youth in a Believing World* (1931); *Faiths Men Live By* (1934, 7th printing, 1948); and *The Sikhs* (1946).

ARCHITECTURE, ECCLESIASTICAL. See ART, ECCLESIASTICAL.

ARCHIVES, ECCLESIASTICAL: I. United States: Archival material for the history of American churches may be found in the official depositories of the denominations and of their subordinate organizations, in the collections of many individual churches, in the collections of state and local historical societies, and, among other libraries, especially in the libraries of Congress, Harvard, Yale, Chicago University, Union Theological Seminary, New York, and the New York Public Library.

Special Collections

Adventists: Seventh-day Adventist Theological Seminary.

Baptists: Crozer Theological Seminary; Colgate-Rochester Divinity School (which now has the Samuel Colgate Baptist Historical Collection); New England Baptist Library, Boston, Mass.; Southern Baptist Theological Seminary; Shurtleff College; Franklin College; Seventh Day Baptist Library, Plainfield, N. J.

Brethren, Church of the: Bethany Biblical Seminary; Brethren Publishing House, Elgin, Ill.; Juniata College.

Congregationalists: Congregational Library in Boston; Chicago Theological Seminary; Yale University; Hartford Theological Seminary.

Disciples: Transylvania University; Disciples Divinity House; Oliver Stockton College.

Episcopalians: Church Missions House in New York; Church Historical Society; Divinity School, Philadelphia, Pa.; Berkeley Divinity School; Maryland Diocesan Library, Baltimore, Md.; General Theological Seminary.

Evangelical and Reformed: Theological Seminary, Lancaster, Pa.; Eden Theological Seminary.

Friends: Friends' Library, Philadelphia, Pa.; Quaker Meeting House, Rutherford Place, New York, N. Y.; Swarthmore College; Haverford College; New York Monthly Meeting, Religious Society of Friends, New York, N. Y.

Jews: Jewish Theological Seminary, N. Y.; Hebrew Union College in Cincinnati.

Lutherans: Lutheran Theological Seminary, Mt. Airy, Phila., Pa.; Concordia Theological Seminary; Augustana Theological Seminary; Gettysburg Theological Seminary; St. Olaf College.

Mennonites: Goshen College.

Methodist: Drew Theological Seminary; Garrett Biblical Institute; Duke University; New England Methodist Historical Society Library in Boston; Methodist Historical Society Library, New York, N. Y.; Emory University Library; Perkins School of Theology.

Moravians: Bethlehem, Pa., Archives: Winston-Salem (N. C.) archives; Moravian Historical Society, Nazareth, Pa.

Mormons: Salt Lake City, Utah, archives; New York Public Library, New York, N. Y.

Presbyterians: Department of History, Witherspoon Building, Philadelphia, Pa.; Historical Foundation, Montreat, N. C.

Reformed: Sage Library, New Brunswick, N. J.

Roman Catholics: Catholic University of America; Notre Dame University; St. Mary's, Baltimore, Md.; Georgetown University; St. Louis University.

Shakers: Western Reserve Historical Society, Cleveland, Ohio; Ohio Archaeological and Historical Society, Columbus, Ohio; Grosvenor Library, Buffalo, N. Y.

Unitarians and Universalists: Congregational Library, Boston; Rhode Island Historical Society, Providence, R. I.; Meadville Theological School; Tufts College.

II. Canada: Archives of the United Church of Canada are at Victoria University in Toronto. The records of the Presbyterian Church of Canada, before union, are at Queen's University Library, Kingston, Ontario, while collections of their presbyteries and synods of the Maritime Provinces are at Pine Hill Divinity Hall Library, Halifax, Nova Scotia. Archives of the continuing Presbyterian Church of Canada may be found at Knox College, Toronto. Early Canadian Baptist records are located at Acadia University Library, Wolfville, Nova Scotia, and in the Baptist Historical Collection at McMaster University, Hamilton, Ontario. Congregational records for the Maritime Provinces are at Mount Allison University Library, Sackville, New Brunswick. The Church of England in Canada has placed its collections at Church House, Toronto; at Divinity Hall, Montreal; and at the headquarters of the ecclesiastical provinces.

See also MISSION RESEARCH.

BIBLIOGRAPHY: W. H. Allison, *Inventory of Unpublished Materials for American Religious History in Protestant Church Archives and other Repositories* (1910) is still useful and merits revision and expansion. Robert B. Downs, *American Library Resources; A Bibliographical Guide* (1951), pp. 69–86, lists references to published inventories and descriptions of some collections, and includes the inventories issued under the auspices of the Historical Records Survey. W. W. Sweet, "Church Archives in the United States," in *Church History*, Vol. 8 (1939), pp. 43–53; Mrs. T. G. Keir, "Theological Libraries in Canada Today," in *Summary of Proceedings, Fourth Annual Conference of the American Theological Library Association* (1950), pp. 8–13; Christopher Crittenden and Doris Godard, eds., *Historical Societies in the United States and Canada: A Handbook*, 1944.

[Sup.] KENNETH S. GAPP.

ARGENTINA: With an area of 1,078,769 square miles, Argentina has a population of 16,550,000 (1949 estimate), largely white and of European background. It is the most prosperous of the South American countries.

In June, 1943, a group of army officers overthrew the conservative government. They were strongly nationalistic and their slogan was "Argentina for the Argentines." Colonel (later General) Juan B. Perón soon asserted leadership and in 1946 was elected president, chiefly through the support of the laboring classes, the Roman Catholic Church, and the army. He was elected for a second term in November, 1951, this being the first time an Argentine president has succeeded himself.

Primary education is free and compulsory for children from 6 to 14. In 1945 there were 14,294 primary schools with 2,064,464 pupils; 505 secondary, normal, and special schools with 163,626 pupils, and 640 incorporated schools with 57,783 pupils. For advanced education there are national universities at Córdoba, Buenos Aires, La Plata, Santa Fé, Tucumán, Corrientes, and Cuvo.

There is no state religion, but the Roman Catholic faith is supported by the state. All other faiths are tolerated and there is freedom of conscience.

According to Article 76 of the Constitution, the president and vice-president of Argentina must be Roman Catholics, and, according to Article 86, the president exercises the right of patronage in the appointment of bishops. He grants or withholds the publication of papal communications. The government claims the right to appoint parish priests. Argentina has 1 cardinal, 7 archbishops, 15 suffragan bishops. There is a seminary in each diocese, and each one is partly supported by state funds. The Apostolic Internunciature to Argentina was raised to a Nunciature in July, 1916, when the centennial of Argentine independence was celebrated.

According to 1948 estimates there were 259,056 Protestants in Argentina. There are thirteen foreign-language churches (i.e., their worship is in languages other than Spanish). The largest Protestant seminary and the largest bookstore in South America are located in Buenos Aires. Both are interdenominational. The Evangelical Confederation of Churches serves many denominations in the River Plate republics of Argentina, Uruguay, and Paraguay.

There are 260,000 Jews in Argentina, and usually they are grouped according to their country of origin. The oldest congregation was founded in 1868. No official body represents the Jews, though there are numerous social institutions.

BIBLIOGRAPHY: Lewis S. Weber, *Argentina from Within*, 1945; J. Merle Davis, *The Evangelical Church in the River Plate Republics*, 1943; J. Lloyd Meecham, *The Church and State in Latin America*, 1934; Edwin Ryan, *The Church in the South American Republics*, 1943; J. P. Howard, *Religious Liberty in Latin America*, 1944; R. Pattee, *Catholicism in Latin America*, 1945; P. M. Dunne, *A Padre Views South America*, 1945.

[Sup.] W. STANLEY RYCROFT.

ARIAS, BENEDICTUS: The polyglot Bible which was prepared under the leadership of Arias appeared at Antwerp in 1569–72 (Christ. Plantin Press), consisting of eight volumes. The title of this work was *Biblia sacra hebraice, chaldaice, graece et latine, Philippi II regis catholici pietate et studio ad sacrosanctae ecclesiae usum.*

BIBLIOGRAPHY: A. Lambert, in *Dict. d'hist. et de géogr. ecclés.*, Vol. IV (1930), col. 129–145.

[Sup.] MATHIAS GOOSSENS.

ARMAGEDDON: The field of final battle between the "kings of the whole world" led by "devil spirits" and the Almighty God (Rev. 16:16). Although there are several variations in the form of the word in the Greek texts (see Hastings' *Dictionary of the Bible*, article "Armageddon"), the most probable etymology is that which derives it from the two Hebrew words "Har" and "Megiddo," meaning "Mount Megiddo." This was the mountain located at the upper end of the Plain of Esdraelon, from which entrance is made onto the great battlefield where Israel's fortune was so often decided. In this region Deborah and Barak defeated the Canaanites in spite of almost insuperable odds (Judg. 5:19); Saul and Jonathan met their death at the hand of the Philistines (I Sam. 31:1); and the fate of Judah was sealed when the good King Josiah fell before the Egyptians (II Kings 23:29). Wars with Damascus and later with Assyria had tortured the valley time and again. Even after Israel ceased to rule the land, Mount Megiddo still presided over this scene of decisive contests. By Esdraelon Alexander entered when he brought Hellenistic culture to Palestine and the east. By the time of the later prophets "Megeddon" had become the symbol of mourning over ruin (Zech. 12:11). Literalists interpret the passage in Revelation to mean that God and the devil will engage in mortal combat at "Armageddon." Apocalyptists take it as symbolical of the finality of the struggle between good and evil by which the victory of God in the broadest spiritual sense, is assured.

See also ESCHATOLOGY.   JULIAN PRICE LOVE.

ARMENIA: The Armenian plateau is composed largely of volcanic debris. Mount Ararat is one of its extinct cones and rests on a base of Devonian and Carboniferous formations. Devastating earthquakes occur. Copper, silver, lead, iron, and coal are found, with traces of ancient gold mines. Oil occurs but is undeveloped. Irrigation, forestation, and hydroelectric development are under way. An outstanding stone culture goes back to the neolithic period and a remarkable metal culture probably to early in the second millennium B.C. The Hurrians appear shortly after 2000 B.C. The Amarna and Boghasköy archives mention the kingdom of Mitanni from about the middle of the second millennium. From Tukulti-Urta I (1243–1206) on Assyrian sources refer to a large number of small states in the Nairi lands. These soon developed into the kingdom of Urartu. Ancient Urartuan inscriptions are only imperfectly read, but a promising key to the language may be provided by the Urartu stone written in both Assyrian and Urartuan, a copy of which was secured by Cameron in 1951. Armenia has had a tragic history during the past half century. In World War I nearly a million lives were lost through massacres and deportations. A Soviet Socialist Republic was created in 1918. Gregorian churches continue to function. The Catholicate has been dispossessed of lands, buildings, and revenues. Foreign missionary activities are not permitted. It is estimated that two and a half million Armenians are still in existence, about half of whom reside in Soviet Armenia.

BIBLIOGRAPHY: Jacques de Morgan, *Histoire du Peuple Arménien*, 1919; C. F. Lehmann-Haupt, *Corpus Inscriptionum Chaldicarum*, 1928–1935; *Armenien einst und jetzt*, 2 vols., 1931; Albrecht Goetze, *Kleinasien*, 1933; A. Salmaslian, *Bibliographie de l'Arménie*, 1946; Leon Arpee, *A History of Armenian Christianity*, 1946; René Grousset, *Histoire de l'Arménie*, 1947.

[Sup.] EDWIN R. THIELE.

ARMSTRONG, WILLIAM PARK: Presbyterian; b. in Selma, Ala., Jan. 10, 1874; d. in Princeton, N. J., March 25, 1944. He studied at Princeton University (A.B., 1894; A.M., 1896); Princeton Theological Seminary (1894–97); and at the universities of Marburg (1897), Berlin (1897–98), and Erlangen (1898). He was instructor in New Testament literature (1899–1903), professor of New Testament literature and exegesis (1903–40), and graduate professor of New Testament exegesis (1940–44), Princeton Theological Seminary.

FREDERICK WILLIAM LOETSCHER.

ARNAULD, ANTOINE: Antoine Arnauld, the Jansenist leader, was also one of the first of the Cartesians in France, the first to teach Cartesianism in the Sorbonne, and one of those most responsible for the strong strain of rationalism in French Catholic thought. Descartes' *Discourse sur la methode* was published in 1637, while Arnauld was still a student at the Sorbonne. Arnauld immediately familiarized himself with the new ideas, and in 1639 used them as the basis for his course of lectures in philosophy in the College of Mons. A few years later he was the only one in the Sorbonne willing to contribute comments on the *Meditations*, and he was the only one among those submitting comments who was wholeheartedly in favor of Descartes' ideas. He liked the novelty of the system and the logical, geometric method of presentation. But most important, he approved of the fact that Descartes tried to make his philosophy conform to Catholic dogma, and yet avoided what Arnauld considered to be the empty formalism of scholasticism. Arnauld pointed out the close connection between the *cogito* and the principles by which St. Augustine sought to distinguish mind and body. Arnauld also approved Descartes' system because he thought that his proofs of the existence of God and of the immortality of the soul were important contributions to theology. He used the Cartesian system to replace the syllogisms and elaborate terminology of scholastic philosophy with a simpler logical method and more common-sense terminology. He based his arguments on the Cartesian proofs of God and the distinction between mind and body, and he used the test of clarity and distinctness of ideas, considering it coequal with the test of authority. Arnauld used all of this rationalist apparatus to support the doctrines of Catholicism. The alliance between Cartesianism and

Jansenism was founded on the work of Arnauld and through this connection it flowed into the main stream of French Catholic thought.

The high point in Arnauld's career came after the peace of Clement IX in 1668 when he was received by the papal nuncio and by Louis XIV. For the first time since 1643 Arnauld was out of hiding, and people came to see him in embarrassing numbers. It was during this period that he was visited by the young Leibniz, a meeting which led later (1686–90) to the well-known correspondence between them. The pressures on the Jansenists, however, increased to the point where by 1679 Arnauld felt that he no longer could remain safely in France and still be free to express his ideas. He fled to the Low Countries where he spent the rest of his life as an exile, most of the time living in Brussels. However, the vicissitudes of the times, especially the frequent invasions by Louis XIV, forced Arnauld several times to seek refuge in Protestant Holland where he received asylum from the so-called Jansenist Church of The Netherlands (q.v.). News of the arrest and lifelong imprisonment of Père du Breuil, a priest of the Oratory, for having received some of Arnauld's books, was convincing proof to Arnauld that France was not a safe place for him. He was joined by other exiles from France at various times, among them being Pasquier Quesnel (q.v., Vol. IX) who succeeded Arnauld as Jansenist leader, and whose *Reflexions morales* were condemned by the Bull *Unigenitus*. Although an object of persecution himself, Arnauld greeted with joy the news of the Revocation of the Edict of Nantes. He never wavered in his vigorous opposition to the Protestants. In spite of this the Jesuit attacks on him and on the Jansenists continued, so that Arnauld wrote the *Fantome du jansenisme* in which he argued that the existence of any sort of organized Jansenist party was a myth. The revolution in England which replaced the Catholic James by the Protestant William horrified Arnauld, who could not understand why all the Catholic powers did not unite in a holy war to restore James. It was with the greatest reluctance that he accepted the fact that even the pope had given aid to William.

During the period of his exile Arnauld carried on a long controversy with Malebranche on the doctrine of grace. The discussion was conducted within the framework of the Cartesian system, and much more metaphysics was discussed than in any of the Jansenist-Jesuit literature. Malebranche had argued that God's activity in the world, including the distribution of grace, was limited to the establishment of general laws which along with secondary causes were productive of all individual events in the world. Arnauld argued against this idea, contending that it made meaningless all Christian

beliefs and practices. In his work, *Des vrais et des fausses idées*, he attacked the epistemological foundations of Malebranche's system, and in his later writings in the controversy showed how they were illogical and contrary to the traditions of the church and the teachings of the fathers. The controversy was ended by the death of Arnauld, on August 8, 1694, in Brussels, where his body was secretly buried. His heart was taken to Port Royal (q.v.).

BIBLIOGRAPHY: Leonard Guelphe, *Relation de la retraite de M. Arnauld dans les Pays-Bas en 1679*, 1733; Nicolas Malebranche, *Recueil de toutes les reponses M. Arnauld*, 4 vols., 1709; Pasquier Quesnel, *Histoire abrégée de la vie et des ouvrages de M. Arnauld*, 1695; Jean la Porte, *La Doctrine de la grace chez Arnauld*, 1922; Noel de Larrière, *Vie de M. Antoine Arnauld*, 2 vols., 1782–1783; Norman D. Kurland, "Antoine Arnauld," Unpublished thesis. University of Michigan, 1952.

[Sup.] NORMAN D. KURLAND.

ARNDT, ELMER J. F.: Evangelical and Reformed; b. at New Orleans, La., Nov. 10, 1908. He studied at Tulane University, Eden Theological Seminary (B.D., 1929), Washington University (M.A., 1930), Union Seminary (S.T.M., 1931), and Yale University (Ph.D., 1943). He joined the faculty of Eden Seminary in 1931 and since 1941 has been professor of historical theology and Christian ethics. He was visiting lecturer, Johannes Gutenberg University, Mainz (1951–52). He is author of: "Conflicts of Power" in *Challenge of Our Culture*, ed. by C. T. Craig (1946) and "Sacramental Fellowship" in *The Heritage of the Reformation*, ed. by E. Arndt (1950).

ARNDT, WILLIAM F.: Lutheran (Mo. Syn.); b. Mayville, Wis., Dec. 1, 1880. He studied at Concordia Seminary, St. Louis, Mo. (B.D., 1903); University of Chicago (M.A., 1923); Washington University (Ph.D., 1935). He was pastor of Lutheran churches at Bluff City, Tenn. (1903–05); St. Joseph, Mo. (1905–10); Brooklyn, N. Y. (1910–12); taught Latin, Greek and Hebrew at St. Paul's College, Concordia, Mo. (1912–21), and has been professor of New Testament at Concordia Seminary, St. Louis, Mo. (1921—). He has been managing editor of *Homiletical Magazine* (1924–26); *Theological Monthly* (1926–30), and *Concordia Theological Monthly* (1938–49). His books include: *Does the Bible Contradict Itself?* (1926); *Siehe, ich stehe vor der Tuer* (1929); *Bible Difficulties* (1932); *Popular Symbolics* (with others) (1934); *Christian Prayer* (1937); *Fundamental Christian Beliefs* (1938); *New Testament History* (1939); *Life of St. Paul* (1944); *From the Nile to the Waters of Damascus* (1949). He is engaged with F. Wilbur Gingrich in the translation and adaptation of Bauer's Lexicon of the Greek New Testament.

ARNOBIUS: *Fl.* A.D. 300; last surviving apologist from the period of the persecutions and in modern times an undeservedly neglected author, was professor of rhetoric at Sicca Veneria in proconsular Africa, Lactantius being among his pupils. If we may believe the debatable statements of St. Jerome, his vigorous opposition to the faith while yet a pagan caused his conversion to be viewed with suspicion by the bishop, and in order to prove his sincerity he composed the seven "most splendid" books *Against the Pagans (Adversus Nationes)*, now preserved for us, together with the *Octavius* of Minucius Felix, in *codex Parisinus* 1661 of the early ninth century. Doubtless influenced by Jerome's rather low opinion, confirmed by the so-called *Decretum Gelasianum* (sixth century), and perhaps nauseated by the exceptional frankness of the description of the pagan cults, modern scholars have too frequently contented themselves with expressing amazement at what they consider bizarre, unorthodox, or even heretical as they meet it in sporadic reading of isolated passages torn from their context. Many fail completely to comprehend the satiric nature of the method, the author's purpose in debating the pagan position upon its own premises, and see in silence concerning many details of the Christian faith a vast ignorance of it. Thus, they are themselves the losers. Book One is devoted to a defence of Christians from pagan charges, chiefly that they are the cause of natural calamities. Book Two, which is Arnobius at his best, is a spirited attack upon philosophy, principally Platonic idealism. In Books Three and Four Arnobius turns his satire on the myths, culminating in Book Five in an exposure of two of them in detail, those of Jupiter Elicius and of Attis and the mysteries. Finally, Book Six examines the temples and images, Book Seven the ceremonies of the cults. Arnobius is a mine of information on the religion which Christianity supplanted. While his style is verbose, his skill as a satirist is superb.

BIBLIOGRAPHY: Latin texts by A. Reifferscheid, *Corpus Scriptorum Ecclesiasticorum Latinorum*, vol. 4, 1875, not yet wholly supplanted by C. Marchesi, *Corpus Scriptorum Latinorum Paravianum*, vol. 62, 1934. For English translation, introduction, and the only modern commentary, see G. E. McCracken, *Arnobius of Sicca, The Case Against the Pagans*, in *Ancient Christian Writers*, vols. 7–8, 1949. On Arnobius and his work, see F. Gabarrou, *Arnobe son oeuvre*, 1921; E. Rapisarda, *Clemente fonte di Arnobio*, 1939, and *Arnobio*, 1945; and F. Tullius, *Die Quellen des Arnobius im 4., 5. und 6. Buch seiner Schrift*, 1934, as well as the bibliography by McCracken, 232–8.

[Sup.] GEORGE E. McCRACKEN.

ARNOLD OF BRESCIA: His career must be seen in the light of the changing social structure which during his lifetime was in full swing. The rise of cities to independence and power began first in northern Italy, where he lived. It was the middle class or bourgeoisie which now became aware of its importance. The third estate in Italy did not have to wait until the French Revolution to acquire prestige. Before the end of the Middle Ages the patricians in the great cities began to wrest from the nobility and the clergy their respective rights and privileges in so far as these seemed out of proportion to their numbers and usefulness. The rigorist Arnold of Brescia went a bit too far, however, for he approached the communist line of thought. He was more for the proletariat than for the middle class. In the field of religious doctrine he has also of late begun to seem rather heretical.

BIBLIOGRAPHY: E. Vacandard, *Arnoud de Brescia*, in *Revue des questions historiques*, 35 (1884), 52–114; G. W. Greenaway, *Arnold of Brescia*, 1931; A. Ragazzoni, *Arnaldo da Brescia nella tradizione storica*, 1937; P. Pedele, *Fonti per la storia di Arnaldo da Brescia*, 1938.

[Sup.] MATHIAS GOOSSENS.

ARNOLDI, BARTHOLOMAEUS:
BIBLIOGRAPHY: L. Boiteux, in *Dict. d'histoire et de géogr. ecclés.* Vol. IV (1930), 583–586. Here is to be found a complete list of Arnold's works. [Sup.]

ART. See AESTHETICS.

ART AND CHURCH: The subject is receiving increased attention today. Church art applies to the fabric and furnishings of the building, the poetry and music in worship, and the liturgy itself. Art consists in skillful handling of design and function, symbolism and ornament, so as to express the desired motifs, all in proper balance. Otherwise, overemphasis here or there leads to the eccentric or the bizarre. Seasonal moods and fancies call for careful study and evaluation in the light of history. The great periods of church art have shown certain relationships, which have varied at different times and are not to be taken as absolute. The first of these relationships, the "latreutic," concerns the liturgy. This does not compete with the purely aesthetic or the plainly pedagogic, but stands as a special requirement. If art bears no relationship to worship, it is merely art (secular, domestic, or commercial, etc.) in the church, but not church art. The use of the organ is a case in point. It should be the servant and ornament of the liturgy, especially the hymns. If the organ becomes an end in itself, and so competes with worship, the servant has tried to become the master.

In its most noteworthy periods and examples church art has profited from the creative efforts of the master artists. If art today is to represent God and aid in his worship, that art should have the highest quality in design, in materials, and in workmanship. After a period marked by much carelessness and ugliness in worship, the church today should again become the friend and patron of the ablest artists in all fields, and claim their handiwork for the glory of the Master Artist. The church is not a museum for the display of the cheap, shoddy, commonplace, but the repository of all that is true and beautiful and of good report. The best art is a delight and an inspiration to those who worship. Art may also educate, by teaching and enforcing the faith of the church at many points. In living forms it can lead the faithful to nobler worship and more devoted service, bringing honor to God, to whom it all is dedicated. Such a renewal of concern about sacred art ought to begin at the theological seminary. Then it will spread out to local churches, where every pastor ought to serve as a home missionary of beauty, in the form of art that promotes the worship of God.

See also JESUS CHRIST, IMAGES AND PICTURES OF.

[Sup.] GEORGE R. SELTZER.

ART, ECCLESIASTICAL: In order to do justice to this subject it will be necessary to discuss not only architecture but also sculpture and painting. For this reason the present article will be divided into three parts—architecture, sculpture, and painting.

I. Architecture: The oldest Christian churches originated for the most part in the reign of Emperor Constantine. The moment he tolerated the Christian religion (311 A.D.) Christian churches were built in large numbers. During the fourth century ecclesiastical architecture rose to great heights.

The typical structure is the basilica, modeled after the Roman building bearing the same name, though used more for secular than religious purposes. A rectangular nave led from the front door to the two new parts, namely the transept and the apse, which were added to make the whole church resemble the form of a cross. The altar was placed in the extreme rear, behind the large transept. To the right and left the building sloped to lower levels and the aisles formed by pillars were much less impressive than was the large and high nave. The apse was either rectangular or formed a semicircle. Above the altar was the *ciborium*, resting upon four short pillars. The choir was as a rule beautifully adorned and constructed near the altar, with two parts to the right and left of the pavement leading to the altar. It was separated from the rest of the building by marble walls, which later were often replaced by wooden partitions, lavishly carved. The complete basilica was constructed around an *atrium*, an open courtyard surrounded by rows of pillars. It also included a front hall called *narthex*, while the tower often stood apart from the rest. Famous churches of the better type are St. Paul Without the Walls, S. Maria Maggiore, S. Clemente, S. Sabina, etc. in Rome; S. Apollinare in Ravenna, and the Church of the Nativity in Bethlehem.

Another type is the round or polygonal structure surmounted by a dome, and used as a *baptisterium* (baptismal chapel) or mausoleum (burial chapel). An excellent example of this kind, definitely not called a basilica, is S. Con-

stanza in Rome, or the mausoleum of Galla Placidia in Ravenna, or S. Giovanni in Fonte in Rome.

The Byzantine style developed out of a combination of several features, including Hellenistic and Oriental, but so well managed by the architects of Constantinople (the former Greek city of Byzantium) that an entirely different type made its appearance as compared with the buildings of Greece or Rome or Persia or Egypt. Byzantine civilization was indeed a mixture of older cultures, well blended and by no means so dull or insipid as has often been imagined by experts in the countries of Western Europe and America. The dome and the elaborate mosaics remind the spectator of classical and Asiatic prototypes. From 330 to 1204 the artists of the Byzantine or East Roman Empire clung rather narrowly to the pattern set by the masters of the fourth and fifth centuries. Unlike the Roman type, that of the Byzantines was constructed to resemble a Greek cross. As a result the buildings were not so long and narrow as were the churches built in and near Rome. The most famous Byzantine church is that known as Hagia Sophia (Holy Wisdom), sometimes called Saint Sophia. In Ravenna, which for a time was under Byzantine rule, a church of the same kind is that known as S. Vitale (sixth century), while Venice, also at one time dominated by Constantinople, boasted of having built St. Mark (eleventh century). The Oriental influence witnessed in the Byzantine structures also spread into Russia, Sweden, Hungary, and even Italy. Here, as we shall see in the next section, the basilica was followed by a new style, less Roman certainly than its name would seem to imply.

The Romanesque style was extensively used in the Germanic-Roman Empire (962–1250), which after the middle of the thirteenth century was usually called the Holy Roman Empire. The Carolingian emperors (800–911) had encouraged the building of large churches and monasteries, but the so-called Carolingian Renaissance contributed little to the fine arts. The church built under Charlemagne's supervision at Aachen, where he afterward was buried, had the dome of the Byzantine style and some mosaics as well. Other churches constructed during the ninth century in Western Europe also indicate the powerful influence of the Byzantine masters. At the same time the basilica type retained some of its popularity. Gradually, however, the architects at the end of the tenth century devised a new type which grew in stature until by 1120 it had reached full maturity. Retaining the general plan of the basilica but without the central courtyard and the narthex, and making more use of the transept than had been done before, the builders of the twelfth century fashioned something stately and dignified that has won the admiration of art critics ever since. Around the altar they often added the *deambulatorium,* which was a semi-circular row of little chapels. Another innovation was the frequent use of geometrical figures. The towers were constructed on the west side or the end of the east side, attached to the main structure, and no longer separate as was the case with St. Mark in Venice. The windows were rather small, the walls heavy, the height of the pillars not above a moderate span. This somewhat somber and severe style appealed strongly to the Benedictine monks who used it to their delight. Many were the abbey churches they built, and the name of Westminster Abbey in London reminds the modern spectator of the artistic accomplishment perfected in the Middle Ages by the Benedictines, whose monasteries were abbeys, and their heads abbots, not priors. Numerous cathedrals still adorn the medieval portions of famous cities in France, Germany, and England. Durham has its great monument, as does Toulouse, Angoulême, Tournay (Belgium), Hildesheim, Mainz, Worms, and Bamberg. The Romanesque style is spiritual, earnest, turned inward. Horizontal lines predominate; the arches are round, not pointed. The pillars and the walls are heavy; the interior is not gaily decorated. It would seem that the builders of these massive structures reflected the sorrows of an age that was passing. The confusion which accompanied the downfall of the Frankish empire, the invasions of the Northmen and the Magyars, the destruction caused by some of the Saracens, and the poverty of both peasants and townsmen must have left their marks upon writers and artists.

Then came the thirteenth century, with the rise of new cities, the revival of trade in Western Europe, the withdrawal of the Saracens from Spain and Sicily, the rise of new national states, and the emancipation of the middle class in the cities. The sunshine of a new intellectual climate proved most refreshing to the builders of homes and churches. The joy of better living and more wholesome thinking pervaded the songs that the troubadours sang and the paintings that the artists fashioned for the merchant princes. Daring explorers sailed to distant shores in southeastern Asia, and scientists began to talk about flying through the air like birds. The Saviour was looked upon as a man of healing powers, not merely the suffering mediator between God and man. His childhood and youth fascinated the artists of the day. They depicted him in the arms of the Madonna; they thought of him as a link between humanity and divinity. No longer satisfied with poorly lighted churches, they built another type, named erroneously Gothic by the Italians, who thought that the men of France and Germany and

England were still somewhat under the cloud of Gothic barbarism, whereas, on the contrary, the Transalpine countries were on the way to intellectual leadership. The windows became larger, the arches pointed upward, the leading lines vertical, the pillars much taller, the whole atmosphere more pleasant. And in place of severe geometrical figures came wonderful statues and stained glass in magnificent rose windows. The thirteenth century was not for nothing lauded by discerning critics throughout the nineteenth century.

The Gothic cathedrals originated for the most part in the vicinity of Paris known as the Isle de France. The earlier structures retained much more of the Romanesque features than did the later types. Notre Dame in Paris, for example, has more heavy horizontal lines than does the cathedral at Rheims or the famous Dom in Cologne.

The cathedrals were the visual synthesis of medieval thought. Plants, animals, human beings, saints, angels, the Virgin Mary, and Christ —all of them together came from God and go back to God. Inscribed in stone and imbedded in stained glass are still to be seen the grand synopsis of thirteenth century civilization in the West. Chartres, Canterbury, Strasbourg, Amiens, and a host of other cities can show the world how deep religious fervor combined with artistic taste for beauty to make visible what Bernard of Clairvaux and Francis of Assisi had in their minds.

Italy did not share in the wealth and profusion of Gothic art. Its people had their backs turned toward the North and West. Classical and East Roman art seemed more respectable to the Italians than the productions of the so-called Goths. They learned to create a new school of art usually termed the Renaissance type, since Italy gave birth to the Renaissance. For the first time in many centuries individual architects arose who planned a whole building, just as they do today. Such had not been the case in France or England. Michelangelo, for example, was largely responsible for the building of St. Peter's in Rome. Other great architects were Brunellesco (1377–1446), Michelozzo (1396–1472), Battista Alberti (1404–72), Bramante (1444–1514), and Michele Sanmichele (1484–1559). As a rule they retained the Byzantine dome, the ornate decorations along the Byzantine pattern, the Greek columns, and the Roman arches. Outstanding examples of Renaissance architecture are the façade of the Carthusian church at Pavia, S. Andrea at Mantua, S. Lorenzo en S. Spirito, Florence, and the dome of the cathedral at Florence.

The period after 1550 produced the later Renaissance type which merged with the baroque. Among the leading architects in this period were Tignola (1507–73), Palladio (1508–80), and

Lorenzo Bernini (1589–1630). These builders emphasized the need for more space and more profuse ornamentation. Typical examples of late Renaissance architecture are S. Maria della Salute, Venice; S. Gesu, Rome; the Basilica at Vicenza, and the façade of St. Peter's in Rome.

During the past three centuries no important styles have developed in the field of ecclesiastical architecture. Formerly the countries in the West were united in a common philosophy of life, and the peoples could create something distinctively new and inspiring. In this manner both Romanesque and Gothic architecture arose. But at the opening of the twentieth century American as well as European architects seemed enslaved by the desire merely to imitate what had been done before their time. They felt that neo-Romanesque or neo-Gothic was the best to be had. There was no use in trying to surpass these styles, since they were so eminently fitted to engender religious fervor in the minds of the worshipers. After World War I a few countries favored the neo-classical style, which even more than the other two revealed the lack of originality among the leaders of the masses. Inasmuch as the practical demand for more light and space called for a new type of building used in the great new cities for railway stations, banks, offices, and stock markets; the idea seemed logical that churches should also be revamped to meet the same demand for light and space. The use of steel and cement easily lent themselves to the desire to have more and larger windows. Strong and wide pillars were no longer necessary.

Striking examples of the "businesslike" church are structures resembling theatres, like that by H. Hofmann (Zurich, 1938) and W. Moser (Zurich-Altstetten, 1941). This type of building is still in the experimental stage. On numerous occasions it has been possible to adjust the modern type of building to the atmosphere of religious worship. Examples are to be found in many countries. In Germany are handsome churches built by Professor Dominikus Boehm (as at Cologne-Riehl, with excellent interior, but not so successful an exterior); also those by H. Herkommer (Frankfurt, 1927; Schneidemuehl, 1930) and M. Weber (Frankfurt, 1926). The French churches of A. and G. Perret with their "glass in cement" walls lack the required atmosphere of rest and quiet (Paris, 1923 and 1925). Daring, but very beautiful interior (of pure cement) is the remarkable feature in the church by J. Droz (Nice, 1932). P. Rouvière (Blois, 1932) perfected a gracious and harmonious building of cement modeled after the ancient basilica. As a matter of fact, many architects in recent times have used the basilica as a model, and for this reason have not escaped the evil of mere imitation. Boosten and Kropholler have built some striking churches closely resembling the basilica, notably those after World War II, while a very interesting church was built in Detmold as recently as 1952. In America there have been similar cases, like the work by Albertson & Association, 1930; while in Mexico there is the type by E. de la Mora. It should be noted that the churches built since 1940 by Catholics and Protestants indicate a close co-operation among painters, glass fitters, silversmiths and workers in stone.

II. Sculpture: During the first four centuries the Christian sculptors made use of classical styles but occasionally added new figures, such as that of the good shepherd. In the Merovingian and Carolingian periods ecclesiastical sculpture was rather poor and lifeless, confining itself largely to ivory work and relief figures on baptismal fonts and sarcophagi. The rise of Romanesque architecture, however, brought with it a revival of superior sculpture. At first this was little more than relief work, but it greatly surpassed the crude figures of earlier times. At the entrances of the new Romanesque cathedrals the heavy walls were beautifully adorned with scenes from Old Testament accounts, like the temptation of Eve, as was done at the portal of Notre Dame at Clermont-Ferrand. Striking were the figures on the tympanums, like that of the Apocalypse at Moinac, the mission of the Apostles (Matt. 28:18) at Vezelay, and Christ seated among the four animals of the Apocalypse at Charlieu. Numerous figures were also carved on pillars in the interior. As a rule these were rather crowded, owing to lack of adequate space. Some outstanding statues are those of Ste. Fay in Avegron, the Madonna in Essen, known as *Sedes Sapientiae,* and the black madonnas at Chartres, Rocamadour, Marseille, etc. Some of these are somewhat pre-Romanesque.

The Gothic sculpture freed itself from the need of merely decorative purposes. It finally reached the point where it equaled the classical perfection with the separate statue representing a deeply spiritual concept. Likewise the wealth of new subjects marked a great advance. A great variety of scenes greeted the eyes of devout worshipers, drawn from both Old and New Testaments. Obviously there were also statues of saints and martyrs, besides medieval views of buildings and landscapes, especially on stained glass. The clothing worn by various persons was gracefully reproduced with all the intricate shades of color and detail in folds and laces. Moreover, the religious ardor shown on the faces of great leaders in the church still wins profound admiration from severe critics today. The figures on the portal royal at Chartres, dating from about 1145, are still somewhat archaic. Gradually, however, the figures became more graceful and meaningful, until they reached the heights of the late thirteenth century, as may be seen in Rheims, Chartres, Amiens, and many other French cities. Particularly striking are *Beau Dieu* and *Vierge dorée* in Amiens, besides the Annunciation and the Visitation in Rheims. The Flemish masters introduced a more realistic type of work, which spread rapidly from Flanders in all directions. A notable example is Moresput at Dyon, by Claus Sluter. In Germany the most important work was done at Bamberg, Magdeburg, and Naumburg. In England may be mentioned the statues at Salisbury and Exeter; in Spain much was accomplished at Toledo, Avila, and Seville. Italian churches do not possess much Gothic sculpture of a high order. But Nicolo Pisano carved notable figures on the pulpit at Pisa (1260), while Giotto fashioned famous reliefs in the campanile of the cathedral in Florence.

Renaissance sculpture strove after true realism rather than idealism. It borrowed much from classical prototypes, but added a wholly new atmosphere of its own. Its center was naturally in Italy. Among the masters in the early Renaissance period were Ghiberti (Baptisterium, Florence), Lucca and Andrea della Robbia (Florence), A. and B. Rossellino, and Benedetto da Majano. Early in the sixteenth century Michelangelo easily surpassed all others in this field. He was also the outstanding architect of the Renaissance, besides being a famous painter. His personality dominated the whole Italian school. Those who still cling to the idea that the fifteenth century was a period of decline for all of Europe certainly should make an exception for Italian civilization. The same may be said for the Low Countries. Among Michelangelo's masterpieces are the David, Moses, Pietà, and the tomb of G. Medici. Other masters were Raf. de Montelupo, Ang. Montorsoli, Bacchio Bandinelli, B. Ammanati, etc. In the Holy Roman Empire were also eminent sculptors, including Pieter de Witte (Dutch), whose Patrona Bavariae (Munich) is well known, and Peter Vischer and sons, noted for the tombstone of Sebaldus in Nuremberg. In France labored Michel Colombe, who depicted the burial of Christ, the coronation and ascension of the Virgin Mary, in the abbey church of Solesmes.

The baroque style was at first strongly influenced by Michelangelo, who is often called the father of the baroque. He was followed by Lorenzo Bernini, whose David (Rome, Villa Borghese) and the tombstone of Pope Urban VIII (Rome, St. Peter's) are characterized by graceful lines and symmetry. Other masters were Niccolo Salvi, Alessandro Algardi, Francis Duquesnoy (Fleming), and Antonio Montanti; and in France Antoine Coysevoic, Jean Antoine Houdon; in Germany Andreas Schluter, Raphael Donner, and Artus Quellinus from Antwerp. In England much was achieved by

Francis Bird and Thomas Banks. The baroque style continued to dominate both architecture and sculpture until the second half of the eighteenth century. Since that time it has shared the field with many other types which need not be mentioned here.

III. Painting: The Christians who used to assemble in the catacombs underneath Rome and vicinity drew much inspiration from the paintings on the walls of their little rooms. Here their artists drew pictures of those scenes which the worshipers found most helpful in their desire to commemorate the deeds of the Saviour. The Last Supper in Jerusalem, the tragedy on Calvary, the healing of the sick, and the work by the Good Shepherd gave them new courage and hope. Unfortunately this early type of painting could not withstand the ravages of the damp atmosphere in the subterranean halls and rooms. Very little is left of the first treasures, but descriptions made by some of the spectators during the second and third centuries can enable the art critics of our time to form a fairly accurate concept of what was accomplished.

Far more elegant than the paintings in the catacombs were those perfected in the ancient basilicas, particularly S. Constanza, the Baptisterium of the Lateran, S. Prudenziana, and S. Maria Maggiore in Rome; and somewhat later in S. Apollinare nuovo and S. Vitale in Ravenna; also the mausoleum of Gallia Placidia. Of the Merovingian mural paintings practically nothing is left, but undoubtedly some very good paintings were produced at Tours, Toulouse, and Cologne. Fortunately, however, precious miniatures have been preserved in Sacramentaria, Evangeliaria, etc. These date from the time of the great Germanic migrations in the fifth and sixth centuries. More numerous are those from the ninth century, when the Northmen invaded the Frankish empire and destroyed many but by no means all the manuscripts. In the monasteries the rich treasures were carefully preserved. It is possible to distinguish among the Frankish, Celtic, and Saxon styles. Famous examples are the Sacramentarium of Gellone, the Evangeliaria of St. Gall in Switzerland and of Echternach in Luxemburg. The Carolingian manuscripts are much more advanced, showing purple background, gold and silver colors of a high order, and more beautiful reproductions of scenes. Among the most valuable miniatures are those in the Bible of Emperor Charles the Bald, the Bible of Bamberg, and the Psalter of Utrecht. Frescoes dating from the ninth century are to be found in the monastery of S. Vincenzo de Volturni in Italy, and from the tenth century in the Church of St. George (St. Georgkirche) at Reichenau. The former are partly Roman and partly Byzantine in style, the latter are more elegant and more realistic.

In the Romanesque churches a large number of mural paintings were perfected with increasing skill. One of the oldest is that of the Last Judgment and the Passion in Saint-Savin (Vienne, eleventh century). The colors are direct and few in number, red, white, yellow, and green. The painting is made up of parallel and concentric lines. Grand simplicity is a notable feature. The best schools of painting were those at Poitevin, Touraine, Cluny (in Burgundy), and Auvergne. In Germany three styles are noted in the following order: the crude, the strong, and the free style. The technical terminology used by the painters and their pupils is to be found in *Diversarum artium schedula* by the monk Theophilus. Examples of early Romanesque paintings have been preserved in Schwarzrheindorf (middle of the twelfth century) with scenes from the Old and New Testaments, Brauweiler, and Hildesheim (ceiling of the Church of St. Michael). In Italy are the famous paintings in S. Angela in Formis, S. Maria in Tratevere; both in Rome. The paintings on glass follow soon after the first mural paintings. The oldest preserved are those of Saint Denis (about 1144), having great iconographic significance, indicating that the Old Testament is the prototype of the New Testament. Symbolical are the quadriga of Aminadab. S. Denis also labored in the cathedral at Chartres. Important also are the paintings in the cathedrals of York, Vendôme, Mans, Angers, and Poitiers. The colors used are blue, orange, red, and green. In numerous cases legends of the saints are depicted.

The greatest height attained was that in Gothic painting. Since the miniatures of the twelfth century follow the Romanesque pattern, it would not be correct to speak of Gothic painting until the thirteenth century is reached. Paris was the chief center, and the first productions of importance still extant are to be found in the two Psalteria of King Louis IX (St. Louis). During the fourteenth century Paris and Flanders share equal honors. Outstanding masters were Jean Pucelle, the brothers van Limburg, and Malvel. The painting on glass was most noteworthy at Chartres, Bourges, Tours, Mans, Sens, Canterbury, Lincoln, Wells, York, Gloucester, and Oxford. The most popular subjects depicted on the stained glass windows were the life of Christ, the Madonna, the legends of the saints, and the prophets.

The Gothic fresco became very beautiful in Italy, where Giotto labored during the fourteenth century, preceded in the thirteenth by Cimabue. Being originally of Byzantine origin and therefore hieratic in character, the fresco was developed more freely in Siena than elsewhere in Italy. Leading masters were Duccio, Guido of Siena, and later Simone Martini. Those who followed the style of Giotto included Taddeo and Angelo Gaddi, Spinello Aretino, and Orcagna. One of the best painters of the whole period was Giotto di Bondone, who in his figures and the proper measurement of space tried to reproduce exactly what he saw. Outstanding are the mural paintings in the churches of S. Francesco, Assisi; Anungiata dell'Arena, Padua; and S. Croce, Florence. All the scenes are drawn from the Christian tradition, both legendary and artistic. In the other areas of Western Europe until the end of the fourteenth century the fresco predominated, together with the work on stained glass.

During the fifteenth century magnificent panel paintings were developed in the Low Countries. Since the altar was the focal point of the religious service, being placed at the rear of the huge nave, it was only natural that the great masters of Flanders should concentrate their energy on the panels attached to the altar. They used the traditional subjects that called forth devotion, such as the birth of Christ, the Crucifixion, and the Madonna. They painted these in large dimensions, very realistic, and full of color. Their oil paint still glistens with a power hardly equaled before or since their time. Now the portrait came into its own. Behind the features there lay a profundity of thought and knowledge. The chief masters were the brothers Van Eyck (the Lamb of God at Ghent, the Last Judgment, and the Hermitage), Rogier van der Weiden, or Weyden (the descent from the cross in Madrid, the altar in Antwerp), Hugo van der Goes (the birth of Christ; the Portinari Altar in the Uffizi Palace, Florence; the Three Kings adoring Christ, panel in the Kaiser Friedrich Museum, Berlin), Dirk Bouts (the Last Supper, Louvain), Memlinc (Shrine of St. Ursula, St. John's Panel, Bruges), Gerard David (Baptism of Christ, Bruges), and Geertgentot Sint Jans (Illuminated Christmas Night, National Gallery, London). The style of the Flemings exerted great influence upon the Germans, including Stephan Lochner (the Three Kings Panel, Cologne) and M. Schongauer (Madonna, Colmar). In other countries also the Flemish school strongly affected the art of painting.

Italian painting during the fifteenth century also served the Christian Church. Here flourished three great schools, namely the Florentine, the Umbrian, and the Venetian. Early Renaissance painting was largely given over to religious subjects. In the work of Fra Angelico da Fiesole religious art in Italy reached its greatest height. Famous are the mural paintings in S. Marco, Florence; his panels were also highly prized. Among the other masters were Masaccio (the Tax Penny, Florence), Sandro Botticelli (the Worshiping Kings, Florence), and Ghirlandajo (the Visitation, Paris).

These exhibited the typical features of Renaissance painting, such as realistic representation, accurate spacing, and proper symmetry.

The later Renaissance, which surpassed the more primitive school of the fifteenth century, brought still more clarity of composition. Outstanding were Leonardo da Vinci (Last Supper, Milan), Rafael da Santi (the Disputation, the Sistine Madonna, Dresden, and numerous other madonnas), and Michelangelo. The latter's masterpiece on the ceiling of the Sistine Chapel has called forth lasting admiration. Here the creation of Adam is depicted with rare acumen, besides other scenes from the book of Genesis. His Last Judgment approaches the baroque style. Emotion and drama vie with each other to attract the eye and the heart. The Venetian school was well represented by Titian (the Tax Penny, Dresden), Giorgione, Palma il Vecchio, and Tintoretto.

The best known painter in Germany was Albrecht Duerer, whose apostle figures are remarkable. They are in Munich, while his Feast of the Rose Wreath in Prague and his woodcuts representing scenes from the Apocalypse, the Passion, and the life of the Virgin Mary also mark him as a distinguished leader in religious art. But gradually art became secularized, together with politics. The portrait became the most popular theme, even in religious art. Now more attention was paid to accurate reproduction than symbolism or religious inspiration. Individualism replaced communal living and thinking. Duerer himself underwent such a process in his own work. His etchings had a tendency to popularize civil rulers rather than saints or popes or priests. The same may be said of Holbein the Younger and Hans Baldung Grien. In the Low Countries religious themes continued to find popular favor, and the Romanists J. Gossaert, Bernard van Orley, Jan van Sorel, Quentin Matsys (Family of St. Anna, Brussels), and H. Bos were actually late medieval in their type of presentation. The first is famous for his madonnas, the last for his painting of the devil and the terrors of the witches. Breughel the Elder is known for his allegories and scenes from rural life. This peasant atmosphere is also seen in his presentation of the worshiping kings.

When at the end of the sixteenth century the Renaissance style merged with the baroque, the Roman Catholic authorities used painting as a weapon to stem the tide of Protestantism in Italy. Reni, Carracci, Domanichini, and Tiepolo labored there with marked success, while in Flanders the celebrated Rubens (the Last Judgment, Munich) aided the clergy with some of his work. In Spain beautiful madonnas were painted by Velasques and Murillo. On the other hand, the Dutch painter Rembrandt showed the world that among the Calvinists the art of painting was by no means despised. His biblical scenes are very moving, but even here the landscape and the garb of the people no longer have that air of religious devotion which marked the paintings of the fifteenth century. Clearly the process of secularization (*q.v.*) went on apace, unseen perhaps by later historians, but nevertheless very effective.

See also AESTHETIC, THE, AND RELIGION.

BIBLIOGRAPHY: Architecture: A. Kingsley Porter, *Lombard Architecture*, 1918; F. Cabrol, *Dictionnaire d'archéologie chrétienne et de liturgie*, 1907–1952; C. Diehl, *Manuel de l'art byzantin*, 1910; R. de Hasteyrie, *L'Architecture religieuse en France à l'époque romane*, 1912; idem, *L'Architecture gothique*, 1927; H. Sedlmayr, *Die Entstehung der Kathedrale*, 1950; H. Woelfflin, *Die klassische Kunst: Eine Einfuehrung in die italienische Renaissance*, 1924.

Sculpture: A. Kingsley Porter, *Romanesque Sculpture of the Pilgrim Roads*, 10 vols., 1923; idem, *Spanish Romanesque Sculpture*, 2 vols., 1928; A. Gardner, *French Sculpture of the Thirteenth Century*.

Painting: Wilpert *Die roemischen Mosaiken und Malereien der kirchlichen Bauten vom IVten bis XIVten Jahrhundert*, 4 vols., 3rd ed., 1924; H. Brehier, *L'Art chrétienne*, 1928; M. Friedlaender, *Die alt-Niederlaendische Malerei*, 1924–1937; K. Smits, *De iconografie der Nederlandse primitiven*, 1933; E. Panofsky, *Early Netherlandish Painting*, 2 vols., 1954; F. J. Mather, *A History of Italian Painting*, 1950.

KAREL SMITS.

ART, HEBREW: Excavations in Palestine have shown that the Hebrews were not so destitute of artistic appreciation as had been supposed. They refused to represent their God pictorially; but, as the description of Solomon's buildings indicates (I Kings 6:23–28; 7:25–36), they were not altogether averse to images. While the Israelite invaders lacked the artistic sense of the Canaanites, after settling they assimilated some of the culture of their neighbors. It is probable that Phoenician craftsmen like Hiram (I Kings 7:13–14) employed Hebrew apprentices who became skilled. Though their patterns were borrowed or adapted from Egypt, Assyria, Babylonia, Phoenicia, and Philistia, Hebrew potters, lapidarians, metal workers, and stone cutters produced objects of beauty. Exquisite ivories found at Megiddo and Samaria, without being slavish copies, show Egyptian motifs, and the proto-Ionic capitals at Megiddo are probably Phoenician. In ceramics the Hebrews developed considerable skill, imitating imported ware and also showing some originality. One development was the Astarte figurine, doubtless used as a charm by Hebrew women. Most of the figurines are crude, but some are well made. Small animal figures, probably horses, are common finds. In the period of the kings, seals, largely in imitation of the Egyptian scarab, became popular. These seals show cherubim, lions, birds, serpents, beetles, and human beings, generally with the owner's name in Hebrew. So it is certain that the Hebrews had artistic sense and some accomplishment, though the flowering of Jewish art did not come until well after the Exile.

BIBLIOGRAPHY: A. Reifenberg, *Ancient Hebrew Arts*, 1950; Paul L. Garber, "Reconstructing Solomon's Temple," *Biblical Archaeologist*, Feb., 1951.

[Sup.] OVID R. SELLERS.

ARTOPHORION. See TABERNACLE.

ARYANS. See RACE RELATIONS.

ASCH, SHOLEM: Jewish, b. at Kutno, Poland, November 1, 1880. He attended the Yeshiva Orthodox Rabbinical College. His attitude upon religion can perhaps best be found in his book, *What I Believe*. His other books are: *The Apostle; In the Beginning; Children of Abraham; East River; Mary; The Mother; Mottke, the Thief; The Nazarene; One Destiny; Salvation; Song of the Valley; Tales of My People; Three Cities; Three Novels; The War Goes On;* and *Moses.*

ASEITY: This term is a philosophical expression for underived or self-contained being. Negatively it connotes independence, that is total absence of dependence upon any other. But the term itself is positive and denotes something containing its whole being within and from itself; (Latin, *ab* from, *se* self). In a universe, this is a quality attributable only uniquely: there cannot be more than one entirely self-sufficient being. Applied to God, it means that God is entirely self-supporting, perfectly self-sufficient. Philosophical or religious monism or absolutism attributes aseity in its simplest form: God not merely enjoys self-sufficiency, but is identical with the universe. From the biblical point of view, the expression approaching nearest to aseity is the divine utterance: I am that I am (Ex. 3:14). But the affinity is more apparent than real, since the Hebrew phrase has none of the static quality of aseity, and might be better translated: I will be what I will be. Here activity is involved. This is borne out by the rest of Scripture, which never conceives God's self-sufficiency as otiose. According to the Christian revelation, God wills not to remain entire and intact. He creates not only the world outside himself as a genuine other, but man with whom he will have communion. God's self-sufficiency must, in the light of revelation, be construed as congruous with divine love. So far from being the expression of an immense self-centeredness, aseity thus becomes the ground and guarantee of the free and unconstrained character of the divine love.

J. K. S. REID.

ASHERA. See GODS AND GODDESSES, PAGAN.

ASHLAND BRETHREN. See DUNKERS.

ASHRAM: In modern usage, a place in which a group undertakes the pursuit of a common religious aim, usually under the direction of a leader who in India is called a *guru*. The word is derived from the Sanskrit root, *śram*, to exert oneself, to practice asceticism. The derived noun, *āśrama*, designates the place where such activities are undertaken. In early Sanskrit literature the word most often refers to the forest hermitages to which men retired on abandoning active life. The word is also used later to indicate the four stages of life of orthodox Hindu theory, those of the student, the householder, the forestdweller, and the sannyasi. In modern times the ashram in the first sense has been revived with new aims, notably at Shantiniketan by the Tagore family for educational purposes, at Sabarmati and Sevagram by Gandhi for the training of political leaders, and at Pondicherry by Arabindo Ghose. The technique of the ashram community has been adapted to Christian use in many places. Among the best known are the Christu-Kula-Ashram at Tirupattur, the Christa-Prema-Seva-Sangha-Ashram at Poona, the Christa-Seva-Ashram in Jaffna, Ceylon, and the Sat Tal Ashram in the foothills of the Himalayas, where Dr. Stanley Jones has called together groups for creative thinking. Through Dr. Jones' influence, the movement has spread to America. Of these groups he writes: "The basic idea of the Christian Ashrams as worked out through the years in India and in America is that of a group which shall try, not to find an answer, but to be the answer in its own corporate life." Another Western venture which bears some resemblance to the Indian ashram ideal is that of the Iona community (*q.v.*) in Scotland.

BIBLIOGRAPHY: P. Chenchiah and others, *Asramas, Past and Present*, 1941. See also the reports of individual ashrams.

MAX HUNTER HARRISON.

ASHTORETH. See GODS AND GODDESSES, PAGAN.

ASMUSSEN, HANS: Lutheran; b. in Flensburg, Germany, Aug. 21, 1898. After serving in the German army (1917–18) and studying in the universities of Kiel and Tuebingen, he was assistant to the rector of the deaconess home in Flensburg (1922–25) and pastor in Albersdorf, Dithmarschen (1925–32), and Altona, suburb of Hamburg (1932–34), when he was dismissed by "German Christians" (see GERMANY, I). He served as adviser of the Confessing Church at Oyenhausen (1934–36) and was on the faculty of the clandestine theological seminary in Berlin (1936–43). After World War II (1945–49) he was head of the chancelery of the Evangelical Church in Germany, and since 1949 he was dean of Kiel in the Church of Schleswig-Holstein (*q.v.*). His works include: *Offenbarung und Amt* (1932); *Seelsorge* (1934); *Politik und Christentum* (1934); *Galaterbrief* (1934); *Gottes-*

dienstlehre (1936); *I. Samuelisbuch* (1938); *Johannesbriefe* (1939); *Rechtglaeubigkeit und Froemmigkeit* (1938); *Bergpredigt* (1939); *Epheserbrief* (1949); *Warum noch Lutherische Kirche* (1950); *Maria, die Mutter Gottes* (1951); *Geheimnis der Liebe* (1952); *Roemerbrief* (1952).

ASSEMBLIES OF GOD: Organized in a constitutional convention at Hot Springs, Ark., April 2–12, 1914, this is one of the largest of the charismatic groups commonly designated "Pentecostal." Its constituency includes approximately 6,000 churches (assemblies) with a membership of 318,478 (1951), a Sunday school enrollment of 599,872, an average attendance of 460,096. As is common with smaller denominations, attendance at church services exceeds enrolled membership.

The organization is based on a combination of congregational and presbyterian principles. Local congregations are autonomous in the choice of pastors and the management of local affairs. The sovereignty of the local congregation was guaranteed in the preamble to the constitution adopted at the first General Council in 1914. At that time the Bible was recognized as the all-sufficient rule for faith and practice. Later (1916) a statement of truth was adopted.

Doctrinally, the denomination is Arminian—following the Methodist pattern, basically. Emphasis is laid on new birth, divine healing, baptism in the Holy Spirit, accompanied by the sign of speaking in tongues (Acts 2:4), and the premillennial return of Christ. It is held that the pattern set forth in Acts is the norm for Christian experience and growth. The denomination is evangelistic and missionary in spirit and practice, spreading over the entire United States and its territories.

Missionary work has been evangelistic rather than institutional. Mission stations are found on every continent and in over fifty different countries, staffed by approximately 670 missionaries and 3,519 native workers. The number of baptized believers in foreign lands exceeds 200,000. The budget for the support of this work exceeds $2,000,000 annually.

All ordained ministers and one lay delegate from each affiliated, co-operative congregation constitute a general council, which meets biennially. The officers of the general council are a general superintendent, four assistant general superintendents, general secretary, general treasurer, and a foreign missions secretary. These officers, together with four others, constitute an Executive Presbytery. To them is committed the management of the various departments of the denomination, including Home and Foreign Missions, Youth, Publications, Education, Benevolences, etc. The Executive Presbytery is supplemented by a General Presbytery, composed of three representatives from each of the District Councils and two from each of the eight foreign language (U.S.A.) branches. These branches report 146 churches using European languages, and about 280 Latin American congregations with a total membership of approximately 15,000, located in about one-third of the states. There are forty-one district councils, the boundaries of which, in the main, follow state lines. They are organized like the general council and meet annually. Foreign language branches have no territorial boundaries and function under the general supervision of the Home Missions Department.

The Assemblies of God is a member of the National Association of Evangelicals (*q.v.*) and of the Pentecostal Fellowship of North America.

See also CHURCH (CHURCHES) OF GOD; PENTECOSTAL CHURCHES.   J. ROSWELL FLOWER.

ASSISTANT PASTOR: Many large Protestant congregations follow the Roman Catholic custom of a multiple ministry. Some church leaders think in terms of one ordained clergyman for every five hundred members, or major fraction thereof. As a rule, the church secures for an assistant a young graduate from the divinity school, who serves an apprenticeship for two or three years and then seeks a parish of his own. Under a wise senior pastor this plan benefits the young minister, but may not prove ideal for the congregation. Hence many church leaders think in terms of a staff, with men and women of various ages, and with longer tenure. Such a plan permits careful division of labor, and development of special provinces, such as pastoral work, counseling, and leadership of young people.

ANDREW W. BLACKWOOD.

ASSOCIATIONISM: A theory of mental structure and functioning which proposes that (1) a mental state is reducible to simple elements and (2) when combined by the laws of the association of ideas, these elements explain the phenomena of mental life. The theory was hinted at in Plato, developed more fully in Aristotle, but was pre-eminently the mark of the British school of psychology of the seventeenth, eighteenth, and nineteenth centuries. Hobbes, Locke, Berkeley, Hume, James Mill, John Stuart Mill, and A. Bain were associationists. David Hartley (1704–57) was the chief exponent of this school of psychology. Influenced by Hobbes, and by Newton's stress on motion as the key to the nature of all physical things, Hartley developed a theory of vibrations in the nervous system to account for mental operations, including memory. He called these slight vibrations *vibratiuncles*. When two sensations occur simultaneously or in close succession, they are likely to become associated, so that whenever one is later re-excited, the other is also. The more complex mental structures are compounds built up from simple elements through the laws of association. All phases of the life of the mind, including the emotions, are under these laws.

Beginning with Plato and Aristotle, the associationists proposed various statements of the laws of association. Contiguity in time and space was the clearest and most universally accepted law. If events A and B happened to me simultaneously, I will recall B if A is brought back to my mind. If I wrecked my car in a blinding rain, each new blinding rain will remind me of that wreck. Similarity is also fairly clear. One ghost story brings on another. Contrast, the other side of the law of similarity, was advanced as a separate law. When two things are quite different, one often brings to mind the opposite. Right reminds of wrong, black of white, Satan of God. Hume included cause and effect as a separate law, but later analysis subsumed it under contiguity.

The later writers specified the importance of recency, frequency, and vividness if an association was to be powerful and permanent. The presence or absence of an inhibitory factor, the general interests of the individual mind, emotional congruity and other subtle angles have been taken into consideration by the later writers.

Today British associationism probably would be categorized as epistemology (q.v.), rather than as psychology.

With the rise of experimentalism, and with the advent of the physiological understanding of mental processes, associationism ceased to be a living school of psychology, but its contribution to the long history of psychology was great. Its empirical approach paved the way for modern experimentalism. The basic laws of association are clearly the ancestors of some of the present "laws of learning," particularly contiguity. Ernest Hilgard in his brilliant study, *Theories of Learning,* sets forth the thesis that at the middle of the twentieth century there are two fundamental schools of learning, the associationist and the field or Gestalt. The learning theories of functionalism, and behaviorism, as well as the connectionism of Thorndike and the conditioned response of Guthrie are considered derivatives of the ancient associationism. While a 1951 discussion of the laws of learning does not contain the word association in the index, it speaks of the same principles that Aristotle had suggested two thousand years before Pavlov and Hull.

Locke coined the phrase "association of ideas" but did not take the theory with full seriousness. The phrase was too narrow for the work of the school, for emotions as well as intellect-ual ideas were discussed. Locke himself, for instance, in writing of the association of ideas, showed how a fear could be inculcated in one's mind by unfortunate experiences. This sounds like very recent work on conditioning.

The associationism of the past centuries has made a real contribution to the present. It is one fundamental stream contributing to our understanding of the learning process. But the whole is more than the sum of all its parts, and Gestalt or field psychology has its own contribution to make to our understanding.

See also PSYCHOLOGY.

BIBLIOGRAPHY: The Histories of Psychology; the standard works of the men mentioned.

HARRY GORDON GOODYKOONTZ.

ASSOCIATION OF CHURCH SOCIAL WORKERS. See SOCIAL SERVICE OF THE CHURCH; SOCIAL WORK, CHURCH.

ASSOUAN PAPYRI. See PAPYRI, BIBLICAL AND EARLY CHRISTIAN.

ASSUMPTION, DOGMA OF THE: The doctrine of the Assumption of Mary, that is, of her being taken, soul and body, to heaven, was defined an article of faith by Pope Pius XII, on November 1, 1950.

I. Early Legends: The earliest account of the death and Assumption of Mary is found in an apocryphal writing commonly known as the *Liber Transitus,* Book of the Passing (of Mary), falsely attributed to Meliton of Sardes. Various recensions of this writing were circulated during the fifth century.

The *Liber Transitus* states that Mary died in Jerusalem, and not, as another tradition has it, in Ephesus, where she was believed to have followed the Apostle John. The Ephesus tradition is endorsed by the synodal letter of the bishops who met in this city for the Universal Council of 431.

The Jerusalem story, as it was told to the pilgrims, may thus be summarized. Mary had a premonition of her death. The apostles, miraculously summoned by angels, attended her last moments. During the funeral procession, a Jew was stricken with the palsy for having laid his hands on the bier. The body of Mary, placed in a new sepulcher, was carried to heaven by angels. The apostles witnessed the miracle, and the Virgin dropped her sash in order to convince Thomas, who had come late, and who was incredulous.

Because of Mary's association with the Twelve, Acts 1:13, Jerusalem Christians used to commemorate the *Dormitio,* or "sleeping-in" of Mary, in the church of Holy Zion, built by Constantine on the site of the presumed meeting place of the disciples after the Resurrection. Between 453 and 458, Juvenal, bishop of Jerusalem, built a church to enshrine what he believed to be the tomb of Mary, at a short distance from the basilica of Gethsemane.

II. Liturgy and Doctrine: Before the close of the fifth century, a feast of the Assumption was observed in Palestine, probably in August. The Egyptians, however, celebrated it in January, and the Gallican Liturgy followed the Egyptian usage until the adoption of the Roman Rite. In the Greek Church, a decision of Emperor Maurice (d. 702) prescribed the celebration of the feast on August 15, and this date prevailed also in Rome.

No extensive reference to the Assumption is found in patristic literature prior to the seventh century. In the West, the sermons of Jerome and Augustine for the feast are spurious. Gregory of Tours (d. 594) simply reproduces the testimony of the Apocrypha.

In the East, the earliest doctrinal developments occur in the writings of Modestus (d. 634), Andrew of Crete (d. 740), and John Damascene (d. 749). The speculations of the Eastern doctors are also based on the testimony of Juvenal and the Apocrypha.

Most of the medieval theologians regard the Assumption as a historical fact, rather than an object of doctrinal speculation. This is particularly noticeable in Aquinas, who takes the Assumption for granted, and studies in its light the sanctification of Mary and such other mysteries.

It is chiefly the post-Tridentine theology which endeavors dogmatically to establish the belief in the Assumption on grounds of convenience, stating that Mary, due to her sinlessness, and in her capacity as the mother of Jesus, was fittingly spared the horrors of the grave.

III. Dogmatic Definition: The doctrine of the Assumption, prior to the definition, rated in the Roman Church as a probable opinion, the denial of which was considered as impious and somehow blasphemous. During the Council of the Vatican, 1869–70, a petition signed by 197 bishops was presented to Pope Pius IX to the effect that the doctrine of the Assumption be declared an article of faith. However, no action was taken then. Later, various petitions addressed to Rome resulted in the appointment of experts to study the whole matter, and in a poll of the members of the Catholic hierarchy as to the possibility and desirability of a dogmatic definition.

The bull *Munificentissimus Deus,* issued on November 1, 1950, points to the unanimous faith and desire of the hierarchy and the faithful as the primary ground for the definition of the dogma. The bull does not consider the testimony of the Apocrypha, but reviews such evidence as may establish that the tradition of the Assumption of Mary was consistently

held in the church throughout the ages. It insists on the harmony which exists between the dogma of the Immaculate Conception and the doctrine of the Assumption.

The dogmatic definition reads as follows: "We declare and define this to be a revealed dogma, namely that the Virgin Mary, the Immaculate Mother of God, when the course of her life was finished, was taken up, body and soul, into the glory of heaven."

Original text of the bull *Munificentissimus Deus* is in *Acta Apostolicae Sedis,* XXXII (1950), 753–773. Various Roman Catholic theological journals have published English translations with commentaries, for instance *The Thomist,* XIV (1951), 1. See also R. Winch, *The Assumption of Our Lady and Catholic Theology,* 1950.

GEORGES A. BARROIS.

ASSUMPTIONISTS, AUGUSTINIANS OF THE ASSUMPTION: Abbreviation A.A. An American province of the order (U.S.A. and Canada) was founded in 1946 with headquarters in Worcester, Mass. The fathers engage in pastoral work and teaching on the secondary and college levels. Fathers: 67. Professed clerics: 24. [Sup.]

ASSYRIA: An important result of archaeological research in recent decades has been to lift the veil from the history of Assyria before 1800 B.C. The possible impression, arising from Gen. 10:9–11, that the civilization of Babylonia (*q.v.*) preceded and gave birth to that of Assyria must now be reversed; for we know that men in the land later called Assyria had made impressive steps in the direction of civilization before even the soil of Babylonia became habitable by human beings. The known prehistory of Assyria now begins at a stone age site called Barda Balka, located in territory just east of that of Assyria proper, but forming part of the Assyrian domain in most periods of its historic development.

I. Early History: From the Acheulean industry of Barda Balka to the painted pottery culture of Hassuna at least four successive prehistoric periods are represented by the recently investigated sites of Hazar Merd, Palegawra, Karim Shahir, and Jarmo, all in the Assyrian realm. In Assyria proper the Hassuna period and the following Halaf period are both earlier than the earliest remains of human life in Babylonia. Excavations at Nineveh, Arpachiyah, and Tepe Gawra in Assyria have shown remains of human cultures paralleling and synchronizing with those of Babylonia from the earliest settlements down to historic times. The basic population of Assyria in earliest historic times appears to have been composed of two elements, one a people called Subarians from the mountains to the north and east, and the other a Semitic people stemming from the upper Euphrates area rather than from Babylonia. The earliest historical culture of the land seems to have been dominated by the Sumerian (q.v.) culture, beginning with the Early Dynastic period in Babylonia.

II. The Assyrian Empire: The name Assyria cannot properly be assigned to this ancient land until the kingdom that was established at the city of Ashur came to dominate the surrounding territory. From the evidence of the king list from Khorsabad a kingdom must have existed at Ashur as early as the Akkad Dynasty in Babylonia (ca. 2400 B.C.). The first king's name was Tudia. From his time until the final fall of Nineveh (612 B.C.) there were five different periods in which the Assyrian kings rose to a position of dominating power over Western Asia, with intervening periods when they were themselves dominated by foreign powers.

After a period in which the Assyrian kings were more or less dominated successively by the kings of Akkad, the people of Gutium, the rulers of the Third Dynasty of Ur, and the Amorite Dynasty of Isin, the Assyrian king, Ilushumma (ca. 1900 B.C.), succeeded in establishing the first Assyrian empire. It reached its greatest power under Sargon I of Assyria, and apparently broke up under fresh attacks from Subartu and Gutium. The second Assyrian empire was set up by Shamshi-Adad I (ca. 1750 B.C.), who controlled also the kingdoms of Mari and Eshnunna. This was an empire of short duration, since it came under the power of Babylonia in the later years of Hammurabi (q.v.). A number of ethnic movements in the middle of the second millennium B.C. produced widespread political changes over all Western Asia. The result for Assyria was subjection to a confederacy of Hurrian (q.v.) states under the leadership of certain Indo-Iranian princes. Ashuruballit I (1362–27 B.C.) succeeded in releasing Assyria from this subjugation and in establishing the third Assyrian Empire. This period was characterized by strong competition for power by Assyria's neighbors, notably the Hittite (q.v.) kingdom on one hand, and the Kassite kingdom of Babylonia on the other. However, it was the hostility of Aramean (q.v.) peoples of the eleventh and tenth centuries B.C. that led to the disintegration of the empire.

A new era of expansion was begun by Adad-nirari II (911–891 B.C.), who may be called the founder of the fourth Assyrian Empire. His grandson, Ashurnasirpal II (883–859 B.C.), had palaces in numerous provincial capitals, and moved the chief capital of the empire from Ashur to Kalhu. The reigns of his successors were marked by unrest in the empire, by political intrigue in high levels of the government, and by friendship between the royal family and the court of Babylon. A new and final era in

Assyrian history, which may be called the fifth empire, was begun by Tiglathpileser III (745–727 B.C.). The dynasty which he founded pushed the power of Assyria to its widest reaches, including virtually all of Western Asia and even reaching into Egypt.

III. Origin of the Name: The meaning and origin of the name of the god Ashur remains uncertain. The earliest known written form of the name is A-shur in the Old Assyrian texts from Kueltepe. The form with the doubling of the sibilant, Ash-shur, appears about the time of the First Dynasty of Babylon. This, however, does not prove that the sibilant was not doubled in Old Assyrian; because it was the custom to write most doubled consonants with only single representation in Old Assyrian time. The writing of the name as A-USAR does not occur until the time of Shamshi-Adad I, contemporary of Hammurabi of Babylon. Still later is the writing AN-SHAR, which came about through the effort of the Assyrian scribes to identify the ancient deity called AN-SHAR in the Babylonian Creation Epic with the Assyrian god Ashur. A writing frequently used about the time of Ashurnasirpal II was the simple sign ASH. See also MESOPOTAMIA.

BIBLIOGRAPHY: Archaeology and Excavations: W. Andrae, Das wiedererstandene Assur, 1938; R. C. Thompson and R. W. Hutchinson, The Excavations on the Temple of Nabu at Nineveh, 1929; idem, "The Site of the Palace of Ashurnasirpal at Nineveh Excavated in 1929–1930 on Behalf of the British Museum," Annals of Archaeology and Anthropology, 18 (1931), 79–112; R. C. Thompson, "The Buildings on Quyunjiq, the Larger Mound of Nineveh," Iraq, 1 (1934), 95–104; R. C. Thompson and M. E. L. Mallowan, "The British Museum Excavation at Nineveh, 1930–1931," Iraq (1932), 55–116; M. E. L. Mallowan, "The Excavations at Nimrud (Kalhu), 1949–1950," Iraq, 12 (1950), 147–183; ibid., 13 (1951), 1–20; D. J. Wiseman, "The Nimrud Tablets," Iraq, 13 (1951), 102–122; G. Loud, Khorsabad, University of Chicago Oriental Institute Publications, Vols. 38, 40, 1936, 1938; S. Lloyd, F. Safar, and R. J. Braidwood, "Excavations by the Iraq Government Directorate General of Antiquities in 1943 and 1944," JNES, 4 (1945), 225–289; M. E. L. Mallowan and J. C. Rose, "Excavations at Tell Arpachiyah, 1933," Iraq, 2 (1935), 1–178; E. A. Speiser, Excavations at Tepe Gawra, I (1935); A. J. Tobler, Excavations at Tepe Gawra, II, 1950; R. F. S. Starr, Nuzi, Report on the Excavations at Yorgan Tepe, 2 vols., 1937–1939; Ann L. Perkins, The Comparative Archaeology of Early Mesopotamia, 1949; R. J. Braidwood, "From Cave to Village in Prehistoric Iraq," BASOR, 124 (1951), 12–18.
History: A. Ungnad, Subartu, Beitraege zur Kulturgeschichte und Voelkerkunde Vorderasiens, 1936; I. J. Gelb, Hurrians and Subarians, 1944; E. A. Speiser, "Hurrians and Subarians," JAOS, 68 (1948), 1–13; S. Smith, "On Hurrians and Subarians . . ." Quarterly Statement of the Palestine Exploration Fund, 81 (1949), 117–126; S. Smith, Early History of Assyria, 1928; A. T. Olmstead, History of Assyria, 1923; W. von Soden, "Der Aufstieg des Assyrreiches als geschichtliches Problem," Der alte Orient, 37 (1937); A. Goetze, Hethiter, Churriter und Assyrer . . . , 1936; E. O. Forrer, Die Provinzeinteilung des assyrischen Reiches, 1920; A. Poebel, "The Assyrian King List from Khorsabad," JNES, 1 (1942), 247–306, 460–492; 2 (1943), 56–90; Reallexikon der Assyrologie, art., "Assur," Vol. 1, 170–227; "Assyrien," 228–303; Vol. 2, "Eponymen."
Religion: E. Dhorme, Les religions de Babylonie et d'Assyrie, 1945; K. Tallqvist, Der assyrische Gott, 1932.
Texts: "Keilschrifttexte aus Assur," Heft 1–13, Wissenschaftlichen Veroeffentlichung der deutschen Orient-Gesellschaft, 16, 28, 34, 35, 37, 50, 1911–1927; G. G. Cameron, "The Annals of Shalmaneser III, King of Assyria," Sumer, 6 (1950), 6–26; F. Safar, "A Further Text of Shalmaneser III from Assur," Sumer, 7 (1951), 3–21; Cuneiform Texts from Babylonian Tablets in the British Museum, 41 parts, 1896–1931.

Translations of Texts: D. D. Luckenbill, *Ancient Records of Assyria and Babylonia*, 2 vols., 1926–1927; E. Ebeling, B. Meissner and E. F. Weidner, *Die Inschriften der altassyrischen Koenige*, 1926; A. G. Lie, *The Inscriptions of Sargon II, King of Assyria*, 1929; E. Ebeling, *Urkunden des Archivs von Assur aus mittelassyrischer Zeit*, 1933; Th. Bauer, *Die Inschriften Assurbanipals*, 1933; A. C. Piepkorn, *Historical Prism Inscriptions of Ashurbanipal*, 1933; J. B. Pritchard, ed., *Ancient Near Eastern Texts Relating to the Old Testament*, 1950.

Language: A. Ungnad, *Grammatik des Akkadischen*, 1949; J. Lewy, *Untersuchung zur akkadischen Grammatik . . .*, 1921; M. Bar-Am, "The Subjunctive in the Cappadocian Texts," *Orientalia Nova Series*, 7 (1938), 12–31.

Special Subjects: G. R. Driver and J. C. Miles, *The Assyrian Laws*, 1935; K. Tallqvist, *Assyrian Personal Names*, 1914; E. Ebeling, *Die Eigennamen der mittelassyrischen Rechts- und Geschaeftsurkunden*, 1939; I. J. Gelb, P. N. Purves, and A. A. MacRae, *Nuzi Personal Names*, 1943; R. C. Thompson, *A Dictionary of Assyrian Chemistry and Geology*, 1936; *idem, A Dictionary of Assyrian Botany*, 1949.

[Sup.] FERRIS J. STEPHENS.

ASTERISK: In the Byzantine liturgies, a dome-shaped frame made of two strips of metal bent and assembled crosswise with a star hanging from the top. The asterisk is placed over the eucharistic bread, so as to prevent its coming into contact with the veil which covers it. A similar instrument is used in the papal mass, when communion is brought to the pontiff at his throne.   GEORGES A. BARROIS.

ASTROLOGY: Astrology is the art—its devotees would call it the science—of divination by reference to the stars and planets. Its practice is very ancient, and out of it eventually grew astronomy, though it was not until Kepler's time that astronomy as a science began to disentangle itself from astrology. It was the astrologers' task to discover the relations of the planets to one another, to the zodiacal signs, and to the observer, and to make deductions therefrom. The first two are in a sense scientific, the latter is based upon ancient lore which has no scientific basis but rests largely upon observed parallelisms between given zodiacal positions and human events.

Nevertheless, the practice of astrology persists into our own age and is probably the major divination technique in current use in the Western world. It is definitely big business, employing the full time of many thousands of astrologers who prepare horoscopes by the millions, for a consideration. There is a national organization in America of about 30,000 astrologers. Any newsstand will be found to carry from one to ten national or local astrological magazines, and slot machines will yield a horoscope for a dime. A great many metropolitan dailies carry regular astrological columns which people evidently continue to read. Many persons will take no important step without first consulting the stars. It is known that individuals occupying important positions in business and public life are subscribers to astrological services, which purport to disclose things to come. Adolf Hitler was a great believer in astrology and had a well equipped astrological laboratory in his Berchtesgaden retreat. See OCCULTISM.

BIBLIOGRAPHY: See articles "Sun," "Moon," and "Stars" in *Encyclopaedia of Religion and Ethics*. Also article "Astrology" in *Encyclopædia Britannica*; Robson, *A Students' Textbook of Astrology*, 1922; De Vore, *Encyclopedia of Astrology*, 1947; Evangeline Adams, *Astrology for Everyone*, 1931.

CHARLES S. BRADEN.

ASTRONOMY. See COSMOLOGY.

ATHEARN, WALTER SCOTT: Disciples of Christ; b. July 25, 1872 at Marengo, Ia.; d. Nov. 13, 1934. He studied at Drake, Iowa, and Chicago. After five years as principal of schools in Delta, Ia. (1894–99), he taught pedagogy at Drake (1900–04); was dean at Highland Park Normal College (1906–09); was professor of religious education at Drake (1909–16); professor of religious education at Boston University (1916–29), where he was also dean of the School of Religious Education and Social Service (1918–29). His latter years he served as president of Butler University (1931–34). In addition to very active participation in the religious education movement he wrote: *The Church School* (1914); *The City Institute for Religious Teachers* (1915); *The Organization and Administration of the Church School* (1917); *Religious Education and American Democracy* (1917); *The Malden Leaflets* (1917); *A National System of Education* (1920); *An Introduction to the Study of the Mind* (1921); *Character Building in a Democracy* (1924); *An Adventure in Religious Education* (1930); and *The Minister and the Teacher* (1932).

RAYMOND W. ALBRIGHT.

ATHEISM, AMERICAN ASSOCIATION FOR THE ADVANCEMENT OF: A non-profit educational organization founded and incorporated in New York in 1925 by Charles Smith, Freeman Hopwood, and Woolsey Teller. Its purpose is to conduct a frontal attack on all religions, chiefly by opposing the God idea. It is "the militant foe of the churches and the clergy." It operates partly through public forums, lectures, and debates, but mainly through the distribution of atheistic literature, chiefly tracts. It believes that religion is so discredited in every field of learning in this age of science that it is a social duty to oppose it as superstition. The writings of such men as d'Holbach, Paine, Voltaire, and Ingersoll are circulated by the association.

BIBLIOGRAPHY: Homer Croy, "Atheism Beckons to Our Youth," *World's Work*, LIV (May, 1927), 18–26.

ROBERT T. HANDY.

ATHEISTS, LEAGUE OF MILITANT: Organized in 1929 from a previously existing group, this body was to carry out the communist aim of destroying the religious foundations of the old society. This was to be done not only by publications (mostly translations of the Western eighteenth and nineteenth century atheistic literature), but also by magazines, by establishing training centers for educating lecturers, by conducting lectures, and by placing atheist teachers in schools. The league reported 5,500,000 members by 1932, in addition to 2,000,000 children. The aim was to increase the membership enormously so that all children and young people would be brought up in atheism.

BIBLIOGRAPHY: Matthew Spinka, *Christianity Confronts Communism*, 1936.

MATTHEW SPINKA.

ATHENAGORAS I (Aristocles Spyrou): Greek Orthodox; b. in 1886 at Vasilikon, Janina, Turkey (now Greece). After preliminary education at Vasilikon he studied at the theological school of Halki, Istanbul (1903–10). He served as archdeacon to the metropolitan of Pelagonia (1910–19), archdeacon to the archbishop of Athens (1919–22), and became metropolitan of Kerkyra and Paxos in December 1922. In August, 1930, he was elected Archbishop of the Greek Orthodox Church of North and South America. He became archbishop of Constantinople, New Rome, and Oecumenical Patriarch on Nov. 1, 1948.

RAYMOND W. ALBRIGHT.

ATKINS, GAIUS GLENN: Congregationalist; b. Mt. Carmel, Ind., Oct. 4, 1868. He studied at Ohio State University (A.B., 1888); Cincinnati Law School (LL.B., 1891); and Yale Divinity School. He was head of department of history at Mt. Hermon Fitting School (1892–95). He served pastorates at Greenfield, Mass. (1895–1900); Burlington, Vt. (1900–06); First Church Detroit (1906–10); Central Church, Providence, R. I. (1910–17); and again First Church, Detroit (1917–27). He was Hoyt Professor of Homiletics and Sociology at Auburn Theological Seminary (1927–39; professor emeritus since 1939). He is the author of *Pilgrims of the Lonely Road, Modern Religious Cults and Movements, Reinspecting Victorian Religion, The Making of the Christian Mind, The Procession of the Gods, Life of Cardinal Newman, Religion in Our Times, Preaching and the Mind of Today, From the Cross—a Study of the Seven Last Words, Resources for Living, From the Hillside,* and contributed to the *Interpreter's Bible.* He is editor of *the Minister's Quarterly.*

ATKINSON, HENRY A(VERY): Congregationalist; b. Aug. 26, 1877, at Merced, Calif. He studied at Pacific Methodist College (1897) and Garrett Biblical Institute. Ordained to the Congregational ministry in 1902, he served as pastor of First Church, Albion, Ill. (1902–04);

First Church, Springfield, O. (1904–08); and Central Church, Atlanta, Ga. (1908–11). After seven years as the secretary of the Special Service Commission of the Congregational Churches in the United States (1911–18), he became general secretary of the Church Peace Union and the World Alliance for International Friendship through the Churches (1918–   ). He has written: *The Church and Industrial Welfare* (1914); *The Church and the People's Play* (1915); *Men and Things* (1918); *Causes of War* (1932); and *Prelude to Peace* (1937).

RAYMOND W. ALBRIGHT.

ATOM BOMB, RELIGIOUS OPINION AND THE: The development of the atom or atomic bomb, its actual employment to hasten (so it is claimed) the end of World War II in its Pacific Ocean phase, the monopoly of it for a time by the United States, its alleged utility in preventing or postponing the outbreak of a World War III, the subsequent development of an effective atomic bomb by Soviet Russia, the failure of all efforts, thus far, to control its manufacture and to prevent or regulate its employment in another war—such events have awakened or accentuated the deepest apprehensions among those who are best acquainted with them, together with a surprising and possibly an alarming apathy among others. The moral and "practical" judgments among men with regard to them have differed, and still differ, very widely. The subsequent development of a hydrogen bomb by the United States, and later the confirmed announcement that Russia also possesses the secret and produced an explosion of this type, accentuated the apprehensions, exacerbated the differences of judgment, but seems neither to have penetrated the popular apathy nor to have introduced any new principles, except, of course, scientific. Finally, we are assured that scientists have begun to envisage a C-bomb (using Cobalt), and that, if it is ever developed and exploded, it threatens at one blow to wipe out all life upon this planet.

Christians, as such, are not concerned with what might be called the purely technical problems of scientific development, military strategy, and statecraft, all of which are profoundly involved in, and affected by, such discoveries and inventions. Their primary interest is in the impact of such things on human character and upon human social relations and upon their task of carrying the gospel of salvation and Christian love to all mankind. If the accentuation of fear and suspicion tends to break down human character, and either to cause men to turn earnestly towards the moral and spiritual quest or to glory in the hatred and power to destroy others, then Christians become vitally interested. They are concerned with the moral and spiritual justification for the use of violence of any kind and degree in the settlement of human problems, and with the spirit in which warfare and statecraft are engaged. It is not clear that the development of the atom bomb and of its even more dangerous successors has introduced any new element, except imminence, into such agelong moral and spiritual problems.

It could be proved, perhaps, that Christians have been characteristically more sensitive to such moral and spiritual problems than has the majority of men, and that, certainly in recent times, they have been more successful in developing and in preserving under the stress of war a humane and loving spirit which at least sought to mitigate the horrors of war and to heal the breach at the termination of the fighting. But it would be difficult to prove that Christians have been historically less ready to sanction and to engage in war, nor have they been noticeably more successful than others in achieving among themselves a unanimity of opinion on the question of the employment of violence in the settlement of human problems and on the conditions in which, and the degree to which, force may thus be used. As a result, it is not apparent that Christian opinion as to the employment of these more powerful forms of force in war is any more uniform than are the opinions of those who make no Christian profession. In short, it is doubtful whether a "Christian opinion" with regard to the atom bomb really exists.

Those Christians who remember that "our side" was first in a race with the Nazi powers and that, if we had been second, the result might well have been the subjugation of the whole world by those men, may perhaps regard our success with some satisfaction and approval. Those who believe that our monopoly, and subsequently our leadership, in atomic weapons has been the sole, or at least the major, restraining influence on Soviet aggression may judge that the hand of "providence" may be seen here. But no sensitive Christian, surely, can make such judgments without, at the same time, experiencing the anxious and deeply disturbing pain of a troubled conscience. Are any men, singly or in groups, wise and good enough to wield such tremendous power? Can any circumstance or combination of circumstances ever justify the widespread and almost indiscriminate slaughter, in one blinding flash, of women and innocent children, the aged and impotent, civilians and military which occurred at Hiroshima and which will inevitably happen again if and when these weapons are employed? Is it not an unpardonable affront to the Creator to employ the forces of his nature in such a manner as this? Are we not caught up in the grip of forces that are truly demonic, and is there any way of escape? Such sad questionings torment those sensitive Christians who yet approve, in some measure and for some reason, of the use of these bombs; but there are always those who, for such reasons, condemn the use of the bomb without going to the length of being pacifists; and there are always those who judge that any attitude other than that of pacifism is alien to Christianity.

BIBLIOGRAPHY: Julia E. Johnsen, comp., *The Atomic Bomb*, 1946; John Hershey, *Hiroshima*; Ronald A. Knox, *God and the Atom*; Wilbur M. Smith, *The Atomic Bomb and the Word of God*, 1945; "Atomic Warfare and the Christian Faith," a report issued by the Federal Council of the Churches of Christ in America, 1946.

ANDREW K. RULE.

ATONEMENT. See SOTERIOLOGY.

ATONEMENT FRIARS: The Franciscan Friars of the Atonement were founded in 1899 by Paul James Francis at Graymoor, Garrison, New York. On Oct. 30, 1909, the friars were received into the Roman Catholic Church, having been an Anglican community for ten years. On June 16, 1910, Father Paul was ordained a Catholic priest. He died in 1940.

The principal aim of the Atonement Friars is to "unite in a common life men who aspire after perfection by the profession of the three vows of poverty, chastity, and obedience." They devote themselves to reconciling sinners to God, winning non-Catholics to the Catholic faith, and the conversion of the heathen.

To further these aims the friars maintain a home for homeless men and direct their own press and publishing house in Peekskill, New York. They also broadcast the *Ave Maria Hour*, a radio program which dramatizes the lives of the saints. The friars also travel as mission preachers throughout the parishes of the country.

BIBLIOGRAPHY: David Gannon, *Father Paul of Graymoor*, 1951.

GILBERT L. ODDO.

ATTWATER, DONALD: Roman Catholic layman; b. in Essex, England, 1892. He was educated in legal studies. He was editor of *Catholic Herald* (England; 1935–36); associate editor of *Eastern Churches Quarterly* (England) and *Orate Fratres* (USA). He edited *A Catholic Dictionary* (1931) and Butler's *Lives of the Saints* (1932–38). He is the author of *St. John Chrysostom* (1939), *Christian Churches of the East* (2 vols., 1947), and has translated early works of N. A. Berdyaev.

AUBREY, EDWIN EWART: Baptist; b. at Glasgow, Scotland, March 19, 1896. He studied at Bucknell University (Ph.B., 1919) and the University of Chicago (M.A., 1921; B.D., 1922; Ph.D., 1926). He taught at Carleton College, Miami University, and Vassar College before returning to the University of Chicago as professor of Christian theology and ethics (1929–

44). After five years as President of Crozer Theological Seminary (1944–49) he went to the University of Pennsylvania to establish the department of religious thought. He wrote *Religion and the Next Generation* (1931); *Present Theological Tendencies* (1936); *Living the Christian Faith* (1939); and *Man's Search for Himself* (1940).

AUBURN AFFIRMATION. See AFFIRMATION, AN.

AUDIO-VISUAL AIDS: The use of motion pictures, television, etc., in Christian education and public worship. The synchronizing of motion pictures and interpretation to make vivid the events of the Bible and the truths of religion, as in dealing with missions. Opinions differ about the value of such devices. Proponents insist that they help to transform religious teaching, and to solve the Sunday evening problem, especially with young people. Up to now the results do not justify sweeping claims. Theoretically, few object to such aids in religious teaching, even occasionally from the pulpit. But many feel that people are surfeited with commercialized amusements all week, and need a complete change when they come to church. Neither in equipment nor in variety of entertainment can the church compete with industry. Devotees of the screen often grow weary of what they see and hear. They find it hard to think about God while using means elsewhere commercial. Many churches still rely mainly on teaching and preaching by "truth through personality" for human needs.

ANDREW W. BLACKWOOD.

AUGER, EDMOND: Because of his eloquent preaching he was called the Chrysostom of France. His catechism had the same success in France that the work of Canisius had in Germany. In Paris alone during eight years some 38,000 copies were sold. But in foreign countries his catechism did not rival that of Canisius.

BIBLIOGRAPHY: *Dict. d'hist. et de géogr. eccl.*, Vol. V '1931), 378 383.

[Sup.] MATHIAS GOOSSENS.

AUGSBURG CONFESSION: For the meeting of the Reichstag (Diet) in 1530 the Protestants had to prepare a declaration about their faith which they could present to Emperor Charles V (*q.v.*) and the Roman Catholic delegates. Elector John of Saxony as early as March 14, 1530, had requested that the theologians at Wittenberg draft an elaborate statement in which they would set forth the differences between their own standpoint and that of the Catholics, not only in the matter of doctrine but also of liturgy and church government. In the electorate of Saxony much use was made of the

Schwabach Articles (*q.v.*, Vol. X), which in the summer of 1529 had been drawn up by the Wittenberg theologians and on Dec. 2 and 3 had been accepted as the official creed at Schwabach by the electorate of Saxony, Brandenburg-Ansbach and Nuremberg. Luther used those articles in shaping his own to be used at the Marburg Conference (Oct. 2–4, 1529); these were called the Marburg Articles. But the fundamental differences in ceremonies were set forth later and called the Torgau Articles.

Melanchthon, after his arrival at Augsburg on May 2, 1530, where he acted as the official leader of the Protestants, because Luther had to remain behind at the Koburg Castle, soon observed that it was necessary to prepare a new confession. This had to contain a much more comprehensive treatment of the creed than that set forth in the Schwabach Articles and also a discussion of the ceremonies, which should be combined with the first. For several weeks he kept on making revisions, some of which are known to us, and just before the official presentation on June 25, 1530, he had the final form ready under the title of Confessio Augustana. Even on June 24 and 25 some lesser changes were contemplated. They help us understand the numerous differences in the manuscript copies still extant.

The Augsburg Confession is not merely, as was originally planned, a confession of the churches in the electorate of Saxony, but of nearly all the Lutherans in the Holy Roman Empire, notably of the government officials known as *Reichsstaende*. It was signed by Elector John of Saxony, Margrave George of Brandenburg-Ansbach, Duke Ernest of Lueneburg, Landgrave Philip of Hesse, Duke John Frederick of Saxony (the son and successor of the elector), Duke Francis of Lueneburg, Prince Wolfgang of Anhalt and the imperial cities of Nuremberg and Reutlingen. Later on (the middle of July) the cities of Windsheim, Heilbronn, Kempten, and Weisenburg (in Bavaria) joined. It is significant to note that the Protestant princes did not merely present a confession drafted by theologians but acted themselves as professing Christians. They had succeeded, in spite of the emperor's protest, in having the confession actually read on June 25 in the German language, which Charles V did not understand very well. Since the windows were open many of the interested spectators outside the building could hear the confession read. The action of the princes in making this bold move was as important as the contents of the document.

The German and Latin texts of the confession were presented to the emperor in person. The original copies have disappeared, and although many searches have been made they could not be recovered. The German text was probably preserved in the Imperial Chancery. An exact duplicate of the original was probably kept in the archives of the archbishop and elector of Mainz, who acted as the archchancellor of the empire. At present it is to be found in the state archives in Vienna. The Latin original was deposited till 1569 in the imperial archives at Brussels, from which it was brought at the request of King Philip II to his Spanish capital, probably by the Duke of Alva in person. The purpose probably was to have it destroyed forthwith. Of the original version in Brussels copies had been made before it was removed, which in recent times have been discovered. From these copies the original Latin text can be restored. It was not until the year 1952 that the Latin original, after much labor, was published in the work known as *Bekenntnis-schriften der evang.-luth. Kirche* (see bibliography below), exactly as it appeared when presented to the Diet in 1530. In the fifty-four German and Latin manuscript copies dating from the year 1530 which have been found thus far there are many variations, some larger and some smaller.

The Latin and the German texts are authentic, and the one is not merely a translation of the other. Both were made by Melanchthon, with the exception of the Preface, which was drawn up in German by Chancellor George Brueck of the Electorate of Saxony, translated into Latin by Justus Jonas (*q.v.*), and revised in the Latin form by Melanchthon. It is now apparent that this Preface was not simply a personal address to the emperor, as Melanchthon had originally planned, but a political instrument. The Protestant leaders at the Diet wished to make use of the imperial invitation dated Jan. 21, 1530, the decisions of the Diet of Speyer in 1526, and the appeal to a general council which had been expressed at the Diet of Speyer.

The text of the confession itself is divided into two parts: Articles of Faith (*Articuli fidei praecipui* I–XXI) and Articles of the Roman Abuses, which have been Eliminated in the Reformed Churches (*Articuli in quibus recensentur abuses mutati* XXII–XXVIII). In the Articles of Faith the first three present those doctrines on which the Protestants agreed with the Roman Catholics (God, original sin, Christ), next those covering justification and the church (IV–VIII), then the sacraments (IX–XIII, in which penance and confession are also treated), church ordinance and political sovereignty (XIV–XVI), and separate problems (XVII–XXI: the second coming of Christ, free will, faith and good works, veneration of saints, etc.). All the Articles of Faith, which in part are classical in their simplicity and clarity, indicate a desire to reach a common ground. In the original version Melanchthon actually went so

far as to say that the *only* (or *whole*) difference lay in the attitude toward abuses in the church. But he changed his position in the first printed version. He believed in agreement with the leaders in the old Roman Catholic Church, going back to the early scholastic authorities. Nevertheless, the Augsburg Confession did not remain silent on the differences, with the exception of some, notably on purgatory, the papacy, etc. In Article X the doctrine of Zwingli on the Eucharist was condemned rather severely. Those dealing with abuses were much more elaborate than the others and dealt with the following points: Communion in both kinds (XXII), celibacy (XXIII), the Mass (XXIV), confession (XXV), fasting (XXVI), monastic vows (XXVII), and the power of the bishops (XXVIII). They were very carefully drafted, revealing a sound understanding of the historical background, and showing that the author wanted to mention only those actual abuses which the Protestants had to remove, preserving everything that was seen to be wholesome and proper in the church of Jesus Christ.

Although this document and the subsequent statements like the Apology (see AUGSBURG CONFESSION, APOLOGY OF THE) did not achieve the purpose intended by the author, namely, the friendly reconciliation with the Catholic authorities, they did have great historical significance, for the confession was so carefully prepared that afterward it often served as a common basis in negotiations between Catholic and Protestant leaders. It was indeed the most ecumenical confession of the Reformation. Its good reputation was later enhanced by Melanchthon, who regarded the document as a sort of private confession of his own and for that reason felt authorized to make important alterations, as in the edition of 1540, called Confessio Augustana Variata. Here Article X was changed to resemble the statement on the Eucharist in the Wittenberg Concordance of 1536. Bitter quarrels resulted among Protestant theologians, which condemned either the Invariata or the Variata. But these quarrels were only of a temporary nature and they have lost their significance in recent times.

BIBLIOGRAPHY: The authentic text, ed. by D. Heinrich Bornkamm in *Die Bekenntnisschriften der evangelisch-lutherischen Kirche*, 2nd ed., 1952 (with historical introduction, critical apparatus, commentary and bibliography); K. Schottenloher, *Bibl. zur deutschen Gesch. im Zeitalter der Glaubensspaltung*, Vol. IV (1938), Nr. 34504 ff., Vol. V (1939), Nr. 51502; W. Guszmann, *Quellen und Forschungen zur Geschichte des Augsb. Glaubensbekenntnisses*, Vol. I (1911). II (1912); T. Kolde, *Histor. Einleitung in die Symbol. Buecher* (J. T. Mueller, *Die symb. Buecher der ev.-luth. Kirche*, 11th ed., 1912); J. Ficker, *Die Originale des Vierstaedtebekenntnisses und die originalen Texte der Augsb. Konf. Geschichtliche Studien fuer A. Hauck* (1916), pp. 240–251; R. Hermann, *Zur theol. Wuerdigung der Augustana*, *Jahrb. d. Luthergesellschaft*, 1930; K. Thieme, *Die Augsb. Konf. und Luthers Katechismen auf theologische Gegenwartswerte untersucht*, 1930; W. E. Nagel, *Luthers Anteil an der Conf. Aug.*, 1930; idem, *Die Augs. Konf. in ihrer ersten Gestalt als Bekenntnis deutscher Reichsstaende*, 1930; J. Ficker, *Die Eigenart d. Augs. Bek.* (Hallische Univ. reden, 47), 1930; P. Althaus,

Der Geist der luth. Ethik in Augs. Bek., 1930; H. Bornkamm, *Der prot. Mensch nach dem Augs. Bek.*, 2nd ed. 1936; G. Hoffmann, *Zur Entstehungsgesch. d. Augustana*, *Zt. f. syst. Theol.* 15 (1938), 419–490; E. Schlink, *Theol. d. luth. Bekenntnisschriften*, 2nd ed. 1946; W. Maurer, *Z. gesch. Verstaendnis der Abendmahlsart. in der Conf. Aug.* (*Festschrift fuer Gerhard Ritter*, 1950), pp. 161–209; F. Brunstaed, *Theologie der luth. Bekenntnisschriften*, 1951; W. Koehler, *Zwingli und Luther*, Vol. II (1953) (*Quellen und Forschungen zur Reformationsgeschichte*, Vol. 7), Chap. 5.

[Sup.] HEINRICH BORNKAMM.

AUGSBURG CONFESSION, APOLOGY OF THE: Melanchthon's Apology of the Augsburg Confession was written in September, 1530, at the Diet (Reichstag) of Augsburg. The Augsburg Confession (*q.v.*) was presented on June 25, and was answered by Emperor Charles V (*q.v.*) in an extensive "Confutation" read before the Protestant delegates on August 3 but not delivered to them. Melanchthon made use of notes which had been made during the reading in composing his Apology, which together with the official protest against the planned manner of closing the diet (*Reichstagsabschied*) was to have been presented on September 22. But the emperor refused to accept it. After Melanchthon had left the diet and had studied a copy of the Confutation he wrote a carefully prepared and lengthy treatise, published first in Latin in the spring of 1531 and next in German translation by Justus Jonas (*q.v.*) (autumn of 1531). Although Melanchthon revised this work on several occasions, the version published in the Book of Concord (1580) was based upon the earliest. The Apology was one of the most profound doctrinal treatises of the Lutheran Reformation and one of the best works by Melanchthon. It is a complement to the Augsburg Confession and carefully answers the arguments of the Roman Catholics. In numerous details it represents the Evangelical position better than the Augsburg Confession does.

BIBLIOGRAPHY: The authentic text was published by H. Bornkamm in *Bekenntnisschriften der evang.-luth. Kirche*, 2nd ed. 1952, with extensive bibliography on p. 158; K. Thieme, *Der Geist der lutherischen Ethik in Melanchthons Apologie*, 1930; H. Engelland, *Melanchthon: Glauben und Handeln*, 1931; E. Schlink, *Theologie der lutherischen Bekenntnisschriften*, 2nd ed. 1946; F. Brunstaed, *Theologie der lutherischen Bekenntnisschriften*, 1951.

[Sup.] HEINRICH BORNKAMM.

AUGSBURG, DIET OF: The Diet of Augsburg held in 1530 differs from the earlier diets in its political constellation. The victorious Emperor Charles V (*q.v.*) had signed peace treaties with his opponents, with Pope Clement VII in Barcelona (June 29, 1529), and with King Francis I of France at Cambrai (Aug. 5, 1529). This insured his rule in Italy, and now the pope could no longer refuse to crown him emperor, which was done on Feb. 24, 1530, at Bologna. On the other hand, the Turks had advanced up to the gates of Vienna (end of Sept. 1529), causing consternation among the

Habsburgs in Austria. These important political developments impelled the emperor to turn his attention once more to the Reformation in Germany. The Edict of Worms (see WORMS, DIET OF), which had been intended to destroy that Reformation, remained without effect. Since 1521 the Lutheran movement had grown mightily. At the Diet of Speyer in 1529 the Protestant princes and cities blocked the attempt made there to enforce the Edict of Worms throughout Germany. They presented the Protest which gave rise to the name "Protestantism," and they made an effective appeal for the calling of a general council.

Emperor Charles V for the first time in nine years attended a meeting of the Reichstag or diet. He faced two possibilities: (1) one more attempt to unite the religious parties, or (2) suppress Lutheranism with the Edict of Worms, as his brother Ferdinand, Archduke of Austria and King of Hungary, had tried to do at the Diet of Speyer. Charles chose the first, and he issued an invitation dated Jan. 21, 1530, requesting that the parties come together in a peaceful state of mind, ready to bury their animosities and differences. Emperor and pope had agreed upon this course of action. If it should fail, Charles and his brother Ferdinand would try to exterminate heresy with force. The papal delegate Campeggio received the assignment to remind the brothers constantly of their sacred duty.

The conciliatory tone of the imperial invitation gave the Protestant princes the hope that at last they would receive the opportunity to express publicly their faith at a diet where they would be heard with dignity and respect. For this reason the Protestant states prepared confessions, and some of them, notably the Electorate of Saxony, sent to the emperor before the meeting articles of faith, in order to help remove his opposition to the principles of the Reformation. But these attempts were fruitless. The fateful decision was postponed until the meeting of the diet. Since Charles arrived two months later than the date he had assigned for his coming, the Protestant delegates had plenty of time to lay their plans of action and to seek a common cause. Melanchthon took the confession made for the Electorate of Saxony and revised it to become the confession for the majority of the Protestant states and cities. This was the Augsburg Confession (*q.v.*). When the emperor immediately after his arrival at the diet (June 5) prohibited the Protestant preaching services, the Lutherans realized that their hope of friendly settlement in their favor had been groundless. They now sought mutual aid among themselves through union and firmness. For this reason the Augsburg Confession was given a new Preface, expressing the position that the Protestant cause had a legal basis and demanding again a general church council. The confession was read in German on June 25, but the difference in the conception of the Eucharist made it impossible for some cities to accept the official confession by Melanchthon. Strasbourg, Constance, Lindau, and Memmingen on July 9 presented a confession by Bucer and Capito called the Confessio Tetrapolitiana. The day before the city council of Zurich had delivered a confession prepared by Zwingli called Fidei Ratio. A group of Roman Catholic theologians drafted a refutation of the Protestant confessions called Confutation, but the emperor considered the first version too sharp and too long. A thoroughly revised copy was presented on August 3 in the name of the emperor, who in this manner made himself the spokesman for the Roman Catholic delegates at the diet.

Since a peaceful solution of the religious differences now seemed out of the question the emperor requested of the pope that a general church council be held as soon as possible. He also threatened to adopt severe measures against the Protestants who refused to come to terms with him and his Catholic supporters. Because the pope refused to call the council at that time, Charles was forced to try once more some method of reconciliation. But negotiations in August and September led nowhere, although Melanchthon made overtures so far-reaching that he aroused the anger and scorn of Luther and the Protestant princes. From the papal point of view the breach also seemed impossible to heal. Charles refused to accept Melanchthon's Apology (see AUGSBURG CONFESSION, APOLOGY OF THE) on September 22, and now the diet suddenly came to an end. The Protestants in their turn saw no sense in accepting the proposal made at the final meeting to wait another six months and then admit that their cause was lost. On September 23 they were informed that their allegiance to the emperor had been terminated, but they remained resolute in their determination to stand by their faith. This was the first step in the forthcoming Schmalkaldic War against them, which would have broken out at once if it had not been for the Turkish threat to the imperial forces from the southeast, the new war with France, and a number of other political complications disturbing Charles V. The renewal of the Edict of Worms on Nov. 19, 1530, compelled the Protestant princes and cities to take steps in their defense. Early in 1531 they formed the Schmalkaldic League.

In addition to the problem of religion the diet also had to consider the aid which the rulers could give the emperor in his fight against the Turks, besides the election of the emperor's brother Ferdinand as king of the Romans, which would mean his future succession to the imperial title. The Roman Catholic and the secular princes were bribed with enormous sums, totaling 1,200,000 gulden (florins or guilders, gold coin). Cardinal Albrecht of Mainz received the largest amount.

BIBLIOGRAPHY: Schottenloher, Bibl. zur deutschen Gesch. im Zeitalter der Glaubensspaltung, Vol. III (1936), Nr. 28011–28067, Vol. V (1939), Nr. 51034; J. von Walter, Die Depeschen des Venezianischen Gesandten Tiepolo vom Augsburger Reichstage, in Abh. d. Ges. d. Wiss. zu Goettingen, Neue Folge, Vol. XXIII Part I, 1928; Joh. von Walter, "Der Reichstag zu Augsburg 1530," in Luther-Jahrbuch (1930), pp. 1–90 (the best treatment thus far); E. W. Mayer, "Forschungen zur Politik Karls V. waehrend des Augsburger Reichstags von 1530," Arch. fuer Reformationsgeschichte, Vol. XIII (1916), pp. 40–73, 124–146; H. von Schubert, "Der Reichstag von Augsburg im Zusammenhang der Reformationsgeschichte," in Schriften d. Ver. fuer Reformationsgeschichte, Nr. 150, 1930; H. von Schubert, "Luther auf der Koburg" in Luther-Jahrbuch (1930), pp. 109–161; J. von Walter, Luther und Melanchthon waehrend des Augsb. Reichstags, 1931; K. Brandi, Kaiser Karl, Vol. I, 1937, Vol. II, 1941; P. Rassow, "Erasmus und der Augsburger Reichstag 1530," in Die politische Welt Karls V. (1942), pp. 40–65; J. Hoess, "Georg Spalatin auf dem Reichstag zu Augsburg 1530 und seine Stellungnahme zur Frage des Widerstandsrechts," in Arch. f. Ref., Vol. XLIV (1953), pp. 64–84.
For many years German scholars have contemplated the publication of the minutes of the diet, but thus far the plan has not yet materialized. For this reason the following printed sources are still of great value: Urkunden buch zu der Geschichte des Reichstages zu Augsburg, ed. by K. E. Foerstemann, Vol. I (1833), Vol. II (1835); Briefe und Akten zu der Geschichte des Religionsgespraechs zu Marburg 1529 und des Reichstages zu Augsburg 1530, ed. by F. W. Schirrmacher, 1876; S. Ehses, "Kardinal Lorenzo Campeggio auf dem Reichstage zu Augsburg 1530," in Roemische Quartalschrift, Vols. 17–21 (1903–07).

HEINRICH BORNKAMM.

AUGSBURG, PEACE OF: Here the strange concept of *Cuius regio eius religio* was expressed for the first time in a definitive and legal way. During the past three decades a number of experts in political science, especially in the United States, have concluded that Martin Luther was largely responsible for the idea that the prince may dictate to his subjects what their religious views must be and what sort of books they shall read in the field of religion. The Treaty of Augsburg in 1555 was, however, the outgrowth of local political conditions and the revival of the study of Roman Law (*Corpus Juris Civilis* by Emperor Justinian). Luther in 1523 published a treatise on the subject that contained exactly the opposite of *cuius regio eius religio* (*On Civil Government: In How Far One Should Obey It*). He as well as his most intimate followers, together with their opponents also, were carried along in the tide toward absolutism, very slowly at first, and after Luther's death much more rapidly.

BIBLIOGRAPHY: E. F. Henderson, A Short History of Germany, Vol. I (1926), Chap. 15; K. F. Reinhardt, Germany 2,000 Years (1950), pp. 208–218; G. Barraclough, The Origins of Modern Germany (1947), pp. 366–378; H. S. Lucas, Renaissance and Reformation (1934), pp. 461–576; E. G. Schwiebert, Luther and His Times (1950), pp. 32–95, 468; Schwiebert points out on p. 468 that there were precedents for the principle of giving the civil rulers a great deal of power over the clergy, as was also indicated in the article by Gerhard Ritter, "Protestantism" in the present encyclopedia (q.v.). See also the famous book by Karl Brandi, The Emperor Charles V, 1939; J. Buehler, Deutsche Geschichte, Vol. III, Das Reformationszeitalter, 1938.

[Sup.] ALBERT HYMA.

AUGUSTINE: The output of literature in connection with the recent anniversary of Augustine's death has been very great.

Some writers continue to follow Windelband's suggestion that Augustine's principle of inwardness makes him the great precursor of modern philosophy. On this interpretation Augustine's orthodox theology is like the trunk of a dead tree, useful only as the support of living and fruit-producing vines.

Others hold that Augustine's basic thought is expressed in his doctrines of the Trinity, temporal creation, historic redemption through the work of Christ, and the sovereign grace by which God saves sinners from their folly and their doom. On this interpretation the main thrust of Augustine's thought makes him the forerunner of Calvin rather than of Descartes. On this view it is granted that Augustine never fully outgrew the Platonism and Neo-Platonism which held him enthralled in his early years. The contention is that in his maturest thought his main concepts of the ontological Trinity, of temporal creation, and of sovereign grace so controlled him that the Platonic view of the potential identity of man with God receded far into the background. Thus his work was of the greatest possible help to Calvin when he developed a more self-consciously biblical epistemology, ontology, and ethics (see CALVINISM).

BIBLIOGRAPHY: Excellent bibliographies dealing with Augustine and his writings are found in the following works of recent date: Jacob Hendrik Koopmans, *Augustinus' Briefwisseling Met Dioscorus*, 1949; Pieter Johannes Couvée, *Vita Beata en Vita Aeterna*, 1947; Geoffrey Grimshaw Willis, *Saint Augustine and the Donatist Controversy*, 1950; John H. S. Burleigh, *The City of God*, 1949; Meyrick H. Carré, *Realists and Nominalists*, 1946; Christopher J. O'Toole, *The Philosophy of Creation in the Writings of Augustine*, 1944; B. Altaner, *Patrologie*, 1950; E. Nebreda, *Bibliografia Augustiniana*, 1928; *Religión y Cultura* (1931), pp. 461–509; *International Bibliography of Historical Sciences*, V (1934), 2496–2531.

[Sup.] CORNELIUS VAN TIL.

AUGUSTINE OF ALVELDT:

BIBLIOGRAPHY: J. H. Sbaralea, *Supplementum et castigatio ad scriptores trium ordinum S. Francisci*, Vol. I, 1907.
[Sup.]

AUGUSTINIANS: When St. Augustine returned to Africa after his conversion he went to Tagaste, where in 388 he founded a monastery for men; in 391 followed the second institution at Hippo. As bishop he used his authority to impose upon the local clergy the common life. At Hippo he also founded a convent for women. During the invasion of the Vandals some of the monks fled into the wilderness, seeking solitude, for which reason they were called hermits. This name has ever since then been used for such persons. Other monks went to Europe, where they founded settlements, so that in the early Middle Ages groups of their followers were to be found in Italy, Spain, and France; later also in Germany.

Popes Innocent IV and Alexander IV directed the labors of all these groups in such manner that they were firmly united into a great monastic organization. This may be gathered from the fact that when in 1256 the official unification took place, there were set up immediately the four provinces of Italy, France with England, Germany, and Spain with Portugal (Iberian Peninsula). These had a total of 122 monasteries. The life of the average Augustinian was (and still is) a *vita mixta*, being a combination of contemplation and action. The order was always distinguished by scholarly labors and missionary activity. A right wing, which wanted sterner discipline, received an independent status in 1912 (the barefooted Augustinians). The French Revolution greatly weakened the order. But since the end of the nineteenth century it has experienced an interesting resurgence. At present it has about 5,000 members, and there exists a second order of cloistered nuns with 140 convents; besides a third order with many branches.

BIBLIOGRAPHY: A great deal of historical material is to be found in Augustinian periodicals: *Analecta augustiniana*, Rome, since 1907; *La vie augustienne*, since 1929; *Bolletino storico agostiniano*, since 1924; the best study is by M. Th. Disdier, in *Dict. d'Histoire et de géogr. ecclés.*, Vol. V (1931), 498–653.

[Sup.] MATHIAS GOOSSENS.

AULÉN, GUSTAF EMANUEL HILDEBRAND: Church of Sweden; b. at Ljungby, county of Kalmar, May 15, 1879. He studied at the University of Uppsala. Docent in 1907, he became professor of systematic theology at the University of Lund (1913–33); and bishop of Strängnäs Diocese (1933–52, retired 1952). His publications are: *Dogmhistoria*, 1917; *Den allmänneliga kristna tron*, 1923; trans. into Dutch and English: *The Faith of the Christian Church*, 1948; *Den kristna gudsbilden* (trans. into German and Dutch); *Den kristna försoningstanken* (trans. into English: *Christus Victor*; and into Dutch, French, and Chinese); and *Church, Law and Society*, 1948.

AUSSENAMT. See EVANGELISCHE KIRCHE IN DEUTSCHLAND.

AUSTRALIA: The executive power of Australia is vested in the British Crown and is exercised by a governor general who is advised by the Federal Executive Council. The governor general is usually an Englishman, but may be an Australian citizen. The Federal Cabinet, consisting of the prime minister and 19 ministers, is in charge of the administration. There is a senate of 10 members from each of the six states, and a house of representatives of 123 members. Since 1911 the legal ties which bind Australia to England have progressively loosened until today Australia is an autonomous nation with full powers and responsibility in foreign affairs. Accordingly Australia has diplomatic representation in most foreign countries and is a member of the United Nations (*q.v.*). The inner bonds to England remain; like other former British dominions, Australia is a member of the British Commonwealth of Nations in which all under the British crown are of equal status with the motherland, all united by a common loyalty to the crown. Since World War II events in the Pacific area and in Southeast Asia have brought Australia and the United States into a close friendship which is being systematically fostered.

A vast immigration scheme of displaced persons and others (see REFUGEES) brought hundreds of thousands of European and British immigrants to Australia after World War II, so that in 1952 the population had risen to about 8,600,000. The religious bodies which benefited most by this influx are the Roman Catholic and the Lutheran. The last census was taken in 1947, and the following table cannot therefore give a complete picture of the extent to which churches have benefited by the immigration.

have strong affiliated bodies in each state, all the major Protestant groups being represented. The Faith and Order Commission in Australia has been very active, and in the World Council of Churches (*q.v.*) most of the churches were charter members. Only the Lutherans have kept aloof, preferring affiliation with the Lutheran World Federation (*q.v.*) or with Lutheran bodies in the United States.

A major event in the Roman Catholic Church was the elevation in 1946 of the archbishop of Sydney to the rank of cardinal—the first in Australia. To the province of Sydney the diocese of Wagga Wagga was added in 1917. In the province of Adelaide the former diocese of Victoria is now known as Darwin, and the archdiocese Perth has been detached to form its own province with the diocese of Geraldton, the Vicariate of Kimberley, and the Abbey Nullius of New Norcia. In the province of Brisbane the dioceses of Toowoomba (1929), Townsville (1930), and Cairns (1941) have been added. The number of female orders and congregations in this church has grown considerably in each province.

	New South Wales	Victoria	Queensland	South Australia	West Australia	Tasmania	Aust. Capital Territory	Northern Territory
Anglican	1,293,964	729,902	388,621	188,151	222,457	123,158	7,091	3,688
Presbyterian	262,166	288,383	121,604	24,304	31,809	12,644	1,944	686
Methodist	246,876	234,595	124,322	170,513	59,194	33,358	1,356	1,211
Baptist	34,935	32,020	16,399	18,431	6,097	5,374	185	86
Church of Christ	10,269	29,722	5,717	16,877	7,043	2,039	49	55
Lutheran	5,915	10,002	21,244	28,713	841	57	18	101
Congregational	19,331	11,374	8,546	13,916	5,950	4,007	72	47
Salvation Army	10,871	10,984	5,734	5,130	3,200	1,612	26	15
Roman Catholic	676,993	416,873	251,952	80,990	96,222	39,844	4,353	2,499

In addition there were 857 Quakers, 1,824 Unitarians, 17,550 Seventh-day Adventists, 13,002 Brethren, 3,499 Latter-day Saints (Mormons), 11,389 Christian Scientists, and 5,019 Christadelphians. The sum total of the Protestant population of the commonwealth in 1947 was 5,103,-210, and there were 1,569,726 Roman Catholics in Australia.

There has been a steady expansion of the Anglican Church since 1900. To the province of Melbourne the diocese of St. Arnaud was added in 1927; in South Australia another extra provincial diocese was established (Willochra, 1914); the new province of Western Australia was created to include the dioceses of Perth (1856), Bunbury (1904), North West Australia (1910), and Kalgoorlie (1913).

The most important development in the life of the Protestant churches has been the growth of interest in the ecumenical movement (*q.v.*). The Student Christian Movement (*q.v.*) and the International Missionary Council (*q.v.*)

The strength of the non-Christian religions in 1947 was as follows: 32,019 Jews, 2,704 Mohammedans, 411 Buddhists, 359 Theosophists, 357 Confucians, 244 Indus, and 10 Shintoists. The figures of those who profess no religion were as follows: 2,764 Rationalists, 1,918 Agnostics, 1,829 Atheists, and 1,339 Freethinkers.

Full blood aborigines in 1947 numbered 46,630 (they are estimated to have numbered 300,000 at the time of the first white settlement in 1788). Missionary activity among them has made big advances. In the far north the Roman Catholics and Anglicans are at work, while in Central Australia the Lutherans and Presbyterians have established important centers. A major problem is to make of the natives useful and self-supporting members of the community. In this respect the Lutherans have had some success at Hermannsburg, where a school of native artists, headed by the well-known Albert Namatjira, has achieved fame with its water colors of Central Australian landscapes.

BIBLIOGRAPHY: *Year Book of the Commonwealth of Australia*, 1951; W. K. Hancock, *Australia*, 1930; E. Scott, *A Short History of Australia*, 4th ed., 1925; B. C. Fitzpatrick, *Australian People, 1788–1945*, 1947; A. P. Elkin, *The Australian Aborigines*, 1948; T. G. H. Strehlow, *Aranda Traditions*, 1947.

[Sup.] SIEGFRIED HEBART.

AUSTRAL OR TUBUANI ISLANDS. See SOUTH SEA ISLANDS.

AUSTRIA: The first half of the twentieth century was important for the development of Protestantism in Austria. From a diminutive group without great influence at the turn of the century, it has become a movement with spiritual influence which is out of proportion to its size (5% of the population in 1950).

Even before World War I Roman Catholics began to drift into Protestantism. Including 100,000 converts, there were about 600,000 Evangelicals in the Austro-Hungarian Empire at the close of World War I, and 177,178 of these remained in the new republic of Austria. The dominance of Roman Catholicism was threatened by the downfall of the Hapsburg rulers, and there was a movement out of the Roman Church (see LOS VON ROM), encouraged by Freethinkers who developed an effective anticlerical (see CLERICALISM) propaganda. In an attempt to recover its influence the Roman Church allied itself with reactionary Austrian Fascists. This maneuver was unsuccessful, for during the civil conflict of 1934 more than 25,000 were added to Protestant rolls. Among these were many National Socialists for whom "German" and "Protestant" were synonymous. Adolf Hitler's annexation of Austria brought with it a new wave of converts. Consequently the Protestant churches grew to 342,000 souls by 1938 (including 40,000 Evangelicals in Burgenland, transferred to Austria from Hungary in 1921), and thus the Protestant membership of the country was doubled in a period of twenty years.

Soon after the establishment of its power in Austria, National Socialism craftily turned anticlerical sentiment into an attack on all churches, including the Evangelical. Many, especially among the educated proletariat, withdrew from the churches, and Protestant membership shrank to 317,331. After World War II the tide shifted again, and although many churches, parsonages, and other buildings were destroyed during the war, there were 140 Evangelical congregations with 411,872 members in 1950. This increase resulted in part from the influx of thousands of refugees (*q.v.*) from eastern Europe. Interchurch aid from the World Council of Churches (*q.v.*) and the Lutheran World Federation (*q.v.*) helped in the reconstruction of church life and, together with ties formed by marriages between Austrians and English and American occupation forces, extended and deepened relations with world Protestantism. Moreover, Austria became less solidly Catholic, and the minority Protestant movement found increasing opportunity to influence the Catholic majority.

Of great importance was the introduction of bishops, the increase in superintendents, and the adoption of a new constitution for the Church of the Augsburg and Helvetic Confessions (1949). Although the constitution no longer requires the sanction of the state, it enjoys legal recognition. The inner life of the church is marked by a tendency toward a more biblical theology. There is a shortage of clergymen and teachers of religion, but the character of the clergy, matured by the profound experiences of World War II, is on a high level. Publication of religious literature remains undeveloped, but inner mission activity is comparatively extensive, and effective use is made of the radio.

BIBLIOGRAPHY: Georg Loesche, *Geschichte des Protestantismus in Oesterreich*, 3rd ed., 1930; Hans Eder, *Die evangelische Kirche in Oesterreich*, 1940; B. H. Zimmermann, *Evangelisch in Oesterreich*, 2nd ed., 1950; B. H. Zimmermann, "Rising Lutheranism in Austria," in *The Lutheran Church Quarterly*, IV (1931), No. 4.

BERNHARD H. ZIMMERMANN.

AUTOCEPHALOUS CHURCH: The word "autocephalous," which is roughly synonymous with "autonomous," applies to some Eastern Christian Churches in two ways.

(1) In the time of the Byzantine Empire, it designated churches whose heads were exempt from the jurisdiction of the metropolitan, and depended immediately on the patriarch. Such privileges were granted by decree from a council, or, for political reasons, by the basileus.

(2) The word "autocephalous" applies also to churches whose historical ties with a patriarchate were entirely dissolved, as, for instance, the Church of Cyprus in the twelfth century. The situation resulting from the Turkish conquest multiplied autocephalous churches on a national or territorial basis. Their heads are called either patriarch, exarch, or archbishop and metropolitan. This diversity of titles does not imply any subordination of their bearers with regard to each other, the relationship between autocephalous bodies being conceived as a communion of federated churches, not as an administrative unity.

BIBLIOGRAPHY: N. Milasch, *Das Kirchenrecht der morgenlaendischen Kirche*, 1905; B. J. Kidd, *The Churches of the Eastern Christendom*, 1927; Seraphim, *Die Ostkirche*, 1950.

GEORGES A. BARROIS.

AUTONOMY: The status of being self-ruled or self-determining, usually attributed to (1) political entities, such as independent nations, and (2) the human will, especially, but not necessarily, as conceived by Immanuel Kant.

According to Kant, the autonomy of the good will consists in the fact that it is itself the source or ground of the moral law to which it subjects itself. In contrast, a *heteronymous* will is determined by a principle "external" to itself, such as sympathy, the desire for happiness, or the command of God. The law the autonomous will prescribes for itself is, according to Kant, the categorical imperative, one version of which is: "act only on that principle which thou canst will should become a universal law."

See also WILL, FREEDOM OF THE.

BIBLIOGRAPHY: Immanuel Kant, *Critique of Practical Reason*, trans. by L. W. Beck, 1949; *Fundamental Principles of the Metaphysics of Ethics*, trans. by T. K. Abbott, 1929; H. J. Paton, *The Categorical Imperative* (1948), Chap. XX.

VINCENT TOMAS.

AUTOSUGGESTION: Autosuggestion is suggestion that comes from within oneself. This process has been familiar for two thousand years or more. "As a man makes evaluation in his own soul, so is he" (Prov. 23:7) is an ancient statement of its essential meaning. I think to myself, "that is too big a job for me, and I may fail," and the probability is that I will fail. Both psychosomatic medicine and the healing cults (*q.v.*) testify to the power of autosuggestion. Functional disturbances may be created or healed by autosuggestion, as a primary factor in the process.

See also PSYCHOLOGY.

HARRY G. GOODYKOONTZ.

AVE MARIA HOUR. See ATONEMENT FRIARS.

AVERROES. See ARABIC PHILOSOPHY.

AVICENNA. See ARABIC PHILOSOPHY.

AVILA, JUAN DE: B. 1500 at Almodovar del Campo. He was declared Blessed in 1894. His work, *Audi filia*, is an extensive treatment of prayer. The first edition of his *Epistolario* appeared in 1578–79 at Madrid and Alcalá. Don Vincente Garcia de Diego prepared a critical edition in 1912, which appeared in the collection, *Classicos Castellanos*.

BIBLIOGRAPHY: J. M. de Buck S.J., *Le bienheureux Jean d'Avila, Lettres de direction*, 1927.

[Sup.] MATHIAS GOOSSENS.

AYER, JOSEPH CULLEN, JR.: Episcopalian; d. Apr. 15, 1944. He was rector at South Groveland, Mass., (1888–90); Keene, N. H. (1893–95); Nantucket, Mass. (1895–99); Sandwich, Mass. (1900–03); and Lexington, Mass. (1903–05). He was professor of ecclesiastical history in the Divinity School of the Protestant Episcopal Church, Philadelphia (1905–36); and was lecturer on history of Christian Thought at the University of Pennsylvania (1927–36); rector of St. Philip's Church, Philadelphia (1929–36); and librarian of the Yarnall Library of St. Clement's Church, Philadelphia. His major work which has appeared in many editions is *A Source Book for Ancient Church History* (1913).

BIBLIOGRAPHY: Leicester Crosby Lewis, "Joseph Cullen Ayer," in *S. Clement's Quarterly*, Vol. VIII, No. 3 (1944).

[Sup.] RAYMOND W. ALBRIGHT.

AYER LECTURES: Founded at Colgate-Rochester Divinity School, Rochester, N. Y., 1928, by Mr. and Mrs. Wilfred W. Fry, of Camden, N. J., in memory of Mrs. Fry's father, Francis Wayland Ayer. The terms of the foundation provide that the lectures are to fall within the broad field of the history or the interpretation of the Christian message. Four lectures are given each year at the Divinity School and are subsequently published in expanded form. WILBOUR EDDY SAUNDERS.

B

BAAB, OTTO JUSTICE: Methodist; b. July 6, 1896. He studied at Hamline University (B.A., 1921); Northwestern University (M.A., 1927); Garrett Biblical Institute (B.D., 1927); University of Chicago (Ph.D., 1928). He was professor of Oriental languages, University of Chicago, and professor of religion, Illinois Wesleyan University (1930–34); and has been professor of Old Testament interpretation at Garrett Biblical Institute (1934–). He wrote: *Jesus Christ Our Lord* (1937); contributed to *The Study of the Bible Today and Tomorrow* (1947); and *The Theology of the Old Testament* (1949).

BAAL. See GODS AND GODDESSES, PAGAN.

BABISM: Furnishes the connection between the eclectic teaching of Bahaism and Islam. 'Alī Muḥammad of Shiraz (1821–50) declared himself to be "the gateway (*bāb*) to knowledge of divine truth." Coming approximately one thousand years after the last of the "representatives" of the Shi'ite imams, he seized the opportunity to exploit a developed millennial longing for the return of the Twelfth Imam. He came as a reformer, advocating changes in Muslim law, writing treatises that were considered divine revelations, and had himself proclaimed as "the mirror of the breath of God." His first disciple succeeded in converting two brothers from Teheran, who came to be known as Subḥi-Ezel and Bahā' Allāh. The Persian government was intolerant of Mirza 'Alī Muḥammad's claims and had him shot in 1850. Subsequently the movement was carried on as Bahaism. See also BAHAISM; SHIʻISM.

BIBLIOGRAPHY: "Bāb," "Bābī," *Ency. of Islam;* Index, *ERE;* Mirza Kazem-beg, "Bāb et les Bābīs," *Jour. As.,* VI, VII, Index; Huart, *La Religion de Bāb,* 1889; Browne, *A Traveller's Narrative,* 1891; Nicolas, *Seyyid ʻAli Muhammad dit le Bāb,* 1905; *idem, Le Beyan arabe,* 1905.

[Sup.] DWIGHT M. DONALDSON.

BABYLONIA: Babylonia is the country which extends from the head of the Persian Gulf to about 34° north latitude, lying between or immediately adjacent to the Tigris and Euphrates Rivers. Babylonia is alluvial land, formed by the deposit of silt by the Tigris and Euphrates, beginning about 20,000 years ago. The land was very productive in ancient times when the irrigation canals were kept in repair, although the average rainfall is only six inches. It contains no building stone, and clay was widely used for making building bricks and tablets on which cuneiform writing was inscribed.

I. History: The earliest civilization in Babylonia is known as the Obeid culture, from discoveries at Tell el-Obeid, a mound four miles northwest of Ur. It dates from about 4000 B.C. Pottery was made by hand or on a hand-turned wheel. Houses were constructed of reeds matted together and plastered with mud. There is evidence of trade relations with the Iranian highlands and possibly India; some of the early inhabitants may well have been Iranians. The next culture is that of Uruk (biblical Erech), of the latter part of the fourth millennium. At this time the potter's wheel and the cylinder seal came into use, the first ziggurat (temple tower), was built, and writing was first done in a pictographic script (see WRITING, ANCIENT HEBREW). The third predynastic period is that of Jemdet Nasr, *ca.* 3000 B.C. Bronze was first used at this time.

The Early Dynastic Period dates from 2800 B.C. to 2360 B.C. The dominant people were the Sumerians (*q.v.*), who had apparently been in the land since the Uruk period. They were a non-Semitic people, highly gifted in many aspects of culture, who laid the basis for much of the culture of Mesopotamia (*q.v.*). They employed an agglutinative language which has no direct relationship with any other known language. Various city-states competed with one another for supremacy and for control of adjacent lands. The best-known phase of the period is that of the First Dynasty of Ur, when Sumerian culture reached its climax. This culture is represented by the discoveries in the "royal cemetery" of Ur by Sir Leonard Woolley. Very remarkable art objects worked in gold, silver, lapis lazuli and other media show that the Sumerians of the third millennium reached a stage of artistic skill not surpassed in the ancient Near East. In several of the tombs

human skeletons were found in such condition as to suggest human sacrifice; the purpose of the sacrifice, however, is not apparent and several theories have been proposed.

Semites probably had come into Babylonia in the fourth millennium, but the first Semitic dynasty was established by Sargon I of Agade, and the Old Akkadian Period, 2360–2180 B.C., was ushered in. Sargon founded the city of Agade; from it the northern half of Babylonia took its name, Akkad, and the Semitic people were designated as Akkadians. The southern half was called Sumer; many a later king proudly called himself "king of Sumer and Akkad." Sargon conquered all of Babylonia and extended his rule as far as Elam on the east and the Mediterranean Sea on the west. At the close of the period Babylonia was overrun by peoples from the land of Gutium on the east (2180–2070 B.C.). After about a century the land experienced a Sumerian revival, in the Neo-Sumerian Period (2070–1960 B.C.), under Gudea of Lagash and the remarkable rulers of the Third Dynasty of Ur. This was followed by a second period of invasions, by the Elamites and by the Amorites (*q.v.*) from the west (1960–1930 B.C.).

The period which ensued was the most brilliant of Babylonian history before the middle of the first millennium. It is known as the Old Babylonian Period, or the First Dynasty of Babylon, 1830–1550 B.C. The dynasty was established by the Amorite Sumu-abu, who gained control of the city of Babylon, at that time an unimportant Akkadian city. The power of this Amorite dynasty grew, and reached its climax in the reign of Hammurabi (*q.v.*), the greatest of all Babylonian rulers. The date of Hammurabi can now be fixed with relative certainty since recent discoveries at Mari show that he was contemporaneous with Shamshi-Adad I of Assyria. The most probable date for Hammurabi is 1728–1686 B.C. Hammurabi was a strong military leader and an administrative genius. He consolidated the power of his dynasty by defeating Rim-Sin of Larsa and made himself king of all Babylonia. He carried on trade relations with the Mediterranean regions. Hammurabi undertook a codification of the laws of his realm, now known in the famous Hammurabi Code, discovered at Susa. It was probably during his reign that the Babylonian epic known as *Enuma elish,* containing the Babylonian account of creation, was composed; it is actually a long poem glorifying Marduk, the god of Babylon whom Hammurabi made the national god of Babylonia. In this period the Sumerian language ceased to be used except as a sacred language, and the Semitic Babylonian came into general use.

After the fall of the First Dynasty of Babylon, the country was ruled by Kassites from the east for about five hundred years. During their rule the horse, a divine symbol to the Kassites, came into general use. The history of the period is obscure. Following the Kassites came another long period which is little known and during which Babylonia was of little political importance. During the Assyrian (*q.v.*) Empire, Babylonia was largely under Assyrian control, though there were occasional revolts, such as that led by the Chaldean Marduk-apaliddina II (Merodach-baladan of II Kings 20:12–19), in the latter part of the eighth century B.C. Upon the death of Ashurbanipal, the kingship of Babylon was seized by Nabopolassar, a Chaldean. The Chaldeans broke the power of the Assyrians by capturing Nineveh in 612 B.C., and defeating the Assyrians and Egyptians in the Battle of Carchemish (605 B.C.). Nabopolassar died soon after the latter battle and was succeeded by his son, Nebuchadrezzar II (605–562 B.C.), the best-known and strongest of the rulers of the Neo-Babylonian Empire.

Nebuchadrezzar took over the Asiatic lands which had been under the control of Assyria or Egypt (*q.v.*). When the Jews revolted, he invaded Judah, and in 587 B.C. captured Jerusalem and exiled many of the Jews to Babylonia. Most of Nebuchadrezzar's inscriptions describe his building activities. He rebuilt Babylon, with its fortifications, palace, sacred buildings and hanging gardens. The Babylon of Nebuchadrezzar is well-known from the excavations by the Deutsche Orientgesellschaft under R. Koldewey. Nebuchadrezzar was succeeded by his son, Amel-Marduk, 562–560 B.C. (Evilmerodah of II Kings 25:27). The last king of the Neo-Babylonian Empire was Nabonidus (556–539 B.C.). Because this king spent much of his time away from Babylon, the actual rule was often exercised by his son, Belshazzar. The city of Babylon fell without a battle to the army of Cyrus the Persian in 539 B.C., and Babylonia thus became a part of the Achaemenian Empire (see MEDO-PERSIA).

II. Religion: Religion played a very important part in the life of the ancient Babylonians, as is shown by numerous inscriptions and the temples excavated in Babylonian sites. Most of the religious conceptions go back to the Sumerians, but the later religion includes Semitic and other elements in addition to the Sumerian. Babylonian religion was polytheistic, including the worship of thousands of deities. Most of the gods were conceived as being anthropomorphic, at least in historical times. Among the Sumerians the higher gods were thought of as constituting the aristocracy of society, with lower deities and human beings as followers and servants. The gods lived in the temples, which were centers of very widespread influence, since the temples often owned large landed estates and carried on much economic activity. Nearly every city included in its temple complex an imposing ziggurat.

Some of the deities were personifications of elements or forces of nature, such as Anu, god of heaven; Enlil, god of the air; Ea (Sumerian Enki), god of the earth and of wisdom; Shamash (Utu), the sun-god and god of justice; Sin (Nanna), the moon-god; and Adad (Ishkur), god of thunder and lightning. One of the principal goddesses was Ishtar (Inanna), a goddess of the planet Venus and of war and sexual love. Some of the deities were patrons of cities, such as Marduk, god of the city of Babylon (perhaps originally an agricultural deity). Tammuz (Damuzi) was the dying-rising god of mythology, and the god of the pasture. Nergal was ruler of the underworld. There were countless other deities associated with aspects of culture, patrons of individuals, and so on.

The Babylonian temples were centers of elaborate religious rites, in which magic and soothsaying played a prominent role. Sacrifices of animals and of agricultural products were offered. The most important and climactic festival was the New Year's festival, the *akitu*. The festival is very ancient, probably going back to ancient Sumerian times, and it was celebrated in many cities. Its rites are best known for the city of Babylon. In the *akitu* (which lasted twelve days), the *Enuma elish* was recited, the king was humbled before the deity but received the insignia of his office anew from the god, the fates for the new year were fixed by the assembly of the gods, and a sacred marriage was celebrated.

Babylonian religion included the belief in a future life in *Arallu,* which like Hades was a place to which all alike went, but was not a place of retribution.

BIBLIOGRAPHY: L. Delaporte, *Mesopotamia*, 1925; S. A. Pallis, *The Babylonian Akitu Festival*, 1926; Edouard Dhorme, *Les religions de Babylonie et d'Assyrie*, 1945; Alexander Heidel, *The Gilgamesh Epic and Old Testament Parallels*, 1946; idem, *The Babylonian Genesis*, 2nd ed., 1951.

[Sup.] JAMES PHILIP HYATT.

BACK TO GOD HOUR: The denominational broadcast of the Christian Reformed Church (*q.v.*), begun in 1939, employs a full-time radio minister since 1946 and a full-time evangelist since 1950. There is a half-hour radio broadcast weekly over 315 stations of the Mutual Broadcasting System, and a fifteen minute television program on some thirty independent stations. The "Family Altar," a monthly booklet of daily devotions, is distributed. The choir is composed of Calvin College students. The messages present the orthodox Reformed position.

JOHN H. KROMMINGA.

BACON, BENJAMIN WISNER: Congregationalist; d. Feb. 1, 1932. In addition to being Buckingham Professor of New Testament criticism and interpretation at the Yale Divinity School (1897–1932) he was the director of the American School of Archaeology in Jerusalem and Syria (1905–06). His additional publications include: *Beginnings of the Gospel Story* (1909); *The Founding of the Church* (1909); *Commentary on Galatians* (1909); *The Fourth Gospel in Research and Debate* (1909); *Jesus the Son of God* (1911); *Making of the New Testament* (1912); *Theodore Thornton Munger, New England Minister* (1913); *Christianity Old and New* (1913); *Is Mark a Roman Gospel?* (1919); *Jesus and Paul* (1920); *The Teaching Ministry for Tomorrow* (1923); *He Opened to Us the Scriptures* (1923); *The Gospel of Mark; Its Composition and Date* (1925); *The Apostolic Message* (1925); *The Story of Jesus* (1927); and *Studies in Matthew* (1930).

[Sup.] RAYMOND W. ALBRIGHT.

BADEN: Part of the province of Wuerttemberg-Baden, Germany. In a population of 2,-811,152 in 1950, 37.9% were Evangelicals, 58.9% Roman Catholics, and 3.2% of other persuasions. All churches are equal before the law.

Since 1821 the Evangelical Church has been a Lutheran and Reformed Union Church (*q.v.*). Together with its 513 congregations, it enjoys autonomy. It is governed by a bishop, provincial synod, and superior church councils. Each congregation has a church council made up of the pastor and of elders elected by the congregation. The congregations are grouped in districts headed by deans, district councils, and district synods. Salaries of clergymen are paid from provincial church taxes; buildings are maintained by taxes raised locally. Relations of church and state are defined in the concordat of 1932.

The Roman Catholics in Baden are subject to the jurisdiction of the archbishop in Freiburg. The relation of the Catholic Church to the state is also defined in a concordat.

See also GERMANY. [Sup.] OTTO FRIEDRICH.

BADER, JESSE M(OREN): Disciples of Christ; b. at Bader, Ill., April 15, 1886. He was educated at the University of Kansas (1905–07) and Drake University (A.B., 1911). After serving as a student pastor for the Disciples of Christ (1905–11) he served the Disciples' church at Atchison, Kan. (1911–18). Following service as a Y.M.C.A. secretary overseas (1918–19) he became a pastor again at Kansas City, Mo. (1919–20). For eleven years he was secretary of evangelism for the Disciples of Christ (1920–31); he became the executive secretary of the department of evangelism of the Federal Council of Churches (*q.v.*) (1931–51) and has been the executive director of the joint department of evangelism of the National Council of Churches (*q.v.*) (1951–).

RAYMOND W. ALBRIGHT.

BAHAISM: The Baha'i cause two decades ago was decreasing in influence in Iran, but is, at present, experiencing remarkable vitality. Some of Iran's finest young people are Baha'is, revealing great missionary zeal and sincerity, but also ignorance of the principles of the religion. As now held, these principles include the establishment of a totalitarian dictatorship over all the world, with governing power concentrated in a House of Justice whose membership is to be limited to acceptable Baha'is.

As at its beginning, the movement has again split into two rival parties. That of Shoghi Efendi, continuing the headquarters of Abdul Baha at Acre (Acca) on Mt. Carmel and at Haifa, now included in the State of Israel, is facing local difficulties with the government.

After Abdul Baha's death in 1921, this group, under Shoghi Efendi as Guardian and authoritative director, promoted first the idea of a Baha'i World Order, then a Baha'i Organization and finally a Baha'i Administration which aimed to have the supreme authority over the National Spiritual Assembly of the Baha'is of the United States and Canada and its hundred or more local Assemblies.

In the nineteen twenties another group of Baha'is, led by Mirza Ahmad Sohrab and others, formed a New History Society, which affirmed the non-organizational character of the religion. The Baha'i Administration excommunicated him, his associates, and the New History Society, but failed in an attempt by a lawsuit, to prevent them from using the term "Baha'i" for themselves and their activities. The same Administration group also excommunicated Shoghi Efendi's cousin and aide, Ruhi Efendi Afnan, even though he also is a great grandson of Baha Ullah, who founded the religion.

In 1948 another difficulty of the Baha'is was disclosed with the private publication of a book by Ruth White, called *Abdul Baha's Questioned Will and Testament*, Beverly Hills, California. This Will, which is the basis of Shoghi's position as Guardian of the Faith, with final and absolute authority residing in himself, is a forgery, says the author.

A summary of Baha' Allah's *al-Kitāb al-Aqdas*, "The Most Holy Book," was published in W. M. Miller's *Baha'ism*, but a full translation into English has not yet been published.

See also BABISM.

BIBLIOGRAPHY: By Baha'is: Mirza Ahmad Sohrab, *Broken Silence*, 1942; *World Order* magazine; *Baha'i World*, year book. By non-Baha'is: J. R. Richards, *The Religion of the Baha'is*, 1932; W. M. Miller, *Baha'ism*, 1931. Articles: "The Baha'i Cause Today," by W. M. Miller, in *The Moslem World*, Vol. 30 (1940), 379–404; "The Spiritual Situation in Iran," by John Elder, in *The Muslim World*, Vol. 38 (1948), 107–109.

[Sup.] EDWIN E. CALVERLEY.

BAHAMA ISLANDS. See WEST INDIES.

BAILLIE, DONALD MACPHERSON: Church of Scotland; b. at Gairloch, Ross-shire,

Nov. 5, 1887. He studied at Edinburgh, Marburg, and Heidelberg; was minister at Bervie (1918–23), St. John's, Cupar (1923–30), St. Columba's, Kilmacolm (1930–34); and has been Professor of Systematic Theology at St. Andrews University since 1935. In theology he occupies a reconciling position between the old liberalism and neo-orthodoxy. He has been active in ecumenical work, especially in the Faith and Order movement. His main publications are *Faith in God* (Kerr Lectures, 1927), and *God was in Christ* (1948).

BAILLIE, JOHN: Presbyterian; b. at Gairloch, Ross-shire, March 26, 1886. He studied at the University of Edinburgh (M.A., 1908; D.Litt., 1928; Hon. D.D., 1930); at New College, Edinburgh; at the Universities of Jena and Marburg. He has been Professor of Christian Theology in Auburn Theological Seminary (1919–27); Professor of Systematic Theology, Emmanuel College, University of Toronto (1927–30); Roosevelt Professor of Systematic Theology in Union Theological Seminary, New York (1930–34); Professor of Divinity, University of Edinburgh (1934–); principal of New College, University of Edinburgh (1950–); convener of Church of Scotland Commission on the Interpretation of God's Will in the Present Crisis (1940–45); moderator of the General Assembly of the Church of Scotland (1943–44); member of Editorial Board of *Religion in Life*. His publications include: *The Roots of Religion in the Human Soul* (1926); *The Interpretation of Religion* (1929); *The Place of Jesus Christ in Modern Christianity* (1929); *And the Life Everlasting* (1934); *A Diary of Private Prayer* (1936); *Our Knowledge of God* (1939); *Invitation to Pilgrimage* (1942); *The Prospects of Spiritual Renewal* (1943); *What is Christian Civilization* (1945); *The Belief in Progress* (1950); *The Human Situation* (1950); *Natural Science and the Spiritual Life* (1951).

BIBLIOGRAPHY: V. Ferm (ed.), *Contemporary American Theology*, 1933.

BAINTON, ROLAND H.: Congregational minister, affiliated member of the Society of Friends; b. at Ilkeston, Derbyshire, England, March 30, 1894. He was brought by his father to Canada in 1898 and to the state of Washington in 1902. He received from Whitman College the degree of B.A. in 1914, and of B.D. and Ph.D. from Yale University in 1917 and 1921. He has been teaching church history at Yale Divinity School since 1920. His chief studies have been in the field of Reformation scholarship. He has written: *Sebastian Castellio Concerning Heretics* (1935); *David Joris* (in German) (1937); *Bernardino Ochino* (in Italian) (1940); *The Church of Our Fathers* (1941); *The Life of George Lincoln Burr* (1943); *The Martin Luther Christmas Book* (1948); *Here I Stand,*

A Life of Martin Luther (1950); *The Travail of Religious Liberty* (1951); *The Reformation of the Sixteenth Century* (1952); *Hunted Heretic, The Life and Death of Michael Servetus, 1511–1553* (1953); *Michael Servet, Hérétique et Martyr, 1553–1953* (1953).

BAKER, OREN H(ULING): Baptist; b. at Alderson, W. Va., on June 10, 1894. He studied at Denison University (Ph.B., 1917), Rochester Theological Seminary (B.D., 1922); and the University of Chicago (Ph.D., 1937). After serving as the assistant principal of the Cabin Creek District High School at Eastbank, W. Va. (1917–18) he was ordained to the Baptist ministry (1919) and became pastor of the First Baptist Church in Morgantown, W. Va. (1922–28); Parsells Ave. Baptist Church, Rochester, N. Y. (1928–35). He has taught applied Christianity and pastoral counselling at Colgate Rochester Theological Seminary (1935– ; dean, 1945–). He was chairman of the conference on the integration of theological education and has been the executive secretary of the American Association of Theological Schools (1951–54). He wrote: *Albert W. Beaven: Pastor, Educator, World Christian.*   RAYMOND W. ALBRIGHT.

BAKHUIZEN VAN DEN BRINK, JAN NICOLAAS: Dutch Reformed; b. at Haskerland, Friesland, May 25, 1896; studied at the University of Leiden (Dr. Theol., 1923), and at the École des Hautes Études at Paris; minister at Nieuw Dordrecht (1920–24), Winterswijk (1924–29), Rotterdam-Kralingen (1929–34); professor of church history and history of Christian doctrine at Leiden (1934); member of the Royal Dutch Academy of Sciences; one of the leaders of the liturgical movement in the Dutch Reformed Church. He wrote: *De Oud-christelijke monumenten van Ephesus* (1923); *Breedevoort tijdens het Anholter pandschap* (1933); *De Romeinsche Catacomben en hare fresco's* (1933); *De Nederlandsche Belijdenisgeschriften* (1940, textcritical); together with Prof. J. Lindeboom, *Handboek der Kerkgeschiedenis*, 2 vols. (1942–45); *Protestantsche Kerkbouw* (1946); *Traditio in de Reformatie en het Katholicisme in de zestiende eeuw* (1952); editor of the quarterlies *Nederlands Archief voor Kerkgeschiedenis* and *Kerk en Eredienst*.

BALFOUR, ARTHUR JAMES: Philosopher and statesman; b. at Whittinghame, near Edinburgh, July 25, 1848; d. near Woking, March 19, 1930. He was educated at Trinity College, Cambridge. He entered Parliament as a Conservative in 1874; was prime minister, 1902–1905; served in other prominent capacities in public life; and became Earl of Balfour in 1922. His philosophic aim was the defence of Christian theism, negatively in *The Foundations* of *Belief* (1895) and *The Defence of Philosophic Doubt* (1899), and positively in *Theism and Humanism* (1923) and *Theism and Thought* (1922–23).   ANDREW K. RULE.

BANES, DOMINGO: The contrast between the doctrine of Banes and that of Molina (*q.v.*) is to be sought in the problem of God's co-operation with man in the process of salvation through grace. Banes emphasized very strongly the omnipotence of God, as well as his determination to control all events; while Molina laid equally great emphasis upon man's free will. This problem in the Roman Catholic Church may be treated in any manner not opposed to the teachings of the Bible, since there is no official doctrine on the subject. But many Roman Catholic authorities have reasoned that Banes did not follow the well-recognized doctrine of authentic Thomism. In order to indicate this, his doctrine is not recognized as Thomistic but as Banesianistic.

BIBLIOGRAPHY: G. Manser, *Das Wesen des Thomismus,* 1935; M. Lepée, *Banez et Ste. Thérèse,* 1947.
[Sup.] MATHIAS GOOSSENS.

BANKS, LOUIS ALBERT: D. June 17, 1933. After serving as an evangelist in union evangelistic meetings after 1911, he concentrated most of his efforts after 1913 in the temperance movement. He was a national lecturer for the Anti-Saloon League of America and also for the World Prohibition Movement (1913–33). Among his later books are: *Live Boys in Oregon* (1897); *The Christ Brotherhood* (1897); *Heroic Personalities* (1898); *The Christian Gentleman* (1898); *John and His Friends* (1899); *My Young Man* (1899); *A Manly Boy* (1900); *Capital Stories of Great Americans* (1905); *Spurgeon's Illustrative Anecdotes* (1906); *The Problems of Youth* (1909); *The World's Childhood* (1910); *The Great Themes of the Bible* (1911); *Ammunition for the Final Drive on Booze* (1917); *The Winds of God* (1920); *The New Ten Commandments* (1922); *Wonderful Bible Conversions* (1923); *Dramatic Stories of Jesus* (1924); *Bible Soul Winners* (1924); *Christ's Soul Searching Parables* (1925); and *Sermons for Reviving* (1928).
[Sup.] RAYMOND W. ALBRIGHT.

BANNS: The public announcement of a prospective marriage to be made by the rector of the parish in which the marriage is to be celebrated. According to modern Roman Catholic discipline, the banns must be read in the church on three consecutive Sundays or feasts of obligation, unless a dispensation intervenes, which the bishop may grant at his own discretion. Canon law empowers bishops to substitute for the reading of the banns the posting of the list of prospective marriages at the entrance of the church on eight consecutive days, two Sundays or feasts

of obligation being included. No banns are to be published in the case of mixed marriages.
[Sup.] GEORGES A. BARROIS.

BAPTISMAL SERVICE: Older controversies about the mode of baptism have largely died away. Believers in immersion as biblical hold their ground, and keep winning adherents, the majority of whom do not look on this mode as essential to salvation. Some Baptist churches admit to membership persons baptized in other ways. Instead of infant baptism, such churches in growing numbers have public services for dedication of infants to God. On the other hand, many churchmen who practice sprinkling, for infants and adults, do so because they believe in the guidance of the church through the Holy Spirit, and not because of a clear warrant from the New Testament. During the past decade or two these matters have assumed new prominence, practically, rather than controversially. On the mission field among newer churches, baptism means a complete break with the past and the beginning of a new life in Christ. As these newer churches have grown stronger they have begun to share with older bodies a sense of baptism as close to the heart of Christianity. On the Continent, also, theologians have in a sense rediscovered Christian baptism. For example, Karl Barth and Oscar Cullmann call on the church to make more out of what in some quarters has become largely a matter of form. About many aspects of baptism, theoretically, such churchmen differ widely, but the majority would agree, practically, that it symbolizes cleansing from sin, uniting with the church, and beginning a new life in Christ. They also insist that pastors and local churches take measures to put baptism in a place of prominence almost equal to that of the Lord's Supper. Why call the latter "The Sacrament," as though there were only one? Details must differ, according to the history and traditions of the local church. Everywhere the ideal calls for sermons about Holy Baptism, not in its controversial aspects, but in its central meaning and glory; more careful instruction of boys and girls in "communicants' classes"; more faithful preparation of adults about to be baptized, and parents about to present their little ones; and solemnity in performing this holy rite so that it will become a memorable part of Christian experience, both for those being baptized and for all who share in the service. For many reasons baptism ought normally to be administered in the church proper, and at a climactic stage of public worship. These ideals call for a new kind of training in practical liturgics by every school of theology.
ANDREW W. BLACKWOOD.

BAPTISTS: Since 1900 wars, nationalistic uprisings in Africa and the Orient, and totalitarian ideologies have combined to unsettle church life, particularly in Europe and among the younger churches on mission fields. Within the churches there also have been tensions arising from theological dissension, from differences in polity and social outlook, and from the blighting influence of secularism (q.v.).

I. British Baptists: In Great Britain, Baptists have maintained a steady leadership among nonconformists as members of the National Free Church Council. At the same time the Baptist Union of Great Britain and Ireland has strengthened its denominational leadership. This organization, although purely advisory in its relation to the churches, became a strongly centralized organ to maintain the efficient co-operation of twenty-seven Baptist Associations under the direction of John Howard Shakespeare, its secretary for more than twenty-six years.

In the face of an emerging ecumenical movement (q.v.), Baptists have maintained a steady witness. In 1920 when the Lambeth Conference (q.v.) of Anglican bishops appealed to all Christian people to consider the subject of church union, the Baptist Union expressed willingness to engage in a federation of equal and autonomous churches, but not in a union which would compromise the Baptist democratic view of the church and its ministry. Twice since then it has reaffirmed this position: in 1929 and 1949.

During World War II, 60 Baptist churches were demolished, 680 damaged. Through a Reconstruction Campaign funds were raised for rebuilding and repairs. Part of the amount was donated to German Baptists for the rehabilitation of their churches. In 1942, in the midst of war, English Baptists contributed a total of £157,677 to support their foreign missions in the Belgian Congo, India, China, and Jamaica, and 257 young people volunteered for foreign missionary service.

Canadian Baptists also have strengthened their witness by establishing a co-ordinating agency for their churches in 1944, called the Baptist Federation of Canada. The Canadian Baptist Foreign Mission Board, organized in 1912, supervised foreign missions in South India and South America.

Baptist work in Australia and New Zealand is still in a pioneer state. The number of Baptists has increased since 1900 from 12,000 to more than 31,000 members. In New Zealand the Baptist membership is over 9,000, but only about 1% of the population.

II. European Baptists: Perhaps nowhere are Baptists bearing a witness at so costly a price as in Europe. Yet they may be found—minorities, to be sure—in nearly every country. Their cause has been supported by Baptists of Great Britain and America. To consolidate and strengthen the Baptist witness in spite of persecution on nearly every hand, the European Baptist Federation was organized in Zurich, Switzerland, in 1949.

III. American Baptists: In the United States, Baptists reflected, at the opening of the twentieth century, much of the concern for greater efficiency of operation which characterized big business. It is not surprising, therefore, to find those of the states north of the Mason-Dixon Line organizing the Northern Baptist Convention in 1907 at Washington, D. C., a corporation with restricted powers to which the churches sent their representatives each year. The national agencies, the state conventions, and the city mission societies remained intact, although affiliated by voluntary action. They relinquished only a degree of self-determinism in the co-operative plan of raising and distributing funds with a unified budget. During the first fifty years of the Convention's existence, changes were made from time to time in its structure in the interest of efficiency and to allay fears that it represented a degree of centralization unbecoming the democratic polity of Baptists. In 1950 its name was changed to the American Baptist Convention, and the office of general secretary was created.

Within the Convention are thirty-four state conventions, sixteen Baptist city societies, thirteen theological seminaries, three training schools for girls, eleven academies, six junior colleges, twenty-nine colleges and universities, eighteen homes for orphaned children, twenty-two institutions for the aged, and six hospitals. Through these agencies and institutions 1,561,073 Baptists in 6,768 local churches co-operatively support missionary, educational, and social service enterprises.

Through the American Baptist Home Mission Society and the Woman's American Baptist Home Mission Society, work is maintained in thirty-four states, Alaska, Central America, Cuba, El Salvador, Haiti, and Puerto Rico. Foreign mission stations are maintained by the American Baptist Foreign Mission Society and the Woman's American Baptist Foreign Mission Society in Burma, Assam, India, China, Japan, the Belgian Congo, and the Philippines through a staff of 376 missionaries.

The Southern Baptist Convention, the largest single body of Baptists in the world, was composed in 1950 of 7,079,889 members in 27,788 churches. Unlike Baptists of the North, the Convention functions through denominational boards for home and foreign missions, Sunday school work, and ministerial relief. The Home Mission Board maintains work in Southern states, in Alaska, Cuba, Costa Rica, Panama, and the Canal Zone. The Foreign Mission Board supports 700 missionaries in twenty-two countries and three continents. The Sunday School Board provides literature for over 4,500,-000 pupils in nearly 26,000 Sunday schools. A marked degree of denominational solidarity is maintained through such training of laymen and through the program of five theological seminaries which are supported and controlled by the Convention. Southern Baptists also support thirty colleges, twenty-three junior colleges, eight academies, twenty-nine hospitals, and twenty orphanages.

Both conventions have national conference centers for the training of leadership and for inspirational gatherings. The American Baptist Assembly, founded in 1944, is located at Green Lake, Wis. In the same year, a conference center at Ridgecrest, N. C., came under the administration of the Sunday School Board as the Southern Baptist Assembly.

The two conventions co-operate along with the two conventions of Negro Baptists in the Baptist World Alliance (*q.v.*) and in the Baptist Joint Committee on Public Affairs. The latter agency was created in 1938 to give expression to Baptist views on religious liberty and separation of church and state. Headquarters are maintained in Washington, D. C.

Negro Baptists, who number approximately 7,000,000, are organized in two major bodies: the National Baptist Convention of the United States of America, Incorporated, and the National Baptist Convention of America. They are thus divided because of a division which occurred in 1915–16 over a dispute concerning convention control of property and publications. The latter body, although the smaller (2,645,789 members in 10,851 churches), by court action retained the original name and so dates its origin from 1895. The former body is the larger (4,445,605 members in 25,350 churches), and was incorporated in 1915 under the laws of the District of Columbia.

Negro Baptists conduct missions in Africa and assist needy churches and schools in the United States. They are aided in support of their educational institutions by the American Baptist Home Mission Society and the Home Mission Board of the Southern Baptist Convention. Their significance in American life is appreciable, for they comprise one-half of the total number of Negroes in America; moreover, their church life offers a significant opportunity for growth that comes from participation in a democratic group life.

Since 1900 Baptists have made some notable strides forward in leadership among their fellow Christians. Perhaps first and foremost has been their pronounced evangelistic program, which has been notable on the mission fields. Through a policy of developing and training national leaders, the mission boards have helped to establish in various countries churches which are now or are becoming self-supporting and self-governing.

In the United States the Southern Baptist Convention has enjoyed a remarkable increase of 4,000,000 members within a single generation. This has been made possible by a number of factors: (1) a continual program of vigorous evangelism; (2) the strong appeal which simple biblical preaching holds for the rank and file of Americans; (3) their success in holding the allegiance of rural people who move to town; and (4) an intense sense of mission. In the North, where Baptists have been confronted by the deterring factors of an urban and highly industrialized society, the gains have been less spectacular.

In the field of Christian education, Baptists have given notable leadership in the institution of the plan for uniform Sunday school lessons in 1871 and of the Graded Lessons Series in 1909. The Daily Vacation Bible School Movement was inspired between 1898 and 1901 by two Baptists, Mrs. Walker Aylett Hawes and Robert G. Boville, of New York City. In a similar manner, the idea of a Cradle Roll connected with Sunday schools was introduced in the Central Baptist Church of Elizabeth, N. J., by two sisters, Mrs. Alonzo Pettit and Miss Juliet E. Demock, between 1877 and 1884. After 1906 the idea of enrolling infants in the church school and collecting pennies for their birthdays to be used for missions, which had spread among Baptists, was taken up by other denominations. Baptists were also first to develop and complete a three-year series of Christian Camping materials for junior, junior-high, and senior grades.

The Baptist Church School Advance, developed in 1940, inspired the interdenominational enterprise known as the United Church School Advance. The Baptist program of "Winning the Children for Christ," which was inaugurated in 1943, has been very influential also. In 1951, Baptists held three offices in the executive direction of the Division of Christian Education of the National Council of Churches of Christ in America.

The social concern of Baptists has grown apace and perhaps, in some cases, gone ahead of that of some denominations, although, to be sure, it has lagged behind the interest and activism of others. Perhaps because of the pressure of urban and industrial problems in the North and East, leaders in the American Baptist Convention have manifested a more progressive outlook than those in the Southern Baptist Convention, where the economy has been more prevailingly rural. However, there, too, a gradual transition has been taking place as the cultural and economic life of the South has undergone change. At the same time, it should be observed that many Baptist churches, both North and South, have become more middle-class in social and economic status. This has meant, in some quarters at least, the lessening of the appeal of Baptists to the plain people with whom they have usually been associated. This phenomenon, however, is more characteristic of other denominations in the United States than of Baptists. In the meantime, the neglected plain people are open to the appeal of Christians of the holiness and pentecostal sects with whom they have a close cultural affinity.

Baptists have maintained a steady opposition to support of sectarian instruction in public and private schools by tax funds, and have led in recent years in the protest against diplomatic representation of the government at the Vatican (q.v.). Their position in defense of separation of church and state has been consistent and inviolable.

BIBLIOGRAPHY: Source materials are available in several collections throughout the country, information concerning which may be secured from the American Baptist Historical Society, Upland Avenue, Chester, Pa. For secondary studies see: Robert A. Baker, *Relations Between Northern and Southern Baptists*, 1948; Henry Cook, *What Baptists Stand For*, 1947; William R. McNutt, *Polity and Practice in Baptist Churches*, 1935; Robert G. Torbet, *A History of the Baptists*, 1950; A. C. Underwood, *A History of the English Baptists*, 1947; Henry C. Vedder, *A Short History of Baptist Missions*, 1927.

[Sup.] ROBERT G. TORBET.

BAPTIST STUDENT UNIONS. See STUDENT ORGANIZATIONS, RELIGIOUS.

BAPTIST WORLD ALLIANCE: A world fellowship of Baptists, founded in London in 1905 as a non-legislative union "to promote the spirit of fellowship, service, and co-operation among them, while recognizing the independence of each particular church and not assuming the functions of any existing organization." In 1908 a congress of European Baptists was held in Berlin. Periodically thereafter a congress of the Baptist World Alliance was held: in Philadelphia, 1911; Stockholm, 1923, the meeting scheduled for Berlin in 1916 having been prevented by World War I; Toronto, 1928; Berlin, 1934; Atlanta, 1939; Copenhagen, 1947; and Cleveland, 1950.

Under a series of able presidents (John Clifford, of London; Robert Stuart MacArthur, of New York; E. Y. Mullins, of Louisville; John McNeill, of Toronto; George W. Truett, of Dallas; J. H. Rushbrooke, of London; C. Oscar Johnson, of St. Louis; and F. Townley Lord, of London) and general secretaries (J. H. Rushbrooke, W. O. Lewis, and Arnold T. Ohrn), the Alliance has done much to unite Baptists throughout the world and thereby to create and express a Baptist world consciousness. The Alliance serves as an agency to safeguard religious liberty, to propagate Baptist principles, to assist various Baptist groups in establishing new fields of world service, including relief during periods of war and distress. Through its promotion of regular contacts between Baptists of Europe, Australasia, Africa, Asia, Canada, and the United States, the Baptist witness has been preserved in the face of totalitarianism

and tragic persecution prior to, during, and since World War II.

BIBLIOGRAPHY: Baptist World Congress, *Proceedings*, 1905–50; Robert G. Torbet, *A History of the Baptists*, 1950.

ROBERT G. TORBET.

BAPTIST YOUNG PEOPLE'S UNION. See YOUNG PEOPLE'S SOCIETIES.

BAR KOKBA: There is no hint that Bar Kokba pursued any selfish end by his acceptance of the Messianic title. His name may have had a very natural derivation. Graetz believes it to be more correctly spelled Bar-Kosiba from the town of Kosiba.

Though all accounts speak of his enormous physical strength none of these accounts attribute any miracles to him. His influence was so great, however, that Samaritans and some heathens joined Jews in a common attempt to throw off the Roman yoke. Jewish Christians alone refused to take part in the war. Regarded as renegade Jews, they were persecuted severely. It is clear, however, that Bar Kokba feared their growing influence, and it was during this period that it was made legal for Jews to pronounce the name of God, IHW, and even to use this sacred name in greetings.

In spite of natural exaggeration, extant accounts indicate that Bar Kokba's revolt met with unusual success at first. As evidence of this it is reported that Tinnius Rufus, governor of Judaea, in one year gave up 50 fortified places together with 985 cities and villages to the rebels. At the height of the revolt the rebellious Jews appear to have controlled all of Judaea, Samaria, and Galilee. So serious at one time was the military situation that Hadrian in his message to the Senate, when mentioning this conflict, omitted the usual formula "Both I and my army are well."

The two most important causes of this uprising appear to have been: (1) the edict of Hadrian confirming the Domitianic prohibition of castration and adding to it a prohibition of circumcision. The penalty for violation was death. (2) The plans of Hadrian to rebuild Jerusalem, naming it Aelia Capitalina and to erect an altar to Zeus on the site of the Temple.

BIBLIOGRAPHY: Heinrich Graetz, *History of the Jews*, 6 vols., 1898; Max Margolis and Alexander Marx, *A History of the Jewish People*, 1927; W. O. E. Oesterley, *A History of Israel*, 1932; Abram Sachar, *A History of the Jews*, 1930; *Ancient Hebrew Arts* (coins of Bar-Kokba), 1950.

[Sup.] CARL HAMILTON MORGAN.

BARLAAM AND JOASAPH: The doubts formerly cast by Zotenberg on the correctness of the attribution of the familiar form of the Greek text of this work to John of Damascus are now seen to be largely unfounded, so the new edition of Boissonade's text in the Loeb Classical Library entitles it, *St. John of Damas-*

cus; Barlaam and Joasaph with an English translation by the late G. R. Woodward and H. Mattingly (1937). The numerous Oriental versions of the tale, however, do not all go back to a Greek original, so that the problem of the source from which they and John himself drew the material still awaits investigation. The Ethiopic version was published by Sir E. A. Wallis Budge, *Barlaam and Yewasef, being the Ethiopic version of a Christianized Recension of the Buddhist Legend of the Buddha and the Bodhisattva* (1923), but we still lack adequate texts of the other Oriental versions.

[Sup.] ARTHUR JEFFERY.

BARMEN, THEOLOGICAL DECLARA-TION OF. See GERMANY, I.

BARNES, GEORGE EMERSON: Presbyterian; b. at Hersey, Mich., May 26, 1882; d. at Philadelphia, Dec. 29, 1948. He studied at the University of Montana (B.A., 1902); Oxford (Rhodes Scholar, 1904–7). He was minister at Coldwater, Battle Creek and Flint, Mich. (1907–22) and Overbrook, Philadelphia (1922–48). Theologically a liberal with conservative tendencies, he was greatly respected for his capacity for leadership and beloved for his friendly eagerness to be helpful.

ALEXANDER MACKIE.

BARON, SALO WITTMAYER: Jewish; b. at Tarnow, Austria, May 26, 1895. He studied at the University of Vienna (Ph.D., 1917; Pol. Sc. D., 1922; Jur. D., 1923) and the Jewish Theological Seminary in Vienna (ordained rabbi, 1920). He taught at the Juedisches Paedagogium in Vienna (1919–25); served as professor of history (1926–30) at the Jewish Institute of Religion, New York; and has occupied the chair of Jewish history, literature and institutions at Columbia University (since 1930); director of the newly established Center of Israeli Studies at Columbia (1950–). He served at the Conference of Jewish Relations (president since 1941); American Academy for Jewish Research; National Jewish Welfare Board (chairman, Commission on Survey, 1946–48); and Jewish Cultural Reconstruction (president since its foundation in 1948). His principal publications include: *A Social and Religious History of the Jews* (3 vols., 1937; rev. ed., Vols. I-II, 1952); *The Jewish Community: Its History and Structure to the American Revolution* (3 vols., 1942); and *Modern Nationalism and Religion* (1947). He has also served as editor of the quarterly *Jewish Social Studies* (since 1939); of *Essays on Maimonides* (1941); and of memorial volumes in honor of George A. Kohut (1935) and of Morris R. Cohen (1951).

BARONIUS, CAESAR: His *Annales* have a double purpose: (1) primarily to serve his church by opposing the teachings of the Centuriators, and (2) to present purely historical facts. But he used the second to bolster the first, since he tried to show that the Centuriators were wrong in alleging that the Roman Catholic Church since the seventh century has been a deviation from the early church. He failed to meet the latter on their own ground.

BIBLIOGRAPHY: P. Polman, *L'Element historique dans la controverse religieuse du XVIe siècle*, 1932; A. Mollen in *Dist. d'hist. et géogr. eccl.*, Vol. VI (1932), 871–882.

[Sup.] MATHIAS GOOSSENS

BARROIS, GEORGES A.: B. at Charleville, France, Feb. 17, 1898. He entered the Dominican Order and studied at the College of Le Saulchoir, Tournai, Belgium. Ordained in 1923, he taught Archaeology and Old Testament Exegesis at the *Ecole Biblique,* Jerusalem, and at the Dominican College, Etiolles, France (1925–39). Converted to Protestantism, he became a Presbyterian minister (1942) and is associate professor at Princeton Theological Seminary. He wrote: *Arslan Tash* (as coauthor) (1931); *Precis d'Archeologie Biblique* (1935); *Manuel d'Archeologie Biblique,* Vol. I (1939), Vol. II (1952).

BARROWS LECTURESHIP: Founded at the University of Chicago in 1894 by Mrs. Caroline E. Haskell and named for John Henry Barrows, Chicago minister whose "catholicity of spirit and prolonged, laborious devotion gave to the Parliament of Religions (World's Columbian Exposition, 1893) in so large a measure its remarkable success." The lectures are given by leading Christian scholars of the world and are intended to present to the scholarly and thoughtful people of India the great truths of Christianity and its harmonies with the truths of other religions.   W. V. MORGENSTERN.

BARTH, KARL: Swiss Reformed; b. at Basel, May 10, 1886. He studied at the universities of Bern, Berlin, Tuebingen, and Marburg; was assistant editor of *Die Christliche Welt* (1908); minister in the German Reformed Church in Geneva (1909); minister in Safenwil (1911–21); professor at Goettingen (1921–25); professor at Muenster (1925–30); professor at Bonn (1930–35) until expelled by Hitler; since 1935 professor of theology at Basel.

Barth has been the acknowledged leader of the "theology of crisis," the "dialectical theology," or "neo-orthodoxy" (*q.v.*), a movement that sought to recall Protestant theology from its nineteenth century alliance with immanental philosophy to a biblical basis. This development has also stressed the Reformation confessions, although Barth's criticism of Calvin's views on predestination and eschatology prevent its being called "neo-Calvinism." The many revisions of the *Roemerbrief* show his own transition from Kierkegaardian existentialist categories (see EXISTENTIALISM) to a "theology of the pure Word of God." His dogmatic volumes, now in mid-course, have covered the doctrines of revelation, of God as Trinity, of creation, election, and freedom. He early battled with E. Brunner (q.v.), denying his natural revelation, and with Gogarten (q.v.) over the theology of the state. He was a leader in the German church struggle with Hitler and provided by his influence the theological rationale for the Barmen (q.v.) Confession, the anchor-point of the German Confessing Church. His more important works include: English translations: *The Romans* (1919); *The Word of God and the Word of Man* (1928); *The Christian Life* (1931); *Theological Existence Today* (1933); *Come Holy Spirit* (1933); *The Resurrection of the Dead* (1933); *God's Search for Man* (1935); *Credo* (1935); *God in Action* (1936); *Doctrine of the Word of God*, Vol. I (1936); *The Holy Ghost and the Christian Life* (1938); *Church and State* (1939); *The Knowledge of God and the Service of God* (1939); *This Christian Cause* (1941); *The Church and the War* (1944); *"NO" in Natural Theology* (1946); *Dogmatics in Outline* (1949); *Teaching of the Church Regarding Baptism* (1948); *Prayer* (1952). Untranslated: *Erklaerung des Philipperbriefs* (1927); *Fides Quaerens Intellectum* (1932); *Die Protestantische Theologie im 19. Jahrhundert* (1947); *Christliche Ethik* (1946); *Die Christliche Lehre nach dem Heidelberger Katechismus* (1948); *Die Kirchliche Dogmatik*, Vol. I: *Die Lehre vom Wort Gottes* (two parts), Vol. II: *Die Lehre von Gott* (two parts), Vol. III: *Die Lehre von der Schoepfung* (four parts).

BIBLIOGRAPHY: F. W. Camfield (ed.), *Reformation Old and New*, 1947; J. McConnachie, *The Significance of K. Barth*, 1932, and *The Barthian Theology and the Man of Today*, 1933; W. Pauck, *K. Barth, Prophet of a New Christianity*, 1931.

WILLIAM J. WOLF.

BARTHOLOMEW OF BRAGA: At the Council of Trent he played an important part in the preparation of the canons which dealt with the reformation of the higher and the lower clergy. His book, *Stimulus pastorum ex sententiis Patrum concinnatis, in quo agitur de vita et moribus episcoporum aliorumque praelatorum*, bears reference to this work. The first edition was put through the press in Rome in 1564 by S. Carolus Borromaeus.

BIBLIOGRAPHY: Quétif-Echard, *Scriptores Ordinis Praedicatorum*, Vol. II; F. de Almeida, *Historia de Igreja em Portugal*, Vol. III, 1915.

[Sup.] MATHIAS GOOSSENS.

BARTON, GEORGE AARON: D. June 28, 1942. He was professor of biblical literature and Semitic languages at Bryn Mawr College (1891–1922); professor of Semitic languages and history of religions at the University of Pennsylvania (1922–32); and professor of New Testament literature and language in the Divinity School of the Protestant Episcopal Church in Philadelphia (1921–37). He was an acknowledged minister of the Society of Friends (Orthodox) (1879–1918) and was ordained in the Protestant Episcopal Church in 1918. He served as the director of the American School of Oriental Research in Baghdad (1921–34). Among his later publications are: *The Haverford Library Collection of Cuneiform Tablets or Documents from the Temple Archives of Telloh* (Part II, 1909; Part III, 1914); *Ecclesiastes* (in *I.C.C.*, 1908); *The Heart of the Christian Message* (1910; 2nd ed., 1912); *Commentary on Job* (in "Bible for Home and School") (1911); *The Origin and Development of Babylonian Writing* (1913); *Sumerian Business and Administrative Documents from the Earliest Times to the Dynasty of Agade* (1915); *Archeology and the Bible* (1916; 7th ed., 1937); *Religions of the World* (1917; 4th ed., 1937); *Miscellaneous Babylonian Inscriptions—Part I, Sumerian Religious Texts* (1918); *The Religion of Israel* (1918; 2nd ed., 1928); *Jesus of Nazareth, a Biography* (1922; tr. in Japanese and Korean, 1938); *Hittite Studies* (No. 1, 1928; No. 2, 1932); *Studies in New Testament Christianity* (1928); *The Royal Inscriptions of Sumer and Akkad* (1929); *A History of the Hebrew People* (1930); *Semitic and Hamitic Origins, Social and Religious* (1934); *Christ and Evolution* (1934); and *The Apostolic Age and the New Testament* (1936). He also wrote for many dictionaries, encyclopedias, and religious journals.

[Sup.] RAYMOND W. ALBRIGHT.

BARTON, WILLIAM ELEAZER: D. Dec. 7, 1930. He was pastor of First Congregational Church, Oak Park, Ill. (1899–1924). In addition to serving as associate editor of *Bibliotheca Sacra*, he was editor of the pastor's department of *The Advance* (1904–12; editor-in-chief, 1913–17). He also served on the staff of *Youth's Companion* (1900–17; 1925–30). He was lecturer on applied practical theology in the Chicago Theological Seminary (1905–09; on ecclesiastical law, 1911–24; trustee, 1900–10). He also lectured on biographical leadership and practical theology at Vanderbilt University (1928–30). He was a delegate to fourteen triennial national councils of the Congregational Churches, the secretary of its commission on polity and principal author of its Kansas City Creed (1913). He was also a delegate to the International Council (1899–1930) and the author of its Constitution (1920). He was a careful student of Lincoln and wrote much about him in his later years. Among his additional books are: *Life in the Hills of Kentucky* (1899); *I Go A-Fishing* (1901); *Four Weeks of Family Worship* (1906); *His Last Week, His Life, His Friends, His Great Apostle* (1906–07, with Sydney Strong and Theodore G. Soares); *Pocket Congregational*

Manual (1910); *The Law of Congregational Usage* (1915); *Congregational Creeds and Covenants* (1917); *The Parables of Safed the Sage* (1917); *Wit and Wisdom of Safed the Sage* (1919); *Safed and Keturah* (1921); *The Life of Clara Barton* (1921); *More Parables of Safed the Sage* (1923); *Fun and Philosophy of Safed the Sage* (1925; these books about "Safed" were largely reprints of his syndicated column in the *Christian Century* published anonymously over the signature "Safed the Sage"); *My Faith in Immortality* (1926); *The Young Folks' Bible Library* (8 vols., 1911).

[Sup.] RAYMOND W. ALBRIGHT.

BASEL, COUNCIL OF: Pope Martin V had appointed Cardinal Cesarini as the legate for this council, which opened on July 23, 1431. The number of delegates was not large, unlike that at Constance, partly because Pope Eugene IV on December 18, 1431, declared the council dismissed. His act was an error, for he had been poorly informed about the intentions of the men present there. When the papal bull about the removal of the council from Basel to Bologna was read on January 13, 1432, all the members left the room. Three bishops, some abbots, and many doctors had assembled. They declared in an encyclical that they would under the guidance of the Holy Spirit continue their meetings. They were supported by Emperor Sigismund, and by France and Venice. Moreover, the Hussites (see HUS, JOHN) won the campaign against the crusaders sent against them at the request of the pope. Cesarini tried in vain to persuade Eugene IV to withdraw his papal bull. The council renewed the antipapal decrees of the Council of Constance, stating that the council was above the pope. It demanded the personal presence of the pope and the cardinals, and it completed its revolutionary action with the giving of a majority voting power to the doctors in the universities and the lower clergy. The latter counted from 500 to 600 members over against 20 bishops. The whole hierarchy was threatened with dissolution, as Cesarini, Cardinal Cusa (*q.v.*) and others decided that a parliamentary form of government should henceforth rule the church. In 1433 Cusa composed his famous work, *De concordantia catholica,* in which he stated that a general church council had power above that of the pope. On December 15, 1433, Pope Eugene IV withdrew his opposition to the Council of Basel; on June 26, 1434, the council reaffirmed the decrees of the Council of Constance. The pope was deprived of the annates and of other taxes, for which the council provided no substitutes. In the meantime a revolution broke out in Rome, which forced Eugene IV to flee to Florence. He was the twenty-sixth pope who fled from Rome, and the last one before Pius IX.

While Eugene IV resided in Florence the Council of Basel became ever more revolutionary. In 1436 it issued orders for the election of another pope, the appointment of various cardinals and the government of the Papal States, or States of the Church. It gave shabby treatment to the papal legates, but no further breach arose until the question came up whether the Western Church should now unite with the Eastern Church. The latter was in dire straits, as the Ottoman Turks pressed very hard against Constantinople and occupied nearly the whole of the Balkan Peninsula. The leaders in the Greek Orthodox Church were so eager for assistance against the Turks that they willingly signed a statement to the effect that the Bishop of Rome was head of the whole Christian Church. Eugene IV suggested that the Greeks be permitted to meet with the others in an Italian city, since Switzerland was so far away. At the Council of Basel the majority of the members voted against this proposal, largely because they wanted to keep the management of affairs in their own hands. Now it was they who were making a bad mistake. During the twenty-fifth session on May 7, 1437, the majority voted for Basel, Avignon, or a city in Savoy; while a minority voted with the papal legates for Florence or Udine. When the pope sided with the minority group, the council replied by stating that he must within thirty days give an account of his disobedience. Now the pope felt strong enough to call another council which met at Ferrara on January 8, 1438. A minority of the members at Basel left for Ferrara, but Cusa remained, together with Aenea Silvio, the later Pope Pius II. The latter was a distinguished humanist, indicating how much was at stake and how nearly the pope's power was reduced to that of a prime minister in a parliamentary state. He wrote a famous work in which he defended the Council of Basel: *Libellus de generalis concilii auctoritate* (1437).

Early in 1439 the other council removed from Ferrara to Florence, chief center of the Renaissance in Italy. Here in succession were present about 150 bishops of the Western Church, besides Emperor John VII Paleologus and several Greek bishops. The two branches of the Christian Church were formally united, which signified a tremendous victory for Eugene IV. Two main currents now appeared in the Western Church: on the one hand were those who wanted to reduce the power of the papacy and have a general church council rule like a parliament. They had their main support in Germany and France. The others were led by prelates and scholars in Spain and Italy. It was not until the Vatican Council that this question was definitively decided in favor of papal absolutism.

In Basel the small group remaining went farther and farther in the direction of open rebellion against the papacy. Led by Cardinal d'Aleman, archbishop of Arles, who was beatified in 1527 by Pope Clement VII, it elected Amadeus of Savoy as Pope Felix V (1439–49, antipope). The latter, however, found little support outside of Savoy and Switzerland. At first King Alfonsus of Aragon assisted him but soon he did not dare to continue on this dangerous course and ordered his subjects to remove from Basel. With this move on his part the Council of Basel was doomed to an early dissolution. Henry VI of England and Duke Philip of Burgundy supported Eugene IV, while France and Germany adopted a peculiar attitude. They recognized Eugene IV as pope and yet they accepted those decrees passed at Basel which suited them. They did not want a papal schism but naturally wanted to take advantage of an opportunity offered them to increase their national interests at home over against those of the higher clergy. In both France and Germany the reformation of the church became a matter of concern for the national government rather than for the clergy.

Of great importance was the decision on the part of King Charles VII to permit his higher clergy to meet at Bourges and draw up there the Pragmatic Sanction of Bourges (1438), stating that all of the twenty-three decrees passed at Basel for the reformation of the church were henceforth binding upon the clergy in France. A general church council would be considered above the pope in Rome. The levying of papal taxes in France was to be restricted by the royal government, while appointments to clerical positions from now on would be largely under the control of the king. This is the high water mark of Gallicanism (q.v.), which during the period of the Reformation inflicted vast damage upon the papacy and the Roman Catholic Church as a whole. In Germany the seven electors declared themselves neutral, though the archbishops of Cologne and Trier were opposed to Eugene IV, who deposed them. This action increased antipapal feeling in Germany and should be studied in line with the success later obtained by Erasmus (q.v.) and Luther (q.v.). In 1447 Eugene IV made concessions to a number of German princes, who signed concordats (q.v.) with the papal chair. This action ruined the Council of Basel. In 1448 Nicholas V signed the Concordat of Vienna with Emperor Frederick III of the Holy Roman Empire. It remained in force until the act of secularization in 1803.

In 1443 the last session at the Council of Basel was held. This council exerted much influence upon the great universities in that here the professors sided with the lower clergy in desiring to give greater powers to the large body of men who served the church in the lower ranks. It

hurt the papacy far more than the Council of Constance had done. Historically it was also much more important than the latter. Papal authority was now damaged beyond repair, and Luther could some day expect to reap his harvest in German lands. The Elector of Saxony would be quick to see the advantage derived from his support of Martin Luther, in spite of the latter's attack on the system of indulgences. The relation between the pious Catholic who ruled Electoral Saxony and Professor Luther cannot possibly be understood without a careful study of the results obtained at Basel by the enemies of Eugene IV and Nicholas V. The latter were forced to make so many concessions to the French and German governments that henceforth a new era would mark the end of the medieval papacy as a world power in itself, that is, in the realm of politics. The concordats of 1447 and 1448 bear eloquent testimony to the decline of the papacy in the fifteenth century. This decline enabled Frederick the Wise in Saxony to save the life of Martin Luther.

Most important of all was the development of the idea expressed in the term *Cuius regio, illius et religio*, or *Cuius regio eius religio*. Eugene IV emerged victorious because his opponents at Basel impelled him to seek the favor of the secular rulers, which is exactly what Luther also did under similar circumstances. In saving the papal claim to primacy the pope sacrificed something far more valuable, namely the former power to rule the kings of Western Europe through the power over the souls of men.

BIBLIOGRAPHY: J. Haller, *Concilium Basilieense: Studien und Quellen zur Geschichte des Konzils von Basel*, 8 vols., 1896–1936; J. Dephoff, *Zum Urkunden- und Kanzleiwesen des Konzils von Basel*, 1930; J. Toussaint, *Les relations diplomatiques de Philip le Bon avec le concile de Bâle*, 1942; J. Schweizer, *Nicolaus de Tudeschi: Seine Taetigkeit am Baseler Konzil*, 1924; N. Valois, *La crise religieuse du XVe siècle: Le pape et le concile (1418–1450)*, 2 vols., 1909; L. Elliott-Binns, *The History of the Decline of the Medieval Papacy* (1934), pp. 206–215; A. Hyma, *Christianity and Politics* (1939), pp. 60–68; G. Hofmann, *Epistolae pontificiae ad concilium Florentinum spectantes*, Part I, 1940; A. Atiya, *The Crusade in the Later Middle Ages*, 1938; L. Mohler, *Kardinal Bessarion als Theologe, Humanist und Staatsmann*, Vol. I, 1920; G. Hofmann, *Documenta Concilii Florentini de unione orientalium*, 3 vols., Rome, 1935–36. The treatment by L. Pastor in Vol. I of his history of the Popes is antiquated. The same is true of many others.

[Sup.] ALBERT HYMA.

BASIL, SAINT, THE GREAT: Basil's place in monastic history has been profoundly studied in the twentieth century. It is generally agreed that he was the true founder of communal, as distinguished from eremitic, monasticism. As to the relative merit of solitude and society in the achievement of sanctity, with even Aquinas exalting solitude, Basil is decisively for society: he is sure that Christian love demands it. It seems certain enough that he gave to Christian monasticism the rule of the permanent or irrevocable vow, even though in his time the vow could not have the power of legality behind it. Basil's work definitely influenced Benedict (cf. Dom Cuthbert Butler, *Sancti Bened. Regula Monachorum* [1912], p. 197).

For Basil's works, we have four volumes of his letters, in the Greek, with parallel English, done by R. J. Deferrari (1926) (Loeb Classical Library). Also, *The Ascetic Works of Saint Basil*, by W. K. L. Clarke (1925); and Saint Basil, *Ascetical Works*, translated by M. M. Wagner (1950). Questions of authenticity still engage textual scholars. For example, Deferrari gives us Letter VIII (in Vol. I: *Letters*) as if it were authentic, but adds a note to Vol. II in which he accepts R. Melcher's decisive rejection of that long theological epistle.

BIBLIOGRAPHY: D. Amand, *L'Ascèse Monastique de Saint Basile*, 1949; O. Bardenhewer, *Geschichte der Altkirchlichen Literatur*, Vol. III (1923), 130–162; G. Bardy, "Saint Basile, évèque de Césarée de Cappadoce," in *Dict. de Spiritualité ascetique et mystique*, I (1937); W. K. L. Clarke, *Saint Basil the Great, A Study in Monasticism*, 1913; E. F. Morison, *St. Basil and His Rule*, 1912; J. Pargoire, "St. Basile de Césarée et Basiliens," in *Dict. d'archéologie chrétienne et de liturgie*, II (1910).

[Sup.] JOHN WOOLMAN BRUSH.

BASILIDES AND THE BASILIDIANS: I. The Sources and Their Evaluation: Though Krueger's treatment of Basilidian doctrine cannot today be accepted without extensive qualification, the central problem of evaluation of the sources available for a reconstruction of this important Gnostic system remains. Most scholars, beginning with Neander and Gieseler, have accorded only secondary importance to Irenaeus' exposition, preferring the accounts of Clement and the fragments in the *Acta Archelai*. Quasten (*Patrology*, 1950), however, is content to base his whole description of the doctrine and the movement on Irenaeus' authority. The Hippolytan *Philosophumena* (preferred by Jacobi, Uhlhorn, Baur, and Hort) Salmon and Staehelin, supported by Hilgenfeld, Lipsius, Harnack, and Krueger, believed to have been based upon forged, corrupted, or later Gnostic works foisted upon the unsuspecting heresiologist. For several decades, then, the fragments of the *Exegetica* preserved by Clement and the compiler of the *Acta Archelai* were accepted as the more authoritative sources. Since Peake's critical examination (*ERE*, 1913) of the arguments advanced by Salmon, Krueger, and others against the genuineness of Hippolytus' document, the testimony of the *Philosophumena* can no longer be completely disregarded.

II. The Systems of Basilides: Three more or less diverse Gnostic systems emerge from the three major sources (Irenaeus, Hippolytus, and the *Acta Archelai*). Since none has won universal acceptance, the accounts of Irenaeus and Hippolytus deserve brief review along with that of the *Acta* set forth in Krueger's article.

A. IRENAEUS' ACCOUNT: Irenaeus' résumé of Basilides' teaching outlines a cosmology oriented to the problem of evil and its origin similar to the speculations of Valentinus. From the uncreated and unknowable Father were begun the generations of Nous, Logos, Phronesis, Sophia, Dynamis, and the (according to Clement) Principalities and Angels. These with the Father constituted the first heaven from which in turn emanated other powers constituting other heavens to the number of 365. Of the powers of the lowest heaven the chief was the Archon, the God of the Jews and Creator of the world. To deliver the Jews from destruction at the hands of the pagan nations, God the Father sent his own first begotten Son (Nous) who appeared on earth as a man. Since he could not suffer death, Simon the cross bearer was transfigured into the likeness of Jesus and was crucified in the place of the First Begotten who ascended again to his Father. Man is delivered from the powers of the world by a Gnosis which only two in ten thousand are able to appropriate. Since only souls can be redeemed, bodies are worth nothing and the sins of the flesh may therefore be regarded as a matter of indifference.

B. HIPPOLYTUS' ACCOUNT: Basilides, according to Hippolytus on the other hand, propounded a doctrine not of emanation but of creation *ex nihilo*. The Absolute Being is here described as Pure Nothing and yet as the creator of the Panspermia which contained the germs of all things and the three Consubstantial Sonships. Here the emphasis is upon evolution and ascent rather than emanation and degeneration. The First Sonship being pure ascended to the Father, the Second Sonship being impeded by a gross nature escaped from the Panspermia only with difficulty and by the assistance of a Wing (the Holy Spirit) from the seed and could not rise higher than the region between the world and heaven, becoming at last the firmament. The Third Sonship, immersed in matter, could not escape from the seed but remained in it as the highest of beings beneath the firmament. Finally the Great Archon, second in the world only to the Third Sonship, emerged from the seed and ascending to the firmament thought himself to be the highest God. His son who was superior in wisdom inspired him to create the ethereal universe above the moon. A second archon, emerging from the seed, rose to the limit of this upper world and with the aid of his son created the world below the moon. Now the son of the Great Archon, having been illumined by the Third Sonship strove toward enlightenment. Reaching this he revealed the truth concerning the Supreme God to his Father and to the Son of the second Archon. The end of this process of enlightenment came when the gospel of the Supreme God reached the seed where it descended upon Jesus, the son of Mary, through whom redemption was accomplished at the cost of the Cross. After his resurrection

Christ ascended to the region of blessed sonship followed by the Third Sonship, now purified, who passed beyond to the region of the Supreme God.

III. Criticism and Conclusions: Krueger's account of the fragments of the *Exegetica* preserved in the *Acta Archelai* (Vol. II, p. 1f.) presents a system basically dualistic and apparently influenced by Persian models. It must be noted, however, that this doctrine is introduced by Basilides in these fragments as the wisdom of the barbarians (Persians?) and favorably contrasted with the foolish notions already examined of other peoples. There is no explicit indication in the quotation cited that Basilides himself held this doctrine. His appeal to it could be explained, as Peake points out, in terms of the support it might afford the milder dualism manifest in Hippolytus' exposition of the notion of the seed with its elements of purity and grossness from which emerged the Archon who thought himself to be the Supreme God. Conclusive arguments for the primacy of any one of these sources are not yet at hand. Several tendencies and conclusions of the more recent criticism of all the sources may, however, be noted. Against Quasten, Irenaeus' exposition of the Basilidian Christology with its story of the crucifixion of Simon of Cyrene is generally rejected, as is also any ascription to Basilides or to his son, Isadore, of the opinion that morality was a matter of indifference. Quasten interprets the fragment in the *Acta Archelai* as a refutation of Zoroastrianism rather than an endorsement of dualism. Peake on the other hand points to the dualistic strain in Hippolytus' account but is not convinced that the fragment in the *Acta* at all indicates that Basilides was pledged to a thoroughgoing Persian dualism. Some interest continues in the more remote sources of Basilides' thought, identified with Greek philosophy where Irenaeus is accepted, with Persian cults and cosmologies on the basis of the *Acta Archelai,* and as Hindu and Buddhist from the account of Hippolytus.

BIBLIOGRAPHY: The best text of the *Philosophumena* is Paul Wendland's *Hippolytus Werke* in *Die griechischen christlichen Schriftsteller,* 1916. Studies: H. Windisch, "Das Evangelium des Basilides," *ZNW* (1906); Scott-Moncrieff, "Gnosticism and Early Christianity in Egypt," *Ch. Q.* (1909), 64 ff.; Peake, "Basilides," *ERE,* II (1913) 426 ff.; J. Drummond, *Character and Authorship of the Fourth Gospel,* 1903; Kruger, "Basilides," *PRE* 3rd ed.; P. Hendrix, *De alexandrijnsche haeresiarch Basilides,* 1926; S. Petrement, *Le dualisme chez Platon, les gnostiques et les manichéens,* 1947; J. Quasten, *Patrology* I, 1950.

[Sup.] NOAH EDWARD FEHL.

BASUTOLAND. See AFRICA.

BATAKLAND. See MALAY ARCHIPELAGO.

BATES, MINER SEARLE: Disciples of Christ; b. Newark, O., May 28, 1897. He studied at Hiram College (B.A.); Oxford University (Rhodes Scholar) (B.A., M.A.); Yale (Ph.D.); and Harvard. He served in the Y.M.C.A. of India, Mesopotamia (1917–18). He was supplied by United Christian Missionary Society to University of Nanking, China, as professor of history (1920–50); professor of missions, Union Theological Seminary (1950–   ); adjunct professor, East Asian Institute, Columbia University (1951–   ). He wrote: *Religious Liberty; An Inquiry; Missions in Far Eastern Cultural Relations; Christianity and Communism* (in Chinese); and *Introduction to Oriental Journals in Western Languages* (in Chinese).

BATTISTA VARANO: Blessed; b. April 9, 1458, at Camerino; d. May 31, 1524. Her christian name was Camilla. She was a daughter of Giulio Cesare Varano (not "da Varano") and Cecchina de Malignis. She was educated in all arts of the Renaissance. Her love with Angelo Perotti is not historical. The preaching of Fra Francesco da Urbino converted her in 1479. In 1481 she entered the monastery of Poor Clares at Urbino. She founded a new convent, St. Maria Nova, at Camerino in 1484. She had visions and extraordinary graces. She wrote *I dolori mentali di nostro Signore Gesu Cristo,* an autobiography, *Vita Spirituale* (1491), *Le istruzioni al discepolo* (1501), *Trattato della purità del cuore, Considerazioni supra la Passione,* and other works. Another convent was founded by her in 1505.

BIBLIOGRAPHY: Editions of her works by M. Santoni, 1894; D. Puliti, *Un' asceta del Rinascimento,* 1915; G. Joergensen, *B. Battista Varano,* 1919; D. Aringoli, *La B. Battista Varano,* 1928; *Camilla Batista Varano,* 1943.

WILIBRORD LAMPEN.

BAUDARTIUS, WILLEM: Dutch Reformed theologian and historian; b. Feb. 13, 1565, at Deinse in Flanders; d. Dec. 15, 1640, at Zutphen. In 1585 he went to Leiden, where he matriculated in the newly founded university. In Feb., 1587, he removed to the University of Franeker, where he studied under the famous Hebrew scholar, Johannes Drusius. In Heidelberg he prepared a comprehensive index for the annotations on the Old Testament translation by Junius and Tremellius; his work was published in 1596. April 28, 1593, he went to Leiden, where on May 20, 1593, he enrolled again. He was pastor at Kampen from 1593 to 1596, at Lisse from 1596 to 1598, and at Zutphen from 1598 to 1640. He was buried in the famous Walburg Church at Zutphen.

Baudartius was the chief leader of the Reformation in the County of Zutphen, in which after the conquest of Groenlo by Prince Maurice (1597) the work commenced on a large scale. He was largely responsible for the orderly setting up of congregations in the Classis of Zutphen. In the rest of Gelderland he was also a prominent figure, particularly in the fight against the Remonstrants. In 1615 and 1616 he attended the meetings of correspondence in Amsterdam. In 1610 the Classis of Zutphen adopted under his guidance an ecclesiastical contract which the preachers had to sign and thus accept the confession and catechism of the Dutch Reformed Church. In 1618 he presided over the meeting of the provincial synod of Gelderland, which declared firmly against the Remonstrants and favored his appeal for the calling of a national synod. But he himself was not chosen to represent Gelderland at the Synod of Dordrecht. The latter, however, honored him with the assignment to share with Johannes Bogerman, President of the synod, the task of translating the Old Testament, assisted by revisors. There was a third translator named Gerzon Burems, but he died on Aug. 17, 1631. From May 1, 1626, to the beginning of 1637 Baudartius had to reside with his family in Leiden, in order to do justice to the important translation. Nevertheless he often visited his flock at Zutphen during this period, and he also participated in discussions at the various synodical meetings.

He wrote several books, chiefly semi-popular works dealing with history. In 1610 he published: *Morgenwecker der vrije Nederlandsche Provintien*, in which he recounted the story of persecution and bloodshed perpetrated by the Spaniards in the Netherlands. More valuable, however, was his larger work, *Memorien ofte Kort Verhael der Ghedenckweerdighste geschiedenissen van Nederlandt ende Vrankrijck principalijck*, covering also important events in Germany, Great Britain, Spain, Italy, Hungary, Bohemia, Savoy, Transylvania, and Turkey. The book first appeared in 1620 as a continuation to some extent of Emanuel van Meteren's great historical work. In 1624 the second edition followed, enlarged in two volumes, covering the period from 1603 to 1624. In this edition the author left the tradition established by Van Meteren and added an extensive account of the religious troubles since 1608. It is the most valuable source for the period of the Twelve Years' Truce (1609–21), containing numerous original documents. Defects are evident, such as poor style, one-sided treatment of events, and omission of material that did not please the author. He was a zealous Calvinist, thoroughly convinced that only Calvinism was true to the orthodox Christian faith. This conviction colored his writings and many of his actions.

BIBLIOGRAPHY: A. J. van der Kemp, "Willem Baudart," in *Arch. voor Ned. kerkgesch.*, VII (1899), 225–277; *Biogr. woordenboek van Prot. Godgel. in Nederland*, Vol. I, pp. 349–355; C. C. de Bruin, *De Statenbijbel en zijn voorgangers*, 1937; O. C. Broek Roelofs, *Wilhelmus Baudartius*, 1947.

D. NAUTA.

BAUER, WALTER: Lutheran; b. in Koenigsberg, Aug. 8, 1877. He studied at Marburg (Lic. Theol., 1902), Berlin, and Strasbourg. He taught New Testament at Marburg (1903–13); at Breslau (1913–16); and since 1916 at Goettingen. His chief works include: *Muendige und Unmuendige bei Ap. Paulus* (1902); *Der Apostolos der Syrer* (1903); *Das Leben Jesu im Zeitalter der neuentestamentlichen Apokryphen* (1909); *Ein Handbuch zum N.T.: Johannes evangelium* (3rd ed., 1933); *Die Briefe des Ignatius und der Polykarpbrief* (1920); in *Die Mischna* (Giessen) *Pea* (1915) and *Dammai* (1931); *Der Wortgottesdienst der Aeltesten Christen* (1930); *Die Oden Solomans* (1933); *Rechtglaeubigkeit und Ketzerei im aeltesten Christentum* (1934); *Griechisch-deutsches Woerterbuch zu den Schriften des Neuen Testaments und der uebrigen urchristlichen Literatur* (4th ed., 1952).

RAYMOND W. ALBRIGHT.

BAUMGAERTEL, FRIEDRICH: B. at Plauen, Germany, Jan. 14, 1888. He began his career at Leipzig (1916–22); was professor of Old Testament at Rostock (1922–28); at Greifswald (1928–37); at Goettingen (1937–41); has held this position at Erlangen since 1941, and was rector of Erlangen university (1948–50).

He belongs to the school of Rudolf Kittel (*q.v.*). Being a conservative theologian he strives to connect the results of modern science of the Old Testament with its value as God's revelation.

He wrote: *Elohim ausserhalb des Pentateuchs* (1914); *Die Bedeutung des Alten Testaments fuer den Christen* (1925); *Ist die Kritik am Alten Testament berechtigt?* (1927); *Die Eigenart der alttestamentlichen Froemmigkeit* (1932); *Der Hiobdialog* (1933); *Zur Frage der theologischen Deutung des Alten Testaments* (*Z.f. syst. Th.*, 15 [1938]).

BIBLIOGRAPHY: *ThLZ.* (1947), Sp. 367–368.

ROBERT STUPPERICH.

BAUMGARTNER, WALTER: Protestant; b. at Winterthur, Switzerland, Nov. 24, 1887. He studied at the universities of Zurich (Dr. Phil., 1913), Marburg (Lic. Theol., 1916) and Giessen; assistant for Hebrew (1915); unsalaried lecturer (1916); a.o. professor of Old Testament at Marburg (1920); professor in ordinary at Giessen (1928); at Basel (1929); lecturer for Semitic languages at Zurich (1947–). In theology he is a liberal evangelical. He wrote: *Kennen Amos und Hosea eine Heilseschatologie?* (1913); *Die Klagegedichte des Jeremia* (1916); *Das Buch Daniel* (1926); and *Israelitische und altorientalische Weisheit* (1933).

BAUMSTARK, ANTON: Roman Catholic, orientalist; b. Konstanz, Germany, Aug. 4, 1872; d. Muenster, May 31, 1948; studied Oriental languages at Heidelberg, Leipzig, Rome, and Jerusalem. After various teaching assignments he became professor of Oriental languages at the University of Muenster (1930) and simultaneously at Utrecht, Holland. He founded and edited since 1905 *Oriens Christianus*. His books include: *Aristoteles bei den Syrern vom 5.–8. Jahrhundert* (1900); *Die Messe im Morgenland* (1906); *Die konstatinopolitanische Messliturgie vor dem 9. Jahrhundert* (1909); *Die christliche Literatur des Orients* (1911); *Geschichte der syrischen Literatur mit Ausschluss der christlich-palaestinensichen Texte* (1922); *Nichtevangelische syrische Perikopenordnungen des ersten Jahrtausends* (1921); *Vom geschichtlichen Werden der Liturgie* (1923); *Sacramenta anni circuli* (1927); *Missale Romanum. Seine Entwicklung, ihre wichtigsten Urkunden und Probleme* (1930); he edited *Die Ostkirche betet. Hymnen aus den Tageszeitender byzantinischen Kirche* (4 vols., 1934–37).   OTTO A. PIPER.

BAUSMAN, BENJAMIN: D. 1909. After serving the First Reformed Church in Reading, Pa. for a decade he founded St. Paul's Reformed Church nearby in 1873 and served as its pastor (1873–1909). He also founded and edited *Reformirte Hausfreund* (1867–1909). [Sup.]

BAVARIA: In a total population (1950) of 9,127,000, 71.08% are Roman Catholics, 26.17% Lutherans, about 2% members of smaller religious bodies, and the rest religionless. The increase in population since World War II resulted from an influx of about 2,200,000 refugees (*q.v.*), of whom 790,000 were Lutheran and the rest Catholic.

The Evangelical Lutheran Church in Bavaria, with 2,390,000 members in 1950, ceased being a state church in 1918. In 1920 it adopted a constitution, according to which elders in local congregations elect delegates to a synod which, in turn, elects the bishop. Between synod meetings a superior church council, consisting of fourteen members and headed by the bishop, possesses administrative powers. The territory of the church is divided into five districts, and these into seventy-two deaneries. Religious instruction in public schools has continued without interruption. Under the leadership of Bishop Hans Meiser (*q.v.*) the church stood firmly on its Lutheran confession during the conflict with National Socialism (see GERMANY, I).

Relations between Lutherans and Catholics are generally peaceful. Hundreds of churches were put at the disposal of one communion by the other in order to provide services for refugees who settled in communities not of their confession. Both communions distinguish themselves sharply from the sects, whose propaganda increased after 1945.

See also LUTHERAN CHURCH IN GERMANY, UNITED EVANGELICAL.

BIBLIOGRAPHY: R. Bauerreiss, *Kirchengeschichte Bayerns [im Mittelalter]*, 2 vols., 1949–50; Matthias Simon, *Evangelische Kirchengeschichte Bayerns*, 2 vols., 1942.
[Sup.] WILHELM-FERDINAND SCHMIDT.

BAVO: Alias Allowin; saint; born of a noble family in the vicinity of Namur; died Oct. 1, 653 or 654; buried in Ghent. At first he led a sinful and worldly life, but under the influence of St. Amandus he was converted, entering the services in the Church of St. Peter, founded in Ghent by Amandus. From this center of missionary work he frequently accompanied Amandus on voyages, but a few years later he retired into an abbey. In the calendar the bishoprics of Ghent and Haarlem have been assigned to him. He is the patron of the Church of St. Bavo in Ghent, which houses the famous painting "The Adoration of the Lamb" by the brothers Van Eyck (1432).

BIBLIOGRAPHY: *Vita Bavonis*, ed. Krusch, *Mon. Germ. Hist. Script. rer. merov.*, IV, 527; *ASB*, 1 Oct., 199; L. van der Essen, *Etude critique et littéraire sur les Vitae des Saints mérovingiens de l'ancienne Belgique*, 1907; R. Prodevijn, *Bavo*, 1945.
MATHIAS GOOSSENS.

BAYNES, NORMAN HEPBURN: B. May 29, 1877, in London. He was educated at Eastbourne College and New College, Oxford. He is emeritus professor of Byzantine history in the University of London. He has published: *The Byzantine Empire* (1925); *Israel Amongst the Nations* (1927, 1928); *Constantine the Great and the Christian Church* (1929); *A Bibliography of the Works of J. B. Bury* (1929); ed. with St. L. B. Moss, *Byzantium, An Introduction to East Roman Civilization* (1948); with Elizabeth Dawes, *Three Byzantine Saints* (1948). He was coeditor of Vol. XII of the *Cambridge Ancient History* (1939).

BEACH, HARLAN PAGE: D. March 4, 1933. He was professor of theory and practise of missions at the Yale Divinity School (1906–21); and lecturer on missions at Drew Theological Seminary (1921–28). Among his later publications are: *Renaissant Latin America* (1916); and *Missions as a Cultural Factor in the Pacific* (1927). He was also the coauthor of *World Atlas of Christian Missions* (1911); *World Statistics of Christian Missions* (1916), and *World Missionary Atlas* (1925).

[Sup.] RAYMOND W. ALBRIGHT.

BEATITUDES. See SERMON ON THE MOUNT.

BEATRIX OF NAZARETH: B. about 1200 at Tienen in the old duchy of Brabant. After the death of her mother she learned the elementary Latin grammar from the Beguines (*q.v.*) at Zout-Leeuw. At the age of nine she joined the Cistercians, first as oblata, later as novice. She lived in three abbeys which had been founded through the generosity of her father. The last was known as Nazareth and situated near the town of Lier. At the time of her death on Aug. 29, 1236, she was prioress of the abbey. Her name is honored among the Blessed. In

her *Vita* it is told that she wrote several treatises in the Flemish language, most of them of
an allegorical nature. She described her own
visions, which are very similar to those of
Hadewych (*q.v.*). One of her works has been
preserved, *Van seven manieren van heiliger
minnen* ("Of Seven Ways of Holy Love"). The
text was known, but not the author, until L.
Reypens S.J.; and J. van Mierlo S.J. proved
her authorship.

See also MYSTICISM AND ASCETICISM IN THE
NETHERLANDS.

BIBLIOGRAPHY: Willem van Affligem, "Vita venerabilis
Beatricis quondam priorisse de Nazareth," Chr. Henriquez
O. Cist., ed., in *Quinque prudentes virgines* (1630), pp. 1–177;
Beatrijs van Nazareth, *Seven manieren van minne*, (L. Rey-
pens S.J. and J. van Mierlo S.J., eds.), 1926; same in
modern Dutch, J. van der Kun S.J., ed., 1929.

M. SMITS VAN WAESBERGHE.

BEAVEN, ALBERT W.: Baptist; b. at Mos-
cow, Idaho, Oct. 21, 1882; d. at Rochester, N. Y.,
Jan. 24, 1943. He studied at Shurtleff College
(B.A., 1906) and Colgate-Rochester Divinity
School (B.D., 1909); was minister of Lake Ave-
nue Baptist Church, Rochester, N. Y. (1909–29)
and president of the Colgate-Rochester Divinity
School (1929–43). A liberal churchman and an
ecumenical leader, he was president of Northern
Baptist Convention (1930–31), president of the
Federal Council of Churches (1932–34), vice-
president of the Baptist World Alliance (1934–
39), president of the American Association of
Theological Schools (1940–42). He wrote: *The
Fine Art of Living Together* (1927); *Putting the
Church on a Full Time Basis* (1928); *Fireside
Talks for the Family Circle* (1928); *Sermons for
Everyday Living* (1933); *The Lift of a Far
View* (1936); *The Local Church* (1937); *Remak-
ing Life* (1940).

BIBLIOGRAPHY: Oren H. Baker (ed.), *Albert W. Beaven:
Pastor, Educator, World Christian*, 1944.

WINTHROP S. HUDSON.

BEAVER, ROBERT PIERCE: Evangelical
and Reformed; b. Hamilton, O., May 26, 1906.
He was educated at Oberlin (A.B. and A.M.,
1928), Cornell (Ph.D., 1933), Munich, Yale, Col-
lege of Chinese Studies at Peking, Union Theo-
logical Seminary, and Columbia. He was pastor
of the Evangelical and Reformed Church of
Oakley, Cincinnati (1932–36); Huber Memorial
Church, Baltimore (1936–38); member of China
Mission, Evangelical and Reformed Church
(1938–47; professor at Central China Union
Theological Seminary); professor of ecumenical
Christianity, Theological Seminary, Lancaster,
Pa. (1944–48); director of Missionary Research
Library (1948–); and is lecturer at Union
Theological Seminary and the Biblical Seminary
in New York.

BECHUANALAND. See AFRICA.

BECKET, THOMAS À: Martyr in the Roman Catholic Church; b. in London, Dec. 21,

1117. His relic shrine in Canterbury was the
richest and most famous in all England, made
of pure gold and adorned with precious stones.
Chief among these was the extremely beautiful
ruby, the "Regal of France," given by Louis
VII in 1179. During the reign of Henry VIII
the shrine was torn down; the gold and precious
stones became the property of the royal treasury. Thomas was branded as a traitor because
of his opposition against King Henry II and
his defense of the hierarchy of Rome. The
English parliament prohibited his *officio* and
prayers in his honor. In 1538 his body was
burned and the ashes scattered to the winds.
The great present-day English poet, T. S. Eliot,
devoted a play to him entitled, *The Murder
in the Cathedral* (1935).

BIBLIOGRAPHY: V. H. Hutton, *Thomas Becket, Arch-
bishop of Canterbury*, 1926; S. Dark, *Saint Thomas of
Canterbury*, 1927; H. Prentout, "Thomas Becket et ses
historiens," in *Société bibliographique et critique de
Normandie* (1929), pp. 370–393; T. Bocenius, *St. Thomas
Becket in Art*, 1932; R. Foreville, *L'Eglise et la royauté
en Angleterre sous Henri II (1154–1189)*, 1943; R.
Speaight, *Thomas Becket*, 1940; French ed., 1949.

[Sup.] MATHIAS GOOSSENS.

BECKMANN, JOACHIM: Lutheran; b. at
Wanne-Eickel (Ruhr Area), Germany, July 18,
1901. He studied at the universities of Marburg, Tuebingen, Muenster (Dr. Phil.) and
Goettingen (Lic. Theol.) from 1920–25. He was
pastor of the Innere Mission at Berlin, Wies-
baden and Soest (1926–33); and, since 1933,
pastor of the Evangelical parish at Duesseldorf.
He is cofounder of the Bekennende Kirche
and member of the Reichsbruderrat of the
German Evangelical Church since 1934. Since
1945 he has been a member of the council of the
Evangelical Church in the Rhineland and lecturer (since 1951 professor) on dogmatics and
liturgics at the Kirchliche Hochschule at
Wuppertal. During the conflict of the church
he published numerous pamphlets against the
Nazi Weltanschauung and the so-called Deutsche
Christen. His publications include: *Vom Sakrament bei Calvin* (1925); *Ruf zum Gehorsam*
(sermons) (1941); *Die Kirchliche Ordnung der
Taufe* (1950); *Die Heilsnotwendigkeit der Taufe*
(1951); he is the publisher of *Kirchenagende
fuer evangelische Kirchen und Gemeinden*
(1949) and *Der Gottesdienst an Sonn- und
Festtagen* (1949). Since the annual set 1933/44,
publisher of *Kirchliches Jahrbuch der Evangelischen Kirche in Deutschland*.

BECKWITH, CHARLES MINNIGERODE:
D. April 18, 1928. He was the fourth bishop of
Alabama (1902–28). In addition he wrote:
Rightly Instructed in God's Holy Word (1902).
[Sup.]

BECKWITH, CLARENCE AUGUSTINE:
D. April 2, 1931. He was professor of systematic
theology in the Chicago Theological Seminary

(1905–26). He was editor of the department of theology, philosophy and ethics for *The New Schaff-Herzog Encyclopedia of Religious Knowledge*, and wrote *The Idea of God* (1922).

[Sup.]

BEDE: Died at Jarrow on May 26 or 27, 735 or 736. His relics were brought to Durham during the ninth century, together with those of Cuthbert. The popular title of "reverend" which he received after the year 800 resulted in his canonization by Pope Leo XIII, who on November 13, 1899, gave him the honorary name of Church Teacher, and he extended his feast day to all parts of the Roman Catholic Church. This day was determined on May 27, his day of death. Bede composed the first "historical" *martyrologium,* the original type of all others that followed. It was published in its exact form and contents by H. Quentin in *Les martyrologes histor. du moyen age,* 1908.

BIBLIOGRAPHY: M. Laistner, *Bedae Venerabilis Expositio Actuum Apostolorum et retractio,* 1939; idem (with the collaboration of H. King), *A Handlist of Bede Manuscripts,* 1943; integral text in the *19th Congrès eucharistique 1908,* 1919; Dom. A. Wilmart, "La collection de Bède le Vénérable sur l'Apôtre," in *Revue bénédictine,* 38 (1926), 16–52; P. F. Jones, *A Concordance to the Hist. Eccl. of Bede,* 1929; C. Jones, *Bedae Pseudepigrapha: Scientific Writings Falsely Attributed to Bede,* 1939; R. W. Chambers, "Bede," *Proc. of the Brit. Acad.,* 22 (1936), 129–156; M. T. A. Carrol, *The Venerable Bede: His Spiritual Teachings,* 1946.

[Sup.] E. STOKMAN.

BEDIKIAN, ANTRANIG ARAKEL: Congregationalist; b. May 30, 1885, Constantinople, Turkey. He studied at Robert College (A.B., 1907); University of Chicago (Ph.B., 1913; M.A., 1914; B.D., 1915). He has been minister of the Armenian Evangelical Church of New York (1951–). He has taught at the University of Chicago and at Columbia University in the Department of Indo-Iranian Languages. He has been coeditor of the oldest Armenian weekly, *Gotchnag.* He published in Armenian *Sketches of the Village of Bardizag* (1950).

BEECHER LECTURES ON PREACHING, LYMAN: Founded in 1872 by a gift of $10,000 from Henry W. Sage, of Brooklyn, N. Y., as a memorial to the great divine, Lyman Beecher (*q.v.,* Vol. II), whose name it bears. The income of the fund is used at Yale Divinity School, New Haven, Conn., for an annual series of lectures, most of which have subsequently been published. Lecturers have included Henry Ward Beecher, Phillips Brooks, William M. Taylor, Washington Gladden, J. A. Broadus, Henry van Dyke, George Adam Smith, Lyman Abbott, P. T. Forsyth, Charles E. Jefferson, George Wharton Pepper, William P. Merrill, Harry Emerson Fosdick, W. R. Inge, George A. Buttrick, Earnest F. Tittle, Willard L. Sperry, Charles Clayton Morrison, Ralph W. Sockman, Paul E. Scherer, Reinhold Niebuhr, Henry K. Sherrill, Leslie Weatherhead.

THEODORE G. TAPPERT.

BEETS, HENRY: D. Oct. 29, 1947. He was pastor of the LaGrave Ave. Dutch Reformed Church, Grand Rapids, Mich. (1899–1915); Burton Heights, Grand Rapids (1915–20); secretary and director of missions of the Christian Reformed Church (1920–39): stated clerk of the denomination (1902–42). He was a member of the joint American and Canadian church committee to revise the Metrical Version of the Psalms (1902–9). He was the associate editor of *Gereformeerde Amerikaan* (Dutch Monthly; 1898–1916); editor-in-chief of *The Banner* (1904–29); and editor and publisher of the *Reformed Review* and *Heidenwerld* (1915–40). Among his later books are: *Life of President McKinley* (in Dutch, 1901); *Life and Times of Abraham Lincoln* (in Dutch, 1909); *Triumphs of the Cross* (in Dutch, 1909, 1914); *Compendium of the Christian Religion Explained* (1915, 1919, 1924); *History of the Christian Reformed Church* (in Dutch, 1918); *The Christian Reformed Church, Its History, Work and Principles* (1923); *Student's Compendium of the Heidelberg Catechism* (1925–29); *The Reformed Confession Explained* (1929); *Bible History, Book by Book* (1934); *The Man of Sorrows* (1935); *Johanna of Nigeria* (1937); *Toiling and Trusting, for Indians and Chinese, Fifty Years of Christian Reformed Mission Work* (1940). He also edited and wrote the Preface to A. Kuyper's *Calvinism* (Stone Lectures, 1931); *Van het groote Goed* (1934); *The Christian Reformed Church, its Roots, History, Schools and Mission Work* (1946).   [Sup.] RAYMOND W. ALBRIGHT.

BEGBIE, HAROLD: B. at Farnham St. Martin, Suffolk, 1871; d. at Ringwood Hants, Oct. 8, 1929. Educated at Merchant Taylors' School, he began to farm, then turned to journalism. Soon he was writing novels, children's stories, and biographical studies. Finally he withdrew from journalism and wrote about movements directed towards religious and social betterment. *Broken Earthenware, Other Sheep,* and his greatest work, the two-volume *Life of William Booth,* was concerned with the Salvation Army; *Life Changers* with the movement led by Frank Buchmann. He visited the United States and Russia during World War I. Altogether he wrote nearly fifty books.   F. W. DILLISTONE.

BEGHARDS AND BEGUINES: The origins of the remarkable institution known as the beguinages must be sought in the religious revival of the twelfth century which accompanied the reforms inaugurated by Pope Gregory VII, the crusades, the founding of new monastic orders, and the application of evangelical poverty. In this manner a new era began in the history of Western Europe. The disorders of the period from 450 to 1050 were followed by the building of national states such as France, England, Bohemia, Hungary, and Denmark. At the same time, Italy and the Low Countries stood at the threshold of religious movements which, even now, are not yet fully appreciated and understood.

As a typical phenomenon in this new age may be mentioned the development of the beguinages in which the *mulieres religiosae* lived together without monastic vows, remaining in the world but devoted to divine services. In France they were generally called *papelardae*, in Italy *humiliatae* or *bizzocchae*, in Germany *coquennunnen*, in the Low Countries beguines. Jacob of Vitry remarks: "With such nicknames people tried to deter those who had determined to live in a state of chastity, to make them give up their holy purpose." Many of these pious women and also some men united in groups for the sake of seeking organized forms of religious life. A number of these institutions were characterized by heretical beliefs and practices, for which reason the Fourth Lateran Council in 1215 took steps to curtail the latter. It decreed that henceforth no new religious orders might be founded except in conformity with those already existing.

The beguinages acquired their most lasting and successful institutions in the southern Netherlands, particularly in Flanders. Notwithstanding the prohibition expressed by the Lateran Council, Pope Innocent III in 1216 permitted the beguinages in this region to retain their rules and customs. Among these were the inclination to imitate the monastic life, the principle of seclusion, and the manner in which the women chose to occupy beguinages as a group or sometimes in separate rooms. Other characteristics were the preference for individual poverty and for chastity, the urge to inculcate virtue in others, the numerous works of charity, notably the teaching of the catechism and the care of the sick. Another feature was the practice of providing for their own expenses through the performance of manual labor. In all of these habits the beguines resembled the Sisters of the Common Life, who at one time had more than one hundred houses, modeled somewhat after the beguinages.

The beguines played an important part in the development of personal piety in what is now Belgium. They were noted for their zeal to meditate upon Christ's humanity and his suffering, the Sacred Heart of Jesus and his childhood. Generally known was their adoration of the Eucharist. They were in the vanguard of those who favored frequent communion services and the sacramental processions. Their mysticism was often of a high order.

Among the most distinguished beguines were Mary of Oignies, Odilia of Liége, Margaret of Ypres, Ivette of Hoei, Eva the hermit, Christina of Stommelen, Christina the Wonderful,

Hadewich and her circle. There were also a number of beguines who later joined the Cistercians, including Beatrice of Nazareth, Aleydis of Schaarbeek, Ida of Zoutleeuw, Ida of Louvain, Ida of Nijvel, and Lutgardis of Tongres (Tongeren). In Belgium there occurred a tremendous upsurge of the beguinages after the sixteenth century. But in the Netherlands to the north of the Belgian frontier only Amsterdam and Breda have retained their beguinages.

BIBLIOGRAPHY: Dayton Phillips, *Beguines in Medieval Strasburg: A Study of the Social Aspects of Beguine Life*, 1941. Alcantara Mens O.F.M. Cap., *Oorsprong en betekenis van de Nederlandse Begijnen en Begardenbeweging: Vergelijkende studie 12e en 13e eeuw*, 1947; J. van Mierlo S.J., *Losse beschouwingen over het ontstaan der Begijnen en Begardenbeweging*, in *Ons Geestelijk Erf*, 23 (1949), pp. 121–149, 247–267.

[Sup.] M. SMITS VAN WAESBERGHE.

BEGUINES. See BEGHARDS AND BEGUINES.

BEHAISM. See BAHAISM.

BEING: Being is the basic notion of classical metaphysics and of metaphysical theology. "Being" is an abstract general name (m) covering the uses of the verb "to be"; e.g. of *implication* (n)—"the interior angles of a triangle *are* equivalent to two right angles": it is implied in their being what they are that they should have such a measure; of *existence* (o)—"Here *are* some triangular objects": instances of "triangular object" are to be found here; of *characterization* (p)—"These pieces of cheese *are* triangular": they have that characteristic rather than the characteristic of being square. Plato took (n) as the standard sense of "being"; there is a realm of timeless truth which is necessarily all that it is. Judged by such a standard, the (o) and (p) senses appear defective: particular physical instances of being (o) may or may not be, only are if they are and while they are, and even while they are their being (p) is inconstant, for their characteristics are relative and alterable. They *are* not beings in their own right; they merely *partake in* being. Plato proceeded further to speak of being as such (m) as the common something expressed in all being. So he obtained the hierarchy of conceptions—(m) Being-as-such, (n) the various forms of timeless being, (o,p) the many instances of changeable being.

Plato's thought is ambiguous. His being-as-such (m) can be conceived of either as empty abstraction, related to particular sorts of being as color-in-general to the several actual colors; or as full actuality, related to the special sorts of being rather as full sunlight to the severally colored rays into which the prism breaks it. Plotinus and the Neo-Platonists decided for the second interpretation. Sheer being (m) is the principle and cause from which first the realm of timeless truth (n) and then the realm of contingent existence (o,p) arises by differentiation, and on which both realms constantly depend.

Most of the fathers of the Greek Church, and St. Augustine among the Latin, were deeply influenced by the Neo-Platonic doctrine. But they substituted creation for emanation: the primary Being did not give rise to secondary being by natural extension, but by free choice. The Latin scholastics, notably Thomas Aquinas, carried on this synthesis between the philosophy of being and the doctrine of creation with the aid of Aristotelian ideas. Thomas taught that in God alone essence is really inseparable from existence. From all other essences their existence is separable; and a determining cause, viz., God's will, is required for the putting together of the two, i.e., for the creation of all other beings outside God himself. A biblical basis for the doctrine was found in God's self-description to Moses, "I am what I am."

The theology of being has been criticized in modern times (1) as logically illegitimate, by the antimetaphysicians (Hume, Kant, present-day positivists), (2) as misleading, by metaphysicians who subordinate being to process or life (Hegel, Bergson) and by theologians, mostly Protestant, who accuse it of depersonalizing God. Thomistic and allied theologians, mostly Catholic, defend it on all counts (e.g., Gilson).

AUSTIN FARRER.

BELGIC CONFESSION: This creedal statement of the Reformed faith was drawn up by Guido de Brès (*q.v.*), a minister of the gospel in the southern, French speaking, areas of the Low Countries. He had it ready for publication in 1559. In that year it was carried by Adrian Saravia to Geneva for approval. Upon his return Saravia reported that Geneva had withheld approval, advising the churches of the Low Countries to adopt instead the French Confession, just then coming out. The full reason for Geneva's veto seems to have been withheld from the public. Two years later, as a result of pressures exerted by Godfrey van Wingen, de Brès' colleague, the Confession was printed nevertheless, at Rouen, and in spite of Saravia's remonstrances. This printing had the approval of the Emden church; endorsement by Geneva had not been given nor asked. This first printing occurred while the Reformed churches in the Low Countries were still "under the cross." Consequently it was contraband; and the authorities took steps to have all copies destroyed. At one time the Regent, Margaret of Parma, was able to confiscate two hundred copies at once. For a long time it was thought that not a single copy had survived. Late in the nineteenth century, however, a copy was found by Jonkheer Trip van Zoutlandt. This text was reproduced by J. J. Van Toorenenbergen in his *Eene Bladzijde in de Geschiedenis der Neder-*

landsche Geloofsbelijdenis. At about the same time and quite independently, Pastor Frossard of Lille printed the same text, presumably from another original, in his *Eglise soubs la Croix pendant la domination Espagnol,* referring to it as *Confession de Anvers.* The original was at once translated into Dutch, possibly by van Wingen (poorly done) and printed in 1562. A copy of this translation has also been located. This copy has been reproduced by Dr. A. van der Linde.

In 1566 a new era began for the Reformed churches in the Low Countries. At that time the conspiring nobles began to court the favor of the consistories. This coalition marked the beginning of the Eighty Years War (1568–1648) at the end of which the Reformed churches came out enjoying what was virtually the status of establishment. No sooner was the coalition seriously considered than a revision of the Confession of the Reformed churches was deemed necessary. A synod was held at Antwerp, in 1566, for this purpose. The leading role at this revision synod was played by the youthful Junius (François Du Jon), just twenty-one. He had been encouraged by the nobles to come to the Low Countries and was their special favorite. At this synod subtle changes were introduced, especially in the wording of Article 36 (which deals with the duties of the civil magistrates toward the kingdom of Christ). In this new form the confession was once more submitted to Geneva for its approval, which was received, and the confession was printed there in 1566. A copy of this printing has also been located recently, at Geneva; it gives the text as we have always had it.

The revision did not enjoy unanimous approval in the Low Countries, however. How little a man like van Wingen relished the changes may be gathered from the fact that in the very year of the revision he reprinted the original text. (A copy in the Hulthem Collection, kept at Brussels, under Number 26451). For some decades there was considerable rivalry between the two versions, each having its set of advocates. The controversy on more than one occasion reached the floor of the major assemblies. Gradually the revised version won out, as did the coalitionism that had brought it about. By 1580 the revised version was in undisputed control. In that year the Walloon churches transcribed it on parchment and required all ministers to sign. This parchment is still in existence and in reasonably good condition. The great Synod of Dordt fixed the text, following the revised version. After that the earlier version was a memory, and a not too clear one, until the discoveries mentioned above.

The Belgic Confession has had a serene time in the churches of Dutch background the world over. No major changes have been necessary. An exception to this should be made for Article 36. Over it there has been a great deal of controversy. All churches that feel themselves bound by this creed have had to adjust the wording of Article 36 to fit present-day convictions. The Reformed Church in America has simply recast the article in what was intended to be a translation, so getting rid of the problem. It is to be regretted that when English translation was needed recourse was not had to an already existing English translation, done in the Refugee Church of London in 1640. (In the Knuttel Collectie; the University of Michigan has a copy.) No sooner had the principle of establishment been shaken by the secessions in the Netherlands of the nineteenth century than the secession churches felt themselves out of step with the tenor of Article 36 as the coalitionists had left it. The Gereformeerde Kerken tried to meet the situation by exscinding the "twenty-one objectionable words." Its daughter, the Christian Reformed Church of America, turned the trick by adding a footnote in which the matters confessed in the text were forthwith repudiated. The *Eglise Chrétienne Missionnaire Belge* allows its candidates for the ministry mental reservation at the point. The end of revision is not yet. With the development of Reformed ecumenicity there is need of a revision satisfactory to all churches holding the Belgic Confession.

The Belgic Confession contains thirty-seven articles and follows the same general order as its French rival and contemporary. That the two are not unrelated is evident; but the genetic relation between them is not clear. It has often been said that de Brès simply followed the French Confession as he wrote. But this is an unwarranted assumption. Dependence upon the French creed is nowhere acknowledged; plagiarism was never charged, not even by those who in 1559 tried to obstruct the printing of it. The two are, as we have seen, strictly contemporary. It is wholly possible that de Brès and Antoine Chandieu (the responsible author of the French creed) met and collaborated up to a certain point.

The Belgic Confession was intended to serve a double purpose, to convince the secular authorities that the Reformed people were not of a piece with seditious Anabaptists and to serve as a standard for the nascent Reformed churches. In keeping with the former purpose a letter to the king, Philip II of Spain, was printed before the creed; and a letter to the lesser magistrates followed. These letters, probably also from the hand of de Brès, constitute a noble apology and rise to prophetic heights—worthy of the hero of faith that wrote the Confession. As early as 1563 the Confession was already a formula of unity among the Walloon churches.

BIBLIOGRAPHY: Best as to text and critical apparatus is J. N. Bakhuizen van den Brink, *De Nederlandsche Belijdenisgeschriften*, 1940. In the English language Schaff is still the best, although obsolete in many points.

[Sup.] LEONARD VERDUIN.

BELGIUM: In 1949 there were 8,602,611 inhabitants, of whom about 100,000 were Protestant. The *Union des Eglises Evangélique* or *Belgische Nationaal Protestantse Kerk,* founded in 1839, has twenty parishes, six preaching stations, with ten ministers for the Walloons (French-speaking), six for the Flemings (Dutch-speaking), and one Scottish clergyman. The synod is made up of a minister and an elder from each congregation. Many of the ministers are of Dutch origin, and in 1950 a Belgian theological seminary was opened with aid from the *Nederlandse Hervormde Kerk* (see HOLLAND).

There is also a free church in Belgium, the *Société Evangélique des Eglises Chrétiennes Missionaires* or *Belgische Christelijke Zendingskerk,* founded in 1849 under the influence of the British and Foreign Bible Society (see BIBLE SOCIETIES). Not so large in membership as the *Union,* the *Société* has thirty congregations, twenty-one ministers, and additional evangelists.

Since 1920 there are five congregations in Belgium attached to the *Gereformeerde Kerken* in Holland (*q.v.*). There are eight Methodist congregations with headquarters in Brussels. The *Belgische Evangelische Zending* has twenty-three stations. Liberal French intellectuals have formed an *Eglise Protestante Liberale;* there is a small union of Baptists, and an active Salvation Army (*q.v.*).

Roman Catholicism is still the dominant religion. In the two world wars resistance against Germans was led by Cardinals Mercier and van Roey. Since 1945 Catholicism has been losing ground in politics and among the people, and Catholic Action (*q.v.*) and propaganda for confessional schools are used to stop the decline. There are (1946) 650 monasteries and 3,000 convents in Belgium, and there are 6,785 Belgian missionaries in various parts of the world.

BIBLIOGRAPHY: E. de Moreau, *Histoire de l'Eglise en Belgique,* 4 vols., 1946–49; S. Axters, *Geschiedenis der Vroomheid in de Nederlanden,* 1950.

[Sup.] WILLEM JAN KOOIMAN.

BELL, BERNARD IDDINGS: Episcopalian; b. at Dayton, O., Oct. 13, 1886. He studied at the University of Chicago (B.A., 1907) and Western Theological Seminary (S.T.B., 1912). After he had been ordained in 1910 he became vicar at St. Christopher's Church, Oak Park, Ill. (1910–13); dean St. Paul's Cathedral, Fond du Lac, Wis. (1913–18); warden St. Stephen's College (1919–33); professor of religion, Columbia University (1930–33); preaching canon St. John's Cathedral, Providence, R. I.; and in recent years has been educational consultant to the bishop of Chicago. He has been a radical independent in politics and a progressive leader for a religious basis for modern education. His books include: *The Good News* (1921); *Post-Modernism and Other Essays* (1925); *Common Sense in Education* (1928); *Beyond Agnosticism* (1929); *Unfashionable Convictions* (1931); *The Holy Week* (1933); *Preface to Religion* (1935); *O Men of God* (1936); *In the City of Confusion* (1938); *The Priestly Way* (1938); *Religion for Living* (1939); *Christian Virtues* (1940); *Understanding Religion* (1941); *Still Shine the Stars* (1941); *The Church in Disrepute* (1943); *The Altar and the World* (1944); and *God Is not Dead* (1945).   RAYMOND W. ALBRIGHT.

BELL, GEORGE KENNEDY ALLEN: Church of England; b. Feb. 4, 1883, at Hayling Island. He was eldest son of Canon J. Allen Bell. He was educated at Westminster and Christ Church, Oxford, where he was subsequently tutor and student (1910–14). Ordained to the ministry of the Church of England in 1907, he was three years assistant curate at Leeds Parish Church. From 1914 to 1924 he was resident chaplain to Randall Thomas Davidson, archbishop of Canterbury, and served as assistant secretary to the Lambeth Conference of 1920. As Dean of Canterbury (1924–29) he founded the Friends of Canterbury Cathedral. In 1929 he was consecrated Bishop of Chichester. Dr. Bell has been prominent as an exponent of the ecumenical movement (*q.v.*), and very active in his contacts with the Lutheran churches of Germany and Scandinavia. On the formation of the World Council of Churches in 1948 at Amsterdam he was elected first chairman of its Central Committee. He is also known as a patron of the arts in connection with the church, especially of mural painting and religious drama. His published writings include: *The Life of Randall Davidson* (1935); *The Church and Humanity* (1946); and *Christian Unity: The Anglican Position* (1948).

BELL, RICHARD: Presbyterian; b. at Cummertrees, Dumfriesshire, Oct. 27, 1876. He studied at the University of Edinburgh (M.A., 1897; B.D., 1900), and after that in Germany. He was made assistant to the professor of Hebrew, Edinburgh University (1901–04); assistant minister at Burntisland (1904–06); and Greenside, Edinburgh (1906); minister of Wamphray (1907–21); lecturer in Arabic, Edinburgh University, 1921–47. He has published *The Origin of Islam* (1926); *The Qur'an Translated* (1937, 1939); and *Introduction to the Qur'an* (1952).

BELL, WILLIAM MELVIN: D. Oct. 6, 1933. He studied at Roanoke (Ind.) Classical Seminary. Ordained in the ministry of the Church of the United Brethren in Christ in 1882, he served pastorates at LaGrange, Lafayette,

Ligonier, and Elkhart, Ind. (1879–92). He was general secretary of home and foreign missions for his denomination (1893–1905). He was elevated to the episcopacy in 1905 and was bishop of the eastern district (1917–29). He wrote: *The Love of God* (1902); *The Social Message of Our Lord* (1909); *Torches Aloft* (1913); and *Biography of Bishop Nicholas Castle* (1923).
                    [Sup.] RAYMOND W. ALBRIGHT.

BELLARMINE, ROBERT: In the process of his canonization objection was raised to the effect that he wrote unreliable facts in his preface to the Sixtine Bible under Clement VIII (Editio Sixto-Clementina, 1592), in which he tried above all things to protect the scholarly reputation of Pope Sixtus V. Afterward it was shown that Bellarmine had been unjustly attacked. His autobiography of 1613 was also mentioned as a reason why he should not be canonized. The process began in 1627, but was soon interrupted. It was frequently resumed, but each time the decision was postponed. Finally, on May 13, 1923, Pope Pius XI pronounced the beatification, although some persons tried to prevent it (P. Baumgarten, I. de Récalde, and later G. Buschbell). In 1930 Bellarmine was declared a saint, and in 1931 proclaimed an ecclesiastical teacher. His body rests in the beautiful main church of the Jesuits, that of St. Ignazio in Rome.

BIBLIOGRAPHY: His *Opera oratoria*, ed. S. Tromp, 9 vols., 1942; *Dict. d'histoire et de géographie ecclésiastique*, VII, (1934), 798–824; J. Broderick, *Robert Bellarmine*, 2 vols., 1950.
                    [Sup.] MATHIAS GOOSSENS.

BELLS: These have for centuries been used within the church and outdoors as signals to indicate the progress of the service, times of day, or to celebrate events in the life of the community. The development of bells as a musical instrument followed two different lines in Britain and on the Continent. The British art of chiming involves a peal of bells tuned to the normal major scale, with perhaps one or two chromatic notes, on which it is possible to play simple tunes, with an occasional second note for harmony. In addition, the art of change ringing causes all the bells of a peal to be rung in succession, the order being determined by rather artificial rules. Unaccustomed ears sometimes experience difficulty in perceiving the musical element in these performances. On the Continent, bell founders gained such skill in tuning that it was possible to play music in full, four-part harmony. Several notable carillons have been installed in our country following the plan of these remarkable instruments of Belgium and the Netherlands. The sound of bells has frequently been imitated by metal tubes, struck by electrically operated hammers. These "tubular chimes" are installed in towers, or, somewhat modified, in organs. Recent developments include the electric amplification of phonograph recordings from bells, and of comparatively feeble bell-like sounds from metal objects. The similarity to the sound of chimes or carillon is sometimes remarkable, depending on the quality of the original installation and its state of repair. [Sup.] PAUL ALLWARDT.

BENDER, HAROLD STAUFFER: Mennonite; b. at Elkhart, Indiana, July 19, 1897. He studied at Goshen College (B.A., 1918), Garrett Biblical Institute (B.D., 1922), Princeton Theological Seminary (Th.M., 1923) and the universities of Princeton (M.A., 1923) Tuebingen, and Heidelberg (D. Theol., 1935). He was ordained to the Mennonite ministry in 1944. He has been professor of church history at Goshen College and Goshen College Biblical Seminary since 1924, dean of the college 1931–44, dean of the Biblical Seminary since 1944. He was founder and has been editor of the *Mennonite Quarterly Review* (1927–) and president of the Mennonite Historical Society (1925–). He was president of the Mennonite World Conference at Basel, Switzerland (August, 1952), and chairman of its Preparatory Commission (1950–). His writings include: *Menno Simons 1496–1561, A Quadri-Centennial Tribute* (1936); *Mennonite Sunday School Centennial* (1940); *Conrad Grebel 1498–1525, Founder of the Swiss Brethren* (1950); and numerous scholarly articles in the *Mennonite Quarterly Review* and other historical journals. His special field is Anabaptist-Mennonite history.

BENEDICT: Benedict I: Correct dates: 575–579.

Benedict II: A saint; his feast day in Rome is May 7. He was born in Rome. He restored Wilfrid to his bishopric of York, from which he had been unjustly ousted.

Benedict III: The mythical pope Joan has often been placed between him and his predecessor Leo IV. Benedict III was a model of virtue, and he strove after the sanctity of married life among the greatest men and women of his time. Among the single he also raised moral standards.

Benedict IV: B. in Rome. In 901 he held a synod in the Lateran. He was responsible for the coronation of Emperor Louis III, who in 902 was forced to give up Italy to Berengar I. He probably was not murdered, though this has often been claimed.

Benedict V: B. in Rome. He was called Grammaticus because of his scholarly attainments.

Benedict VI: B. in Rome. He confirmed against the claims of Pilgrim of Passau through a document of questionable accuracy the right of the archbishop of Salzburg to rule Noricum

and Pannonia. He also ratified the privileges of the archbishop of Trier.

Benedict VII: He was elected through the intervention of a representative of the emperor, Count Sicco, who drove out the intruder Franco (afterward Pope Boniface VII).

Benedict VIII: The Synod of Pavia in 1022, under his supervision, attacked the abuse of simony and repeated the prohibition of marriage among the clergy.

Benedict IX: Was installed at the age of twelve.

Benedict XI: Was the son of a notary. He favored the college of cardinals and the friars, improved the papal finances, and fostered missionary activities in Mongolia, Persia, and Armenia. Among his learned works are commentaries on part of the Psalms and on the Gospel of Matthew. He was declared a saint (*beatus*) by Pope Clement XII on April 26, 1736.

Benedict XII: Saint; his feast day is April 25. He established the office of apostolical secretary for the secret political correspondence, regulated the qualifications and functions of the attorneys and procurators of the Rota, and gave the Penitentiary a new organization through the Bull *In agro Dominico*. He increased the papal treasury from 748,672 to 1,117,000 florins. He promoted interest in schools and provided a better organization for the Benedictines.
See also POPES.   [Sup.] ALBERT HYMA.

Benedict XV (Giacomo della Chiesa): Pope (1914–22). He was born at Genova, Nov. 21, 1854. His family belonged to the titled aristocracy of feudal Italy. He completed his academic preparation for a church career as a student of the Capranica College, Rome, and as a member of the Pontifical Academy of Noble Ecclesiastics, obtaining the degree of Doctor of Theology in 1882. Ordained a priest in 1878, he followed Mgr. Rampolla (*q.v.*, Vol. IX), to the papal nunciature in Spain, in the capacity of private secretary. Back in Rome, when Mgr. Rampolla was created cardinal and became secretary of state to Pope Leo XIII (*q.v.*, Vol. VI), he entered the Section of Ordinary Ecclesiastical Affairs of the Secretariat of State (1887), and was sent abroad on several missions, particularly to Vienna, Austria (1889–90). Pope Pius X (*q.v.*, Vol. IX) made Mgr. della Chiesa archbishop of Bologna (1907) and created him cardinal, May 25, 1914.

After the death of Pius X on Aug. 20, 1914, Cardinal della Chiesa was elected pope on Sept. 3, 1914, and took the name Benedict XV, nearly one month after the outbreak of World War I. He appointed Cardinal Gasparri his secretary of state. Benedict's early appeals for peace were ignored by the belligerents, and the entry of Italy into the war on the side of the Entente powers (1915) made it plain that, at least for the time being, the pope would have to limit his efforts to counteracting the most disastrous effects of the war. The Vatican successfully negotiated the exchange of disabled war prisoners and the repatriation of interned civilians unfit for service in the armed forces, in co-operation with neutral Switzerland and the International Red Cross. Information about missing persons was also collected with a view of bringing about the reunion of scattered families, and the pope manifested his personal interest in the plea of suffering populations and starving children in initiating and promoting organizations of relief in occupied or war-torn countries.

In the fall of 1917, Benedict XV made public a specific plan for a negotiated peace, in which he stressed the moral force of right over against the brutal force of arms, recommended the restitution of occupied territories, and suggested that the legitimate aspirations of peoples be given due weight in view of solving difficult problems of irredentism, such as in Poland, Alsace-Lorraine, and the territory of Trieste. The pope's plan was presented to Emperor Wilhelm II on June 29, 1917, by Mgr. Pacelli, then nuncio in Bavaria, and who was to become pope Pius XII (*q.v.*). It was politely laid aside by the emperor, and turned down by the powers of the Entente.

The diplomatic activity of Benedict XV toward the end of World War I and after its conclusion aimed at the normalization of the relations between the secular powers and the Holy See. A *modus vivendi* was established with the French government, and Mgr. Cerretti was appointed to the nunciature in Paris, 1921. In Poland, Mgr. Ratti (the future Pius XI [*q.v.*]), and, in Germany, Mgr. Pacelli, negotiated the preparations for a series of concordats (*q.v.*) which, however, were not concluded until the pontificate of Pius XI.

Benedict XV promulgated the *Codex Juris Canonici* (*q.v.*), the compilation of which had been ordered by Pius X, on May 27, 1917, and decreed that the new canon law would take effect on the day of Pentecost, May 19, 1918. A new impulse was given to Scripture studies, in the encyclical *Spiritus Paraclitus* (*q.v.*) (1920). The principal encyclicals of Benedict XV are listed under ENCYCLICALS (*q.v.*). Benedict XV died on Jan. 22, 1922.

BIBLIOGRAPHY: P. Quirico, *Cor paternum (Storia documentata dell'opera di Benedetto XV durante la guerra)*, 1918; H. le Flock, *La politique de Benoit XV*, 1920; F. Vistalli, *Benedetto XV*, 1928; "Benedetto XV," in *Enciclopedia Cattolica*, Vol. II, 1949. The official documents of the pontificate of Benedict XV are found in the *Acta Apostolicae Sedis*. Cf. M. Claudia Carlen, *A Guide to the Encyclicals of the Roman Pontiffs from Leo XIII to the present day, 1878-1937*, 1939.

GEORGES A. BARROIS.

BENEDICTION: In most evangelical churches the benediction comes at the close of public worship, to crown it with the blessing of God. The minister pronounces the words while standing with arms uplifted and palms toward the people, as a symbol of mercies coming down. In some places the people also stand, but custom favors having them kneel or bow down, and then remain in silent prayer. Not magically but by faith they receive the blessing God bestows and conveys through his ministering servant. In many churches the benediction seems to be only a polite way of putting a period to an hour full of other things important. To remedy such irreverence the leader can utter the words impressively. After a pause, waiting for silence, he can speak deliberately, with low tones, and the right sort of prose rhythm. Occasionally, also, he can preach on one of the benedictions, such as the Apostolic (II Cor. 13:14). In keeping with the tone color of various services he can use other benedictions, such as the Priestly (Num. 6:24-26), the Covenant (Heb. 13:20, 21), and the Peace Benediction (derived from Phil. 4:6, 7). Any lover of the Bible and the Church Fathers can make a long list of benedictions and use them so that this part of the service will not suffer from sameness. Often it suffers from carelessness in prefixing the word "May," translating a benediction into a petition. No one has ever "improved" a benediction from the Bible. At some other climactic stage in worship one can employ a doxology, such as Jude 24, 25. In a doxology one raises the palms toward heaven, as a symbol that one is addressing God. Custom calls for a benediction at the end of public worship. Then silence!

[Sup.] ANDREW W. BLACKWOOD.

BENEDICTION OF THE BLESSED SACRAMENT: A devotion most popular in the Roman Catholic Church, and which was adopted by some Uniate Churches. It consists in the exposition of the consecrated Host displayed in a monstrance or ostensorium (*q.v.*), by means of which the priest blesses the people, in tracing over them the sign of the Cross. The benediction of the Blessed Sacrament is often added to the celebration of Vespers or Compline. It is also given regularly at the end of a procession of the Blessed Sacrament, or whenever the Sacrament has been exhibited in the monstrance during the celebration of the Mass.

GEORGES A. BARROIS.

BENEDICTUS: (1) The Latin name of the Canticle of Zachary, Luke 1:68-79, from its opening words in the Vulgate, *Benedictus Dominus Deus Israel*, "Blessed be the Lord God of Israel." It is recited daily in the office of Lauds (*q.v.*, Vol. VI). This use of the *Benedictus* in the Roman liturgy parallels that of the *Magnificat* (*q.v.*, Vol. VI), and of the *Nunc dimittis* (*q.v.*).

(2) In the Roman liturgy, the last verse of the *Sanctus* (*q.v.*) from Matt. 21:9. At high Mass, it ought to be sung by the choir only after the consecration of the Eucharist.

GEORGES A. BARROIS.

BENNETT, JOHN COLEMAN: American theologian who has specialized on theological problems related to social ethics. B. 1902 at Kingston, Canada. Educated at Williams College, Union Theological Seminary, Oxford University. Ordained Congregational minister. Has taught at Auburn Theological Seminary, Pacific School of Religion and, since 1943, has been Professor of Christian Theology and Ethics at Union Seminary. He was secretary of one section of the Oxford Conferences (1937) and of Amsterdam Assembly of World Council of Churches (1948), on staff of World Council in Geneva 1946. Traveled to Asian countries in 1950–51 for International Missionary Council to discuss issues created by communism. Chairman of Congregational Council for Social Action, 1942–44. Member of Economic Life, and International Justice departments of National Council of Churches. Member editorial board *Christianity and Crisis.* Author of *Social Salvation; Christianity and Our World; Christian Realism; Christian Ethics and Social Policy; Christianity and Communism.*

BENSON, LOUIS FITZGERALD: Presbyterian; b. July 22, 1855, at Philadelphia, Pa.; d. Oct. 10, 1930. He studied at the University of Pennsylvania (A.B., 1874; A.M., 1877) and Princeton Theological Seminary (graduated 1887). He practiced law (1877–84). Ordained in 1888, he became pastor of the Church of the Redeemer, Germantown, Pa. (1888–94), after which he resigned to edit hymnals and also edited the *Journal of the Presbyterian Historical Society* (1903–11). He wrote: *Hymns and Verses* (1897); *The Best Church Hymns* (1898); *Best Hymns—A Handbook* (1899); *Studies of Familiar Hymns* (1903; 1923); *The English Hymn—Its Development and Use in Worship* (1915); *Hymns Original and Translated* (1925); and *The Hymnody of the Christian Church* (1927). He collected a private library of 9,000 volumes on hymnology and also edited the Presbyterian (1895) and Congregational (1896) hymnals and was a member of the committee which prepared the Presbyterian *Book of Common Worship.* RAYMOND W. ALBRIGHT.

BENZ, ERNST: B. Nov. 17, 1907. He was educated at Tuebingen (Dr.Phil.), Berlin (Lic. Theol.) and Marburg (D.Theol., 1931). He has taught church history and dogmatics at Halle (1931–35), and at Marburg (1935–); and has been dean of the theological faculty (1946–47). He has written: *Das Todesproblem in der* *stoischen Philosophie* (1929); *Marius Victorinus und die Entwicklung der abendlaendischen Willensmetaphysik* (1932); *Ecclesia spiritualis: Kirchenidee und Geschichtstheologie der franziskanischen Reformation* (1934); *Der vollkommene Mensch nach Jakob Boehme* (1937); *Nietzsches Ideen zur Geschichte des Christenthums* (1938); "Leibniz und Peter der Grosse" in E. Hochstetter's *Leibniz. Zu seinem 300. Geburtstag* (1947); *Swedenborg in Deutschland* (1949); *Emanuel Swedenborg: Naturforscher und Seher* (1948); *Westlicher und oestlicher Nihilismus in christlicher Sicht* (1948); *Jung-Stilling in Marburg* (1949); *Wittenberg und Byzanz* (1949); *Die abendlaendische Sendung der oestlich-orthodoxen Kirche* (1951); *Die Monologe des Judas Ischarioth* (1951).

RAYMOND W. ALBRIGHT.

BERDIAEV, NICOLAS: Eastern Orthodox; b. in Kiev, Russia, March 6, 1874; d. at Clamart, near Paris, March 24, 1948. He studied science at the University of Kiev and philosophy at Heidelberg. All his life he lived as a private writer and journalist, except for a brief period after the Russian Revolution, when he lectured on philosophy at Moscow University. Because of his strong spiritual resistance to the new régime, he was in 1923 exiled from the Soviet Union, and the rest of his years he spent at Berlin and finally at Paris. He organized there free courses in philosophy and religion, under the name of an "Academy" and in 1925–40 was editor of a magazine in Russian, *Put* ("The Way"), with the collaboration of a wide group of Russian scholars and thinkers in the emigration. His main work was always in writing books and articles. He was a prolific writer. He began as a Marxist, but very soon abandoned this position under the strong influence of German idealistic philosophy, of Kant first of all, to which, at a later date, another German influence was added: the mysticism of Jacob Boehme (*q.v.*). Berdiaev was well and widely read in various fields and he wrote usually in response to some external challenge. Polemical dialectics is a distinctive feature of his thought. His main problem was always the problem of man, and his main emphasis was on man's freedom. He strongly insisted on the "prophetical" character of his thinking and did not pretend to be an accurate exponent of any confessional tradition. He was very much concerned with the problem of Russian destiny and insisted on the "critical" meaning of the present historical age. He wrote always in Russian, but most of his books (especially those written abroad) are available in various translations.

BIBLIOGRAPHY: Matthew Spinka, *Nicolas Berdyaev: Captive of Freedom,* 1950; see "Selected Bibliography," pp. 209–215. The English translation of Berdiaev's autobiography, *Dream and Reality,* is unfortunately unreliable (unavowed omissions and tendentious editing); O. Fielding Clarke, *Introduction to Berdyaev,* 1950; George

Seaver, *Nicolas Berdyaev: An Introduction to His Thought*, 1950.

GEORGES FLOROVSKY.

BEREAN REFORMED CHURCH. See CHRISTIAN REFORMED CHURCH.

BERENGAR OF POITIERS:

BIBLIOGRAPHY: *Dict. d'hist. et géogr. eccl.*, Vol. 8 (1935), cols. 379–380; R. Klibansky, "l'Épitre de Bérenger de Poitiers contre les Chartreux," in *Revue Moyen Age latin*, Vol. 2 (1946), pp. 314–316.   [Sup.]

BERENGAR OF TOURS: It is now well established that he denied the doctrine of transubstantiation. The older school of theologians (for example, Thomas Aquinas, *Summa theol.*, III a, qu. 75) were of the opinion that he also denied the real presence, believing only in a figurative presence or an intellectual concept. But the later school (for example, Mabillon, *Acta Sanct. Ord. S. Ben., Saec.* VI, Part II, pp. xxii-xxxi; and Franzelin, *Tractatus de ss. eucharistiae sacramento et sacrificio* [2nd ed., 1873], p. 196), doubts very much that he went so far.

BIBLIOGRAPHY: H. Macdonald, *Berengar and the Reform of Sacramental Doctrine*, 1930; M. Capuijns, *Dict. d'hist. et geogr. ecclés.*, Vol. 8 (1935), col. 385–407; H. de Lubac, *Corpus mysticum L'Eucharistie et l'Eglise au moyen âge*, 1944.

[Sup.] E. STOKMAN.

BERGENDOFF, CONRAD JOHN IMMANUEL: Lutheran; b. Shickley, Nebraska, Dec. 3, 1895. He studied at Augustana College and Augustana Theological Seminary, Rock Island, Ill., and the universities of Pennsylvania, Columbia, Chicago (Ph.D.), Uppsala, Lund (Sweden), and Berlin. He was pastor, Salem Lutheran Church, Chicago (1921–31); dean, Augustana Theological Seminary (1931–35); president Augustana College and Theological Seminary (1935–48); president, Augustana College (1948–). He served with Religious Affairs Division, American Army Occupation, Germany (1949), visiting German universities. He has been a member of the Joint Commission on American Lutheran Liturgy since 1945. He is editor, *The Lutheran Quarterly*. He wrote: *Olavus Petri and the Ecclesiastical Transformation in Sweden* (1928); *I Believe in the Church* (1937); and *Christ as Authority* (1947).

BERGER, DANIEL: D. Sept. 12, 1920. He studied in the Ohio Methodist Episcopal School in Springfield, Ohio, and taught in a private academy for three years. Afterward he studied at Ohio State University (M.A., 1856). During his pastorate of six years he served the last year as minister of the First United Brethren Church in Dayton, Ohio (1864). His *History of the United Brethren in Christ* (1897) was for a generation the definitive work in its field.

[Sup.] RAYMOND W. ALBRIGHT.

BERGGRAV, EIVIND: Lutheran; b. in Stavanger, Norway, Oct. 25, 1884. He studied at the universities of Oslo, Copenhagen, and Marburg, and as a graduate student at Oxford, Cambridge, and Oslo. His dissertation was entitled *The Threshold of Religion*, tr. into German as *Durchbruch der Religion*.

He was headmaster of a Folk-school (1909–19); minister at Hurdal (1919–25); at the Oslo prison (1925–28); bishop of northern Norway (1929–37); and bishop of Oslo and primate of the Church of Norway (1937–50, imprisoned 1942–45). He is the president of the United Bible Societies and one of the presidents of the World Council of Churches, having been active in ecumenical movements since 1917. His major interests have been in psychology of religion, the contacts between Christianity and culture, especially as this gave him opportunity to lead the resistance against Nazi occupation of Norway, and he has been a promoter of greater spiritual freedom in the Church of Norway.

He is editor of the monthly journal, *Kirke und Kultur*, and has written thirty-four books, many of which have been translated into French, German, Finnish, and English. His better known works in English are *The Prisoner's Soul and Our Own* (1932); *The Land of Suspense* (1943); and *Man and State* (1951).

BIBLIOGRAPHY: Odd Godal, *Eivind Berggrav, Leader of the Christian Resistance*, 1949; and Sven Stolpe, *Eivind Berggrav, Norwegens Bischof*, 1951.

RAYMOND W. ALBRIGHT.

BERGSON, HENRI LOUIS: B. 1859; d. 1941. French philosopher of intuition, creativity, and freedom. Born of Jewish parents, he became a "Catholic of intent" although never baptized. At the École Normale Superieure, his *alma mater*, and at the Collège de France he became famous as a brilliant lecturer, 1900–14, and exerted powerful influence on the artists, writers and philosophers of his time. His books were scientific and philosophic studies of successive problems: psychology, biological evolution, sociology of religion. He opposed the positivism of his day, declaring that scientific knowledge is the refinement of a broader intuitive faculty, without whose imaginative flexibility it is incapable of learning the truth about spirit, change and God.

Bergson's interest in psychology and religious mysticism led to friendship with William James, and to the presidency of the Society for Psychical Research (1913). He lectured in Great Britain and America, starting a series of Gifford Lectures which were interrupted by the war of 1914. His most influential book, *Creative Evolution* (1907) appeared at the time of the Roman Catholic "Modernist" controversy, with which many of his friends and students were associated. His major books were placed on the Index in 1914.

Honored by his admission to the French Academy in 1914, he won the Nobel Prize for literature in 1927. He says in his last book, *The Two Sources of Morality and Religion* (1932) that as man is the freest, most creative product in nature, so the Christian saint is the highest development within humanity.

GEORGE FREDERICK PARKER.

BERGSON, THE PHILOSOPHY OF: Henri

Bergson (1859–1941) contends that metaphysics requires intuition (*q.v.*) as well as intellect. The rigid concepts of intellect are adapted to grasp magnitude and juxtaposition. But when applied to life, these concepts divide the continuous flow of duration into a succession of discrete states, just as a movie camera divides living action into a series of "stills." Only intuition permits us to enter and coincide with what is unique in the object of knowledge. It is thus we know ourselves. Intuition reveals life to be not spatial, but temporal, a creative flow in which perception melts into accumulating memory (see TIME). Memory is the self. The brain filters into consciousness just those memories which are relevant to current perception, thus enabling the body to act in its environment of space and matter. Matter is the "still" of the moment, a spatial concept of the intellect, and true enough for practice. But reality is the duration disclosed by intuition. The duality of intellect and intuition is illustrated by the contrast between the fixed morality of "closed societies" analogous to intellect, and the creative morality of "open societies," analogous to intuition. In aesthetics (*q.v.*), the incongruity of intellect and intuition suggests a theory of the comic: we feel that movement should be flowing; hence, we laugh at the stiff and pompous.

If duration is freely creative, as intuition declares, there is no problem of mechanism (*q.v.*) and teleology (*q.v.*). Creativity cannot be mere fulfilment of a program. The *élan vital* must and does find its own way, whether in vegetative torpor, the instinct of the bee, or the intellect and intuition of man. God (*q.v.*) is the living center from which worlds shoot out like rockets. He is no *thing,* but a continuity of free action such as we intuit ourselves to be. The goal of the mystics (see MYSTICISM) is to know and partly to coincide with God: they report that God is love and the object of love (*q.v.*). Human survival after death is probable, for intuition shows that "mental life overflows cerebral life." The brain simply sluices into action a thin stream of the durational flow. Destruction of the sluice should merely release the flood; hence the onus of proof is with those who deny survival.

BIBLIOGRAPHY: Bergson's principal works (excluding those listed under BERGSON, Vol. XII, p. 549) are: *Introduction à la métaphysique,* 1903; Eng. transl. by T. E. Hulme, *Introduction to Metaphysics,* 1912; *Les deux sources de la morale et de la religion,* 1932, Eng. transl. by R. Audra, C. Brereton, and W. Carter, *Two Sources of Morality and Religion,* 1935; *La pensée et le mouvant,* 1934, Eng. transl. by M. L. Andison, *Creative Mind,* 1946. H. W. Carr, *The Philosophy of Change,* 1914; G. W. Cunningham, *The Philosophy of Bergson,* 1916; J. Chevalier (Eng. tr. by L. Clare), *Henri Bergson,* 1928; A. Cresson, *Bergson, sa vie, son oeuvre,* 1941; B. Scharfstein, *Roots of Bergson's Philosophy,* 1943. [Sup. to Vol. XII, pp. 549–550.]

GEORGE ALFRED CLARK.

BERKHOF, LOUIS: Christian Reformed; b. Oct. 13, 1873, Emmen, Netherlands. He studied at: Calvin College and Seminary; Princeton Theological Seminary (B.D., 1904); and the Divinity School of the University of Chicago (1904–06).

He was pastor at Allendale, Mich. (1900–02); and Oakdale Park Church, Grand Rapids, Mich. (1904–06). He has taught at Calvin Seminary, Grand Rapids, Mich., exegetical theology (1906–14); New Testament exegesis (1914–26); dogmatic theology (1926–44); and was president (1931–44). He is the author of: *Het Christelijk Onderwijs en Onze Kerkelijke Toekomst* (1905); *Beknopte Bijbelsche Hermeneutiek* (1911); *Christendom en Leven* (1912); *The Church and Social Problems* (1913); *Life Under the Law in a Pure Theocracy* (1914); *Biblical Archaeology* (1915; 3d ed., 1928); *New Testament Introduction* (1915); *Paul the Missionary* (1915); *The Christian Laborer in the Industrial Struggle* (1916); *Subjects and Outlines* (1918); *Pre-millennialisme* (1918); *De Drie Punten in Alle Deelen Gereformeerd* (1925); *The Assurance of Faith* (1928; 2nd ed., 1939); *Reformed Dogmatics* (4 vols., 1932–37; 3d ed. of Dogmatics proper, 2 vols., 1946); *Manual of Reformed Doctrine* (1933); *Vicarious Atonement through Christ* (1936); *Summary of Christian Doctrine* (1938); *Principles of Biblical Interpretation* (1950); *The Kingdom of God* (1951); *Aspects of Liberalism* (1951); and *The Second Coming of Christ* (1953).

BERNARD OF CLAIRVAUX: Even in his childhood he was noted for agility of mind and religious fervor. His mother's death made such a strong impression upon him that he gave up all ambition to seek worldly honor or fame. He persuaded his uncle Gaudry and all his brothers, besides some other relatives and friends, to do the same and forsake all frivolity and vanity. About thirty Burgundian noblemen joined him and Abbot Stephanus Harding at the monastery of Citeaux, which had just started upon its course of reforming a host of other institutions. Another distinguished friend of Bernard was William of Champeaux, the former teacher at Paris, who recognized in Bernard great talents and organizing ability. The latter exerted tremendous influence upon the Benedictines of Cluny, the Knights Templar, for whom he issued a constitution or rules, and the Carthusians, whom he encouraged to retain strict discipline and for whom he composed his famous work, *De diligendo Deo*. His *Apologia* of 1125 also had a powerful effect, while in the work *De conversione* he insisted upon high moral standards for priests and bishops. At the request of Pope Eugene III, a former Cistercian abbot of humble character, he composed *De consideratione*, which may be regarded as a manual for the reformation of the papal office. He pointed out the great dangers involved in the high position enjoyed by the pope in the twelfth century.

At the Council of Etampes (1130) he put an end to the schism caused by Anacletus II. He also checked the rebellion of Arnold of Brescia (1142). In 1146 he preached vigorously in France to arouse pilgrims to undertake the Second Crusade. On this occasion he did much for the protection of the Jews, taking bold steps to restrain anti-Semitism (*q.v.*). He attacked the propositions of the learned and skeptical Abelard and of Gilbert de la Porrée (1148). Moreover, he actively opposed the Manichaeans in all parts of France. But the failure of the Second Crusade and severe stomach trouble finally sapped his seemingly boundless energy. Like Peter Damiani, he was not a friend of secular learning and art, nor did he approve of Neo-Platonic speculation on the part of St. Augustine and Dionysius the Areopagite. His religion was simple and practical, hence widely followed in the later Middle Ages. He explained many difficult passages in the Bible along the lines of allegory and sound mysticism. Humility was the proper way to union with God, so he argued; while love is the most powerful element in religion: "God is known as far as he is loved." He also emphasized strongly the reverence demanded for Mary, Christ's mother. In this field his influence was very great.

BIBLIOGRAPHY: E. Vacandard, *Vie de S. Bernard*, 5th ed., 1927; Ailbe Luddy, *Life and Teachings of Saint Bernard*, 1923; R. Linhardt, *Die Mystik des Hl. Bernards*, 1923; J. Leclerq, *S. Bernard mystique*, 1948; Watkin Williams, *S. Bernard Abbot of Clairvaux*, 1935; M. Slotemaker de Bruine, *Het ideaal der navolging van Christus ten tijde van Bernard van Clairvaux*, 1926.
[Sup.] A. R. M. KIEVITS.

BERNARDIN OF SAHAGUN: Missionary, archaeologist; b. about 1500 at Sahagun, Spain. Joined the Franciscans at Salamanca and offered to help establish a mission in Mexico, where he labored for sixty years. He was very familiar with the language and culture of the Aztecs, and he published thirty treatises on catechetical, ascetic, and hagiographic subjects, besides various books dealing with the language and history of Mexico. Of particular importance is his work, *Historia general de las cosas de Nueva España* (ed. C. M. Bustamente, 3 vols., 1829; see also *Mexican Antiquities*, Vols. V and VII, 1831).

BIBLIOGRAPHY: *Dict. d'histoire et de géographie eccl.*, Vol. VIII (1935), 799, with excellent bibliography.
MATHIAS GOOSSENS.

BERNARDIN OF SIENA: He was the chief apostle or disseminator of the devotion of the Sweet Name of Jesus, hence the monogram of I. H. S. The reverence which he evoked everywhere for this name led to the introduction of the Feast of the Holy Name, the Sunday between January 1 and the Feast of the Three Kings. Well known also are his sermons devoted to the Virgin Mary, in which, among other things, he emphasized the share which she was said to have in the dispensation of divine grace. Moreover, his sermons dealing with purgatory are significant. He pointed not only to the sufferings but still more to the joys experienced there. He mentioned twelve in particular and said: "Although those who are in purgatory suffer grievous torments, nevertheless, their condition is more felicitous than that of those who are upon the earth."

BIBLIOGRAPHY: *Opera omnia Bernardini Senensis*, editio critica, Quarrachi, Florence 1951; D. Pacetti O.F.M., *De St. Barnardini Senensis operibus, ratio criticae editionis*, Quarrachi, Florence 1947; F. Vernet, *Dict. Theol. Cath.*, Vol. 2 (1923), cols. 787–791; H. Schmidt O.F.M., "Bernardin-Literatur 1939–1949," in *Franziskanische Studien*, Vol. 32 (1950), pp. 388–418.
[Sup.] E. STOKMAN.

BERNEUCHEN MOVEMENT. See ST. MICHAEL, EVANGELICAL BROTHERHOOD OF.

BERNHARDT, OSKAR ERNST. See MESSIAHS, FALSE.

BERTHOLET, ALFRED: D. at Basel, Aug. 24, 1951. He was professor of Old Testament at Basel (1905–13); Tuebingen (1913–14); Goettingen (1914–28); and Berlin (1928–43). His works include: *Kulturgeschichte Israels* (1919); *Kultur und Religion* (1924); *Die Religion des Alten Testaments* (1932).

BIBLIOGRAPHY: W. Baumgartner *et al.*, *Festschrift Alfred Bertholet zum 80. Geburtstag*, 1950.
[Sup.] E. E. FLACK.

BERTOCCI, PETER ANTHONY: Methodist; b. at Elena, Italy, May 13, 1910. He studied at Boston University (A.B., 1931; Ph.D., 1935), University of Cambridge, England (1934–35). He taught psychology and philosophy at Bates College (1935–45), and is professor of philosophy at Boston University (1945–). He was secretary of the American Theological Society (1947–51). He has written: *The Empirical Argument for God in Late British Thought* (1938); *The Human Venture in Sex, Love, and Marriage* (1949); and *Introduction to the Philosophy of Religion* (1952).

BETHEL. See ARCHAEOLOGY, BIBLICAL.

BETHEL BEI BIELEFELD. See BODELSCHWINGH, FRIEDRICH, in Vol. II.

BETH-SHEAN. See ARCHAEOLOGY, BIBLICAL.

BETH-SHEMESH. See ARCHAEOLOGY, BIBLICAL.

BETHUNE-BAKER, JAMES FRANKLIN: Anglican; b. Aug. 28, 1861, Birmingham; d. 1951. He was educated at Pembroke College, Cambridge. Ordained in 1888, he was dean of Pembroke College, Cambridge (1889–1906); and Lady Margaret's Professor of Divinity, Cambridge University (1911–35). He edited the *Journal of Theological Studies* (1903–35). He wrote: *An Introduction to the Early History of Christian Doctrine* (1908); *The Faith of the Apostle's Creed* (1918); *The Way of Modernism* (1927); *Early Traditions about Jesus* (1929); *The New View of Christianity* (1930).
[Sup.] F. W. DILLISTONE.

BETH-ZUR. See ARCHAEOLOGY, BIBLICAL.

BETTS, GEORGE HERBERT: Methodist; b. April 1, 1868, at Clarksville, Iowa; d. Dec. 8, 1934. Educated at Cornell, Iowa (A.B., 1899), Chicago (Ph.M., 1904), and Columbia (Ph.D., 1909), he taught psychology at Cornell, Iowa (1901–18); was professor of religious education at Boston University (1918–19), the University of California (1921–22), and at Northwestern University (1919–21; 1922–26; professor of education and director of research, 1926–34). Among his publications those of greatest interest are: *The Mind and Its Education* (1906); *Function and Distribution of Mental Imagery* (1909); *Social Principles of Education* (1912); *How to Teach Religion* (1919); *The New Program of Religious Education* (1921); *The Curriculum of Religious Education* (1921); *Laboratory Studies in Educational Psychology* (with E. M. Turner, 1924); *Method in Teaching Religion* (with M. O. Hawthorne, 1925); *The Beliefs of 700 Ministers* (1929); and *Character-Outcome of Present Day Religion* (1931).
RAYMOND W. ALBRIGHT.

BEWER, JULIUS AUGUST: Congregationalist; b. at Ratingen, Germany, Aug. 28, 1877; d. Sept. 1, 1953. He studied at Union Seminary, (B.D., 1898); Columbia University (Ph.D., 1900) and the universities of Basle, Halle, Berlin (1899–1901). He was professor of Old Testament at Oberlin Theological Seminary (1902–04), Union Theological Seminary (1904–45; emeritus, 1945–53); lecturer in biblical literature, Teachers College (1912–28) and a member of Faculty of Philosophy, Columbia University (1913–45). He was also a member of the revision committee of the American Standard Version (1937–53). In theology he was a liberal evangelical of the critical school in biblical interpretation. He was the author of a critical and exegetical commentary on *Obadiah* and *Joel*

(1911), *Jonah* (1912), in "International Critical Commentary"; *Der Text des Buches Ezra* (1921); *The Literature of the Old Testament* (1922); *Ezechiel* (in Kittel; *Biblia Hebraica*) (1932); *The Book of the Twelve Prophets* I, II (1949); *Isaiah* I, II (1950); *Jeremiah* I, II (1951–52).

BEZA, THEODORE: I. Beza as Poet: Beza's early delight in poetry and epigram continued after his conversion (1548). "I still cannot repent of it," he wrote in 1550, introducing his play, *Abraham sacrifiant*. He had deeply repented of the moral laxity reflected in his *juvenilia*, and of his irresolute behavior when first he faced the new light of the Reformation. "God came to seek me by means of a serious illness," he states. "After interminable sufferings of body and soul, God had pity on his fugitive servant." Unlike Calvin, he did not become a theological writer until ten years after his conversion, but remained a classical scholar and man of letters. His *Abraham*, as P. F. Geisendorf points out, is the one instance of the successful fusion of the two traditions of a Greek tragedy and the medieval mystery play. This play went through thirty-six reprintings to 1928, a record by which Beza surpasses all save one of the (French) playwrights of his century. In 1595 he presented a group of canticles with music of his own composition.

II. Beza and Notable Opponents: Beza's contacts with the Reformed were in general harmonious. His refusal to have Peter Ramus, the anti-Aristotelian philosopher, as a colleague in the Geneva Academy (1570) is a revealing exception to this. Jacob Arminius first diverged from Beza by espousing the philosophy of Ramus. He subsequently imbibed Beza's supralapsarian theology, only to depart from it (*ca.* 1590) to lay the foundations of "Arminianism." Efforts by St. Francis de Sales and others to convert him, and recover Geneva to Roman Catholicism, were met by Beza with equal firmness and courtesy.

III. Authenticity of Writings: The *Ecclesiastical History* ascribed to Beza is probably in the main the work of an associate. On the other hand, he was evidently the principal compiler of the *Harmony of the Confessions* (1581) circulated under the name of Jean François Salvard.

BIBLIOGRAPHY: The biography by P. F. Geisendorf, *Théodore de Bèze* (1949) is more ample than that of H. M. Baird (1899) but creates a similar impression of the personality. His list of works cited, and Th. Dufour's "À propos de la bibliographie de Théodore de Bèze" in his *Le Secret des textes* (1925), pp. 86–97, should be consulted. Special phases are discussed in R. Lebègue, *La tragédie religieuse en France: les debuts*, 1929; L. Romier, *Catholiques et huguenots à la cour de Charles IX*, 1924; B. F. Paist, "Peter Martyr and the Colloquy of Poissy," *Princeton Theological Review*, XX (1922), 212–31, 418–47, 616–46; J. Viénot, *Histoire de la Réforme Francaise: Des origines à l'Édit de Nantes*, 1926; H. Vuilleumier, *Histoire de l'Église réformée du Pays de Vaud sous la régime bernois*, I, 1927.

[Sup.] JOHN T. MCNEILL.

BIBLE CONFERENCES. See SUMMER BIBLE CONFERENCES.

BIBLE, THE, IN CHRISTIAN EDUCATION: Before Christ the contents of our Old Testament were used in teaching truth and duty, and in apostolic days the contents of both Testaments. In medieval times Bible teaching went partially into eclipse, but pre-Reformation sects and mystical groups (such as the followers of John Wycliffe, John Huss, and Peter Waldo) recovered the Bible. Through preaching and teaching they insisted on lay knowledge of Scripture. The Reformation restored the Bible to the laity, through translations into the vernacular, with constant biblical preaching and teaching. The great catechisms (Lutheran, Heidelberg, Westminster, etc.) formulated the faith for laymen, and supported it with biblical references. Later the translation and distribution of Scripture became an astonishing aspect of church history. In the state schools of Europe (except in France and Russia, since their revolutions) the Bible has been the chief text in religious courses. The publicly supported schools of England use an "agreed syllabus," prepared by the various Protestant bodies, and containing basic materials from the Bible. In our colonies the first materials were the *Horn Book* and the *New England Primer*, both full of Bible content. Later, during the rise of Sunday schools, the Bible became the chief source of the curriculum, and so continued until the changes caused by the newer interpretations, the use of extra-biblical materials, and the pupil-centered emphasis.

Since about 1900 liberalizing forces have led to less emphasis on content than on personal and social experience. Today the struggle between content and experience-centered educators continues, with more of a desire for a position holding to both. Four positions now seem to obtain: the conservative, the liberal, the neo-orthodox, and the neo-liberal. Under the World Council and the National Council a more ecumenical approach is being attempted. Several new curricula (e.g., Presbyterian, U.S.A., Reformed and Evangelical, and others) devote an entire year to a study of the Bible, accepting the results of historical and literary studies. It is now regarded less as a static volume of proof texts than as an authentic record of God's redemptive acts in history, centering in the person and work of Christ. The Bible is the source of all our knowledge of God's unique work for man's salvation, and the guidebook for the Christian in all his faith and practice.

ELMER G. HOMRIGHAUSEN.

BIBLE INSTITUTES AND COLLEGES: When, toward the close of the nineteenth century, the preaching of men like Dwight L. Moody awakened new interest in the Bible, Bible institutes emerged. In 1882 the first classes of what later became the Missionary Training Institute of Nyack were held in a New York theater by Albert B. Simpson. Moody himself founded the Chicago school which now bears his name, in 1886.

At first the purpose was to train "gap" men who might stand between pastor and people in local Protestant churches. Gradually, however, men and women were trained to serve as missionaries and as pastors in independent congregations or churches of smaller denominations. Married men, converted too late to pursue the normal college and seminary courses, enrolled in the Bible schools. Later the average entrance age dropped. Children of alumni entered directly from high school, and during World War II the Youth for Christ (*q.v.*) movement influenced hundreds of others to enroll immediately after high school "to establish their faith" before going to a secular college. Meanwhile the schools extended their curricula; from the original one or two years the course was expanded to three, four, and five years of study after high school.

In October, 1947, with the counsel of John Dale Russell and Carroll Newsom, the Accrediting Association of Bible Institutes and Bible Colleges was organized with headquarters in Providence, R. I. Of 36 schools examined the first year, 12 were accredited in the collegiate division. A lower intermediate division was formed to include 6 of the schools examined. The Association, which has come to include all the larger and older Bible schools, is recognized by the U. S. Office of Education, the American Council on Education, the National Education Association, and similar groups.

The names "Bible Institute" and "Bible College" are synonymous. Popularly the terms describe anything from an evening study class in a local church to a fully accredited day college. In the more circumscribed sense in which the terms are used here, Bible Institutes and Colleges are undergraduate schools (in distinction from the graduate study in theological seminaries, *q.v.*) in which the instruction is Bible-centered.

Before 1900 there were only nine schools of this type. Fourteen more were founded before 1910, fifteen more by 1920, twenty more by 1930, thirty-five more by 1940, and by 1950 there were one hundred fifty in the United States and Canada.

Following are the accredited schools (1952) in the collegiate division: *California*: Bible Institute of Los Angeles; Pacific Bible College; Pacific Bible Institute; Southern California Bible College. *Colorado*: Rockmont College (Denver Bible Institute). *Georgia*: Toccoa Falls Institute. *Illinois*: Moody Bible Institute. *Indiana*: Fort Wayne Bible College. *Iowa*:

Chicago Evangelistic Institute. *Kansas:* Manhattan Bible College. *Michigan:* Owosso Bible College. *Minnesota:* Minnesota Bible College; St. Paul Bible Institute. *Missouri:* Central Bible Institute. *Nebraska:* Grace Bible Institute. *New York:* Missionary Training Institute (Nyack). *Ohio:* Cleveland Bible College. *Pennsylvania:* Messiah [Bible] College; Philadelphia Bible Institute. *Rhode Island:* Providence Bible Institute. *South Carolina:* Columbia Bible College. *Texas:* Southwestern Bible Institute (Bible College Division). *Manitoba, Canada:* Mennonite Brethren Bible College.
See also REVIVALS OF RELIGION.

TERRELLE B. CRUM.

BIBLE READING BY THE LAITY, RE-STRICTIONS ON. See ROMAN CATHOLIC LAWS ON BIBLE READING.

BIBLES, ANNOTATED: Only those annotated Bibles are included in which the English text of the whole Bible is presented. Unless otherwise noted the text is the King James Version.

Analytical Holy Bible, edited and arranged by A. Roberts. Egyptian Publishing Co., Carbondale, Ill., 1906.
The Modern Reader's Bible (English Revised Version) in modern literary form. Edited with introduction and notes by Richard G. Moulton, Macmillan, New York, 1907.
The Student's Bible, with marginal and explanatory footnotes and references, by Orville J. Nave and Anna S. Nave, Abingdon Press, New York, 1907, and republished since in seventy-nine editions.
The Marginal Chain-Reference Bible, compiled and edited by Frank Charles Thompson. Chain Reference Bible Publishing Co., Mt. Morris, N. Y., 1908, and reissued in 1917 (Eaton and Mains, New York), and in 1934 (Kirkbride Bible Co., Indianapolis, Ind.).
The Scofield Reference Bible. Topical references with annotations, edited by C. I. Scofield and seven consulting editors. Oxford University Press, New York, 1909; new and improved ed., 1917.
The Self-Interpreting Bible. A new edition with John Brown's notes. Introduction by John H. Vincent. Bible Educational Society, St. Louis, Mo., 1909.
The Cross-Reference Bible. American Standard Version, with variorum renderings and readings, topical analyses, and cross-references. Edited by Harold E. Monser. Cross-Reference Bible Co., New York, 1910.
The New Indexed Bible, comprising biblical biography, geography, history, teaching. John A. Dickson Publishing Co., Chicago, 1913. Also issued in 1923 and 1941.

The Companion Bible. With structures and notes; critical, expository, and suggestive. Six volumes. Oxford University Press, New York, 1909–21. New one volume edition in 1953.
Wilmore's New Analytical Reference Bible. Comprehensive helps, revised and edited between 1891 and 1918 by Philip Schaff. A complete analysis of the Holy Bible, edited by Roswell D. Hitchcock. Cruden's Concordance, revised by John Eadie. Funk & Wagnalls Co., New York, 1921.
The Bible for Today. With introductory paragraphs, headlines, and footnotes, by John Stirling. Illustrated by Rowland Hilder. Introduction by William Lyon Phelps. Oxford University Press, New York, 1941.
The Concordia Bible. Edited by John Theodore Mueller, with notes, introductions, explanations, instructions, and references. Concordia Publishing House, St. Louis, Mo., 1943.
The Westminster Study Edition of the Holy Bible. Paragraphed. Introductory articles and prefaces with footnotes, concordance, and maps. The Westminster Press, Philadelphia, 1948.
The Pilgrim Edition of the Holy Bible. With notes especially adapted for young Christians. Edited by E. Schuyler English. Oxford University Press, New York, 1948.
The Interpreter's Bible. With the King James and Revised Standard Version, and with general articles, as well as introduction, exegesis, and exposition for each book of the Bible. Edited by G. A. Buttrick and others. Twelve volumes. Abingdon-Cokesbury Press, New York, 1951– .

BIBLIOGRAPHY: Readers who desire a more complete list are referred to the *Historical Catalogue of the Printed Editions of Holy Scripture,* in the Library of the British and Foreign Bible Society, compiled by T. H. Darlow and H. F. Moule, 2 vols., 1903 (a new edition of this catalogue is in preparation); *A Catalogue of Books Represented by Library of Congress Printed Cards,* issued to July 31, 1942, Vol. 14 (1943), pp. 1–255; *British Museum General Catalogue of Printed Books,* Vol. 16 (1936), Vol. 17 (1937), Vol. 18 (1937).

[Sup.] HOWARD TILLMAN KUIST.

BIBLES, ILLUSTRATED: The German edition of the Bible published by the Evangelische Buecherverein (1855) contains 327 woodcuts by old Italian and German masters. A similar work is the edition by G. Schiller, *Bilder zur Bibel* (1938), while the work by W. Bredt, the Rembrandt Bible (*Rembrandt-Bibel*) published in 1927–28, contains 240 illustrations. The edition of Julius Schnorr (1852–60) has had numerous reprints in the twentieth century. Somewhat different is the edition by R. Seeberg and P. Petersen, which as far as clothing and landscape are concerned, is more realistic than the others.

BIBLIOGRAPHY: W. Neusz, "Bibel-Illustration," in *Reallexicon zur deutschen Kunstgeschichte,* II (1948), 478–517: with extensive bibliography; A. M. Hind, *An Introduction to a History of Woodcut,* 2 vols., 1935.

[Sup.] MATHIAS GOOSSENS.

BIBLE SOCIETIES: The basic purpose of Bible societies continues unchanged—the most widespread diffusion of the Scriptures in the languages of all peoples in forms and at prices suitable to their condition. But translations in more languages have been published (see BIBLE VERSIONS), new measures of co-operation and integration have taken place, and circulation has considerably increased.

Impelled by the unwisdom of separate but essentially similar operations in mission lands, the British and Foreign Bible Society and the American Bible Society began in 1932 to integrate their work in various countries. In each case a single budget and staff, supported by both societies, carries on the work under supervision of one or the other society, and in some cases joint supervision. By 1946 the distribution of Scriptures in all of South America, in the Near East from Bulgaria and Greece to Iraq and the Sudan, and in China and Japan was so administered. The National Bible Society of Scotland has joined these integrations in Japan and China. In Singapore the NBSS and the BFBS have united their work. In Indonesia the work of these two societies and that of the Netherlands Bible Society has been integrated under the latter's administration.

New national Bible societies have appeared, usually growing from advisory councils established by the BFBS and ABS for the joint agencies. Thus were founded the China Bible House (or Society) in 1937 (full development was hindered by World War II), the Japan Bible Society in 1938, the Bible Society of Brazil in 1948. Other societies were begun in areas not under joint operations. Under the pressure of war the Korean Bible Society in 1940 continued the work of the BFBS there. The BFBS combined its auxiliaries in India to form (1944) the Bible Society of India and Ceylon, now of India, Pakistan, and Ceylon. Plans for forming the United Bible Societies (see below) led to the creation of new units of co-operation in Europe: Austria Bible Committee (1947), Belgian Bible Society (1946), Czechoslovak Bible Society (1947), Alliance Biblique Française (1946), Federation of Swiss Bible Societies (1947), and Union of Evangelical Bible Societies in Germany (1948). The formation of these national societies has not meant a cessation of support from the BFBS and ABS, but generally the administration of such support, plus contributions from the country concerned, by a national board of directors, usually with representatives of the BFBS and ABS as counselors.

This expanding co-operation had its natural climax in the formation, at Elfinsward, England, in 1946, of the United Bible Societies, a world fellowship of twenty-four national societies, bringing in not only the societies named above but also the societies of Norway, Sweden, Denmark, Finland, Iceland, Ireland, and the BFBS bodies in Australia, Canada, and New Zealand. The United Bible Societies works in the common interest of all societies, assembling data, studying problems, providing services, making contact with other ecumenical bodies. Its council or standing committee meets annually. Its office is in London.

There has also been a vast increase in Scripture circulation. The total BFBS issues in the 103 years to 1907 were 203,931,768 Bibles, Testaments, Gospels, etc. In the next 34 years (to 1941) 328,572,256 more were issued. Similarly, to the ABS total of 82,366,323 in the first 91 years there were added, in the following 44 years (to 1950), 324,055,687. Circulation rose during each war and did not recede to prewar levels in the postwar period. The United Bible Societies' annual summary gives the total circulation by all Bible Societies in 1950 as 2,497,-208 Bibles, 3,424,748 Testaments, 15,878,271 Gospels and other portions; a total of 21,800,227. This is an increase of more than 4,000,000 over the 1948 figures. It is estimated that the circulation of the last 25 years has been in over 650 languages. However, the annual circulation has not yet been able to overtake the annual increase in literate persons.

A factor of much importance in the postwar period has been the mutual aid given by Bible Societies. During World War II and the years immediately following the ABS expended more than $1,000,000 for Scriptures for German prisoners of war and civilians and for raw materials and machinery for the German Bible Societies, and about $1,250,000 for similar aid to Japan. The British Society also made large contributions.

The contributions received by the principal Bible Societies are reported by the United Bible Societies for 1950 as follows (not including income from invested funds or sales): United States $1,908,000; England and Wales $936,000; Canada $370,000; Australia $101,000; New Zealand $87,000; the Netherlands $84,000; South Africa $79,000; Scotland $50,000. See also GIDEONS; POCKET TESTAMENT LEAGUE.

BIBLIOGRAPHY: Eric M. North, ed., *The Book of a Thousand Tongues*, 1938; *Bulletin* (quarterly) of the United Bible Societies; annual *Reports* of the several societies.

[Sup.] ERIC M. NORTH.

BIBLE TEXT: I. The Old Testament: In recent decades archaeology and research have brought marked advances in the textual criticism of the Old Testament in uncovering new sources of knowledge and in providing a better text.

A. NEW MATERIALS: The list of modern discoveries which throw light on the Hebrew Bible includes: Aramaic incantation texts from Nippur, which reflect pre-Masoretic Hebrew characters used in Babylonia; a Hebrew text of Jeremiah 48:11, found on a jar stamp; the Lachish Letters (q.v.), which exhibit Hebrew script from the time of Jeremiah (589 B.C.); and the Dead Sea Scrolls (q.v.), embracing among other Hebrew writings the Book of Isaiah, a commentary on Habakkuk, and fragments of Leviticus. In addition, the Ras Shamra (q.v.) Inscriptions and the Mari Letters (q.v.) contribute richly to our knowledge of epigraphy, paleography, and comparative Semitic philology.

Among fragments which afford new insights into the text of the Greek Bible are: the manuscripts in the Freer Collection on Deuteronomy, Joshua, the Psalms, and Minor Prophets; the Chester Beatty Biblical Papyri (q.v.), which embrace parts of several books of the Old Testament in Greek antedating the leading uncials; the John Rylands Library Papyri, which afford us in portions of Deuteronomy (23–28) our earliest extant witness to the Septuagint, dated to the second century B.C.; and the John H. Scheide Papyri, representing a Greek text of Ezekiel earlier than any hitherto known.

B. TEXTUAL RESEARCH: Recent Old Testament textual criticism has included: re-evaluation of older discoveries in the light of the new; studies in comparative Semitic philology, prose, prophecy, and poetry; the alphabet, its origin, forms, consonantal mutations, and vowel values; the vocabulary, including the claims as to the composite character of Hebrew and Aramaic; pre-Masoretic and Masoretic vocalization; re-examination of the theory (Lagarde) of the archetype in the Masoretic text; efforts toward the recovery of the *Urtext*, the original Greek text of the Septuagint, and the determination of the character of the Septuagint-*Vorlage,* the text used by the translators; and intensive study of the versions.

C. CRITICAL TEXTS: Until recently all editions of the Hebrew Bible, including the first and second editions of Kittel's work (1905, 1912), were based on the printed text of Jacob ben Chayyim (1524–25). Through the work of Paul Kahle a manuscript (Leningrad Codex B 19a) of the Ben Asher text (tenth century) was made the basis of the third edition of Kittel's *Biblia Hebraica* (ed. by P. Kahle, A. Alt, and O. Eissfeldt, 1929–37). This is a better text than that appearing in the edition of C. D. Ginsburg (*The Old Testament Diligently Revised According to the Massorah and the Early Versions . . .* , 1926). Among other researches, Kahle's studies of manuscripts discovered in the Cairo Geniza have contributed much toward a better knowledge of the Hebrew text.

Progress toward the completion of the critical Cambridge edition of the Septuagint (*The Old Testament in Greek*, ed. by A. E. Brooke, N. McLean, and H. St. John Thackeray, 1906–)

has been slow. This edition, following that of H. B. Swete, carries the text of the Codex Vaticanus, but with more extensive apparatus. In his complete edition of the Greek Bible (*Septuaginta*, 1935) A. Rahlfs provided a reconstructed text based largely on Codices Sinaiticus, Vaticanus, and Alexandrinus. The more ambitious Goettingen edition, designed by Rahlfs, is still incomplete.

BIBLIOGRAPHY: H. Bauer and P. Leander, *Historische Grammatik der hebraeischen Sprache*, 1922; A. E. Cowley, *Aramaic Papyri of the Fifth Century B.C.*, 1923; F. X. Wutz, *Die Transkriptionen von der Septuaginta bis zu Hieronymus*, 1925; idem, *Systematische Wege von der Septuaginta zum hebraeischen Urtext*, I, 1937; H. St. John Thackeray, *Some Aspects of the Greek Old Testament*, 1927; F. G. Kenyon, *The Chester Beatty Biblical Papyri*, 1933–38; idem, *The Text of the Greek Bible*, 1937; idem, *Our Bible and the Ancient Manuscripts*, 1948; L. H. Gray. *Introduction to Semitic Comparative Linguistics*, 1934; O. Eissfeldt, *Einleitung in das Alte Testament* (1934), 693 ff.; H. L. Ginsberg, *The Ugaritic Texts*, 1936; H. I. Bell, *Recent Discoveries of Biblical Papyri*, 1937; H. Torczyner, *The Lachish Letters*, 1938; A. C. Johnson, H. S. Gehman, and E. H. Kase. eds., *The John H. Scheide Biblical Papyri: Ezekiel*, 1938; C. H. Gordon, *Ugaritic Grammar*, 1940; E. Brenno, *Studien ueber hebraeische Morphologie und Vokalismus*, 1943; D. R. Ap-Thomas, *A Primer of Old Testament Text Criticism*, 1947; Paul Kahle, *The Cairo Geniza*, 1947; G. R. Driver, *Semitic Writing*, 1948; D. Diringer, *The Alphabet*, 1948, 2nd ed., 1949; H. M. Orlinsky, *The Septuagint*, 1949; D. W. Thomas, "The Textual Criticism of the Old Testament," in *The Old Testament and Modern Study* (1951), 238–263; B. J. Roberts, *The Old Testament Text and Versions*, 1951.
[Sup.] ELMER E. FLACK.

II. The New Testament:

A. THE MANUSCRIPTS: The number of Greek witnesses to all or part of the New Testament, according to the latest official lists (published by Ernst von Dobschuetz in *Eberhard Nestle's Einfuehrung in das griechische Neue Testament*, 4te Aufl. 1923; and in *ZNTW*, XXIII [1924], 248–264; XXV [1926], 299–306; XXVI [1927], 96; XXVII [1928], 216–222; and XXXII [1933], 185–206; and by K. Aland in *TLZ* [1953], 465–496) are: papyri, 63; ostraca, 25; talismans, 9; uncial manuscripts, 232; minuscule manuscripts, 2440; and lectionaries, 1678.

The oldest known fragment of the New Testament is a tiny scrap of papyrus (designated P[52]) measuring 2½ by 3½ inches and now at the John Rylands Library at Manchester. It contains John 18:31–33, 37–38, and has been dated by competent palaeographers within A.D. 100–150 (so C. H. Roberts, who published the fragment in 1935, and F. G. Kenyon, W. Schubart, H. I. Bell, A. Deissmann, and W. H. P. Hatch).

From the third century come the three important papyri acquired by A. Chester Beatty of Dublin and edited by Sir F. G. Kenyon (1933–37). P[45] comprises portions of thirty leaves of a papyrus codex, which originally contained all four Gospels and Acts. Matthew and John are the least well preserved, each being represented by only two fragmentary leaves. Six leaves of Mark, seven of Luke, and thirteen of Acts remain of these books. P[46] contains eighty-six leaves (all slightly mutilated) of a papyrus codex which originally embraced ten epistles of Paul in the following order: Rom., Heb., I and II Cor., Eph., Gal., Phil., Col., I and II Thess. P⁴⁷ comprises ten slightly mutilated leaves of the Book of Revelation. Of the original codex, estimated to have been thirty-two leaves in length, only the middle portion remains, containing the text of 9:10–17:2. (For other papyri see B. M. Metzger, "Recently Published Greek Papyri of the New Testament," *Smithsonian Report for 1948*, pp. 439–452; and the exhaustive list of the New Testament papyri by G. Maldfeld and B. M. Metzger in *JBL*, LXVIII [1949], 359–370. See also PAPYRI, BIBLICAL AND EARLY CHRISTIAN.)

Among the more important uncial manuscripts discovered during the twentieth century are the following. Codex W, now in the Freer Collection of the Smithsonian Institution in Washington, apparently dates from the late fourth or the fifth century. It contains the Gospels in the so-called "Western" order, namely Matthew, John, Luke, Mark. The type of text changes markedly in strata, and its editor Henry A. Sanders (1912) suggested that the manuscript is descended from an ancestor made up of fragments from different rolls of the Gospels pieced together after Diocletian's attempt to destroy all Bibles.

Codex *Theta* (Koridethianus), dated by its editors, G. Beermann and C. R. Gregory (1913), in the ninth century, contains the four Gospels written in an inelegant hand by a scribe who was clearly not familiar with Greek script. Formerly it belonged to the monastery of Koridethi near the Caspian Sea, and is now in Tiflis. Its type of text (particularly in Mark) is related to that used by Origen in the third century at Caesarea. For recent discoveries of uncial fragments, see B. M. Metzger in *Expository Times*, LXIII (1951–52), 309–311, and W. H. P. Hatch in *HTR*, XLV (1952), 81–86.

B. CRITICAL EDITIONS OF THE GREEK NEW TESTAMENT: The editors of the Oxford series of Greek and Latin classics invited Alexander Souter to prepare a critical edition of the Greek New Testament with a selected critical apparatus of variant readings. His *Nouum Testamentum graece* (Oxford, 1910; ed. sec., 1947) gives the Greek text which, by inference, lies behind the English Revised Version (1881). The chief strength of the apparatus lies in the relatively full evidence from the Latin Fathers.

The most monumental edition to appear after Tischendorf's *editio octava critica maior* (1869–72) was Hermann von Soden's *Die Schriften des Neuen Testaments in ihrer aeltesten erreichbaren Textgestalt*, I. Teil: *Untersuchungen*, 1, 3 Abteilungen, 1902–10; II. Teil: *Text mit Apparat*, 1913. In the first part von Soden surveys the entire history of the transmission of Greek manuscripts (excluding Greek lectionaries). According to his textual theory, most New Testament witnesses fall into one of three families, the Hesychian,

Jerusalem, and Koine. He also invented a new system of sigla which indicate the age, contents, and type of text of each manuscript. Because of its complicated nature most textual critics have refused to adopt this nomenclature. His textual theory has also been criticized as involving several basic errors, such as grouping together in the Jerusalem family quite heterogeneous witnesses, and, still more serious, elevating the Koine group to a rank co-ordinate in importance with the other two groups (see K. Lake's critique in *Review of Theology and Philosophy*, IV [1908], 201–217 and 277–295). Von Soden also published a Handausgabe, *Griechisches Neues Testament, Text mit kurzen Apparat*, 1913. Two useful lists which transpose von Soden's nomenclature into the Gregory-Dobschuetz system are Friedrich Krueger's *Schluessel zu von Sodens Die Schriften des Neuen Testaments . . .*, 1927, and Benedikt Kraft's *Die Zeichen fuer die wichtigeren Handscriften des Neuen Testaments*, 2te Aufl., 1934.

The edition prepared by Heinrich J. Vogels, *Novum Testamentum graece* (1920), makes special use of evidence derived from Old Latin, Old Syriac, and Tatianic sources. A second edition appeared in 1922; in the same year a Greek-Latin edition was published (3rd ed., 2 vols., 1949–50). For its size, August Merk's useful edition, *Novum Testamentum graece et latine* (1933; 7th ed., 1951), contains a relatively large amount of evidence of variant readings. Special attention is given to witnesses to Tatian's Diatessaron (see HARMONY OF THE GOSPELS [TATIAN'S]), but without the one-sided judgment characteristic of von Soden.

In 1935 the Oxford Press issued the first fascicle of a critical apparatus which was intended to be as comprehensive for its generation as Tischendorf's eighth edition was for his. The editor, S. C. E. Legg, published only two fascicles, *Nouum Testamentum graece secundum textum Westcotto-Hortianum; Euangelium secundum Marcum*, 1935; . . . *Euangelium secundum Matthaeum*, 1940. In 1948 the enterprise was reorganized as the International Project to Establish a Critical Edition of the Greek New Testament, with headquarters at the Universities of Chicago and Oxford.

The text of José M. Bover's *Novi Testamenti biblia graeca et latina* (1943; 3rd ed., 1953) is an eclectic one, departing frequently from an Alexandrian type of text and approaching a Western or Caesarean type. Thus it is closer to von Soden's text than to Westcott and Hort's. The apparatus, which includes the opinions of six modern editors, supplies evidence of the manuscripts on only the more important variants. (See B. M. Metzger, "Recent Spanish Contributions to the Textual Criticism of the New Testament," in *JBL*, LXVI [1947], 401–424.)

Nestle's convenient pocket edition of the

Greek Testament, first published in 1898, has gone through twenty-one editions (1952). Its text is based on the readings supported by two of the following three critical editions, Tischendorf, Westcott and Hort, B. Weiss. The apparatus contains a useful and relatively full conspectus of variant readings. Graeco-Latin and Graeco-German editions have also been published.

C. DEVELOPMENTS IN TEXTUAL CRITICISM: During the twentieth century attempts were made to discover groups of manuscripts belonging to texts, families, and subgroups. K. Lake isolated family 1 (comprising manuscripts 1, 118, 131, and several others; see *Texts and Studies,* VII, 1, 1902), and several scholars have added to family 13 (comprising manuscripts 13, 69, 124, 346, 543, and others). Von Soden, despite certain methodological errors in his edition, made several noteworthy contributions, particularly in tracing the history of the text in Byzantine manuscripts. In 1924 B. H. Streeter proposed his theory of "Local Texts" (*The Four Gospels,* pp. 27–78), namely that at the great sees of antiquity there developed special, characteristic texts. They may be identified in Greek manuscripts by discovering agreements with the earliest versions and with the quotations in the earliest fathers. Streeter's findings, in abbreviated form, are as follows. The primary and secondary authorities for the five local texts: (1) Alexandria: primary = B; secondary = *aleph,* L, Sahidic, Bohairic; (2) Antioch: prim. = Sinaitic Syriac; sec. = Curetonian Syriac; (3) Caesarea: prim. = *theta,* 565 in Mark; sec. = fam. 1, fam. 13, 28, 700, W in part of Mark, Old Georgian; (4) Italy and Gaul: prim. = D; sec. = b and a; (5) Carthage: prim. = k in Matthew and Mark; sec. = W in part of Mark, e.

Streeter's work in identifying the Caesarean text was generally (though not totally) confirmed and supplemented by a monograph entitled, "The Caesarean Text of the Gospel of Mark," by K. Lake, R. P. Blake, and Silva New (*HTR,* XXI [1928], 207–404). Not the least important part of these scholars' work was the attention they give to certain oriental versions, namely the Old Armenian, the Old Georgian, and the Palestinian Syriac, all of which, in their opinion, are witnesses to the Caesarean text.

Subsequent investigation, particularly after the discovery of the Chester Beatty Biblical Papyri, has tended to modify these opinions in the direction of dividing the Caesarean text into the primitive or pre-Caesarean group (including P45, W, fam. 1, 28, and fam. 13), and the recensional or Caesarean group proper (including *theta,* 565, 700, Origen, Eusebius, the Sinaitic Syriac, Old Armenian, and Old Georgian); see especially Teófilo Ayuso in *Biblica,* XVI (1935), 369–415. For a survey of the problems up to

1945, see B. M. Metzger, "The Caesarean Text of the Gospels," *JBL,* LXIV (1945), 457–489; subsequent treatments include A. H. White, "The Problem of the Caesarean Text," *Journal of the Manchester University Egypt and Orient Society,* XXIV, 1942–45 (published in 1947), 39–59; Francesco Russo, "I manoscritti del gruppo 'Ferrar,'" *Bollettina della badia greca di Grottaferrata,* N.S. III (1949), 76–90; and Lars-Olov Almgren, "Diskussionen om den caesarensiska texttypen," *Svensk exegetisk årsbok,* XV (1950), 81–100.

Another area which hitherto has been almost totally neglected by textual critics, the Greek Gospel lectionaries, has recently begun to receive more attention (see LECTIONARIES, NEW TESTAMENT GREEK, and H. Greeven, *ThLZ,* LXXVI [1951], cols. 513–522).

The so-called Western text remains the *bête noire* of New Testament textual critics. In reaction to the generally unfavorable regard which Westcott and Hort had for this type of text, certain scholars (e.g., J. R. Harris, F. C. Burkitt, Hans von Soden, A. C. Clark, H. J. Vogels, Alexander Souter, H. A. Sanders, C. H. Turner), held in varying degrees to the general superiority of the Western text. At present textual critics of the New Testament recognize that the Western text undoubtedly contains some original readings not present in other types of text, but few would agree (with A. C. Clark and H. A. Sanders) that its readings are almost always to be preferred. On the contrary, they would either continue to regard (with K. Lake, J. H. Ropes, W. H. P. Hatch) the Neutral or Alexandrian form of text as generally superior to all others, or would be (with L. Vaganay, H. Pernot, and E. C. Colwell) frankly eclectic. See A. F. J. Klijn, *A Survey of the Researches into the Western Text of the Gospels and Acts,* 1949 (with additional bibliography by Metzger in *Theologische Zeitschrift,* VII [1951], 330). On methodology in general see Metzger, "Trends in the Textual Criticism of the Iliad, the Mahābhārata, and the New Testament," *JBL,* LXV (1946), 339–352.

BIBLIOGRAPHY: Handbooks of New Testament textual criticism include: Caspar René Gregory, *The Canon and Text of the New Testament,* 1907; Edward A. Hutton, *An Atlas of Textual Criticism,* 1911; F. G. Kenyon, *Handbook to the Textual Criticism of the New Testament,* 2nd ed., 1912; Alexander Souter, *The Text and Canon of the New Testament,* 1912; E. Jacquier, *Le Nouveau Testament dans l'église chrétienne,* II, *Le texte du Nouveau Testament,* 10th ed., 1913; P. G. Groenen, *Algemeene inleiding tot de heilige schrift,* II, *Geschiedenis van den tekst,* 1917; August Pott, *Der Text des Neuen Testaments nach seiner geschichtlichen Entwicklung,* 2nd ed., 1919; Ernst von Dobschuetz, *Eberhard Nestle's Einfuehrung in das griechische Neue Testament,* 4th ed., 1923; H. J. Vogels, *Handbuch der neutestamentlichen Textkritik,* 1923; A. T. Robertson, *An Introduction to the Textual Criticism of the New Testament,* 1925; 2nd ed., 1928; K. Lake, *The Text of the New Testament,* 6th ed., rev. by Silva New, 1928; Giuseppe Sacco, *La koinè del Nuovo Testamento e la trasmissione del sacro testo,* 1928; Leon Vagnay, *Initiation à la critique textuelle neotestamentaire,* 1934, Eng. trans., *An Introduction to the Textual Criticism of the New Testament,* 1937; M. J. Lagrange, *Introduction à l'étude du Nouveau Testament;*

II, *Critique textuelle*, 2, *La critique rationnelle*, 1935;
F. G. Kenyon, *The Text of the Greek Bible, A Students' Handbook*, 1937. For 1200 additional works, see
B. M. Metzger, *Annotated Bibliography of the Textual Criticism of the New Testament*, 1955. See also BIBLE
VERSIONS, I; and HARMONY OF THE GOSPELS (TATIAN'S).

[Sup.] BRUCE M. METZGER.

BIBLE UNION OF CHINA. See CHINA.

BIBLE VERSIONS: The versions dealt with
in this article are divided into two principal
groups, ancient and modern. The ancient versions include all the known versions produced
down to the close of the tenth Christian century; so far as practicable these are arranged in
approximate chronological order. The modern
versions include those of the principal languages
of Europe and America, arranged in alphabetical
order. These are concluded with a cross reference
to an article which treats Bible versions on the
mission field.

In addition to the special bibliographies supplied for individual versions, the following books
are of general importance.

T. H. Darlow and H. F. Moule, *Historical
Catalogue of the Printed Editions of Holy Scripture in the Library of the British and Foreign
Bible Society* (2 vols., 1903–8); R. Kilgour, *The
Gospel in Many Years* (1929); O. M. Norlie, *The
Bible in a Thousand Tongues* (1935); British
Museum, *General Catalogue of Printed Books*,
Vols. XVI–XVIII (1936–37); Eric M. North, *The
Book of a Thousand Tongues* (1938); R. Kilgour,
The Bible Throughout the World (1939); F. G.
Kenyon, *Our Bible and the Ancient Manuscripts*,
(4th ed., 1939); H. W. Robinson (ed.), *The Bible
in Its Ancient and English Versions* (1941); Ira
M. Price, *The Ancestry of Our English Bible*
(2nd rev. ed., by W. A. Irwin and A. P. Wikgren, 1949; corrected ed., 1951); B. M. Metzger,
"The Evidence of the Versions for the Text of
the New Testament," in M. M. Parvis and A. P.
Wikgren (eds.), *New Testament Manuscript
Studies* (1950), pp. 25–68 and 177–208; Bleddyn
J. Roberts, *The Old Testament Text and Versions* (1951); B. M. Metzger, *Annotated Bibliography of the Textual Criticism of the New Testament* (1955), pp. 27–65; Arthur Vööbus, *Early
Versions of the New Testament, Manuscript
Studies (Papers of the Estonian Theological Society in Exile, No. 6, 1954).*

I. Ancient Versions:

A. THE SEPTUAGINT: See article, SEPTUAGINT,
THE.

B. LATIN VERSIONS: 1. THE LATIN BIBLE BEFORE JEROME: The suggestion by several scholars
(e.g., D. S. Blondheim, *Les parlers judéo-romans
et la Vetus Latina*, 1925; A. Baumstark, *ZDMG*,
N.F. XIV, 89–118), that alleged Semitic influence upon the Old Latin translations of the Old
Testament indicates that they were made originally from the Hebrew or the Aramaic Targums,
has not been accepted by most investigators,

who continue to hold that Christians made the
version from the Septuagint. Despite others' assertions that the Old Latin of the Old Testament is markedly "Lucianic," J. A. Montgomery
found no evidence of characteristic Lucianic
doublets in Daniel (*Commentary*, pp. 45–46).
On the other hand, his analyses corroborated
Burkitt's dictum that Old Latin citations by the
fathers are distinctly pre-Hexaplaric. Among
suggestions as to the place of origin of the Old
Latin (North Africa, Antioch in Syria, and
Rome), the most recent research points to Rome
(G. Bardy, *La question des langues dans l'église
ancienne*, I, 1948; Christine Mohrmann, "Les
origines de la latinité chrétienne à Rome," *VC*,
III, [1949], 67–106, and 163–183). Besides the two
main types of pre-Jerome Latin translations
(African and European), traces of another, much
nearer the Septuagint, are to be found in quotations by Augustine (Burkitt in *JTS*, XI, [1910],
258–268).

In the New Testament the textual complexion
of the Old Latin is typically Western, and as a
rule the African form offers the larger divergencies, the European the smaller. The remarkable variations among the Old Latin manuscripts may perhaps be explained on the supposition that the scribes regarded their work not
in terms of mechanical transmission, but as producing a "Targum" which incorporated their
own and others' traditions. That is to say, the
Old Latin was a living creation constantly growing even after the publication of Jerome's Vulgate (see Montgomery, *Daniel*, p. 45; von Soden
in Juelicher's *Festgabe* [1927], p. 273; H. H.
Glunz, *History of the Vulgate in England*
[1933], pp. 14 ff.).

Three important series of publications of Old
Latin evidence are in the course of production:
A. Juelicher's edition of the *Itala; Das Neue
Testament in altlateinischer Ueberlieferung nach
den Handschriften*, I: *Matthaeus* (1938); II:
Markus (1940); III: *Lukas* (1955); and the
Benedictine *Vetus Latina; Die Reste der altlateinischen Bibel nach Petrus Sabatier neugesammelt und herausgegeben von der Erzabtei
Beuron*, of which there have been published
Verzeichnis der Sigel (1948), and the first part of
Genesis (ed. B. Fischer, 1951); and Teófilo
Ayuso, *La Vetus Latina Hispana*; I: *Prolegómenos* (1953).

BIBLIOGRAPHY: Old Testament: A. Amelli, *Liber Psalmorum juxta antiquissimum latinam versionem*, Rome, 1912;
P. (later Bernard) Capelle, *Le texte du psautier latin en
Afrique*, 1913; A. Dold, *Konstanzer altlateinische Propheten und Evangelienbruchstuecke*, 1923 (26 folios of
Ezekiel, Daniel, and Minor Prophets); A. V. Billen, *The
Old Latin Texts of the Heptateuch*, 1927; A. Allgeier,
Die altlateinische Psalterien, 1928; B. Motzo, *La versione
latina di Ester secondo i LXX*, 1928; A. Allgeier, "Das
afrikanisches Element im althispanischen Psalter," *Spanische Forschungen*, II (1930), 196–228; H. Degering and
A. Boeckler, *Die Quedlinburger Itala Fragmenta*, Berlin,
1932 (new fragments of Samuel and Kings); D. De
Bruyne, "Les plus anciennes versions latines du Cantique," *R. Bén*, XXXVIII (1926), 97–115; A. Dold, *Neue
St. Galler vorhieronymische Propheten-Fragmenta*, 1940;
J. Schildenberger, *Die altlateinische Texte des Proverbien-*

buches, 1941; R. Weber, *Les plus anciennes versions latines du II⁰ livre des Paralipomènes*, 1945; B. Bischoff, "Neue Materialien zum Bestand und zur Geschichte der altlateinischen Bibeluebersetzungen," *Miscellanea G. Mercati*, I (1947), 410 ff.

New Testament: A. Reichardt, *Der Codex Boernerianus der Briefe des Apostel Paulus*, 1909; E. S. Buchanan, *The Four Gospels from the Codex Veronensis*, 1911; H. J. Vogels, *Codex Rehdigeranus. Die vier Evangelien nach der lateinischen Handschrift 169 der Stadtbibliothek Breslau*, 1913; C. Cipolla, *Il codice evangelico "k" della biblioteca universitaria di Torino*, 1913; A. Gasquet, *Codex Vercellensis*, Rome, 1914; A. Juelicher, "Kritische Analyse der lateinischen Uebersetzungen der Apostelgeschichte," *ZNTW*, XV (1914), 163–188; H. J. Vogels, *Untersuchungen zur Geschichte der lateinischen Apokalypsenuebersetzungen*, 1920; C. H. Milne, *A Reconstruction of the Old Latin Text or Texts of the Gospels Used by St. Augustine*, 1926; H. J. Vogels, *Evangelium Palatinum, Studien zur aeltesten Geschichte der lateinischen Evangelienuebersetzung*, 1926; A. Bakker, *A Full Collation of Codex Evang. Bobbiensis (k)*, 1933; G. Godu, *Codex Sarzanensis, fragments d'ancienne version latine du quatrième évangile*, 1936; T. Ayuso Marazuela, "Una importante colección de notas marginales de la Vetus Latina Hispana," *EB*, IX (1950), 328–378.

On the linguistic phenomena of the Old Latin (besides Blondheim's work cited above), see A. Allgeier, "Vergleichende Untersuchungen zum Sprachgebrauch der lateinischen Uebersetzungen der Psalmen und der Evangelien," *ZATW*, XLVI (1928) 34–49; P. W. Hoogterp, *Étude sur le latin du Codex Bobbiensis (k) des évangiles*, 1930; W. Suess, *Studien zur lateinischen Bibel*, I: *Augustins locutiones und das Problem der lateinischen Bibelsprache*, 1932; W. Matzkow, *De vocabulis quibusdam Italae et Vulgatae christianis quaestiones lexicographicae*, Berlin, 1933; Robert C. Stone, *The Language of the Latin Text of Codex Bezae*, 1946.

2. THE LATIN VULGATE: The Vulgate text of the Old Testament is far from being uniform; in the historical books Jerome's skill and originality as translator of the Hebrew are most conspicuous, whereas in the Prophets and Psalter he often deliberately accepted the rendering of the Greek versions (cf. F. Stummer, *Einfuehrung in die lateinischen Bibel* [1928], pp. 99–110). Contrary to A. Condamin's denial of the influence of Jewish tradition on Jerome (*RSR*, V [1914], 1–21), C. H. Gordon found ample evidence in Proverbs to substantiate the generally accepted view that Jerome frequently followed current Rabbinical interpretations (*JBL*, XLIX [1930], 384–416). With regard to Jerome's revisions of the Psalter, De Bruyne maintained that the so-called *Psalterium Romanum* is not the work of Jerome (whose revision made for Pope Damasus has been lost), but is an Old Latin Psalter erroneously attributed to Jerome (*R. Bén.*, XLII [1930], 447–482). This was refuted by A. Allgeier, who, inverting the sequence customarily proposed for Jerome's three revisions of the Psalter, held that the first was *Psalterium iuxta Hebraeos*, the second *Psalterium Gallicanum* (both based on the Hexaplaric Greek text of Origen), and the third *Psalterium Romanum* (A. Allgeier, *Die altlateinischen Psalterien*, 1928; and *Die Psalmen der Vulgata*, 1940).

The Vulgate text of the New Testament poses many problems for the textual critic. No unanimity of opinion prevails as to the type of Greek text which Jerome chose as a standard by which to revise the Old Latin. Von Soden believed that it was like the archetype of his own three great recensions, *I, H,* and *K* (*Die Schriften des Neuen Testaments*, I, iii [1910], 1524–1532). Vogels maintained that in the Gospels Jerome utilized what is called the Koine type of Greek text (*Vulgatastudien* [1928], pp. 55–80). Burkitt, however, denied that Jerome consulted only one type of Greek text, and held that he depended on at least two, one similar to that found in codex Vaticanus, and the other similar to that found in codex Alexandrinus (*JTS, XXX* [1929], 408–412). Lagrange agreed with Burkitt in part, but thought that Jerome was influenced by the type of text represented by codex Sinaiticus even more than by that in codex Alexandrinus (*Critique textuelle* [1935], 287 ff.).

In the Acts Ropes found that the Vulgate agrees most often with codex Alexandrinus (*The Text of Acts* [1926], p. cxxvii).

De Bruyne proposed the startling thesis that what is commonly taken to be Jerome's Vulgate text of the Pauline Epistles is none other than the work of Pelagius (*Revue Biblique*, N.S. XII [1915], 358–392). Cavallera went still further and denied that Jerome had any part in making the Vulgate text of the Acts, Epistles, and Apocalypse (*Bulletin de littérature ecclésiastique* [1920], 269–292). Against these views the traditional opinion was upheld by Buonaiuti (*ET, XXVII* [1915–16], 425–427), Souter (*JTS, XVI* [1915], 105), Mangenot (*RB*, N.S. XV [1918], 244–253), and Chapman (*JTS, XXIV* [1923], 33–51).

For the Catholic Epistles of the Vulgate there exists a distinctive type of text of great importance for the textual critic (von Harnack, *Zur Revision der Principien der neutestamentlicher Textkritik*, 1916).

The most thorough study of Jerome's text of Revelation is that by Vogels, who found many resemblances of the Vulgate to codex Sinaiticus (*Untersuchungen zur Geschichte der lateinischen Apokalypsenuebersetzung*, 1920).

Several scholars have attempted to disentangle the complicated strands of national types of Vulgate text which emerged during the Middle Ages; e.g., Hans Glunz, *Britannien und Bibeltext, der Vulgatatext der Evangelien . . .* (1930); *idem, History of the Vulgate in England from Alcuin to Roger Bacon . . .* (1933); L. J. Hopkins-James, *The Celtic Gospels . . .* (1934); J. M. Bover, "La Vulgata en España," (*EB*, seg. época, I [1941–42], 11–40, 167–185; cf. VIII [1948], 161 f.).

In 1907 Pope Pius X appointed Abbot (later Cardinal) Gasquet, president of the English Benedictines, as head of a commission entrusted with the revision of the text of the Vulgate. The so-called *règle de fer* for evaluating variant readings, which Dom Henri Quentin elaborated for the textual criticism of the Vulgate (*Mémoire sur l'établissement du texte de la Vulgate*,

1922), was subjected to devastating criticism by E. K. Rand (*HTR*, XVII [1924], 197–264), Chapman (*R. Bén.*, XXXVII [1925], 5–40, 365–403), and Stummer (*ZATW*, N.F., IV [1927], 141–151). Thus far nine volumes have been published: Genesis (1926); Exodus, Leviticus (1929); Numbers, Deuteronomy (1926); Joshua, Judges, Ruth (1939); Samuel (1944); Kings (1945); Chronicles (1948); Ezra, Tobias, Judith (1950); Esther, Job (1951).

The edition of the New Testament, begun by Wordsworth and White in 1879, with the publication of Matthew in 1889, has now been completed by H. F. D. Sparks (1954).

BIBLIOGRAPHY: F. Amann, *Die Vulgata Sixtina von 1590*, 1912; H. Hoepfl, *Beitraege zur Geschichte der Sixto-Klementinischen Vulgata*, 1913; A. Juelicher, "Kritische Analyse der lateinischen Uebersetzungen der Apostelgeschichte," *ZNTW*, XV (1914), 163–188; Ambrosius Amelli, *Cassiodoro e la Volgata*, 1917; J. M. Harden, *Psalterium iuxta Hebraeos Hieronymi*, 1922; Henri Quentin, *Essais de critique textuelle*, 1926; idem, *La Vulgate à travers les siècles et sa révision actuelle*, 1926; C. H. Turner, *The Oldest Manuscript of the Vulgate Gospels . . .*, 1931; Alban Dold, *Zwei Bobbienser Palimpseste mit fruehestem Vulgatatext*, 1931; G. Sacco, *La Volgata latina e il testo del Nuovo Testamento*, 1933; N. Greitemann, *De Windesheimse Vulgaatrevisie in de vijftiende Eeuw*, 1937; Pierre Salmon, *La révision de la Vulgate*, 1937; Hans Rost, *Die Bibel im Mittelalter*, 1939; J. Ziegler, *Die juengeren griechischen Uebersetzungen als Vorlagen der Vulgata in den prophetischen Schriften*, 1943–44; Jan O. Smit, *De Vulgaat*, 1948. On the language of the Vulgate, see John J. Jepson, *The Latinity of the Vulgate Psalter*, 1915; W. E. Plater and H. J. White, *A Grammar of the Vulgate*, 1926; M. Stenzel, "Zum Wortschatz der NT Vulgata," *VC*, VI (1952), 20–27; as well as the studies listed at the close of the preceding bibliography on the Old Latin.

3. LATER LATIN TRANSLATIONS: In 1529 there was published at Wittenberg a revision of part of the Latin Vulgate, made by unknown translator(s)—Luther; Melanchthon; Bucer?—on the basis of the original texts and Luther's German version. It embraced only the Pentateuch, Joshua, Judges, the Books of Kings, and the New Testament. According to Eberhard Nestle, who edited the reprint for the Weimar edition of Luther's *Werke* (*Die Deutsche Bibel*, Vol. 5, 1914), in the New Testament the version frequently improves upon Jerome's Latinity and at the same time comes closer to the Greek text (Nestle in *Philologus*, LXXI [1912], 314–317).

In 1941 Pope Pius XII assigned to the Pontifical Biblical Institute in Rome the task of preparing a new Latin translation of the Psalms directly from the Hebrew. This *Liber Psalmorum* was completed in 1944, and a second edition with the seventeen canticles from the Old and New Testaments which are used in the Psalter of the Roman Breviary appeared in 1945. The translators sought to be faithful to the original while having a careful regard for "the venerable Vulgate" and other ancient versions (*Acta Apostolicae Sedis*, XXXVII [1945], 65–67). See also Augustinus Bea, *Il nuovo salterio latino* (2nd ed., 1946), also in French (1947) and German (1949) translations.

In 1950 Bea published his Latin translation of *Liber Ecclesiastae . . . qui ab Hebraeis appelatur Qohelet.*

BIBLIOGRAPHY: For a discussion of Latin versions of the sixteenth century, see Hugh Pope, *English Versions of the Bible* (1952), 99–128.

C. SYRIAC VERSIONS: 1. THE OLD SYRIAC: Though Torrey has argued for Palestine as the origin of this version (*Documents of the Primitive Church* [1941], pp. 345–370), most scholars continue to regard Edessa as its birthplace. Vööbus' research has revealed the persistence of sporadic Old Syriac variants in ecclesiastical authors down to the twelfth century. From the form of quotations in Ephraem's commentaries on the Acts and Pauline Epistles, extant in Armenian, it appears that an older form of the Syriac text for these books preceded the Peshitta, even though no manuscript of this has survived (Conybeare in J. H. Ropes, *The Text of Acts* [1926], 373–453; Joseph Molitor, *Der Paulustext des hl. Ephraem . . .*, 1938). See also HARMONY OF THE GOSPELS (TATIAN'S).

2. THE PESHITTA: The Peshitta of the Old Testament, at least in the Pentateuch, is thought to be of Jewish or Jewish Christian origin (J. Bloch, *AJSL*, XXXV [1919], 215–222; A. Baumstark, *Geschichte der syrischen Literatur* [1922], p. 18; R. H. Pfeiffer, *Introduction to the Old Testament* [1941], p. 120). Some books of the Old Testament, e.g., Genesis (Haenel), II Samuel (Englert), the Psalms (Berg), reveal influence from the Septuagint. Esther is a careful but not slavish rendering of the Hebrew. Chronicles has the paraphrastic characteristics of a Targum. Proverbs is free but, on the whole, faithful to the original (Pinkuss, *ZATW*, XIV [1894], 65–141; Chajes, *JQR*, XIII [1901], 86 ff.). Lamentations and Ezra follow the Masoretic text carefully (Abalesz; Hawley).

Whether Rabbula, Bishop of Edessa (411–435), made the Peshitta of the New Testament (so Burkitt and many following him), appears to be somewhat less certain in view of Vööbus' researches (yet see Matthew Black's critique in *Bulletin of the John Rylands Library*, XXXIII [1951], 203–210, and in *Bulletin* of *Studiorum Novi Testamenti Societas* [1950], 51–62). As to text type, Gwilliam found that, in Matt. 1–14, the Peshitta agrees with the *textus receptus* 108 times and with Vaticanus 65 times, while in 137 cases it differs from both, usually with the support of the Old Syriac or the Old Latin (*Studia Biblica et Ecclesiastica*, V [1903], 187–237). In Acts the Peshitta preserves many Old Syriac readings in a text substantially like that of the Old Uncials (J. H. Ropes, *The Text of Acts*, pp. 291–316).

3. THE PHILOXENIAN AND/OR HARCLEAN SYRIAC: The problem whether the Philoxenian Syriac version was reissued by Thomas of Heraclea or whether the second was an entirely new version has not yet been solved. In any case, the Harclean marginal variants in Acts are second only to codex Bezae in importance for the Western text.

John Gwynn edited *The Apocalypse of John in a Syriac Version Hitherto Unknown* (being the first Syriac book issued from the Dublin University Press, 1897), which he identified as the Philoxenian version. He also edited *The Four Minor Catholic Epistles* (II Peter, II and III John, Jude) of the same version (1909). In the same volume there are included also the *pericope de adultera* (in two recensions) and fragments of the Syro-Hexaplar version of the Septuagint (Gen., Lev., I and II Chron., Neh.). Zuntz finds influence in the Harclean version from the Caesarean type of text, but the reliability of his work has been questioned by Kilpatrick and McHardy (*JTS*, XLVIII [1947], 92–99).

4. THE PALESTINIAN SYRIAC: The view commonly held is that the Pentateuch in this version was made from the Septuagint. Baumstark, however, maintained that it goes back to a Jewish Palestinian Pentateuch Targum (*OC*, 3te Serie, X, 201–224). In the Gospels the version appears to be a witness of the Caesarean text (so Lake-Blake-New, *HTR*, XXI [1928], 312–323). For literature down to 1924, see Friedrich Schulthess, *Grammatik des christlichpalaestinischen Aramaeisch* (1924). Additional fragments were published by Hugo Duensing, in *ZNTW*, XXXVII (1938), 42–46; Matthew Black, *Bulletin of the John Rylands Library*, XXIII (1939), 201–214; Duensing, *Nachrichten der Ak. der Wiss. in Goettingen*, phil.-hist. Kl. (1944); and Black, *A Christian Palestinian Syriac Horologion* (1954).

BIBLIOGRAPHY: J. F. Berg, *The Influence of the Septuagint on the Peshitta Psalter*, 1895; A. Abalesz, *Die syrische Uebersetzung der Klagelieder . . .*, 1895; J. Haenel, *Die aussermasoretischen Uebereinstimmungen zwischen der Septuaginta und der Peshitta in der Genesis*, 1895; C. A. Hawley, *A Critical Examination of the Peshitta Version of the Book of Ezra*, 1922; M. J. Wyngarden, *The Syriac Version of the Book of Daniel*, 1923; Leo Haefeli, *Die Peschitta des Alten Testaments mit Ruecksicht auf ihre textkritische Bearbeitung und Herausgabe*, 1927; C. Moss, "The Peshitta Version of Ezra," *Le Muséon*, XLVI (1933), 58–110; Franz Rosenthal, *Die aramaistische Forchung seit Th. Noeldeke's Veroeffentlichungen*, 1939; P. A. H. de Boer, *Research into the Text of I Samuel I–XVI* (1938), pp. 22–43; Guenther Zuntz, *The Ancestry of the Harklean New Testament*, 1945; J. van der Ploeg, "Recente Pesitta-Studies (sinds 1927)," *Jaarbericht van het Vooraziatisch-Egyptisch Gezelschap, Ex Oriente Lux*, X (1948), 392–399; Donald M. C. Englert, *The Peshitto of Second Samuel*, 1949; Arthur Vööbus, *Studies in the History of the Gospel Text in Syriac*, 1951; A. Vogel, "Studien zum Peschitta-Psalter," *Biblica*, XXXII (1951), 32–56, 198–231, 336–363, 481–502.

D. THE SAMARITAN PENTATEUCH: This text (which, being Hebrew written in Samaritan characters, is not strictly a version) differs from the Masoretic text in about 6,000 places, in more than 1,900 of which it agrees with the Septuagint (Kahle in *Theologische Studien und Kritiken*, LXXXVIII [1915], 399–439). Some of the grammatical differences may be explained by the hypothesis that the Samaritan text preserves North Israelitic dialectal peculiarities, while the Masoretic text perpetuates a Judaean dialectal

recension (so A. Sperber, *Hebrew Union College Annual*, XII-XIII [1937–38], 151 ff.). When the Septuagint diverges most from the Masoretic text, the Samaritan follows the latter with great fidelity (so H. M. Wiener, *The Expositor*, 8th Series, II [1911], 200–219, who criticizes Gesenius' methodology in his analysis of the Samaritan text).

Early in the Christian era the Samaritan Pentateuch was translated into the Aramaic dialect of the Samaritans. This version, called the Samaritan Targum, is a colloquial rendering which is distinguished from the Palestinian-Jewish Targums by lacking the literalism of the latter (E. Robertson, in *Saadya Studies*, pp. 166–176). The exegesis is popular and without influence from Jewish sources. See also E. ARAMAIC VERSIONS (TARGUMS), below.

There was also a Greek translation of the Samaritan Pentateuch (known as the Samaritikon), about fifty quotations of which are preserved in the notes on Origen's Hexapla. What its exact relationship to the Septuagint is has been debated, but the discovery of fragments of the version (Gen. 37; Deut. 24–29; ed. P. Glaue and A. Rahlfs, *Mitteilungen des Septuaginta-Unternehmens*, II, 1911) reveals that it was made from the Samaritan Pentateuch by translators familiar with the Septuagint.

Several Arabic translations of the Samaritan Pentateuch were made in the eleventh to the thirteenth century (P. Kahle, *Die arabischen Bibeluebersetzungen*, pp. x f.; and *The Cairo Geniza*, pp. 36–39).

BIBLIOGRAPHY: A. Rahlfs, *Fragmenta einer griechischen Uebersetzung des samaritanischen Pentateuchs*, 1911; A. von Gall, *Der hebraeische Pentateuch der Samaritaner*, 5 vols., 1914–18; Chaim Heller, *The Samaritan Pentateuch, an Adaptation of the Masoretic Text*, 1923; M. Gaster, *The Samaritans*, 1925; D. S. Sassoon, *Descriptive Catalogue of the . . . Samaritan MSS. in the Sassoon Library*, 1933; C. W. Dugmore, "Two Samaritan MSS in the Library of Queens College, Cambridge," *JTS*, XXXVI (1935), 131–147; Lea Goldberg, *Das samaritanische Pentateuchtargum*, 1935; E. Robertson, *Catalogue of the Samaritan Manuscripts in the John Rylands Library*, 1938.

E. ARAMAIC VERSIONS (TARGUMS): Five substantial fragments (dated *ca.* A.D. 700–900) of a Palestinian Pentateuch Targum, not Onkelos, were discovered in the famous Genizah of a synagogue in Old Cairo. The new Targum is often a free paraphrase with haggadic additions and occasionally presupposes an underlying Hebrew consonantal text differing from the Masoretic text. The language of the fragments is thought by Kahle to be first century Aramaic and, as such, to represent a much earlier stage in the history of the Targums than that of the other Targums. There is, however, no generally accepted dating of the various Targums.

According to Stenning, the Hebrew text presupposed by the Targum of Isaiah differs very slightly from the Masoretic text. In addition, the translation is generally faithful to the Hebrew; a notable exception, however, is the Targumist's bias when he "actually rewrites ch. 53, replacing it by one bearing no resemblance to the original" (P. Churgin, *Targum Jonathan* [1927], p. 84). See also D. THE SAMARITAN PENTATEUCH.

BIBLIOGRAPHY: M. Neumark, *Lexikalische Untersuchungen zur Sprache der jerusalemischen Pentateuch-Targume*, 1905; A. Levy, *Das Targum zu Koheleth nach suedarabischen Handschriften*, 1905; Emil Brederek, *Konkordanz zum Targum Onkelos*, 1906; P. E. Kahle, *Masoreten des Westens*, Vols. I and II, 1927. 1930; Aapeli Saarisalo, "The Targum to the Book of Ruth," *Studia Orientalia* (Societas orientalis fennica), II (1928), 88–104; S. Silverstone, *Aquila and Onkelos*, 1931; A. Marmorstein, "Bemerkungen zu den neuentdeckten Fragmenten des jerusalemischen (palaestinensischen) Targums," *ZATW*, N. F. VIII (1931), 231–242; P. Churgin, "The Targum and the Septuagint," *AJSL*, L (1933), 41–65; A. Sperber, "The Targum Onkelos in its Relation to the Hebrew Masoretic Text," *Proceedings of the American Academy for Jewish Research*, VI (1934–35), 309–351; idem, "Peschitta und Onkelos," *Jewish Studies in Memory of G. A. Kohut* (1935), pp. 554–564; S. Wohl, *Das palaestinische Pentateuch-Targum*, 1935; V. Hamp, *Der Begriff "Wort" in den aramaeischen Bibeluebersetzungen*, 1938; C. J. Kosowski, *Otzar ha-Targum* (A Concordance to the Targum of Jonathan), 1940; Allen Wikgren, "The Targum and the New Testament," *JR*, XXIV (1944), 89–95; P. Churgin, *Targum Kethubim* (in Hebrew), 1945; J. F. Stenning, *The Targum of Isaiah*, 1949.

F. COPTIC VERSIONS: The largest collection of Coptic biblical manuscripts made available is the *Bibliothecae Pierpont Morgan codices coptici photographice expressi* . . . (1922, 56 vols. in 63). For a list of the contents of these volumes, as well as information regarding other biblical texts, see Winifred Kammerer, *A Coptic Bibliography* (1950). This latter now supplants A. Vaschalde, *Ce qui a été publié des versions coptes de la Bible* (1922) (originally published in *RB*, XXVIII–XXXI [1919–22]).

Gehman's study of Daniel reveals that the Sahidic version was translated from the Greek text of Theodotion with influence from Origen's Hexapla on a Hesychian background, and that the Bohairic version was made from the Hesychian form of the Hexaplaric Greek.

The Sahidic version of the Gospels reveals a complex character, combining elements found in the Alexandrian and Western families, and agreeing as well with certain of the readings of P[45]. In the Acts the Sahidic shows a close affinity with the type of text in Codex Vaticanus (B). In the rest of the New Testament this version belongs to the Alexandrian recension.

In all parts of the New Testament the Bohairic version is freer from Western readings than is the Sahidic, and agrees closely with the Alexandrian recension.

The Qau papyrus codex of the Gospel of John in the sub-Achmimic dialect, dated by its editor in the third quarter of the fourth century, agrees most frequently with B, *aleph*, and L.

BIBLIOGRAPHY: Herbert Thompson, *The Coptic (Sahidic) Version of Certain Books of the Old Testament from a Papyrus in the British Museum*, 1908; Sir Herbert Thompson, *A Coptic Palimpsest Containing Joshua, Judges, Ruth, Judith and Esther in the Sahidic Dialect*, 1911; E. A. Wallis Budge, *Coptic Biblical Texts in the Dialects of Upper Egypt*, 1912; George Horner, *The Coptic Version of the New Testament in the Northern Dialect* . . . , 4 vols., 1898–1905; idem, *The Coptic Version of the New Testament in the Southern Dialect* . . . , 7 vols., 1911–24; Sir Herbert Thompson, *The Gospel of St. John According to the Earliest Coptic Manuscript*,

1924; W. H. Worrell, *The Coptic Manuscripts in the Freer Collection*, 1923; H. S. Gehman, "The Sahidic and Bohairic Versions of the Book of Daniel," *JBL*, XLVI (1927), 279–330; W. Till, *Die achmimische Version der Zwoelf Kleinen Profeten*, 1927; W. H. Worrell, *The Proverbs of Solomon in Sahidic*, 1931; F. H. Hallock, "The Coptic Old Testament," *AJSL*, XLIX (1932–33), 325–335; A. Boehlig, *Untersuchungen ueber die koptischen Proverbientexte*, 1936; Willem Grossow, *The Coptic Version of the Minor Prophets*, 1938; M. Malinine, "Fragment d'une version achmimique des Petits Prophètes," *Coptic Studies in Honour of W. E. Crum* (1950), pp. 365–416.

G. THE GOTHIC VERSION: In 1908 a vellum leaf from a bilingual Gothic-Latin codex was discovered at Antinöe in Egypt (Paul Glaue and Karl Helm, *ZNTW*, XI [1910], 1–38). Wilhelm Streitberg edited all the extant fragments of both Old Testament and New Testament and reconstructed the Greek *Vorlage* (*Die gotische Bibel*, 1908; 3rd ed., 1950). According to Michael Metlan, Streitberg's Greek text is in need of revision (*Journal of English and Germanic Philology*, XXXII [1933], 530–548). The University Library at Uppsala published a magnificent photographic facsimile of Codex Argenteus (*Codex argenteus Upsaliensis* . . . , 1927).

BIBLIOGRAPHY: P. J. Odefey, *Das gotische Lukas-Evangelium* (Diss. Kiel), 1908; Adolf Juelicher, "Die griechische Vorlage der gotischen Bibel," *ZDAL*, LII (1910), 365–387; Erich Mayr, *Die gotische Bibel, I: Matthaeus*, 1913, 2te Aufl., 1928; Hans Lietzmann, "Die Vorlage der gotischen Bibel," *ZDAL*, LVI (1919), 249–278; W. Limke, *Das gotische Markusevangelium*, 1920; G. W. S. Friedrichsen, *The Gothic Version of the Gospels, A Study of Its Style and Textual History*, 1926; idem, *The Gothic Version of the Epistles, A Study of Style and Textual History*, 1939; J. de Vries, *Wulfilae codices Ambrosiani rescripti epistularum evangelicarum textum Goticum exhibentes*, Florence. 1936; Fernand Mossé, "Bibliographia Gotica, A Bibliography of Writings on the Gothic Language, to the End of 1949," *Mediaeval Studies*, XII (1950), 237–324 (pp. 255–264 deal with the biblical version).

H. THE ARMENIAN VERSION: In general the Armenian version of the Old Testament is thought to follow carefully the Hexaplaric recension of the Septuagint. Gehman's research on Daniel reveals its affinities with an Origenian-Constantinopolitan type of text, with agreements also with the Hesychian witnesses and the Syriac.

It has been disputed whether the Armenian New Testament was translated from the Syriac (so J. A. Robinson, Conybeare, Merk, Blake, Baumstark) or directly from the Greek (so Macler, Lyonnet, and Colwell). As to type of New Testament text represented by the Armenian, Blake, Colwell, Lyonnet, and Williams find evidence of Caesarean traits.

Recently Lyonnet has investigated more thoroughly certain suggestions made by Baumstark, Peradze, and Essabalean that behind the present Armenian text of the Gospels there was an Armenian Diatessaron. As for the Apocalypse, Conybeare discerned five revisions.

BIBLIOGRAPHY: Artasches Abeghian, *Vorfragen zur Entstehungsgeschichte der altarmenischen Bibeluebersetzungen*, 1906; F. C. Conybeare, *The Armenian Version of Revelation*, 1907; Frédéric Macler, *Le texte arménien de l'évangile d'après Matthieu et Marc*, 1919; August Merk, "Die armenische Evangelien und ihre Vorlage," *Biblica*, VII (1926), 40–70; H. S. Gehman, "The Armenian Version of the Book of Daniel and its Affinities," *ZATW*,

N.F. VII (1930), 82–99; E. C. Colwell, "The Caesarean Readings of Armenian Gospel Manuscripts," *Anglican Theological Review*, XVI (1934), 113–132; idem, "Slandered or Ignored: The Armenian Gospels," *Journal of Religion*, XVII (1937), 48–61; C. S. C. Williams, "Syriasms in the Armenian Text of the Gospels," *JTS*, XLIII (1942), 161–167; St. Lyonnet, *Les origines de la version arménienne et le Diatessaron*, 1950.

I. THE GEORGIAN VERSION: According to Blake the manuscript tradition of different parts of the Georgian Old Testament is not uniform. The original translations and later revisions were made at different times and from varying archetypes, namely, Armenian and Greek (Septuagint). The relation of the edition printed at Moscow in 1743 to the Armenian texts, in the Prophets at least, is much closer than has previously been supposed, being presumably a revision of a direct translation from the Armenian. In the New Testament modern non-critical editions reproduce a Georgian text prepared in the tenth or eleventh century. The earliest known manuscripts of the Gospels are the Adysh manuscript (A.D. 897), Opiza manuscript (A.D. 913), and Tbet' (A.D. 995) which preserve two strains of Old Georgian text, both of which belong to the Caesarean family. A manuscript of Acts (A.D. 965, so Ropes, *The Text of Acts*, p. clxxxiii, n. 2), tested in four chapters, reveals many Western readings. The Book of Revelation, according to Lyonnet, appears to have been first translated into Georgian by St. Euthymius, the Athonite (ca. A.D. 978).

BIBLIOGRAPHY: F. C. Conybeare, "The Growth of the Peshitta Version of the New Testament illustrated from the Old Armenian and Georgian Versions," *AJT*, I (1897); idem, "The Old Georgian Version of Acts," *ZNTW*, XII (1911), 131–140; Franz Zorell, "Ursprung und Eigenart der georgischen Bibeluebersetzung," *Handes Amsorya*, XLI (1927), 669–680; R. P. Blake, *The Old Georgian Version of the Gospel of Mark, from the Adysh Gospels with the Variants of the Opiza and Tbet' Gospels* (=*Patrologia Orientalis*, XX, 3), 1929; . . . of Matthew (=*Patr. Orientalis*, XXIV, 1), 1933; . . . of John (with M. Brière) (=*Patr. Orientalis*, XXVI, 4), 1950; R. P. Blake, "Ancient Georgian Versions of the Old Testament," *HTR*, XIX (1926), 271–297; idem, "The Athos Codex of the Georgian Old Testament," *HTR*, XXII (1929), 33–56; idem, "Khanmeti Palimpsest Fragments of the Old Georgian Version of Jeremiah," *HTR*, XXV (1932), 225–272; cf. P. L. Hedley's corrections in *JTS*, XXXV (1933), 392–395; Stanislas Lyonnet in M. J. Lagrange, *Critique textuelle* (1935), 375–386, 460–463, 625; R. P. Blake and Sirarpie Der Nersessian, "The Gospels of Bert'ay; an Old Georgian Ms. of the Tenth Century," *Byzantion*, XVI (1942–43), 226–285; A. Shanidze, *Two Old Recensions of the Georgian Gospels according to Three Shatberd Manuscripts* (A.D. 897, 936, 973) (in Georgian), 1945; J. Molitor, "Die georgischen Bibeluebersetzung," *OC*, 4th Ser., I (1953), 23–29; idem, "Das Adysh-Tetraevangelium," ibid., 30–55.

J. THE ETHIOPIC VERSION: It is estimated that outside Abyssinia there are today about 1,200 manuscripts of various parts of the Ethiopic Bible, most of them belonging to the sixteenth to eighteenth centuries. From a sampling of these it appears that the overwhelming majority present a form of text which was Arabicized in the fourteenth century. Very few manuscripts are older than this date. According to Gehman, in I Kings the Ethiopic text is based on a Greek text like that in B (Codex Vaticanus) with a strong Lucianic influence. There is no evidence, however, for a single unified text of the Ethiopic Bible, influenced throughout by the same Greek source. To the contrary, Gleave's research supports Charles' view (based on Malachi and Lamentations) that the Ethiopic is indebted to Symmachus and other portions of the Hexapla.

In the New Testament the original translators at times followed the Greek text slavishly, and at other times, perhaps where the Greek proved too difficult for them, they paraphrased wildly (so Montgomery). An analysis of sporadic quotations of the Synoptic Gospels in several Ethiopic ecclesiastical writers seems to reveal kinship with the Old Syriac text (so Vööbus).

BIBLIOGRAPHY: August Heider, *Die aethiopische Bibeluebersetzung* . . . , I: *Bibelkritische Abhandlung*, 1902; F. M. E. Pereira, *Job* (*Patrologia Orientalis*, II, 5), 1905; *Esther* (*P.O.*, IX, 5), 1911; *Esdras et Néhémie* (*P.O.*, XIII, 5), 1919; J. Oscar Boyd, *The Octateuch in Ethiopic*, I and II (Gen., Ex., and Lev.), 1909–1911; F. M. E. Pereira, "O livro do profeta Amós e a sua versão etiopica," *Academia das sciencias de Lisboa; Boletim da segunda classe*, XI (1918), 472–534; Francesco da Bassano edited the Ethiopic Bible at Asmara, 5 vols., 1911–21, 2nd ed. of New Testament, 1934; Oscar Loefgren, *Die aethiopische Uebersetzung des Propheten Daniel*, 1927; idem, *Jona, Nahum, Habakuk, Zephanja, Haggai, Sacharja und Maleachi aethiopisch*, 1930; S. A. B. Mercer, *The Ethiopic Text of the Book of Ecclesiastes*, 1931; H. S. Gehman, "The Old Ethiopic Version of I Kings and Its Affinities," *JBL*, L (1931), 81–114; James A. Montgomery, "The Ethiopic Text of Acts of the Apostles," *HTR*, XXVII (1934), 169–205; H. C. Gleave, *The Ethiopic Version of the Song of Songs Critically Edited*, 1951; Arthur Vööbus, *Die Spuren eines aelteren aethiopischen Evangelientextes im Lichte der literarischen Monumente*, 1951. For excellent annotated bibliographies see George F. Black, "Ethiopica and Amharica," *Bulletin of the New York Public Library*, XXXII (1928), 443–481, 528–562; C. Conti Rossini in *Aevum*, I (1927), 459–624 (covers 1915–27); *Aevum*, X (1936), 467–587 (covers 1927–36); *Rassegna di studi etiopici*, IV (1944–45), 1–132 (covers 1936–45); J. Simon in *Orientalia*, XXI (1952), 47–66 (covers 1946–51). See also Silvio Zanutto, *Bibliografia etiopica*, 1932; K. J. Luethi in *Gutenbergmuseum*, XXII, 5–38, reprinted with additions in his *Aethiopisch in der Schweiz*, 1936.

K. THE NUBIAN VERSION: During the sixth century the northern kingdom of Nubia (the land between Egypt and Abyssinia) received Christianity from Monophysite missionaries. Portions of an Old Nubian lectionary for Christmastide survive, dating from the tenth or eleventh century and containing for each day pericopes from the Apostolos and the Gospel (namely, short sections from Romans, Galatians, Philippians, Hebrews, Matthew, and Luke).

BIBLIOGRAPHY: For the history of Nubian Christianity, see G. Roeder, *ZKG*, XXXIII (1912), 364–398; and Ugo Monneret de Villard, *Storia della Nubia cristiana*, 1938. The fragments were edited first by H. Schaefer and K. Schmidt in *SBA*, phil.-hist. kl. (Nov. 8, 1906), 774–785; and definitively re-edited by F. L. Griffith, *Abhandlungen der koeniglich Preussischen Akademie der Wissenschaften*, phil.-hist. Kl. (1913), no. 8.

L. THE SOGDIAN VERSION: The Sogdian language, the easternmost member of the Indo-European family of languages, flourished in Central Asia during the second half of the first millennium of the Christian era. Portions of Matthew, Luke, and John in the form of a lectionary, as well as small fragments of I Corinthians and Galatians, have been discovered in this Iranian dialect. According to a study by Peters, the Gospel material was translated from a Syriac base substantially identical with the Peshitta, but containing several noteworthy variations.

Portions of Psalms 94–99, 118 (119), and 121–136 (122–137) have been discovered in Pahlavi, an Iranian language related to Sogdian, dating from about the seventh century (edited by F. C. Andreas and Kaj Barr in *SBA*, 1933, 91–152).

BIBLIOGRAPHY: F. W. K. Mueller, "Neutestamentliche Bruchstuecke in soghdischer Sprache," *SBA* (1907), 260–270; *idem, Abhandlungen der koeniglich Preussischen Akademie der Wissenschaften*, phil.-hist. Kl. (1912). no. 2; J. R. Harris, *Side-Lights on N. T. Research* (1908), pp. 116–124; Curt Peters, *OC*, 3te Serie, XI (1936), 153–162.

M. THE OLD SLAVIC VERSION: On the basis of an examination of 500 readings in the Old Slavic Psalter, Josef Vajs found that 449 preserve a Lucianic (Greek) type of text, and that the others were influenced by the Latin Vulgate (*Byzantinoslavica*, VIII [1939–46], 55–86).

It appears certain that the Old Slavic Gospels existed first in lectionary form, having been translated from a Greek Gospel lectionary. Later additions were made in order to embrace the full text of the Gospels. According to analyses made by Vajs, the textual type of the Gospels is fundamentally Byzantine in which are embedded many Palestinian and Caesarean readings. (The work of Schweigl, who found strong Alexandrian influence, *Biblica*, XXIV [1943], 289–303, is vitiated by an imperfect acquaintance with textual methodology). The Apostolos, according to Jagić, presents a text substantially like that of the Greek *textus receptus*. The Apocalypse stands apart from the rest of the version, not having been translated until the twelfth century (so Oblak).

Whether influence from the Latin Vulgate can be detected in the Old Slavic has been debated, Pogorělov (*Sborník fil. fak. Univ. Komenského, Bratislavě*, III, 32 [1925], 207–216) arguing for such influence; Meillet (*Revue des études slaves*, VI [1926], 39–41), against it. See also **II. Modern Versions: W. SLAVIC VERSIONS.**

BIBLIOGRAPHY: V. Oblak, "Die kirchenslavische Uebersetzung der Apokalypse," *Archiv fuer slavische Philologie*, XIII (1891), 321–361; V. Jagić, "Zum altkirchenslavischen Apostolus," in *Sitzungsberichte d. Ak. d. Wiss. in Wien*, phil.-hist. Kl., 191, 2 (1919); Andrej Snoj, "Veteroslavicae versionis evangeliorum . . . momentum," *Biblica*, III (1922), 180–187; Josef Vajs, *Evangelium sv. Matouše. Text rekonstruovaný*, 1935; . . . *Marka*, 1935; . . . *Lukáše*, 1936; . . . *Jana*, 1936; R. P. Casey and Silva Lake, "A New Edition of the Old Slavic Gospels," *JBL*, LV (1936), 195–209; J. Hamm, "Ueber den gotischen Einfluss auf die altkirchenslavische Bibeluebersetzung," *Zeitschrift fuer vergleichende Sprachwissenschaft*, LXVII (1942), 112–128; J. Bonfante and B. M. Metzger, "The Old Slavic Version of the Gospel according to Luke," *JBL*, LXXIII (1954), 217–236 (with a survey of previous investigations).

N. THE ARABIC VERSIONS: In opposition to the prevailing opinion, several scholars have argued in favor of a pre-Islamic date for the earliest Arabic versions (e.g., Anton Baumstark, *Islamica*, IV [1931], 562–575; *OC*, 3te Serie, IX [1934], 165–188, and 278–279; and Curt Peters,

Acta orientalia, XVIII [1940], 124–137; *Revista degli studi orientali*, XX [1942], 129–143).

As regards the Pentateuch, Rhode found that two Christian Arabic versions were current in Egypt: a version from the Bohairic used by the Jacobites and one from the Sahidic used by the Melchites; both were influenced by the Hebrew and Samaritan texts.

According to Vaccari (*Biblica*, II [1921], 401–423; III [1922], 401–423; cf. IV [1923], 312–314) the Arabic text of the prophetic books in the Paris Polyglot was translated at Alexandria by the priest El-Alam (ninth or tenth century) from a Greek text close to Codex Alexandrinus. Gehman's study of the Arabic version of the Book of Daniel in the Paris and London Polyglot Bibles shows that it was rendered from a Greek Hexaplaric text of Constantinople in a recension superior to Codex Alexandrinus and all other witnesses.

In the New Testament Peters, who tested sample passages from all four Gospels in a group which Guidi found to be translated from Greek, discovered not a few Tatianisms (*OC*, 3te Serie, XI [1936], 188–211). Levin's analysis of Matthew and Mark in two Arabic manuscripts translated from Greek discloses that in addition to Tatianisms many readings characteristic of the Caesarean text are also present. See also **D. THE SAMARITAN PENTATEUCH.**

BIBLIOGRAPHY: P. E. Kahle, *Die arabische Bibeluebersetzungen*, 1904; H. Spiegel, *Saadia al-Fajjûmî's arabische Danielversion*, 1906; J. C. Hughes, *De Lagarde's Ausgabe der arabischen Uebersetzung des Pentateuchs*, 1920; J. F. Rhode, *The Arabic Versions of the Pentateuch in the Church of Egypt*, 1921; H. S. Gehman, "The 'Polyglot' Arabic Text of Daniel and its Affinities," *JBL*, XLIV (1925), 327–352; P. E. Algermissen, *Die Pentateuchzitate Ibn Ḥazm*, 1933; O. Löfgren, *Studien zu den arabischen Danieluebersetzungen mit besonderer Beruecksichtigung der christlichen Texte*, 1936; Bernard Levin, *Die griechisch-arabische Evangelien-Uebersetzung . . .*, 1938; George Graf, *Geschichte der christlichen arabischen Literatur*, I (1944), 85–195; P. E. Kahle, *The Cairo Geniza*, 1947.

O. THE ANGLO-SAXON VERSION: Investigation of the type of Latin text underlying the Anglo-Saxon version reveals that it was a mixture of various recensions of the Vulgate (with Alcuin's and the Irish recensions prominent) along with continuing strains of Old Latin texts. It may even be (so Peters) that the Anglo-Saxon preserves a Tatianic element, transmitted via the Old Latin. In any case, the view advocated by Drake, L. M. Harris, and Bright, that the type of text in Matthew differs from that in Mark and Luke, and both from that in John, is based on an incomplete examination of the data; Glunz's thorough analyses reveal no marked differences of type of text among the four Gospels.

BIBLIOGRAPHY: Allison Drake, *The Authorship of the West Saxon Gospels*, 1894; Robert Handke, *Ueber das Verhaeltnis der westsaechsischen Evangelien-Uebersetzung zum lateinischen Original*, 1896; L. M. Harris, *Studies in the Anglo-Saxon Version of the Gospels*, Part I: *The Form of the Latin Original . . .*, 1901; James W. Bright. *The Gospel of Saint John [Matthew, Mark, Luke] in West-Saxon . . .*, 1904–6; S. J. Crawford (ed.), *The Old*

English Version of the Heptateuch . . . , 1922, Hans Glunz, *Die lateinische Vorlage der westsaechsischen Evangelien-Version,* 1928; G. P. Krapp, *The Junius Manuscript* [of Caedmon's paraphrases], 1931; *idem, The Paris Psalter and the Meters of Boethius,* 1932; Curt Peters, "Der Diatessaron-text von Mt. 2, 9 und die westsaechsische Evangelien-version," *Biblica,* XXIII (1942), 323–332.

II. Modern Versions:

A. AFRIKAANS VERSION. See **E. DUTCH VERSIONS.**

B. BOHEMIAN (CZECH) VERSIONS, and **BULGARIAN VERSIONS.** See **W. SLAVIC VERSIONS.**

C. CELTIC VERSIONS: In 1932 the Reverend Ernest E. Joynt of the Irish Methodist Church published at Dublin his revision of Mark in present-day Irish. Other portions of the New Testament followed, and the entire New Testament appeared in 1951. The final revision of the manuscript of Joynt (who died shortly before the work was completed) was undertaken by the Reverend C. W. Quin. In the opinion of Douglas Hyde, expressed in a letter to the Hiberian Bible Society, Joynt's version is superior to previous ones, and "gives the sense of the Greek without any circumlocution whatever and still in a language quite intelligible."

BIBLIOGRAPHY: Hibernian Bible Society, *Report* (1933), p. 8; R. W. Jackson, *The Bible in Ireland* (1950), pp. 18–19.

D. DANISH VERSIONS. See **V. SCANDINAVIAN VERSIONS.**

E. DUTCH VERSIONS: H. C. Voorhoeve and N. A. J. Voorhoeve prepared for the use of Plymouth Brethren in The Netherlands their translation of the New Testament (1877). This was based on the Greek text underlying J. N. Darby's version. A third edition appeared in 1931. A second edition of Kuenen and Oort's version of the New Testament was published in 1915. A. M. Brouwer and H. Th. Obbink, of the University of Utrecht, published three large volumes of selections of their translation of the Bible (Amsterdam, 1917–27).

A good translation by Roman Catholic scholars (R. Jansen, B. Alfrink, J. Cools, *et al.*) was published in honor of Petrus Canisius in five volumes (Amsterdam, 1936–39). Another Roman Catholic translation, *De katholieke Bijbel,* less satisfactory than the "Canisius" edition, was prepared by two Franciscan scholars, Laetus Himmelreich and Crispinus Smits, who translated the Old Testament and the New Testament respectively (Bruegge, 1938).

In 1928 an interdenominational committee with F. W. Grosheide as chairman, which had been at work since 1911, was sponsored by the Netherlands Bible Society and commissioned to produce a version in accord with modern Dutch idiom and based upon the oldest attainable text. The New Testament was published at Amsterdam in 1939; the Bible in 1951.

Afrikaans, which is a Dutch dialect that was reduced to written form about 1872, became the medium of a version of Genesis (Paarl, 1893),

translated by S. J. Du Toit and others. A committee, including D. G. Du Toit, J. D. Kestall, and B. B. Keet, prepared a translation of the Bible which the British and Foreign Bible Society published at Capetown in 1943. Before the Bible had actually been issued 30,000 copies had been ordered and paid for; 300,000 copies were sold within the first two years of its publication.

BIBLIOGRAPHY: C. C. De Bruin, *De Statenbijbel en zijn voorgangers,* 1937.

F. ENGLISH VERSIONS: 1. PROTESTANT (AND OTHER) TRANSLATIONS:

A group of about twenty scholars, whose identity was not disclosed beyond the fact that they represented various sections of the Christian Church, prepared *The Twentieth Century New Testament,* translating Westcott and Hort's Greek text. This was published at London in three parts between 1898 and 1901, and a revision in 1904. Within general subdivisions the books were arranged in what was regarded as their probable chronological order (thus, Mark precedes Matthew).

James Moffatt's *Historical New Testament* (Edinburgh, 1901) is a new translation, in traditional "biblical" English, of the books of the New Testament "arranged in the order of their literary growth and according to the dates of the documents" (as determined by the critical hypotheses prevalent at the beginning of the century).

A. S. Way, the noted translator of Homer, Vergil, and other classics, published his rendering of *The Letters of St. Paul to Seven Churches and Three Friends* (London, 1901). The second edition (1903) contained also the *Letter to the Hebrews.* The translation is marked by a judicious use of expansion, particularly of transitional connectives.

In 1903 Richard F. Weymouth, formerly head master of the Mill Hill School, produced *The New Testament in Modern Speech,* edited and partly revised by E. Hampden-Cook. It is a dignified and idiomatic translation into everyday English which seeks to render with great exactness the tenses of the Greek verb. (See Weymouth's pamphlet, *On the Rendering into English of the Greek Aorist and Perfect Tenses* . . . , 1894). The underlying Greek text is Weymouth's Resultant Greek Testament, based on the best critical scholarship of the time. The first American edition, newly revised by J. A. Robertson, was published at Boston in 1943.

The Corrected English New Testament, A Revision of the "Authorized" Version (by Nestle's Resultant Text) was prepared by Samuel Lloyd (New York, 1905).

In 1912 the American Baptist Publication Society issued an "Improved Edition" of the Bible Union Version of 1864. Where the word "baptize" occurs it is followed by the word "immerse" enclosed in parentheses. In several passages the translation anticipated the rendering of the Revised Standard Version (1952), as, e.g., the translation of 'almah in Isa. 7:14 as "young woman." Instead of italics, brackets are used to indicate words not in the original but supplied because of the requirements of English idiom.

James Moffatt's second translation (Edinburgh, 1913) was based upon von Soden's edition of the Greek New Testament, with several transpositions of verses, paragraphs, and chapters. In 1924 he published a translation of the Old Testament. Following the practice of several French translations and Matthew Arnold, Moffatt rendered the divine name ("Lord," "Jehovah") by "the Eternal." Both Testaments are characterized by a certain freshness of phraseology and sentence structure. In 1935 a "revised and final edition" of the Moffatt Bible was published.

The New Testament, An American Translation, utilizing the common language of everyday life, was prepared by Edgar J. Goodspeed (Chicago, 1923), based on the Westcott and Hort Greek text. *The Old Testament, An American Translation* appeared in 1927, prepared by T. J. Meek (University of Toronto), Leroy Waterman (University of Michigan), A. R. Gordon (University of Montreal), and J. M. P. Smith (University of Chicago), who was responsible also for the general editorial oversight. This edition contains an appendix of 91 pages listing emendations of the Hebrew which the translators preferred to the Masoretic text. In 1931 Goodspeed's New Testament was published with the Old Testament translation as *The Bible, An American Translation.* In 1939 there appeared *The Complete Bible, An American Translation,* consisting of T. J. Meek's stylistic revision of the Old Testament, Goodspeed's new translation of the Apocryphal books, and Goodspeed's New Testament.

The Riverside New Testament was translated by William G. Ballantine from Nestle's Greek text (1923; revised ed., 1934). It is an eclectic rendering with acknowledged dependence upon several previous translations.

G. C. Martin and T. H. Robinson edited ten pamphlets of *Books of the Old Testament in Colloquial Speech,* translated by various scholars and published by the National Adult School Union (London, 1923 ff.).

To mark the first hundred years of service of the American Baptist Publication Society, Mrs. Helen B. Montgomery, of Rochester, N. Y., published *The Centenary Translation of the New Testament* (2 vols., Philadelphia, 1924). She supplied her modern speech translation with colloquial subject headings, e.g., "A 'Close-up' of Sin," "Paul's Swan Song," and "Orchestrate Your Virtues."

A professor of Greek at Union University (Tennessee), Charles B. Williams, published *The New Testament, A Translation in the Language of the People* (Boston, 1937; reprinted, Chicago, 1950), based on Westcott and Hort's Greek text. Williams paid strict attention to the exact shades of meaning of the Greek tenses, especially with regard to the verbal "aspects" (*Aktionsarten*), but in so doing he occasionally overtranslated the Greek.

The Berkeley Version of the New Testament (Berkeley, California, 1945) is the work of Gerrit Verkuyl, who for many years was on the Board of Christian Education of the Presbyterian Church, U.S.A. Using chiefly Tischendorf's eighth edition of the Greek text (1869–72), Verkuyl's aim was to produce "a translation less interpretative than Moffatt's, more cultured in language than Goodspeed's, more American than Weymouth's, and freer from the King James Version than the Revised Standard [proved to be]" (Verkuyl, in *The Bible Translator,* Vol. II, No. 2 [April, 1951], 81).

The New Testament in Basic English (Cambridge, 1941) is a translation prepared by a committee under the direction of S. H. Hooke, Professor of Old Testament in the University of London. Basic English, which has a vocabulary of 850 words, was in this case supplemented by the addition of 50 special biblical words and 100 other words listed as giving most help in the reading of English verse. *The Old Testament in Basic English* was completed in the year 1950.

The New Testament Letters, prefaced and paraphrased by J. W. C. Wand, Bishop of London (Oxford, 1946), is a dignified rendering which expands the more difficult passages.

The New World Translation of the Christian Greek Scriptures is a more or less faithful rendering of Westcott and Hort's Greek text into vernacular English, published by the Watchtower Bible and Tract Society for the use of Jehovah's Witnesses (Brooklyn, 1950). The footnotes contain a certain amount of technical information regarding variant readings in manuscripts and early versions, but this is mingled with totally irrelevant information from various translations into Hebrew, made in the sixteenth and succeeding centuries. These latter are thought to give authority for the introduction of "Jehovah" into 237 passages in the New Testament. One of the characteristics of the version is an attempt to render each major Greek word always by the same English equivalent, irrespective of the requirements of the context. (For a critique of its Unitarianism, see B. M. Metzger, *TT,* X [1952], 65–85). The first of three projected volumes of the Witnesses' rendering of the Old Testament was issued in 1953. Among other characteristics, it follows Robert Young's idiosyncrasy in deliberately ignoring the force of the waw consecutive.

The Revised Standard Version of the New Testament, published in February, 1946, is a revision (authorized by churches through their educational boards associated in the International Council of Religious Education) of the American Standard Version (1901). It was prepared by a committee of translators from more than twenty theological seminaries and universities, with Luther A. Weigle as chairman. The work of revision was begun in 1930, suspended in 1932 because of lack of financial support, and resumed in 1937. The aim of the committee was to produce a version which retained more of the literary beauty of the King James Version than did the Revision of 1901, and at the same time to make such alterations as were deemed necessary in the light of increased knowledge of the text, vocabulary, and grammar of the Scriptures. The Old Testament was published in September, 1952. This differs from the 1901 revision in returning to the King James' use of "Lord" (instead of "Jehovah") and in a somewhat greater reliance upon variant readings supported by ancient versions, as against the Masoretic Hebrew text. A revision of the Apocryphal books is in progress. (See two pamphlets of essays issued by members of the Revision Committee, *An Introduction to the Revised Standard Version of the New Testament*, 1946; and *An Introduction to . . . the Old Testament*, 1952.)

J. B. Phillips, an Anglican priest, prepared a rendering of the New Testament Epistles (*Letters to Young Churches*, New York, 1948), characterized by frequent expansion and paraphrase couched in flowing vernacular English. It is based on Souter's edition of the Greek text which inferentially lies behind the 1881 English Revision. Phillips also published *The Gospels Translated into Modern English* (New York, 1953).

E. V. Rieu, translator of several Greek and Latin classics and editor of the Penguin Classics since 1945, published his rendering of the Gospels in the Penguin series (1952); this had been preceded by his privately printed rendering of Mark (1951). The translation is characterized by dignified simplicity.

In 1937 the Society for the Promotion of Christian Knowledge asked Charles Kingsley Williams to prepare a translation of the New Testament in simplified English (involving the vocabulary of about 2000 common words listed by a group of educators in the *Interim Report on Vocabulary Selection,* 1936). Williams entitled his rendering of Souter's Greek text, *The New Testament, A New Translation in Plain English* (London, 1952).

2. ROMAN CATHOLIC TRANSLATIONS: With Cuthbert Lattey, S.J., as the general editor, there began to appear in 1913, *The Westminster Version of the Sacred Scriptures,* based on the original Hebrew and Greek. The New Testament was finished in 1935, and several books of the Old Testament have been published.

Shortly before his death in 1913 Francis A. Spencer, O.P., completed a rather free translation of the Greek New Testament; this was edited and published by C. J. Callan and J. A. McHugh (New York, 1937). Vulgate readings when different from the Greek are given in brackets or in footnotes.

A revision of the Challoner-Rheims version, resting upon the Latin Vulgate, was published by a group of twenty-seven Roman Catholic scholars under the patronage of the Episcopal Committee of the Confraternity of Christian Doctrine (Paterson, N. J., 1941). Where the Latin and the Greek differ, a rendering of the latter is given in footnotes. Under the patronage of the same Episcopal Committee a group of members of the Catholic Biblical Association of America is at work translating the Old Testament from the Hebrew. The Book of Genesis was published in 1948; the Psalms and Canticles in 1950; and the books from Genesis to Ruth, 1952. A curious typographical error appears in the first printing of the last-named volume. In Lev. 11:30, among the list of lizard-like animals forbidden as food, there is listed the "skunk," a misprint for "skink."

Monsignor Ronald A. Knox's rendering of the Vulgate New Testament (London, 1944) and of the Old Testament including Apocrypha (two volumes, 1949), is a fresh, sagacious, and skillful piece of work. (See Matthew P. Stapleton, "Catholic Bible Translations," *JBR,* XIV [1946], 198–202).

3. JEWISH TRANSLATIONS: Claude G. Montefiore, a liberal Jewish scholar, published in two volumes in 1896 and 1899 nearly the whole of the Old Testament in his *Bible for Home Reading.* He also included a version of the Synoptic Gospels in his two-volume commentary on *The Synoptic Gospels* (1911; 2nd ed., 1927).

In 1917 the Jewish Publication Society of America issued *The Holy Scriptures According to the Masoretic Text, A New Translation,* which was prepared by a committee of Jewish scholars with Max L. Margolis as editor-in-chief. It aims to combine the spirit of Jewish tradition with the results of biblical scholarship. (See M. L. Margolis, *The Story of Bible Translations,* 1917; and Alexander Sperber, "A New Bible Translation," *Alexander Marx Jubilee Volume,* Eng. Section [1950], pp. 547–580.)

See also BIBLES, ANNOTATED.

BIBLIOGRAPHY: J. G. Carleton, *The Part of Rheims in the Making of the English Bible,* 1902; M. W. Jacobus, *Roman Catholic and Protestant Bibles Compared,* 1905; Henry Barker, *English Bible Versions,* 1907; A. W. Pollard, *Records of the English Bible,* 1911; Joseph H. Penniman, *A Book About the English Bible,* 1919; Laura H. Wild, *The Romance of the English Bible,* 1929; P. Marion Simms, *The Bible in America, Versions that have*

Played Their Part in the Making of the Republic, 1936;
H. W. Robinson (ed.), *The Bible in Its Ancient and Eng-
lish Versions*, 1940; C. C. Butterworth, *The Literary
Lineage of the King James Bible*, 1941; David Daiches,
The King James Version of the English Bible, 1941; Har-
old R. Willoughby, *Soldiers' Bibles through the Cen-
turies*, 1944; Ira M. Price, *The Ancestry of Our English
Bible*, 2nd rev. ed., by W. A. Irwin and A. P. Wik-
gren, 1949, corrected ed., 1951; Luther A. Weigle, *The
English New Testament from Tyndale to the Revised
Standard Version*, 1949; A. P. Wikgren, "The Use of
Marginal Notes in the English Bible," *Crozer Quarterly*,
XXVII (1950), 143–153; Stanley Rypens, *The Book of
Thirty Centuries*, 1951; Herbert Gordon May, *Our Eng-
lish Bible in the Making*, 1952; Hugh Pope, *English
Versions of the Bible*, revised and amplified by S. Bul-
lough, 1952.

G. FINNISH VERSIONS: In 1891 Ludvig Enk-
vist published at Porvoossa his translation of
St. John's Gospel. This was the first portion of
Scripture to appear in roman type. Since about
1910 Scripture editions have generally been in
roman character, except those in the Karelian
dialect. These latter, which were published by
the Russian Orthodox Missionary Society, use
the Cyrillic characters. In the twentieth century a scholarly revision of the Finnish Bible, on
the basis of the oldest accessible texts of the
original languages, was prepared by a group of
professors. The New Testament was finished
in 1913 and was tentatively approved by the
Lutheran Church Assembly. Tentative editions
of various parts of the Old Testament were
issued up to 1930. As few criticisms were received, the whole was re-examined by the committee in 1931 and a final text prepared. In
1933 the Lutheran Church Assembly tentatively
approved the Old Testament, and both Testaments were approved fully in 1938. They were
published by the Finnish Bible Society at Helsinki in 1939.

BIBLIOGRAPHY: Arthur Hjelt, "Mikael Agricola, der erste
finnische Bibeluebersetzer," *Theologische Studien, Theodor
Zahn . . . dargebracht* (1908), pp. 91–106; O. M. Norlie
(ed.), *The Translated Bible* (1934), pp. 158–166; A. F.
Puukko "Die Lutherbibel und die finnische Bibeluebersetzung," *Zeitschrift fuer systematische Theologie*, XVIII
(1941), 68–75; idem, "Mikael Agricola som finsk Bibel-
översättare," *Festskrift tillägnad hovpredikanten Isaac
Béen . . .* (1948), pp. 13-28.

H. FRENCH VERSIONS: Among Protestant
translations are the following. Pastor A. De-
coppet published (Paris, 1903) a rendering of
Westcott and Hort's edition of the Greek New
Testament, which is less modern in style than
Stapfer's translation (1889). A revision of the
Ostervald text, prepared under the direction of
the Synod of the Reformed Churches and published by the Bible Society of France, appeared
in 1910. This has been revised several times.
Maurice Goguel, Henri Monnier, and several
other scholars published their modern vernacular
version of the New Testament in 1929. It contains notes regarding variant readings in manuscripts and ancient versions. The Bible du
Centenaire de la Jeunesse, based on the latest
results of modern scholarship and published by
the Protestant Bible Society of Paris, appeared
in 1947.

Among Roman Catholic translations are the
following: M.-J. Lagrange of the École Biblique
at Jerusalem, published translations of the Gospels in his commentaries (1921–29). In 1932
the Pieuse Société Saint Paul issued a version
of the Bible based upon the Vulgate. The
Belgian scholar, Bernard Botte, O.S.B., published a translation of the Greek text of the
New Testament, with notes that deal with textual and exegetical difficulties (Turnhout, 1944).

A translation which may supplant the widely-
used version by Abbé Crampon (1905) is being
issued in several small volumes under the direction of the École Biblique of Jerusalem (the
Gospels were published at Paris in 1948). The
rendering, which is not so literalistic as Crampon's, was made from the original languages
and is accompanied by two series of notes, one
justifying the variant readings adopted, and the
other explaining difficult passages. Paul George
Passelecq, a Benedictine at Maredsous who,
while in a concentration camp during World
War II, formed the resolve to bring the Bible
to Roman Catholics in the vernacular, published
his translation of the Gospels (Brussels, 1946),
the New Testament (1948) and the Bible (1950).
The rendering follows somewhat Segond's (Protestant) version, but is simpler and more colloquial.

BIBLIOGRAPHY: D. Lortsch, *Histoire de la Bible en
France . . .* , 1910.

I. GERMAN VERSIONS: A translation of the
Bible by F. E. Schlachter was published at Biel,
Switzerland, in 1903–4. In 1920 Ludwig Albrecht, a Free Church pastor at Bremen, finished
his rendering of the New Testament (6th ed.,
1938). The translation, which is free, clear, and
idiomatic, has been used widely in Bible classes
for the laity and in schools for advanced pupils.

The "Menge Bible" is generally recognized as
one of the very best German versions of the
Bible. Hermann Menge worked tirelessly for
twenty years on his translation, finishing it on
his eighty-fifth birthday. It was published by
the Privilegierte Wuerttembergische Bibelan-
stalt of Stuttgart in 1926. Like Luther, however,
Menge continued to improve his work, and, a
few months before his death on January 8, 1939,
in his ninety-seventh year, he gave to the Bibel-
anstalt his final revision, which was incorporated
in the eleventh edition and represents the "textus receptus" of the Menge Bible.

Theodor Daechsel, a Silesian pastor, published
in 1928 a rendering of von Soden's Greek text
under the following title, *Die Schriften des
Neuen Testaments nach ihrem urspruenglichen
Wortsinn in die deutsche Sprache der Gegenwart wort- und sinngetreu uebertragen*. Despite the aim expressed in the title, Daechsel's
work is marred occasionally by anachronisms,
fanciful opinions, and poor German.

After twenty-five years of work a committee,
appointed by the Synod of Churches of the
Canton of Zurich, issued a revision of the Old

Zwingli version, on the four hundredth anniversary of the death of Zwingli (Zurich, 1931). It is considered by many to be one of the best modern German translations, particularly for the Old Testament.

In 1931 Adolf Schlatter published at Stuttgart his translation of Nestle's Greek text, accompanied by a few notes.

Under the Nazis, Wilhelm Teudt made a revision designed to remove "Jewish taints." The Psalms, thus Germanized, were published at Leipzig in 1934. The Gospel of John was made more palatable to anti-Semites by omitting or altering Hebrew words and Old Testament references (Leipzig, 1936). In 1934–35 Wilhelm Michaelis published in *Kroeners Taschenausgabe,* Band 120/121 (Leipzig), his translation of the New Testament. This provides in parentheses alternative translations of words and phrases.

A revision of Luther's version of the New Testament and Psalms, prepared by a committee appointed by the German Bible Societies and by the German Evangelical Church, was published (Stuttgart, 1938) as a *Probe-Ausgabe* ("test edition"). The aim of the committee was to give the church a reliable version, based on Nestle's Greek text, presenting Luther's understanding of the Bible and keeping as far as possible the unique treasure of Luther's language. The Old Testament was also issued as a *Probe-Ausgabe* (Stuttgart, 1951). After the Bible has been in circulation for several years, a committee will give consideration to criticisms by those who have used the version, and a revised form will then be submitted to the Landeskirche (regional Evangelical Churches) for official approval.

In 1939 a so-called Concordant version of the New Testament was published at Stepenitz, prepared under the direction of A. E. Knoch. In this version each Greek word is always translated by the same German equivalent. Friedrich Pfaefflin issued a rendering of the New Testament in modern vernacular German (Heilbronn, 1938; 2nd ed., 1949).

In 1946 Ludwig Thimme, a Lutheran pastor, published at Stuttgart a translation of the New Testament in beautiful, fluent German.

Among Roman Catholic translations are the following: Jakob Ecker, professor at Priesterseminar, Trier, published a translation of the New Testament based on the Vulgate text (Trier, 1915). Peter Ketter's rendering of the New Testament was made at the request of the then Bishop of Rottenburg, Paul Wilhelm von Keppler (Stuttgart, 1915). It was revised in 1937 on the basis of Merk's Greek text; a third edition appeared in 1948. Fritz Tillmann translated Vogels' Greek text (Muenchen, 1927; 7th ed., 1947). J. E. Niederhuber, Hochschulprofessor at Regensburg, published a translation of

the Greek New Testament in 1931. Two members of the Order of Capuchian Monks, Konstantin Roesch and Eugen Henne, published a translation, the former rendering the New Testament (Paderborn, 1932), the latter the Old Testament (1936).

In 1944 Johann Perk published at Koeln a translation of the New Testament which in some respects resembles that of Roesch, but in general is more literalistic. The series, *Das Neue Testament uebersetzt und kurz erklaert,* is an original and scholarly translation from the Greek by Josef Schmid, Alfred Wikenhauser, and others; the concluding volume (ninth, containing Revelation) appeared in 1947. P. Riessler and R. Storr translated respectively the Old and the New Testaments (Mainz, 1949). J. F. Allioli and K. Thieme rendered the New Testament from the Vulgate, making comparison with the Greek (Feiburg/B, 1949); this is called "Herders Laienbibel." In 1950 O. Karrer translated and annotated the New Testament (Muenchen). Seeking since 1919 to put inexpensive portions of the Scripture in the vernacular into the hands of the laity, Pius Parsch, a monk at Klosterneuburg, Austria, finished his rendering of the entire Bible in 1952 (see *TT*, X [1953], 45 ff.).

A special group of German versions are those printed in Hebrew characters. It was Moses Mendelssohn, whom the *Jewish Encyclopedia* calls "the 'Third Moses,' with whom begins a new era in Judaism," who produced a German translation of the Pentateuch, printed in Hebrew characters, which came to be warmly admired by German-speaking Jews (Berlin, 1780–83). He translated the Psalter in 1783; the Song of Solomon in 1789. Luther's version of the New Testament was transliterated into rabbinic characters by Judah D'Allemand (London, 1820). Mendelssohn's work was continued by Salomon Kasselberg, who published the Old Testament at Basel in 1825. A translation by H. Arnheim and M. Sachs aided by J. Fuerst and L. Zunz (all under the editorship of Zunz), was published in Berlin in 1937. See also **Y. YIDDISH (JEWISH-GERMAN) VERSIONS.**

BIBLIOGRAPHY: Hans Rost, *Die Bibel im Mittelalter,* 1939; Hermann Strathmann, "Ueber einige moderne deutsche Uebersetzungen und Bearbeitungen des Neuen Testaments," in *Theologische Blaettern* (1940), cols. 330 ff.; Wilhelm Michaelis, *Uebersetzungen, Konkordanzen und konkordante Uebersetzung des Neuen Testaments,* 1947; G. Eis, *Fruehneuhochdeutsche Bibeluebersetzungen; Texte von 1400–1600,* 1949.

J. GREEK VERSIONS, MODERN: Under the auspices of Olga, Queen of the Hellenes, a Modern Greek version of the Gospels was published at Athens in 1900. The ancient Greek text was printed in parallel columns. In the following year Professor Alexander Pallis published a frankly vernacular version of Matthew's Gospel in an Athenian newspaper (*The Acropolis*). What was felt to be undue license in his version aroused bitter hostility, which extended to Queen Olga's version. The populace connected the latter book with a supposed Panslavist conspiracy, and riots occurred in the streets of Athens. This agitation led to the prohibition of the use of any modern Greek version of the New Testament. The prohibition was repealed in 1924. Pallis' completed version of the Gospels (based on the Vatican codex, B) was published at Liverpool in 1902.

In 1946 K. Phrilingos published at Athens a new translation of the Psalms. The Professor of Old Testament at the University of Athens, B. Vellas, has begun publishing (Athens, 1947—) a commentary on the Minor Prophets, which includes his own rendering of the Hebrew text into modern Greek. Instead of the usual "kyrios" of the Septuagint for the Hebrew tetragrammaton, Vellas uses a transliteration of Yahweh. Poetic passages are printed in strophes.

K. HEBREW TRANSLATIONS OF THE NEW TESTAMENT: J. M. P. Bauchet, O.C.D., has begun to revise Delitzsch's Hebrew New Testament (which in later editions was made to conform to the Greek *textus receptus*) on the basis of M. J. Lagrange's work in establishing a critical Greek text. Two editions of Matthew have been published (Jerusalem, 1950), one with and one without vowel points. Mark was issued with vowel points (1950).

BIBLIOGRAPHY: S. R. Driver, "Two Hebrew New Testaments (Delitzsch's and Salkinson's)," *Expositor*, Third Series, III (1886), 260–275. See also Y. YIDDISH VERSIONS.

L. HUNGARIAN (MAGYAR) VERSIONS: The revision of the Old Testament in the classic Károli version (1590), published in 1898, aroused so much adverse criticism that another committee, under the leadership of Elek Petri, undertook further revision in order to bring it into general accord with the English Revised Version. The work of this committee resulted in so many alterations of the time-honored text that many felt it to be misleading to call this a revision of the Károli translation. At the same time, many linguistic archaisms which were permitted to remain prevented the revision from gaining general acceptance.

Among several attempts to produce a more satisfactory translation, the following may be mentioned: In 1903 István Kecskeméthy published at Budapest his version of St. Mark's Gospel. A Jewish translation was prepared by an editorial committee of V. Bacher, J. Bánóczi, and S. Krausz, and published in four volumes (1898–1907), by the Jewish Hungarian Literary Society (Vols. 8, 12, 18, and 24 in its series). In 1923 Stefan Barcy, a former burgomaster of Budapest, published with ecclesiastical approbation his translation of the four Gospels. This was arranged in the form of a single narrative, ordered chronologically, in eleven chapters, hav-

ing from one to twenty-one sections each. A revised and illustrated edition was published by the British and Foreign Bible Society (Budapest, 1935). Dr. Bernat Frenkel translated the Old Testament (Budapest, 1927). Aladár Hornyánszky translated Amos (printed in strophic form; Bratislava, 1936), as well as Job, Romans, I Thessalonians, and Hebrews. Ladislaus Farkas translated the Gospels and Acts (Debrecen, 1938).

It was, however, work by two representative scholars, Pastor Alexander Czeglédy of the Reformed Church of Hungary, and Bishop Alexander Raffay of the Lutheran Church, which laid the foundations for a revision which, it is hoped, will prove to be satisfactory to all Hungarian Protestants. In 1929 the Luther Society of Budapest published Raffay's translation of the New Testament. Next, the British and Foreign Bible Society published Czeglédy's version of the New Testament (Budapest, 1930). Czeglédy, aided by a certain Rabbi Klein, prepared a translation of the Old Testament, which was published with Raffay's version of the New Testament (Budapest, 1938). In 1943 the British and Foreign Bible Society authorized the publication in Hungary of a Bible with the 1938 Old Testament slightly revised by Czeglédy and with Czeglédy's rather than Raffay's translation of the New Testament. Because of increasing criticisms leveled against the work of these two outstanding scholars, who died during the war years, a Joint Bible Commission of the two representative Protestant churches was appointed in 1947, formed of seven Old Testament and seven New Testament scholars. Through a newly (1949) constituted Hungarian Bible Council of the Evangelical churches of Hungary, other Protestant Churches (Baptist, Methodist, Brethren, Adventists) also have a certain responsibility for the revision. The latest editions of Kittel's Hebrew Bible and of Nestle's Greek Testament form the textual basis, and a literal translation is attempted, avoiding the frequent euphemisms and paraphrases of the previous revisions, and retaining in modern Hungarian all that is still alive in the idiom of the Károli translation. Long sentences are broken up, and the orthography follows new official rules. Where the critical Greek text departs from the *textus receptus* (particularly in familiar passages) the variants are given in brackets or in notes. In the Old Testament the tetragrammaton is rendered by ÚR (Lord) in capital letters. The copious use of marginal references and explanatory notes (bearing upon the continuity of revelation and "saving history") resembles the old Károli Bible. A trial edition of Genesis appeared in 1951. The New Testament was completed in 1952.

BIBLIOGRAPHY: The introduction to the trial edition of Genesis (in English, German, and Hungarian); and Ladislaus M. Pákozdy, "The New Revision of the Hungarian

Bible," in *Bulletin of the United Bible Societies*, No. 6 (1951), pp. 11-15. For the classical Vizsoly Bible, see the essays in the Festschrift in honor of its translator, Károli: *Károlyi Emlékkönyu* . . . , ed. Béla Vasady, 1940.

M. ICELANDIC VERSIONS. See **V. SCANDINAVIAN VERSIONS.**

N. ITALIAN VERSIONS: Most of the Italian translations made by Roman Catholic scholars are based on the Latin Vulgate, and all are provided with notes and comments. The S. Girolamo Society Version of the Gospels and Acts, prepared by P. Clementi, was published at Rome in 1902. Monsignor Antonio Martini's version, revised and corrected, appeared at Turin in 1920. The Compagnia di S. Paulo Version of the Bible was prepared by Giuseppi Ricciotti and a company of scholars and was published by the Cardinal Ferrari Society (Florence, 1929). Although based on the Vulgate, variations from the Hebrew and Greek are noted in the margin. In 1929 Giovanni Re, S.J., translated the Gospels from Vogels' Greek text. Marco Sales, O.P., Maestro del S. Palazzo Apostolico, published his rendering of the Vulgate at Turin in 1931. Dain Cohenel's translation appeared in parts (1930-33), at Gravina de Puglia. The "Bibbia di Firenze" under the care of the Pontifical Biblical Institute, directed by Alberto Vaccari, S.J., began to appear in 1922. It is in a modern, flowing, dignified, and simple Italian. The introduction and notes are brief and non-argumentative. The translators depart from the traditional text (Vulgate) only "when it is morally certain that the text is corrupt and what the original reading must have been." Another translation of the original texts with the Latin Vulgate printed opposite has appeared under the direction of S. Garofalo (Turin, 1948). Salvatore Quasimodo published his translation of John's Gospel (Milan, 1950) with the Greek text on the opposite page.

Among Protestant scholars Giovanni Luzzi (of the Waldensian theological faculty, Rome) has been the most active. He published his version of the New Testament at Rome in 1911, and of the Bible in 1930. He also headed a committee revising the old Diodati version; the New Testament was published by the British and Foreign Bible Society in 1916; the Bible in 1925. Subsequently, at the request of Seventh-day Adventists, the rendering of Rev. 1:10, "nel giorno della Domenica," was changed to "nel giorno del Signore."

O. LITHUANIAN AND LETTISH VERSIONS: In 1904 A. Eynars of Memel published at Berlin a revision of the New Testament in the Samogit dialect of Lithuanian. A reprint of J. A. Giedraitis' 1816 version, with orthographic changes, was published at Shenandoah, Pa., in 1906. It was edited by S. Pautienins, a Roman Catholic priest of Mahanoy City, Pa. Another Roman Catholic edition of the Bible in the Samogit dialect was prepared by Bishop Juoz-

apas Skvireckas and was published in six volumes (Kaunas, 1922) as a memorial to the five hundredth anniversary of the Samogit Bishops (1421-1921).

In 1930 the Synod of the Reformed Church of Lithuania appointed Povalis Jakubenas and Adomas Sernas to prepare a revision of the New Testament. The Gospels were published at Memel in 1934, and the work on the New Testament was completed by A. Jurenas of Canada (British and Foreign Bible Society, *Popular Report* [1951], p. 82).

In 1898 R. Auning, a pastor at Sesswegen, and others appointed by the Evangelical Synods of Courland and Livonia, published at Riga a revision of the Lettish version of the Bible. This, with further revisions of the New Testament in accordance with Westcott and Hort's Greek text, was published at Leipzig in 1902. A translation of the Gospels by a committee of pastors was published by the British and Foreign Bible Society at Riga in 1933. This was the first edition to appear using roman characters. The New Testament was published in 1937.

BIBLIOGRAPHY: Paul Salopiata, *Das Verhaeltnis der Evangelien-Texte in den aeltesten katholisch-litauischen Drucken*, 1929.

P. NORWEGIAN VERSIONS. See **V. SCANDINAVIAN VERSIONS.**

Q. PERSIAN VERSIONS: A sixteenth century Persian Harmony of the Gospels, copied from a parent manuscript of the thirteenth century, throws new light on the history of the Gospels in Persia. The manuscript (edited by G. Messina) not only reveals many Tatianic readings, but also appears to be closely related to the Pococke manuscript which provides the Persian text in Walton's Polyglot Bible.

Fischel's study of the history of Bible translations in Persia reveals that the Pentateuch translation of Jacob ben Tarus (1546), so far from being, as has been long believed, the first and only such translation by Persian Jews, stands at the end of a long chain of Judaeo-Persian translations.

The most recent translation into modern Persian is the version of Wm. M. Miller and Ahmed, printed in Leipzig and published in Teheran by the Intermission Literature Committee: Acts (1932); Luke (1934); etc.

BIBLIOGRAPHY: Eduard Sachau, "Vom Christentum in der Persia," in *SBA*, phil.-hist. Kl., XXIX (1916), 971 ff; Giuseppe Messina, *Notizie su un Diatessaron persiano tradotta dal siriaco*, 1943; Bruce M. Metzger, "Tatian's Diatessaron and a Persian Harmony of the Gospels," *JBL*, LXIX (1950), 261-280; G. Messina, *Diatessaron persiano*, 1951; Walter J. Fischel, "The Bible in Persian Translation," *HTR*, XLV (1952), 3-45.

R. POLISH VERSIONS. See **W. SLAVIC VERSIONS.**

S. PORTUGUESE VERSIONS: In 1902 a group of Franciscans began to prepare a translation of the New Testament, publishing it in parts at Bahia, Brazil. Huberto Rohden, a Roman Catholic scholar with leanings toward theosophy, began to translate the New Testament while studying at Innsbruck in 1924–27, finishing it after returning to Brazil (Petropolis, 1934). Based on the Greek texts edited by Nestle and by Vogels, the rendering has been widely praised as clear, smooth, and esthetically agreeable. The third edition (1942) seems to have been revised according to Roesch's German version.

A revision of the d'Almeida version, designed especially for use in Brazil, was prepared by a committee of Brazilians and Protestant missionaries representing several denominations. The New Testament was published at Rio de Janeiro in 1910; the Bible in 1914; corrected edition, 1926. This Versão Brasileira, patterned largely upon the American Standard Version of 1901, has never been able to supplant the popular d'Almeida rendering. Beginning work in 1941, a commission of Baptist scholars published a rigorous revision of the d'Almeida New Testament (Rio de Janeiro, 1949), following the Nestle Greek text. In 1951 the Bible Society of Brazil published an "authorized revision" of the d'Almeida New Testament which seeks to preserve in modern orthography much of the familiar phraseology of the older rendering. A certain amount of information about variant readings in the Greek is given in footnotes. The revision of the Old Testament is expected to be ready by 1955.

T. ROMANY VERSIONS: Gypsies in Spain were the earliest of their race to possess a book of Scripture in their own tongue, Gitano or Spanish Romany. This was the Gospel of Luke translated in 1837 by George Borrow, then agent of the British and Foreign Bible Society at Madrid. A revised form was published at Madrid in 1872. Besides the Spanish form of Romany, some portion of Scripture now exists in no fewer than ten other forms of the Romany tongue, namely Central Bulgarian, South Eastern Bulgarian, North German, South German, Hungarian, Italian, Lettish, Moravian (spoken by approximately 50,000 gypsies in Czechoslovakia and Ukrainia), Scottish, and Yugoslav.

U. RUSSIAN VERSIONS. See **W. SLAVIC VERSIONS.**

V. SCANDINAVIAN VERSIONS: 1. DANISH VERSIONS: The translation of the New Testament by Bishop T. Skat Rördam (Copenhagen, 1886), which retained much of the traditional Danish Biblical language, was made from a Greek text established by modern scholarship. This translation became very popular. In 1897 another translation of the New Testament was published by Bishop A. S. Poulsen and J. L. Ussing. Frants Buhl, the famous Hebrew scholar of Copenhagen, with the assistance of other scholars, published a rendering of the Old Testament which departs frequently from the Masoretic text in preference for readings supported by ancient versions.

The current text is the 1907 revision of the New Testament and the 1931 revision of the Old Testament. This was prepared by a Royal Commission consisting of the most prominent Danish scholars, and has been authorized to be read in churches. In 1942 a "test revision" of the New Testament was issued, looking forward to an authorized revision.

2. ICELANDIC VERSIONS: In 1897 the Icelandic Bible Society made arrangements to revise thoroughly the version of Gudbrandur Thorláksson, Bishop of Hólar, which had been frequently reprinted, sometimes with minor revisions, since its first publication at Holum in 1584. Specimens of the revision of various Old and New Testament books were published. After consideration had been given to various criticisms, the complete Bible was published by the British and Foreign Bible Society at Reykjavik in 1908.

3. NORWEGIAN VERSIONS: Special linguistic changes within Norway have necessitated frequent revisions of the vernacular versions. After four centuries of union with Denmark, the official Norwegian written language had become quite Danish, and in the middle of the nineteenth century an effort was made to return to the genuine Norwegian language. A composite of various rural dialects was made and called *Landsmaal* or New Norwegian. Both the official Norwegian written language and New Norwegian have been becoming more like each other, and consequently translations of the Bible in each form of the language require frequent revision.

Noteworthy revisions include the following: Under the guidance of Professor H. J. M. A. Seippel, portions of the Scriptures have appeared in *Landsmaal;* the Gospels (Oslo, 1915–20); the Acts (1923); Samuel and Kings (1930). The Students' Folkemaal Society of Oslo published a translation of the Bible in 1921. A committee of two theologians (Alanaes and Messel) and two professors (Odland and Seippel) revised the Old Caspari version to make the language more Norwegian. This revision was published by the Norwegian Bible Society at Oslo in 1930. At the end of the Bible is a list of passages omitted by many manuscripts. In 1938 the Norwegian Bible Society published a revised version of the Bible in New Norwegian, prepared by Pastor R. Indrebö.

4. SWEDISH VERSIONS: At the end of the last century, O. F. Myrberg published at Stockholm his translation of the New Testament (1890) and of most of the Old Testament (1887–1899). A Roman Catholic version of the New Testament, translated by J. P. E. Benelius, was published at Stockholm in 1895. J. August Edman's scholarly rendering of the New Testament, printed at Göteborg, was published at Stockholm in 1900.

In 1773 Gustavus III appointed a Bible Commission of leading biblical scholars to revise the "Charles XII's Bible" of 1703. The revisers and their successors submitted many specimens of their work to the Church Diet, but none of them met with final approval until 1917. In that year a revision of the 1903 translation of the Old Testament and of the 1907 translation of the New Testament was finally accepted and recommended to the king for his authorization.

BIBLIOGRAPHY: O. M. Norlie, *The Translated Bible, 1534–1934* (1934), pp. 122–157; *Festskrift utgiven av teologiska fakulteten i Uppsala 1941 till 400-årsminnet av bibelns utgivande på svenska*, 1941; R. Gyllenberg (ed.), *Våra fäders Bibel 1541–1941. Minnesskrift utgiven av teologiska fakulteten vid Åbo akademi*, 1941; J. Lindblom and H. Pleijel, *Observationes Strengnenses*, 1943; B. Molde, *Källorna till Christian III:s Bibel 1550. Text filologiska studier i reformationstidens danska bibelöversättningar*, 1949; P. Otzen, *Hvorledes danskerne fik deres Bibler*, 1949; B. Molde (ed.), *Bidrag till den danske Bibels Historie. Festskrift in Anledning af den danske Bibels 400 Aars Jubilaeum*, 1950.

W. SLAVIC VERSIONS: 1. BOHEMIAN (CZECH) VERSIONS: F. Zilka, a pastor of the Evangelical Church of the Czech Brethren and professor on the Hus Theological Faculty, Prague, published his version of the New Testament at Prague in 1933. J. Hejčl's revision of J. L. Sykora's edition of the New Testament was published at Frýdek in 1946. Another translation of the New Testament by R. Col was issued at Velehrad in 1947.

Sporadic and superficial studies in the nature of the Old Bohemian version suggest that a complete knowledge of this text might yield results of much importance for the "Western" text (so J. H. Ropes, *The Text of Acts* [1926], p. cxli). For a résumé of various studies of this version, especially in relation to other Slavic versions, see Josef Vraštil, S.J., "Quomodo sacri codicia bohemici iubilaeum quingentorum annorum digne celebrandum sit; conspectus recentiorum de antiqua bibliorum versione bohemica litterarum et consilia," *Acta academiae velehradensis*, IX (1913), 31–44.

2. BULGARIAN VERSIONS: A revision of the New Testament, made by a committee headed by Robert Thomson, was published at Sofia in 1921; the Bible, in 1923. In 1891 a committee appointed by the Synod of the Bulgarian Orthodox Church, under the leadership of the Metropolitan Boris, Exarch of Bulgaria, began work on a version of the Scriptures. After five committees had worked successively on the project, the translation was published at Sofia in 1925.

3. OLD CHURCH SLAVONIC; see **I. Ancient Versions: M. OLD SLAVIC VERSION.**

4. POLISH VERSIONS: The Wujek version, which is the standard Roman Catholic Bible in Polish, was revised most recently in 1935. One of the best Protestant versions is that prepared by Jan Szersuda, a minister of the Lutheran Church in Poland. A translation of the New Testament was published by the Mariasite archbishop, O. J. M. Michal Kowalski (Plock, 1928).

5. RUSSIAN VERSIONS: Count Leo Nikolaevich Tolstoy drew up a Gospel Harmony (Geneva, 1890). In 1946 Joseph Schweigl, S.J., prepared a translation of the New Testament for the Russian Pontifical College of Rome to use in missionary work.

A translation of the New Testament and Psalms in White Russian, prepared by A. Luckiewicz and D. Malej, was published by the British and Foreign Bible Society at Helsingfors in 1931.

The Ukrainian (or Ruthenian) version of the Bible, translated by P. A. Kulisch, D. I. Puluj, I. C. Levitsky, and revised for printing by Alexander Sluszarczyk, was published in Russian characters at Vienna in 1903. Yaroslav Levitsky's translation of the New Testament, revised by a committee of professors and officials of the Orthodox Church, was published at Žolkief (near Lemberg) in 1921.

6. SERBIAN, CROATIAN, AND SLOVENIAN VERSIONS: Serbs, Croats, and Slovenes are united politically in Yugoslavia. The first two speak the same language; the last two, being Roman Catholic, use the Roman alphabet; the Serbs, being Orthodox, use the Cyrillic alphabet. Dr. Lujo Bakotić, a minister of high cabinet rank, published his revision of the Vuk-Daničić version of the New Testament (in Roman characters) at Belgrade in 1930; the Bible, 1933. His translation has been termed "inescapably lucid." Dimitri Stefanović, professor of New Testament exegesis at the University of Belgrade, published at Belgrade in 1934 his version of the New Testament (in Cyrillic characters).

Two revisions of the Slovenian Bible were made during the twentieth century. The British and Foreign Bible Society published Anton Chraska's version of the New Testament at Laibach in 1908; of the Bible, 1914. Dr. Antona Bonaventura Jegliča, Bishop of Ljubljana (Laibach) translated the New Testament (1929).

7. SLOVAK VERSIONS: Catholic Slovaks (not to be confused with the Slovenes), first received the Scriptures in their own tongue in the nineteenth century when Jiři Palkovič, a canon of Gran, translated the Latin Vulgate Bible (Gran, 1832). His version was replaced in 1926 by the work of the Vojtech Union. This version was translated by Ján Donoval and a group of Roman Catholic scholars, and was revised by Richard Oswald. The New Testament was published in 1913; the Bible in 1928.

A Lutheran pastor, Josef Rohaček, translated from the original languages first the New Testament, which the British and Foreign Bible Society published at Budapest in 1913, and later the complete Bible (Prague, 1936). In 1946 Stefan Žlatoš and Anton Jan Surjanský published their translation of the New Testament at Trnava.

X. SPANISH VERSIONS: The classic version of Cipriano de Valera (1602) has been frequently republished with minor revisions. The text of current editions was prepared in 1909 by J. B. Cabrera and C. Tornos. This is now being revised again by a committee of representatives from Spain and all parts of Latin America. The revision is not to be a heavy one, but such as will remove archaisms and crudities, without affecting the quality of this much-loved version.

In 1909 a Jesuit, Juan José de la Torre, published at Freiburg a Greek and Spanish edition of the New Testament, of which a third edition appeared in 1939.

The "Hispano-Americana" New Testament (Madrid, 1916) was produced by a committee of Spanish and South American translators meeting in Spain, who used the Nestle Greek text and sought to make available in a joint version the advances in knowledge of text and language expressed in the English Revised Version.

Guillermo Juenemann, a Roman Catholic whose theology approached that of Protestantism, published in 1928 at Concepción (Chile) an extremely literal translation of the New Testament in everyday Spanish. Its text is based on the early Greek manuscripts (B, *aleph*, A), and contains no notes favorable to Romanism.

A Jesuit, José J. Réboli, revised the old Amat version (1825) of the Gospels, taking into account modern critical editions of the Greek text (Buenos Aires, 1944).

The first complete translation of the Bible into Spanish from the original languages made by Roman Catholic scholars is that of Canon Eloíno Nácar Fuster and Alberto Colunga. This quite modern translation was prepared under the auspices and direction of the Pontifical University of Salamanca (Madrid, 1944; 4th ed., 1951). The notes specially related to passages which prohibit idolatry appear to be less defensive than those which occur in earlier Roman Catholic versions (e.g., the Scio San Miguel and the Amat versions).

In 1944 Monsignor Juan Straubinger began to publish the first Spanish version of the Greek Gospels made in America (Buenos Aires, 1944); Acts (1946); Romans to Hebrews (2 vols., 1948). His version is based on Merk's Greek text compared with Nestle's.

Francisco Cantera and José Maria Bover, S.J., published their version at Madrid in 1947. The Old Testament is based on Kittel's Hebrew Bible, and the New Testament on Bover's edition of the Greek text. The aim of the translators was to provide a rendering marked by fidelity to the original, clarity, and "hispanidad."

BIBLIOGRAPHY: C. W. Turner, *La Biblia en América Latina*, 1951.

Y. YIDDISH (JEWISH-GERMAN) VERSIONS: Yiddish is a conglomerate language based on Middle High German mixed with Hebrew (both biblical and postbiblical) and with varying elements of Slavic dialects of Lithuania, Poland, Bessarabia, etc., depending upon the locality of the speakers. The first publication of the New Testament (without the Book of Revelation) appeared at Cracow in 1540, translated by Johann Harzuge. The Old Testament, translated by Jekuthiel ben Isaac Blitz and revised by Meir Stern, was published at Amsterdam in 1676–78. Subsequently, besides the translation of parts of the Scriptures (which are not mentioned here), the New Testament was translated by Christian Moeller (Frankfurt a.d. Oder, 1700), and by Johann Heinrich Reitz (Offenbach, 1703).

The Old Testament was translated by Naphtali Hirz b. Suesskind and Menahem b. Solomon Levi (Amsterdam, 1725–29). In 1732 J. H. Callenberg published at Halle his translation of the New Testament. The New Testament in rabbinic characters, translated by Benjamin Nehemiah Solomon, was published by the London Jews Society (London, 1821). P. I. Hershon's translation of the New Testament (London, 1878) was revised by J. Rabinowitz, W. I. Nelom, and Joseph Lerner (Berlin, 1901) in an attempt to combine Lithuanian, Bessarabian, and Galician forms. J. A. Adler published his translation of the New Testament at London in 1895. In 1908 the British and Foreign Bible Society published the Bible translated by Mordecai Samuel Bergmann of the London City Mission and revised by Aaron Bernstein of the London Jews Society. The New Testament was revised again in 1912 by Bergmann, Bernstein, A. S. Geden, S. H. Wilkinson, and R. Kilgour, and the Old Testament in 1927. C. Neuhausen, A. H. Charlap, and others edited the Hebrew of the Old Testament with a Yiddish translation on opposite pages (4 vols., New York, 1919). Solomon Bloomgarden (under the pseudonym Jehoash) published his translation of the Old Testament (New York, 1926–36).

A fresh problem relating to Yiddish Scriptures grows out of the inevitable linguistic modification of the language of Central European Jews who have migrated to English speaking countries, particularly the United States, where gradually English words and idioms have supplanted certain Yiddish expressions. Henry Einspruch attempted to meet this problem with his *American Translation of the New Testament into the Yiddish Language* (Brooklyn, 1941). See also **K. HEBREW TRANSLATIONS OF THE NEW TESTAMENT.**

BIBLIOGRAPHY: W. Staerk and A. Lietzmann, *Die Juedisch-Deutschen Bibeluebersetzungen von den Anfaengen bis zum Ausgang des 18. Jahrhunderts*, 1923; S. Noble, "Sacred and Secular in the Language of the Yiddish Bible Translation," in *Yivo Annual of Jewish Social Science*, I (1946), 274–282.

Z. BIBLE VERSIONS FOR THE MISSION FIELD: See article, MISSION FIELD, BIBLE VERSIONS FOR THE.   [Sup.] BRUCE M. METZGER.

BIBLICAL ARCHAEOLOGY. See ARCHAE-
OLOGY, BIBLICAL.

BIBLICAL COMMISSION: Official name:
Pontificia Commissio de Re Biblica. It was instituted by Pope Leo XIII for the promotion
and direction of scriptural studies, with a view
to restraining intemperate higher criticism (cf.
Acta Sanctae Sedis, 35 [1902–3], pp. 234–238).
The commission is composed of several cardinals and consultants selected from the secular
and regular clergy, and from whose number a
permanent secretary is appointed.

Since Feb. 23, 1904, the commission functions
also as an examining body for granting special
degrees in Holy Scripture to be conferred upon
priests having previously obtained academic degrees in theology, and preparing to teach biblical subjects at the graduate level. Two degrees
were first granted, namely: *Prolytatus* (a master's degree), and *Laurea* (doctorate) *in Sacra
Scriptura.* A decree published in 1951 modified
the program of the examinations and divided
the *Prolytatus* into two parts, viz., baccalaureate
and license.

The decrees published from time to time by
the commission deal with problems of literary
or historical criticism. They are given in form
of answers to *dubia,* i.e., questions bearing on
controversial issues. They are not dogmatic in
character, but rather tend to delimit the positions which may or may not be held by teachers,
with regard both to the general principles of
Roman Catholic doctrine and to the actual
status of biblical science.

Here is the list of the decrees of the commission in chronological order: implicit quotations
extant in Scripture (1903); scriptural books or
passages having the appearance of history (1905);
authenticity of the Pentateuch (1906); authenticity and historicity of the Fourth Gospel
(1907); character and authorship of Isaiah
(1908); historical character of Gen. 1–3 (1909);
the author of Psalms and the time of their composition (1910); Matthew (1911); Mark and
Luke (1912); problem of the Synoptics (1912);
Acts of the Apostles (1913); Pastoral Epistles
(1913); Epistle to the Hebrews (1914); the second coming of Jesus in the Pauline Epistles
(1915); reasons for condemning Dr. Schmidtke's
book *Die Einwanderung Israels in Kanaan*
(1934); public use of versions made on the
original texts (1934).

To these should be added: an instruction to
the Italian hierarchy on the teaching of Scripture in seminaries (1941), and a letter to the late
Cardinal Suhard for further clarification of the
decrees on the Pentateuch and Genesis (1948).

The text of those decrees, as well as of the
documents pertaining to the organization and
work of the commission, may be found in the
Acta Sanctae Sedis and *Acta Apostolicae Sedis,*
and in the *Enchiridion Biblicum,* published by
the Vatican Press.   GEORGES A. BARROIS.

BIBLICAL CRITICISM: I. Old Testament:
In contrast to the general agreement on most
major critical issues which obtained a generation ago, the field today exhibits a remarkable
fluidity. Many conclusions, once regarded as
assured, have been called into question. As regards the Hexateuch, the documentary hypothesis continues to find wide acceptance. Further
redivision of J (Smend, Eissfeldt, Morgenstern,
Mowinckel, Pfeiffer) and of P (von Rad) has
been suggested. The elimination of E (Volz,
Rudolph) and of P (Volz) as literary sources
has been urged. A seventh-century date for D
continues to hold favor, although dates much
later (Hoelscher *et al.*) and earlier (Welch *et
al.*) have been argued. The attempt to extend
the Hexateuch sources into the historical books
(Eissfeldt *et al.*) is countered by Noth, who
denies their presence (except D) beyond Numbers. But although certain scholars (Engnell
et al.) would abandon it in the interests of oral
tradition, and although fundamentalists continue to reject it, the documentary hypothesis
is still widely accepted.

There is, however, a tendency to a decidedly
less skeptical attitude regarding the historical
value of the various traditions than was formerly the case. As knowledge of the ancient
Orient has increased, not a few scholars have
broken completely with the developmental pattern in which the Wellhausen criticism sought
to explain the origins of Israel's religion. Some
(notably Albright) have argued strongly for
Mosaic monotheism. It has become increasingly evident that the task of criticism cannot
end with literary analysis: that to date a document says nothing regarding the origin and
value of the material contained in it. Gunkel
and his school (Gunkel's application of the
method of Form Criticism to the Psalms became basic to subsequent research) early showed
that the Bible must be studied in comparison
with the literature of the ancient Orient. The
work, for example, of Alt and his school on
certain lists, laws, and traditions in the Hexateuch, of Albright and his pupils on certain
lists and poems, plus new archaeological evidence and the recognition of the importance of
oral tradition, has made it plain that even the
latest documents may contain old and valuable
material. Importance of oral tradition has been
given due stress especially by certain Scandinavian scholars (Nyberg, Mowinckel, Engnell
et al.). Although some of them have pressed it
to extremes, it remains a factor of importance,
as most recent work on the Pentateuch and the
prophetic books shows.

As regards the prophetic books no uniform
trend may be charted. On the one hand, books

such as Ezekiel, which a generation ago seemed to present no problem, have been accorded extremely radical treatment (Hoelscher, Torrey, Irwin, Messel), though not without reaction. On the other hand, many of the more radical tendencies of an earlier day, such as the arbitrary emendation of the text and the relegating of eschatological passages to an exilic date, would find fewer advocates today. In general, there seems to be a trend toward a clearer realization of the problems with which criticism must deal, and a more balanced approach to them than formerly.

BIBLIOGRAPHY: General: H. R. Willoughby (ed.), *The Study of the Bible Today and Tomorrow*, 1947; H. H. Rowley (ed.), *The Old Testament and Modern Study*, 1951; W. F. Albright, *From the Stone Age to Christianity*, 1940; O. Eissfeldt, *Einleitung in das Alte Testament*, 1934; R. H. Pfeiffer, *Introduction to the Old Testament*, 1941, 2nd ed., 1948; A. Bentzen, *Introduction to the Old Testament*, 2 vols., 1948–49. Specific treatments: A. Alt: *Der Gott der Vaeter*, 1929; idem, *Die Urspruenge des israelitischen Rechts*, 1934; P. Volz and W. Rudolph, *Der Elohist als Erzaehler: Ein Irrweg der Pentateuchkritik?*, 1933; G. von Rad, *Das Formgeschichtliche Problem des Hexateuchs*, 1938; M. Noth, *Ueberlieferungsgeschichtliche Studien I*, 1943; S. Mowinckel, *Psalmenstudien I-VI*, 1921–24; idem, *Prophecy and Tradition*, 1946; G. Widengren, *Literary and Psychological Aspects of the Hebrew Prophets*, 1948.

[Sup.] JOHN BRIGHT.

II. New Testament. See ACTS OF THE APOSTLES; HEBREWS, EPISTLE TO THE; JAMES, EPISTLE OF; JOHANNINE EPISTLES; JUDE, EPISTLE OF; PAUL THE APOSTLE; PETER THE APOSTLE; REVELATION, BOOK OF; NEW TESTAMENT STUDIES, TWENTIETH CENTURY TRENDS IN.

BIBLICAL HISTORY. See ISRAEL, HISTORY OF, BIBLICAL.

BIBLICAL INTRODUCTION: I. Old Testament: Fifty years ago, as the methods and results of literary criticism made their impact on Old Testament studies, the task of introduction was conceived largely in terms of that discipline: to present the problems of composition, date, and authorship which attach to the various books, and to show how those books reached their present form. This viewpoint, to a large degree, still obtains, as a survey of recent introductions (e.g., Oesterley and Robinson, Eissfeldt, Pfeiffer) would indicate. Although chapters are given to text and canon, and brief sections devoted to the message of each book, the bulk of the space is concerned with matters of literary criticism. Other treatments approach the subject chronologically, rather than book by book (e.g., Bewer, Hempel, Lods), but here, too, literary criticism is given paramount importance. These two approaches reflect the fact that the Old Testament may be viewed either as a body of canonical writings or as a developing literature, so that an introduction to it may proceed from either viewpoint, or both.

But a decided tendency to broaden the scope of the subject may be observed. As other ancient literatures have been made available, and

as the value of form-critical studies and the importance of oral tradition have become apparent, more attention has been given in recent works to the history of the literary types and the traditions which underlie the finished documents. Introductions of the conventional type give this feature little or no attention, but it finds increasing place in recent treatments (notably that of Bentzen). In another direction, since the line between the two is sharp, there is increasing tendency to include under Old Testament introduction a discussion of non-canonical Jewish writings (so Eissfeldt, Bentzen, Weiser, Lods). At the same time, perhaps because the field has grown so large, special introductions to various subjects, the prophets, the Apocrypha, the text, etc., appear in great number.

Although it is perhaps beyond the limits of Old Testament introduction strictly defined, it has become increasingly plain that the task of introduction is not finished with a discussion of the formation of the Old Testament literature itself. An introduction is needed to the world of the Old Testament, its history and culture, in short to everything that makes the biblical record more understandable. This feeling has produced collections of ancient texts relevant to the Bible (Gressmann, Pritchard), introductions to biblical archaeology, works of synthesis treating the thought world of the ancient Orient and of Israel (Frankfort, Pedersen), as well as numerous efforts to set forth the distinctive features of the Old Testament faith and their abiding validity. One senses in this last a dissatisfaction with a discipline which provides introduction to critical problems but gives scant attention to the message of the books and of the Old Testament as a whole. Is the task of introduction to be broadened, not only to lay the basis for further critical and exegetical study, but to provide the groundwork for biblical theology as well?

BIBLIOGRAPHY: Introductions to the books: Oesterley and Robinson, 1934; O. Eissfeldt, 1934; R. H. Pfeiffer, 1941, 2nd ed., 1948; A. Bentzen, 2 vols., 1948–49; A. Weiser, 2nd ed., 1949.
Introductions to the literature: J. A. Bewer, *The Literature of the Old Testament*, 2nd ed., 1933; J. Hempel, *Die althebraeische Literatur*, 1930; A. Lods, *Histoire de la littérature hébraïque et juive*, 1950.
The Old Testament, its leading ideas and its environment: H. Gressmann (ed.), *Altorientalische Texte und Bilder zum Alten Testament*, 2 vols., 1926–27; J. B. Pritchard (ed.), *Ancient Near Eastern Texts Relating to the Old Testament*, 1950; W. F. Albright, *Archaeology and the Religion of Israel*, 1942; H. Frankfort et al., *The Intellectual Adventure of Ancient Man*, 1946; J. Pedersen, *Israel: Its Life and Culture*, 2 vols., 1926, 1940; H. H. Rowley, *The Rediscovery of the Old Testament*, 1946; G. E. Wright, *The Old Testament Against Its Environment*, 1950.

[Sup.] JOHN BRIGHT.

II. New Testament. See ACTS OF THE APOSTLES; HEBREWS, EPISTLE TO THE; JAMES, EPISTLE OF; JOHANNINE EPISTLES; JUDE, EPISTLE OF; PAUL THE APOSTLE; PETER THE APOSTLE; REVELATION, BOOK OF; NEW TESTAMENT STUDIES, TWENTIETH CENTURY TRENDS IN.

BIBLICAL THEOLOGY: I. Old Testament: In attempting to present the chief articles of biblical faith we must state at the outset that the Bible is primarily a literature in which history and historical traditions are taken seriously because they are interpreted as the handiwork of God, or of man in revolt against God. Hence biblical theology cannot be understood as propositional dogmatics, arranged in an abstract manner and divorced from history. To describe God is to tell a story about what God has done, while man is understood by what he has done in response to the lordship of God. Biblical theology, therefore, must be defined as the confessional recital of the acts of God in a particular history, together with the inferences drawn therefrom. While this story began with creation, its particular focus is in the story of Israel as the chosen people and of the new people of God established in Jesus Christ, who was and is the climactic event in the series of divine acts for the redemption of the world.

A. THE REDEMPTIVE ACTS OF GOD: The central confession of the people of Israel was somewhat as follows: God, who created the world, and man upon it as its ruler, chose the fathers (patriarchs) and promised to make of their progeny a nation in possession of a land and of a blessing in which all peoples of the world would find their own blessing (Genesis). In fulfillment of these promises he delivered Israel from Egyptian slavery with remarkable proofs of his power, made the people into a nation in covenant with himself at Mt. Sinai (Exodus-Deuteronomy), and gave them a land in which to dwell (Joshua).

The central event in Israelite history was looked upon as the Exodus, or deliverance from slavery. The inferences concerning God which were made from this event were as follows: (1) The Power which had saved them was the same as the God of the fathers. (2) This God was the greatest of all powers in the world because he was able to make both the greatest monarch on earth (the august Pharaoh) and as well the forces of nature serve him. His mighty acts in Egypt were a testimony to the world as to his identity, power, and sovereignty (e.g., Exod. 7:1–5; 15:11–18). (3) Yet quite as remarkable as his power was the completely unmerited demonstration of his grace toward a weak and outcast people. His was a righteousness, unknown hitherto, which evidently had within it a special concern for the weak who had no other savior. Even his severity, therefore, had redemption within it. (4) The object of this unmerited love, Israel, could only infer that for some reason known only to himself God had chosen her; she was the chosen people. Since God had shown himself to be the Lord of events, the purpose of his choice was to be made clear in history. His seeming favoritism did not

contravene his righteousness because his chosen people was given a responsible vocation in history. His work with, and revelation to, Israel was to the end that the latter play a role in his establishment of the world as his kingdom. Hence the conception that God had a purpose in history was understood to involve his choice of human agents, of whom the central and special "servant" was Israel. Historical choice involved historical vocation and a grave responsibility.

The conception of the conquest of Canaan as God's gift of the land was a further indication and acknowledgment of his lordship over history and his direction of events for his own ends. In this case his agent's hopes were rewarded in conquest, though in subsequent centuries others were called against Israel, and the tables were turned (cf. Deut. 9:1–6; Judg. 3; Isa. 10:5 ff.). The land as God's gift meant that there could be no idea of the natural right of private property. All that one owned was given as a conditional loan and to be used faithfully as though one were a steward (e.g., Lev. 25:23). Since the righteousness of God was specially concerned, not only with evil, but with the need of the needy, one's administration of God's property must have the same ends in view.

The conceptual language, by means of which the relation of God and people was kept clear, was drawn from common law. The religious vocabulary thus abounded with legal terms. God was conceived to have made a compact with Israel, one which was most frequently called a "covenant" (though Hosea likened it to a marriage pact). This covenant rested upon a political anthropomorphism which furnished the basic religious vocabulary. In it God appeared as the actual Ruler or Lord of the people, who ruled by means of leaders whom he provided (judges, kings, priests), by means of his revealed law, and by royal heralds or messengers whom he sent (prophets). The people, on their part, freely accepted his leadership and acknowledged themselves to be his subjects or servants whose task was to hearken to him and to obey him. Righteousness was thus covenant-keeping while sin was more than infraction of law; it was disobedience, rebellion, and betrayal of commitment to the Ruler. The attempt was constantly made, however, to transcend the legalism of the relationship by the appeal to the unmerited grace of God in the Exodus and Conquest, a grace which should bind the people to him with an attachment stronger than legal bonds could portray. In the deepest reaches of Israelite faith gospel preceded law without negating the latter's necessity, even as was the case in the early church.

B. THE CREATIVE ACTS OF GOD: God was affirmed as the Creator because he was known to be the Lord of history and of nature. As such he was believed to stand in a completely free, unconfined and unlimited relationship to all that exists as his creation. His will is the basis of the world's unity and of the inner relationship between nature and history. This meant that no dualism of opposing forces was needed to explain the world, and it excluded also every form of pantheism in which deity and world are in any measure identified or in which the divine is believed to be immanent in the evolving process.

The center and climax of God's creative work was seen to be man. He alone of the creatures of earth had a special relationship with God. It was a relationship which acknowledged man's dependence, his capacity to hear and obey (i.e., his free nature), and his responsibility to assume a God-given vocation. To the Priestly writer of Genesis 1 this involved a similitude between God and man which could be expressed by the metaphor "image" (man "in the image of God"). Yet this likeness was not such as to permit confusion between the two. God remained Lord, and man his servant. The latter, however, was no automaton; his freedom and power were given to enable him to work out his vocation, but he could also misuse them by trying to make himself "like God."

God as Creator and Lord thus preserved a gulf between himself and his world, which could be bridged only as he himself chose. The means by which he chose to reveal himself were many. The "signs and wonders" of nature and of history were always viewed as his handiwork and to be interpreted for their meaning. Nature, however, was no focus of concern in itself, as in polytheism. God used it as the handmaiden of his historical work. The latter was the chief means by which and in which he revealed his will and purpose; and at every juncture of history he was believed to provide for his people spokesmen, or prophets, to whom he revealed his interpretative Word. These men were raised up and empowered by his Spirit, whom he sent into the world as an extension of his presence. Similarly, in describing past events, the writers employed the category of heavenly messengers (angels) as a means whereby God actively governed the world and revealed himself to men. So direct was God's control over the world he created and so manifold his manner of exercising that control that the problem of immanence and transcendence was not acute, in the sense that it later became acute. Only in the skepticism which was peculiarly biblical was the divine transcendence so emphasized that his control over history could be doubted. This, however, was considered the skepticism of the sinner who wished to remain in his sins (cf. Jer. 5:12; Zeph. 1:12).

C. THE WRATH AND SALVATION OF GOD:
Inasmuch as God is primarily known by what he does, and the knowledge of which acts involves an interpretation of history, it was understood in Israel that God's righteousness encompassed crisis and tragedy, wrath and judgment. The compromises of history were seen as sins against the Lord which were visited by his judgment. This viewpoint furnished the means by which the history of Israel among the nations was interpreted (especially in Judges, I-II Kings, I-II Chronicles). Historical crisis was searched for meaning in the context of sin and judgment, and the imperialism of the nations was used by God to effect his judgment. This involved a view of sin as both an act of will on the part of man and a state in which he lived. It was something man did which was accompanied or followed by a disruption of his well-being ("peace") in his social and material life (God's judgment). It was occasioned by a "stiffnecked," "hardhearted," or "uncircumcised" spirit which not only violated one's dependent relationship to God, on which life was based, but also the covenant relationship with the neighbor. Every sin was both willful and a burden to be borne. Consequently, the search for release and security was often desperate and always intense. The pathways chosen were many. One was idolatry, a compromise with neighboring religions which made fewer demands upon the will. Others were faith in king, state, and political alliances, in the exterior observances of cultus and temple, and even in a prudential wisdom which purported to teach the golden mean between extremes (Proverbs). The last mentioned was acclimated to the faith, though not without theological controversy as illustrated by Job and Ecclesiastes.

Yet the prophets proclaimed true security to exist in God alone and not in any substitute for him and his law. He alone could relieve men from the burden of evil, and it was confidently asserted that, inasmuch as he was the righteous Lord of history, he had not promised in vain but would do what he had promised. Consequently, to the prophets the Assyrian and Babylonian crises were the Day of the Lord, the beginning of his fulfillment of history in which the present orders of the world would be destroyed and, beyond that, restoration in his kingdom. Beyond the suffering of the present with its purging of evil there would be the new covenant (Jer. 31:31 ff.), the gift of a new heart and a new spirit (Ezek. 36:26), the new heavens and earth (Isa. 65:17 ff.), and the new Jerusalem as the capital of the world (Isa. 2:2-4; 60). The promises of God to the Davidic king as preserved in the theology of kingship were recalled by certain of the prophets and seen fulfilled in this goal of history. God would raise up his true Anointed (Messiah), and so empower him with his spirit that the government of the world-kingdom would be upon his shoulders to the end that justice and peace would finally be achieved (e.g., Isa. 9, 11). God the Lord could not be defeated by sin, but would accomplish what he purposed (cf. Isa. 43:11–13; 45:23). It was thus characteristic of his nature to instill hope, not in man's capacity to save himself, but in his own righteous power. He alone controlled and interpreted the history which proved the death of the nation's gods (cf. Isa. 41:21–29).

D. THE WORSHIP AND SERVICE OF GOD: Because God's first requirement in the covenant was an unreserved and undivided loyalty to himself as Lord, he demanded a worship based upon: (1) a holy fear or reverence which acknowledged complete dependence; (2) faith in his complete control of all things so that the faithful could obey and wait upon him in confidence and without anxiety; and (3) a love which his own grace called forth and which made all obedience a matter of response in gratitude rather than simply a matter of duty. This deep, inner basis of worship meant rejection of the overt practices of magic which dominated pagan worship, while it meant a reinterpretation of the sacrificial cultus which Israel shared with her neighbors. This cultus with its variety of practice and ritual had no automatic efficacy, though of course it was often interpreted in a pagan way. But in the official theology it was God's gift whereby he could be formally worshiped by gifts from the worshiper's substance, by prayers, by confession and praise. It was valid, however, only for faithful members of the covenant community who possessed true reverence and true faith. Their unwitting sins could find atonement in the cultus (e.g., Lev. 4:2; 5:15). But the cultus had no efficacy for flagrant covenant-breakers, who believed they could live as they chose and find security in splendid worship. When the means of worship were used in this manner, the prophets claimed that they became practices which God hated and would destroy.

As for daily life in God's service, it may be observed that, in the covenant, common law became religious law and religious law became common law; that is, there was no separation of sacred and secular. The society as ruled by God was a religious, a chosen, society of divine formation. Hence all law was covenant law, given to the nation as its guide to life, much of it as in the Decalogue addressed to individuals in whom and by whom decisions were made ("thou shalt"). All life was responsible, obedient life, and God's claim upon both individual and society was unconditional. Individual life, therefore, possessed a dignity and meaning unknown elsewhere because in God's "Thou shalt" each person was singled out as the recipient of God's personal address. At the same time,

man's life and law must reflect the righteousness of God. This meant that his institutions must function without regard for the community status of individuals and that justice was distributive according to need rather than according to class, power, ability or possessions. For this reason, the most surprising thing about Israelite law in its ancient setting was its conception of the function of economic life. That function was not profit but the fulfilling of need, based upon the principle of neighborly love (cf. Lev. 19). It thus exhibited a deep concern for the victims of exploitation and a violent distrust of the rich and the powerful who turned the weakness of the weak into an occasion for profit.

Hence, Israel's worship and service of God were the response to the divine nature as it had been revealed in the redemptive history. This response took its form in overt practices, many of which had their counterpart in paganism. Yet behind them was a faith and spirit which transformed their inner meaning.

Bibliography: Millar Burrows, *An Outline of Biblical Theology*, 1946; H. Wheeler Robinson, *Inspiration and Revelation in the Old Testament*, 1946; Walther Eichrodt, *Theologie des Alten Testaments*, 1948; G. Ernest Wright, "The Faith of Israel," *Interpreter's Bible*, Vol. I, 1952; *God Who Acts: Biblical Theology as Recital*, 1952.

[Sup.] G. Ernest Wright.

II. New Testament: A. THE POINT OF VIEW: Fruitful study of New Testament theology rests on certain basic convictions: (1) The unity of the Bible. Without denying or minimizing the Bible's diversity of literary form and thought, we may hold that a central theme binds the whole together. It is this unity of theme that justifies the formation of the canon. The books of the New Testament especially are united in explicit statement of the one basic gospel. (2) God is the axiomatic fact for every New Testament writer and speaker. The New Testament is a book about God, and specifically about what he has done through Christ and the Spirit. (3) Hence Christ is central. The gospel story and teaching focuses on him and on the effects of his work. (4) This reminds us that history is essential in the New Testament gospel, which does not present timeless truths but reports and interprets the working of God in a series of purposeful events. (5) Since history is involved, diligent critical study of that history is necessary. The study of New Testament theology includes honest historical investigation. (6) But the eye of faith is equally necessary. This group of writings gives a unified witness to the working of God, which only the believer can discern and understand. Pure objectivity, in the sense of neutrality, is impossible in God's world, and particularly in dealing with the story of God's redemptive working. (7) The gospel is God's answer to man's sin rather than to his intellectual curiosity.

B. CHRIST THE RISEN LORD: No book of the New Testament is satisfied to present Jesus merely as a great teacher, noble example, or powerful personality. Every book presents Him as the risen Christ who is the living Lord of His church. The Resurrection is the key fact of the story, and every New Testament Christian accepts it. It is the interpreting center from which every phase of the gospel can be rightly understood.

The Resurrection interprets the Cross. Only in the light of the Easter story did the Christians understand the Cross as God's way to effect his redemptive purpose. The ministry also, with its patient friendship, its authoritative teaching, its healing power, and its faithfulness under opposition, is rightly understood only when seen as part of the total working of God through Christ; He carries God's purpose to victory through humble service and voluntarily accepted suffering.

The Resurrection results in the active lordship of Christ over his church. It does not speak to believers merely of His personal survival. Christ risen is exalted to the right hand of God; so say eleven New Testament books by seven different writers. As Lord, He rules actively now in this time of conflict with evil, and His followers are assured that he will "reign until He has put all His enemies under His feet" (I Cor. 15:28). Thus the Resurrection interprets the earlier career of Christ and opens the way to His further victorious working.

C. CHRIST AND THE FATHER: While every New Testament writer, and every book except the Epistles of John, call Jesus Lord, no New Testament Christian regards Him as a rival of God the Father. Rather, it is always taken for granted that God the Father was involved in and behind whatever Christ did. "All this is from God" (II Cor. 5:18). God is known most fully through the works of Christ. Christ is sent by God in the divine redemptive work. He is called by many significant titles: prophet, Messiah, Son of Man, King, Lord; his unique relation to the Father comes to expression in the frequent reference to him as Son or Son of God.

The New Testament clearly recognizes Christ's (pre-existent) activity in creating and sustaining the world. This teaching begins early; it plainly is no late development (I Cor. 8:6; Col. 1:13 ff.; Heb. 1:1-3; John 1:1-18). But the New Testament puts no great emphasis on this fact. It prefers to stress the redemptive work which Christ in his historical career began and as Lord is now carrying to completion.

D. CHRIST AND ISRAEL: The history in which Jesus of Nazareth was central was not unprepared. It was the climax of God's work with Israel: he chose Israel, freed her, bound her to himself in covenant, and persisted in his faithfulness to her even when she proved stubborn and rebellious. This Old Testament story is unfinished. It leaves Israel at a crossroads: either she will draw back within herself and seek in isolation the fulfillment of God's promises, or she will open her eyes and heart to the world vision that challenges her in su h writings as Second Isaiah and Jonah. Chr'st comes to climax that Old Testament story. He fulfills the promises made to Israel; as the Messiah of God's chosen people he calls them to become God's instrument in effecting his full purpose. Thus the work of Christ and the mission of the church continue, fulfill, and expand the work of God with Israel. The biblical story is one story; the entire message has its center in Christ and its basic unity in this one ongoing purpose of God that opens into a world mission.

This unity explains why Jesus and the church inevitably accepted and used the Scriptures of Israel. From the outset the Old Testament was their possession. The New Testament holds that it is the Christians who rightly see the meaning and connection of the Old Testament; this is the church's book, and it is a witness to Christ. Even though some New Testament interpretations of Old Testament passages are strained, yet the truth remains that the work of Christ and the apostles carries forward the Old Testament story. The church rightly inherits the Old Testament as Christian Scripture.

E. CHRIST AND THE CHURCH: The New Testament church is not an entirely new creation. It continues and enlarges the Old Testament people of God; it finds the basis of its fellowship in faith in Christ, who fulfilled the Old Testament promises. The church is not a voluntary human association, for it is God who builds the church. Through the historical work of Jesus Christ he gathered together a nucleus. He exalted the risen Christ to lordship and made him Head of the Church. The gift of the Holy Spirit, sent by the Father, or by Christ for the Father (John 14:16, 26; 15:26; 16:7; Acts 2:33), brings God's active presence, guidance, and power to the church. Thus the church looks back to God's work in Israel and especially in Christ, but its life and unity never rest solely on past events; Christ's present lordship and the Holy Spirit's active work direct its life.

The fellowship of the church is called by many names: the disciples, those of the Way, the Israel of God, the body of Christ, the temple of the Spirit, etc. Because the church has one Lord, it is one. It belies its true nature when it splits into parties. The church's task is to worship in gratitude, to maintain unity in brotherly fellowship, to witness to the Gospel in the world, to foster growth in faith and good living in its members, and to live in confident hope of the full, final triumph of the cause of God.

F. CHRIST AND THE CHRISTIAN: Behind all the redemptive working of God is the sin and need of man. Whether in brief reference, as in words of Jesus, or in explicit discussion, as in Rom. 1–3, the fact that all men sin, cannot save themselves, and need redemption is common New Testament teaching. The gospel is God's answer to that universal need. The God who, through his Son, created man and cares for him in daily providence also redeems man through the life, death, resurrection, and living power of Christ, who continues his work through the Spirit.

Man must accept what he can never earn or deserve. He must turn in repentance from his sin, accept in faith the freely offered salvation, and live in grateful worship and loyal obedience. He lives in the fellowship of the church, but he is personally responsible for growing loyalty to his Lord. Through the Holy Spirit he is enabled to believe, to pray, to live in love, and to witness to Christ. In the church he hears God's word in Scripture and the preaching of the Gospel, shares in the sacraments of baptism and the Lord's Supper, and accepts his share of the church's task. In daily life he walks by the Spirit, with love for his neighbor. God's grace in Christ is not a substitute for moral fruitfulness; its creative working makes possible good living otherwise beyond human reach; the fruit of the Spirit working in the believer is love and all its expressions.

G. CHRIST AND THE WORLD: The basic task of church and Christian is evangelistic and missionary, to witness to the gospel as widely as possible. The world is the scene of this witness. But the world is not a neutral stage. Forces of evil are active, and the church is in conflict with agencies that openly or subtly resist its witness. The church may rejoice at every sign of advance, but cannot expect constant success or easy victory. The New Testament church is a persecuted church, and these writings treat opposition and ill-treatment as inevitable. Christ is the Lord of all men; he has won the essential victory over the hosts of evil; his final triumph is certain and will be complete. But not all men are aware of the lordship of Christ, opposition still continues, and faithful witness to God's grace in Christ is the church's constant task; therefore the church does not quail or surrender when trouble comes.

Christians give the witness of active living for the right in personal and social situations. But God's working is their essential resource, and they do not expect that social plans without spiritual conversion can effect radical and permanent improvement in society. The early Christians were a small minority, living in a totalitarian system. But they fixed on the essential thing, the necessity of faith, of renewal, of obedience to God, and of a life of Christian love as the basis of a durable and wholesome fellowship.

H. CHRIST AND THE FINAL GOAL: The New Testament breathes confidence that full victory will rest with Christ's cause. This hope rests on what God has already done in the past. In the work of Jesus Christ he has defeated sin and evil and determined the outcome of the struggle. The risen Christ carries forward this work, and God's full purpose will be realized. Most New Testament writers expected this victory rather soon, but they never attempted to fix the exact time, nor did they undertake to describe in specific detail the conditions of the time to come. It would be blessed life with God and Christ (John 17:3); it would be the permanent joy of all who have been faithful to God and looked for his kingdom. This new order began with the coming and work of Jesus Christ; the life of faith, under the guidance of the Spirit, is the foretaste of what is to come. The final defeat of evil, the final judgment, and the establishment of the eternal kingdom will thus not be a totally new order; it will but complete and free from conflict that life which the people of Christ know even now.

See JESUS CHRIST; MARANATHA.

BIBLIOGRAPHY: W. Bousset, *Kyrios Christos*, 1913, 3rd ed., 1926; J. G. Machen, *The Origin of Paul's Religion*, 1921; E. Hoskyns and N. Davey, *The Riddle of the New Testament*, 1931; A. Schweitzer, *The Mysticism of Paul the Apostle*, Eng. tr., 1931; C. H. Dodd, *The Apostolic Preaching and Its Developments*, 1937; E. W. Parsons, *The Religion of the New Testament*, 1939; E. Stauffer, *Die Theologie des Neuen Testaments*, 4te Aufl., 1948; F. V. Filson, *One Lord, One Faith*, 1943; M. Burrows, *An Outline of Biblical Theology*, 1946; O. Cullmann, *Christ and Time*, Eng. tr., 1950; F. C. Grant, *An Introduction to New Testament Thought*, 1950; P. S. Minear, *The Kingdom and the Power*, 1950; R. Bultmann, *Theology of the New Testament*, Eng. tr., 1951.

[Sup.] FLOYD V. FILSON.

BIBLICISM: The practice of those medieval scholastics who depended on a strictly literal interpretation of the Bible for their line of argument. The biblicists were among the formal rationalists who employed Aristotle's system and method in dealing with biblical thought. Their finespun theories proved sterile, but biblicism is to be found in all ages. Its essence lies in adhering to the letter of the Scripture and often ignoring the context or historical situation. Thus, a true biblicist abjures oath-swearing and turns the other cheek when smitten, as commanded (Matt. 5:34, 39). The tendency toward biblicism is seen most markedly in two related lines: millennialism (see MILLENNIUM) and fundamentalism. Millennialists tend to emphasize a literal use of biblical references to eschatological events, such as Jeremiah's prediction of the seventy years of the captivity (Jer. 25:11; 29:10), or Jesus' description of the physical phenomena that accompany the end of the age (Mark 13:24–25), or the seer's reference to the thousand years of blessedness (Rev. 20:1–10). Fundamentalists have certain basic beliefs which they defend largely on a literal interpretation of statements of Scripture. Those who oppose biblicism point to Paul's dictum that the letter kills while the spirit gives life (II Cor. 3:6) and to his principle of testing and holding fast that which is good (I Thess. 5:21).

JULIAN PRICE LOVE.

BICKERMAN (BIKERMAN), ELIAS J.: He studied at St. Petersburg, Russia (M.A.), Berlin (Dr. Ph.), École des Hautes-Études, Sorbonne (Éleve diplômé). He was formerly professor at the École Pratique des Hautes Études (Sorbonne), New School of Social Research (New York); visiting professor at Columbia University (New York), and University of Judaism (Los Angeles, Cal.). His publications: *Institutions des Séleucides* (1938); *The Maccabees* (1949); "The Foundations of Post-Biblical Judaism," in L. Finkelstein (ed.), *The Jews*, Vol. I (1950).

BIDDING PRAYER: In one of various forms the bidding prayer calls for a few brief statements by the leader, each statement followed by silent petitions or intercessions on the part of the people. In praying for rulers, in a time of crisis, he may begin with those who govern the home community. Then he mentions those in the state, in the nation, and in the world. He could do the same with world missions, or world peace. This kind of devotion appeals to many young people and others who have attended conferences. The effectiveness depends largely on the skill and care of the leader. He prepares as carefully as for three minutes of pastoral prayer, so as to state each "directive" clearly and tersely. Then he waits in silence, perhaps thirty seconds. After five or six periods of "directed silence" he may close with a collect. Such a prayer lends itself to the needs of many a special occasion.

[Sup.] ANDREW W. BLACKWOOD.

BIEL, GABRIEL: I. Life: B. about 1418, Spires; d. Dec. 7, 1495. Matriculated University of Heidelberg (1432; A.B., 1434; A.M., 1438). Entered University of Erfurt for short stay (1442–43) but made full matriculation, it seems, first in 1451 in theological faculty. Also matriculated University of Cologne (1453). Received Licentiate in Theology, probably from Erfurt.

Further activities unknown until 1462 when he reappears as cathedral preacher and vicar-general for the archbishop of Mainz. Took active part on papal side in struggle between chapter candidate Diether v. Isenburg and papal-supported candidate Adolf v. Nassau for archiepiscopal seat and wrote tract "In Defense of Papal Obedience" (*Defensorium obedientiae apostolicae*), contending that the decrees of a

legally elected pope must be obeyed when they do not contravene Holy Scriptures or natural law.

Sometime during these years Biel came under influence of the *Devotio Moderna*. As vicar-general, he aided in introducing the Brethren of the Common Life into Upper-Rhenish Germany; in 1468 he joined the Brethren-House Marienthal near Griesheim and soon thereafter he was made prior of the newly founded Brethren-House St. Mark's in Butzbach. During this time he composed a treatise "On the Common Life of Clerks" (*De commune vita clericorum*), defending ably the practices of the *Devotio Moderna*. "We confess simply and freely that we are no order because we are neither monks, nor do we take vows, nor do we assume the habit of the religious," is his dictum.

Under his leadership St. Mark's prospered. In 1469 the house joined the union of German brethren-houses known as the Muenster Colloquium, and in 1471 Biel undoubtedly led in organizing a General Chapter of Brethren-Houses in Upper-Rhenish Germany. Eventually this chapter counted ten houses in southwestern Germany.

In 1477 Biel with collaborators, was invited by Count Eberhard I of Wuerttemberg to transform, according to papal approval, the city parish church St. Amandus in Urach into a chapter church of the Brethren of the Common Life. Two years later he became prior of the chapter. During the remainder of his life he was intimately associated with every effort to improve religious conditions in Wuerttemberg, after 1484 as professor of theology in the lately founded University of Tuebingen, and after 1492 as prior of the unique Brethren-House St. Peter's in Schoenbuch where he remained until death.

II. Theology: Biel was the last important exponent of the *via moderna*. His fame rests primarily upon two works: (1) *Exposition of the Sacred Canon of the Mass* (*Sacri canonis missae expositio*); (2) *Commentary on the Sentences of Peter Lombard* (*Epithoma pariter et collectorium circa quattuor sententiarum libros*). Both were originally delivered as series of lectures at Tuebingen. The first came in 1488 and was published immediately in Reutlingen under Biel's direction. The second, where Biel chose Occam for his guide, he never completed for publication. His disciple and fellow-brother of the common life, Wendel Steinback, did so and published it in 1501.

Biel's theological point of departure is the assertion by Occam: only where there is evidence can there be real knowing. True knowing can come only from perception of the senses or intuition. General concepts constitute no reality since they cannot be intuitively apprehended, hence the conclusions derived from a logical connection of such concepts cannot be considered as proven or called scientific knowing. On this postulate Biel formulates his theory of universals. Intuitive knowing can only be directed toward an object present. As intuition perceives more and more objects it fuses or abstracts them into a collective concept, the universal, which is the last act in knowing. Universals, then, constitute the basis for opinions, definitions and conclusions.

The entire process of knowing Biel placed under control of the will, which operates in the simplest act of perceiving. Will, mind, intellect are one and the same thing and function freely of their own volition, but they cannot take us far toward certainty in the knowing process. Belief and faith must implement the will. Man may, to be sure, establish by intellect the existence of God from the concept of the first cause; he may even arrive at a measure of understanding about God but such attributes as his omnipotence, omnipresence, unlimited freedom of action, and creative power can be grasped only by faith. Here reason must remain silent. Things most unreasonable can be objects of faith.

God is limited only by the so-called contradictory antithesis. He has no rule to which he must conform, for his divine will is the rule of all contingency. His fiat or disposition is final and supreme. Our highest norms of morality and spirituality are purely arbitrary dispositions on his part. He might have decreed otherwise. Thus he might have opened heaven to sinners and hell to saints, or he might have established sin in place of good. Hence morals, truth and faith are dispositions of God. Human reason is inadequate, yea helpless. Man's greatest good lies in ascertaining God's dispositions as found in Holy Writ of which the church is the expositor. Man must, in turn, submit to the church without reservation as the only certainty in a world of human uncertainty and weakness.

With the aid of the church man can attain to justification. At this point Biel departs from his own logic and now assigns to human will a large share in process of justification. Reason can aid man in recognizing the existence and omnipotence of God and assists man in acquiring faith necessary to justification. The moment man recognizes God's existence, power and trinity he receives grace like a medicine and aided by the will, directs his life toward serving his creator. The process is completed in the sacrament of baptism which, however, does not empower man to live perfectly. He needs continuous renewal in justification which he obtains in the sacrament of penance. In penitence Biel stressed hatred and detestation of sin as all-important. The act of absolution was essential as conveying to the penitent the all-justifying grace of God, but Biel did not strongly emphasize this act or the priest's part in absolution.

BIBLIOGRAPHY: In addition to works mentioned, important sources are found in Hauptstaatsarchiv Stuttgart; Staatsarchiv Darmstadt; Parish church archives Butzbach. Still valuable among earlier studies: Linsenmann, "Gabriel Biel, der letzte Scholastiker, und der Nominalismus," Theologische Quartalschrift, 47, (1865), 449–481, 601–676; G. Plitt, Gabriel Biel als Prediger, 1879. Recent studies: Anatriello, La Dottrina di Gabriele Biel sull' Eucaristia, 1937; G. Feckes, Die Rechtfertigungslehre Gabriel Biels, 1925; Joh. Haller, Die Anfaenge der Universitaet Tuebingen (1927), Pt. I, pp. 153–172, Pt. II. pp. 54–64; W. M. Landeen, "Gabriel Biel and the Brethren of the Common Life," Church History, XX (1951), 23–36.

[Sup.] WILLIAM MARTIN LANDEEN.

BIGAMY: A polygamous marriage limited to two wives (bigyny) or two husbands (bi-andry). It was practised among the ancient Hebrews, associated with concubinage, and the law did not condemn it. It began to disappear after the exile but continued into the Christian era. The rare cases of bigamy among early Christians probably were entered into prior to conversion. Polygamy among primitive peoples is rarely concupiscent; it reflects the need for domestic labor and for progeny. Christian asceticism rejects both bigamy and digamy (remarriage of a widowed spouse). This prohibition was later applied only to clergy, and then became a policy of clerical celibacy in a double-standard morality as between clergy and laity. Some post-Reformation Catholic moralists have argued that monogamy is a part of the "natural law," but this is disputed by most Protestant scholars. Jesus' ethical sayings do not touch on the issue of polygamy vs. monogamy. Neither do St. Paul's, but I Cor. 7 seems to assume monogamy. Modern legal codes enforce monogamy.

BIBLIOGRAPHY: G. E. Howard, A History of Matrimonial Institutions, 3 vols., 1904; E. Westermarck, A History of Human Marriage, 3 vols., 1921; idem, Christian Morals, 1939; M. Cronin, The Science of Ethics, 2 vols., 1939.

JOSEPH FLETCHER.

BILLING, EINAR MAGNUS: B. at Lund, Sweden, Oct. 6, 1871; d. at Västerås, Dec. 17, 1939. He studied at the University of Uppsala, and became professor of systematic theology there (1908–20). He was bishop of the diocese Västerås (1920–39). Einar Billing inaugurated a revival of the Luther-investigation in Sweden. His analysis of the idea of the church was pioneering. Most important, however, was his dramatical view of revelation as presented in his penetrating biblical investigations. Through his remarkable theological work Billing helped to create a new, vigorous Swedish theology. He wrote: Luthers lära om staten (1900); De etiska tankarna i urkristendomen (1907; new edition, 1936); Försoningen (1908; translated into English); Vår kallelse (1909; translated into German and Chinese); Herdabrev (1920); Den svenska folkkyrkan (1930); Kyrka och stat (1942).

BIBLIOGRAPHY: Einar Billing in Memoriam, 1940; E. Montan, Einar Billing, 1943; A. Ihrmark, Från Einar Billings ungdomstid, 1945.

RAYMOND W. ALBRIGHT.

BINATION: The privilege to celebrate mass twice on the same day, granted to a priest by the Holy See or by the local bishop, in order to make it easier for the faithful of a parish to attend mass on Sundays and feasts of obligation. The general rule is that a priest can say mass only once a day, except at Christmas and on All Soul's Day (*q.v.*), when he is permitted to say mass three times.   GEORGES A. BARROIS.

BIRTH CONTROL. See SEX, ETHICS OF.

BISHOP: The Code of Canon Law reserves to the pope the exclusive right of appointing bishops and archbishops to vacant churches, even in countries and dioceses where the government, or some civil or ecclesiastical body, retains the privilege of electing or presenting candidates to vacant bishoprics. The tendency of the Roman Catholic Church is to do away with any form of lay patronage or local interference in the nomination of its officers. Residential bishops are declared by canon law to be the responsible pastors of their respective dioceses, over which they exercise ordinary and immediate jurisdiction. They are under obligation of habitually residing in their diocese, even if they are assisted by an auxiliary bishop or a coadjutor. Canon law makes it a duty for all residential bishops to report to the pope every five years on the state of their church. Since Jan. 1, 1911, these reports rotate according to geographic order. Reports from Italy and Mediterranean islands are due the first year of every quinquennial; from western Europe, including Great Britain and Ireland, the second; from central and eastern Europe, the third; from America, the fourth; and from Africa, Asia, and Australia, the fifth. European bishops are requested to visit the pope every five years, others every ten years.   [Sup.] GEORGES A. BARROIS.

BISHOP, AUXILIARY: In the Roman Church, any bishop appointed to help a residential bishop on account of his incapacity to meet the duties of his charge, because of age, ill health, or of an excessive working load. Canon law distinguishes the auxiliary bishop from the coadjutor, the latter being granted right of succession to the bishop whom he assists. Auxiliaries and coadjutors are consecrated with a title to a church not having a residential bishop. See also IN PARTIBUS INFIDELIUM.
GEORGES A. BARROIS.

BISHOPRIC. See DIOCESE.

BISMARCK ARCHIPELAGO. See SOUTH SEA ISLANDS.

BIXLER, JULIUS SEELYE: Congregationalist, educator; b. in New London, Conn., April 4, 1894. He studied at Amherst (A.B., 1916),

Yale (Ph.D., 1924), and also at Harvard, Chicago, Union Seminary, University of Freiburg and the University of Zurich. He was instructor in American College, Madura, India (1916–17), American University, Beirut, Lebanon (1920–22). He taught religion and biblical literature at Smith College (1924–33) and was Bussey professor of theology, Harvard (1933–42). He has been President of Colby College, Waterville, Maine, since 1942. Author: *Religion in the Philosophy of William James* (1926); *Immortality and the Modern Mood* (Ingersoll Lecture) (1931); *Religion for Free Minds* (Lowell Lectures) (1939); *Conversations with an Unrepentant Liberal* (Terry Lectures) (1946); *A Faith that Fulfills* (Ayer Lectures) (1951). He was Inglis Lecturer at Harvard (1951) and is also author of over a hundred articles in theological journals.

BLACK, HUGH: Presbyterian; d. April 6, 1953. He was the first incumbent of the graduate chair of homiletics at Union Theological Seminary, New York (1906–38; emeritus, 1938–53). Recognized as one of the world's great preachers he was called widely to preach during these years. Among his additional publications are: *Edinburgh Sermons* (1906); *Christ's Service of Love* (1907); *Happiness* (1911); *Three Dreams* (1912); *According to My Gospel* (1913); *The Open Door* (1915); *The New World* (1916); *The Cleavage of the World* (1920); *The Adventure of Being Man* (1929); and *Christ or Caesar* (1938).   [Sup.] RAYMOND W. ALBRIGHT.

BLACK, JAMES MACDOUGALL: Presbyterian; b. Rothesay, Isle of Bute, Jan. 25, 1879; d. Oct. 18, 1949. He was educated at Glasgow University; Marburg; United Free Church College, Glasgow. Ordained in 1903, he was minister of Broughton Place Church, Edinburgh (1907–21) and St. George's West, Edinburgh (1921–49). He was also moderator of the General Assembly (1938–39). He wrote: *The Mystery of Preaching; The Dilemmas of Jesus; New Forms of the Old Faith;* and *His Glorious Shame.*   F. W. DILLISTONE.

BLACK JEWS. See CHURCH OF GOD AND SAINTS OF CHRIST.

BLACKWOOD, ANDREW WATTERSON: Presbyterian; b. Clay Center, Kan., Aug. 5, 1882; educated at Harvard and Princeton. He taught Bible at Louisville Presbyterian Seminary (1925–30); homiletics, Princeton Seminary (1930–50); Temple University School of Theology (1950–). Among his books are: *The Fine Art of Preaching* (1937); *The Fine Art of Public Worship* (1939); *Preaching from the Bible* (1941); *Evangelism in the Home Church* (1942); *The Funeral; A Source Book for Minis-*

ters (1942); *Planning a Year's Pulpit Work*
(1942); *This Year of Our Lord* (1943); *Pastoral
Work, a Source Book for Ministers* (1945);
Preaching in Time of Reconstruction (1945);
Preaching from Samuel (1946); *The Protestant
Pulpit* (1947); *The Preparation of Sermons*
(1948); *Pastoral Leadership* (1949); *Preaching
from Prophetic Books* (1951); *Expository
Preaching for Today* (1953); *Biographical
Preaching for Today* (1954).

BLAKE, EUGENE CARSON: Presbyterian;
b. St. Louis, Mo., Nov. 7, 1906. He studied at
Princeton University (A.B., 1928); New College,
Edinburgh University; Princeton Theological
Seminary (Th.B., 1932). He taught at Forman
Christian College, Lahore, India (1928–29); and
was visiting lecturer in religion at Williams College (1938–40). He was assistant pastor, Collegiate Church of St. Nicholas, New York City
(1932–35); pastor, First Presbyterian Church,
Albany, N. Y. (1935–40); and pastor, Pasadena
Presbyterian Church (1940–51). He was stated
clerk of the Central Assembly of the Presbyterian Church in the U.S.A. (1951–) and president of the National Council of the Churches of
Christ in the U.S.A. (*q.v.*) (1955–).

BLAKE, ROBERT PIERPONT: B. at San
Francisco, Cal., Nov. 1, 1886; d. at Cambridge,
Mass., May 9, 1950. He studied at the University of California and at Harvard (Ph.D.,
1916). He studied and taught for several years
in Russia and in Georgia. He taught at Harvard for thirty years on the economic development of the ancient and medieval Mediterranean world and on the Byzantine and Ottoman empires. He taught also Georgian and
Armenian. His most notable publications are
his editions of various Armenian and Georgian
texts, including, though partly unpublished at
the time of his death, the Old Testament
Prophets and the Gospels. He took part in the
search for manuscripts or archaeological remains
in expeditions to Athos, Sinai, Samaria and Van.
He served from 1928 to 1937 as Director of the
Harvard University Library. In 1938 he was
exchange professor to the University of Sorbonne.

BIBLIOGRAPHY: *Harvard University Gazette*, XLVI, No. 6
(1950–51), pp. 34 f.

HENRY J. CADBURY.

**BLESSED SACRAMENT, CONGREGA-
TIONS OF THE:** Several religious congregations in the Roman Church have as their particular objective to foster the devotion to the
Blessed Sacrament. The Priests of the Most
Blessed Sacrament, abbreviation S.S.S., have established the headquarters of their American
province in New York (1900). Fathers: 36;
scholastics: 33.
Various congregations of women practice the

"Perpetual Adoration" of the Blessed Sacrament which is exposed permanently in their
chapels, and offer special prayers in reparation
of blasphemies and sacrileges against the Eucharistic presence, as the Nuns of the Perpetual
Adoration of the Blessed Sacrament the Religious of the Perpetual Adoration of the Blessed
Sacrament, and the Sacramentine Nuns (Religious of the Order of the Blessed Sacrament
and of Our Lady).

A similar worship is given in several monasteries of nuns affiliated with monastic or mendicant orders, as the Benedictine Sisters of Perpetual Adoration, the Dominican Nuns of the
Second Order of Perpetual Adoration, and the
Franciscan Nuns of the Most Blessed Sacrament.

In contrast with the above nuns and sisters,
who live in cloistered or semi-cloistered monasteries, several congregations also devoted to
the special worship of the Sacrament lead an
active life, as the Sisters of Perpetual Adoration
of Guadalupe, founded first in Mexico and represented in the archdiocese of San Antonio,
Tex. (300 professed sisters), and the Sisters of
the Blessed Sacrament for Indians and Colored
People, founded in the United States in 1891,
with a motherhouse at Cornwell Heights, Pa.
(476 professed sisters).

GEORGES A. BARROIS.

**BLIND, RELIGIOUS LITERATURE FOR
THE:** Out of approximately 200,000 blind in
the United States and Canada, only 25% read
braille and less than 5,000 read New York Point
or Moon Type.

In 1874 the Society for Providing Evangelical
Religious Literature for the Blind was organized. First on its own and later in co-operation
with the Sunday School Union and the American Bible Society (see BIBLE SOCIETIES), this
Society published, in New York Point and/or
in braille, Sunday School lessons, a hymnal,
and fifteen devotional books, most of them supplied without charge. In 1919 the income of
this Society fell so low that all embossed publications ceased, and for almost a decade blind
Protestants were without any current religious
reading matter except for hand-brailled copies
of books which kind-hearted individuals provided.

In 1925 the Home Missions Council of North
America published 100 copies of George Mathe-
son's *Day Unto Day* in braille. About this
time a number of religious bodies (Churches
of God, Seventh-day Adventists, Christian
Scientists, Mormons) started modest publication programs of their own in response to urgent
appeals from their blind constituencies. Among
larger denominations to pioneer were Episcopalians and Lutherans. In 1926 the Lutheran
Synod of Missouri started publishing *The Lutheran Messenger* and followed with Luther's
Small Catechism and other devotional material.

Today this body operates a loan library of religious books in braille. Other loan libraries under independent auspices also exist.

As early as 1900, Roman Catholics founded the Xavier Society for the Blind with headquarters in New York. Here the *Catholic Review* is published bi-monthly (1,800 copies in 1951), and a loan library of 1,600 titles, most of them brailled by hand, is maintained. In some Roman Catholic dioceses special workers, both lay and clerical, are appointed to carry on a pastoral ministry among blind communicants.

Hebrew religious leaders were not far behind in the provision of religious literature in braille for their constituents.

In 1928, four years before the Revised Standard English Braille was officially adopted, more than fifty Protestant denominations, then constituting the International Council of Religious Education and the North American Home Mission Council, realizing the high cost of embossing literature for their respective constituencies and the resulting duplication, united to form the John Milton Society, an interdenominational non-sectarian agency, and delegated to this society the task of publishing religious literature for the blind.

The activities of the John Milton Society are world-wide. Its two monthly magazines and its Sunday school quarterly are mailed free of charge each month to more than 8,000 readers in the United States and Canada and to blind readers in sixty-two foreign countries. Through correspondence it carries on a wide pastoral ministry. In the fall of 1951 it published its first religious periodical in talking book form. It aids thirty schools and homes for the blind on mission fields and now publishes Christian literature in six foreign braille systems.

In a study made by the John Milton Society in 1950 it was found that there were then twenty religious magazines for adults in braille, six for children, five Sunday school lesson periodicals, and two daily devotional publications—a total of thirty-three religious periodicals in braille. In addition there were two religious monthlies published in New York Point (750 copies) and one in Moon type (600 copies).

A few of the larger Protestant denominations have recently embossed hymnals, catechisms, liturgies, and prayer books for the use of their respective communicants. The American Bible Society has pioneered in the publication of the Bible both in braille and in other embossed systems. A limited number of religious titles is published in braille or recorded on talking book records by the United States Library of Congress (Blind Department).   MILTON T. STAUFFER.

B'NAI B'RITH. See ANTI-DEFAMATION LEAGUE.

BOARDS, DENOMINATIONAL: The name comes from the "board," or table, where officials sit to confer. In a collective capacity they manage and control such work as foreign missions or Christian education, subject to the authority of the denomination. The board maps the over-all strategy, devises ways and means, enlists personnel, promotes the cause in local churches, and raises necessary funds. The executive secretaries incur criticism for supposed autocratic methods, and financial extravagance. On the other hand, ever since the formation of the American Board (1810), denominations in the United States have owed a large part of their progress to the zeal and skill of these boards. See also MISSIONS, PROMOTION OF.
          ANDREW W. BLACKWOOD.

BOAS, FRANZ: Anthropologist; b. July 9, 1858 at Minden, Westphalia; d. Dec. 21, 1942. He studied at Heidelberg, Bonn, and Kiel (Ph.D., 1881). He explored Baffin Land (1883–84) and made investigations in Mexico and Puerto Rico (1886–1931). In addition to giving much time to scientific societies and numerous museums he taught at Berlin (1885–86); Clark (1888–92); and Columbia (1896–1937). Among his many publications those of interest to students of religion are: *The Growth of Children* (1896); *The Mind of Primitive Man* (1911, 1938); *Primitive Art* (1927); *Anthropology and Modern Life* (1928–38); and *Race, Language and Culture* (1940). RAYMOND W. ALBRIGHT.

BODY. See MAN, DOCTRINE OF.

BOE, LARS WILHELM: Lutheran; b. at Calumet, Mich., Dec. 27, 1875; d. at Northfield, Minn., Dec. 27, 1942. He was graduated from St. Olaf College, Northfield, Minn. (M.A., 1898) and from Luther Theological Seminary, St. Paul, Minn. (1901). He was pastor at Lawler, Iowa (1901–4); president, Waldorf College, Forest City, Iowa (1904–15); member Iowa Legislature (1909–11); state senator (1913–15); executive secretary, board of trustees and board of education, United Norwegian Lutheran Church (1915–17); general secretary, Norwegian Lutheran Church of America (1917–18); president, St. Olaf College (1918–42).   ERIK HETLE.

BOEHME, JACOB: B. at Alt Seidenberg, April 24, 1575; d. at Goerlitz, Nov. 17, 1624. He combined the devotional impulses of medieval piety with the nature philosophies of the Renaissance in one single system marked by bold, unindoctrinated pious speculative vigor.

Boehme flourished in an age and region when ideas were in ferment. He was exposed to creative Lutheranism, Crypto-Calvinism, Schwenkfeld, Paracelsian medical theories, Weigel, the apocalyptic of folk prophets, the doctrines of the *Rosenkreutzer,* and the deepest that the ancient church had to offer. In 1600, having been awakened by his devout pastor, Martin Moller, the first of the Pietists, he experienced the conflict of these fermenting ideas which gave him "many a hard blow and repulse." He managed to resolve the contradictions in what must be called a mystical experience which in a fire-flaming "quarter of an hour" brought him new knowledge—the speculative understanding that, as he said, "in Yes and No all things consist." This insight, which he claimed to have gotten from contemplation in the traditional sense, became the principle of his real dialectic and it dominated the work of his life.

In 1612 he started to write his first book, *The Aurora, or Day Spring* . . . , in which his as yet confused ideas poured themselves forth to fill thirty folios of insight and confusion. A neighboring nobleman, Carl von Ender, discovered the manuscript, had it copied, circulated it among his friends until it fell into the hands of the churlish Gregory Richter, a vindictive watchdog of Lutheran orthodoxy. The town council forbade Boehme to write more books. He silently obeyed until 1619, when, urged by his growing circle of admiring friends, he again took up his pen and in five years produced over twenty-five works of amazing profundity.

These works show the growth of a restless mind, one which was admittedly childish when the *Aurora* was written but which can be compared in its final moments with the best philosophical, theological, and devotional minds of the age. Stages are discernible, and, had he lived longer, his final position would have been unpredictable. The earlier period was dominated by alchemical imagery which was even then only superficial decoration for fundamentally sound ideas. His profound work, *The Signature of all Things*, although full of alchemical language, really marks the end of European alchemy. His devotional period served as a purgative for the two great works of his middle period, *On the Election of Grace* and *The Mysterium Magnum*, in which he achieved a preliminary maturity. These works were followed by a group of works which lead to a final period which never came because he died before his thought became static. All periods, however, are attempts to solve the speculative difficulties which his mystical *gnosis* created: the reconciliation of the Yes and No in all reality. This central insight posed his speculative problems, and that on all levels of his thought.

First, his problem was theogonic, to explain how out of the *Ungrund* (a characteristic Boehme word) the trinitarian God arose. To describe the process of generating the Trinity he set up his Seven Spirits of God, including his interesting notion of Heavenly Wisdom, or Sophia, the counter-image of the Divine Logos. These Seven Spirits produce a dynamic God far removed from the classic Unmoved Mover.

Second, his problem was metaphysical, to explain how out of One the world of myriad ideas arose. To describe the process of generating what he called Eternal Nature he set up the Seven Natural Principles which by dialectic interaction produce the variegated world of eternal ideas. (Hegel and other Boehme students, even in the face of Boehme's clear warnings, mistakenly identified the Seven Spirits of God with the Seven Natural Principles and the confusion was disastrous.)

Third, his problem was cosmological, to describe how out of chaos this manifold world was made in seven days and how each "day" had clear metaphysical implications. This gave him a world in which all things were made up of his Yes and No.

Having thus gotten his bifurcated world, his focus changed. This schizoid trend of his speculation marks all of Boehme's writing, and he approached solution only near the end of his life. The key to bridge the gap was the idea of the indwelling Logos, or of the signature within each created thing which could be seized for the purposes of knowledge and hence of regeneration. Thus Boehme was a Neo-Platonist in that creation contained its own inherent principle of regeneration, an outgoing and ingoing force which, even in his later writings, are never quite brought together.

Boehme's soteriology rejected forensic, legal views and re-established the Pauline doctrine of Christ in us in place of the Tertullian-Anselmic Christ for us. But Boehme made this inner Christ both subjective and objective: subjective by combining it with the old medieval mystical *Fuenklein*, or indwelling inner divine spark or "inner light," and objective by identifying this inner Christ with the alchemical notion of the signature which is the inward form of all created things. So Christ becomes both a personal (psychic) and metaphysical principle as well as an all-inclusive epistemological principle from which regeneration proceeds. And the regeneration of individual man is at once the regeneration of a fallen world.

Boehme's speculation was marked by an empirical boldness and a freedom which is understandable only from the fact that Boehme's was the first unshackled mind of front-rank stature which tackled the problems of Scripture, nature, and redemption freed from medieval indoctrination. He knew no Aristotle, no Lombard, no Anselm, no Tertullian; and only little of Luther, Schwenkfeld. He purposely rejected the contemporary philosophers who were seeking to base modern science on mathematics. Boehme's was the first really modern mind in the sense that he approached ancient problems with but little ancient baggage.

Although he founded no sect, his influence has been as continuous as it has been pervasive.

And reaction to Boehme himself has also involved the Yes and the No: he has been seen as a baroque Faust and been venerated as a persecuted saint. Yet the line of people, important in the cultural history of the West, who have found in Jacob Boehme deep comfort is impressive. In this group are poets, writers, philosophers, radicals, and unorthodox thinkers of many kinds. Among them are Angelus Silesius, Gottfried Arnold, Tieck, Schelling, Hegel, Steffens, von Baader, the early Quakers, the Cambridge Platonists, Thomas Traherns, Henry Vaughan, John Milton, Isaac Newton, John Byrom, Coleridge, Browning, Yeats, Nicolas Berdyaev, and many others. For Boehme has been the continuing fountainhead for that stream of modern thought which has rebelled against the mechanistic philosophies of the Cartesian tradition. He was the first modern exponent of a true *Lebensphilosophie*, which is as the term indicates, a life philosophy.

BIBLIOGRAPHY: The most serviceable edition of Boehme's works is the ten volume one published in 1730 in Leyden and edited by Johann Wilhelm Ueberfeld from many newly-discovered manuscripts: *Theosophia Revelata: Alle Goettliche Schriften* . . . *Jacob Boehmens*. English translations made before 1920 are all based on those of the Commonwealth period which were in turn made from Dutch translations and not from the original German. Modern translations by Earle and Stoudt are satisfactory. New biographical materials discovered in 1924 in the Goerlitz Archives make all old biographies useless. These materials were embodied in W. E. Peuckert's *Das Leben Jacob Boehmes*, 1924; and in Richard Jecht's *Jakob Boehme: Gedenkgabe der Stadt Goerlitz*, 1924. Other and older works are based on unreliable materials. The best comprehensive work, with excellent bibliography, is A. Koyré's, *La Philosophie de Jacob Boehme*, 1929. The best English work, though unsatisfactory because it does not have the new biographical materials, and because it does not recognize Boehme's amazing growth, is Howard Brinton's *The Mystic Will*, 1930.

[Sup.] JOHN J. STOUDT.

BOEHMER, HEINRICH: Lutheran; b. in 1869 at Zwickau, Saxony. After studies in theology and history he served on the editorial board of *Monumenta Germaniae Historica*. He taught church history in Leipzig (1898–1903), at Bonn (1903–12), at Marburg (1912–15) and again at Leipzig (1915–27). He died March 25, 1927. He wrote: *Kirche und Staat in England und der Normandie im 11. und 12. Jahrhundert* (1899); *Die Faelschungen des Erzbischofs Lanfrank von Canterbury* (1902); *Die Bekenntnisse des Ignatius von Loyola* (trans. 1902); *Analekten zur Geschichte des Franziskus von Assisi* (1904); *Die Jesuiten* (1921); *Luther im Lichte der neuern Forschung* (1918); *Urkunden zur Geschichte des Bauernkrieges und der Wiedertaufer* (1921); *Luthers Romfahrt* (1914); *Studien zur Geschichte der Gesellschaft Jesu* (1914; newly published under the title *Ignatius von Loyola*, 1941); *Loyola und die deutsche Mystik* (1921); *Luthers erste Vorlesungen* (1924); *Der junge Luther* (1925, 1951; tr. into English by Doberstein and Tappert under title *Road to Reformation*); *Gesammelte Aufsaetze* (1927); and *Thomas Munzers Briefwechsel* (1931). He

also brought out Vol. V of Albert Hauck's *Kirchengeschichte* (1920).

RAYMOND W. ALBRIGHT.

BOETHIUS, ANICIUS MANLIUS SEVERINUS: Boethius, often described as the last of the Roman philosophers and the first of the scholastic theologians, produced many treatises in the field of the humanities (of which the most famous is his *De Consolatione Philosophiae*) and translated into Latin the works of several ancient Greek authors (notably Aristotle).

One of the problems connected with research on Boethius arises from the difficulty of determining the genuineness of certain works traditionally ascribed to him. Thus, the translations of Aristotle's *Analytica Priora et Posteriora*, the *Topica*, and *Elenchi Sophistici*, ascribed to Boethius in the Basel (1546) edition of his works (reprinted by Migne, *Patrologia Latina*, LXIV), are now regarded as spurious; see M. Grabmann, *Die Geschichte der scholastischen Methode*, I (1909); and F. Ueberweg, *Grundriss der Geschichte der Philosophie*, Vol. II (1928). Furthermore, many critics doubt the genuineness of the *Ars Geometriae*.

On the other hand, recent scholarly opinion has moved in the opposite direction regarding the five theological tractates traditionally ascribed to Boethius. Contrary to the view expressed in the original article on Boethius (*q.v.*, Vol. II), their authenticity is now recognized to be established by the strongest manuscript evidence.

During the Middle Ages the influence of Boethius on the thought and literature of the West was immense and widespread. In more modern times his *Consolation of Philosophy* has been translated into practically all the civilized languages of Europe.

BIBLIOGRAPHY: A. P. McKinlay, "Stylistic Tests and the Chronology of the Works of Boethius," *Harvard Classical Studies*, XVIII (1907), 123-156; B. L. Jefferson, *Chaucer and the Consolation of Philosophy of Boethius*, 1917; E. K. Rand and H. F. Stewart, *Boethius, The Theological Tractates*, and *The Consolation of Philosophy* ("Loeb Classical Library"), 1918; F. Klingner, *De Boethii Consolatione Philosophiae*, 1921; Lane Cooper, *A Concordance of Boethius. The Five Theological Tractates and the Consolation of Philosophy*, 1928; H. H. Harper, *Boethius and Dante, with Echoes and Love Laments of the Early Italian Renaissance*, 1930; H. R. Patch, *The Tradition of Boethius, A Study of His Importance in Medieval Culture*, 1935; V. Schurr, *Die Trinitaetslehre des Boethius im Lichte der "Scythischen Kontroversen,"* 1935; E. S. Duckett, *The Gateway to the Middle Ages*, 1938; Helen M. Barrett, *Boethius; Some Aspects of His Time and Work*, 1940; Karl Duerr, *The Propositional Logic of Boethius* ("Studies in Logic and the Foundations of Mathematics"), 1951.

[Sup.] BRUCE M. METZGER.

BOGHASKÖI. See HITTITES.

BOHEMIAN MORAVIAN BRETHREN. See SLAVIC MISSIONS IN THE UNITED STATES.

BOHLEN LECTURES: Endowed by John Bohlen with a trust fund of $10,000, two or

more lectures are given in Philadelphia on subjects similar to the Bampton Lectures of Oxford, or any other subject connected with the
Christian religion. Qualified persons are selected by the bishop of Pennsylvania, the rector
of Holy Trinity Church, and the professors of
biblical learning, systematic divinity, and ecclesiastical history in the Divinity School of the
Protestant Episcopal Church in Philadelphia.
                                    FRANK D. GIFFORD.

BOHLIN, TORSTEN BERNHARD: Swedish
bishop; b. 1889; d. 1950. He became professor
of systematics at Åbo in 1925 and at Uppsala in
1929; bishop of Härnösand in 1934. Bohlin's
dogmatic and ethical writings are distinguished
by a liberal-theological and Christian-humanis-
tic attitude. He is best known as one of the
foremost apologists of Christianity in Sweden.
Bohlin was a zealous and inspiring supporter
of youth work, popular education, and the
Christian temperance movement.

BIBLIOGRAPHY: *Torsten Bohlin. En minnes—och vänbok,*
1950.
                                 CARL-GUSTAF ANDRÉN.

BOISEN, ANTON T.: Congregationalist; b.
Bloomington, Ind., 1876. Educated at Indiana
University (A.B., 1897); Yale Forest School
(M.F., 1905); Union Theological Seminary
(B.D., 1911); Harvard (M.A., 1923). He was
instructor in Romance languages, Indiana University (1899–1903); forest assistant, U.S. Forest
Service (1905–8); field investigator, Presbyterian
Department of Country Church Work (1911–
12); rural pastor, Congregational Church, Wa-
baunsee, Kan. (1913–15); North Anson, Me.
(1915–17); Y.M.C.A., A.E.F. (1917–19); supervisor, North Dakota Rural Survey, Interchurch
World Movement (1919–20); chaplain, Worcester (Mass.) State Hospital (1924–32); Elgin
Illinois State Hospital, since 1932; research associate and lecturer, Chicago Theological Seminary
(1925–42); lecturer, Boston University School of
Theology (1929–31); research consultant, Council for Clinical Training of Theological Students,
since 1945. He edited *Hymns of Hope and
Courage* (4th ed., 1950); and wrote: *Exploration of the Inner World* (1936); and *Problems
in Religion and Life* (1946).

BOKSER, BEN ZION: Rabbi and author;
b. Poland, 1907. He was ordained as a rabbi
at the Jewish Theological Seminary (1931) and
studied at Columbia University (Ph.D., 1935).
He has been rabbi of the Forest Hills (New
York) Jewish Center since 1933. He wrote:
Pharisaic Judaism in Transition (1935); and
The Legacy of Maimonides (1950).

BOLIVIA: Precise calculations of the area of
Bolivia (estimated 416,040 square miles) are
impossible because of boundary disputes with

neighboring countries. The population (1949
estimates) is 3,990,000. More than 50% of these
are Indians, and 25% of mixed blood.

Bolivia has five universities. In 1944, 1513
rural schools had 110,000 pupils, 1740 primary
schools had 144,056 pupils, and 55 secondary
schools had 17,496 pupils. About 80% of the
people are illiterate. Protestants have initiated
literacy campaigns. Under supervision of the
Ministry of Education, religious instruction is
free.

According to Article 2 of the Constitution, the
Roman Catholic religion is recognized and supported by the state, but the public exercise of
all other forms of worship is permitted.

There are 73 Roman Catholic convents (36
for men and 37 for women), 400 secular priests,
2 archbishops, 5 bishops, and 5 apostolic vicars.
In 1946 there were 38 American priests and nuns
in the country. The state pays 121,108 bolivianos ($48,500) for the support of the church,
23,820 bolivianos ($9,500) of this being used for
propagating the Catholic faith among the Indian population. Since March, 1912, all marriages must be celebrated by civil authorities.
Bolivia has an envoy extraordinary and minister plenipotentiary at the Holy See. A Papal
Internuncio resides at Sucre, the capital.

Twenty Protestant missionary societies (North
American, British, and internationally-sup-
ported) have work in Bolivia. The Protestant
community in 1948 was 14,211. The work of
some of these societies among the Indians is
outstanding, especially around Lake Titicaca.

BIBLIOGRAPHY: W. Stanley Rycroft (ed.), *Indians of the
High Andes*, 1946; P. M. Dunne, *A Padre Views South
America*, 1946; Webster E. Browning, *West Coast Republics of South America*, 1930; see ARGENTINA for general
works on South America.
                            [Sup.] W. STANLEY RYCROFT.

**BOLLAND, JAN, AND THE BOLLAND-
ISTS:** Since 1891 the *Bulletin des publications
hagiographiques* is inserted in the *Analecta Bollandiana*. Publications which are too large for
the *Analecta* are published in the *Subsidia
hagiographica*. After the death of Karel de
Smedt, Hippolytus Delehaye was for many years
the leading man among the Bollandists. Paulus
Peeters succeeded him. In 1925 the last volume
was issued; it deals with the saints whose day
is Nov. 10. The work now runs to sixty-four
volumes.

BIBLIOGRAPHY: Hippolytus Delehaye, *A travers 3 siècles.
L'oeuvre des Bollandistes, 1615–1915*, 1920; P. Peeters,
L'oeuvre des Bollandistes ("Mémoires Acad. Royale de
Belgique"), 1942; P. Peeters, *Figures bollandiennes contem-
poraines*, 1948.
                            [Sup.] WILLEM JAN KOOIMAN.

BOLSHEVISM. See COMMUNISM (MARXIAN).

BONAVENTURA:

BIBLIOGRAPHY: E. Gilson, *La philosophie de S. Bonaventure*, 1924; H. Spettmann, *Die Erkenntnislehre der
mittelalterlichen Franziskanerschule von Bonaventura bis*

Skotus, 1925; B. Luyckx, *Die Erkenntnislehre Bonaventura's*, 1923; E. Lutz, *Die Psychologie des heiligen Bonaventura*, 1919; B. Rosenmoeller, *Religioese Erkenntnis nach Bonaventura*, 1925; D. Dobbins, *Franciscan Mysticism, St. Bonaventura*, 1927; C. Noelkensmeier, *Ethische Grundfragen bei Bonaventura*, 1932; St. du Chambon-Feugerolles, *La dévotion à l'humanité du Christ dans spiritualité de S. Bonaventura*, 1932; J. Bissen, *L'exemplarisme divin selon S. Bonaventure*, 1929.

[Sup.] ALBERT HYMA.

BONIFACE:

Boniface VIII: After he had received prebends in Italy and France, he went with Cardinal Ottobuona to England in 1265, attempting to reconcile King Henry III with the barons. Soon after that he was appointed attorney and notary at the papal court. In 1281 he became cardinal-deacon, and in 1291 cardinal-priest. The famous poet Dante became acquainted with him while he was on a political mission in Rome. He considered this pope far too ambitious and referred to him as the "Prince of the New Pharisees." In his opinion Boniface was so wicked that "in His Vicar Christ was made a captive," with the result that He "was mocked a second time." The pope was a diligent patron of the fine arts, and he took great pains to improve and enlarge the Vatican Library.

Boniface IX: In the Papal States he succeeded in restoring the authority of the pope, though at first he experienced great difficulties and employed means at his disposal (such as the imposition of certain dynasties) that aroused much adverse criticism. In 1403 he recovered Bologna for the States of the Church. He also accomplished much in bolstering the papal finances, which during the period of the so-called Babylonian Captivity had suffered dismal blows. His most significant achievement was the formal introduction of the annates, together with other regular sources of income. In the field of higher education he accomplished much, encouraging both scholarship and art. In 1398 he founded the University of Ferma.

See also POPES.   [Sup.] ALBERT HYMA.

BONIFACE, SAINT: In 716 he landed at the Dutch town of Wijk-bij-Duurstede, but an uprising of the Frisians against him rendered further preaching on his part impossible. He returned to England, where he was chosen abbot of his monastery, but he refused to remain there. In the winter of 718–719 he was in Rome, asking for a missionary field from Pope Gregory II, who orally assigned Germany to him, particularly Thuringia. He did his best in the latter region, but was unable to overcome the hostility of certain local potentates. When he learned that King Radboud of the Salian Franks had died, he decided once more to preach among the Frisians. For two years he labored under Willibrord (*q.v.*), but his promise made to the pope to work in central Germany induced him to go back once more to Thuringia. First he preached in Hesse, where the heathen still predominated.

His success was so great in the year 721 that he was planning to make Hesse and a part of Thuringia a bishopric. For this step he had to have the permission of the pope and of Charles Martel, ruler of the Franks, though not the actual king. From the latter he obtained a letter of protection, from the former the position of missionary bishop of Germany east of the Rhine, without a permanent residence (722). He became the chief organizer of the German church and the chief reformer of the Frankish church. Each time he had to make an important move he consulted the papal chair, thus winning for himself powerful support against local rivals. During his work in Hesse and Thuringia from 723 to 735 he forced numerous clergymen to give up their wives and accept the state of celibacy. In 738 he paid his third visit to Rome, where he received the title of German Legate of the Apostolic Chair. He founded bishoprics in Hesse, Thuringia and Bavaria.

Charles was succeeded in 741 by his two sons Carloman and Pippin. The former received Austrasia, the latter the rest of the Frankish kingdom. In 747 Carloman entered a monastery, leaving his brother the title to his domains. But before this date Carloman was aware of the sad state of affairs in the church of Austrasia, and he urged Boniface to reform the clergy. In 742 the latter presided over a synod in a German town whose name is not known to us, while the second synod was held at Leftine in Hainault (743–744). Pippin also wanted help in his territory, and at Soissons in Neustria Boniface held a synod in 744, where the synodical decisions of Austrasia were largely accepted. At all of the synods mentioned lay nobles were present. Strict discipline was imposed on the clergy, who were not permitted to have any woman in each of their homes except their mother or sister or niece. They were prohibited from wearing arms and from hunting or warfare. After Pippin became sole ruler of the Frankish kingdom he was reluctant to call frequently upon the services of Boniface, who was becoming too powerful to suit Pippin, with the pope in Rome always ready to back him. Protestants have often accused him of having been too friendly with the pope and too much inclined to neglect his duties toward the civil ruler. On the other hand, as Hauck has shown in his great church history of Germany (Vol. I, p. 593), he derived his great strength from his friendship with the pope. Moreover, historians generally point to the great favor which was bestowed upon Pippin by the pope, for he was crowned king by the pope when he was still only a mayor of the palace, as his father had been before him. The two churches of France and Germany were brought into close contact with the papal chair and with classical civilization. St. Boniface was one of the greatest figures in medieval history.

BIBLIOGRAPHY: S. Crawford, *Anglo-Saxon Influence on Western Christendom, 600–800,* 1933; W. Levison. *England and the Continent in the Eighth Century,* 1946; C. de Clercq, *La législation réligieuse franque de Clovis à Charlemagne,* 1936; L. Duchesne, *Les premiers temps de l'Etat Pontifical,* 3rd ed., 1911; R. Macaigne, *L'Eglise Merovingienne et l'Etat Pontifical,* 1929; K. Jaentere, *Die roemische Weltreichsidee und die Entstehung der weltlichen Macht der Paepste,* 1936; W. Lampen, *Willibrord en Bonifacius,* 1939.

[Sup.] ALBERT HYMA.

BOOK CLUBS, RELIGIOUS. See BOOK PUBLICATION, RELIGIOUS.

BOOK OF THE DEAD: The Egyptian Book of the Dead never existed as a "canonical" book of sacred scriptures comparable with the Bible. It was a collection of approximately 150 funerary spells of different dates and varying character, which were designed solely to insure the welfare of the deceased in the hereafter. The modern but inappropriate title of the book was invented by the German Egyptologist, Richard Lepsius, who in 1842 published the first collection of such texts and who also assigned to the different spells the chapter numbers which for convenience are now universally retained. The Egyptian title of most of these is "Spell of Coming Forth [from the Tomb] by Day."

Some of the spells in the collection go back to the Coffin Texts, which are texts of similar purpose written on the wooden coffins of the Middle Kingdom and earlier, and, in some instances, to the Pyramid Texts, which originated in the early dynastic era for the benefit of the Egyptian kings after their death (it not having been considered at that time that mere commoners could qualify for such benefits).

Examples of the Book of the Dead are usually preserved in the form of hieroglyphic (sometimes hieratic) documents written on rolls of papyrus and frequently illustrated with appropriate pictures or vignettes, often both colorful and beautiful. Nearly every surviving roll contains a different selection of spells. In this form the "book" appears to have developed from the early Eighteenth Dynasty or shortly before. Rolls of greater or less excellence of craftsmanship or length were usually prepared in special "studios" for sale to individuals to be used in their burials. The name of the purchaser was commonly added later in blank spaces left for the purpose by the scribe.

Beginning with the late Eighteenth Dynasty, numerous hymns to the sun-god Re were added to the collection. These were often carved or painted on either side of the tomb entrance; eventually numerous other spells and accompanying illustrations from the "book" were employed in the decoration of the tomb.

Whether supplied to the deceased in the form of a papyrus roll or as a portion of the decoration of his tomb, the spells were believed to enable him magically to pass in safety through the judgment of his soul before Osiris, to emerge

daily from the tomb in order to partake of the food deposited for him by his survivors, to assume any form that he desired, to avoid the manifold obstacles believed to beset a dead man in the netherworld, and the like.

No truly satisfactory translation of the collection exists, as the language is often obscure and the text corrupt, even the ancient copyists not always understanding what they were writing.

BIBLIOGRAPHY: Edouard Naville, *Das aegyptische Todtenbuch der XVIII bis XX Dynastie,* 3 vols., 1886; E. A. W. Budge, *The Chapters of Coming Forth by Day,* 3 vols., including translation, 1898; Sethe, "Die Sprueche fuer das Kennen der Seelen der heiligen Orte" (critical study of Chapters 107–109, 111–116), in *Zeitschrift fuer aegyptische Sprache,* Vols. LVII–LIX; A. W. Shorter, *Copies of the Book* pr(t)-m-hrw *from the XVIIIth to the XXIInd Dynasty* ("Catalogue of Egyptian Religious Papyri in the British Museum"), Part I, 1938.

KEITH C. SEELE.

BOOK PUBLICATION, RELIGIOUS: Since the invention of printing from movable type and the production of the "Gutenberg Bible" (*ca.* 1455), religious titles have occupied a prominent place in book publishing. The first dated book printed in England (1477), *The Dictes or Sayengis of the Philosophers,* was in the general field of religion; and "the function of the first printer in the New World was to print devotional books for the instruction of natives in the Christian religion."

This was the work of Juan Pablos, beginning in 1539 in Mexico City. A century later, in 1640, Stephen Daye produced in Cambridge, Mass., the first book to be published in British North America, *The Whole Booke of Psalmes Faithfully Translated into English Metre,* commonly called "The Bay Psalm Book." America's first book publishers gave first place in their output to religious books. Thirty-seven per cent of the books for all American presses from 1639 to 1763 were theological in character. In the last years of the eighteenth century book publication increased rapidly, and religious book production exceeded the average rate of growth, being 6.6 times as great in 1798 as in 1778. In this same period, however, books in the areas of literature and political science were increasing twelvefold.

The nineteenth century saw the birth and rise of many firms publishing religious books which continued to flourish in the twentieth century. In 1890, 4,560 new books and pamphlets were published in the United States and 467, or 10.2%, were religious in character. In the twentieth century the percentage fluctuated but tended to move downward. In 1900, 6,356 new titles and editions were published; and 448, or about 7%, were religious. In 1922, 6,863 new books and new editions were published; 593, or about 8.6%, being religious. The largest number of religious books to appear in a single year in the first half of the twentieth century was 843, in 1940, which was about 7.5% of a total of

11,328 titles released that year. A decade later the number of new religious books and new editions had fallen to 727, which was 6.6% of the 11,022 titles published. Nevertheless, by 1950 religious books ranked first among non-fiction categories in number of new titles and new editions being issued. Only fiction and juvenile issues appeared in greater volume of titles, and publishers reported a growing interest in their books.

Religious books in America represent all the concerns of religious life and church organization and the areas of theological education. All Protestant viewpoints, as well as those of Roman Catholics, Jews, and other religious groups, are covered. Books are designed to appeal to the interests of various audiences, including lay people, students, ministers, church workers, and scholars. These books are issued by general book publishers either through religious book departments or incidentally in general non-fiction lists, by textbook publishers, by independent publishers specializing in religious books, by publishing agencies related to religious denominations or organizations, by university presses, and by private and author-subsidized agencies. Some general publishers have for many years maintained religious book departments; and in the twentieth century a large number of other general publishers have begun to enter the religious field. A large number of religious books appears through the auspices of publishing agencies officially related to churches or other religious organizations, such as the Y.M.C.A., the Y.W.C.A., and the Joint Commission on Missionary Education. In 1950 the Abingdon-Cokesbury Press, sponsored by the Methodist Church, was first among denominational publishers in number of titles issued—48; the Westminster Press (Presbyterian Church in the U.S.A.) was second with 43; the Broadman Press (Southern Baptist) third with 32; and the Beacon Press (Unitarian) fourth with 31. Publishers specializing in books for Roman Catholics and for Jews generally are not related officially to these religious groups but often co-operate closely with their interests and programs.

The interests of general Protestant and Roman Catholic publishing agencies are promoted by the Religious Publishers' Group of the American Book Publishers' Council. Twenty-four Protestant publishing houses, producing books and church and church school supplies for 35,000,000 members, joined in 1951 to promote their common interests in the Protestant Church-Owned Publishers' Association, and other houses joined subsequently. The National Association of Catholic Publishers and Dealers in Church Goods claims a membership of 150. Independent publishers of Protestant books often serve particular clienteles, notably conservative and fundamentalist groups not fully served by denominational agencies. There are no accurate reports or statistics available to describe the scope and influence of private and author-subsidized religious book publishing.

Religious books in America are distributed through bookstores, by mail order, through book clubs, and by individual colporteurs and agents. Many general bookstores and department store book departments devote a section to religious books, and stores specializing in religious books are sponsored both by church agencies and by private concerns, catering either to a broad clientele or to particular religious groups. There are between 1,500 and 2,000 retail outlets for religious books in the United States. Most denominational bookstores report a much larger volume of business through mail orders from catalogs than from customers coming to the stores.

Book clubs usually offer members, who agree to purchase annually a certain number of books, book "bonuses" or discounts. The Religious Book Club, organized in 1927, the oldest and largest club of its kind in the U.S.A., distributes books to 30,000 members, of whom 85 per cent are Protestant clergymen. The Pulpit Book Club, organized in 1938, provides Protestant clergymen with books of professional interest to them. Some clubs, such as the Pastoral Psychology Book Club, the Club of Inspirational Books, and the Sword Book Club, appeal to particular interests of readers. Some Protestant denominations provide special book clubs or purchase plans for ministers in their own communions. The Thomas More Book Club distributes Catholic books to its members; and the Catholic Book Club, although not exclusively a religious book club, distributes fiction and non-fiction titles of interest to Catholic readers. The Jewish Book Guild of America serves Jewish readers.

BIBLIOGRAPHY: E. L. Bradsher, "Book Publishers and Publishing," *The Cambridge History of American Literature*, Vol IV, 1921; Hellmut Lehmann-Haupt, *The Book in America*, 1939; Douglas C. McMurtrie, *The Book, The Story of Printing and Bookmaking*, 1943; *Publishers' Weekly*, *The American Book Trade Journal*.

PAUL L. MEACHAM.

BOOTH, CARLTON. See YOUTH FOR CHRIST.

BOOTH, EVANGELINE CORY: B. Dec. 25, 1865; d. July 17, 1950. The daughter of General William Booth, founder of the Salvation Army (*q.v.*), she was educated in London and soon took a leading place in the Army. She was field commissioner in London for five years; principal of the International Training Colleges; commanded the Army in Canada for nine years; and was commander-in-chief in the United States (1904–34). Then she served as general of the world Army and resided in London (1934–39). Upon retiring, she returned to the United States. She wrote many songs of the Army and published *Songs of the Evangel* (1927). Among her other books are: *Love Is All* (1925); *Towards a Better World* (1928); *Woman* (1930); and with Grace Livingstone Hill she wrote *The War Romance of the Salvation Army* (1919).

RAYMOND W. ALBRIGHT.

BOOTH, WILLIAM: Commander-in-chief of the Salvation Army (*q.v.*). D. Aug. 20, 1912.

BIBLIOGRAPHY: Harold Begbie, *The Life of General William Booth*, 2 vols., 1920.

[Sup.]

BORNEO. See MALAY ARCHIPELAGO.

BORNKAMM, HEINRICH: Lutheran; b. at Wuitz, Kr. Zeitz, Saxony, on June 26, 1901. After studying at the universities of Jena, Tuebingen and Berlin (D. Theol.) he became privatdozent for church history at Tuebingen; ord. professor at Giessen (1927); Leipzig (1935); and Heidelberg (1948–). His major interests are Luther, the Reformation, mysticism, eighteenth century church history and modern Catholicism. Since 1935 he has been president of the Evangelischer Bund. In 1948 he was named head of the Verein fuer Reformationsgeschichte and is a coeditor of *Archiv fuer Reformationsgeschichte* (1938–). He has written: *Luther und Boehme* (1925); *Mystik, Spiritualismus und die Anfaenge des Pietismus im Luthertum* (1926); *Der protestantische Mensch nach dem Augsburgischen Bekenntnis* (1930; 2nd ed., 1936); *Das Wort Gottes bei Luther* (1933); *Eckhart und Luther* (1936); *Die Einfuehrung der Reformation in Leipzig* (1939); *Luthers geistige Welt* (1947); *Luther und das Alte Testament* (1948); *Grundriss zum Studium der Kirchengeschichte mit Zeittafeln zur Kirchengeschichte* (1949); *Die Staatsidee im Kulturkampf* (1950); and *Das Verhaeltnis der Konfessionen im heutigen Deutschland* (1951). He has also published *Die Augsburger Konfession und die Apologie* ("Bekenntnisschriften d. ev. luth. K.," 1930; 2nd ed., 1952); *Imago Dei, Beitraege zur theologischen Anthropologie* (1932); Heinrich Boehmer's *Der Junge Luther* (3rd ed., 1939; 4th ed., 1951); and he was coeditor of *Zeitschrift fuer Kirchengeschichte* (1928–32).

RAYMOND W. ALBRIGHT.

BORROMEO, CARLO: After the death of Pius IV (1565) he devoted himself very largely to his bishopric of Milan. Through his forceful application of the reforms recommended by the Council of Trent in his own diocese, he was acclaimed "teacher of the bishops." At the numerous episcopal synods which he convened from time to time he took concrete steps to carry through the general decrees and recommendations of the said council. The decisions made by these synods were published in the *Acta ecclesiae Mediolanensis,* which were made known

in many countries and served as models for other bishoprics. His enormous correspondence with all parts of the world, filling 300 folio volumes, is preserved in the Ambrosian Library in Milan.

BIBLIOGRAPHY: *Acta ecclesiae Mediolanensis . . .* (A. Ratti, ed.), 4 vols., 1890; L. Pastor, *Charakterbilder katholischer Reformatoren des XVI. Jahrhunderts*, 1924; C. Orsenigo, *Vita di S. Carlo Borromeo*, 3rd ed., 1929.

[Sup.] MATHIAS GOOSSENS.

BOSANQUET, BERNARD: Anglican; b. at Alnwich, England, June 14, 1848; d. at London, Feb. 8, 1923. Educated at Balliol College, he became a fellow and tutor at University College, Oxford (1871–81), then lived in London (1881–1903) where he worked with his wife in behalf of the Charity Organization Society, and finally served as professor of moral philosophy at St. Andrews University (1903–8). He delivered the Gifford Lectures in 1911 and 1912. Though he wrote several works on logic, ethics, and aesthetics, his main contribution to religious thought was in his attempt to develop from the Christian doctrine of the Holy Spirit a philosophical conception of the dynamic unity of the world. He is best known for his insistence that the Absolute is impersonal. His principal works dealing with religion were: *The Civilization of Christendom* (1893), *The Principle of Individuality and Value* (1912), *The Value and Destiny of the Individual* (1913), *What Religion Is* (1920), *The Meeting of Extremes in Contemporary Philosophy* (1920).

BIBLIOGRAPHY: Helen Bosanquet, *Bernard Bosanquet: An Account of His Life*, 1924; J. H. Muirhead, *Bernard Bosanquet and His Friends*, 1935.

EDWIN E. AUBREY.

BOSCO, ST. JOHN: Giovanni Melchior Bosco, founder of the Salesian Society, was born in a small Italian hamlet of poor parents on Aug. 16, 1815. In 1841 he was ordained. The incident which changed his life occurred on Dec. 8, 1841, the feast of the Immaculate Conception (*q.v.*, Vol. V). He befriended a young street urchin and began instructing him. By 1846, drawn by St. John's kindness, the number of boys under his charge grew to 400. With the approval of Archbishop Franzoni of Turin, two rooms were secured. They were turned into a chapel and dedicated to St. Francis of Sales (*q.v.*). Don Bosco's mother, known as "Mama Margaret," joined her son and devoted herself and her meager belongings to the sustenance of this first Salesian home. Don Bosco devoted his life to the education of poor boys. In a vision or a dream which it is said he had in his early years, these words became impressed upon Don Bosco: "Not with blows, but with charity and gentleness, must you draw these friends to the path of virtue." Don Bosco's method of study knew nothing of punishment. Observance of rules was obtained by instilling a true sense

of duty and by removing all occasion for disobedience. His chief object was to form the
will and to temper the character. He was canonized a saint in 1934.

BIBLIOGRAPHY: *Don Bosco's Apostolate and Other
Sketches*, 1901; Henri Gheon, *St. John Bosco*, 1935.
                                    GILBERT L. ODDO.

BOSLEY, HAROLD A.: Methodist; b. at
Burchard, Nebr., Feb. 19, 1907. He studied at
Nebraska Wesleyan University (B.A., 1930) and
the University of Chicago (B.D., 1932; Ph.D.,
1933). He was director of religious activities at
Iowa State Teachers College in Cedar Falls,
Iowa (1934–38); pastor of Mount Vernon Place
Church in Baltimore (1938–47); dean of the
Divinity School, Duke University, Durham,
N. C. (1947–50); pastor of the First Methodist
Church, Evanston, Ill. He is author of: *The
Quest for Religious Certainty* (1939); *The Philosophical Heritage of the Christian Faith* (1944);
On Final Ground (1946); *Main Issues Confronting Christendom* (1948); *A Firm Faith for Today* (1950); *The Church Militant* (1952).

BOSNIA AND HERZEGOVINA. See YUGO
SLAVIA.

BOSWORTH, EDWARD INCREASE: Congregationalist; b. Jan. 10, 1861 at Dundee, Ill.;
d. July, 1926. He studied at Oberlin (1879–
81; B.D., 1886; A.M., 1893); Yale (A.B., 1883);
Leipzig; and Athens. After a pastorate at Mt.
Vernon, Ohio (1886–87) he taught New Testament at Oberlin (1887–1926), serving as dean of
the School of Theology (1921–23) and acting
president of Oberlin College (1918–19). Among
his books are: *Studies in the Acts and Epistles*
(1898); *Studies in the Teaching of Jesus and
His Apostles* (1901); *Studies in the Life of
Jesus Christ* (1904); *New Studies in Acts* (1908);
Christ in Everyday Life (1910); *Thirty Studies
about Jesus* (1917); *Commentary on Romans*
(1919); *What it Means to be a Christian* (1922);
and *Life and Teaching of Jesus According to
the First Three Gospels* (1924).
                              RAYMOND W. ALBRIGHT.

BOURGEOIS (BOURGEOYS), LOYS: B. *ca.*
1510 at Paris; date of death unknown; lived
1541–52 in Geneva as precentor under Calvin.
He was the principal architect of Huguenot
melody. He is the author of four psalteries
and a pedagogical treatise, *Le Droict Chemin
de Musique.* See also GOUDIMEL, CLAUDE.

BIBLIOGRAPHY: Fétis, "Bourgeois," *Bibliographie univ.
des musiciens*, 1865; F. Bovet, *Histoire du Psautier des
églises réformées* (1872), 60 f.; G. Becker, *La Musique en
suisse* (1874), 48 f.; O. Douen, *Clément Marot et le
psautier huguenot* (1878–79), I, 600 f., II, 3 f. and 635 f.;
Th. Dufour, "Critique du livre de M. Douen," *Revue
critique d'Histoire et de Littérature* (1881), 7 f. and 15 f.;
A. Cartier, *Arrêts du Conseil de Genève sur le fait de
l'imprimerie et de la librairie de 1541–1550* (1893), 150 f.;
P. André Gaillard, *Loys Bourgeoys*, 1948; idem, *Die Musik
in Geschichte und Gegenwart* (1951), 161 and 162.
                          M. P. ANDRÉ GAILLARD.

BOUSSET, JOHANN FRANZ WILHELM:
D. 1920. Following his professorship at Goettingen he taught New Testament at Giessen until
his death. With special emphasis on the sources
of the New Testament and the early church he
became a leader of and contributor to the religious-historical group of scholars and in this
became associated with J. F. H. Gunkel (*q.v.*)
and others. His later publications include *Die
Religion des Judentums im neutestamentlichen
Zeitalter* (1903; 3rd ed. by H. Gressmann, 1926);
*Kyrios Christos. Geschichte des Christenglaubens
von den Anfaengen des Christentums bis auf
Irenaeus* (1913; 2nd ed. by G. Krueger and R.
Bultmann, 1921; 4th ed., 1935); *Das Wesen der
Religion* (1903; 4th ed., 1920); and *Jesus* (1904;
4th ed., 1927).

                    [Sup.] RAYMOND W. ALBRIGHT.

BOVER, JOSEPH M.: Roman Catholic, Jesuit; b. at Vinaroz Castellon, July 15, 1877. He
studied at the Gregorian University of Rome
(Ph.D., 1895) and later at Collegium Maximum of Tortosa (Th.D., 1911). He was appointed to teach Latin, Spanish, and Greek
literature at Veruela, Zaragoza (1899–1901,
1903–7); Gregorian University (1919–22). He
now teaches Sacred Scriptures at Collegium
Maximum Sancti Francisci a Borgia, S. Cugat,
Barcelona, being counsellor of the Pontifical
Biblical Commission of Rome, and consultive
of the Consejo Superior de Investigaciones
Cientificas. He has written: *Las Epistolas de
San Pablo* (1940); *San Pablo maestro de la vida
espiritual* (1941); *Deiparae Virginis consensus,
Corredemptionis ac mediationis fundamentum*
(1942); *Evangeliorum concordia* (1943); *Novi
testamenti biblia graeca et latina* (1943); *Maria
mediadora universal, o Soteriologia Mariana*
(1946); *Evangelio de San Mateo* (1946); *Teologia de San Pablo* (1946); *Asunción* (1947);
Sagrada Biblia; with Francis Cantera's collaboration he wrote: *Nuevo Testamento* (1948);
and *El sermon de la Cena* (1951).

BOWER, WILLIAM CLAYTON: Disciple;
b. Wolcottville, Ind., Feb. 6, 1878. He was
educated at Tri-State, Butler, and Columbia.
He specialized in functional nature of religion,
experience curriculum, creative method, value
content of public education. He served pastorates in Indiana, New York and California.
He was professor of religious education at Transylvania and the College of Bible (1912–26);
University of Chicago (1926–43). He was advisor to the Kentucky Department of Education on Moral and Spiritual Values. His publications include: *Survey of Religious Education
in the Local Church* (1919); *Educational Task
of the Local Church* (1921); *Curriculum of Religious Education* (1925); *Religious Education
in the Modern Church* (1929); *Character
through Creative Experience* (1931); *Religion*

and the Good Life (1933). He was editor of and contributor to *The Church at Work in the Modern World* (1935); *The Living Bible* (1936); *The Disciples and Religious Education* (with Roy G. Ross), 1936; *Christ and Christian Education* (1943); *Church and State in Education* (1944); *Protestantism Faces Its Educational Task Together* (with P. R. Hayward), 1949; *Moral and Spiritual Values in Education* (1951).

BOWIE, WALTER RUSSELL: Episcopalian; b. at Richmond, Va., Oct. 8, 1882. He studied at Harvard University (B.A., 1904; M.A., 1905); Union Theological Seminary and Virginia Theological Seminary (B.D., 1908). He has been rector, Greenwood Parish, Va. (1908–11); St. Paul's Church, Richmond, Va. (1911–23); Grace Church, New York (1923–39); professor of practical theology, Union Theological Seminary, N. Y. (1939–50) and dean of students (1946–50); professor of homiletics, Virginia Theological Seminary (1950–); Lyman Beecher Lecturer at Yale, and Hale Lecturer at Seabury Divinity School. He was chaplain in France, World War I. He is the author of *The Master, a Life of Jesus Christ; The Story of the Bible; On Being Alive*, and more than twenty other books. He is associate editor of *The Interpreter's Bible*.

BOWMAN, THOMAS: D. March 19, 1923. In 1875, in his fortieth year, he was elected a bishop of the Evangelical Association. When he retired from the episcopate in 1915 he had served in this capacity for forty years, a record unequalled in American church history. During this incumbency he had also served at the Union Biblical Institute (now Evangelical Theological Seminary) at Naperville, Ill. (1891–1911). He served on major boards of his church and frequently represented the denomination in national and world gatherings. Among his publications are: *The Great Salvation* (1909); *Historical Review of the Disturbances in the Evangelical Association* (1894); *Die Stoerung in der Evangelischen Gemeinschaft*, tr. by W. W. Horn (1894); *Der Kleine Katechismus* (1909); *A Reply to a Pack of Lies* (1894); and *The Revised Catechism of the Evangelical Association* (1905).

[Sup.] RAYMOND W. ALBRIGHT.

BOWNE, BORDEN PARKER: Methodist; d. 1910. A disciple of Martin Ulrici, and especially of Lotze (*q.v.*, Vol. VII), Bowne developed independently a form of Lotzean idealism which has come popularly to be known as Personalism (*q.v.*). He sometimes described his views as transcendental empiricism or Kantianized Berkleianism. At Boston University where he spent most of his life he taught phi-

losophy from 1876; and served as dean of the graduate school (1888–1910). His additional works include *Personalism* (1908); *Studies in Christianity* (1909); and *Kant and Spencer* (posthumous, 1912).

BIBLIOGRAPHY: Francis J. McConnell, *Borden Parker Bowne*, 1929.

[Sup.] RAYMOND W. ALBRIGHT.

BOY SCOUTS. See SCOUTS, BOY AND GIRL.

BRADEN, CHARLES SAMUEL: Methodist; b. Sept. 19, 1887, Chanute, Kan. He was educated at Baker University (A.B., 1909); Union Theological Seminary (B.D., 1912); University of Chicago (Ph.D., 1926). Ordained in 1914, he was a missionary in South America (1912–22) and assistant secretary, Methodist Board of Foreign Missions (1923–25). At Northwestern University he has taught history and literature of religions (1926–). He is author of: *Religious Aspects of the Conquest of Mexico* (1930); *Modern Tendencies in World Religions*; (with G. G. Atkins), *Procession of the Gods* (1936); (ed.), *Varieties of American Religions; World's Religions* (1939); *Man's Quest for Salvation* (1941); *These Also Believe* (1949); and *Sacred Literature of World's Religions* (1952).

BRADLEY, FRANCIS HERBERT: B. 1846; d. Sept. 18, 1924. Educated at Cheltenham and Marlborough, Bradley spent most of his life as a fellow of Merton College, Oxford, where his activity was limited by ill health. Opposed to utilitarianism and naturalism he sought, as an objective idealist and in a somewhat neo-Hegelian way, to reconcile the heroic and worshipful God demanded by religion with an absolute and infinite deity. His published works include: *The Presuppositions of Critical History* (1874); *Ethical Studies* (1876); *The Principles of Logic* (1883); *Appearance and Reality* (1893; 1914); *Essays on Truth and Reality* (1914); and *The Principles of Logic*, revised with Commentary and Terminal Essays (1922).

BIBLIOGRAPHY: C. A. Campbell, *Scepticism and Construction, Bradley's Sceptical Principle as the Basis of Constructive Philosophy*, 1931; H. Rashdall, *The Metaphysic of F. H. Bradley*, 1912; R. G. Ross, *Scepticism and Dogma; a Study in the Philosophy of F. H. Bradley*, 1940; and T. K. Segerstedt, *Value and Reality in Bradley's Philosophy*, 1934.

RAYMOND W. ALBRIGHT.

BRAHMANISM (THE NEW BRAHMANISM): Brahmanism in the twentieth century has undergone developments peculiar to its genius. Without the restraint of a canon of scripture authoritative to all, and within which all recasting of thought must take place, there has been a new synthesis analogous to other creative periods of thought. This synthesis has as a framework the philosophy of the Vedanta.

The elements of the "new" Brahmanism are: (1) a reaffirmation of the essential thought of the Upanishads; (2) a reaffirmation and recasting of the doctrine of Karmasamsara; (3) a disregard or denial of a religious basis for the social institutions of the joint family and caste; (4) the affirmation after the principles of Sri Ramakrishna of the unity of all religions within the framework of a philosophy which recognizes Ultimate Reality as spiritual and all material as only relatively real if not illusory. The differentia between the religions is conceived as arising only from historical and cultural accidents, and a differing interpretation of the same fundamental experience of the "Perennial Philosophy." The modern Hindu is therefore likely to think in terms of religion rather than Hinduism, or, conversely, of Hinduism as a universal religion into whose mold all others can be poured. In this sense there is an "evangelistic" aspect to their thinking and their writing.

Some of the more conspicuous names in this movement are: (1) Sarvepalli Radhakrishnan (1888–   ). Professor Radhakrishnan has been probably the most eminent interpreter of Hinduism to the rest of the world, principally in his writings and the long periods as professor in Oxford University. In common with all modern Hindu philosophers he meets the problem of the correlation of Ultimate Reality, the Absolute, with the necessity of a declaration concerning the validity of moral law, the freedom of man, a real purpose of his being, and intense participation in an active life. This is a difficult synthesis to achieve and perhaps Professor Radhakrishnan has been as successful as any. He has said, "When the incarnation of God is realized not only in a few individuals but in the whole of humanity, we will have new creation, a new race of men and women, mankind transformed, redeemed and reborn, and a new world created anew. This is the supreme spiritual ideal. It alone can rouse our deepest creative energies, rescue us from cold reason, inspire us with constructive passion and unite us mentally, morally and spiritually in a world fellowship." The identification with Reality is only possible when our souls are first purified through moral action. Goodness then becomes not an essential part of Reality itself, but an attribute of God who in himself is only relatively real, for when the ultimate is reached all things relative will disappear. Professor Radhakrishnan accepts and expands the Hindu cyclical view of history. The criterion of authority is the intuitive experience of the sages.

(2) Sri Aurobindo (1872–1951). Aurobindo was himself a mystic living the life of a recluse after a colorful participation in modern life. The world to him is real, and the individual self is eternal. His was a Western education, "protected" from things Indian. There followed an intense political career in India's approach to national independence; finally came retirement in Pondicherry in an Ashrama with some three thousand disciples where he sought to discipline himself and them in the way which would bring the realization of the divine life within the human soul. His was a theistic Vedanta, "the descent of the supermind, the divinization of body and mind, the formation of a gnostic community and the emergence of a higher species of man."

There have been others who have profoundly influenced the thought of India and attracted others to themselves as embodying the precepts of the "new" Hinduism with its emphasis both on radical social reform and on the Vedantic philosophy. One of these is Bhagavan Sri Ramana Maharshi who in South India has taught many the way of life prescribed by the older Hinduism with its adaptations to the present. The writings of Rabindranath Tagore, the poet, and D. S. Sarma, the teacher and philosopher, among others, have been very influential.

See also INDIA.   [Sup.] MALCOLM S. PITT.

BRAHMO SAMAJ, THE: The Brahmo Samaj with its provincial affiliates has consistently maintained a unitarian theism coupled with an advanced program of social reform. Its function during the first half of the twentieth century has been to inspire the totality of Hinduism with demonstrated modification of traditional patterns of Hindu society. There is no longer the necessity of such reform standing without the recognized social institutions—the Brahmo Samaj has won its case and is now a small worshiping community after the manner of the denominations of Christendom.

Much of the social reform embodied in the Hindu sections of legislation under the Constitution of the Republic of India is attributable to the steady influence of the Brahmo Samaj in social affairs. This reform is in the realm of the position of woman in society (the abolition of purdah, child marriage and polygamy, with the possibility of widow remarriage, higher education for all), the relaxation of the rigidities of caste, intercaste dining and free travel without defilement. These have all been practiced by the Brahmo Samaj and may stand as permanent contributions to Hindu renaissance.

The most significant name associated with the Brahmo Samaj in later times is that of the poet, Rabindranath Tagore (1861–1941). His work transcends the denominational aspect of the organization, but his thought and religious position owed much to his heritage within the Samaj. Other influences upon him were the Vaishnava groups in Bengal with their bhakti as expressed in music and their devotional worship patterns. The religious thought of the poet may be seen summarized in *The Religion of Man;* his is a religious humanism with devotional emphasis—this devotional emphasis finds expression supremely in the Gitanjali and other poetic works.

The Brahmo Samaj movement is a member body of the International Association for Liberal Christianity and Religious Freedom, joined in this organization with the American Unitarian Association and the Unitarian churches of various nationalities.

See also HINDUISM; INDIA.

BIBLIOGRAPHY: Manilal C. Parekh, *Brahmo Samaj,* 1929; J. N. Farquhar, *Modern Religious Movements in India,* 1918; Sivaneth Sastri, *History of the Brahmo Samaj,* 2 vols., 1911; Rabindranath Tagore, *Collected Poems and Plays,* 1937; *idem, The Religion of Man,* 1930; and his other works.

[Sup.] MALCOLM S. PITT.

BRANSCOMB, (BENNETT) HARVIE: Methodist; b. at Huntsville, Ala., Dec. 25, 1894. He was graduated from Birmingham-Southern College (A.B., 1914) as Rhodes scholar from Alabama; Oxford University (B.A. and M.A., 1914–17); and Columbia University (Ph.D., 1924). During World War I he was with the commission for relief in Belgium (1914–15) and served as private in the Fifth Replacement Regiment, F.A., O.T.S. (1918). He began teaching in the department of philosophy at Southern Methodist University (1919–20). He taught New Testament at the Divinity School, Duke University (1921–45; dean, 1945–46). Since 1946 he has been chancellor of Vanderbilt University. A liberal in theology, he has also taken part in a wide range of cultural projects. He was chairman of the Commission of the American Library Association to Brazil (1945), as well as of the United States Advisory Committee for Educational Exchange (1947–51). He wrote: *The Message of Jesus* (1925); *Jesus and the Law of Moses* (1930); *The Teaching of Jesus* (1931); *The Gospel of Mark* (1937); and *Teaching with Books* (1940). From 1943 to 1946 he was editor of *The American Oxonian.*

BRUCE M. METZGER.

BRANT, SEBASTIAN: His *Narrenschiff* ("Ship of Fools") was very popular. It appeared in 1494 and went through at least fifty editions, including thirty-two published in the fifteenth century (*incunabula*). The latter are listed in *Gesamtkatalog der Wiegendruecke,* Vol. IV, Nos. 5019–5072. There have been two Latin editions (1497 and 1505), three French, two English, one Dutch, and one Low German.

BIBLIOGRAPHY: A. Pompen, *The English Versions of the Ship of Fools,* 1925; H. Gumbel, *Brants Narrenschiff und Freidanks Bescheidenheit,* 1938.

[Sup.] MATHIAS GOOSSENS.

BRAZIL: The United States of Brazil have an area of 3,288,240 square miles and a population of 52,000,000. Of these 63.5% are whites, 14.6% Indians, 21.1% mulattoes, and the rest Asiatics. Brazil has attracted large numbers of immigrants; the chief groups, numerically speaking, have been Portuguese, Italians, Spaniards, Japanese, Germans, and Syrians, in that order. The two largest cities are Río de Janeiro and São Paulo, with over 2,000,000 inhabitants each.

The official language is Portuguese, though German and Italian are widely used in the southern states. During World War II the use of any language but Portuguese was forbidden in schools and churches.

Education is compulsory. According to the 1940 census, 43.6% of the population over 18 years of age could read and write, an increase of 73% over the 1920 figures. The government has an active literacy campaign in which Protestant churches cooperate. Brazil has eight universities; in addition, there are two Catholic universities and one Protestant. In 1948 there were 66,641 primary schools with 4,745,914 pupils. In 1946, 1,344 secondary schools had 297,508 pupils; 3,970 commercial and vocational schools had 216,954 pupils; and 339 upper schools had 28,404 pupils.

Freedom of worship is granted by the constitution. In 1889 church and state were separated; in 1934 the relationship was restored, but in 1946 it was again abolished. No sect or church receives subsidy from, or is dependent upon, the government. No citizen is to be deprived of his civil or political rights by reason of his religious beliefs. Brazil has a representative at the Vatican.

The republic is divided into twelve Roman Catholic metropolitan sees, and the hierarchy consists of 2 cardinals, 19 archbishops, 59 bishops, 25 prelates, and 2 apostolic prefects. According to 1946 figures, there were 5,383 priests.

According to the government census of 1940, there were 1,074,857 Protestants, 37,953 Orthodox Christians, 123,353 Buddhists, 463,400 Spiritualists, and 87,330 atheists. There are 55,000 Jews in Brazil, mostly in the large cities, particularly Río de Janeiro and São Paulo. Synagogues, communal organizations, and libraries exist in smaller Jewish communities throughout the country.

Protestant churches have grown rapidly in recent years; 1950 estimates gave over 2,000,000 Protestants, double the number ten years previously. The Evangelical Confederation of Brazil, with headquarters in Río de Janeiro, is a strong organization in which several Protestant denominations work together. The Presbyterian, Methodist, Episcopal, and Baptist Churches are autonomous and indigenous.

BIBLIOGRAPHY: Fernando de Azevedo, *Brazilian Culture,* 1950; Erasmo Braga and Kenneth G. Grubb, *The Republic of Brazil,* 1932; J. Merle Davis, *How the Church Grows in Brazil,* 1943. See ARGENTINA for general works on South America.

[Sup.] W. STANLEY RYCROFT.

BREASTED, JAMES HENRY: Historian and orientalist; b. Aug. 27, 1865 at Rockford,

Ill.; d. Dec. 2, 1935. He studied at North Central College (A.B., 1888); Chicago Theological Seminary (1888-90); Yale (A.M., 1892) and Berlin (Ph.D., 1894). Thereafter he was associated with the University of Chicago, teaching Egyptology, Semitic languages, and Oriental history (1894-1933). From 1895 he was associated with the Haskell Oriental Museum and was its director (1901-31). He led many research projects in the Near East and in the museums of Europe. He was relieved of all responsibility for teaching after August, 1925, in order to make it possible for him to take charge of the Oriental Institute of which he was the director (1919-35). Among his many publications those of greatest interest to students of religion are: *Egypt through the Stereoscope* (1905); *A History of Egypt* (1905; 1909); *Ancient Records of Egypt, Historical Documents* (5 vols., 1906); *The Temples of Lower Nubia* (1906); *A History of the Ancient Egyptians* (1908); *Development of Religion and Thought in Ancient Egypt* (1912); *Survey of the Ancient World* (1919); *Conquest of Civilization* (1926); and *The Dawn of Conscience* (1933).

RAYMOND W. ALBRIGHT.

BREBEUF, JEAN DE: Jesuit missionary; b. March 25, 1593, in Normandy. In 1617 he entered the Society of Jesus as a scholastic. His studies curtailed because of ill-health, he set out to do missionary work in French Canada. With another Jesuit he established his first mission near Georgian Bay. He met with little success. In July, 1629, Champlain surrendered to the British and Brebeuf and other French missionaries returned to France. Four years later the colony was restored to France and Brebeuf returned to Canada.

In 1640 he set out to evangelize the Neutres Indians who lived north of Lake Erie. At that time the war between the Iroquois and the Hurons was at its height. After many hazards Brebeuf reached the Huron country and tried to establish a mission. In 1648 the Iroquois attacked the Huron territory and fresh disasters befell the missionaries—their churches and schools were burned and many of them were slaughtered. On March 16, 1649, the Iroquois seized Brebeuf. He was inhumanly tortured and murdered. His remains were afterwards gathered and are still kept as a relic at the Hotel Dieu in Quebec. He was canonized a saint in 1930, and his feast day is September 26.

BIBLIOGRAPHY: J. G. Shea, *The Catholic Church in Colonial Days*, 1888; Francis Talbot, *Saint Among the Hurons*, 1949.

GILBERT L. ODDO.

BREEN, QUIRINUS: Presbyterian; b. at Orange City, Iowa, March 3, 1896. He studied at Calvin College and Theological Seminary (A.B., 1920) and University of Chicago (Ph.D., 1931). He was minister of Twelfth Street Chris-

tian Reformed Church, Grand Rapids (1921-24), and Downers Grove Presbyterian Church (1926-31). He taught history in Hillsdale College (1931-33), Albany (Ore.) College (1933-38), University of Oregon (1938-). He is best known for his book, *John Calvin; A Study in French Humanism* (1931). Since then his more important publications are studies on Melanchthon, G. Pico della Mirandola, Ermolao Barbaro, Celio Calcagnini, mainly for their work as humanists.

BREMEN: The free Hanseatic city includes (1952) Bremen and Bremerhaven with 558,619 inhabitants. Of these 474,192 are Evangelicals, 49,721 Roman Catholics, 106 Jews, 34,224 Freethinkers (*q.v.*, Vol. IV) and others. The Evangelical Church of Bremen embraces all the Protestant congregations in Bremen and one congregation in Bremerhaven. The other Protestant congregations in Bremerhaven belong either to the Church of Hanover (*q.v.*) or to the Reformed Church in Northwest Germany. The Evangelical Church of Bremen, which has no defined confessional position, is governed by a council of twelve elected representatives.
See also GERMANY.   [Sup.] KURD SCHULZ.

BREMNER-RIND PAPYRUS. See PAPYRI, BIBLICAL AND EARLY CHRISTIAN.

BRENNER, SCOTT FRANCIS: United Presbyterian; b. at Harmony, Pa., Dec. 8, 1903. He studied at Ursinus College (A.B., 1926); the Theological Seminary, Lancaster, Pa. (B.D., 1930); the Divinity School of the Protestant Episcopal Church, Philadelphia, Pa. (Th.M., 1935; Th.D., 1938). He ministered in the following parishes: Schwenksville-Limerick, Pa. (1930-37); St. Paul's Memorial Reformed, Reading, Pa. (1937-47); the First United Presbyterian, Carnegie, Pa. (1947-). He wrote: *The Way of Worship* (1944); *Let Us Pray* (1945). He is also coauthor of *A Handbook On Worship* (1941); and of *The Book of Worship of the Evangelical and Reformed Church* (1945).

BRENT, CHARLES HENRY: Episcopalian; d. March 27, 1929. After service as bishop of the missionary district of the Philippine Islands he was elected bishop of Western New York on Oct. 2, 1917, assuming his duties on Feb. 6, 1919. He was also in charge of the Protestant Episcopal churches in Europe (1926-28). He was very largely instrumental in promoting and conducting world church conferences, beginning with the first conferences at Stockholm and Lausanne. Brent's idea of Christian unity was analogous to the unity in the British empire where personal loyalty to the monarch rather than organic, constitutional, or legislative ties bind vastly different groups into one whole. He felt that every Christian group could contribute something to all others in such a great church which would become the heir of all the spiritual, moral, and intellectual wealth of the Christian centuries. Bishop Brent's additional publications are: *Adventure for God* (1905); *With God in Prayer* (1907); *The Mind of Christ in the Church of the Living God* (1908); *Leadership* (1908); *The Sixth Sense; Its Cultivation and Use* (1911); *Presence* (1914); *Prisoners of Hope and Other Sermons* (1915); *The Inspiration of Responsibility, and Other Papers* (1915); *The Revelation of Discovery* (1915); *The Conquest of Trouble and the Peace of God* (1916); *A Master Builder, Being the Life and Letters of Henry Yates Satterlee* (1916); *The Mount of Vision* (1918); *Understanding* (1925); *A Victor, Nathaniel Bowditch Potter* (1930); *The Commonwealth; Its Foundation and Pillars* (1930); and *Adventures in Prayer* (arranged and edited by S. S. Drury, 1932).

BIBLIOGRAPHY: Alexander C. Zabriskie, *Bishop Brent, Crusader for Christian Unity*, 1948.

[Sup.] RAYMOND W. ALBRIGHT.

BRENZ, JOHANNES: B. 1499; d. 1570. Supported Lutheranism in southwest Germany against doctrines of Bucer, Zwingli, and Calvin. Educated at Heidelberg, where he attended Luther's Disputation (1518). Ordained 1520. Published *Syngramma Suevicum* (1524) defending Lutheran interpretation of the Eucharist. Represented his region at Marburg (1529), Augsburg (1530), Schmalkalden (1537), Regensburg (1546), and Trent (1552) for which he produced the *Confessio Wirtembergica*.

BIBLIOGRAPHY: Walther Koehler, *Bibliographia Brentiana*, 1904; Julius Hartmann, *Johannes Brenz, Leben und ausgewaehlte Schriften der Vaeter und Begruender der lutherischen Kirche*, 1862; J. G. Pahl, *Ueber Johann Brenz, seinen Charakter und seine Verdienste* (1814). 163–199; G. Bossert, "Zu den Missverstaendnissen ueber die Rechtfertigungslehre des Johannes Brenz," *Theologisches Literaturblatt*, XX (1899), 153–158, 169–171; Christa Mueller, "Die Lehre des Johannes Brenz von Kirchendienst und Kirchengesang," *Monatsschrift fuer Gottesdienst und kirchliche Kunst*, XXXIX (1934), 220–228.

[Sup.] ERNEST G. SCHWIEBERT.

BRÈS (brê), **GUIDO DE** (Guy de Bray): Guido de Brès, minister of the gospel, reformer, author of the Belgic Confession (*q.v.*) was born at Mons in Hainault about 1522; executed, by hanging, on May 31, 1567, at Valenciennes. Of his youth and family background little is known. Tradition has it that he was reared by a fervently Roman Catholic mother and was converted to Calvinism at about twenty-five. But this tradition, though old, rests on questionable grounds. It grew out of a literal reading of a cryptic sentence occurring in a letter he wrote to his mother from prison shortly before his execution. Comforting her he bids her ponder the goodness of God who has heard her prayers and has given her more than she asked. He reminds her how that shortly before

she gave him birth she had followed "a certain Italian Jesuit" who was preaching in the streets of Mons. Deeply touched by the man's preaching she had prayed that God might give her a son who would so preach the Word of God. This prayer has been heard and above it God has given her a martyr for the faith. It is patently impossible however to take this reference to "a certain Italian Jesuit" at face value—for the quite sufficient reason that in 1521 there were as yet no Jesuits. What are we to make of this passage? There must have been preaching and the subsequent petition, for one cannot comfort another by the use of bare fiction. If the preaching occurred in the streets it was probably clandestine. And if so the adjective Italian leads us to think of some migrant Waldensian; for the Waldensians had their headquarters in the Piedmont. We know that Waldensians had been very active in the vicinity of Mons for centuries. If indeed de Brès' mother had Waldensian sympathies it would incriminate her to indicate it in the son's letter which had to pass through the hands of the prison authorities. That de Brès had his tongue in his cheek when he wrote "a certain Italian Jesuit" is likely; for a little farther down in his letter he informs his mother as to what Jesuits are. Many known facts fit admirably if we may assume that de Brès grew up in a home already estranged from the Roman church. We read of no conversion from Catholicism; in his lengthy debates with representatives of the Catholic Church he does not so much as hint that once he, too, held to their views. Nor do we read of any conversion in his mother's life—although it is unquestionably true that she shares his evangelical and Protestant convictions. Moreover, all the other children in the family, at least four brothers and one sister, were ardent Protestants—a situation not likely in a home as Catholic as tradition has made it. And there are expressions in de Brès' writings that have a strangely Waldensian flavor. He asserts, for example, in his first book *Baston de la Foy* (1555) that men err if they go exclusively to the Scriptures to prove their point seeing that the most ancient fathers and church councils are quite as authoritative (the Waldensians fairly doted on the earliest fathers and councils, repudiating all that came after Sylvester). He holds also that the truth in things religious has reached us through the Eastern Church (another Waldensian postulate). De Brès' admiration for martyrdom is strongly reminiscent of the pre-Reformation dissenters. He revels in it.

As to de Brès' conversion to Calvinism it may be said that his mature thought shows considerable indebtedness to the great reformer. But it is quite certain that de Brès was already a refugee for his non-Catholic convictions before the name of John Calvin was much more than a name in the southern Low Countries. About 1548 de Brès fled to England. Here he was theologically formed, in the Refugee Church at London, known contemporaneously as "Zwinglian." By 1552 he was back in his native land, assisting the nascent Protestant churches. Lille (Rijssel) and Tournai (Doornik) were his headquarters. Late in 1561 this period of activity came abruptly to an end, when flocks of the populace led by Huguenot agitators from across the border staged the *Chanteries* (nocturnal singing of the Psalms as versified by Marot). De Brès had no part in these seditious activities, denounced them roundly. The investigations that followed them made it necessary for de Brès to flee once more. Before his departure he caused a copy of the Belgic Confession to be thrown over the wall of the outer court of the castle in the vain hope that the reading of it would convince the authorities that he and his followers were not seditious people. He also left instructions with one of his flock to burn all his papers left in the garden hut that had served as his study should the danger become so great as to warrant it. This arrangement did not work out well for de Brès; for the man blunderingly set fire to the hut, the neighbors rushed out to put it out, officers of the law put in their appearance, and all de Brès' carefully guarded secrets were known. Also that he was the author of the confession that was tossed over the wall—for the handwriting of the letter accompanying it was the same as that of the papers. Unable to lay hand on him, for he had successfully escaped, they burned him in effigy and put a reward on his head, dead or alive.

We find him next at Sedan, under the protection of the Duke of Bouillon, Henri Robert de la Marck, that champion of freedom of conscience. De Brès seems to have made occasional visits to his homeland, however; in 1564 he was at Brussels for a conference with the Prince, William of Orange. There is every reason to think that de Brès looked with disfavor upon the increasingly seditious activities of the Protestants in his homeland, influenced as they were by the spirit of Huguenotism.

In the stormy Year of Wonders (1566) we find him, in his eagerness to get into the fray to head off a development that displeased him utterly, soliciting an invitation to come back to Antwerp "to oppose the Anabaptists who are spoiling so many of our people." This expression is strange, seeing that the danger of Anabaptist inroads is not mentioned again. The expression is in all probability a veiled reference (it stands in a letter to the "Consistory of Capernaum," i.e., Antwerp) to the seditionists that were taking the reins in hand, so that if the letter fell into enemy hands (as indeed it did) there would be nothing in it to incriminate the Protestants of Antwerp. After a few weeks

at Antwerp we find de Brès at Valenciennes, again "to oppose the Anabaptists." The *Hagepreeken* (field preachings) were just coming into vogue when he arrived. His presence seems to have had a quieting effect; for after his first service there was a cessation of the volley of pistol shots with which these services were being concluded, the reason being "because the minister has forbidden it."

But things were already out of hand in Valenciennes. A country-wide celebration of the Lord's Supper was planned. Fifteen or twenty thousand were expected from all over Flanders and from across the border in France. When de Brès and his party opposed so manifestly seditious a thing, cries went up, "We want the Lord's Supper; and if we don't get it we will cut the throats of all priests and seize their properties." Happily, in this instance the part of wisdom prevailed; for the celebration was cancelled. The regent, thinking to make Valenciennes an object lesson, agreed to the suggestion to declare the city in rebellion and to lay siege, in December, 1566. De Brès tried his utmost, at the head of the saner element of the citizenry, to bring men to reason and to receive the garrison which the regent wanted quartered there to restore order. But de Brès' fellow minister, Peregrin de la Grange, a Frenchman imported for this very purpose, had the common people on his side and, master rabble rouser that he was, made de Brès' labors vain. There were many stormy sessions at which the two parties in the city faced each other, so that Margaret's agents were fully aware of a "division within." The city was forced to capitulate in March. La Grange and de Brès together with a few other leading men managed to escape the city shortly after it fell. After several days of hiding in the woods hunger drove them out. Discovered in an inn where they had ordered food they were imprisoned, first at Tournai and then at Valenciennes. After hearings they were sentenced to death, by hanging, as rebels against the crown.

The execution took place on May 31, 1567. De Brès' last words were an exhortation to his followers to obey duly constituted authorities. The expression of such sentiment being unwelcome, the official in charge gave the signal to dispatch him. A violent tumult arose within the soldiery at the time of de Brès suspension. Several soldiers and bystanders were killed, a dozen others wounded. When order was restored the executions were concluded. At evening the soldiers moved the bodies to the morgue for burial. They buried de Brès without incident; but the body of La Grange they resuspended and riddled it with bullets before they interred it, "for being the cause of the delay in the capitulation of the city."

De Brès' last words, an exhortation to obey the magistracy, gave to Catholic reporters of the execution occasion to aver that de Brès died with his faith wholly shaken. And a legend sprang up to the effect that de Brès' faith had failed him at the end. The truth in the matter is that Catholic reporters, unable to visualize a person theologically a dissenter but wholly non-seditious the while, concluded from the man's repudiation of sedition that he had recanted his theological dissent.

So ended the life of one of the most intriguing characters of an age that produced them in quantity. Guido de Brès was deeply devout, a man of mild temper and broad, almost liberal, sympathies. Without the benefit of a formal education in theology he revealed an astounding knowledge of the literature, quoting endlessly and from memory, the ancient writers. He had mastered Latin, Greek, and Hebrew. His earthly possessions were few. (The inquisitors were told to be on the lookout for a "tall man with a shabby overcoat"), but in the things of the spirit he was rich, as his writings, especially his letters to his wife and mother written from prison, show abundantly.

BIBLIOGRAPHY: L. A. Van Langeraad, *Guido de Bray, zijn Leven en Werken,* 1884; Daniel Ollier, *Guy de Brès,* 1883.

[Sup.] LEONARD VERDUIN.

BRETHREN, CHURCH OF THE. See DUNKERS.

BRETHREN, GERMAN BAPTIST. See DUNKERS.

BRETHREN IN CHRIST, UNITED. See UNITED BRETHREN IN CHRIST.

BRETHREN OF THE COMMON LIFE. See COMMON LIFE, BRETHREN OF THE.

BRETHREN, RIVER. See RIVER BRETHREN.

BREVIARY: The disposition of the Roman breviary was changed in 1911 by order of Pope Pius X. The psalms of the office were redistributed in such a way that the whole Psalter might be read within one week. Likewise the rubrics were modified in order to prevent the feasts of the saints from usually taking precedence of the office of the day. On March 24, 1945, a decree of Pius XII authorized the use of the new version of the psalms from the Hebrew, prepared by the Pontifical Biblical Institute, in the recitation of the divine office. Cf. *Acta Apostolicae Sedis,* III (1911), 633–651; XXXVII (1945), 65–67.

[Sup.] GEORGES A. BARROIS.

BREYFOGEL, S(YLVANUS) CHARLES: D. Nov. 24, 1934. For thirty-nine years he served as a bishop of the Evangelical Associ-

ation (Church after 1922) and was especially helpful in guiding the arrangements for the union of the United Evangelical Church and the Evangelical Association to form the Evangelical Church (*q.v.*) in 1922. From 1930 until the time of his death he was bishop-emeritus. He was largely responsible for the foundation of the denomination's Board of Church Extension, The Pension Fund, and its eastern seminary, The Evangelical School of Theology, Reading, Pa., of which he was the president from its beginning in 1905 until 1934. At his death he left unpublished a survey of church law and trends in denominational life.

BIBLIOGRAPHY: Raymond W. Albright, "Bishop S. C. Breyfogel—His Life and Contribution to the Evangelical Church," *Bulletin of the Evangelical School of Theology,* Vol. XI, No. 1.

[Sup.] RAYMOND W. ALBRIGHT.

BRIDGES, RONALD: Congregationalist; b. at West Pembroke, Maine, Nov. 23, 1905. He studied at Bowdoin College (A.B., 1930) and Harvard University (M.A., 1932). He was associate professor of English, Arizona State College (1942–45); president, Pacific School of Religion, Berkeley, California (1945–50); and is executive director, Broadcasting and Film Commission, National Council of Churches of Christ in U.S.A., New York (1950–). He is chairman of the Joint Religious Radio Committee and president, American Board of Commissioners for Foreign Missions (1950).

BRIDGET, SAINT, OF SWEDEN: During the fifteenth and sixteenth centuries the Brigittine Order was widely spread throughout Europe. There were about eighty monasteries; see the complete list in *Lexikon fuer Theologie und Kirche,* which also gives the present number, Vol. 2, col. 367. In 1935 a group of nuns began again the Brigittine rule at Vadsténa in Sweden, while in the same country since 1923 there have been Brigittine Sisters at Vilohem, founded under the direction of Elisabeth Hesselband in Rome; with a second house at Norrköping, founded in 1929.

BIBLIOGRAPHY: E. Pearcy, *Saint Brigitte of Sweden,* 1984; F. Vernet, *Dict. d'hist. et géogr. ecclés.,* Vol. X (1937), col. 719–731; Heimbucher, *Orden und Kongregationen,* 3rd ed., Vol. I (1933), pp. 620 ff.; N. Söderblom, *Brigitte och reformationen,* 1917.

[Sup.] E. STOKMAN.

BRIGGS, CHARLES AUGUSTUS: D. June 8, 1913. His additional contributions are largely in the field of biblical criticism which he produced at Union Seminary where he taught until his death. In his own defense at his trial for heresy before the Presbyterian Church Committee he wrote *The Case of Dr. Briggs* (3 parts, 1892). The record of the appeal before the General Assembly was compiled by John J. McCook, as *The Appeal in the Briggs Heresy Case,* 1893. Dr. Briggs's additional books include: *Church Unity;* and *The Papal Commission and the Pentateuch* (joint author, 1906). With Francis Brown and S. R. Driver he wrote the *New Hebrew Lexicon.* He was also an editor of The International Theological Library and of the International Critical Commentary.

[Sup.] RAYMOND W. ALBRIGHT.

BRIGHTMAN, EDGAR SHEFFIELD: Personalistic philosopher and author; b. at Holbrook, Mass., Sept. 20, 1884; d. Feb. 25, 1953. He studied at Brown University (A.B., 1906 and A.M., 1908); Boston University (S.T.B., 1910; Ph.D., 1912) and in Germany. He taught philosophy and Greek at Brown (1906–8); he was professor of philosophy and Bible at Nebraska Wesleyan University (1912–15); of ethics and religion at Wesleyan University (1915–19); and of philosophy at Boston University (1919–53). Ordained, New England Conference of the Methodist Church; Fellow of American Academy of Arts and Sciences, and of Conference on Science, Philosophy and Religion; past president: American Philosophical Association, Eastern Division; American Theological Society, Eastern Branch; and National Association of Biblical Instructors. He was pupil of Everett, Meiklejohn, Bowne, Knudson, Harnack, Riehl, Herrmann, and Natorp. His chief interests were epistemology, metaphysics, axiology, philosophy of religion, Hegelianism, Latin-American and Indian philosophy. He defended coherence, vs. irrationalism, pragmatism and logical atomism; epistemological dualism; theistic personalism, vs. naturalism and positivism; organic pluralism, vs. monistic absolutism and atomistic pluralism.

His chief contribution was to an empirical personalism, resulting in the idea of a temporalistic, "finite" God within whose eternal unified personality will is limited by eternal experiences called the rational and the nonrational Given. God is then Controller of the Given.

Among the lectureships he held are Ingersoll (1925); Lowell Institute (1925, 1934); Boston University (1951).

His chief works are *Sources of the Hexateuch* (1918); *Introduction to Philosophy* (1925, 1951); *Religious Values* (1925); *Philosophy of Ideals* (1928); *Moral Laws* (1933); *Philosophy of Religion* (1940); *Nature and Values* (1945). He edited *Personalism in Theology* (in honor of A. C. Knudson) (1943); wrote articles for V. Ferm (ed.), *Encyclopedia of Religion* (1945); *History of Philosophical Systems* (1950); and W. R. Inge (ed.), *Radhakrishnan* (1951).

See also PERSONALISM.

BRILIOTH, YNGVE: Lutheran; b. at V. Ed, Sweden, July 12, 1891. He studied at the University of Uppsala (Ph.D., 1916). Ordained in Uppsala in 1918, he became lecturer in church history in Uppsala (1919), professor of church history at Åbo University (1925), professor of practical theology at the University of Lund and dean of Lund (1928). He was bishop of Växjö (1937–50); Archbishop of Uppsala (1950–). He is a member of Central Committee and Executive Committee of World Council of Churches and chairman of the Commission On Faith and Order of World Council of Churches. His publications are: *The Anglican Revival* (1925); *Eucharistic Faith and Practice* (1930); "The Church of Sweden in its Relations to the Anglican Church" in *Church Quarterly Review* (1920); *Three Lectures on Evangelicalism and the Oxford Movement* (1934); and *Landmarks in the History of Preaching* (1950).

BRING, RAGNAR: Swedish Lutheran; b. in Skara, July 10, 1895. He studied at Uppsala (fil. kand., 1917) and at Lund (teol. lic., 1926; teol. d., 1930). He also studied in Germany (Goettingen, Marburg and Erlangen, 1928–32) and in England (1936). Bring was librarian at the University of Lund (1925–33) and became lecturer in systematic theology in the university (1929). He taught dogmatics, history of dogma, ethics and philosophy of religion at Åbo (Finland) (1930–34). He was professor of systematic theology at Lund, succeeding Bishop G. Aulén (1934–). He has written: *Dualismen hos Luther* (1929); *Förhållandet mellan tro och gärningar inom luthersk teologi,* D. 1–2 (1933); *Till frågan om den systematiska teologiens uppgift med särskild hänsyn till inom svensk teologi föreliggande problemställningar* (1933); *Theologi och religion* (1937); *Luthersk bibilsyn* (1947); and *Kristendomstolkningar* (1950).

BIBLIOGRAPHY: *Särtyck ur Lunds universitets matrikel,* (1949–50), 72 f.

RAYMOND W. ALBRIGHT.

BRINTON, HOWARD HAINES: Society of Friends; b. West Chester, Pa., July 24, 1884; was educated at Haverford, Harvard and University of California. He has taught at Guilford, Earlham and Mills colleges. Since 1936 he has been director of Pendle Hill Graduate School, Wallingford, Pa. He is author of *The Mystic Will; Creative Worship; A Religious Solution to the Social Problem; Divine-Human Society; Quaker Education; Sources of the Quaker Peace Testimony; A Guide to Quaker Practice; Critique by Eternity; The Quaker Doctrine of Inward Peace; Prophetic Ministry;* also editor and contributor to *Children of Light,* and *Byways in Quaker History.*

BRITISH COUNCIL OF CHURCHES: A fellowship of Churches in England, Scotland, Wales, and Ireland, constituted on the same theological basis as the World Council of Churches (*q.v.*)—acceptance of our Lord Jesus

Christ as God and Saviour. Its creation in 1942 was the outcome of influences generated by the Ecumenical Conferences on Life and Work and Faith and Order at Oxford and Edinburgh in 1937.

The Council exists for the following declared purposes: (1) To facilitate common action by the churches in evangelistic enterprise, in promotion of international friendship, in stimulating a sense of social responsibility, and in guiding the activities of the churches for the welfare of youth; (2) to facilitate such other common action as may later be determined; (3) to promote co-operation in study and to ensure adequate British participation in the studies promoted by the World Council of Churches; (4) to assist the growth of ecumenical consciousness in the members of all churches and generally to promote Christian unity.

The Council consists of 118 members (62 English, 13 Scottish, 7 Welsh, 6 Irish, 10 representing interdenominational organizations, and 20 co-opted). Its president is the archbishop of Canterbury. The Council works by Departments for Faith and Order, International Affairs, Social Responsibility, Youth, etc.

BIBLIOGRAPHY: *Christian Year Book*, 1950.

EVELYN CLIFFORD URWIN.

BRITISH-ISRAEL. See ANGLO-ISRAEL.

BROSS FOUNDATION: Established by William Bross at Lake Forest University, Lake Forest, Ill., in 1879 to provide (1) for series of lectures in the university and (2) for competitive awards to stimulate the writing of books of distinction in the field of religion.

BROTHERHOOD MOVEMENT: Founded by John Blackham, a Congregational deacon, at West Bromwich, England, in 1875. Originally known as the "P.S.A." Movement (from Blackham's "Pleasant Sunday Afternoon" Bible Class for young men), it gathered 100,000 members in ten years, and in twenty was established throughout the country. In 1891 the first women's P.S.A.'s and P.M.E.'s ("Pleasant Monday Evenings") inaugurated the Sisterhood side of the movement. In 1906 the first National Conference was attended by 500 delegates representing 250,000 members. The movement took its present name officially in 1910, and in 1919 became an incorporated body. Its organization includes local societies (Brotherhoods, Sisterhoods, P.S.A.'s, etc.), county and area federations, separate Brotherhood and Sisterhood Councils, various social service departments, and a National Conference. It is non-sectarian, but mostly holds its meetings on church premises, where it seeks to form "a bridge between the pavement and the pew." Its motto is: "One is your Master, even Christ, and all ye are brethren." Its membership in 1951 numbered 75,000.

Headquarters are in Wealdstone, Middlesex. Monthly magazine: *Outlook*.

PHILIP SAVILLE WATSON.

BROTHERHOOD OF MAN: The conception of a fundamental kinship between all mankind has origins in both Greek and biblical thought. Greeks of the classical period divided the human race into Greeks and non-Greeks, described the latter as barbarians, and regarded them as an inferior stock. Plato said that all barbarians were enemies by nature, and Aristotle believed that they lacked the qualities of freemen, being destined by nature to serve as slaves. Although this view was occasionally challenged and a more cosmopolitan outlook was expressed, especially by the Cynics, it is to the Stoics that we owe the first expressions of human brotherhood as an inspiriting ideal of conduct. In Zeno's *Republic* all distinctions of earthly rank and race have been abolished, and there is neither Greek nor barbarian in his world-city, from which only the unworthy are excluded. In the writings of the later Stoics, Epictetus and Marcus Aurelius, Zeus is regarded as the father of all mankind, and men are therefore brothers, possessing a common reason, and alike subject to the universal law of nature which prescribes their mutual obligations and establishes their freedom and equality. Epictetus demands that a master should refrain from anger with a neglectful slave on the grounds of their common kinship: "Slave, will you not bear with your own brother, who has Zeus for his forefather, and is born as a son of the same seed as you and of the same heavenly descent? . . . Will you not remember what you are and whom you are ruling? that they are kinsmen, born your brothers, children of Zeus?" (*Discourses* i. 15)

In the Old Testament there is much emphasis on the ties of kinship that bind together the Israelites, and on the unique bond that unites them as the chosen people of Yahweh. There is, however, an incipient universalism in the book of Amos, where neighboring nations stand equally under the judgment of Yahweh; in Deutero-Isaiah, where Israel is to be the instrument for the conversion of the Gentiles; and in the short books of Ruth and Jonah, where national exclusiveness is transcended. The accounts of the creation and the flood in Genesis clearly indicate that all men are descended from a common stock, and the sons of Noah are regarded as the progenitors of the various races of mankind. Yet the symbol of brotherhood is never extended explicitly beyond the limits of Israel, and, although Yahweh is occasionally referred to as a Father, it is always in relationship to the nation. At the same time, mercy and kindness are to be shown not only to the poor and needy of Israel, but especially to slaves and foreigners within her borders, and the Messianic kingdom is to initiate universal peace for all mankind.

In the New Testament, the prevailing sense of the word "brother" (*adelphos*) is "fellow-Christian," and the community of believers is called the "brotherhood" (*adelphotēs*, I Peter 2: 17; 5:9). "Brotherly love" (*philadelphia*) is the duty of Christians towards each other (I John 2:9 ff; 3:10, 14; I Thess. 4:9; etc.). Beyond this more intimate circle of discipleship, however, there is also a universal bond uniting all men in a natural brotherhood, which is generally assumed rather than asserted. Jesus refers to God as "Father" without any restrictions upon the term's sphere of reference, and also uses "brother" in the general sense of "fellowman" (Matt. 5:22, 23; 7:3; 18:15, 35; 23:8). It is probably to the Stoic Cleanthes that Paul refers when he uses at the city of Athens the quotation "For we are also his offspring" (Acts 17:28).

The reason for this ambivalence in the New Testament is that sin has alienated men from God and from their fellows, so that the relationship is more potential than real. So Jesus has come to establish a *new* brotherhood of those who are obedient to God's will (Mark 3:32–35); Paul speaks of being *adopted* into sonship through God's grace (Rom. 8:15); and the Fourth Gospel says that those who receive Christ are given the right "to *become* children of God" (John 1:12). This brotherhood is, however, quite universal in its scope: "For ye are all sons of God, through faith, in Christ Jesus. . . . There can be neither Jew nor Greek, there can be neither bond nor free, there can be no male and female: for ye are all one man in Christ Jesus" (Gal. 3:26, 28). The Christian's relation to his fellows is marked by an outgoing love which is given unconditionally to every "neighbor" and is not withheld even from his enemies, because it has its origin in the love of God himself; "for he maketh his sun to rise on the evil and the good, and sendeth rain on the just and the unjust." It is in this way that the disciples show that they are sons of their Father in heaven (Matt. 5:43–48).

The concept of human brotherhood has exercised a potent influence on Western thought and action which it would be difficult accurately to assess. It has been an ideal of personal ethics, stimulating acts of charity and attitudes of brotherly love. It has at times served as an ideal to challenge social inequalities and injustices, especially the institution of slavery, to condemn national exclusiveness, and to mitigate the barbarity of warfare. In the eighteenth century Enlightenment the universalism of Stoicism blended with Christian idealism in forming the concept of man's natural right to freedom and equality, which powerfully influenced the American and French Revolutions, and the slogan of the latter included "fraternity" as one of its objectives.

In the liberal theology (see LIBERALISM) of the latter half of the nineteenth century the "kingdom of God" (*q.v.*) in the Gospels was interpreted to imply the brotherhood of man and the Fatherhood of God, and these were the ideals which inspired the Social Gospel (*q.v.*) at the beginning of the present century. A vigorous protest was made against social inequalities and the injustices of *laissez-faire* capitalism (*q.v.*), and pacifism (see PEACE MOVEMENTS) became widely accepted as the only Christian attitude to international tensions. The neo-Reformation reaction to liberalism has been less concerned with man's natural brotherhood than with his innate selfishness and his need of redemption (see SOTERIOLOGY). The kingdom of God will never be fulfilled within history, and the Christian must therefore pursue the more modest social aim of achieving a tolerable justice between men's competing interests.

See also ETHICS.

BIBLIOGRAPHY: W. J. Oates, ed., *The Stoic and Epicurean Philosophers*, 1940; W. W. Tarn, *Alexander the Great and the Unity of Mankind*, 1933; Shailer Mathews, *The Social Teaching of Jesus*, 1897; Walter Rauschenbusch, *Christianizing the Social Order*, 1914.

ANTHONY S. CHADWICK.

BROTHERHOOD OF THE KINGDOM. See SOCIAL GOSPEL.

BROTHERS, RICHARD. See MESSIAHS, FALSE.

BROWN, ARLO AYRES: Methodist; b. April 15, 1883, at Sunbeam, Ill. He received his education at Northwestern University (A.B., 1903) Drew Seminary (B.D., 1907) and Union Theological Seminary. After serving as an associate at the Madison Avenue Church in New York City (1907–9) and pastor of the Mount Hope Church, New York (1909–12) he became the agent for the Board of Foreign Missions of the Methodist Church in Jerusalem (1912–13); an executive of the Newark District of his church (1913–14); superintendent of teacher training of the Board of Sunday Schools of the Methodist Church (1914–21); president of the University of Chattanooga (1921–29) and president of Drew University (1929–47). He has written: *Studies in Christian Living* (1914); *Primer of Teacher Training* (1916); *Life in the Making* (coauthor, 1917); *A History of Religious Education in Recent Times* (1923); and *Youth and Christian Living* (1929).

RAYMOND W. ALBRIGHT.

BROWN, CHARLES REYNOLDS: D. Nov. 28, 1950. He was pastor of the First Congregational Church, Oakland, Cal. (1896–1911) and became the dean of the Yale Divinity School (1911–28; emeritus 1928–50) where he had a distinguished career as teacher, preacher and administrator. He also wrote: *The Strange Ways of God* (1908); *The Young Man's Affairs* (1909); *Faith and Health* (1910); *The Modern Man's Religion* (1911); *The Latent Energies in Life* (1912); *The Quest of Life* (1913); *Yale Talks* (1919); *The Master's Way* (1919); *Living Again* (1920); *The Religion of a Layman* (1921); *The Greatest Man of the Nineteenth Century* (1921); *The Art of Preaching* (1922); *Why I Believe in Religion* (1923); *What Is Your Name* (1924); *Where do You Live* (1925); *Ten Short Stories from the Bible* (1925); *These Twelve* (1926); *The Making of a Minister* (1927); *The Gospel for Main Street* (1929); *My Own Yesterdays* (1931); *Have We Outgrown Religion?* (1932); *They Were Giants* (1934); *Finding Ourselves* (1935); *The Master's Influence* (1936); *Being Made Over* (1939); and *Dreams Come True* (1944).

[Sup.] RAYMOND W. ALBRIGHT.

BROWN, WILLIAM ADAMS: D. Dec. 15, 1943. He served as Roosevelt Professor of Systematic Theology in Union Theological Seminary (1898–1930) and as research professor in applied theology (1930–36; emeritus, 1936–43). He was acting provost of Yale University (1919–20) and chairman of the Committee on Educational Policy at Yale (1919–30). He also gave much time to the work of the Federal Council of Churches, the Board of Home Missions of the Presbyterian Church, and the ecumenical movement (*q.v.*), participating in its early major assemblies. He was a distinguished leader in the liberal theological movement. His additional books include: *Life of Morris K. Jesup* (1910); *The Christian Hope* (1912); *Modern Theology and the Preaching of the Gospel* (1914); *Is Christianity Practicable?* (1916); *Modern Missions in the Far East* (1917); *The Church in America* (1922); *Imperialistic Religion and the Religion of Democracy* (1923); *The Creative Experience* (1923); *The Life of Prayer in a World of Science* (1926); *The Quiet Hour* (1926); *Beliefs that Matter* (1928); *Pathways to Certainty* (1930); *God at Work* (1933); *Ministerial Education in America* (Vol. I, 1934); *The Church, Catholic and Protestant* (1935); *Finding God in a New World* (1935); *Church and State in Contemporary America* (1936); *The Minister—His World and His Work* (1937); *The Case for Theology in the University* (1938); *A Teacher and His Times* (1940); *A Creed for Free Men* (1941); and *The New Order in the Church* (1943).

[Sup.] RAYMOND W. ALBRIGHT.

BROWNE, LAURENCE EDWARD: B. at Northampton, England, April 17, 1887. After study at Sidney Sussex College, Cambridge, he served for over eleven years overseas, in India and the Middle East. His first line of scholarship was in the Old Testament, from which he turned to the study of Islam and then to the comparative study of religions. He was professor of comparative religion at Manchester University (1941–46), and professor of theology at the University of Leeds (1946–52). His books include *Early Judaism* (1920); *From Babylon to Bethlehem* (1926); *Eclipse of Christianity in Asia from the Time of Muhammad to the Fourteenth Century* (1933); *Prospects of Islam* (1944); *Where Science and Religion Meet* (1950); *Ezekiel and Alexander* (1952).

BROWNE, LEWIS: Author; b. June 24, 1897, in London, Eng.; d. Jan. 3, 1949. He was educated at the University of Cincinnati (B.A., 1919), Hebrew Union College, Rabbinical Seminary (B.H., 1920), and Yale (1920–22). He served as rabbi of Temple Israel, Waterbury, Conn. (1920–23); Free Synagogue of Newark, N. J., where he was associated with Stephen S. Wise (1924–26); after which he resigned his rabbinate to devote his time to lecturing and writing. Among his noteworthy books are: *Stranger than Fiction* (1925); *This Believing World* (1926); *The Graphic Bible* (1928); *Why Are Jews Like That?* (1929); *Since Calvary* (1931); *Blessed Spinoza* (1932); *How Odd of God* (1934); *All Things are Possible* (1935); *The Wisdom of Israel* (1945); and *The World's Great Scriptures* (ills. by author, 1946).

RAYMOND W. ALBRIGHT.

BROWNE, ROBERT, AND THE BROWN-ISTS:

BIBLIOGRAPHY: C. Burrage, *The Early Dissenters*, 2 vols., 1912; J. B. Black, *The Reign of Elizabeth* (1936), pp. 163-164; A. F. Pearson, *Thomas Cartwright and Elizabethan Puritanism*, 1925; J. G. de Hoop Scheffer, *History of the Free Churchmen Called the Brownists, Pilgrim Fathers and Baptists in the Dutch Republic, 1581-1701*, 1922. [Sup.]

BRUNNER, EMIL: Swiss Reformed; b. at Winterthur, Zurich, Switzerland, Dec. 23, 1889. He studied at the universities of Zurich (Lic. Theol., 1913) and Berlin, and also at Union Theological Seminary, New York. He taught languages in England (1913–14); was pastor of the mountain parish of Obstalden, Glarus (1916–24) and has been professor of theology at Zurich (1924–53) and at Christian University, Mitaka, Tokyo, Japan (1953–).

He is known as one of the founders of the so-called "Dialectical School" of theology and a collaborator of Karl Barth. He has lectured widely at universities in Europe and the United States. He was guest professor at Princeton Theological Seminary (1938–39) and Gifford lecturer in 1947 and 1948. He participated in the preparation of the theological materials for the ecumenical assemblies at Oxford and Amsterdam.

Among his most important books, many of which have been translated into English, Japanese and European languages, are: *Die Mystik und das Wort* (1924); *The Mediator* (1926); *The Divine Imperative* (1932); *Man in Revolt* (1936); *The Divine-Human Encounter* (1937); *Revelation and Reason* (1942); *Justice and the Social Order* (1944); *Christian Doctrine* (in process, Vol. I, 1946; Vol. II, 1949); *Christianity and Civilization* (Gifford Lectures) (1948, 1949).

BIBLIOGRAPHY: *Das Menschenbild im Lichte des Evangeliums*, edited for his sixtieth birthday (1949).

RAYMOND W. ALBRIGHT.

BRUNO I OF COLOGNE: Was regarded as a saint from the very beginning, but not until 1870 did the Papal Curia grant permission to have his cultus accepted for the archdiocese of Cologne.

BIBLIOGRAPHY: H. Schroers in 1910 published in Vol. 88 of the *Annalen des historischen Vereins fuer den Niederrhein* a German translation of the *Vita Brunonis* by Ruotger, and in 1911 in Vol. 91 of the same periodical he published the testament of Bruno with a translation and commentary.

[Sup.] MATHIAS GOOSSENS.

BRUNO, GIORDANO: As a former Dominican he was thoroughly familiar with theology and obviously interested in ecclesiastical affairs. No doubt the only reason why he left the order was that he taught opinions that appeared heretical to his superiors. His main interest, however, was in philosophy, and many scholars have called him the first of the modern philosophers. He reflected the culture of the Italian Renaissance (*q.v.*), the daring attitude of the skeptic who loved to exploit all human talents and study all systems of religion and philosophy. He lectured with great success in Paris and at Oxford and Wittenberg, his main subjects being astronomy and philosophy. His semipantheism was taken over by Spinoza and Leibnitz. Even in the field of pure literature he had his pupils and admirers. The highly influential Schelling named one of his works after him: *Bruno, or the Natural and Divine Principle of Things*. He introduced the hypothesis of the ether and had an extremely involved and learned theory of relativity. In the cosmos, he argued, there are countless stars, planets, worlds, and suns, since the universe is infinite in all directions. Not one of them is truly central. He actually peered beyond the scope of modern astronomy, beyond the limits of the telescopes and other material instruments. His intuition seems to have been extraordinary. For years he carried on an intellectual fight with the officials in the Roman Inquisition. Finally, when they grew weary of argumentation they took recourse to persecution and had him burned at the stake. Egon Friedell has called him with much reason a human volcano.

BIBLIOGRAPHY: A nearly complete bibliography of Bruno's works is the following: V. Salvestrini, *Bibliografia delle opere di Giordano Bruno, e degli scritta ad esso attinenti*, 1926; other works: X. Atanassievitch, *La doctrine métaphysique et géométrique de Bruno*, 1923; W. Boulting,

Giordano Bruno, 1916; E. Cassirer, *An Essay on Man*, 1944; A. Corsano, *Il pensiero di Giordano Bruno*, 1940; S. Greenberg, *The Infinite in Giordano Bruno*, 1950; E. Namer, *Les aspects de Dieu dans la philosophie de Giordano Bruno*, 1926; A. Wolf, *History of Science, Technology, and Philosophy in the Sixteenth and Seventeenth Centuries*, 1935.

[Sup.] ALBERT HYMA.

BRUNO OF QUERFURT: From his pen there has been preserved in a letter addressed by him to Emperor Henry II a valuable account of ecclesiastical policy. With St. Adalbert he is the patron of Prussia. He was martyred in 1009 near Braunsberg, which place was named after him, that is, the Mountain of Bruno.

BIBLIOGRAPHY: *Dict. d'histoire et de géogr. eccl.*, Vol. X (1938), with excellent bibliography, including the latest Polish sources described by J. Ostrowski.

[Sup.] MATHIAS GOOSSENS.

BRUNSWICK: With the abdication of the duke, who as "emergency bishop" was head of the church as well as of the German duchy, the Evangelical Lutheran Church of Brunswick (*Braunschweig*) became independent of the state at the conclusion of World War I. A new constitution was adopted in 1922 according to which the church was divided into districts, a bishop was placed at the head of the ecclesiastical administration, and legislative power was committed to a synod.

The church was disturbed during the period of National Socialism, when (1933) the ecclesiastical districts were rearranged to conform with the districts of the state, considerable church property was confiscated, churchmen were limited in their activity or completely silenced, children were alienated from the church, and the ancient cathedral in Brunswick was turned into a "national shrine" (see GERMANY, I). Not until the close of World War II was the independence of the church restored. A complete reorganization took place in 1951, when the synod (*Landessynode*) was again given legislative authority. Each congregation elects its own council and sends representatives to a district synod (*Propsteisynode*). The district synods in turn elect 44 members, in addition to 4 members appointed by the bishop, to the *Landessynode*, and this synod elects the members of the ecclesiastical administration. Elections are free, secret, and limited to active members of congregations rather than open (as was the case under National Socialism) to the masses of the population.

In 1942 Holzminden and several other small parts of the church were transferred to the Church of Hanover (*q.v.*) in return for the territory around Goslar and Salzgitter. The major part of the district of Blankenburg was cut off by the boundary of the occupation zones, and so an independent administration was set up although this territory remains a part of the Church of Brunswick. Evangelical refugees (q.v.) who settled in Brunswick after World War II were automatically added to the church rolls and helped to revitalize church life. As a matter of fact, all areas of church life—work among men and women, the youth movement (q.v.), and the Inner Mission—were quickened again after they had been suppressed under National Socialism.

Among the sects and cults (q.v.), the New Apostolic Church (q.v.), Christian Science (q.v.), the Mormons (q.v.), and adherents of Anthroposophy (q.v.) were most active. Roman Catholicism grew in strength as a result of the influx of refugees. According to the census of 1950 there were 651,717 Evangelicals, 147,985 Roman Catholics, and 67,054 unchurched or members of sects in that part of Brunswick belonging to the West German Republic. There were no figures for the population in the Russian zone.

The Evangelical Lutheran Church of Brunswick is a member of the United Evangelical Lutheran Church (q.v.) in Germany and of the Evangelical Church in Germany (see GERMANY, I).

BIBLIOGRAPHY: Johannes Meyer, *Kirchengeschichte Niedersachsens*, 1939; Ernst Rolffs, *Evangelische Kirchenkunde Niedersachsens*, 2nd ed., 1938.

[Sup.] ERNST-GEORG WOLTERS.

BUBER, MARTIN: Jewish; b. Vienna, Feb. 8, 1878. The grandson of the noted scholar, Solomon Buber, from whom he received his early education, he studied philosophy and history of art from 1896 to 1900 at the Universities of Vienna, Leipzig, Berlin, and Zurich; was Zionist political writer and editor of the Vienna *Welt* in 1901; studied philosophy of religion in Berlin (1906). From 1916 until 1924 he was the editor of *Der Jude*, a periodical for German-speaking Jews which he had founded. He held the first chair of Jewish philosophy of religion and ethics in Germany at Frankfort-Main from 1923 to 1933. After his exile from Germany in 1938, he emigrated to Israel and became professor of social philosophy at Hebrew University. One of the outstanding religious thinkers of our time, he was a leader of the German religious socialist movement, and is noted for his reinterpretation of Hasidism, a philosophy which has had a profound influence on Western thought. His early Zionist activities were partly responsible for the transforming of Zionism from a purely political to a cultural movement as well. He is the author of over twenty volumes dealing with all aspects of Jewish life, and his writings contain some of the most profound, original studies in Judaism and in the philosophy of religion in general. Together with Franz Rosenzweig, and later alone, he made a most revolutionary translation of the Bible into German. His influence has been widely felt, not only in Central Europe but throughout the world. Among his most significant works are: *I and Thou* (1937); *Moses* (1944); *For the Sake of Heaven* (a novel) (1945); *Tales of Hassidism* (2 vols., 1947); *Between Man and Man* (1947); *Israel and the World* (1948); *Prophetic Faith* (1949); *Two Types of Faith* (1951).

LOUIS FINKELSTEIN.

BUCER (BUTZER), MARTIN: At the age of fifteen he was accepted as an inmate of the Dominican monastery at his native town of Schlettstadt. At the end of 1516 he removed to the monastery in Heidelberg. As a direct result of meeting Luther in April, 1518, he changed from a follower of Erasmus into a Lutheran. In April, 1521, he was able to leave the monastery, and for a short time he was a pastor at Landstuhl, where the local parish belonged to Franz von Sickingen. His Protestant affiliation was first demonstrated in the Alsatian town of Weiszenburg, from which he soon had to flee as a married man to Strassburg (May, 1523). Largely as a result of his personal influence the introduction of Protestantism as the leading religion occurred in March, 1524, while the ecclesiastical ordinance of 1534 was also for the most part his work.

He tried to convert the Anabaptists to his faith through disputations, and he disapproved of the death penalty against them then in vogue, recommending instead banishment. His campaign against the Anabaptist religion convinced him that there should be a strong church discipline, but the magistrates refused to heed his request. His last proposal was that of 1546, when he suggested that there be small groups in a congregation which were to submit to the discipline of elders and pastors elected by the people. These *ecclesiolae in ecclesia* became a model for Spener about 150 years later: the *collegia pietatis* used by the famous Pietists. But only in Hesse was Bucer able (thanks to the aid of the count Philip in his fight against the Anabaptists) to introduce his church discipline and the office of elders.

In the struggle between Luther and Zwingli he tried to establish a compromise on the doctrine of the Eucharist, but Luther strongly opposed his view (1527–30). Finally, however, Luther relented his attitude, and in 1536 Bucer succeeded in obtaining the Wittenberg Concord between Luther and the South German reformers. It meant the union of the Protestants in southern Germany under the banner of moderate Lutheranism, but also the eventual schism between German and Swiss Protestantism. Emperor Charles V appointed him to lead the discussions in 1540 and 1541 which he hoped would produce a compromise between Roman Catholics and Protestants, but the formula proposed by Bucer did not prove acceptable to either Luther or the Pope. Charles V after his victory over the Schmalkaldic League, commissioned Bucer to help arrive at the Augsburg Interim, but he opposed any weakening of the Lutheran creed and so lost the support of the magistrates in Strassburg, who in 1549 dismissed him.

Archbishop Cranmer of Canterbury offered him a position which he preferred above any in Germany. He assisted in the revision of the Prayer Book, which was partly based upon the liturgy of Archbishop Herman of Cologne, completed in 1543. Although he favored the moderate Anglican position, he won many followers among the early Puritans, who studied with him at Cambridge. They derived from him their biblical theology and the concept of a living congregation with strong discipline. Unfortunately, excessive labors resulted in a serious illness which quickly caused death on February 28 or March 1, 1551. He was buried in the Great St. Mary's Church in Cambridge, where five years later Queen Mary's officials removed his bones and after a charge of heresy against him burned them in public. At the ascension of Queen Elizabeth a ceremony was held to restore him to a position of honor.

Being strongly influenced by Erasmus, Luther, and Zwingli, he does not belong to any of the great denominations of the sixteenth century. He was, in fact, one of the leading spirits who sought to establish reunion. The Protestants of southern Germany, the Church of England, and the Reformed churches owe much to him. For the Diet of Augsburg in 1530 he fashioned with Capito the *Confessio Tetrapolitana* of Strassburg, Constance, Memmingen, and Lindau. Through an enormous correspondence with theologians, princes, city councils, etc., he advanced the cause of the Reformation with boundless energy. An edition of his collected works has not yet made its appearance, but in 1577 a volume of his later works, *Scripta Anglicana fere omnia*, was published at Basel. His letters have also been published only in part.

BIBLIOGRAPHY: R. Stupperich and Ernst Steinborn, "Bibliographia Buceriana," in *Schriften des Vereins fuer Reformationsgeschichte*, No. 169 (1952); G. Anrich, *Martin Butzer*, 1914; Wilhelm Pauck, *Das Reich Gottes auf Erden*, 1928; Hastings Eells, *Martin Bucer*, 1931; Jacques Courvoisier, *La notion de l'église chez Bucer*, 1933; A. Lang, *Puritanismus und Pietismus*, 1941; Constantin Hopf, *Martin Bucer and the English Reformation*, 1946; Heinrich Bornkamm, "Martin Butzers Bedeutung fuer die europaeische Reformationsgeschichte," in *Schr. d. V. fuer Reformationsgeschichte*, No. 169 (1952); important discussions in Otto Ritschl, *Dogmengeschichte des Protestantismus*, III, 1926; Walther Koehler, *Zwingli und Luther*, I, 1924; II, 1952; W. Koehler, *Zuericher Eheegericht und Genfer Konsistorium*, 1942; Ernst Bizer, *Studien zur Geschichte des Abendmahlsstreits*, 1940.

[Sup.] D. HEINRICH BORNKAMM.

BUCHMAN, FRANK NATHAN DANIEL: B. at Pennsburg, Pa., June 4, 1878. He studied at Muhlenberg College (A.B., 1899; A.M., 1902), and Mt. Airy Lutheran Seminary, Philadelphia. He never married. After a brief period as pastor of a struggling church in a Philadelphia suburb he resigned, had a conversion experience, and then acted for seven years as student Christian worker at Penn State College. In 1919 he returned from a tour of the Orient to lecture on personal evangelism at Hartford Theological Seminary. After one year there he set out on his own, to "change lives and enlist life-changers" in a First Century Christian Fellowship. By emphasizing problems of sex, private confession, the house-party technique and strong mysticism (guidance), he alienated many people, but in spite of ups and downs he has won (and lost) many adherents in all parts of the world. Annual international house parties at Oxford gained the title "Oxford Groups" for his following (see OXFORD GROUP MOVEMENT). At the end of the 1920's the name was changed to Moral Re-Armament and social problems were attacked, yet still through the personal role and by means of appeal to the wealthy and prominent rather than to the poor or humble. He still retains "the four absolutes of honesty, purity, selflessness, and love," and aims at "personal, social, racial, and supernational change." Of eight publications the best known are *You Can Defend America* (1941); *Moral Rearmament* (1938); *Re-Making the World* (1948); and *The World Rebuilt* (1951). Since 1920 Mr. Buchman has traveled almost constantly throughout the world to and from his "groups" of "key" people.

JOSEPH FLETCHER.

BUCKLER, FRANCIS WILLIAM: Layman, Church of England; b. Aug. 10, 1891, at Groby, Leicestershire, Eng. He studied at Cambridge (B.A., 1913; M.A., 1920; Allen scholar, 1921). He taught history in the Christian College, Madras, India (1913–14); Muir Central College, Allahabad, India (1914–16); was lecturer at Cambridge (1920–25); professor of church history in Oberlin Graduate School of Theology (1925–51), and returned to England in 1951. He wrote: *Harunu'l-Rashid and Charles the Great* (1931); and *The Epiphany of the Cross* (1938).

RAYMOND W. ALBRIGHT.

BUDDHISM: Was only partly continuous with Brahmanism, whose center was some 1000 miles west, and was probably the religion of the ruling class of its area in which it remained for 200 years until Asoka.

Asoka made Buddhist lay ethics the basis of his edicts much as Shotoku did later in Japan, largely because the Buddhist ethic was individual as opposed to that of caste and clan. In China Confucian clan solidarity permitted adoption of only such aspects of Buddhism as clan religion lacked, so that a Chinese might be at the same time Buddhist, Taoist and Confucianist. Laymen are seldom, in any land, exclusively Buddhist adherents.

The "missions" of Asoka were more diplomatic than missionary, an extension beyond his frontiers of the work of his new travelling officials. Religion was relevant, for rulers had magical and divine functions. This pattern continued, for an early sutra used in Japan was "Benevolent Kings Protecting their Countries" to give peace, cause rain, stop pestilence and avert evil omens. It was not the teaching of such sutras that was valued, for the "turning and reading" method was used in Japan, reading some lines in the beginning, middle and end. Contemporary Japanese propaganda literature emphasizes "Buddhism guarding the land."

Buddhism provided super-magic when indigenous magic failed. Printing was invented in Buddhist monasteries in China in order to increase the effect of scriptures by multiplying them, and in Japan an empress printed a million copies of the "great magic formula of stainless pure light."

In China Taoism had developed "sitting in forgetfulness" and early translations were manuals giving Buddhist techniques for meditation and trance. Scholars became interested in Buddhist philosophy, and Chinese sects developed. Tientai made an encyclopedic rearrangement of the mass of scriptures and reduced its philosophy to two main concepts. Hwa Yen was typically Chinese in relating one phenomenon to another, whereas previous schools had related phenomenon to noumenon. Zen discovered sudden enlightenment, by-passed learning, made Buddhism an individual inner experience, and became the prevailing sect. This constituted a Chinese revolt against Indian philosophy. However, these sects supplied cosmology and philosophy which Confucianism lacked, and profoundly influenced Chinese thought, resulting in neo-Confucianism, which has replaced Confucianism for the last 700 years. After this Buddhist philosophical sects declined.

Co-operation with commerce aided the entrance into northwestern China where monasteries provided warehouses and banking facilities. Later in Japan they sponsored business, owned ships and engaged in foreign commerce.

Early Japanese sects were official, aristocratic, magical. A tenth century monk became the first street preacher and began a reformation resulting in the distinctive Japanese sects which are more like churches and include a majority of Japanese Buddhists.

The Mahayana was the most missionary. Hinduism spread widely, usually based on colony or conquest. The Hinayana spread chiefly where there was previous indianization, Hindu or Mahayana. The Mahayana celibate monk, with monasteries along the main routes, achieved an unprecedented mobility.

In India, Buddhism disappeared: partly because of Mahayana creative influence on Hinduism—Shankara's Vedanta being "largely a compound of . . . Buddhism with the Upanishad notion of the permanent self super-added," and partly because its monasteries were conspicuous and easily suppressed by the invading Muslims, and the laity was a loose group centering around the monastery, and disappeared with it.

In Hinayana lands the monastery school is an important asset, but tends to decline with the progress of public education. Confucian schools forestalled this development in China and Japan. Chinese Buddhism has seminaries, but little modern scholarship. Japan has a number of government-recognized Buddhist universities, and modern-trained scholars.

The last forty years have been marked by archeological finds and the editing and translation of manuscripts. Recent discoveries have added to the Mahayana canon and tend to place it alongside the Hinayana as another phase of early Buddhism. The chief scholarship has been French, Japanese and Indian, and concerned not only with philosophy but emphasizing history and institutions.

BIBLIOGRAPHY: An outstanding event has been the publication of the Taisho edition of the *Tripitáka*, 56 vols., 1940; *Bibliographic Bouddhique*, I–XX (in 7 vols., ca. 950 pp.) (1930–49), has outlines of Japanese works.

[Sup.] Earl Herbert Cressy.

BUDÉ, GUILLAUME: French humanist; b. Paris, Jan. 26, 1468, the son of an ennobled royal officer; d. Aug. 23, 1540. After legal studies at Orléans, he turned to the study of Greek, ancient literature, and theology. His scholarly writings and family connections won him the patronage of Francis I, who sent him on a diplomatic mission to Rome in 1515 and who appointed him royal librarian and *maître des requêtes* in 1522. He was several times *Prévôt* of Paris. He worked zealously for the royal patronage of humanists and was largely responsible for the founding by Francis I of the Collège de France. Several years before Luther, he criticized the sale of indulgences and ignorance, luxury, corruption, and neglect in the Catholic Church, which he hoped might be reformed by the College of Cardinals or Pope Leo X. Opposed to the Lutherans and to any break with Rome, he nevertheless was critical of the persecution of Protestants. Against clerical accusations that humanist studies were heretical, Budé claimed that they stimulated virtue and were useful in the study of Christian theology, particularly in the understanding of Scripture. Nine years after he died, his wife, Roberte Le Lieur, moved to Geneva. His major works include: *Annotationes . . . Pandectarum* (1508); *De Asse et partibus ejus* (1515); *De Studio litterarum recte et commode instituendo* (1527); *Commentarii linguae graecae* (1529); *De Transitu Hellenismi ad Christianismum* (1535).

BIBLIOGRAPHY: Best work: Louis Delaruelle, *Guillaume Budé. Les Origines, Les Débuts, Les Idées Maîtresses,*

1907. Also see Eugène de Budé, *Vie de Guillaume Budé*, 1884; Delaruelle, *Répertoire Analytique et Chronologique de la Correspondance de Guillaume Budé*, 1907; Jean Plattard, *Guillaume Budé et les Origines de l'Humanisme Français*, 1923; D. Rebitté, *Guillaume Budé, Resturateur des Études Grècques en France*, 1846.

[Sup.] NATALIE ZEMON DAVIS.

BUDGET, CHURCH: From the French, *bougette*, a bag or wallet. The commonly accepted meaning: a financial statement of estimated income and expenses for a certain period, usually a year. The year may be that of the calendar, or may begin at any other date. On the basis of budget figures, plans are devised so that anticipated receipts will equal necessary expenses. In making a budget for the coming year the officers work several months in advance. On the basis of past experience, and in view of evident needs, they decide to increase the budget, decrease it, or leave it much as before. The ensuing program, such as an every-member canvass, is of more concern than the budget, but the two belong together. Fortunate is the church whose officers know how to prepare the budget and then raise the funds, so that the church gains the reputation of doing the Lord's work in ways that please businessmen. See CHURCH, LOCAL; RECORDS, CHURCH.

ROBERT CASHMAN.

BUEHRING, PAUL HENRY: Lutheran; b. at Elkhorn, Wis., July 5, 1880. He studied at Wartburg College (A.B., 1898); Capital University Seminary, Columbus, O.; Divinity School of the University of Chicago (A.M., 1923); and Augustana Seminary (B.D., 1927). Ordained in 1905, he was pastor at St. Marys, O. (1905–11); president of Hebron (Nebr.) Academy (1911–19); and since then has been professor of historical theology and dean at the Columbus Seminary (1936–46). He has been chairman of the Board of Foreign Missions of the American Lutheran Church since 1930. He wrote *Christian Ethics* (with J. Michael Reu, 1935) and *The Spirit of the American Lutheran Church* (1940).

BUGENHAGEN, JOHANNES: Was called Doctor Pomeranus by Luther and other contemporaries because he was born in Pommern (Pomerania). In the heated controversy about the Eucharist he sided with Luther against Zwingli. He aided Luther particularly with the following of his writings: *Contra novum errorem de sacramento corporis et sanguinis Jesu Christi* (1525) and *Publica de sacramento corporis et sanguinis Christi confessio* (1528). He was very devout and well qualified to aid those who were suffering from various spiritual disorders. Even Luther himself often went to him for confession, strange though this may seem, inasmuch as Luther had recommended the abolition of the Sacrament of Penance which began with confession. Luther freely discussed with him his own weaknesses and temptations. He was the pastor who married Luther and Catherina von Bora in 1525. It is to be regretted that his theology and exegesis have never been adequately treated, nor has there been published a collection of his works. Many of them remain unpublished.

BIBLIOGRAPHY: K. Schottenloher, *Bibl. zur deutschen Gesch. im Zeitalter der Glaubensspaltung*, Vol. 5 (1939), pp. 33 ff.; G. Geisenhof, *Bibliographie der Druckschriften des Dr. J. Bugenhagen*, Vol. 6 of "Quellen und Darstellungen des Reformationsjahrhunderts," 1908; Emil Sehling, *Die evang. Kirchenordnungen des 16. Jahrhunderts*, 5 vols. (1902–13): contains Bugenhagen's church ordinance; H. Lietzmann (ed.), *Braunschweiger Kirchenordnung 1528*, 1912; E. Michelson (ed.), *Die Schleswig-Holsteinsche Kirchenordnung von 1542*, 1909, 1920; Bugenhagen, *Predigten*, (G. Buchwald, ed.), 1885; *Katechismuspredigten 1525–1532*, in "Quellen u. Darst. aus dem Reformationsjahrhundert," Vols. 9 and 13, 1909, 1910; Otto Heinemann (ed.), *Pomerania*, Vol. 4 of "Quellen zur pommerschen Geschichte," 1900; J. R. Rost, *Die paedagogische Bedeutung Bugenhagens*, 1890; W. Leege, *Bugenhagen als Liturgiker*, 1925; W. M. Ruccius, *John Bugenhagen Pomeranus: A Biographical Sketch*, 1925; E. Wolf, "Johann Bugenhagen, Gemeinde und Amt," in *Joh. Bugenhagen, Feier der Kirchengemeinde Wittenberg zur 450. Widerkehr des Geburtstages ihres ersten evang. Stadtpfarrers* (1935), pp. 10–30; O. Dibelius, "Bugenhagens daenische Sendung," in *Die Furche*, 23 (1937), 50–65; H. Wolfgang Beyer, *Johann Bugenhagen, Leben und Wirken*, in "Der Heiland," Heft Nr. 54 (1939); W. Koehler, *Zwingli und Luther, Ihr Streit um das Abendmahl*, Vol. I (1924), *passim*.

[Sup.] D. HEINRICH BORNKAMM.

BULGAKOV, SERGIUS: Eastern Orthodox; b. in Livny, Russia, June 16, 1871; d. in Paris, July 12, 1944. He studied in the University of Moscow, where he received a Doctorate in National Economy (1912). After a two-year research trip to Western Europe he became professor of national economy in the Polytechnical Institute, Kiev (1901), and in 1906 at the Moscow Institute of Commercial Science; in 1917 he was elected to the same chair at Moscow University. He began as a Marxist, but very soon abandoned this position, under various philosophical influences, and gradually came back to the faith of the Eastern Orthodox Church. Religious and theological interests became dominant in his studies and in his writing. In 1906 he was member of the Governmental Duma (representing Moscow). In 1917 he was member (and a very active one) of the All-Russian Church Council, and was elected to the Supreme Church Board. In 1918 he took holy orders. For political reasons he left Moscow in the same year and settled in Symperopol, Crimea, where he was for some time professor at the university. In 1923 he was expelled from Russia by the government and went to Prague, Czechoslovakia, to become professor of political economy at the Russian Graduate School of Law. In 1925 he went to Paris and became professor of divinity at the newly founded Orthodox Theological Institute; later on he was appointed its dean. He has actively participated in the ecumenical movement as well as in the Anglo-Russian Fellowship of St. Sergius and St. Alban (in England). His most important books were written in his last years. His ambition was to give an inclusive and comprehensive interpretation of all main traditional doctrines of the Christian Church from a particular point of view: in the light of the doctrine of "Sophia," the Holy Wisdom. His ideas met with strong opposition in certain quarters and his orthodoxy was challenged. Yet no close examination of his views was ever made. Two books only are available in English: *The Orthodox Church* (1935); *The Wisdom of God, A Brief Summary of Sophiology* (1937). Two volumes of his theological trilogy are available in French: *Du Verbe Incarne* (1943); *Le Paraclet* (1946). One of the books was published only in German: *Die Tragoedie der Philosophie* (1927). See also RUSSIAN ORTHODOX CHURCH.

BIBLIOGRAPHY: L. A. Zander: *God and the World—The System of Father Sergius Bulgakov*, 2 vols., 1948 (in Russian, a full list of Bulgakov's writings is given): a brief biographical article by P. B. Anderson, in *The Living Church* (November 9, 1935).

GEORGES FLOROVSKY.

BULGARIA: After the Young Turk's Revolution of 1908, Bulgaria secured full political independence. Prince Ferdinand proclaimed Rumelia fully independent of Turkey and assumed the title of tsar. This act also freed Bulgaria of the last vestiges of the ecumenical patriarch's jurisdiction.

The position of Exarch Joseph, who had his see in Constantinople, became exceedingly difficult, particularly during the First Balkan War (1912) which Bulgaria, Serbia, and Greece waged against Turkey. He moved to Sofia while his exarchal see was reduced to the rank of a bishopric.

Exarch Joseph died in 1915, during World War I, in which Bulgaria participated on the side of the Germans. No elections for his successor were held because of disturbed conditions. Metropolitan Stephan of Sofia assumed leadership, but was not elevated to the exarchal see until 1945.

When World War II broke out, Bulgaria, under Tsar Boris, tried to remain neutral, but by 1941 it signed a pact with Germany and allowed German troops to occupy the country. With Nazi defeat certain, the government decided to withdraw from the war. But before this could be done, Russia declared war on Bulgaria and occupied the country Thereupon it fell (1945) under Soviet influence.

The Bulgarian Orthodox Church, with Exarch Stephan at its head, submitted to the new masters without a fight and called upon its members to support the new regime (1947). Stephan likewise obediently accepted the leadership of the Moscow patriarch and supported him in his efforts to secure "primacy." But his subserviency did not save him; he resigned in 1948 for "reasons of health." Thereupon the government forced through legislation separating church and state; nevertheless, shortly afterwards, the church was restored to the rank of a state church but was prohibited from educating youth and sharing in social services.

Roman Catholics, Protestants, and Jews were treated as foreign elements and prohibited from maintaining any sort of connection with their coreligionists abroad. Their activity was greatly restricted, and in some instances entirely prohibited. Fifteen Protestant leaders of four denominations were placed on trial; thirteen of them were sentenced to prison terms ranging from five years to life.

BIBLIOGRAPHY: Matthew Spinka, *A History of Christianity in the Balkans*, 1933.

[Sup.] MATTHEW SPINKA.

BULLARIUM ROMANUM: The *Bullarium Magnum Romanum*, known as *Bullarium* of Turin, covers the years 440–1758, from Leo I to Benedict XIV. It consists of twenty volumes printed in Turin (1857–72), and five volumes printed in Naples (1867–85). The collections of which the *Bullarium* is an enlarged edition were continued by a series of nineteen volumes (Rome, 1835–57), and another of ten volumes (Prato, 1843–67), which contain acts of the Popes from Clement XIII to Gregory XVI. These collections are neither official nor complete. [Sup. to BRIEFS, BULLS, AND BULLARIA]

GEORGES A. BARROIS.

BULLETIN, CHURCH: Almost every local church in the United States has a weekly bulletin, or calendar, printed or mimeographed. Bulletins from abroad contain little more than the order of service, with a few "intimations," often attractively displayed. In the United States bulletins assume many forms, some wooden and a few sensational. Even when well planned abundance of church news may distract from worship. On the other hand, the right sort of bulletin, or weekly news letter, may go to the ends of the earth, and become the most effective publicity agent at home.

ANDREW W. BLACKWOOD.

BULLINGER, HEINRICH:

I. Personal Data: Professor Blanke in his study of Bullinger's early years finds no evidence that he was instructed by Brethren of the Common Life at Emmerich. His first meeting with Zwingli was apparently in the autumn of 1523. His wife, Anna Adlischweiler, a former nun, supported his work by tasks of household hospitality, which was extended to countless refugees and unfortunates. Six sons and five daughters were born to them. Zwingli's widow and children, left without support in 1531, lived in Bullinger's home for years. Zwingli's distinguished son Ulric (*ca.* 1571) married Bullinger's daughter, Anna.

II. Writings and Influence: Bullinger's writings were extensive and varied, and many of them were widely circulated in Eastern as well as Western Europe. Through his *Decades* (50 theological sermons, 1547) authorized by Archbishop Whitgift in Convocation, December, 1586, and previously well known in England, through his personal friendship with and influence upon English exiles such as John Hooper, John Jewel, Edmund Grindal, Laurence Humphrey and John Parkhurst, and by a constant flow of letters, after 1558, to persons in England, Bullinger must be regarded as one of the most potent outside influences in the English Reformation and early Puritanism. His extant letters number nearly 12,000 (three times Luther's number). They remain largely unpublished, but have furnished much material to A. Bouvier in his study of Bullinger's ecumenical relationships. He emerges as a figure of great steadfastness and charity, somewhat hesitant, especially toward the Lutherans, in ecumenical interchanges, indubitably an international figure of importance but too cautious and circumspect to be a highly effective ecumenical leader.

BIBLIOGRAPHY: F. Blanke, Der junge Bullinger 1504–31, 1942; A. Bouvier, Henri Bullinger, réformateur et conseiller oecuménique, le successeur de Zwingli, 1940; W. Kolfhaus, "Der Verkehr Calvins mit Bullinger," in Calvinstudien (1909), 27–125; T. Schiess, "Der Briefwechsel Heinrich Bullingers," Zwingliana V (1933) 396–408; F. J. Smithen, Continental Protestantism and the English Reformation, 1927.

[Sup.] JOHN T. MCNEILL.

BULTMANN, RUDOLF KARL: Lutheran; b. Aug. 20, 1884, at Wiefelstede, Oldenburg, Germany. After attending the Volksschule in Rastede (Oldenburg 1892–95) and the Gymnasium in Oldenburg (1895–1903) he studied at the Universities of Tuebingen, Berlin, and Marburg (1903–7) and was promoted to Lic. Theol. on Nov. 7, 1910. He was Privatdozent in New Testament at Marburg (1912–16); Professor of New Testament at Breslau (1916–20); Giessen (1920–21); and at Marburg (1921–). His publications include: Der Stil der paulinischen Predigt und die kynisch-stoische Diatribe (1910); Die Geschichte der synoptischen Tradition (1921, 2nd ed., 1931); Jesus (1926, 3rd ed., 1951); Glauben und Verstehen (1933); Das Evangelium des Johannes (1941, 2nd ed., 1950); Die Theologie des Neuen Testaments (I, 1948; II, 1951); Das Urchristentum im Rahmen der antiken Religionen (1949). See also MYTH IN THE NEW TESTAMENT.

BIBLIOGRAPHY: Coniectanea Neotestamentica (VIII, 1944) —Bibliographia Dibeliana atque Bultmanniana.

RAYMOND W. ALBRIGHT.

BUND, EVANGELISCHER ("Evangelical Union"): About 1900 the Los-von-Rom (q.v.) movement in Austria and Bohemia confronted the German Evangelical Union with a new task. By sending preachers and giving financial support to poor congregations, the Union helped many to become Protestants. In counteracting Roman propaganda in Germany, it published 16,000,000 tracts, 4,500,000 pamphlets, and 1,000,-000 books in a period of 50 years. In 1942 its headquarters in Berlin, with an unusually valuable library, was bombed. Present headquarters are in Bensheim (Hessen), Germany.

BIBLIOGRAPHY: F. von der Heydt, Gute Wehr. Werden, Wirken und Wollen des Ev. Bundes, 1936; H. Bornkamm, Das Verhaeltnis der Konfessionen im heutigen Deutschland, 1951.

[Sup.] HEINRICH BORNKAMM.

BURCHARD OF WORMS: Bishop of Worms; d. Aug. 20, 1025. He was a Hessian by birth, and was educated at Coblenz, and also under the famous Olbert in the Flemish monastery of Laubach. Willigis of Mainz ordained him and employed him in a number of important affairs. Otto III gave him the bishopric of Worms (1000). In 1014 Henry II gave him secular jurisdiction over the inhabitants. His fame rests chiefly upon his Decretum, a complete, practical, and systematic collection of canon law of his time. Its principal aim is to establish and even increase the episcopal power; apocryphal sources are quoted and true sources are adapted to ideas of his own. For practical reasons the Decretum or parts of it had a very wide circulation, not only in Germany but also in France and Italy. Yet it had no influence upon the reformation of Pope Gregory VII aiming at centralization of the church by establishing papal authority.

BIBLIOGRAPHY: The Decretorum libri viginti are in M.P.L., CXL; J. Pétrau-Gay, "Burchard de Worms," in Dict. de Droit Canonique, 2 (1937) col. 1141–1157.

MATHIAS GOOSSENS.

BURLEIGH, JOHN HENDERSON SEAFORTH: B. Ednam, Scotland, May 19, 1894. He was educated at the Universities of Edinburgh (M.A., 1915; B.D., 1920), Strasbourg, and Oxford (B.Litt., 1923). He was minister of the Church of Scotland; Fyvie Parish, Aberdeenshire (1924–28); St. Enoch's Parish, Dundee (1928–31); professor of ecclesiastical history, University of Edinburgh (1931–37); at Aberdeen (1937); he edited the Evangelical Quarterly (1943–49). He wrote The City of God (1945).

BURMA: Before 1948 the country remained under British imperial control with increasing political evolution. Its administration was separated from India in 1937. Japanese invasion and military occupation, 1942–45, were accompanied by chaotic breakdown. National independence, with a presidential-parliamentary and socialistic constitution, was established in January, 1948, and was followed by insurgency and social and economic disorder. The population probably totaled 18,000,000 in 1951.

Buddhism maintained cultural and religious dominance and claimed 84% of the population. Buddhist monks were active politically from 1920; monks and laity promoted youth improvement, rural uplift, educational and moral reform movements. The 1947 constitution claimed freedom for religion, did not recognize Burma as an official Buddhist state. Buddhist missions to animists, begun after World War II, met little early success. On the other hand, the accession of non-Burman animists to Christianity continued. Burman Buddhism continued to challenge Christian evangelism; about one Burman per thousand is in the Christian community.

The Christian population was reckoned at 525,000 in 1948 (Burma Christian Council reports). The proportion rose from 2% to 3% of the whole population. After World War II missionary personnel and residential stations reached about half the prewar strength. Growth in national Christian responsibility paralleled that in other Asiatic countries. The Christian community comprised 383,000 Baptist, 128,000 Roman Catholics, 14,000 Anglicans, Methodists, and others. Karens were the impressive majority of the Christians.

Education declined seriously during and after World War II. Christian schools retained relative popular favor, but the government refused sanction to reopen Judson College. Karen insurgency, provoked by local persecutions, aroused some popular Burman suspicion and resentment against Christianity. Violent, insurgent Communism and Marxist indoctrination seemed to attract more attention and support among Burmans than Christianity.

BIBLIOGRAPHY: J. L. Christian, *Modern Burma*, 1942; H. J. Harwood, "Christianity in Present-Day Burma," in *World Dominion*, Nov.–Dec., 1949.

[Sup.] HARRY J. HARWOOD.

BURNEY, CHARLES FOX: Anglican; b. Nov. 4, 1868; d. April 15, 1925. He studied at St. John's College, Oxford (M.A.), gaining many university distinctions. He was fellow of St. John's College until 1914, Oriel Professor of the Interpretation of Holy Scripture at Oxford (1914–25). He was a noted authority on Semitic languages and wrote: *Outlines of Old Testament Theology* (1899); *Israel's Settlement in Canaan* (1918); *The Book of Judges* (1918); *The Aramaic Origin of the Fourth Gospel* (1922).

F. W. DILLISTONE.

BURROWS, MILLAR: Professor. B. Cincinnati, Ohio, Oct. 26, 1889. Educated at Cornell University (B.A., 1912); Union Theological Seminary (B.D., 1915); and Yale University (Ph.D., 1925). Taught biblical literature and history of religion at Tusculum College (1920–23); Brown University (1925–34); professor of biblical theology, Yale University Divinity School since 1934. President, American Schools of Oriental Research (1934–48). Director, American School of Oriental Research at Jerusalem (1931–32, 1947–48). Fellow of the American Academy of Arts and Sciences. Author: *Founders of Great Religions* (1931); *Bible Religion*

(1938); *The Basis of Israelite Marriage* (1938); *What Mean These Stones?* (1941); *Outline of Biblical Theology* (1946); *Palestine Is Our Business* (1949). Editor: *Dead Sea Scrolls of St. Mark's Monastery* (1950–).

BURTON, ERNEST DE WITT: D. May 26, 1925. He was professor of New Testament Literature and Interpretation and head of this department and of biblical and patristic Greek (1892–1923) at the University of Chicago where he also served as director of the University Libraries (1910–23). He became president of the University of Chicago in 1923 and served until the time of his death. His additional books include: *Biblical Ideas of the Atonement* (with J. M. P. and G. B. Smith, 1909); *Harmony of the Synoptic Gospels in English* (with Edgar J. Goodspeed, 1917); *Spirit, Soul and Flesh, in Greek Writings from the Earliest Period to 180 A.D.* (1918); *Harmony of the Synoptic Gospels in Greek* (with E. J. Goodspeed, 1920); *Commentary on Paul's Epistle to the Galatians* (in *ICC* 1920); and *Sourcebook for the Study of the Teaching of Jesus* (1923).

[Sup.] RAYMOND W. ALBRIGHT.

BURY, JOHN BAGNELL: Historian; b. in the county of Monaghan (Ireland) Oct. 16, 1861; d. in Rome, June 1, 1927. He studied at Trinity College, Dublin, became fellow of Trinity College (1885) and professor of modern history in Dublin (1893) and Regius Professor of Modern History in the University of Cambridge (1902). Bury is best known for his work on the history of the Byzantine Empire, but readers of this encyclopedia will probably be specially interested in *A History of Freedom of Thought* (1914); *The Life of St. Patrick* (1905) and *The Idea of Progress* (1924).

BIBLIOGRAPHY: N. H. Baynes, *A Bibliography of the works of J. B. Bury* (with a memoir), 1929; Harold Temperley, ed., *Selected Essays of J. B. Bury*, 1930.

NORMAN H. BAYNES.

BUTTERFIELD, HERBERT: Methodist; b. at Oxenhope, Yorks., Oct. 7, 1900. He was educated at the Trade and Grammar School, Keighley, Yorks.; and later (Scholar) at Peterhouse, Cambridge, England, of which college he has been a fellow since 1932. In 1923–24 he was Proctor Visiting Fellow at the Graduate College, Princeton, N. J. From 1930 he was lecturer and from 1944 has been professor of modern history in the University of Cambridge. From 1938 until 1952 he edited the *Cambridge Historical Journal*. In 1949 he again visited Princeton as a member of the Institute for Advanced Study. Apart from technical historical work he has written chiefly on the relations of the historian with Christianity, modern science and problems of political morality. His published writings are: *The Historical Novel* (1924); *The*

Peace Tactics of Napoleon, 1806–08 (1929); *The Whig Interpretation of History* (1931); (ed.) *Select Documents of European History,* Vol. III, 1715–1920 (1931); *Napoleon* (Great Lives) (1939); *The Statecraft of Machiavelli* (1940); *The Englishman and his History* (1944); Inaugural Lecture on *The Study of Modern History* (1944); *George III, Lord North and the People* (1949); *Christianity and History* (1949); *The Origins of Modern Science* (1949); *History and Human Relations* (1951); *Christianity in European History* (1951); *Liberty in the Modern World* (1952).

BUTTRICK, GEORGE ARTHUR: Presbyterian; b. March 23, 1892, at Seaham Harbour, Northumberland, Eng. He studied at Lancaster Independent College, Manchester (grad. 1915) and at Victoria University where he graduated with honors in philosophy in 1915. Ordained in the Congregational Church in the United States in 1915. He became pastor of the First Union Congregational Church in Quincy, Ill. (1915–18); First Congregational Church, Rutland, Vt. (1918–21); First Presbyterian Church, Buffalo, N. Y. (1920–27); and served with marked distinction as pastor of the Madison Ave. Presbyterian Church in New York City 1927–54. In addition he has taught homiletics at Union Theological Seminary, lectures and preaches widely and has been one of the editors of *The Interpreter's Bible.* In 1954 he became Plummer Professor of Christian Morals and chairman of the Board of Preachers at Harvard University where he also teaches homiletics in the Divinity School. His publications include: *The Parables of Jesus* (1928); *Jesus Came Preaching* (1931); *The Christian Fact and Modern Doubt* (1934); *Prayer* (1942); *Christ and Man's Dilemma* (1946); and *So We Believe So We Pray* (1951). RAYMOND W. ALBRIGHT.

BUTZER, MARTIN. See BUCER, MARTIN.

BYZANTINE RITE: The system of prayers and ceremonies developed at first in the Patriarchate of Byzantium (Constantinople) for public worship and the administration of the sacraments, and which is used today throughout the four patriarchates of Constantinople, Alexandria, Antioch, and Jerusalem, as well as in the Church of Cyprus, and such national bodies as the Russian, Greek, Bulgarian, Serbian, Roumanian, Georgian, and Polish Orthodox Churches. The Byzantine rite should be distinguished from the other Eastern rites, as for instance the Coptic, Syrian, or Armenian rites, in spite of some analogy of form and ceremonial.

The churches of the Byzantine rite make use of the so-called liturgies of Saint John Chrysostom and of Saint Basil for the celebration of the Eucharist, for which the liturgy of the Presanctified, also known as the liturgy of Saint Gregory, is substituted during Lent, except on Saturdays and Sundays. The original language is Greek, but national or missionary churches outside the Greek-speaking area had the liturgy and the divine office translated into their own tongue; thus the Russian Church uses old Slavonic as its liturgical language.

The architecture and decoration of church buildings of the Byzantine rite have the following characteristics: The nave of the church is preceded by a narthex or vestibule. The sanctuary, with the altar in the middle and the *prothesis* and *diakonikon* (*qq.v.*), on either side, is divided from the nave by the *ikonostasis,* which is a screen or wall decorated with images of Christ, of the Virgin, and of the saints, distributed in a traditional order in the panels separating the three doors through which the officiating ministers gain entrance into the sanctuary. Statues are prohibited, as well as the use of musical instruments. The laity partakes of both elements in the Eucharistic communion.

Such fractions of the churches of Byzantine rite as seceded from their parent church and acknowledged the authority of the pope, thus passing to the Roman communion, generally were allowed to retain their original language and ceremonial.

BIBLIOGRAPHY: F. A. Brightman, *Liturgies, Eastern and Western: I, Eastern Liturgies,* 1896; B. J. Kidd, *The Churches of Eastern Christendom,* 1927; S. Salaville, *An Introduction to the Study of the Eastern Liturgies,* 1938. GEORGES A. BARROIS.

C

CABALA: Closer acquaintance with the texts and a better understanding of the development of theosophical and mystical speculation within the Jewish community have of necessity changed the older hostile attitude towards the Qabbala. It is no longer possible to regard it as wholly a movement of reaction against philosophic rationalism, for it is clear that there were several streams of relatively early speculation on these matters which went into its formation, and which, in all probability, would have produced much the same result even had there been no rationalistic movement against which piety found it necessary to react. On the other hand, research has made it abundantly clear that the *Zohar,* its most famous monument, has as such no claim to antiquity. There is still no critical edition of the *Zohar,* though a useful text, with parallels from Rabbinic sources, was published by Reuben Margulies in three volumes (1940–46). Partial translations are given in Sperling and Simon's *The Zohar* (5 vols., 1931–34; reprint, 1949), and Ernst Mueller's *Der Sohar: das heilige Buch der Kabbala* (1932) and there is a volume of selections edited by G. Scholem, *Zohar: the Book of Splendour: selected and edited* (1949). These completely supersede the faulty and misleading French version by Jean de Pauly (6 vols., 1906–12). Moreover important texts such as the *Bahir,* and the works of Abraham Abulafia, Moses of Burgos, Isaac ben Jacob and Joseph Gikatila have been closely studied and made available, so that we can now see much more clearly the curious development of Qabbalism after the expulsion of the Jews from Spain, the new direction given by the work of Moses Cordovero, Isaac Luria, Israel Sarug along with their followers in the Safed School, and its significance both for the antinomian Sabbatianism and for the gentle pietism of the Hassidic movement.

BIBLIOGRAPHY: The most important work embodying the results of modern study is Gershom Scholem's *Major Trends in Jewish Mysticism,* lectures delivered in New York in 1938 but published in Jerusalem in 1941. Scholem had earlier published a *Bibliographia Kabbalistica* (1927), which is an invaluable introduction to the literature about the Qabbala, and since 1942 has been publishing with the Schocken Publishing Company at Jerusalem *Studies and Texts in Jewish Mysticism.* Bernard Pick, *The Cabala: its Influence on Judaism and Christianity* (1913), Ariel Bension, *The Zohar in Moslem and Christian Spain* (1932) and Joseph Blau, *The Christian Interpretation of the Cabala in the Renaissance* (1944), have sketched the external influence of the Qabbala; and such studies as Ernst Mueller's *Der Sohar und seine Lehre: Einleitung in die Gedankenwelt der Kabbala* (2nd ed. 1923), A. Z. Aescoly-Weintraub's *Introduction à l'étude des hérésies religieuses parmi les juifs: la Kabbale, le Hassidisme* (1928) and Henri Sérouya's *La Kabbale: ses origines, sa psychologie mystique, sa metaphysique* (1947), are attempts to make the Qabbalistic doctrine more generally intelligible. At Leipzig in 1923 there commenced to appear a journal devoted to these studies, *Kabbala: Quellen und Forschungen zur Geschichte der juedischen Mystik.*

[Sup.] ARTHUR JEFFERY.

CABOT, RICHARD CLARKE: Unitarian; b. at Brookline, Mass., May 21, 1868; d. at Cambridge, Mass., May 8, 1939. After graduation from Harvard (A.B., 1889; M.D., 1892) he taught clinical medicine at Harvard Medical School (1899–1929), social ethics at Harvard College (1920–34), natural theology at Andover Newton Theological School, Newton Centre, Mass. (1935–39). He founded Medical Social Work at Massachusetts General Hospital, Boston, in 1905. A pioneer in religion and health, he urged physicians to tell their patients their true condition; he wrote "A Plea for a Clinical Year for Theological Students" (*Survey-Graphic,* Dec., 1925) and founded (1925) Council for Clinical Training under leadership of the Rev. Anton T. Boisen (*q.v.*), Protestant Chaplain at Worcester State Hospital, Worcester, Mass. He was noted in the field of medicine as a teacher and diagnostician, and he originated the now internationally accepted method for teaching

diagnosis, known as clinico-pathological conference. He wrote: *Physical Diagnosis* (1901); *Social Service and the Art of Healing* (1909); *Differential Diagnosis* (1911); *What Men Live By* (1914); *Laymen's Handbook of Medicine* (1916); *Social Work* (1919); *Facts on the Heart* (1926); *Adventures on the Borderlands of Ethics* (1926); *The Meaning of Right and Wrong* (1933); *The Art of Ministering to the Sick* (with Russell L. Dicks, 1936); *Christianity and Sex* (1937).

ROLLIN JONATHAN FAIRBANKS.

CABRINI, FRANCES XAVIER: Known to American Roman Catholics as Mother Cabrini, she was born in St. Angelo, Italy, July 15, 1850. She is the first American citizen to be canonized a saint of the Catholic Church. St. Cabrini arrived as an immigrant to the United States in 1889. Originally St. Cabrini had wanted to go to the Far East to do missionary work, but at the behest of Pope Leo XIII she came instead to the United States to work among her fellow Italian immigrants. In America she founded many hospitals, schools, nurseries, and other welfare institutions. In 1952 her order of Catholic sisters, Missionaries of the Sacred Heart, had 4,000 members who take care of ninety-seven welfare institutions all over the world. St. Cabrini died in Chicago Dec. 22, 1917, and she was canonized in 1946.

BIBLIOGRAPHY: Theodore Maynard, *Too Small a World,* 1945.

GILBERT L. ODDO.

CABROL, FERNAND: Roman Catholic scholar; b. at Marseille, 1855; d. 1937; Benedictine monk since 1878; afterwards prior of the celebrated Abbey of Solesme (dép. Sarthe, Fr.); since 1909 abbot of Farnborough (G. Br.). An eminent liturgist, he edited since 1900 the *Monumenta ecclesiae liturgica* together with his fellow-scholar Henri Leclercq and since 1903 was with the same scholar, editor of the standard work, *Dictionnaire d'Archéologie chrétienne et de Liturgie.* Other publications: *Histoire du Cardinal Pitra* (1893); *Études sur la Peregrinatio Silviae* (1895); *Les livres de la Liturgie latine* (1903); *Les origines liturgiques* (1906); *Introduction aux études liturgiques* (1907); *L'Angleterre avant les Normands* (1909); *Le livre de la Prière antique* (1910, 1921); *La prière pour la France* (1916); *La prière des anciens chrétiens* (1929); *La Messe en Occident* (1932).

R. WILL.

CADBURY, HENRY JOEL: B. at Philadelphia, Pa., Dec. 1, 1883; educated in the classics and biblical studies at Haverford College (A.B., 1903) and Harvard (Ph.D., 1914). He taught the Bible at Haverford College (1910–19) and at Bryn Mawr College (1926–34). At Harvard he taught the New Testament (1919–26; 1934–

54), holding latterly the Hollis professorship of divinity. A member by birth of the Religious Society of Friends (Quakers) he was active particularly in the work of the American Friends Service Committee, serving as chairman between 1928 and 1934, and again after 1944. His writings include articles on both biblical and Quaker history and the following books: *Style and Literary Method of Luke* (1920); *National Ideals in the Old Testament* (1920); *The Making of Luke-Acts* (1927); *The Beginnings of Christianity* (with Kirsopp Lake), Vols. IV and V (1933); *The Peril of Modernizing Jesus* (1937); *The Annual Catalogue of George Fox* (edited 1939); *Jesus: What Manner of Man* (1947); *George Fox's Book of Miracles* (1948).

BIBLIOGRAPHY: See "Towards a Bibliography of Henry Joel Cadbury," in *Harvard Divinity School Bulletin* (1954), pp. 65–70.

CADMAN, S(AMUEL) PARKES: D. July 12, 1936. During his distinguished pastorate at Central Congregational Church, Brooklyn, N. Y. (1901–36) this church became one of the leading churches in the country. Dr. Cadman also served widely beyond his congregation. He was acting president of Adelphi College (1911–13); president of the Federal Council of Churches (*q.v.*) (1924–28) and its radio minister (1928–36). He lectured at many colleges and seminaries and actively helped to promote the ecumenical movement (*q.v.*). His publications include: *William Owen, A Biography* (1912); *Three Religious Leaders of Oxford* (1916); *Ambassadors of God* (1920; 2nd ed., 1921); *Christianity and the State* (1924); *Lure of London* (1925); *Imagination and Religion* (1926); *The Christ of God* (1929); *Every Day Questions and Answers* (1930); *The Parables of Jesus* (1931); *The Prophets of Israel* (1933); and *The Pursuit of Happiness* (1935).

RAYMOND W. ALBRIGHT.

CADOUX, CECIL JOHN: Congregational; b. Smyrna, Turkey-in-Asia, May 24, 1883; d. Oxford, Aug. 16, 1947. Educated at King's College, London, and Mansfield College, Oxford, he became professor of New Testament criticism and theology, Yorkshire United Independent College (1919–33) and Mackennal Professor of Church History, Mansfield College (1933–47). He wrote: *The Early Christian Attitude to War* (1919); *The Early Church and the World* (1925); *Catholicism and Christianity* (1928); *The Case for Evangelical Modernism* (1938); *The Life of Jesus* (1947). F. W. DILLISTONE.

CAEDMON: The Old Testament poems in the Anglo-Saxon language, as preserved in the Junius manuscript at Oxford are written in a beautiful hand, decorated with forty-eight drawings (illuminations), for the most part realistic presentations of the eleventh century in the style of the Winchester School. They are strongly influenced by the Utrecht Psalterium (see BIBLES, ILLUSTRATED).

BIBLIOGRAPHY: C. W. Kennedy, *The Caedmon Poems* (text and illustrations), 1915; A. H. Smith, *Three Northumbriam Poems*, 1927; I. Gollancz, *The Caedmon MS. of Anglo-Saxon Biblical Poetry* (in facsimile), 1927; G. P. Krapp, *The Junius Manuscript*, 1931.

[Sup.] MATHIAS GOOSSENS.

CAERULARIUS, MICHAEL: He saw in the alliance of the pope and the Byzantine emperor against the Normans (about 1050) a threat to his own position as an independent ruler of an ecclesiastical state. This fear inspired his actions throughout. His career indicates clearly that the separation of the Western and the Eastern Churches was not caused so much by religious as by other factors, such as political considerations and racial and linguistic barriers. Constantinople (Byzantium) wanted to rule Rome, reminding the world of its former position in the Italian peninsula, particularly under Emperor Justinian and his great generals. But by 1050 Byzantine power in Italy was but a shadow of its former self.

BIBLIOGRAPHY: A. Michel, *Lateinische Aktenstuecke und Sammlungen zum griechischen Schisma*, in *Hist, Jahrbuch*, Vol. 60 (1940); A. Michel, *Humbert und Kerullarios*, 2 vols., 1925–30; J. M. Hussey, *Church and Learning in the Byzantine Empire 867–1185*, 1937.

[Sup.] MATHIAS GOOSSENS.

C.A.I.L. See SOCIAL GOSPEL.

CAILLIET, EMILE: Professor of Christian Philosophy, Princeton Seminary. B. in 1894 and educated in France (Ph.D., Th.D.); National Fellow, French Academy of Colonial Sciences. He is an authority on Pascal, and has also contributed to the literature of symbolism and mysticism. His most important works include *The Clue to Pascal* (1943); *Pascal, Genius in the Light of Scripture;* and *Great Shorter Works of Pascal* (1948).

CAIN, KENITES: None of the recently advanced theories about the Kenites has met with general acceptance. It cannot be proved that Cain and Kenan are variant names of one person or that either was the ancestor of the Kenites. In fact, the name may signify that the Kenites were coppersmiths and have nothing to do with an eponymous ancestor. Seeming inconsistencies in the Cain story (Genesis 4) do not necessarily indicate differing documents; the Hebrew story tellers were not bound to explain logically how Cain found his wife or how he could be both a vagabond and a city builder. It has been proposed that Moses first learned of Yahweh from his father-in-law, Kenite-Midianite Jethro or Reuel. Julian Morgenstern has developed an elaborate hypothesis of a basic Kenite document, part of which was incorporated in the Hexateuch. This hypothesis has met with varied response. The Kenite document is supposed to have contained the story of Moses from his birth to his successful presentation of the covenant to Israel. The ritual code of Exodus 34, the precursor of the Decalogue, is part of the presumed Kenite material.

BIBLIOGRAPHY: Julian Morgenstern, "The Oldest Document in the Hexateuch," *Hebrew Union College Annual* IV (1927), 1–138; Adolph J. Feinberg, "Kenite Document," *The Universal Jewish Encyclopedia*, 1942; Robert H. Pfeiffer, *Introduction to the Old Testament*, 1941, pp. 224–226; Theophile James Meek, *Hebrew Origins*, rev. ed., 1950, pp. 95–99.

[Sup.] OVID R. SELLERS.

CAJETAN, THOMAS: Was a greater figure in the field of literature than in politics. He was a typical humanistic scholar, counting among his personal friends many humanists. His Latin style was almost purely classical, somewhat dull and polished but not throbbing with emotion or zest of joyful living. In the history of Thomism he constituted a bridge from medieval to modern times. Even during his lifetime he was often called the "second Thomas." He was the outstanding Roman Catholic theologian in the period of the Reformation, and his writings were, as a rule, the basis for discussions at the Council of Trent. His significance as a theologian was derived from his Aristotelian philosophy, which excelled in several respects. Like Aristotle, he was profoundly interested in the natural sciences and medicine, acquiring a tremendous body of knowledge in these fields. This he used to great advantage in perfecting his own type of philosophy and ethics. Furthermore, he made a lasting contribution to canon law, exegesis, and moral theology.

BIBLIOGRAPHY: Cajetan, *Scripta theologica*, ed. V. Pollet, 1936; *Registrum litterarum Fr. Thomae de Vio Cajetani*, ed. A. de Meyer, in *Monumenta Praedicatorum Historiae*, XVII, 1935; *Dict. d'hist. et de géogr. eccl.*, XI (1949), 248–252.

[Sup.] MATHIAS GOOSSENS.

CALENDAR, MUSLIM. See MUSLIM CALENDAR.

CALHOUN, ROBERT LOWRY: Congregationalist; b. Dec. 30, 1896, at St. Cloud, Minn. He studied at Carleton College (B.A., 1915); and at Yale (B.D., 1918; M.A., 1919; Ph.D., 1923). He taught philosophy and education at Carleton (1921–23) and since 1923 has been teaching historical theology at Yale. He has written: *God and the Common Life* (1935); *What is Man?* (1939); *Religious Realism* (1931); *The Nature of Religious Experience* (1937); *Church and State in the Modern World* (1937); *The Christian Understanding of Man* (1938); *The Meaning of the Humanities* (1938); *Religion and the Modern World* (1940); *God and the Day's Work, Christian Vocation in an Unchristian World* (1943).

RAYMOND W. ALBRIGHT.

CALL, THE MINISTER'S: In a more or less gradual or sudden stirring of religious consciousness a person feels from God an absolute imperative that he become God's representative to spend his full time serving his generation in the church of his choice. Many Christians think of the call as solely between a man and God. Others stress the role of the church in determining who should or should not be ministers. In one extreme there is lack of ecclesiastical authority; in the other, a rigid system of authority ecclesiastically applied. Consequently communions range themselves on a graduated scale between gross individualism and hardened ecclesiasticism. Why has no clear voice yet given Christian theology an adequate doctrine of Christian vocation?

For an understanding of the matter see Acts 13:2–4. Paul and Barnabas personally had felt the moving by the Holy Spirit, leading them to go as the first Christian missionaries from a church. Then the Spirit spoke to the church at Antioch and led them to send the two. In calling individuals the Spirit does not work apart from the body of Christ in the church. In speaking to the church He does not vest wisdom in a few members, but rather causes the body of Christ to be of "one mind and one heart." Ideally, a call to the ministry assumes a place of importance second only to the experience of regeneration through faith in Christ. According to a recent anthropological survey, both experiences tend to fade in any church body as it gains prestige in its local community.

WAYNE E. OATES.

CALVERLEY, EDWIN ELLIOTT: Missionary to Muslims, teacher, editor; b. at Philadelphia, Pa., Oct. 26, 1882. He studied at Princeton University (B.A., 1906; M.A., 1908), Princeton Theological Seminary (1909), and Hartford Seminary Foundation (Ph.D., 1923). Ordained by Philadelphia Presbytery, Nov. 29, 1908, he joined the Arabian Mission of the Reformed Church in America, arriving at Bahrain, Persian Gulf, Dec. 31, 1909. He served also at Basrah and Amarah in Iraq but mostly at Kuwait, Arabia, until 1930, when he became a teacher of Arabic and Islamics in the Kennedy School of Missions of the Hartford Seminary Foundation. He published *The Arabian Readers* (1920), *Worship in Islam* (1925), and articles on missionary and Islamic subjects in the *Royal Central Asian Society Journal* and elsewhere but chiefly in *The Moslem (Muslim) World*. In 1938 he became coeditor with Dr. Samuel M. Zwemer (*q.v.*) of *The Moslem World*, editor (1947–52), and coeditor with Dr. A. Kenneth Cragg (1952–54), the title of the journal being changed to *The Muslim World* in 1947. He became professor emeritus in 1951. He was visiting professor, School of Advanced International

Studies, Johns Hopkins University, Washington, D. C., 1953–54.

CALVIN, JOHN: The article CALVIN in Vol. II requires correction and expansion in the following particulars.

I. Family: Calvin was the fourth son in the family of Gérard Calvin. Two of the older brothers died very young; the other, Charles, a canon of Noyon, died excommunicate in 1537. The fifth son, Antoine, was to be associated with the reformer in Geneva. One of the half-sisters, Marie, also joined Calvin in Geneva and became the wife of a Geneva citizen.

II. Calvin's Law Teachers: The statement that Alciati was "more to Calvin's taste" than de l'Étoile should be reversed. Andrea Alciati of Milan came on the invitation of Marguérite d'Angoulême to Bourges as professor of Roman law. Attracted by his reputation, Calvin and several of his friends left Orleans to study with him in Bourges. Calvin was displeased by Alciati's contempt for Pierre de l'Étoile and wrote (1529) the preface to Nicholas Duchemin's *Antapologia* (published 1531) in defense of de l'Étoile.

III. Psychopannychia: The *Psychopannychia* was written in 1534, but was withheld from publication, possibly on the advice of Oecolampadius, until 1542.

IV. Cop's Rectorial Address: Opinion among Calvin scholars has moved away from the view that Calvin was the author of Nicholas Cop's rectorial address of Nov. 1, 1533; and many would regard the address itself, not as a consciously Protestant declaration, but as a bold manifesto of the party of Marguérite d'Angoulême and Lefèvre against the Sorbonne. Cop was eminent and competent, and it is not likely that he would hand over to another the preparation of a public utterance of first importance. He had induced the university to oppose the Sorbonne's condemnation of Marguérite's book, *The Mirror of a Sinful Soul.* Calvin, his close friend, would not improbably have seen the address in advance and discussed it with Cop: but it is not written in Calvin's style. Calvin was not charged with its authorship, but was looked upon as guilty by association with the author. It contains an invocation of the Virgin Mary, and does not criticize the papacy. Calvin's connection with it would not prove that at the time he was a Protestant. There is no real evidence that his attachment to the Roman Church was broken prior to his visit to Lefèvre at Nérac early in April, 1534, and his surrender of his benefices at Noyon which followed promptly after this interview (May 4). These events seem to set as nearly as possible the date of his "sudden conversion."

V. Renée: Renée, duchess of Ferrara (1510–75), was the daughter of Louis XII of France, and felt the influence of Lefèvre, Marguérite, and the Christian humanism of France. Her husband, Ercole II d'Este, was a son of Lucrezia Borgia. Renée favored the religious refugees, but soon after Calvin's visit to Ferrara Ercole made the situation untenable for them. Renée fell under Calvin's religious influence and guidance, was in occasional correspondence with him until his death, and promoted Protestantism in France.

VI. Communion and Discipline: It is important to recognize the relationship between communion and discipline in Calvin's church order. The central point of discipline was fitness or unfitness to partake of the Eucharist. "It is certain," wrote Calvin, in the Articles of January, 1537, "that a church cannot be called well-ordered and regulated unless in it the Holy Supper of Our Lord is often celebrated and attended—and this with such good discipline that none dare to present himself at it save holily and with singular reverence. And for this reason the discipline of excommunication, by which those may be corrected who are unwilling to govern themselves lovingly and by the Holy Word of God, is necessary in order to maintain the church in its integrity." This point is reverted to later in the same document, where it is said that the members of the church are united to Christ and to one another in the Lord's Supper, and that "for this reason our Lord has placed in his church the discipline of excommunication." The need of discipline, then, arises from the necessity of protecting the Eucharist from profanation. It is not a consequence of a determination to impose a legally conceived pattern of moral conduct. Nevertheless, in the development of the discipline legalism tended to assert itself strongly.

VII. The Strasbourg Period: Discipline: Calvin's Strasbourg period (1538–41) was of the utmost significance both for his personal development and for his achievement in reform. The success of his pastorate in Strasbourg was a vindication of the principles of church order and discipline that he had unsuccessfully attempted to apply in Geneva. He was in the position of the leader of a refugee congregation separated by language from the citizens—the situation that Knox later occupied in Geneva and John à Lasco in London. In these cases the foreign congregation enjoyed a considerable autonomy, and opportunity to develop its worship and polity with unusual freedom. Calvin was able, as the German-speaking Strasbourg ministers were not, to exclude offenders from communion without the action of the magistrates. Yet the Strasbourg system made its impact upon him and the "Little French Church." In the Strasbourg polity three lay church officers (*Kirchenpfleger*) in each parish assisted the ministers, within limits permitted by the magistrates, in discipline, visitation and the guidance of souls. His own congregation elected these officers, and they were confirmed in office by the magistrates. Their powers and functions helped to clarify Calvin's notion of the lay eldership, and Bucer's view of their office as scripturally authorized may be reflected in Calvin's *Ordonnances ecclésiastiques* of 1541, in which the elders (*anciens*) are a divinely authorized order along with pastors, teachers and deacons.

VIII. Worship: In Strasbourg also we first see the essentials of Calvinist public worship. Calvin's liturgy, *The Form of Prayers and Manner of Ministering the Sacraments according to the Use of the Ancient Church,* appeared at Strasbourg in 1540, but the 1542 edition is the earliest extant. It is indebted to Farel's Montbéliard liturgy of 1525, known from its abbreviated title as *La Maniere et fasson,* which was used in Geneva during Calvin's first period there; but the indebtedness is confined to minor features. It is mainly a French version of the 1539 edition of Bucer's Sunday Morning Service, which was based upon the translation and Lutheran modification of the Roman Mass made by Diebold Schwarz, a young Strasbourg cleric, in 1524. Calvin's liturgy thus bears the marks of the structure of the mass. It was his desire to have the Lord's Supper celebrated each Sunday. The Strasbourg authorities, however, permitted it only monthly, and in Geneva, much against Calvin's wishes, its celebration was confined to the seasons of Christmas, Easter, Pentecost and the first Sunday in September.

IX. Principles of Government: The tendency in civil government in Geneva was to enhance the power of the Little Council at the expense of that of the other governing bodies. This Council of Twenty-five had the sole power of initiating legislation. The General Council of Citizens retained the right to elect the syndics, but only from a list of nominees presented to it by the Two Hundred. At the same time, however, the basis of eligibility for the eldership was broadened by the admission of members of the Council of Two Hundred, regardless of their membership in the Council of Sixty or the Little Council (1560). Also, the names of elders chosen were posted in the churches so that anybody might file objections with a syndic before final action (1561). Thus if the trend in the state was aristocratic, in the church it was in some sense democratic. Calvin objected, however, to a proposal by Jean Morelli for the French Protestant Church by which each congregation would have unrestricted power to elect its minister and its officers (1562).

Calvin's political teaching grows out of his sense of God's complete sovereignty over all mundane things. Kings and rulers are to be obeyed as ministers of God; their failure to behave as such subjects them to criticism but does not justify revolt. The secular government is for Calvin a proper sphere of the Christian's activity. Litigation is permitted if entered into in charity. The ruling power takes responsibility for the protection of the visible church, and the maintenance of justice and equitable laws. Positive law is to be based upon the moral law, which while summarized in the Commandments is a testimony of the natural law (*naturalis legis testimonium*)—an "interior law . . . imprinted on the heart of everyone." He has been represented as basically favorable to monarchy; but his works abound in caustic criticisms of kings and rulers, ancient and modern. He praises universal suffrage, the election of rulers by the ruled, and the maintenance of a regulated and enduring liberty. Yet he uniformly decries violent revolution, and habitually insists upon patient obedience to existing rulers, except where magistrates have been constitutionally provided to restrain them (*Institutes* IV, xx, 31), and saving always the obedience due to God. Where princes seek to grasp "the rights of God," "we ought rather utterly to defy them than to obey them" (thirtieth lecture on Daniel).

X. Economic Ethics: Calvin's influence in modern economic development has been much discussed since 1904 when Max Weber began to publish his studies that took shape as *The Protestant Ethic and the Spirit of Capitalism.* Both Weber's own unfamiliarity with Calvin's teaching, and subsequent misconceptions of Weber's thesis, have left the subject somewhat confused. Weber does not ascribe to Calvin, but to Calvinistic Puritans, the specific teaching of an ethic of capitalism, but he regards this as due to an impulse from Calvin's doctrine of predestination. This, in disregard of Calvin, he associates with an "unprecedented inner loneliness of the single individual" from which, together with the enforcement of scriptural injunctions to industry and frugality, he derives the religious sanction of accumulation, investment and business enterprise. Numerous studies designed to test, refute or modify Weber's thesis appeared, and the issues are still much debated. Certainly Calvin spoke highly of vocation as service to God and man, approved diligence and thrift, and loathed waste of time and goods. His sanction of interest on loans was guarded by strict rules of equity, protecting the poor from exploitation, and making the public good a necessary condition of the transaction. His introduction of the silk industry in Geneva was motivated by a desire to give a livelihood to unemployed and distressed refugees. Contrary to statements sometimes made, he did not regard business success or worldly prosperity as evidence of God's favor. It is a view that he repeatedly condemned, ascribing it to "the ungodly." "For we see daily," he wrote in his Sermons on Job (clviii), "the state of the faithful more miserable than the state of the despisers of God." On Deut. 8:12 he notes: "The Israelites laughed at all reproof because God seemed propitious, as though he manifested his favor by prosperity. . . . This is a common evil."

BIBLIOGRAPHY: The following bibliographical studies should be consulted: Peter Barth, "Fuenfundzwanzig Jahre Calvinforschung, 1509–1534," *Theologische Rundschau*, Neue Folge, VI (1934), 161–175, 246–267; T. H. L. Parker, "A Bibliography and Survey of the British Study of Calvin, 1900–1940," *Evangelical Quarterly*, XVIII (1946), 123–131; J. T. McNeill, "Thirty Years of Calvin Study," *Church History*, XVII (1938), 207–240. The last-named contains 258 titles. Émile Doumergue's monumental *Jean Calvin, les hommes et les choses de son temps* was completed in seven volumes (1899–1927). Scholarly biographies in English include those of W. Walker (1909), H. Y. Reyburn (1914), R. N. C. Hunt (1933), J. Mackinnon (1936), P. Imbart de la Tour in Vol. IV of his *Les Origines de la Réforme* (1935) offers an outstanding treatment from the viewpoint of a Roman Catholic layman. Probably the best study of the Servetus case is found in E. M. Wilbur's *A History of Unitarianism: Socinianism and its Antecedents* (1945). S. Zweig's *Castellio gegen Calvin* (1936), in English, *The Right to Heresy* (1936) is unreliable and extremely hostile to Calvin. He has been followed by J. Schorer, *Jean Calvin et sa dictature* (1948). Many of Calvin's works have been republished in the original or in translations during the present century. Notable are the *Calvini opera selecta* edited by P. Barth and W. Niesel (5 vols., 1926–36). and the edition of the French *Institutes* of 1542 by J. Pannier and associated scholars (4 vols., 1936–39). P. T. Fuhrmann has presented in English Calvin's first book of lay instruction, *Instruction in Faith, 1537* (1949). For the history of Calvin's *Form of Prayers* W. D. Maxwell's *John Knox's Geneva Service Book* (1931) is indispensable. Other books useful for the materials of the present supplement are the following: E. Choisy, *Calvin, éducateur des consciences* (1925); Léon Wencelius, *L'Esthétique de Calvin* (1937); W. S. Pratt, *The Music of the French Psalter of 1562* (1939); M. Weber, *The Protestant Ethic and the Spirit of Capitalism*, translated by Talcott Parsons (1930); E. Troeltsch, *Social Teaching of the Christian Churches*, translated by O. Wyon from the third German edition (1931); H. Hauser, *Les Débuts de Capitalisme* (1927); H. M. Robertson, *Aspects of the Rise of Economic Individualism; A Criticism of Max Weber* (1933); A. Hyma, *Christianity, Capitalism and Communism* (1937); H. D. Foster, *Collected Essays* (1929); Q. Breen, *John Calvin: A Study in French Humanism* (1931); G. Harkness, *John Calvin, the Man and His Ethics* (1931); J. Courvoisier, *La notion d'Église chez Bucer dans son développement historique* (1933); G. Bohatec, *Calvin und das Recht* (1934) and *Calvin's Lehre von Staat und Kirche* (1937); M. E. Chenèviere, *La Pensée politique de Calvin* (1937); R. H. Murray, *Political Consequences of the Reformation* (1936); H. Baron, *Calvins Staatsanschauung und das Konfessionelle Zeitalter* (1924) and "Calvinist Republicanism and Its Historical Roots," *Church History*, VIII (1939). 30–42; J. T. McNeill, *John Calvin on God and Political Duty* (texts with introduction) (1949); F. Busser, *Calvins Urteil ueber sich selbst* (1950).

JOHN T. McNEILL.

CALVINISM: I. Epistemology: Calvinism maintains without qualification the Protestant conception of Scripture as self-authenticating. The God of the Bible cannot appeal to anything beyond himself to corroborate the truth of his Word. Even in paradise man, made in the image of God, surrounded by the universe, itself a revelation of God, needed the self-authenticating, supernatural revelation from God. As all men see the revelation around and within them, so all men, through Adam (Rom. 5:12) representing them, have heard the voice of God. All men, therefore, know the true God, their

Creator (Rom. 1:19–20; 2:14–15). Men cannot escape knowing their responsibility to God.

Yet, having sinned in Adam, all men seek to suppress this knowledge, devising systems by which it becomes dependent upon the autonomous human will and the movements of time. Only if God in sovereign grace and providence brings men into contact with the gospel and, through the regenerating power of the Spirit, enables them to receive this gospel will men accept the truth.

In apologetics, therefore, Calvinism does not, like Romanism and varying forms of Evangelical Protestantism, begin with "natural theology," to lead on to the "mysteries" of the faith. Such a procedure presupposes the autonomy of man. On the contrary, Calvinism asks men to presuppose God as the one through whose revelation, natural plus supernatural, any human knowledge has significance.

II. Ontology: Calvinism maintains without qualification the Protestant conception of God as self-dependent and of the creature as God-dependent. Man's knowledge is inherently analogical of God's knowledge because his being is analogical of God's being (see ANALOGY).

Calvinism stands opposed, therefore, to the Romanist conception of the "analogy of being," according to which God and his creatures are subject to a common species of being; to the dialectical notion of the "analogy of faith" according to which God and man exist as aspects of the one Event called Christ; and to varying forms of Evangelical Protestantism which, by virtue of a measure of ultimacy or autonomy attributed to human being, make concessions to the Romanist or to the dialectical idea, or to both.

III. Ethics: Calvinism maintains without qualification the Protestant doctrine of self-conscious submission to the revealed will of God. Man's ethical reaction is inherently analogical. But, as a sinner in Adam, the "natural man" seeks to suppress the originally proper reaction of his will. He seeks to be a law unto himself. Only on the basis of the substitutionary work of Christ and by the regenerating power of the Holy Spirit can the sinner do the will of God.

Calvinism is therefore opposed to the Romanist scheme of ethics, based upon the "analogy of being"; to the ethics of dialectical theology whereby the will of God and the will of man are reduced to unity in the Event of Christ; and to the varying schemes of Evangelicalism to the extent that they, because of their views of the autonomy of the human will, make concessions to Romanism and dialecticism.

BIBLIOGRAPHY: For recent bibliography consult G. Brillenburg-Wurth, *Het Calvinisme Vandaag*, 1948; L. Van der Linde, *De Leer van den Heiligen Geest by Calvyn*, 1943; H. Henry Meeter in *God-Centered Living*, 1951.

[Sup.] CORNELIUS VAN TIL.

CAMEROONS. See AFRICA.

CAMILLIANS: Nicknamed "Agonizants," abbreviated as O.S.Cam. Headquarters of the North American province in Milwaukee, Wis.; fathers: thirteen. Professed brothers: six. In charge of two hospitals. [Sup.]

CAMPANIUS, JOHN: Pioneer Lutheran missionary to American Indians; b. in Stockholm, Sweden, Aug. 15, 1601; d. Sept. 17, 1683; clergyman in Swedish churches on the Delaware, 1642–48, where he became interested in the Delaware Indians, learned their dialect, and translated Luther's Small Catechism into their tongue. After his return to Sweden Campanius was pastor in Upland, where he revised his translation, published posthumously by the king in 1696: *Lutheri Catechismus öfwersatt på American-Virginiske Språket.* The work of Campanius and his successors, who used his Catechism, is more notable for the concern manifested than for the converts won.

BIBLIOGRAPHY: Facsimile edition of Campanius' Catechism published in 1937; Albert Keiser, *Lutheran Mission Work among the American Indians,* 1922; Nils Jacobsson, *Svenskar och Indianer,* 1922.

THEODORE G. TAPPERT.

CAMPBELL, EDWARD FAY: Presbyterian; b. McDonald, Pa., Nov. 2, 1894. He studied at Yale (B.A., 1918; S.T.B., 1924). He was secretary, Yale Christian Association (1918–19); traveling secretary for Student Volunteer Movement (1919–21); general secretary, Yale Christian Association (1921–42); and has served with the division of higher education, board of Christian Education, Presbyterian Church in the United States of America, since 1942. He is editor and coauthor of *To Glorify God.*

CAMPENHAUSEN, HANS FREIHERR V.: Lutheran; b. Mar. 16, 1903, at Rosenbeck (Livland, Russia). He studied theology in Marburg and Heidelberg (Dr. Theol., 1926) and also in Goettingen. He taught church history in Heidelberg (1945–), later assuming the field of New Testament. His major interest has been in early church history and his works include: *Ambrosius von Mailand als Kirchenpolitiker* (1928); *Die Passionssarkophage* (1930); *Die Idee des Martyriums in der alten Kirche* (1936); 3. Auflage der *Kirchengeschichte* von Karl Mueller I, 1 (1941); *Polykarp v. Smyrna und die Pastoralbriefe* (1951); *Der Ablauf der Osterereignisse und das leere Grab* (1952); *Kirchliches Amt und geistliche Vollmacht in den ersten drei Jahrhunderten* (1953).

RAYMOND W. ALBRIGHT.

CAMPION, EDMUND:

BIBLIOGRAPHY: B. Camm, *Lives of the English Martyrs,* 2 vols., 1904; R. Simpson, *Edmund Campion,* 2nd ed., 1907; E. Waugh, *Edmund Campion,* 1935. [Sup.]

CAMPS, SUMMER: Since 1881, when Camp Chocorua was organized at Holderness, N. H., camping has grown into a major aspect of the American educational and cultural pattern. The *National Camp Directory and Marketing Guide* (1951) listed 4,000 camps with approximately 3,000,000 children in attendance. Included are private and organizational camps: Boy and Girl Scouts (*q.v.*), Y.M.C.A. (*q.v.*), Y.W.C.A. (*q.v.*), Boys' Clubs, Camp Fire Girls, Catholic Youth Organization, Jewish Center, 4-H Clubs, settlements (see SETTLEMENT MOVEMENT) and neighborhood houses (*q.v.*), schools, municipalities, industries, labor unions, fraternal organizations, service clubs, churches. The original impulse came from the recognition that the home environment is unnatural, with little opportunity for developing self-reliance, all-around skills, and living together as once provided by large pioneer families. Three stages mark the development: (1) recreational, with emphasis primarily on rugged outdoor life; (2) educational, with scientifically oriented programs of character development; (3) social orientation and responsibility, with schools and communities attempting to integrate camping into their total program of democratic living. A typical program stresses at-homeness in the out-of-doors, safe and healthful living, constructive use of leisure, personality development, democratic group and community living, spiritual meanings and values, thus reflecting the general educational trends.

BIBLIOGRAPHY: H. S. Dimock, ed., *Administration of the Modern Camp,* 1948; *Camping Magazine,* organ of the American Camping Association, Plainfield, N. J.

MARTIN J. HEINECKEN.

CAMUS, JEAN PIERRE: The addition of de Pont Carré to his name is erroneous, since it stems from a confusion with Jacques Camus de Pont Carré, who was born in 1584 in Bordeaux and was from 1614 until his death in 1651 bishop of Séez.

BIBLIOGRAPHY: H. Bremond, *Histoire littéraire du sentiment religieux en France,* 2nd ed. (1924), I, 149–186, 273–298, 525–534, VII, 140 ff.; G. Joppin, *Jean Pierre Camus évêque de Belly,* 1938; *Dict. de spiritualité,* II (1947), 62–73.

[Sup.] MATHIAS GOOSSENS.

CANAAN, CANAANITES: Discovery of the Ras Shamra (*q.v.*) Inscriptions and related documents, researches in Ugaritic, and recent excavations in Palestine have provided fresh insights into the history, language, literature, mortuary practices, and cultus of the Canaanites, who occupied Syria-Palestine centuries prior to the Hebrew conquest. A composite people closely related to the Amorites, Hittites, Phoenicians (*qq.v.*) and other Semitic groups, they manifest a culture much older and richer than has hitherto been recognized. Many of their cities (e.g., Jerusalem, Jericho, Ai) were important centers prior to 3,000 B.C. By 1400

B.C. they were remarkably well advanced in their civilization, exhibiting vast wealth in gold, silver, ivory, brass, iron, and other commercial products. Since Canaan, by reason of its geographical location, was the bridge over which many peoples of the ancient world passed in their successive conquests, it exerted a marked influence through long centuries over wide areas of culture. Evidences of its linguistic influences are still observable in many languages of the West.

The Israelites probably absorbed more from the Canaanites than from any other neighboring peoples. As a comparison of Hebrew and Ugaritic reveals, they imitated their language, literature, poetry, music, art, architecture, and even their religion, which centered in Baal worship. The infiltration of fertility cult practices into Israel was a constant concern of the prophets of Yahweh (see FERTILITY CULTS; GODS AND GODDESSES MENTIONED IN THE OLD TESTAMENT, PAGAN). It was only by divine power and direction that the higher culture of the Hebrews prevailed.

BIBLIOGRAPHY: W. F. Albright, "The Role of the Canaanites in the History of Civilization," in *Studies in the History of Culture* (Leland Memorial Volume, 1942), 11–50; idem, *From the Stone Age to Christianity*, 2nd ed., 1946; *The Archaeology of Palestine*, 1949; G. Ernest Wright and Floyd V. Filson, *The Westminster Historical Atlas to the Bible*, 1945; C. H. Gordon, *Ugaritic Literature*, 1949; T. J. Meek; Hebrew Origins, 1950; H. H. Rowley, ed., *The Old Testament and Modern Study*, 1951.
[Sup.] ELMER E. FLACK.

CANADA: Canada has grown both in area and in population since 1910. Its area is 3,845,144 square miles, and its population (1951 census) 14,009,429. Canada also grew in other ways—in national production, trade and commerce, self-government, and political importance. Notable has been its development to full autonomy as a member of the British Commonwealth of Nations. Canada is bound to the mother country by sentiment, community of tradition, similarity of institutions, and common allegiance to the same Crown, but it is completely self-governing. Equally notable has been its rise to a position of some influence in international affairs.

There are ten provinces in Canada. Newfoundland (q.v.) joined the Confederation to become the tenth province in 1949 and thereby increased the area of Canada. Other changes were made in the map of the country by the addition of certain areas to the provinces and reduction in the number of territories and districts. One territorial council now governs the Yukon Territory, and another the Northwest Territories, the latter now including the Districts of Franklin, Keewatin, and Mackenzie.

The increase in population is the result of immigration, natural increase, and the addition of Newfoundland. The urban proportion of the population has increased greatly. The provinces of Ontario and Quebec continue to be the most thickly populated and the most highly industrialized. Ontario has the largest population and Quebec the second largest, together constituting 61.75% of the population of the country.

The largest religious denominations in Canada had the following adherents in 1951: Roman Catholic, 6,069,496; United Church of Canada, 2,867,271; Church of England in Canada, 2,060,720; Presbyterian, 781,747; Baptist, 519,585; Lutheran, 444,923; Jews, 204,836; Ukrainian (Greek) Catholic, 190,831; Greek Orthodox, 172,271; Mennonite, 125,938.

These ten denominations include 96% of the population. Other religious bodies comprise 571,811 souls. There is a considerable disparity between these census figures of the religious professions of the people and the smaller numbers of members, children, and adherents reported by the churches themselves as actually under their pastoral care.

Roman Catholics constitute 43.3% of the population of Canada. They are most numerous in Quebec, where they comprise almost 88% of the provincial population. The Roman Church has an apostolic delegation at Ottawa, and is organized in fourteen ecclesiastical provinces, with fifty-nine dioceses. In addition to these, the archdiocese of Winnipeg is immediately subject to the Holy See. If the Ukrainian (Greek) Catholics in Canada be added, the combined numbers constitute 44.68% of the total population.

The United Church of Canada (q.v.) is the largest Protestant church in the country. Enrolling 20.46% of the population, it was instituted in 1925 by the union of Congregational, Presbyterian, and Methodist Churches.

The Church of England in Canada (q.v.) receives the adherence of 14.7% of Canadians. It is organized in four ecclesiastical provinces, with twenty-nine dioceses.

A minority of Presbyterians declined to concur in the union of 1925. Presbyterians are 5.6% of the population. The General Assembly of the Presbyterian Church in Canada meets annually, and the offices of the church are located in Toronto.

Baptists comprise 3.7% of the Canadian population. The principal Baptist Churches are those of the three Conventions (Maritime Provinces, Ontario and Quebec, and Western) which are allied in the Baptist Federation of Canada (see BAPTISTS).

Lutherans make up 3.17% of the total population. There are ten bodies of Lutherans (q.v.) working in Canada, all with their headquarters in the United States.

Anglicans, Baptists, Lutherans, Presbyterians, and United Church adherents together constitute 47.6% of the total population.

Other denominations include the Evangelical United Brethren (*q.v.*), the Churches of Christ (see DISCIPLES OF CHRIST), the Salvation Army (*q.v.*), the Society of Friends (*q.v.*), the Pentecostal Assemblies (*q.v.*), and many others.

Several Canadian churches are associated in the Canadian Council of Churches (*q.v.*).

All major churches carry on extensive mission work, at home and overseas. They have well organized boards of evangelism, social service, missions, and education. All maintain educational institutions—secondary schools, university colleges, and theological seminaries.

Education in Canada is under provincial jurisdiction. There are therefore ten sets of statutes and regulations. In the province of Quebec there is a dual system of schools based on religious belief. In Ontario, Saskatchewan, and Alberta there are separate Roman Catholic schools. There are no separate schools in Manitoba, Nova Scotia, New Brunswick, and Prince Edward Island. In Newfoundland the schools are operated and staffed by the religious denominations under provincial regulations regarding financial support and the training of teachers. Throughout Canada the prevailing approach is that of co-operation between church and state. The regulations regarding religious exercises and religious instruction in the schools vary from province to province.

BIBLIOGRAPHY: W. Stewart Wallace, *The Encyclopedia of Canada*, 6 vols., 1948; A. Shortt and A. G. Doughty, eds., *Canada and its Provinces* (Vol. XI, 1913). See articles on the several churches.

[Sup.] W. J. GALLAGHER.

CANADIAN COUNCIL OF CHURCHES: A council of Canadian churches for fellowship, consultation, and co-operation. Its members are the Baptist Federation of Canada, Churches of Christ (Disciples), Church of England in Canada, Evangelical United Brethren Church, Presbyterian Church in Canada, Reformed Episcopal Church, United Church of Canada, Salvation Army, and Society of Friends. The United Lutheran Church in America is in friendly association with the Council. The Student Christian Movement of Canada, the National Y.M.C.A., and the National Y.W.C.A. are affiliated members. Affiliated members have limited voting privileges. The control of the Council rests with its member churches.

Organized in 1944, the Council united a number of previously existing interchurch groups under a fresh mandate from their constituent churches. It has no authority over its member bodies, but is representative of them and responsible to them. It provides an instrument for their co-operation within Canada (*q.v.*), and by agreement it is also the Canadian agency of the World Council of Churches (*q.v.*).

The Council held annual meetings from 1944 to 1951. Thereafter it met biennially. Under the supervision of its Executive Committee it carries on its work through Departments of Evangelism, Christian Education, Social Relations, and Ecumenical Affairs, and Committees on University Christian Missions, Faith and Order, International Affairs, Immigration of Refugees, Christian Stewardship, Chaplain Service in the Forces. Steps were also taken to set up a Department of Overseas Missions.

Any communion in Canada which "accepts our Lord Jesus Christ as God and Saviour" may become a member of the Council by resolution of its governing body and acceptance by the Council, or upon invitation of the Council and resolution of the communion's governing body. Acceptability depends upon autonomy, Canadawide organization, and other pertinent considerations.

The Council maintains offices and permanent secretarial staff in Toronto.

W. J. GALLAGHER.

CANISIUS, PETRUS: Often called the second apostle of Germany, the first having been St. Boniface. He achieved much in enforcing the decrees of the Council of Trent in German-speaking regions. He prepared three versions of his famous catechisms. The large one (1555) was intended for instruction in theology, the shortest (1556) for young people ("ad captum rudiorum"), and the other (1558) is generally named after the edition published at Cracow: *Institutiones Christianae*, or *Christian Institutes*. The latter was the most widely used of the three, running up to 200 editions in his own lifetime; before 1700 there were some 400 editions. Translations have appeared in German, English, French, Spanish, Italian, Polish, Greek, Ethiopic, Japanese, Indian, etc. In 1925 Canisius was canonized and proclaimed ecclesiastical teacher.

BIBLIOGRAPHY: Canisius, *Epistolae et acta*, ed. O. Braunsberger, 8 vol., 1896–1923; O. Braunsberger, *Petrus Canisius: Ein Lebensbild*, 1916; J. Metzler, *Der hl. Petrus Canisius und die Neuerer seiner Zeit*, 1927; J. Tesser, *Petrus Canisius als humanistisch Geleerde*, 1932; J. Brodrick, *Saint Peter Canisius*, 1935 (German edition, 1950).

[Sup.] MATHIAS GOOSSENS.

CANNON, JAMES: Methodist; b. at Farmville, Va., Nov. 30, 1892. He was educated at the Webb School, Bell Buckle, Tenn.; Trinity College (now Duke University) (A.B., 1911); Princeton University (A.M., 1917); Princeton Theological Seminary (Th.B., and Th.M., 1925).

He has taught at Trinity College and Duke University since 1919, holding the Ivey chair of history of religion and missions in the Divinity School of Duke University since 1926; dean of the Divinity School (1951–).

He is the author of *The History of Southern Methodist Missions* (1926).

CANON LAW. See CODEX JURIS CANONICI.

CANON OF SCRIPTURE: I. Old Testament:
In the course of its history the term "canon" (Greek, *kanōn*, "rod"; Hebrew, *qāneh*, "reed") has acquired a variety of meanings. Originally a straight rod, it came to signify anything straight—a rule, standard, model, measure, criterion, or norm. Then it came to mean a rule of faith. While the Hebrews regarded their Scriptures as inspired, they did not refer to them as "canonical." Church fathers in the fourth century A.D. first applied the term to the sacred Scriptures to distinguish them as the authoritative writings recognized by the church. The crystallization of what is now the Old Testament was a long and complicated process, marked by several stages. Modern research has thrown considerable light on the process.

A. THE FIRST STAGE: Cultic interests in Israel contributed much toward the recognition of sacred writings. The religious community gradually crystallized, collected, and preserved early songs, narratives, laws, annals, psalms, prophecies, and other literary remains (see Ex. 40:20; Deut. 31:24–26). Men of God gave forth utterances recognized at once as inspired. So there was no early demand for a formal canonization. The first public recognition which the Hebrews gave a sacred document seems to have taken place in 621 B.C. when "the book of the law" which Hilkiah found in the temple was formally made regulative by pronouncement of King Josiah (II Kings 23:1 ff.) This marked the beginning of the subtle process which in time brought public recognition of the tripartite canon. Scholars are not agreed as to the time each of the three parts received formal approval. Pfeiffer, e.g., suggests that the canonization of the Law took place *ca.* 400 B.C.; the Prophets, *ca.* 200 B.C.; and the Hagiographa, finally *ca.* A.D. 90. Oesterley and Robinson, following Hoelscher, find no canon of the Old Testament before the Council of Jamnia, *ca.* A.D. 90. G. R. Driver questions the theory that the issue was settled at Jamnia. Rowley and many others feel that the fixation of the canon was by general consent and not by formal decision.

Doubtless, the Torah (*q.v.*) acquired earliest recognition as authoritative. Long after the crystallization of the Prophets and the Writings the primacy of the Pentateuch prevailed. The fixation of the literary strata and eventually the books of the Pentateuch (*q.v.*) was an involved process. Apparently it was complete by the time of Nehemiah (432 B.C.), for when the Samaritans withdrew from Judaism (Neh. 13:28 f.), they adopted the Pentateuch as their sole canon. At least by *ca.* 250 B.C., when the Torah was translated into Greek (the Septuagint, *q.v.*), it had become the Bible of Judaism. In all the synagogues the Law was read and regarded as authoritative.

B. THE PROPHETIC COLLECTION: Continued in the "Former Prophets" is the historical narrative begun in the Pentateuch. Within this prophetic framework numerous documents sprang up only to be lost in the process of selection, evaluation, assimilation, and preservation (I Kings 11:41; 14:19, 29; I Chron. 29:29). Evidently the Deuteronomists organized, adapted, and edited these materials during the Exile (*ca.* 550 B.C.) to preserve the prophetic record of the history and faith of Israel, which had become vitiated by the fall of Jerusalem in 587 B.C. Later hands made numerous alterations in the text.

The "Latter Prophets" had a somewhat different development. Projected for the most part independently and limited in their early use by reason of the primacy of the Law, the writings of the prophets acquired public recognition slowly. During the Exile, under the influence of Ezekiel (*q.v.*) and the Second Isaiah (*q.v.*), who projected great hopes for Israel's future, there sprang up a revival of interest in prophecy, particularly predictive passages envisioning the coming of a Deliverer and the overthrow of Israel's enemies. As reverence for the written Law increased, there came also a growing appreciation of the word of the prophet. But in spite of this, countless interpolations were made in the text to bring books up to date and to enhance their values for current religion and morality. The presence of late sections in some prophecies and the absence of the Book of Daniel (*q.v.*) from the collection place the fixation of the prophetic canon late, *ca.* 200 B.C. Writing *ca.* 180 B.C., Ben Sira reveals a recognition of "the Law and the Prophets" (Ecclus. 44–49). In 132 B.C. the grandson of Ben Sira refers repeatedly to these two divisions, both of which by that time had been translated into Greek.

C. THE HAGIOGRAPHA: The process by which the "Writings" attained canonical status was much more imperceptible than that attending the Law and the Prophets. This was due to their independent character, varied contents, and loose connection. About all that they had in common was the claim of inspiration. Each faced its own problem of survival. Wide appeal and circulation insured their ultimate preservation. Some of the books, such as Psalms and Proverbs, include separate collections. By 132 B.C. there existed a fluid grouping, for Ben Sira's grandson refers to "the Law and the Prophets and the rest of the books." But while the third division in general had become crystallized before the beginning of the Christian era (see Luke 24:44), some of the books, such as Esther (*q.v.*), Ecclesiastes (*q.v.*), and the Song of Solomon (*q.v.*), remained long under dispute. The fate of Jerusalem in A.D. 70, the disorganization of Judaism, controversies over the status of certain books, and the influence of Christianity led to the fixation of the canon of twenty-four books (twenty-two, with Ruth combined with Judges and Lamentations with Jeremiah). The formal recognition of the complete Old Testament is usually regarded as having taken place at the Council of Jamnia, ca. A.D. 90, though the general pattern appeared much earlier and some books came into question later.

D. THE GREEK BIBLE: Besides the twenty-four canonical books (thirty-nine in the English Bible), there are numerous documents of the last centuries B.C. and the first century A.D. classified as the Apocrypha and Pseudepigrapha of the Old Testament (qq.v.). In recent decades these writings have become the object of considerable research. It has been observed that Jews in Alexandria handled Scripture more loosely than did those in Palestine. The latter held that prophecy ended in the time of Ezra (Neh. 8 f.), thus precluding admission to canonical standing of any document recognized as later; the former, on the other hand, held to the continuity of inspiration and the sanctity of books translated from Hebrew or Aramaic into Greek. Hence they included in their loose collection not only the books of the Hebrew canon but also the Apocrypha, which they interspersed among the canonical writings and made numerous other alterations in the text. But apparently they did not set up a special Alexandrian canon. The witness of the Septuagint is to the effect that the Old Testament canon had not become fixed when the Greek version was projected. Bentzen, following Kahle, suggests that the Greek Bible was the creation of the Christian Church.

E. CHRISTIAN USAGE: The New Testament bears testimony to the free use of Scripture on the part of early Christians. It includes, besides numerous quotations from each of the three parts of the Old Testament, adduced largely, though not exclusively, from the Septuagint, several references to or reminiscences of writings lying outside the Hebrew canon (see Heb. 11:35–37; James 1:19; Jude vv. 5, 14–16.) This practice of employing a larger collection obtains also in the writings of the apostolic and early church fathers. While the Septuagint was the Old Testament long used by the church, the acceptance of the Apocrypha was by no means universal. There was, in fact, considerable variation in usage in both East and West. Jerome, e.g., protested vigorously against the inclusion of these books, but Augustine and the Roman Church, following him, accepted them. At the time of the Reformation the Protestant churches returned to the original Palestinian canon as the basis for doctrine, but retained the arrangement of books as handed down by the Septuagint and the Vulgate, which leave no distinction between the second and third divisions of the tripartite canon. In his German

Bible of 1534 Luther placed the Apocrypha at the end of the Old Testament, with the notation that they were inferior but "good and useful for reading."

Modern research has brought fresh appreciation of the intertestamental literature and likewise a better understanding of the complex process by which the canon of Scripture became established under divine direction.

BIBLIOGRAPHY: M. L. Margolis, *The Hebrew Scriptures in the Making*, 1922; H. E. Ryle, *The Canon of the Old Testament*, 2nd ed., 1925; S. Zeitlin, *An Historical Study of the Canonization of the Hebrew Scriptures*, 1933; Otto Eissfeldt, *Einleitung in das Alte Testament* (1934), pp. 614–630; W. O. E. Oesterley and T. H. Robinson, *An Introduction to the Books of the Old Testament* (1934), pp. 1–10; R. H. Pfeiffer, *Introduction to the Old Testament* (1941), pp. 50–70; Aage Bentzen, *Introduction to the Old Testament*, Vol. I (1948), pp. 20–41; Artur Weiser, *Einleitung in das Alte Testament* (1949), pp. 243–256; H. H. Rowley, *The Growth of the Old Testament*, 1950; Gunnar Ostborn, *Cult and Canon: A Study in the Canonization of the Old Testament*, 1951; Arthur Jeffrey, "The Canon of the Old Testament," *The Interpreter's Bible*, Vol. I (1952), pp. 32–45.

[Sup.] ELMER E. FLACK.

II. New Testament: A. DOCUMENTS AND LISTS RELATING TO THE CANON: (1) The Marcionite Prologues to the (ten) Pauline Epistles. In 1907 Donatien De Bruyne showed ("Prologue biblique d'origine marcionite," *RBén*, XXIV, 1–16) that the Prologues or prefatory statements regarding the authorship, place of origin, purpose, and occasion of writing, which are found widely spread in certain Vulgate manuscripts of the Pauline Epistles, originated in Marcion's canon of "the Apostolos," comprising originally Galatians, Corinthians, Romans, Thessalonians, Laodiceans, Colossians, Philippians, and Philemon. Characteristically the Prologues lay great stress on Paul's work in correcting the teaching of "false apostles." At once J. R. Harris (*ET*, XVIII [1907], 393–394), A. von Harnack (*TLZ* [1907], cols. 138–140), and F. C. Burkitt (*The Gospel History and Its Transmission* [2nd ed., 1907], pp. 353–357) acclaimed the brilliance of De Bruyne's investigation and adduced evidence for believing that the Prologues were written originally in Greek. Later the Catholic Church took over these Prologues practically unaltered, substituted "Ephesians" for "Laodiceans," and added Prologues to II Corinthians, II Thessalonians, I Timothy, II Timothy, and Titus. Last of all (probably not before A.D. 350–380) a Prologue was provided for Hebrews; the wording of this differs markedly among the manuscripts, at least six different forms being extant.

The attempt by W. Mundel ("Die Herkunft der 'marcionitischen' Prologe," *ZNTW*, XXIV [1925], 56–77) to prove that these Prologues are not of Marcionite origin, but are probably dependent upon Ambrosiaster (q.v.), has failed to carry conviction (see Harnack's refutation, *ZNTW*, XXIV [1925], 204–218; cf. also E. Barnikol, "Marcions Paulusbriefprologe," *Theologische Jahrbuecher*, VI [1938], 15–16).

The text of the original Prologues, with an English translation, is given by Burkitt, *op. cit.*, and reprinted by John Knox, *Marcion and the New Testament*, 1942.

(2) The Anti-Marcionite Gospel Prologues. These Prologues to the Gospels of Mark, Luke, and John (the Matthean Preface has been lost) are extant in 12, 33, and 10 Latin manuscripts respectively, dating from the fifth to the tenth century. In addition, the Prologue to Luke is extant also in Greek, preserved in two manuscripts from the tenth and eleventh centuries. In 1928 Donatien De Bruyne ("Les plus anciens Prologues latins des Évangiles," *RBén*, XL [1928], 193–214) perceived their anti-Marcionite tendency and argued that they were written originally in Greek between A.D. 160 and 180 in opposition to Marcion. Harnack immediately adopted De Bruyne's findings and pointed out further implications of statements in the Prologues bearing on the Lucan authorship of Acts, the Johannine and apostolic authorship of Revelation, and Luke's relation to Paul ("Die aeltesten Evangelien-Prologe und die Bildung des NTs," *SBA*, phil.-hist. Kl., XXIV [1928], 322–341). The statement in the Prologue to the Gospel of John, that Papias in his (lost) *Expositions* asserted that the Fourth Gospel was written in the lifetime of John and taken down at his dictation by Papias, has aroused much discussion. (a) W. F. Howard ("The Anti-Marcionite Prologues to the Gospels," *ET*, XLVII [1935–36], 534–538) favored Lightfoot's conjecture that an ambiguous form of the Greek verb was wrongly taken to mean that Papias was John's amanuensis. (b) Robert Eisler (*The Enigma of the Fourth Gospel*, 1938) emended the Prologue to make it assert that John dictated his Gospel to Marcion (see H. Burnaby's refutation, *JTS*, XLI [1940], 295–300). (c) F. L. Cross (in a letter to *The* [London] *Times*, February 10, 1936) thought that the Prologue, in its presumed original form, "asserted that the Fourth Gospel was written by John the Elder at the dictation of John the Apostle when the latter had reached a very old age." (d) Engelbert Gutwenger, S.J. ("The Anti-Marcionite Prologues," *ThSt*, VII [1946], 393–409) denied the identity of authorship of the three Prologues and found no reason to date the Prologue to John before 300. See also B. W. Bacon, "The Latin Prologues of John," *JBL*, XXXII (1913), 194–212; "Marcion, Papias, and 'The Elders,'" *JTS*, XXIII (1921–22), 134–160; "The Anti-Marcionite Prologue to John," *JBL*, XLIX (1930), 43–54; and R. M. Grant, "The Oldest Gospel Prologues," *ATR*, XXIII (1941), 231–245 (who gives the text, translation, and commentary).

(3) The Muratorian Canon. Scholars have continued to debate the date, authorship, and literary character of this anonymous fragment.

The view of Lightfoot, that its author was Hippolytus, was supported, with additional arguments, by T. H. Robinson (*Exp.*, Seventh Series, II [1906], 481–495), T. Zahn (*NKZ* XXXIII [1922], 417–436), M. J. Lagrange (*RB*, XXXV [1926], 83–88; and XLII [1933], 161–186). On the other hand, V. Bartlet thought Melito was its author (*Exp.*, Seventh Series, II [1906], 210–224); C. Erbes attributed it to Rhodon, who drew it up about A.D. 220 (*ZKG*, XXXV [1914], 331–362; and J. Chapman attempted to prove that it was part of Clement of Alexandria's *Hypotyposes* (*RBén*, XXI [1904], 240–264; see also 369–374 and XXII [1905], 62–64). Harnack maintained that it was an official list intended for the whole church, very probably of Roman origin with the authority of either Pope Victor or Pope Zephyrinus behind it (*ZNTW*, XXIV [1925], 1–16; cf. H. Koch's article condemning Harnack's reasoning but supporting his conclusions, *ZNTW*, XXV [1926], 154–160).

On the puzzling reference (lines 3 f. of the Canon) to Luke and Paul, see E. Nestle (*ZNTW*, X [1911], 177) and E. Klostermann (*ZNTW*, XXII [1923], 308 f.).

For other treatments, see E. S. Buchanan, "The Codex Muratorianus," *JTS*, VIII (1907), 537–545; H. Lietzmann, ed., *Das muratorische Fragment* (*KlT*, no. 1) (1902, 4th ed., 1933; reprinted by F. W. Grosheide in *Some Early Lists of the Books of the New Testament*, Leiden, 1948); A. Donini, "Il canone muratoriano," *Ricerche religiose*, II (1926), 127–138; S. Ritter, "Il frammento muratoriano," *Rivista di archeologia cristiana*, III (1926), 215–268; H. Leclercq, "Muratorianum," *DACL*, XII, 1 (1935), cols. 543–560 (with facsimile of the manuscript).

(4) The Priscillianist (or Monarchian) Prologues. These Latin Prologues, previously termed Monarchian and dated during the pontificate of Zephyrinus, A.D. 198–217 (so Corssen, *TU*, XV, 1, 1896), may be the work of either the Spanish heretic Priscillian of the latter part of the fourth century (so John Chapman, *Notes on the Early History of the Vulgate Gospels* [1908], pp. 217–288), or Instantius who defended Priscillian at the Council of Bordeaux in A.D. 384–385 (so G. Morin, *RBén* [1913], 153–173). These Prologues, having been reworked in an orthodox interest, were held in such high repute that they were incorporated in the Vulgate. H. Lietzmann edited the Monarchian Prologues in his *KlT* series, no. 1, 1902, 4th ed., 1933. See also Gutwenger, *ThSt*, VII (1946), 403 ff.

(5) A Latin Version of the Eighty-fifth Apostolic Canon. C. H. Turner discovered (*JTS*, XIII [1912], 511–514) a Latin manuscript (Verona 51, fifth or sixth century) containing the Eighty-fifth Apostolic Canon (which concludes the eighth book of the Apostolic Constitutions),

which presents a different list of New Testament books from that preserved in the Greek form of this Apostolic Canon. The Greek text, it should be noted, rests on manuscripts which are later by some centuries than this Latin manuscript. After enumerating by name the four Gospels and grouping the fourteen Epistles of Paul in one item, the list proceeds, "one Epistle of Peter, one Epistle of John, two Epistles of Clement, and these present constitutions . . . and the Acts of us the Apostles." Turner concludes, "At a rather later date than the *Apostolic Constitutions*, the Peshitta still knows only of three Catholic Epistles, I Peter, I John, and James; and I do not doubt that more critical texts of our fourth century authorities will tend to show that the full canon of seven Catholic Epistles only attained recognition at a later date than has hitherto been supposed" (*op. cit.*, p. 512).

(6) The Decretum Gelasianum. This document was previously thought to be an official statement, containing a list of canonical books, which embodied the decrees of the Council of 382 held at Rome under Pope Damasus. As the result of E. von Dobschuetz's research, however, it is now regarded as the private work of a cleric in Italy during the first half of the sixth century (Dobschuetz, *Das Decretum Gelasianum*, 1912; see also E. Schwartz, *ZNTW*, XXIX [1930], 161–168).

J. Chapman made an unsuccessful attempt to defend the traditional view of the Decretum (*RBén* [1913], 187–207, 315–333; cf. Amann in *RB* [1913], 602–608).

(7) A New Stichometrical List. C. H. Turner edited "An Unpublished Stichometrical List from the Freisingen MS of Canons" (*JTS*, II [1900–1], 236–253), in a manuscript of the eighth century, in which the epithet "canonical" is applied to the seven Catholic Epistles, and the title "Zelotes" is applied to Jude. This last agrees with the statement in the so-called Decretum Gelasianum, with Matt. 10:3 in certain Old Latin manuscripts, and with the mosaics of the great Baptistry at Ravenna.

(8) The Canon in the Syrian Church. The statement of Zahn (*Schaff-Herzog*, II, 398) that "Ephraem was familiar with all the Catholic epistles" (a view held also by J. A. Bewer, *The History of the New Testament Canon in the Syrian Church*, 1900 [reprinted from *AJT*, IV (1900), 64–98, 345–363]) goes beyond the reliable evidence so far as the Minor Catholic Epistles are concerned (Walter Bauer, *Der Apostolos der Syrer* [1903], pp. 40–53).

Three pieces of evidence have come to light bearing upon the canon of the Nestorian Church. Two corroborate the consensus of testimony that the Nestorian canon lacked II Peter, II and III John, Jude, and Revelation. (a) An anonymous Arabic chronicle of the ninth or tenth century

testifies that the Babylonian Nestorians maintained their canon of twenty-two books (G. Rothstein, *ZDMG*, LVIII [1904], 634–663, 700–779). (b) An Arabic circular letter of A.D. 821 lists the New Testament books accepted by Nestorians as the four Gospels, Acts, and fourteen epistles of Paul (L. Rost, *ZNTW*, XXVII [1928], 103–196). Apparently opposed to this evidence is the testimony of the famous Nestorian monument erected A.D. 781 at Hsian-fu, China, which speaks of "the twenty-seven standard works of His [Christ's] Sutras" (Saeki's translation). In spite of its contradiction of all that is known elsewhere of the Nestorian canon, most scholars have felt that this must be interpreted as referring to the twenty-seven books of the New Testament. Sten Bugge, however, disputes the legitimacy of this interpretation, pointing out, *inter alia*, that nothing in the inscription alludes directly to *canonical* books ("Den syriske kirkes nytestamentlige kanon i China," *NTT*, XLI [1940], 97–118). On the monument in general, see P. Carus, *The Nestorian Monument*, 1909; P. Y. Saeki, *The Nestorian Monument in China*, 1916; A. C. Moule, *Christians in China Before the Year 1550*, 1930; W. Gummell's new translation of the Chinese text in Glasgow Oriental University Society, *Transactions*, VII (1934–35), 28–39; P. Y. Saeki, *The Nestorian Documents and Relics in China*, 1937; Gerhard Rosenkranz, *Die aelteste Christenheit in China*, 1938.

For information regarding the four Minor Catholic epistles and Revelation in the Philoxenian Syriac version, see John Gwynn, *The Apocalypse of St. John*, 1898, and *Remnants of the Later Syrian Versions of the Bible*, 1909.

In a hagiographical Syriac manuscript of A.D. 875, now in the British Museum (Wright, *Catalogue*, p. 1105), there is the statement that "in one of the villages of the Samaritans . . . those of the heresy of the Herodians . . . receive only Mark the Evangelist and three letters of Paul and four books of Moses . . ." (F. Nau, "Le canon biblique samaritano-chrétien des Hérodiens," *RB*, XXXIX [1930], 396–400).

B. APOCRYPHAL BOOKS: Only those apocryphal books are mentioned here for which serious claims to canonicity were made in the early church; for others, see APOCRYPHA, N.T. English translations, with brief introductions, are available in M. R. James, ed., *The Apocryphal New Testament*, 1924. See also E. J. Goodspeed, *Strange New Gospels*, 1931 (deals with modern forgeries), and K. L. Schmidt, *Kanonische und apokryphe Evangelien und Apostelgeschichten*, 1944.

(1) The Acts of Paul. Carl Schmidt's publication (*Acta Pauli*, 1936) of eleven pages of a Greek papyrus codex, written about A.D. 300, supplies a major portion hitherto lacking of this second-century apocryphon. One of the epi-

sodes in the papyrus tells of Paul's fighting wild beasts in the arena at Ephesus; the lion which is let loose on him, however, proves to be the same one which had previously been converted and baptized as the result of Paul's preaching (for translation and discussion, see B. M. Metzger, "St. Paul and the Baptized Lion," *Princeton Seminary Bulletin*, XXXIX, 2 [1945], 11–21). See also Rosa Soeder, *Die apokryphen Apostelgeschichten und die romanhafte Literatur der Antike*, 1932.

(2) Paul's Third Epistle to the Corinthians. This document, which for some time enjoyed canonical status in Syrian and Armenian churches, is contained in the apocryphal Acts of Paul. It deals with the status of early Christian prophets, the birth of Christ from the Virgin Mary, the human nature of Christ, and the resurrection of the flesh. See L. Vouaux, *Les actes de Paul et ses lettres apocryphes*, 1913; B. Pick, *IJA* (January, 1913), 9–13; and K. Pink, *Biblica*, VI (1925), 68–91. A. von Harnack edited the Epistle in Lietzmann's *Kleine Texte* series, No. 12, 2nd ed., 1931, and De Bruyne (*RBén*, XLV [1933], 189–195) and H. Boese (*ZNTW*, XLIV [1952–53], 66–76) published additional manuscripts containing the apocryphon.

(3) The Epistle to the Laodiceans. Several additional Latin manuscripts containing this apocryphon were edited by E. J. Goodspeed (*JBL*, XXIII [1904], 76–78; *AJT*, VIII [1904], 536–538). Harnack's idea (*SBA* [1923], 235–245) that this Epistle was a Marcionite forgery of the second half of the second century has not commended itself to other scholars. The most convenient edition is by Harnack in Lietzmann's *KlT* series, No. 12, 2nd ed., 1931. See also B. Pick, *IJA* (October, 1912), 73–76; and K. Pink, *Biblica*, VI (1925), 179–192.

(4) The Apocalypse of Peter. The complete text of the Ethiopic version of this book, held in high esteem by some in the early church, was published in 1910 (S. Grébaut, *ROC*, XV [1910], 198 ff., 307 ff., 425 ff.). Dating from the second century (it is mentioned in the Muratorian Canon), this Apocalypse continued to be used in the Liturgy of Good Friday in some churches of Palestine (Sozomen, *Hist. Eccl.*, vii, 19). It consists mainly of visions describing the beauty of heaven and the torments of hell. A later Arabic version was published by A. Mingana (*Woodbrooke Studies*, III, 2, 1931).

C. THE INFLUENCE OF ROLL AND CODEX ON COLLECTIONS OF NEW TESTAMENT BOOKS: The maximum length of a scroll convenient to handle (approximately thirty-one to thirty-two feet) could contain the equivalent of either the Gospel of Luke or Acts. As long as Christians used the roll in the transmission of their sacred books, the four Gospels or the Pauline Epistles could be collected in an external way only by assembling several rolls in the same box or chest

(*capsa*; cf. *Acts of Scillitan Martyrs*, A.D. 180, for evidence regarding Paul's Epistles). When, however, the codex or leaf-form of books was adopted, many or even all the separate documents of the New Testament could be more closely assembled in one book.

Evidence recently collected shows that the Christians made almost exclusive use of the codex form for the transmission of their Scriptures at a much earlier date than was heretofore thought probable (C. H. Roberts, "The Christian Book and the Greek Papyri," *JTS*, L [1949], 155–168). It has been suggested (Roberts, *JTS*, XL [1939], 257; elaborated by Peter Katz, *JTS*, XLVI [1945], 63–65) that the Gentile Christian church, in opposition to the Synagogue, may have deliberately substituted the codex for the traditional Jewish scroll. However this may be, considerations of economy (using both sides of the writing material) and ease in the consultation of proof-texts would certainly have encouraged Christians to adopt this format for their sacred books. See also Hugo Ibscher, "Der Kodex," *Buch und Schrift, Jahrbuch der Einbandkunst*, X (1937), 3–15; W. Schubart, "Das antike Buch," *Die Antike*, XIV (1938), 171–195.

D. PROBLEMS REGARDING THE CANON: Although the recognition of the canon of the New Testament was one of the most important developments in the early church, there is a surprising absence of contemporary references to (1) the order in which the various parts of the New Testament achieved general currency, and (2) the reasons which led the church to make the selection that ultimately prevailed. The following are some representative theories on both these matters.

(1) Harnack held that the Gospels were the nucleus of the canon, and that the Pauline Epistles followed. The Acts of the Apostles was added chiefly to vindicate the authority of Paul and to join his writings to the Gospels (for a sharp critique, see H. C. Vedder, "The Origin of the New Testament," *The Union Seminary Review* (Richmond), XXXVIII [1926–27], 146–158).

According to E. J. Goodspeed the first collection of New Testament books was made by a Christian, perhaps at Ephesus, whose interest in Paul had been roused by reading the recently published Acts of the Apostles (shortly after A.D. 90). This admirer of the Apostle composed a prefatory encyclical (Ephesians) and published the corpus of ten letters (i.e., all but the Pastorals), which in turn called forth the composition of other letters, namely Rev. 1–3, Hebrews, I Peter, and I Clement. See, among several publications where Goodspeed advanced these theories, his *New Solutions of the New Testament Problems* (1927), and "The Editio Princeps of Paul," *JBL*, LXIV (1945), 193–204; cf. A. E. Barnett, *Paul Becomes a Literary In-*

fluence, 1941. John Knox conjectured that the collector and publisher of the preliminary Pauline corpus was Onesimus (*Philemon among the Letters of Paul,* 1935).

Hans Windisch thought that the Book of Revelation, because it contained words of Jesus Christ, history of the Kingdom, and letters, supplied the pattern for the canonization of documents in each of these three areas ("Der Apokalyptiker Johannes als Begruender des neutestamentlichen Kanons," *ZNTW,* X [1909], 148–174).

The question whether the church's canon preceded or followed Marcion's canon continues to be debated, but in view of the consistent representation in the Fathers that Marcion *rejected* certain books, the great probability is that the church's canon was anterior to Marcion's rival canon (so C. H. Turner, *JTS,* X, 357 f.; J. Chapman, *RBén,* XXIX [1912], 252; J. Moffatt, *Introduction to the New Testament,* p. 60; E. C. Blackman, *Marcion and His Influence* [1948], p. 32).

John Knox proposed the elaborate hypothesis that Marcion had a kind of proto-Luke which the church later enlarged in the interest of anti-Marcionite polemic, producing our present Luke sometime after A.D. 150 (*Marcion and the New Testament, An Essay in the Early History of the Canon,* 1942). Knox fails, however, to show that after A.D. 150 conditions prevailed in the church to render possible the immediate general acceptance of a newly redacted Gospel (see also C. Kraeling, *CQ,* XX [1943], 159–161).

Taking up a suggestion made by J. Chapman ("The Earliest New Testament," *Exp.,* Sixth Series, XII [1905], 119–127), J. H. Ropes hazarded the theory that the formation of the basic canon took place early in the second century, perhaps at Antioch. The "Western" text (found today in such manuscripts as Codex Bezae, the Old Latin manuscripts, and other witnesses) "was the text of the primitive 'canon' (if the term may be pardoned in referring to so early a date), and was expressly created for that purpose" (Ropes, *The Text of Acts* [1926], p. ix). Later the "Western" text was "supplanted by a 'pre-canonical' text of superior age and merit [i.e., the Neutral or Alexandrian or Old Uncial]" (*ibid.,* p. ccxlv).

(2) Various answers have been given to the question why the church approved certain books and rejected others. According to Harnack, the canon constituted one of the three barriers (the other two were the creed and the bishops) which the church erected in its struggle with heresy, particularly Gnosticism. The process involved essentially the competition of many and the survival of the fittest. Juelicher, on the other hand, stressed the importance of *anagnosis,* or "[public] reading," of New Testament documents along with Old Testament documents,

already regarded as canonical, with the consequent impartation of the authority of the latter to the former. Conflict, so far from decreasing the canonical material by selection, actually worked to increase the amount subsequently canonized by widening the church's acquaintance of acceptable literature. According to Westcott, the formation of the canon was among the first instinctive acts of the Christian society, resting upon the general confession of the churches and not upon the independent opinions of its members. The canon was not the result of a series of contests; rather, canonical books were separated from the others by the intuitive insight of the church.

E. THE THEOLOGY OF THE CANON: Discussion of the canon should distinguish between the ground of canonicity and the grounds of conviction of canonicity. The latter were variously apprehended in different parts of the ancient church. In some areas (e.g., Alexandria) the process of canonization proceeded by way of selection, moving from many to few; in other areas (e.g., Syria) the church was content with a canon of twenty-two books. The ground of canonicity, on the other hand, rests ultimately upon what God has accomplished through Christ and the Spirit. Luther recognized as canonical those writings which preach Christ. (For a systematic treatment from this point of view, see Martin Albertz, *Botschaft des Neuen Testamentes,* I, ii, *Die Entstehung des apostolischen Schriftkanons,* 1952.) Calvin defined the authority of the Scriptures in terms of the activity of God's Spirit (*testimonium Spiritus Sancti internum*). According to a modern Reformed theologian, "The concept of the canon is bound up with the concept of God. . . . God is *ho kanōn*" (F. W. Grosheide, *Algemeene canoniek van het Nieuwe Testament* [1935], pp. 9 f.). In this sense, the church did not create the canon, but came to recognize and acknowledge the self-authenticating quality of the canonical documents, which imposed themselves as such upon the church.

BIBLIOGRAPHY: In addition to works mentioned above: I. Guidi, "Il canone biblico della chiesa copta," *Revue Biblique,* X (1901), 161–174; E. C. Moore, *The New Testament in the Christian Church,* 1904; Paul Ewald, *Der Kanon des Neuen Testaments,* 1906; Hans Lietzmann, *Wie wurden die Buecher des Neuen Testaments heilige Schrift?,* 1907; U. Fracassini, "Le origini del canone del N.T.," *Rivista storica-critica,* IV (1908), 349–368, 433–445; R. H. Gruetzmacher, "Die Haltbarkeit des Kanonbegriffes," *Theol. Studien. Th. Zahn dargebracht* (1908), pp. 47–68; Johannes Leipoldt, *Geschichte des neutestamentlichen Kanons;* II, *Mittelalter und Neuzeit,* 1908; Henry C. Vedder, *Our New Testament: How Did We Get it?,* 1908; C. H. Turner, "The Growth of the Idea of the Canon of the New Testament," *JTS,* X (1909), 13 ff., 160 ff., 354 ff.; E. Jacquier, *Le Nouveau Testament dans l'église chrétienne;* I, *Préparation, formation et définition du canon du Nouveau Testament,* 3rd ed., 1911; P. Dausch, *Der Kanon des Neuen Testaments,* 1910, 4th ed., 1921; G. F. Moore, "The Definition of the Jewish Canon and the Repudiation of Christian Scriptures," *Essays in Modern Theology and Related Subjects . . . A Testimonial to C. A. Briggs* (1911), pp. 99–125; Alexander Souter, *The Text and Canon of the New Testament,* 1913; A. von Harnack, *Die Entstehung des Neuen Testaments und die wichtigsten Folgen der neuen Schoepfung,*

1914; Eng. tr., *The Origin of the New Testament and the Most Important Consequences*, 1925; E. von Dobschuetz, "The Abandonment of the Canonical Idea," *AJT*, XIX (1915), 416–429; I. Haenel, *Der Schriftbegriff Jesu. Studie zur Kanongeschichte*, 1917; Ed. Koenig, *Kanon und Apokryphen*, 1917; A. Fridrichsen, *Den nytestamentlige skriftsamlings historie*, 1918; W. S. Reilly, "Le canon du N.T. et le critère de la canonicité," *Revue Biblique*, XXX (1921), 195–205; Sigurd Odland, *Det nytestamentlige Kanon*, 1922; Johannes Bestmann, *Zur Geschichte den neutestamentlichen Kanons*, 1922; E. J. Goodspeed, *The Formation of the New Testament*, 1926; H. Hoepfl, "Canonicité," *Dictionnaire de la Bible, Supplément*, I (1928), cols. 1022–1045; Albert Maichle, *Der Kanon der biblischen Buecher und das Konzil von Trient*, 1929; N. B. Stonehouse, *The Apocalypse in the Ancient Church*, 1929; G. M. Perrella, *De apostolico et prophetico munere et inspirationis et canonicitatis criterio altero pro N. altero pro V.T.*, 1931; M. J. Lagrange, *Histoire ancienne du canon Nouveau Testament*, 1933; H. Strathmann, *Die Entstehung des Neuen Testaments*, 1936; H. Oppel, *Kanōn*, 1937; S. M. Zarb, *Il canone biblico*, 1937; J. Brinktrine, "Nach welchen Gesichtspunkten wurden die einzelnen Gruppen des neutestamentlichen Kanons geordnet?" *Biblische Zeitschrift*, XXIV (1938–39), 125–135; D. W. Riddle, "Factors in the Formation of the New Testament Canon," *Journal of Religion*, XIX (1939), 330–345; O. Cullmann, "Die Pluralitaet der Evangelien als theologisches Problem im Altertum," *Theologische Zeitschrift*, I (1945), 23–42; T. W. Manson, "The Johannine Epistles and the Canon of the New Testament," *JTS*, XLVIII (1947), 32–33; A. C. Cotter, "Lost Books of the Bible?" *Theological Studies*, VI (1945), 206–228; Olaf Moe, "Hebreerbrevets betydning innenfor den nytestamentlige kanon," *Korsets ord og troens tale, Festskrift til . . . O. Hallesby* (1949), pp. 92–102; W. C. van Unnik, "De la règle *mēte prostheinai mēte aphelein* dans l'histoire du canon," *VC*, III (1949), 1–36; W. C. Kuemmel, "Notwendigkeit und Grenze des neutestamentlichen Kanons," *Zeitschrift fuer Theologie und Kirche*, XLVII (1950), 277–313.

Many handbooks on introduction to the New Testament have sections dealing with the canon. Special studies on the canon in ecclesiastical writers (arranged in chronological order) include the following: *The New Testament in the Apostolic Fathers*, edited by a Committee of the Oxford Society of Historical Theology, 1905; Aguado Esteban, "San Teófilo de Antioquía y el canon del N.T.," *E.B.*, VI (1934), 290–326; A. Camerbynk, *Saint Irénée et la canon du N.T.*, 1896; J. Hoh, *Die Lehre des hl. Irenaeus ueber das N.T.* (*Neutestamentliche Abhandlungen*, VII), 1919; H. Kutter, *Klemens Alexandrinus und das N.T.*, 1897; P. Dausch, *Der neutestamentliche Schriftkanon und Klemens von Alexandrien*, 1899; J. Ruwet, "Les 'antilegomena' dans les oeuvres d'Origène," *Biblica*, XXIII (1942), 18–42; XXIV (1943), 18–58; XXV (1944), 311–334; *idem*, "Le canon alexandrin des écritures, Saint Athanase," *Biblica*, XXXIII (1952), 1–29; T. Zahn, *Athanasius und der Bibelkanon*, 1901; *idem*, "Das N.T. Theodors von Mopsuestia und der urspruengliche Kanon der Syrer," *NKZ*, XI (1900), 788–806; C. Baur, "Der Kanon des hl. Joh. Chrysostomus," *TQ*, CV (1924), 258–271 (of about 11,000 citations from the N.T., there is none from II Pet., II and III Jn, Jude. and Rev.); V. Tzortzatos, *Hé peri tōn hagiōn graphōn didaskalia tou Chrysostomou*, Athens, 1947; H. H. Howorth, "The Influence of St. Jerome on the Canon of the Western Church," *JTS*, X (1909), 481–496; XI (1910), 321–347; XIII (1912), 1–18; C. J. Costello, *St. Augustine's Doctrine on the Inspiration and Canonicity of Scripture*, 1930; *idem*, "St. Augustine's Canon of Scripture and His Criterion of Canonicity," *Revue de l'Université d'Ottawa* (1932), pp. 125*–138*; A. Tapia Basulto, "El canon escriturístico en S. Isidore de Savilla," *Ciencia Tomista*, LVIII (1939), 364–388; C. van der Borne, "De canone biblico S. Bonaventurae," *Archiv franc. hist.*, XVIII (1925), 313–317; P. Synave, "Le canon scripturaire de Saint Thomas d'Aquin," *RB*, XXXIII (1924), 522–533; H. H. Howorth, "The Origin and Authority of the Biblical Canon According to the Continental Reformers," *JTS*, VIII (1907), 321–365; IX (1908), 188–230; X (1909), 183–232; *idem*, "The Bible Canon of the Reformers," *IJA* (October, 1913), pp. 66–70; A. Maichle, *Der Kanon der biblischen Buecher und das Konzil von Trient* (*Freiburger theologische Studien*, XXXIII), 1929; H. H. Howorth, "The Origin and Authority of the Biblical Canon in the Anglican Church," *JTS*, VIII (1907), 1–40.

[Sup.] BRUCE M. METZGER.

CANTERBURY ASSOCIATION, NATIONAL. See STUDENT ORGANIZATIONS, RELIGIOUS.

CAPITALISM: In economics, capital may be defined as wealth, created by work, held back from immediate consumption, and used, at more or less risk of ultimate loss, in the process of creating more wealth. Because of the self-deprivation involved in the creation of capital, and of the investment of time and talent, the continued self-deprivation, and the risk of loss involved in its use, it is normally insisted and conceded that a reward is justified, in the form of rent, interest, or profit. It is also urged that, without a reasonable assurance of such rewards in sufficient amount, no such self-deprivement and self-investment would occur or continue; but the large measure of truth in this contention should not be permitted to obscure the presence of other motivations.

So far, the problem of definition has been easy; but now, as we proceed, difficulties begin to emerge. In accordance with this definition of capital, a capitalist would be anyone who withholds part of his wealth from immediate consumption and employs it for productive purposes; and capitalism would be a form of economic organization which relies on capital. As the latter terms are commonly employed, however, such definitions of them would be too broad. For example, a person who is predominantly a laborer, but who saves part of his income and invests it in stocks and bonds or who buys and rents a house, is not normally classified as a capitalist, though he is sometimes so designated for purposes either of argument or of humor. Usually the term "capitalist" is reserved for one whose major economic activity is the ownership and use of capital in large amounts. Strictly regarded, the borders of such a definition are flexible and unclear, but the usage works well enough in practice.

Commonly, also, an economy such as the "American" is distinguished, as capitalism, from a socialist or communist economy, which is not capitalist. But capital is employed in the latter economies also. Indeed, "to *any* advance in the arts of industry or the comforts of life, a rate of production exceeding the rate of consumption, with consequent accumulation of resources, or in other words, the formation of capital, is indispensable" (article "Capital" in *Encyclopedia Britannica*, 9th edition, Vol. V, p. 64; italics added). Thus, if capitalism were defined as suggested above, a socialist and a communist economy would also be capitalistic, and the distinction drawn in this way between them and the American economy would be invalid. Sometimes, the distinction is described as one between "private" capitalism, on the one hand, and "state" or "public" capitalism, on the other. This comes nearer to the truth; but it also requires qualification because, on the one hand, private capitalists are not absent either from recognized socialist theory and practice or from the present "socialist" stage of the Soviet economy, and, on the other hand, capital is both privately and publicly owned and controlled in America. The real difference, then, is one of proportion and of specific programs—what proportion of the economy and what specific economic programs and institutions should be privately controlled and what publicly, and how may each kind of ownership and control be exercised so as to bring about the highest level of productivity, the right amount and kind of personal freedom and prosperity, and the greatest personal and social security and attainment of culture?

Hunt points out that "for nearly two thousand years European civilization has rested upon a contradiction—between a philosophy and a religion which teach that all men are brothers, and an economic system which organizes them as masters and servants" (*The Theory and Practice of Communism* [1950], p. 3). It is not surprising, therefore, that, as he also points out, "in almost every century men have sought to resolve the contradiction by demanding a readjustment of the social order" (*ibid.*, p. 3). The criticisms of capitalism have been theoretical and practical, superficial and profound; the proposed remedies have ranged, and still range, all the way from comparatively minor readjustments and "improvements" of capitalism to sweeping, utopian, or more sober and practical, demands for its abolition. Practically all of the more sweeping criticisms and programs of improvement have rested upon an estimate of man's rational and moral stature which is probably too high—apart, at least, from man's regeneration; and upon an estimate of the cause of man's predicament which does not recognize the true location of the trouble or its profound seriousness. Most of them have been intellectually unclear and practically unworkable, due in part probably to the white heat of emotion in which they were generated.

The claim that the most thorough of these proposals, both theoretically and practically, is that of the communists is probably just (see COMMUNISM [MARXIAN]). Marx saw clearly enough certain real dangers in modern capitalism, especially perhaps its inherent tendency to concentrate, in the hands of the few, power which would inevitably be or become socially irresponsible, in several ways—e.g., the increase of the misery of the proletariat involving the exploiting of women and children and the destruction of the home; the competition for raw materials and for markets, eventually on a world scale, leading to destructive wars; the cycle of "boom and bust"; and so forth. What he did not allow for, because there was little to suggest it in the society of his time, was the inevitable, subsequent development of controls, such as the spreading of ownership through the establishment of joint-stock, limited liability companies; the strengthening of the middle classes; the more or less successful expedients of democratic governments; the various movements looking to the establishment and preservation of world peace, and possibly leading in the future to some form of world government.

In religious circles, the "liberal movement," with its "Christian socialisms" (*q.v.*) and its "social gospel" (*q.v.*), was perhaps the most earnest indictment of the "profit motive" and of other "evils" in capitalistic society, and the most widespread effort to think out and to apply remedies. That movement is, for the present, in eclipse (see LIBERALISM). But Christianity, with its doctrine of brotherhood in Christ and its essential sympathy for all who are oppressed, can never surrender its function of criticism of all systems erected by finite and sin-perverted man; and it is to be hoped that the objectives of the "social gospel" will presently be revived, on more realistic theological and sociological foundations and with more practical programs.

Along with this religiously motivated criticism of capitalism, there has been a persistent effort to lay the blame for capitalism, or for its "evils," upon Protestantism, and more specifically upon John Calvin and his followers. Its first expression was an essay of Max Weber's (1904–5), later translated into English by T. Parsons, and published with the title *The Protestant Ethic and the Spirit of Capitalism* (1930). But the theory, along with criticisms and modifications of Weber's formulation and exposition of it, had already been made familiar to English readers through R. H. Tawney's *Religion and the Rise of Capitalism* (1926). It has been widely and learnedly discussed, in America, in Britain, and in Europe; but the student who is not a specialist may find a brief and adequate consideration of it in *John Calvin: The Man and His Ethics*, by Georgia Harkness (1931, Chapter IX). It is true that Protestantism did contribute to the rise of modern capitalism by justifying the relief of industry from ecclesiastical, especially monastic, control; by announcing and defending the legitimacy of interest and credit; by emphasizing individualism and the so-called "economic virtues." As a result, "there is a historical correlation, which cannot be explained by an accidental conjunction, between the growth of Calvinism and the growth of capitalism" (*John Calvin* etc., p. 190). But, on the other hand, "before Calvin was born, forces were at work which were calculated inevitably to bring about a transition to a new economic order" (*ibid.*, p. 191); "capitalism existed, both in form and spirit, before Calvin's day" (*ibid.*, p. 187); and Calvin labored to instil a religiously sanctioned ethic which, had it been followed, would largely have obviated the formation of that soulless, godless, greedy system which is all that the more extreme critics see, apparently, in capitalism.

Some, in their effort to rebut Weber's charge, appear to agree that capitalism is an evil thing, but deny that Protestantism had any significant part in its development. Perhaps more commonly, Protestants regard capitalism, with all its acknowledged faults, as the best economic system now available. They hope for and confidently expect a progressive remedying of its more obvious defects; they point out that, human nature being what it now is, competition is useful and necessary, and may be carried out under conditions which at least greatly minimize its potentially destructive character; and they expect no substitution of the very different spirit of Christian *agape* (*q.v.*) for it, in the economic order, until the Kingdom of God (*q.v.*) has come, or at least until a much closer approach to it has been achieved than seems likely in the near future.

BIBLIOGRAPHY: The character of contemporary discussion of various aspects of capitalism may be sufficiently discovered by reading F. M. Stern, *Capitalism in America*, 1951; G. Spiro, *Marxism and the Bolshevik State*, 1951; Rosa Luxemburg, *The Accumulation of Capital*, translated from the German by A. Schwarzschild, 1951; F. Sternberg, *Capitalism and Socialism on Trial*, 1952; and V. A. Demant, *Religion and the Decline of Capitalism*, 1952.
ANDREW K. RULE.

CAPITULATIONS: (1) Those agreements by which the persons having part in the election of a bishop or pope imposed upon the candidate conditions to be fulfilled after his taking office. The practice of episcopal capitulations became universal in Germany during the Middle Ages and the Renaissance, in spite of its being condemned repeatedly by the popes. Similar capitulations, tending to restrain the rights of the future pope with regard to the nomination of cardinals or the appointment of dignitaries, were entered into at the election of several popes, especially during the fourteenth and fifteenth centuries. Cf. L. Pastor, *History of the Popes*, Vols. I–VI, London, 1891–1901.

(2) Treaties by which the sultans of Turkey, since 1536, conferred the privilege of extraterritorial jurisdiction within the boundaries of the Ottoman Empire on some subjects of Western Christian powers. Thus, Christians of the Latin rite were placed under French protectorate. The capitulations were drastically modified after World War I, when various provinces of the former Ottoman Empire were administered under mandate from the League of Nations. The accession of several of those countries to full sovereignty since World War II virtually terminated the regime of the capitulations inasmuch as the new states were concerned.
GEORGES A. BARROIS.

CAPUCHINS: They literally followed the rule of St. Francis and insisted that they must wear exactly the same clothes as he had had, including the *capuccio*, or hood. They remained under the supervision of the Franciscan Conventuals, until in 1619 Pope Paul V gave them complete independence. In 1637 they counted 1,337 monasteries with 21,573 members. At the beginning the group experienced a severe crisis. The first vicar-general (Bassi, who was one of the two founders) returned to the Observants, the second (Louis of Fossombrone, the other founder) was deposed in 1536 and the fourth (Ochino) in 1542 became a Protestant.

BIBLIOGRAPHY: Fr. Cuthbert, *The Capuchins: A Contribution to the History of the Counter Reformation*, 1928; *Monumenta historica ordinis minorum Capucinorum*, Vol. I, Assisi, 1937; *Liber memorialis Ordinis Fratrum Minorum Capucinorum 1528–1928*, Rome, 1928.
[Sup.] ALBERT HYMA.

CARDINALS, COLLEGE OF: The rules governing the creation and status of cardinals, either residing in the Curia, or actually the heads of dioceses and ecclesiastical provinces, are found in the *Codex Juris Canonici*, canons 230–241, where the earlier legislation is reproduced without notable changes. The powers of the Sacred College during a vacancy of the Holy See are defined in the constitution *Vacante Sede Apostolica* of Pius X, modified by the decree *Cum proxime* of Pius XI, and the constitution *Vacantis Apostolicae Sedis* of Pius XII (see POPE).

Since the consistory held by Pius XII on Feb. 18, 1946, the Sacred College had become depleted by successive deaths, and numbered only forty-six cardinals on Nov. 29, 1952, when the pope decided to fill the vacancies by nominating twenty-four new cardinals, whose names were announced unofficially. One of the nominees, Mgr. Carlo Agostini, patriarch of Venice, died on Dec. 28, 1952, and was replaced on the original list by Mgr. Valerian Gracias, archbishop of Bombay. The new cardinals were created in the secret consistory of Jan. 12, 1953, and solemnly invested on Jan. 15.

After the consistory, there were twenty-six Italian cardinals. In 1954 four cardinals belonged to the Roman hierarchy in the United States, namely the Cardinals Mooney, archbishop of Detroit; Stritch, archbishop of Chicago; Spellman, archbishop of New York, and McIntyre, archbishop of Los Angeles, who was created in the 1953 consistory; two cardinals belonged to the Roman hierarchy in Canada, namely the Cardinals McGuigan, archbishop of Toronto, and Léger, archbishop of Montreal, who was created in the 1953 consistory. The deaths of several Italian cardinals since the consistory of 1953 modified again the composition of the Sacred College. [Sup. to CURIA, I, in Vol. III.]   GEORGES A. BARROIS.

CAREW LECTURES: Founded in 1873 by Joseph Carew and his wife, of South Hadley Falls, Mass., through a gift to the Hartford Theological Seminary (then the Theological Institute) of which he was a trustee. Lectures "for the benefit of the students and the public" are provided annually. Among the lecturers: Cyrus Hamlin, Henry Drummond, Woodrow Wilson, Talcott Williams, Kenyon L. Butterfield, William M. Ramsay; more recently, Herbert H. Farmer, Henry J. Cadbury, Louis Finkelstein, George H. C. MacGregor, George F. Thomas.

TERTIUS VAN DYKE.

CARILLON. See BELLS.

CARITAS: Founded in 1924, Caritas is a combination of Roman Catholic charitable organizations in Central Europe and Scandinavia. Under the direction of a general secretary in Luzerne, Switzerland, the work of the organization is administered by thirteen technical commissions which contain all the various fields of assistance and welfare. In 1949 the Holy See authorized Caritas as the representative of Catholic organizations to the United Nations.

Paralleling the growth of Catholic Charities (q.v.) in the United States has been the development of Caritas throughout Germany, Switzerland, Austria, Poland, Czechoslovakia, Denmark, Norway, and Sweden. Acting not only as a relief agency, these Caritas units have supported an extensive child welfare program while sponsoring such social welfare projects as social security (q.v.) and housing.

In most of these countries Caritas has achieved far-reaching contributions in the development of co-operative housing programs. Caritas-organized German co-operatives (q.v.) have constructed about 25,000 housing units since the war.

For years the various Caritas groups in the different European nations have been endeavoring to set up an international Catholic Charities organization. The secretariat, initiated by the Swiss Caritas, is looked upon as a primary step to such a federation. See also HILFSWERK, EVANGELISCHES.

THOMAS J. MCCARTHY.

CARLSTADT: His real name was Andreas Bodenstein of Karlstadt am Main. He was often wrongly interpreted, both in his own and in more recent times. Even today the experts are still experiencing great difficulties in trying to understand him properly. From 1505 he taught at Wittenberg, where in 1510 he received the degree of Th.D. and the position of archdeacon in the Allerheiligenstift. Staupitz at first and Luther later on induced him to turn more and more to St. Augustine. This can be seen in his 151 theses of April 26, 1517, published by Kolde in 1890 in *Zeitschr. fuer Kirchengeschichte,* Vol. XI, pp. 450 ff. They were intended as a sort of program or platform for the newly established faculty of theology. Even

more clearly can Augustine's influence be seen in his work, *Commentary on Augustine's De spiritu et littera,* written in 1517–19, and published in fragmentary form in 1905 by Barge, and in complete form by Ernst Kaehler in 1952. In this treatise Carlstadt departs from scholasticism and draws from Augustine, who was his chief source now, spiritual sustenance and thought leading to his later aptitude for mysticism and a desire to seek the "inner word" in various texts. In this manner his symbolical views of the sacraments were developed. A series of theses in 1518 led to an attack on Eck (q.v.) and his part in the dispute of 1519 at Leipzig, in which Carlstadt did not win fame. He was the first among Eck's opponents to take the floor, but failed to hold his own against his subtle adversary. In the first years of the Reformation he acted more radically than did Luther (q.v.), particularly after he had composed his work, *Von paepstlicher Heiligkeit,* which happened in 1520. His fight against celibacy and monasticism, especially against the Mass, through the introduction of a stormy administration of the communion service along supposedly Evangelical lines, disturbed Luther, who was then at the Wartburg (Dec. 25, 1521).

Luther attacked Carlstadt with pamphlets and letters, and finally an iconoclastic uprising in Wittenberg instigated by Carlstadt forced Luther to return home. The Zwickau prophets (q.v.) also had a hand in this affair. According to Luther, his colleague had done an injustice to those members of the local congregation who had clung to the time-honored respect for statues and paintings in the church buildings. With the exception of the ordinance for the City of Wittenberg of January 24, 1522, Carlstadt in his reformatory activities was largely dependent upon Luther, rather than being free to do as he saw fit. After the rift with the latter, Carlstadt in 1523 withdrew to the parish of Orlamuende, and in 1524 was expelled from the Electorate of Saxony, after having tried to force through his radical reforms in his local congregation. Luther in 1525 wrote his treatise, "Wider die himmlichen Propheten," against Carlstadt's mysticism and his symbolical interpretation of the communion service. Carlstadt did not actively support the Peasants' Revolt (see PEASANTS' WAR). After some tumultuous years and a temporary residence in the Electorate of Saxony, he removed in 1530 to Switzerland, and in 1534 became a professor at the University of Basel. There he propagated Zwinglian theology and church rites.

Both his personality and his theology have thus far been inadequately treated. The biography by Barge does contain much useful source material, but it is highly uncritical, for which reason it has been rather severely attacked by Karl Mueller and others. Carlstadt was a complicated figure with an undisciplined will but at times a great desire to win respect for himself. In his earlier years he was offensively rude and sharp, but later he became more moderate and considerate. His theology was a mixture of conservative, critical, and rationalistic thought, with ingredients of mystical and Lutheran trends. Its core was a true devotion to biblical precept and law determined by the desire to restore the primitive Christian church in its simplicity. Through his mystical writings he exerted a powerful influence on the Anabaptists and on Protestants who placed spiritual thought and values far above material. But he refused to join any of the sects.

BIBLIOGRAPHY: Schottenloher's bibliography, Vol. I (1933), 9616–9649, Vol. V (1939), 47138–47149; E. G. Schwiebert, *Luther and His Times*, 1950; R. Bainton, *Here I Stand, A Life of Martin Luther*, 1950; E. Freys and Herman Barge, "Verzeichnis der gedruckten Schriften des Andreas Bodenstein von Karlstadt," in *Zentralbl. fuer d. ges. Bibl. Wesen* (1904), pp. 153–179, 209–243, 305–331; Karl Mueller, *Luther und Karlstadt*, 1907; N. Mueller, *Die Wittenberger Bewegung 1521–1522*, 1911; W. Friedensburg, *Geschichte der Universitaet Wittenberg*, 1917; K. Bauer, *Die Wittenberger Universitaetstheologie und die Anfaenge der deutschen Reformation*, 1928; E. Hertzsch, *Karlstadt und seine Bedeutung fuer das Luthertum*, 1932; E. Kaehler, *Karlstadt und Augustin, Hallische Monographien*, No. 19, 1952.

[Sup.] D. HEINRICH BORNKAMM.

CARMELITES: As a result of the persecutions by the Seljuk Turks and the Saracens, the Carmelites about the middle of the thirteenth century departed for Europe, where, after a difficult period of adjustment (under the guidance of H. Simon Stock, Nicholas Gallus, and others), their golden age commenced. Among their outstanding scholars may be mentioned Gerard of Bologna, Guido Terreni, Sibert van Beek, Robert Walsingham, Joannes Baconthorp, and Michael of Bologna. They could also boast of saintly characters and authors of important religious compositions. Near the close of the Middle Ages a period of decline set in, and during the period of the Renaissance several attempts were made to reform the order as a whole or in part. An example of local reform is the work done by the Congregation of Mantua (led by the famous author Baptista Mantuanus), and the labors of Joannes Soreth. The latter in 1452 founded the second order of Carmel, the Carmelitesses. Gradually the devotion of the scapular developed into a popular custom. In this period flourished Arnoldus Bostius (Mariology), Franciscus Amelry (mystical treatises), Joannes Pascha (famed for his exercises in the way of the cross), and numerous other leaders.

About the year 1600 the two most important reforms took place. That of Saint Teresa of Avila and Saint Juan de la Cruz originated in 1562 in Spain, and in 1593 it led to the division of the order into two parts: the Carmelites With Shoes (Old Observation) and the Carmelites Without Shoes (Reform of Teresa).

The two authors just mentioned became models to many others in later times, exerting a powerful influence throughout the whole Roman Catholic Church. Among Carmelites Without Shoes their works were the basis of a large school of religious writers, including John of Jesus-Maria, Thomas of Jesus, Joseph of Jesus Maria, and Joseph of the Holy Spirit. The second reform was that of the French Carmelites, begun in 1609, with headquarters in Touraine. It remained confined to the Old Observation. This renewal of religious fervor was intended as a revival of the old tradition, particularly in connection with the practice of contemplation and the veneration of the Virgin Mary. The first great leader was Brother Jean de St. Samson, who wrote many mystical treatises, and taught the following: Dominicus a Sto. Alberto, Maurus a Puero Jesu, Marcus a Nativitate, and Leo a Sto. Jeanne. In Belgium, where the reform movement attained great success, the most influential leaders were Michael a Sto. Augustino, Daniel a Virgine Maria, and Maria a Sta. Theresia. The reform gradually was extended throughout the whole Old Observation.

In addition to the Touraine Reform Movement may be mentioned the influential writers and leaders in other regions, including S. Maria Magdalena de Pazzi, and Seraphina di Dio in Italy, and Michael de la Fuente in Spain, as representatives of the Old Observation. After a period of decline in the nineteenth century a new revival of religious power and fervor developed in the present century. There are now two new provinces in the United States. Among the leading representatives of recent times are Joannes Brenninger and Titus Brandsma, both of whom died in World War II; Brandsma suffered horrible persecutions at the hands of the Nazis just before he was about to publish the works of Gerard Zerbolt (*q.v.*) of Zutphen. The Reform of Teresa also has expanded in the past four decades, and it has one province in the United States. Among its great personalities are Edith Stein, Thérèse de Lisieux, Elisabeth de la Trinité, and Chrisogono a Jesu.

BIBLIOGRAPHY: J. Brenninger, O. Carm., *The Carmelite Directory of Spiritual Life*, 1951; T. Brandsma, O. Carm., *Carmelite Mysticism*, 1936; W. P. Mustard, *Eclogues of Baptista Mantuanus*, 1911; S. M. Bouchereaux, *La Réforme des Carmes en France et Jean de St. Samson*, 1950; A. Peers, *St. John of the Cross*, 1946; *Complete Works of Saint Teresa of Jesus*, ed. by A. Peers, 3 vols., 1946; Thérèse de Lisieux, *Collected Letters*, transl. by F. Sheed, 1948; Siverio O.C.D., *Historia del Carmen Descalzo en España, Portugal y América*, 14 vols. thus far, 1939– ; Antoine-Marie de la Présentation OCD, *Le Carmel en France*, 6 vols., 1936–39.

[Sup.] P. CANISIUS JANSSEN.

CARMICHAEL, AMY WILSON. See DOHNAVUR FELLOWSHIP.

CARNIVAL: The days of popular feasting and merrymaking previous to the beginning of the fast on Ash Wednesday. The name comes from the Latin *carnem levare,* "to take away the meat." In England, the carnival is called Shrovetide, ending on Shrove Tuesday, from the verb "to shrive," viz., "to make confession." In spite of this etymology, Shrovetide is also regarded as a time for lively rejoicing. Frequent excesses committed during carnival, especially in Latin countries, have prompted the Roman Church to institute ceremonies of propitiation, like, for instance, the forty hours (*q.v.*)

[Sup.] GEORGES A. BARROIS.

CAROLINE ISLANDS. See SOUTH SEA ISLANDS.

CARPOCRATES AND THE CARPOCRATIANS:

BIBLIOGRAPHY: E. Buonaiuti, *Gnostic Fragments* (1924), 51–57; E. de Faye, *Gnostiques et Gnosticisme* (1913), 391–397; H. Leclerq, *Dict. d'Archéologie Chrétienne et de Liturgie,* article "Carpocratiens," 1910; H. Leisegang, *Die Gnosis* (1924), 257–270; W. Voelker, *Quellen zur Geschichte der Christlichen Gnosis,* 1932.
[Sup.] JOHN WOOLMAN BRUSH.

CARTHUSIANS: At present there are eighteen monasteries for men and four convents for women. No institutions were founded outside of Europe. The order was noted particularly for its emphasis upon contemplation and prayer. Solitude and silence have always been characteristic. They always live in separate huts or houses, in which each member spends a large part of the day. The whole day is scrupulously divided into periods in accordance with strict rules. Although the members are essentially hermits, they do take part in communal exercises. During Lent and on important holidays they devote more time than is customary to prayer. The normal procedure is as follows: Arise at 5:45; perform various spiritual exercises before the noon meal which is served at 10:30, and during Lent at 11:30; next some recreation and study till 3:00; then more spiritual exercises till 4:30, when the evening meal is served; after this study and prayer till 7:00, when all go to bed; at 10:30 or 11:00 arise for the night vigil until 2:00 or 2:30. Meat is never consumed by them. Lent lasts from Sept. 15 to Easter, and during that period no dairy products or eggs are eaten, while on Fridays only bread and water are used. Silence is strictly enforced, but on Sundays for an hour and also during the walk on the other days the members may talk. On Christmas, Easter, Whitsunday, and White Thursday silence is maintained all day.

The chief purpose of the Carthusian rule is the union of the soul with God. Solitude and silence are means employed toward reaching this goal. The first consideration is purity of heart and surrender of all worldly attachments; the second simplicity, or the reduction of all things into One, which is God; the third the

negation of ambition and notoriety, so that on each grave only a white cross is erected but no name given, and no steps are taken that may lead to the declaration that any one member is or was a saint upon earth: *Cartusia sanctos facit sed non patefacit.* The fourth step is inner joy; the cultivation of this joy is a heritage of the founder.

BIBLIOGRAPHY: Guigo I, *Consuetudines,* in *Patr. Lat.,* Vol. 153; Henry of Calcar, *Ortus et decursus Ordinis cartusiensis,* ed. by H. B. C. W. Vermeer, 1929; Le Couteulx, *Annales Ordinis Cartusiensis,* 1887–91; N. Molin, *Historia Cartusiana,* 1903–6; C. Boutrais, *La grande Chartreuse par un Chartreux,* 7th ed., 1930; A. de Meyer and J. M. de Smet, *Guigo's "Consuetudines" van de eerste Kartuizers,* 1951.

[Sup.] A. R. M. KIEVITS.

CARTWRIGHT, THOMAS: Cartwright's birthplace was probably Royston, Hertfordshire, though he inherited a farm in Whaddon, Cambridgeshire. At Cambridge he came under the influence of Thomas Lever, Master of St. John's College and probably of Martin Bucer who was lecturer in Divinity, 1549–51. C. Borgeaud has found clear evidence of his being in Geneva, 1571–72. Cartwright shows no knowledge of the "Presbytery of Wandsworth" (1572), the existence of which rests on a later questionable statement by Richard Bancroft on the basis of an examination of John Field's papers. Cartwright was not the author of the First, nor, probably, of the Second, Admonition to Parliament of 1572. His period in Guernsey (1595–1601) was fruitful in the unification (1596) and strengthening of the Presbyterianism of Guernsey and Jersey, but the Form of Discipline there introduced by him and Edmund Snape is not to be identified with the Guernsey Discipline of 1574 with which he had no connection. His works of edification include a number of letters of counsel, of which *Two Godly and Comfortable Letters* published in 1589, on the themes of repentance and the confession of sins, are of special interest; *The Holy Exercise of a True Fast;* and a *Short Catechism,* which treats primarily of "the law and the gospel otherwise called the covenant of works and the covenant of grace." These are included, with his *Treatise on the Oath Ex-officio,* in *Cartwrightiana* by A. Peel and L. H. Carlson. A. F. S. Pearson has called attention to Cartwright's firm political Aristotelianism, which was brought into play in his debate before Elizabeth in 1564 and in his later controversies. In this he is in accord with his admiring mentor, Beza, but not with his friend, Andrew Melville.

BIBLIOGRAPHY: Three works by A. F. S. Pearson, *Der aelteste englische Presbyterianismus,* 1912; *Thomas Cartwright and Elizabethan Puritanism, 1535–1603,* 1935; and *Church and State: Political Aspects of Sixteenth Century Puritanism,* 1928, have greatly enlarged our knowledge of Cartwright. In the last-named book there is a valuable section on "Aristotelianism in Puritanism." D. J. McGinn, in *The Admonition Controversy,* 1949, gives an abridgment of the controversy with Whitgift (nearly 400 pages) and treats Cartwright as a controversialist in an unfavorable light. A. Peel and L. H.

Carlson in *Cartwrightiana*, 1950, have edited important texts of Cartwright's, with some of which his authorship is in doubt. See also C. Borgeaud, *Histoire de l'Université de Genève*, Vol. I, 1934.

[Sup.] JOHN T. McNEILL.

CARUS, PAUL: D. Feb. 11, 1919. In addition to his active editorial life, Carus wrote: *Karma; Nirvana; Eros and Psyche; Crown of Thorns; The Chief's Daughter; Godward; Nature and State; Sacred Tunes; Amitabha; Rise of Man; Story of Samson; Bride of Christ; God, an Enquiry into Man's Highest Ideals; The Pleroma, an Essay on the Origin of Christianity; Truth on Trial; Personality and the Interpersonal; Nietzsche and Other Exponents of Individualism; Mechanistic Principle and the Non-Mechanical; Principle of Relativity from the Standpoint of the Philosophy of Science; Truth and Other Poems; K'ung Fu Tze; Goethe;* and *The Venus of Milo*.

[Sup.] RAYMOND W. ALBRIGHT.

CARVER, WILLIAM OWEN: Theologian; b. Wilson County, Tenn., April 10. 1868; d. May 24, 1954. He studied at Boyle College, Tenn.; Richmond College, Va. (M.A., 1891); Southern Baptist Theological Seminary (Th.D., 1896); and in Europe (1908–09). He was ordained to the Baptist ministry (1891); and served in the pastorate (1889–1907). He was professor of philosophy and ancient languages at Boscobel College, Nashville, Tenn. (1893–95); and taught New Testament Interpretation at Southern Baptist Theological Seminary (1896–1923) and was also professor of comparative religion and missions (1899–1943; retired 1943); acting professor (1947–48); Norton Lecturer (1933–34, 1945–46). He was managing editor of the *Review and Expositor* (1919–42); contributing editor of *The Commission;* and author of *History of New Salem Church* (1903); *Baptist Opportunity* (1908); *Missions in the Plan of the Ages* (1909); *Missions and Modern Thought* (1910); *Acts Commentary* (1916); *All the World in All the Word* (1918); *The Bible a Missionary Message* (1921): *The Self-Interpretation of Jesus* (1926); *Thou, When Thou Prayest* (1928); *The Course of Christian Missions* (1932); *How the New Testament Came to be Written* (1933); *The Rediscovery of the Spirit* (1934); *The Furtherance of the Gospel* (1935); *Sabbath Observance* (1940); *Christian Missions in Today's World* (1942); *If Two Agree* (1942); *Why They Wrote the New Testament* (1946); *The Glory of God in the Christian Calling* (Ephesians) (1949).

WILLIAM A. MUELLER.

CASE, ADELAIDE TEAGUE: Episcopalian; b. at St. Louis, Mo., January 10, 1887; d. at Cambridge, Massachusetts, June 19, 1948. She studied at Bryn Mawr (A.B., 1908) and at Teachers College, Columbia (Ph.D., 1924), where she taught from 1919–41. She was Professor of Christian Education at the Episcopal Theological School (1941–48). She wrote: *Liberal Christianity and Religious Education* (1924); *As Modern Writers See Jesus* (1927); *Seven Psalms* (1935); *The Servant of the Lord* (1940); and contributed to *Religion: The Dynamic of Education* (1929); *Our Children* (1932); *Liberal Catholicism and the Modern World* (1934) and *The Church through Half a Century* (1936). CHARLES L. TAYLOR.

CASE, SHIRLEY JACKSON: Baptist; b. at Hatfield Point, New Brunswick, Canada, Sept. 28, 1872; d. at Lakeland, Florida, Dec. 5, 1947. He was educated at Acadia University (A.B., 1893; A.M., 1896; D.C.L. 1928); Yale (B.D., 1904; Ph.D., 1906; D.D., 1917), Marburg (1910). He taught in academies in New Brunswick and New Hampshire (1893–97); was instructor in New Testament Greek, Yale (1905–06); professor of history and philosophy of religion, Bates College (1906–08); taught New Testament interpretation at the University of Chicago (1908–17); and the history of early Christianity (1917–38); dean, Divinity School (1933–38). After retirement from the University of Chicago he became professor of religion and dean of School of Religion, Florida Southern College. He edited the *American Journal of Theology* (1912–20); and the *Journal of Religion* (1927–39). A theological liberal, he made distinguished contributions in the field of the historical study of the New Testament and the history of the early church, particularly stressing the environmental influences. Among his numerous books the most notable are *The Historicity of Jesus* (1912); *Evolution of Early Christianity* (1914); *The Millennial Hope* (1918); *The Revelation of John* (1919); *Social Origins of Christianity* (1923); *Jesus, A New Biography* (1927); *Experience of the Supernatural in Early Christian Times* (1929); *Jesus through the Centuries* (1931); *The Social Triumph of the Early Church* (1933). WILLIAM W. SWEET.

CASTELLIO, SEBASTIAN: Sebastian Castellio (1515–63) was one of the most intrepid champions of religious liberty in the sixteenth century and his denunciation of the execution for heresy of Michael Servetus in 1553 served more than aught else to precipitate the toleration controversy among Protestants. Castellio's views on the subject of tolerance were by that time already well matured. He was an exile for religion from France, who, having been associated first with Calvin during his exile at Strassburg, accompanied him on his return to Geneva and was assigned to the post of school teacher. In this capacity he produced a very lively dramatization of biblical stories which enjoyed an immense vogue. In them, one finds protests against the cruelty of Pharaoh and of

Joseph's brethren. Castellio left Geneva because he was denied ordination to the ministry on two doctrinal counts. He did not accept Calvin's interpretation of the descent of Christ into Hell nor could he regard *Song of Songs* of Solomon as an inspired book. Castellio went to Basel where he supported himself by manual labor until he was able to bring out his translations of the Bible into classical Latin and colloquial French. The Latin dedicated to Edward VI of England and the French to Henry II of France were both eloquent pleas for religious liberty. Castellio was rewarded for these labors by appointment to the professorship of Greek in the University of Basel.

Then came the execution of Servetus. The following year, 1554, Castellio brought out under the pseudonym of Martin Bellius a work entitled *De Haereticis, Concerning heretics and whether they are to be punished by the sword of the magistrate*, in which he assembled the opinions of many eminent Christians to the contrary and in several pseudonymous sections amplified his own objections. Prevented thereafter from publishing anything but classical works, he continued to compose books which found only a posthumous publication. The *Contra Libellum Calvini* came out in Holland in 1611. The *De Arte Dubitandi* was not published until 1937 by Elizabeth Feist (Mrs. Felix Hirsch). Castellio's reply to Calvin's associate, Beza, was only recently discovered by Professor Becker of Amsterdam and awaits publication at his hands.

The arguments of Castellio were essentially Erasmian, a combination of ethical, rational, and mystical elements. He contended that in the eyes of God creeds are not as important as deeds and that creed is to be adjudged the best which produces the best men. A second consideration was rational, an appeal to ignorance. Here a distinction was made between the essentials and the non-essentials for salvation, and those tenets alone, according to Castellio, could be considered essential which can be known and readily understood by all. The points over which heretics were burned in his day were precisely the most obscure and intricate, such as the doctrine of the Trinity. In the third place, he contended that religion is so inward in character and requires such heart-felt and sincere devotion that constraint is utterly futile to produce the desired attitude. Above all else, sincerity is requisite even though applied to erroneous ideas. The religious response must be spontaneous and cannot be constrained. All that force can do is to break down conviction and convert heretics into hypocrites. It may increase the quantity and diminish the quality of the church. It may even advertise heresy and provoke sedition. Finally, Castellio appealed in impassioned apostrophes to Christ,

the compassionate, to know whether he countenanced such deeds in his name.

BIBLIOGRAPHY: Ferdinand Buisson, *Sebastian Castellion*, 2 Vols., 1892; Étienne Giran, *Sebastien Castellion*, 1914; Roland H. Bainton, *Concerning Heretics*, 1935; idem, "Sebastian Castellio, Champion of Religious Liberty" in *Castellioniana*, 1951. Modern editions of Castellio's works: *Dialogues Sacrés*, 1932; *Traité des Hérétiques*, ed. Choisy, 1913; "De Arte Dubitandi," ed. E. Feist (Hirsch) in *Per la Storia degli Eretici Italiani*, Reale Accademia d'Italia VII, 1937.

[Sup.] ROLAND H. BAINTON.

CASUS RESERVATI. See RESERVATION OF SINS AND CENSURES.

CATECHISM, ROMAN: Also called Catechism of Trent, inasmuch as the Council, session 24, chapter 7, and session 25, recommended the publication of a handbook of Christian doctrine, as a help to pastors in their preaching and catechizing office. A commission of four theologians, under the direction of Cardinal (Saint) Carlo Borromeo, prepared the text which was published in 1566 under the full title *Catechismus ex decreto Concilii Tridentini ad parochos*. It was translated into Italian, French, German, and Polish, by order of Pope Pius V. Recent translations and adaptations have been composed since, the latest being an Italian version by L. Andrianopoli, *Il catechismo Romano del Concilio di Trento* (1946).

The Roman Catechism is divided in four parts: The Creed; the Sacraments; the Commandments; the Lord's Prayer. Its dogmatic authority is regarded as secondary to the decrees and canons of the Council, but it stands higher than catechisms composed by private persons, with the possible exception of Bellarmine's *Dottrina cristiana breve* (1597), and *Dichiarazione più copiosa della dottrina cristiana* (1598), which were chosen by the Vatican Council of 1870 as models for the intended compilation of a "Catechism Universal." The *Catechismus Catholicus* of the late Cardinal Gasparri (1930), in spite of its author's intention, was not approved for official use in the whole church, and, therefore, remains a private work.

BIBLIOGRAPHY: S. L. Skibniewski, *Geschichte des roemischen Katechismus*, 1903; P. Paschini, *Il catechismo Romano del Concilio di Trento: Le sue origini e la sua prima diffusione*, 1923.

GEORGES A. BARROIS.

CATECHISMS, LUTHER'S. See LUTHER'S TWO CATECHISMS.

CATECHUMENATE: Roman Catholic scholars like Dom B. Capelle and Dom P. de Puniet and the Protestants Michael Reu and Lewis J. Sherrill have given attention to the catechumenate in recent times. The importance of this institution in the life of the early church has been duly emphasized. "People the church had not hitherto known come to her each day in increasing numbers" (Lebreton and Zeiller). To integrate these into the life and thought of the church she developed the catechumenate early in the second century. By A.D. 450, it had reached its height, by A.D. 600, it had declined. It was designed for the perpetuation of pure teachings, against heretical influences, and for the development of high moral standards among the converts.

BIBLIOGRAPHY: Dom B. Capelle, "L'Introduction du catéchuménat à Rome," in *Recherches de Théologie ancienne et médiévalle*, Vol. V, 1933; Julius Leberton and Jacques Zeiller, *History of the Primitive Church*, Vol. II, 1947; Dom P. de Puniet, "Catechumenat," in *Dictionnaire de archéologie chrétienne et de liturgie*; Lewis J. Sherrill, *The Rise of Christian Education*, 1947; J. Michael Reu, *Catechetic, or Theory and Practice of Religious Education*, revised edition, 1927.

[Sup.] RUDOLF G. SCHADE.

CATENAE: I. Meaning of the Term:

The term "catenae" designates extracts selected from exegetical commentaries of older ecclesiastical writers, sometimes including Philo and Josephus, as St. John of Damascus did in his *Sacra Parallela*. Such commentaries, as a rule, were also called *exegeseis* or *exegetica*. Formerly, the fragments drawn from them were called *exegeticai eclogai;* they aimed at offering a consistent explanation of the Bible, thus saving the trouble of perusing original works. The term "catenae" does not seem to have been used previous to the late thirteenth century; very likely it comes from the title usually employed to designate the *Expositio continuata* on the Gospels by Thomas Aquinas.

Originally, *eclogai* were distinguished from scholia, a scholion being specifically an isolated explanation, a comment elucidating a difficult or obscure passage or an uncommon phrase, without any connection with what comes before or after. The making of scholia may be traced as far back as pre-Christian antiquity; Origen revived their use and they are to be found in the works of Cyril of Alexandria, Olympiodorus, Photius, in *Doctrina Patrum*, and in the thirteenth century in Nicephorus Blemmydes' works. Nowadays, this term might be accurately enough translated as "remarks" or "footnotes," thus plainly indicating the unconnected or fortuitous characteristic of such explanations. But as time passed on, partly owing to the reduced extent of both, no less than to a common fragmentary appearance, it came about that to the extracts from commentaries (eclogai) were gradually added such fortuitous notes (scholia); some copyists even gave to exegetical miscellanies the title of *synopsis scholicè*, so that without much danger of error, we may call "scholiasts" the last authors or compilers of catenae.

Catenae do not belong to the same literary category as dogmatic florilegia, these latter having been written with a view to prop a doctrinal thesis on the argument of tradition. Their growth is closely connected with the history of theological controversies, whereas catenae are not much concerned about the orthodoxy of the authors they borrow from. They do not care either about schools or their tendencies; catenae are valuable in reconstructing the exegesis of the Alexandrian and Antiochian schools, but their authors do not seem to have ever thought of opposing one to the other, or even to distinguish one from the other; it only happens, now and then, that in writing out an extract the copyist feels surprised or indignant, and lets the reader know about it.

II. Origin: Between the most ancient catena, which may be dated as far back as Procopius (sixth century) and the most recent one, which very likely is that of Macarios Chrysocephalos (fourteenth century), a long time elapsed during which the very conception of catenae, as well as their reciprocal connections and their external forms were more than once modified. Some consist of extracts directly quoted from patristic commentaries and put together without a break; others are appended round a central core which is either a commentary or a treatise about exegetical points, or a collection of homilies whose purely exegetical part was arranged in the form of questions and answers; some others are primarily a summary of a first compilation, and added to such abstracts are other fragments borrowed from different commentaries.

III. Form: Among the different forms under which catenae appear, the most frequent are: (1) The Scripture is placed in the middle of the page, quotations surrounding it; (2) the Scripture fills the middle of the page and extracts occupy the external margin; (3) the Scripture fills the page in a series of extracts and the chain comments on them in the same order; (4) the Scripture and extracts are disposed in two columns. The name of the author supporting each extract (lemma) is made apparent, most often being written in large, red letters, in the genitive. It is, as a rule, abbreviated, or reduced to consonants; hence there are often some difficulties in interpreting it. But it also happens that the lemma is missing, extracts having been copied out without a break with nothing to distinguish one from the other; such is the origin of pseudo-commentaries, as those of Peter of Laodicea.

IV. Value: To appreciate the value of a catena accurately, it is necessary to find out the first materials from which it was built up, then to discover the bases from which the different types and families sprang and grew up. Catenae appear in a different form from one Bible to another. It is therefore necessary to trace backwards in each of them the work of agglutination in its formation during centuries, so as to come back to the point it started from, and then to evaluate one by one the materials which were successively inserted into the whole building.

BIBLIOGRAPHY: R. Devreesse, "Chaînes exégétiques grecques," in *Dictionnaire de la Bible*, Supplément, I, 1928, coll. 1084–1233; G. Zuntz, "Die Aristophanen-Scholien der papyri," *Byzantion*, XIII (1938), 631–690; XIV (1935), 545–614. Octateuch: R. Devreesse, "Les commentateurs grecs de l'Octateuque," *Revue Biblique*, XLIV (1939), 166–191; XLV (1936), 364–384; H. Lewy, "Neue gefundene griech. Philonfragmente," *SBA*, 1932, 79–84. Psalms: R. Devreesse, *Le commentaire de Théodore de Mopsueste sur les Psaumes (I–LXXX)* (*Studi e Testi*, 93) 1939, Città del Vaticano. Isaiah: R. Devreesse, "L'édition du commentaire d'Eusèbe de Césarée sur Isaïe." *Revue Biblique*, XLII (1933), 540–555. Gospels: J. Reuss, *Matthaeus- Marcus- und Johannes-Katenen*, 1941; Klostermann-Benz. *Origenes Werke*, XII (1941) (Matthew); R. Devreesse, "Essai sur Théodore de Mopsueste." *Studi e Testi*, 141 (1941), 289–419 (John). Paul: Karl Staab, *Pauls Kommentare aus der griech. Kirche aus Katenenhandschriften gesammelt und herausgegeben*, 1933. On different books: M. Richard, "Les fragments exégétiques de Théophile d'Alexandrie et de Théophile d'Antioche," *Revue Biblique*. XLVII (1938), 387–397; E. M. Buytaert, "L'héritage littéraire d'Eusèbe d'Emése," *Bibliothèque du Muséon*, 24, 1949. Louvain.

[Sup.] ROBERT DEVREESSE.

CATHOLIC. See also ROMAN CATHOLIC.

CATHOLIC ACTION: In its most obvious sense Catholic Action is simply an act conformable to the principles of the Roman Catholic religion. In his letter *Quae Nobis* to Cardinal Betram of Breslau, Nov. 12, 1928, Pope Pius XI wrote: "Catholic Action is a true apostolate in which Catholics of every social class participate, and thus come to group themselves, in thought and in work, around centers of sound doctrine and manifold social activity, legitimately constituted, and assisted and sustained accordingly by the authority of the bishops."

Catholic Action can be understood in a wide or in a narrow sense. For Catholic Action to exist in the wider sense it is sufficient that an association or a specific work of Catholics should have an apostolic scope and that it be approved by the proper ecclesiastical authority. For example, Catholics working on behalf of the educational theater, for the stimulation of the fine arts, for a society on behalf of the Catholic press, in an anti-blasphemy league, or in an organization striving to improve public morals—these are all examples of Catholic Action by the apostolate for the application of Catholic teaching to a wide scope of social endeavor.

Catholic Action, in the more narrow sense, is action by laymen in which they carry out every form of apostolate for the direct assistance of the ecclesiastical hierarchy. Not only is this form of Catholic Action carried on by the laity at the behest of the hierarchy, but it is also carried on under the direct supervision of the clergy. When endowed with these requisites Catholic Action can call itself official in the sense that it is officially willed and recognized by the church.

Both in the wide and narrow sense, however, Catholic Action constitutes apostolic activity of laymen in conformity with the principles of the Catholic faith.

BIBLIOGRAPHY: Luigi Civardi, *A Manual of Catholic Action*, 1943.

GILBERT L. ODDO.

CATHOLIC APOSTOLIC CHURCH: Since the death in 1901 of the last "divinely called apostle," there have been no ordinations in this religious body which is popularly called Irvingite. On this account, as well as on account of the absence of missionary activity, there has been no growth. The U.S. religious census of 1936 reported seven congregations with 2,577 members. More vigorous is the New Apostolic Church of North America (*q.v.*), which claims to continue the original teachings of the movement.

BIBLIOGRAPHY: P. E. Shaw, *The Catholic Apostolic Church, Sometimes Called Irvingite*, 1946.

[Sup.] THEODORE G. TAPPERT.

CATHOLIC CHARITIES, NATIONAL CONFERENCE OF: Organized in 1910, the Conference represents an initial effort to fuse all the varied social organizations that are engaged in Roman Catholic charitable work throughout the United States. The Conference has provided advice to local agencies of the Catholic Charities through special bulletins and surveys together with regional and national congresses. Active in serving Catholic religious communities engaged in charitable work, the National Conference has attempted to unify their labors through frequent meetings so as to discuss and implement their mutual activities. An important information bulletin is distributed to diocesan agencies by national headquarters offering counsel on current problems.

A distinguishing feature of the Catholic Charities program has been the development of central diocesan bureaus, the first of which was established in 1903. There were (1952) some 265 diocesan Catholic Charities centers in the United States.   THOMAS J. McCARTHY.

CATHOLIC EVIDENCE GUILD: Originated in England in 1918 as a lay movement for the diffusion of Roman Catholic truth through outdoor speaking. Guild work in the United States was formally introduced in 1931. The Guild talks are always designed to define and explain Catholic beliefs and not to criticize or attack other religions. Guildsmen are enjoined to speak only on a subject that is readily known to them and never to give an answer of which they are uncertain. Priests often avail themselves of Guild platforms and direct the society's regular program of devotions.

THOMAS J. McCARTHY.

CATHOLIC HOUR: One of the oldest nationwide religious radio programs in the United States. Inaugurated March 2, 1930, the half-hour presentation is heard over 130 stations of the National Broadcasting Company on a free time basis. Leading Roman Catholic speakers, outstanding choirs, and special features are offered in the program produced by the National Council of Catholic Men, Washington, D.C.

THOMAS J. McCARTHY.

CATHOLICITY. See MARKS OF THE CHURCH.

CATHOLIC LAYMEN'S ASSOCIATIONS: Two state-wide bodies of Roman Catholic laity organized to publicize the truth of Catholicism in predominantly non-Catholic areas.

The Association of Georgia was founded in 1916 to refute false charges against the Catholic Church by publishing thousands of pamphlets and newspaper advertisements designed to present the truth about misunderstood Catholic practices and beliefs. In 1920 the Association began regular publication of a newspaper, the *Bulletin,* which is circulated among Catholics and non-Catholics in Georgia.

In order to promote friendship between the Catholic and non-Catholic elements, the North Carolina Association was formed by Bishop Vincent S. Waters in 1946. Following the guidance of the Georgia organization, the North Carolina unit now publishes the *North Carolina Catholic,* a weekly newspaper.

THOMAS J. McCARTHY.

CATHOLIC REFORMATION. See COUNTER REFORMATION.

CATHOLIC SOCIAL GUILD. See SOCIAL GUILD, CATHOLIC.

CATHOLIC STUDENTS, INTERNATIONAL MOVEMENT OF. See PAX ROMANA.

CATHOLIC UNITY LEAGUE. See UNITY LEAGUE, CATHOLIC.

CATHOLIC WELFARE CONFERENCE, NATIONAL. See WELFARE CONFERENCE, NATIONAL CATHOLIC.

CAUSALITY: Is the relation between cause and effect. The term cause has two different, though related and occasionally identified, meanings. In scientific usage cause means any antecedent or contemporary event or complex of events invariably followed or accompanied by some other event or complex of events known as the effect. Metaphysically, cause means the power or efficient agent producing any event, complex of events, or thing. The concept of cause probably arose from man's experienced activity in producing results and his observation of analogous sequences of environmental events.

Leucippus (*ca.* 450 B.C.) first stated clearly the principle of causality: "Nothing happens at random but everything through a cause and necessity." Aristotle distinguished four types of causes: (1) material cause, that out of which something is made; (2) formal cause, the form or pattern used in making it; (3) efficient cause, the power or force producing an effect; and (4) final cause, the end or purpose for which something is made. Aristotle did not succeed, however, in making clear either the basis for the assumption of causal relationship in nature or the character of the efficacy of natural causes in producing effects. Aenesidemus followed by Sextus Empiricus challenged the validity of the concept by pointing out that the terms cause and effect as correlatives have only circular meaning, and that we actually do not experience causal relation in nature.

The advent of modern science re-enforced the concept of causality as necessary relation. The correlations obtained between mathematical formulation and empirical observation, particularly in the work of Newton, led to the assumption that the physical world is governed by necessary mathematical relations. Laplace expressed the classical ideal by contending that a superhuman mathematician knowing the position and momentum of every atom at any one time could calculate all past and future occurrences. The assumption that the cause must be like and equal to or greater than the effect found metaphysical application among rationalists like Descartes and empiricists like Locke in their arguments for the existence of God.

Hume in analyzing the meaning and experiential base of the concept of causality undermined both philosophic and scientific faith in knowledge of necessary causal relation. We do not experience any relation between objects that is rightly called necessary connection. All we observe are repeated sequences of sense impressions which lead the mind through custom or habit to expect their repetition in the future. But such expectation is rationally unwarranted, for "we have no reason to draw any inference concerning any object beyond those of which we have had experience." With certain causal knowledge also disappeared certain prediction and induction. The necessity for finding a new foundation for scientific procedure and the imperiled physics of Newton seemed imperative.

Kant accepted Hume's challenge and sought a new foundation by shifting investigation from the data of knowledge to its presuppositions. Scientific knowledge including causal relations is not given in sensation but is the result of the synthetic activity of the mind in interpreting sense-data coherently. According to Kant, causality is a category of the understanding, i.e., one of the a priori forms or principles by means of which the mind spontaneously orders its experience and without which intelligible experience would be impossible. Kant thus gave warrant for continued use of causality either as a principle of interpretation or as a principle of economy of thought (methodological justification), but not for the assumption of certain knowledge of a closed causal physical system independent of the human mind.

As a result of the work of Hume and Kant and advances in physics, it has become progressively evident that science (q.v.) is not concerned with productive relations between events but with descriptive generalizations of their uniform sequences. Scientific causality has become restricted to those uniform sequences which admit of possible extrapolation or prediction. The criterion of causality is successful extrapolation but with the recognition that causation may not be provable in any particular case. The applicability and relevance of the principle has been further restricted by the development of quantum physics and the discovery of Heisenberg's Uncertainty Principle which states the impossibility of extrapolation within certain well defined limits on the subatomic level. Accordingly, some investigators, e.g., Eddington, insist that the principle of causality must be abandoned in science. Others, e.g., Schlick, hold that its applicability is unchanged except on subatomic levels. Still others, e.g., Planck and Einstein, hold to causality as a scientific ideal and heuristic principle guiding the direction of scientific investigation.

The problem of metaphysical causality (the power in, or giving rise to, events) becomes more acute in the light of the scientific restrictions of the term. While positivists (q.v.) maintain that knowledge is limited to the uniform sequences of science, other thinkers contend that enumeration of the members of a uniform sequence and their time order is no explanation of the sequence. How and why events follow in sequence is as important as the fact that they do. Answers to the problem have varied from materialistic accounts in terms of impact and transmission of "force" by inert bodies to pantheistic and absolute idealistic assertions that all agency is the immanent activity of God or the Absolute. Excepting materialists and positivists, most metaphysical investigators recognize the relevancy of human experiences of willing, feeling, striving, thinking, and purposing as well as sensing as data in the causal problem. Any adequate account of productive causality in the universe must include human experience plus any evidence of direction, kind of organization, and types of integration discoverable in wider areas.

BIBLIOGRAPHY: Aristotle, *Metaphysics;* Sextus Empiricus, *Outlines of Pyrrhonism,* I, 17, and III, 4, 5; Hume, *Treatise of Human Nature,* III; Kant, *Kritik der reinen Vernunft;* B. P. Bowne, *Metaphysics,* 1882; A. N. Whitehead, *Process & Reality,* 1929; Moritz Schlick, "Causality" in *University of California Publications in Philosophy* 15, 1932; L. S. Stebbing, *Philosophy and the Physicists,* 1932; A. S. Eddington, *New Pathways in Science,* 1933; Max Planck, *The Philosophy of Physics,* 1936;

Albert Einstein, *Out of My Later Years,* 1950; C. J. Ducasse, *Nature, Mind, and Death,* 1951; Hans Reichenbach, *The Rise of Scientific Philosophy,* 1952.

RICHARD MARION MILLARD.

CAVERT, SAMUEL McCREA: Presbyterian; b. at Charlton, N. Y., Sept. 9, 1888. He studied at Union College (B.A., 1910), Columbia University (M.A., 1914), and Union Theological Seminary (B.D., 1915), and was a fellow of Union Theological Seminary in the Orient (1916–17). He was a chaplain in the United States Army (1918–19). In 1919 he joined the staff of the Federal Council of the Churches and in 1921 was elected general secretary, serving through 1950, when it united with other agencies to form the National Council of the Churches of Christ in the U. S. A., of which he became the first general secretary. He was chairman of the committee on arrangements for the first assembly of the World Council of Churches held in Amsterdam in 1948. He was executive officer for the United States of the World Council of Churches (1953–   ). He wrote *Securing Christian Leaders for Tomorrow* (1926), *The Adventure of the Church* (1927) and (with H. P. Van Dusen) edited *The Church through half a Century* (1936).

CELANO, THOMAS OF: In 1214 he became Friar Minor, in 1222 superior of the Franciscan monasteries in Germany, notably at Mainz, Cologne, and Worms. In 1223 he returned to Italy. In 1228 he wrote the *Vita prima* of St. Francis of Assisi, next the *Vita secunda, Tractatus de miraculis, Legenda S. Clarae.* He was rector of the convent of Clarissa sisters at Varro near Tagliacorso, where he died and was buried. On his tombstone it was recorded that he wrote *Dies Irae* and was named *Beatus.* The year of his death is still unknown.

BIBLIOGRAPHY: *Analecta Franciscana,* Vol. X, 1927; M. Bihl, "Disquisitiones Celanensis" in *Archivum Franciscanum historicum,* XX (1927), and ff., P. Hoonhout, *Het Latijn van Thomas van Celano, biograaf van S. Franciscus,* 1947; V. Facchinetti, *Tomasso da Celano,* 1918.

[Sup.] WILLIBRORD LAMPEN.

CELE, JOHANNES (JAN): His school at Zwolle was discussed at great length by A. Schoengen, archivist at Zwolle. Its importance in the history of the Northern Renaissance and the Reformation is tremendous. Hans Baron, in his well-known article which appeared in 1925 in *Historische Zeitschrift,* tried to minimize this importance, arguing that the enrollment figures given in all the sources must be interpreted in the light of humanistic exaggeration. He was entirely mistaken, and Henry S. Lucas, in his textbook, *Renaissance and Reformation,* repeats correctly the figures for the schools at Zwolle and Deventer. Of particular significance is the study of the Bible in the elementary public schools, begun for the first time on a large scale by Cele and other men connected with the

Brethren of the Common Life. That is the reason why the parents of Thomas à Kempis, Erasmus, and Luther sent these young men to Deventer and Magdeburg, in order to receive the new type of instruction.

BIBLIOGRAPHY: A. Schoengen, *Die Schule zu Zwolle von ihren Anfaengen bis zu dem Auftreten des Humanismus*, 1898; Albert Hyma, *The Brethren of the Common Life*, 1950.

[Sup.] ALBERT HYMA.

CELEBES. See MALAY ARCHIPELAGO.

CELSUS: Celsus writes just after the Christian martyrdoms of 177; his work can be regarded as the literary or propagandist justification of the political action. He represents the religious Middle Platonism with which most of the apologists (whose works he does not know) were trying to come to terms. Origen calls him an Epicurean, but this is probably a term of abuse. Celsus relies on Jewish sources (perhaps including Philo) for some of his criticisms of the Old Testament and of the Christian gospel. He is acquainted with some of the Christian heresies, such as those of Marcion and of the Ophites, but he is usually able to distinguish them from the "Great Church." He has no sympathy with either. On the other hand, Origen attacks Celsus rather bitterly because his own theology is essentially Christian but makes use of Middle Platonic language in its formulation.

BIBLIOGRAPHY: O. Gloeckner, *Celsi* ΑΛΗΘΗΣ ΛΟΓΟΣ, 1924; A. Miura-Stange, *Celsus und Origenes*, 1926); R. K. A. Bader, *Der* ΑΛΗΘΗΣ ΛΟΓΟΣ *des Kelsos*, 1940; A. Wifstrand, "Die Wahre Lehre des Kelsos," *Bull. de la soc. royale des lettres à Lund* (1942), 391–431; P. de Labriolle, *La réaction païenne*, 2nd ed., 1942, 111–69; W. Nestle in *Archiv fuer Religionswiss.*, XXXVII (1942), 51–100 (on Celsus, Porphyry, and Julian).

[Sup.] ROBERT M. GRANT.

CELTIC CHURCH IN BRITAIN AND IRELAND:

BIBLIOGRAPHY: Additional information may be found in G. F. Browne, *The Christian Church in These Islands before Augustine*, 2nd ed., 1895; C. Plummer, *Vitae Sanctorum Hiberniae*, 2 vols., 1910; J. E. Lloyd, *A History of Wales, from the Earliest Times to the Edwardian Conquest*, 2 vols., 1911; A. B. Scott, *The Pictish Nation; Its People and Its Church*, 1918; J. Macnaught, *The Celtic Church and the See of Peter*, 1927; J. F. Kenney, *The Sources for the Early History of Ireland: an Introduction and Guide*, Vol. I, *Ecclesiastical*, 1929; L. Gougaud, *Christianity in Celtic Lands*, 1932; W. D. Simpson, *The Celtic Church in Scotland*, 1935; W. D. Simpson, *Saint Ninian and the Origins of the Christian Church in Scotland*, 1940. [Sup.] HARRY KIMBER.

CENSORSHIP: According to the actual discipline of the Roman Church, the following categories of books and periodicals are to be submitted to the judgment of ecclesiastical authorities before being printed: Bible texts and studies; devotional and theological books; books whose subject matter is formally related to religion and morals; devotional pictures; documents concerning procedures of beatification or canonization not yet terminated; lists of current indulgences; collections of decrees from the Roman Congregations; liturgical books; versions and new editions of books already approved.

The responsibility of presenting such writings for examination rests with the author and publisher, but not with the printer. The ordinary of the author, or the bishop in whose diocese the publishing house or the printing shop is located, are generally competent in granting the imprimatur, by which permission is given to print the book submitted for approval.

Writings printed in violation of the above rules, as well as any books blasphematory, obscene, or fostering heresy, may not be read by unauthorized Roman Catholics, even though such books are not actually inscribed in the *Index Librorum Prohibitorum*, i.e., the catalogue of books listed by the Congregation of the Holy Office as notorious and subversive of Christian faith and morals. Cf. *Codex Juris Canonici*, can. 1384–1405. [Sup.] GEORGES A. BARROIS.

CENSURES: In Roman canon law, penalties inflicted on baptized Christians for sinful acts committed deliberately and with obstinacy against public order in the church. The purpose of such penalties is to vindicate the inviolability of church laws, and induce delinquents to amend their ways. In order to achieve this goal, the transgressor is deprived of some spiritual privileges otherwise enjoyed by the faithful, until he is absolved from the censure, upon condition of recanting. The privileges of which delinquents are commonly deprived by censures are the following: reception of the sacraments, participation in or attendance at the ceremonies of the church, any public ecclesiastical office or dignity, the reception of income from benefices, and the exercise of functions proper to ordained clerics. It is to be noted that censures and their absolution belong to the *forum externum* or external order of the church, and are distinct from the administration of the sacrament of penance, which belongs to the *forum internum* or order of conscience.

Canon law distinguishes two kinds of censures according to the manner in which they are inflicted. Some are individually notified following a judicial sentence, whenever a previous admonition has failed to elicit a favorable response from the transgressor. They are known as censures *ferendae sententiae*. Others are prescribed once and for all as prospective sanctions of specific infractions described by the Code of Canon Law, no admonition nor sentence being necessary. They are called censures *latae sententiae*.

Censures fall into three categories, viz., excommunication, by which individual transgressors are more or less rigorously withdrawn from the communion or consortium of the faithful; interdict, a collective penalty by which an entire group, while remaining in the communion of the church and still enjoying the essential ministrations of religion, is deprived of the external pomp and solemnity with which the liturgical ceremonies are normally conducted; suspension, which is pronounced against a cleric, and deprives him of his office or benefice, or both.

Although the absolution from censures is an act of jurisdiction *in foro externo,* i.e., of administrative concern, priests simply empowered to receive confessions may nevertheless absolve penitents from ordinary censures. However, the authority competent *in foro externo* may demand proof that the absolution was actually granted.

Special faculties are required to absolve from censures inflicted by decision of an ecclesiastical superior, also known as censures *ab homine,* and of censures "reserved" by law. The absolution from the former belongs to the one who inflicted the penalty, his delegate, or successor. The absolution from the latter is reserved to the ordinary or, in proportion of the offense, to the Holy See, "commonly," "specially," or "most specially."

A penitent in danger of death may be absolved from any censures by any priest. Should he recover, however, he is under strict obligation of notifying within a month the authority which pronounced the sentence in the case of a censure *ab homine,* or, in the case of a censure *latae sententiae* reserved "most specially" to the Holy See, the Roman tribunal of the *Sacra Poenitentiaria.*

BIBLIOGRAPHY: *Codex juris canonici,* canons 2241-2285; F. M. Cappello, *Tractatus canonico-moralis de censuris,* 1933; "Censura," III, in *Enciclopedia Cattolica,* III, 1949.

GEORGES A. BARROIS.

CENSUS: It is now widely admitted that a census, as described in Luke 2:1 ff., (1) may have taken place in Herod's reign, (2) may have involved the return of everyone to his original home, (3) may have formed part of an empire-wide enrollment, (4) may have been held during Quirinius' first governorship of Syria. It is rare, however, to find all four admissions made by the same person; cf. Lily Ross Taylor, *AJP,* LIV (1933), 120 ff., who allows the first three but does not think Quirinius was legate of Syria at the time.

For (1) we have the statements of Josephus that towards the end of Herod's reign Augustus treated him as a subject rather than a friend, and all Judaea took an oath of allegiance to Augustus and Herod (*Antiqq.* xvi, 9, 3; xvii, 2, 4). Cf. the census imposed in A.D. 36 on the client kingdom of Antiochus (Tacitus, *Annals* vi, 41).

For (2) we have a papyrus of A.D. 104, where the prefect of Egypt orders Egyptians to return home that the customary census by household may be carried out (Frederic G. Kenyon and

H. Idris Bell, *Greek Papyri in the British Museum,* III [1907], No. 904). Luke "seems to have been recording a custom familiar in Judaea when he says that everyone was ordered to go to his own city" (L. R. Taylor, *op. cit.,* 131).

For (3) we have scattered evidence of censual activity in various parts of the empire between 11 and 8 B.C., the evidence for a census in Egypt in 10–9 B.C. being practically conclusive (cf. U. Wilcken, *Papyruskunde,* I [1912], 192 ff.).

For (4) the evidence is more disputable. Sir William M. Ramsay adduced inscriptional evidence, additional to the Lapis Venetus (*CIL,* III, 6687) and Titulus Tiburtinus (*CIL,* XIV, 3613), suggesting that Quirinius commanded the Homanadensian campaign as legate of Syria between 12 and 6 B.C. (*Bearing of Recent Discovery* . . . [1915], 223 ff.; *JRS,* VII [1917], 271 ff.). (Cf. similar use of Syrian provincial troops against the Clitae in A.D. 36 and 52 [Tacitus, *Annals* vi, 41, xii, 55]. But this is not universally agreed. It is difficult to fit a Syrian governorship of Quirinius within these years; some think he subdued the Homanadensians as *legatus extraordinarius* of Syria (Ramsay, Lodder); others, as legate of Galatia (Syme, Roos). Certainty must await further evidence. Solutions which require alteration of basic texts are suspect. B. S. Easton (*Commentary on Luke* [1926], 20 ff.) and J. W. Jack (*ET,* XL [1928–9], 496 ff.) read "Saturninus" for "Quirinius" in Luke 2:2, and similarly unconvincing emendations and rearrangements of Josephus' narrative have been proposed by F. Spitta, *ZNTW,* VII (1906), 281 ff.; W. Weber, *ZNTW,* X (1909), 307 ff.; W. Lodder, *Die Schaetzung des Quirinius bei Flavius Josephus,* 1930; T. Corbishley, *JRS,* XXIV (1934), 43 ff., *Klio,* XXIX (1936), 81 ff., *Scripture,* I (1946), 77 ff.

See further M. J. Lagrange, *Rev. Bibl.,* VIII (1911), 60 ff.; W. M. Calder, *Discovery,* I (1920), 100 ff., *Class. Rev.,* XVI (1927), 151; F. Bleckmann, *Klio,* XVII (1921), 104 ff.; E. Groag, Pauly-Wissowa's *Realencyclopaedie,* Ser. II, 4 (1931), *s.v.* "Sulpicius (90)," 822 ff.; R. Syme, *Klio,* XXVII (1934), 131 ff.; A. G. Roos, *Mnemosyne,* Ser. III, 9 (1941), 306 ff.

[Sup.] FREDERICK FYVIE BRUCE.

CENSUS, RELIGIOUS. See STATISTICS, ECCLESIASTICAL.

CENTER PARTY: A political party in Germany which reflected and espoused the interests of the Roman Catholic Church. Several unsuccessful or short-lived attempts had been made to form such a party before the Center Party came into being in 1870. It was strengthened during the subsequent *Kulturkampf* (see GERMANY, I, 3, in Vol. IV), and from then until the rise of National Socialism the party controlled an average of about 100 seats in the *Reichstag.* Inasmuch as Catholic bishops sponsored the election of its candidates, the party exposed itself to the charge of being a confessional rather than a political party.

BIBLIOGRAPHY: F. K. Krueger, *Government Politics of the German Empire*, 1915; L. K. Goetz, *Das Zentrum eine konfessionelle Partei*, 1911; L. Bergstrasser, *Der politische Katholizismus, 1815–1914*, 2 vols., 1921–23; Joseph N. Moody (ed.), *Church and Society: Catholic Social and Political Thought and Movements, 1789–1950*, 1953.
THEODORE G. TAPPERT.

CENTRAL AMERICA: The Census of the Americas (1950–51) reported Central America's population to be 8,835,357, practically doubled since 1900: Costa Rica, 800,875; El Salvador, 1,858,656; Guatemala, 2,787,030; Honduras, 1,-533,625; Nicaragua, 1,053,189; Panama, 801,982.

In these preponderantly Indian and mestizo agricultural republics, the white or near white minorities still largely direct their destinies, but the Indian is receiving greater attention and has been taking a more important place since the organization, in 1940, of the Inter-American Indian Institute under the leadership of the Mexican Evangelical statesman, Moses Saenz. The Indians of El Salvador have become adapted most to modern dress and life; the Guatemalans least. Panama, with its more primitive Indians, is still the least developed, except along the Canal, having barely ten percent of its tillable soil under cultivation.

Impelled by changing world conditions, five ministers of foreign affairs of these respective countries, undaunted by past failures to federate, signed on Oct. 14, 1951, the historic Charter of San Salvador. (The door has been left open for Panama.) This was a new step toward federation through a sort of UNESCO program, within the framework of the United Nations rather than by way of international law.

Economic conditions in many parts of Central America are described by such familiar phrases as, single product economy, two-product Central America (bananas and coffee), paternalistic plantation production, subsistence farming, low-wage peonage, or, Ernest Galarza's phrase, ". . . . a penthouse of free enterprize on the adobe foundation of feudalism." In happy contrast is Costa Rica's proprietary agriculture, a healthy situation where two-thirds of the people live on farm lands in a healthy climate on the central plateau. The hastening chain reaction forces which are ending political colonialism portend the same fate for economic colonialism, even in Central America.

Latest U.N. statistics, reported by the Golden Rule Foundation (*q.v.*), show that the annual per capita income in all Central America is only $108: Costa Rica, $125; El Salvador, $92; Guatemala, $77; Honduras, $83; Nicaragua, $89; Panama, $183.

A steadily growing Evangelical movement has a constituency of 150,000 with some 500 churches. Schools, increasingly evangelistic, are crowded, though expensive for the poor and strongly opposed by the Roman Church. Modern methods are being used: airplanes save time and lives; evangelical radio programs are increasing in number and efficiency; denominations co-operate in National Evangelical Councils. In the Canal Zone are six union churches with nine denominations co-operating.

Both Roman Catholic and Evangelical missions in Guatemala have been surveyed recently by the Catholic historian Mary P. Holleran. Her frank, objective report, entitled "Today's Picture," affords an opportunity for Evangelicals and Catholics to understand each other's point of view and the task in Guatemala and other similar fields.

The author sees in the physical deterioration of Catholic church property a symbol of social, spiritual, and political deterioration. The people have suffered spiritually from having been too long without teaching and guidance: expropriation of schools and other institutions brought about a "deterioration, disintegration, and devastation that is well nigh fatal." The Indian persists in integrating rites and customs of his Mayan ancestors with his Roman Catholicism, as may be seen daily at the famous church in Chichicastenango. For nearly 3,000,-000 people there are only 120 priests, mostly foreign, who know no Indian language. The native priest, often "ignorant or dirty or greedy," is very poor because the church is poor and he is not, and cannot be expected to be, a product superior to his social and economic environment.

Marriage for Catholics requires two ceremonies, one civil and one religious. Both require money, of which the Indian has very little. He also fears contact with government officials, and the priest comes only about once a year; so very few Indians get married, possibly as few as two percent in some parts.

Anticlericalism (*q.v.*) is in reality a civil conflict. One of history's greatest lessons ". . . is that when the Church acts like a political party it will be treated as one."

Another sad situation is pointed out: that of ". . . a chasm of separation deep and complete" between Catholic and Evangelical. They neither fraternize nor co-operate in any work for the community. In recent years it has been easier for Evangelical missionaries to enter the country than for Catholic priests. They do not wear priestly garb, and come to teach or nurse. Their organization is growing but there is no great increase in permanent conversions. Their programs seem not well adapted to the social climate. But they have done a good deal of pioneering in the Indian language problem. The author has praise for many Evangelical missionaries and their various types of service to the country. In conclusion, she considers that the state-church conflict is still far from settled.

BIBLIOGRAPHY: Mary P. Holleran, *Church and State in Guatemala*, 1949; M. Searle Bates, *Religious Liberty: An Inquiry*, 1945; J. Lloyd Mecham, *Church and State in Latin America*, 1934; Kenneth G. Grubb and E. J. Bingle, *World Christian Handbook*, 1949.

[Sup.] JAY CARLETON FIELD.

CERTAINTY: F. R. Tennant emphasizes the distinction between certitude and certainty, the former being the convincedness of the believer, a state of mind, and the latter being an objective character assigned to propositions (*Philosophical Theology* I, p. 290). John Dewey, on the other hand, urging the necessity of ending the false segregation of action and thought, maintained that certainty is a will-o'-the-wisp, and that we can hope at the most for a clarification of the possibilities of experience (*The Quest for Certainty*). In the sphere of morals, doubt has been cast on the idea of certainty by Oswald Spengler (*The Decline of the West*), by the Marxists, and by many others; but others base a conviction that certainty is attainable in morals on the experience of the "ought" which is "a primary and unique meaning, as little derivable from another as blue from bitter" (*The Idea of the Holy,* ch. VII, by Rudolf Otto).

A Christian doctrine of religious certainty has its scriptural basis chiefly in Rom. 8:15 ff. and Gal. 4:6 where it is said that the divine Spirit bears witness within the spirit of man. A familiar term is "full assurance" (Col. 2:2; I Thess. 1:5; Heb. 6:11; and Heb. 10:22). What is presented to us is not a rational certainty, but the certainty of encounter. It is more than knowing *what* we believe. We know *whom* we have believed (I John 4:16; II Tim. 1:12). It is impossible for us by any observation or any thinking of our own to reach what God is and wills. We are thrown back on his own revelation. There are differences in the mode of conceiving the impact of this revelation.

I. Certainty is based on the luminous quality of an inner experience. It is not necessarily implied that there should be any minimizing of the value of Scripture or of the church, but the tendency is to adopt a subjective standard of certainty. The case is fairly stated by Robert Barclay (*An Apology:* Proposition Second). The work of the Lutheran, Frank of Erlangen, is most appropriately considered here (*System of Christian Certainty*) since he pointed to the convincingness of one particular inner experience, that of regeneration, which is beyond all questioning and free from all dubiety. Nevertheless, Frank did not rest in that subjective experience, for the consciousness of being reborn leads to other certainties.

II. Certainty is based on some form of authority. Augustine (in the Commentary on St. John's Gospel, XXIX, 6), makes use of the principle contained in the Septuagint version of Isaiah 7:9, "Unless you believe, you will not understand." At one point (*Contra Epistolam Manichaei quam vocant Fundamenti,* Sec. 6) he even declares, "I would not believe the gospel unless the authority of the Catholic Church compelled me thereto." It should be noticed, however, that this was spoken in the heat of controversy and is nowhere repeated; that "authority" here means "testimony" (see Warfield, *Tertullian and Augustine,* and J. H. S. Burleigh, *The City of God,* pp. 57 ff.); and that, even if the sentence were taken at its face value, it would still be necessary to inquire, What is the Catholic Church? The truth in this doctrine of authority lies in the contention of Aquinas that God seldom makes use of direct assurance. There are lonely souls who have passed beyond all dubiety in their religious life and yet seem to owe little to the church; but it is also true that it is unusual, in many cases impossible, to have certainty in isolation from the fellowship of Christian people.

III. Certainty is based on Scripture and the Holy Spirit. Luther put the testimony of the Holy Spirit in the forefront of his teaching, as (1) guarantor of Scripture and (2) guarantor of personal certainty. Thus he broke through the error of the church in which it had sought for premature certainty by the way of doctrine declared on authority to be infallible. No authority can do that; certainty can come only through a more than human source. Calvin developed the doctrine of the *testimonium Spiritus Sancti internum* in *The Institutes,* Book III, and in Chapter XXIV anchored the doctrine in election and God's hidden decree. Many Calvinists realize that there is the suggestion of a circular movement in the argument at this stage. Man cannot have assurance until he has—assurance; and it is seen that there is as much room for doubt and despair here as in certain aspects of the Roman system. In both, men may rest in doubt rather than in assurance, in one case because there is ambiguity in our interpretation of the eternal divine decree, in the other because the final decision seems to lie in the power of the church in its aspect of a human organization.

Conclusion. The divine speech can become historically clear only in the existential situation: the voice of God can be heard only in the sublime moments. But the existential situations do arise: the sublime moments do occur, and God does indicate when he is "making a special announcement." He may do so through special clarity in the soul, and we speak of vision; or through his prophets, and we look on them as inspired; or by the testimony of his church; or by his Word in Scripture speaking with inescapable force. The witness of the luminous moment will be found to coincide with the evidence received from sound authority and tradition, from the Bible, the church, and the Christian fellowship, and that coincidence will provide the highest form of religious conviction.

BIBLIOGRAPHY: W. Adams Brown, *Pathways to Certainty*, 1930; E. Brunner, *Revelation and Reason* (1947), pp. 166 ff.; John Dewey, *The Quest for Certainty*, 1929; E. P. Dickie, *Revelation and Response*, 1938; Karl Heim, *Das Gewissheitsproblem*, 1911; *Glaubensgewissheit*, 1920; *God Transcendent*, 1935; F. R. Tennant, *Philosophical Theology* (2 vols., 1928–30), I, p. 290; Westminster Confession of Faith, ch. xviii.

EDGAR PRIMROSE DICKIE.

CHAFER, LEWIS SPERRY: Presbyterian; b. at Rock Creek, Ohio, Feb. 27, 1871; d. Aug. 22, 1952. He studied at New Lyme (Ohio) Academy (1885–88) and at Oberlin (Ohio) College (1889–92). He also studied under Frank E. Fitch, Buffalo, N. Y. (1900). He was a traveling evangelist (1900–14); an internationally known Bible teacher and lecturer (1914–24); founder, president and professor of systematic theology of Dallas (Tex.) Theological Seminary (1924–); editor, *Bibliotheca Sacra* (1940–). He wrote *Satan* (1909); *True Evangelism* (1911); *The Kingdom in History and Prophecy* (1915); *Salvation* (1916); *He That Is Spiritual* (1918); *Grace* (1922); *Major Bible Themes* (1926); *The Ephesian Letter* (1935); *Systematic Theology* (8 vols.—1948).

CHANCE. See GAMBLING.

CHANCEL: In a church edifice the space beyond the nave and transepts, reserved for the altar, or communion table, the minister, and the choir. In Roman churches, often known as "the sanctuary." The altar stands against the wall (usually the eastern) farthest from the congregation, and serves as the focal point of interest. A communion table, if in use, stands away from this wall, so that the minister can stand behind it and face the people. Except when ministering at the lectern or in the pulpit he sits near one of the side walls, so as not to turn his back towards the altar, or table, with its surmounting cross. For the same reason members of the choir sit in two sets of parallel pews facing each other, rather than the people. All this symbolizes the worship of God, not the entertainment of an audience. Even in bodies not liturgical the chancel arrangement is becoming common. In time it may practically supplant the central pulpit (*q.v.*)

[Sup.] ANDREW W. BLACKWOOD.

CHANDIEU, ANTOINE DE LA ROCHE: He participated in the 1560 Conspiracy of Amboise. He served as interim director and professor of theology at the Lausanne Academy, 1577–79.

BIBLIOGRAPHY: Henri Naef, "La Conjuration d'Amboise et Genève," *Memoires et Documents publiés par la Société d'histoire et d'archéologie de Genève*, XXXII (1922), 327–730; Henri Vuilleumier, *Histoire de l'église réformée du Pays de Vaud . . .* 4 vols., 1927–33.

[Sup.] ROBERT M. KINGDON.

CHANGE OF CONFESSION: State laws regarding the obligation for persons transferring from one Christian church to another to notify the civil authority, have been abrogated in most democratic countries holding the principle of separation of church and state, with a few exceptions; namely, in those states in which ministers of religion act as officers of vital statistics, or in which the payment of school taxes is made on a confessional basis.

[Sup.] GEORGES A. BARROIS.

CHANNING FOUNDATIONS. See STUDENT ORGANIZATIONS, RELIGIOUS.

CHANTEPIE DE LA SAUSSAYE, PIERRE DANIEL: Protestant scholar; b. at Leeuwarden, Netherlands, April 9, 1848; d. at Bilthoven, April 20, 1920. He taught at the universities of Amsterdam and Leiden (1878–1916). He is known chiefly for his *Lehrbuch der Religionsgeschichte*, published first in 1887–89, and whose last edition was completely revised under the direction of A. Bertholet and E. Lehmann.

[Sup.] GEORGES A. BARROIS.

CHAPEL: A term variously employed to indicate (1) a small church building, in Britain usually nonconformist; (2) a small place for worship under the same roof and control as the vast cathedral to which it belongs, such as that of St. John in New York City; (3) a room set apart for worship in a hospital, or other institution; (4) the recognized center for public worship at a university, such as Oxford or Yale, the man in charge being known as the dean; (5) under the same roof and control as the main "sanctuary," a smaller room for private devotions, weddings, funerals and other occasions not attracting numbers. This last may take the place of the old-time prayer meeting room. Except at a university, the term chapel suggests a place of worship, small and intimate, without being unchurchly.

[Sup.] ANDREW W. BLACKWOOD.

CHAPLAIN: Since 1914, with two world wars, the work of army and navy chaplains has attained new importance. Never have so many clergymen served church and state at the same time. Usually they represent three groups: Protestants (as a unit), Roman Catholics, and Jews. The effectiveness of a chaplain's work depends much on the attitude of his commanding officer, who may keep the man of God busy with secular concerns, such as supervising sports and other amusements. Most chaplains have had few complaints. With some exceptions they have rendered valiant service, often heroic. A few have been sent home because of irregularities with money, liquor, or women. All find it hard to maintain habits of study and prayer;

also to keep from becoming militarized and professionalized. In times of peace many of the ablest prefer to labor among civilians. Hence the armed forces suffer from lack of religious leadership. In war or in peace the work consists partly in speaking before groups of men, and more in personal counseling about problems religious and secular. As an officer the chaplain mingles freely with other officers, and less freely with enlisted men. Many ordained men serve as chaplains in schools of learning, hospitals, and other institutions, and a few in factories. The "industrial chaplain" has not met with signal success. He finds it hard to finance the work without being supported by the corporation, and suspected of representing the employers. A chaplain anywhere today engages in a difficult and delicate ministry calling for ability and training, with character and grace.

[Sup.] Andrew W. Blackwood.

CHAPLAINS, THE ASSOCIATION OF MENTAL HOSPITAL. See Mentally Ill, Care of the.

CHAPMAN, J. WILBUR: D. Dec. 25, 1918. He spent the last fifteen years of his life as a representative-at-large for the Evangelistic Commission of the Presbyterian Church. His later books include: *The Lost Crown; The Secret of a Happy Day; The Surrendered Life; Spiritual Life of the Sunday School; Chapman's Pocket Sermons* (1911); *Revival Sermons* (1911); and *When Home Is Heaven* (1917).

[Sup.] Raymond W. Albright.

CHAPTER: Latin *capitulum.* In some religious orders of the Roman Catholic Church, the assembly in which the election of conventual, provincial, or general superiors takes place, as well as the discussion of other matters pertaining to administration and discipline. These assemblies are distinct from the *capitulum culparum,* in which monks and nuns or friars confess publicly their external infractions against the rule and constitutions of the order.

[Sup.] Georges A. Barrois.

CHARITY, BROTHERS AND SISTERS OF: The name "Brothers of Charity" is given sometimes, though improperly, to the Order of St. John of God, whose American province, with headquarters in Los Angeles, counts twenty-seven professed brothers (and fathers). Another congregation of Brothers of Charity, of Belgian origin, has its American headquarters in Montreal; 240 professed brothers.

The original institute of the Daughters of Charity, founded by St. Vincent de Paul in France in 1633, and first established in the United States in 1809, has two American provinces with headquarters at Emmitsburg, Md., and Normandy, Mo.; 2160 professed sisters.

A foundation from Emmitsburg to Canada became independent in 1856 under the title, Sisters of Charity of St. Vincent de Paul, Halifax; 1339 professed sisters.

These institutes are distinct from the congregation of the Sisters of Charity of St. Vincent de Paul, which has regional centers in New York, Cincinnati, Convent Station, New Jersey, and Greensburg, Pennsylvania, with 4732 professed sisters.

In addition to these sisters, who conduct schools, including schools for the deaf and otherwise disabled, hospitals, asylums, orphanages, homes for convalescent and the aged, several congregations of women also known as Sisters of Charity, of foreign or American origin, are engaged in similar occupations on a diocesan or regional basis. [Sup.] Georges A. Barrois.

CHARITY, CHRISTIAN: With the rise of Protestantism, Christian charity was subjected to conceptual reformulation and redirection. The reformers sharply criticized the selfish motives which prompted much of the almsgiving in the medieval church, viz., merit for penance and the gaining of heaven. They called for a recapture of the impulse of Godly love which had prompted the early church to care not only for its own poor but for broken and destitute humanity wherever found. Such teaching, combined with the unsettled state of affairs in the sixteenth century, led to a temporary disruption of charitable activities among Protestants. But in the next three centuries the Protestant ethic gradually created a fervency, in Christian concern for men's physical and spiritual needs, that produced a wondrous proliferation in the extent and modes of Christian charity.

Protestantism, especially in its Reformed tradition, affected Christian charity in still another way. It stimulated the ideal of Christianizing social, economic, and political institutions. It condemned any otherworldly attitude which encouraged complacent acceptance of non-Christian social practices and institutions. The general effect on charity was to put everyone to self-supporting work and to encourage thrift, thus eliminating in large measure those strata of society which previously had been the object of so much Christian charity.

As great nations took shape, however, and as religious toleration grew and the line between Christian church and secular society was sharpened, the conditions of Christian charity changed radically. Masses of physically and spiritually impoverished people mushroomed in the new industrial societies. The first emergency reaction of Christians, both Roman and Protestant, was to fall back on direct benevolence and charitable institutions, the latter brought up to date to meet new problems. But the Protestant ideal reasserted itself, being well stated by Thomas Chalmers: "If you wish to combat poverty, combat it in its first elements. If you confine your beneficence to the relief of actual poverty you do nothing. Dry up, if possible, the springs of poverty, for every attempt to intercept the running stream has failed."

In the nineteenth and twentieth centuries this ideal attempted in two directions to meet the needs of the new industrial world. Some Christians emphasized the indirect approach by attacking the spiritual sources of human grief in the unchristian moral principles and social attitudes of the upper classes. The practical effect of this effort was to inspire large-scale, paternalistic philanthropy by the industrial magnates. Other Christians, in terms of the so-called "social gospel" (q.v.), attacked the problem chiefly in an effort to transform the socio-economic structure of society. With its optimistic faith in the possibility of a thoroughly Christian culture, this movement contributed to the gradual removal of charitable activities from the direct promotion and supervision of the church and the assumption of them by secular social organizations or governmental bureaus. This led in time to the cutting away of the peculiarly Christian, theological foundations of charity and to their replacement by an empirical ethic guided by detached scientific objectivity.

But as the optimism of liberal Christianity (see LIBERALISM) was shattered by war, depression, and ideological conflict with Fascism and Communism (q.v.), a reborn Christian orthodoxy brought to bear on the needs of men a more complex and critical "dialectical" approach (see DIALECTIC THEOLOGY) which stressed the need of both an individual-spiritual and a socio-structural resolution of the evils which beset mankind, insisting at the same time that all resolutions will be relative and imperfect until God brings his kingdom (q.v.) in its fullness. What new specific modes of the expression of Christian charity will be dictated by this new Christian mentality is not yet clear. But that Christian charity will again be rooted in Christian love and the life of the church is certain. See also ETHICS.

BIBLIOGRAPHY: K. S. Latourette, Three Centuries of Advance (1939), pp. 403–408; The Great Century, pp. 152–162, 384–410; F. H. Stead, The Story of Social Christianity; J. C. Bennett, Christian Ethics and Social Policy, 1946; C. H. Hopkins, The Rise of the Social Gospel in American Protestantism, 1940; Report of the Conference at Oxford, 1937.

[Sup.] ARNOLD B. COME.

CHARITY SCHOOLS: An educational enterprise launched in behalf of the children of the German settlers in Pennsylvania in the mideighteenth century by benevolent Protestant leaders in England and Scotland. An appeal by Michael Schlatter (q.v., Vol. X.), missionary superintendent appointed by the Reformed synods of Holland to oversee the German

churches in the English colonies, so impressed David Thomson, pastor of the English Church in Amsterdam, that he inaugurated a campaign in Great Britain to meet the need. Funds were raised, probably to the amount of $20,000, and Schlatter was appointed supervisor of the schools. Eight of these were reported by William Smith (q.v.) to have been in operation in 1760 in six counties of Pennsylvania. The project, however, was bitterly attacked by Christopher Sower (q.v., Vol. XI), Germantown publisher, as an attempt by the English to eliminate German churches, language, and culture. He also charged that the appeals for funds had depicted the Germans as near-savages. Schlatter, discouraged by the rising tide of opposition, resigned, and the schools, with their sources of income drying up, were soon abandoned.

BIBLIOGRAPHY: S. E. Weber, Charity School Movement. 1905.

DAVID DUNN.

CHARLEMAGNE: Authorities have long debated the question as to the possibility of the emperor's coronation by Pope Leo III having been a surprise to Charlemagne. The latest experts are inclined to believe that both men had discussed the matter beforehand. Charles himself entertained a theocratic conception of his reign. Church and state were one, and he was the ruler of both, thus having been ordained and called by God. This idea of his later led to the investiture struggle, which had its roots in the consolidation of the emperor's power. After his death he became a legendary hero, as described for example in the Song of Roland and the novels written about his career.

BIBLIOGRAPHY: C. Russell, Charlemagne, 1937; L. Halphen, Études critiques sur l'histoire de Charlemagne. 1921; J. Calmette, Charlemagne, 1945; E. Eichmann, Die Kaiserkroenung im Abendland, 2 vols., 1942; K. Seiler, Der Erziehungsstaat Karls der Groszen, 1937; R. Folz, Charlemagne: Le souvenir et la légende dans l'empire germain médiéval, 1950.

[Sup.] H. GOOSSENS.

CHARLES I (1625–49): B. Nov. 19, 1600, at Holyrood, the royal palace in Scotland, son of King James VI (q.v.) and Anne of Denmark. He had an older brother, Henry, who was born in 1594 and died in 1612. His sister Elizabeth in 1613 married Frederick, count of the Palatinate, who for a short time was also king of Bohemia and candidate for the position of emperor in Germany.

In 1616 Charles became prince of Wales. His father hoped he would marry the Spanish infanta, believing that Spain was still the greatest power in Europe, and worrying not at all about the fact that Spain happened to be the most loyal of all nations to the papacy. Charles and his most intimate friend, the duke of Buckingham, traveled incognito to Spain in 1623. They were not very diplomatic and failed to satisfy the demands of King Philip III, who insisted that Charles make England thoroughly Catholic. When Charles and Buckingham after a long absence finally returned to England, they were greeted with huge bonfires and the pealing of church bells, for the rank and file of English citizens were delighted to hear that the heir to the throne had not fallen under the power of the Roman Catholic potentates. But Charles soon married Henrietta Maria, daughter of King Henry IV of France. It was not Spain but France that would henceforth most seriously threaten the safety of England.

From 1624 to 1628 Charles and Buckingham plunged England into five wars, all of which ended disastrously for England. As the famous British historian G. M. Trevelyan explains in his masterpiece, England under the Stuarts, at no time did the fortunes of England sink so low as in those four dismal years. English naval power suffered terrible blows, but in the days of Oliver Cromwell a new era was begun which saw England rise to the top among the nations. The king's French wife added to the difficulties, for she brought both of her sons up to detest Protestant doctrines, particularly those that implied the right of individuals to challenge authority in state or church. Moreover, she carried on secret intrigues with French and Dutch agents, causing her husband great harm and loss of prestige.

Charles I, like his father before him, relied on the power of the bishops to keep the masses in check. When King James I exclaimed one day that without bishops there could be no king, he was telling the truth as far as his own and his son's positions were concerned. Puritanism was getting so strong that Charles nearly lost control of the situation. Archbishop Laud (q.v.) performed excellent service in his behalf, but the policy which he pursued in persecuting the Puritans could not fail to arouse tremendous popular opposition. The latter combined with the Scotch army and the Scotch Presbyterians to overthrow Charles, whose two sons had to flee to Holland in order to escape from the wrath of the great majority of their father's subjects.

The king and Laud, Archbishop of Canterbury, disliked the way in which Puritans conducted their church services, showing little respect for ancient usage and rites. As Laud said in 1637, " 'Tis superstition now-a-days for any man to come with more reverence into a church, than a tinker . . . into an ale-house." The government was attempting to enforce a degree of liturgical uniformity in all the churches. The bishops, who lived lives of luxury, exerted powerful influence upon the civil government, and openly defended the theory that kings rule by divine right. The Puritans soon discovered that opposition to the bishops was construed at the royal court as sedition. Godfrey Davies has

correctly summarized the whole situation as follows on p. 69 of his book, The Early Stuarts (1937): "The Stuart system of government would have collapsed ignominiously early in the century but for the support of the hierarchy." The bishops, on their part, would have been called upon to answer charges long before the Long Parliament finally took that step in 1640, if it had not been for the royal protection given to them by both James I and Charles I. Francis Bacon, the famous philosopher, said that religion was the chief bond of human society, and Laud argued that if unity was lost in the church there could be no unity in the state. It became Laud's great concern to take away from the Puritans freedom of the press and of speech even in their own church buildings. Criticism of the monarchy was denounced by the bishops and their supporters as blasphemy. The pro-Spanish foreign policy of James I and the behavior of Henrietta Maria in public and private, with her pro-French and pro-papal utterances and gestures, created an extremely difficult situation. Queen Elizabeth had given her two successors an example they gladly followed. She used to "tune the churches, as her saying was." In 1622 the government issued instructions to the effect that preachers should adhere strictly to the texts they used for their sermons. Many of them had taken the liberty to dwell on political topics and interesting news items, which caused great concern to Laud and his royal master. The afternoon sermons, so read the government instructions, must be confined to a part of the catechism, or a text from the creed, or the Ten Commandments, or the Lord's Prayer. This order resulted in a tremendous upheaval among the Puritans. They resented the royal measures all the more when they observed that the Arminians did not suffer any restrictions of that sort. John Rushworth, speaking of the proclamation issued in 1626, said: "The effects of this proclamation how equally soever intended, became the stopping of the puritans mouths, and an uncontrolled liberty to the tongues and pens of the Arminian party." Things went from bad to worse, and the end was not unexpected by the king's enemies. On January 30, 1649, Charles was beheaded.

BIBLIOGRAPHY: G. Davies, The Early Stuarts 1603-1660 (1937), pp. 32-44, 64-95, 103-104, 119-121, 140-157, 217-218, bibl. pp. 414-436; G. Huehns, Antinomianism in England, 1951; Fr. E. Pamp, Jr., Doctoral Dissertation at Harvard on the influence of Hugo Grotius and Arminianism in England, 1951; G. Albion, Charles I and the Court of Rome, 1935; H. Ross Williamson, Charles I and Cromwell, 1946. In 1951 appeared an interesting volume on Charles I entitled The Age of Charles I, by David Matthew. This author has featured the discussion of various groups of people, held together by occupation, kinship, or neighborhood. But Puritanism is not adequately treated, nor is foreign policy. Fr. Madan, A New Bibliography of the Eikon Basilike of King Charles the First, 1950; R. Bouvier, Comédie royale: Le mariage manqué du Prince des Galles Charles avec l'infante Maria, 1949; J. Brookes, A Vindication of Charles the First, 1931; C. V. Wedgwood, King Charles I, 1649-1949, 1949; E.

Wingfield-Stratford, *Charles King of England*, 1949; *idem, King Charles and King Pym, 1637–1643*, 1943; *idem, King Charles the Martyr*, 1950; J. Mackay, *Little Madam: A Biography of Henrietta Maria*, 1939; Charles I, *Works*, several editions beginning with the year 1650, printed in London by Roger Norton with a false The Hague imprint, containing his speeches, messages for peace, letters, the *Eikon Basilike* (see MILTON), the Henderson Papers, the New-Port Papers, and six prayers.

ALBERT HYMA.

CHARLES V, EMPEROR: A central weakness in European politics in the time of Charles V was the growth of the Ottoman Empire, extending in 1529 to Vienna and threatening to go beyond that bulwark of Christendom. As Joseph Lortz has stated in his admirable work on the German Reformation, Islam "was officially the enemy of Christian Europe. In reality is it shown nowhere more mercilessly how far the loss of unity had gone in political and religious theatres of action, and how shameful the selfish policies of the individual nations had become, than in the reaction by the German princes to the danger of the Turkish onslaught." First came the strange action on the part of Pope Alexander VI, next that of Pope Clement VII (though sporadically) then that of Venice, of Zapolya in Hungary and his Bavarian ally, and of the French. It was a picture of egoism and faithlessness which made the idea of Christian unity seem a derision. The disunity of the German princes was a second weakening factor in the time of Charles V. Each insisted on having his own army, currency, and customs duties. Nobody seemed to care about common dangers and common duties. If the Elector of Saxony suddenly decided to help France against the emperor, and if he felt that he must invade the lands of his own cousin, that was his privilege.

A third source of weakness confronting Charles V was the low moral code in the homes of the princes, both secular and ecclesiastical. When Luther reached Rome in the winter of 1510–11 he was astonished at the lack of religious fervor. Later certain critics of his noted the same thing at the court of certain German princes who were no longer reprimanded by Luther. After the Peasants' War the ethics of the German princes were notorious. It has become a practice in Germany today to distinguish between the Luther of Worms and the Luther after the Peasant War. The contrast is great.

The results of these three weaknesses soon appeared. Germany did not become united until the nineteenth century in the time of Bismarck, and even then it took still more effort to obliterate particularism. While Spain, France, England, and the Dutch Republic built empires and gained great wealth through sea-borne trade, the Germans gave up their chance to develop sea power and great commercial institutions. One reason why the reign of Charles V

is so important in Germany history is that it became a sign of patriotism among the German princes to weaken the power of the emperor. They were so afraid of his overwhelming political power that they did not think of their common duty in building a great German nation. As long as they were opposing Rome they were drawn together by common interests, but Charles was not a real German and became more and more a Spaniard. He could never depend fully upon any of the German princes, for they all had the same objective, to increase the power and prestige of each individual state at his expense.

Charles V was so busy with his wars against the king of France and so immersed in Spanish and Italian politics that he neglected his duties in Germany. He misunderstood Luther at first and never sought to use adequate diplomacy in trying to prevent what soon followed. As long as Luther was identified with the anti-foreign policy of the German princes he fared well. But after 1530 his career became involved in dynastic intrigues. The emperor missed his mark several times in his attempts to solve the problem of Lutheranism.

Moreover, his policies in the Low Countries antagonized many good Catholics. Largely because the Calvinists could take advantage of the anti-Spanish sentiment they almost unwittingly attracted the support of a great many Roman Catholics, who did not realize that in this way they were aiding the cause of Protestantism. It was not until after the Dutch Republic had been established and the Calvinists had begun to some extent to persecute Catholics that the latter saw what they had done to their church. Although the final contest came after 1555, the whole anti-Spanish wave of sentiment started long before that date. Charles had brought back with him from Spain certain counselors whose interest in the Netherlands was very limited. Moreover, his son Philip II should have been told to spend several years in the Low Countries before his father's abdication, in order to win the love and respect of his subjects in that wealthy region. But Charles did not realize the nature of his errors. He should at least have known that the strong demand for personal liberties in the Netherlands would express itself in a revolt, unless the Spanish rulers were diplomatic enough to counteract the popular uprising. The religious policy of Charles also added to the feeling of disappointment in all the provinces. Many prominent citizens objected to his persecutions primarily on the ground of decent government.

German historians in recent times have interpreted the career of Charles by saying that as early as 1519, when he became emperor, his attitude was that of a Spaniard. This erroneous analysis has been corrected by Paul Joachimsen in his, *Die Reformation als Epoche der deutschen Geschichte* (published posthumously in 1951, and edited by Otto Schottenloher), where he mentions the obvious fact that Charles at the age of nineteen was mindful of his Burgundian ancestry and his residence of sixteen years in what is now Belgium. It was his Burgundian policy that involved him in five wars with France. What he wanted to accomplish first was to recover the ancient Duchy of Burgundy, which King Louis XI in 1477 had taken from Mary of Burgundy, Charles' grandmother. He also remembered well how Charles the Bold, Mary's father, had almost succeeded in establishing the Kingdom of Burgundy by adding Lorraine and Luxembourg to his dominions. Such a state would have given Charles more pleasure than a victory over the Protestant princes in Germany. He expected upon his accession to complete the plans of Charles the Bold. As Joachimson correctly intimated (pp. 79–80), Charles wanted to make this kingdom the center of his campaigns and cultural activities.

BIBLIOGRAPHY: R. B. Merriman, *Charles V and the Spanish Empire*, 1939; W. Tritsch, *Karl V*, 1935; P. Rassow, *Die politische Welt Karls V*, 1942; K. Brandi, *Karl V*, 1937 (the best work up to 1937, with trans. into English and Dutch); J. Babelon, *Charles-Quint*, 1947.

[Sup.] ALBERT HYMA.

CHARLES, ROBERT HENRY: D. Jan. 30, 1931. At Westminster Abbey he was both canon (1913–31) and archdeacon (1919–31). He was Speaker's lecturer in biblical studies, Oxford (1910–14) and lecturer in advanced theology, London (1913). He contributed articles to the *Encyclopaedia Biblica*, Hastings' *Dictionary of the Bible*, and the *Encyclopaedia Britannica;* and was the general editor of and a contributor to *The Apocrypha and Pseudepigrapha of the Old Testament* (Translation and Commentary, 1913). In addition to printing three volumes of sermons, he has written, edited, or translated, among other works, the following: *Fragments of a Zadokite Work* (edited and translated, 1912); *The Book of Enoch or I Enoch* (Ethiopic text revised and translated, 1912); *Immortality* (1912); *Studies in the Apocalypse* (1913); *A Critical History of the Doctrine of a Future Life in Israel, in Judaism, and in Christianity* (2nd ed., 1913); *Religious Development Between the Old and the New Testaments* (1914); *The Chronicle of John, Bishop of Nikiu* (Ethiopic text translated, 1916); *A Critical and Exegetical Commentary on the Revelation of St. John* (1920); *The Teaching of the New Testament on Divorce* (1921); *Lectures on the Apocalypse* (1922); *The Decalogue* (1923); *Divorce and the Roman Dogma of Nullity* (1927); *A Critical and Exegetical Commentary on the Book of Daniel* (1929).

BIBLIOGRAPHY: *Courage, Truth, Purity,* 1931. This volume of sermons by Canon Charles contains a memoir

of the author by the Most Rev. C. F. D'Arcy. W. F. Howard, *The Romance of New Testament Scholarship* (1949), pp. 105–110.

[Sup.] RAYMOND W. ALBRIGHT.

CHARRON, PIERRE: The sceptical tendency in his philosophy went back to his teacher Montaigne. On this scepticism he based his need of revelation for religion. But more important than religion in life he considered morality or good morals, which does not consist in a human conformity to a moral code but to an inward state of mind or soul.

BIBLIOGRAPHY: *Lexikon fuer Theologie und Kirche*, Vol. II, 842 ff.

[Sup.] H. GOOSSENS.

CHARTISM: The Chartist movement in England dated from 1838, with the appearance of the People's Charter and its six points: universal suffrage, a secret ballot, annual parliaments, equal representation, no property qualification, and payment of Members of Parliament. Politically, the Charter was the work of classes still unenfranchised after the 1832 Reform Bill. It provided a political formula for a variety of local working-class agitations throughout England. Chartists used the movement to express social and economic grievances. It was at its most violent in years of bad harvests and economic distress, 1838–42 and 1846–48.

The Charter was the work of William Lovett and the London Working Men's Association, too small and idealistic to start a national agitation on their own. Chartism owed its organization, based on a National Convention, to Thomas Attwood and the Birmingham Political Union, whose efforts produced the first of three Parliamentary Petitions in 1839. Militant, or "physical force," Chartism developed in the North under the leadership of Feargus O'Connor in *The Northern Star*. It was this militant section which gradually dominated the movement, superseding the "moral force" of Lovett. From 1845 O'Connor advocated a scheme of Land Reform which divided rather than aided Chartism. With the failure of the Petition of 1848, Chartism ceased to be effective.

Never solely a political or economic movement, Chartism had important religious aspects. In Birmingham, Christian Chartist Churches appeared. Chartists generally copied the Methodist class-meeting (*q.v.*), and in the North there were many cases of Chartist camp meetings (*q.v.*). EVELYN CLIFFORD URWIN.

CHASIDIM: Hasidism is an extraordinarily interesting development of Jewish mysticism that continues to be a closed book to most students as the greater part of its literature, and many important studies thereof, are accessible only to those who read Hebrew. The best introduction to the modern interpretation of Hasidism is that in chapters III and IX of

Gershom Scholem's *Major Trends in Jewish Mysticism* (1941), the former of which studies its beginnings in medieval Germany, and the latter its further development in Eastern Europe. He gives the essential bibliography. Martin Buber's earlier work is useful, but his later studies, e.g., *Hasidism* (1948), lie under suspicion of reading into Hasidic texts a good deal that does not belong there.

[Sup.] ARTHUR JEFFERY.

CHASTITY: A self-imposed regulation or moderation of sexual intercourse, associated from primitive times with various taboos of pregnancy, lactation, menstruation, pre-nuptiality, or ritual cleanliness. In Christian ethics it is a virtue, a form of temperance in the use of sex. Sometimes it is confused with continence (*q.v.*) or complete abstinence from sex. The Catholic "vow of chastity" does so. Roman Catholics assert also that chastity is an "evangelical counsel" calling for celibacy in the clergy and the "religious": another confusion of terms and ideas, since celibacy is renunciation rather than moderation. The celibacy ideal finds two warrants in the New Testament (none in the Old): Jesus' saying (Mt. 19:12) that some "made themselves eunuchs for the kingdom of heaven's sake," and Paul's, "it is good for a man not to touch a woman" (I Cor. 7:1). However, in the Matthean passage, "eunuch" is certainly used metaphorically; and in the Pauline passage the context reveals that he favored continence because "the form of this world is passing away." Luther set the Protestant principle by: 1) doing away with the double morality as between minister and layman, thus undermining celibacy, and by (2) exhorting all Christians alike to observance of chastity while leaving continence to the individual's sense of vocation. A marked tendency towards ethical dualism, and the idea that material-physical things are evil, has encouraged some chastity among Christians, but more often as an inhibiting check than as a positive or ethical self-denial. This dualism is often attributed to Paul; yet his constant interchange of the words *sarx* (flesh) and *soma* (the whole person) suggests that he really felt that the flesh (with its sex component) is not inherently evil but only (as a result of the "Fall") more subject to the powers of evil (which are spiritual) than is the mind (cf. Rom. 7:22). From the beginning, the Christian ideal has been continence outside wedlock and chastity within it. The sex drive is not in itself evil but it must be kept "under" as a means to moral and spiritual ends; otherwise there is unchastity in deed (I Cor. 6:15), in word (Eph. 5:3, 12), or in thought (Mt. 5:28). Christian marriage is a protection of chastity (I Cor. 7:1–7), but no guarantee of sexual purity (*castitas*), as I Pet. 3:1–7 explains; the guidance and strength of the Holy Spirit are required (Rom. 8:13, Gal. 5:22–23), added to the Christian's own self-discipline (I Cor. 9:27, Eph. 4:29, Phil. 4:8, I Tim. 5:22). For a theological reason ("resurrection of the body"), a pure use of the body was vital; not because the body is evil but because it is a part of the whole scheme of redemption. Unlike Stoicism and Manichaeism, Christianity gave chastity a positive rather than a negative meaning and motive.

BIBLIOGRAPHY: H. C. Lea, *The History of Sacerdotal Celibacy*, 2 vols., 1907; Robert Briffault, *The Mothers*, 3 vols., 1927; W. E. H. Lecky, *The History of European Morals*, 2 vols., 1927; Oscar Hardman, *The Ideal of Asceticism*, 1924.

[Sup.] JOSEPH FLETCHER.

CHASUBLE: The ancient forms of the chasuble, Latin *casula,* are being revived in the Roman Church. They are derived from the *paenula,* a mantle worn by men in the Roman empire. The chasuble à l'antique is fuller in shape than the stiff vestment of the seventeenth century. It extends to the wrists of the priest, and is eventually so ample that it hangs all around in long supple folds. Another name for the chasuble is the *planeta,* Italian *pianeta,* used in Rome preferably to *casula.* Some Anglican priests and others make use of the chasuble for the celebration of the Eucharist. The chasuble corresponds to the *phelonion* of the Byzantine priests. [Sup.] GEORGES A. BARROIS.

CHAUTAUQUA INSTITUTION: In the first quarter of the twentieth century cultural and religious assemblies, similar to those held on Chautauqua Lake, were conducted by itinerant speakers and artists during summer months in towns throughout the United States. In 1924, when interest was at its height, the tents of "Chautauquas" were set up in 12,000 towns. Then the competition of motion pictures and radio brought a quick end to the assemblies. However, the original Chautauqua Institution, at Chautauqua, N. Y., continued, as before, to offer extensive programs of religious services, courses of instruction, and lectures on religious and other subjects during the summer months.

BIBLIOGRAPHY: M. G. Scott, *Chautauqua Caravan*, 1939; V. and R. O. Case, *We Called It Culture*, 1948.

[Sup.] THEODORE G. TAPPERT.

CHAUVINISM: The term comes from the name of one of the officers of Napoleon, Nicolas Chauvin of Rocheford, whose attitude of unquestioning loyalty to Napoleon was so exaggerated that it awakened ridicule even among his comrades. Thus it came to mean blind devotion to any lost cause. This wider, popular use of the term was probably due to the name of a character in Cogniard's vaudeville, *La Cocarde Tricolore* (1931). In current usage, the idea of a lost cause has fallen into the background; although, as the term is usually employed, it has not been entirely eliminated. Chauvinism primarily signifies exaggerated patriotism; but those who most commonly employ the term usually wish to suggest that the patriotism which was possibly a virtue in the past is now out of date, i.e., that it is blind devotion to a lost cause.   ANDREW K. RULE.

CHAVE, ERNEST JOHN: Religious educator; b. Woodstock, Ontario, May 4, 1886. He studied at McMaster University, Toronto, (A.B., 1906; B.Th., 1910); and the University of Chicago (A.M., 1920; Ph.D., 1924). He taught in religious education at the Divinity School, University of Chicago (1926–52). His chief interests have been in progressive educational philosophy and methods, with such publications as *The Junior, Supervision of Religious Education, Measurement of Attitudes, Measure Religion, Personality Development in Children, A Functional Approach to Religious Education,* and *Curriculum Construction.*

CHENG HO: Muslim; b. in Yunnan in fourteenth century; d. 1431. Commanded seven expeditions to littoral states of China Sea and Indian Ocean; in 1405 sailed to Cambodia and Siam. In 1408 and 1412 he conducted naval expeditions to Ceylon, enroute inducing states to send envoys to China. He conducted further expeditions in 1415, 1421 and 1424. In 1431 he visited Hormuz.

BIBLIOGRAPHY: P. Pelliot, in *T'ung Pao,* 1933; J. J. Duyvendak, in *Hollandsche uitgeversmaatschappij,* 1933; Chin Yun-ming, *Cheng Ho Ch'i Tz'u Hsia Hsi-yang Nien-yueh K'ao-cheng,* 1937.
CLAUDE L. PICKENS, JR.

CHEROUBIKON: In the Byzantine liturgies, the so-called "Hymn of the Cherubim," which is sung by the choir, whereas the priest and the deacon recite it three times prior to entering the sanctuary to place the elements of bread and wine on the altar in view of the celebration of the Eucharist. The *Cheroubikon* expresses the union of the church with the angelic choirs in the worship of the Holy Trinity.
GEORGES A. BARROIS.

CHESTER BEATTY PAPYRI. See PAPYRI, BIBLICAL AND EARLY CHRISTIAN.

CHESTERTON, GILBERT KEITH: B. in London, May 29, 1874; d. at Beaconsfield, June 14, 1935. He studied at Saint Paul's School, and audited various university courses, making journalism his profession. After a period of doubts, he sought the guidance of the Church of England, and was converted to Roman Catholicism in 1922. His leading thought is that the church, which he finally identified with the Roman Church, is the only institution in which

a true humanism can develop. He wrote polemic and apologetic essays: *Orthodoxy* (1908); *Tremendous Trifles* (1909); *Fancies versus Fads* (1923); *The Thing: Why I Am a Catholic* (1929); *Resurrection of Rome* (1930); *The Well and the Shallows* (1935). He also wrote monographs on *Robert Browning* (1903); *Charles Dickens* (1905); *George Bernard Shaw* (1909); *Saint Francis of Assisi* (1923); *Chaucer* (1932); *Saint Thomas Aquinas* (1933). His autobiography was published in 1936.

BIBLIOGRAPHY: H. Belloc, *The Place of Chesterton in English Literature,* 1937; M. Ward, *Gilbert Keith Chesterton,* 1944; D. Attwater, *Modern Christian Revolutionaries,* 1947.
GEORGES A. BARROIS.

CHICAGO SCHOOL OF THEOLOGY, THE: The Chicago School of Theology applies to the group of men in the Divinity School of the University of Chicago who, under Shailer Mathews, developed the socio-historical method of interpreting the Christian religion. The principal participants, besides Mathews, were Shirley Jackson Case, Gerald Birney Smith, and J. M. P. Smith.

This method assumed that the resources basic to an understanding of doctrines, ceremonies, and institutions were history and the social sciences. History unfolded the drama of religious development before the student; social psychology equipped him with the conceptual facilities to enable him to analyze what he envisaged. The method assumed, further, that religion is, and basically has been, a social movement of a particular people or culture in process of development; consequently whatever informed the development of social movements generally could be considered applicable to the study of religion. The method held also that religion is pre-eminently a phenomenon of the social experience within a given cultural period. Religious beliefs, it claimed, arose as explicit functions to enable individuals and groups to come to terms with "objective activities" under circumstances peculiar to the cultural environment. Accordingly, it conceived religion to be always a vital response which can never be contained within any ecclesiastical formula or interpreted through the abstractions of philosophy.

Consistent with its view of religion, the Chicago School concerned itself solely with the functional import of religious doctrines and institutions. In pursuing the historical study of doctrines, they asked: Why did the doctrine arise? What social tensions lay behind the religious formula? What environmental factors influenced religious people of this period to meet the problem at issue in this manner?

In assessing the validity of a religious belief, they again considered its functional worth: How does it meet the demands of the social experience of the people who held it? In foregoing the apologetic task, the Chicago School felt it had opened the way for dealing faithfully with inherited doctrines, and for permitting the historic faith to speak for itself out of its full, variegated context. Continuity with the past, they argued, is to be sought, not in any conformity to doctrinal systems, but in "the life process of actual people who have created institutions and dogmas in accordance with the deepest convictions of Christians throughout the evolving course of history" (Case). These convictions rooted in an attitude of loyalty to Jesus' ideals and to God (Mathews). Readiness to let the past speak authentically out of its social experience, they argued, released the modern person from bondage to the past on the same principle that he thinks and lives within a social context, in terms of which he must be his authentic self.

See also LIBERALISM.

BIBLIOGRAPHY: G. B. Smith, editor, *A Guide to the Study of the Christian Religion*, 1916; also *The Journal of Religion*, esp. 1920–45. Representative works of this school include: S. J. Case, *The Social Origins of Christianity*, 1912; *The Evolution of Early Christianity*, 1923; *Jesus: A New Biography*, 1928; G. B. Smith, *Social Idealism and the Changing Theology*, 1913; J. M. P. Smith, *The Prophets and Their Times*, 1925; Shailer Mathews, *The Faith of Modernism*, 1924; *The Atonement and the Social Process*, 1930; *The Growth of the Idea of God*, 1931.

BERNARD EUGENE MELAND.

CHILD PSYCHOLOGY: Child psychology is that branch of general psychology (*q.v.*) whose concern is with the growth of human beings from conception to the beginning of adolescence. This definition includes life from its inception, as an increasing, though balanced, emphasis is being placed on the prenatal period. It would take advantage of such facts as have been discovered by any of the related sciences. Biology, anthropology, sociology, psychiatry, pediatrics— all have contributed to a better understanding of the child as a whole in his total environment. University research centers like those at California, Chicago, Minnesota, and Yale have greatly advanced knowledge in this field, and have made child psychology more and more scientific, though it may never become an exact science. While we have better knowledge of childhood than of any other period of life, Dr. Arnold Gesell warns that it will take a century of patient research before there will be anything like a clear understanding of the factors that make childhood what it is. Today there are many divergent viewpoints and it is difficult to sift out fact from opinion.

Certain trends can be noted about which there is a fair amount of agreement: (1) The child's body, mind, thinking, feeling, willing are bound together in an indissoluble unity. Psychosomatic medicine has emphasized the relation between them, stressing especially the place of the emotions in his life. (2) Gesell and his associates have shown that children in their growth follow definite gradients, which, while somewhat different for the individual, must be considered by those who would guide them aright. (3) While most psychologists would not go as far as Freud and Adler, who held that life's problems are caused and its patterns fixed before the child goes to school, they would emphasize the meaning of the early years to the rest of life. (4) The child is not born into a vacuum, but into a world of things and people. Persons are the creative influence in his life. (5) Facts do not seem to sustain a mechanistic conception of the child. (6) Religious teaching begins not when the child learns to talk, but at the moment of birth. It is the family, not the church, that lays the child's religious foundations. This is done effectively not by the words spoken, but by the attitudes and conduct of the parents in relation to each other, the child, those outside the home, the natural world, and God. The basic need for a child's wholesome growth is an atmosphere of love created by his parents' love for each other and for him. If he is loved and loves in return it is not hard for him to learn to respond to a God who is love.

BIBLIOGRAPHY: Ruth Strang, *An Introduction to Child Study*, 1951; A. T. Jersild, *Child Psychology*, 1947; Marian E. Breckenridge and E. Lee Vincent, *Child Development*, 1949; Arnold Gesell and Frances Ilg, *Child Development*, 1949; Grace Langdon and Irving W. Stout, *These Well-Adjusted Children*, 1951; Lewis Joseph Sherrill, *The Opening Doors of Childhood*, 1939.

WILLIAM TALIAFERRO THOMPSON.

CHILDREN AT WORSHIP: Since worship is largely a matter of habit, church leaders have devised three ways of promoting the attendance of boys and girls: (1) The separate Junior Church has seldom proved satisfactory. (2) The special Junior Sermon is good, especially when children remain for the entire service. (3) The Family Idea calls for worship that appeals to the family as such, with something for the little ones in each main part of the service. To many observers this seems most nearly ideal. Adults gain much from public worship when it appeals to children.

The character of a child's worship depends largely on the adults with whom he lives, and the children with whom he mingles. Both at home and in the church school adults should teach him to follow the forms of the church to which his parents belong. Early in his life they should lead him to revere the church and its ways of worship, also developing his inner life so that he will want to express himself in songs and in prayers, in contemplation of things holy, and in silence. Under skillful leadership, and in the presence of others whom he loves, he can learn by engaging actively in the public worship of God. This approach by way of experience assumes that the individual and the group can best grow in Christian living as they are led to express their thoughts and feelings in acts of worship. While the ecclesiastical approach has its place, the main reliance must be on this growing experience, as the child responds to the leadings of the Holy Spirit.

Teachers and parents, with pastors and other leaders, find that as children advance into the teen-age this approach by way of experience helps them to become more firmly rooted. Instead of withering, their personal and corporate devotional lives tend to flourish. But the beginnings ought to come early in life, years before the teen-age. At home little ones should learn to worship as members of the group, with appropriate songs, readings, prayers, and confessions of faith. The end result will depend on whether or not the growing child has become a Christian. Has he learned to know God in Christ for himself, or merely learned to follow forms of worship in which others engage? Like little Samuel in the temple, every growing lad needs to discover God. Then forms will begin to have new meaning.

Leaders of children's work have gained a new understanding of boys and girls, religiously, with appreciation of their God-given capacities for worship. Instead of the sentimental ditties that filled such books at the turn of the century, newer books of praise for children strive to make a synthesis out of songs arising from children's experience, and those that come as a heritage from yesterday.

See also CHILDREN'S WORK.

EDITH LOVELL THOMAS.

CHILDREN, CARE OF: The first half of the twentieth century witnessed a considerable growth in the emphasis of churches on services to children apart from institutional care. In America this has been evidenced by the creation of church welfare agencies, many on a statewide basis, primarily offering services of child placement. The interest of churches in having their own children placed in homes of their own denomination has been one of the strong contributing factors in the development of services of child placement.

Churches have found it easy to accept the social welfare proposition that when a child must find placement because he has been denied the privileges of a proper home, such placement should be in an environment most nearly approximating a natural home. In preference to institutional placement church agencies utilized the membership of congregations to provide foster family care. Churches have also looked to their members for adoptive homes where the custody of children has been relinquished by their natural parents. Along with the program of child placement has naturally developed a service to unmarried mothers.

Some churches have developed day-care programs, settlement work (see SETTLEMENT MOVEMENT), and summer camps (see CAMPS, SUMMER) for children with special needs. Delinquency among children has been a concern, and

church agencies have accepted commitments from juvenile courts and followed children into training schools with the services of institutional chaplains (see CHAPLAIN). After World War II church agencies have also assisted in the resettlement in America of homeless children from Europe (see REFUGEES).

Churches have gradually, though not completely, come to the acceptance of the need for professionally trained social workers (see SOCIAL WORK, CHURCH) in providing for their work of child care. In many areas their child welfare services have related themselves to the community, county, and state in which they operate. Many agencies receive funds from Community Chests and accept reimbursement from county or state for the care of children of indigent parents. Representatives from church agencies participated in community planning and have accepted licensure from the state.

See also CHILDREN'S INSTITUTIONS.

BIBLIOGRAPHY: Inter-Agency Committee on Child Welfare, *The Nation's Children, the Church's Responsibility*, 1950; Child Welfare League, *Standards for Children's Organizations Providing Foster Family Care*, 1941.

LEON N. ZAHN.

CHILDREN'S INSTITUTIONS: Before the twentieth century the interest of the church in the care of children took the form primarily of institutions known as orphan asylums or homes. Under the auspices of churches, these institutions were organized to provide shelter, protection, and education for orphans and other dependent and neglected children. See SOCIAL SERVICE OF THE CHURCH, Vol. X.

With the development of standards in social service has come a change. Institutions for the care of children gradually began using professionally trained caseworkers to study the histories of children applying for admission, for treatment of children within the institutions, and for proper placement at the time of discharge. This use of casework service has tended to make of the institution a study home for children of special needs. Church institutions have gradually accepted the fact that foster-family home-placement for children who are able to establish meaningful relationships with adults is the best substitute for the child's own home. In view of this it has become necessary for many institutions to redefine their policies and make changes in their programs. This transition has not been easy for some because of capital investments, endowment funds, and the slow process of educating constituencies to accept this development in the practice of social welfare. Where, however, institutions have changed their program to offer a service for the physical, mental, and emotional study and treatment of children of special needs they have found an increasing number of requests for service. Some church institutions have employed the services of one or more social caseworkers and have adopted a program of foster-family placement using the institutions as a receiving home for children. Others have developed a program of temporary care for children who can best be served in an institution. Such children are those who, because of lack of emotional preparedness on their own part or on the part of their parents or for other reasons, are not immediately able to accept foster-family placement.

Some church institutions have maintained their service only for those who were members of their own denomination. Others have accepted children on the basis of their needs. Christian worship and instruction have been emphasized in church institutions, thus distinguishing them from non-church institutions where religious worship and instruction are incidental to the program.

See CHILDREN, CARE OF.

BIBLIOGRAPHY: Howard W. Hopkirk, *Institutions Serving Children*, 1944.

LEON N. ZAHN.

CHILDREN'S WORK: Ever since Bible days the chief factor in Christian education has been the home, and experience with adults. At the Reformation the Bible became the chief authority. Luther and Commenius (d. 1671) advocated teaching in the vernacular. The latter, a pioneer, emphasized respect for the child's personality, use of visual processes, and functional methods of teaching. He was so far ahead of his time that many religious educators have not yet caught up with him. Pestalozzi (d. 1827), Herbart (d. 1841), and Froebel (d. 1852) made large advances toward understanding children. Meanwhile, in colonial America the Bible was the supreme authority. Between 1787 and 1847 there was a gradual withdrawal of religious materials from public school curricula, so that the teaching of religion became increasingly the responsibility of the churches. Between 1790 and 1815, teaching in the Sunday School centered in the catechism, and numerous churches still continue to stress this. By the second decade of the nineteenth century emphasis had shifted to Bible study. Children memorized large portions of Scripture, to be recited each Sunday with little supervision, and with prizes as the chief incentive. This plan was followed by the use of Bible selections without much regard to the capabilities of the children. By the third quarter of the nineteenth century a plan was developed to give some attention to their capacities, but unfortunately the same Bible passages were used for all ages. The Uniform Lessons continued until 1910 when a modified form of Bible study was developed, with closely graded lessons, and later with group graded lessons. Many children are still being taught through uniform lessons.

Many graded lesson materials are biblical.

They tend toward moralizing and the "trait theory" of teaching. Weekday religious classes attended by nearly two million children have been generally biblical. Often Bible stories have been used with little reference to children's limited knowledge, and verbalization has been confused with education. More recent pioneers have stressed building in early childhood proper foundations for later religious education. Young children are guided to think religiously in terms of their own world and experiences. Meanings and motives are regarded as more important than verbalization of adult ideas and incidents. Christian conceptions of God are fostered in connection with the child's actual experiences with persons, the church, and the world around him. More direct Bible study is provided some time after the third grade, when children are becoming conversant with geography, time, and foreign affairs. Such courses usually begin with the New Testament and are taught in long units, to provide an understanding of Jesus as a real person in His own world. Vivid kinds of experiences are provided, and questions are encouraged, so that children gain more knowledge and better understanding. Using sound biblical and psychological scholarship such teachers prepare for later childhood, when attention is given to friendship with varied cultural and racial groups, to study of the local church and other churches in the community, and to lessons about creation, the universe, life and death, and the practice of prayer and worship. The practice of Christian living precedes the theoretical teaching of a faith. Thus prepared, adolescents seem more ready to progress through courses in Bible, church history, worship, Christian vocations, and other practical subjects involving Christian service.

See also CHILDREN AT WORSHIP.

EDNA M. BAXTER.

CHILE: Area, 286,396 square miles; population, 5,760,571 (1950 estimate). One-fifth of the population lives in Santiago. Infant mortality in Chile is high, being 169.0 per 1,000 live births.

There are two state universities, two Catholic universities (one in Santiago and one in Valparaiso), and a school of technology. Primary schools in 1948 had 518,446 pupils and secondary schools 70,622 pupils; private and municipal schools had 149,802 pupils. Both Catholics and Protestants maintain good schools.

The Roman Catholic Church was disestablished in 1925. The hierarchy consists of one cardinal-archbishop, two archbishops, fifteen bishops, and two vicars apostolic. The constitution guarantees the public exercise of all religious beliefs, freedom of conscience, and the free exercise of all forms of worship.

According to 1948 estimates there were 354,440 Protestants in Chile, 202,000 of these being Pentecostals (*q.v.*). Protestantism has made its greatest gains among the humble classes, among whom the Protestants have a reputation for honesty and sobriety. Alcoholism is one of the curses of Chile. There is a National Evangelical Council in which various denominations cooperate. Religious bodies include: Methodists, Presbyterians, Baptists, Pentecostals, Salvation Army, Christian Missionary Alliance, Seventh-day Adventists, Anglicans, and Roman Catholics. The South American Missionary Society (Anglican) and the Methodists maintain educational, medical, and church work among the Mapuche Indians in the south. The Methodists also maintain an important agricultural school and experimental station at Angol in the south of Chile.

BIBLIOGRAPHY: *Guía Eclesiástica de Chile*, 1944; R. C. Moore, *Piety and Poverty in Chile*, 1946. See ARGENTINA for general works on South America.

[Sup.] W. STANLEY RYCROFT.

CHINA: I. Political Revolution: From 1910 to 1952 China experienced a thoroughgoing revolution in all aspects of her life. The political revolution of 1912, caused by the impact of the Occident, replaced the empire established on Confucian ideals with a so-called republic. Sun Yat-sen with his Three People's Principles stimulated the development of Chinese nationalism. General Chiang Kai-shek emerged in the 1920's, fought the Communists who had made a start in South China, and forced them into the Northwest. He became the first president of the Nationalist Government established in 1928.

Consolidation of China was accompanied by growing tensions with outside countries, especially Japan. Treaties were revised and in 1930 extraterritoriality was abrogated. Japanese encroachments in northeast China led in 1937 to open war. Chiang, driven back, established his wartime capital in Chungking. Puppets governed the occupied areas.

After Japan surrendered, relations with the Communists worsened (see COMMUNISM). Low morale of the Nationalist army and political leaders, confiscatory financial methods, serious inflation, failure to effect land reforms, and war weariness gave Communist propaganda its chance. The Communists with a disciplined army waged full-scale war, taking Manchuria and North China in 1947–48 and completing the conquest of the mainland in 1950. Nationalist China was confined to Formosa. The People's Republic formed in Peking in 1949 was recognized by nineteen nations. The United States withdrew its officials in 1950. The propaganda against American "imperialism" increased with Chinese entrance into the Korean War. At the end of 1952 the People's Republic, under Mao Tse-Tung and backed by Russia, seemed firmly established.

II. Educational and Social Revolution: This was marked by language reform, the introduc-

tion of scientific method and the democratic process into the educational system, a new concern for the common man, and increased education for girls and women. Relations between the sexes became freer, divorce more prevalent. The Communists, while announcing protection of women's rights, attacked the filial relations of the family system. Narrow family loyalties gradually gave way to loyalty to the nation. Under the Communists devotion to Marxism and "democratic centralism" became the supreme loyalty.

The "New Life Movement," sponsored by General and Madame Chiang, aimed to renovate life by promoting simplicity and modesty in dress and manner, correctness of behavior in the army, and honesty in political life. Economical mass weddings, wearing of cheap uniforms, somewhat improved army discipline, and the banning of some Western social practices resulted.

A more critical attitude toward religion resulted in the anti-religion movement with its anti-Christian turn in 1922. Christianity was accused of being superstitious, unscientific, and imperialistic. Twenty-five years later the Communists repeated these accusations.

III. The Christian Movement: A. EVANGELISM: The Protestant churches witnessed through preaching in churches and markets, through student evangelistic campaigns and conferences, through circulation of the Mandarin Bible and tracts, and through three-year and five-year movements to increase membership and deepen spiritual life. The Clark Evangelistic Bands in Shantung, rural service unions, city industrial programs, and missions to the hinterland reached new people. Indigenous groups—Bethel Band, Little Flock, Spiritual Grace, Jesus Family (173 organized families or villages reported in 1950) —sprang up. Most of the 10,000 churches were rural, with widely scattered membership. Figures indicate steady growth in church membership from 254,431 in 1914 to 750,000 in 1948.

The Roman Catholic Church aimed at Christianizing whole families and villages. Rural programs were emphasized. Zealous laymen helped propagate the faith. Catholic Action (*q.v.*) reported by 1933 the baptism of 250,000, mostly infants, and the opening of twenty churches and chapels. Statistics, not limited to baptized adults, were: 1912, 1,406,659; 1949, 3,251,374. Yet in 1950 the total Catholic and Protestant constituency was less than 1% of the population.

B. PERSONNEL AND DEVOLUTION: The number of Protestant China missionaries fluctuated from 5,000 in 1910 to 8,325 in 1936; 1,000 in China in 1945, 4,000 in 1948, and fewer than 20 at the end of 1952.

Meanwhile, theological schools were preparing Chinese leaders. The number of ordained ministers rose from 764 in 1915 to 2,196 in 1936. The Christian Associations put foreign personnel under Chinese national committees and Chinese general secretaries. Episcopally organized denominations elected Chinese bishops. Moderate devolution proceeded until the Communists stopped entirely the use of foreign personnel and funds.

The foreign staff of the Roman Catholic Church increased from 2,355 in 1912 to 5,835 in 1939. By 1942 about 650 Americans were serving in China, more than in any other country. At the end of 1952 several hundred Catholic missionaries were still in China.

The Chinese staff increased proportionately more rapidly than the foreign. In 1912 there were 2,236 Chinese priests, lay brothers, and sisters; and by 1939, 6,555. In 1926, six Chinese priests were raised to the episcopacy and consecrated by the pope in Rome. Some European priests served under Chinese bishops. The Catholic hierarchy was set up in China (1944–46) with a Chinese cardinal, archbishops, and bishops.

C. INSTITUTIONAL WORK: Protestant missions emphasized *education:* elementary schools, which by 1929 numbered 7,000 with 241,000 students; middle schools, of which there were, in 1938, 269 with 47,940 students; higher education, with all thirteen of the associated colleges organized and operating by 1924. Every year they "sent out into the service of church and nation young men and women of marked abilities and tested character, deeply impregnated with Christian principles and life-motives, furnished with the Christian educational equipment for leadership."

Government registration after 1927 abolished compulsory courses in religion and compulsory chapel attendance, separated theological schools from arts colleges, and required two-thirds of the board members and the heads of institutions to be Chinese. Some Christian schools objected to these requirements and the Sun Yat-sen memorial services. Some refused to register. The number of Protestant elementary schools dropped to 3,000 in 1936 with 6,000 kindergartens. Eventually most Protestant colleges and middle schools registered. The Roman Catholic schools objected to the curbs on religious instruction but were not averse to Chinese control.

The Roman Catholic Church gave increasing attention to education, especially for the training of the priesthood. They founded hundreds of orphanages, and in 1936 had 4,283 primary schools, 103 colleges and middle schools, and 3 universities.

Medical work developed rapidly and made an immense contribution to the Christian movement. By 1936 there were 306 hospitals (*q.v.*) with 21,578 beds. In that year Protestant missions had three-fourths of all the hospitals in China, half of the doctors (963), and a majority of the trained nurses (1,982)—nearly half of the total trained nurses for all mission fields. By 1948 the war had reduced the hospitals to 216, with 6 medical schools and 79 nursing training centers.

Roman Catholic hospitals and dispensaries were more numerous than in any other country in Asia and gave more treatments in China than did the Protestants. The Catholic Medical Service, organized in 1935 in Peking, coordinated their medical activities.

D. CO-OPERATION AND UNITY: The 1907 Centenary Conference urged the unification of Chinese churches holding the same denominational order. In 1912 churches growing out of the Episcopal missions came together; several Lutheran bodies united in 1917; other denominational unions followed.

In 1922 Chinese church leaders proposed corporate unity. The most significant church union across denominational lines was the Church of Christ in China. Negotiations started in 1918. By 1950 Chinese churches related to 16 missionary societies had joined. With 175,000 members it was much the largest church in China, active and well-organized. Under pressure from the outside, churches of all denominations united. This occurred in the occupied areas under the Japanese, and now under the People's Republic.

The National Christian Council was formed in 1922 of mission boards and agencies representing three-fifths of the Protestant constituency. It served the Christian movement by representing it in ecumenical and governmental relationships, by promoting new projects and experiments in rural, industrial, and family life fields, in nation-wide evangelistic campaigns, anti-opium and anti-footbinding efforts, and relief programs.

E. THE WAR YEARS (1937–48): Millions of students and others migrated to the West. As many as 117 middle schools and most of the Protestant colleges established themselves in Free China. After the war they returned to rehabilitate their original plants. Churches and schools suffered losses in trained leadership and in demoralization from war. Occupied China had a legacy of fear, hatred, suspicion, and widespread ethical breakdown. Nevertheless, by 1948 there were 250 middle schools and a college enrollment of 12,121, and Protestant church membership had increased over 30%.

F. INCREASING COMMUNIST INFLUENCE AND CONTROL (1948–52): The church under Communist pressure tried to adapt itself to conditions, stressing its social program, the loyalty of its members to the government, its desire to be independent of all foreign control while continuing loyal to Jesus Christ. A careful report indicates these stages of the developing situation: (1) Period of mutual friendliness. Christian leaders exhibited a friendly attitude toward the new regime because everybody was dissatisfied with the old, obvious improvements had been made, freedom of religious belief was promised, and special consideration was shown to Protestants in the People's Consultative Conference of Representatives of Historical Religions. (2) Period of self-clearance from foreign domination with the adoption of the so-called Christian Manifesto and launching of the Three-Self Movement. (3) Period of open attack against foreign missions. The Peking National Conference of Christian leaders (April, 1951) condemned all world Christian organizations as agents of American imperialism and asked Christian organizations to sever all international connections. Individual Christians, Chinese and foreign, were "accused" on political grounds. (4) Period of complete submission. Christian educational and medical institutions were absorbed by the government. Theological seminaries were brought into line. All Christian publications were censored. Church members were urged to pledge support to the Communist Party. All Christian organizations were required to participate in the Resist-America Aid-Korea Movement, in politics, and in parades.

The People's Republic succeeded in bringing Protestant churches together and in enlisting their public support. Country churches suffered acutely; many were closed, others conducted only limited programs. Propaganda turned youth against Christianity, causing concern for the next generation.

Roman Catholics suffered most severely because of their connections with the Catholic hierarchy, large real estate holdings, less participation in the self-clearance movement and in the accusation meetings, and the church's pronounced stand against Communism. From 1945 to 1950, twenty-nine foreign missionaries and eighty-one Chinese leaders suffered martyrdom because of their loyalty to the church.

In the country in which there had been the largest investment of foreign personnel and funds, a mission era was ended. The remarkable achievements outlined in this survey did not prevent the church from yielding ground to a powerful non-Christian force. The Communists think that the history of Nestorianism will be repeated, that Christianity, with its world-wide connections broken, will wither away. Chinese Christians are suffering terribly as they make their decision on how much can be compromised without disloyalty to Jesus Christ. The Chinese church will undoubtedly become "more Chinese, less Western, perhaps also less Christian."

We have learned from what has happened in China that: our denominational divisions are tragic; our program must answer human needs; all of life must be Christianized; we must keep clear of Western imperialism; there must be clear, sound theological teaching to meet the impact of Communist teaching and rapid devolution within the church.

A missionary statesman goes further and asks whether, in "facing an age-old and highly developed civilization with well-thought-out culture embodied in established institutions" like China's, "missionary Christianity, relying solely on its methods of evangelistic persuasion, education, and witness through service, can ever win."

The China situation requires that we learn these lessons and face that question while we remember the words of a China missionary: "A church which, like her Lord, refuses the world's way of power, must always seem to fail, even when it bears the seeds of future triumph."

BIBLIOGRAPHY: D. J. Dallin, *Soviet Russia and the Far East*, 1948; John K. Fairbank, *The United States and China*, 1948; L. C. Goodrich, *A Short History of the Chinese People*, revised ed., 1951; C. P. Fitzgerald, *Revolution in China*, 1952; K. S. Latourette, *A History of the Expansion of Christianity*, Vol. VII, *Advance Through Storm*, 1945; *China Committee Reports; China Bulletin*, semi-monthly publication of the Far Eastern Joint Office, National Council of Churches; *China Missionary Bulletin*, bi-monthly of the Roman Catholic Church.
[Sup.] ROWLAND MCLEAN CROSS.

CHOIR: The establishment of a school for the training of choristers before the reign of Gregory the Great indicates the high value placed upon well-trained choirs in early Christian times. Before the Reformation, fine voices were in such demand that the kidnapping of boy choristers was a not uncommon practice. Adult choristers were frequently members of at least minor orders of clergy. Except in convents, women did not ordinarily take part in church choirs, and even now important cathedrals and parishes frequently prefer choirs of men and boys. Wealthy congregations often employ professional singers in choruses, which are expected to render, in addition to the usual service music, excerpts from oratorios at services devoted principally to music. The high cost of such choirs, as well as a desire to cultivate a more general participation of the congregation in church music, has led to the formation of several choirs in a parish, designed for the training of designated age groups, with degrees of skill in the performance of music suitable to the several divisions of the church school, or the special services of the congregation. Several services each year are planned to require the participation of all the choirs. See D. D. Kettring, *Steps toward a Singing Church* (1948), for a discussion of the organization and administration of a multiple-choir program.   [Sup.] PAUL ALLWARDT.

CHORLEY, EDWARD CLOWES: Episcopalian; b. at Manchester, England, May 6, 1865; d. at Cold Spring, N. Y., Nov. 2, 1949. He studied at Richmond College (B.A., 1888), and the Philadelphia Divinity School (B.D., 1904). In 1915 he was appointed Historiographer of the diocese of New York, and in 1919 he was made Historiographer of the Episcopal Church. He was the founder and editor of *The Historical Magazine of the Protestant Episcopal Church* from its inception in 1932 until his death. His writings include: *The New American Prayer Book, Its History and Contents* (1929); and *Men and Movements in the American Episcopal Church* (1946).

BIBLIOGRAPHY: *Historical Magazine of the P.E. Church,* Dec. 1949; *The Living Church,* Nov. 9, 1949.

MASSEY H. SHEPHERD, JR.

CHRISTADELPHIANS: This Adventist-Unitarian group has experienced little growth. It has about 100 congregations or *ecclesias* with approximately 2,500 members in twenty-six states of the U.S.A., usually meeting in rented halls. The members regard themselves as being "called out of the world," hence they do not vote, hold public office, or participate in war. Polity is strictly congregational, with no overhead organization, and there is no missionary work in the accepted sense, although Christadelphians are found in several countries. A periodical, *The Faith,* is published at Waterloo, Ia.

[Sup.] ELMER T. CLARK.

CHRISTENDOM MOVEMENT. See KINGDOM OF GOD, LEAGUE OF THE.

CHRISTENGEMEINSCHAFT: During the last phase of his life, Rudolf Steiner (see ANTHROPOSOPHY) interpreted Christianity in terms of his anthroposophic philosophy. Under his influence the former pastor, Friedrich Rittelmeyer, of Berlin, started the Fellowship of Christians in 1923. Congregations were organized all over Germany, and a few appeared in other European countries and the United States. Their influence is increasing steadily.

The biblical Christ is viewed as a "high spiritual being," head of the "cosmic hierarchies" of spirits. Salvation is interpreted as *gnosis* of higher worlds, death as the path to reincarnation. The Fellowship's liturgy, received by Steiner in a special "revelation," resembles the Roman Mass. Its baptism is no longer (1950) acknowledged as valid by the churches in Germany. Its ministry, teachings, and sacraments are separated from those of Protestant churches.

BIBLIOGRAPHY: F. Rittelmeyer, *Meine Lebensbegegnung mit Steiner,* 1925; *Christus aller Erde,* a series, since 1924.

HANS CHRISTOPH VON HASE.

CHRISTIAN: The name arose in the Greek-speaking world. The use of the ending *-ianos,* of Latin origin, on the stem of the Greek *Christos* (often confused by pagans with *chrēstos,* "good," "serviceable") could not occur in an Aramaic-speaking situation. Origin of the designation at Antioch in Syria (Acts 11:26) was fitting. There, for the first time, the disciples included with Jews a considerable number of Gentiles; the group could no longer be regarded as a Jewish sect. A new name was needed, and since the disciples baptized "in the name of Christ," the name Christian was apt. We need not seek its origin at Rome (Gercke); Roman influence was prominent at Antioch, where lived later the first non-canonical Christian writer to use the title (Ignatius). The name was not originated by the disciples themselves (Bickerman). Nor did it arise in the offices of the provincial administration (Paribeni), to describe the group as revolutionary (Peterson). It probably arose among the people of Antioch, who heard the new group confess Christ as Lord and so coined the title. Nothing proves that its original intent was abusive, but as the Christian group grew, and people and rulers saw clearly its threat to pagan faith and ways, the term inevitably acquired a note of reproach. The Christians at first preferred other names, but in the second century they gradually adopted and defended it.

BIBLIOGRAPHY: A. Gercke, "Der Christenname ein Scheltname," *Festschrift zur Jahrhundertfeier der koenigl. Universitaet zu Breslau* (1911), 360–373; R. Paribeni, "Sull' origine del nome Christiano," *Nuovo Bullettino di Archeologia Christiana,* XIX (1913), 37–41; P. de Labriolle, "Christianus," *Bulletin du Cange,* V (1929–30), 69–88; E. Peterson, "Christianus," *Miscellanea Giovanni Mercati,* I (1946), 355–372; E. J. Bickerman, "The Name of Christians," *HTR,* XLII (1949), 109–124.

[Sup.] FLOYD V. FILSON.

CHRISTIAN AMENDMENT MOVEMENT. See POLITICAL ACTION, THE CHURCHES AND.

CHRISTIAN AND MISSIONARY ALLIANCE: The Board of Managers has been increased to twenty-four persons. The work of the Alliance is departmentalized and, with the officers, six executive secretaries lead the work of the respective departments. There are nearly one thousand branches and churches in North America, where the work is divided under the leadership of district superintendents.

Foreign work is largely evangelistic, although some educational and simple medical work is carried on. The Alliance recognizes a responsibility for the evangelization of some eighty million people in areas where, in most instances, other societies are not working. These fields are in Asia, Africa, Latin America, and the Islands. In 1950, 610 foreign missionaries, with some 2,000 indigenous workers in about 3,000 centers, had a record of over 7,000 baptisms. There are 87,000 active members in churches abroad. Twenty-five Bible training schools abroad had, in 1950, 1,200 students taking a full course covering several years, and over 4,000 students taking shorter periods of training. The budget of the Alliance, excluding local church expenses, has reached nearly two million dollars per year.

Five Bible schools in North America had a total enrollment (1950–51) of 1,332.

[Sup.] WILLIAM F. SMALLEY.

CHRISTIAN BIOGRAPHY LECTURES:
The Tipple Foundation of Drew University provides for an annual series of lectures on some phase of Christian biography. The fund was established by the late President and Mrs. Ezra Squier Tipple. Dr. Tipple's chief scholarly interest was in the realm of Christian biography. He was author of a book on Bishop Francis Asbury and a collector of Wesleyana, the latter now in possession of Drew University. Lecturers have included: Kenneth Scott Latourette, G. Bromley Oxnam, and Wilbert F. Howard.

FRED G. HOLLOWAY.

CHRISTIAN BROTHERS: A religious Congregation of teaching Brothers founded in 1680 by St. John Baptist de la Salle for the purpose of giving Christian education to Roman Catholic boys, especially those of the working classes.

The Brothers conduct both private and parochial schools, including high schools, trade schools, and colleges. Two of their colleges, St. Mary's, Moraga, Calif., and La Salle, Philadelphia, are among the most prominent of Catholic institutions of higher learning in the United States.

The members of the Institute of the Brothers of the Christian Schools take the vows of poverty, chastity, and obedience. Candidates who have graduated from high school spend a year in novitiate before attending college to prepare themselves for the teaching life. In America this scholasticate is De La Salle College, located at Washington, D. C., and associated with Catholic University. The entire congregation is governed by a superior general, elected for life by the general chapter.

The Christian Brothers were introduced into the United States in 1846, at Baltimore. It is estimated that the Brothers teach over 300,000 pupils throughout the world.

[Sup.] THOMAS J. McCARTHY.

CHRISTIAN CATHOLIC APOSTOLIC CHURCH IN ZION: The fundamentalist-premillennarian communal theocracy established at Zion City, Ill., in 1896, by John Alexander Dowie, has undergone the vicissitudes of bankruptcy, fire, and ridicule which have almost completely altered its character. Private enterprise and other churches have entered, the strict puritanical pattern of personal conduct has been modified, and the former colony has become a typical town of its class. The group attracted wide attention by its claim that the world is flat, which was not relaxed even when Dowie's successor, Wilbur Glenn Voliva, made a trip around the world. The sect has not spread, but membership figures are not available.

BIBLIOGRAPHY: E. T. Clark, *The Small Sects in America*, rev. ed., 1949; Frank S. Mead, *Handbook of Denominations*, 1951; *The Final Warning* (periodical).

[Sup.] ELMER T. CLARK.

CHRISTIAN CHURCH. See CHURCHES OF CHRIST; CONGREGATIONAL-CHRISTIANS; CONGREGATIONALISTS; DISCIPLES OF CHRIST.

CHRISTIAN CONGREGATION: Formed March 10, 1887, near Kokomo, Ind. The incorporation of this religious body was revised Oct. 18, 1898. It is devoted to the proclamation of the new commandment of Christian love (John 13:34–35) which its members accept as their standard of Christian conduct, doctrine, organization, union, and fellowship with one another and with God in Christ. Although titles of "bishop" and "pastor" are used, the polity of the body, formed by the voluntary association of individuals and local assemblies, is strictly congregational. Doctrinal agreements and creeds are not used. Forms of worship resemble those of other Christians. In 1951 there were 68 parishes, 71 ministers and Bible colportage representatives, and 6,120 members. Publishing and corresponding office is in Augusta, Tex. [Sup. to MISCELLANEOUS RELIGIOUS BODIES.]

OSCEOLA J. READ.

CHRISTIAN EDUCATION. See EDUCATION, CHRISTIAN.

CHRISTIAN ENDEAVOR, THE INTERNATIONAL SOCIETY OF: An interdenominational, interracial organization founded by Francis E. Clark on February 2, 1881, in the Williston Congregational Church, Portland, Me., for the purpose of training young people in the duties of church membership and the activities of Christian life. The principles include open confession of Christ, active service for him, loyalty to his church, and fellowship with his people. Today thousands of societies are found in almost eighty different denominations and in practically every country on the globe. The active membership is estimated at almost three million. The organization has a graded system, with societies adapted to all ages, beginning with juniors and including adults, with graduate members known as alumni. In addition to local societies there are C.E. unions—local, district, state, provincial, and national—with the World's C.E. Union as the over-all organization. The International Society of C.E. takes in bodies throughout North and South America, and serves as a clearing house for all sorts of C.E. activities. It publishes and circulates varied literature, including *The Christian Endeavor World* as the official magazine. Headquarters of the International Society and of the World C.E. Union are at 1201 East Broad Street, Columbus, Ohio. [Sup. to YOUNG PEOPLE'S SOCIETIES, Vol. XIII.]

GENE STONE.

CHRISTIAN REFORMED CHURCH IN AMERICA: In 1952 the Church numbered 389 congregations, 38,887 families, 165,801 souls, and 92,204 communicants. There were twenty-one classes, comprising the one synod. Growth has been primarily internal. Rapid expansion is under way in Canada, due to immigration from the Netherlands. Fifty-three new immigrant congregations were organized in Canada between 1948 and 1951, forming two all-Canadian classes.

The degree to which doctrinal orthodoxy has been maintained calls for comment. The language isolation which once protected this position is now gone. With the exception of a few "extra" services, all of the regular church services in the long-established congregations are now English. Rapid Anglicization is under way in the Canadian congregations also. But the doctrinal position remains substantially unchanged. During the years 1918–24, it was defended in church trials against premillennialism, "modernism," and other deviations. During these controversies, numerical losses were experienced in the formation of the Berean and Protestant Reformed Churches. Membership in the Federal Council of the Churches of Christ (q.v.) was maintained for only two years; it was terminated in 1924 on doctrinal grounds, as was membership in the National Association of Evangelicals (q.v.), after eight years, in 1951. Fellowship with other orthodox Reformed Churches is sought in the Alliance of Reformed Churches. Emphasis on doctrinal instruction, catechism preaching, home visiting, etc. are maintained, but hymns were introduced in worship in 1934. Conservative positions have been adopted on such matters as divorce, worldly amusements, and birth control.

The mission work of the church has been expanded to reach China, 1920; South America, 1934; Africa, 1939; Ceylon, 1947; Japan and India in the year 1950. The work among the American Indians (q.v.) has been expanded also. Home mission work is preoccupied chiefly with Canada, but church extension in the United States still goes on. Follow-up evangelism in the Back to God Hour (q.v.) and work among Negroes began more recently. Many radio broadcasts are supported and much city mission work carried on through local auspices. The church publishes its own Sunday school lesson material and encourages tract evangelism through a denominational tract committee.

In 1952 Calvin College had 1,200 students and a faculty of 60. Calvin Seminary had 120 students and a faculty of eight. The Reformed Bible Institute has been maintained in Grand Rapids, Mich., since 1942. The work of three psychopathic hospitals, numerous homes for the aged, and several other agencies of mercy is given substantial support. The church has re-luctantly come to tolerate the big labor unions, but gives moral and financial support to the Christian Labor Association. Support of a Christian school system is more consistent and enthusiastic than ever before.

The strength of this denomination lies in its literal subscription and loyal adherence to its historic creeds, which serve both to stabilize its position and broaden its outlook. There is a growing awareness of a distinctive position and a broad mission in the American environment. Despite numerical limitations, the denomination feels itself to be an outstanding representative of Reformed orthodoxy on the North American continent, with the duty and desire to maintain that position to the profit of the environment as a whole.

BIBLIOGRAPHY: H. Beets, *The Christian Reformed Church*, 1946; *Classis Holland Minutes, 1848–1858*, 1943; J. C. De Korne, ed., *Navaho and Zuni for Christ*, 1947; A. Hyma, *Albertus C. Van Raalte*, 1947; D. H. Kromminga, *The Christian Reformed Tradition*, 1943; J. H. Kromminga, *The Christian Reformed Church*, 1949; J. Schaver, *The Polity of the Churches*, Vol. II, 1947.
[Sup. to REFORMED CHURCH, CHRISTIAN.]

JOHN H. KROMMINGA.

CHRISTIAN SCIENCE: Long before the death of Mrs. Eddy in 1910 she had largely withdrawn from active direction of the movement she had founded. But she reserved to the end her right to, and not infrequently did, intervene in its direction through some suggestion or rule which was incorporated into the *Church Manual*. She had set up two legal corporations, the Board of Directors and the Trustees of the Publishing Society, to carry on the work of the church, and in her will constituted a group known as the Trustees under the will of Mrs. Eddy, charged with the publication and sale of her own writings. At present the Board of Directors are also the Trustees under the will. Difference of opinion as to the conduct of affairs developed between the Board and the Trustees of the Publishing Society. About a decade after the death of their leader, the Board undertook to remove one of the three Trustees. The Trustees resisted by an appeal to the courts, thus initiating the Great Litigation. The lower court found in favor of the Trustees, but the Supreme Court of Massachusetts reversed the decision and the final authority of the Board of Directors was upheld. Their control has been increasingly solidified across the years.

No successful rival movement has thus far developed. During Mrs. Eddy's lifetime the famous Stetson case occurred and the founder of the great First Church of Christ Scientist of New York City was excommunicated. For several years her loyal followers carried on, but the group has now disappeared. Another movement of revolt was begun by Mrs. Annie C. Bill, aided by a former member of the Board of Directors who was excommunicated, Mr. John V. Dittemore; but this group, too, has practically disappeared. Individuals such as Mr. Herbert Eustace, who led the fight for the Board of Trustees, have continued, outside the church, to teach, practice, and publish. Others have been Mr. John Doorly, onetime lecturer, teacher, and prolific writer; Arthur Corey, author of a widely circulated book, *Christian Science Class Instruction;* and quite recently Mrs. Margaret L. Laird; but none has created a formidable rival organization. Most of them have conceived a fundamental distrust of organization because of their experience within the highly authoritarian Mother Church.

The Board of Directors regards itself as the custodian of Mrs. Eddy's thought, and the central aim of headquarters has been to preserve the original purity of her teachings from dilution or alteration. They consider that they are carrying out faithfully Mrs. Eddy's intention in permitting no deviation from the government which she herself set forth. Not a few, however, insist that the insertion of numerous "estoppel clauses" in the *Manual,* requiring her consent or signature, was meant to bring the whole material organization to an end, and so the end of the highly authoritarian control of the church. It must be said that quotations can be found in Mrs. Eddy's writings which support both positions.

Since the church does not disclose its membership, the only clue to its growth is in the number of churches and societies reported in the *Journal,* and the number of practitioners. At Mrs. Eddy's passing, there were 1,229 branch churches and societies. In 1951 there were 3,049. In 1910 there were 4,661 practitioners; in 1951 there were 10,503. Christian Science churches are now found in Europe, Asia, Africa, and Australia as well as the Americas.

Christian Science healing has been recognized legally by all state legislatures in the United States, and the right of the individual to rely on spiritual healing without interference by public authority, in the way of compulsory medical examination or treatment, particularly at the adult level, has come to be recognized in most states.

BIBLIOGRAPHY: Hugh Studdert-Kennedy, *Christian Science and Organized Religion,* 1930; Edwin F. Dakin, *Mrs. Eddy,* 1929; Lyman Powell, *Mary Baker Eddy,* 1930; Arthur Corey, *Christian Science Class Instruction,* 1945; Charles S. Braden, *These Also Believe,* 1949.

[Sup.] CHARLES S. BRADEN.

When news was announced of Mrs. Eddy's demise in 1910, many people predicted that the Church of Christ, Scientist would disintegrate. Instead, it grew steadily in numbers, stability, scope of activity, and fellowship with other Christian denominations. Its unique form of government under Mrs. Eddy's *Manual of the Mother Church,* which was sustained by the highest court of Massachusetts, rules out personal domination and insures government by

law rather than by men. Despite the defection of a few individuals or small splinter groups (see below), the unity of the great body of Christian Scientists was overwhelming. *The Christian Science Monitor,* established by Mrs. Eddy in 1908, achieved widespread recognition as one of the world's great newspapers and has given notably sympathetic and effective publicity to the ecumenical movement (*q.v.*). Christian Scientists served as chaplains in the United States armed services, and the huge Christian Science war relief activities, extended to those of all faiths, won commendation from many governments.

The Christian Science Publishing Society in Boston sent out a stream of literature to every quarter of the globe. *The Herald of Christian Science* was published, monthly and quarterly, in ten different languages, and short articles and pamphlets in nineteen. The evangelistic activities of the Mother Church included a weekly radio program over 800 stations on three continents. Its philanthropic activities included a permanent home for Christian Science workers of advancing years, at Concord, N.H.; sanatoriums at Boston and San Francisco for Christian Scientists needing temporary care; and widespread disaster relief. Extensive organized activities in the armed services and the striking growth of Christian Science organizations at universities and colleges evidence the movement's concern with youth. With all this, however, the vital emphasis in Christian Science remains on individual spiritual growth and emulation of Christ Jesus' example.

BIBLIOGRAPHY: C. P. Smith, *et al., Permanency of the Mother Church,* 1954; *The Story of Christian Science Wartime Activities, 1939–1946,* 1947; Norman Beasley, *The Cross and the Crown,* 1952; Vergilius Ferm, ed., *Religion in the 20th Century,* 1948.

[Sup.] WILL B. DAVIS.

CHRISTIAN SOCIALISM: Used only in areas where the religious tradition is Protestant, the term is employed loosely to denote Christian theory and practice marked by a strong social emphasis. Since 1910 Christians have shown growing concern for greater justice in the relations between economic groups, increasing sympathy with socialist thought (see SOCIALISM) and labor movements, and have attempted to formulate what would constitute a genuinely Christian socialism.

Indicative of this changing social emphasis in Britain were the National Mission of Repentance and Hope (1916); the Fifth Report of the Archbishop's Committee on Christianity and Industrial Problems (1918), which showed that the church could no longer be counted on as a bulwark of existing social arrangements; the Conference on Christian Politics, Economics, and Citizenship (*q.v.*); the interdenominational Society of Socialist Christians (1924) which, proclaiming that it was socialist because it was

Christian, was affiliated with the Labor Party; the pan-Protestant Christian Social Council (1928) and the Roman Catholic Social Guild (1932); the Malvern (*q.v.*) Conference (1940); the formation of the World Council of Churches (*q.v.*), one responsibility of which was the study of social problems from a Christian perspective. Important leaders were Charles Gore (*q.v.*), G. A. Studdert-Kennedy, William Temple (*q.v.*), George Lansbury, Clement Atlee, and Stafford Cripps.

There were also parallel movements on the continent of Europe. In Germany Friedrich Naumann (1860–1919) was a leader; in Holland Slotemaker de Bruine (b. 1869) was most prominent in social reform; in Denmark J. Sadolin organized a Christian Socialist League. Such men engaged in political action, largely in behalf of the workingman.

Developments of social Christianity in America followed the same general pattern, but several decades later. Important points were the organization of the Federal Council of Churches (1908, *q.v.*), which promulgated "The Social Ideals of the Churches," the National Catholic Welfare Conference (1918, *q.v.*), and the social action departments of various denominations. All of these furthered the study of industrial, financial, and political problems from Christian perspectives and with increased sympathy for labor unions. Protestant organizations also fostered sympathetic understanding of socialism. Influential have been Reinhold Niebuhr (*q.v.*), John Bennett (*q.v.*), Charles C. Morrison (*q.v.*), and Francis McConnell (*q.v.*).

See also SOCIAL GOSPEL; INDUSTRY, THE CHURCH AND; LABOR, THE CHURCH AND.

BIBLIOGRAPHY: James Dombrowski, *The Early Days of Christian Socialism in America*, 1936; Wilhelm Luetgert, *Der christliche Sozialismus*, 1927; M. B. Reckitt, *The Church and Society in England from 1800*, 1940; M. B. Reckitt, *Maurice to Temple: a Century of the Social Movement*, 1947.
[Sup.] ALEXANDER C. ZABRISKIE.

CHRISTIAN UNION, THE: Organized in Columbus, Ohio, on Feb. 3, 1864, by independent congregations which withdrew from Methodist, Presbyterian, Baptist, and United Brethren Churches as a protest against "political preaching" during the Civil War and against what were deemed intolerant restrictions on Christian liberty. Although avoiding creeds, congregations of the Union hold doctrines which, on the whole, are common to evangelical churches. Baptism is administered according to the mode desired by individual candidates. Ordination is accessible to women as well as men. The polity is strictly congregational. A general council, made up of clerical and lay delegates from state councils, meets quadrennially. In 1938 there were 220 congregations, mostly in Ohio, Indiana, and Missouri, with 15,400 members.

[Sup.] THEODORE G. TAPPERT.

CHRISTIAN UNION, YOUNG PEOPLE'S. See YOUNG PEOPLE'S SOCIETIES.

CHRISTIAN WORKERS FOR FELLOWSHIP. See CHURCH (CHURCHES) OF GOD.

CHRISTMAS SERVICES: In non-liturgical churches, the celebration of Christmas has tended to be a family affair rather than an ecclesiastical function. This may be due, in part, to Puritan opposition to stated church feasts, associated, as they sometimes were, with extreme types of merriment. Many congregations now celebrate Christmas by anticipation on the Sunday before. In some cases, the children of the church prepare their own service of carols and readings, bringing gifts for a stated cause. Elsewhere, services consist of the choral performance of carols from many sources. Frequently lighting is limited to candles except where electric lighting is absolutely necessary. Local customs have developed in the older parishes, such as in the church school at the Chapel of the Intercession in New York, with the decoration of the grave of Clement Moore, the author of "A Visit from St. Nicholas." Some churches set up a crèche and give opportunity for the children and others to have devotions nearby. Elsewhere services are planned to mark the lighting of important public out-of-door Christmas trees, such as the annual lighting of a tree in Washington, D. C., by the President.   PAUL ALLWARDT.

CHRISTOLOGY: The last half century has been a period of considerable activity in the field of Christology. While the old problems have continued to engage interest and the old answers have found stalwart defenders, the period has been marked by the emergence of new problems, largely as a result of the use of newer methods of biblical and historical criticism, and by attempts at reformulation and reinterpretation of the orthodox formulas.

I. The Jesus of History Movement: The early years of the century were dominated by "the rediscovery of the Jesus of history" and a comparative eclipse of Christology. A variety of factors combined to bring this about: a widespread revulsion against ecclesiastical dogma, which was ascribed to an intrusion of Greek intellectualism on the primitive simplicity of the original Galilean gospel; a new appreciation of the teaching of Jesus, which had been so strangely neglected throughout the centuries until Sir John Seeley drew attention to its significance (*Ecce Homo*, originally published anonymously in 1865); a desire to find a place in Christology for an authentic human life, which was foreshadowed in the kenotic theories of the nineteenth century; and, above all, a belief that the apology for Christianity in an age of declining faith was to be sought, not in the abstract, metaphysical person of the ancient creeds, but in the warm, human personality of the historical Jesus of Nazareth. The most arresting statement of the new attitude was given by Harnack in his *Wesen des Christentums* (1901; Eng. tr., *What is Christianity?* 1904). Harnack drew a radical distinction between the gospel *about* Jesus and the gospel *of* Jesus, which he reduced to a simple proclamation of the Fatherhood of God and the infinite value of the human soul. The shift of interest was reflected in a stream of popular books on the historical life of Jesus, in which he was portrayed as the supreme teacher, the genius, the hero, the martyr, whose true significance as an historical figure had been obscured behind the metaphysical screen of orthodox dogma.

II. Return to Christology: The assumption that it is possible to recover a portrait of the historical Jesus free of Christology, which had already been questioned by Martin Kaehler (*Der sogennannte historische Jesus und der geschichtliche biblische Christus,* 1892), was challenged in a sensational manner by Albert Schweitzer, who demonstrated that the whole mission and teaching of Jesus were set in an eschatological framework which could not be stripped away without mutilating the picture beyond recognition (*Von Reimarus zu Wrede,* 1906; Eng. tr., *The Quest of the Historical Jesus,* 1910). It has been further undermined by the application to the Synoptic Gospels of the new critical method known as *Formgeschichte* (Form Criticism, *q.v.*). According to the Form critics, the Gospel narratives acquired their form in the preaching and teaching of the primitive church and were shaped by homiletical rather than by biographical interests; "the telling of the story of Jesus was Christological through and through from the start" (D. M. Baillie).

III. Neo-orthodox Christology: A strong reaction against the Jesus of history movement on more definitely theological grounds was led by Karl Barth and Emil Brunner who contend that not the historical appearance of Jesus but only the Christ who is discerned by the eye of faith is the vehicle of the revelation of God. Their vigorous advocacy of a Christology on orthodox lines is thrown into relief by an apparent lack of interest in the words and deeds of the historical Jesus, for which they have been widely criticized. At the same time, Brunner has become increasingly critical of the terms of the Chalcedonian definition; he holds that it is sufficient to affirm the divinity and the humanity of Christ and that the attempt to define the relation between them in terms of two natures or in any other way exceeds the competence of human thought.

IV. Philosophical and Psychological Christology: Following in the philosophical tradition

of English theology, a small but significant group have sought to interpret the Incarnation in the light of a philosophical view of the universe. The most notable product of this school is *The Incarnate Lord* by Lionel Thornton (1928), where an attempt is made to integrate the doctrine with the organic philosophy of A. N. Whitehead. William Temple in an earlier work (*Christus Veritas,* 1924) sought to find a place for the Incarnation in the context of an evolutionary view of the universe. These interpretations are open to the criticism that they tend to give Christ the role of a cosmic principle rather than that of a Saviour from sin.

It is curious that in a period marked by the rise to prominence of psychology and allied sciences so few theologians looked to this quarter for light on the mystery of the person of Christ. A notable exception was William Sanday, who sought a solution of the apparent psychological dualism of the Chalcedonian definition in the theory that the divinity of Christ was located in the subliminal consciousness (*Christologies Ancient and Modern,* 1910). Further use of the enlarged conceptions of personality, which have emerged from modern psychological research, has been urged in a recent essay by W. R. Matthews, who suggests that Jung's theory of the racial unconscious may help us to understand Christ's liability to temptation and the racial significance of his saving work (*The Problem of Christ in the Twentieth Century,* 1950).

V. Christological Thought in America: For the greater part of the last half century there has been "something like a moratorium on the doctrine of Christ in American religious thought" (W. M. Horton). The last decade, however, shows a marked revival of interest in Christology, as echoes of European discussions have reached America and provoked American reactions. One point on which there is general agreement is that the insights gained by the rediscovery of the Jesus of history must receive an integral place in the Christology of the future. W. L. Sperry has passed severe strictures on the neo-orthodox theologians for their "studied neglect of Jesus" and particularly for their cavalier treatment of his recorded words and deeds. W. M. Horton emphasizes the historical record of the whole lifework of Jesus as the ground of our faith in him as our Eternal Contemporary, and from a reinterpretation of the threefold office in terms of Leader, Saviour, and Victor (on lines suggested by Karl Heim) Horton draws Christological conclusions which point in the direction of Nicaea and Chalcedon. John Knox pleads for the view that the meaning of Christ is to be found not merely in his birth or his death or his resurrection, but in the whole closely knit series of events of which he forms the center and which comprises not only the facts concerning Jesus himself but also the response he awakened, the coming of the Spirit, and the creation of the new community. The meaning of Christ must therefore be stated in terms of action rather than of nature, and Knox argues that the ancient creeds are to be understood as attempts to express symbolically God's unique revelatory act in Christ rather than as metaphysically accurate descriptions of the nature of his person. Similarly, W. Norman Pittenger, while keeping more closely to the traditional formulas, seeks to replace the static conceptions of the patristic period with a dynamic interpretation of the incarnation as God's decisive act in Christ.

VI. Christology and History: A new approach to the Christological problem has been made by a small group of theologians who seek to interpret Christ as the key to the meaning of history. While Otto Piper combines a view of Christ as the turning point of history and the inauguration of the new aeon with a biblical realism which accords full value to the categories of orthodox Christology, Paul Tillich regards these categories as mythical and allows them only a symbolic significance. Reinhold Niebuhr is also critical of the orthodox formulas on the ground that they attempt to state the significance of Christ in "ontic" terms and verge on logical nonsense; to him, as to Tillich, the presence of the eternal from beyond history in an historically conditioned person can only be expressed symbolically.

See also EXALTATION OF CHRIST; GOD; JESUS CHRIST; PRE-EXISTENCE; SOTERIOLOGY; THEOTOKOS; THEOLOGY, TWENTIETH CENTURY TRENDS IN.

BIBLIOGRAPHY: P. T. Forsyth, *The Person and Place of Jesus Christ*, 1910; R. H. Mackintosh, *The Doctrine of the Person of Christ*, 1912; S. Cave, *The Doctrine of the Person of Christ*, 1925; G. K. A. Bell and A. Deissmann, *Mysterium Christi*, 1930; L. W. Grensted, *The Person of Christ*, 1933; J. K. Mozley, *The Doctrine of the Incarnation*, 1936; J. S. Lawton, *Conflict in Christology*, 1947; D. M. Baillie, *God was in Christ*, 1948. *In re* Section I: A. Harnack, *What is Christianity?* 1904; T. R. Glover, *The Jesus of History*, 1917. II: A. Schweitzer, *The Quest of the Historical Jesus*, 1910; R. Bultmann, *Jesus and the Word*, 1929. III: E. Brunner, *The Mediator*, 1927; K. Barth, *Kirchliche Dogmatik*, I, 2 § 15, 1938; *idem*, *Dogmatics in Outline*, 1949; W. A. Visser 't Hooft, *The Kingship of Christ*, 1947; H. Vogel, *Christologie*, I, 1949. IV: W. Temple, *Christus Veritas*, 1924; L. S. Thornton, *The Incarnate Lord*, 1928; W. Sanday, *Christologies Ancient and Modern*, 1910; W. R. Matthews, *The Problem of Christ in the Twentieth Century*, 1950. V: W. M. Horton, *Our Eternal Contemporary*, 1942; W. N. Pittenger, *Christ and Christian Faith*, 1941; John Knox, *On the Meaning of Christ*, 1947; W. L. Sperry, *Jesus Then and Now*, 1949. VI: Otto Piper, *God in History*, 1939; Paul Tillich, *The Interpretation of History*, 1936; *idem*, *Systematic Theology*, I, 1951; Reinhold Niebuhr, *The Nature and Destiny of Man*, II, 1943.
[Sup.] GEORGE S. HENDRY.

CHRIST'S SANCTIFIED HOLY CHURCH, COLORED. See CHURCH (CHURCHES) OF GOD.

CHRONICLES, BOOKS OF: It is widely held that Chronicles, Ezra and Nehemiah were originally one work, written by the Chronicler somewhere between the time of Nehemiah (444 B.C.) and Ben Sira (180 B.C.). Pfeiffer dates the work about 250 B.C., whereas Albright holds to a date some time between 425 B.C. and 405 B.C., with a re-editing of the material possibly a few years later. For this early dating he adduces some cogent archaeological and linguistic arguments which are difficult to refute.

According to Torrey, Pfeiffer and a few others, the Chronicler was a poor historian who modified canonical sources to suit his purpose and fabricated stories out of his own mind. Pfeiffer says, "It is an error to consider the Chronicler as a writer of history. It is futile to inquire seriously into the reality of any story or incident not taken bodily from Samuel or Kings.... The Chronicler is utterly devoid of historical sense . . . " (*Introduction* . . . , p. 806).

It is true that the Chronicler did write history with a definite religious view and purpose in mind, as is shown by the way he incorporates the doctrine of individual retribution into his material (cf. the accounts of Manasseh and Josiah in *Kings and Chronicles*), his emphasis on the direct action of God in history, and his interest in the religious activity of the Temple. The size of the military forces mentioned by him is generally regarded as exaggerated (II Chron. 13, 14, 17, 26), and his description of the religious reforms of Asa, Jehoshaphat, and Hezekiah does not seem to coincide with the record in Kings. But in spite of these observations, evidence has been accumulating during the past quarter of a century from archaeological discoveries (Albright) and from a thorough study of the historical passages peculiar to the Chronicler (A. Alt and his school) which shows that the work of the Chronicler cannot be summarily dismissed as apocryphal or fictitious, but that it must be taken seriously as an historical document.

The vocabulary and idiom of the Chronicler in those sections where he does not quote from known ancient sources have been thoroughly studied by E. L. Curtis (*Chronicles* [ICC], pp. 27–36), and Torrey has shown conclusively that the language of the Chronicler and that of the Ezra Memoirs are nearly identical. It is on the basis of the studies of Torrey that Albright, following ancient Jewish tradition, equates the Chronicler with Ezra (see EZRA AND NEHEMIAH, BOOKS OF).

The Chronicler knew the whole Pentateuch, for he explicitly refers to "the book of Moses" (II Chron. 35:12). The influence of P on the Chronicler is quite obvious, according to Pfeiffer, and recent studies (M. Noth and G. von Rad) point out that the Chronicler's view of history was strongly colored by Deuteronomistic ideology (D).

BIBLIOGRAPHY: C. C. Torrey, *The Composition and Historical Value of Ezra-Nehemiah*, 1896; *idem*, *Ezra Studies*, 1910; A. C. Welch, *The Work of the Chronicler*, 1939; R. H.

Pfeiffer, *Introduction to the Old Testament*, 1941; A. Bentzen, *Introduction to the Old Testament*, Vol. II, 1949; W. F. Albright, "The Judicial Reform of Jehoshaphat," in *Alexander Marx Jubilee Volume* (1950), 61-82.

[Sup.] CHARLES T. FRITSCH.

CHRONOLOGY, OLD TESTAMENT: The presentation of a complete, consistent, and convincing chronology of the Bible is still an unachieved goal of scholarship. Much progress has been made in recent years, however: correlations with Egypt and Mesopotamia have set the biblical data firmly in the framework of Near Eastern chronology; and a number of dates have been fixed within a year or two.

I. From Earliest Times to the Establishment of the Monarchy: A. THE PATRIARCHAL PERIOD: Scientific biblical chronology properly begins with the patriarchs. The historical validity of the stories of Genesis is now generally recognized; these sources reflect the Middle Bronze Age, and the patriarchs may safely be located in this period (twenty-first to sixteenth centuries B.C.). Within these broad limits there is a great deal of uncertainty. A more precise date might be secured if the kings of Genesis 14 could be identified and fixed historically, but that problem has not been solved.

B. THE SOJOURN: According to Exodus 12:40 the sojourn lasted 430 years. In view of the certain thirteenth century date for the Exodus, this would place the descent into Egypt around 1700 B.C., in accord with the traditional view connecting Jacob and his sons with the Hyksos invasion. On the other hand many scholars hold that the sojourn was not nearly so long; the genealogies indicate that there were only four or five generations from the descent to the Exodus. This argument, however, rests on the assumption that the genealogies are complete. Unfortunately, the Joseph story has not provided the necessary link with Egyptian dynastic chronology.

C. THE EXODUS AND CONQUEST: The date of the Exodus has been one of the focal problems of biblical chronology, and remains so, though the range of possibility has been narrowed considerably. The traditional fifteenth century date, though still proposed, can no longer be defended; it is virtually certain that Moses led the Israelites out of Egypt some time in the thirteenth century (XIX Dynasty). Unless the tradition of a generation's wandering in the wilderness is to be abandoned, the Exodus must be placed in the first half of the century.

D. THE JUDGES: The limits of this period are fixed by the close of the main phase of the conquest (early twelfth century) and the establishment of the monarchy (late eleventh century). In considering the biblical data it is clear that many of the judges overlapped and that the numbers are generally approximate. Some fairly definite dates can be given: (1) The victory over Sisera and the Canaanites (*ca.* 1125

B.C.), celebrated in the Song of Deborah (Judg. 5); (2) Gideon and Abimelech (*ca.* 1100–1050); (3) Jephthah (early eleventh century); (4) The battle of Ebenezer and the destruction of Shiloh by the Philistines (*ca.* 1050 or a little later); (5) Samuel (third quarter of the eleventh century).

II. From the Establishment of the Monarchy to the End of the Old Testament Period: Beginning with the monarchy there is considerably more data, both biblical and non-biblical, and a greater degree of precision is possible. There are important areas of disagreement among scholars nevertheless, and a number of unsolved problems remain.

A. THE UNITED KINGDOM (*ca.* 1020–922): While no figure is given for Saul, a reign of about twenty years seems reasonable. The forty-year reigns of David (1000–961) and Solomon (961–922) are well attested in biblical sources, though the figures may not be exact. The usual dates for Solomon are 970–931 B.C. But the *Tyrian Annals* provide synchronisms with biblical chronology which support the lower date. Hiram, who was a contemporary with both David and Solomon, reigned from 969 to 936. This means that David's reign must have extended considerably beyond 970. Furthermore, according to Josephus, the *Annals* date the building of the Temple at Jerusalem in the twelfth year of Hiram (= the fourth year of Solomon), 958.

B. THE DIVIDED MONARCHY: The chronology of the divided kingdom presents many complex problems. Taking biblical evidence in the light of many variable factors (e.g., ante-dating, post-dating, Nisan or Tishri commencement of the civil year, coregencies), it is clear that there will be an element of uncertainty with regard to many of the dates. From external sources (particularly Assyro-Babylonian records) we have a number of fixed dates. These form a rigid framework in the light of which biblical data must be interpreted:

(1) From the division of the kingdom to the accession of Jehu (922–842/1): There are three important synchronisms for this period: (1) the invasion of Judah by Shishak of Egypt in the fifth year of Rehoboam. The chronology of the XXII Dynasty has not been precisely fixed, but in any case Breasted's figures for Shishak must be reduced. (2) The battle of Qarqar (853 B.C.), in which Ahab of Israel took part; (3) The payment of tribute by Jehu to Shalmaneser III (841 B.C.).

(2) From the accession of Jehu to the fall of Samaria (842/1–722/1): Synchronisms with Uzziah (Azariah) of Judah (742) and Menahem of Israel (738) are supplied by the annals of Tiglath-pileser III (744-727). The fall of Samaria is fixed in the accession year of Sargon II (722/721).

(3) From the fall of Samaria to the fall of Jerusalem (722/1–587/6): A number of dates are fixed by Assyro-Babylonian synchronisms, e.g., the invasion of Judah by Sennacherib (701 B.C.), the fourteenth year of Hezekiah (715–687). For the last fifty years of Judah virtually fixed dates have been secured; only one year separates the two principal schemes: Josiah, 640/639–609/8; Jehoahaz, 609/8; Jehoiakim 609/8–598/7; Jehoiachin, 598/7; Zedekiah, 598/7–587/6. The higher chronology seems preferable although the biblical evidence does not appear consistent, and the Babylonian data is not decisive.

C. FROM THE EXILE TO THE END OF THE OLD TESTAMENT: Fixed dates for this period are: (1) the Edict of Cyrus, 538; (2) the rebuilding of the temple, 515. The period of Ezra and Nehemiah remains an acute problem. Nehemiah's mission belongs to the reign of Artaxerxes I (Neh. 1:1). Ezra's arrival in Jerusalem is dated in the seventh year of Artaxerxes, either 458 (Artaxerxes I) or 398 (Artaxerxes II). A number of scholars emend Ezra 7:7 to read "the thirty-seventh year of Artaxerxes" (I). This would bring Ezra to Jerusalem after Nehemiah, and at the same time do justice to the passages which link the two men (Neh. 8:9; 12:26, 36).

BIBLIOGRAPHY: W. F. Albright, "The Chronology of the Divided Kingdom," BASOR, No. 100 (1945), 16–22; "The Old Testament and the Archaeology of Palestine," The Old Testament and Modern Study, ed. by H. H. Rowley (1951), 5–7; H. H. Rowley, "Recent Discovery and the Patriarchal Age," Bulletin of the John Rylands Library, 32:1 (1949), 3–38; From Joseph to Joshua (1950), p. 164 ff.; E. Thiele, The Mysterious Numbers of the Hebrew Kings (1951), pp. 254–255.

DAVID NOEL FREEDMAN.

CHRYSOSTOM: Chrysostom's place in the history of Christian education is assured by his address On Vainglory and the Right Way for Parents to Bring Up Their Children, translated with a commentary by M. L. W. Laistner (Christianity and Pagan Culture, 1951). His greatest importance, however, lies in his rhetorical skill; he was the greatest preacher of the Greek church. After his death more than 500 sermons were wrongly ascribed to him. Many of these are still unpublished. His interest in grammar and rhetoric is also reflected in his relatively literal and historical exegesis of the Bible. Though like Theodore of Mopsuestia (q.v.), he was a pupil of Diodorus of Tarsus, his teaching was not attacked as theirs was by Cyril of Alexandria (q.v.).

BIBLIOGRAPHY: C. Baur, Johannes Chrysostomus, 1929–30; D. Attwater, St. John Chrysostom, 1939; G. Bardy in Dict. de théol. cath., VIII, 660–90; H. Lietzmann in Pauly-Wissowa-Kroll, Real-Encyclopaedie der classischen Altertumswissenschaft, IX, 1811–28. On his rhetoric cf. E. Norden, Die antike Kunstprosa (1898), 550–72; H. M. Hubbell in Class. Philol., XIX (1924), 261–76. A sixth-century papyrus excerpt: P. Sanz, Mitteilungen aus der Papyrussammlung der National-bibl. in Wien, IV (1946), 124–26; a ninth-century palimpsest: J. E. Powell in JTS, XXXIX (1938), 132–40. Full bibliography in B. Altaner, Patrologie (2nd ed., 1950), 278–89.

[Sup.] ROBERT M. GRANT.

CHURCH AND STATE: I. Significance of the Contemporary State for the Church: Great changes have taken place since 1910 in actual relationships between church and state in many countries of the world, and also in thought and attitudes on such relationships. The state has changed much, the church somewhat. States of modern type have greatly extended their functions, dominating large fields of human activity and dwarfing church efforts in education, medicine, and other services. Masses of citizens have come to feel that only the state has the material resources and the numerous technicians required for adequate meeting of human needs —apart from a narrow strip designated as spiritual or religious. In the minds of many, not merely the church but even God himself is displaced by the state, which appears to be the providence of daily bread, of healing, of moral standards, of hope for a better ordering of community life.

The state is the collective representation of secularized man. But the state goes on to shape man himself by universal education, now extended even to maturity, fashioning him for its own type of nationalism and industrialism, in peace and in war. No wonder the most frequent issue in church-state relations is that of the purpose and method of education, whether youth is to be trained only by and for the state, or with some educative claim for God on the part of family and church.

Since World War I, the national state has reached hysterical intensity in Fascist Italy, National-Socialist Germany, and lesser imitations such as Franco Spain and Peronist Argentina, all learning techniques from the Communist Russia they professed to abhor. Revolutionary Russia, for a time concealing both its nationalistic quality and its rigid absolutism of state power, has come to stand clearly as the complete totalitarianism; and through military and political extension its Communist system now includes one-third of mankind.

In this scientific-secular age so favorable to the growth of state power, church influence has, in many countries, declined. The religious training of home and church has been overpowered by the totality of public education and mass suggestion from press, film, and radio, mass labor, mass housing, mass amusements. On the other hand, important elements of leadership have awakened to the danger, and are now conducting the rank and file toward a new consciousness of the church as a unique fellowship of faith working within the community but set over against its secularism (q.v.). The crisis was dramatized in the remarkable, if tardy and incomplete, Christian response of the German churches, and the substantial resistance of the churches, in occupied lands, to the pressures of the Nazi power. Lutheran thought, notably in

Germany and in Scandinavia, has brought forth in fresh emphasis Martin Luther's assertion of the spiritual independence of the church, diminishing the tradition of obedient dependence upon state authority.

II. Change in Church-State Relationships: Major Cases: The picture of a generation's changes must now be made more concrete. The Orthodox state churches, save in Greece, have lost their historic character, and are sad victims of Communist conscription and abrasion, but still alive. In divided and uncertain Germany (*q.v.*), the state tentatively continues to support the churches lest it lose public approval; but in the Soviet Zone the Communist authorities employ the schools and special organizations to take the young from the churches.

The Roman Catholic record is mixed, with the church appearing collaborative or submissive toward totalitarian regimes, but now standing intransigent before those which are thoroughly hostile; seeking in Austria (1934) or Portugal (1933) a "corporative" version of "the Christian state," but reconciling itself to a state neutral and tolerant in varying degrees of benevolence, as in Chile (1925) or Eire (1921, 1937). Captious criticism should be withheld, in view of the wide variety of situations, the severe state changes from period to period, and the inconsistent hesitations present also in Protestant opinion. It seems that Roman Catholic leadership has been trying to conserve principles in a world uncongenial to its ancient system, and yet to make the best adjustments possible in each case, suffering harsh lessons from Mussolini and others.

The Republic of Italy continues the Lateran Treaty (*q.v.*) of 1929, which ended the long *dissidio* between the national state and the papacy by establishing the Vatican State and a contentious mutual support in education. Portugal (*q.v.*) represents juridically a friendly separation of church and state, in fact an agreed co-operation without mutual control, succeeding the anticlerical revolution of 1911. Spain's (*q.v.*) alternations of anticlerical swings with clerical reactions seem to have paused in the semi-Catholic Franco regime. In Latin America clericalism has continued to beget liberal or revolutionary anticlericalism (*q.v.*), sometimes countered by clerical reaction, sometimes resulting in compromise.

At the mid-century there appears to be a rally of the Roman Catholic system to press for alliance with the state in education, whether or not constitutional separation exists. In the United States, persistent development of Roman Catholic schools is coupled with efforts to secure direct or indirect public subsidy for all private schools—of which Roman Catholic schools are so large a fraction; and with depreciation of the traditional public schools as irreligious, varied in certain localities by efforts to capture the public schools for Roman Catholic personnel and policies. Without general agreement among themselves as to the right policy for public schools in regard to religion, Protestants are roused to oppose present and possible use of tax funds and of public institutions for sectarian purposes. In Great Britain and in the British states overseas, the state-church relationship in education is less acutely controversial, because of frequent local co-operation for agreed programs of religious training in or associated with the government schools, and because of the tradition of public grants-in-aid to private schools.

The outstanding instance of the old territorial type of Protestant state-church, in Sweden (*q.v.*), is cautiously relaxing its integration of the community and increasing the rights of religious minorities—though of course basic toleration has long been practiced. The Church of Scotland (*q.v.*), reunited in 1929, is both national and free, while other religious bodies in that land enjoy entire liberty and show no resentment over public recognition of the one widely accepted form of Christianity. The Church of England (*q.v.*) approaches that position, though its practical autonomy is under the ultimate sanction of Parliament; the remnants of history are more prominent—such as the presence of bishops in the House of Lords—and the Church itself no longer has a communicant membership equal to one-half even of the church-related fraction of the total population.

The decline of colonial systems removes from the scene several governments which were linked to churches or were benevolently neutral toward them, replacing these governments by states recognizing religions other than Christian, or constitutionally secular but with a socio-cultural leaning toward such religions. India (*q.v.*), Pakistan (*q.v.*), Burma (*q.v.*), and Indonesia are conspicuous examples, involving nearly 500,000,-000 persons. Among surviving colonial regimes, the Portuguese is the chief instance of active state preference for a church—the Roman Catholic.

III. Separation or Co-operation? The Instance of the United States: "Separation of church and state" is a common principle or slogan employed variously for drastic attacks upon churches or religions by anticlerical or antireligious states, for friendly modernizations of historic unions, and for continuing situations popularly regarded as those of mutual independence. If the United States is taken for instance, it will be discovered that church and state are actually in contact through many relationships, some of them amounting to significant aid and co-operation despite apparent conflicts of duty and of financial interest. Many of these relationships appear, with appropriate variations, in other countries.

The churches, or their religion, are recognized by law and by government custom in various public ceremonies and in observance of Sunday (*q.v.*). Chaplains are provided at public cost, not only for the armed services, but also for many prisons, hospitals, and public institutions. Church properties, whether defined strictly or most comprehensively, are exempted from general taxation. The exemption amounts in total to an enormous subsidy, increasing as rates of taxation are increased. Social security benefits are made available to important classes of church employees, and are accepted by many, though not usually by clergymen.

The governments of some of the respective states prescribe the reading of the Bible in publicly supported schools, some permit it, some forbid it; commonly they authorize the release of school children at specified hours for religious instruction provided on private premises by the various churches. On grounds of need and of equity, public aid is given, directly or through their beneficiaries, to some church-operated schools, hospitals, and social agencies, despite the generally declared principle that no sectarian organizations should benefit from tax funds. The president of the United States for some years maintained a personal representative at the Vatican (*q.v.*), disregarding widespread criticism of the preferential prestige thus bestowed upon one church not renowned for reticence in politics. The state gives special consideration to young men who have substantial religious scruples against military service, particularly those taught by certain church bodies, and exempts clergymen from the general requirement.

There is a large body of special legislation and of judicial precedent which facilitates and protects the particular interests of churches, even of individual church bodies. The state accepts churches as wholesome organizations whose spiritual-ethical, educational, and benevolent functions are not only approved by the community, but carry part of the moral and social load of the state. At the same time, churches and their members come under the requirements of ordinary law as to fire prevention, sanitation, responsibility for criminal acts, and so on. But the state does not concern itself with the religious life and practices of the churches, and assumes that they are self-directing and self-disciplining to a high degree.

In a democratic society it is evident that the churches and the state are composed of the same people acting in different capacities and in differing degrees of inclusiveness. Distinction of function, not antiseptic abhorrence, is the true principle of "separation." Indeed, as the social services and manifold activities of the modern state have developed, deeply relating the state to the total well-being of the community and of every person within it, the ethical teachings of the churches are bound increasingly to discern not merely the rights but also the duties of their members vis-à-vis the state and in the workings of the state.

See also POLITICAL ACTION, THE CHURCHES AND; PROPERTY, ECCLESIASTICAL; LIBERTY, RELIGIOUS.

BIBLIOGRAPHY: A. Keller, *Church and State on the European Continent*, 1936; N. Ehrenstrom, *Christian Faith and the Modern State*, 1937; J. H. Oldham, *The Oxford Conference: Official Report* (Conference on Church, Community and State), 1937; International Missionary Council, The Madras Series, Vol. 6, *The Church and the State*, 1939; L. Sturzo, *Church and State*, 1939; P. Hutchinson, *The New Leviathan*, 1946; H. A. Rommen, *The State in Catholic Thought*, 1947; C. Garbett, *Church and State in England*, 1950; A. P. Stokes, *Church and State in the United States*, 3 vols., 1950; C. F. G. Zollmann, *American Church Law*, 1933.

[Sup.] MINER SEARLE BATES.

CHURCH ARMY: Prebendary Wilson Carlisle founded the Church Army in England in 1882 as an organization of lay missionaries and evangelists within the Church of England. Arranged along military lines, both men and women wear uniforms and are known as "Captains" and "Sisters." Working under the direction of the bishops, they engage in parochial work, conduct missions, and care for many social agencies. The English branch has been especially active in moral welfare, work in prisons, evangelistic preaching among the armed forces, and hostels for both youth and the aged. The American branch was constituted in 1927. Both branches conduct training schools. The English headquarters is in London; the American headquarters is in New York.

[Sup.] NELSON RIGHTMYER.

CHURCH ASSOCIATION. See CHURCH SOCIETY.

CHURCH ASSOCIATION FOR THE ADVANCEMENT OF THE INTERESTS OF LABOR. See SOCIAL GOSPEL.

CHURCH (CHURCHES) OF GOD: There are numerous sects in America that bear the name of Church of God or variations of the same. Nearly all are holiness bodies and most of them are of the pentecostal type (see PENTECOSTAL CHURCHES). The following may be mentioned.

1. The Church of God (Anderson, Ind.) originated in 1880 when a group led by Daniel S. Warner seceded from the Church of God in North America, General Eldership. The dissidents held to the theory of sanctification as a distinct work of grace subsequent to justification and believed that Church of God is the only scriptural name for any church. While the body does not keep statistics, it has about 1,500

churches and 90,000 members. The second coming of Christ is expected, and immersions and the washing of feet (see FEET WASHING) are practiced. This body rejects "the gift of tongues." Its headquarters are at Anderson, Ind., where it has a publishing house and an educational institution.

2. The Church of God (Apostolic) is a holiness body organized under the name of Christian Faith Band Church by Thomas J. Cox at Danville, Ky., in 1897. The name was changed in 1915. The group teaches that in it the "true church" has been reinstituted. Sanctification and spiritual gifts are prominent, and foot washing is practiced. It reports about 50 churches and 3,000 members.

3. The Church of God as Organized by Christ resulted from a schism in the Mennonite Brethren in Christ (see MENNONITES) in 1886. It holds that church membership and ordination are special divine gifts, but it opposes sanctification as a second work of grace. The body opposes denominational co-operation, tobacco, lodges, war, going to law, Sunday schools, revivals, shouting, speaking in tongues (q.v.), theaters, jewelry, creeds, salaried ministers, and other forms of what it regards as worldliness. It has about a dozen churches and 2,000 members.

4. Negro Churches of God are numerous. They are usually of the Holiness and Pentecostal type. The Church of God in Christ was founded by C. H. Mason at Memphis, Tenn., in 1895; in 1936 it reported 750 churches and 30,000 members. The Free Church of God in Christ, with about 20 churches and 900 members, was organized at Enid, Okla., in 1915 by J. H. Morris; divine healing and speaking in unknown tongues are emphasized. The Church of God, Holiness, was formed by K. H. Burrus in Atlanta, Ga., in the 1890's and claims 35 churches and 6,000 members. The Church of God, Holiness, U.S.A., is a little larger; it was organized at Selma, Ala., in 1894. There are two Churches of the Living God; one is the Christian Workers for Fellowship and the other is the Pillar and Ground of Truth. The original body resulted from a revelation to William Christian at Wrightsville, Ark., in 1889. There have been various splits in the parent group, caused mainly by disputes over leadership. These churches are of the Holiness, near-Pentecostal type and teach that Jesus and many other biblical characters were Negroes. The Apostolic Overcoming Holy Church of God is a similar sect which was formed at Mobile, Ala., in 1916, by W. T. Phillips. Other small Negro churches of this type are the Sought Out Church of God in Christ and Spiritual House of Prayer, Inc., (Brunswick, Ga., 1947); Triumph the Church and Kingdom of God in Christ (q.v.; Birmingham, Ala., Ca. 1936); United Holy Church of America (Raleigh, N. C., 1886); Latter House

of the Lord for All People and the Church on the Mountain, Apostolic Faith (Cincinnati, O., 1938); House of the Lord (Detroit, Mich., 1925); House of God, etc. (Washington, D. C., 1914); National David Spiritual Temple of Christ Church Union (q.v.; Kansas City, Mo., 1932); Christ's Sanctified Holy Church, Colored (West Lake, La., 1903); Fire-Baptized Holiness Church of God of the Americas (Anderson, S. C., 1908).

5. Churches of God (Tomlinson). Around forty or fifty Churches of God, all of the Holiness-Pentecostal type, originated directly or indirectly from the work of A. J. Tomlinson, leader of the so-called "Latter Rain Revival." Tomlinson took over in 1903 a movement (characterized by high emotionalism, sanctification as a second work of grace, and speaking in tongues) which had been started in the mountain area of North Carolina and Tennessee by R. G. Spurling. Establishing headquarters at Cleveland, Tenn., Tomlinson promoted the revival with vigor, and it spread all over the country. The individualist nature of the movement and the strict control exercised by Tomlinson resulted in several splits, and when the leader died in 1943 rivalry between the followers of his two sons and other leaders caused the movement to fall apart. There are four independent Churches of God with headquarters at Cleveland, Tenn., one of them being under the leadership of M. A. Tomlinson. Another has headquarters at Chattanooga. A third is the Church of God (World Headquarters), with headquarters in Queens Village, N. Y., of which Homer A. Tomlinson is bishop (see CHURCH OF GOD).

Among the various bodies there is little variation in doctrine. The distinctive feature is always sanctification and spiritual gifts, especially glossolalia. There is a non-trinitarian wing which is broken into "Jesus Only" and "Father Only" groups over the nature of the baptismal formula. The movement has made considerable progress among Negroes and Spanish-speaking groups in the United States and has spread to Europe and South America. Some of the churches do not keep membership lists, and statistics are difficult of access, but there are undoubtedly thousands of congregations and hundreds of thousands of adherents. Several bodies are indirect products of the Tomlinson movement and represent mergers of various Latter Rain churches. This is true of the largest of all the groups, the Pentecostal Assemblies of God (q.v.), General Council, which has headquarters at Springfield, Mo., and enrolls nearly a quarter of a million members in 5,000 congregations.

The following is a partial list of the bodies which grew directly or indirectly out of the Latter Rain movement, with such approximate statistics for the United States, as were available in 1953:

Church	Congre-gations	Mem-bers
Church of God (Ceveland, Tenn.)	2,542	126,844
Church of God (Tomlinson)	1,989	111,011
Church of God (World Head-quarters)	1,550	56,188
Original Church of God	75	6,000
Italian Churches of God	120	12,000
Bible Church of God		
Church of Jesus (Bishop Officer)		
Church of God (Bishop Poteat		
Church of God, Holiness	32	20,700
Church of God in Christ	3,600	328,304
Church of God, Incorporated		
Church of God (Mother Horn)		
Church of God (Mother Robin-son		
Church of God (Mountain As-sembly		
Glorified Church of God		
Justified Church of God		
Holstein Church of God		
Latin American Churches of God		
Non-Digressive Churches of God		
Remnant Church of God		
Faith Tabernacle (California)		
Garr Auditorium (Charlotte, N.C.)		
Jesus and Watch Mission		
Churches of Our Lord Christ of Apostolic Faith	175	50,000
Forward Movement Bible School and Headquarters		
Apostolic Church of Jesus Christ		
School of the Prophets		

BIBLIOGRAPHY: Elmer T. Clark, *The Smalll Sects in America*, rev. ed., 1949; Homer A. Tomlinson, *Diary of A. J. Tomlinson*, 1949; S. H. Frodsham, *With Signs Following, the Story of the Latter-Day Pentecostal Revival*, n.d. Periodicals: *Church of God Evangel; Gospel Trumpet; The Church of God*.

[Sup.] ELMER T. CLARK.

CHURCH, CONSTITUTION OF, IN EARLY CHRISTIANITY: Some hold that the church began with Adam and was redeemed by Jesus (*Scots Confession* [1560] Art. v; C. T. Craig in *Man's Disorder and God's Design* [Amsterdam Assembly 1948 Series] I. 33); but it is everywhere recognized that the ministry of Jesus marked a decisive stage in the history of God's people and even that the Christian Church strictly speaking is "the church of the ascended Christ whose Body it is" (J. A. F. Gregg, *Man's Disorder, etc.*, I. 59; Aulén and Florovsky, *ibid.*, 18 f., 45; R. N. Flew, *Jesus and His Church*, 19; Zeiller and Lebreton, *History of the Primitive Church*, I. 83). I prefer to keep the word church for the post-Resurrection society, whilst recognizing a measure of continuity with Israel (see *The Church in the New Testament*, 56). Whatever view be held concerning the church's origin, the primary fact for matters of organization is that after Jesus' death a new community arose. We must now ask whether the twelve disciples who first proclaimed the Resurrection had received from the Lord a commission of lawful authority to organize and govern the community.

I. The Twelve: Were assistant missionaries of the Kingdom, chosen by Jesus and representative of the tribes of Israel (Mark 3:14 f., 6:7 ff.). They were forbidden to desire rank or use titles like rabbi and father (Mark 10:42–45; Matt. 23:8–10), yet are to judge Israel in the final realization of the Kingdom (Luke 22:30; perhaps not to be taken too literally in the light of Mark 10:40, 13:32). There are good grounds for doubting the historicity of Matt. 16:18 (O. Linton, *Das Problem der Urkirche*, gives the various theories); John 20:22 f. need not confer legal authority; therefore it is unlikely that Jesus transmitted governing powers. Matt. 28:19 reflects the fact that the twelve did lead in preaching and baptizing, for to them the risen Messiah had appeared (I Cor. 15:5). To this act of forgiveness, their companionship with Jesus, and their earlier mission they owed their pre-eminence; and as recipients of the Spirit they became witnesses (Acts 2; cf. John 15:27). Matthias's election (Acts 1:21 ff.) shows that they were necessarily a closed group. Hence the twelve could have no successors. Later tradition, however, exalted them as The Apostles (Luke 6:13), adding Paul and James the Lord's brother who also had "seen" the risen Christ (Gal. 1:19; I Cor. 15:7 f.), and making them foundation stones of church or Kingdom alongside Messiah himself (Eph. 3:20, 4:11; Rev. 21:14. Matt. 16:18 goes even farther in Peter's case). In line with this Acts 8:14 ff., 19:6 implies that apostolic ordination of new members is essential for receiving the Spirit.

II. Before A.D. 70: Eschatological expectations that Jesus would return quickly as judge and king dominated the earliest society (Acts 3:21, 10:42; I Thess. 1:9 f.; I Cor. 4:5, 15:24 f.), and, modified perhaps, continued into the sixties (Phil. 4:5; Col. 3:4) so that constitutional concerns were not paramount. An institutional element was present, of course (I Cor. 14:40), and some had to lead (*prohistamenoi*, I Thess. 5:12). Paul's ideal "lay somewhere between the military rigour of Macedonia and the democratic license of Corinth" (W. M. Macgregor, *Christian Freedom* [1931], 224). Membership was open first to Jews, then equally to Gentiles, on a confession of faith in Jesus followed by the rite of baptism (Acts 2:38, 11:17 f.; Rom. 5:1, 6:3 ff., 10:9).

Acts shows Peter as spokesman for the church and as such dangerous to Herod and Judaism (3:11, 12:3 ff.; cf. Gal. 1:18, 2:9; John 21:15 ff.).

On the death of James bar-Zebedee Peter left Jerusalem and the Lord's brother assumed a new standing. He was no missionary nor a menace to the régime, but more probably leader of the Judaisers who opposed Paul and Peter (Acts 11:2, 15:1; Gal. 2:12). Karl Holl (*Gesammelte Aufsaetze* [1927], II. 54) and others go too far in calling James the resident head of the Jerusalem church, exercising a divine prerogative (see also Flew, *op. cit.*, 185 ff.). For Acts 15:13 (a dubious source) need not imply his presidency; 21:18 indicates that Jerusalem had presbyters; so James was perhaps an *archisynagogos*. Thus a dynastic principle emerged in Jewish Christianity and lasted till Trajan's reign (Eus., *H.E.*, III. xx. 1-8; xxxii. 3-6). The Seven of Acts 6 are an *ad hoc* group, not deacons; the passage may illustrate a typical ordination to new ministries (H. J. Carpenter). Congregational choice is mentioned in 6:3, 5.

Paul speaks once of bishops and deacons (Phil. 1:1); once doubtfully of a deaconess (Rom. 16:1; cf. I Tim. 3:11?). Linguistic usage, Greek and Syriac, proves that "bishops" and "presbyters" are identical, so that Acts 14:23 (appointment of presbyters in Pauline churches) is corroborated, with the modification required by the Spirit's directive (Acts 20:28; I Cor. 12:7 ff.). This is good practice on a mission field. If character and spiritual gift warranted, first converts might be chosen (I Cor. 16:15 f.; I Clem. 42:4), but the rule could not be absolute. Paul also names delegates of the churches (apostles), prophets, and teachers of the Word who deserve support (II Cor. 8:23, 11:8; Gal. 6:6), as well as other workers who cannot be identified by title (I Cor. 12; Rom. 12). In I Cor. 12 the wider meaning of "apostles" is preferable (I Cor. 15:5, 7; Rom. 16:7; cf. Acts 14:4, 14). There is no hierarchical order here; all ministries are given to the church by God through the Spirit in his freedom and intended to edify the Body of Christ. R. Sohm is right to emphasize this (*Kirchenrecht* [1892], I). There are no laymen, for each is granted his gift and priestly office (cf. Rom. 12:1, 15:16). Paul as the founder chosen directly by the Lord has authority (II Thess. 3:9), but the local bishops govern the congregations each of which is autonomous within the unity of the whole.

III. After A.D. 70: Later New Testament documents (Pastorals excluded) tell little more; they stress the preaching, teaching and pastoral work (John 10:16, 17:18, 20; Heb. 13:7, 17; James 3:1; I Pet. 5:2 on which see Macgregor, *op. cit.*, 189). In James 5:14 presbyters pray over the sick and anoint them. It is unsafe to deduce monarchical episcopacy from the title "the elder" (II, III John), for we do not know its significance. Diotrephes (III John 9 f.) may be a local bishop or a party leader (Dodd *in loc.*, *Moffatt Comm.*). As the new Israel the

church in I Pet. 2:4-9 and Rev. 1:6 is a priestly society. Heb. 6:4 deals with apostasy.

Until the middle of the second century the evidence shows presbyter-bishops ruling and teaching in local churches assisted by deacons: e.g., at Rome, Alexandria and Philippi, though not Asia Minor (Hermas, *Vis.* iii. 5, 9; *Sim.* IX. xxv ff., X. iv. I; Jerome, *Epp.* cxlvi; Polyc., *Phil.* 5:3, 6:1). Deacons served at the Lord's Supper (Justin, *I Apol.* 65, 67) and probably cared for the needy. Widows formed some kind of order (to work with women and children?) or were enrolled separately (Ign., *Smyrn.* 13:1; I Tim. 5:9 f.; Tert., *de virg. vel.* 9, *de pudic.* 13; Hipp., *A.T.* 11). According to the Roman church, bishops or presbyters supervised the congregation and offered the gifts (sacrifices?): I Clem. 42:4, 44:4 f., 47:6, 54:2, 57:1; they owed their appointment to the apostles or their delegates ("approved men," 44:3, an obscure reference). Ministers are distinguished from the laity and by Old Testament typology equated with priests (40 f., 44:4).

The New Testament Pastorals (date uncertain; *ca.* A.D. 115-35) speak of presbyter-bishops also, though Timothy and Titus appear as apostolic delegates with quasi-archiepiscopal jurisdiction (but note I Tim. 4:14; II Tim. 1:6; Timothy belongs to the ordaining presbyterial order). There are useful directions on status and character, little on clerical functions (I Tim. 3:1-13, 5:17; II Tim. 2:2; Tit. 1:5-9).

The *Didache* cannot be dated with accuracy (scholars offer A.D. 60-70 or a Montanist date a century later with equal diffidence). So far as it goes it agrees with the view adopted here. Too much should not be made of the itinerant, charismatic prophets, who seem to include "apostles" (11:5).

IV. Non-Episcopacy: Wholly different are the letters of Ignatius, martyred under Trajan or Hadrian. Each church *must* be ruled by a bishop, representing the Father or Christ; advised by a council of presbyters, representing the apostles; assisted by deacons, representing the ministering Saviour (*Eph.* 4 f.; *Magn.* 2, 6; *Trall.* 2 f.; *Smyrn.* 8). In the "catholic" (i.e., universal and orthodox) church the bishop refutes heresy and presides at all meetings with full authority. (Note the failure to address any bishop at Rome.) This novel threefold order in Asia quite probably evolved from the norm by the elevation of one presbyter (or prophet?), though the stages are hidden from us. Perhaps Ignatius thought it had apostolic sanction (*Magn.* 13; *Trall.* 3, 7). Between A.D. 140 and 225 this system spread to Italy, Greece, North Africa and South Gaul (Iren., *adv. her.* III. 2 f., IV. 26; Eus., *H.E.* IV. xxxiii, V. xxiv. 14 ff.; Tert., *Apol.* 39; *de Bapt.* 17; *prescript. her.* 41; *monog.* 12; *exh. cast.* 7). Tertullian mentions the reader, and early councils in Greece. Irenaeus further emphasizes the apostolic succession of the bishops as teachers of apostolic doctrine. His lists of bishops, like those in Eusebius, are very dubious in view of above evidence.

V. Summary: The church is a loose confederation united under Christ its Head; neighboring bishops ordain with the local presbyters (Hipp., *A.T.* 2, 9) and exchange letters; a sacred canon is growing up (e.g., the *Muratorianum*). The system is "episcopal," but the bishop is a parish minister; or "presbyterian," for the elders rule, teach and share in administering the sacraments; nevertheless congregational autonomy was preserved within the framework of one apostolic family. The rise of heresies, natural growth, the complexity of business, liturgical demands, secular Hellenistic influence—and the controlling wisdom of the Spirit, all helped to form this late second century constitution.

BIBLIOGRAPHY of books not cited: Histories by Elliott-Binns and Lietzmann; B. S. Easton, *The Pastoral Epistles*, 1947; M. Goguel in *The Ministry and the Sacraments*, ed. Dunkerley, 1937; M. Goguel, *L'Église primitive*, 1947; *idem, La Naissance du Christianisme*, 1946; Ph.-H. Menoud, *L'Église et les ministères selon le Nouveau Testament*, 1949; James Moffatt, *The First Five Centuries of the Church* (1938), pp. 229 f.; A. Harnack, *Constitution and Law of the Church*, 1910; *The Apostolic Ministry*, ed. K. E. Kirk, 1947; T. W. Manson, *The Church's Ministry*, 1948; *A Theological Word Book of the Bible*, ed. A. Richardson, 1950; K. L. Schmidt, *The Church*, 1932, English Translation, 1950.

GEORGE JOHNSTON.

CHURCH DISCIPLINE. See DISCIPLINE, CHURCH.

CHURCHES OF CHRIST: As here used, "Churches of Christ" is a term applied to certain local congregations, not to different denominations.

The Churches of Christ do not regard the Reformation as a restoration of the "ancient order of things" but rather as an attempt to correct errors and abuses in existing religious communions. Early in the nineteenth century there was a movement in America to discard all human creeds and inventions in religion and go back to the Bible as the sole and complete source of authority. This movement was led by such men as Thomas and Alexander Campbell (*q.v.*, Vol. II), Walter Scott, and Barton W. Stone (*q.v.*, Vol. XI). They proceeded according to the principle, "Where the Bible speaks, we speak; where the Bible is silent, we are silent." One after another they rejected denominational tenets and practices until they thought they occupied New Testament ground in teaching, worship, organization, and life. They did not seek to originate a new religious sect or denomination; they sought to restore the church of Christ, the church of the New Testament, in its original purity. In a letter to the editor of the *Commercial Bulletin*, of New Orleans, Alexander Campbell wrote: "You have done me, gentlemen, too much honor in saying

that I am the 'founder' of the denomination, quite numerous and respectable in many portions of the West, technically known as 'Christians,' but more commonly as 'Campbellites.' I have always repudiated all *human heads* and *human names* for the people of the Lord, and shall feel very thankful if you will correct the erroneous impression which your article may have made in thus representing me as the founder of a religious denomination."

The Churches of Christ look upon Campbell and his colaborers as restorers and not founders of the church of Christ. They think of Christ as the founder, head, and saviour of the church. The Word of God, they contend, is the seed of the kingdom, or church, and when it is preached, without any admixture of human opinions or teachings, it will produce Christians, or a church of Christ.

It is not correct to think of the Churches of Christ as having a peculiar "body of divinity." They accept the Old and New Testaments as being inspired of God. The New Testament is regarded as the only rule of faith and practice; no humanly devised creed or confession of faith is accepted. Faith, repentance, confession (of faith in Christ), and baptism (a burial) are the conditions of salvation. The items of worship, engaged in each Lord's day, are singing, teaching, contribution of money, prayer, the Lord's Supper. Instrumental music and missionary societies are rejected. Each congregation is autonomous in character, presided over by elders and served by deacons. Preachers are under the oversight of the elders of the church for which they preach.

The Churches of Christ have been slow to file census reports. Their numbers are much larger than the government census would indicate. From the best available private sources of information, it is safe to say that their membership is approximately 1,000,000. There are about 15,000 preachers and 16,000 congregations. Members of the Churches of Christ operate a number of publishing houses, orphanages, and colleges. Missionaries have gone to carry the gospel to many foreign countries.

See also DISCIPLES OF CHRIST.

BIBLIOGRAPHY: M. M. Davis, *How the Disciples Began and Grew*, 1947; W. E. Garrison and A. T. De Groot, *The Disciples of Christ*, 1948; Robert Richardson, *Memoirs of Alexander Campbell*, 1868; Earl West, *The Search for the Ancient Order*, 2 vols., 1949.

B. C. GOODPASTURE.

CHURCHES OF CHRIST IN CHRISTIAN UNION. See HOLINESS CHURCHES.

CHURCHES OF CHRIST, WORLD CONVENTION OF: The World Convention of Churches of Christ was organized in 1930 as the largest fellowship agency of those churches known as Disciples of Christ (see DISCIPLES OF CHRIST) in America and mission countries, but as Churches of Christ in Great Britain and the Dominions.

The purpose of the World Convention is fellowship, inspiration, and mutual helpfulness. It does not seek to regulate the theology of the churches, direct their polity or policy, or take any action that would interfere with their autonomy. In normal times it meets every five years. It is not a convention of national assemblies of the various countries, but a convention of brethren located in thirty-four nations who have a common history and common goals.

The first gathering was held in Washington, D. C., in 1930, with over 8,000 delegates registered; and the second in Leicester, England, in 1935. The third, scheduled for Toronto, Canada, in 1940, was postponed because of World War II and was not held until 1947, at Buffalo, N. Y.; delegates from thirty nations were present. The fourth world convention was scheduled for August 5-10, 1952, in Melbourne, Australia. From the beginning the general secretary of the World Convention was Jesse M. Bader. The World Convention of the Churches of Christ is not to be confused with the separate group known as Churches of Christ (see CHURCHES OF CHRIST).

A. T. DeGROOT.

CHURCH, DOCTRINE OF THE (Teaching concerning the nature of the Christian community): There has been little change in the dogma of ecclesiology since the Reformation formulations of the church visible and the church invisible and the action of the Vatican Council of 1870 firmly establishing papal infallibility as a Roman Catholic principle (Volume III, pages 77–83).

Roman Catholic doctrine of the church remains essentially the same dedication to the Roman power system. The church is the extended infallible body of Christ with an infallible body of doctrine in apostolic succession. For example, Henri De Lubac holds the given nature of the church to be precisely the Roman form. One is to look for no authority beyond that given to the church forever. This authority is manifest in the papal pronouncement of two Marian dogmas obligatory for the faithful: the immaculate conception (1853) and the assumption of the Virgin (1950). Here is the ark of salvation for all men. An unofficial spokesman like Maritain can suggest pluralism in form of the church. The official position is that there is no salvation outside the Roman Church, though some not now in the visible church may be Roman Catholics by intention, desire, or inculpable ignorance. This is not to say there is no vigor in Roman Catholic consideration of the nature of the church. Rather, the drive is to implement the now established doctrine of the church in such areas as politics, economics, social relations, and science. An example is Eric Voegelin's *The New Science of Politics* (1952)

which vindicates the Roman Church as representative and articulator of ultimate or divine truth from which all governments must draw their precepts and their very identity.

Among non-Roman students there has come a resurgence of interest in the nature of the church. Part of this has been due to the rebellion of some Continental confessional churchmen against a culture-dominated church. They concluded that the church must be the church free to judge and proclaim whatever the cost. Part of it has been due to the ecumenical impetus toward unity (see ECUMENICAL MOVEMENT). Ever since the protest of Bishop Charles Brent that matters of faith and order could hardly be exempt from ecumenical discussion, and the subsequent initiation of the World Conference on Faith and Order, most large ecumenical gatherings have featured a solemn conclave considering the nature of this divided church which is really one. Notable studies of the nature of the church were issued under ecumenical auspices in 1945, 1948, 1952, and 1954. Still another part of this new interest in the doctrine of the church springs from the despair of church historians who try to present the history of a church in the midst of denominational fragmentation. They are driven to consider what this church may be which they are to portray.

Protestant students of the nature of the church have not adhered closely to the time-honored denominational lines. Congregationalist Daniel Jenkins urges that Protestants overcome the kind of anemia springing from denial of tradition as though God's Spirit were absent from his church from the closing of the canon until denominational founding day. Reformed theologian Brunner attacks the traditional Reformed concepts of the visible and invisible church and declares the church to be a "fellowship of the Holy Ghost" which "has nothing to do with an organization and has nothing of the character of an institution about it."

Barth can speak of the divine mysterious nature of the church which is hidden. The given nature of the church for him is its position as bearer and proclaimer of God's Word. The church is the fellowship or community in which the Word is proclaimed. There is ever a danger that men will set the church on some authority of their own and so falsify it. The church undergoes constant reformation and has repeatedly become the church anew by decision. Tillich places little emphasis upon the historical founding of the church or upon the historical institution of the sacraments. The crucial thing for him is the church as a community of today open to the "Gestalt of grace"—the whole complex of God's personal revelation. Then all of secular society, shaped by the church, will be related to the Gestalt of grace as its spiritual center.

T. W. Manson holds that ministry is the cue to an adequate doctrine of the church. Thus the church is the remnant—Christ's version of the ministering Messiah personified. The church is indeed the body of Christ, that is the corporate group of his followers all imbued with his Spirit and continuing his ministry. L. S. Thornton also stresses the church as the body of Christ but for him the best cue to its nature is the mystical union of the believer with God in Christ: "In the beginning the Church entered a baptismal life corresponding to her confession of faith. The essence of this life consists in eucharistic worship, prayer and fraternal love, grounded upon, sustained by, and manifesting union with the divine-human priest-victim in his eternal sacrifice and in his regnant glory."

These constitute a sampling of the twentieth-century concentration on the nature of the church. Out of all this emerges no new Protestant dogma of ecclesiology. Yet, from the interchange comes a new enriched appreciation for some truths of long standing. The church is essentially a community of believers. Its community is based in God's gift of salvation. This church is a historic community, rich in tradition, yet ever fresh at its growing edge. It is a community involved in culture, yet never surrendered to it. It is a congregation of saints marked by the gospel rightly taught and the sacraments rightly administered. In polity and in doctrine this community is sorely divided. Yet there is in fact one Holy Catholic Church.

BIBLIOGRAPHY: For the Roman Catholic doctrine of the church the best sources are the authoritative official utterances such as the declarations of the Council of Trent and the Vatican Council and the encyclicals of various modern Popes (see ENCYCLICAL LETTERS). Helpful monographs include H. Dieckmann, *De Ecclesia*, 1925; Karl Adam, *One and Holy*, 1951; idem, *The Spirit of Catholicism*, 1929; Henri De Lubac, *Catholicism*, 1950.
Under auspices of the World Council of Churches (*q.v.*) there appeared in 1948 a four volume study of the church entitled *Man's Disorder and God's Design*. Perhaps the most useful single volume issued by the World Council on this subject is *The Nature of the Church* (1952) edited by R. N. Flew. This includes the report of the American Committee published under the same title by Willet, Clark and Company in 1945. *The Christian Hope and the Task of the Church* (1954) was issued as a source book for the meeting of the World Council of Churches at Evanston. Additional works by more than one author include *The Catholicity of Protestantism* (1951) edited by R. N. Flew and R. E. Davies; *The Apostolic Ministry* (1947) edited by K. E. Kirk; *This Is the Church* (1952) edited by Anders Nygren; *The Ministry of the Church* by Stephen Neill, et al.; *The Church and Organized Movements* (1946) edited by Randolph Crump Miller.
Recent monographs include Karl Barth, *The Knowledge of God*, 1939; F. W. Dillistone, *The Structure of the Divine Society*, 1951; T. W. Manson, *The Church's Ministry*, 1948; L. S. Thornton, *The Common Life in the Body of Christ*, 1942; Paul Tillich, *The Protestant Era*, 1948; R. N. Flew, *Jesus and His Church*, 1938; C. T. Craig, *The One Church*, 1951; Emil Brunner, *The Misunderstanding of the Church*, 1953; Daniel Jenkins, *The Nature of Catholicity*, 1942; idem., *Tradition, Freedom and the Spirit*, 1951; J. R. Nelson, *The Realm of Redemption*, 1951; E. L. Mascall, *Christ, the Christian and the Church*, 1946.

[Sup.] LA VERE CHRISTIAN RUDOLPH.

CHURCH HISTORY: Among the notable compendia of Church History produced in America since 1900, the following may be singled out as representative: Albert Henry Newman's two-

volume *Manual of Church History* (1900) and Williston Walker's excessively condensed *History of the Christian Church* (1918). Cyril Richardson's *The Church Through the Centuries* (1938) has a doctrinal aim. The missionary work of the church received a scholarly treatment in K. S. Latourette's monumental *History of the Expansion of Christianity* (7 vols., 1937–45).

Of the outstanding historians belonging to the social environmental school Shirley Jackson Case may be chosen as the most representative. Among his chief works are: *Evolution of Early Christianity* (1914); *Social Origins of Christianity* (1923); *Jesus, a New Biography* (1927); *Experience with the Supernatural* (1929). In his *Christian Philosophy of History* (1943) he undertook to survey the whole range of historical theology. Another liberal scholar of the school of Adolf Harnack (*q.v.*, Vol. V) was Arthur Cushman McGiffert, whose *History of Christianity in the Apostolic Age* (1899) created a storm of opposition on account of its "critical" conclusions. One of the most valuable contributions in this field is C. N. Cochrane's *Christianity and Classical Culture* (1944).

Among medievalists, John T. McNeill's most important works are *The Celtic Penitentials* (1923), *Medieval Handbooks of Penance* (1938), *The Makers of Christianity, from Alfred the Great to Schleiermacher* (1935), and *Books of Faith and Power* (1947). Rufus M. Jones contributed a volume on *The Flowering of Mysticism* (1947). S. Harrison Thomson published a book on *The Writings of Robert Grosseteste* (1940), and Matthew Spinka contributed a study on *John Hus and Czech Reform* (1940). Ray C. Petry published his *Francis of Assisi* (1941) and a selection of medieval sermons, *No Uncertain Sound* (1948). Albert Hyma contributed his valuable studies of *The Christian Renaissance* (1924) and *The Youth of Erasmus* (1930).

The Reformation period attracted many American scholars; this represented a renewed interest in Calvin, Luther, and the "Left-Wing of Reformation." A Society for Reformation Research was organized (see HISTORICAL ASSOCIATIONS). Besides, important works in this field were published in this country: the earliest was A. C. McGiffert's *Martin Luther* (1910). Among the later works are Roland H. Bainton's *Here I Stand* (1950) and E. G. Schwiebert's monumental *Luther and His Times* (1950). Swedish researches in this subject are reflected in E. C. Carlson's *The Reinterpretation of Luther* (1948).

Calvin studies likewise engaged the attention of several American scholars. John T. McNeill's comprehensive knowledge of this subject is reflected in his "Thirty Years of Calvin Study" (*Church History*, Sept., 1948). One of McNeill's students, Quirinus Breen, published *John Calvin: A Study of French Humanism* (1932).

Georgia Harkness contributed *John Calvin: the Man and His Ethics* (1931).

Of great interest are the original researches into the hitherto neglected and consequently misunderstood subject of the Anabaptists. Pioneers in this field are American Mennonite historians, under whose auspices the *Mennonite Quarterly* was published since 1927. Among them may be mentioned John Horsch, whose *Menno Simons* was published in 1916, and especially Harold S. Bender, who contributed his *Menno Simons' Life and Writings* (1936) and *Conrad Grebel, the Founder of the Swiss Brethren* (1950). Roland H. Bainton's interest resulted in his publication of "David Joris," in *Archiv fuer Reformationsgeschichte* (1937), and *The Travail of Religious Liberty* (1951).

Other phases of the Reformation were treated by Earl Morse Wilbur, who wrote *A History of Unitarianism* (1945), and Roland H. Bainton, who contributed his *Bernardino Ochino* (1940) and *Sebastian Castellio, Concerning Heretics* (1935).

Among the notable contributions to the study of the English Reformation may be mentioned Winthrop S. Hudson's *John Ponet* (1942); W. K. Jordan's four volumes on *The Development of Toleration in England* (1932–40); M. M. Knappen's *Tudor Puritanism* (1939); and W. Haller's *The Rise of Puritanism* (1938).

Seventeenth-century studies yielded monographs dealing mainly with the unionist movements. Among these were John T. McNeill's *Unitive Protestantism* (1935); J. Minton Batten's *John Dury* (1944); and Matthew Spinka's *John Amos Comenius* (1943).

Eighteenth-century studies centered about John Wesley. F. J. McConnell contributed *John Wesley* (1939); Umphrey Lee published *The Historical Background of Early Methodist Enthusiasm* (1931); and W. R. Cannon *The Theology of John Wesley* (1946).

Since the multiplicity of interests characteristic of the latest period is reflected in the literature dealing with it, a survey of this literature is more easily arranged in topical order. In the first place, American Church History studies have come into their own only within the last thirty years. Formerly the majority of such studies were of a denominational character. Among the pioneers in this field was Frank Hugh Foster, who contributed his *Genetic History of New England Theology* (1907) and other similar works. Peter Mode's *Source Book and Bibliographical Guide for American Church History* appeared in 1921. A more determined start was made by William Warren Sweet, who held, from 1927, the first chair of American Church History in a Protestant divinity school. His *Story of Religion in America* (1930) has been published in several editions. His other most important writings include four volumes of *Re-*

ligion on the American Frontier, 1783–1850 (1931–46), which deal with hitherto unpublished sources of Presbyterians, Baptists, Congregationalists, and Methodists. His *Religion in Colonial America* (1942) and *Religion in the Development of American Culture* (1952) are to be followed by two other volumes. Perry Miller likewise greatly enriched this field by his various studies: *Orthodoxy in Massachusetts* (1933); *The New England Mind* (1939); *The Puritans* (1938); and *Jonathan Edwards* (1949). O. E. Winslow likewise contributed a biography of *Jonathan Edwards* (1940). H. Richard Niebuhr dealt with *The Kingdom of God in America* (1937). Willard L. Sperry published his *Religion in America* in 1946. Anson Philips Stokes contributed a three-volume work on *Church and State in the United States* (1951). C. H. Hopkins published *The Rise of the Social Gospel in American Protestantism* in 1940, and James H. Nichols *Democracy and the Churches* (1951). Among the denominational histories, too numerous to include adequately, may be mentioned *The Journals of Henry Melchior Muhlenberg* (3 vols., 1942–55), edited by T. G. Tappert and J. W. Doberstein; Leonard Trinterud's *The Forming of American Tradition* (1949); and W. C. Barclay, *History of Methodist Missions* (6 vols., 1949 ff.).

The rise of the Soviet Union to world power has stimulated interest in Eastern Orthodoxy. Matthew Spinka published his *Church and the Russian Revolution* (1927); *History of Christianity in the Balkans* (1933); and *Nicholas Berdyaev* (1950). George P. Fedotov edited *A Treasury of Russian Spirituality* (1948) and published a book on *The Russian Religious Mind* (1946). Robert P. Casey wrote on *Religion in Russia* (1946).

Among the works dealing with various aspects of the life of the church may be listed John T. McNeill's *A History of the Cure of Souls* (1951).

Church History, the first American quarterly devoted exclusively to professional studies in this whole field of Church History (1932 ff.), contains a large number of valuable articles. For the first seventeen years it was edited by Matthew Spinka and Robert Hastings Nichols.

BIBLIOGRAPHY: S. J. Case, ed., *A Bibliographical Guide to the History of Christianity*, 1931; George H. Williams, "Church History," in Arnold S. Nash, ed., *Protestant Thought in the Twentieth Century*, 1951; Francis X. Curran, *Major Trends in American Church History*, 1946.
[Sup.] MATTHEW SPINKA.

CHURCH HISTORY, AMERICAN SOCIETY OF. See HISTORICAL ASSOCIATIONS.

CHURCH LEAGUE FOR INDUSTRIAL DEMOCRACY. See CHURCH SOCIALIST LEAGUE.

CHURCH LEAGUE, NATIONAL. See CHURCH SOCIETY.

CHURCH, LOCAL, THE: This constitutes the unitary body in Christianity. The plan seems to have originated with the synagogue (*q.v.*, Vol. XI), the organization of which the early church largely adopted. In promoting the work of the kingdom Paul and others established and strengthened local churches. From that day to this the welfare of the church at large and of individual members has depended much on the spiritual health and vigor of the home church. Whatever the over-all plan for the church in its wider concerns, the most important activities all center in the local church; e.g., public worship, Christian education, pastoral nurture, evangelism, and missions. Ideally, every such body would have its own pastor, residing in the community and remaining long enough to do constructive work. Actually, many congregations suffer from absentee or intermittent leadership. In some communities a small number of congregations too weak for self-support form a group under a single pastor as a sort of "circuit rider." According to the "Larger Parish" plan five or six neighboring congregations may co-operate under the leadership of "experts" in various sorts of pastoral leadership, such as young people's work, and the ministry of music. All this has to do mainly with rural churches. In country and city alike many communities suffer from the presence of too many weak, competing bodies. Under competent leadership any one of them might prosper. In certain cases, owing to shifting population, some kind of local church union, or affiliation, seems to be the only remedy; but often it is easier to unite large churches than small ones. Frequently the local body suffers from individualism, which may result in failure to meet changing conditions with suitable methods. On the other hand, the local body may try to imitate a metropolitan church, where the community seems to need a church swimming pool. In recent times, partly for reasons financial, few churches have engaged in such activities. Local leaders feel increasingly that while they ought to show concern about everything that affects the community, the congregation should engage primarily in work different from that of other local agencies. "Let the church be a church!" On the welfare of the local body seems to depend the progress of the kingdom at home and abroad; but strangely historians of the church and some teachers have paid little attention to local units. Perhaps as a consequence, many a starry-eyed young idealist has gone out to "save the world" while neglecting the local church, and its individual members. Such work calls for the humility and perseverance of an indefatigable undershepherd (I Pet. 5:1-4).

See BUDGET, CHURCH; DOWNTOWN CHURCH; MISSIONS, PROMOTION OF; OFFICIAL BOARD; PUBLICITY, CHURCH.

ANDREW W. BLACKWOOD

CHURCH OF CHRIST IN CHINA. See CHINA.

CHURCH OF CHRIST, SCIENTIST. See CHRISTIAN SCIENCE.

CHURCH OF DANIEL'S BAND. See DANIEL'S BAND, CHURCH OF.

CHURCH OF ENGLAND. See ENGLAND, CHURCH OF.

CHURCH OF ENGLAND IN CANADA: While a constituent part of the Anglican communion throughout the world, this church is a self-governing body. Its beginnings go back to 1710, when the first service according to the use of the Church of England was held in Port Royal (now Annapolis Royal), Nova Scotia. The oldest Anglican church in Canada was erected in Halifax in 1749.

In 1787 Charles Inglis (*q.v.*) was appointed the first Anglican bishop in Canada. The early settlers were provided with a ministry by the Society for the Propagation of the Gospel. The Society for the Promotion of Christian Knowledge also aided by providing books and means to build churches, and the Colonial and Continental Church Society provided missionaries and teachers.

Since the early British settlement of Canada, immigration and natural increase contributed to the growth of the church. Its territory extends from the Atlantic to the Pacific, and north to the Arctic Ocean. Its membership totals about 1,000,000, half of them confirmed. There are about 1,700 parishes and between 1,800 and 2,000 clergy.

There are twenty-eight dioceses, each with its bishop and its diocesan synod, over which the bishop presides. These dioceses are distributed among four ecclesiastical provinces, each with its archbishop and provincial synod. Over all these is a general synod, organized in 1893, with its primate. There have been eight primates since 1893, the incumbent (1952) being Walter Foster Barfoot, archbishop of Edmonton, Alberta.

While the work of the church as a whole generally comes under the direction of the general synod (subject, however, to certain limitations in relation to provincial synods); yet the general synod, for the sake of efficiency, delegates to certain bodies, constituted by itself, special parts of the church's work. At present there are three main departments of general synod dealing with missionary, educational, and social work. (1) Overseas missionary work is carried on in Pakistan (*q.v.*), China (*q.v*), and Japan (*q.v.*). There is also missionary work among the Indians (*q.v.*) and Eskimos in Canada. (2) The church has ten theological colleges and four universities which, to a large extent, supply the candidates for the ministry. There are also eighteen residential schools for boys and girls in addition to parish education. (3) The social service department promotes the care of immigrants and their training in citizenship, and works toward the maintenance of just living conditions and the formation of Christian public opinion.

Doctrinal standards of the church are the Apostles' and Nicene Creeds and the Thirty-nine Articles (*q.v.*, Vol. XI) as printed in the Book of Common Prayer (see COMMON PRAYER, BOOK OF).

BIBLIOGRAPHY: Charles W. Vernon, *The Old Church in the New Dominion*, 1929; W. Bertal Heeney, ed., *Leaders of the Canadian Church*, 3 vols., 1918–43.
ROBERT ARTHUR HILTZ.

CHURCH OF GOD: The Church of God, with headquarters in Cleveland, Tenn., was founded in 1886 by a small group of Methodists and Baptists in eastern Tennessee and western North Carolina because of discontent with these denominations. Leaders in the revival movement were R. G. Spurling, R. G. Spurling, Jr., both ministers in the Baptist Church, and W. F. Bryant, a Baptist deacon.

The group was of the holiness variety (see HOLINESS CHURCHES) and in 1896 experienced an outbreak of what it termed the "baptism of the Holy Ghost," making it one of the earliest Pentecostal organizations (see PENTECOSTAL CHURCHES). The revival was pressed in the southeastern section of the United States, then to the Bahama Islands and Jamaica. From this region it spread into all states of the U.S.A. but remains strongest in the southeastern states.

The Church of God, in keeping with most holiness and pentecostal bodies, is ultra-fundamentalist, strongly Arminian in doctrine, interprets the Bible literally, and emphasizes the gifts of the Spirit, speaking in tongues as "the initial evidence of the baptism of the Holy Ghost," and divine healing. Its ordinances are baptism (by immersion) and the Lord's Supper, which is generally followed by washing one another's feet (see FOOT WASHING).

The organization has maintained headquarters in Cleveland, Tenn., since 1908. It operates Lee College, a Bible school with a junior college division, regional schools in North Dakota, California, and Saskatchewan, and two orphanages. In 1954 it sponsored mission stations in 54 countries and had more than 250,000 members. In 1949 it amalgamated with the Full Gospel Church in South Africa.

Several groups have stemmed from the Church of God—particularly in 1923, when A. J. Tomlinson was impeached as general overseer and organized what was designated as the Tomlinson Church of God. At his death in 1943 his organization was split between his sons. One of these factions also has headquarters in Cleve-

land, Tenn., and is known as the Church of God of Prophecy. The other has headquarters in Queens Village, N. Y.

See also CHURCH (CHURCHES) OF GOD.

BIBLIOGRAPHY: Charles W. Conn, *Like A Mighty Army*, 1955; E. L. Simmons, *History of the Church of God*, 1938.
CHARLES W. CONN.

CHURCH OF GOD (ANDERSON, IND.). See HOLINESS CHURCHES.

CHURCH OF GOD AND SAINTS OF CHRIST. See CHURCH (CHURCHES) OF GOD.

CHURCH OF GOD (APOSTOLIC). See HOLINESS CHURCHES.

CHURCH OF GOD AS ORGANIZED BY CHRIST. See CHURCH (CHURCHES) OF GOD.

CHURCH OF GOD (OREGON, ILL.). See ADVENTISTS.

CHURCH OF GOD (SEVENTH DAY). See ADVENTISTS.

CHURCH OF REVELATION: Founded 1930 in Long Beach, Calif., by Janet Stine Lewis Wolford; eleven congregations with 1,050 members were reported in 1951. Ministers receive no salaries. Divine healing is practiced.
T. G. TAPPERT.

CHURCH OF THE NAZARENE. See NAZARENE, CHURCH OF THE.

CHURCH OF THE NEW JERUSALEM. See NEW JERUSALEM, CHURCH OF THE.

CHURCH PEACE UNION. See PEACE MOVEMENTS.

CHURCH REGISTERS: Roman Catholic Church law prescribes the keeping of the following registers. In the diocesan archives: register of ordination. In every parish: register of baptisms; register of confirmation; register of marriages; and register of the dead. If a person is confirmed, marries, is ordained to major orders, or takes solemn vows of religion, the fact must be notified to the rector of the parish, in which such person was baptized, to be made a part of his, or her, baptismal record.
[Sup.] GEORGES A. BARROIS.

CHURCH SOCIALIST LEAGUE: Organized by members of the Church of England in 1906; an off-shoot of the same name was organized by Episcopalians in the U.S.A. in 1911. Their aim was to pioneer in social theory and action in directions in which the great bulk of their fellow-churchmen were not willing to follow. Leading spirits in England were Lewis Donaldson (who summed up the League's position: "Christianity is the religion of which socialism is the practice"), P. E. T. Widdington, James Adderley; and in America were B. I. Bell, Lyford Edwards, and Bishop Spaulding, who called himself a Christian Marxist. The League never exerted influence in the Protestant Episcopal Church, partly because the term socialist was equated in most minds with anti-American tenets, partly because some of its leaders were pacifists. It was absorbed by the Church League for Industrial Democracy in 1919. See also CHRISTIAN SOCIALISM.

ALEXANDER C. ZABRISKIE.

CHURCH SOCIETY: An organization for the promotion of Anglican Evangelicalism mainly by education, evangelism, publication, and youth work; it was formed in June, 1950, by the amalgamation of the Church Association, organized in 1865, which had supported most of the prosecutions for ritualism until the failure of the Lincoln Case in 1892, and the National Church League, organized in 1906 by the union of a number of groups devoted to more positive methods of evangelical propaganda.

BIBLIOGRAPHY: *Official Yearbook of the Church of England*, annual; Ollard, Crosse, and Bond, *Dictionary of English Church History*, 3d ed., 1948, *s.v.* Societies, Ecclesiastical.

EDWARD ROCHIE HARDY.

CHURCH UNION. See UNION OF THE CHURCHES.

CHURCH UNION, THE: Formed Jan. 1, 1934, by the union of the English Church Union and the Anglo-Catholic Congress. The E.C.U. had been since 1860 a center of fellowship, propaganda, and defense for Anglo-Catholics; it provided the defense in most of the ritualistic trials. Its leading figure was Lord Halifax, president 1868–1919 and 1927–33; his final achievement was the negotiation of union with the A.C.C., which sponsored the Anglo-Catholic Congresses of 1920–33 and other modern evangelistic efforts. The Union continues the activity of both organizations in the fields of church defense, prayer, social action, and youth work, and publishes *The Church Observer* (under various names since 1861).

BIBLIOGRAPHY: J. G. Lockhart, *Charles Lindley, Viscount Halifax*, 2 vols., 1935–36; *Official Yearbook of the Church of England*, annual.

EDWARD ROCHIE HARDY.

CHURCH WORLD SERVICE: Created in May, 1946, to integrate and carry forward the work of three emergency relief organizations established by the Protestant churches of the United States: (1) Church Committee for Re-

lief in Asia, an expansion of Church Committee for China Relief, begun in 1938; (2) Church Committee on Overseas Relief and Reconstruction, succeeding the Committee on Foreign Relief Appeals in the Churches, organized in 1938, developing a program of contributed relief supplies; (3) Commission for World Council Service, organized in 1945 to carry on relief and reconstruction services in Europe in connection with the World Council of Churches (*q.v.*), then in process of formation. Later, Church World Service absorbed the American Committee for Christian Refugees.

During its separate existence, Church World Service, Inc., received cash contributions of $19,202,304 directly and through Protestant and Orthodox denominations, and contributions of relief supplies valued at $36,504,998. It disbursed these in relief activities in Europe and Asia, and also in its program for the resettlement of 51,000 Protestant and Eastern Orthodox displaced persons in the United States.

On January 1, 1951, it became a department of the newly established National Council of the Churches of Christ, U.S.A.

IVANE SAULPAUGH.

CHURCH YEAR: For the background see CHURCH YEAR, Vol. III. The present article deals only with churches traditionally not liturgical. In the break with Rome the reformers discarded many customs that had come to seem synonymous with papal idolatry and corruption. Only such sacraments, celebrations, and observances as had a biblical basis were to be retained. Although the limitations were severe, they did not in principle represent a rejection of liturgical and seasonal observances. Luther showed a lively concern about the art of worship, maintained the Christian year, and prepared manuals founded upon ancient forms. Zwingli retained certain ceremonies not authorized in Scripture. With the exception of Geneva, Continental Protestantism developed liturgical forms, and made much use of the traditional Christian calendar, reinterpreted in the light of Protestant theology. The Genevan Liturgy, prepared by Calvin, limited its observance to the Lord's day and became the pattern for the Scottish Liturgy, published by Knox. In contrast with elaborate Catholic forms, and Lutheran and Anglican revisions, Presbyterian ways of worship seemed severely simple, but maintained a strong sense of order and dignity. Anabaptists, Quakers, Separatists, and Brownists went all the way in abandoning the idea of a church calendar, at times even picketing established churches with "No Easter" and "No Christmas" banners. American Protestantism from the first was characterized by variety and informality, including extreme experimentalization by revivalistic sects.

At present Free Churches tend toward a Protestant-modified, somewhat Americanized version of the classic Church Year. Most churches observe the main seasons and events in the first half of the traditional year, from Advent and Christmastide, through the Epiphany season, Lent, Holy Week, Easter, to Pentecost, with observance of many days and weeks more recently introduced in the civil calendar. The National Council of Churches and practically all denominational headquarters encourage this by supplying appropriate materials. Official hymnals, worship manuals, and plan books give information about the scheme of the year, and to some extent follow it in organizing their services.

Recent influences tending to bring the Church Year back into Protestant consciousness are: (1) Revival of interest in the nature of worship, its architecture, symbolism, and theology; (2) The ecumenical movement, with emphasis on the nature of the church, broadened sympathy among its various branches, and recognition of the practical necessity for unity; (3) The deepening devotional search in crisis times, leading toward recovery of classic means of grace in ancient lectionaries and observances of the Church Year; (4) Emphasis on long range planning of program and preaching, with the year as the unit.

While this renewal of concern about classic modes of worship has widely influenced usages in local churches, the Christian Year remains for Protestants a guide, not an authority.

BIBLIOGRAPHY: G. M. Gibson, *The Story of the Christian Year*, 1945; Jn. Dowden, *The Church Year and Kalendar*, 1910; F. M. Wilson, *An Outline of the Christian Year*, 1941; *A Manual of Worship for the Free Churches*, 1948; books of worship in various Churches.

GEORGE MILES GIBSON.

CIBORIUM: In the Roman Catholic Church, a liturgical vessel of precious metal in which the wafers for the communion of the faithful are kept permanently. It has usually the shape of a chalice with a lid. It is covered with a veil of silk and placed in the tabernacle (*q.v.*). [Sup.]

CIVILIAN PUBLIC SERVICE. See CONSCIENTIOUS OBJECTORS.

CIVILIZATION, CHRISTIANITY AND: Civilization is, abstractly, the act or process of civilizing; and, more concretely, the society which is judged to be civilized. It is in the latter sense that the term is employed here. The term "to civilize" comes from the Latin, "civilis," which means: (1) of, or belonging to, a citizen, and consequently (2) conduct or a form of life which belongs to, in the sense of befitting, a citizen. The implied or explicit contrast is with the conduct or manner of life of a barbarian. Thus, "to civilize" is to bring out of

a state of barbarism, to train in the arts of polite (from "polis," a city, as contrasted with the "boorishness" of the country) or cultured life, to refine or enlighten. And civilization is constituted by that society in which the conduct and tastes of men are judged to be thus refined, enlightened, polite.

Cultural anthropologists have differed as to the time and place of the first society that could be called civilized, the Nile Valley and the Mesopotamian Valley being the leading contenders for that honor. Certain it is that civilization long antedated Christianity, and that civilizations have arisen, since the birth of Christianity, which owed nothing to Christianity. For this historical reason, as well as for others later to be mentioned, Christianity and civilization cannot be equated.

Christianity arose and had its first creative period in the Mediterranean basin, in the midst of a civilization which may be roughly called Greco-Roman, though it represented the break-up and the continuation of many older civilizations: the Egyptian, the Cretan, the Persian, the Mesopotamian, the Indian and possibly others. Towards this civilization, as normally towards all others which it encounters, Christianity adopted, for reasons later to be indicated, a dual attitude. On the one hand, it was bitterly critical, hostile and exclusive; on the other hand, it was appreciative and appropriative, and contributive. Just as it made use of the Greek and later the Latin languages, rejecting such terms (e.g., the Greek *eros*) as inevitably conveyed meanings which it regarded with horror, making use of, and sometimes reviving, others which it could, however, fill with its own distinctive meanings; so it persistently chose and rejected and transformed the forms and spirit of the Greco-Roman civilization until, by the time of the death of Augustine of Hippo (A.D. 430) it had achieved what might be called, with some necessary qualifications, a Christianized Greco-Roman culture or a Greco-Romanized expression of Christianity. This was firmly embedded in its external forms (its organization, its administration, its discipline, its forms of worship, its art and architecture, its doctrinal expressions), in its world view, and in its inner spirit. So firmly built was this civilization within a civilization that it alone was able to stand, though with some damage to its outer forms and inner spirit, before the assaults of the invading barbarians. Presently it took the initiative against the depravity and chaos of barbarian life, becoming the "schoolmaster" to the barbarians; and thus, though once more at a price to herself, the architect, or certainly one of the chief architects, of modern Western civilization. Within that civilization it has continued to be both champion and critic. Through its missionary activities, organized Christianity has been a major, and perhaps the most wholesome and constructive, factor in carrying that civilization, in varying degrees of effectiveness, over the face of the earth.

The dual relation which Christianity maintains toward any and every civilization springs from the very nature of Christianity, on the one hand, and of human civilization, on the other. That they are by their very nature different, and at least potentially opposed, has appeared repeatedly and from both sides. From the religious side the consciousness of difference and potential hostility is early expressed by the fact that, in Genesis 4:21, 22, the invention of the arts of civilization is attributed, not to the godly line of Seth, but to the ungodly line of Cain. The classical expression of this awareness on the side of Christianity is Augustine's *City of God,* in which the earthly "city" is certainly civilized but is contrasted most vividly with the heavenly. That this awareness of potential hostility is not an expression of otherworldly morbidity merely, or a weakness in Christianity, or in some Christians, which could be corrected to advantage is shown by the "crucial experiment" of nineteenth century theological liberalism (see LIBERALISM). It was definitely an attempt to remove the hostility by accommodating Christianity to the culture and civilization of that time and place. In the judgment of later friendly (cf. W. M. Horton, *Realistic Theology,* etc.) and unfriendly (cf. J. G. Machen, *Christianity and Liberalism,* etc.) critics, it succeeded only too well. As a result, it (1) sacrificed the function of critical judgment which is essential to Christianity's constructive purpose, and (2) it became out-of-date with the passing of that historical era.

These criticisms of liberalism suggest some of the reasons why a tension between Christianity and civilization is natural, inevitable and valuable. (1) Christianity is presented as a revelation of and from the "absolute" of eternity to the relativities of time, while civilization belongs to the latter. It may very well be that the currently popular distinction between absolutes and relativities is too starkly drawn, and that time and eternity are correlative contraries rather than the absolute contradictories which, for example, Barthian thought represents them to be (see ETERNITY; TIME; CRISIS, THE THEOLOGY OF; DIALECTICAL THEOLOGY); but certainly there is a difference and a potential hostility between civilization, which belongs to the temporal and relative, and Christianity, which belongs primarily to the eternal and absolute. (2) The "salvation" which Christianity offers to man is primarily a gracious gift of God, while civilization is a human achievement. The distinct and proper difference at this point may, of course, be conceived and expressed in a manner that is a misrepresentation of Christianity. It may be

maintained, as it was by certain of the Gnesio-Lutherans in sixteenth-century Germany, that human good works, which are constitutive of civilization, are indifferent to, or even injurious to, salvation. It may also be maintained, especially by humanists of the atheistic or secular type, that Christianity has no place in, or is a danger to, civilization. Thus John Dewey contended at one time, in harmony with his instrumentalist epistemology and his evolutionary conception of the growth of culture, that, while religion was once true in the sense that it was a necessary support for the spirit of ignorant and powerless man, it is now no longer true, since science serves that purpose much more effectively, and it is harmful since it diverts man's attention from science. The tension is not as complete as that; but it is real nevertheless. Christianity, when it is fully self-conscious, cannot accept as adequate to it even the role ascribed to it by such humanists as the authors of the chapters in *Humanism and America,* (Norman Foerster ed.), for whom Christianity is a useful aid in elevating man's self-estimate and thus making him welcome and strive to attain the classical cultural standards. Luther was not wrong in refusing to be restrained by the humanistic program and conceptions of Erasmus, or even in insisting that his spirit and that of Zwingli were not the same. A basic reason is that Christianity looks ultimately for salvation to a gift of God, while civilization looks to the work of man (see SOTERIOLOGY). This difference is accentuated and exacerbated (3) by the fact that, for Christianity, all human achievements, including the finest fruits of civilization, are sullied by the sin from which it is the purpose of Christianity to redeem man; and indeed, when they are done by unregenerated men, are a fruit of sin. That is why Augustine characterized the finest virtues of the Greeks as simply "splendid vices."

For such reasons, civilization and Christianity can never be simply equated; nor can civilization be regarded, without qualification, as one of the fruits or desired goals of Christianity. But the relationship is not only one of tension and potential opposition. From the point of view of humanism Christianity can be, and as we have seen has been, regarded as an ally. And the proper function of Christianity with regard to civilization is, under certain conditions, to commend and promote as well as to judge and condemn. The doctrine of common grace (*q.v.*) permits and requires the Christian to regard every good human achievement as, in some real sense, a gracious gift of God, the Holy Spirit; and it was this consideration which led some of the greatest thinkers of the early church, as well as some later thinkers, to characterize such men as Socrates and Plato as "Christians before Christ." The proper Christian attitude towards everything good in human society is thankfulness to God and gratitude towards its human creators, a prayerful effort to baptize these things into the authentic spirit of Christianity, and thus endeavour to use and extend them for the glory of God and the welfare of men. The very affecting picture which, in his autobiographical chapter in *Contemporary American Theology* (ed. by Vergilius Ferm), J. G. Machen, often misunderstood as representing a very different spirit, gives of his parents, who were authentic Christians and, as such, enjoyed and commended the good things of life and culture—this is a sound Christian attitude.

Christianity, then, claims allegiance for its own sake, or for the sake of Christ, and will not submit to becoming merely a device for "getting society out of a scrape." It approaches every civilization in judgment on its inadequacies and perversions and injustices, and as such is a dynamic revolutionary force. It rejects as sinful the human autonomy which is characteristic of all historical civilizations. But it approves and seeks to improve and further the good, baptizing it into its own spirit.

BIBLIOGRAPHY: W. F. Albright, *From the Stone Age to Christianity*; Herbert Butterfield, *Christianity and History*; Arnold J. Toynbee, *A Study of History*, abridgement by D. C. Somervell; Charles D. Eldridge, *Christianity's Contributions to Civilization*; McNeill, Spinka and Willoughby, eds., *Environmental Factors in Christian History*.

ANDREW K. RULE.

CLAPHAM SECT: Not a sect in the strict sense (see SECT AND CULT), but a movement within Anglican Evangelicalism at the close of the eighteenth and beginning of the nineteenth century. Named after Clapham, a village outside of London where John Venn (1759–1813) was rector, an intimate and influential circle of Evangelicals was formed which included such prominent laymen as William Wilberforce (*q.v.*, Vol. XII). Wealth and public position were placed in the service of a puritanical piety which expressed itself in social reform and missions.

BIBLIOGRAPHY: J. W. Bready, *England: Before and After Wesley*, 1938; see also bibliography under ANGLICAN EVANGELICALISM.

THEODORE G. TAPPERT.

CLARE OF ASSISI: Saint, virgin, foundress of Poor Clares; b. July 16, 1194, at Assisi; d. Aug. 11, 1253. She was a member of the noble family Dei Sciffi. St. Francis persuaded her to lead an ascetic life. On March 18, 1212, she took the vows of obedience, chastity and poverty, but her family resisted her, except her sister Agnes, who followed her later. St. Francis prepared a refuge for her at St. Angelo, later at San Damiano, where the community rapidly increased. Her mother Hortulana and her sister Beatrice also entered. For forty years, of

which twenty-seven were in illness, she governed the convent, living solely of alms. Her mortification and prayer obtained many miracles. Her order was spread the world over. She was canonized in 1250. Her body is now in Santa Chiara at Assisi. In art she is represented with the Blessed Sacrament, because with its aid she helped Frederick II to defeat the Saracens.

BIBLIOGRAPHY: Thomas a Celano, *Legenda S. Clarae*, 1908; *Acta Sanctorum Aug.*, II. 754–67; P. Robinson, "The Writings of St. Clare of Assisi," *Arch. Franc. Hist.*, 1913.

WILLIBRORD LAMPEN.

CLARES POOR, or SECOND ORDER OF ST. FRANCIS: The order was founded by St. Francis and St. Clare of Assisi and approved by Pope Innocent III in 1215 or 1216. This pope permitted the order to live without property. St. Clare gave to her order a Rule in twelve *Capitula*, which were approved two days before her death. The first convents had followed the rules of St. Benedict and the customs of San Damiano, the first convent of St. Clare. In 1219 convents were founded at Burgos and Barcelona, and in 1220 at Reims. In Bohemia the order was introduced by Agnes of Prague and in Belgium by Ermentrude. When St. Clare died, there were seventy convents; in 1335 the first one was founded in the Netherlands. Each one of these was self-supporting. The way in which they were organized was variable. Pope Gregory IX nominated Francis as General Superior of the Poor Clares and permitted many convents to have some property. Pope Innocent IV gave a new Rule in 1247. A third Rule was given in 1253. Blessed Isabella, sister of St. Louis, gave another Rule, approved by Alexander IV (Alexandrists). Another new Rule was given by Urbanus IV; he obliged all sisters to follow it, and permitted them to have property (Urbanists). Some convents were excepted. In the fifteenth century a reformation was needed. St. John of Capistrano worked for it. The Council of Trent prescribed that the order should have some revenues. Today there are 12,000 sisters in about 550 convents.

BIBLIOGRAPHY: L. Oliger, "De origine regularum S. Clarae," in *Arch. Franc. Hist.*, 5 (1913); *St. Franciscus*, 27 (1912), 65–112.

WILLIBRORD LAMPEN.

CLARK, ELMER TALMAGE: Methodist; b. in Randolph County, Ark. September 9, 1886. He was educated at Hendrix College, Birmingham, Southern College (A.B.), Vanderbilt University, Temple University (B.D., S.T.D.), and George Peabody College (M.A.). He served pastorates in Saint Louis and during the first World War was a foreign correspondent for the *New York Tribune* and *St. Louis Republic*. He subsequently became a missionary secretary of The Methodist Church in charge of literature and editor of *World Outlook*. He is president and executive secretary of the Association of Methodist Historical Societies (U.S.A.), secretary of the International Methodist Historical Society, and member of the Ecumenical Methodist Council. Among his best known books are: *The Psychology of Religious Awakening, The Small Sects in America, Social Studies of the War, The Chiangs of China,* and *The Warm Heart of Wesley.*

CLARK, FRANCIS E(DWARD): D. May 25, 1927. After a very successful pastorate in Portland, Me., he founded the United Society of Christian Endeavor (*q.v.*) to which he subsequently devoted forty-four years of his life. He travelled around the world five times in the interest of this work and also served as the president of the World's Society of Christian Endeavor. His later books include: *Fellow Travelers* (1898); *The Great Secret* (1895); *Training the Church for the Future* (1902); and *The Christian Endeavor Manual* (1903). He edited *The Continent of Opportunity; Old Homes of New Americans* (1912); *The Holy Land of Asia Minor* (1914); *Christ and the Young People* (1916); *In the Foot-Steps of St. Paul* (1917); *Our Italian Fellow-Citizens* (1919); and *The Gospel of the Out-of-Doors* (1920).

[Sup.] RAYMOND W. ALBRIGHT.

CLARK, SIDNEY J. W. See WORLD DOMINION MOVEMENT.

CLARKE, CHARLES PHILIP STEWART: Anglican; b. at Whiteshill, Glos., in 1871. He was educated at Clifton College and Christ Church, Oxford; d. Dec. 18, 1947. Ordained in 1895, he served Eastleigh, Hants; Christ Church Mission, Poplar (1898–1901); Vicar of High Wycombe (1910–16); Donhead St. Andrew's and Examining Chaplain to Bishop of Salisbury, subsequently becoming a prebend in Salisbury Cathedral. In 1934 he became archdeacon of Chichester. Publications: *A Short History of the Christian Church; The Oxford Movement and After; Everymans' Book of Saints; Church History from Nero to Constantine; Via Media.*

EDWIN OLIVER JAMES.

CLARK FOUNDATION: Enables Pomona College, Claremont, Cal., to invite a lecturer in the field of religion anually. Income from an endowment of $10,000 is available for this purpose. Recent lecturers have included Bernard D. Meland, D. Elton Trueblood, and Douglas Horton. E. WILSON LYON.

CLASS MEETING: John Wesley divided the membership of Methodist societies into classes, each composed of twelve members and a class leader. He developed the weekly class meeting to provide opportunities for worship, fellowship,

instruction, discipline, and group discussion of religious problems. English Methodists still regard it as an indispensable institution in their churches. In America class meetings, though used effectively for a century, were gradually discarded after 1866. Most branches of American Methodism have replaced the class meeting by other agencies designed for the specific religious needs of varying age and interest groups.

BIBLIOGRAPHY: O. P. Fitzgerald, *The Class-Meeting,* 1889.

[Sup.] JOSEPH MINTON BATTEN.

CLAY, ALBERT TOBIAS: Orientalist; b. at Hanover, Pa., Dec. 4, 1866; d. New Haven, Conn., Sept 14, 1925. He studied at Franklin and Marshall College (A.B., 1889); Mt. Airy Seminary (1892); University of Pennsylvania (Ph.D., 1894). He taught Semitics at the University of Pennsylvania (1893–95; 1899–1910); Chicago Lutheran Seminary (1895–99); and at Yale University (1910–25). His works include: *Amurru, the Home of the Northern Semites* (1910); *The Empire of the Amorites* (1919); *The Origin of the Biblical Traditions* (1923).

ELMER E. FLACK.

CLÉMANGES, NICHOLAS POILLEVILLIAN OF: Since he was a very capable master of style the University of Paris chose him as a mouthpiece for its conciliar policy and teachings, as well as its standpoint regarding the Papal Schism. In his writings he turned against the wrong use of dialectics, the excessive feast days in the church, and simony among the higher clergy.

BIBLIOGRAPHY: P. Hemmerle, *Das religioese und kirchenpolitische System des pariser Theolog Nicolaus Poillevillain, genannt Nicolaus von Clémanges,* 1911; A. Simon, *Studien zu Nicolaus von Clémanges,* 1930; *Dict. de Théologie Catholique,* Vol. XI (1931), col. 597–600, where the works are mentioned which are not listed in his *Opera omnia.*

[Sup.] H. GOOSSENS.

CLEMENT: Clement II. Belonged to a noble Saxon family; in 1401 he became bishop of Bamberg and chancellor of Emperor Henry III, whom he accompanied on a trip to Italy. After his death Leo IX sent Clement's body to Bamberg, where it was buried in the cathedral.

Clement V. B. *ca.* 1264. He was elected pope because he had the support of the Italian party, Boniface VIII, and the French cardinals, being a Frenchman himself. By appointing nine French cardinals, he obtained a majority of Frenchmen in the College of Cardinals. Another favor bestowed upon France was the removal of the papal court from Rome to Avignon, thus initiating the so-called Babylonian Captivity of the papacy.

Clement VI. Was born in 1291 at Maumont in the province of Limousin. At an early age he joined the Benedictine Order, studied at the University of Paris, was appointed prior of St.

Baudil, then abbot of Fecamp, then bishop of Arras. He served under King Philip IV as chancellor of France and also became archbishop of Sens and later of Rouen. Having accused the king of Poland (Casimir) of adultery, he excommunicated him and compelled him to amend his ways. But as pope he himself was not without serious faults, being guilty of gross nepotism and excessive taxation. On the other hand, he won much admiration for his theological learning, affable personality, and eloquence.

Clement VII. When in May 1532 German soldiers plundered Rome, Clement was besieged and had to provide funds for his ransom, besides a promise to convoke a church council which would deal with the dangers posed by Protestantism. Since he was largely dependent upon the support of Emperor Charles V (*q.v.*), he did not wish to annoy the latter by granting the request made by Henry VIII (*q.v.*) of England for a divorce from Catherine of Aragon, the aunt of Charles V. His vacillating course of action so strongly offended the English monarch that the latter inaugurated the profound breach between the royal house of England and the papacy which since 1558 has never been healed.

BIBLIOGRAPHY: E. Casanova, *Lettere di Carlo V a Clemente VII*, 1893; E. Rodocanachi, *Les pontificats d'Adrien VI et de Clément VII*, 1933.

Clement VIII. Born in 1536 at Fano of a prominent Florentine family that had been exiled by the house of Medici. In order to ward off the Turks in central Europe he dispatched an army to Hungary, which did not, however, meet with much success. He had hopes of making England Catholic through the friendship of James VI of Scotland, who in 1603 became king of England. The latter's wife, Anna of Denmark, did enter the Roman fold, but James remained a staunch Calvinist. Clement practised nepotism, providing distinguished scholars, including Baronius and Bellarmin, with the cardinal's hat. He was a very pious man and attended scrupulously to his manifold clerical duties. Owing to a feeble constitution, he had to work slowly, and during a long illness of his the papal finances suffered a relapse.

Clement VII. Antipope. In 1361 he became bishop of Thérouanne, in 1368 archbishop of Cambrai, in 1371 cardinal. From 1376 to 1378 he served as papal legate in northern Italy, where he in 1378 suppressed a rebellion. In 1378 he was chosen antipope to replace Urban VI, being supported mainly at Fondi by a large number of French and several Italian prelates. In 1379 he returned to Avignon, where he became entirely dependent upon the French court.

BIBLIOGRAPHY: K. Hauquet, *Documents rel. au grand schisme*, Vol. I, *Suppliques de Clément VII*, 1924.

Clement VIII. Antipope. Alfonso of Aragon supported him because he wanted to oust Mar-

tin V, who had objected to his claims to the kingdom of Naples. But before long Alfonso and Martin V became friends and thus impelled Clement VIII to abdicate. Thereupon he spent his remaining years as bishop of Majorca. See also POPES.   [Sup.] ALBERT HYMA.

CLEMENT OF ALEXANDRIA: Various attempts to find Clement's sources in earlier lost writings have proved fruitless, as in Bousset's ascription of parts of the *Eclogae* and *Excerpta* to Pantaenus and in Gabrielsson's theory that Clement's reading was largely confined to the encyclopedist Favorinus. Clement's reading, like his writing, resembles a multi-colored carpet. His thought, too, is derived from various strands. W. Bauer has argued that some of his ideas come from an early period when he was a Gnostic, perhaps a Valentinian; his ideas about the body of Jesus seem to reflect a development away from Gnostic theories. Again, the mystical element in his thought has sometimes been exaggerated, but it was real. His "Gnosticism" was not only philosophical but based on revelation and on secret tradition. In spite of (or perhaps because of) these various elements in his thought, Clement is essentially Christian.

BIBLIOGRAPHY: The edition of Staehlin, finished in 1909, was supplemented by an invaluable index (1936). See also R. B. Tollinton, *Clement of Alex.*, 1914; W. Bousset, *Juedisch-christlicher Schulbetrieb aus Alex. und Rom*, 1915; J. Munck, *Untersuchungen ueber Klemens von Alex.*, 1933; R. P. Casey, *The Excerpta ex Theodoto of Clement of Alex.*, 1934; E. Molland, *The Conception of the Gospel in the Alexandrian Theology*, 1938; W. den Boer, *De Allegorese in het Werk van Clemens Alex.*, 1940; M. Pohlenz in *Nachrichten . . . Goettingen* (1943), 3, 103–80; C. Mondésert, *Clément d'Alex.*, 1944; P. Camelot, *Foi et Gnose*, 1945. The ascription to Clem. of a papyrus scrap is most uncertain; cf. H. St. J. Thackery in *JTS*, XXX (1928–29), 179–89; W. Voelker, *Der wahre Gnostiker nach Clemens Alexandrinus* (Texte und Untersuchungen, LVII), 1952.

[Sup.] ROBERT M. GRANT.

CLEMENT OF ROME: The problem of church order, with which in the interest of harmony and unity I Clement is primarily concerned, remains difficult. The author describes the apostles' appointment of "bishops and deacons" in various places (xlii. 4) and their provision for the future succession of "approved men" to the episcopate (xliv. 2). When he speaks of the "elders" who have already died (xliv. 5), he apparently has in mind the age of the bishops, not their status as "presbyters" (cf. i. 3). Are the "presbyters" mentioned later (xlvii. 6, liv. 2, lvii. 1) simply older men or simply presbyters, or are they "presbyter-bishops"? The Corinthian trouble-makers have evidently removed some (one? not necessarily more, in spite of xliii. 6) from the episcopate, and Clement urges those responsible to accept voluntary exile for the sake of the church (liv-lv). The view that they represent an older ministry of wandering prophets cannot be established, although admittedly prophets were known at Rome about this time (cf. Hermas). Too often, as in B. H. Streeter's *The Primitive Church,* Clement's epistle is read in the light of some other document rather than investigated for what it says.

I Clement marks an important step in the Hellenization of Christian literature. It is written by a man who has been trained in rhetoric; he knows how to use rhetorical and philosophical commonplaces, which he adapts by combining them with examples taken from the Old Testament. Note his encomium of the Corinthians (i) and of Peter and Paul as Christian athletes (v), his Stoicizing picture of cosmic harmony (xx, xxxiii), his description of the phoenix as a proof of resurrection (xxv), his comparison of the church to an army and (from 1 Cor. 12) a body (xxxvi), and the commonplaces about voluntary exile (liv–lv). Such commonplaces are often found in Hellenistic Jewish literature, but Clement usually seems to be drawing them directly from his rhetorical training.

The Latin translation of the letter is most important for the history of "Christian Latin." Two different Coptic translations have been found in recent years.

Bibliography: R. Knopf, *Die apostolischen Vaeter*, 1920; B. H. Streeter, *The Primitive Church*, 1929, 200–21; A. Harnack, *Einfuehrung in die alte Kirchengeschichte*, 1931; L. Sanders, *L'hellénisme de saint Clément de Rome et le paulinisme*, 1943; J. A. Kleist, *The Epistles of St. Clement of Rome*, 1946; W. C. van Unnik in *Vigiliae Christianae*, IV (1950), 181–89; C. Mohrmann, *ibid.*, III (1949), 67–106, 163–83; C. Eggenberger, *Die Quellen der politischen Ethik des I. Klemensbriefes*, 1951.

[Sup.] Robert M. Grant.

CLERICALISM: Especially in Roman Catholic countries, but also occasionally in Protestant countries, the exercise by clergymen of influence which extends beyond what is deemed their proper sphere. Intervention of the clergy in affairs of state is the most common form of clericalism. Opposition to clerical pretensions, and sometimes hostility to the church itself, is called anticlericalism. See, for example, Spain; Portugal; Center Party.

Theodore G. Tappert.

CLINICAL TRAINING: Anton T. Boisen and Russell L. Dicks have pioneered in this development. A group of theological students, usually not more than twelve, reside in a hospital, mental or general, or a penal or correctional institution, serving as assistants to a clinically trained chaplain. They work for a' maximum of twelve weeks (Council for Clinical Training), and a minimum of six (Institute of Pastoral Care). For half his day a student normally visits and interviews patients or inmates, during the other half writing records, conferring with the chaplain, and attending regular seminar discussions. He studies the life situations of those with whom he counsels—"the living human documents" (Boisen). This work usually comes in summer when the student can give it full time.

Several thousand students have received such training, now available as follows: Institute of Pastoral Care, under Rollin J. Fairbanks, Andover Hall, Cambridge, Mass.; Council for Clinical Training, Frederick Kuether, 2 E. 103 St., N. Y. C. 29; Andover-Newton Seminary, Philip Guiles and John Billinsky, Newton Centre, Mass., co-operating with Boston City Hospital; Boston University School of Theology, Paul E. Johnson; Duke Divinity School, Russell L. Dicks, co-operating with Duke Hospital, Durham, N. C.; Drew Theological Seminary, Paul B. Maves, Madison, N. J.; Garrett Biblical Institute, Carroll Wise, Evanston, Ill.; Iliff School of Theology, co-operating with Denver General Hospital; Southern Baptist Seminary, Wayne E. Oates, Louisville 6, Ky., co-operating with Norton Memorial Infirmary Psychiatric Clinic, and also with five other hospitals.

This work was formerly conducted apart from seminaries, but with their co-operation. The trend now is for each school to have on the staff a clinically trained professor to develop such a program, which becomes an integral part of a student's curriculum. Some seminaries, however, turn such work over to a special agency, such as one of those above. Seminaries are engaged in suitable course building, and special agencies are struggling for adequate financial resources. The movement is divided ideologically. One group, represented by leaders of the "Council," adopts an esoteric variation of psychoanalysis, known as "Reichian organotherapy." Another group (the "Institute") stays largely within the historic tradition of pastoral care. A third group keeps fairly close to denominational traditions.

A moot question in the minds of most men with extensive experience is this: How far should the pastor go in adopting the specific techniques of a given school of psychotherapy, and how can he best define the unique role and function which he as a pastor should play in the life of his people? Another problem which follows this question is that of the amount and kind of personal psychotherapeutic treatment a minister should receive in training, and the role that teachers in this type of training should have in administering that treatment.

The purpose of this article is not to settle these questions in a few words, but to inform the reader as to the methodology, resources, strategic difficulties, and ideological differences existing in this field at the middle of the century.

See Pastoral Theology.

Wayne E. Oates.

CLOISTER, CLAUSURA: This article will outline the laws of the Roman Church concerning the seclusion of religious persons of either sex living in community. The Code of Canon Law states that no women may enter the precincts of religious houses of men with the exception of the chapel, parlors, and eventually guest quarters.

Contemplative orders of women taking solemn vows are subject to similar regulations, the law making allowance for the admittance of maintenance workers, or of physicians and confessors called to a sick bed. Novices as well as professed nuns are not permitted to leave the monastery at any time.

The application of the above laws is under papal jurisdiction, *clausura papalis major.* The constitution *Sponsa Christi* (cf. *Acta Apostolicae Sedis,* 43 [1951], pp. 1–24, and the subsequent instruction, pp. 37–46), extend the papal *clausura* to communities of women having solemn vows, but engaging in some active ministry within the precincts of the convent, the rules concerning communication with strangers being modified accordingly, *clausura papalis minor.* These laws do not apply to institutes of sisters having only simple vows.

GEORGES A. BARROIS.

CLOUD OF UNKNOWING:
BIBLIOGRAPHY: English edition, 1924; American ed., 1950; French ed., *Le nuage de l'inconnaissance,* 1923.

CLUNY: This monastery was placed under the protection of the apostles Peter and Paul, which meant that the only superior power above it was the papacy in Rome. It was done in defiance of the rule laid down at the Council of Chalcedon in 451 and at Aachen in 802. Fulda in 751 had received the same privilege, and after the founding of Cluny other monasteries were similarly blessed. The Congregation of Cluny about the year 1100 counted some 2000 houses, but still greater was the number under Petrus Venerabilis (1122–56).

BIBLIOGRAPHY: G. de Valous, *Le monachisme clunisien des origines au XVe siècle,* 2 vols., 1935; P. Champly, *Histoire de l'abbaye de Cluny,* 3rd ed., 1930; J. Evans, *Monastic Life at Cluny,* 1931; C. Letonnellier, *L'abbaye de Cluny et le St. Siège,* 1923.

[Sup.] ALBERT HYMA.

COADJUTOR. See BISHOP, AUXILIARY.

COCHLAEUS (DOBNECK, WENDELSTINUS), JOHANNES: B. at Wendelstein, he chose the name of Cochlaeus in imitation of other humanists, the name being derived from *cochlea,* a winding staircase—*Wendeltreppe* in German. He was a voluminous writer, being the author of some 200 publications, among them editions with notes or commentaries of liturgic manuscripts. His influential work, *Commentaria de actis et scriptis Martini Lutheri* is polemical but not vehement. It de-

rives its importance from the accumulation of pertinent facts and the manner in which many Catholic writers used it later in their controversial writings against Luther and other Protestants. He was not a warlike person, but more genteel and refined than many of his contemporaries, resembling Erasmus to some extent. But he was not nearly as profound as the latter, nor as far-reaching in his polemics.

BIBLIOGRAPHY: H. Jedin, *Des Johannes Cochlaeus Streitschrift De libero arbitrio,* 1927; P. Polman, *L'Elément historique dans la controverse religieuse du XVIe siècle,* 1932; A. Herte, *Das katholische Lutherbild im Bann der Lutherkommentare des Cochlaeus,* 3 vols., 1943; *Lexikon fuer Theologie und Kirche,* Vol. II (1931), col. 998 ff., where some of the later editions of his works are listed.

[Sup.] H. GOOSSENS.

COCKBURN, JAMES HUTCHISON: Church of Scotland; b. at Paisley, Scotland, Oct. 29, 1882. He studied at Glasgow University (M.A., B.D) and was ordained in 1908. After ministries at Mearns (1908–14), and Battfield (Glasgow, 1914–18) he became minister of Dunblane Cathedral (1918–); and was also chaplain to His Majesty King George VI. He was moderator of the General Assembly of the Church of Scotland (1941); and has held lectureships on pastoral theology at St. Mary's and St. Andrews (1931–34); William Belden Noble (Harvard, 1942); Warrack (Edinburgh, 1944–45); and Otts (Davidson, 1951). RAYMOND W. ALBRIGHT.

CODEX JURIS CANONICI: The Code of Canon Law of the Roman Catholic Church, promulgated in 1917 by order of Pope Benedict XV. It supersedes the old *Corpus juris,* which contained several collections of church laws of various origin and of unequal authority, such as the *Decretum Gratiani,* the *Extravagantes* of John XXII, and the *Extravagantes communes,* all of a private character; and the official, but incomplete compilations known as the *Decretales* of Gregory IX, the *Liber sextus* of Boniface VIII, and the *Clementinae* of Clement V. The basic *Corpus juris* was supplemented by partial collections such as the *Liber septimus decretalium* of Petrus Matthaeus, the *Institutiones* of P. Lancelot, and another *Liber septimus* or compilation of decretals published under the name of Clement VIII. (See CANON LAW, Vol. II.)

Unavoidable duplications and contradictions, as well as problems of interpretation arising from conflicts with local customs or statutes, called for a thorough revision which was put on the agenda of the Council of the Vatican (1869), but could not be carried on because of the political difficulties which interrupted the work of this assembly. The project was resumed under the reign of Pius X, who ordered the constitution of a commission of cardinals and of consultors, in his *motu proprio* "*Arduum sane munus,*" March 19, 1904 (cf. *Acta Pii X,* I [1905], pp. 219–222). Monsignor (later Cardinal) P. Gasparri (*q.v.*), was appointed secretary to the commission. It was early felt that a systematic compilation would not be satisfactory, and the commission started to work on an entirely new codification, after the manner of modern codes of civil law. The redaction of the *Codex Juris Canonici* was achieved under the pontificate of Benedict XV. The instrument of promulgation, viz., the constitution *"Providentissima Mater Ecclesia,"* May 27, 1917 (Pentecost), announced that the new canon law would take effect on the day of Pentecost, May 19, 1918.

The *Codex Juris Canonici* is divided into five books, viz.: I. General principles and rules; II. Of persons (clerics, religious, laymen); III. Of things (sacraments, places and times of worship, teaching office of the church, benefices, church possessions); IV. Procedure of ecclesiastical courts; V. Penal law. Mere liturgical regulations or dogmatic pronouncements as such are not included in the *Codex.* The precision of the terminology, the organic relationship of single canons to the unity of the whole, and the clarity of purpose apparent throughout the *Codex* make it an outstanding piece of legislation, as was often recognized by competent jurists of the most various cultural or denominational background. The canons of the *Codex* have force of law in the Roman Catholic Church only. They do not bind members of the Uniate Churches (*q.v.*), who continue to be ruled by their own statutes, while a special commission for the codification of the canon law of the Eastern Churches has been instituted in 1935 by Pope Pius XI for the purpose of achieving a desirable uniformity in the discipline of the autonomous church bodies in communion with the Holy See.

In spite of the masterly redaction of the *Codex Juris Canonici,* it was unavoidable, however, that some doubts should arise from time to time concerning the interpretation of the new church laws. In order that such doubts be solved in an authoritative manner, Pope Benedict XV, in his *motu proprio "Cum juris canonici,"* September 15, 1917, announced the creation of a permanent commission for the authentic interpretation of the *Codex Juris Canonici* (cf. *Acta Apostolicae Sedis,* 9 [1917], pp. 483–484).

The source material used by the editors of the *Codex,* inasmuch as it was not already included in the *Corpus juris,* the *Acta* of the Council of Trent, and the rubrics of the liturgical books, was recently collected and published under the title *Fontes Juris Canonici* (8 vols.), by Cardinal Gasparri and Cardinal Seredi.

Bibliography: I. Noval, *Codificationis iuris canonici recensio historico-apologetica,* 1918; P. Gasparri, *Storia della codificazione del diritto canonico,* in *Acta congressus iuridici internationalis,* IV (1937), 3–10; "Codex iuris canonici," in *Enciclopedia Cattolica,* III, 1949.

Georges A. Barrois.

COEDUCATION. See Education, The Churches and Higher.

COFFIN, HENRY SLOANE: Presbyterian; b. New York City, Jan. 5, 1877; d. Nov. 25, 1954. He was educated at Yale (B.A., 1897; M.A., 1900), Edinburgh University (1897–99), Union Theological Seminary, N. Y. (1899–1900; B.D.). He was pastor at Bedford Park, New York City (1900–5); Madison Avenue, New York (1905–26). He also taught practical theology at Union Theological Seminary (1904–26), and became Brown Professor of Homiletics and Pastoral Theology (1926–45; president of the faculty). He has been a Fellow of the Corporation of Yale University (1921–45). He wrote: *The Creed of Jesus* (1907); *Social Aspects of the Cross* (1911); *University Sermons* (1914); *The Ten Commandments* (1915); *Some Christian Convictions* (1915); *In a Day of Social Rebuilding* (Lyman Beecher Lectures, 1918); *A More Christian Industrial Order* (1920); *What is there in Religion* (1922); *Portraits of Jesus Christ* (1926); *What to Preach* (Warrack Lectures, 1926); *The Meaning of the Cross* (1931); *What Men are Asking* (1933); *God's Turn* (1934); *Religion Yesterday and Today* (1940); *The Public Worship of God* (1946); *God Confronts Man In History* (1947); *Communion Through Preaching* (1952); and "II Isaiah" in *The Interpreter's Bible.*

COFFIN TEXTS. See Book of the Dead.

COLE LECTURES: Instituted in 1894 by Col. E. W. Cole of Nashville, Tenn., through a gift to Vanderbilt University for the endowment of "a perpetual lectureship in connection with the School of Religion of the University, to be restricted in scope to a defence and advocacy of the Christian religion." The lectures, six in number, are delivered annually in connection with an interdenominational convocation of ministers and churchmen and are published by the university.   John Keith Benton.

COLET, JOHN: B. 1469; d. 1519. English humanist and foremost of the Oxford Reformers. It was accepted previously that the year of Colet's birth was 1466. New evidence on the life of Erasmus, however, has revealed that these two, of the same age within two or three months, were born in 1469. Colet was the son of Sir Henry Colet—twice mayor of London, 1486 and 1495. Between 1493 and 1496 Colet travelled in Germany, France, and Italy, where it is believed he was influenced by such humanist figures as Ficino and Savanarola. When Erasmus met Colet on his first visit to England, he doubtlessly found in him the embodiment of his earlier ideals patterned after the *Devotio Moderna,* for Colet was obviously a man whose religious principles and character were beyond reproach. Colet's outstanding sermons on public occasions reveal his views on clerical, religious, and political matters. The convocation sermons in 1511 and 1512 were appeals for reform among members of the clergy and for a rededication of their lives to the vows of their profession; the sermon upon the approaching departure of the king on his French expedition in 1513 reflected his disapproval of foreign wars launched for material gain and vainglory rather than in the cause of Christianity; the sermon at the installation of Wolsey as cardinal in 1515 was one of direction to the new cardinal in which his Christian responsibilities were plainly stated. In these sermons are reflected Colet's sincerity and lack of pretense. Despite his refusal to compromise any one of his principles to clergy or state, Colet was held in highest regard by such men as Henry VIII and Archbishop Warham. In 1517 Colet made his last public appearance at the Lenten services of the season.

BIBLIOGRAPHY: A. Hyma, "Erasmus and the Oxford Reformers (1493–1503)," in *Nederlandsch Archief voor Kerkgeschiedenis*, XXV (1933), 69–92, 97–132; J. A. R. Marriott, *The Life of John Colet*, 1933.

[Sup.] GRACE LARSEN.

COLETA: Known also as Nicolette Boillet of Boellet. B. Jan. 3, 1381, at Cerbie; d. March 6, 1447, at Ghent. She was at first a beguine (*q.v.*), but later became a recluse, and in 1406 joined the Clarissas, among whom she persuaded many to return to the strict rules of the original order. She founded eighteen new convents herself, some of which are still in existence and are known as the Clarissas Coletine. She has often been incorrectly considered the founder also of the Franciscan Conventuals called the Coletanes. She is often invoked in Belgium by pregnant women who hope for a speedy and painless delivery.

BIBLIOGRAPHY: The *Vita* written by her spiritual guide Petrus de Vaux was published in *A.S.B. Mart.* I, Part 3, 538–88; another *Vita* by Petrus de Balma in same source, 600–19; on both see U. d'Alençon, *Les vies de S. Colette*, 1911; H. Lippens, *Jean Capestran en Bourgogne*, in *Archivum Franciscanum historicum*, Vol. 35 (1942), 113–32, 254–95.

H. GOOSSENS.

COLIGNY, GASPARD DE: B. Feb. 16, 1519, third son; Vaucelles truce was Feb. 5, 1556; Cateau-Cambrésis treaty; Fontainebleau Assembly, Aug. 21–26, 1560; Henry of Navarre was eight years old, 1562–63; Poltrot de Meré shot Guise Feb 18, 1563; Guise died Feb. 24; St. Germain edict, Aug. 8, 1570; Charles IX visited Coligny Aug. 22, 1572; d. at no. 134 rue de Rivoli.

Coligny encouraged colonization in Brazil (1555) and Florida (1562), partly to provide refuge for Huguenots. Both settlements were soon destroyed. The St. Batholomew Massacre may have been plotted by the Guises from April, 1572; it occasioned many anti-monarchical Protestant political pamphlets.

See also HOTMAN, FRANCIS.

BIBLIOGRAPHY: A. W. Whitehead, *Gaspard de Coligny . . .*, 1904; Lucien Romier, *Les Origines politiques des guerres de religion*, 2 vols., 1913–14; *Le Royaume de Catherine de Médicis . . .*, 2 vols., 1922; *La Conjuration d'Amboise . . .*, 1923; *Catholiques et Huguenots à la cour de Charles IX . . .*, 1924; John Viénot, *Histoire de la Réforme française . . .*, Vol. I. 1926. On the St. Bartholomew Massacre see Lucien Romier, "La Saint-Barthélemy, les événements de Rome et la premeditation du massacre," *Revue du seizième siècle*, I (1913), 529–60; Sylvia L. England, *The Massacre of St. Bartholomew*, 1938.

[Sup.] ROBERT M. KINGDON.

COLLADON, NICOLAS: French Protestant pastor and theologian, d. 1586. Nicolas Colladon was the son of a prominent lawyer in La Châtre (Berry) near Bourges in France. In 1549 he came to Lausanne to study under Jean Ribit and in 1550 he moved to Geneva where he worked for three years as a teacher in the Collège de Rive. In 1553 he was named pastor to the church of Vandoeuvres in the Geneva countryside and in 1557 he was recalled to a post in the city churches and made a "bourgeois" of the city. From 1561 to 1571 he served as secretary of the Geneva Company of Pastors and handled a voluminous correspondence especially in 1561, mostly pertaining to requests from French churches for pastors. He was a close friend of Calvin and wrote an extremely laudatory biography of Calvin shortly after Calvin's death. Unlike almost all the other Geneva pastors, he never returned to his native country. He and Calvin were about the only pastors in French Switzerland who did not return to France in the crucial year of 1561.

After Calvin's death Colladon assumed some professorial duties alongside his pastoral cares. From 1564 to 1566 he was rector of the University of Geneva. From 1566 to 1571 he shared with Beza (*q.v.*) the chair of theology Calvin had occupied. In 1570 Colladon served for six months as minister to the plague victims in Geneva. But from 1568 Colladon had been making a series of violent attacks on the municipal councils from his pulpit. In 1571 he attacked them so violently for violating their own anti-usury edicts by setting up a new state bank authorized to charge ten percent on loans, that he was deposed from his ministry with the consent of most of the ministers.

Colladon first took refuge in Heidelberg and then was appointed full-time professor of theology at the Lausanne Academy by the Berne government. The Geneva Company of Pastors continued to make trouble for him, for he had carried off their official registers with his private papers. This quarrel was finally settled after an appeal to Berne.

Colladon taught in Lausanne until his death in 1586. In 1581 he finished Calvin's project of preparing commentaries on every book in the New Testament by printing a *Commentaire sur l'Apocalypse* which quickly ran through three editions. He also published with Beza the *Correspondance latine de Calvin* and a new Latin edition of Calvin's *Institutes*. In 1576 he was elected rector of the Lausanne Academy. He got into trouble with the local government again in 1581. He and his printer were scolded and fined for not submitting the book on the Apocalypse to Berne for censorship.

BIBLIOGRAPHY: Eugène and Émile Haag, *La France Protestante* (2nd ed., 1877–88), IV, 512–13, is very brief. H.-V. Aubert, "Nicolas Colladon et les Registres de la Compagnie des Pasteurs et Professeurs de Genève," *Bulletin de la Société d'histoire et d'archéologie de Genève*, II (1898–1904), 138–63, has much more information. See also references in Henri Heyer, *L'Eglise de Genève* . . . , 1909; Henri Vuilleumier, *Histoire de l'église réformée du pays de Vaud* . . . , 4 vols., 1927–33; Charles Borgeaud, *Histoire de l'Université de Genève* (1900), I, 1559–1798; Jean-Antoine Gautier, *Histoire de Genève* . . . , 8 vols., 1896–1914.

ROBERT M. KINGDON.

COLLEGES, RELIGION IN THE: The Christian church brought higher education to North America. Starting with Harvard, a large number of colleges were founded by the church, in the first instance to provide an educated ministry for the colonies. During the nineteenth and early twentieth centuries a large number of public-supported universities were established by states and municipalities. It is impressive, however, to note that sixty-seven percent of the colleges in the United States today were founded by the church.

In the United States there are three main types of higher education. Let us examine the place of the Christian faith in each one of them.

I. Private Colleges and Universities: Founded by the church, but often quite secular in their educational philosophy. Such colleges are largely an American phenomenon. From their founding until about 1920, these colleges maintained a rather formal Christian character. Following World War I, most of them began to give up the pretense of being religious in orientation. World War II was a shock to the intellectual world. The mid-century finds the fine old prestige colleges and universities much more ready to look again at their Christian heritage. Bible Departments are being strengthened and chapel services are being taken much more seriously.

II. Public-Supported Universities: Because of the separation of church and state in the United States, it has always been hard to define clearly the place of religion in the public-supported university. In some great state universities there are good courses in religion given for credit, which have proved very profitable and extremely popular with students. In other state universities there is no instruction in religion available to the students. In the mid-century one can say: (1) More experimentation is needed. Perhaps more can be done by state universities in religious instruction if they will only try. (2) The churches and Christian lay movements have learned how to work effectively in these public-supported universities.

III. The Church-Related Colleges: There are in the United States about 476 colleges related to the Protestant Churches and about 229 related to the Roman Catholic Church. They were all founded on the principle that the Christian faith has a stake in the intellectual life. The Christian church will continue to support its colleges because: (1) Freedom is a Christian ideal. Truth is of God, and only men who believe in God will persistently battle for freedom to find the Truth. The church will never give up the struggle for academic freedom. (2) The Bible is the central book of knowledge. The Church will never be content to see educational institutions ignore the Bible. (3) The Christian faith is concerned with culture. The state may be satisfied with training technicians.

All over the western world the intellectuals are being humbled by the task they face. Academic responsibility has not always gone with academic freedom. Religion faces a new openmindedness in the college world today.

E. FAY CAMPBELL.

COLLEGES, ROMAN CATHOLIC. See ROMAN CATHOLIC COLLEGES, UNIVERSITIES, SEMINARIES, AND SCHOOLS.

COLLEGIATE CHURCH: In Great Britain, a church served by a college, or group, of clergymen as colleagues. In America, an ecclesiastical corporation which controls a college, or group, of churches whose ministers are colleagues.

The most famous collegiate church in America is officially known as the Reformed Protestant Dutch Church (Collegiate) of the City of New York. Its history goes back to 1628, when, under the leadership of Jonas Michaelius, the first Dutch Reformed Church was established in America. Located on the southern tip of Manhattan Island, this church, and others that were built to serve the expanding population, acquired valuable land rights confirmed by Royal Charter on May 11, 1696.

The corporation issues an annual yearbook, averaging approximately 175 pages, covering the main events of the year. A comparison between the yearbooks of 1910 and 1951 is instructive. In 1910 there were six churches, three chapels, and two missions; fifteen ministers were in charge. In 1952 there were five churches and one chapel. Population shifts are largely responsible for this seeming decline. The combined communicant membership in 1910 was 4,509, with contributions for benevolent objects totaling $91,280.82. In 1951 communicants totaled 5,457 and contributions for benevolent objects $41,205.00 (a very serious decline). These collegiate churches support fourteen domestic and foreign missionaries.

Few churches in America are better known than the Marble Collegiate Church. It has a clinical staff of thirteen psychiatrists and psychologists, who during 1950 gave 2,550 interviews in the way of counseling. Each week the minister delivers a radio message over a national broadcasting chain.

BIBLIOGRAPHY: W. L. Brower and H. P. Miller, *Collegiate Reformed Protestant Dutch Church of the City of New York*, 1928.

MILTON J. HOFFMAN.

COLLEGIUM RUSSICUM: Russian College of St. Theresa of the Child Jesus, founded in the Vatican, Aug. 15, 1929. Under the direction of the Jesuit Fathers, the college trains candidates as priests to serve Russian expatriate communities throughout the world. The college is preparing for the time when Russia will again be opened to Catholic priests by instructing Russian-speaking students for ordination as priests. The Rev. G. A. Wetter, S.J., was rector of the college in 1952.

THOMAS J. MCCARTHY.

COLLIN, NICHOLAS: Lutheran; b. Aug. 2, 1746, in Fundbo, Sweden; d. Oct. 7, 1831, in Philadelphia, Pa. Educated in the University of Upsala, Collin set out for Philadelphia in 1770 to minister to the Swedish and Finnish Lutherans on the Delaware River, where he remained until his death. By ministering to his Anglicized parishioners in English, he prepared the way for the transfer of the Lutheran congregations to the Protestant Episcopal Church. A member of the American Philosophical Society, Collin made contributions in fields of natural science, medicine, history, and philology.

BIBLIOGRAPHY: Amandus Johnson, *The Journal and Biography of Nicholas Collin*, 1936.

THEODORE G. TAPPERT.

COLLOQUY: From the Latin *colloquium*, "conversation," "conference." In the early usage of Reformed Churches, this term often applies to ecclesiastical courts composed of ministers and elders, and is roughly synonymous with "classis" or "presbytery."

COLOMBIA: Area, 439,830 square miles; population, 11,015,210 (1949 estimate). The bulk of the population lives at altitudes varying from 4,000 to 9,000 feet above sea level. Bogotá, the capital, lies at 8,703 feet above the sea. It boasts that the Spanish spoken there is the purest in South America.

There are five national or government universities and a number of private institutions of higher learning. Primary instruction is free but not compulsory. According to 1946 figures there were 732,371 children in primary schools, and 45,678 pupils in high schools. In the whole school system there were 828,210 students. A law passed in 1934 requires that at least 10% of the national budget be devoted to education.

According to a concordat with the Vatican, education in state schools is under the control of the Roman Catholic Church. Colombia is the most Catholic and least tolerant country in South America. The religion of Colombia is Roman Catholic, but the exercise of other forms of worship is allowed, so long as they are "not contrary to Christian morals nor to the law." There are four archbishops and seven suffragan bishops.

The Presbyterian Church, U.S.A., began work in Colombia in 1856 on the indirect invitation of the government at that time. In 1948 there were 25,655 Protestants in the country. In 1950 a Confederation of Evangelical Churches was formed with a membership of eighteen denominations.

BIBLIOGRAPHY: Kenneth G. Grubb, *Northern Republics of South America*, 1931. See ARGENTINA for general works on South America.

[Sup.] W. STANLEY RYCROFT.

COLOR CASTE. See RACE RELATIONS.

COLORED METHODIST EPISCOPAL CHURCH. See METHODISTS.

COLORS, LITURGICAL: Western liturgical usage prescribes certain standard colors for the vestments worn during altar functions by the officiating ministers. In the Roman rite, white is the festive color, which may be replaced by gold or silver brocade on solemn occasions; red is worn at Pentecost and on the feasts of martyrs; green is employed on ordinary Sundays and non-festive days throughout the year; violet is reserved for Sundays and non-festive days in Advent and Lent; rose color may be substituted for violet on the third Sunday in Advent and the fourth Sunday in Lent. Black is used for the office of the dead and on Good Friday. The draperies of the altar generally match the color of the vestments

GEORGES A. BARROIS.

COLOSSIANS, EPISTLE TO THE. See PAUL THE APOSTLE.

COLVER LECTURESHIP, NATHANIEL: Established at the University of Chicago in 1894 by Jesse L. Rosenberger and Susan E. Colver, his wife, of Chicago. It is a memorial to Nathaniel Colver, noted Baptist minister and abolitionist who aided in founding what is now the Divinity School of the University of Chicago. The income from the fund is used to defray the expenses of lectures or lecture courses, preferably given under the auspices of the Divinity School, by authorities on religious, biblical, moral, sociological, or related fields.

W. V. MORGENSTERN.

COLWELL, ERNEST CADMAN: Methodist; b. at Hallstead, Pa., Jan. 19, 1901. He graduated from Emory University (A.B., 1923; B.D., 1927); and the University of Chicago (Ph.D., 1930). He taught the New Testament in the Divinity School of the University of Chicago (1930–44; Dean 1938–45). He organized the faculties of four theological schools into the Federated Theological Faculty of the University. He is the Chairman of the Editorial Board now laboring to produce a new edition of the manuscript evidence for the Greek New Testament. In 1943, he entered the general administration of the university and rose to be its President, from which office he resigned in 1951 to join the faculty of Emory University. Among his works are: *The Greek of the Fourth Gospel* (1931); Editor: *Prolegomena to the Study of the Lectionary Text of the Gospels* (with D. W. Riddle) (1933); *A Greek Papyrus Reader* (with E. J. Goodspeed) (1935); *John Defends the Gospel* (1936); *The Four Gospels of Karahissar*, Vol. I (1936); *The Study of the Bible* (1937); *A Hellenistic Greek Reader* (with J. R. Mantey) (1939); *The Elizabeth Day McCormick Apocalypse*, Vol. II (1939); *An Approach to the Teaching of Jesus* (1947).

COMFORT, WILLIAM WISTAR: Society of Friends; b. at Philadelphia, Pa., May 27, 1874. He studied at Haverford College, Harvard University, and in Europe; taught at Cornell University and Haverford College; now president emeritus of Haverford College. He is the author of *Just Among Friends* (1941); *Stephen Grellet* (1942); *William Penn: A Tercentenary Estimate* (1944); and *Quakers in the Modern World* (1949).

COMFORT IN SORROW: "Comfort" is derived from the Latin (con-fortis). The original Greek word also stresses strength from God to unify the soul, rather than consolation, passively received. Especially in days after war, multitudes in grief seek comfort from churches and ministers. In dealing with adults the church can render no more fruitful service than in preparing for grief sure to come, and in bringing Christian comfort to those already in sorrow. In public worship such a ministry calls for hymns full of hope, prayers breathing assurance, sermons pointing to God, and communion feasts in the spirit of the mountaintop. In the home and in the counseling room the pastor relies largely on sympathetic listening, on Holy Scripture, one passage at a time, and on prayer. He may also use a hymn or other poem about the beyond. John Watson rendered such a ministry of comfort in Liverpool, and Peter Green in Manchester; Theodore L. Cuyler in Brooklyn, and Maltbie D. Babcock in Baltimore. In recent times some churches and ministers have failed to stress Christian comfort, but many signs indicate that the church of tomorrow will rediscover what William Sanday taught in Ox-

ford, that in the New Testament the center of gravity lies beyond the grave.
ANDREW W. BLACKWOOD.

COMITE INTERMOUVEMENT AUPRES DES EVACUES. See REFUGEES.

COMMANDMENTS OF THE CHURCH: In Roman Catholic terminology, a summary of the principal laws of the church, the observance of which is made the responsibility of all the faithful. There are some variations in the number and the formulation of the precepts as they were drafted in the lists of Antoninus of Florence (1439), Peter Canisius (1555), Martin Aspilcueta (1586), and Bellarmine (1589).

According to the Baltimore Catechism (1885), the commandments of the church are: (1) Attending Mass and abstaining from servile works on Sundays and specified holy days; (2) fasting and abstaining from meat on prescribed days; (3) going to confession at least once a year; (4) taking communion at least once a year at Easter time; (5) contributing to the financial support of the church; (6) observing the restrictive rules of the church with regard to marriage within a certain degree of kindred. The *Catechismus Romanus* of Cardinal Gasparri (1930) lists only the first five precepts, omitting the sixth. This, however, does not imply any alteration of the provisions of canon law concerning Christian marriage.

BIBLIOGRAPHY: Vacant, "Commandements de l'Église," *Dictionnaire de Théologie Catholique.*
GEORGES A. BARROIS.

COMMENTARIES, HOMILETICAL. See HOMILETICAL COMMENTARIES.

COMMITTEE ON CO-OPERATION IN LATIN AMERICA. See LATIN AMERICA, COMMITTEE ON CO-OPERATION IN.

COMMITTEE WORK: In most churches the work is done mainly by committees. Details differ according to the laws of the denomination, the customs of the parish, and the desires of the pastor. In some cases he appoints the committee, at least the chairman. More often committees represent various societies. The effectiveness depends largely on care and skill in selecting each chairman, and on giving the committee something worthwhile to do. Ordinarily three or five members function better than a larger number. In case of need the chairman confers with the pastor. Ordinarily the plan should relieve him of concern about details. The principles appear in a booklet, *Committees in Organization*, by Lyndall Urswick, 1937. See also OFFICIAL BOARD.　　ANDREW W. BLACKWOOD.

COMMON GRACE: I. Nature of the Concept: The concept of common grace has its historical origin in the theology of Calvin (Herman Kuiper, *Calvin on Common Grace,* 1928). In modern times Charles Hodge, Herman Bavinck, and especially Abraham Kuyper sought to develop the idea of common grace as a part of the Calvinist philosophy of history and culture. "Through this doctrine of *gratia communis* the Reformed [theologians] have, on the one hand, maintained the specific and absolute character of the Christian religion and, on the other hand, have been second to none in their appreciation of everything good and beautiful that God has given to sinful men" (Herman Bavinck, *De Algemeene Genade,* 1894).

Common grace, like special or saving grace, says Kuyper, presupposes the idea of total depravity. But whereas special grace regenerates the hearts of men, common grace: (1) restrains the process of sin in mankind and (2) enables mankind positively to develop the latent forces of the universe and to do works of "civil righteousness." Without common grace there would be no field of operation for special grace. Yet the purpose of common grace is not exhausted by serving as the historical basis for special grace. According to the principle of *Heteregonie der Zwecke,* common grace has as its *Nebenzweck* the general development of human culture (Abraham Kuyper, *De Gemeene Gratie,* 3 vols., 1902).

II. Recent History: During the second decade of the present century opposition arose among Reformed theologians to the idea of common grace. It was said to tone down the doctrine of total depravity and to be, of necessity, a steppingstone toward the Arminian idea of grace as God's desire to save all men. This opposition has been expressed with vigor in a number of publications on the part of the Reverend Herman Hoeksema and others. It is currently set forth in connection with his exposition of *The Heidelberg Catechism.*

In 1924 the Synod of the Christian Reformed Church affirmed the idea of common grace under three heads pertaining to: (1) a favorable attitude of God toward mankind in general; (2) the restraint of sin in the life of the individual and in society; and (3) the performance of civic righteousness by the unregenerate.

III. Relation to Natural Theology: In the Netherlands Valentine Hepp developed the views of Kuyper and Bavinck in the direction of a natural theology similar to that of scholasticism. He sought for an area of knowledge and ethical response where there is commonness without difference between the believer and the unbeliever (*Het Testimonium Spiritus Sancti*). Accordingly, he developed a method of apologetics in which appeal is made to an area of knowledge (general truths about God, man, and the world) that unbelievers have in common with believers. The great stress that Calvin

lays on the fact that by their systems of philosophy unbelievers seek to suppress their own inescapable knowledge of God as their creator and judge is not denied but largely ignored by Hepp (*Gereformeerde Apologetick,* 1920). The views of Hepp are currently being advocated by William Masselink (*Common Grace and Christian Education,* 1952).

IV. Integration with Other Doctrines: Thus the pendulum is swinging back and forth between the two extremes of a total denial of common grace (difference without sameness) and a scholastic affirmation of common grace (sameness without difference). On either position it is impossible to integrate the idea of common grace with the genius of Calvinism. According to Calvinism, the self-sufficient God of Scripture works out his purpose for mankind covenantally, that is, by way of challenge and response. At the beginning of history God gives mankind life and favor. He offers mankind still higher life and favor on condition of obedience (covenant of works). Thus sameness is basic to the idea of the conditional as the conditional is constitutive of the covenantal, and the covenantal is the means by which God accomplishes the differentiation between the "vessels of mercy" and the "vessels of wrath."

After mankind fell into sin, God continues his conditional dealings with mankind. He continues to give life and favor, and he restrains man in his path "unto death," so that man gives some measure of externally favorable response to the striving of God's Spirit with him. Thus, in spite of his hatred of God, the sinner is bound to respond with some measure of respect for the laws and favors of God. Every fact about and within him speaks to man of the goodness of God. Every fact is to the sinner a call to repentance for sinning against the goodness of God. Every fact says to him, "Do this and thou shalt live; do that and thou shalt die." Only thus is civilization to be accounted for. And thus the stage is set daily for the "vessels of mercy" and for the "vessels of wrath," each to react significantly in his own way, in faith or in disobedience, toward his own ultimate destiny.

Thus the idea of common grace is integrally related to the idea of God as the sovereign determiner of the ultimate destinies of men, of the genuine meaning of history, and of the conditional in relation to human choice. Only thus can Calvinism be distinguished as a life and world view from all systems based on the "autonomy" of man. Thus Calvinism is shown to be theism and Christianity come to its own, a life and world view on the basis of which human history has genuine significance. For thus it is possible to prevent falling into the idea of absolute identity (univocism) or into the idea of absolute difference (equivocism) between God and man. Progress on the idea of common grace is likely to come with progress on the idea of analogy (*q.v.*), based on the idea of God as sovereign, over against the Romanist-Evangelical idea of analogy of being and the dialectical idea of analogy of faith.

CORNELIUS VAN TIL.

COMMON LIFE, BRETHREN OF THE: This organization was founded by Gerard Groote (*q.v.*), as the original sources clearly show. David of Augsburg was not a member. See GROOTE, GEERT; ZERBOLT, GERARD; GANSFORT, WESSEL; MYSTICISM; DEVOTIO MODERNA.

BIBLIOGRAPHY: Albert Hyma, *The Brethren of the Common Life*, 1950.

[Sup.]

COMMON PRAYER, BOOK OF:

BIBLIOGRAPHY: Reprints or facsimile reproductions which are noteworthy are: *Book of Common Prayer from the original MS. attached to the Act of Uniformity of 1662*, 1892; *Book of Common Prayer of 1549*, facsimile, 1896; *Prayer Book of Queen Elizabeth, . . . from Originals*, 1898; *First Prayer Book of Edward VI.*, 1903, 1905; *Second Prayer Book of King Edward VI.*, 1905. Consult: J. H. Blunt, *Annotated Book of Common Prayer*, 1890; E. Cardwell, *The Two Books of Common Prayer set forth . . . in the Reign of Edward VI.*, 1852; C. E. Hammond, *Liturgies Eastern and Western*, 1878; W. M. Campion and W. J. Beaumont, *Prayer Book Interleaved*, 1880; William Palmer, *Origines Liturgicae or Antiquities of the English Ritual*, 2 vols., 3d ed., 1839; W. Maskell, *Ancient Liturgy of the Church of England*, 1882; A. T. Wirgmann, *The English Reformation and the Book of Common Prayer, 1531–1662*, 1887; F. A. Gasquet, *Edward VI and the Book of Common Prayer*, 1928; J. Cornford, *Book of Common Prayer with Explanatory Notes*, 1897; J. C. Jones, *Concordance to the Book of Common Prayer*, 1898; J. Dowden, *Workmanship of the Prayer Book*, 1902; L. Pullan, *History of the Book of Common Prayer*, 1900; E. Daniel, *Prayer-Book; its History, Language and Contents*, 1901; H. Gee, *Elizabethan Prayer Book and Ornaments*, 1902; F. Procter and W. H. Frere, *New History of the Book of Common Prayer*, 1914; A. R. Fausset, *Guide to the Study of the Book of Common Prayer*, 1904; M. McColl, *The Royal Commission and the Ornaments Rubric*, 1906; F. E. Brightman, *The English Rite*, 2 vols., 1915; W. K. L. Clarke, *Liturgy and Worship*, 1950; S. Morison, *English Prayer Books*, rev. ed., 1945 (best account of the Anglican liturgy); G. Dix, *The Shape of the Liturgy*, 2d ed., 1947; H. C. White, *The Tudor Books of Private Devotion*, 1951.

[Sup.] HARRY KIMBER.

COMMUNISM. III, see COMMUNISTIC SOCIETIES.

COMMUNISM (MARXIAN): Social theories which may properly be characterized as communist, and efforts to translate them into practice, have appeared in Western history, with impressive frequency, at least since the time of Plato. For a brief account of some of them, see the article "Communism" in this Encyclopedia (Vol. III, 182 ff.). Those responsible for them have not been uniformly simple-minded or wicked people. They have indeed included men of outstanding character and intellect, such as Plato and Thomas More. R. N. Carew Hunt explains this phenomenon by saying, "For nearly two thousand years European civilization has rested upon a contradiction—between a philosophy and a religion which teach that all men

are brothers, and an economic system which organizes them as masters and servants," thus involving "inequalities of human life" which "are seen largely to derive from private property" (*The Theory and Practice of Communism*, [1950], 3). In general it may be said that the several theories have not won serious allegiance on a large scale or for long; the experiments have been local and short-lived; and the attitude of others towards both theories and experiments has commonly been easy tolerance and good-humored rejection.

But when communism is mentioned in America today, it is not these theories and experiments of the past but the Marx-Engels-Lenin-Stalin succession that is referred to; and the attitude expressed, if it is not a devotion which approaches religious veneration, is one of intense hostility and fear or of bewilderment and frustration. In some other Western nations the emotion revealed in the usual public reaction is not so intense, but the same responses of attachment, or of uncertainty, or of rejection, appear. In Asia, apart from China, and in Africa, the ignorance of, and uncertainty towards, the claims of communism are much more widespread; but there is a small, but apparently growing, area of intense devotion, and the intense opposition is not much in evidence. Apart from a "hard core" of devoted communists which has persisted in every Western nation (comparatively large in some, almost insignificant in others), the West has passed through a "honeymoon period" with communism into one of growing disillusionment and hardening opposition. Something like the experience of the six contributors to *The God that Failed* (edited by R. Crossman and A. Koestler, 1950) has been shared by the governments and by many of the common people of the West. Apparently, also, the relatively stable numerical strength of the Party and its "fellow-travellers" in America has been maintained only by the constant flowing into it and out again of numerous inarticulate people who must therefore also have shared the experience of attraction and subsequent disillusionment. It is claimed that many more would like to leave the Party, but are prevented from doing so, partly by a realization of the intense spiritual suffering which almost all the former communists have found to be involved in making such a break, and partly by the combination of persecution pressures from their former comrades and the lack of an intelligent, understanding inducement on the part of non-communist society. On the other hand, communism has been able to win, and to retain to the point of imprisonment, ruin, and even death, the allegiance of many whose education, social, and financial status, and future prospects in non-communist society, were much above the average. Witness Judy Coplan, the Rosenbergs and at least some of the American prisoners of the communists in the Korean war who have refused repatriation.

Marxian communism is thus a very challenging phenomenon—challenging in several senses of the word. In its first formulation, and in the adherence to it of much of its subsequent leadership, it appears as a missionary movement of certain intellectuals on behalf of the oppressed proletariat, a movement in which a genuine social sympathy and the pangs of conscience accusing the person for his undeserved privileges both seem to play a part in varying proportions. But certainly also adherence to it may be due to the lust for self-vindication on the part of people who feel themselves to be failures, the lust for power over others, an intense desire to "belong" to a devoted group, a liking for a "cloak and dagger" life, a hatred for organized society, or to any of a number of similar questionable motivations; as membership in it may also issue in such motivations.

The theory was hammered out by Karl Marx (1818–83) in association with Friedrich Engels (1820–95), and in an environment of constant, intense co-operation with, and dissention from, other revolutionaries on the basis of the philosophy of such left-wing Hegelians as Ludwig Feuerbach (1804–72), the writings of the classical, mainly English, economists, and some acquaintance with English social conditions in that comparatively early stage of the industrial revolution when its socially disruptive effects were much in evidence and the remedial measures had not yet begun to take effect. Engels, who had operated mills in England, was much more aware of the latter than was Marx, whose mind remained largely Continental to the last. The "catechism" of Marxian communism is *The Communist Manifesto*, the work of Marx and Engels, first published in German in February, 1848. Its "bible" is Marx's *Capital*, the first volume of which was published in German in 1867, the second, by Engels, in 1885 after Marx's death. For direct access to their views, in translation, the two-volume Marx-Engels *Selected Works* (1950) will suffice, except for specialists.

The history of this movement has been characterized throughout by internal controversy, as a result of which numerous people who thought of themselves as true and loyal communists have been constantly expelled from the Party, often, though not always, for theoretical divergencies, and often also through party manipulation rather than through the winning of theoretical arguments. The agreement within the triumphant faction has often been achieved without those who participated knowing what it was that they were agreeing on. For a revolting example of this, see Ignazio Silone's report in *The God that Failed*, 3 ff. It is therefore very difficult for the dispassionate student to decide whether the officially orthodox developments at the hands of Lenin and Stalin are a true expression of the spirit of the original or not. This has been a hotly debated, and a bloodily contested, question; especially in the case of Stalin, as witness such events as the contest between him and Trotsky and such books as *Stalin versus Marx* by Klaus Mehnert (1952). It is not difficult to agree with Spolansky's assertion that Marx, if he were alive today, would totally fail to understand the discussions in contemporary communist groups (*The Communist Trail in America*, 1951). However that may be, within the Party the works of Lenin and of Stalin (unless, as is suspected by some, the latter is now in a slow process of repudiation) are regarded also as authoritative. For all but specialists, they may be consulted by a process of sampling; and perhaps a reading of Lenin's *The Teachings of Karl Marx* (1914), and of Stalin's *Dialectical and Historical Materialism* (1938) will be sufficient. The widely accepted view of the relation of their work to that of their predecessors is expressed by Hunt as follows: "Lenin developed Marxism in more than one direction, but broadly speaking it is true to say that his most important contribution was in the field of Party organization and tactics; and that Stalin's contribution has been his theory of 'Socialism in one country' with all that this implies" (*op. cit.*, p. 8).

Communist theory was little more than a ferment, and their activity only a "nuisance," within the labor movement until, in 1917, Lenin was transported in a closed railway car across Germany by the German High Command, from his exile in Switzerland to Petrograd, in the hope that his activity there might hasten that disintegration of Russia which had already begun, and thus take Russia out of World War I. Under his inspiration and guidance, the Kerensky government, which had taken over at the time of the Czar's abdication in March, was overthrown. There followed a long and bitter struggle to reclaim Russia from domestic and foreign military opposition, to hammer out a consistent Soviet policy, and to clamp its hold upon the country as a whole (see E. H. Carr, *The Bolshevik Revolution, 1917–1923*, 1951). Events connected with World War II severely tested the security of Russia and the stability of the Soviet regime; but the test was met and ultimately Soviet power was vastly extended, so that now it controls approximately one third of the human race. That expansion seems now to have been halted, for the present at least, though the goal of ultimate world conquest has not been abandoned. There has also been one notable defection, not indeed from communist theory and practice within a state, but from the Kremlin's policy of complete domination from Moscow, on the part of Jugoslavia (see V.

Dedijer, *Tito,* 1953), and the communists have been forced, mainly by American pressure, to withdraw from penetrations of northern Iran and of southern Korea. For apparently authentic information as to contemporary conditions, policies and events in Soviet-dominated countries, a detailed source is the magazine "News from behind the Iron Curtain," published monthly by the Research and Publications Service, National Committee for a Free Europe Inc., 110 W. 57th Street, New York, 19, New York.

Marxian communism is essentially a program based on, and guided by, a philosophy of violent revolution in which, so it is confidently believed, the proletariat will ultimately seize power on a world-wide basis. After this revolution there will be an intermediate "socialist" period in which, under the "dictatorship of the proletariat," all remnants of "bourgeois" thinking and practice, and those who entertain them, will be ruthlessly exterminated. When this has been accomplished the communist stage of history will have been achieved, the classless society will be finally ushered in, all exploitation of man by man will disappear, each will voluntarily contribute according to his ability and receive according to his needs in a situation of plenty for all, and the state, which is essentially coercive power in the hands of a few, will wither away.

The inevitability of this outcome is guaranteed by the dialectical character of historical evolution, through the class conflict. This theory of "historical materialism" rests on the belief that the principle which ultimately conditions all human relationships is the production of the material means to support life. It is believed that a primitive communism, on a low social level, was disrupted by the institution of private property. Though a disruption, it was also an advance. But a society so organized has within it the seeds of its own destruction and of the creation of a higher social stage because it divides mankind into two warring classes: the owners and exploiters, on the one hand; and the larger and growing class of the dispossessed, on the other. Thus the class struggle is inevitably generated. The dominating class develops, by conscious and unconscious processes, a superstructure of culture, including political institutions and theories, ethics, religion and philosophy, the real purpose of which is self-justification, and which is therefore relative purely to the interests of the class. The exploited class presently begins to do the same. Since the dominant class will never willingly yield up its privileges, and since it controls for the time being the means of power, the transition from one stage of historical evolution to another will always involve violence. It is believed that history has thus passed from the

primitive communism to a slave economy; from that to feudalism; and from that to capitalism (see CAPITALISM). The latter is the present stage of history. It must develop all of its potentialities for good before the inner contradictions will destroy it and usher in the final victory of the proletariat. It was this latter belief which caused considerable confusion in communist minds when power came to them, not as was anticipated in the most advanced industrial societies, but in the mainly peasant economy of Russia. The problem was whether they should first develop an advanced, capitalist society in Russia before their communism could really take hold there; or perhaps mark time in Russia until the expected revolution should take place in Germany; or proceed to communize Russia at once, and, if so, how that could be done.

But this "historical materialism" itself rests, in communist theory at least, upon a more ultimate philosophy of "dialectical materialism" which, so it is maintained, is the only real alternative to idealism (see IDEALISM; MATERIALISM). The latter is the philosophy of the bourgeois society, and all the current philosophies of bourgeois society which seem to be opposed to idealism are really disguised forms of it (see *In Defence of Philosophy,* by M. Cornforth). Such a philosophy the communists strenuously reject and combat. Their philosophy must be "scientific" which means, for them, that it must be materialistic, and its laws must be those of, or similar to, the classical physics. At the same time, it must be able to guarantee that development is in the direction of the desired revolution and to provide a guide to revolutionary action. This seemed to mean that its laws must be dialectic in character. There must be opposites, which are yet interconnected, so that they will conflict and result in revolutionary change. Whether any philosophy could satisfy such requirements may well be doubted, but Marx was sure that his dialectical materialism could. "With me," he wrote in the introduction to the first volume of *Capital,* "the ideal is nothing else than the material world reflected by the human mind and translated into terms of thought." But, it may be asked, if matter is ultimate, and if matter is conceived, as Marx thought that he conceived it, in the manner of nineteenth century physics, what is the character of this "human mind," where did it come from, how can it translate the material world into terms of thought, and how can we be sure that thereby objective truth may be known? Marx himself, apparently, became impatient with such questions. They are, he says, not questions of theory at all, but practical questions. We may agree that practical life does answer them; but that a theoretical answer is desirable also in a philosophy of any kind would seem to be obvious, and also that that answer must be in harmony both with the practical answers and with the philosophical theory. It cannot be admitted that Marxism meets this test.

Furthermore, as a revolutionist, Marx had to find a justification in his philosophy for his conviction that human free choice influences the on-go of events, and a guide to such choice. He and Engels, like their successors, are for ever urging the proletariat to exercise their free choice and to unite for revolution, and assuring them that the resultant action will influence the course of history; and the former bitterly condemned the proletariat for their lethargy and refusal. But if matter is primary and if it is the matter of the classical physics, how could beings having freedom of choice have come into existence and, if they did, how could their free actions influence an evolution which is determined by iron laws? The compromise often suggested is that human free action can hasten, or delay, but that it cannot otherwise change the inexorable outcome. But that is an evasion, not a solution, of the problem.

Some characteristic and essential features of this theory and program call for further emphasis: (1) World-wide revolution by violence belongs to its essence. Marx came repeatedly into contact with those who advocated revolution by means of gradualism and constitutional procedures. He always and emphatically repudiated such ideas. Only violent and bloody revolution would work. Every responsible organ of communist expression has reiterated this judgment, openly and many times. Any retreat from this view, such as the suggestions of Stalin and Malenkov that communism and capitalism can have a peaceful coexistence, are purely strategic and intended for outside consumption to aid the world revolution by disarming opposition. The communists entertain, and openly express, nothing but contempt for those well-meaning individuals who think that they can be persuaded to compromise this issue, or to abandon this program. The "subversive" activities in other countries are intended only to soften them up and thus prepare the way for the inevitable bloody revolution there. Stalin's "socialism in one country" is also simply a strategic and temporary retreat.

(2) Communist theory acknowledges, and its procedures admit, none of our ethical and religious restraints upon either their subversive activities, their international diplomacy, their domestic administration, or the violent revolution. Our ethics belongs to the bourgeois superstructure and is purely relative to it; their ethics belongs to their superstructure and consists, at present, of anything which actually aids their cause. Thus deceit and untruth, when practised by them and not against them, is a virtue so long as it is successful. Religion not only belongs to our superstructure and is in the interest simply of bourgeois dominance, as an "opiate of the people"; it is also repudiated by their materialism, which is aggressively atheistic. In the last year of his life, 1895, Engels did recognize that Christianity had once proved to be, not an opiate, but a marvellously successful revolutionary force (see The Marx-Engels *Selected Works*, Vol. I, 126 f.). Presumably, if it played that role once, it could do so again, as of course it has repeatedly. But this acknowledgement and its implications have played no part in communist theory or practice. They will tolerate the church, as a temporary strategy, if and in so far as they think it to be necessary and can use it for their own purposes (see *Religious Freedom in Eastern Europe*, by J. Hutchison Cockburn, 1953); but they have not abandoned, and will not abandon, their essential atheism, and their goal is the destruction of the church.

(3) Communist theory, and much of communist practice, involves no respect for present individuals. The outlook is so futuristic that present standards of living and present individuals are cheerfully sacrificed in the supposed interest of the future; and the individual is merged in, and readily sacrificed to, the group. Thus, though the communists commonly describe themselves as democratic, the term as they use it means something very different from our understanding of the word (see DEMOCRACY). They have toyed with the idea that the classless society will be a pure democracy, without any coercion and even without any delegated authority. Lenin seems to have thought, when he wrote his pamphlet "How to Organize Competition" in January, 1918, that something approaching this would work in the Russia of that time; but by April of that year, when his "Immediate Tasks of the Soviet Government" appeared, he had begun to change his mind. Stalin seems to have completely repudiated the whole idea. The country is ruled by one man or by a few men at the top; the Party, as Stalin openly acknowledged, is a mere "transition belt" (see *How Russia is Ruled*, by Merle Fainsod, 1953). Their claim to be democratic seems to mean that they aim at the welfare of all reliable members of Soviet society (together with the elimination of all others), and particularly at their economic security (not economic equality).

BIBLIOGRAPHY: For further reading the following may prove helpful: John C. Bennett, *Christianity and Communism*, 1951; I. Deutscher, *Stalin: A Political Biography*, 1949; Hyde, *From Communism towards Catholicism*; A. Koestler, *The Yogi and the Commisar*, 1946; M. Lovell, *The Soviet Way of Life*, 1948; G. V. Plekhanov, *Fundamental Problems of Marxism*; idem, *In Defence of Materialism*; D. Runes, *The Soviet Impact on Society*, 1953; R. Schlesinger, *Marx: His Time and Ours*; L. Schwarzschild, *The Red Prussian*, 1947; V. Venable, *Human Nature, The Marxian View*, 1946.

ANDREW K. RULE.

COMMUNISTIC SOCIETIES: Most of the communistic groups described in Volume III, pp. 182–190, have disappeared or are dwindling. Two other religious groups, not there included, have real vitality: the Dukhobors in Canada and the Hutterite Brethren in the United States and Canada.

I. Dukhobors: The Dukhobors are now divided into three sects, the Orthodox, the Named Dukhobors, and the Sons of Freedom. The last is an extremist group which has given the Canadian government a great deal of trouble. As a method of protest they have appeared nude in processions, thus offending public taste, and have also burned a school and other buildings. A recent general conference of Dukhobors urged the adoption of a new code, outlawing such extreme methods of protest against the enforcement of the civil law. The groups are communistic, make no use of money within the group, worship in homes rather than churches, and have no paid ministry. Serious financial and property losses have occurred in some of the communities, and signs of disintegration begin to appear. See also DUKHOBORS.

II. Hutterians: The American Hutterites or Hutterian Brethren, descendants of Swiss Anabaptists, settled in Bon Homme, S.D., in 1874, establishing a thoroughgoing communal settlement, and, from this mother group, have spread to some twenty other colonies in the United States, while there are 10,000 or more Hutterites in Canadian communities in Manitoba, Saskatchewan, and Alberta. The communes are agricultural. All land, tools, and equipment are owned in common, and all work for the common good. Families live together, but all meals are communal. Only the pastor who is the head of each commune may have his meals in his own home.

Conflict has sometimes arisen between their neighbors and the communes. Attempts have been made to prevent their further purchase of land. Questions have been raised as to the labor policies within the group, and requirements made concerning the education of their children. Some Canadian Hutterites have returned recently to the Dakotas, and investigation of the possibility of removal of some of them to Mexico has been made. What they desire is freedom from compulsion in matters military and educational, and opportunity to preserve, without interference, their chosen way of life.

III. Zionists: In Palestine, almost 200 Zionist communistic settlements have been founded. While they differ in some respects, some consisting of only 20 to 30 families, others of 200 to 300, most of them are agricultural and they follow a fairly uniform pattern. All machinery and tools are drawn from a common pool. There is no private ownership even of clothing or fur-

niture. Married couples have a private room allotted to them but eat in a common dining room. Children live together in cottages apart, but can be seen at any time by their parents. Educated in settlement schools, at the age of eighteen they are given money and allowed to leave the community for a year, but may return if they wish. Most young people do. Recreation is provided by the group, but if one desires to go outside for diversion occasionally, one is given spending money. No money is required within the group. The community products are sold, and the money belongs to the group as a whole. The organization is simple and democratic, the business, the allotment of labor, and the discipline of the community resting in the hands of an annually elected committee. In distinction from the Russian *Kolkhoz,* which is compulsory, the communal villages are entirely voluntary.

IV. Communities of Work: Among the most interesting recent expressions of communalism are the Communities of Work which have developed chiefly in France, most of them since World War II. These differ from other communistic societies chiefly in the fact that they do not necessarily involve communal living. Their central features are the common ownership, generally, of the factory or land or at least the tools or machinery with which they work, and the group sharing of the fruits of labor in equitable fashion. Some of the societies are industrial, some agricultural; some are quite small, not over a dozen persons or so, while others have hundreds of members. But the primary aim is not economic. According to Claire Hutchet Bishop, the emphasis is not on acquiring together but on "working together for a collective and personal fulfillment." She sums up what this means in four points: (1) that a man needs to enjoy the whole fruit of his labor, (2) he must be able to educate himself, and to do this he must (3) pursue a common endeavor within a group, and (4) be actively related to the world as a whole.

Boimondau will serve as an example. Here are associated together 133 workers engaged in manufacturing watch cases. Started by Marcel Barbu, the former owner of the factory, the group has now completed purchase of the plant. In addition, it has acquired a farm of 235 acres on which everyone, including wives, has to work three periods of ten days each annually. In addition, each worker has a full month's vacation with pay, so that he works in the factory but ten months of the year. Since education is regarded as necessary, they have shortened the working day by one hour and give the last hour of the day to classes conducted in the factory.

Management of group activities is vested in a General Assembly, which elects a chief of community to be the executive for a period of three years. It also elects a General Council of seven members plus heads of departments. There is also a Council of Direction which, with the chief of community, meets weekly. There is an Assembly of Contact, which includes all members of the group and also meets once a week to keep the members abreast of what is happening in the community. Neighborhood groups, composed of five or six families who live in an area, meet regularly. They come together in the evenings and over a cup of coffee thrash out issues facing the group. The chief of community visits the various units from time to time on invitation. A principle running through all the groups at Boimondau, and all the other communities, is that all decisions must be reached unanimously.

Membership of many of the communities of work is open. Generally the candidate for admission is accepted for a probationary period of three months simply as a wage worker. He may then become a *postulant*. After a time he may be accepted as a novice for a year, during which period he is paid according to his total human value. He may be held for a second year before being fully admitted.

BIBLIOGRAPHY: A. J. F. Zieglschmid, *Das Klein-Geschichtsbuch der Hutterischen Brueder*, 1947; Marcus Bach, *Faith and My Friends*, 1951; Edwin Samuel, "The Jewish Communal Villages in Palestine," *Political Quarterly*, Vol. XVIII, 143–160; Claire Hutchet Bishop, *All Things Common*, 1950; Marguerite F. Melcher, *The Shaker Adventure*, 1941; John S. Duss, *The Harmonists*, 1943; Robert A. Parker, *A Yankee Saint: John Humphrey Noyes and the Oneida Community*, 1935; A. E. Bestor, *Backwoods Utopias*, 1950; Jacob J. Sessler, *Communal Pietism among Early American Moravians*, 1933; Alice F. Tyler, *Freedom's Ferment: Phases of American Social History to 1860*, 1944; R. V. Hine, *Utopian Colonies in California*, 1953; E. Andrews, *The People Called Shakers*, 1953.

[Sup. to COMMUNISM.] CHARLES S. BRADEN.

COMMUNITIES AND ORDERS, PROTESTANT: At the time of the Reformation Protestants were moved by their emphasis upon the priesthood of all believers and by their abolition of the double standard of "religious" and "secular" vocations to do away with the monastic communities and orders (see MONASTICISM, II, in Vol. VII) on which the power of the pre-Reformation Western Church had largely depended. Not until the nineteenth century was there a revival of communities and orders among Protestants, notably by the reintroduction of the office of deaconess (*q.v.*).

Strongest emphasis in this revival has been among Anglicans. By 1900 there were twenty-five Church of England communities. By 1950 there were in the provinces of Canterbury and York eight communities of men and forty-six of women, many with branch houses scattered throughout the Anglican Communion. The first community in the Protestant Episcopal Church in the U.S.A. was established in 1865, the Community of St. Mary for women, founded by Harriet Starr Cannon with the ap-

proval of Bishop Horatio Potter (*q.v.*, Vol. IX) of New York. The first community for men in this church was the Society of Mission Priests of St. John the Evangelist (Cowley Fathers; see Vol. IX, 288) established in 1870 by three of the English branch of the community. By 1950 there were twenty-three Episcopalian communities, nine for men and fourteen for women, most of them with mother houses in or near Boston and New York City.

Other Protestant movements for reclaiming group discipline and ordered devotional life have been founded or revived in the past few decades. These include resident communities such as the Amana Society in Iowa; the Dukhobors in North Dakota, Montana, and western Canada; the Bruderhof in Paraguay, England, and other countries; the Macedonia Community and Koinonia Farm in Georgia; the Kingwood Community in New Jersey; the Celo Community in North Carolina; and the St. Michael's Brotherhood (*q.v.*) in Germany. See also COMMUNISTIC SOCIETIES.

"New Life Centers," such as the Iona Community (*q.v.*) in Scotland, Kirkridge (*q.v.*) in Pennsylvania, and Parishfield in Michigan, have some monastic disciplines but exist primarily for the extension of devotional life throughout the churches rather than for devotional intensification for persons of monastic profession.

BIBLIOGRAPHY: W. M. Horton, *Centers of New Life in European Christendom*, 1950; *Religious Communities in the American Episcopal Church*, 1945; Friedrich Parpert, *Das Moenchtum und die evangelische Kirche*, 1930.

WILLIAM ANTHONY CLEBSCH.

COMMUNITIES OF WORK. See COMMUNISTIC SOCIETIES.

COMMUNITY CHURCHES: A growing phenomenon in American religious life since 1900 has been the rise of Protestant churches without denominational affiliation. Such churches were originally called union or federated churches (*qq.v.*). They came into existence most frequently through the merger of small, competing congregations in communities inadequate for the proper maintenance of several separate church plants, staffs, and programs. In some instances, as in the case of the Union Church of Berea, Kentucky, they were originally founded, as long ago as the middle of the nineteenth century, as non-sectarian congregations in cosmopolitan centers where breadth of view and diversity of religious background were marked.

The mingling of men of all faiths in the armed services during World War I, and the rapid emergence of new communities where families of many religious backgrounds were thrown together, accentuated the demand for a type of church fellowship where inherited denominational differences could be transcended in a religious fellowship centered about the great central Christian convictions and expressed in terms of the nature and needs of the individual community. The name community church became a name to conjure with, and such nonsectarian congregations sprang up spontaneously throughout the land. The movement was accelerated by similar factors during and following World War II and by the growing recognition, throughout Christendom, of the imperative need of unity among Christian believers.

The first systematic roster of community churches in 1921 included 713 such congregations. Later a mailing list of 2,000 non-denominational churches was compiled, and an inclusive roster of all known community churches numbered well over 3,000 in 1952. Many of these remain unrelated to other churches. Three distinct groups, however, eventually formed informal fellowships for purposes of mutual helpfulness and missionary outreach. These were the Biennial Council of Negro Churches; the National Council, an interracial group; and the English Language Churches in foreign lands. In a convention at Lake Forest, Ill., on Aug. 16, 1950, in which these three groups as well as independent native churches in several foreign countries were represented, there was formed the inclusive fellowship of the International Council of Community Churches, with headquarters in Columbus, Ohio, and with J. Ruskin Howe as its first president.

The International Council holds and desires no authority whatever over any local congregation and explicitly disavows any purpose to become, itself, a denomination. Its sole purpose is to provide a co-operative fellowship of free churches, "as comprehensive as the teachings of Jesus and as inclusive as the love of God," devoted to mutual helpfulness in Christian worship and service and to missionary outreach free from divisive creeds and barriers.

BIBLIOGRAPHY: David R. Piper, *Community Churches*, 1928; J. Ruskin Howe, ed., *That They All May Be One*, n.d.; Ralph A. Felton, *Cooperative Churches*, 1947.

J. RUSKIN HOWE.

COMMUNITY CHURCHES, INTERNATIONAL COUNCIL OF. See COMMUNITY CHURCHES.

COMPARATIVE RELIGION: An enormous amount of valuable work has been done in this field since 1910, but within the limits imposed here it is impossible to do more than indicate the essential bibliography. Discussion and exposition of the comparative method as applied to the study of religion will be found in G. Foucart, *Histoire des religions et méthode comparative*, 1912; J. Estlin Carpenter, *Comparative Religion*, 1913; H. Pinard de Boullaye, *L'Étude comparée des Religions: Essai critique*, 2 vols., 1922–25; A. G. Widgery, *The Comparative Study of Religion*, 1923; H. Frick, *Vergleichende Religionswissenschaft*, 1928; E. O. James,

Comparative Religion, 1938; Gustav Mensching, *Vergleichende Religionswissenschaft*, 1938; Mircea Eliade, *Traité d'Histoire des religions*, 1949; A. C. Bouquet, *Comparative Religion, a Short Outline*, 1950. Of particular interest in regard to this question of method are R. Pettazzoni's *Svolgimento e carattere della storia delle religioni*, 1924; two essays by Joachim Wach, "Zur Methodologie der allgemeinen Religionswissenschaft" in *Zeitschrift fuer Missionskunde* for 1923, and *Religionswissenschaft: Prolegomena zu ihrer wissenschaftstheoretischen Grundlegung*, 1924, and Jean Przyluski's article, "Y a-t-il une science des religions?" in the *Revue de l'histoire des religions* for 1936.

I. Periodicals: Though there is no journal exclusively devoted to the comparative study of religion there are many important periodicals which serve this study. Among the more important are: *L'Année sociologique* and its successor *Annales sociologiques* (Paris); *Anthropos* (Vienna); *Archiv fuer Religionswissenschaft* (Leipzig); *Bilychnis: Rivista di studi religiosi* (Rome); *Credo* (Uppsala-Stockholm); *Harvard Theological Review* (Cambridge, Mass.); *Eranos Jahrbuch* (Zurich); *Hibbert Journal* (London); *Journal of Religion* (Chicago); *Missionswissenschaft und Religionswissenschaft* (Muenster); *Le Muséon* (Louvain); *Recherches de science religieuse* (Paris); *Religio: Rivista di studi religiosi* (Rome); *Religion och Kultur* (Uppsala); *Review of Religion* (New York); *Revue de l'histoire des religions* (Paris); *Revue d'histoire et de littérature religieuses* (Paris); *Revue des sciences religieuses* (Strasbourg); *Storia delle religioni* (Turin); *Studi e materiali di storia delle religioni* (Bologna); *Svensk teologisk Kvartalskrift* (Lund); *Zalmoxis: Revue des études religieuses* (Paris); *Zeitschrift fuer Missionskunde und Religionswissenschaft* (Muenster-i/W); *Zeitschrift fuer Religions- und Geistesgeschichte* (Erlangen).

The *Transactions* of the International Congress for the History of Religions, though not strictly a periodical, ought to be mentioned here, and in the *Transactions* of the various Academies and Learned Societies, as well as in the *Journals* devoted to the study of particular religions or particular cultures, there is an abundance of material germane to this study constantly appearing.

II. Encyclopedias: Almost all the Encyclopedias and larger Dictionaries have articles on the various religions which suggest comparative study. Of those more directly concerned with religion, Hasting's *Encyclopaedia of Religion and Ethics*, 12 volumes, 1908–22, with Index volume, 1927, still holds pride of place, though many of its articles are now antiquated. A one volume *Encyclopaedia of Religions* was produced by Maurice A. Canney in 1921, and in the same year appeared *A Dictionary of Religion* *and Ethics*, by S. Mathews and G. B. Smith. There is also a *Dictionary of Religion and Religions*, by R. Ince, 1936. The second edition of *Die Religion in Geschichte und Gegenwart*, by Gunkel und Zscharnack, 5 vols., 1926–32, contains material of fundamental importance. There is much useful comparative material in the ten volumes of the *Handbuch des deutschen Aberglaubens*, 1927–42; in Bricourt's *Dictionnaire pratique des connaissances religieuses*, 7 vols., 1925–33; and in the Danish *Illustreret Religionsleksikon*, 3 vols., 1949–50. Here should be mentioned also Hans Haas' *Bilderatlas zur Religionsgeschichte*, 1924 ff.; K. Streit's *Religionskarte der Erde*, 1929; and the *Histomap of Religions*, 1951.

III. Bibliography: Elements of a bibliography of the subject will be found in the various volumes of L. H. Jordan on Comparative Religion; in L. Salvatorelli's *Introduzione bibliografica alla scienza della religioni*, 1914; in Carl Clemen's *Religionsgeschichtliche Bibliographie*, of which five parts have appeared; and in the bibliographical section of Friess and Schneider's *Religion in Various Cultures*, 1937. A history of the discipline has been attempted by G. Mensching, *Geschichte der Religionswissenschaft*, 1948; and its prospects are discussed in Forrell-Frick-Heiler, *Religionswissenschaft in neuer Sicht*, 1951; while Gerhard Rosenkranz, *Evangelische Religionskunde: Einfuehrung in eine theologische Schau der Religionen*, 1951, has made an extremely interesting attempt to show how even the treatment of Christian theology may benefit from a parallel discussion of how other religions have dealt with the various problems with which it is concerned.

There are several lectureships devoted primarily to studies in this field, notably the *Hibbert Lectures* in England, the *Haskell Lectures* at Chicago and Oberlin, the *Lamson Lectures* at Hartford Seminary, the lectures at the Musée Guimet in Paris, published in its *Bibliothèque des études* and *Bibliothèque de vulgarisation* (*diffusion*), the *Olaus-Petri Lectures* at Uppsala, the *American Lectures on the History of Religions*. Also several series have been devoted to this discipline. In Paris the École pratique des Hautes Études has a "Section des sciences religieuses" whose researches are published in the *Annuaire* and the *Bibliothèque* of the School. Leroux' *Bibliothèque historique des religions* has been appearing at Paris since 1914 and the series *Mythes et religions*, edited by Couchaud, since 1939. Pettazzoni's *Testi e documenti per la storia delle religioni* has been appearing since 1921 at Bologna; the Giessen *Religionsgeschichtliche Versuche und Vorarbeiten* since 1903; the Tuebingen *Religionsgeschichtliche Volksbuecher* since 1906, of which Reihe III is devoted to "Allgemeine Religionsgeschichte (Religionsvergleichung)"; Streitberg's

Religionswissenschaftliche Bibliothek at Heidelberg since 1910; the *Quellen der Religionsgeschichte* at Goettingen since 1910; the University of Leipzig's *Veroeffentlichungen des Forschungsinstitut fuer vergleichende Religionsgeschichte*, since 1917; the Bonn *Untersuchungen zur allgemeinen Religionsgeschichte*, commenced by Carl Clemen, and the "Religionswissenschaftliche Reihe" of the series *Aus der Welt der Religion* at Giessen from 1924. The two most recent of such Series are the section on "World Religions" edited by E. O. James in Hutchinson's *University Library*, 1949 ff., and the *Collection Mana: Introduction à l'histoire des religions*, published by the Presses Universitaires de France, 1944 ff.

IV. Source Material: Max Mueller's fifty volumes of translations of the *Sacred Books of the East*, 1879–1910, are now for the most part antiquated, and there is great need for a new series of translations of the sacred writings of the various religions. A beginning has been made for the older religions in *Ancient Near Eastern Texts*, translations edited by J. B. Pritchard, 1950. The second edition of Bertholet's *Religionsgeschichtliches Lesebuch*, 1926 ff., offers a considerable amount of material in reliable translations. N. Söderblom edited four volumes of *Främmande Religionsurkunde i urval och öfversättning*, 1908. The important task of collecting the material in the classical authors on the ancient religions was commenced by Carl Clemen in 1920 at Bonn in a series of *Fontes historiae religionum ex auctoribus graecis et latinis*.

V. Surveys: Of the numerous survey volumes on comparative religion it would be unwise to use anything earlier than G. F. Moore's *History of Religions*, 2 vols., 1920; reprinted 1949. There is a second edition of A. Jeremias' *Allgemeine Religionsgeschichte*, 1924, and of Julius Richter's *Die Religionen der Voelker*, 1927. Other summaries which are still useful because of some individual point of view are H. Th. Obbink's *De Godsdienst in zyn Verschyningsvormen*, 1923; R. E. Hume's *The World's Living Religions: an historical Sketch with special reference to their Sacred Scriptures, and in comparison with Christianity*, 1926; Blum-Ernst's revision of Wurm's *Handbuch der Religionsgeschichte*, 1929; the Tiele-Söderblom *Kompendium der Religionsgeschichte*, 1931; D. Cinti, *Storia delle religioni: I culti di tutti i popoli antiche e moderni: Dottrine, iti, usanze*, 2 vols., 1934–36; A. G. Widgery, *Living Religions and Modern Thought*, 1936; John B. Noss, *Man's Religions*, 1949; G. Mensching, *Allgemeine Religionsgeschichte*, 1949; G. Bardy, *Les religions non-chrétiennes*, 1949.

The more important survey books, however, are those in which an editor has assembled the contributions of a number of expert collaborators. The fourth edition of Chantepie de la Saussaye's *Lehrbuch der Religionsgeschichte* as edited by Bertholet and Lehmann, 2 vols. 1924–25, is one of the best of these though some of its articles are now antiquated. In 1927 Carl Clemen edited a one volume work *Die Religionen der Erde: ihr Wesen und ihre Geschichte*, which was translated as *The Religions of the World*, 1931, and has now appeared in a new edition, 1949. Thirteen Professors of the University of Vienna collaborated to produce *Die Religionen der Erde in Einzeldarstellungen*, 1929, and P. Tacchi Venturi had more than a dozen collaborators for his *Manuale di Storia delle Religioni*, 2 vols., 1944. More recent cooperative surveys are those edited by G. Mensching, *Handbuch der Religionswissenschaft*, 1948 ff.; by G. van der Leeuw, *De Godsdiensten der Wereld*, 2 vols., 1948; Johs. Pedersen, *Illustreret Religionshistorie*, 1948, and Gorce et Mortier, *Histoire générale des religions*, 5 vols., 1947–1950. Survey volumes of a somewhat different character are the essays edited by E. H. Sneath in *The Evolution of Ethics as revealed in the Great Religions*, 1927; the enormous mass of material collected in J. G. Frazer's *Golden Bough*, 12 vols., 1915; by Wm. Schmidt in *Der Ursprung der Gottesidee: eine historisch-kritische und positive Studie*, 9 vols., 1926–49, and in the survey by G. van der Leeuw in his *Phaenomenologie der Religion*, 1933.

Introductions to the study of Comparative Religion are numerous. Among the more important are F. B. Jevons, *An Introduction to the History of Religion*, 1908 and later reprints, and the same author's *Comparative Religion*, 1913; R. Dussaud, *Introduction à l'histoire des religions*, 1914; C. H. Toy, *Introduction to the History of Religions*, 1921; J. W. Hauer, *Die Religionen: ihr Werden, ihr Sinn, ihre Wahrheit*, 1923; G. van der Leeuw, *Inleiding tot de Godsdienstgeschiedenis*, 1924; N. Söderblom, *Einfuehrung in die Religionsgeschichte*, 1928; E. E. Kellett, *A Short History of Religions*, 1934; G. Graneris, *La Religione nella storia delle religioni*, 1935; A. E. Haydon, *Man's Search for the Good Life*, 1937; R. Callois, *L'Homme et le sacré*, 1939; T. H. Robinson, *An Outline Introduction to the History of Religions*, new edition, 1951.

VI. Origin and Development of Religion: Theories as to the origin of religion and the principles of its development are too numerous to mention in detail, but the discussions in the following books published since 1910 will cover most of them. Beuchat et Hollebecque, *Les religions: étude historique et sociologique du phénomène religieux*, 1910; H. Cunow, *Ursprung der Religion und des Gottesglaubens*, 1913; R. R. Marett, *The Threshold of Religion*, 1914; R. Otto, *Das Heilige*, 1922 and later editions, translated as *The Idea of the Holy*, 1926; E. W.

Hopkins, *The Origin and Evolution of Religion*, 1923; G. F. Moore, *The Birth and Growth of Religion*, 1924; R. Kreglinger, *Études sur l'origine et le développement de la vie religieuse*, 3 vols., 1919–22; N. Söderblom, *Das Werden des Gottesglaubens*, 1926, and *Der lebendige Gott im Zeugnis der Religionsgeschichte*, 1942, translated from an earlier edition as *The Living God*, 1939; Wm. Schmidt, *Ursprung und Wesen der Religion*, 1930, translated as *The Origin and Growth of Religion*, 1931; J. Baruzi, *Problèmes d'histoire des religions*, 1935; G. van der Leeuw, *Der Mensch und die Religion*, 1941; John Murphy, *The Origin and History of Religions*, 1949.

Primitive religion is a special problem which has a peculiar interest of its own and has given rise to a large literature. Adequate discussion of its problems from various points of view will be found in A. le Roy, *The Religion of the Primitives*, 1922; F. Graebner, *Das Weltbild der Primitiven*, 1924; R. R. Marett, *Faith, Hope and Charity in Primitive Religion*, 1932, and *The Sacraments of Simple Folk*, 1933; M. P. Nilsson, *Primitive Religion*, 1934; B. Malinowski, *The Foundations of Faith and Morals*, 1936, and *Magic, Science and Religion*, 1948; G. van der Leeuw, *De primitieve mensch en die Religie*, 1937; P. Radin, *Primitive Religion*, 1937; G. Mensching, *Volksreligion und Weltreligion*, 1938; and his *Gut und Boese im Glauben der Voelker*, 1950; Ruth Benedict, *Patterns of Culture*, 1946; K. H. Ratschow, *Magie und Religion*, 1947; R. H. Lowie, *Primitive Religion*, 1948; E. O. James, *Primitive Ritual and Belief*, 1917, and his *The Beginnings of Religion: an Introductory and Scientific Study*, 1947.

The other important special problem of comparative study is that of the sociology of religion. No religion functions save in the life of a social group. Every religious tradition is handed on by well-known social procedures. Participation in religious activities is always socially conditioned, so that recognition of the significance of this social functioning of religion has led to considerable interest in this aspect of the study of comparative religion. It was Robertson Smith who in his *Kinship and Marriage in Early Arabia*, 2nd ed., 1907, and *Lectures on the Religion of the Semites*, 3rd ed., 1907, brought out in striking fashion the group significance of the sacred; and this social approach has been applied fruitfully to both simpler and more advanced religions. One may refer to L. Lévy-Bruel, *Les fonctions mentales dans les sociétés inférieurs*, 1910; Emile Durkheim, *Les forms élémentaires de la vie religieuse*, 1912; translated 1926, and his *L'Education morale*, 1925; I. King, *The Development of Religion: a Study in Anthropology and Social Psychology*, 1910; F. Schleiter, *Religion and Culture*, 1919; Max Weber, *Gesammelte Aufsaetze zur Religionssozi-*

ologie, 3 vols., 1922–23, and his *Wirtschaft und Gesellschaft*, 1925; Maurice Besson, *Le Totémisme*, 1929; Gerald Heard, *The Social Substance of Religion*, 1931; Joachim Wach, *Einfuehrung in die Religionssoziologie*, 1931, and *Sociology of Religion*, 1945; N.Bastide, *Éléments de sociologie religieuse*, 1935; A. Bros, *L'Ethnologie religieuse*, 1936; J. Hasenfuss, *Die moderne Religionssoziologie und ihre Bedeutung fuer die religioese Problematik*, 1937; E. O. James, *The Social Function of Religion*, 1940, and Wm. J. Goode, *Religion among the Primitives*, 1951.

[Sup.] ARTHUR JEFFERY.

COMPARATIVE RELIGION, TWENTIETH CENTURY TRENDS IN THE STUDY OF: The supplementary article on Comparative Religion (*q.v.*) reveals the strong and widespread interest in this subject. It mentions scores of works in numerous languages, and many more could have been added. As will be noticed, the material presents the scholar's idea of the way to study the subject: learn first how other scholars have dealt with religion in the world; then choose or devise one's own research procedure and method of presentation of facts and conclusions.

It would not be too much to expect all the works mentioned to be available in the libraries of institutions specializing in Comparative Religion and the History and Philosophy of Religion. Teachers devoting their lives to the subject will want to work through the literature. Undoubtedly in the works mentioned there is much repetition, so that in many cases it will be the viewpoints of the writers that will be the new and interesting features.

It will also be noted that several classes of literature appear because it may be taken for granted that they will be read. One class is specifically missionary literature, books by and about missionaries, histories of missions, magazines and news letters published by missionary societies. Works such as the *Jesuit Relations* and Moravian records written several hundreds of years ago have historical and sociological value. In time, the reports of other missions will receive similar recognition. Harvard University has that foresight and is giving library care to the records of the American Board of Commissioners for Foreign Missions.

Another kind of information that deserves study is the propaganda literature of other religions. There is no international journal of Comparative Religion. Similarly there is no journal nor indeed any book published on Comparative Missions. Only three of the important world religions profess the missionary principle of world-wide expansion; namely, Buddhism (*q.v.*), Christianity and Islam (see MUHAMMAD). There is more than scholarly interest, there is vital need, to know what the protagonists of

Buddhism and Islam and other religions and also Communism have to say against Christianity and in defense of their own dogmas. Accurate information about what people believe about their own religion and the religion of others is best found in what they say to each other. Often there is special value in the viewpoints of heretical sects splitting off from parent bodies and claiming validity for their own emphases or asserting that their own is the original and true doctrine. That has frequently been the case in Islam. Hundreds of years ago Ismāʿīlī missionaries were trained to convert other Muslims to their sect. The first Assassins were missionaries with special methods of dealing with opponents. Those methods reveal the political and social, rather than the religious, nature of Islam. Numerous other groups, large and small, within Islam have justified their own views to their own communities, defended themselves against the criticisms of others, and sought to expand in numbers and power. Much about particular religions and religion in general can be learned from the history and propaganda literature of sects.

It is generally maintained that Judaism is not missionary in principle. But Judaism has ever been totalitarian in the sense that it embraces all the interests and activities of its adherents. Many Hebrews, however, gave up the political and even the social aspects of Judaism, retaining its purely religious and spiritual teachings. The Zionist movement revived the old elements of Judaism and made strong efforts to enlist the support of all Jews for the political and civil Judaism now realized in the State of Israel.

Buddhism (*q.v.*) offers students of Comparative Religion unusual study problems in that it was abandoned in its original home and flourished along different lines in other lands. There are British and American Buddhists with doctrinal emphases of their own. Recently relics of the original Buddha have been welcomed back into India and in 1952 a Buddhist monastery was established in New York State.

During this century thousands of Muslims have become residents of this country, increasing the varieties of religious experience to be found here (see MUSLIMS IN THE U. S. A). But only a few of the Sunni Muslims have had missionary objectives. Most of the groups have been content to carry on their own meetings in makeshift mosques. Only during the current decade has a Sunni mosque been erected in Washington. There are, however, two groups, considered heretical by the majority or Sunni Muslims, that have missionary aims and activities. These are the Bahāʾī Cause (see BAHAISM) and the Ahmadiyyah Movement. The former is Persian in origin and the latter Indian. Both are split into factions that are bitterly hostile to each other. There are also in America families of Muslim origin, retaining important social attitudes of Islam, but allowing their members to belong to Christian churches.

Since the former edition of the *Schaff-Herzog Encyclopedia of Religious Knowledge* was published, a number of marked experiences have been described in the articles RELIGION, RELIGION IN LITERATURE and the PHILOSOPHY OF RELIGION as well as in the articles upon the various religious systems.

The two Supplementary Volumes contain notable articles dealing with developments during this century in non-christian religions. These accounts describe the political and social, as well as the religious events that have affected the followers of these other religions. They report also the increase in knowledge of these other faiths and any changes in attitudes towards them, both within and without the communions themselves. For instance, the effect of World War II upon Shinto (*q.v.*) in Japan is explained: a god that fails, fails to hold followers. There is danger that the religion of the conquerors will win new adherents who do not understand the spiritual requirements of that religion. Missionary work in Japan is flourishing because of Japan's defeat. Therefore the spiritual nature and requirements of Christianity need special emphasis.

Great changes have taken place also in Western and Southern Asia. The articles on PAKISTAN and INDIA, on ABABIA, IRAQ, IRAN, ISRAEL, JORDAN, LEBANON, SYRIA, and TURKEY describe these changes. The religions of the peoples of these lands likewise have new articles, supplementing those in the previous edition of this Encyclopedia, presenting important new information. These include the articles on the religions of the new India (*q.v.*), such as the new BRAHMANISM, HINDUISM, JAINISM, SIKHISM, and ZOROASTRIANISM. Similarly the religions of the Near and Middle East have new and important material. Attention may be called to the accounts of MUHAMMAD, ARABIC PHILOSOPHY, BABISM, DRUSES, SHI'ISM, SUFISM, the TUAREG, WAHHABIS, YAZIDIS and the ZAR. There is new material on AFGHANISTAN, CONFUCIANISM, the MONGOLS, SHAMANISM and TURKESTAN. There are also articles on abandoned religions, persistent superstitions, minor but continuing religious movements, supplementary and new biographical sketches of important religious personalities. In this category may be mentioned the scholarly articles on JOHN OF DAMASCUS, DIVINATION, FOLKLORE, ISAAC OF NINEVEH, MAGIC, MAIMONIDES, MANI, GANDHI, SADHU SUNDAR SINGH, and TAGORE.   EDWIN E. CALVERLEY.

COMPASSION: The word is derived from the Latin *cum*, i.e., "with," and *patior*, i.e., "I suffer," and it is etymologically the exact equivalent of *sympathy*, from *sum*, i.e., "with" and

pascho, i.e., "I suffer." But the English term "sympathy" (*q.v.*) has widened its meaning to include any fellow-feeling with another, in joy as well as in suffering, while the term "compassion" has retained exclusively the narrow meaning. Thus compassion is the feeling, often expressing itself in overt action, of one who is not in personal trouble but who vicariously makes the suffering of another his own.

In ethical discussion, compassion is seldom dealt with directly or extensively, but is normally referred to, often without the use of the term, as one form of the wider "sympathy." The translators of the Scriptures into English, however, found it appropriate to employ the term quite frequently, and in each testament it represents several different roots.

Thus, in the Authorized (King James) Version, it is employed in Ex. 2:6; I Sam. 23:21; II Chron. 36:15, 17; Ezek. 16:5, to translate the root *chamal*, which means to commiserate, or to spare. In Deut. 13:17; 30:3; I Kings 8:50; II Kings 13:23; Mic. 7:19, it translates *racham*, which means first to fondle, to love; then, by an extension, it means a maiden, and by a further, possibly psychological, extension, the womb. In various Psalms it is used to translate *rachum*.

In the New Testament this word is employed to translate *splagchnizomai*, from *splagchnon*, which means "the intestine," expressing the fact, already indicated, that there was in the past a widespread tendency to locate emotions in the abdominal area as their seat. It also translates *eleos* which means compassion; and *oiktermos* which means pity or mercy; and *metriopatheo*, meaning to be moderate in passion, and thus gentle, and thus compassionate; and *sumpathēs*, meaning to have a fellow-feeling for someone.

By bringing together the various root-meanings here indicated, one may readily discover the kind of human attitude to which specific compassion belongs. It should be noted, however, that, from the scriptural point of view, compassion is not confined to man; God also feels and exercises compassion. Nor, in man, is it simply a human attainment or virtue; it is a divine gift. In so far as it is a human attainment, it is an "imitation of Christ," or of the Father of mercies.   ANDREW K. RULE.

CONCORDATS: The concordat between the Holy See and the government of Serbia (1914), was the only one concluded under the pontificate of Pope Pius X. It dealt with the erection of new Roman Catholic dioceses and with the freedom of the Roman Church, her schools and institutions. World War I held up the execution of the concordat. Since then, Rome has pressed the execution of most of its provisions, often in spite of a lively opposition, under the rule of the Yugoslav government.

Political and social conditions prevailing in

Europe after World War I brought about a marked change in the relations between the Holy See and the nations. While the policy of separation of church and state continued to be favored by the civil rulers, the anticlericalism of the first decade of the twentieth century had abated, and several governments felt the desirability of closer relations with the Holy See. On the other hand, Pope Benedict XV, in a consistorial allocution on November 21, 1921, declared himself ready to treat with foreign powers for the amiable solution of problems concerning both church and state.

The recent concordats and accords thus concluded between the Holy See and civil governments uphold the independence of the Roman Catholic Church and seek to safeguard the liberty of her administration, worship, and educational institutions. They eventually strive to maintain privileges previously recognized, such as the exemption of churches, chapels and religious houses from taxation, as well as the immunity of clerics or their exemption from military service. In countries predominantly not Roman Catholic, they tend to solve problems resulting from the modification of ecclesiastical circumscriptions or from the creation of new bishoprics.

The following concordats and accords were concluded between the Holy See and foreign powers in execution of the general policies defined by Pope Benedict XV and continued by his successor Pope Pius XI. Concordats with Latvia (1922) and Lithuania (1927). Solemn convention with Poland (1925). *Modus vivendi* with Czechoslovakia (1927). Concordat with Rumania (1927), and accord for the solution of difficulties arising from the execution of the same (1932). Concordat with Austria (1933). Concordats with Bavaria (1924), Prussia (1929), and Baden (1932). Solemn agreement with the *Reich*, supplementing the existing concordats with several German states, and aiming to achieve uniformity in political relations between the Holy See and Germany (1933). Accords of the Lateran, between the Holy See and the Italian government, to supplement the recognition of the City of the Vatican as a sovereign state, and to define the situation, rights and privileges of the Roman Catholic Church in her relations with the Kingdom of Italy (1929). Accords with Portugal (1928–29), followed by a solemn convention (1940). *Modus vivendi* with Spain (1941), to replace the concordat of 1851, which became obsolete after the fall of the monarchy. While the concordat of 1801, initiated by Napoleon, had been denounced by the French Republic in 1905, its dispositions continued in Alsace-Lorraine after the reunion of this province to France in 1918. In consequence of renewed diplomatic relations between France and the Holy See, accords were signed concerning

the so-called "associations cultuelles diocésaines" for the administration of ecclesiastical property, approved by Pope Pius XI and recognized by French law (1924). Similar accords defined the status of French representatives and civil officials in various countries of the Near East which had been part of the Ottoman Empire and were administered by mandate from the League of Nations (1925). These accords have become obsolete since the countries under mandate have proclaimed their independence after World War II.

The conditions of political instability which prevailed generally after World War II were not favorable to the conclusion of concordats between civil governments and the Holy See. The first comprehensive treaty signed in the name of Pius XII is the concordat with Spain, Aug. 27, 1953, the official text of which (Italian and Castilian) is given in the *Acta Apostolicae Sedis*, XXXV, 13 (Oct. 27, 1953).

It proclaims that Roman Catholicism is the only religion of the Spanish nation. It confirms the procedure previously agreed upon by Rome and Madrid for the nomination of Spanish bishops. It initiates a wholesale revision of ecclesiastical circumscriptions in order to aline them, as far as possible, with the administrative divisions of the country, and it calls upon the cooperation of the state for the dotation of new dioceses, or for the redistribution of church properties. The concordat maintains the general principle of the exemption of clerics from secular courts (*privilegium fori*), and from military service. It establishes, however, the competence of secular courts in purely civil or criminal matter in which clerics may be involved or called as witnesses, from the consent of the diocesan ordinary. It claims for ecclesiastical tribunals an exclusive competence with regard to the annulment of marriages, the separation of married persons, and the application of the so-called "privilege of the Apostle" (see MARRIAGE, ROMAN CATHOLIC LAWS ON). The concordat states that religious instruction in public schools and institutions of learning of all degrees must be given according to the principles of the dogma and the morals of the Roman Catholic Church.

A concordat with the Dominican Republic was signed on June 16, 1954, the official text of which (Latin and Castilian), was published in the *Acta Apostolicae Sedis*, XXXVI, 11 (Aug. 20, 1954). It states that Roman Catholicism is the religion of the Dominican nation. The nomination of bishops and church dignitaries, as well as the creation of new ecclesiastical circumscriptions, is the exclusive privilege of the church, which enjoys an unlimited right of association, subject only to notifying the civil government, whose silence shall be construed as approval. In the selection of incumbents for ecclesiastical charges or benefices, the church shall give priority to Dominican citizens, while retaining the right of calling foreigners if no acceptable candidates can be secured from the ranks of the national clergy. The provisions of the concordat for the exemption and privileges of clerics, the respective competence of courts, ecclesiastical, civil, and criminal, the laws concerning marriage and religious education, are generally similar to those of the concordat with Spain.

BIBLIOGRAPHY: A. Mercati, *Raccolta di concordati su materie ecclesiastiche tra la S. Sede e le autorità civili*, 1919; A. Perugini, *Concordata vigentia notis historicis et iuridicis declarata*, 1934; J. M. Restrepo, *Concordata regnante SS. Pio PP. XI inita*, 1934; A. Giannini, *I concordati postbellici*, 2 vols. 1936; E. Lange Ronneberg, *Die Konkordate*, 1929; Y. de Brière, *Aspect général de la politique concordataire du pontificat de Pie XI*, 1930; H. Wagnon, *Concordats et droit international*, 1935.

[Sup.] GEORGES A. BARROIS.

CONCUPISCENCE: The thought of this term is more often expressed in modern speech by the words "lust" and "sensuality." It refers technically to the concepts centering around *concupiscentia* in the Latin theologians and *epithumia* in the New Testament, especially Paul. Concupiscence, in keeping with its etymological derivation, can quite properly refer to the simple and natural act of desiring a thing for the satisfaction to be derived therefrom. In this sense of the term, Pelagians maintain that concupiscence is perfectly natural, normal and therefore good. Concupiscence becomes evil only in excess because any excess violates the principle of moderation dictated by reason.

The Pauline-Augustinian tradition has held that the Pelagian view is too simple and too Hellenistic. According to it, the satisfaction of physical desire in man is indeed not evil in itself since it is inherent in the constitution of man as created by God. But the Pelagians fail to recognize that the nature of man as created by God is corrupted by sin (see MAN, DOCTRINE OF). Although sin is primarily spiritual, it manifests itself also in the corruption of all phases of man's physical nature. So thirst becomes an excuse for drunkenness; hunger, for gluttony; sex, for lust. Because these forms of sin are more obvious, they have sometimes been thought of as an independent kind of sin or even as the essence of sin itself. The Pauline contrast between "spirit" and "flesh" is taken to mean that physical desire and its satisfaction is evil in itself and is the source of sin. This latter view has found expression especially in some of the statements on sex in the Augustinian-Catholic tradition. But even this tradition at its heart recognizes that sin is essentially spiritual and that physical sins are derivative and secondary in nature.

The exact relation, however, between spiritual and physical sin is obscure and not easy to analyze. It can be said with Paul (Rom. 1:26–30) that, because men refused to worship God, He "gave them up to vile passions," and so the spirit became subservient to the flesh, became *kata sarka* instead of *en sarki* (II Cor. 10:3). Or it may be said that because man in self-love sinned against God with a consequent disintegration in their relationship, so man in sensuality now sins against himself with a consequent disintegration in his own nature. However, the apparent independence and initiative of sensuality as a principle of sin in man's life requires a definition of it as something more than an extension of self-love. This has been done (R. Niebuhr) by indicating that sometimes sensuality actually deifies or idolizes something or someone outside the self in a vain attempt to escape the self; and further, as a last resort, it sometimes is an attempt at resignation of both self and world to a common dissolution in the depths of the impersonal ocean of subconsciousness. But it must be stressed that concupiscence, whatever its motive, has a great variety of forms and consists of "any inordinate devotion to a mutable good," of which sexual license is only the most striking example.

See also SEX, ETHICS OF.

BIBLIOGRAPHY: R. Niebuhr, *The Nature and Destiny of Man* (1941), Vol. I, Chap. 8; Vol. II, Chap. 5; A. Harnack, *History of Dogma* (1900), Vols. III, V, VI, VII, cf. Index; R. Seeberg, *History of Doctrine* (1905), 2 vols., cf. Index; O. Piper, *The Christian Interpretation of Sex* (1941), Chap. 2, 16, 17; N. P. Williams, *The Ideas of the Fall and Original Sin* (1927), cf. Index; T. Aquinas, *Summa Theologica*, II. i, Q. 23, art. 1; Q. 52, art. 2; Q. 26, art. 4; Q. 30; Q. 82, art. 3.

ARNOLD B. COME.

CONDÉ, LOUIS DE BOURBON, PRINCE OF: The first great Huguenot leader; b. May 7, 1530; d. March 13, 1569. Condé was a cadet son of the House of Bourbon and closely related to the Valois kings of France. After the usual young aristocrat's education he appeared at the French Court in 1549 and was made gentleman of the chamber of King Henri II. Condé early showed fine fighting aptitudes and from 1551 to 1558 distinguished himself in many battles in the north of France and in Italy. Meanwhile he became interested in the Protestant faith which was beginning to make headway in France. In 1555, on his way back from an Italian campaign, he stopped at Geneva to attend a Calvinist service and to find out more about the new doctrines. He also developed a strong antipathy to the Guises, chief royal favorites and bulwarks of the Catholic power in France. Their control of the royal treasury meant that Condé only got a fraction of the revenues that the other principal courtiers enjoyed, and yet his high birth forced him to maintain a high position at the court.

When the Guises assumed control of the regency of the young King Francis II and used their power to renew repression of Protestantism, Condé decided to act. He was the "silent chief" of the Conspiracy of Amboise, a daring attempt to kidnap the king and get rid of the Guises, hatched in 1560 by a number of young noblemen. The plot was discovered and suppressed with great bloodshed. Condé in a dramatic public statement denied any connection with it. Condé then retired to Guienne with another group of nobles, and demanded the convocation of the Estates-General. When the Guises not only accepted this proposal but also took steps to control the deputies to the Estates-General, Condé hatched another plot. This one had not only the same general purposes as the Amboise conspiracy but also aimed at the surprise capture of a number of big French cities. A young nobleman named Maligny, from Condé's suite, actually tried to seize Lyon. Condé was immediately summoned to court, thrown in jail, tried and convicted of treason and sentenced to death. Only the unexpected death of Francis II saved him. The queen-mother Catherine de Medici immediately assumed the regency of the new King Charles IX and had Condé released, had him reconciled in public to the Duke of Guise and made him governor of Picardy. Catherine went on to call the Colloquy of Poissy (q.v.), the first real opportunity for the Calvinists to state their views in public, and launched a policy of royal toleration with the edict of January, 1562.

The Massacre of Vassy in March, 1562, convinced Condé and many other Protestants that the Guises were going to make a new bid for power and insist on repression of Protestantism. Condé and Theodore Beza (q.v.) left Paris, vainly tried to win control of the persons of the king and queen-mother, seized Orléans, issued a call to arms and published a manifesto. More than thirty-five important French cities immediately declared for Condé and large detachments of noblemen poured into Orléans. Condé dispatched a series of special ambassadors to German princes, to Switzerland and to England, to justify his recourse to arms and to ask for money and military help. Calvin, Beza, and other leading ministers did their best to help his foreign negotiations and to keep Huguenot soldiers in France loyal to him. A series of further negotiations with the French court collapsed and open war began. The first big pitched battle at Dreux in Normandy resulted in Condé's capture. In prison he signed the Treaty of Amboise, March 12, 1563, which abandoned the fight for tolerance of Calvinism in many parts of France, and made Coligny (q.v.) and the ministers furious. In the ensuing period of uneasy peace Condé further scandalized the ministers by a series of illicit love affairs.

The second war of religion began in 1567 after the failure of another attempt to seize the persons of the king and queen-mother, this time engineered by Coligny. Condé again took the lead in negotiations and led the Huguenot armies to the battle of Saint-Denis which was indecisive but resulted in the mortal wounding of the Catholic leader Constable Montmorency. The peace of Longjumeau, signed March 13, 1568, was unsatisfactory to both sides and was never really observed. Rumors of a plot to kidnap Coligny and Condé led them both to flee to La Rochelle where they organized a new army, sent diplomatic missions to England, Germany, and the Low Countries, and after further negotiations with the court, again plunged into war. This third religious war climaxed in the battle of Jarnac where Condé was again captured and treacherously shot while being led off the field of battle. Condé's fighting abilities had made French Calvinism a political power, but his use of typical contemporary methods of intrigue stained the purity of the Calvinist cause.

A great many of Condé's state papers and documents relating to the first war of religion are contained in the *Memoires de Condé* . . . , which was first published in Strasbourg (3 vols., 1565–1566) with his personal authorization. The most complete edition is that of Secousse (London, 6 vols., 1743–1744) which includes a sixth volume on Henri IV. A defense of Condé's activity in the third war of religion and a description of his death is contained in the *Literae Illvstriss. Principis, Lvdovici Borbonii, Principis Condaei, &c. Ad Carolum IX Galliae regem* . . . (n.d., but apparently published soon after his death).

BIBLIOGRAPHY: The only full-length biography is included in the Duc d'Aumale's *Histoire des princes de Condé*, Vols. I, II, 1863. See also Eugène and Émile Haag, *La France Protestante*, Vol. II (2nd ed., 1877–88), 1038–66. Standard histories of the French wars of religion contain a great deal of material on Condé. See especially Lucien Romier, *La Conjuration d'Amboise* . . . , 1923; and *Catholiques et Huguenots à la cour de Charles IX* . . . , 1924. For his relations with Swiss Protestants see Jean-Antoine Gautier, *Histoire de Genève* . . . , Vols. III, IV, V (1896–1914), *passim*; Edouard Rott, *Histoire de la représentation diplomatique de la France auprès des cantons suisses, de leurs alliés et de leurs confédérés*, Vol. II (1902), *passim*.

ROBERT M. KINGDON.

CONDREN, CHARLES DE: B. Dec. 15, 1588, at Vaubun near Soissons; d. Jan. 7, 1641, in Paris. Studied at the Sorbonne in Paris. In 1614 he was ordained priest, and in 1617 joined the newly founded Oratorium of Pierre de Bérulle, whom he succeeded as superior-general in 1629. He was one of the chief leaders of the Counter Reformation in France and accomplished a great deal for the reform of the higher clergy, as well as the education of the younger men. Many sought his advice, and he was particularly eulogized for his concept of sacrifice in the whole structure of theology and personal religion. Unfortunately the historians of the period since 1700 have neglected him; which is remarkable, since his contemporaries had the highest praise for him, notably Jeanne de Chantal, Vincent de Paul, and even Cardinal Richelieu.

BIBLIOGRAPHY: D. Amelote, *La vie du père Charles de Condren . . . composée par un prêtre*, 1643; *Lettres du P. Charles de Condren*, ed. P. Auvray and A. Jouffray, 1943; H. Brémond, *Histoire, littéraire du sentiment religieu en France*, Vol. III, 1921; A. Molien, "Condren," in *Dict. de spiritualité*, 1373–1388, Vol. II (1949).

H. GOOSSENS.

CONFERENCE OF MISSIONARY SOCIETIES IN GREAT BRITAIN AND IRELAND:

Founded in 1912, following the World Missionary Conference at Edinburgh in 1910. The Conference brings together in regular consultation representatives of some fifty British missionary societies, including societies especially concerned with the Christian approach to the Jews. It forms the recognized center for British missionary co-operation, united planning and negotiations with British and other governments, and is also the British member-organization of the International Missionary Council (*q.v.*). A Standing Committee acts as the executive of the Conference between its annual meetings. The work is carried on through area committees —for the Far East, India and Pakistan, Africa, the Middle East, the West Indies, and the home base—in co-operation with the Christian Literature Council and the Advisory Board for Medical Missions. The Conference works in association with the British Council of Churches (*q.v.*) through a liaison committee and through the mutual representation of interests on appropriate committees. The former Joint Committee on Religious Liberty has been amalgamated with the International Department of the British Council of Churches. During World War II the Conference secured special recognition by the British government and was entrusted with considerable responsibility for the representation of missionary interests in relation to several ministries and government departments, notably the Ministry of Information, the Ministry of Labor, and the Colonial Office. The secretariat of the Conference is in London.

PHILIP SAVILLE WATSON.

CONFERENCE ON CHRISTIAN POLITICS, ECONOMICS, AND CITIZENSHIP (COPEC):

The Interdenominational Council of Social Service Unions, believing that the social ethics of Christianity had been neglected with disastrous results to individuals and society and that Christian faith could provide the vision and power required by the problems of modern corporate life, convened commissions of leading Christian authorities on political, international, industrial, agricultural, financial, recreational, housing, and other problems in Britain. Four years were spent assembling, co-ordinating, and evaluating material, and in promoting study groups throughout the nation.

The Conference of 1,400 delegates, which met at Birmingham for a week in April, 1924, began a new stage in Christian social thinking in Great Britain and contributed to the Ecumenical Movement (*q.v.*), especially to the formation of the British Council of Churches (*q.v.*). Among its significant leaders were William Temple (*q.v.*), Charles E. Raven (*q.v.*), Lucy Gardiner, and Malcolm Spencer. ALEXANDER ZABRISKIE.

CONFERENCE ON SCIENCE, PHILOSOPHY, AND RELIGION:

Founded in 1940 through the efforts of Louis Finkelstein, president of the Jewish Theological Seminary of America, with the aid of about a hundred leaders in American academic and intellectual life, headed particularly by Lyman Bryson and Harlow Shapley. The annual meetings of the Conference have been held each year—generally in September—since 1940. Its constitution has changed gradually, and there are now a body of fellows, selected from among the convoking members and participants of earlier years, and a board of directors. Many different religious groups—Protestant, Catholic, and Jewish—and all shades of philosophical approach are represented in the papers which are read and published annually. Finkelstein was president of the Conference from 1940 to 1951.

BIBLIOGRAPHY: Proceedings of each annual conference, 1941 ff.

WILLIAM F. ALBRIGHT.

CONFERENCES, SUMMER BIBLE. See SUMMER BIBLE CONFERENCES.

CONFESSING CHURCH. See GERMANY, I.

CONFESSIONAL, SECRECY OF THE. See SECRECY OF THE CONFESSIONAL.

CONFESSION, CHANGE OF. See CHANGE OF CONFESSION.

CONFESSOR: (1) In the Roman liturgy, a beatified or canonized male saint who did not die a martyr. (2) In the Roman Church, a priest who hears confessions. He must hold faculties from the bishop in whose diocese he is to exercise the ministry of confession. But every ordained priest, even if not holding faculties, may validly receive the confession of a dying person. Lay persons are free to confess to any confessor. Special rules apply to the confessors of nuns and sisters. See also SECRECY OF THE CONFESSIONAL. GEORGES A. BARROIS.

CONFRATERNITY OF UNITY:

Founded in 1926, this society is composed of members of the Anglican Communion who believe that the See of Rome is the center of unity for all churches. The Confraternity therefore seeks, through corporate action within the Anglican Communion, a basis of reunion with the Holy See which will not be prejudicial to her own sacramental life. Membership in the Confraternity is open to clerical and lay communicants of any Anglican church who accept the credenda of the Confraternity. Members pray daily for reunion with the Apostolic See. Clerical members say Mass weekly for reunion.

SHEAFE WALKER.

CONFUCIANISM: A rationalization of the Chinese social order, defining the relationships within the kinship structure of the clan, and between king and minister. From this arise its practicality and omission of metaphysics and religion.

Confucius was the first to accept pupils regardless of rank. The curriculum covered the culture of the time, and Confucianism came to be identified with Chinese learning as a whole, other schools being considered partial and sectarian.

It is doubtful whether Confucius wrote or edited the books traditionally attributed to him, which are largely composite. The "mandate of heaven" was probably Chou propaganda to make the more civilized Chinese of the Shang dynasty accept the Chou conquest of 1027 B.C. Confucius' statement of the importance of the Book of Changes was probably interpolated in the analects when this ancient book of divination was being philosophized during the Han Dynasty (206 B.C.–A.D. 220).

The empire established 221 B.C. was on the basis of the realistic Legalist School. Its extent led the first Han emperor to seek and examine able men. This soon had to be delegated and fell to the Confucian scholars, who set examinations, established a university to train for them, and edited text books. In a few generations Confucianists controlled the government.

Confucian clan ethics in national government contributed to the fall of the Han Dynasty through emphasis on filial piety, which gave the mother of the emperor and her clan too great power in the state. Confucianism then went into eclipse for four centuries of disturbance, Taoism flourished and Buddhism entered, spread, and became influential. When the Tang Dynasty consolidated the empire, Confucianism regained control and broke Buddhism in a series of persecutions but adopted Buddhist and Taoist metaphysics and cosmology to form the neo-Confucianism of the Sung Dynasty. Two trends developed: Lu-Wang continued a mystical tendency; Chen-Chu remained humanistic and dominated education until recently.

BIBLIOGRAPHY: H. G. Creel, *Confucius, The Man and the Myth*, 1949; Fung Yu-lan, *History of Chinese Philosophy*, 1937; idem, *Short History*, 1948; Arthur Waley, *Three Ways of Thought in Ancient China*, 1939; Homer Dubs, *Hsüntze, the Moulder of Ancient Confucianism*, 1927.

[Sup. to CONFUCIUS] EARL HERBERT CRESSY.

CONGO. See Africa.

CONGREGATIONAL AND CHRISTIAN CHURCHES, COMMISSION ON INTERNATIONAL RELATIONS OF THE. See PEACE MOVEMENTS.

CONGREGATIONAL CHRISTIANS: The merging of the National Council of the Congregational Churches of the United States with the General Convention of the Christian Church in 1931 brought into existence a single national organization, the General Council of the Congregational-Christian Churches of the United States of America. The Congregational Churches in 1930 numbered 5,381, with 943,569 members and 5,609 ministers; while the Christian Churches in the same year numbered 981, with 97,706 members and 756 ministers. The two older national organizations with their affiliated societies continued their corporate identity, but the affairs of the two denominations were, so far as practicable, entrusted to the new Council. Since the churches of both groups were organized on the principle of congregational polity, the formation of the General Council did not affect the independent status of the individual churches, Congregational or Christian. In most cases, the corporate name of the local churches remained unchanged, the merger operating only at the state and national levels. The basic unit in the Congregational-Christian denomination is the local church, which is completely autonomous and controls all of its internal affairs, financial and ecclesiastical. These local churches are organized into voluntary fellowships of neighboring churches, known as Associations. In most states there is a State Conference embracing the churches and associations within its borders. Finally, the General Council brings together the local churches, associations, and state conferences into a voluntary national organization for promoting national and international matters.

Ordination rests with the local churches, but customarily the association and often the state conference are requested to assist in the examination and approval of ministerial candidates. Ministerial standing, although stemming from ordination by a local church, ordinarily vests, for denominational purposes, in the associations. Candidates for ordination are examined by an ecclesiastical council, summoned by a local church by letters missive to the other churches of its association, or, rarely, to a selected number of churches irrespective of associational membership. The latter procedure constitutes a "council of the vicinage" but is not recommended by the body of Congregationalism since it seldom results in as representative a council and has in former times been subject to a considerable amount of abuse. Ministerial candidates are expected to submit evidence of a genuine purpose of Christian service and a sound understanding of Christian history and doctrine, which are set forth in a formal paper and by oral examination. In addition, college and seminary training are expected.

The General Council meets biennially in various parts of the United States, and, concurrently with it, the various independent Congregational and Christian societies, among them the American Board of Commissioners for Foreign Missions and the Board of Home Missions. The former society carries on the foreign missionary work of the denomination while the latter embraces educational, missionary, and publication activities within the United States.

Inasmuch as each local church is autonomous, the denomination has no official creedal statement, but suggested formulations of belief, such as the Kansas Confession of Faith adopted by the National Council in 1913, have from time to time been recommended to local churches for adoption as the basis of church membership. In general, Congregational-Christian churches are trinitarian and evangelical, but in recent years little emphasis has been placed upon theological conformity and heresy trials are almost unknown. Most churches embrace a considerable divergency of theological opinion within themselves, and even greater from church to church.

The General Council was working on a merger with the Evangelical and Reformed Church (q.v.), and although the General Council gave strong support to the plan, legal difficulties were encountered and the matter was (1951) being held in abeyance pending the result of an appeal from the decision of the Supreme Court of New York.

The membership of the denomination in 1950 was 1,227,527, with 5,651 churches and 5,728 ministers. The total budget of the churches was $50,538,509.

BIBLIOGRAPHY: G. G. Atkins and F. L. Fagley, *History of American Congregationalism*, 1942; *The Year Book of the Congregational-Christian Churches*, 1930–50.

RICHARD D. PIERCE.

CONGREGATIONALISTS: The nineteenth century in American Congregationalism has been characterized by the multiplication of independent boards and societies for every sort of religious cause from ministerial pensions to the spiritual welfare of the freedman. The early years of the twentieth century brought the realization that consolidation was necessary to more effective work within the denomination. In 1911 a Committee of Nineteen was appointed by the National Council to bring in recommendations for more effectively administering the activities of the several national societies. In 1913 the report of the committee was adopted, thereby greatly diminishing duplication of effort among the societies both in their work and in the solicitation of funds. In 1917 an Annuity Fund for ministerial pensions was proposed and adopted

by the National Council. Further consolidations in the financial organization of the denomination and its agencies were adopted in 1919, 1925, and 1927, particularly missions.

Another movement was in the direction of interdenominational unity. As a result of a proposal to unite the Cleveland Presbytery and the Cleveland Union of Congregational Churches, which was under discussion in 1923, a similar proposal was brought before the General Assembly of the Presbyterian Church in the U.S.A. and the National Congregational Council. "Sincere approval" was expressed but no further action resulted. In 1925 the Evangelical Protestant churches, consisting of some twenty-three churches, became affiliated with the Congregationalists and were admitted on a parity with the state conferences. About this time a more tenuous affiliation was made with the German Congregational Church, numbering some 250 congregations and about 25,000 members. A proposal for union with the Universalists was discussed in 1925 and 1927, but it failed to receive sufficient support and was laid upon the table in the latter year. A similar effort looking toward a merger with the Christian denomination proved more successful, and after nine years of discussion was finally consummated in 1931, thereby constituting the General Council of Congregational-Christian (*q.v.*) Churches of the United States.

In England, the Congregational Union of England and Wales celebrated its centennial in 1931 with appropriate observances emphasizing its expanding program and growth. The toll of World War II was yet in the future; subsequently it was to cripple the work of the Union, but the Union has carried forward and in 1950 numbered 3,173 churches, 229,825 members, and Sunday school enrollments of 225,788.

Congregational work is carried on in every continent, but the United States and Britain continue to be the chief centers of the movement, both domestically and through their foreign missionary boards in other lands.

BIBLIOGRAPHY: G. G. Atkins and F. L. Fagley, *History of American Congregationalism*, 1942; Albert Peele, *Three Hundred Years*, 1931.

[Sup.] RICHARD D. PIERCE.

CONGREGATIONAL UNION LECTURES: Three series of lectures were delivered on this lectureship: 1833–51, 1855–62, and 1873–98. Thirty volumes of lectures were published between 1833 and 1898. Through 1862 they were designated the Congregational Lectures and were sponsored by the Congregational Library of England. In 1873 they came under the direct control of the Congregational Union and were renamed "The Congregational Union Lectures." No lectures have been given since 1898.

BIBLIOGRAPHY: Albert Peele, *Three Hundred Years*, 1931.

RICHARD D. PIERCE.

CONGREGATION OF GOD IN THE SPIRIT. See GRUBER, JOHN ADAM.

CONGREGATION OF THE TRUE INSPIRATION. See GRUBER, JOHN ADAM.

CONGREGATIONS, ROMAN: The various departments or agencies of the papal administration. These are, to date: *The Congregation of the Holy Office,* which replaced the so-called *Roman Inquisition* in 1908, and whose competence extends to all matters of faith and morals, and to questions concerning the validity of the sacraments. *The Congregation of the Consistory,* having jurisdiction over bishops and other ordinaries, and to which it pertains to create new dioceses or to modify ecclesiastical circumscriptions. *The Congregation for the Eastern Church,* having jurisdiction over the Uniate Churches and, since 1938, over the Catholics of the Latin rite throughout the Near East. *The Congregation of the Sacraments,* whose functions are to supervise the correct administration of the sacraments, to grant dispensations from matrimonial impediments, and since 1939, to control the handling of matrimonial cases in ecclesiastical courts. *The Congregation of the Council,* which rules in matters pertaining to ecclesiastical administration, such as church property, benefices, pious foundations, etc. The *Congregation of Religious,* having jurisdiction over religious orders and congregations, tertiaries (*q.v.*), and since 1947, over secular institutes whose members strive to achieve the state of Christian perfection while taking no vows. *The Congregation of the Propaganda* (see PROPAGANDA, CONGREGATION OF THE), having jurisdiction over foreign missions. *The Congregation of Rites,* which has competence in matters pertaining to the liturgy, and in the procedures of beatification and canonization of the saints. *The Congregation of Ceremonies,* viz., papal ceremonies, which regulates the public functions of the pontifical court. *The Congregation for Extraordinary Ecclesiastical Affairs,* which has exclusive competence with regard to the erection, division, or provision of dioceses, wherever these actions require negotiations with the civil government. *The Congregation of Seminaries and Universities,* having jurisdiction over ecclesiastical institutions of learning, including, since 1931, seminaries formerly controlled by the *Propaganda* and *The Congregation for the Eastern Church. The Congregation of the Fabric of St. Peter, i.e., of the Vatican Basilica.*

BIBLIOGRAPHY: *Codex Juris Canonici,* can. 246–257; V. Martin, *Les Congrégations romaines,* 1930; N. del Re, *La Curia Romana,* 1941; "Congregazioni Romane" in *Enciclopedia Cattolica,* IV, 1950.

[Sup. to CURIA, 4.] GEORGES A. BARROIS.

CONGRESS, EVANGELICAL SOCIAL: During World War I the work of the Congress in bringing together German Protestants for dis-

cussion and action in social questions was interrupted. The Congress was reorganized in 1923 under the leadership of Johannes Herz, the general secretary. Thereafter annual Congresses were held, Proceedings and the periodical *Evangelisch-Sozial* (to 1944) were published, and an Evangelical Social Institute (destroyed in an air raid, 1943) was established in Leipzig. The work of the organization was impeded by National Socialism and the outbreak of war. After World War II only provincial meetings were held.

BIBLIOGRAPHY: J. Herz, "Protestantismus und soziale Frage," in *Der Protestantismus der Gegenwart,* ed. by O. Schenkel, 1926; *Evangelisches Ringen um soziale Gemeinschaft: 50 Jahre Evang. Soz. Kongress,* 1940.

[Sup.] GEORG WUENSCH.

CONGRUISM: One of the hypotheses devised to reconcile the predetermination of God with the freedom of man, especially with regard to saving grace. Congruism is associated with Francisco Suarez, a Jesuit scholastic (1548–1617), who, in swinging back toward Augustinianism from Molina's (relatively) free-will doctrine, developed this theory. According to congruism, the nature or essence of grace that saves (efficacious grace) is not specifically different from that which does not save (sufficient grace, to use the Thomist word). Efficacious grace is so *ex eventu,* from its effect. According to Molinism, the effectiveness of grace comes in the last analysis from the free choice of him who avails himself of it. According to congruism (which, according to Garrigou-Lagrange, is "whitewashed Molinism"), its effectiveness comes from the foreseen congruity or precise suitability of the grace, the person involved, and the circumstances. As a congruist sees it, God knows in the case of every man infallibly what combination of circumstances and motives will induce him to turn to God and be saved; and therefore, for the elect, God predetermines those circumstances which are "congruent" with his choosing the highest good, and bestows his grace under those precise circumstances.

Congruism is not accepted by Reformed theologians, who teach that saving grace is not only essentially different from any other kind of grace, but is irresistible. It is rejected also by strict Thomists in the Roman Catholic church, but is current as a minority view and has never been specifically condemned, though it seems to be in conflict with, e.g., Canon 9 of the Council of Orange: "Whatever good we do, God operates in us and with us that we may operate." See "Congruism" in the *Catholic Encyclopedia.* For a neo-thomist critique of congruism, see R. Garrigou-Lagrange, *Grace,* Vol. VI, 1952.

KENNETH J. FOREMAN.

CONNELL, FRANCIS J.: Catholic educator; b. Boston, Mass., Jan. 31, 1888. He was educated at Boston Latin School, College, Mt. St.

Alphonsus Seminary, and the University of Angelico, Rome. He is a member of the Redemptorist Order (1908–). He was professor of Dogmatic Theology, Seminary of Mt. St. Alphonsus, Esopus, N. Y. (1915–21, 1924–40). He has taught Moral Theology at the Catholic University of America (1940; Dean of School of Sacred Theology, 1949–). He is author of *Morals in Politics and Professions,* and *De Sacramentis Ecclesiae.*

CONOVER, ELBERT MOORE: Methodist; b. Harrisonville, N. J.; d. Nov. 17, 1952. He studied at Dickinson College and Drew Theological Seminary. He studied architecture in Europe in 1926 and 1932. He was secretary, Department of War Emergency and Reconstruction of the Methodist Episcopal Church (1919–24); assistant superintendent, Department of Church Extension, Methodist Church (1920–24); director of the Bureau of Architecture of the Methodist Episcopal Church (1924–34); director, Interdenominational Bureau of Architecture of the Home Missions Council of North America (1934–50); executive director, Bureau of Church Building and Architecture, National Council of Churches in the United States of America (1951–53). He is author of *Building the House of God* (1928); *The Church Builder* (1948); *The Church School and Parish House Building; Planning Church Buildings; Planning the Small Church; Building for Worship; Ministers' Homes: How to Plan and Build Them; Church Building Finance; Rebuilding the Town and Country Church;* and *Church Building Guide.*

CONRAD OF GELNHAUSEN:
BIBLIOGRAPHY: V. Martin, "Comment s'est formée la doctrine de la superiorité du concile sur le Pape," in *Revue des sciences religieuses,* Vol. 17 (1937), 121–143, 261–289, 405–427.   [Sup.] H. GOOSSENS.

CONRAD OF MARBURG: Belonged to the secular clergy of the diocese of Mainz. He was harsh to himself and others, and even Catholic scholars condemn his injustice and cruelty. But it should be borne in mind that he directed his energies toward the extinction of a group of heretics who taught that Lucifer should be worshiped as God was. They actually went so far as to predict that Lucifer would emerge victorious in the contest with God, and they also were guilty of improper ritual. They probably never became a well organized sect. The first signs of their activity in Germany date from about 1224.
BIBLIOGRAPHY: Art. by E. Amann in *Dict. de Théol. Cath.,* Vol. IX (1926), col. 1044–1056; L. Foerg, *Die Ketzerverfolgung in Deutschland unter Gregor IX,* 1932.   [Sup.] H. GOOSSENS.

CONSCIENTIOUS OBJECTORS: Although the Waldenses (*q.v.*) and others before the Reformation were conscientious objectors to war, the modern Christian objection to participation in armed conflict has its roots in the Reforma-

tion. The peaceful wing of the Anabaptists (*q.v.*) in their desire to recapture the spirit and practices of the New Testament church adhered to the view of Conrad Grebel (*q.v.*), their founder, who declared, "The Gospel and those who accept it are not to be protected with the sword, neither should they thus protect themselves."

The spiritual descendants of these peaceful Anabaptists furnished large numbers of conscientious objectors during the past four centuries. Although the problem of compulsory military service did not become an acute one for European conscientious objectors before the Napoleonic era, several thousand Mennonites (*q.v.*), spiritual heirs of Anabaptism, came to colonial Pennsylvania, where they were guaranteed religious liberty, including exemption from military service. After the Napoleonic wars Mennonites, along with other objectors, migrated to the United States to escape compulsory service. Following the militarization of Prussia, Mennonites left that country and settled in southern Russia, where they were granted exemption from military service. When Russia threatened to withdraw this exemption, more than 15,000 Mennonites emigrated to North America in the 1870's. In the United States and Canada the official position of the various Mennonite bodies has consistently been a witness of conscientious objection to war, although not all members of these churches adhered to the official position.

The Society of Friends (see FRIENDS, RELIGIOUS SOCIETY OF) throughout its history has taken the leadership in obtaining governmental recognition for freedom of conscience on military service. William Penn's "Holy Experiment" in Pennsylvania was designed not only to serve as a haven for those who could not participate in warfare but here an attempt was made to operate a state on a pacifist basis. The Church of the Brethren likewise maintained a witness against Christian participation in war. These three denominations are often referred to as the "historic peace churches," although smaller groups, such as the Brethren in Christ, are affiliated with them in peace conferences.

During America's wars, various official methods of dealing with religious objectors were devised. These experiments, particularly those of World War I, led to the plan of Civilian Public Service under which objectors were drafted to work camps under the United States draft law of 1940. Between 1941 and 1947 nearly 12,000 conscientious objectors to war were drafted under the Selective Training and Service Act of 1940 and assigned to Civilian Public Service camps where they performed "work of national importance." Of these 4,664, 38% were Mennonites, 1,353 were members of the Church of the Brethren, 951 were Friends, and 673 were

Methodists. More than eighty-five religious denominations had three or more conscientious objectors in the United States Civilian Public Service Camps.

The most active interdenominational peace group, the Fellowship of Reconciliation (q.v.), championed the cause of objectors in many countries where they are not given legal recognition.

The Canadian government has been liberal in its treatment of conscientious objectors. During World War II, Canadian objectors served in Alternative Service Work Camps. In March, 1944, a report indicated that 8,932 conscientious objectors had been given postponement of World War II military service in Canada. Of these, approximately 63% were Mennonites, 20% Dukhobors (q.v.), and 10% Plymouth Brethren (q.v.).

During World War II England had 67,000 men provisionally registered as conscientious objectors. Her laws covering objection were liberal. Belgium has no provisions for conscientious objectors. France has few conscientious objectors and no legal provisions for them. The German constitution has legal provisions for conscientious objectors, who since World War II have increased in numbers. The number of objectors in Holland, too, is increasing, where they are given special consideration by law. Italy and Switzerland do not exempt objectors from military service, but the Scandinavian countries have exemption laws. Paraguay, Uruguay, Mexico, and Brazil, where many Mennonites have settled, allow exemption from military service, but Argentina has no such provision.

BIBLIOGRAPHY: Leslie Eisan, Pathways of Peace: A History of the Civilian Public Service Program Administered by the Brethren Service Committee, 1948; Melvin Gingerich, Service for Peace, A History of Mennonite Civilian Public Service, 1949; Guy F. Hershberger, War, Peace, and Nonresistance, 1944; M. Q. Sibley and Philip Jacob, Conscription and Conscience: The American State and the Conscientious Objector, 1940–1947, 1952; Norman Thomas, The Conscientious Objector in America, 1923; Selective Service System, Conscientious Objection, Vols. I and II, 1950.

MELVIN GINGERICH.

CONSERVATISM. See LIBERALISM.

CONSTANCE, COUNCIL OF: The second of the three councils of the Conciliar Movement. The previous Council of Pisa (q.v., Vol. IX), having deposed both the Roman (Gregory XII) and the Avignon (Benedict XIII) popes and elected Alexander V, had, because the deposed popes refused to acknowledge the depositions, left Christendom with three popes instead of two, and the whole of Europe demanded that the scandalous situation be remedied. The emperor of the Holy Roman Empire, Sigismund, aware of public opinion, took the initiative and obliged Pope John XXIII (q.v., Vol. VI), the Pisan successor of Alexander V, to call a general council to meet at Constance. The most vocal

of the supporters of the idea of a council as a body competent to settle the troubles in the Church were Pierre D'Ailly and Jean Gerson (q.v.) who, as heads of the French delegation, were to be the dominant factors in the deliberations and decisions of the council. The theory of conciliar supremacy over the monarchic head of the church had indeed been vigorously discussed since before the return of the papacy to Rome in 1378, but its advocacy by these two high churchmen of great prestige had widened the popular support of the idea with the passage of time and the increasingly distasteful sight of three contending heads of the church.

Constance, which met in forty-five plenary sessions from Nov. 5, 1414, to April 22, 1418, ranks as the best attended of all ecumenical councils. As delegates there attended at least 3 patriarchs, 29 cardinals, 33 archbishops, 150 bishops and almost 200 other prelates of the church, abbots, doctors, etc., all with some or many attendants. The small city of Constance, normally of about 6000 population, entertained with remarkable efficiency almost 50,000 visitors of various sorts, respectable and otherwise. Aside from the principal protagonists, the popes and the emperor, Hus and Jerome, Gerson and D'Ailly, the most impressive participants were Cardinal Robert Hallum, Bishop of Salisbury and his successor from September, 1417 as head of the English "nation," Henry Beaufort, Bishop of Winchester; and the cardinals, Zabarella and Fillastre.

The tasks before the council, by common consent, were primarily three: (1) the healing of the schism (q.v., Vol. X); (2) the condemnation of the Wyclyfite-Hussite heresy (see WYCLYF, JOHN, and HUS, JOHN); (3) the initiation of reform in head and members. Though Pope John had formally convoked the council to meet on Nov. 1, 1414, and was himself with his curia in Constance on Oct. 28, he had done so reluctantly and because he was indebted to Emperor Sigismund for help against King Ladislaus of Naples who had successfully invaded papal territory in Italy. Invitations were sent to the other two popes by the emperor; and Gregory, at least, was represented by two high ranking delegates, yet without thereby recognizing the authority of the council.

The two first tasks of the council, the healing of the schism and the eradication of heresy were attacked almost simultaneously. Problems of procedure had first to be settled, and it was decided, against the wish of John, on Feb. 7, 1415, that voting should be by nations, similarly to the traditional government of the University of Paris. Here the nations of England, France, Italy, and Germany were each given a vote. It was not until 1417 that a fifth vote was given to the Spanish nation. To this extent, and perhaps more, the conciliar movement could be regarded as a transfer to ecclesiastical polity of the principle of political representation, to which Europe, by the early fifteenth century had become somewhat accustomed. Already sentiment at the council that John would have to resign had begun to crystallize, and on Mar. 2, 1415, he publicly promised to do so provided that the other two "pretenders," Benedict and Gregory, do likewise. His sincerity was widely doubted, and his flight from Constance, March 20, and recapture at Breisach, April 23, deprived him of any further credit with the council. On April 6 the council formally declared that its authority came directly from Christ, and that it was superior to any pope or ecclesiastical judicatory outside itself. John was thereupon tried, found guilty of numberless crimes and sins, some doubtless real, others ridiculous, and deposed (May 29, 1415). Imprisoned for a while, he was later (1419) raised to the cardinalate. With John deposed, the way was clear for the resignation or deposition of the two popes who had refused to come to Constance.

In the meantime the trial of John Hus (q.v.) for heresy was under way. As his heresy was related, in the minds of members of the Council with the heresies of John Wyclyf (q.v.) whose works were so popular in Bohemia, it was deemed expedient to condemn the English heresiarch first. At the eighth general session (May 4, 1415), the condemnations of forty-five articles from Wyclyf's writings by the archbishop of Canterbury, the universities of Paris and Prague and the Council of Rome (1412) were reaffirmed. Hus could then be tried upon a background of previous canonical action. Preliminary hearings made it certain that he would not recant, particularly what he had not said or did not believe, and there was nothing left for the council to do but condemn him. The final hearing and condemnation and his burning all took place on the same day (July 6, 1415). Jerome of Prague, on trial for similar doctrines, first recanted and abjured his Wyclyfite ideas (Sept. 11, 1415), but at a public rehearing of his case on May 23, 26, and 30, 1416, withdrew his recantation and heroically suffered burning at the stake. Thus, with the condemnation of Wyclyf's writings and the burning of Hus and Jerome of Prague the second task of the council was discharged.

The schism was not yet healed. Though John had been deposed in May, 1415, there were still two popes. Gregory XII was persuaded that the via cessionis was necessary for him and sent Carlo Malatesta, Lord of Rimini, his last political supporter, to Constance to negotiate a graceful resignation, accepted by the council on July 4, 1415. His cardinals were seated in the council and Gregory given the title of cardinal-bishop of Porto. He died Oct. 18, 1417. Benedict XIII was of sterner stuff. He steadfastly

refused to acknowledge the authority of the council, and was still in 1415 supported by Spain, Portugal, and Scotland. It was important to the legally minded council that, if possible, Benedict resign of his own volition. The Emperor Sigismund, acting as a representative of the council, went to Narbonne and Perpignan to meet Benedict. Discussions lasted for several months, but Sigismund's efforts were in vain and in December, 1415, almost all Benedict's own cardinals, weary of his inflexibility and influenced by King Ferdinand of Aragon, signed the Capitulation of Narbonne (Dec. 13, 1415) supporting a plan for Benedict's deposition by the Council at Constance. Thus strengthened, the council, after ratifying the capitulation (Feb. 4, 1416) and inviting the Spaniards to join the council, repeated its summons to Benedict (Mar. 8, 1417) and listing Benedict's delicts, formally deposed him at the thirty-seventh session (July 26, 1417).

By previous understanding the matter of reform, which had dragged along desultorily in Sigismund's absence (July 18, 1415, to Jan. 27, 1417), was now to be taken up in earnest. Some of the most serious griefs of the church, involving privileges and perquisites of the whole upper clergy, presented inherent difficulties. In the course of the deliberations the zeal of the Italians for reform, never very ardent, cooled, and the German nation also seemed to lose some of its passion for the clerical austerity that reform would involve. The cardinals, whose position in this matter was most vulnerable, gradually gained back some of their prestige, but they were not anxious to punish themselves. Pressures from several quarters for the early election of a pope, now that the previous three were gone or deposed, led to a feeling that the difficult and thorny question of reform would best be the chief task of the new pope, whoever he might be. Yet several reform measures were passed, of which the decree Frequens (Oct. 9, 1417) was the most important. It provided that another general council should convene in five years, a second after seven years, and thereafter regularly every ten years. Other decrees provided for limitation of the number of cardinals (to twenty-four), the curtailment of their habitual nepotism, the limitation of the pope's control over the procurations properly belonging to the bishops, and the pope's disposition of the income of bishoprics during the vacancy of the see. Compared with the hopes of Christendom and the hopes of the elements that wanted reform these were extremely modest achievements. On Oct. 30, 1417, the Council decreed (Sacrosancta generalis synodus) that the pope who was to be elected must assume the task of reforming the church "in head and members" and detailed eighteen heads under which this reformatory work was to be initiated and effected. A goodly proportion of this reform touched vitally the pope's own prerogatives and revenues. Ten days later (Nov. 11, 1417) one of the cardinals who, along with all the other cardinals, had sworn to support and, if elected, carry out this reform program, Odo Colonna, became Pope Martin V. He was a moderate and, not previously active in intrigue, acceptable to the whole Council. Until this election Sigismund had been the dominant factor in the council, and his demands for reform were responsible for whatever was accomplished to correct the admitted abuses. But once a new pope was elected and unity of the church was assured, Sigismund naturally gave way to Martin V.

High hopes for Martin's reform zeal and the implementation of his pre-election promises were almost immediately dashed. His first pontifical act was to issue (though kept secret for some months) the rules by which the papal chancery would function; his rules were almost identical with those of John XXIII which had systematized abuses to the profit of the pope and the cardinals. This was a virtual cancellation of the council's reformatory efforts. Factions and fatigue made it evident that no real reform would be accomplished. Sigismund had himself by now lost interest in the whole question. Several lesser questions came before the pope, among them the demand of the Poles that their dispute with the Teutonic Knights (q.v.) be formally and favorably judged by the pope. Martin, playing for time in the awareness that the council was rapidly disintegrating, avoided making any real decision. The Poles have always since felt that German political pressure had deprived them of justice in their case. Lingering pressures for reform were satisfied by the device of concordats made with the several nations (approved by the whole council on Mar. 21, 1418). But these concordats were basically innocuous. The last session of the council was on April 22, 1418, and Martin left Constance for western Switzerland and Italy on May 16. The third aim of the council, reform, was not carried out in any substantial way, but the schism had been ended and the church could begin to gather its strength for the struggles ahead.

BIBLIOGRAPHY: Basic documents are in H. van der Hardt, Magnum et oecumenicum Constantiense concilium, 6 vols., 1696-1700; Mansi, Conciliorum amplissima collectio, Vols. XXVI, XXVII; Ulrich von Richental, Chronik des Constanzer Concils, 1882; H. Finke, Acta Concilii Constantiensis, 4 vols., 1896-1928. Monographic studies: J. Lenfant, Histoire du Concile de Constance, 2 vols., 1728; J. H. Schwab, Johannes Gerson, 1858; P. Tschackert, Peter von Ailli, 1877; H. Finke, Forschungen und Quellen zur Geschichte des Konstanzer Konzils, 1889; B. Bess, Zur Geschichte des Konstanzer Konzils, 1891; J. H. Wylie, Council of Constance to the death of John Hus, 1900; N. Valois, La France et le Grand Schisme d'Occident, Vol. IV, 1902; E. J. Kitts, Pope John the Twenty-Third and Master John Hus of Bohemia, 1910; Hefele-Leclercq, Histoire des Conciles, Vol. VII, Part I, 1916; G. C. Powers, Nationalism at the Council of Constance, 1927; J. L. Connolly, John Gerson, Reformer and Mystic, 1928; L. Salembier, Le Grand Schism d'Occident, 5th ed., 1922; J. P. McGowan, Pierre D'Ailly and the Council of Constance, 1936; H. Heimpel, Dietrich von Niem 1340-1418, 1932; E. F. Jacob, Essays in the Conciliar Epoch, 2nd ed., 1953. The older accounts of Pastor, History of

the Popes, Vol. I, and M. Creighton, History of the Papacy, Vol. I, can still be consulted with profit. The most convenient bibliography is that in the Cambridge Medieval History, Vol. VIII.
[Sup.] S. HARRISON THOMSON.

CONSTANTINE THE GREAT AND HIS SONS: The legendary frescoes in the chapel of San Silvester, depicting Constantine as summoning Silvester for a cure and his subsequent baptism by Silvester, are but part of the maze of myth that developed in rapport with his genuinely apocalyptic disposition. Legend seems to have seized upon his baptism (by Eusebius of Nicomedia) in an attempt to trace subordination of the state to the church back to the first Christian emperor.

The exact reasons for the execution of Crispus and for the death of Fausta will probably never be known.

BIBLIOGRAPHY: De mortibus persecutorum, ascribed to Lactantius; Orations of the Panegyrici, vi–x; Aurelius Victor, De Caesaribus; Eutropius, Breviarium historiae romanae; J. B. Firth, Constantine the Great, 1905; Cambridge Mediaeval History, I. 1, 1911; F. J. Doelger, Konstantin der Grosse und seine Zeit, 1913; C. B. Coleman, Constantine the Great and Christianity, 1914; O. Seeck, Geschichte des Untergangs der Antiken Welt, I. 4. Auflage, 1921; J. Burckhardt, Das Zeitalter Konstantin des Grossen, 4. Auflage, 1924; V. Burch, Myth and Constantine the Great, 1927; E. Stein, Geschichte des spaetroemischen Reiches, I. 1928; G. P. Baker, Constantine the Great and the Christian Revolution, 1931; E. Schwartz, Kaiser Constantin und die christliche Kirche, 1936; L. B. Holsapple, Constantine the Great, 1942; J. d'Elbée, Constantin le Grand, 1947; A. Alfoeldi, The Conversion of Constantine and Pagan Rome, trans. by H. Mattingly, 1948; A. H. M. Jones, Constantine and the Conversion of Europe, 1948; J. Vogt, Constantin der Grosse und sein Jahrhundert, 1949.
[Sup.] DANIEL JOHANNES THERON.

CONSTITUTION OF CHURCH IN EARLY CHRISTIANITY. See CHURCH, CONSTITUTION OF, IN EARLY CHRISTIANITY.

CONTARINI, GASPARO: One of the greatest Roman Catholic contemporaries of Luther, very scholarly and talented. His kindly, irenic temperament and his gentle optimism exerted a favorable influence upon many friends and foes. He was eminently qualified to train a new school of future cardinals who shared his views. Among them was Pope Pius V and also some of his successors. They became superb leaders of the Catholic Church in the period of the Counter or Catholic Reformation, when this church emerged in a manner well worthy of the best intellects.

BIBLIOGRAPHY: H. Rueckert, Die theologische Entwicklung G. Contarinis, 1926; Fr. Huenermann, Gasparo Contarini, Gegenreformatorische Schriften, 1923.
[Sup.] H. GOOSSENS.

CONTEMPLATION: For Aristotle the life of the philosopher was one of "seeing," and Latin writers translated his bios theoretikos as contemplatio. In the Nicomachean Ethics he states that contemplation is the highest activity of which human nature is capable, since it is the sole activity of God, and brings with it the most enduring satisfaction (10. 7). For him, as for Greek thought generally, the primary significance of "contemplation" is the active investigation of intellectual problems and meditation upon the truth which is thus attained. Yet Aristotle gives the name of "theology" to the highest branch of contemplation, and this seems to imply a meditation upon the divine nature which is akin to worship (Met. 5.1). It is in the thought of Plato however that contemplation assumes most clearly the character of religious aspiration, and it is in him that the main stream of Western mysticism has its origin. The philosopher is the "true lover" who recollects the glimpses he had of the supersensuous world in his pre-natal existence: "He forgets earthly interests and is rapt in the divine . . . and when he sees the beauty of earth, is transported with the recollection of true beauty" (Phaedrus 249D). He begins with the love of beautiful forms, but ascends through the love of beautiful actions to beautiful notions, until at last he reaches "absolute Beauty." "This . . . is that life above all others which man should live . . . beholding Beauty with the eye of the mind, he will be enabled . . . to become the friend of God and be immortal, if mortal man may" (Symposium 212A).

In Neo-Platonism the material world is regarded as an emanation from the One, the body is a prison, and salvation consists in an escape from the world back to God. Its ultimate goal is a union with God in a state of ecstasy in which the subject-object relationship which is characteristic of discursive reason has been transcended. Pseudo-Dionysius united the thought of Plotinus with Christianity in a mysticism which emphasized the "way of negation," enjoining a type of contemplation which renounced the activity of the intellect as well as the world of the senses, in its effort to achieve union with "that which is beyond all seeing and understanding" (Myst. Theol. 1:1, 2).

The anti-intellectualism of Pseudo-Dionysius may be contrasted with the mysticism of the school of St. Victor in which the vision of God requires not only purity of heart, intensity of love, and moral effort, but intellectual travail as well. Although the goal of contemplation is an ecstatic union with God, the road to it lies through "reflection" and "meditation," which includes a study of the works of God, and of the order and harmony of the universe. For Thomas Aquinas, too, contemplation involves a life of study and a passion for truth; and the intuitive and immediate vision of God is never fully realized in this life at all, but is reserved for eternity.

Bernard of Clairvaux distinguished "consideration" from "contemplation," the object of the former being the sensible world, and of the latter the supersensuous world of the angels and of the Divine Being. Consideration must be the steppingstone to contemplation; we must know the sensible world before we can know God. The distinction of Bernard however is in the prominence which he gave to the earthly life of Jesus as the fitting object of Christian meditation. He returns to the theme of the Fourth Gospel in his insistence that we have the vision of God "in the face of Jesus Christ." The glorified Christ, who is the "Bridegroom of the soul" is to be known through a loving meditation on the incidents in his earthly life. This "Christ-mysticism," as it has been called, has had an enduring influence on Catholic piety, and in the work of the Franciscans and in the devotional writings of St. Francis de Sales, and Ignatius of Loyola.

Protestantism has tended to depreciate the contemplative life and to reject the mystical approach to God. Friedrich Heiler (q.v.) has drawn a sharp distinction between two types of religion, the "mystical" and the "prophetic," and maintained that the former is not distinctively Christian, even though it has had its finest examples among Christian mystics, but the latter is "biblical" and "evangelical," and is represented very clearly by the piety of Luther. Justification by faith is opposed to the conception of man's ascent to God by the mystical ladder of purgation, illumination, and union, and so prayer consists chiefly in petition and thanksgiving rather than in meditation and contemplation.

In seventeenth century pietism there emerged on Protestant soil a type of mysticism whose distinctive feature is an emphasis upon the indwelling of the Holy Spirit in the heart of the believer. This "Spirit-mysticism" is distinguished by its dynamic character from mysticism of the Oriental or "classical" type, and stress is laid upon action rather than contemplation. The spiritual rebirth which is the height of the believer's experience cannot be induced by any human effort, but is entirely the work of the Spirit.

The contemporary Protestant theologians who have been influenced by the neo-Reformation thought of Barth (q.v.), Brunner (q.v), Nygren (q.v.), and Niebuhr (q.v.) have agreed with Ritschl (q.v.) in attacking mysticism. (See NEO-ORTHODOXY.) In *Agape and Eros* Nygren maintains that mysticism is an alien intrusion of the motif of Eros into Christian theology, and that it is basically egocentric in its attempt to raise up the soul to God. The true motif of Christianity is Agape, which is the descending love of God bestowed freely on man, in spite of his sinfulness which he can in no way remedy by his own effort or aspiration.

It remains true, however, that many modern Protestants have turned to the devotional writings of the great Catholic mystics for inspiration for prayer and worship, and many of them, especially within the Anglican communion, have sought to combine contemplation with an active life of service, without abandoning their Protestant heritage.

See also MYSTICISM AND ASCETICISM IN THE NETHERLANDS; MYSTICISM, MEDIEVAL.

BIBLIOGRAPHY: Kenneth E. Kirk, *The Vision of God*, 1931; Edward C. Butler, *Western Mysticism*, 1922; Rufus Jones, *Studies in Mystical Religion*, 1928; Evelyn Underhill, *Mysticism*, 1930; Friedrich Heiler, *Prayer*, Eng. tr., 1932; Anders Nygren, *Agape and Eros*, Eng. tr., 1937–39.

ANTHONY S. CHADWICK.

CONTINENCE: Abstinence from sexual intercourse; not to be confused with chastity (*q.v.*) nor with celibacy (the unmarried state, in which there may be neither continence nor chastity). This confusion is to be seen in the Roman Catholic vow of "chastity" taken by "religious," which really means continence. From primitive times it has often been a policy of cults to require continence of the charismatic figures (priests, priestesses, shamai, fakirs, etc.), because of the psychosexual tendency to find an opposition between "holiness" and sexuality. The Hebrew priests were an exception. For all others, continence has ordinarily been regarded as unnatural and antisocial, except in the prenuptial state. Deviation from this norm has been found only in extreme ascetical movements demanding continence of their followers. Jesus' words in Matt. 19:12, that some "made themselves eunuchs for the kingdom of heaven's sake," are often taken as a scriptural basis for continence. But only the most absolute literalism would take this to mean emasculation; "eunuch" is most obviously a metaphor meaning a self-denying son of God who is prepared to forego even good things, if need be, out of loyalty to God's will. St. Paul in I Cor. 7 seems to recommend (but not to require) continence, but this is to be seen as uttered in an apocalyptic context. See also BIGAMY and SEX, ETHICS OF.

JOSEPH FLETCHER.

CONTRITION: Contrition is essentially a Roman Catholic term. Its meaning for Roman theology was thoroughly elaborated at the Council of Trent. It is always linked with their doctrine of doing penance and becomes efficacious for salvation when united with the sacrament of penance; or, in the absence of this sacrament, when the sinner makes an "effort to elicit a perfect act of contrition." This is, of course, salvation by the works of man, not by the grace of God.

The word contrition does not occur in the Bible. The "contrite heart" spoken of (Psalms 34:18, Isaiah 57:15) is the heart crushed or bruised by its sense of guilt. Such a heart God does not despise but rather forgives, not because it merits forgiveness but because of his grace.

There is, in the New Testament, a godly sorrow for sin (II Cor. 7:7–10) which leads to repentance, but it is never linked to a sacrament. It never earns forgiveness for the sinner. It does enable him to receive the grace of God in forgiveness apart from any sacrament.

For further discussion from the Roman Catholic point of view, see *Catholic Encyclopedia*, Vol. IV. W. D. CHAMBERLAIN.

CONVENTICLE ACT: In 1726 Sweden published a strict edict against Pietism and conventicles, threatening transgressors with fines, imprisonment, and even banishment. The act did not destroy the Pietistic movement, and in time it became a dead letter, although it remained on the statute books until 1858. The severity of this law must bear a large share of responsibility for the cleavage between revivals and the church in Sweden.

In Norway and Denmark (then united) a conventicle act was enacted in 1741 by a Pietistic court (Christian VI). Its purpose was to promote and regulate conventicles and to guard against sectarianism. It admonished pastors to be active in promoting spiritual life. Conventicles in homes were to be led by pastors. Other gatherings in private houses for mutual edification were permitted. But attendance at such gatherings was limited to only a few people besides members of a household, men and women separately, and food or drink were not to be served. Those who disturbed such gatherings were threatened with punishment. Travel on the pretext of edification or revival was prohibited, as was usurpation of the teaching ministry belonging to clergymen. It was under this last provision that Hans Nielsen Hauge (*q.v.*, Vol. V) suffered imprisonment. In Norway the act was repealed in 1842 after much opposition by Haugeans and political liberals. In Denmark the same act was repealed when full religious liberty was granted in 1849.

[Sup.] IVER IVERSEN.

CONVERSION: Writers on the psychology of religion (*q.v.*) paid not nearly as much attention to conversion during the second quarter of the century (see EMPIRICAL THEOLOGY). Perhaps this was a reflection of changing religious mores and ideas. After the middle thirties, the word "conversion" was used popularly with reference to ideologies as well as to religion. Alcoholics Anonymous (*q.v.*) made it evident that freedom from alcoholism involves a conversion. At mid-century, conversion was coming back into its own, with its insights refined. These points seemed clear:

(1) Conversion means a turning around, a changing of the way of life, a reversal of goal, a new center of orientation. For Christians, that new center of orientation is Jesus Christ, the

way, the truth and the life, the revelation of the Father (John 14:6).

(2) Conversion may be dramatic or developmental, sudden or gradual, cataclysmic, or a peak moment in a life that has always been Christian. The line between these two basic types is not razor-sharp. The sudden conversion has antecedents, and the quiet conversion has some deep emotions connected with it.

(3) Conversion may occur at any age. Political conversions, and the conversions wrought by the aid of the psychiatrist or Alcoholics Anonymous are adult conversions. The same psychological process sometimes results in a religious conversion for adults. Whereas Starbuck (q.v.) and Coe at the turn of the century found the average age of conversion was 16.4, E. T. Clark in 1929 found the average age to be 12.7. While there were a goodly number of conversions among the men in the armed forces during 1940–45, probably the age of conversion at midcentury lay in the junior high school years, ages 12–14.

(4) Both the type of conversion and the time thereof are greatly influenced by custom, social expectation, and training. In isolated mountain areas, some folk still expect to be converted twice annually, and that with shoutings and groanings and other cataclysmic phenomena. In city churches for the middle class, conversions are not highly emotional or overly dramatic. In the churches, as distinguished from the sects (q.v.), conversion comes during the junior high school years, as the natural climax of Christian nurture in family and in church.

(5) Conversion does not occur in a vacuum. Even in a Damascus road experience, the psychologist can clearly discern antecedents. The individual is prepared for his conversion, be it sudden or gradual, by the experiences of his life. The theologian believes in the guidance of the Holy Spirit (q.v.), in the prevenient grace of God, as the inner cause of these experiences. The psychologist, qua psychologist, cannot use such terms, but the things he describes as the preparation for the conversion are best seen through the eyes of faith. In any religious conversion there have been some external causes, such as the plea of a preacher or the loving word and deed of a parent or sudden danger, and there have been internal causes, which may be described dynamically. The converted person is one who has been changed, and where there is change there is release from conflict and tension, a unified self takes the place of a divided self, life is re-evaluated, and new purposes motivate.

(6) Theologically, such religious conversion is the result of a new birth. Conversion is the human response to regeneration. It results, therefore, for the religious, in a vital new relationship with God, so that "life becomes new,"

God is one's supreme joy, Christ one's Saviour, and, with Masefield's Saul Kane, one desires "to brother all the souls on earth." Light takes the place of darkness; assurance of pardon overcomes self-condemnation; peace is where strife was; Christ, not self, is now central; and one desires to share with all men this joy.

(7) Conversion is not the end, for the religious life is a process. The sudden conversion may be to the consciousness the beginning of the life of religion, but there will follow growth, and plateaus of stagnation, and backslidings, but the more real the conversion, the more certain the over-all steady growth. In the gradual conversion, rather than one peak moment, there may be a series of peak moments when great decisions are made. There is a sense in which a person may have not one, but many conversions, as new areas of his life are brought into line with the will of God. Yet all of these grow out of the original conversion. Or, more properly, in the eyes of faith, out of the regenerating grace of God expressing itself in that initial conversion.

See also CONTEMPLATION; CONVICTION OF SIN; FORGIVENESS.

BIBLIOGRAPHY: E. T. Clark, The Psychology of Religious Awakening, 1926; G. A. Coe, The Psychology of Religion, 1916; Paul Johnson, The Psychology of Religion, 1946; J. B. Pratt, The Religious Consciousness, 1920; John Masefield, The Everlasting Mercy.

[Sup.] HARRY G. GOODYKOONTZ.

CONVICTION OF SIN: The state of moral certainty or persuasion that one is a sinner. It is not itself an experience of conversion (q.v.), but is a path leading in that direction. It may come quietly as the result of deep contemplation, or it may burst upon the soul suddenly in anguish of fear or remorse. It is often induced by a weariness with sin (q.v.) which has long been practiced, and by a growing hatred of its power. In its more terrifying forms it is typical of those who have come through experiences of stubborn resistance, as Paul, or of gross wrongdoing, as Augustine. Conviction may soon find relief in an assurance of the regenerating work of God, or it may continue for some time before the sense of forgiveness (q.v.) assuages its grief. Especially during revival meetings of high emotional appeal, it may be attended by prolonged physical and mental sufferings (see REVIVALS OF RELIGION; EXPERIENCE, RELIGIOUS). An inner struggle against conviction is frequent when the conscience is aroused in teen-age youth.

Scripture teaches that conviction of sin is essentially the work of the Holy Spirit (q.v.) (John 16:8–10), and must be followed by conviction of righteousness and of judgment before that work is finished. God uses various means to bring the individual to a conviction of sin. Thus the Bible can speak of it as the work of the Lord (Jude 1:5) and especially of the law

(Titus 1:9). So also a spiritually minded church or preacher can be said to bring conviction of sin, the sense of moral blame being awakened by public refutation (Acts 18:28; I Cor. 14:24). The need for conviction of sin is universal, the unique exception being Jesus who challenged anyone to convict him (John 8:46).

JULIAN PRICE LOVE.

CONWELL, RUSSELL HERMAN: D. Dec. 6, 1925. During the last third of his long life, Conwell saw the fruits of his vision and labor mature in the development of the very strong congregation at the Baptist Temple in Philadelphia (1891–1925), and in the phenomenal growth of Temple University of which he was founder and president (1888–1925). Most famous of his lyceum lectures was the *Acres of Diamonds*, first published in 1888, the income from which was used entirely in developing his university, largely by providing generous aid for needy students. His other publications include: *Observation* (1916); *What You Can Do With Your Will Power* (1917); *Effective Prayer* (1920); *The Angel's Lily* (1920); *Sermons for Occasions* (1921); *Unused Powers* (1922); *Why Lincoln Laughed* (1922); and *Borrowed Axes* (1923).

[Sup.] RAYMOND W. ALBRIGHT.

CONYBEARE, FREDERICK CORNWALLIS: D. Jan. 9, 1924. Among other works he wrote: *Myth, Magic, and Morals: a Study of Christian Origins* (1909); *History of New Testament Criticism* (1910); *The Ring of Pope Xystus together with the Prologue of Rufinus: now first rendered into English with an Historical and Critical Commentary* (1910); *The Historical Christ* (1914); *Russian Dissenters* (1921). In 1896 he contributed to *Studia Biblica et Ecclesiastica* an edition of the *Acta Pilati*, and in 1905 edited both *Letters and Exercises of the Elizabethan Schoolmaster, John Conybeare* and, with St. George Stock, selections from the LXX. In 1907 he edited and translated an Armenian version of Revelation. He translated several Greek romances, among them (in 1912) *The Life of Apollonius* by Philostratus. In 1922 he prepared the section on Old Armenian liturgies for *Patrologia Orientalis*. From 1913 until his death he was instrumental in cataloguing Armenian manuscripts, first in the British Museum, then in the Bodleian Library at Oxford, and finally at the Vatican.

[Sup.] RAYMOND W. ALBRIGHT.

COOK, STANLEY ARTHUR: B. at Kings Lynn, April 12, 1873; d. at Cambridge, Sept. 20, 1949. He studied at Cambridge, where he became a Fellow of Gonville and Caius College (1904–49). He was Lecturer in Hebrew (1904–32), and in Comparative Religion (1912–20), and Regius Professor of Hebrew (1932–38). He was a pupil of W. Robertson Smith, with whom

he collaborated in working on the *Encyclopaedia Biblica* and whose influence he always showed. His range of interests was extraordinarily wide, and his power to stimulate and encourage younger scholars exceptional. His publications include: *A Glossary of the Aramaic Inscriptions* (1898); *The Laws of Moses and the Code of Hammurabi* (1903); *Critical Notes on Old Testament History* (1907); *The Religion of Ancient Palestine in the Second Millennium B.C. in the light of Archaeology and the Inscriptions* (1908); *The Study of Religions* (1914); *The Old Testament: A Reinterpretation* (1936); *The "Truth" of the Bible* (1938); *The Rebirth of Christianity* (1942); *An Introduction to the Bible* (1945). In addition he completed W. Wright's *A Catalogue of the Syriac Manuscripts preserved in the Library of the University of Cambridge* (1901), edited a new edition of W. R. Smith's *Religion of the Semites* and a posthumous volume of essays by R. H. Kennett. He was joint editor of the *Cambridge Ancient History*, for which he wrote a number of chapters. His work for the *Encyclopaedia Britannica* (11th ed.) received far less notice than it deserved. A volume of essays was prepared in his honour, but was not published until after his death, under the title *Essays and Studies* presented to Stanley Arthur Cook by members of the Faculty of Divinity and Oriental Languages in the University of Cambridge, Edited by D. Winton Thomas (1951).   H. H. ROWLEY.

COONEYITES: A sect founded about 1885 in Northern Ireland by William Irvine and George Walker but later dominated by Edward Cooney. Also called Go-Preachers (Mark 16:15), its traveling exhorters attacked churches and clergymen, education and luxury, smoking and drinking. It spread to other parts of Great Britain and to North America but gradually declined.   THEODORE G. TAPPERT.

CO-OPERATIVE: A voluntary association of individuals carrying on non-profit-making self-managed economic activities. Voluntary economic societies have been present throughout history. Two British co-operative associations, the Sheerness Economical and the Lennoxtown Victualing Societies, have unbroken histories from the period of the Napoleonic Wars. But the modern co-operative movement dates from the establishment in 1844 of the Rochdale Co-operative Society, organized by twenty-eight workers, the majority of them flannel weavers and Owenites.

The end of the eighteenth and the beginning of the nineteenth centuries was a period of great industrial development and considerable economic distress for the masses of workers in Great Britain. Robert Owen (*q.v.*, Vol. VIII), who at the age of twenty-one was a partner in a group of mills in Scotland, became distressed at the care given machines and at the ruthless exploitation of their human operators. He instituted reforms without launching the co-operative movement. However, he did contribute to economic theory and practice the concept of "co-operation." Owenism became the leaven giving rise, via Rochdale, to a movement which, in 1951, had more than 150,000,000 members engaged in a variety of co-operative economic activities throughout the world.

Co-operatives are strongest in Great Britain and Scandinavia. In North America the movement has not been uniformly successful. Among the more spectacular recent gains were those sustained by co-operative credit unions which added new associations at the rate of more than 100 per month during 1951.

The more popular enterprises maintained by the societies are stores, laundries, gasoline filling stations, houses, restaurants, insurance companies, health services, banks, credit unions, power lines, and agricultural operations.

Underlying and essential to all such activities are: (1) ownership of the enterprises by the consumer or producer members; (2) economic democracy based on one vote per member; and (3) nonprofit operation. These have been cardinal principles of co-operatives ever since 1844.

The movement has received support from many Protestant denominations in addition to the following major religious bodies: the Federal Council of Churches of Christ in America (q.v.), the National Catholic Welfare Conference (q.v.), the United Church of Canada (q.v.), and the Oxford Conference on Church, Community, and State (see ECUMENICAL MOVEMENT).

BIBLIOGRAPHY: P. H. Casselman, *The Co-operative Movement and Some of Its Problems*, 1952; G. D. H. Cole, *A Century of Co-operation*, 1945; M. Digby, *The World Co-operative Movement*, 1950; B. Fowler, *The Co-operative Challenge*, 1947; G. Mladenatz, *Histoire des Doctrines Coopératives*, 1933.

CHARLES GARABED CHAKERIAN.

COPE, HENRY FREDERICK: Baptist; b. June 17, 1870, at London, Eng.; d. Aug. 3, 1923. He was educated privately in England and after arrival in the United States studied at Ripon College (A.B., 1908) and at the Southern Baptist Theological Seminary. After ordination to the Baptist ministry in 1893 he served pastorates in Rochester, N. Y. (1894–95); Plano, Ill. (1895–98); and Dillon, Mont. (1898–1903). For two years he taught and lectured in Chicago and thereafter was associated with the Religious Education Association (assistant secretary, 1905–07; general secretary, 1907–23). In addition to editing *Religious Education* (1906–23) he wrote: *The Modern Sunday School in Principle and Practice* (1907); *Levels of Living* (1908); *The Friendly Life* (1909); *The Efficient Layman* (1910); *Efficiency in the Sunday School* (1912); *Religious Education in the Family* (1915); *The*

Modern Sunday School and its Present-Day Task (1916); *Religious Education in the Church* (1917); *The School in the Modern Church* (1919); *Parent and Child* (1921); *The Week-Day Church School* (1921); and *Principles of Christian Service* (1921).

RAYMOND W. ALBRIGHT.

COPEC. See CONFERENCE ON CHRISTIAN POLITICS, ECONOMICS, AND CITIZENSHIP.

CORINTHIANS, EPISTLES TO THE. See PAUL THE APOSTLE.

CORNELISZ (CORNELII), ARENT: B. Jan. 14, 1547, at Delft; d. June 5, 1605, at Delft. He was also called Croesius or Kroese (Crusius). He studied at Heidelberg under Ursinus and at Geneva. He was pastor at Frankenthal (1571–73) as colleague of Van der Heyden (q.v.) and at Delft (1573–1605). Twice he declined the offer of a professorship at Leiden. For some time he was perhaps the outstanding Calvinist in the province of Holland. He presided over the national synod at Middelburg in 1581, and acted as secretary at the synods of Dordrecht in 1574 and 1578, while at the national synod at The Hague in 1586 he was assessor. He also was called upon to perform other tasks, such as that of translator of the Bible upon the death of Marnix of St. Aldegonde in 1598, working with Helmichius. He was a member of the committee that was called together by the provincial estates of Holland to prepare a church ordinance (1583), and again in 1591 for the same purpose. In 1578 he and Donteclock held a debate with Coornhert concerning the Reformed and Roman Catholic denominations. From March 5 to 8, and May 25 to 29, 1577, he and his colleague Thomas Filius disputed with a Lutheran preacher at Woerden about the doctrine of baptism, continuing the dispute in pamphlets. In 1584 he baptized the young prince Frederick Henry, and on Aug. 3, 1584, he delivered the funeral sermon for William of Orange, who had been assassinated in Delft. The Reformed Church in Delft flourished greatly under his leadership. He translated the Belgic Confession into Dutch (a translation which was published in 1583 at Dordrecht); he also translated some commentaries of Calvin. He was a moderate Calvinist, opposing those who sought to make much of little points in the creed. For example, he disapproved of the supralapsarianism of Beza, whom on the whole he revered. His thoughtful and careful consideration of disputed problems in an age of vehement outbursts of anger and vituperation gave further height to his stature.

BIBLIOGRAPHY: *Biogr. Woordenboek van Prot. Godgeleerden in Nederland*, in Vol. V, with bibliogr.; H. J. Jaanus, *Hervormd Delft ten tijde van Arent Cornelisz*, (1573–1605), 1950.

D. NAUTA.

CORRUPTION: In biblical thought the idea of corruption is similar to that of pollution. Corruption is both a manifestation and a result of sin. God made man perfect and placed him in a perfect environment. But by sinning against God, man became guilty (subject to condemnation) and corrupt or vile. The idea of guilt and corruption are supplemental. By virtue of sin man is loathsome in his guilt and guilty in his vile estate. Moreover, the idea of ethical corruption in man and physical corruption in his environment are supplemental.

In non-biblical thought there was no perfect creation of man or the world. Thus the corruption of man does not involve guilt. Nor is the corruption of the universe directly dependent upon human sin. Corruption is an inherent aspect of reality.

In biblical thought, the Son of God has come to remove corruption from the heart of man and, eventually, in the "regeneration of all things," from the cosmos. He does so by dying for his own, removing their guilt, meriting eternal life for them. Thus, the corruption of their hearts is, in principle, removed. And, in the new heavens and on the new earth, all corruption in man and in the cosmos will have disappeared.

The biblical point of view must be accepted on the authority of Scripture. Then it appears that only on its basis is there any firm distinction between perfection and corruption or any solid foundation for human hope.

See Young's *Concordance* for biblical references and works on dogmatics for doctrinal discussions.   CORNELIUS VAN TIL.

CORSON, FRED PIERCE: Methodist bishop; b. in Millville, N. J.; April 11, 1896. He is a graduate of Dickinson College and Drew University. After serving as a district superintendent (1929–34), he became president of Dickinson College (1934–44) and a bishop of the Methodist Church (1944–). He has written *The Dilemma of the Liberated; Free Masonry and the Framing of the Constitution; The Education We Have and the Education We Need; The Pattern of a Church; Your Church and You; Introduction to Wesley's New Testament; Living Successfully;* and *The Education of a Christian.*

CORVEY: After 1820 the building complex of Hessen-Rotenburg was constructed. The ruler established here a library, in which later the famous Hoffmann von Fallersleben was librarian (1860–74). He was buried in the church. Of the old church building the ninth-century Romanesque west front has been preserved. About the year 1100 this was increased with the bell tower and enclosed by two square towers. The entrance is baroque (end of the seventeenth

cent.), while the nave, which looks Gothic, was constructed from 1667 to 1675.

BIBLIOGRAPHY: P. Lehmann, *Korveyer Studien,* 1919; W. Effmann-Fuchs, *Die Kirche der Abtei Korvey,* 1929.
[Sup.] H. GOOSSENS.

COSMOLOGY: Cosmology, the science of the form of the physical world, is based on the principle that the world has a form and so is a cosmos, not a chaos. Its development has passed through four stages marked by four theories of space—space as having an absolute up and down, space as spherical, space as homogeneous and infinite, and space as heterogeneous and finite.

I. Space as having an absolute up and down: The most obvious law of the physical world is that we fall down, not up, when unsupported. That the three-dimensional space in which we live is characterized by two directions, one way up and the opposite way down, is a universal fact of experience. Early cosmological theories, assuming without question that space has an absolute up and down, explained in terms of this principle the great phenomena of the world— the daily cycle of the sky which causes day and night, the monthly cycle of the moon's phases, the annual cycle of the sun around the zodiac which brings the seasons, and the complicated yet regular motions of the planets. They described the world as being what it appears to be, a dome-shaped structure with heaven above and earth below. The Babylonians believed that below the flat earth on which we live is a subterranean ocean ("the waters under the earth") and below that the underworld home of the dead; and that above the sky where the stars shine is a supercelestial region of light and above that the "third heaven" where God dwells.

Scientific cosmology was founded by Anaximander of Miletus (610–545 B.C.), who, defying all common sense, asserted that "the earth is a heavenly body supported by nothing." He thus introduced the scientific notion of the earth as being a body in the universe, not itself the base of the universe. He explained that the earth, which he described as a cylinder with diameter three times its thickness, does not fall down "because of its equal distance from all things," and this suggestion that the earth is somehow at the center, rather than the bottom, of the world pointed the way to the next stage of cosmology.

II. Space as Spherical: Philolaus of Tarentum (5th century B.C.), a cosmologist of the Pythagorean School, established the second era of cosmology by his insight that the daily motion in which all celestial bodies concur can best be explained as an apparent motion due to a real motion of the earth from which they are observed. This implies that up and down are not absolute directions in space, for the direction which is up at any time will be down twelve hours later. He supposed the earth to revolve daily about a central point, keeping one flat surface always toward this point and the other (on which we live) always away from it. This point is the center of a spherical universe: all directions toward it are down, and all directions away from it are up. Since the revolving earth must also rotate, and it is the rotation which actually explains the apparent motion of the heavenly bodies, Philolaus' followers recognized that the theory of revolution could be dispensed with, without failing to save the phenomena, by thinking of the earth as spherical and rotating on its own axis. This geocentric theory, that the earth is a sphere at the center of space, dominated cosmological thought for two thousand years.

The theory of spherical space required a new consideration of the celestial bodies. Eudoxus of Cnidos (406–353 B.C.) showed that the apparent motions of the planets can be analyzed into a number of unaccelerated circular motions around the earth, and he described this analysis by the hypothesis of twenty-seven concentric spheres, which rotate in a regular way relative to one another, and to seven of which the planets are attached.

Aristotle (385–322 B.C.), who treated cosmology as part of an all-embracing system of philosophy, denied that the earth rotates. The combined problem of the daily motion of the whole sky and the special motions of the planets he solved by reinterpreting Eudoxus' hypothetical spheres as material spheres (invisible because transparent) actually rotating around the earth. They are composed of a "fifth element" which naturally moves in circles, unlike earth, water, air, and fire, which naturally move straight down or up. The outermost sphere of the fixed stars is moved immediately by God, and its motion is transmitted to the lower ones. This theory survived for a long time in popular and literary cosmology, and found a classical expression in Dante's (q.v.), *Divine Comedy*, where the devil is placed at the center of space, head and feet both extending upward, and the saints are distributed among the celestial spheres according to their respective merits.

The theory of spheres was soon replaced in scientific thought, however, by the theory of epicycles proposed by Apollonius of Perga (250–200 B.C.). He gave a new analysis of planetary motion based on the hypothesis that each planet moves on a circle ("epicycle") the center of which moves on a larger circle ("deferent") around the earth. This theory was elaborated by Hipparchus (2nd century B.C.) and Claudius Ptolemy (A.D. 100–170) into the "Ptolemaic system" by which future positions of all planets could be predicted.

Observed deviations from calculated positions could only be explained, on this theory, by assuming subordinate epicycles moving on the principal epicycle, and the accumulation of such observations led to an intolerable complication of the system. Finally Nicolaus Copernicus (1473–1543) proposed that the observed motions could be explained and predicted with equal accuracy and greater simplicity by considering that the sun is fixed at the center of space, that the earth revolves around it once a year, and that the other planets likewise revolve in circular orbits around the sun (except the moon, which clearly revolves around the earth). The apparent motion of the planets is then explained as being due partly to their own real motion around the sun and partly to the observer's motion on the earth. This implies that the fixed stars, which show no annual displacement, are very distant, and consequently that their daily motion must be due to the earth's rotating. The practical advantages of the heliocentric theory were obvious, but its cosmological difficulties were considerable. Copernicus still considered space to be spherical, with the sun at the center and the fixed stars at the periphery, but the force of gravity by which things fall on the earth had to be considered a local phenomenon not to be explained by the structure of space.

The way for a new cosmology was prepared by two brilliant scientists. John Kepler (1571–1630) demonstrated by an analysis of accurate observations that the orbit of each planet is not a circle but an ellipse with the sun at one focus, and that a planet's velocity and period of revolution are functions of its distance from the sun. These empirical laws involved a radical departure from previous cosmological theory, which had always assumed that celestial motions are, in some way or other, circular. Galileo Galilei (1546–1642), by using a telescope, discovered that there are many more stars than the 5,000 visible to the naked eye, their number seeming to be unlimited and to depend only on the power of the telescope.

III. Space as homogeneous and infinite: The third cosmology was associated with the modern classical system of mechanics developed by Isaac Newton (1642–1727). Bringing terrestrial and celestial mechanics into a single science (as against Aristotle's theory that they have different laws), he formulated the law of universal gravitation and by it explained both terrestrial phenomena and the motions of the planets. The cosmological implications were revolutionary. Gravitation depends on mass, not place, being determined by the propinquity of massive bodies, not by the structure of space. Space itself, consequently, is homogeneous, with no fixed direction or fixed point which is down. Having no center, it has no periphery, but is of infinite extent.

Cosmology, hitherto concerned primarily with

the solar system, was extended to the fixed stars by the new science of spectroscopy, developed especially by Joseph von Fraunhofer (1727–1826). The spectroscope shows that the stars are composed of the same kinds of matter known on earth, and that the sun is a typical star. It also provides a technique for calculating the distance of a star. The nearest stars are found to be twenty-five trillion miles or four light years away (as compared with the moon, distant 240,000 miles or one light second). Other stars have distances reckoned in thousands of light years. Some are believed to be hundreds of millions of miles in diameter. Other observed objects include nebulae hundreds of light years across and clusters containing millions of stars themselves a light year or so apart.

The Milky Way, inside which we are, was shown to be a disc-shaped universe of billions of stars, thousands of light years in diameter. A still vaster perspective on the physical world came with the discovery that the Andromeda "Nebula" is a galaxy comparable in size with the Milky Way itself, containing billions of stars, and a million light years away. Millions of such galaxies, each containing millions of stars, are known to astronomers. More recently supergalaxies, which are systems containing many galaxies, have been observed in numbers and at distances which seem limited only by the power of our telescopes. It would seem that the physical world consists of an infinite number of stars, arranged in an infinite number of galaxies, distributed throughout an infinite space.

Meanwhile other approaches to cosmology appeared in the writings of Immanuel Kant (1724–1804), who argued that the laws of science are subjective and therefore apply only to phenomena of experience, and Nikolai Lobachevski (1793–1856), who suggested that the the a priori system of Euclidean geometry (taken for granted by all cosmologists) need not necessarily apply to real space, which can only be known by experience. These points of view presaged the advent of a new cosmology.

IV. Space as heterogeneous and finite: Progress in cosmology has consisted in progressive freedom from limitations due to the special position of the observer. The cosmology of absolute up and down is valid for a small region of the earth's surface, that of spherical space for the earth as a whole, and that of classical mechanics for observers anywhere who have the same motion. The new cosmology, valid for all observers regardless of their motion, is associated with the relativity mechanics of Albert Einstein (b. 1879). This system, based on the principle of operational definition, that a physical concept must be defined in terms of the operation by which its phenomena are observed, rejects as meaningless concepts not so definable and stresses the relativity of concepts definable

only in relation to a given observer, such as length and mass. Its implications for cosmology are far-reaching. Space, described in terms of observable phenomena, is heterogeneous, since these phenomena, such as acceleration of bodies and direction of light, are determined by the propinquity of massive bodies. That is, mass is considered a property of space and mathematically formulated as curvature. Euclidean geometry (approximately correct for any small region) is rejected in favor of a geometry in which parallel lines intersect at a certain distance. Space, consequently, although boundless, is finite, including only a certain number of cubic miles. Its size remains an unsolved problem, but its circumference must be greater than the distance of the most distant objects observed by astronomers. Finally, since distant events can be observed only through the medium of light, which has a finite velocity, the space of experience cannot be described in abstraction from time, and so the cosmos must be regarded as a four-dimensional continuum of space and time, in which the distinction between them, being determined by the observer's motion, is not absolute but relative. The distinction between static and dynamic phenomena is lost, and an objective account of the world can consider it only *sub specie aeternitatis*.

See also CREATION AND PRESERVATION OF THE WORLD; SCIENCE.

BIBLIOGRAPHY: T. Heath, *Aristarchus of Samos*, 1913; A. S. Eddington, *The Nature of the Physical World*, 1928; H. T. Stetson, *Man and the Stars*, 1930.

GEORGE BOSWORTH BURCH.

COSTA RICA. See CENTRAL AMERICA.

COUNSELING, PASTORAL: A term now reserved for a specific kind of interpersonal relationship, somewhat formal, in which a layman with a felt need of help seeks a conference with a pastor skilled in the theory of personal adjustments, and in the technique of counseling. The plan calls for a series of appointments, moving from superficial levels of insight to deeper ones. This is the most formal and intensive type of pastoral care that a minister renders. It is distinguished from more casual and informal ministries of visitation, etc., in that the initiative lies mainly with the counselee. Such counseling is nothing new among Christian pastors. See *A History of the Cure of Souls* (1950), by John T. McNeill, and *Physicians of the Soul* (1947), by Charles F. Kemp. See also *The Reformed Pastor* (1656), by Richard Baxter. Jonathan Edwards (d. 1758) also had his full share of "seekers" whom he counseled in the Lord.

The influence, however, of modern psychological theories of personality and the techniques of psychotherapy have led to revoluntionary interpretations of pastoral counseling. The reproduction of the parent-child situation of both pastor and parishioner through the "transference of affect" is emphasized. Also, the relation between mind and body, as set forth in recent psychosomatic research, has led pastors to move co-operatively toward psychiatric specialists, with respect for their diagnostic and therapeutic skills. The value of a "listening ministry" by pastors has led many to take seriously the indirect, non-directive, or client-centered counseling described by Carl R. Rogers in his valuable researches at the University of Chicago.

The increased status of military chaplains during World War II and afterwards has done much to clarify and emphasize the work of pastoral counseling in general. With preaching and education reduced to a minimum, wartime chaplains were pushed into personal counseling, and many proved of invaluable aid to officers and enlisted men as advisees. Soldiers returned to civilian life expecting a counseling ministry from their pastors, and chaplains enrolled in seminaries for specialized training in counseling.

Since 1936 several new emphases have been introduced. In *The Art of Ministering to the Sick* (1938), by R. C. Cabot, and R. L. Dicks, pastoral counseling appears in connection with the visiting of the sick. In *The Exploration of the Inner World* (1936), Anton Boisen relates pastoral counseling to the spiritual plight of acutely psychotic persons. Thus far, however, there was little help for the pastor in dealing with emotionally disturbed persons in office or study, apart from the controlled conditions of a hospital. Hence, *The Art of Counseling* (1939), by Rollo May, stressed for pastors a consciously psychoanalytic concept of personality, the necessity of establishing rapport, or empathy, in counseling, and the need for personality wholeness in the pastor himself.

In 1938 J. S. Bonnell wrote *Pastoral Psychiatry* and in 1948 *Psychology for Pastor and People*. He interprets the role of the pastor as analogous to that of the psychiatrists, if not identical with it. His books provide interesting reading, but pastors have found difficulty in using his methods without his experience as the son of a psychiatrist and as a close student of other psychiatrists since childhood. In 1948 Seward Hiltner published *Pastoral Counseling* and for the first time viewed it in the context of the pastorate itself. He also discusses "precounseling," which means that a pastor has many informal and formal contacts with people, which serve as a preparation for counseling situations. Hiltner is obviously dominated by the ideas of "non-directive" psychotherapists, and follows them in what he calls "eductive counseling." He also stresses the inseparability of counseling from the administrative and other functions of the pastor. Hiltner sees the situation clearly and as a whole.

Two recent books deal with our subject. My own work, *The Christian Pastor* (1951), analyzes counseling in terms of different levels of relationship between a pastor and another. A given person affords the pastor a role—as friend, comforter, teacher, father-confessor, or psychiatrist in a non-medical sense. Every such relationship calls for a shift in technique, as well as for adequate resources with reference to other members of a "community team." In *Pastoral Counseling: Its Theory and Practice* (1951) Carroll A. Wise has done the most recent and thorough work in clarifying the nature of pastoral counseling. He turns the reader toward a more profound philosophy of counseling and makes a significant contribution to pastoral theology, per se. He makes clear the main issue in all such work: How can the pastor draw upon the resources of secular schools of counseling and psychotherapy and at the same time keep in focus his own unique and distinctive task and contribution to the care and cure of individual souls? See PSYCHIATRY.　　WAYNE E. OATES.

COUNTER REFORMATION (CATHOLIC REFORMATION): The Counter Reformation or Catholic Reformation deserves much fuller attention than was previously devoted to it in the present work. It obviously was more than a collection of individual enterprises, and it originated before the Reformation began its course. Much misunderstanding of this powerful movement can be eliminated among Protestants and Roman Catholics when the facts are known.

Historical custom does not always operate with precision. We speak of Gothic architecture, knowing full well that it was not in any sense of the word Gothic. Similarly, we now understand that the Catholic Reformation or Counter Reformation was much more than a reaction to the Reformation. Numerous attempts have indeed been made, even by some Protestant historians, to replace the name "Reformation" by another name, preferably, "Protestant Revolution." It is true that the Reformation was to a large extent a revolt against the authorities and practices in the Roman Catholic Church. But the old name is so widely used in Europe that American scholars might as well bow to established custom.

The name "Counter Reformation" causes considerable difficulty, since it was at first applied chiefly by Protestants who saw in the movement merely political measures adopted after 1550 by the Austrian and south German princes to check Protestantism. There were also historians who talked of "Counter Reformations" (*Gegenreformationen*). Gradually, however, the term was used to describe spiritual or intellectual measures employed by the Roman Catholic authorities in both church and state. The religious or intellectual opposition to Protestantism has been defined more and more in the sense of a renewal of Catholic piety and religious reform from within the church, not merely in a small area of Central Europe but as an international phenomenon, extending over many important countries, even continents.

In recent historiography the term "Counter Reformation" has acquired a double meaning, namely that of opposition to Protestantism and that of positive restoration of former piety and wholesome reform. This is in marked contrast to the attempt made by Carlton Hayes of Columbia University and E. M. Hulme of Stanford University, who in their influential textbooks sought to abolish entirely the terms "Reformation" and "Counter Reformation." These two American scholars were fully justified in their disappointment with these shopworn words, but they did not reckon with the power of tradition among European historians. A similar failure resulted when Professor H. O. Taylor of Harvard University tried to drop the term "Renaissance."

The following measures used by Roman Catholic authorities in modern times are negative in character: political actions, such as the prohibition of study by students in certain foreign universities, the discharge of magistrates suspected of harboring heretical opinions, and the exile of preachers and certain influential laymen; juridical steps like the censoring of books and inquisitions in courts resembling somewhat the Spanish Inquisition; pedagogical measures such as polemical books, and a series of decrees adopted at synodical conferences and church councils. These constitute truly a Counter Reformation, a counter attack upon the Reformation of the past.

On the other hand, all scholars are fully aware of the fact that the Counter Reformation includes much more than mere counter measures. The elements of renovation, restoration, and sanctification are certainly present, as they have always been, even in the worst period of the Middle Ages. Among the traditional means employed are the teaching of the catechism, as is also done often in great Protestant denominations, the preaching of sermons, care of the poor and the sick, visits to persons in jails and other institutions, missionary activity in foreign countries as well as domestic missions, instruction in parochial schools (which is far more extensive than in Protestant regions), the maintenance of a dignified liturgy and ritual, the activation of personal piety within the home through suitable ascetic and mystical books, pamphlets and periodicals, and stern measures against the old abuses. Those who wish to include all of this under the concept of a mere Counter Reformation are of course mistaken.

The Protestant Reformation and the Catholic Reformation ran parallel to each other. It must be admitted, however, and this is unfortunately seldom done by Catholic apologists, that from 1450 to 1550 the measures adopted by the Catholic authorities were very largely of a local and scattered character, not directed as before 1450 and after 1550 by the Vatican.

The worthy reformers of the fifteenth century must not be overlooked. The labors of the Bursfeld Congregation, the Brethren of the Common Life (q.v.), the Franciscans (q.v.), the Congregation of Windesheim, and similar bodies show clearly what was done within the ranks of the clergy before Luther appeared.

As has been indicated elsewhere (see RENAISSANCE), the humanists of the fourteenth and fifteenth centuries contributed heavily to the coming of the Reformation. The same is true of many mystics and reformers who remained Roman Catholics but exposed abuses in their church. Erasmus and Lefèvre are notable examples. Luther was steeped in medieval theology. He was not fully aware of his own background, while many of his modern biographers have likewise misinterpreted this background. In France, Italy, Spain, the Low Countries, England, and the German lands a powerful demand for reform was generated at the very time that Luther grew up in Mansfeld and Eisenach. He drew upon the same sources that did so much for the Jesuits as well as for the Calvinists.

The movement originated for the most part in the countries we have just mentioned. It owed a great deal to Luther's work, for the Roman Catholic Church was in need of correction and constructive criticism. After Luther's denunciations it became increasingly difficult to place a wicked man on the papal chair in Rome. Again, under pressure from the shaping of creeds like the Confession of Augsburg (see AUGSBURG CONFESSION) the Catholics felt that they should establish a creed of their own. It is no doubt true that the Orthodox Church in Russia would have been more fruitful than it was if it had been forced to compete strongly with rivaling organizations. In short, a combination of long standing beliefs and practices, together with a tremendous reaction to Luther's work, helped to produce the Counter Reformation.

In general, it may be stated that a transition occurred from liberal to conservative tendencies. During the fifteenth century some of the humanists could freely give expression to their contempt for certain members of the clergy. Moreover, justification by faith was taught by some in the fifteenth century, but caused little stir. The Bible was freely translated into German, but few of those who read the German version were molested for this. About the middle of the sixteenth century, on the other hand, certain inquisitors were so disturbed when they found an unacceptable translation that they had no peace until all the copies were destroyed. Nevertheless, it must no longer be assumed that Bibles were destroyed simply because they were vernacular Bibles.

In the political sphere of action the process of nationalism harmed the church much more than has been recognized generally. (See FREDERICK THE WISE; WORMS, DIET OF; PHILIP OF HESSE; MAURICE OF SAXONY; HENRY VIII; MARY TUDOR; and JAMES, KING OF SCOTLAND AND ENGLAND.) Particularly illuminating is the latest literature on Emperor Charles V and Cardinal Richelieu (qq.v.). Moreover, the process of secularization (q.v.) was far-reaching in its influence. Luther did try his best to convert the politicians, but it can hardly be said that he obtained much of a hearing.

In the realm of economics and sociology the picture is also very disappointing. The Commercial Revolution resulted in many changes which injured the cause of personal piety. Rural property lost in value and hordes of peasants moved to the villages and new towns, away from the strictly rural scene. The paupers blame the monks for their poverty, and a facetious humanist like Erasmus has a tremendous appeal for numerous rebels. In the *Utopia* of Thomas More we also see a reflection of this new trend of affairs. The secular powers take away from the clergy the bulk of their charitable work and their pupils. New city schools and public libraries greatly weaken the hold which the clergy had wielded for centuries. Moreover, the Papal Schism, the Babylonian Captivity, the worldly lives of many clergymen, and the strange manners of the Renaissance popes combined to sharpen the pens of Protestants and humanists.

The Counter Reformation covered much space and time. It began before the fifteenth century, and it had not yet run its course when the Treaty of Westphalia in 1648 ended the last of the religious wars. It operated in all the countries of western and central Europe, causing some reverberations also in the colonies of Spain, Portugal, and France. In the realm of politics it added the power of the sword to that of the pen. In the great universities it fought battles of an intellectual type. Its four chief weapons were (1) the Spanish Inquisition and the Roman Inquisition, (2) the Index, (3) the Council of Trent, and (4) the Society of Jesus (Jesuits).

BIBLIOGRAPHY: Pierre Janelle, *The Catholic Reformation*, 1949; G. G. Coulton, *Five Centuries of Religion*, Vol. IV, 1950, deals with late medieval monasticism; Gerhard Ritter, *Die Neugestaltung Europas im 16. Jahrhundert: Die kirchlichen und staatlichen Wandlungen im Zeitalter der Reformation und der Glaubenskaempfe*, 1950; Theodore Maynard, *The Crown and the Cross: A Biography of Thomas Cromwell*, 1950; E. de Moreau, *Histoire de l'Eglise en Belgique*, Vol. IV, 1949, deals with the period from 1378 to 1559; W. Schenk, *Reginald Pole:*

Cardinal of England, 1950; Paul Faure, *La Renaissance*, 1949; Albert Hyma, *Renaissance to Reformation*, 1951; Leonardo Olschki, *The Genius of Italy*, 1949; Maynard H. Smith, *Henry VIII and the Reformation*, 1948; Augustin Renaudet, *Préréforme et humanisme à Paris, 1494–1517*, 1916. The recent works contain further bibliographical information.

[Sup.] ALBERT HYMA.

COUNTER REFORMATION IN SWITZERLAND: Raverta, Papal Nuncio to Switzerland, 1554–60, started Catholic reform work there. His successor, Nuncio Volpe, 1560–64, 1565, 1573, continued this work by persuading Swiss Catholics to co-operate more in the Council of Trent and to form closer political alliances. Borromeo was appointed "Protector of the Swiss Nation" in 1560 and began to follow Swiss events closely. The Swiss Nunciate lapsed in 1566 but Jost Segesser of Lucerne, Captain of the Swiss Guard in Rome, assumed many of its duties. Counter Reformation began in earnest when a 1567 Constance Synod: (1) enacted strict doctrinal and disciplinary statutes; (2) laid plans for a Seminary; (3) ordered semi-annual visitations. Bishop Jacob Christoph Blarer of Basle (see BISHOP JACOB, Vol. VI) adopted a similar program on the urging of German Nuncio Portia, 1576. Apostolic Commissioner Sporeno, 1576, Nuncio Ninguarda, 1578, and finally Nuncio Bonhomini, 1579–81, helped enforce these reforms. Rome guided the entire movement. Recent scholars barely mention Cysat. For the Counter Reformation in French Switzerland, see FRANCIS, SAINT OF SALES, Vol. IV.

BIBLIOGRAPHY: Heinrich Reinhardt and Franz Steffens, *Die Nuntiatur von Giovanni Francesco Bonhomini, 1579–81, Einleitung*, 1910, and *Dokumente*, 3 vols., 1906–29; Karl Fry, *Giovanni Antonio Volpe und seine erste Nunziatur in der Schweiz, 1560–64*, 1931, and *Dokumente*, 1935; *Zeitschrift fuer Schweizerische Geschichte*, passim. Both *Dokumente* collections are rich sources.

[Sup. to JACOB CHRISTOPH]
ROBERT M. KINGDON.

COURTS, ECCLESIASTICAL: The Roman Catholic Church claims full judicial power upon its members. The court of first instance is the court of the bishop, who delegates his jurisdiction to a judge-official, assisted eventually by vice-officials, and who is competent in matrimonial causes, in causes involving the validity of ordinations, and in matters of discipline and ecclesiastical privileges. The court of appeal is that of the metropolitan.

In addition, anyone may appeal to the tribunals of the Roman Curia, namely: the *Rota*, which, among other functions, judges matrimonial causes appealed from diocesan or metropolitan courts; the *Poenitentiaria*, which grants absolution from censures and dispensations; the *Signatura*, which acts as Supreme Court (Cf. *Codex Iuris Canonici*, can. 1569–1607).

GEORGES A. BARROIS.

COVENANT CODE. See PENTATEUCH; LAW CODES, ANCIENT.

COVENANT THEOLOGY: I. Meaning of the Term: Covenant theology sprang up naturally as the most consistent expression of Calvinism, in which the idea of the self-sufficient, ontological Trinity is the final reference point in all predication. It is this idea that lies at the center of covenant theology. The three persons of the Trinity have exhaustively personal relationship with one another. And the idea of exhaustive personal relationship is the idea of the covenant.

II. Covenant of Works: Since the internal relationships of the triune God are covenantal, God's relation to mankind is also covenantal. God dealt covenantally with mankind through its representative head, Adam (Rom. 5:12). As made in the image of God, Adam received supernatural, positive communication from God (Geerhardus Vos, *Biblical Theology,* 1948). God promised a reward for fully self-conscious obedience and threatened with punishment for disobedience. Thus man was called upon to think God's thoughts after him and to obey God's will. Man was, in short, expected to think and act analogically (see ANALOGY). Man's task was as wide as the universe. He was asked to subdue the powers of the created world. He was to do all to the glory of God. As philosopher, as scientist, as artist, in short, as man with all the gifts God had bestowed, he was to act analogically or covenantally.

III. The Sinner as Covenant-Breaker: When Adam disobeyed the behest of God he broke the covenant. In him mankind broke the covenant. Men are therefore covenant-breakers, are under God's wrath, and are corrupt in nature.

As covenant-breakers men assume that they are not created by God. The covenant-breaker makes himself the final reference point in all predication. In theology he reduces God to a projection of man. In philosophy he holds that ultimate coherence lies in Reality, enveloping God and man. In science he assumes that reality is: (1) non-structural in nature (irrationalism); and (2) that God is subject to the structure of reality (rationalism).

IV. Covenant of Grace: However the sinner, as covenant-breaker, cannot succeed. His program is inherently destructive. But the sovereign God rules. Covenant theology holds that whatsoever comes to pass does so by virtue of the ultimate plan of God.

Accordingly, even the "wrath of man" must praise God. God sees to it that mankind fulfils its task. He sends his Son, through whom the world was made, into the world as the Saviour. He dies for his own and merits life for them. Thus he maintains the covenant of works, fulfils its obligations, and thereby assures the accomplishment of the covenantal task of mankind. Through Christ man knows God truly and knows the universe truly. Thus not only theology, but also philosophy and science are saved. Those in Christ are covenant-keepers.

V. The Covenant of Common Grace: But not all men are covenant-keepers. Many have never heard of Christ. Others, having heard of him through the general offer of the gospel of grace, have rejected him. Still others, born within the fold of the church, given in a special sense the promises of the covenant of grace, with Esau break the covenant and crucify the Son of God afresh. They are "covenant-breakers" in the narrower sense of the term.

Even so, God, through Christ, restrains the wrath of men as covenant-breakers. Through his Holy Spirit, God strives with men, withholding them from fully expressing their hostile, self-frustrating policy as covenant-breakers. In the depths of their minds all covenant-breakers know that they should be covenant-keepers. They know that only so will they succeed. God keeps this consciousness of himself as creator and judge alive in men's minds, however much they, as covenant-breakers, seek to suppress it (Rom. 1). As a result, though in principle covenant-breakers, they yet can make great contributions to the work and program of Christ, through whom mankind fulfills its covenant responsibilities and reaps its covenant rewards.

VI. History: The idea of covenant theology has only in modern times been thus broadly conceived. As the term indicates, the idea of the covenant has usually been limited to theology. And among covenant theologians there has been a difference of opinion on the nature and extent of the covenant. Some hold that God made his covenant of grace with the elect only, while others hold that God made his covenant with "believers and their seed." The former stress the "unconditional" or sovereign character of the promises of God. The latter stress the "conditional" character of the promise given to "children of believers" as a class. But such differences do not in the least undermine the common presuppositions of Calvinism, especially that of the counsel of God as controlling whatsoever comes to pass. Even those who stress the conditional character of the covenant maintain that back of the will of man is the ultimate, all-determinative will of God.

In his work on *De Verbondsleer in de Gereformeerde Theologie* (1891), Geerhardus Vos traces the history of this doctrine. See also Peter Y. De Jong, *The Covenant Idea in New England Theology,* 1945; H. H. Kuyper, *Hamabdil,* 1907; G. Ch. Aalders, *Het Verbond Gods,* 1939; William Hendriksen, *The Covenant of Grace,* 1932, for additional bibliographies. The subject is discussed in all major works on systematic theology by Reformed theologians.

CORNELIUS VAN TIL.

COVETOUSNESS: The term came into English, through the Old French *cuveitier,* from the Latin *cupere,* to desire. Desire, of course, may be good or bad, according to the character of the object and to the circumstances in which, and the degree to which, it is desired. But desire so easily gets out of hand that the derivatives of *cupere,* in Latin and in other languages, early came to express an evil connotation. Thus covetousness came to mean a desire for anything which was inordinate in degree, or a desire for something, especially for money (e.g., Latin *cupiditas,* English cupidity), particularly if it rightfully belongs to another. Another derivative, concupiscence, came to mean primarily inordinate sexual desire, lust, though the term is also used more broadly to constitute, along with pride, the twin bases of moral evil (cf. Dietrich Von Hildebrand, *Christian Ethics* [1953], especially pp. 408 ff.).

The discussion of covetousness is seldom given primary emphasis in works of naturalistic ethics. In works on Christian ethics which follow the Roman Catholic tradition, however, very considerable attention is paid to this vice, probably because the ascetic, other worldly point of view which made monasticism such a prominent feature of the life and thought of this branch of the church served to render covetousness a serious and keenly felt temptation. In those ethical works of Protestantism which either employ the exegetical method or philosophize on the basis of scriptural doctrine, covetousness also receives considerable attention because of the frequency of the prohibition and condemnation of this vice in the Scriptures.

The terms "covet," "covetousness" are used to translate at least three different Hebrew roots in the Old Testament, meaning respectively: to delight in, to wish for, and to plunder; and in the New Testament they translate five different Greek roots, meaning respectively: to long for, to have warmth of feeling for or against, to reach out after, to be fond of silver, and to be avaricious. Such roots are thus translated in the Scriptures at least thirty times.

ANDREW K. RULE.

COX MEMORIAL LECTURESHIP: This lectureship was established in 1947 by the Warren Memorial Methodist Church, Denver, Col., in the Iliff School of Theology, in memory of Frederick John Cox (1891–1947), pastor of Warren Memorial Church from 1928 until his death in 1947. The lectureship is designed to bring to Iliff School leaders in fields in which Dr. Cox was interested. It has been held by Russell L. Dicks, Van Denman Thompson, and Eric Baker.

WILLIAM H. BERNHARDT.

CRAIG, CLARENCE TUCKER: Methodist; b. at Benton Harbor, Mich., June 7, 1895; d. Aug. 20, 1953. He studied at Morningside College (A.B., 1915), Boston University (S.T.B., 1919; Ph.D., 1924), Harvard, Basel, and Berlin Universities. After serving Methodist pastorates in Cincinnati and Brooklyn, he was New Testament professor at the Oberlin Graduate School of Theology (1928–46); Yale Divinity School (1946–49); and became Dean of Drew Theological Seminary in Madison, N. J. (1949–). After serving on the American Standard Bible Translation Committee, he spent six months as its educational representative in 1946. He has participated extensively in the Faith and Order work of the World Council of Churches. In addition to editing and contributing to five volumes, he has written: *The Christian's Personal Religion* (1925), *Jesus in our Teaching* (1931), *We Have an Altar* (1934), *The Study of the New Testament* (1939), *The Beginning of Christianity* (1943), *One God, One World* (1943), *The One Church* (1951).

BIBLIOGRAPHY: L. A. Weigle, "Clarence Tucker Craig, 1895–1953," in *Religion in Life,* XXIII (1954), 451–457.

CRALOG. See RELIEF, RECONSTRUCTION, AND INTER-CHURCH AID.

CRAM, RALPH ADAMS: Author and architect; b. Dec. 16, 1863, at Hampton Falls, N. H.; d. Sept. 22, 1942. An architect since 1889 he was supervising architect at Princeton (1907–29); and construction architect at Bryn Mawr and Wellesley colleges. Among his many books on art are: *The Decadent, Black Spirits and White, Church Building* (1901); *The Ruined Abbeys of Great Britain* (1906); *The Gothic Quest* (1907); *Excalibur* (1908); *The Ministry of Art* (1914); *Heart of Europe* (1915); *The Substance of Gothic* (1917); *The Nemesis of Mediocrity* (1918); *The Great Thousand* (1918); *The Catholic Church and Art* (1929); *The Cathedral of Palma de Mallorca* (1933); *Convictions and Controversies* (1935); and *My Life in Architecture* (1936). RAYMOND W. ALBRIGHT.

CRANMER, THOMAS: That Cranmer was among the group who met at the White Horse Inn, Cambridge, to discuss projects for an English Reformation is unlikely, although he became a keen biblical student. When his treatise on Henry's divorce was completed, manuscript copies were given to the heads of Cambridge University, and Cranmer personally defended his arguments. He made such an impression as to gain many supporters for the king's cause. As archbishop, Cranmer was an Erastian: he strongly upheld the royal supremacy, and slavishly ministered to Henry's wishes. He and Gardiner were bitter rivals. In 1536, he preached at St. Paul's against the pope, purgatory, and indulgences. He secured the printing of the first official English Bible, and himself wrote the Preface. In spite of his opposition to the

Six Articles, they were passed as law. His Book of Homilies, published in 1547, shows Lutheran influences. That his Eucharistic beliefs had also become Lutheran during the last years of Henry's reign, revealed itself when, in 1548, he drew up a form altering the Mass into a Communion Service. His other liturgical reforms, notably the services of Morning and Evening Prayer, show him to have been a follower of Cardinal Quinonez. By this time, he no longer accepted all the seven sacraments, and was anxious to abolish clerical celibacy. After Edward's accession, Cranmer was responsible for bringing over to England a group of Continental reformers, including Bucer, Martyr, and à Lasco (qq.v.). How he himself came under their influence was apparent in the striking changes made between the Prayer Book of 1549 and that of 1552, by which time Cranmer had adopted an almost Zwinglian theological outlook. When Northumberland made his desperate attempt to alter the succession to the English throne, Cranmer acquiesced, though with reluctance.

BIBLIOGRAPHY: J. D. Mackie, *The Earlier Tudors*, 1953; P. Hughes, *The Reformation in England*, Vol. I, 1950, Vol. II, 1953; H. Maynard Smith, *Henry VIII and the Reformation*, 1948; G. Constant, *The Reformation in England*, Vols. I and II, 1941; F. M. Powicke, *The Reformation in England*, 1940; C. H. Smyth, *Cranmer and the Reformation under Edward VI*, 1926; A. C. Deane, *Thomas Cranmer*, 1927.

[Sup.] GORDON HUELIN.

CRAWFORD, PERCY. See YOUTH FOR CHRIST.

CREATION AND PRESERVATION OF THE WORLD: Recent work in astrophysics, while tremendously expanding our knowledge of cosmic structure, has complicated rather than solved questions of creation and preservation of the cosmos (see COSMOLOGY).

Physically, man inhabits a lesser planet rotating around a lesser star in a star cluster towards an edge of a rotating galaxy approximately 150,000 light years across and 25,000 to 40,000 light years thick in its central area. Our galaxy is but one of countless nebulae extending in all directions from us on an average of 2,000,000 light years apart and receding from each other at incredible speeds which increase with distance.

In spite of distances and speeds the expanding cosmos gives some indication as to its age and extent although investigators disagree both on the indications and their interpretation. The age of the earth as shown by the amount of lead in uranium deposits is about 2,000 million years. Earlier, on the basis of assumed evolution (q.v.) of star types and loss of energy the age of the sun was estimated at five to eight million million years and the age of the cosmos, in a state analogous to the present, an indefinite or infinite time, but the rate of cosmic expansion contradicts both estimates. If acceleration of

nebulae has been constant, 200,000 million years ago the cosmos would have been concentrated in a masspoint the size of a pin head. Present evidence, on a purely scientific basis, seems to place the age of our cosmos at about 2,000 million years also. Science describes the process as follows. At that time the nebulae or their materials were compressed in a relatively small region of space in our neighborhood in a state of unstable equilibrium. Something happened. Expansion began. The present universe should be spherical in shape with a radius of not more than 2,000 million light years (Whitrow). What the state of affairs was prior to the critical age remains unanswered.

The problems of origin and preservation are increased by the second law of thermodynamics which, taken alone, seems to indicate that our cosmos began at a finite time with a maximum organization of available energy and will end in total disorganization of energy at some finite future date. On the other hand, cosmic radiation plus the possibility that star energy comes from increasing complication instead of annihilation of matter has led some investigators to assume that a counterbalancing creative process is also occurring. De Sitter and Tolman suggest the cosmos is pulsating, expanding then contracting. Tolman has developed a relativistic thermodynamics to account for this.

While increasing astrophysical knowledge adds data for interpretation, the creation and preservation of the cosmos remains a metaphysical rather than a scientific problem.

See also SCIENCE, NATURAL.

BIBLIOGRAPHY: W. deSitter, *Kosmos*, 1932; A. S. Eddington, *The Expanding Universe*, 1933; E. A. Milne, *Relativity, Gravitation, and the World Structure*, 1935; H. S. Jones, *Worlds without End*, 1935; W. H. Werkmeister, *A Philosophy of Science*, 1935; E. Hubble, *The Observational Approach to Cosmology*, 1937; J. H. Jeans, *The Universe Around Us*, 1944; H. Shapley, *Galaxies*, 1943; J. W. N. Sullivan, *The Limitations of Science*, 1949; G. J. Whitrow, *The Structure of the Universe*, 1949.

[Sup.] RICHARD MARION MILLARD.

CREMATION: From *cremare*, "to burn." Cremation has long been common among Indo-European peoples. It used to be so in England, but under the influence of Christianity cremation gave way to burial. In recent times, in the United States as elsewhere, cremation has become common, especially in cities. It is difficult and costly to secure land for burial. Roman Catholic authorities uniformly oppose the practice. Protestants usually prefer burial, but with few exceptions leave such matters open, as adiaphora. The pastor may favor burial, but he leaves such decisions to the friends concerned. If they wish cremation he stands ready to invoke the blessing of God on those in sorrow. The services, public or private, may proceed much as prior to burial, being held at the home the evening before cremation, or at the crematory, before the body is dissolved. The officiant avoids saying "fire," or "flame." He may declare: "We commit this body to be dissolved." If the ceremony comes after cremation: "We commit the ashes to this resting place." The ashes may be strewn at a spot dear to the departed. More often they repose in an urn, perhaps with others in a "columbarium," named after a dovecote. Whatever the procedure, cremation seems not to affect belief in the resurrection of the body. Whether it be "lost" at sea, or consumed by fire, the God who made it can create another body, wholly spiritual, adapted to the life beyond. The same holds with "incineration," where the body is exposed to intense heat, but not to the flames, so that only three per cent remains in the form of gray ashes.

ANDREW W. BLACKWOOD.

CRESSY, EARL HERBERT: Baptist; b. Lacon, Ill., 1883. He studied at the University of Minnesota (B.A., 1907), and Rochester Theological Seminary (B.D., 1910). While missionary in China (1910–48) he was executive secretary, Council of Christian Colleges (1926–48), associate general secretary, National Christian Council; honorary secretary, Royal Asiatic Society. He became professor of Chinese studies, Hartford Seminary Foundation (1947–). He wrote: *Christian Higher Education in China* (1929), *Yellow Rivers* (1932), *Christianity Meets the Cultures of East Asia* (1948).

CRIME: Any form of conduct prohibited and punishable by the statutes or ordinances of any governmental unit. In modern societies there has been a tendency to restrict the term so as to exclude acts committed by juveniles and mentally abnormal individuals.

Crime is a universal phenomenon. Treason, murder, and extreme types of deviant sex behavior are more or less generally classified as crimes in most cultures. However, the character of many crimes varies from culture to culture, and from time to time within the same culture.

The extent of crime is difficult to determine because of the absence of uniform systems of reporting. In recent years, minor offenses against public order have tended to rise sharply, offenses against property have increased less abruptly, while violent crimes have shown a tendency to decline slightly.

In no society are all crimes detected and reported. Also, there is an enormous discrepancy between the number of arrests and the number of convictions. Between 25 and 30% of those apprehended are released without prosecution.

More crimes are committed in urban centers than in rural districts. And in the cities, the ecological concentration of crime is largely in the underprivileged areas inhabited by minorities where law enforcement policies and practices are likely to be strict. Women constitute a very small, though a growing, minority of the criminal population of most nations.

Criminological explanations of the causes of crime have led to a variety of theories: evil spirits, sin, disease, heredity, economic maladjustment, family breakdown, emotional disturbances. The trend now is to replace particularistic approaches by eclectic theories.

In the treatment of criminals the emphasis used to be on physical punishment in the form of the death penalty, whipping, the stock, or the pillory. By the end of the eighteenth century incarceration in prisons became the chief means of punishment. John Howard (*q.v.*, Vol. V) and Jeremy Bentham fought for reforms in both the criminal law and prisons of Great Britain. The Quakers of Pennsylvania substituted imprisonment for corporal punishment and abolished capital punishment except for first degree murder. (See also Vol. X, pp. 472, 473.)

More recently the punitive character of treatment has been further modified and the indications are that increasingly the emphasis will be on rehabilitation and prevention. A variety of developments is combining in bringing about this change: rise of humanitarianism, impact of religion, advances in the social, psychological, and biological sciences, the work of private agencies, such as the American Prison Association and the National Council of Churches (*q.v.*).

Even though the lag between theory and practice is considerable, there are evidences of progress: increasing use of parole and probation; more reliance on the findings of social workers, of medical and psychiatric consultants; addition of chaplains to the official administrative and policy-making staffs of institutions; establishment of new types of institutions, farms, or colonies, such as the Bostal Prison at Kent, England, and the California Institution for Men at Chino.

Great advances have been made in the handling of juvenile delinquents, child offenders, by the juvenile courts which originated at the beginning of this century. Such courts are interested not in the conviction but in the rehabilitation of the maladjusted child. Free use of medical, psychiatric, social welfare, and religious resources of the community is made by the more progressive court and correctional institution.

Among the very recent advances in the treatment, control, and prevention of delinquency are the use of foster homes, informal supervision, and the greater co-ordination and integration of community resources.

BIBLIOGRAPHY: M. A. Elliott, *Crime in Modern Society*, 1952; S. & E. Glueck, *Unraveling Juvenile Delinquency*, 1950; K. J. Scudder, *Prisoners Are People*, 1952.

CHARLES GARABED CHAKERIAN.

CRISIS, THE THEOLOGY OF: The phrase, Theology of Crisis, refers to a way of interpreting the Christian faith which had a definite effect upon Protestant theological thinking during the first half of the twentieth century. Certain ideas about God's self-revelation in Jesus Christ and a certain method of theological analysis were put together and put forward with sufficient distinctiveness and force to mark a new theological movement. The phrase, Theology of Crisis, is often used interchangeably with two other phrases to denote this theological movement, namely, *dialectical theology,* and *neo-orthodoxy.* This loose usage, however, may be rendered more precise, and thus may serve to clarify what the Theology of Crisis is.

Dialectical theology denotes the *method* of theological analysis which is characteristic of the Theology of Crisis. Dialectical thinking in the Western intellectual tradition is as old as Socrates. Such thinking tries to arrive at truth by setting opposites over against each other. The opposites with which the theologians of crisis are concerned are not statements (as in the case of Socrates and the Sophists); not the antithetical rhythm of thought regarded as the ultimately real (Hegel); but the contradictions of human existence (Kierkegaard) as these contradictions are sharpened when they are considered in the context of God's self-revelation in Jesus Christ (See DIALECTICAL THEOLOGY). *Neo-orthodoxy* denotes the *historical* position of the Theology of Crisis in the course of theology since the Protestant Reformation. The theologians of crisis are *orthodox* in the sense that they accept the central conceptions and the doctrinal formularies of the sixteenth century Reformation as reliable guides to the understanding of what the Bible says about God's action in Jesus Christ for man's salvation and the world's redemption. But they are also *neo-*orthodox because the theologians of crisis regard it as a primary responsibility of theology to give to the doctrinal conceptions and creeds of the past a contemporary formulation and significance. They consider it the business of theology not to restate truths as they have once been stated, but to make room for fresh thinking and fresh statements for the living Truth to which all authentic theological thinking points. The Theology of Crisis, strictly considered, denotes the theological movement which seeks—by dialectical thinking and in the light of the central theological insights and concerns of the sixteenth century Reformation—to give contemporary meaning and relevance to the interpretations of the relations between God and man and the world, established and illuminated by God's self-revelation in Jesus Christ.

It is not yet possible accurately to assess the permanent contribution of the Theology of Crisis to Christian theology in the twentieth century. Nevertheless, it is possible to distinguish the narrower from the broader boundaries

of the movement. The pivotal date is the year 1919, when Karl Barth published the first edition of his now celebrated commentary on the letter by Saint Paul to the Romans (*Der Roemerbrief*). The broader boundaries would then include those antecedent tendencies and movements in post-Reformation theology which tried with varying degrees of authenticity and effectiveness to interpret the central insights of the Reformation (see LIBERALISM), and those ways in which, since 1919, the thought of Barth and his more intimate associates have affected the theological thinking of their contemporaries. The narrower boundaries may be drawn around the original collaborative work of Barth and his more intimate associates, that is, between the publication of the *Roemerbrief* in 1919 and the cessation of the publication of the initial periodical series, *Zwischen den Zeiten* (*Between the Times*) in 1933. Since 1933, the apparently inevitable parting of the ways which overtakes creative cultural movements set in upon the Theology of Crisis and its continuing story is the story of divergent accents from the unfolding thoughts of those who first set the movement going or of those chiefly influenced by them.

The Theology of Crisis is a theology of the parish rather than of the schools. It was inspired by the predicament of the Christian minister under the weekly obligation of preaching a sermon. Karl Barth (*q.v.*), the creative genius of the movement, was a pastor in the village of Safenwil, in the canton of Aargau, in Switzerland. Eduard Thurneysen (*q.v.*), Barth's intimate friend and most constant and consistent associate, was a pastor in a neighboring village (Leutwil). The *Roemerbrief* grew out of the searching conversations of these two friends as they tried to take seriously their responsibilities as Christian ministers towards Bible from which they spoke each Sunday in their pulpits, and for the people assembled with them as a congregation of believers in Jesus Christ. It was not long until they were joined in their common search and emerging common orientation by another Swiss pastor from Obstalden in the canton of Glarus, Emil Brunner (*q.v.*); and still later, by two Germans, Friedrich Gogarten (*q.v.*), a professor of Theology at Breslau, and Rudolf Bultmann (*q.v.*), a professor of New Testament at Marburg on the Lahn. Barth, Thurneysen, and Brunner were members of the Reformed Church of Switzerland; Gogarten and Bultmann of the Evangelical Lutheran Church of Germany. Owing to the vitality and substance of their writings, Barth and Brunner moved from the parish ministry to theological professorships, while Thurneysen added a professorship in practical theology in Basel (1935) to his preaching and pastoral duties at the Muenster there (since 1927). Brunner began at Zurich in 1924, where he remained until his retirement in 1953, when he joined the faculty of the newly formed International Christian University at Tokyo. Barth was called in 1921 to the professorship of Reformed theology at Goettingen; in 1925, to the chair of theology at Muenster in Westphalia; and in 1929 to the Protestant faculty at Bonn. Owing to the totalitarian National-Socialist government of Germany under Adolf Hitler, Barth was compelled to leave Bonn, and since 1935 has occupied the chair of theology at Basel, where, in 1953, he is at work trying before his retirement to complete his major theological work.

The controversy among the theologians of crisis is the outgrowth of the characteristic doctrines of the movement. Among these doctrines the following may be mentioned:

(1) The sovereign freedom of God. God is free and sovereign in and over the world which he has created and redeemed, particularly in the freedom to reveal himself or to withhold himself, according to the mystery of his being and activity.

(2) God's self-revelation. God's revelation is always both a dynamic act of self-disclosure and a free gift of grace.

(3) The Word of God. The knowledge of God and of his self-revealing activity comes through Jesus Christ and in a threefold form characteristic of the life of the church in the world. This threefold form of revelation is the Word of God and the church in the world is the fellowship of believers in the Word. According to the order of God's self-revelation, there is first of all the historical life of Jesus Christ: his birth, ministry, death, and resurrection, which point to his ascension and exaltation, his pre-existence and his second advent. Jesus Christ is the Word of God in the sense that he is God's personal giving and communicating of himself in personal involvement and encounter with men in the world. In short, Jesus Christ is the "Word made flesh." Then, there is the Bible. The Bible is the Word of God because it is the report of Jesus Christ, the Word. As in the theology of the reformers, so in the Theology of Crisis, the maxim of the Sola Scriptura is pragmatically, and in principle, the point of departure for and the norm of theological thinking and interpretation. And thirdly, there is the proclamation of the church in the sermon. The sermon is God speaking in and to the fellowship of believers through human words. What distinguishes the Word of God from the word of man in the sermon is the faithfulness of what is said in the pulpit to the biblical report of Jesus Christ, and the degree to which the human words become the vehicle of God's Holy Spirit, that is, God's contemporary self-communication.

(4) The crisis of human existence. Crisis means both turning point and decision. According to the Theology of Crisis, when man is confronted through the preaching of the gospel by the self-revealing God, the actual character of human existence, individually and totally, is exposed. The actual character of human existence is its alienation from God and consequent internal disorder and disintegration. A radical turn about is the only way to wholeness and to health. It is God in his dynamic activity of self-revelation in his Word who requires the decision to turn about and who gives the power to make the decision. Thus, crisis is the central characteristic of the relations between God and man.

(5) The paradox. The relations between man and God can be described appropriately only in paradoxical terms. This is the case, first of all, because the Bible describes God's activity paradoxically. God is holy love. Man is the forgiven sinner. Jesus Christ is the God-man. And then, human existence is paradoxical. Man is both believer and unbeliever; obedient and disobedient; child of death and of eternal life.

Sooner or later the question of how these paradoxical facets of God's relations with men are to be interpreted was bound to arise. And over this question the Theology of Crisis fell apart. In how far, and in what ways are these paradoxes to be referred to God's self-revealing activity as Redeemer or as Creator? In how far, and in what ways is man prepared beforehand to respond to, or to apprehend the meaning of Jesus Christ? Barth, and Thurneysen with him, has remained adamantly Christocentric. Gogarten, however, found it necessary to go his own way by stressing creation, according to an elaborate doctrine of the "orders of creation." Brunner and Bultmann have been more concerned to stress the problems involved in the knowledge of God. The debate between Brunner and Barth centered on the problem of the "point of contact" (Anknuepfungspunkt); between Bultmann and Barth on the problem of the preparatory knowledge of God, that is, preparatory to the revelation in Christ (Vorverstaendnis). Obviously as the divergences have widened, other significant issues of disagreement have emerged.

Whatever may be the ultimate significance of the Theology of Crisis, certain impressive contributions have already become plain. The Theology of Crisis has given fresh and contemporary understanding to the initiative and sovereignty of God, so that once again it is possible to think about the world and about human life in the world in the context of clearly formulated apprehensions of the divine activity. The Theology of Crisis, while taking full account of the higher criticism of the Scriptures, has restored the sense of the unity of the Bible, and opened the way for the instruction and guidance of religious faith through the inner logic of biblical events and ideas. The Theology of Crisis has given significant emphasis to the Christian church as the fellowship of believers in which a continuing creative conversation is going on in two directions. On the one hand, the church is engaged in a living conversation with itself, that is, with the faith and thoughts of those who in all the times and places of the church's history have given faithful and creative witness to God's self-revelation in Jesus Christ. Perhaps the most striking fact about the Christian church in the twentieth century is its movement toward ecumenical unity (see ECUMENICAL MOVEMENT). Such a unity requires a common mind, which transcends the particular formulations of the separate confessional traditions. And no single theological influence has been more operative in the emergence of an ecumenical theology than the Theology of Crisis. On the other hand, the church is engaged in a living conversation with those outside the church, whose creative labors of mind and spirit determine the making and the remaking of culture. There are those who believe that it is largely owing to what the Theology of Crisis has contributed to the restoration of theology as an independent science, that Christian thought in the twentieth century can participate constructively and critically in the cultural enterprise as it has not been able to do since the high Middle Ages.

But these contributions have also raised certain problems which point beyond the Theology of Crisis, and for the solution of which the insights and the method of the Theology of Crisis are inadequate. Chief among these problems are: (1) The problem of biblical interpretation or hermeneutics. How shall the unity of biblical faith and thought, and the diversity of biblical experience and development be meaningfully related and understood? (2) The problem of revelation. What is the relation between revelation as act and revelation as knowledge? Some answer to this question must be worked out along lines which transcend the hitherto fruitless correlation or juxtaposition of natural and revealed theology. (3) The problem of Christianity and culture. Can theology discharge its cultural responsibility without an ontology? And if not, what are the nature and terms of a theological ontology? It is with these problems that the next chapter of Protestant theology in the twentieth century promises to be concerned. And the theologians who are dealing with these problems most constructively are the theologians who have been at once the severest critics of the Theology of Crisis, and the most deeply influenced by it.

See also DIALECTICAL THEOLOGY; EXISTENTIALISM; PHILOSOPHY.

BIBLIOGRAPHY: Since Karl Barth and Emil Brunner are the principal architects of the Theology of Crisis, it must suffice in this connection to mention only the very major works of the two theologians named. As already noted, Barth's Roemerbrief was published in 1919 (2d ed., 1922; 5th ed., 1926). The great systematic interpretation of the Christian faith is Barth's Kirchliche Dogmatik. Three volumes, each in several large books, have already been completed; the fourth volume is under way, and a fifth volume is projected. The volumes by Karl Barth are as follows: I/1, Kirchliche Dogmatik: Prolegomena, die Lehre vom Worte Gottes, 1932. This volume is a revision of the Christliche Dogmatik im Entwurf, the first half of Vol. I, 1927. There is an English translation by G. T. Thomson, The Doctrine of the Word of God, 1936. A complete English translation of the entire Dogmatik is currently being made by a group of translators under the sponsorship of the publishers T. & T. Clark, Edinburgh. I/2, Kirchliche Dogmatik: Prolegomena, die Lehre vom Worte Gottes, 1938. This volume is a revision of the second half of the Christliche Dogmatik im Entwurf. II/1, Kirchliche Dogmatik: die Lehre von Gott, 1940; II/2, Kirchliche Dogmatik: die Lehre von Gott, 1942 (Predestination); III/1, Kirchliche Dogmatik: die Lehre von der Schoepfung, 1945; III/2, Kirchliche Dogmatik: die Lehre von der Schoepfung, 1948 (Anthropology); III/3, Kirchliche Dogmatik: die Lehre von der Schoepfung, 1950 (Providence); III/4, Kirchliche Dogmatik: die Lehre von der Schoepfung, 1951 (Ethics); IV/1, Kirchliche Dogmatik: die Lehre von der Versoehnung, 1953.

The major works of Emil Brunner are the following: Der Mittler, 1927, second edition unaltered, 1937, English translation by Olive Wyon under the title, The Mediator, 1947; Das Gebot und die Ordnungen, 1933, English translation by Olive Wyon under the title, The Divine Imperative, 1947; Der Mensch im Widerspruch, 1937, English translation by Olive Wyon under the title, Man in Revolt, 1947; Offenbarung und Vernunft, 1941, English translation by Olive Wyon under the title, Revelation and Reason, 1946; Dogmatik: I, die christliche Lehre von Gott, 1946; II, die christliche Lehre von der Schoepfung und Erloesung, 1950; English translations by Olive Wyon under the titles, I, The Christian Doctrine of God, 1950; II, The Christian Doctrine of Creation and Redemption, 1952.

Three periodical series should also be noted: Zwischen den Zeiten, edited by Georg Merz in collaboration with Karl Barth, Friedrich Gogarten, Eduard Thurneysen, 11 vols., 1923-33; Theologische Existenz Heute (Theological Existence Today), edited by Karl Barth and Eduard Thurneysen, Numbers 1-46; edited by Eduard Thurneysen, Numbers 47-62, 1933-39; new series, 1946, edited by K. G. Steck and Georg Eichholtz; Theologische Studien (Theological Studies), Numbers 1-36, 1953, continuing, edited by Karl Barth. The two last-named series have appeared after the break between Karl Barth, on the one hand, and, for different reasons, Emil Brunner and Friedrich Gogarten, on the other.

Among the general discussions of the Theology of Crisis, the most instructive come from the early days of the movement. Walter Lowrie, Our Concern with the Theology of Crisis, 1932; John McConnachie, The Significance of Karl Barth, 1931; John McConnachie, The Barthian Theology and the Man of Today, 1933; Wilhelm Pauck, Karl Barth: Prophet of a New Christianity?, 1931. There is a voluminous literature in books and periodicals dealing with the thought of individual theologians of crisis and with various specific problems. No general discussion of the Theology of Crisis in its later development and no appraisal of the movement as a whole is available, owing in part at least to the continuing theological ferment occasioned by the Theology of Crisis, and to the fact that its leading representatives are still at work. Among the more recent sources, however, F. W. Camfield: Reformation Old and New, 1947 may be mentioned. Attention is also called to the discussion by the distinguished Jewish scholar, Martin Buber: Between Man and Man, 1947; and to the widely discussed critical discussion of Karl Barth's significance for Roman Catholicism by a Roman Catholic author, Hans Urs von Balthazar: Karl Barth: Darstellung und Deutung seiner Theologie, 1951.

PAUL L. LEHMANN.

CROCE, BENEDETTO: Italian philosopher, historian, and critic; b. at Pescasseroli (Aquila), Italy, Feb. 25, 1866; d. at Naples, Nov. 20, 1952. He studied briefly at the University of Rome and in later life received honorary degrees from Oxford, Freiburg and Marburg universities but was largely self-educated. He developed a "philosophy of the spirit" in which philosophy was identified with history and history eventually with liberty, and in which four grades or realms of spirit are distinguished: the aesthetic, logical, economic, and ethical. He founded and edited the influential journal *La Critica* (1903–44) and its continuation *Quaderni della Critica* (1945–). In politics he long remained independent but joined the Liberal Party in 1924 and was its president for a time after World War II. He was a senator since 1910, and was minister of education in Giolitti's cabinet in 1920–21 and minister without portfolio in the cabinets of Badoglio and Bonomi in 1944. In 1946 he founded the Italian Institute of Historical Studies, a postgraduate school adjoining his library at Via Trinita Maggiore 12, Naples. Though critical of both Catholicism and Protestantism in all their present forms, he explained "Why We Cannot Help Calling Ourselves Christians" (in *My Philosophy* [1949], pp. 37–47), and thought of himself as having continued the work of philosophers like Vico, Kant, Fichte, and Hegel, who "succeeded in giving critical and speculative range to the idea of the Spirit which Christianity had substituted for ancient realism" (*loc. cit.,* p. 44). Some of his more important philosophical works in English translation are: *Philosophy of the Spirit,* 4 vols.; *Aesthetic,* (1909, 2d ed. 1922); *Philosophy of the Practical* (1913); *Logic* (1917); *Theory and History of Historiography* (1921); *The Philosophy of Giambattista Vico* (1913); *Historical Materialism and the Economics of Karl Marx* (1914); *What is Living and What is Dead of the Philosophy of Hegel* (1915); *History as the Story of Liberty* (1941).

BIBLIOGRAPHY: H. Wildon Carr, *The Philosophy of Benedetto Croce,* 1917; Raffaello Piccoli, *Benedetto Croce, An Introduction to His Philosophy,* 1922; Benedetto Croce, *An Autobiography,* 1927; D. Mack Smith, three articles on Croce's politics in *The Cambridge Journal,* Vols. I, II (1947–49).

MAX H. FISCH.

CROMWELL, OLIVER:

BIBLIOGRAPHY: W. C. A. Abbott, *A Bibliography of Oliver Cromwell,* 1929; idem, (ed.), *Cromwell's Writings and Speeches,* 4 vols., 1937–47; G. Davies, *The Early Stuarts 1603–1660* (1937), pp. 188–234, 345–346; G. K. Fortescue, *Catalogue of the Pamphlets, Books, News-papers, Collected by George Thomason, 1640–1661,* 1908, contains four-fifths of the works produced between the dates mentioned; R. M. Jones, *Mysticism and Democracy in the English Commonwealth,* 1932; L. F. Brown, *The Political Activities of the Baptists and Fifth Monarchy Men in England during the Interregnum,* 1912; J. Buchanan, *Oliver Cromwell,* 1944; H. R. Williamson, *Charles I and Cromwell,* 1946; C. H. Firth, *Oliver Cromwell and the Rule of the Puritans,* 1947; H. Kittel, *Oliver Cromwell: Seine Religion und seine Sending,* 1928; P. O. Lapie, *Cromwell,* 1949; M. T. Blauvelt, *Oliver Cromwell: A Dictator's Tragedy,* 1937; M. Ashley, *Oliver Cromwell the Conservative Dictator,* 1937; C. V. Wedgwood, *Oliver Cromwell,* 1947; R. W. Ramsey, *Richard Cromwell,* 1935; D. Grosheide, *Cromwell naar het oordeel van zijn Nederlandse tijdgenoten,* 1951. See also MILTON; PURITANISM; INDEPENDENTS; CHARLES I; LAUD.

[Sup.] ALBERT HYMA.

CROMWELL, THOMAS: B. in 1485, executed

July 28, 1540. His father was a blacksmith in Putney, and also a brewer noted for his bad ale.

He often had bitter quarrels with his son, who confessed later that in his youth he was a ruffian. Thomas travelled extensively on the Continent, but finally settled down in London. In 1524 he became a member of Grays Inn, and before long was entrusted with the management of the personal affairs of Wolsey (*q.v.*), who also employed him to suppress certain religious houses in order to build his colleges, a task which gave Cromwell experience for his later exploits in this field. Cromwell made himself useful to both king and chancellor when the House of Lords passed a bill of attainder against Wolsey and the House of Commons was about to concur. His eloquence and force of persuasion were such that the bill was defeated. During his first interview with the king, he advised Henry VIII (*q.v.*) to divorce Catherine of Aragon, marry Anne Boleyn, and renounce his allegiance to the pope. All of these measures the king gladly enacted, thus sacrificing Wolsey, breaking with the papacy, and acquiring a vivacious young wife. They were most important steps in the religious history of England. Cromwell was sufficiently astute not only to survive his master's downfall, but even to gain from the king a position in the Privy Council, and a little later he became secretary of state. When Sir Thomas More (*q.v.*), Chancellor of England since Wolsey's disgrace in 1529, was deprived of office and later executed for his refusal to admit that the king was supreme head of the Church of England, Cromwell profited from this and became chancellor in More's place. He guided Henry in his efforts to despoil the church, and was appointed vicar-general for the purpose of suppressing the monasteries. His zeal in this work earned for him the title of "malleus monachorum." He himself received six abbeys, while his nephew, Sir Richard Cromwell, great-grandfather of Oliver Cromwell (*q.v.*), obtained other desirable pieces of real estate. But great was his fall in 1540 when, in order to promote a political alliance with the German Lutheran princes, he urged the king to marry Anne of Cleves. That lady's physique repelled the fastidious connoisseur of female charms, and Cromwell lost his head as the result. Cromwell had studied most carefully Machiavelli's "Prince," and adopted the line of action set out in that book, a policy which was selfish and unscrupulous to the very last degree.

BIBLIOGRAPHY: R. B. Merriman, *Life and Letters of Thomas Cromwell,* 2 vols., 1902; J. D. Mackie, *The Earlier Tudors,* 1952; G. B. Constant, *The Reformation in England,* Vol. I (translated by R. E. Scantlebury), 1934; H. Maynard Smith, *Henry VIII and the Reformation,* 1948; P. Hughes, *The Reformation in England,* 1950; M. H. and R. Dodds, *The Pilgrimage of Grace, 1536–1537,* 1915.

[Sup.] ALBERT HYMA.

CRONIN, JOHN FRANCIS: Roman Catho-

lic; b. at Glens Falls, N. Y., Oct. 4, 1908. He studied at Holy Cross College, Worcester, Mass., and at Catholic University of America, Washington, D. C. (A.B., 1927; M.A., 1928; S.T.B., 1931; Ph.D., 1935). He was ordained a priest in 1932. He taught as professor of economics, St. Mary's Seminary, Baltimore, Md., 1932–45, and has been assistant director, Department of Social Action, National Catholic Welfare Conference, Washington, D. C., since 1946. In the economic field he has stressed labor-management co-operation and has often served as arbitrator and conciliator in labor disputes. He has written: *Cardinal Newman, His Theory of Knowledge* (1935); *Economics and Society* (1939); *Economic Analysis and Problems* (1945); *Catholic Social Action* (1948); and *Catholic Social Principles* (1950).

CROSS, FRANK LESLIE: Anglican; b. Jan. 22, 1900. Educated at Balliol College, Oxford, and Marburg and Freiburg Universities. He was ordained in 1925. He was tutor at Ripon Hall, Oxford (1924–27); librarian of Pusey House, Oxford (1927–44); Wilde Lecturer in Natural and Comparative Religion (1935–38); Lady Margaret Professor of Divinity and Canon of Christ Church, Oxford since 1944. He has written: *Religion and the Reign of Science* (1930); *Anglicanism* (with P. E. More, 1935); *St. Athanasius: De Incarnatione* (1939); and *Life of Darwell Stone* (1943).   F. W. DILLISTONE.

CROSS, SIGN OF THE: Roman Catholics make it by touching successively their forehead, their breast, their left shoulder, and their right shoulder with their right hand, while saying these words: "In the name of the Father, and of the Son, and of the Holy Ghost. Amen." Christians of the Byzantine rite cross themselves from right to left with the thumb and first two fingers joined.

The sign of the cross is made usually at the beginning and the end of private or public prayers, on entering the church, or when being blessed by the priest or the bishop, etc. Eastern Christians often repeat the sign of the cross while praying before the images or during the liturgy, bowing deeply each time.

In the Latin liturgies, the officiating minister and the attendants make the sign of the cross at the opening words of each canonical hour, at the first verse of the canticles *Benedictus, Magnificat,* and *Nunc dimittis,* as well as before and after the reading of the Gospel of the Mass.

The bishop or the priest trace the sign of the cross with the right hand while blessing persons and objects, absolving penitents in the confessional, or over the Eucharistic elements during the celebration of the Mass.

GEORGES A. BARROIS.

CROZER LECTURESHIP, SAMUEL A.: Founded in Crozer Theological Seminary, Chester, Pa., in 1880 to bring to the campus special lectures on subjects of interest and value in the field of the Christian ministry. The lecturers may be selected from any denomination termed evangelical, from laymen as well as ministers, or from citizens of foreign countries.

SANKEY L. BLANTON.

CRUSADES: In several recent works on the crusades the question has been asked about their origins. Some authorities argue with C. Erdmann that they constituted a *bellum sacrum,* or holy war; in other words the Christian counterpart to the Mohammedan "djihad." In the early Middle Ages the church was opposed to warfare, since the Christian religion was regarded as one of love, not hatred or strife. This outlook was altered largely by the conversion of the Germanic tribes and the task they performed in defending the church against infidels and robbers. In the time of Charlemagne political fighting which aided the church was regarded as a holy war. Afterward this idea was extended to the defense of local churches, monasteries, and bishoprics against Northmen, Magyars (Hungarians), and Moors. In the subsequent developments the church considered itself a great unit which stood definitely opposed to the heathen foe. This unit or unity required defense; when the secular powers did not produce it the church provided it. For centuries the fight against unbelievers was looked upon as a good work. Gradually the fight against heretics and excommunicated persons was considered a part of the whole problem, as the career of Pope Gregory VII indicates.

After this evolutionary process the results are reflected in ecclesiastical legislation: that of the twelfth, thirteenth, and fourteenth centuries recognizes the idea of a holy war. The concept of a militia Christi led to the crusades and also to the founding of the knightly orders (*q.v.*). M. Villey, in his important work, *La croisade, théorie juridique* (1942), regards the crusades in a broader sense. He and his followers are correct in seeing in them also the formerly accepted ingredient of the pilgrimage, which affected numerous crusaders. The latter had in mind chiefly a pilgrimage to the Holy Land, and they made a vow to worship the Saviour there. This was why the Franciscans obtained possession of Gethsemane.

Among the results of the crusades must be noted particularly the influence exerted upon religious life in Western Europe after 1200. The Christocentric outlook upon life brought forth in its train an increased attention toward the humanity of Jesus Christ, as seen in the works of St. Bernard (*q.v.*), the monks of St. Victor, and the Franciscan (*q.v.*) friars. This factor exerted an incalculable influence upon the authors of devotional treatises, the most powerful of which was *The Imitation of Christ* (*q.v.*), which in turn was based largely upon the work of David of Augsburg, a Franciscan friar.

BIBLIOGRAPHY: Among recent contributions made by writers in the United States: *The Crusades and Other Historical Essays Presented to D. C. Munro*, 1928; D. C. Munro, *The Kingdom of the Crusaders*, 1935; R. B. Yewdale, *Bohemond I, Prince of Antioch*, 1924; P. Throop, *Criticism of the Crusade: A Study of Public Opinion and Crusade Propaganda*, 1940; idem, "Some Criticism of Papal Crusade Policy in old French and Provencal," in *Speculum*, Vol. 13 (1938), 379–412; J. L. LaMonte, "To What Extent was the Byzantine Empire the Suzerain of the Crusading States?" in *Byzantion*, Vol. 7 (1932), 253–264; M. Baldwin, "The Papacy and the Levant during the Twelfth Century," in *Bulletin of the Polish Institute of Arts and Sciences in America*, Vol. 3 (1944), 277–287; J. L. LaMonte, "The Lords of Sidon in the XIIth and XIIIth Centuries," in *Byzantion*, Vol. 17 (1944–45), 183–211; A. C. Krey, "Urban's Crusade: Success or Failure?" in *American Historical Review*, Vol. 53 (1948), 235–250; A. A. Vasiliev, *History of the Byzantine Empire*, 2 vols., 1st ed., 1928–29, 2nd ed., 1952; M. Baldwin, "Some Recent Interpretations of Pope Urban II's Eastern Policy," in *Cath. Hist. Review*, Vol. 25 (1940), 459–466. One of the most thorough works on the Crusades is Steven Runciman, *A History of the Crusades*. Vol. I, 1951. covers only the First Crusade, and has an extensive bibliography. Vol. II, 1952, appeared under the title *The Kingdom of Jerusalem and the Frankish East, 1100–1187*. Unfortunately both Runciman and Grousset failed to note the contents of the admirable American publication, *Raymond III of Tripolis and the Fall of Jerusalem*, 1936. in which it is shown that the old legend contained in the continuation of William of Tyre in the French language covering the events from 1181 to 1184 is unreliable. while the account by William of Tyre himself gives the correct chronology.

[Sup.] ALBERT HYMA and H. GOOSSENS.

CUBA. See WEST INDIES.

CULLMANN, OSCAR: B. Strasbourg, Feb. 25, 1902. He studied at the University of Strasbourg (B.Th., 1924). Upon completion of his study of the relation between Gnosticism and Jewish Christianity, *Le Probléme littéraire et historique du roman pseudo-Clémentin* (Paris, 1930), he became lecturer in New Testament exegesis at the University of Strasbourg. In 1938 he became Professor of New Testament exegesis and early Christianity at the University of Basel. Besides teaching in Basel he lectures at the Sorbonne in Paris and the Waldensian Seminary in Rome. His publications which have been translated into English include: *Christ et le Temps* (1946); *Le baptême des enfants et la doctrine biblique du baptême* (1948); *Les Premiéres Confessions de foi Chrétiennes* (1948); and *Peter, Disciple, Apostle, Martyr* (1953).

CULT. See SECT AND CULT.

CULTURAL AND SOCIAL CONDITIONS, HEBREW: As the semi-nomadic Israelites invaded the land of Canaan and became settled, there was a resulting friction between two cultures. The Canaanites had developed a comparatively high civilization, while the Hebrews, with a clan organization of their society, brought no art and no written literature. Whatever military unity they have possessed under Joshua soon was lost and, at the beginning of the period of the Judges, they were separate tribes, raising their flocks and beginning to cultivate their recently acquired land interspersed among the Canaanite-Amorite cities.

I. Pastoral Life: Throughout Old Testament times the Hebrews to a large extent remained pastoral, and the Bible abounds in laudatory allusions to the good shepherd, from Abel to Jesus. While there was some raising of large cattle, sheep and goats were the main source of meat, cloth, and milk. There may have been varieties of sheep, but probably the fat-tailed predominated (Ex. 29:22; Lev. 3:9). As pictured in Ps. 23, the shepherd would lead his flock to good pastures and watering places. He would heal the wounded and carry a weak lamb. At intervals he would return the sheep to their fold. Often sheep would be family pets. In both city and country the shepherd with his pipes, his sling, and his staff was a familiar and respected person.

II. Agriculture: As soon as they settled, the Hebrews engaged in agriculture. The Coastal Plain, the Plain of Esdraelon, Lower Galilee, parts of the Jordan Valley, and even many of the hills are fertile. Wheat, millet, dura, barley, lentils, flax, cucumbers, peas, and beans were valuable products. Implements in Bible times were much the same as those still in use: the simple plow, the mattock, the wooden pitch fork, the sickle, the flail, the threshing sledge, and the sieve—the most efficient tools in land that is hilly and stony. Women participated in reaping, gleaning, and the grinding of the threshed grain. The Hebrews enjoyed the agricultural life, and the time of harvest called for general celebration. In the Book of Ruth is a picture of a happy group on an agricultural estate. Distinction between pastoral and agricultural should not be exaggerated. A family would possess both field and flock.

III. City and Village: The Hebrews naturally entered into the Canaanite pattern of urban life, and the complications of city living soon became problems. Trade, industry, and commerce developed. Private ownership superseded community ownership. There were mansions and slums. The Hebrew city was on top of a hill and surrounded by a heavy stone wall; for it had to withstand invading armies. Jericho, the exception, could not endure a siege. Houses were built on stone foundations often with wooden superstructures. Only in the lowlands was mud brick employed. For a well-to-do family there was an open court in the center with separate rooms opening on it. Streets were narrow and crooked. Generally the city gate was complex, so that it could be defended, and inside there was an open area, where the elders sat and judgment was pronounced. In time the cities became more crowded and the private houses more cramped. Each city had a number of dependent villages, groups of dwellings with no surrounding walls. In time of war the villagers would come into the cities for safety.

IV. Dress and Ornament: Though there is little archaeological evidence to tell how the Hebrews dressed, we know that they had garments of wool, flax, camel's hair, and goat's hair. The climate of Palestine demands full covering for protection against sun in summer and cold in winter. So the Hebrew, both male and female, doubtless wore a full, long skirt. The headdress was of cloth, possibly similar to the kaffiyeh worn by Arabs today. There are references to rings, bracelets, anklets, necklaces, and precious stones. The number of these objects found in excavations shows that the Hebrews were fond of personal adornment. Bowls for cosmetics are common finds.

V. Handicrafts: The first Hebrews to settle in Palestine were farmers and shepherds; but soon some of them took up more specialized occupations. Doubtless the building operations of Solomon and Omri stimulated the learning of masonry, carpentry, and metal work. Excavations have shown centers for weaving, dyeing, and the making of pottery. The Bible mentions smiths, potters, fullers, and the makers of images (see ART, HEBREW).

VI. Transportation: Palestine always has been a thoroughfare. So the Hebrews were acquainted with means of travel. There were four-wheeled wagons, two-wheeled ox-carts, chariots, and palanquins. The first recorded large scale use of camels for transport was that of the Midianite army which Gideon defeated (Judg. 6:5). Later the Hebrews used camels on their farms and camel caravans often passed through the land. Horses were fairly common from the time of Solomon. The mule was an animal for royalty. The most common animal for transportation was the donkey.

VII. The Family: In the early days family solidarity was an important element. While a man might have a plurality of wives and concubines (e.g., Gideon, Judg. 8:30), he was the master and there was strong loyalty to the unit (see FAMILY AND MARRIAGE RELATIONS, HEBREW in Vol. IV). But, as estates were divided and small landholders dispossessed, cities became crowded and families were disrupted. When Solomon organized his empire as a totalitarian state and forced many of his subjects into slave labor, family life suffered. Ideally a Hebrew was not a slave; but as property became personal rather than communal, Hebrews went into bondage because of inability to pay their debts. Hence, there emerged legislation about the treatment of slaves, widows, orphans, and poor persons. A Hebrew slave was not supposed to be held more than six years (Deut. 15:12), though this regulation apparently was ignored (Jer. 34: 8–11). Even after the Exile, Nehemiah found

the old process of mortgage, foreclosure, and bondage operating among the Jews (Neh. 5:1–13).

BIBLIOGRAPHY: Madelaine S. and J. Lane Miller, *Encyclopedia of Bible Life*, 1944; Louis Wallis, *God and the Social Process*, 1935; W. F. Albright, *From the Stone Age to Christianity* (rev. ed.), 1946; Earle B. Cross, *The Hebrew Family*, 1927.

OVID R. SELLERS.

CUNERUS PETRI: Bishop of Leeuwarden (Friesland); b. at Brouwershaven in 1530; d. at Cologne on Feb. 15, 1580. He studied theology at Louvain. In 1568 he became rector of the university and in the next year the first bishop of Leeuwarden. He worked for the promulgation of the Council of Trent and for a diocese-synod. He was accused of avarice and worldly life, but without reason. He had to endure much opposition from the convents, the goods of which he incorporated in the *mensa episcopalis,* and from the praepositus of Utrecht who lost a part of his jurisdiction by the newly erected diocese of Leeuwarden. The stadhouder Rennenberg imprisoned him. After his liberation he became professor of Holy Scripture in Cologne. His tomb is in the cathedral of Cologne.

BIBLIOGRAPHY: E. Bruna and others, *Bijdrage tot de Kerkgeschiedenis van Friesland*, 1951; B. A. Vermaseren, *De katholieke Nederlandse geschiedschrijving in de xvie en de xviie eeuw over de opstand*, 1941.

WILLIBRORD LAMPEN.

CUNINGGIM, MERRIMON: Methodist; b. at Nashville, Tenn., May 12, 1911. He studied at Vanderbilt (A.B., 1931), Duke (M.A., 1933), Oxford (Rhodes Scholar; B.A., 1935 and Diploma in Theology, 1936), and Yale (B.D., 1939; Ph.D., 1941). Positions held include: director of religious activities, Duke (1936–38); professor of religion at Emory and Henry College (1941–42), at Denison University (1942–44), and at Pomona College (1946–51); dean, Perkins School of Theology, Southern Methodist University (1951–   ). He wrote *The College Seeks Religion* (1947).

CUNNINGHAM, JOHN ROOD: Presbyterian; b. at Williamsburg, Missouri, July 3, 1891. He studied at Westminster College, Fulton, Missouri (A.B., 1914), and Louisville Presbyterian Seminary (B.D., 1917). After serving with the War Work Council, Presbyterian Church (1918–19), he was minister of Grenada, Mississippi, Presbyterian Church (1919–23); First Presbyterian Church, Gainesville, Florida (1923–28); First Presbyterian Church, Bristol, Tennessee (1928–30); First Presbyterian Church, Winston-Salem, North Carolina (1926–41). After serving as president of Louisville Presbyterian Theological Seminary (1930–36) he became president of Davidson College (1941–   ).

CURIA. See CARDINALS, COLLEGE OF; CONGREGATIONS, ROMAN.

CURRIE LECTURES, THOMAS WHITE:
Founded in 1945 by the Austin Presbyterian
Theological Seminary, Dallas, Tex., the lectures
are named in honor of a former president of the
seminary. It is the purpose of the lectureship
to enable ministers in the southwestern states to
hear outstanding Christian leaders and to publish their lectures. These have included Ernest
Trice Thompson, Josef Hromádka, Paul Scherer,
D. Elton Trueblood, H. Richard Niebuhr, Paul
Minear, and G. Ernest Wright.

DAVID L. STITT.

CUSA, NICHOLAS OF: Aeneas Silvius (Pope
Pius II) called him "eugeniarorum omnium Hercules," for he was a very pious and irenic person who sought to promote the cause of unity
in the church. His aim was to reconcile church
with state through the exercise of popular sovereignty. By emphasizing the main doctrines in
the church which both Arabs and Jews could
accept he hoped to satisfy these groups to such
an extent that they would join the church in
due course of time. Faith and knowledge he
tried to synthesize on a higher plane where
dogma would also become involved and elevated, while the whole body of truth would be
understood in a supersensory mystic vision.
Although subjectively within the bounds of
Catholic doctrine, his philosophy did come very
close to pantheism.

BIBLIOGRAPHY: H. Bett, *Nicholas of Cusa*, 1932; *Nicolai
de Cusa opera omnia*, ed. Acad. Heidelb., Leipzig 1932 ff.;
P. Rotta, *Il Cardinale Nic. d. Cusa*, 1928; M. de Gandil-
lac, *La philosophie de N. de C.*, 1941; R. Haubst, *Das
Bild des Einen und Dreieinen Gottes in der Welt nach
Nik. von Kues*, 1952.

H. GOOSSENS.

CUSTODY: See HOLY LAND.

CUSTOM: Latin *consuetudo*. The Roman
Church attributes to custom an interpretative
and subsidiary function with regard to ecclesiastical law. According to the Code of Canon
Law, any reasonable custom, which is not contrary to divine or natural law, or which is consistently observed for at least forty continuous
years, may obtain strength of law from the consent of the competent ecclesiastical superior or
of a corporation having juridical personality.
Customs explicitly reproved by the canons are
deemed unreasonable, and have no binding
power. Bishops may, in their own prudence,
tolerate century-old customs at variance with
church statutes, and not positively reproved by
law. Cf. *Codex Juris Canonici*, can. 5, 25–30.

GEORGES A. BARROIS.

CUTTS, EDWARD LEWES: Anglican; b.
March 2, 1824, Sheffield, Eng., d. 1901. Educated
Queen's College, Cambridge, and ordained in
1848, he became Vicar of Haverstock Hill (1871)
and remained there until his death on Sept. 2,

1901. He was appointed to visit the Syrian and
Chaldean Churches in 1876 and described his
travels in *Christian under the Crescent in Asia*
(1887). His books include: *A History of Early
Christian Art; Turning-Points of General Church
History*; and *Augustine's Canterbury*.

F. W. DILLISTONE.

CYPRIAN: The relation of Cyprian to Tertullian is clearly portrayed in Jerome's story
(*De vir. inlustr.* liii) that a day never passed
without Cyprian's saying to his secretary, "Give
me the [books of the] master"—Tertullian. The
fact that both men had had a legal education
contributed to Cyprian's admiration. Their
minds worked in somewhat similar ways.

Cyprian's work *De ecclesiae catholicae unitate*,
written in the difficult year 251, argues that the
true note of the Catholic church is sounded by
its unity. The fourth chapter presents difficulties, for its text has been transmitted in two
forms, one of which lays stress on the primacy
of the Roman bishop, the other of which does
not. It has been argued that the "primacy"
passage is an interpolation, but the style and
thought are so Cyprianic that this argument
seems unsound. Both forms probably come
from Cyprian himself, and to judge from the
history of his controversies with Rome, it is
likely that he later removed the "primacy" passage when his relations with the pope deteriorated. It was under these circumstances that
he reached his theory, supposedly based on the
Bible, of the unity of the church as based on
the unity of equal bishops.

Our understanding of the persecution under
Decius in 250 and the *libellatici* has been improved by the discovery of numerous papyrus
libelli which all inhabitants of the empire had
to obtain. They give greater actuality to Cyprian's apologetic work and his sources, recently
discussed by Pellegrino. Cyprian relies primarily
on Tertullian and Minucius Felix, but he contributes a new note of theological, confessional
piety. The treatise *Quod idola dii non sunt* was
written by Cyprian (Koch, Pellegrino).

The pseudo-Cyprianic works deserve special
mention. A tenth-century manuscript (the
"Cheltenham list," originally compiled in the
fourth century) contains the names of only two
of these spurious treatises: *Adversus Judaeos*
and *De laude martyrii*. Many of these works
were written in his time but not by him; examples are *De montibus Sina et Sion, Ad Nova-
tianum, De pascha computus, De rebaptismate*,
and *De singularitate clericorum*. The treatises
De spectaculis and *De bono pudicitiae* were
written by Novatian. Harnack once argued that
Adversus aleatores was written by Victor of
Rome, but later abandoned his theory. It probably comes from some African bishop at the end
of the third century.

BIBLIOGRAPHY: A. d'Alès, La théologie de saint Cyprien, 1922; H. Koch, Cyprianische Untersuchungen, 1926; J. Schrijnen-C. Mohrmann, Studien zur Syntax der Briefe des heiligen Cyprian, 1936–37; M. Bévenot, St. Cyprian's De Unitate Chapter IV in the Light of the Manuscripts, 1937; A. Beck, Roemisches Recht bei Tertullian und Cyprian, 1930; J. C. Plumpe, Mater Ecclesia, 1943, pp. 81–108; M. Pellegrino, Studi su l'antica Apologetica, 1947, pp. 107–149.

[Sup.] ROBERT M. GRANT.

CYRIL OF ALEXANDRIA: Recent studies of Cyril's theology have brought out its essential Platonism. It starts from Platonism and loses itself in abstractions, while his Antiochene opponents, more Aristotelian, lay emphasis on concrete facts, especially "facts" derived from the New Testament. The principal difficulty in his thought lies in: (1) his lack of clarity in definition and (2) his inability to work out the logical consequences of his own statements. He anathematizes Nestorius (q.v.) without taking the trouble to understand him. In turn the accusation of Monophysitism sometimes brought against Cyril considers his language rather than his intention.

Many citations from Cyril's works are found in the Liber contra impium Grammaticum by the Monophysite Severus of Antioch (ed. J. Lebon, 1929–38), and a sixth-century papyrus codex of his De adoratione et cultu is divided among libraries in Dublin, Paris, and Vienna (cf. P. Sanz, Mitteilungen aus der Papyrussammlung der Nationalbibl. in Wien IV [1946], pp. 111–124).

BIBLIOGRAPHY: J. Mahé in Dict. de théol. cath. III, 2476–2527; R. V. Sellers, Two Ancient Christologies, 1940; B. Altaner, Patrologie (2d ed., 1950), pp. 243–247; H. du Manoir du Juaye, Dogme et spiritualité chez saint Cyrille d'Alexandrie, 1944; A. Kerrigan, St. Cyril of Alexandria, Interpreter of the Old Testament, 1952.

[Sup.] ROBERT M. GRANT.

CZECH-MORAVIAN BRETHREN OF NORTH AMERICA, EVANGELICAL UNITY OF: Religious body organized at Granger, Texas, in 1903, by immigrants whose ancestors had belonged to the early Unitas Fratrum. (See UNITY OF THE BRETHREN). The more immediate European background had been Lutheran and Reformed. The Unity is in close fraternal relations with the Moravian Church, the two being drawn together by common tradition and doctrine. It is a member of the National Council of Churches (q.v.). There were in 1951 5,188 members in thirty-two congregations served by six ministers.

BIBLIOGRAPHY: Joseph Barton, The Texas Brethren, 1949.

[Sup. to MISC. RELIGIOUS BODIES: Evangelical Union of Bohemian and Moravian Brethren.]

JOHN R. WEINLICK.

CZECHOSLOVAKIA: When the Czechoslovakian Republic was established in 1918, its founder and first president, Thomas Garrigue Masaryk, infused his liberal spirit into its institutions. Politically, Czechoslovakia became a model of democratic organization. Religiously, the new republic aimed at equal treatment of existing ecclesiastical bodies; but owing to the fact that Roman Catholics constituted approximately 90% of the population, and held political and economic advantages of which they could not be dispossessed, the aim was not reached. Slovakia was far more staunchly Catholic than Bohemia-Moravia, but it was not freed from the jurisdiction of the Hungarian primate of Esztergom until 1937.

Because Roman Catholicism had traditionally supported the Habsburg monarchy, opposition to it often rested on nationalistic grounds. In 1920 nationalistic aspirations were supplemented by modernist demands for reform. The papal curia curtly rejected them, whereupon the proponents of reform organized a strongly anti-papal, nationalistic Czechoslovak Church. Since this body retained an episcopal organization, it attempted to secure from the Serbian Orthodox Church an agreement whereby its clergy could be educated and ordained under the auspices of the Serbs. The conditions laid down by the latter proved unacceptable to the modernist faction of the Czechoslovak Church and were therefore rejected. This majority group thereupon organized itself autonomously, although it retained episcopal polity and elected a patriarch as head of the church. A small Orthodox minority remained in communion with the Serbs. By 1930 the Czechoslovak Church numbered some 800,000, the Orthodox only 145,000.

The Protestant Churches of the country likewise underwent radical changes. The two major Evangelical communions—Reformed and Lutheran—united to form the Evangelical Church of Czech Brethren (1917). A large number of accessions doubled the size of the new church (in 1930 about 300,000). Several new denominations, some of them results of American missions, arose: Congregationalists, Methodists, Baptists, Unitarians.

When the Nazis invaded Czechoslovakia in March, 1938, they divided the country, making Bohemia-Moravia a protectorate, and setting up Slovakia as a puppet state under the leadership of a Roman Catholic prelate, Josef Tiso. Religious bodies suffered repression calculated to subordinate them to the new masters. Msgr. Beran, later archbishop of Prague, was interned in the concentration camp at Dachau. The Orthodox Church was entirely destroyed. In Slovakia the Protestant minorities were harshly dealt with by Slovak Catholics.

With Allied victory the regime of President Eduard Benes was restored (1945), but under greatly changed circumstances. He had negotiated a pact with the Soviet Union and had given a prominent place to Czech Communists led by Klemment Gottwald. Ruthenia was integrated into the Soviet Union, and thus Czechoslovakia lost the majority of its Orthodox population. But the former boundaries of Bohemia-Moravia were restored, although the majority of the German population was expelled (see REFUGEES).

Communists tolerated the coalition government for three years. When threatened with loss of power in the elections of 1948, they engineered a *coup d'état*. After establishing themselves in power, they began an attack upon religious bodies, particularly Roman Catholic. The non-Catholic bodies—Protestant and Czechoslovak alike—accepted the new regime voluntarily (to all appearances). The insignificant Orthodox Church was raised to the metropolitanate, on equality with Moscow, Kiev, and Leningrad. But the Roman Catholic Church resisted, particularly after the regime passed a law subjecting religious bodies to the state financially and administratively. Archbishop Beran was isolated from his clergy and people and relegated to an obscure monastery. The Vatican threatened excommunication to all who accepted

the new laws, but a priest, Josef Plojhar, became minister of health. The aim of the regime was to establish an autonomous national Catholic Church. In 1951 seven bishops were reported as having taken the oath of loyalty and were placed as administrators in charge of the church. Nevertheless, 3,000 of the 7,000 priests were reported in jail or prevented from active service; 70% of the churches were vacant (1951). Old theological seminaries were closed and replaced by state-controlled schools. New "Catholic Action" was organized. Many monasteries were closed, church lands confiscated, and control over youth transferred to the state. See also LOS VON ROM.

BIBLIOGRAPHY: Matthew Spinka, "The Religious Situation in Czechoslovakia," in R. J. Kerner, ed., *Czechoslovakia*, 1940; Gary MacEoin, *The Communist War on Religion*, 1951.

[Sup. to AUSTRIA; HUNGARY.]

MATTHEW SPINKA.

CZECHOSLOVAK NATIONAL CHURCH. See SLOVAK MISSION IN THE UNITED STATES.

D

DAGON. See GODS AND GODDESSES, PAGAN.

DAHL, GEORGE: Congregational-Christian; b. Jan. 11, 1881. He studied at Yale University (B.A., 1908; M.A., 1909; Ph.D., 1913), and in Germany (1909–10). He taught Old Testament in the Yale Divinity School (1912–49). He edited the *Journal of Biblical Literature* (1921–41) and has been a member of the Old Testament committee of the Revised Standard Version since 1940. He is the author of *Materials for the History of Dor* (1915); and *Heroes of Israel's Golden Age* (1923).

DAHOMEY. See AFRICA.

D'AIREBAUDOUZE, PIERRE, SIRE D'AN-DUZE: Sixteenth century French nobleman and Calvinist minister. Pierre d'Airebaudouze was one of the leaders in organizing Calvinist Protestantism in southeast France. After his conversion he served for a time as archdeacon of the Reformed Church of Nîmes. In 1553 he moved to Geneva; in 1555 he was appointed minister to the Jussy church in the Geneva countryside and in 1560 he became one of the Geneva city ministers. He apparently had substantial private means since he bought his own house, bought his way into the select group of Geneva "bourgeoisie," and took occasional trips at his own expense. In 1561 he was temporarily loaned to the Lyon Reformed Church and on November 25, 1561, he presided over a Provin-

cial Synod of the Lyonnais, Dauphiné and Burgundy churches meeting in Lyon. From 1561 to 1563 he kept up an extensive correspondence with churches in southeast France, particularly around Nîmes. Churches in this area often wrote to him instead of to Calvin or to the Geneva Company of Pastors, when they wanted new pastors or when they were sending students to Geneva to be trained for the ministry. Letters to the Company of Pastors and to Calvin often gave d'Airebaudouze as a reference regarding local conditions and people. In 1563 the Geneva municipal Council granted d'Airebaudouze to the Montpellier Reformed Church for one year. He stopped off at Nîmes for a long visit on the way, and after his stay in Montpellier returned to Nîmes where he seems to have served as pastor until the end of his life. In 1569 he was condemned to death "par contumace." In 1570 he appeared at the Nîmes Synod to propose a system for regular payment of ministers. He probably died soon thereafter.

BIBLIOGRAPHY: Very little has been published on Pierre d'Airebaudouze. See Eugène and Émile Haag, *La France Protestante*, Vol. I (2nd ed., 1877), pp. 63–64; Henri Heyer, *L'Eglise de Genève* . . . (1909), p. 418; *Bulletin de la Société de l'histoire du protestantisme français*, *passim;* and references in . . . *Calvini Opera* . . . , 1863–1880.

ROBERT M. KINGDON.

DAMASUS II: Was born in Bavaria. Before he could gain wide acceptance he had to overcome the opposition of the antipope Benedict IX. He held the papal office for only 23 days, whereupon he fell ill and died.   [Sup.]

DANIEL. See RAS SHAMRA.

DANIEL, BOOK OF: The view stated by Buhl that the Book of Daniel is an apocalyptic work coming from the period of the Seleucids is now generally adopted, although the article requires modification in details. The stories of Daniel chapters 1–6 belong in the literary context of the narratives of Jewish heroes and heroines in Esther, Judith, Tobit, Ahikar and Greek Esdras. The apocalyptic chapters 7–12, like the Apocalypse of John (which gave its name to this class of writings), are part of a large group of writings which present their messages in the form of symbolic visions ascribed to an ancient seer, and which were written chiefly in the last two centuries B.C. and the first century A.D. (Ethiopic Enoch, Jubilees, Testaments of the Twelve Patriarchs, Assumption of Moses, Slavonic Enoch, IV Ezra, etc.).

Critical opinion is still divided as to the unity of the book. The absence of any suggestion in chapters 1–6 of the Maccabean persecution, the relatively friendly attitude to foreign monarchs and the indications of a Babylonian rather than of a Palestinian background, are taken by many to indicate the existence of this cycle of stories before the addition of the apocalyptic chapters. The connection in thought between chapters 2 and 7 and the fact that the Aramaic ends with chapter 7 would then suggest that in an intermediate stage the book comprised chapters 1–7 in Aramaic. Following this interpretation, this appears to have been connected by glosses in chapter 7 with the Hebrew chapters 8–12 when the latter were appended, and 1:1–2:4a then to have been translated into Hebrew to make the whole a Hebrew book with an Aramaic enclosure.

Further light has been shed on some disputed points. Belshazzar was coregent with his father Nabonidus during the greater part of his father's reign (556–539 B.C.); Nabonidus possibly was Nebuchadrezzar's son-in-law. But no success has yet attended the efforts to discover a "Darius the Mede" preceding "Cyrus the Persian," or to identify this person with Gobryas-Gubaru who actually took Babylon and remained as its governor under Cyrus. The Darius who took Babylon and "received the kingdom" was the Darius I Hystaspis who reasserted Persian authority there in 521 B.C. after the city had revolted; that he then came with his army from Media may have led to his being called in some circles "the Mede."

BIBLIOGRAPHY: (Conservative) C. Boutflower. *In and Around the Book of Daniel*, 1923; R. D. Wilson, *Studies in the Book of Daniel*, 1917; (Liberal) W. Baumgartner, *Das Buch Daniel*, 1926; J. A. Montgomery, *The Book of Daniel*, 1927; R. H. Charles, *A Critical and Exegetical Commentary on the Book of Daniel*, 1929; R. P. Dougherty, *Nabonidus and Belshazzar*, 1929; M. A. Beek, *Das Danielbuch*, 1935; H. H. Rowley, *Darius the Mede and the Four World Empires*, 1935; idem, *The Relevance of Apocalyptic*, 1944; A. Bentzen, *Daniel*, 1937; H. L. Gins-berg, *Studies in Daniel*, 1948; (Roman Catholic) C. Lattey, *The Book of Daniel*, 1948; J. Steinmann, *Daniel*, 1950.

[Sup.] R. B. Y. SCOTT.

DANIEL'S BAND, CHURCH OF: Classed as an "evangelistic association," it sprang from the Methodist class meeting (*q.v.*) idea at Marine City, Mich., in 1893, and is a holiness church (*q.v.*). It has had no growth, and in 1952 had only three churches and about 130 members, all in Michigan, though some missionary work in Canada was reported.

[Sup. to Vol. VII, p. 391.] ELMER T. CLARK.

DANTE, ALIGHIERI: Has correctly been styled the creator of the modern Italian language as a literary vehicle, and his influence has been truly enormous, especially in the fields of literature and art. The original manuscript of the *Divina Comedia* has been lost, but there are more than 500 manuscript copies. The first edition dates from 1472. It was frequently issued during the fifteenth and sixteenth centuries, but after 1800 the work became more highly esteemed than ever before. During the nineteenth century there were more than 400 editions. It was translated into many languages, and in German alone more than 50 different translations have been published. A great many commentaries have also appeared. According to some critics, only the Bible has received more attention from the experts. In several countries Dante societies have been founded, such as the *Società Dantesca Italiana* (1888) in Italy, the *Deutsche Dante-Gesellschaft* in Germany (1865), which was later revived as the *Neue Dante-Gesellschaft* (1914), and the Dante Society in England (1895). There is also a Dante Society in the United States, founded in 1890. The freely translated Italian version of the *Romance of the Rose,* which under the title of *Il Fiore* was often ascribed to Dante, most certainly was not composed by him.

BIBLIOGRAPHY: Modern critical editions by the Soc. Dant. Ital. (Florence since 1921), and the revision of the Oxford-Dante (1923); periodicals: *Il Giornale Dantesco*, 1893–1927, since 1929 as year book; *Deutsches Dante Jahrbuch*, 1867–77, 1920, 1928 ff.; new commentaries: A. Momigliano, 3 vols., 1947; M. Stefnai Ignodi, 3 vols., 1949. Some new monographs: B. Croce, *La poesia di Dante*, 1921; P. Gauthier, *Dante le Chrétien*, 1931; G. Papini, *Dante vivo*, 1932; P. Mandonnet, *Dante le théologien*, 1935; E. Gilson, *Dante et la philosophie catholique*, 1939; B. Nardi, *Dante e la cultura medievale*, 1949; R. Guardini, *Der Engel in Dantes Goettiche Komoedie*, 2nd ed., 1951.

[Sup.] H. GOOSSENS.

D'ARCY, MARTIN: Roman Catholic; b. at Bath, Somerset, June 15, 1888. He studied at Stonyhurst College and Oxford University (M.A.). Ordained priest of the Society of Jesus (1921); he became master of Campion Hall, Oxford (1932–45) and lectured on philosophy. He was appointed graduate dean of philosophy, Fordham University (1939–40); lecturer at Institute of Advanced Study, Princeton

(1941–42), and English provincial of the Society of Jesus (1945–50). His writings include: *The Mass and the Redemption* (1925); *Catholicism* (1928); *The Spirit of Charity* (1929); *Mirage and Truth* (1930); *The Nature of Belief* (1931); *Christ as Priest and Redeemer* (1933); *Thomas Aquinas* (1935); *Christian Morals* (1937); *The Problem of Pain* (1938); *Death and Life* (1942); *Belief and Reason* (1943); *The Mind and Heart of Love* (1945).

DARGAN, EDWIN CHARLES: D. Oct. 26, 1930. After a pastorate in the First Baptist Church, Macon, Ga. (1907–17) he became editor of the Sunday School Lesson Helps of the Sunday School Board of the Southern Baptist Convention, Nashville, Tenn. (1917–27). His later publications include: *A History of Preaching* (Vol. I, 1905; Vol. II, 1912); *Harmony Hall; Recollections of an Old Southern Home* (1912); *An Exposition of the Epistle to the Romans* (1914); *The Changeless Christ and Other Sermons* (1918); *The Hope of Glory and Other Sermons* (1919); *The Art of Preaching in the Light of History* (1922); and *The Bible our Heritage* (1924).

[Sup.] RAYMOND W. ALBRIGHT.

DARLINGTON, JAMES HENRY: D. Aug. 14, 1930. In addition to his busy life as bishop of the Diocese of Harrisburg he was chairman of the Protestant Episcopal committee to confer with the Eastern Orthodox Churches and the Old Catholic Church (1910–25), and represented his church at ecumenical gatherings. His publications include: *In Memoriam; Little Rhymes for Little People; Verses by the Way* (1923; 4th series, 1929); and in addition to editing *The Hymnal of the Church* (1900) he composed hymn tunes, songs, instrumental music and a symphony, *The Sea and the Sea Gulls* (1929).

[Sup.] RAYMOND W. ALBRIGHT.

DAUGHTERS OF THE KING. See YOUNG PEOPLE'S SOCIETIES.

DAVID: Through a brilliant biography (see SAMUEL, BOOKS OF) we are better informed about David (*ca.* 1000 B.C.) than about any other Old Testament personality. David, son of Jesse, was born in Bethlehem (Judea) and became court musician, armor bearer, and son-in-law of King Saul. Jealous of his popularity, Saul forced David to become first a freebooter, then a vassal of Achish, the Philistine king of Gath. If David had been allowed to fight in the Philistine ranks at the battle of Gilboa, in which Saul died, he would never have become king of Israel. David composed a superb elegy over the death of Saul and Jonathan (II Sam. 1:17–27). For seven years he ruled as king of Judah (at Hebron) and, after the assassination of Ishbaal,

son of Saul, became king of united Israel. After conquering Jerusalem, his new capital, he delivered Israel from Philistine oppression and founded, through the weakness of Egypt, Babylonia, and Assyria, a short-lived empire, which disintegrated after the death of his son Solomon.

BIBLIOGRAPHY: R. Kittel, *Geschichte des Volkes Israel*, Vol. II, 6th ed., 1925; W. O. E. Oesterley and T. H. Robinson, *A History of Israel*, 1932; A. Lods, *Israel*, 1932; M. Noth, *Geschichte Israels*, 1950.

[Sup.] ROBERT H. PFEIFFER.

DAVID SPIRITUAL TEMPLE OF CHRIST CHURCH UNION U.S.A., NATIONAL.—See NATIONAL DAVID SPIRITUAL TEMPLE OF CHRIST CHURCH UNION, U.S.A.

DAVIES, HORTON: Congregationalist: b. at Cwmavon, Port Talbot, South Wales, U.K., Oct. 3, 1916. He was educated at Silcoates School, Wakefield, Yorks; Edinburgh (M.A., B.D.) and Oxford (D. Phil.) Universities; Yorkshire United Independent College; Bradford and Mansfield College, Oxford. He was minister of the Wallington and Carshalton Congregational Church, Surrey (1942–46), and is foundation professor and first head of the new interdenominational department of divinity at Rhodes University, Grahamstown, South Africa (1946–   ). His published works include: *Christian Worship, Its Making and Meaning* (1946); *The Worship of The English Puritans* (1948); *Towards an Ecumenical Theology and a United Church* (1948); *Great South African Christians* (1951); and *The English Free Churches* (1951).

DAWSON, CHRISTOPHER: B. at Hay Castle, Breconshire, Oct. 12, 1889. He was educated at Winchester and Trinity College, Oxford. (M.A., F.B.A., F.R.H.S.) He joined the Roman Catholic Church in 1913. He lectured on the history of culture, University College, Exeter (1925–33). In 1940 he took part with Cardinal Hinsley in the foundation of the Sword of the Spirit (*q.v.*) movement. His publications include: *The Age of the Gods* (1928); *Progress and Religion* (1929); *Christianity and the New Age* (1931); *The Modern Dilemma* (1932); *The Making of Europe* (1932); *The Spirit of the Oxford Movement* (1933); *Enquiries into Religion and Culture* (1934); *Mediaeval Religion* (1935); *Religion and the Modern State* (1935); *Beyond Politics* (1939); *The Judgement of the Nations* (1943); *Religion and Culture* (Gifford Lectures, 1948); *Religion and the Rise of Western Culture* (Gifford Lectures, 1950); *Understanding Europe* (1952).

DAY, ALBERT EDWARD: Methodist; b. Euphemia, O. He studied at Taylor University (A.B., 1904; D.D., 1918); University of Cincinnati (M.A., 1916). Ordained to the ministry of the M.E. Church (1904), he served as pastor at

Bellefontaine, Ohio (1904–06); Cincinnati (1913–16); Delaware, O., (1916–19); Canton (1919–25); Christ Church, Pittsburgh, Pa. (1925–32); Mount Vernon Place Church, Baltimore, Md. (1932–37; and since January, 1948); First Methodist Church, Pasadena (1937–45). He was director of New Life Movement of the Methodist Church (1945–47); and founded the Disciplined Order of Christ (1945). He is the author of: *Present Perils in Religion* (1928); *Revitalizing Religion* (1930); (with others) *Whither Christianity* (1929); (with others) *Contemporary Preaching* (1931); *Jesus and Human Personality* (1934); *God in Us—We in God* (1938); *The Evangel of a New World* (1939); *The Faith We Live* (1940); *Discipline and Discovery* (1946); and *An Autobiography of Prayer* (1952).

DAYTON, TENNESSEE. See SCOPES TRIAL.

DEACONESS: The work of deaconesses in twentieth century Protestantism has moved in two complementary directions: (1) It has built upon its nineteenth century foundations in terms of motherhouse and other forms of organization, and of types of service in health, welfare, education, parish and community work. (2) It has fostered closer relations with various other women's activities in the church (see WOMEN'S WORK) which express the New Testament ideal of diaconal service.

Specialized deaconess work in 1950 included over 60,000 women. Most of them Lutheran, there were also deaconess organizations in the Anglican, Episcopalian, Presbyterian, Reformed, Methodist, and Baptist Churches. Of the total membership, Germany (despite severe losses) claimed 46,000 deaconesses. Other countries included the Scandinavian countries and Finland; England and Scotland; the Netherlands, France, and Switzerland; Austria, Czechoslovakia, Hungary, Poland, Rumania; India and Australia. Of the United States' 1,500 deaconesses, over 800 were in the Methodist Church, 470 in Lutheran bodies, 130 in the Protestant Episcopal Church, 74 in the Evangelical and Reformed.

The International Federation of Deaconess Associations, popularly called "Diakonia," was organized in 1946 under Dutch leadership. Diakonia has endeavored to draw this diversified women's diaconate into a co-operative ecumenical partnership. Without supplanting the older German-dominated Kaiserwerth General Conference of Deaconess Motherhouses, it utilizes a broader organizational base, a wider denominational outreach, and a spirit reflecting the World Council of Churches (*q.v.*) and the concern of that body for the more effective implementation of the services of women in the life and work of the church.

In most countries deaconess work has been grappling with problems of readjustment. Such matters as educational standards in deaconess training, working conditions, salary, social security, the garb, the motherhouse type of organization, have received serious attention, with modifications ensuing. Other questions include: full theological training for women; ordination to the ministry (see WOMEN, ORDINATION OF); the extension of the diaconal ideal into vocations employing women, such as teaching, nursing, welfare work.

BIBLIOGRAPHY: Kathleen Bliss, *The Service and Status of Women in the Churches*, 1952; Inez Cavert, *Women in American Church Life*, 1948; Fritz Hoch, ed., *Vom Dienst der Frau in der Kirche der Gegenwart*, Reports of Diakonia, 1949; Charlotte von Kirschbaum, *Die Frau in der Wortverkuendigung*, 1950.

[Sup.] E. THEODORE BACHMANN.

DEAD SEA SCROLLS: I. The Discovery: The manuscripts known as the Dead Sea Scrolls were discovered by an Arab goatherd early in 1947 in a cave near the northwest corner of the Dead Sea. Five were sold to Mar Athanasius Yeshue Samuel, the Syrian Orthodox Metropolitan, at St. Mark's Monastery in Jerusalem, six to Professor E. L. Sukenik of the Hebrew University. Each purchased also several fragments of manuscripts.

The cave was visited by individuals, but not until the early months of 1949 was it scientifically excavated by G. L. Harding of the Department of Antiquities of Jordan and Father R. de Vaux of the Dominican École Biblique at Jerusalem. No more manuscripts were found, but hundreds of fragments were uncovered. Other fragments have since been acquired by the Palestine Museum at Jerusalem.

Two of the scrolls bought by the Syrian Metropolitan are parts of the Manual of Discipline of a Jewish sect. One is a complete copy of the book of Isaiah; another contains a commentary on Habakkuk. The fifth is in bad condition and has not been unrolled. One column has been detached; it is in Aramaic and consists of apocalyptic material, possibly from the lost Apocalypse of Lamech. The fragments purchased by Archbishop Samuel include two from the book of Daniel. Of the scrolls bought by Professor Sukenik, one contains part of the book of Isaiah, one a composition called the War of the Sons of Light with the Sons of Darkness, and the other three psalms of thanksgiving. The fragments excavated include bits of Genesis, Deuteronomy, and Judges, four in an archaic script from Leviticus, and a scrap of the book of Jubilees in Hebrew. Among the fragments purchased by the Palestine Museum are portions of the Manual of Discipline.

II. Date: The date of the manuscripts is disputed, but evidence of several kinds is available. The excavation showed that the manuscripts had been placed in large jars of the Hellenistic period. A few pieces of Roman pottery suggested that the cave had been entered during the Roman period. The manuscripts may have been more or less ancient than the jars; the excavators believe, however, that all were deposited in the cave before 100 B.C. Other archaeologists lower the limit to about 25 B.C.

The materials used afford a general indication of date. The radiocarbon method of dating ancient materials cannot be applied to the scrolls themselves because it involves the destruction of the material; some of the linen in which the scrolls were wrapped has been examined by this process, however, and dated between 167 B.C. and A.D. 233.

Two literary references to similar discoveries in the same region have been noted by scholars. Eusebius says that a manuscript used by Origen was found in a jar at Jericho; nothing is said of a cave, and the text in question was not Hebrew but Greek. A discovery of Hebrew manuscripts in a cave near Jericho about A.D. 800 is related in a letter of Timotheus, Metropolitan of Seleucia. This may have been the same cave that was discovered in 1947.

Paleography provides evidence of the age of the scrolls. Lack of exactly dated material for comparison prevents precise dating on this basis, but the material is sufficient to make wholly improbable a date earlier than 150 B.C. for the oldest of the scrolls (except perhaps the Leviticus fragments in archaic script) or later than A.D. 150 for the youngest of them.

The original compositions are of course older than the manuscripts containing them. Aside from the books of the Old Testament, when the writings contained in the scrolls were composed must be determined by internal evidence, including references to historical persons and events. The War of the Sons of Light with the Sons of Darkness gives directions for a conflict which may be either historical or eschatological but cannot be identified with any known war. The Kittim in this document seem to be the Macedonian rulers of Egypt and Syria. In the Habakkuk Commentary, however, the Kittim are the Romans. The Commentary, like the Damascus Document, speaks of a Teacher of Righteousness. He was persecuted by a Wicked Priest. A Man of the Lie is mentioned also, and a group called the House of Absalom is condemned for not helping the Teacher of Righteousness. Many attempts to identify all these have been made, but none as yet is convincing. A passage in the Habakkuk Commentary is interpreted by Dupont-Sommer as referring to the capture of Jerusalem by Pompey in 63 B.C., but his interpretation is unacceptable. The historical references have not yet yielded any clear clue to the date of the compositions.

The language of the documents tells something of their place in the history of the Hebrew language. In general it is similar to that of the latest books of the Old Testament, but goes farther than any of them or any other extant Hebrew literature.

In religious terminology and sometimes in extended passages the documents are closely related to the Damascus Document and evidently come from the same group. Affinities with the Apocrypha and Pseudepigrapha, with the rabbinic literature, and even with that of the medieval Karaites have been noted. In the religious ideas and practices and the moral ideals of the group may be found evidence concerning its place in the history of Judaism. The interpretation of Scripture, the calendar, the organization and rites of the group, its apocryphal and messianic ideas, its dualism and angelology, and its attitudes toward war, marriage, and wealth are all significant. Even these, however, do not enable us to establish the chronological position of these writings in Jewish history.

The group represented by the Dead Sea Scrolls and the Damascus Document has been identified by scholars with the pre-Maccabean Hasidim, with some branch of the Pharisees in the Hasmonean period, with the Essenes, with an obscure group called Magharians (cave people), with the followers of Zadok the Pharisee at the time of the destruction of the temple, and with the Christian Ebionites, not to mention the Karaites. Much research will be necessary before the evidence and arguments for all these theories can be sifted and the possibilities and probabilities duly weighed.

III. Significance: Meanwhile it is clear that the scrolls are important in many ways. The Isaiah manuscripts and to a lesser extent some of the other documents are important sources for the textual criticism of the Old Testament. In the Syrian Isaiah manuscript especially we have now a pre-Masoretic Hebrew text, poorly copied and full of errors but containing also real variants, some of which may be superior to the Masoretic readings. These manuscripts afford entirely new knowledge of the vulgar forms of the Old Testament text which circulated alongside the more carefully guarded quasi-official tradition.

For the history of Judaism the significance of the scrolls is great, even though we cannot precisely date them or exactly identify the group which produced them. They testify to the variety and richness of Jewish beliefs, traditions, and practices in the period between the completion of the Old Testament and the definite establishment of "normative" orthodox Judaism. The covenanters of Judea were one of many lateral branches of the family tree of Judaism which did not survive but which bore fruit for later periods of the religion.

The bearing of the documents on Christian origins and early history is important also, though it has been exaggerated by a few scholars. Antecedents and parallels for terms and ideas which appear in the New Testament and other Christian writings appear in the scrolls. In general, however, it is just the importance of the scrolls for Judaism in the Hellenistic or Roman period which makes them most important for Christian history.

BIBLIOGRAPHY: The periodic literature on the scrolls is already enormous. Only book titles are given here. Millar Burrows, John Trever, and William Brownlee, *The Dead Sea Scrolls of St. Mark's Monastery*, I, 1950; II, fasc. 2, 1951; A Dupont-Sommer, *Aperçus préliminaires sur les Monuscrits de la Mer Morte*, 1950; *Observations sur le Commentaire d'Habacus découvert près de la Mer Morte*, 1950; *Observations sur le Manuel de Discipline découvert près de la Mer Morte*, 1951; Paul Kahle, *Die Hebraeischen Handschriften aus der Hoehle*, 1951; E. L. Sukenik, *Megillot Genuzot*, I, 1948; II, 1950; Mier Wallenstein, *Hymns from the Judean Scrolls*, 1950.

MILLAR BURROWS.

DEARMER, PERCY: Anglican; b. in London, Feb. 27, 1867; d. May 29, 1936. He was educated at Christ Church College, Oxford (B.A., 1890; M.A., 1896; B.D.). He was rector of St. Anne's, South Lambeth (1891–94); St. John the Baptist, Great Marlborough (1894–97); Berkeley Chapel, Mayfair (1897); St. Mark's Marylebone Road (1898–1901); and Vicar of St. Mary the Virgin, Hampstead (1901–15). From 1914 to 1918 he was a chaplain to the British Red Cross and from 1919 to 1931 was lecturer in art and professor of ecclesiastical art in King's College, London. He became canon of Westminster (1931–36) and also served there as librarian (1933–36). A leading liturgiologist, he was a major authority in this field and his books are still widely used in these studies. He tried to recall the church to the native English traditions in liturgy and ceremonial and also to improve church music. He wrote: *The Parson's Handbook* (1899); *Highways and Byways in Normandy* (1900); *The English Liturgy* (1903); *The Server's Handbook* (1904); *The Sanctuary* (1905); *Body and Soul* (1909); *Everyman's History of the English Church* (1909); *Reunion and Rome* (1910); *Fifty Pictures of Gothic Altars* (1910); *The Dragon of Wessex* (1911); *Illustrations of the Liturgy* (1911); *Everyman's History of the Prayerbook* (1912; rev. as *The Story of the Prayerbook*, 1933); *The English Carol Book* (1913); *The Art of Public Worship* (1919); *Power of the Spirit* (1920); *Lessons on the Way* (Vols. I–V, 1921–25); *The Church at Prayer* (1923); *Art and Religion* (1924); *The Truth about Fasting* (1928); *The Sin Obsession* (1929); *The Legend of Hell* (1929); *A Short Handbook of Public Worship* (1931); *Our National Church* (1934); *Sanctuary* (1923) *Linen Ornaments of the Church* (1919); *Eight Preparations for Communion* (1923); *The Ornaments of Ministers* (1911); *The New Reformation; The Church of England and the Fellowship of Churches* (1934) and an early work *Religious Pamphlets* (1898). He also edited: *The English Hymnal* (1906); *The Necessity of Art* (1924); *Songs of Praise* (1925; enlarged ed., 1931); *Affirmations: God in the Modern World* (1928); *Oxford Book of Carols* (1928); *Songs of Praise for Boys and Girls* (1929); *Songs of Praise Discussed* (1933); and *Christianity and the Crisis* (1933).

BIBLIOGRAPHY: Nan Dearmer, *Percy Dearmer*, 1940.

RAYMOND W. ALBRIGHT.

DeBENNEVILLE, GEORGE: First American Universalist; b. in London, July 26, 1703, the son of a Huguenot refugee and his wife who was a relative of one of Queen Anne's ministers, Sir George Granville. After a youth of travel in Africa, France, Germany, and Holland, including the study of medicine, deBenneville went to the Duchy of Wittgenstein, where he developed friendship with the editors of the famous mystical Bible of Berlenberg. In 1741 deBenneville came to Pennslvania, arriving just as a pestilence broke out, and he put his medical skill to work in Germantown, where he also helped the printer, Christopher Sower (*q.v.*, Vol. XI), edit his works. In March, 1742, he went to the Oley Valley in Pennsylvania, where he lived with Jean Bartolet, whose daughter Esther became deBenneville's wife in 1745. While living in Oley, deBenneville made the acquaintance of Pennsylvania sectarian leaders, and he seems to have been the leading spirit in getting Sower to print many of the books he brought out. In 1747 deBenneville moved to Philadelphia, where he maintained an apothecary shop and practiced medicine, ministering to the wounded during the Revolution. The rediscovered deBenneville religious and medical manuscripts place him in the forefront of colonial religious leaders, marking him as an astute man, uniting religious devotion with practical ministry. He died March 19, 1793.

BIBLIOGRAPHY: Albert D. Bell, *The Life and Times of Dr. George deBenneville*, 1953.

JOHN JOSEPH STOUDT.

DE BIVORT DE LA SAUDEE, JACQUES: Roman Catholic priest; b. at Roisin, Belgium on Feb. 15, 1900. He joined the Society of Jesus in 1918 and was priested in 1930. In 1948 he left the Jesuits to join the Oratory. In 1951 he was appointed the Belgian corresponding member for the preparation of *The Scientific and Cultural History of Mankind*. His chief publications are: *Anglicans et catholiques:* t. I, *Le Problème de l'Union anglo-romaine (1833–1933)*; t. II, *Documents sur le Problème de l'Union anglo-romaine (1921–27)* (1949); *Essai sur Dieu, l'Homme et l'Univers* (1951; Italian ed., 1952; Eng. ed., 1952); and *L'Antireligion communiste (1917–37)* (1937; Eng. ed., 1939).

RAYMOND W. ALBRIGHT.

DE BLOIS, AUSTEN KENNEDY: Baptist; b. Dec. 17, 1866, at Wolfville, N. S.; d. Aug. 10, 1945. He studied at Acadia College (1886); in

Europe; at Brown (A.M., 1888; Ph.D., 1889); and at the Newton Theological Institute (1889). He was principal, Union Baptist Seminary, St. Martins, N. B. (1892–94); president, Shurtleff College, Alton, Ill., (1894–99); pastor of First Baptist Church, Elgin, Ill. (1899–1902); First Baptist Church, Chicago, Ill. (1902–11); First Baptist Church, Boston, Mass. (1911–26); editor, *The Watchman-Examiner* (1926–28); and president of the Eastern Baptist Theological Seminary, Philadelphia, Pa. (1926–36; emeritus, 1936–45). He has written: *Bible Study in American Colleges* (1899); *The Pioneer School* (1900); *Imperialism and Democracy* (1901); *History of the First Baptist Church in Boston, 1665–1915* (1916); *Life of John Mason Peck, Prophet of the Prairies* (1917); *The Message of Wisdom, Studies in the Book of Proverbs* (1920); *Some Problems of the Modern Minister* (1928); *John Bunyan, The Man* (1928); *Fighters of Freedom* (1929); *Evangelism in the New Age* (1933); *The Church of Today—and Tomorrow* (1934); *The Making of Ministers* (1936); *Christian Religious Education: Principles and Practice* (1939); and he also edited and translated Borelius' *Grundrisse der jetzigen Lage in der deutschen Philosophie.*   RAYMOND W. ALBRIGHT.

DE BRÈS, GUIDO. See BRÈS, GUIDO DE.

DEBRUNNER, ALBERT: Reformed; b. in Basel, Switzerland, Feb. 8, 1884. He studied at the universities of Goettingen and Basel (Dr. Phil., 1907). He has taught Indo-Germanic philology at Zurich (1917–18); Greifswald (1918–20); Bern (1920–25); Jena (1925–35); and Bern (1935–). He has been a member of the synod of the Evangelical-Reformed Church of the Canton of Bern (1938– ; president, 1946–50). He is coauthor with Friedrich Blass of *Grammatik des neutestamentlichen Griechisch* (4th to 8th eds., 1913–50).   RAYMOND W. ALBRIGHT.

DECALOGUE: The Decalogue appears in Exodus 20:2–17 and Deuteronomy 5:6–21 in different forms. The deviations, however, concern only the last of the basic commandments; they are more numerous in the explanations which are added to some of them. From this it would appear that both compositions are secondary and that the Decalogue originally consisted only of the commandments proper. The statements about murder, adultery, robbery, and false witness are kept in their original form.

The reconstructed Ur-Decalogue belongs in form and content to the pattern of apodictic compositions frequently appearing in the Old Testament. They served, as the fully-preserved example of Deut. 27:15–26 (cf. 31:10 ff.) shows, to renew at great cultic assemblies the obligation of Israel to Jahweh's categorical will of right. They indicate only the heaviest crimes, and accordingly they are formulated regularly as prohibitions. The Decalogue also seems to have been shaped originally in all its sentences as prohibitive.

Within this pattern the Decalogue occupies an exceptional position, first of all in that it opens with a self-predication of Jahweh in an I-style corresponding to the You-style in the address in the following sentences. This reveals the situation in the act of concluding or renewing the covenant between Jahweh and Israel (cf. Ps. 81:10 f.). Secondly, the Decalogue does not aim at a formal symmetry of the single sentences. Thereby there is attained an absolute formulation on which to a large extent the incomparable effect of the Decalogue depends.

From all appearances the pattern of apodictic compositions goes back to the beginnings of the history of Israel. A more accurate dating of its individual expressions, as for instance the Decalogue, is impossible and in fact of no particular importance.

BIBLIOGRAPHY: R. H. Charles, *The Decalogue*, 1923; H. Meinhold, *Der Dekalog*, 1927; S. Mowinckel, *Le décalogue*, 1927; L. Koehler, *Der Dekalog*, *TR*, N.F. 1, 1929; A. Alt, *Die Urspruenge des Israelitischen Rechts*, 1934, p. 52 ff.
     [Sup.] ALBRECHT ALT.

DECAPOLIS: An ancient league of Hellenistic cities, formed probably in the first century B.C. and lasting until at least the second century A.D. All except Scythopolis lay east of the Jordan River. It originally included ten cities (the name combines the Greek words *deka*, "ten," and *polis*, "city"); Pliny the Elder's list mentions Damascus, Philadelphia, Raphana, Scythopolis, Gadara, Hippos, Dion, Pella, Galasa (Gerasa), and Canatha (*Historia Naturalis*, v. 16). Later additional cities joined. A second century inscription shows that Abila was a member, and Ptolemy (*Geography*, v. 14) lists eighteen members; he includes all that Pliny names except Raphana, and adds nine others, including Abila. While the first extant mention of the Decapolis occurs in the second half of the first century A.D. (Mark 5:20, 7:31; Matthew 4:25; Josephus, *Wars*, III. 9.7), the league probably originated shortly after 64–63 B.C., when Pompey "liberated" the Hellenistic cities of Palestine from Jewish control and placed them under the Roman governor of the province of Syria.

The league provided more adequate defense against desert tribes, kept an alert watch against Semitic aggression and influence, encouraged Hellenistic ways of life, and fostered mutual trade relations between members. Extensive ruins at Gerasa, Philadelphia, and Gadara illustrate the Hellenistic plan and architecture of these cities, with impressive walls, forum, temples, theaters, and colonnades. Located on the eastern border of the Roman Empire, the Decapolis helped maintain a Graeco-Roman frontier in a dominantly Semitic region.

BIBLIOGRAPHY: G. A. Smith, *Historical Geography of the Holy Land*, 25th ed. (1931), Chap. 28; H. Guthe, *Die griechischroemischen Staedte des Ostjordanlandes* 1918; E. Schuerer, *History of the Jewish People in the Time of Jesus Christ*, English trans., Division II, Vol. I (n.d.), pp. 18–20, 94–122; C. Kraeling, *Gerasa*, 1938; G. E. Wright and F. V. Filson, *Westminster Historical Atlas to the Bible* (1945), pp. 83–86.

FLOYD V. FILSON.

DECLARATION OF HUMAN RIGHTS, UNIVERSAL. See LIBERTY, RELIGIOUS.

DECLARATION OF INDULGENCE: The 1672 Declaration, possibly the work of Clifford, came as a relief to suffering Nonconformists. They were allowed a number of licensed buildings for worship, while Roman Catholics could meet in private houses. But fear of popery, and the refusal to allow that the king could override the law, compelled its withdrawal. James II hoped by issuing the Declarations of 1687 and 1688, to win over to his side the Nonconformists, and unite them with the Roman Catholics against the Established Church. With, however, one or two exceptions, notably William Penn who highly approved his action, James had no support.

BIBLIOGRAPHY: F. Bate, *The Declaration of Indulgence, 1672*, 1908; G. N. Clark, *The Later Stuarts* (1934), pp. 21, 56. 75, 119. 120; C. E. Whiting, *Studies in English Puritanism, 1660–1688*, 1931; A. A. Seaton, *The Theory of Toleration under the Later Stuarts*, 1911; F. C. Turner, *James II* (1948), pp. 395–404; G. P. Gooch, *Political Thought in England from Bacon to Halifax* (1946), pp. 168–70, 176–77.

[Sup.] GORDON HUELIN.

DECLARATORY ACT: An enactment by the highest legislative court of a Presbyterian Church, stating that Church's attitude to its confessional standards. The first such act was passed by the Synod of the United Presbyterian Church in Scotland in 1879, and it decreed that ministers and elders of that church would no longer be required to subscribe literally to the Westminster Confession (see WESTMINSTER STANDARDS, Vol. XII), but would enjoy liberty of interpretation in such matters as did not enter into the substance of the faith. The Free Church of Scotland passed a similar act in 1892, and the established Church of Scotland in 1910. In America the Presbyterian Church in the U.S.A. adopted a similar measure in 1903.

BIBLIOGRAPHY: J. R. Fleming, *The Church in Scotland, 1875–1929*, 1933.

NORMAN V. HOPE.

DE CLERQ, CHARLES: Roman Catholic priest; b. in Antwerp on January 15, 1905. He studied history at Louvain (Ph.D.); in the Oriental Institute at Rome, and canon law at Paris. He has been lecturer at the American College, Louvain, Toulouse, Paris and Quebec. He organized a center of documentation for the history of sacramental and ecclesiastical law at Antwerp. He wrote: *Les Eglises unies d'Orient*

(1934); *La législation religieuse franque de Clovis à Charlemagne* (1936); *Le mariage en droit canonique oriental* (1936); *Catalogue des manuscrits du Grand Séminaire de Malines* (1937); *Ordre, Mariage, Extrême Onction* (1939); *Dix siècles d'histoire byzantine* (1946); *Des Sacrements* (1948); *Conciles des Orientaux catholiques, 1575–1949* (2 vols., 1949, 1952).

RAYMOND W. ALBRIGHT.

DECREE, DIVINE. See SOTERIOLOGY.

DEEMS, MERVIN MONROE: Congregationalist; b. Baltimore, Md., Feb. 22, 1899. He studied at Johns Hopkins University (A.B., 1921), the Southern Baptist Theological Seminary (Th.M., 1924), and the University of Chicago (Ph.D., 1928). He was assistant professor of history, William Jewell College (1924–26); assistant professor of history and religion, Carleton College (1928–31); Waldo professor of ecclesiastical history and missions, Bangor Theological Seminary (1936–43); and professor of the history of early Christianity and missions, The Chicago Theological Seminary and the Federated Theological Faculty, the University of Chicago (1943–). He was pastor of the Second Congregational Church, Norway, Maine, 1932–36. He has done research in early Christian asceticism and in Augustine. He is assistant secretary of the American Society of Church History. He is editor of The Chicago Theological Seminary *Register*.

DEFENSOR VINCULI. See DEFENDER OF THE MARRIAGE TIE, in Vol. III.

DEFERRARI, ROY JOSEPH: Roman Catholic; b. Stoneham, Mass., June 1, 1890. He studied at Dartmouth (A.B., 1912) and Princeton (M.A., 1913; Ph.D., 1915); he was instructor in classics at Princeton (1915–17); taught Greek and Latin at Catholic University of America (1918–49); Dean of Graduate School (1930–37), director of summer session (1929–), secretary general (1937–), director of workshops (1946–). He is author, editor, translator of Concordances of *Prudentius* (1931), *Ovid* (1939), *Lucan* (1940), *Statius* (1942); *Lexicon of St. Thomas* (1949–52); tr. *De Sacramentis*, Hugh of St. Victor (1951); editorial director, *Fathers of the Church Series* (1949–).

DEFINITOR: In some religious orders, title given to assistants of the superior provincial or general, and to elected representatives to the provincial or general chapters.

DEHN, GUNTHER KARL: Lutheran; b. April 18, 1882, at Schwerin (Mecklbg.) Germany. After studying languages, history and theology at Halle, Bonn, and Berlin (1900–05) he became assistant pastor of the Berlin cathedral and associate and examiner of the ministerial candidate school there (1907–11). After eighteen years (1912–30) as pastor of the Reformation congregation in Berlin he became professor of practical theology in Halle in 1931, serving until his dismissal in March, 1933. After eight years as theological teacher of the confessional church in Berlin (1933–41) he was under arrest (1941–42) and became pastoral administrator in Ravensburg (Wuertt.) (1942–45). Since 1946 he has been professor of practical theology in Bonn. He has written: *Proletarierjugend* (1911); *Grossstadtjugend* (1921); *Die religioese Gedankenwelt Proletarierjugend* (1924); *"Ich bin der Herr, dein Gott"* (1924); *Kirche und Voelkerversoehnung* (1931); *Proletarische Jugend* (1931); *Man and Revelation* (1936); *Predigtmeditationen* (2 vols., 1937–40); *Erklaerung des Galaterbriefes* (Gesetz oder Evangelium) (1938); *Jesus Christus, Gottes Sohn* (1940); *Die Zehn Gebote fuer Kinder erklaert* (1950); *Unsere Predigt heute* (1946); *Die Amtshandlungen der Kirche* (1950).

RAYMOND W. ALBRIGHT.

DE JONG, JOHANNES CARDINAL: Archbishop of Utrecht; b. at Nes on the isle of Ameland, Sept. 10, 1885. He was educated in seminaries at Culemborg and Rijsenburg and ordained Aug. 15, 1908. He continued his studies in theology and philosophy at the papal Gregorian University at Rome (Th.D. and Ph.D., 1911). He served as vicar at Amersfoort (1911–12); conrector of the mother institution of the Sisters of Our Holy Lady at Amersfoort (1912–14); professor of ecclesiastical history in the seminary Rijsenburg at Dreibergen (1914–31; president, 1931–35); titular archbishop of Rusio and coadjutor to the archbishop of Utrecht (1935–36); archbishop of Utrecht (1936–); and was elevated to the cardinalate in 1946 with San Clemente at Rome as his titular church. During the occupation of the Netherlands by the Nazis (1940–45) Cardinal de Jong was the leader of the ecclesiastical-religious resistance. He has published: (with W. Knuif) *Philippus Rovenius en zijn bestuur der Hollande Missie* (1925); and *Handboek van de Kerkgeschiedenis* (4 parts; 1929–32; fourth edition 1945).

RAYMOND W. ALBRIGHT.

DE LA BEDOYERE, MICHAEL: Roman Catholic; b. 1900. He studied at Stonyhurst College (Lancashire) and Oxford University (M.A., 1929). He was assistant lecturer in University of Minnesota (1930); assistant editor of *Dublin Review* (1931–34); editor of the *Catholic Herald* since 1934. He is the author of many books, including *Christianity in the Market Places; Christian Crisis; No Dreamers Weak*, and biographies of Lafayette, George Washing-

ton, St. Catherine of Siena, and Baron von Huegel.

BIBLIOGRAPHY: Matthew Hoehn (ed.), *Catholic Authors*, 1948.

DELEGATE, APOSTOLIC: The title of some representatives of the pope. The nature of their office is described summarily in the *Codex Juris Canonici*, canon 267, par. 2. Apostolic delegates are usually titular archbishops assigned permanently to represent the papal government in its relations with the hierarchy of a given country. It should be emphasized that their functions are not of a diplomatic character, since they are not accredited to the sovereign of a nation, as nuncios and internuncios are (see LEGATES AND NUNCIOS, Vol. VI). However, they may have to deal occasionally with political matters, and they are often granted semi-diplomatic privileges by civil governments. The ordinary duties of apostolic delegates are to ascertain that the laws of the church are observed correctly, to inform the Holy See of the state and progress of the church in their circumscription, to communicate special instructions of the pope to ordinaries (*q.v.*) and to grant papal dispensations, absolutions, etc., within the limits of their faculties, or to transmit petitions and appeals to the proper Roman agencies. There are actually twenty-three apostolic delegations, of which five depend on the Congregation of the Consistory, eight on the Congregation for the Eastern Church, and eleven on the Congregation of the Propaganda (see CONGREGATIONS, ROMAN). The apostolic delegation in the United States was founded in 1893. Cf. "Delegato Apostolico," in *Enciclopedia Catolica*, IV, 1950.

GEORGES A. BARROIS.

DELEGATION: According to Roman Catholic canon law, those who, by virtue of their office, enjoy ordinary jurisdiction, may, under conditions fixed by statute, delegate their power generally or in view of particular objects. In the latter case, the terms of the delegation are to be strictly interpreted. Jurisdictional actions exceeding the powers bestowed upon the delegate are null and void. Cf. *Codex Iuris Canonici*, can. 200–207.

GEORGES A. BARROIS.

DELINQUENCY. See CRIME.

DEMOCRACY: In its primary meaning, democracy is government (Greek *kratos*, "rule") by the people (Greek *demos*). In Abraham Lincoln's happy and famous words, it is government "of the people, by the people, and for the people." Such a definition of the term, however, is not universally accepted in our times. Since the Russian communist leaders regard theirs as already a democratic government, they would apparently reject the phrase "by the people," and regard the other two as a sufficient and complete definition, the third being really definitive. Theirs is said to be a democratic government on the alleged ground that it is for the people, and the government of the United States is declared not to be democratic on the alleged ground that it is "for Wall Street." Stalin at least openly acknowledged that his was not by the people, though some superficial bows are made in the direction of that phrase too by the holding of elections (but with only one slate of candidates) from time to time, and by calling "representatives" of the people into a show of consultation occasionally (see COMMUNISM, MARXIAN).

As this very fundamental difference will suggest, the term democracy, in its connotation and even more in its denotation, is by no means easy to define, and it is very commonly employed more as a term of emotional approval or disapproval than as a strictly defined description. If we say that democracy is "a form of government in which sovereignty resides in the people as a whole and is exercised either directly by them or by officers elected by, and responsible to, them," it will be replied by some that you have democracy only when sovereignty is exercised by the people as a whole directly. When authority is delegated to elected officials, so it will be maintained, you have a republic, not a democracy. Others would agree that both forms are democratic, while yet revealing a measure of agreement with the former by characterizing government without delegation of authority as pure democracy. Apparently they regard government through delegation of authority as democracy but not pure democracy.

Some appear to judge that democracy requires a more extensive equality than simply "equality before the law," and deny that Great Britain, for example, is a democracy, though it has representative government based on universal adult suffrage and observes the principle of equality before the law (except for the person of the sovereign), on the ground that Britain is a monarchy and retains some feudal forms and privileges. The French revolutionists emphasized equality (without defining it) in their slogan, and they experimented with it in practice; but their experience with it, and the subsequent instability of French society, shows that they have not succeeded in solving the problem. Lenin and Stalin had to face the problem, particularly in its economic aspect; and they have rejected equalitarianism, though it is not clear that such a solution has satisfied all their coworkers. The problem is, in essence, that democracy requires a large measure of individual liberty, and that this in turn requires some kind and degree of equality; but, on the other hand, unrestricted individual liberty is impossible in a social situation, and anything approaching complete

equality is unnatural. It cannot be justly admitted that any precise solution of this problem, in theory or in practice, is available.

It is generally agreed that an undue restriction of the franchise is undemocratic, but a commonly accepted definition of "undue restriction" has not been achieved. People whose spirit is undoubtedly democratic, but who regard the protection of property rights as the main, or the sole, function of government, have seen no challenge to democracy in a property qualification. Others have proposed some kind of educational or intelligence restriction. Others have advocated, and practised, a "racial" restriction. Until recently, and still in some countries, democracies saw no contradiction in restricting the franchise to adult males. Now it is being suggested that the age restriction of twenty-one years is undemocratically high. The problem here is that democracy calls for as little restriction as possible, while the exercise of the franchise calls for a reasonable measure of responsibility.

Obviously, especially as states become larger, democratic processes may be slow, blundering, and, however effective in the long run, quite wasteful, in some respects, in their proximate operation. It has been judged by some that, for this reason (alone or along with others), no democracy could long survive. Others have felt that democracy could function securely only if there were delegated to a strong, central government powers which, in the judgment of others, were inimical to the rights of individuals or of lesser governmental units within the state, and so extensive as to call in question the right of such a state to be called democratic. Others have contended, and this seems to be upheld by experience, that a strong central government is necessary in times of internal or external stress, but that in less pressing circumstances the "emergency powers" may and should be reclaimed and surrendered. In any case, here is another problem with regard to which no theoretical solution seems to be at hand.

Democracy also attributes to the individual, and demands of him, a comparatively high level of mental capacity and attainment, and of moral responsibility. At the same time, it is usually recognized that men are commonly all too lacking in knowledge and wisdom, in moral reliability and in earnestness of desire to acquire such qualifications. People who are most strongly impressed with the frailty of man, and not convinced of the reliability of the law of compensation even where large numbers of individuals are involved, usually decide that, for that reason also, democracy cannot be a stable form of government. Others, who cannot accept such a conclusion, must still admit the frailty of man and recognize that, in order to succeed, a democratic government must provide certain safeguards, negative and positive. Typical of the negative safeguards are the American constitutional system of checks and balances, the provision for appeal to the electorate at stated, relatively frequent, times, and, in some instances, for referendum and recall. Typical of positive safeguards is the strong emphasis, characteristic of democracies, on free, universal education, freedom of the press, freedom of assembly, and so forth.

A high evaluation of the individual, such as this, also requires a supporting and guiding philosophy. Democracy, it is said, is not simply a form of government; it is a way of life. Historically, in ancient Athens and in the modern West, that philosophy has prevailingly been a humanism of a more or less naturalistic type. It is frequently contended, however, that such a philosophy is itself not stable, and that it needs to adopt, or to become aware of, religious roots. This view is supported by negative and positive historical arguments. On the one hand, the ruin of democracy in Athens is attributed to the abandonment of religious sanctions; and the recent serious challenge to it in the West, marked by open opposition to and temporary abandonment of it in Germany and in Italy, is attributed to the progressive secularization of European culture. Positively, we find an argument such as that of James Hastings Nichols (*Democracy and the Churches*, 1951), who seeks to show historically that modern democracy has been really at home only where the Reformed branch of Protestant Christianity has been strong. Nichols acknowledges only the Scandinavian countries, prevailingly Lutheran, as exceptions to this generalization, and there he finds exceptional circumstances at work.

There does seem to be a profound affinity between democracy and a Christianity of this type, which incidentally, without denying the right of other expressions of Christianity, regards itself as the most complete and authentic expression of the Christian revelation. But, if so, this affinity must not be pressed too far, as some do who, in incautious enthusiasm, appear to teach that the establishment of democracy was the sole or central purpose of Christ's incarnation. It is justly pointed out that recognizable forms of Christianity do not themselves possess or desire a democratic form of organization; that Christianity can and does work effectively in any form of social organization; and that the incarnation had purposes much more fundamental than this.

BIBLIOGRAPHY: From an extensive literature the following ancient and very modern discussions may be consulted: Plato's *Laws;* Aristotle's *Politics;* Alf Ross, *Why Democracy?* translated by David Gatley-Philip, 1952; W. H. Riker, *Democracy in the United States,* 1953; A. Brady, *Democracy in the Dominions,* 2d ed., 1952; R. M. MacIver, *Democracy and the Economic Challenge,* 1952; L. Smith, *American Democracy and Military Power,* 1951; A. T. Vanderbilt, *The Doctrine of the Separation of Powers and its Present-Day Significance,* 1953; Einaudi and Goguel, *Christian Democracy in Italy and France,* 1953; Paul Blanshard, *Communism, Democracy and Catholic Power,* 1951; F. Somary, *Democracy at Bay,* 1952.
ANDREW K. RULE.

DEMON, DEMONISM: The prominence of demons in popular Hebrew thought is partly indicated by worship practices outside the true Yahweh cultus. The religious degradation in the Northern Kingdom included worship of the *se'irim,* with appointed priests (II Chron. 11:15). The prohibition of such sacrifice in Leviticus 17:7 indicates that the people in the Southern Kingdom practiced it too. This corruption probably is indicated also in II Kings 23:8, reading, by a slight alteration of the Hebrew, "the high places of the *se'irim*" rather than ". . . of the gates."

Some scholars find desert demons in serpent form in the fiery serpents of Numbers 21:6 (Heb. *seraphim,* "burning ones," referring to the burning pain caused by the bites). It is further suggested that the heavenly beings called *seraphim* in Isaiah 6:2 were a thought development from such serpent demons (or deities), but this is uncertain. The words in the two passages may be entirely independent. Other animal demons, or animals in which demons supposedly were incarnated, are named in Isaiah 34:13, 14 (also 13:21, 22). Wild beasts, ostriches, wolves, jackals, hyenas (some of the words are rather obscure) are there associated with *Lilith* and *se'irim.* Apparently demonic beings and not ordinary animals are meant.

In Job 18:14 "the king of terrors" may refer to the archfiend living in Sheol; but some scholars interpret this simply as "death." In Psalm 12:8 the Hebrew is corrupt; the Targum preserves a variant reading, "like the leech (the demonic *'alukah* or vampire) which sucks the blood of men." And some scholars think that smearing blood on the doorposts in the Passover (Ex. 12:7) was originally a rite to protect from night demons.

According to the *Testaments of the Twelve Patriarchs,* Beliar is the chief of a host of evil spirits; this is not a naive demonism but a personification of evil tendencies in man. The rabbis have legends picturing *Lilith* as Eve's rival; the offspring of Adam and *Lilith* included a host of demons. In the teaching of Hermas each person has an evil angel inciting to sin, as well as a good angel.

BIBLIOGRAPHY: George A. Barton, *The Religion of Israel,* 1928; *ERE,* iv. 578–583, 594–601, 612–615; W. O. E. Oesterley and T. H. Robinson, *Hebrew Religion,* 1937; Edward Langton, *Essentials of Demonology,* 1949.
HAROLD L. CREAGER.

DE MOREL, FRANÇOIS, SIRE DE COLLONGES: Sixteenth century French nobleman and Calvinist minister. François de Morel came from an Angoumois noble family and early became a disciple of Calvin. His noble blood and breeding made him especially useful as a minister to important French aristocrats. In 1554 Calvin sent him to serve as chaplain to the influential Duchess of Ferrara, daughter of a former King of France. In 1556 he became minister of the Ste. Marie-aux-Mines church in the Vosges mining district. Later that year he visited Paris and in 1557 he came to Geneva and became a member of the Geneva pastoral corps and of the elite Geneva "bourgeoisie." But late in 1558 the Geneva Company of Pastors sent him back to Paris to replace their earlier envoy Jean Macar in that critical position. His many reports to Calvin from Paris show him more occupied with political intrigue than with his religious duties. He apparently had devious ways of getting secret information from the court. He reports details on the release of the Calvinist Prince d'Andelot, on the death of Henri II and the subsequent establishment of the Guise regency which he tried to prevent, and on the trial and execution of the prominent lawyer and member of the Paris Parlement, Anne du Bourg. In 1559 de Morel presided at the highly secret first National Synod of the French Reformed Churches held in Paris. This synod adopted a confession of faith modelled closely on one Calvin had drafted in 1557 and also an order of ecclesiastical discipline which established a nation-wide church organization with careful regulations for the selection of ministers and other church officials and for the resolution of any ecclesiastical disputes. Calvin was kept informed on the progress of the deliberations and even sent his personal envoy, Nicolas des Gallars (q.v.), with suggestions for the delegates. By 1560 de Morel had become so well known in Paris that his usefulness was ended and he returned to Geneva. He served the Geneva church for one year and then returned to France, to serve as a delegate at the Colloquy of Poissy, to serve again as chaplain to the Duchess of Ferrara, and to organize a church in her home city, Montargis. He apparently stayed there until his death sometime before 1569.

BIBLIOGRAPHY: There is little material published on de Morel. See Eug. and Em. Haag, La France Protestante . . . , Vol. VII (1846–58), p. 500; Henri Heyer, L'Eglise de Genève . . . (1909), p. 494; Bulletin de la Société de l'histoire du protestantisme français, passim; . . . Calvini Opera . . . (1863–80), passim.

ROBERT M. KINGDON.

DEMYTHOLOGIZATION, DEMYTHOLOGIZING. See MYTH IN THE NEW TESTAMENT.

DENMARK: According to the census of 1950 Denmark has a population of 4,251,500. Roughly 97% of the population is Lutheran; other confessions include 25,000 Roman Catholics, 7,000 Jews, 22,000 Baptists, and a few Methodists, Irvingites, Adventists, Episcopalians, and Reformed. Since Iceland (q.v.) gained independence in

1944, Greenland (q.v.) is Denmark's sole colony; the Faroe Islands are an autonomous community within the Danish kingdom. In addition to the university in Copenhagen, a university was founded in Aarhus (1942) with its own theological faculty.

Influenced by the Inner Mission, the Lutheran Church in Denmark engaged in extensive social activity, especially in rapidly growing Copenhagen, since 1900. The Magdalene House (Magdalenehjemmet) was founded as a home for vagrant girls. The Court Mission started work in the slums. The Church Army (q.v.) sent missionaries into inns and public houses. In 1878 the YMCA and YWCA had been transplanted onto Danish soil, associations growing up within the Church in a form corresponding to the American Luther League (q.v.); rapid growth was due to the leadership of Olfert Ricard (d. 1929).

Among other social institutions founded by Lutherans was the Co-operative Congregational Relief Work (De samvirkende Menighedsplejer), started in 1902, which engaged in Christian social work among the aged, poor, sick, children, babies, and mothers with the help of deaconesses (q.v.), pastors, and lay workers. In 1898 a Danish physician founded a "city of brotherly love," Filadelfia, with a hospital for epileptics, an insane asylum, and a sanatorium for nervous people. This hospital has a capacity of 1,000 patients and has its own homes for deaconesses and deacons.

The rapid growth of Copenhagen had a disastrous effect on church life. At the turn of the century many congregations numbered 50,000 to 80,000 souls. In 1896 seven laymen established the Copenhagen Church Fund (Kobenhavns Kirkefond) to erect new churches and provide two pastors for each church, so that no church should have more than 10,000 souls and no pastor more than 5,000 to minister to. By 1946 (within fifty years) the fund made possible the erection of thirty-nine churches.

Six currents can be discerned within Danish Lutheranism in the middle of the twentieth century: (1) The Inner Mission, led by the Rev. Christian Bartholdy (1951), was still advocating social action and revivals. (2) N. F. S. Grundtvig (q.v., Vol. V) experienced a renaissance during World War II, reflected in the erection (1939) of the Grundtvig Memorial Church, the reading of his books, and the singing of his hymns; 286 out of a total of 806 hymns in the new Danish hymnal are by Grundtvig. (3) The Church Center (Kirkeligt Centrum), a party following in the footsteps of such men as J. P. Mynster (q.v., Vol. VIII) and H. L. Martensen (q.v., Vol. VII) has taken a mediating position between the two above parties and has shown much theological interest. Dating from the period between the last two wars were three additional movements: (4) A renaissance of Sören Kierkegaard, together with the antihumanistic postwar currents and the study of Karl Barth (*q.v.*), influenced many younger clergymen, but few laymen, in Denmark. (5) The Oxford Group Movement (*q.v.*) appeared in Denmark shortly after World War I and won many clergymen and laymen. (6) The Oratorians are a group of clergymen and laymen who, influenced by the Swedish and Anglican Churches, introduced a liturgical movement with an emphasis on ritual.

BIBLIOGRAPHY: Jens C. Kjaer, *History of the Church of Denmark*, 1945; J. Oskar Andersen, *Survey of the History of the Church in Denmark*, 1930; E. H. Dunkley, *The Reformation in Denmark*, 1948; Hal Koch and Bjorn Kornerup, *Den danske kirkes historie*, 1951.

[Sup.] K. E. JORDT JORGENSEN.

DENNEY, JAMES: Principal United Free Church College, Glasgow (1915). D. June 12, 1917. *Jesus and the Gospel* (1908); *The Way Everlasting* (1911); *War and the Fear of God* (1916); *The Christian Doctrine of Reconciliation* (1917).

BIBLIOGRAPHY: T. H. Walker, *Principal James Denney*, 1918; James Moffatt, ed., *Letters of Principal James Denney to W. Robertson Nicoll*, 1920; *Letters of Principal James Denney to his Family and Friends*, n.d.

[Sup.] RAYMOND W. ALBRIGHT.

DENTAN, ROBERT CLAUDE: Episcopalian; b. at Rossville, Ind., Nov. 27, 1907. He is a graduate of Colorado College (B.A., 1928) and Berkeley Divinity School (B.D., 1932), studied at the American School of Oriental Research (1932–33), and Yale University (Ph.D., 1946). He was professor of Old Testament in Berkeley Divinity School (1943–54), professor of Old Testament in the General Theological Seminary, New York (1954–   ), and editor of the *Journal of Biblical Literature* (1950–54). He has written *Preface to Old Testament Theology* (1950) and *The Holy Scriptures* (1950).

DEPRAVITY: The witness of Scripture to the depravity of fallen mankind is consistent and pervasive. No more incisive and comprehensive indictment is found than in Genesis 6:5: "And the Lord saw that the wickedness of man was great in the earth, and that every imagination of the thoughts of his heart was only evil continually." The implications respecting the intensity, inwardness, inclusiveness, exclusiveness, and continuousness of the evil are to be distinctly noted. The witness of the Scripture throughout, particularly of our Lord and the apostle Paul (cf. Mark 7:15–23; John 3:6; Rom. 3:9–15, 8:6–8), is to the same effect. To try to evade the conclusion that depravity is total would be futile. Man as depraved is destitute of all that is well-pleasing to God—"they that are in the flesh cannot please God" (Rom. 8:8); "there is none that doeth good, no, not so much as one" (Rom. 3:12). And, more positively, man as depraved is in a condition of active enmity towards God and his law—"the mind of the flesh is enmity against God; for it is not subject to the law of God, neither indeed can it be" (Rom. 8:7). This condition is universal (cf. Rom. 3:9–18), and no one indicates this more plainly than our Lord himself when he says that "that which is born of the flesh is flesh" (John 3:6). That which is propagated by human nature is human nature controlled and dominated by sin. It is not proper to speak of degrees of total depravity. But it is necessary to recognize that there are degrees of development and manifestation of this depravity with which all are equally afflicted. It is this fact of depravity that establishes the necessity of regeneration as the only way of appreciating the things of the Spirit of God and of entrance into the kingdom of God (cf. I Cor. 2:14, 15; John 3:3, 5). See also MAN, DOCTRINE OF.

JOHN MURRAY.

DEPRESSION, THE CHURCHES AND THE ECONOMIC: The history of economic depressions in the United States shows that, previous to the great depression of the 1930's, the general effect of widespread distress has been a contributing cause of an increased interest in religion. Thus the great revival of 1857–58 had a definite tie with the great financial panic of that year, and the revival reaped its largest results where the depression hit the hardest. The depression of the early 1890's also had a definite effect on the revivals of Dwight L. Moody, J. Wilbur Chapman, and B. Fay Mills. However, contrary to predictions of religious leaders, the depression of the 1930's, the most disastrous depression of modern times, did not drive men to God. That this was true of the larger denominations is demonstrated by a study of membership statistics during and immediately following the depression years.

One of the direct consequences of the depression was the rapid growth of holiness, pentecostal, and millennial sects (see HOLINESS CHURCHES; PENTECOSTAL CHURCHES) throughout the nation. Preaching of premillennialism was stimulated. The following explanation is sometimes given. Premillennialism is always a particularly effective doctrine among poor people disastrously affected by depressions. Such doctrines are sometimes called poor men's doctrines. Seeing little chance for better things in this life, poor people look forward longingly to the second coming of Christ which will put an end to poverty and injustice. Such church bodies held that the sufferings, privations, and catastrophes which accompany depressions are but signs of the last days and indications that the second coming of the Lord is imminent. The rapid growth of these bodies during the depression years is illustrated by the increase in membership of the Assemblies of God (*q.v.*), and the Church of the Nazarene (*q.v.*). The former had a membership of 48,000 in 1926, and this increased to 175,000 in 1937; the latter doubled its membership during the same period. Numerous new pentecostal and premillennial sects also arose during the depression years, as A. T. Boisen showed in a study of the effect of the depression on the above sects made in three localities in Indiana.

The depression had a disastrous economic effect upon all churches. The easy money of the prosperous twenties stimulated great building programs. Congregations all over the country, especially in the cities, built costly buildings which they were unable to carry financially when the period of economic collapse came in the 1930's and there were numerous foreclosures. Church budgets sharply declined, resulting in reduction of ministers' salaries and the cutting down of benevolent giving. The episcopal fund of the Methodist Church, for instance, was so depleted that bishops' salaries were cut in half. The enrollment in denominational colleges sharply declined, as did income from gifts and endowments, which in many instances led to the sweeping dismissal of instructors, many of whom were compelled to go into other kinds of work. The depression also created new duties for ministers, especially in the area of counseling, due to the crises created by the depression in homes of numerous church members. Large churches were compelled to reduce their staff of paid workers, which placed increased burdens on the ministers and volunteer workers. In numerous instances ministers' attitudes toward economic and social questions became more liberal, resulting in the formation of unofficial social agencies in larger Protestant bodies, and also stimulated the formation of official social agencies among Roman Catholics.

See also UNEMPLOYMENT; CHRISTIAN SOCIALISM; SOCIAL SECURITY.

BIBLIOGRAPHY: Samuel C. Kincheloe, *Research Memorandum on Religion in the Depression*, 1937.

WILLIAM WARREN SWEET.

DESCARTES, RENÉ. See EPISTEMOLOGY; SCEPTICISM.

DESERET CLUBS OF THE CHURCH OF THE LATTER DAY SAINTS. See STUDENT ORGANIZATIONS, RELIGIOUS.

DES GALLARS, NICOLAS, SIRE DE SAULES: French nobleman and Calvinist pastor; b. *ca.* 1520 near Paris, d. sometime after 1580. Nicolas des Gallars was one of Calvin's most important aides and disciples. His noble birth made him useful in politically important pastorates. Des Gallars cut short legal studies and the promise of a brilliant career in Paris to study under Calvin in Geneva in 1544. He was an enthusiastic student, took careful notes of

Calvin's lectures and later helped Calvin in preparing works for publication. In 1551 he was admitted free to the elite "bourgeoisie" of Geneva. In 1553 he was made minister of the Jussy church in the Geneva countryside. Care of his own estates near Paris often took him back to France on business and his trips were used by the Geneva church to maintain contact with the struggling group of Paris faithful. In 1557 des Gallars volunteered to serve the Paris church as their minister. He was there during the tragic St. Jacques street affair which resulted in the imprisonment of many leading Parisian Protestants. His detailed reports to Geneva on the affair helped make possible the organization of a special intercessory embassy to Berne and to the Protestant princes of Germany who in turn interceded with French King Henri II to obtain release of the prisoners. But des Gallars soon became too well known to be useful in Paris and Jean Macar was sent from Geneva to replace him early in 1558. Des Gallars served the Geneva Church for two years and then was dispatched in 1560 by the Geneva Company of Pastors to head the newly organized French refugee church in London. The Colloquy of Poissy (*q.v.*) brought him back to France in 1561. Des Gallars headed the delegation of French Protestant ministers at Poissy until Beza arrived, and played a prominent part in the unsuccessful negotiations that followed. He then returned to London where he may have aided in negotiations between the Huguenot armies and the English crown during the first war of religion. In 1563 he became pastor and professor in the church of Orléans. In 1565 he presided over the Fifth National Synod of the French Reformed Churches, held in Paris. In 1571 he served as secretary to the La Rochelle Synod, and helped draw up a confession of faith and several answers to polemical attacks for that synod. Immediately afterwards the Queen of Navarre asked him to become her private chaplain and he was confirmed in this position by the 1572 Nîmes Synod. After the queen's death in 1572 des Gallars decided to continue his ministry in her home territory of Béarn and served as one of the first theology professors in the Lescar (Béarn) Academy.

Des Gallars published thirteen books including at least three Latin translations of books by Calvin and several books defending Calvin. He also collaborated in the writing of the *Histoire ecclésiastique des églises réformées au Royaume de France* (1580), the most authoritative contemporary history of the beginnings of French Calvinism. As organizer, writer and diplomat he was one of the most important implementators of Calvin's theological and ecclesiastical ideas.

BIBLIOGRAPHY: Eugène and Émile Haag, *La France Protestante*, Vol. V (2nd ed., 1877-88), pp. 298-305, contains a fairly detailed sketch of des Gallars' life. See also Henri Heyer, *L'Eglise de Genève . . .* 1909; *Bulletin de la Société de l'histoire du protestantisme français, passim.*

ROBERT M. KINGDON.

DES MARETS, SAMUEL. See MARESIUS, SAMUEL.

DETERMINISM. See WILL, FREEDOM OF THE.

DEUSDEDIT, CARDINAL: The latest authorities deny his authorship of the *Dictamen pape,* which contains twenty-seven propositions or theses on the privileges of the pope and the church.

BIBLIOGRAPHY: P. Fournier and G. le Bras, *Histoire des collections canoniques en Occident depuis les Fausses Décrétales jusqu'au Décret de Gratien,* Vol. II, 1932; A. Fliche and V. Martin, *Histoire de l'Eglise,* Vol. VIII, 1946; C. Lefebvre, art. "Deusdedit" in *Dict. du droit canonique,* IV (1949), 1186–1191.

[Sup.] H. GOOSSENS.

DEUSDEDIT, POPE: Was later called Adeodatus I. He was a son of the subdeacon Stephanus. This pope was noted for his righteousness and love of peace.   [Sup.]

DEUTERO-ISAIAH. See ISAIAH, BOOK OF.

DEUTERONOMIC CODE. See PENTATEUCH; LAW CODES, ANCIENT.

DEUTERONOMY, BOOK OF: See PENTATEUCH.

DEUTSCHER EVANGELISCHER KIRCHENBUND. See GERMANY.

DEVOLUTION: 1. Procedure for the filling of ecclesiastical offices in case of a vacancy protracted beyond the time limits set by statute. Modern canon law has generally incorporated the earlier rules (see DEVOLUTION, Vol. III).

2. In France the word *devolution* is used in connection with the transmission of ecclesiastical properties which were taken over by the French state after Pope Pius X refused to approve the so-called *associations cultuelles* which had been provided for the administration of such properties. The law of Feb. 15, 1941, authorizes the devolution of properties not yet disposed of to diocesan associations constituted in France with the approval of Pope Pius XI, Encyclical *Maximam,* Jan. 18, 1924.

[Sup.] GEORGES A. BARROIS.

DEVOTIO MODERNA: A religious movement, long neglected by Dutch historians but now attracting much attention. See also RENAISSANCE; MYSTICISM; GROOTE; ZERBOLT; IMITATION OF CHRIST.

BIBLIOGRAPHY: Albert Hyma, *The Brethren of the Common Life,* 1950; idem, *Renaissance to Reformation,* 1951; R. R. Post, *De Moderne Devotie,* 1950.

[Sup.]

DEVOTIONAL LITERATURE: The situation here seems highly paradoxical. The field of religious writing which is in many ways the richest has become the least known. Most religious leaders are acquainted with famous works of doctrine, such as Calvin's *Institutes* and Butler's *Analogy of Religion,* but not with the *Prayers and Devotions* of Lancelot Andrewes or the *Pensées* of Blaise Pascal. Thousands who know the secular writings of Samuel Johnson, such as *The Rambler* and *The Dictionary,* are unaware that the great lexicographer left at least a hundred prayers of profound and enduring devotional appeal.

The most striking feature of all devotional classics is the degree to which they are independent of time and changing social conditions. Old books about science seem quaint, works about theology are easily dated, but writings that reveal the depths of religious experience are remarkably the same through the generations. Those who wrote these classics never moved faster than a horse could run, but their relationship to God, when genuine, was essentially the same as that of persons who can go five hundred miles an hour.

Major classifications are four. First, and perhaps the largest group, the strictly biographical writings. Eminent examples, *The Confessions of St. Augustine, The Autobiography of Richard Baxter,* Cardinal Newman's *Apologia pro Vita Sua,* and various Quaker *Journals,* notably those of George Fox and of John Woolman. In each case, the author bares his soul, showing how God has dealt with his life. This is pre-eminently the literature of witness.

Second, admonitions and spiritual counsels. Men who have lived wisely and well share their wisdom, sincerely and humbly, with all who listen. Eminent examples are such writings as *The Imitation of Christ,* Jeremy Taylor's *Holy Living* and *Holy Dying,* and William Law's *Serious Call to a Devout and Holy Life.*

Third, scattered thoughts, with the work of Pascal as the best-known and best-loved example. On pieces of paper of all sizes Pascal wrote down ideas just as they came, leaving to others after his early death the task of organization. This is powerful writing, chiefly because it is unadorned and never toned down for publication. Some of S. T. Coleridge's writing is similar.

Fourth, actual prayers. Here is devotional literature at its most intense level. God is addressed in the second person, and not mentioned in the third. The prayers of the great Bishop Andrewes, who helped with the Authorized Version of the Bible, have long been loved by those fortunate enough to own copies. Now these prayers are available to all. Any religious leader will grow in spiritual life by acquaintance with such writings. At most other points he must rest content with books *about* religion; in devotional literature he finds books *of* religion. The difference is crucial.

D. ELTON TRUEBLOOD.

DEWEY, JOHN: B. Oct. 20, 1859, at Burlington, Vt.; d. June 1, 1952. He studied at the University of Vermont (A.B., 1879) and Johns Hopkins (Ph.D., 1884). He taught philosophy at Michigan (1884–88; 1889–94); Minnesota (1888–89); Chicago (1894–1904; director of the school of education, 1902–04); and at Columbia for the remainder of his distinguished career. His philosophy of "progressive education" more than any other has influenced teachers and schools across the nation to new adventures in education in the past generation. His "progressive education" is based on the theory of learning by doing. His teaching methods, which permitted students to select subjects appealing to them, first were put into practice at the University of Chicago High School. Soon "new" schools and "progressive" methods were announced, tried, and sometimes grossly distorted. In his later years Dewey said that progressive education had been distorted into a belief that he sanctioned unlimited freedom from discipline for pupils. His major contributions to education include such ideas as that the child is more important than the subject matter, learning must be related to its time, schools should be democratic and not authoritarian in spirit, discipline comes from within and not from without, learning can be taught by experience, education must aim at developing character, and an adequate philosophy of education must underlie the whole educative process. In his system the teacher is a social servant maintaining proper social order and securing right social growth. Many religious leaders and educators feel that his materialistic and humanistic approach to education has been inimical to religion and that because he failed to take religion seriously into his purview his educational philosophy is inadequate. He wrote: *Psychology* (1886); *Leibnitz* (1888); *Critical Theory of Ethics* (1894); *Study* (1894); *School and Society* (1899); *Studies in Logical Theory* (1903); *How We Think* (1909); *Influence of Darwin on Philosophy and Other Essays* (1910); *German Philosophy and Politics* (1915; rev. ed., 1942); *Democracy and Education* (1916); *Reconstruction in Philosophy* (1920); *Human Nature and Conduct* (1922); *Experience and Nature* (1925); *The Public and Its Problems* (1927); *The Quest for Certainty* (1929); *Art as Experience* (1934); *A Common Faith* (1934); *Liberalism and Social Action* (1935); *Logic: The Theory of Inquiry* (1938); *Culture and Freedom* (1939); *Education Today*; and *Problems of Man* (1946). See also INSTRUMENTALISM; POSITIVISM.

RAYMOND W. ALBRIGHT.

DE WITT, JOHN: B. Oct. 10, 1842; d. Nov. 19, 1923. He was professor of church history at Princeton Theological Seminary (1892–1912). He was a member of the Presbyterian General Assembly's committees that drafted the revisions of the Westminster Confession of Faith (1901–2) and that prepared the Book of Common Worship (1903–6). While modestly maintaining anonymity, he was editor-in-chief of *The Princeton Theological Review* (1903–8), and was a trustee of Princeton University (1904–19).

BIBLIOGRAPHY: Frederick W. Loetscher, "John DeWitt," in *The Princeton Theological Review*, XXII (1924), 177–234.

[Sup.] LEFFERTS A. LOETSCHER.

DeWOLF, L. HAROLD: Methodist; b. Columbus, Nebraska, Jan. 31, 1905. A.B., Nebraska Wesleyan; S.T.B. and Ph.D., Boston.

He has held teaching positions in the field of philosophy and logic in Boston University since 1933; since 1944, he has been professor of systematic theology, Boston University School of Theology.

In philosophy he is a personalistic theist, in theology an Arminian evangelical liberal, in politics an independent liberal.

He is the author of: *The Religious Revolt Against Reason* (1949); chapter, "The Doctrine of the Church" in *Methodism* (ed. Wm. K. Anderson).

DHORME, EDOUARD: Member of l'Institut de France; b. at Armentières (Nord), France, Jan. 15, 1881. He was professor in l'Ecole Biblique et Archéologique Française de Jerusalem (1905–31); at present he teaches in two schools in Paris, l'Ecole des Hautes Etudes, Sorbonne (1933–) and Collège de France (1945–). He was director of the *Revue Biblique* (1922–31); since 1934 he has been editing the *Revue de l'Histoire des Religions* and also, since 1944, the *Revue d'Assyriologie et d'Archéologie Orientale.* His publications include: *Choix de textes religieux assyro-babyloniens* (1907); *La religion assyro-babylonienne* (1910); *Les livres de Samuel* (1910); *Les pays bibliques et l'Assyrie* (1911); *L'emploi métaphorique des noms de parties du corps en hébreu et en accadien* (1923); *Le livre de Job* (1926); *Langues et éncritures sémitiques* (1930); *La poésie biblique* (1931); *La religion des Hébreux nomades* (1937); *La littérature babylonienne et assyrienne* (1937); *Les religions de Babylonie et d'Assyrie* (1945); and in *Les premières Civilisations* (1950) the chapters on "la Babylonie," "l'Assyrie," "les Féniciens" and "les Hébreux." RAYMOND W. ALBRIGHT.

DIAKONIA. See DEACONESS.

DIAKONIKON: In Byzantine churches, the part of the sanctuary to the right of the altar, where the ministers put on their liturgical vestments, and where the sacred vessels are kept.

DIALECTICAL THEOLOGY: Dialectic is as old as philosophy, for philosophy does not exist, but only assertion, until the possibility of another point of view is acknowledged. In his friendly discussions in the market place Socrates carried it to a high level, being convinced that truth could be found—in contrast to the Sophists who generally argued merely for the sake of argument. Socrates fought not for victory but for the truth. Among his last words (*Phaedo* 91) were, "Pay little attention to Socrates, but much more to the truth." For Aristotle, dialectic is contrasted with metaphysic, because of its tentativeness, and with sophistic, which is the pretense of knowledge without the reality (*Meta.* 2, 1004. b.); and whereas disciplines like mathematics can give certainty, there is much in human experience which allows only discussion. Abelard, who "preferred the strife of disputation to the trophies of war," by his *Sic et Non* won a permanent place for reverent but thorough enquiry into matters of faith, on the ground that "by doubting we are led to inquire, by inquiry we perceive the truth." Every question can be argued for or against. He thus anticipated the "modern dialectic" in which Aquinas followed the practice of Aristotle, whose works had been newly translated into Latin. The dialectic of Kant was chiefly concerned with the problem of knowledge and the limitations of knowledge. He was the "old pedant guarding the frontier against the trespassing of reason." For Hegel the very nature of reason is the thinking out of contradiction; and to think out contradiction is to abolish it. The higher truth contains and fulfils the contradictions out of which it emerges; the conclusion is a "both . . . and . . . ."

At this point Kierkegaard joins issue. Like Marx with dialectical materialism, he reverses Hegel's system, but in a very different fashion. For "both . . . and . . . ." he substitutes "either . . . or . . . ." You do not get the "yes" by thinking out the implications of the "no." That must be given as something new. The positive is not discovered by reason, but is received through revelation. There is no clear-cut argument in all man's intellectual treasury that will lead man to God. Man has urgent need of God, because every instant is wasted when he has Him not. Dialectical contradiction brings man's passion to despair and helps him, by means of "the category of despair" which is faith, to embrace God (*Unscientific Postscript* and *Philosophical Scraps*).

Thus the dialectical theology, notably connected with the name of Karl Barth, denies the existence of an analogy of being (*analogia entis*) and the doctrine that creation is a similitude of God's being. Fr. Przywara, in *Polarity,* a reply to Barth, indicates the limits of the application of the idea as given in the Fourth Lateran

Council, 1215, cap. 2, *Inter creatorem et creaturam non potest tanta similitudo notari, quin inter eos major sit dissimilitudo notanda.* Barth made use of the phrase *finitum non capax infiniti,* indicating that since we are still *in via* and not *in patria,* we can make no theological pronouncement that can claim finality, but must proceed by statement and counterstatement. In Augustine's words, our life on earth is a watch night between dusk and dawn; between our Lord's Ascension and his Return. (The organ of the theological group, which included Emil Brunner, Friedrich Gogarten, Edward Thurneysen and others, was called "Between the Ages.") Indeed the situation is much worse than that. We are not only finite; we are sinners. And Barth soon replaced *finitum non capax infiniti* by *homo peccator non capax Verbi Divini.* Every human thought concerning what we are contains its opposite in the thought of what we are not. We know the image of God only because we are sinners; and the glory of nature only because of its opaqueness. This is the negative standpoint taken by Barth (*Das Wort Gottes und die Theologie,* 1925). The thought, however, can be applied in a positive direction to indicate that we would not know our unredeemed condition if we were not within the redemption; and we should not, as Pascal said, be seeking for God at all, if we had not already found him.

Dialectical theology thus takes paradox (*q.v.*) and makes it the pattern of theological thinking, as everyone must do when he speaks of the timeless entering time, or of the beyond that is within, or of eternity as a present possession. But in his *Dogmatics* (E.T., p. xii) Barth explicitly rejects the claim to present the case of "dialectical theology." He would wish to be indebted to no human philosophy and to form no "school"; so that a better name for the movement is now perhaps the "Theology of Crisis" (*q.v.*) or best of all the "Theology of the Word." Like all Calvinism, it seeks to build up a system of theology developed under the dominating idea of the absolute sovereignty of God. We can learn about God, not by interpreting our experience, but by turning away from it to revelation. Our human values do not reveal God; but we are driven to him by our ignorance, vanity, poverty, infirmity, depravity and corruption. A recent American writer (Professor Brightman) has expressed it by saying that Calvinism is "uncontaminated by human hypotheses."

It is natural, therefore, that the Calvinistic heritage of the dialectical theology should be strongest in the account which it gives of natural theology. Calvin directs attention to the self-revelation of God in nature, in history, and in human experience, but there is a qualification which goes right to the depths. The opera tive words in this vital and necessary caution are those of *Institutio* I.2.1, "if Adam had remained innocent"; but Adam did not. To an innocent mind, the works of God in nature and in providence would speak of God's essential attributes; but to perverted man no such message is conveyed. True, the image of God was not altogether blotted out in man (I.15.4), yet what remained was wretched and miserable. The faculty for perceiving God in creation and in history is not just weakened: it is lost. Must we not go, for insight into the nature of God, to the revelation through which God undertook the work of restoring the fallen world and redeeming sinful man? Must we not go, in fact, to the history of Israel, the Scriptures, and the life and death and resurrection of Jesus? It is argued with great cogency that the name of *revelation* is too noble to be accorded to those weak and frail suggestions of the divine which the sinner can apprehend in creation.

The controversy between Karl Barth and Emil Brunner on this point can be followed in its earlier stages in *Natural Theology* (translated by Peter Fraenkel). Its later stages are to be seen in Barth's *Dogmatik* II.1 and Brunner's *Revelation and Reason*. Barth seeks to draw a distinction between "natural theology" and "Christian natural theology"; between a doctrine of revelation through creation which can be gathered from mere observation of the created world and one which can be gathered only from the Scriptures. Brunner believes that this introduces a confusion. Created things do bear the divine stamp upon them; they do not first have to acquire it through the historical revelation given in Christ. It is of course true that we cannot see the truth of these analogies without the historical revelation in Christ and the faith which it creates. Barth is defending an important element in Reformed theology against Thomism: the *analogia entis* does not give a sound basis for the construction of a natural theology; for when man is left alone with these analogies he will certainly interpret them wrongly, and in a pantheistic sense; but it is foolish, Brunner considers, to go further and say that the analogies only exist because of faith. It would be better to say that they become visible only to faith. (See further C. C. J. Webb, *Religious Experience;* Hendrick Kraemer, *The Christian Message in a Non-Christian World;* Nicol Macnicol, *Is Christianity Unique?*)

Since, according to the dialectical theology, God is always Subject, when we presume to treat of him as Object—as we necessarily do both in preaching and in theology—we are using reason to abstract; we are looking on him as the other member of an I-object relation and not, as we ought, as the one who addresses us; and therefore we are bound to fall into paradox and contradiction. Brunner has said the latest,

if not the last, word on this subject from the side of dialectical theology in indicating that theology stands very close to the Word of God, but is not itself that Word. "The Devil would pass the most rigorous examination in dogmatic and Biblical theology with distinction." The Christian faith can take root only in the heart which recognizes its need as desperate. Then Christ can conquer the reason and make it free to serve.

See also Crisis, The Theology of; Existentialism.   EDGAR PRIMROSE DICKIE.

DIATESSARON, TATIAN'S. See Harmony of the Gospels (Tatian's).

DIBELIUS, (FRIEDRICH KARL) OTTO: Lutheran; b. May 15, 1880, in Berlin, Germany. He was educated at the University of Berlin, studying law and theology. After having served in various congregations he was appointed "Generalsuperintendent der Kurmark" in 1925. When the German Government dismissed him from this office in 1933, he became one of the leaders of the "Confessional Church" and organized the opposition against the German Nazi Church Government. In 1945 he was elected Evangelical bishop of Berlin and in 1949 president of the Council of the Evangelical Church in Germany, the highest position in the administration of the German Church. Bishop Dibelius attended nearly all important ecumenical meetings during the last decades and was one of the presidents of the World Council of Churches (1954–). He wrote: *Das Jahrhundert der Kirche* (1927); *Friede auf Erden* (1928); *Vom Erbe der Vaeter* (1941); *Grenzen des Staates* (1949); and *Vom ewigen Recht* (1950).

Bibliography: "Otto Dibelius" in *Die Stunde der Kirche,* 1950.

DIBELIUS, MARTIN FRANZ: Lutheran; b. Sept. 14, 1883, in Dresden, Saxony; d. Nov. 11, 1947, in Heidelberg. He studied at the universities of Neuchatel, Leipzig, Berlin, Tuebingen (Dr. Phil., 1905). He taught at Berlin (1908–15) and was professor of New Testament in Heidelberg (1915–47). He was a pupil of Harnack and Gunkel; founder of the *formgeschichtliche Schule* of biblical criticism, which calls for the treatment of Gospel accounts as separate units, inasmuch as the present composition of the New Testament was made at a time subsequent to the writing of the accounts themselves. Among his many pupils, the best known was Professor Ernst Lohmeyer. He wrote: *Die Geisterwelt im Glauben des Paulus* (1909); *Die urchristliche Ueberlieferung von Johannes dem Taeufer* (1911); *Die Formgeschichte des Evangeliums* (1919); *Geschichte der christlichen Literatur* (1926); Commentaries on the small epistles of St. Paul; *Evangelium und*

Welt (1929); *Jesus* (1939); *Paulus* (1951); *Aufsaetze zur Apostelgeschichte* (1951).

MRS. MARTIN DIBELIUS.

DICHOTOMY: From the Greek, *dichotomia,* meaning a "cutting in two." In logic, dichotomy is the division of a class into two subclasses, which are mutually exclusive and collectively exhaustive. A dichotomous argument is one which proceeds by that method: e.g., A is either B or C, but C is either D or F, and so forth. In biology, dichotomy is a form of branching in which each step is a division into two. The term appears in the history of theology as the name for the conviction that human personality is composed of two ultimate, mutually exclusive but collectively exhaustive, principles, the material and the spiritual. Compare trichotomy (*q.v.*). If dichotomy is correct, then such terms as mind, soul, and spirit all refer to one and the same principle, characterizing it in somewhat different aspects. ANDREW K. RULE.

DICKINSON, CLARENCE: Presbyterian; b. at Lafayette, Ind., May 7, 1873. He studied at Miami University Preparatory School and Northwestern University (M.A.; Mus. Doc.). A founder of the American Guild of Organists (1896), he was organist and director of music, Church of the Messiah (1892-98); St. James Episcopal Church (1902-9); and The Sunday Evening Club, Orchestra Hall (1906-9), all in Chicago; and The Brick Presbyterian Church, New York (1909-). He was the founder and conductor of the Musical Art Society, Chicago; conductor of the Bach Choir, Dubuque, Iowa; Aurora Oratorio Society; English Opera Society, Chicago; Mendelssohn Glee Club, New York; and the Bach Festival Choir, Montclair, N. J. He was lecturer and director of sacred Music, Union Theological Seminary (1928-45; director emeritus, 1945-). His published works include: (1) Music: Storm King Symphony, for organ (1919); The Coming of the Prince of Peace, a Nativity Play in Ancient Christmas Carols (1919); Book of Antiphons (1920); Historical Organ Recital Series (Vol. I, 1920; Vol. II, 1939); Sacred Solos for Voice (1930); (2) Books: (with his wife, Helen A. Dickinson, M.A., Queens University, Canada; Ph.D., Heidelberg University, Germany) *German Masters of Art* (1914); *Excursions in Musical History* (1917); *The Troubadours and Their Music* (1920); *The Technique and Art of Organ Playing* (1921); *Choirmasters Guide* (1924); *A Treasury of Worship* (1927); *Choir Loft and Pulpit* (1943); *Sacred Choruses Ancient and Modern;* and editor of *The Hymnal* for the Presbyterian Church, U. S. A. (1933); and *The Hymnal* for the Evangelical and Reformed Church (1941).

DICKS, RUSSELL L.: Methodist; b. at Stillwater, Oklahoma, Sept. 30, 1906. He studied at the University of Tulsa, University of Oklahoma (A.B., 1930) and Union Theological Seminary (B.D., 1933). He served as Protestant chaplain at the Massachusetts General Hospital, Boston, 1933-38; chaplain Presbyterian Hospital, Chicago, 1938-41; chaplain Wesley Memorial Hospital, Chicago, 1944-48; associate professor of pastoral care, Duke University Divinity School (1948-). He is coauthor with Richard C. Cabot, *The Art of Ministering to the Sick* (1936); and has written *Meditations for the Sick* (1938); *And Ye Visited Me* (1939); *When You Call on the Sick* (1940); *Your Self and Health* (1941); *Who Is My Patient* (1942); *Thy Health Shall Spring Forth* (1943); *Pastoral Work and Personal Counseling* (1944); *Comfort Ye My People* (1946); *You Came Unto Me* (1951); *My Faith Looks Up* (1950). He is the general editor of the Westminster Pastoral Aid Books; and serves upon the advisory committee of *The Sex Knowledge Inventory;* and upon the editorial board of *Pastoral Psychology.* He is the founder and editor of *Religion and Health.*

DICTIONARIES, NEW TESTAMENT. See LEXICA OF THE GREEK NEW TESTAMENT.

DIDACHE: The debates over the Didache and its meaning have continued unabated for the last forty years. They revolve around its date, sources, purpose, and meaning; and since these problems are obviously interrelated no single or simple solution has been found for any of them. On the first point, recent studies have shown that a date as late as 180 is not impossible, and the number of scholars who accept a date not only after the Epistle of Barnabas but in the middle of the second century seems to be increasing. On the second point, the vigorous defence of the "Two Ways" as the source of chapters i-vi by E. J. Goodspeed has won many adherents; on this view the *Doctrina apostolorum* is a Latin translation of a source of the Didache, not an abbreviated version of the whole book. The third and fourth problems remain almost insoluble. An increasing number of scholars regards the Didache as (paradoxically) either Montanist or anti-Montanist, but its confusing attitude toward "prophets" contributes to their confusion. On the one hand, it attacks prophets who like Montanists ask for money; on the other, it urges Christians not to "test" prophets, for to do so is to sin against the Holy Spirit. Perhaps we may compare the somewhat ambiguous attitude of Irenaeus (*q.v.*) toward Montanism.

The references to "prophets and teachers" may reflect Acts 13:1, while "bishops and deacons" may be derived from Phil. 1:1 or 1 Clem. 42: 4-5. In this case the picture of the ministry in the Didache may be a deliberate work of archaism, and may be valueless for our reconstruction of the ministry of the late first century. It remains striking, however, that in Hermas (*Mand.* xi) similar (pre-Montanist) tests of false prophets are provided, and that the foundation stones of the church are "apostles and bishops and teachers and deacons" (*Vis.* iii. 5. 1), a group very similar to that which is found in the Didache.

If we attempt to date the book by the sixteenth (apocalyptic) chapter, we shall find that the new notes in an otherwise conventional prophecy are struck by references to the "world-deceiver" (perhaps a parody of the imperial title, "world-ruler") and the unheard-of iniquities which he performs. To judge from second-century apologetic literature, these "unheard-of" events are the persecutions which the emperor Marcus Aurelius approved in Gaul in 177. The fiery trial mentioned would be the burning of martyrs at this time. Unfortunately, the last chapter of the Didache may be an appendix, added after the rest of the book was compiled.

When we regard it as a compilation, however, we come closer to understanding it. The "Two Ways" of the first six chapters is, undoubtedly, derived from Jewish or Christianized Jewish tradition; it ends with a reference to idols as "dead gods," a theme developed in late second-century apologetics and in the martyr-acts of Carpus and others. Two chapters on baptism, fasting, and prayer are purely Christian and could come from any time in the second century. The eucharistic prayers of chapters ix and x are derived from Hellenistic Judaism and point toward the Eucharist, which is not described. Then follow chapters on teachers, apostles, false or dubious prophets, wandering missionaries, and true prophets (xi–xiv). Finally we return to the Eucharist (xiv. 1–3, xv. 3–4) in a discussion interrupted by a later insertion about bishops and deacons (xv. 1–2). The apocalyptic chapter (xvi) ends the book. Can such a compilation be exactly dated? Or do not the various sections come from various times or even various places? Their precise historical environment cannot now be discovered, and the whole book may even represent a Montanist tractate taken over and edited by the Catholic Church, for example at Antioch, perhaps about 180.

Our conclusions may seem somewhat negative. They are negative. The Didache should not be used in efforts to explain the catechetical, liturgical, or hierarchical constitution of the early church, precisely because of the different dates of the materials used in it. These dates can never be precisely recovered. It is by no means clear that Clement of Alexandria regarded the treatise as Scripture, and even had he done so, such use would prove almost nothing in view of

Clement's lack of discrimination between canonical and non-canonical books.

Since Harnack's time a papyrus fragment (fourth—fifth century) of Did. i. 3–4, ii. 7—iii. 2, has been found in Egypt (P. Oxy. xv. 1782), and we have also a Georgian version, an Ethiopic version, and a Coptic version (probably fifth-century, including a prayer over chrism at the end of chapter x and "Hosanna to the *house* of David" in x. 6). Only the Georgian version is complete.

BIBLIOGRAPHY: Rudolf Knopf, *Die Lehre der zwoelf Apostel*, 1920; J. Muilenburg, *The Literary Relations of the Epistle of Barnabas and the Teaching of the Twelve Apostles*, 1929; F. E. Vokes, *The Riddle of the Didache*, 1937; M. Dibelius in *ZNW*, XXXVII (1938), 32–41; E. J. Goodspeed, *The Apostolic Fathers* (1950), pp. 285–310 (reprinted from *Anglican Theol. Rev.*, XXVIII [1945], 228–247); E. Peterson, "Ueber einige Probleme der Didache-Ueberlieferung." in *Rivista di archeologia cristiana*, XXXVII (1952), 37–68. From 1911 to 1945 almost every volume of the *Journal of Theological Studies* contains articles on the Didache from various points of view. Those by Connolly, Creed, and Telfer deserve special attention.

[Sup.] ROBERT M. GRANT.

DIEM, HERMANN: Lutheran; b. Feb. 2, 1900, in Stuttgart, Germany. He studied in Tuebingen and Marburg (1910–23). He is a pastor in the state church of Wuerttemberg (Ebersbach/Fils) and is a part-time lecturer in the University of Tuebingen. He was a leading member of the Confessional Church, cofounder of Kirchlich-theologische Arbeitsgemeinschaft fuer Deutschland, the Kirchlich-theologische Sozietaet in Wuerttemberg, and the Gesellschaft fuer Evangelische Theologie. Theologically he stands close to Karl Barth and is a well known writer about Kierkegaard. He is especially concerned with major theological questions, practical theology and church organization. He has written: *Philosophie und Christentum bei Sören Kierkegaard* (1929); *Kritischer Idealismus in theologischer Sicht* (1934); *Warum Textpredigt?* (1939); *Restauration oder Neuanfang in der evangelischen Kirche?* (1946); *Luthers Predigt von den zwei Reichen* (1947); *Der Abfall der Kirche Christi in die Christlichkeit* (1947); *Die Kirche zwischen Russland und Amerika* (1947); *Amerika-Eindruecke und Fragen* (1949); *Grundfragen der biblischen Hermeneutik* (1950); *Lutherische Volkskirche in West und Ost* (1951); *Die Existenzdialektik von Sören Kierkegaard* (1950); *Theologie als kirchliche Wissenschaft* (1951); and *Das Problem des Schriftkanons* (1952). RAYMOND W. ALBRIGHT.

DIETRICH, CHRISTIAN: Evangelical National Church of Germany; b. at Gschwend, Germany, 1844; d. at Stuttgart, 1919. He was rector of the Evangelical Daughter-Institute at Stuttgart. As president of the old pietistic associations of Wuerttemberg he worked for their close unification. Open to the influences of the younger Free Church movements of Evangelicals, nevertheless he knew how to preserve the sane heritage of the Swabish Pietism and to make it influential within the groups of Evangelicals inside the National Church of the larger Germany. He was editor of *Philadelphia*, a periodical of the national church Evangelicals.

REINHOLD KUECKLICH.

DIETRICH OF NIEHEIM: B. about 1340 at Brakel in Westphalia; d. at Maastricht as canon on March 22, 1418. He was called by Finke the greatest journalist of the later Middle Ages. But his works are in part one-sided, and in many cases they exaggerate the evil conditions in society. That happens frequently in rapidly written pamphlets and newspapers. Nevertheless, they throw much light on the period of the Great Schism in the Western Church (1305–78).

BIBLIOGRAPHY: W. Mulder, *Diederik van Nieheim*, 2 vols., 1907; H. Heimpel, *Eine unbekannte Schrift Dietrichs von Nieheim*, 1929.

[Sup.] H. GOOSSENS.

DIEU, LUDOVICUS DE:
BIBLIOGRAPHY: *Nieuw Nederlandsch Biografisch Woordenboek*, Vol. VIII (1930), 396. [Sup.]

DIGGERS: In April, 1649, a small body of men, led by William Everard, an ex-soldier, and Gerrard Winstanley, a cloth-merchant, arrived at St. George's Hill near Cobham, Surrey, armed with spades wherewith they began to dig the uncultivated land, and to prepare it for sowing vegetables. On being questioned, the leaders maintained that they intended to restore the liberties of the people, lost by the coming of William the Conqueror, and claimed that they had been commanded by God in a vision, to take the common land and to make it fruitful. They were fined, but went back and continued with their digging. When the authorities later destroyed the settlement, the "Diggers" as such, came to an end. Winstanley however, who was something of a religious mystic, and the real prophet of the movement, issued a number of publications, the most important being "The Law of Freedom" (1652). This utopia of the Diggers contains the most revolutionary principles, and beside it, the experiment at Cobham was of minor significance.

See also LEVELLERS.

BIBLIOGRAPHY: G. H. Sabine, *The Works of Gerrard Winstanley*, 1941; L. H. Berens, *The Digger Movement*, 1906; E. Bernstein, *Cromwell and Communism*, 1930; D. W. Petegorsky, *Left Wing Democracy in the English Civil War*, 1940; G. P. Gooch, *Political Thought in England from Bacon to Halifax* (1946), pp. 94–101; W. K. Jordan, *The Development of Religious Toleration in England*, Vol. IV (1940), pp. 196–202.

[Sup.] GORDON HUELIN.

DILLENBERGER, JOHN: B. in St. Louis, Mo., 1918. He studied at Elmhurst College (graduated, 1940); Union Theological Seminary (B.D., 1943); and Columbia University (Ph.D., 1948). Ordained in the Evangelical and Reformed Church (1943), he served as chaplain in the

United States navy. He taught religion at Princeton University (instructor, 1948–49); at Columbia University (assistant professor and associate professor, 1949–54); and theology at Harvard Divinity School (associate professor, 1954–). He is author of *God Hidden and Revealed* (1953) and coauthor of *Protestant Christianity* (1954).

DILLISTONE, FREDERICK WILLIAM: Anglican; b. at Sompting, Sussex, May 9, 1903. He studied at Brasenose College and Wycliffe Hall, Oxford (M.A., 1928). He was ordained in 1927 and became Vicar of St. Andrew's Parish, Oxford, in 1934. He was professor of systematic theology at Wycliffe College, Toronto (1938–45) and at the Episcopal Theological School, Cambridge, Mass. (1947–52). He became Chancellor of Liverpool Cathedral, England, in 1952. He has written: *The Significance of the Cross* (1944), *The Holy Spirit in the Life of To-day* (1946), *The Structure of the Divine Society* (1951), *Jesus Christ and His Cross* (1953), and was joint editor of the *Westminster Study Bible*.

DIOCESE: The Code of Canon Law of the Roman Catholic Church assimilates territories under the ordinary jurisdiction of an abbot or of a prelate *nullius* (see PRELATE), to dioceses or bishoprics. Dioceses are divided into parishes and eventually into regional circumscriptions bearing various names, such as vicariates, decanates, archpresbyterates, etc.

[Sup. to BISHOPRIC.]

DIONYSIUS OF ALEXANDRIA: Two important writings of Dionysius reflect the rising level of Christian philosophical and literary culture. The first is his treatise *On Nature*, part of which is preserved by Eusebius. It is directed against Epicurus and Epicurean doctrines, and takes over materials which Stoics had collected in favor of providential government of the universe. The second is his treatise *On Promises*, in which he attacks millennarian doctrines prevalent in Egypt by a detailed examination of the vocabulary, style, and theological doctrines of the Fourth Gospel as compared with those of the Apocalypse. He ascribes them to different authors.

BIBLIOGRAPHY: F. H. Colson in *JTS*, XXV (1923–24), 364–77.

[Sup.] ROBERT M. GRANT.

DIONYSIUS THE CARTHUSIAN: B. 1402; d. March 17, 1472. He may have been called Van Leeuwen after his own family or Van Ryckel after his birthplace, but generally he was referred to as *doctor extaticus*. First he studied at the school attached to the Church of St. Mary in St. Trond (southern Netherlands, now Belgium), and after that in the famous school at Zwolle, where John Cele had attracted hundreds of boys. At the age of eighteen he wanted to join the Carthusians, but he was too young at the time for that (the age limit being twenty), and the prior of the Carthusians at Roermond advised him to study at the University of Cologne, which he did. Three years later he obtained his M.A. degree. In 1424 he entered the Carthusian monastery at Roermond. In 1451 he accompanied Cardinal Cusa on his trip to a large number of monasteries that needed reformation. In 1465 he founded a new monastery at Vught near 's-Hertogenbosch, returning in 1469 to Roermond, where he died in 1472. He was widely known for his saintly life, great learning, and enormous capacity for work. The Carthusian rules require eight hours of meditation and prayer each day, but he devoted eleven or twelve hours to this. He gave valuable advice to a large number of persons, including some in the higher classes. His superior officers also entrusted him with onerous tasks, but he still had time left to write ascetic and mystical treatises in such volume that they fill forty-two folio volumes in the modern edition. He had a most tenacious memory and robust health, which enabled him to take only four hours of sleep each night.

His works deal with philosophy, theology, exegesis, canon law, mysticism, and asceticism. He is generally considered one of the last scholastic philosophers.

BIBLIOGRAPHY: *Opera omnia,* 42 vols., 1896–1912; this is largely a reprint of the Cologne edition, edited by the Carthusians of Montreuil-sur-Mer; P. Teeuwen, *Dionysius de Karthuizer en de philosophisch-theologische stroomingen aan de Keulsche Universiteit,* 1938; G. E. M. Vos de Wael, *De Mystica theologia van Dionysius Mysticus in de werken van Dionysius Carthusianus,* 1942.

A. R. M. KIEVITS.

DIOTHELETISM: When, in the course of the Christological controversies through which the early church was seeking to define her doctrine of the Person of Christ, it became clear that she must decide, as she did at Chalcedon in 451, that Jesus Christ is unitary as to "person" and dual (human and divine, without intermixture) as to "nature," problems began to arise as to which functions must be assigned to the "person" so that they appeared singly in him, and which must appear doubly because they belonged to a "nature." The effort to settle such questions was, in effect, an attempt to define more specifically the meaning of "person" and "nature."

In the sixth century arose monotheletism (from Greek *monos,* meaning "single," and *thelema,* meaning "will"), which asserted that, though Christ has a human nature, he has only one will, which is a divine will. The history of this quite complicated part of a very complicated and controversial discussion may be found in any of the larger works on church history or on the history of doctrine. The sixth general council at Constantinople in 680 condemned monotheletism, declaring that Christ had two wills, a human and a divine. This is diotheletism.

ANDREW K. RULE.

DIRECTOR OF RELIGIOUS EDUCATION: An important development during the twentieth century. The director leads in the teaching ministry of the church, while the pastor engages in preaching and pastoral work. Schools of various grades offer training courses. The number of churches employing such leaders reached a peak in the 1920's. During the following depression curtailed budgets led to the dismissal of many such leaders, but after World War II there was a resurgent demand for them.

J. DONALD BUTLER.

DISCIPLES OF CHRIST: In the first half of the twentieth century the Disciples of Christ increased their membership from 1,120,000 in 1900 to 1,913,192 in 1950, a gain of 71%. This advance was achieved in spite of the loss of a portion of the original movement which withdrew in and around 1906 into the separate Churches of Christ (*q.v.*). The Disciples of Christ were in 1950 the seventh Protestant body in size in the United States (fifth among white Protestants).

In 1909 the movement celebrated, in Pittsburgh, its centennial, dating from the publication of Thomas Campbell's "Declaration and Address." An attendance of 25,000 observed the Lord's Supper in Forbes Field—the largest Protestant Eucharistic celebration in American history. The sense of cohesiveness resulting therefrom initiated a new era of effective organization for Christian work. A brotherhood publishing house, the Christian Board of Publication, was inaugurated in 1909. A Board of Church Extension, begun in 1888, had assets of $6,000,000 by 1951.

The United Christian Missionary Society was formed in 1920, co-ordinating most of the activities other than those of the local churches. The boards which merged to form this Society represented seventy years of prior co-operation. Its Foreign Division in 1951 worked in 12 foreign fields having 100,122 members, 213 missionaries sent from the United States, and 2,193 trained native workers. The Home Division operates two standard colleges for Negroes, institutions and work among Indian, Mexican, French-Acadian, and Japanese groups. The United Society expended over $3,000,000 in 1951. The National Benevolent Association operates fifteen homes for orphans and aged.

The Board of Higher Education, formed in 1914, has seen the assets of its constituent colleges and its Bible chairs at state universities multiply nearly twenty times to approximately $60,000,000 in 1950. Such well known universities as Butler (Indianapolis), Drake (Des Moines), Texas Christian (Fort Worth), and Phillips (Enid, Oklahoma), and ten colleges like Bethany (West Virginia), and Hiram (Ohio) are institutions of the Disciples of Christ.

An effective Pension Fund for the ministry began functioning in 1930. Over 3,000 recruits for Christian life service, primarily in the various types of church ministry, were gained during the Crusade for a Christian World, 1947–50. There were 8,208 ministers serving in 1951.

The modern religious education program, which is such a large and effective arm of the major church bodies in America, has received much attention from this communion. The Disciples produced the executive secretary of the International Council of Religious Education (interdenominational) in 1936, who remained as such to its merging with the National Council of Churches (q.v.) in 1950. Other Disciples were the American secretary of the World Sunday School Association, from 1928 to 1938, and the secretary of an interdenominational committee of seven that formulated the dominant curriculum theory of co-operative Protestantism today.

The emphasis of the Disciples of Christ upon the congregational principle of the independence of the local church is balanced by a growing sense of responsibility for effective co-operation in affairs of larger outreach. The International Convention of Disciples of Christ was created in 1917. It is (somewhat like the United States system) a two-house body: one small and delegated from the several State conventions, the other a mass meeting open to all who care to register. Both houses must agree on any action before it becomes the representative voice of the Convention.

From the International Convention has emerged an increased interest in the ecumenical movement. The spirit which now expresses itself through the Convention was long resident—indeed, the goal of church co-operation and unity has been one of the primary motivations of the Disciples throughout their history. Isaac Errett and B. B. Tyler represented them on the International Uniform Lessons Committee (interdenominational) from 1884 to 1908. Disciples seconded the federation proposal issued by the Presbyterian General Assembly in 1891. In the early formative proposals of the Federal (now National) Council of Churches (q.v.) the Disciples gave approval by convention vote in 1902 and became a constituent member at its organization in 1908. A World Convention of Churches of Christ (q.v.) was formed in 1930. The International Convention (United States and Canada) is pursuing closer relations with the American (Northern) Baptist Convention. In 1952 the two conventions were scheduled to meet in Chicago at the same time and hold some joint sessions. In 1947 the Disciples be-

came the first official supporters of the call of the Congregational General Council, which has resulted in the so-called Greenwich Plan for the union of all churches "recognizing each other's ministries and sacraments." Into the larger enterprises of the International Missionary Council (q.v.) and the World Council of Churches (q.v.) the Disciples have poured much concern and support. It was directly from one of the Disciple papers, *The Christian Union Quarterly*, later transformed into *Christendom* and made interdenominational, that there emerged the present primary organ of the World Council of Churches, *The Ecumenical Review*.

BIBLIOGRAPHY: Charles A. Young, *Historical Documents Advocating Christian Union*, 1904; W. E. Garrison, *Religion Follows the Frontier*, 1931; W. E. Garrison and A. T. DeGroot, *The Disciples of Christ: A History*, 1948; W. Robinson, *What Churches of Christ Stand For*, 1926; Peter Ainslie, III, *The Message of the Disciples for the Union of the Church*, 1913.

A. T. DeGroot.

DISCIPLINE, CHURCH: This term is used in two senses, one relating to the regulation of church members, the other to correction. In earlier times almost every branch of the church had its Book of Discipline, or some other means of regulating beliefs, conduct, and worship. Today most of this lies in abeyance. There is a feeling that church members show lack of discipline as good soldiers of Christ. Various churches also had corrective measures, for admonition, punishment, or expulsion of members who broke the laws of God and the church. Seldom today does any local body discipline a member, even for gross iniquity. Occasionally the church at large rebukes or silences a clergyman. In every case the welfare of the church ought to take precedence over individual feelings. Better still, each congregation should take loving measures to "discipline" her members, especially the young, in the sense of training them for Christian life and service. See also OFFICIAL BOARD. [Sup. to CHURCH DISCIPLINE.]

ANDREW W. BLACKWOOD.

DISCIPLINE OF THE SECRET. See ARCANI DISCIPLINA, IN VOL. I.

DISPENSATIONALISM: Dispensationalism is the name given to that movement which was begun among the Plymouth Brethren. John Nelson Darby (q.v., Vol. III), born in 1800, was their most prominent leader. Their doctrines are being preached from a number of pulpits and taught in many Sunday Schools in the evangelical Christian churches. The chief medium for disseminating dispensational ideas is the Scofield Reference Bible.

In contrast to historic Christianity, which always recognized two dispensations in the Bible, dispensationalism identifies seven: Innocency, Gen. 1:28–3:13; Conscience, Gen. 3:22–7:23;

Human Government, Gen. 8:20–11:9; Promise, from the call of Abraham to the giving of the Law, Gen. 12:1–Exod. 19:8; the Law, extending from Exod. 19:8 to Matt. 27:35; Grace, John 1:17, Heb. 9:3–8, 10:19, 20; the Fulness of the Times, Eph. 1:10. This seventh and last dispensation is said to be identical with the kingdom covenanted with David (II Sam. 7:8–17), being yet to come.

This movement professes to build its theology directly on the word of God and to be not "in bondage to the opinion of men." Their opponents, however, claim that their tenets rest upon a few passages taken out of their context, and that their theology is therefore arbitrary and unbiblical. The kingdom they expect is a racial, nationalistic, Jewish kingdom.

Dispensationalism distinguishes between the kingdom of the gospel and the kingdom of grace. According to this, the kingdom of the gospel is for the Jews and requires repentance only; the kingdom of the grace of God is for the Gentiles and requires faith only.

One other example must suffice: Acts 15:13–17 is said to be "dispensationally" the "most important passage in the Bible" (*Scofield Reference Bible*, p. 1169). It is supposed to refer to God's plan to save the Gentiles and then to save the Jews. For proof of this doctrine, Scofield refers to Rom. 11:24–27, instead of Acts 15:7, where Peter (Simeon) had just "declared how God had visited" the Gentile Cornelius to claim him for the kingdom.

The logical outcome of dispensational methods is seen in the statement: "The New Testament is a covenant made with the Jewish nation" (Kenneth Wuest, *Hebrews in the Greek New Testament* [1947], p. 14).

See also ESCHATOLOGY.

BIBLIOGRAPHY: Oswald T. Allis, *Prophecy and the Church*, 1945; James E. Bear, "Dispensationalism and the Covenant of Grace," *Union Seminary Review*, July, 1938; Lewis Sperry Chafer, "Dispensationalism," *Bibliotheca Sacra*, Vol. 93, 385–449; *Scofield Reference Bible;* Kenneth Wuest, *Hebrews in the Greek New Testament*, 1947; A. D. Ehlert, "A Bibliography of Dispensationalism," *Bibliotheca Sacra*, CI (1944), 95–101, 199–209, 319–328.

WILLIAM DOUGLAS CHAMBERLAIN.

DISPLACED PERSONS. See REFUGEES.

DIVINATION: Or divining, is the discovery and foretelling for men the will and operation of the supernatural. It assumes a realm of spirit, for example, the *mana* of primitives, not an entity, but a dynamism which permeates the universe; the *ch'i*, perhaps, of the Chinese, an item in their classical tradition; and, to some degree, the *pneuma* of western thought, and the *anima* of Hinduism. It assumes spirits and gods also, in great numbers, whose will and works are subject to interpretation by signs and acts of theirs and whose meanings may be "read" by diviners.

On man's part, charms are much in use as guarantees of divine behavior favorable to the wearers. Divining rods and horoscopes are used, as among the Hindus, subject to examination and decision with reference to marriage, fortunate times for agriculture, the attitude of stars, as for a journey, and appropriate times for ceremonies for the dead. Diviners usually prepare these charms.

Divination is of low or high degree, but places emphasis on man's own responsibility for the avoidance of evil and adherence to the good.

BIBLIOGRAPHY: C. H. Toy, *Introduction to the History of Religions*, 1913; H. L. Friess and H. W. Schneider, *Religion in Various Cultures*, 1932; R. H. Lowie, *Primitive Religion*, 1924.

[Sup.] JOHN CLARK ARCHER.

DIVINE DECREES: The decrees of God have reference to that which God willed to be and therefore to all that is comprised in the works of creation and providence. They do not denote, however, the actions of God in creation and providence but only the eternal counsel of God respecting all that comes to pass in these spheres. Decrees are distinct from their execution—they are eternal, the execution is temporal. Eternity as predicated of the decrees is to be distinguished from eternity as it applies to God Himself. The decrees arise from God's sovereign will, but God did not will Himself to be. Decrees are not to be identified with the commandments of God—decrees refer to what God has determined to come to pass, commandments to what he has revealed to be the rule of thought and action for rational and responsible creatures. Events in contravention of divine command are nevertheless embraced in the divine decree (Acts 2:23). JOHN MURRAY.

DIVINE, FATHER. See FATHER DIVINE'S PEACE MISSION MOVEMENT.

DIVINE OFFICE. See BREVIARY.

DIVINE SCIENCE: One of several New Thought (*q.v.*) groups, Divine Science owes its inception to Mrs. Malinda Cramer, who in 1885 had a remarkable healing through the realization of God's presence. The Divine Science College of Denver was incorporated in 1898, and the first Divine Science Church was founded in Denver by three sisters, Alethea B. Small, Fannie B. James, and Nona L. Brooks, in 1899. The college in Denver trains and ordains most of the workers in the field, though there are other colleges also. Local churches are largely autonomous, each governed by a democratically elected board of trustees. A recent issue of the official periodical, *Aspire to Better Living,* lists thirty-six churches with one or more ministers and forty-six registered workers, meaning teachers and/or practitioners similar to those in Christian Science.

Their beliefs are not significantly different from those of the New Thought Movement as expressed in the statement of principles of the International New Thought Alliance. Their literature stresses the characteristic New Thought emphases (health, prosperity, and happiness) and the power of mind or Spirit to achieve these goods.

BIBLIOGRAPHY: H. W. Dresser, *History of the New Thought Movement*, 1919; Charles S. Braden, *These Also Believe*, 1949; *Divine Science Principles*, 1950.

CHARLES S. BRADEN.

DIVINI REDEMPTORIS: Encyclical of March 19, 1937, in which Pope Pius XI (*q.v.*) condemns Bolshevist Communism (*q.v.*) for its materialism, its conceptions of man and society, and its atheism and terrorism. The Catholic Church has a better plan for reconstructing the social order (see QUADRAGESIMO ANNO). "There would be neither Socialism nor Communism today if the rulers of the nations had not scorned the teachings and material warnings of the Church." Spiritual renewal and Catholic Action (*q.v.*) are recommended as counter-measures.

BIBLIOGRAPHY: Latin text in *Acta Apostolicae Sedis*, Vol. XXIX, pp. 65–106; English in Joseph Husslein, *Social Wellsprings*, Vol. II (1942), pp. 341–374.

THEODORE G. TAPPERT.

DIVINO AFFLANTE SPIRITU· Encyclical of Pope Pius XII, issued on September 30, 1943, on the best means of promoting the study and diffusion of Holy Scripture. It outlines a complete program of scientific investigation of the Bible, starting from the necessity for the exegete to be thoroughly acquainted with the principles of modern linguistics and the methods of textual criticism. It stresses the importance of patristic, ecclesiastical, and profane literatures for a theological interpretation of the sacred text. While acknowledging the necessity of taking into account the literary patterns and formulas used by the inspired writers, it recommends some caution in appraising the bearing of the same upon the substance of the Biblical message.

Original text in *Acta Apostolicae Sedis*, Vol. XXXV (1943), pp. 297–325. English translation in J. E. Steinmueller, *A Companion to Scripture Studies*, Vol. I (1946), pp. 460–483.

GEORGES A. BARROIS.

DIVORCE: A problem in every age (see DIVORCE, Vol. III), most of all today, especially in Russia, Japan, and the United States. Once a stigma, divorce has become accepted as a part of our national life. Among many causes are the impact of world war, the loss of biblical ideals, the breakdown of morals, the growth of secularism, the general feeling of unrest, and in most states, the laxity of laws relating to marriage and divorce. For these conditions the theater, picture magazines, novels, motion pictures and television are partly to blame. The most frequent causes of divorce are disputes about sexual relations (including adultery), about money, and about children, or the absence of children. The facts have become so confusing that government bureaus of late seldom issue official statistics. The peak year seems to have been 1946, following World War II, with 610,000 divorces, over against 2,291,045 marriages (National Office of Vital Statistics). Since then the number of divorces has been lower, but it is still appalling.

To this peril the churches are awake. Both in legislative assemblies and locally they have been demanding more adequate laws about marriage and divorce, and they have been striving to inculcate more Christian ideals. There has been growing admiration for the position of the Protestant Episcopal Church, which does not sanction remarriage by the Church for a person who has been divorced. There is a tendency, however, to allow exceptions, even in the Roman Church, where the authorities can declare a marriage null and void, so as to permit marriage within the laws of the church. No longer do ministers of most churches feel free to remarry divorced persons without restrictions. In the Methodist and Presbyterian Churches, for example, a pastor when in doubt about his remarriage of a divorced person, must now secure the approval of superiors. All the while, everyone recognizes that the fault lies not in the divorce court but in the original marriage. When two Christians are married they do not seek a divorce.

The present age will go down in church history partly for the new emphasis on pastoral counseling, especially about marriage and divorce. Whenever the opportunity comes, the pastor counsels privately with one or the other party, preferably with both together, who apply for divorce. Without lowering his Christian standards he listens with understanding and sympathy. Never does he advise or encourage anyone to secure a divorce. Rather does he take the opposite course. He may explain that under certain extreme conditions divorce for the innocent party is permissible without sin, but that it is not mandatory. He encourages the two persons to seek and find reconciliation, it may be on their knees. He stresses the forgiveness of sins, with the forgiveness of wrongs. In an exceptional case a minister can even bring about the remarriage of two persons divorced through misunderstanding. If he had prevailed on them to postpone the divorce, and live apart for six months of probation, they might have discovered that they loved each other, and no one else in any evil way. In an extreme case he may feel that a legal separation alone will serve, but this need not involve remarriage. Both publicly and privately he makes clear the Bible teachings about the remarriage of a divorced person. On the other hand, many spiritually-minded pastors believe that adultery or wilful and permanent desertion can kill a marriage as surely as though the guilty party were in his grave.

The divorce evil calls for constructive Christian teaching and preaching by parents and pastor, from the cradle to the grave. (See MARRIAGE.) Home and church can train boys and girls, young men and women, so that they will marry in the Lord and then live together by his grace, with never a thought of divorce, which always means sin by one party and often by both.

BIBLIOGRAPHY: R. H. Charles, *Divorce and Nullity*, 1927; W. Goodsell, *A History of Marriage and the Family*, rev. ed., 1934; E. R. Groves, *Conserving Marriage and the Family*, 1944; H. M. Luckock, *The History of Marriage*, 2nd ed., 1910; W. A. Maier, *For Better Not for Worse*, 1939; G. E. Lenski, *Marriage in the Lutheran Church*, 1936; H. J. Wilkins, *The History of Divorce and Remarriage*, 1910; E. Westermarck, *The Future of Marriage in Western Civilization*, 1936; W. Westermarck, *A Short History of Marriage*, 1926.

[Sup.] WILLIAM GOULOOZE.

DIX, GEORGE EGLINTON ALSTON: Anglican Benedictine monk known as Dom Gregory; b. Oct. 4, 1901; d. at Nashdom Abbey, Bucks, May 12, 1952. He was educated at Merton College, Oxford and Wells Theological College. Ordained in 1924 he was history lecturer at Keble College, Oxford, before joining the Nashdom community in 1926. His special interest was the development of Christian thought and its manifestation in liturgical usages. He was sharply critical of certain Anglican movements towards reunion. He wrote: *The Apostolic Tradition of Hippolytus* (1937); *A Detection of Aumbries* (1942); *The Shape of the Liturgy* (1944); and contributed to *The Apostolic Ministry*.   F. W. DILLISTONE.

DOBBINS, GAINES STANLEY: B. Langsdale, Miss., July 29, 1886. He studied at Mississippi College (B.A., 1908); Southern Baptist Theological Seminary (Th.D., 1914); and Columbia University (M.A., 1925). He was ordained in the Baptist ministry (1914); and served pastorates at Gloster, Miss. (1914) and New Albany, Miss. (1915). He was a member of the editorial staff of the Southern Baptist Sunday School Board (1915–20); and was professor of religious education and church administration at Southern Baptist Theological Seminary (1920– ; treasurer, 1933–42; acting president, 1950–52). Among his writings are the following: *Building Better Churches* (1947); *Evangelism According to Christ* (1949); *The Church Book* (1951); *Winning the Children* (1953).   WILLIAM A. MUELLER.

DOBSCHUETZ, ERNST (ADOLF ALFRED OSKAR ADALBERT) VON: He was professor of New Testament at Halle (1913 until his death

in 1934; rector, 1922–23); exchange professor at Harvard (1913–14). His work assumed an international character when he succeeded C. R. Gregory in the task of assigning official numbers to newly found manuscripts of the New Testament (published in *ZNTW*) and when he became director of a projected *Corpus Hellenisticum zum N. T.* (see *ZNTW*, XXIV [1925], 43 ff.).

Representative publications include *The Eschatology of the Gospels* (1909); *Die Thessalonicherbriefe, Meyers Kommentar* (7th ed., 1909); "Bible in the Church," (*HERE*, II [1910], 579–615); *The Apostolic Age* (1910); edited (with O. von Gebhardt) *Die Akten der Edessenischer Bekenner; Gujas, Samonas, und Abibos* (*TU*, XXXVII, 2, 1911); *The Influence of the Bible on Civilization* (1914); *Nestles Einfuehrung in das griechische Neue Testament* (4th ed., 1923); *Der Apostel Paulus* (2 vols., 1926–28); *Das Neue Testament* (1927); *Das Apostolicum in biblisch-theologischen Beleuchtung* (1932); *Die Bibel im Leben der Voelker* (1934).

BIBLIOGRAPHY: Erich Stange, ed., *Die Religionswissenschaft der Gegenwart in Selbstdarstellungen*, Vol. IV (1928), pp. 31–32 (with picture and full list of publications); obituary notice, *JBL*, LIV (1935), vi.

[Sup.] BRUCE M. METZGER.

DOCK, CHRISTOPHER: Mennonite schoolmaster (?–1771) of colonial Pennsylvania, writer of the first scientific American treatise on pedagogy, *Eine einfaeltige und gruendlich abgefasste Schulordnung*, written in 1750 but first published at Germantown, Pa., in 1770. Dock, who probably arrived in America from Hesse-Cassel, Germany, about 1714, was a teacher in the schools at Skippack and Salford in Montgomery County, Pa. (and Germantown, four terms) ca. 1718–28 and 1738–71. He practiced a strikingly modern pedagogy based on pupil interest and motivation, noteworthy also for its successful integration of religious education and Christian character building with secular teaching materials. He was also a skillful artist in *Fractur-Schriften* (illuminated mottoes and texts), using them as rewards for pupil achievement and as copy-models for writing instruction. Dock was a close friend of Christopher Sauer and a contributor to the latter's *Geistliches Magazien* (1764 ff.), where his "Hundred Necessary Rules of Conduct for Children" appeared.

BIBLIOGRAPHY: M. G. Brumbaugh, *Life and Works of Christopher Dock*, 1908; Quintus Leatherman, "Christopher Dock, Mennonite Schoolmaster, 1718–1771," in *Mennonite Quarterly Review*, XVI (Jan., 1942), 32–44; Karl Massanari, "The Contribution of Christopher Dock to Contemporary Christian Teaching," *ibid.*, XXV (April, 1951), 100–115.

HAROLD S. BENDER.

DOCTRINAL PREACHING: The pulpit interpretation of Christian truth for practical ends. Preaching may be doctrinal directly or indirectly. At the core every message ought to have such a truth as God's Providence. Directly, at times, a man should preach on some aspect of such a truth, or he may have a series about sin, or faith. Such "preaching" began with the prophets. "Jesus came preaching the Kingdom." The apostles preached doctrine, and many of the early Fathers. The Reformation brought a return to the practice. In later times pulpit doctrine gave way to "inspiration." Robert W. Dale, Charles E. Jefferson, J. D. Jones of Bournemouth showed how to use doctrine in their day. More recently, Karl Barth and Emil Brunner have led to such preaching, both among followers and critics. Such preaching calls for mastery of the truth, clarity of thought, sturdiness of structure, simplicity of style, and ability to meet human needs. For examples see James S. Stewart, *The Strong Name* (1940). Instead of holding forth about God's omniscience, omnipresence, omnipotence, and transcendence, the popular preacher deals with one such truth in thought-forms of today. He may teach about God as Light, Life, Love, Spirit (Person), or Father. Usually the beginner attempts too much. Instead of compressing into a sermon the entire truth about the Holy Spirit, why not deal with Him as Teacher (John 16:13)? Literature about doctrinal preaching is scant and disappointing. Every book about "what to preach" has such a section, often scholastic or hortatory. Few lecturers or writers try to answer the question, How? For an exception see *The Servant of the Word,* by H. H. Farmer (1942). Also a book less practical, *Positive Preaching and the Modern Mind,* by P. T. Forsyth (1907). Because of present doctrinal concern in seminaries, the church should witness a revival of such preaching, to alleviate "religious illiteracy." ANDREW W. BLACKWOOD.

DODD, CHARLES HAROLD: Born at Wrexham, North Wales, April 7, 1884. He graduated at Oxford (University College) in Literae Humaniores (1906). In the following years he spent a semester at Berlin, pursued research in ancient history and archaeology there and at Magdalen College, Oxford, and, turning to theology, became a student at Mansfield College, Oxford. Ordained in 1912, he served as minister of the Independent or Congregational Church at Warwick (1912–15, 1918–19). Recalled to Mansfield College, he taught New Testament there until 1930, when he became Rylands Professor of Biblical Criticism and Exegesis at Manchester. In 1935 he was elected Norris-Hulse Professor of Divinity at Cambridge, and later fellow of Jesus College. He retired in 1949. His published works include: *The Authority of the Bible* (1928); *The Bible and the Greeks* (1935); *Parables of the Kingdom* (1935); *The Apostolic Preaching and its Developments* (1936); *History and the Gospel* (1938); *Gospel*

and Law (1951); *According to the Scriptures* (1952); *The Interpretation of the Fourth Gospel* (1953); and commentaries on the *Epistle to the Romans* (1932); and the *Johannine Epistles* (1946).

DOHNAVUR FELLOWSHIP: A fellowship of Indian and Western Christian workers which has grown out of the lifework of Miss Amy Wilson Carmichael at Dohnavur, Tirunelveli (Tinnevelly) District, South India. Miss Carmichael reached India as a missionary of the C.E.Z.M.S. in 1895. In 1901 she found a distinctive task in rescuing girls who had been dedicated to a life of servitude in Hindu temples. This led to the establishment of a home for children at Dohnavur which has gradually expanded until the present, when, according to a recent statement, the community embraces 922 persons, including six from Western countries. Among its activities are listed the maintenance of homes and schools for boys and girls of all ages; agriculture and other vocational work; a hospital; and evangelism in the neighbouring area. The Fellowship, which began as part of Miss Carmichael's work under her Mission, was registered as an independent society in 1927. Miss Carmichael died in 1951 after sixty years of unbroken service in India. Among other leaders of the Fellowship has been Dr. G. Webb Peploe, who joined it in 1928.

BIBLIOGRAPHY: A brief portrayal of Miss Carmichael's character will be found in G. S. Eddy, *Pathfinders of the World Missionary Crusade,* 1945. An account of the Fellowship down to 1932 is given by Miss Carmichael, *Gold Cord,* 1932.

MAX HUNTER HARRISON.

DOLEANTIE MOVEMENT: The Doleantie was part of a revival of Calvinism against well-intrenched rationalism in nineteenth century Holland, the outcome of a struggle waged particularly since the 1870's. Abraham Kuyper (*q.v.*) was the central figure, along with F. L. Rutgers, De Savornin Lohman, and many others.

"Doleantie" is used in distinction from "separation" to indicate an attempt to reform the church through duly constituted authorities. The *doleerenden* believed that the synodical organization had departed from the Reformed Confessions and ceased to be the church. The movement embodied such ideas as the autonomy of the local congregation, literal subscription to the Reformed Confessions, pluriformity of the church, and defense of the church order of Dort (see DORT, SYNOD OF, Vol. III).

The occasion for the break was a conflict between synodical regulations and the Confession. The conservative Amsterdam Consistory refused in 1886 to admit to confessing membership those free-thinking young people who wished to make confession of faith before liberal ministers. The ministers protested, and the Provincial Board and the Synod opposed the consistory. The conservative ministers, elders, and deacons, Kuyper included, were deposed. Thousands of members followed them into a new church organization. Similar struggles arose elsewhere. Ownership of property was hotly contested.

The movement contributed to the spread of Calvinism in other countries. It developed Calvinism as a world and life view, influencing such spheres as statesmanship, learning, art, journalism, and social uplift. In 1892 the Doleantie Churches united with the Christian Reformed Churches to form the Reformed Churches in the Netherlands, a denomination which numbered 531 congregations and 491,451 members in 1900.

BIBLIOGRAPHY: P. Kasteel, *Abraham Kuyper*, 1938; A. Kuyper, *Separatie en Doleantie*, 1890; *Tractaat van de Reformatie der Kerken*, 1883; *Winkler Prins' Geillustreerde Encyclopaedie*, s.v. Kuyper, A., and *Gereformeerde Kerken in Nederland*; J. C. Rullmann, *De Doleantie*, 1929.

JOHN H. KROMMINGA.

DOMINIC, SAINT, AND THE DOMINICAN ORDER: The official name of the Dominican order is *Ordo fratrum Praedicatorum;* sometimes also called Jacobins, after the monastery of St. Jacques in Paris. St. Dominic owed much to the prior Diego, later the bishop of Osma, where Dominic was canon in the cathedral. Diego and Dominic in 1204 reformed the chapter of this church in accordance with the rule of St. Augustine. Dominic was at first one of the Augustinian canons secular. The Fourth Lateran Council in 1215 had forbidden the founding of new religious orders, so Dominic chose to adopt the Augustinian rules for his followers, adding some features which he borrowed from the Norbertines. In 1220 at the general chapter of the order the constitution was adopted. It included the obligation to renounce the ownership of property, but the emphasis upon evangelical poverty was less pronounced than that among the Franciscans (*q.v.*). The order was not permitted to own land, though it might acquire monasteries and churches. In 1221 the order counted sixty houses. Jordanus of Saxony, the second general (1222–1237), won more than 1000 novices. At the opening of the fourteenth century the order had 21 provinces and 562 houses. The Second Order originated in the convents of La Prouille (originally intended as a Cistercian house for women in 1206) and of St. Sixtus in Rome (1217). It received from Dominic the Augustinian rule with some additions. At the height of its success this order counted some 350 houses. The Third Order was founded during the career of Dominic; both men and women could join it. In 1285 the general Munio de Zamora provided a rule for it.

BIBLIOGRAPHY: R. Bennett, *The Early Dominicans*, 1937; B. Jarrett, *The English Dominicans*, 1921; E. Formoy, *The Dominican Order in England before the Reformation*, 1925; new biographies of Dominic by C. Barbieri,

Milan, 1922; H. Petitot, S. Maximin, 1925; L. Rambaud, Paris, 1926; H. Scheeben, Freiburg, 1927; P. Mandonnet and H. Vicaire, *St. Dominque, l'idée, l'homme el l'oeuvre*, 2 vols., 1938; B. Altaner, *Der heilige Dominikus: Untersuchungen und Texte*, 1922; idem, *Die Beziehungen des heiligen Dominikus zum heilgen Franziskus*, 1922; R. Zeller, *La vie Dominicaine*, 1927; P. Mortier, *Histoire des maîtres généraux de l'ordre des frères Prêcheurs*, 8 vols., 1903–20.

[Sup.] ALBERT HYMA.

DONALDSON, DWIGHT M.: American Presbyterian foreign missionary in Meshed, Iran (1915–40), and principal of the Henry Martyn School of Islamic Studies, Aligarh, India (1940–50). He is the author of *The Shi'ite Religion* (1933); *Studies in Muslim Ethics* (1952); and is associate editor of *The Muslim World*.

DONATISM: Its rigidity appealed to the peasants, and to some extent, as borne out by recent archaeological discoveries, the Catholic and Donatist division was one between town and country. The Catholics were stronger in Proconsular Africa. The Donatists were rather numerous in Consular Numidia. The Donatists were later joined by the socially discontented, the oppressed, and the rebellious, the Circumcelliones.

Donatism was mainly limited to North Africa, but in A.D. 318 the Donatists established contact in Rome and established a rival bishop, Victor or Garba. In the Council of Sardica-Philopoppolis A.D. 342 (?), the Donatists joined the Semi-Arians. This division in North Africa lasted for about three centuries, until all succumbed to Islam.

BIBLIOGRAPHY: S. Simpson, *Saint Augustine and the African Church Divisions*, 1910; Edward Frank Humphrey, *Politics and Religion in the Days of Augustine*, 1912; H. von Soden, *Urkunden zur Entstehungsgeschichte des Donatismus*, 1913; A. Berthier, *Les vestiges du Christianisme antique*, 1942; G. G. Willis, *Saint Augustine and the Donatist Controversy*, 1950; W. H. C. Frend, *The Donatist Church*, 1952.

[Sup.] DANIEL JOHANNES THERON.

DOSTOIEVSKI, FEODOR MIKHAILOVICH: B. 1821; d. 1881; great Russian novelist whose work, like that of Kierkegaard, constitutes the critical divide of nineteenth century thought. His novels, notably *Poor Folk, The House of the Dead, The Insulted and Injured, Crime and Punishment, The Idiot, The Possessed, A Raw Youth, The Brothers Karamazov*, are distinguished by penetrating character studies (especially in the realm of the abnormal, where he anticipated the most extreme findings of depth psychology), acute self-analysis, and profound sympathy for the poor and defeated.

His fundamental theological significance lies in his influence upon modern dialectical theology (*q.v.*) through Karl Barth (*q.v.*) and others. His work, which influenced the theology of crisis (see CRISIS, THE THEOLOGY OF), belongs to the literature of crisis. His impact is greatest at the point of anthropology, for his crisis was a reaction against intellectualist-idealist humanism (*q.v.*). His characters, who so frequently personify morbid impulses and irrational forces (see IRRATIONALISM), contradict the thesis that human nature is fundamentally rational and good, for these impulses and forces are either quiescent or active in the soul of every man. Even the strong man is a divided being, a "miserable louse."

The clue to Dostoievski's anthropology may be found in the circumstances of his own life (the details of which are readily available elsewhere) and the inner conflict of his own chaotic, tortured, paradoxical being. The characters of the novels, incredible yet real people, facing human impotence, doubt, despair, satanic temptations, demonic powers, find the meaning of life only in the hope of being born again in the image of Christ, the resurrection. The weak, the sick, the foolish, the insane, even murderers and prostitutes, are nearer to salvation because they know they cannot save themselves. Humanity, imprisoned in self-worship, recognizing nothing higher than itself, is condemned to the mental isolation of the insane. Men find themselves in the great solidarity of sin and guilt, but repentance remains, and the leap of faith, and the Kingdom that is coming with power. See also RUSSIAN ORTHODOX CHURCH.

BIBLIOGRAPHY: *The Novels of Feodor Dostoievski*, tr. by Constance Garnett, 12 vols., 1912–20; Andre Gide, *Dostoevsky*, 1949; Rene Fueloep-Miller, *Fyodor Dostoevski, Insight, Faith, and Prophecy*, 1950; William Hubben, *Four Prophets of our Destiny*, 1952; Janko Lavrin, *Dostoievski*, 1947; Eduard Thurneysen, *Dostojewski*, 4th ed., 1930.

JOHN W. DOBERSTEIN.

DOUBT: Doubt is a state of uncertainty as to the truth or reality of something, or as to the reliability of a person. It may involve a factual and disinterested recognition that sufficient evidence is lacking, but there may also be coupled with this a more positive element resulting in either a wavering of opinion or a tendency to acceptance or rejection which, however, cannot become a conviction. Especially if the object is a person, the tendency to rejection may take the form of suspicion, mistrust, or fear.

The term is sometimes employed in a purely descriptive sense, expressing or implying no evaluation of the attitude of the doubter. An example is the statement (Acts 2:12) that some of those who witnessed the outpouring of the Holy Spirit "were in doubt, saying one to another, What meaneth this?" More commonly, however, some evaluation of the attitude of doubt is indicated or implied.

In the Scriptures, and in the Christian tradition, the evaluation of doubt is usually unfavorable. "Thy life shall hang in doubt before thee" (Deut. 28:66) is one of the disabilities which is predicted for failure to observe the law of God. "Dissolving of doubts" is one of the virtues of Daniel (Dan. 5:12). Jesus censured

Peter for doubting (Mt. 14:31). To deal with the doubts of Thomas, the evidence which he demanded is presented, but he is commanded "be not faithless, but believing" and others are commended who shall believe without such evidence (John 20:24–29). In Christian ethics, doubt has commonly been classified as a sin and we have been assured that "doubt is of the devil" and that the cure for it is prayer of confession and petition. The reason is that the Christian life is one of humble reliance on God through Christ. All the fruits of this life flow from trust in him. Doubt, lack of such trust, frustrates such a life. Christianity also maintains that man was made by God for such a life of trust, that refusal to trust constituted the first sin and that our failure to trust is the fruit of sin.

But doubt has also been highly commended, especially when it involves a refusal to accept anything on the basis of untested authority and is a first, negative, step in the quest for truth. This sort of positive, epistemological doubt was characteristic of Socrates, and, though it brought upon him the condemnation of contemporary authority, it has also earned for him the approbation of subsequent ages. Doubt of ecclesiastical authority was basic to both the Renaissance and the Reformation. Doubt of any belief not founded on precise observation and sound reasoning is basic to science. Descartes became the "father of modern philosophy" through his methodological determination to doubt everything that could be doubted, always convinced, however, that thus he would reach an indubitable foundation for his system.

As an epistemological method, therefore, doubt is of the highest value so long as, for pathological or other reasons, it does not degenerate into a "doubt for doubt's sake."

ANDREW K. RULE.

DOUGHERTY, DENNIS JOSEPH: Cardinal; b. at Honesville, Pa., Aug. 16, 1865; d. at Philadelphia, May 31, 1951. He studied at Saint Mary's College, Montreal; at Saint Charles Borromeo Seminary, Overbrook, Pa.; and at the North American College, Rome. Ordained to the priesthood in 1890, he served on the faculty of Saint Charles Borromeo Seminary (1890–1903). He was appointed successively Bishop of Nueva Segovia (1903), and of Jaro (1908), in the Philippine Islands. He was called back to the United States as Bishop of Buffalo, N.Y. (1915), and he became archbishop of Philadelphia (1918). He was created cardinal on March 7, 1921, under the pontificate of Benedict XV. GEORGES A. BARROIS.

DOUGLAS, LLOYD CASSEL: Minister and novelist; b. in Columbia City, Ind., on Aug. 27, 1877; d. Feb. 13, 1951. He was the son of the

Rev. Alexander Jackson and Sarah Jane (Cassel) Douglas. He took the A.B. degree at Wittenberg College (1900). After receiving the B.D. degree at the Hamma Divinity School, Springfield, Ohio (1903), he served in various pastorates from 1903 to 1933, including the Luther Place Memorial Church, Washington, D. C. (1908–11); the First Congregational Church, Ann Arbor, Michigan (1915–21); the First Congregational Church, Akron, Ohio (1921–26); the First Congregational Church, Los Angeles, California (1926–29); and St. James United Church, Montreal (1929–33).

In 1929 he published *Magnificent Obsession*, the first of a number of novels with religious themes, many of which found a very large audience. These include *Forgive Us Our Trespasses* (1932), *Green Light* (1935), *The Robe* (1942), and *The Big Fisherman* (1948). He spent his later years in Los Angeles, and in Las Vegas.

Douglas assigned his narrative ability to his experience when a child of riding out with his father on pastoral calls and hearing him tell stories of his rural parishioners.

AMOS N. WILDER.

DOUGLASS, HARLAN PAUL: Congregational Christian; b. at Osage, Iowa, Jan. 4, 1871; d. April 14, 1953. He studied at Grinnell College (1891). Following Congregational pastorates in the Midwest, he was for eleven years executive secretary of the American Missionary Association. He was editor of *Christendom* (1938–48). He was part time consultant in the newly organized Department of Research and Survey of the National Council of the Protestant Episcopal Church (1951–).

DOWIEISM. See CHRISTIAN CATHOLIC APOSTOLIC CHURCH IN ZION.

DOWNTOWN CHURCH: The term here refers to a large congregation in the heart of a city: e.g., the Methodist Temple of Chicago or Tremont Temple of Boston. Such a church is probably the most important and most difficult pastoral charge. Few members live within walking distance. They come from all parts of the metropolitan area, passing smaller churches in need of support. Such work calls for a man with a striking personality, ability to dramatize, and willingness to advertise. In most cities Protestantism has suffered through failure to maintain strong churches downtown. With the right sort of leadership, and adequate financial support, such a church can affect the whole city, and appeal to transients who carry its influence to the ends of the earth.

ANDREW W. BLACKWOOD.

DRAGON: In the Babylonian creation myth the gods struggle to conquer Tiamat. In Genesis 1:2 the primeval waters are designated *t⁶hom*, a word cognate to Tiamat though not derived directly therefrom. The Babylonian ideas are absent, no warfare occurs here to achieve mastery, and *t⁶hom* is not really a dragon. References to such conflict do occur, however, with Rahab as the hostile dragon (Job 26:12; Ps. 89:10; Isa. 51:9); these are merely literary allusions, not formal teachings, glorifying Yahweh by ascribing the familiar victory to him. The mythical dragon is also called Leviathan, and Yahweh's victory over it figuratively designates his victory over Egypt (Ps. 74:14). The name appears also in Ugaritic mythology, where Anat conquers the monster. See also DEMON.

BIBLIOGRAPHY: George A. Barton, *Archaeology and the Bible*, 7th ed. rev., 1937; W. F. Albright, *Archaeology and the Religion of Israel*, 1942.

[Sup.] HAROLD L. CREAGER.

DRAGUET, RENÉ: Roman Catholic; b. at Gosselies, Belgium, Feb. 13, 1896. He studied at Louvain (M.D., 1924) and has been professor there (1925–), teaching Syriac, Old Slavonic, and ancient Christian Oriental literatures. His main research field is the documents of early Oriental monasticism. He is editor of the *Corpus Scriptorum Christianorum Orientalium* of Louvain-Washington (1948). His works include: *Julien d'Halicarnasse* (1924), *Histoire du dogme catholique* (1947), *Les Pères du Désert* (1942).

DRAMA, RELIGIOUS: Drama has rightly been called the handmaiden of religion. From the Aristotelian meaning of "imitation" to the modern church dramatist's contention that "a play is religious if it has a religious effect upon the audience," drama has consistently had its place in the corporate worship of world religions. Holy books and writings are dramatic treatises, and worship is the drama of man's relationship with God. In Christianity drama's position has been especially significant. The development of the Eucharist in Catholic and Anglican churches, the Sacrament of the Altar in Lutheranism, the observance of the Lord's Supper in Presbyterian and Reformed tradition, no less than rites of baptism, foot washing, and the agape, where these are observed, have been inherently dramatic, and have continued to represent in action both didactic and thaumaturgic aspects of the Christian faith. The early mystery, miracle, and morality cycles were classical forms of religious drama, which drew within their orbits a closely related field of histrionic presentations. They attracted audiences, taught moral and religious principles, stimulated the spiritual life, impressed the intellect, and directed conduct.

In seeking to achieve like results, modern religious drama has reached high importance in contemporary life. There is a growing demand for "plays for the church," religious drama clubs are being organized, leaders in religious drama are being trained, writers are being urged to turn their talents to the preparation of scripts with a distinctive spiritual message. This resurgence of interest in drama for the churches' program shows clearly defined tendencies, such as: (1) Liturgical Drama, designed as a unitive expression of the history, doctrine, development, and spirit of worship; (2) Church Chancel Drama, consisting of presentations that bear the imprint of spiritual appeal and are worthy of incorporation in a service of worship; (3) Plays for the "second service of the day," and sometimes known as Vesper Dramas, including secular plays with a religious emphasis. In this category are constructive and attractive dramatizations for Sunday evening services, young people's fellowships, and mid-week services. Several of America's newer religious movements have taken plays of this type "on the road," presenting them in churches, community buildings, and theaters across the nation: (4) Propaganda Plays in the field of inter-religious relations; (5) Plays for holy days and church festivals; (6) Pageants, tableaux, and dramatic spectacles built around religious figures and historic movements; (7) Dramas for radio and television, based on parables, lives of saints, and biblical sequences; (8) Motion pictures for the church, sponsored by denominational boards or religious film foundations.

While the extensiveness of audience interest in worthwhile religious drama is attested by statistics and by surveys on the field, the immediate need is for qualified leadership in the realm for writing and production, as well as essential equipment to bring religious drama to the highest standards of religious art. In order to be religious, drama must impart spiritual values to the player through study and self-expression, and to the spectator through excellence and receptivity in aesthetic form.

MARCUS BACH.

DREISBACH, JOHN: Evangelical United Brethren; b. June 5, 1789; d. Aug. 20, 1871. Won to the new religious movement begun by Jacob Albright (q.v., Vol. I) in 1800, he began to assist this leader when but seventeen years of age, and at the age of twenty-five was chosen first presiding elder of the new body, then called the Evangelical Association. Frequently he was chosen presiding officer of the annual and quadrennial conferences of his church. Dreisbach was elected a member of the legislature of Pennsylvania for 1828 and 1829. He wrote no less than thirty-five German hymns, others in English, in addition to compiling a hymnal in 1821 and editing many of the official editions of the hymnal of his denomination. He

founded the publishing house of the denomination at New Berlin, Pa., and was its first manager (1820–27). He was also editor of *The Evangelical Messenger* (1855–59). He edited the denomination's first *Catechism* (1809) and was the first to advocate its educational institutions.

RAYMOND W. ALBRIGHT.

DRIVER, SAMUEL ROLLES: d. at Oxford, Feb. 26, 1914. He was regius professor of Hebrew and canon of Christ Church, Oxford (1882–1914). He was a mediating critic. His *Introduction to the Literature of the Old Testament* (rev. ed., 1913) was long a standard text.

BIBLIOGRAPHY: Francis Brown, *Biblical World*, 43 (May, 1914) 291–294.

[Sup.] ELMER E. FLACK.

DRUMMOND, JAMES: D. June 13, 1918. He succeeded Dr. Martineau as principal of New College, Manchester, in 1885 and moved with the college to Oxford in 1889. After his retirement in 1906 he continued his literary work, publishing: *The Pauline Benediction* (1897); *Some Thoughts on Christology* (1902); *Studies in Christian Doctrine* (1908); *The Transmission of the Text of the New Testament* (1909); *Johannine Thoughts* (1909); *Lectures on the Composition and Delivery of Sermons* (1910); and *Paul: His Life and Teaching* (1911). [Sup.] RAYMOND W. ALBRIGHT.

DRURY, AUGUSTUS WALDO: D. Feb. 18, 1935. He was professor of systematic theology in the Bonebrake Theological Seminary, Dayton, O. (1892–1935). He was also a trustee and president of the board of the United Brethren Publishing House, Dayton. His additional publications include: *Baptism, Its Place in the Church Visible* (1902); *History of the Church of the United Brethren in Christ* (1924; 2nd ed., 1931); and *Outlines of Doctrinal Theology* (1914; rev. ed., 1926).

BIBLIOGRAPHY: Marion R. Drury, *The Life of Augustus Waldo Drury*, 1936.

[Sup.] RAYMOND W. ALBRIGHT.

DRURY, CLIFFORD MERRILL: Presbyterian, U.S.A.; b. Nov. 7, 1897, Early, Iowa. He studied at Buena Vista College (B.A., 1918); San Francisco Theological Seminary (B.D., 1922; S.T.M. 1928); and Edinburgh University (Ph.D., 1932). He was pastor of the Community (American) Church, Shanghai, China (1923–27); pastor, First Presbyterian, Moscow, Idaho (1928–38); and is professor of church history, San Francisco Theological Seminary, (1938–). He was commissioned in U. S. Naval Reserve as chaplain in 1933 and served 1941–46. He wrote *History of the Chaplain Corps, U.S. Navy* (2 vols., 1949, 1950), and *United States Navy Chaplains, 1778–1945* (1948). Other books include, *Henry Harmon Spalding, Pioneer of Old*

Oregon (1936); *Marcus Whitman, M.D. Pioneer and Martyr* (1937); *Elkanah and Mary Walker, Pioneers Among the Spokans* (1940); *A Tepee in His Front Yard, a Biography of Henry T. Cowley* (1949); *Presbyterian Panorama, One Hundred and Fifty Years of National Missions History* (1952).

DRURY, MARION RICHARDSON: D. Feb. 21, 1939. He was pastor of United Brethren churches in Toledo, Iowa (1898–1907); Oakland, Calif. (1907–10); and Cedar Rapids, Ia. (1917–19). He served as president of Philomath College (Oregon) (1910–13) and of Leander Clark College, Toledo, Ia. (1913–16). After being student secretary for Coe College (1919–22) he spent his latter years as a missionary for his denomination at Ponce, Puerto Rico (1922–39). His later publications include *After Eighty Years* (1930); *Memorial Record Western College Class of 1872* (1930); *Reminiscences of Early Days in Iowa* (1931); and *Life of Augustus Waldo Drury* (1936).

[Sup.] RAYMOND W. ALBRIGHT.

DRUSES: The Druses entered Lebanon (*q.v.*) from the south in the eleventh century, and flourished in full measure under their emir Fakhr al-Dīn al-Maʻni II (1590–1633). Alienated from the body of orthodox Islam and isolated in their mountain retreat, they maintained a tradition of insularity and a sense of solidarity and independence bordering on that of nationhood. They lived in peace with their northern neighbors, the Maronites, until the mid-nineteenth century. The disturbances that began in 1841 ended in the civil war of 1860, after which Lebanon was constituted an autonomous state guaranteed by the West European powers. Since then the feudal organization of the Druse community began to show signs of breaking down but has managed to survive to the present under the headship of two families, the Arislāns and the Janbalāṭs. The first governor general of autonomous Lebanon established in 1862 at ʻAbayh, in the Druse district, an educational institution which remained until World War I the only secondary school in the country supported by government funds. In 1931 it passed into denominational Druse hands.

In the eighteenth and nineteenth centuries Druses migrated not so much into the West as into Ḥawrān, where they so flourished as to give their name to the district Jabal (mountain of) al-Duruz. In this and other parts of Syria they numbered in 1946 95,749 as against 77,023 in Lebanon. The French mandate encouraged the separatist spirit of the Druses and allowed them in Ḥawrān a special regime (1921–36) under direct French control. The national Syrian uprising of 1925 against the French was led by Syrian Druses.

BIBLIOGRAPHY: Frederick J. Bliss, *The Religions of Modern Syria and Palestine*, 1912; Philip K. Hitti, *Origins of the Druze People and Religion*, 1928; A. H. Hourani, *Minorities in the Arab World*, 1947.

[Sup.] PHILIP K. HITTI.

DUBOSE, WILLIAM PORCHER: B. 1836; d. 1918; South Carolina born, a philosophical and biblical theologian, he taught at the University of the South from 1871 until his death. Profoundly affected by arresting meetings with God, by the experiences of the Civil War (in which he was wounded and captured), the death or maiming of many close friends, the Reconstruction era, he required real, not formal or traditional, answers to the problem of evil and to the questions raised for Christian faith by the discoveries of biologists and psychologists. The material for his answers came from the New Testament and human experience, his method from Aristotle. The theologians whose positions are closest to his are Hort and Westcott.

DuBose's books are: *The Soteriology of the New Testament* (1892); *The Ecumenical Councils* (1896); *The Gospel in the Gospels* (1906); *The Gospel According to St. Paul* (1908); *High Priesthood and Sacrifice* (1908); *The Reason of Life* (1911); *Turning Points in My Life* (1911).

BIBLIOGRAPHY: Murray, *DuBose, Prophet of Unity*, 1924; and Bratton, *Apostle of Reality*, 1936, are excellent books; of some value is Marshall, *The Word Was Made Flesh: The Theology of William Porcher DuBose*, 1949.

ALEXANDER C. ZABRISKIE.

DUBS, HOMER H.: Philosopher, theologian, sinologist; b. Deerfield, Ill., 1892. He studied at Yale University (B.A., 1914); Columbia University (M.A., 1916); Union Theological Seminary (B.D., 1917); University of Chicago (Ph.D., 1925); Oxford University (M.A., 1947). He was a missionary in the China Mission of the Evangelical Church in Hunan, China (1918–24); instructor in philosophy, University of Minnesota (1925–27); professor of philosophy, Marshall College (1927–34); director, Translation of Chinese Histories Project of American Council of Learned Societies (1934–37); acting professor of philosophy, Duke University and Duke Divinity School (1937–43); visiting professor of Chinese, Columbia University (1944–45); professor of Chinese studies, Kennedy School of Missions, Hartford Seminary Foundation (1945–47); professor of Chinese, Oxford University (1947–). He wrote: (with B. H. Niebel) *Evangelical Missions* (1919); *Rational Induction: An Analysis of the Method of Philosophy and Science* (1926).

DUCK RIVER AND KINDRED ASSOCIATIONS OF BAPTISTS: Preferring this name rather than one which should give them the semblance of a denomination, seven associations of moderately Calvinistic Baptist churches in Tennessee, Alabama, Georgia, and Mississippi have been so united since 1890 or earlier. The original association of churches known as the Duck River Association of Baptists was an offshoot of the Elk River Association, organized in 1808. There are 91 churches with an inclusive membership of 7,951. There is no general organization. [Sup. to MISCELLANEOUS RELIGIOUS BODIES.]　　　　　　　　ROBERT G. TORBET.

DUDLEIAN LECTURES: In 1751 Paul Dudley, fellow of Harvard College and chief justice of the province of Massachusetts Bay, left a sum of money to Harvard College for "the erecting, maintaining, supporting & continuing an Anniversary Sermon or Lecture to be held or preached at the said Colledge once every year successively," for which three subjects are now prescribed in rotation: (1) Natural Religion, (2) Revealed Religion, (3) The Validity of Non-Episcopal Ordination. These annual lectures are printed in the *Harvard Divinity School Bulletin*.
　　　　　　　　　　　　　　G. WHITE.

DUDLEY, LORD ROBERT, EARL OF LEICESTER: B. in 1533; d. Sept. 4, 1588. He was the son of John Dudley, Viscount Lisle, Earl of Warwick and Duke of Northumberland, who in the reign of Edward VI had acted as one of the young king's regents. The father had endeavored to secure the crown for Lady Jane Grey, his daughter-in-law, by persuading Edward to appoint her as his heir. But Northumberland's plot had miscarried, and he had been burned at the stake.

The son was sent with his father to the Tower in London, but was spared. Early in the reign of Queen Elizabeth he won her favor. On p. 43 of the seventh volume in the *Oxford History of England* (the volume by Professor J. B. Black of the University of Aberdeen, *The Reign of Elizabeth*) appears this striking statement: "Cecil . . . was still more perturbed . . . to find her sunk in amorous dalliance with one who bore the most tainted name among the aristocracy of England. After solemnly assuring her first parliament that she intended to live and die a virgin . . . she had apparently become infatuated with the charm of Lord Robert Dudley, son of the archtraitor Northumberland." The distinguished author goes on to say that the forthcoming marriage with Dudley was practically certain in Elizabeth's mind. There was one obstacle in her way, namely the fact that Dudley had married one Amy Robsart. Amy Robsart perished in a horrible manner; she was poisoned and her neck broken to indicate that she had fallen down a staircase. A German scholar, E. Bekker, author of a learned volume entitled, *Elisabeth und Leicester (Giessener Studien*, Vol. V, 1890) has established the fact that Elizabeth was an accomplice in the murder of Amy Robsart. But the English ruler shrank from so bold a step as marrying Dudley.

Elizabeth's foreign policy soon enabled Dud-

ley to profit from the turn of events. In the first religious war in France, started in 1562, she agreed to ally England with the French Protestants. In the secret Treaty of Richmond she stipulated that England was to receive Le Havre as a pledge until Calais was recovered (Mary Tudor had lost Calais in 1558). But the Huguenots were badly beaten; their leader Condé in 1563 signed the Treaty of Amboise, obtaining thereby freedom of religion for the Huguenots but depriving the English of Le Havre. Elizabeth was deeply distressed and humiliated, but another opportunity presented itself to her when in 1584 William of Orange, founder of the Dutch Republic, was assassinated and in the next year Antwerp fell into the hands of the Spanish. Once more Elizabeth allied with Calvinists on the Continent, and again she obtained some land there with a fine port, this time Flushing (Vlissingen) at the mouth of the Scheldt. She supplied the Dutch with several thousand soldiers, and out of an annual income of 300,000 pounds she spent 126,000 to help the Dutch fight Spain. She appointed Robert Dudley, now Earl of Leicester, her governor in the northern Netherlands, hoping that he would check the Spanish armies. At first he was cordially received by the Dutch leaders, but he proved to be a poor statesman and military leader. His English forces rapidly dwindled until he was suddenly withdrawn by the irate Queen. He returned to England in November 1586, but seven months later Elizabeth sent him back with 5,000 newly recruited men and 30,000 pounds sterling. Once more he failed to acomplish anything important. In November 1587 he left the Netherlands again, but in spite of his repeated failures he did not lose favor with the Queen. In 1588, when the Spanish Armada was being prepared for the expected invasion of England, Leicester was put at the head of the English forces at Tilbury.

Leicester became the titular political chief of the Puritans in England. He was able on numerous occasions to obtain favors for them at the Court. He was appointed chancellor of the University of Oxford. In 1571 he secured for it a permanent incorporation, which relieved the institution of having to seek incorporation at the accession of each king or queen. He also supplied the university with a new printing press. As a prominent member of the Privy Council he wielded great power in both domestic and foreign policies.

BIBLIOGRAPHY: J. E. Neale, *Queen Elizabeth*, 1934; L. Lemonier, *Elisabeth d'Angleterre, la reine vierge?* 1947; E. Sitwell, *Fanfare for Elizabeth*, 1947; A. B. Allen, *The Spacious Days of Queen Elizabeth*, 1950; *Leicester Correspondence, 1586–87*, ed. Camden Soc., 1844; Ernst Bekker, *Elisabeth und Leicester, Giessener Studien*, Vol. V, 1890; Aubrey Richardson, Mrs., *The Lover of Queen Elizabeth: Being the Life of Robert Dudley, Earl of Leicester 1533–1588*, 1907; F. Chamberlin, *Elizabeth and Leycester*, 1939; M. Waldman, *Elizabeth and Leicester*, 1945.

　　　　　　　　　　　ALBERT HYMA.

DUELING IN THE UNITED STATES: A duel is a private combat with deadly weapons between two persons, fighting by prearrangement and under agreed conditions to settle a personal quarrel. It is distinguished from the wager of battle by its illegality, from an ordinary fight by its formality and prearrangement. Under American law, these are essential. A shooting affray in sudden heat and passion, even after a verbal challenge, is not legally a duel. By almost universal custom, a duel was preceded by a written challenge from the person who considered himself offended and a written acceptance from his opponent. The person challenged had the choice of weapons. Negotiations between the duelists, called principals, were carried on by representatives, called seconds. The seconds were supposed to try to adjust the quarrel and avert the duel. Failing in that, they regulated the fighting and enforced the rules. They were usually armed, and custom supported their wounding or even killing a duelist who violated their instructions.

Dueling was apparently not a separate offense under common law, although duelists could be punished for homicide, assault and battery, or breach of peace. It was, however, soon made a statutory crime by the various states. A duelist who kills an opponent may be punished as a murderer, and other participants as aiding and abetting the crime. Even where there is no bloodshed, some states punish duelists by prison sentences, and in some a man who has taken part in a duel cannot practice law or hold public office.

Nevertheless, duels were common, especially in the South before 1860. A contemporary listed the foremost dueling states as Kentucky, Tennessee, Georgia, and South Carolina, but duels were frequent in other Southern states, and in California during the decade 1850–60. Introduced from the mother country, dueling was practiced in the colonies almost from the beginning, but was uncommon until the mid eighteenth century. It waned in the North after the Revolution and died out in the South also after the War for Southern Independence.

During the golden age of dueling, public opinion would not allow antidueling laws to be enforced. Grand juries would not indict duelists or petit juries convict them so long as the fight was fair. Judges, lawyers, and public officials not only countenanced dueling, but participated in it themselves. A list of American duelists would include Aaron Burr, Alexander Hamilton, Andrew Jackson, Henry Clay, John Randolph, Albert Sidney Johnston, and many others scarcely less distinguished.

Strictly speaking, there was never a universally accepted dueling code; but it was soon recognized as highly desirable to have some set of rules for the instruction of duelists and their seconds. There were several such codes, perhaps the most influential being the South Carolina Code, drawn up by Governor John Lyde Wilson in 1838. These codes sought to regulate dueling and to mitigate as much as possible the cruelty of an institution which their authors considered a regrettable necessity. In practice, however, American duelists were more savage than European, less interested in vindicating their honor than in killing their enemies.

Duels were fought under various conditions and with many different weapons, including knives and shotguns. After the Revolution, swords were rarely used, as firearms were considered fairer. The classical duel of the golden age was fought with long, single-shot, muzzle-loading pistols at from ten to twenty paces (roughly yards); longer distances were customary only with rifles. Shots were exchanged until the principals were satisfied or the seconds stopped the duel.

Marksmanship was very poor: even at ten paces two or three shots were often exchanged without effect. Surviving specimens indicate that this was not the fault of the pistols. Some duelists no doubt missed because of haste or nervousness or fired wide from humanitarian scruples, but misses were common even with cool and ruthless men who fully intended to kill. Apparently few people then knew the basic principles of accurate pistol-shooting. They certainly had opportunity and incentive to practice.

Generalization is difficult because many duels, perhaps most, were kept secret or escaped with the barest notice. The evidence suggests that most duelists were professional men—politicians, lawyers, physicians, editors, and army and navy officers. Businessmen and planters were perhaps involved more often than the records show. The lower classes must generally have settled disputes less formally.

Men who refused a challenge faced the disgrace of being publicly "posted" as cowards, though popular opinion sometimes supported a man of known courage in his refusal. Men also sometimes avoided a duel with a joke when the pretext for the quarrel seemed trivial. There were always people who condemned dueling as barbarous, stupid, and unchristian. Others, however, argued that a man who defended his honor was fighting in self-defense and was thus justified. It was further urged that dueling actually saved lives by preventing sudden, murderous brawls, and allowing time for reflection and peacemaking before fighting. Even some modern writers have seen merit in this last argument, as applied to the tumultuous period before 1860. But dueling could hardly survive in more settled and law-abiding communities, and it disappeared almost entirely by the close of the nineteenth century.

BIBLIOGRAPHY: Don C. Seitz, *Famous American Duels,* 1929; W. O. Stevens, *Pistols at Ten Paces,* 1940; Harnett T. Kane, *Gentlemen, Pistols and Pistols,* 1951; Thomas Gamble, *Savannah Duels and Duellists,* 1923. See also "Duelling," *Corpus Juris Secundum,* XXVIII (1941).
[Sup. to WAGER OF BATTLE, DUEL.]

LAURENCE LEE HOWE.

DUGMORE, CLIFFORD WILLIAM: Church of England; b. at Moseley, Birmingham, May 9, 1909. He studied at Exeter College, Oxford (B.A., 1932; M.A., 1935; B.D., 1940) and Queens' College, Cambridge (M.A., 1936). He was assistant curate at Holy Trinity Church, Formby (1935–37); sub-warden of St. Deiniol's Library, Hawarden (1937–38); rector of Lugestre-with-Tixall (1938–43); chaplain of Alleyn's College, Dulwich (1943–45); rector of Bredfield-with-Boulge and director of religious education in the diocese of St. Edmundsburg and Ipswich (1945–47); lecturer in ecclesiastical history in the University of Manchester since 1947. His publications include *Eucharistic Doctrine in England from Hooker to Waterland* (1942); *The Influence of the Synagogue upon the Divine Office* (1944). In 1944 he edited *The Interpretation of the Bible,* and since 1950 he has been editor of *The Journal of Ecclesiastical History.*

DUHM, BERNHARD: D. 1928. He was professor of Old Testament theology at Basel and also instructor in Hebrew at the gymnasium there (1889–1928). His efforts were directed toward the internal criticism and understanding of the content and meaning of the prophetic literature. In addition to his excellent commentaries on Isaiah, Jeremiah, Job, and the Psalms he later wrote: *Israels Propheten* (1916).

[Sup.] RAYMOND W. ALBRIGHT.

DUKHOBORS (Wrestlers with the Spirit): Originated in the first half of the eighteenth century in the Ukrainian province of Kharkov. Basically, they stressed the mystical doctrine of the indwelling of God in the human soul. The Khlysty influence is discernible in the claim of the leaders to be the "Christ." This claim was first made by Hilarion Pobirokhin of Tambov, who surrounded himself with twelve "angels" and twelve "archangels." After his deportation to Siberia, he was succeeded by Sabellius Kapustin, a non-commissioned officer, who taught that Christ has remained in the world and has incarnated himself first in the Roman popes, later in various saints, and lastly in the Dukhobor leaders. But he changed the order of succession by establishing a "Christ" dynasty in his own family. The last of the line was the widow of Kapustin's greatgrandson, Glycera Kalmykov, who died in 1886. She tried to pass on the succession to her cousin, Peter Verigin, but this attempt caused a schism; only a minority adhered to his leadership.

The Dukhobor community was transported by the government to Crimea, where they settled at Molochnye Vody, and established a commune. They soon became very prosperous. The government once more ordered them to remove, and those who remained faithful took up lands in Transcaucasia, while those who "apostatized" to Orthodoxy were granted the entire communal property at Molochnye Vody.

Peter Verigin, the leader of the minority who acknowledged him as a successor to Glycera, became embued with the teaching of Count Leo N. Tolstoy, and incorporated much of it into the Dukhobor doctrine. Thus his group adopted pacifism, rejection of the state, of private property, denial of the deity of Christ and of immortality.

In 1898–99 Verigin decided to migrate to Canada, a project in which he was financially aided by Count Tolstoy and the American Society of Friends. Some 7,400 of them succeeded in reaching Canada and settled in the western provinces. But because of their anarchistic views—particularly their refusal to send their children to school—they soon came into conflict with the Canadian government. The "non-resisting" methods they adopted greatly embarrassed the officials. Only with difficulty was an adjustment made.

Verigin died in 1939, and since then the body which at the time comprised about 17,000 split up into several groups, the most extreme of which were near-communist. Many moderates among them joined the United Church of Canada, and the rest of this group may follow.

See also COMMUNISTIC SOCIETIES.

BIBLIOGRAPHY: Serge Bolshakoff, *Russian Nonconformity,* 1950; J. F. C. Wright, *Slava Bohu, The Story of the Dukhobors,* 1940.

[Sup.] MATTHEW SPINKA.

DUN, ANGUS: Episcopalian; b. New York, N. Y., May 4, 1892. He studied at Yale University (B.A., 1914); at The Episcopal Theological School, Cambridge, Mass. (B.D., 1917); and at the universities of Oxford and Cambridge; was minister of St. Andrew's Church, Ayer, Mass. (1917–18); was instructor and professor of theology at The Episcopal Theological School (1920–40) and dean (1940–44); has been Bishop of Washington, D. C., since 1944. He was chairman of the commission of the Federal Council of Churches (*q.v.*) that produced the report on "The Christian Conscience and Weapons of Mass Destruction" (1950). He is the chairman of the Commission on Ecumenical Relations of the Protestant Episcopal Church and a member of the Central Committee of the World Council of Churches (*q.v.*). He has written: *The King's Cross* (1926); *Christian Marriage* (1931); *We Believe* (1934); *Not by Bread Alone* (1942); and *Prospecting for a United Church* (1948).   WILLIAM J. WOLF.

DUNBAR, HELEN FLANDERS: B. Chicago, Ill., in 1902. She is a graduate of Bryn Mawr College and Columbia (M.A., Ph.D., and Med. Sc.D.); Union Theological Seminary, New York (B.D.), and Yale (M.D.). She received clinical training at the Worcester (Mass.) State Hospital and the hospitals of the Universities of Vienna and Zurich. She has been associated with the College of Physicians and Surgeons (Columbia University), Presbyterian Hospital and Vanderbilt Clinic, Bellevue Hospital (New York), and the Greenwich (Conn.) Hospital. She helped found the Council for Clinical Training of Theological Students and was its first director. As practicing psychiatrist and psychoanalyst she has pioneered particularly in psychosomatic medicine. She inaugurated and was editor-in-chief of *Psychosomatic Medicine* (1938-47). Publications: *Symbolism in Medieval Thought; Emotions and Bodily Changes;* and *Psychosomatic Diagnosis.*

ROLLIN J. FAIRBANKS.

DUNCAN LECTURESHIP: Established at Andover Newton Theological School by Mrs. Margaret Duncan Phillips and Mrs. Samuel W. Duncan and her son, in memory of the Hon. James H. Duncan, trustee from 1940 to 1869, and the Rev. Samuel W. Duncan, Class of 1864. This lectureship brings to the school from time to time prominent authorities in the field of comparative religion and in the Christian missionary enterprise. HERBERT GEZORK.

DUNKARD BRETHEN. See DUNKERS.

DUNKERS (DUNKARDS, TUNKERS): This word identifies various branches of Baptist Brethren. The original group, founded in Schwarzenau, Germany, in 1708, was known as the German Baptist Brethren.

The German Seventh Day Baptists chose to have their small group classified within the Seventh Day Baptist Church. Their celebrated Ephrata Cloister has become a Pennsylvania state historical monument.

The "Progressives" of the 1882 separation were called the Brethren Church. In 1941 they divided further into two almost equal groups: (1) The Grace Brethren have headquarters and a theological school at Winona Lake, Ind. They carry most of the former mission program of the church and publish *The Brethren Missionary Herald.* In 1946 they had 101 churches with 16,077 members in America and 7,458 in Africa and Argentina. (2) The Ashland Brethren have headquarters and the college at Ashland, Ohio. Their periodical is *The Brethren Evangelist.* In 1947 this branch had 109 churches and 17,687 members.

The Old German Baptist Church (Old Order Brethren) shows an increase in membership,

reaching 3,589 in 1950. They publish *The Vindicator* in Brookville, Ohio.

The central branch (Conservatives) changed their name in 1908 to Church of the Brethren. Their membership reached 186,201 in 1950. They still cherish the idea of being founded upon the New Testament and regard it as the adequate rule of faith and practice. There is a marked shift from free ministers to paid pastors. After several years as licentiates, qualified young men are ordained to the ministry. The third level of the ministry is the eldership. Deacons are elected. The work of lay members has grown.

The pattern of architecture and worship in the local churches has become less distinctive. The programs of education, evangelism, and co-operative participation have shown vigorous development. Mission work was opened in China in 1908, Africa in 1922, Eduador in 1946. The traditional non-participation in war resulted, during World War II, in Civilian Public Service camps for conscientious objectors (*q.v.*). These were maintained co-operatively with Mennonites and Quakers. Following the war vigorous work was done in relief in destitute areas. Its celebrated aspect is the "heifer project" which provides milk for children. Rehabilitation is fostered in Germany and elsewhere in Europe.

Besides six liberal arts colleges (at Bridgewater, Va., Elizabethtown, Pa., Huntingdon, Pa., LaVerne, Cal., McPherson, Kans., and North Manchester, Ind.), the church maintains in Chicago its graduate theological school, Bethany Biblical Seminary. The Brethren Publishing House at Elgin, Ill., publishes *The Gospel Messenger* and other church literature.

The church headquarters are also in Elgin. In 1941 the Brethren Service Committee was added to other boards of missions, ministry, and Christian education to further peace education, social action, youth service projects, relief (*q.v.*) and rehabilitation. In 1947 the various national boards merged into the General Brotherhood Board, which administers the various aspects of the church program. It is chosen by and works under the Annual Conference of the church.

In 1926 a small group withdrew from the Conservatives and called themselves the Dunkard Brethren. Their membership in 1950 is estimated to be 1,000. They publish the *Bible Monitor* at Covington, Ohio.

BIBLIOGRAPHY: Rufus D. Bowman, *The Church of the Brethren and War, 1708–1941,* 1944; Floyd E. Mallott, *The History of the Church of the Brethren,* 1952; D. L. Miller *et al., Two Centuries of the Church of the Brethren,* 1908; Otho Winger, *History and Doctrines of the Church of the Brethren,* 1919.

[Sup.] WILLIAM M. BEAHM.

DUNSTAN, SAINT: From 956 to 957 he lived in the Abbey of St. Peter at Ghent. From there he took back with him to England the complete Benedictine tradition, which had been forgotten in his native land. In the political field he aimed at the amalgamation of various races and the formation of national unity. For a long time he was the most popular saint in England, as the many legends indicate; but after the martyrdom of Thomas à Becket the latter replaced him in this respect.

BIBLIOGRAPHY: J. A. Robinson, *The Times of Saint Dunstan*, 1923.

[Sup.] MATHIAS GOOSSENS.

DURIE, JOHN: In the English colony at Elbing, near the great Hanseatic port of Danzig, he was in contact with the Swedes through James Spens (1627), who was an English agent engaged in obtaining mercenaries for Sweden in Scotland and elsewhere. Durie's great plan of having all orthodox Protestants unite in a common front owed much to David Pareus of Heidelberg, the author of the widely read *Irenicum*. Durie was correct in pointing out that the large Protestant denominations had very much in common, and they could well afford to emphasize less those differences which had caused so much polemics. Pareus had recommended a general synod of Lutheran and Reformed (Calvinist) churches, under the patronage of both Christian IV of Denmark and James I of England and Scotland. This scheme was revived by Durie, while Hugo Grotius (*q.v.*) favored this policy of friendly co-operation. Durie made a favorable impression on Axel Oxenstierna, the leading minister of the Swedish queen. Moreover, Sir Thomas Roe in England attracted the attention of Archbishop Abbot, of the powerful Laud (*q.v.*) and of Williams. Roe hoped that this policy would induce King Charles I of England to pursue a more active foreign policy. Durie paid a long visit to Sweden from 1636 to 1638, where he became intimately acquainted with a court chaplain named Johannes Matthiae Gothus. At the University of Uppsala he also carried on an active propaganda for his scheme, but unfortunately for him the Lutheran theologians were for the most part very reluctant to fraternize with Calvinists or Baptists.

BIBLIOGRAPHY: G. Westin, *John Durie in Sweden*, 1936; idem, *Negotiations About Church Unity 1628–1634*, 1932; G. H. Turnbull, *Hartlib, Dury and Comenius*, 1947; C. Williams, *James I* (1934), pp. 41–44; J. M. Batten, *John Dury Advocate of Christian Reunion*, 1944.

[Sup.] ALBERT HYMA.

DUTY. See ETHICS.

DYNAMISM: (1) A term applied to any philosophical theory which holds that the ultimate constituents of the material universe involve, or are of the nature of, force or activity rather than mass or extension. The classic representative of this view is Leibniz, who held that matter is not constituted by geometrical properties alone; "there must be joined to it some higher or metaphysical notion, to wit: that of *substance, action* and *force.*" Leibniz' dynamic conception of matter may be contrasted with the geometrical, or mechanistic, conception of Descartes.

(2) The theory, expounded by James, Bergson, and Whitehead, that the distinction of past, present, and future indicates an objective and fundamental characteristic of the world. This theory is incompatible with the idealistic view that the distinction expresses merely a subjective mode of experiencing the world. According to James, it is also incompatible with "the notion of eternity being given at a single stroke to omniscience." The theory is frequently expressed by saying that "change and becoming are real."

(3) A conception of logic, sometimes held in connection with (2), according to which the fundamental principles of Aristotelian logic—e.g., the laws of identity and excluded middle—are too "static" to be applicable to reality.

BIBLIOGRAPHY: J. E. Erdmann, ed., *Leibnitii Opera Philosophica*, Vol. I (1840), pp. 112–113, 121–125; William James, *A Pluralistic Universe* (1909), Appendix C; idem, *The Will To Believe* (1896), p. 181; Henri Bergson, *L'évolution créatrice* (1907), Chap. I; A. N. Whitehead, *Concept of Nature* (1920), Chap. III.

RODERICK M. CHISHOLM.

E

EADMER: On reliable authority it may be stated that he was the author of the following treatise which is important in the history of dogma: *Tractatus de conceptione B. Mariae Virginis.* The same is true of the treatise discovered by Dom Wilmart: *De sanctorum veneratione et obsecratione.*

BIBLIOGRAPHY: The *Tractatus* was edited and published by H. Thurston and Th. Slater, 1904; Wilmart published the other treatise in *Revue des sciences religieuses*, Vol. 15 (1935), pp. 184 ff., 354 ff.

[Sup.] MATHIAS GOOSSENS.

EARL LECTURESHIP FOUNDATION: Established in 1901 by Edwin T. Earl "to aid in securing at Berkeley, the seat of the University of California, as the center of secular learning for California, the adequate presentation of Christian truth, by bringing to Berkeley, Calif., year by year, eminent Christian scholars to lecture upon themes calculated to illustrate and disseminate Christian thought, and minister to Christian life, thus serving the purpose of a high evangelism."

STUART LEROY ANDERSON.

EASTER: The date of Easter is incipiently related to the question whether Jesus died on the fourteenth (Synoptists) or on the fifteenth of Nisan (John). The main solutions are: John was mistaken (Dalman). He was symbolizing so that Jesus would die with the paschal lambs (W. Bauer). The Synoptists were mistaken and John is correct (M. Dibelius, Lietzmann, Streeter, etc.). There is no contradiction. John represents the Sadducean custom and the Synoptists that of the Pharisees who celebrated Passover earlier when it would coincide with the Sabbath (Strack-Billerbeck).

April ninth is frequently accepted as the date of the resurrection. But since the Sanhedrin arbitrarily inserted an intercalary month into the lunar year, this date is uncertain.

The Eastern and Western Churches usually celebrate Easter separately since the former did not adopt the Gregorian calendar correction.

A stabilized Easter date has recently been considered by various churches.

BIBLIOGRAPHY: J. Bach, *Monatstag und Jahr des Todes Christi*, 1912; A. F. Chauve-Bertrand, . . . *La question de pâques et du calendrier* . . . , 1936; Norval Geldenhuys, *Commentary on* . . . *Luke*, 1951, pp. 649–670; K. A. H. Heinrich, *Heortologie* . . . , 3. Auflage, 1911; F. H. Meyer, *The Crux of Chronology* . . . (1942), pp. 546–599; J. Schmid, *Osterfestberechnung in der abendlaendlichen Kirche* . . . , 1907; H. L. Strack and P. Billerbeck, *Kommentar zum Neuen Testament* . . . , Vol. II (1924), pp. 812–853.

[Sup.] DANIEL JOHANNES THERON.

EASTER COMMUNION: According to Roman canon law, Christians who have come to the age of discretion are under obligation of taking communion at least once a year at Easter time, that is, from Palm Sunday to the first Sunday after Easter. Bishops are permitted to extend the time for Easter communion at their discretion. It is advisable, though not mandatory, that one should partake of Easter communion in the church of one's own parish.

[Sup.] GEORGES A. BARROIS.

EASTER EVEN: The English equivalent for Holy Saturday, celebration of the Vigil of Easter being advanced from the night of the Resurrection to Saturday morning (see EASTER, Section I, 4, 3, in Vol. IV; and HOLY WEEK, Section 6, in Vol. V).

EASTERN ORTHODOX CHURCHES: These churches, which at present comprise twenty-two autocephalous or autonomous bodies (some of them not fully recognized) with a membership estimated at 160,000,000, form a federation of churches, bound together not so much by a submission to some one supreme administrative center (such as the Patriarchate of Constantinople), but rather by the common adherence to the dogmatic and canonical decisions of the first seven ecumenical councils. Otherwise, each of the constituent autocephalous bodies is self-governing, the supreme authority usually taking

the form of the Holy Synod composed of bishops, one of whom is chosen as the administrative head of the communion. The bodies which have not reached the autocephalous stage are autonomous, but under the supreme jurisdiction of one of the autocephalous churches, usually that of the ecumenical patriarchate of Constantinople. These churches employ in their liturgical services either the native language of a given country, or in the case of some Slavic churches, the Church Slavonic. The liturgy in ordinary use is that of St. James, revised by St. John Chrysostom, or on special occasions the liturgy of St. Basil or some other.

Historically, the Church of the Eastern (Byzantine) Empire is the most important. It survived the downfall of Constantinople (1453). In fact, the Turkish sultans, beginning with Mohammed II, the Conqueror, not only confirmed the patriarch in his ecclesiastical jurisdiction and functions, but even expanded his powers by adding to them the political office of the "ethnarch," i.e., the head of all the Orthodox Christians in the empire. For since the Koran was the source of the civil as well as the religious legislation for the Moslems, and hence such legislation was not applicable to non-Moslems, the Christians necessarily had to be segregated into a separate group which would be governed by their own laws.

It was because of these special privileges it enjoyed that the Patriarchate of Constantinople ultimately extended its jurisdiction not only over the historic and by that time moribund, patriarchates of Alexandria, Antioch, and Jerusalem, but also over the Balkan patriarchates of Serbia and Bulgaria, and the metropolitanates of Greece and Moldavia-Wallachia. It was not until the nineteenth century that the disintegration of the Turkish Empire was accompanied with the similar loss of jurisdiction of the Patriarchate of Constantinople over the liberated territories.

Accordingly, the modern phase of the history of such Orthodox churches as had formerly been subjected to the ecumenical patriarchate begins in the nineteenth century. The Eastern Orthodox Churches as a whole may be divided into the Greek, Slavic, and miscellaneous other groups. Besides, a separate section is given to such of these churches as are found in the United States and Canada.

I. The Greek Churches: First of all may be named the Church of Greece. Its organization goes back to the year 1833, when after the successful Wars of Liberation (1821–30), whereby the Greek people at last threw off the Turkish yoke, the Orthodox Church of Greece set up its autonomous organization, declaring itself free from the Patriarchate of Constantinople. This separation was necessary, since the patriarch, as ethnarch of the Greek population within the

Turkish Empire, was required by his office to oppose the liberation of Greece as a rebellion. In fact, Patriarch Gregory V was strangled by the order of the Sultan because of suspicion that he sympathized with the Greek revolt. Hence, it was not until 1850 that the patriarchate recognized the Church of Greece as autocephalous, independent of its authority.

When during World War II the Germans occupied Greece, Archbishop Chrysanthos was deprived of his office because of his non-compliance with their policies. But his successor, Damaskinos, proved himself equally patriotic. After the expulsion of the Nazis, he became regent of the country until King George II assended the throne (1946). The Church of Greece, which at present numbers some 8,000,000 members, sustained heavy losses during the war. Some 800 churches were destroyed and about 600 priests were killed; during the subsequent struggle with the communist guerrillas, 270 additional priests were put to death. Nevertheless, the church has since made a remarkable recovery, although some 400 churches lack priests (1953). The Zoe Movement and other similar lay organizations have produced a remarkable awakening within the church and among the people. It publishes a magazine, *Zoe*, which has some 150,000 subscribers, and conducts 1,500 Sunday Schools.

The Patriarchate of Constantinople, which is still accorded "pre-eminence of honor" (although not of jurisdiction), has fallen upon evil days. Its size has steadily diminished during the nineteenth century; and when Mustafa Kemal Pasha seized power from the feeble hands of the last of the sultans, the patriarchate but narrowly escaped total extinction. For King Constantine of Greece had chosen to invade Asia Minor, to regain that portion of the ancient Byzantine Empire, and Patriarch Meletios chose to support him. Constantine was disastrously defeated, and Meletios was expelled from Turkey. Thereupon, Kemel would have abolished the patriarchate altogether, had it not been for the intervention of some European powers. He relented sufficiently to allow the patriarchate's continued existence, but deprived it of many of its former powers. The patriarch ceased to exercise his authority as ethnarch over the Greeks in Turkey; all Greeks (and Armenians) were expelled from Turkey with the exception of Constantinople and its immediate environs: about 1,500,000 Greeks were settled in Greece proper. Thus the patriarchate is reduced in numbers to some 100,000 members. But as has already been mentioned, the patriarch exercises jurisdiction over any Orthodox group anywhere in the world which does not possess autocephaly and is not subject to some other jurisdiction. During the very unsettled period after World War I, when a considerable number of new Orthodox churches arose, Constantinople sponsored the Churches of Finland, Poland, Lithuania, Latvia and Esthonia. At present, the hegemony of Constantinople is challenged by the Patriarchate of Moscow; should the struggle result in the latter's favor, we would witness one of the most far-reaching and historic changes in Eastern Orthodoxy.

The remaining two Greek patriarchates, Alexandria and Jerusalem, are but a shadow of their ancient glory. In Alexandria Greeks possess about a two-thirds majority; thus their leadership is relatively safe. But the patriarchate of Jerusalem is dominated by about 100 Greek monks who are barely holding their privileged position against some 40,000 native Arabs. The establishment of Israel in Palestine further complicates the situation.

As for Cyprus and Mt. Sinai, all that needs to be said is that these ancient churches (the latter of which consists of the Monastery of St. Catherine) have so far succeeded in preserving their autocephalous status.

II. The Slavic Churches: This is numerically the largest group of Orthodox Churches, and hence plays the most important role. The Russian Church is treated in a separate article (see RUSSIAN ORTHODOX CHURCH). The Serbian Orthodox is the next largest among them, comprising more than a half of the population (7,500,000 in 1931) of the present Yugoslavia. Although the Serbian Church had been granted the patriarchal rank in 1346, it lost it in 1766 when the church was subjected to the patriarchate of Constantinople. But in 1832, as the result of the Wars of Independence (begun in 1804), the church, still ranking as a metropolitanate, secured conditional autonomy, which in 1879 was at last converted into autocephaly (although the Serbian Church with headquarters in Sremsky Karlovtsy, Hungary, ranked as patriarchate). When after World War I the Kingdom of the Serbs, Croatians, and Slovenes was created, the Serbian Church was greatly enlarged by the consolidation of six formerly separate jurisdictions. Thereupon, the patriarchal rank was restored.

The most important patriarch of recent times was Gavrilo, elected to the office in 1937. He was among the leaders of those patriotic Serbs who repudiated the deal which had been entered into by the regent, Prince Paul, and Hitler, whereby Yugoslavia was to surrender to the Germans without opposition. In order to denounce the treaty, these Serbs placed young King Peter II on the throne. When Germans thereupon invaded the country (1941), they promptly imprisoned the stalwart patriarch, Gavrilo, along with Bishop Nikolai (Velimirovich). Upon the evacuation of Yugoslavia, the Germans placed the two hierarchs in the Dachau concentration camp. They were released at the intervention of an anti-communist Serbian patriot, Dimitrije Lyovich, who co-operated with the Germans against the communist partisans. But Gavrilo did not immediately return to Yugoslavia, because of his opposition to the Tito regime. Later he was induced to return in order to make possible the election and consecration of new bishops, in place of those who had lost their lives or were imprisoned. But even then he stood, as far as possible, against the anti-ecclesiastical policies of the regime, and hence was several times placed under house arrest. He died in 1950 while under arrest. He was succeeded by Vikentije who, although he does not possess Gavrilo's qualities, has shown himself not devoid of courage. But the relations between the state and the church have improved since Tito's break with Stalin, for Tito has to lean on the Western powers for aid. Nevertheless, he has not given up his ultimate aim of eliminating the church from public life. This is indicated by the recent exclusion of the three theological faculties from their respective universities.

The Bulgarian Church likewise has a long and distinguished past, having been the first of the Balkan Slavic churches to have secured autocephaly. It was granted the patriarchal rank in 917, but lost it in 1767 when the Church fell under the jurisdiction of Constantinople. In 1872 the Turkish authorities granted it autonomy against the vigorous protest of the ecumenical patriarch, who even proclaimed the Bulgarian Church schismatic. This strained situation lasted until 1945. Then Metropolitan Stephan assumed the rank of exarch, and endeavored to keep peace with the new communist masters of the country. But despite all he could do, he proved unacceptable to them, and in 1948 was forced out of office by the Holy Synod which acted under pressure from the government. He was imprisoned in a monastery. He was succeeded by Kyrill, who was raised, in 1952, to the rank of patriarch. This action was favored by Patriarch Alexei of Moscow. The Law of 1950 completely subjugated the church to the state, and even granted the state a voice in the election of the patriarch.

As for the small Czechoslovak Orthodox Church, reconstituted from the insignificant remnants of that Communion which had been practically destroyed by Hitler (who held that body responsible for sheltering the assassins of Reinhard Heydrich), it plays a role wholly incommensurate with its size. It has a Russian hierarch, Elevfery, at its head. It was granted autocephaly, and the rank of an exarchate. In this way, for political reasons, this insignificant body is equated with, in fact exceeds in rank, the Roman Catholic Church. But these pretentious claims have not so far been recognized by the

other Orthodox churches outside the Moscow orbit.

The Polish Orthodox Church is in a similar dependent relation in regard to the Moscow patriarchate, although it is officially regarded as autocephalous. It was organized in 1924 by Metropolitan Dionysius, although the membership was mostly Ruthenian. When Galicia was incorporated into the Soviet Union, only a small minority of the Orthodox population remained in Poland. The present Archbishop, Timothy, is in virtual dependence upon the Patriarch of Moscow.

III. Other Orthodox Churches: Among the remaining Orthodox churches, the Rumanian is the largest. It was raised to the patriarchal rank in 1925. After World War II, as the result of the territorial loss suffered by Rumania, the membership was reduced from about 13,000,000 to 9,000,000. But when in 1948 the communist regime unilaterally abrogated the concordat with the Vatican and integrated the Uniate population (see UNIATE CHURCHES) with the Orthodox Church, the latter gained 1,500,000 new members. In that same year, under the pressure of the government, Justinian, who as a priest had been a member of the Communist Party, was elected patriarch.

IV. Eastern Orthodox Churches in the United States and Canada: The beginnings of Eastern Orthodoxy in the present territory of the United States go back to 1741, when Captains Vitus Behring and A. Chirikov landed on one of the Aleutian Islands. A mission comprising eight monks was sent to Alaska in 1794. But the most extensive and successful missionary work was conducted by Father John Venyaminov (1823 on), who was consecrated bishop in 1840, and became archbishop ten years later.

When Alaska was purchased from Russia in 1867, the episcopal see was moved to San Francisco (1872), and later its jurisdiction was enlarged by the inclusion of Canada and the Atlantic seaboard. Archbishop Tikhon (who was later—1917—elected patriarch of the Russian Church) transferred the see to New York.

All this was changed by the events of 1917: the all-Russian Sobor restored the patriarchate; and the October Revolution made basic changes in the relations between church and state. The American metropolitanate found itself leaderless, for Archbishop Evdokim left to attend the Sobor; but having joined the "Living Church," was not expected to return. Thereupon, under the leadership of the Senior vicar, Bishop Alexander, the American clergy at a Sobor declared their church "temporarily autonomous" (1919). But this condition was changed in 1921, when Metropolitan Platon (who had headed the American metropolitanate, 1906–14), returned to the United States and two years later was appointed its administrator by Patriarch Tikhon (then already in prison). Under these conditions, the All-American Sobor held in Detroit (1924) once more declared the church "temporarily autonomous," but confirmed Platon in the position assigned him by Patriarch Tikhon. This action forms the canonical basis of the autonomy of the American metropolitanate.

But the canonicity of this action is denied by the Synod of Bishops Outside Russia, which claims sole jurisdiction over all Russian congregations beyond the borders of the Soviet Union. This body was originally composed of the Russian emigré hierarchs, headed by Metropolitan Antony. It was organized in Constantinople, with the ecumenical patriarch's consent, as the Supreme Church Administration. At that time, Metropolitan Platon was a member of the body, and in 1921 was sent by it to North America. For this reason the Supreme Administration has claimed jurisdiction over the American Church ever since. But in 1926 Platon broke with this body (renamed by this time Synod of Bishops Outside of Russia, and its headquarters removed to Sremsky Karlovtsy in Yugoslavia), and asserted the temporary autonomy of his metropolitanate in accordance with the action taken in Detroit, in 1924. But the Synod sent over some bishops who organized separate parishes of those who now broke away from Platon: thus there were established two parallel jurisdictions in this country.

Metropolitan Theophilus, who succeeded Platon after the latter's death (1934), attempted to reach an agreement with the Karlovtsy Synod, then headed by Metropolitan Anastasy, and signed an accord with the latter (1935). Hence, the double jurisdiction was abolished and all dioceses in the United States and Canada were placed under Theophilus' administration. The Synod of Bishops interprets this action as the canonical submission, on the part of the American metropolitanate, to its jurisdiction; consequently, its repudiation in 1946 is an uncanonical act of revolt. The American metropolitanate, on its part, regards the accord of 1935 as having "more moral than administrative significance, for it shows our accord and our unity, but does not bind us" (A. Schmeman, "The Canonical Position of the Russian Orthodox Church in North America," in *1953 Year Book and Church Directory,* 1953).

A crisis in the relations between these two bodies was reached in 1946, when Patriarch Alexei of Moscow made a determined effort to regain direct jurisdiction over the Russian Churches throughout the world. At the All-American Sobor held in Cleveland, it was voted to sever relations with the Synod of Bishops (which in the meantime had transferred its headquarters to Munich, Germany), and to reaffirm its autonomy. Thereupon, Metropolitan Theophilus entered upon negotiations with the

Moscow Patriarch. But the conditions laid down by the latter proved utterly unacceptable. Hence, the American metropolitanate suspended all further negotiations. Thus at present there exist three Russian Orthodox jurisdictions in North America: the Russian Orthodox Greek Catholic Church of North America, under the leadership of Metropolitan Leonty (who succeeded Theophilus in 1950). This is the largest group, comprising (in 1952) 309 clergy and monks. This church has recently opened a seminary for the training of the clergy, The St. Vladimir Orthodox Theological Seminary under the deanship of the most outstanding theologian of Orthodoxy, Dr. Georges Florovsky. The second is the Synod of Bishops, headed by Metropolitan Vitaly, which has its headquarters at Mahopac, N.Y. Besides the churches in North America (it reported sixty-eight priests and monks in 1952), it has jurisdiction over most of the Russian churches throughout the world. It also conducts an American mission which is headed by Archbishop James. It has likewise opened a small seminary in Jordanville, N.Y. The third Russian jurisdiction is that of Patriarch Alexei of Moscow, exercised through Exarch Makary. The number of clergy of this jurisdiction is given as fifty-nine.

As for the other Orthodox bodies in North America, the largest among them is the Greek, headed at present by Archbishop Michael. He has under his jurisdiction about 300 priests. The liturgical language is exclusively Greek, the English not yet being allowed in services. The church conducts a theological seminary in Brookline, Mass. The Serbian Orthodox Church is still in communion with its mother church. It is administered by Bishop Dionisije, whose headquarters are in Libertyville, Ill. The second bishop of the Serbian Church is Nikolai, who had gained prominence in Serbia and had been imprisoned by the Nazis along with Patriarch Gavrilo. The Syrian Antiochenian Church is administered by Archbishop Antony. The Bulgarian Orthodox Church, still an eparchy of the Patriarchate of Bulgaria, is headed by Bishop Andrey. Besides these, the Orthodox Communions of this country comprise the Albanian, Carpatho-Russian, Estonian, Rumanian, and Ukrainian churches.

See also SLAVIC MISSIONS IN THE UNITED STATES; METAXAKIS, MELETIOS; STRENOPOULOS, GERMANOS; TAVEEV, MICHAEL; TIKHON (BELLAVIN); VARNAVA (ROSSITCH); LITURGICAL WORSHIP, RECENT TRENDS IN.

BIBLIOGRAPHY: Matthew Spinka, "Christianity and the Churches" in *The Interseminary Series,* Vol. IV, 1946; Bishop Theophilus, *A Short History of the Christian Church and the Ritual of the Eastern Orthodox Churches,* 1934; J. Hutchinson Cockburn, *Religious Freedom in Eastern Europe,* 1953; *Church Life* (in Russian), ed. by Prot. George Grabbe, The Synod of Bishops Outside Russia; Alexander Schmeman, "The Canonical Position of the Russian Orthodox Church of North America" in

1953 Year Book and Church Directory, Russian Orthodox Greek Catholic Church of North America.
[Sup. to EASTERN CHURCH.]
MATTHEW SPINKA.

EASTMAN, FRED: Congregationalist; b. Lima, Ohio, July 11, 1886. He studied at College of Wooster (A.B., 1908); Columbia University (1909–11); and Union Theological Seminary. He was pastor, Reformed Church, Locust Valley, N. Y., (1912–17); business manager *Red Cross Magazine* (1917–19); director educational work, Board of Home Missions Presbyterian Church in U.S.A., (1919–23); managing editor *Christian Work* (1924–26); contributing editor *Christian Century* (1926–36); professor biography and drama, Chicago Theological Seminary since 1926, and Federated Theological Faculty, University of Chicago, since 1943. In addition to many plays he has written: (with Louis Wilson), *Drama in The Church* (1933; revised, 1942); (with Edward Oullette), *Better Motion Pictures* (1936); *Books That Have Shaped the World* (1937); *Men of Power* (5 vols., 1938–40); (with Bailey, Conant, and Smith), *The Arts and Religion* (1944); *Christ in the Drama* (1947); and *Writing the One-Act Religious Drama* (1948).

EASTON, BURTON SCOTT: Anglican; b. at Hartford, Conn., Dec. 4, 1877; d. at New York City, Mar. 7, 1950. He was educated at the University of Pennsylvania (B.S., 1898; Ph.D., 1901), University of Goettingen, and Philadelphia Divinity School (1906). Ordained in 1905, he taught New Testament first at Nashotah House, then at Western Theological Seminary, Chicago (1911–19), and from 1919 to 1948 at General Theological Seminary, New York, where he was also Sub-Dean and Librarian. He was most eminent as an exegete; his commentaries on *Luke* (1926) and the *Pastoral Epistles* (1947) and his translation and interpretation of *The Apostolic Tradition* of Hippolytus (1934) are works of the first rank in scholarship.

BIBLIOGRAPHY: Frederick C. Grant (ed.), *Memorial Volume of New Testament Essays,* 1954.
FREDERICK C. GRANT.

EBERHARDT, PAUL: Evangelical National Church of Germany; b. at Strausberg, Mark Brandenburg, 1876; d. at Berlin, 1923. He was philosopher of religion. As a mystically thinking free author (Romance: *Wohin der Weg? Das Jahr einer Seele,* 1920) he penetrated the depths of non-Christian, especially Eastern, religions. Their most sublime products he tried to make available for home-devotion through *Das Buch der Stunde* (1916 and 1920). With his series of publications, *Der Aufbau, Blaetter fuer Suchende* (1914), he influenced his contemporaries ethically and religiously. In the same way

he worked after 1919 through pamphlets and the journal, *Der deutsche Pfeiler* (1921 ff).
REINHOLD KUECKLICH.

EBERLIN, JOHANN: B. *ca.* 1470 at Guensburg; d. Oct., 1533, at Leutershausen. He studied at Ingolstadt and Basel. In his vehemently polemical and anti-Catholic pamphlets of 1521 he expressed a deep hatred of the pope and the Church of Rome, as well as of monasticism and the priesthood. But a few years later he became much more moderate and more interested in purely literary works. Near the end of his life he was occupied primarily with a translation of *Germania* by Tacitus.

BIBLIOGRAPHY: *Lexikon fuer Theologie und Kirche,* Vol. III (1931), pp. 514–515; E. Kurten, *Franz Lambert von Avignon und Nikolaus Herborn* (1950), pp. 39 ff.
[Sup.] MATHIAS GOOSSENS.

ECCLESIASTES, BOOK OF (HEBREW, KOHELETH): During the latter half of the nineteenth century solutions to the manifold problems involved in the understanding of *Ecclesiastes* had generally been sought by assuming multiple authorship (Siegfried), or the disarrangement of leaves in the manuscript (Bickell, Van der Palm). The most popular theory maintained that the book, originally heterodox and unconventional, had been subjected to wide and persistent interpolation (Jastrow, Barton). These additions were regarded as emanating from two schools, one that of a *Hasid* or pious believer, the other a *Hakam,* or conventional expounder of practical Wisdom, both of whom were determined to contravene the unpalatable ideas of the author.

Twentieth-century research has set the biblical Wisdom books within the framework of Oriental Wisdom. It has disclosed the existence of a basic school of practical Wisdom teachers, concerned with the mundane problems of success and well-being (the authors of *Proverbs* and *Ben Sira*), and of a group of dissidents who grappled with the more fundamental issues of the purpose of life, the problems of evil, the basis of morality, the nature of truth. The literary products of this group are *Job* and *Ecclesiastes* (see WISDOM LITERATURE). The relationship between the main school and the dissidents is far from being merely that of antagonism. The writers of *Job* and *Ecclesiastes* were undoubtedly trained in the Wisdom academies, and perhaps taught there themselves. That conditioning affected their style and thought-processes ever after.

I. Integrity and Style: The key to the understanding of *Ecclesiastes* lies in recognizing several fundamental stylistic traits: (1) The author's use of a *conventional religious vocabulary* to express his unconventional ideas. Such terms as "sin" (7:26) "reverence" (7:18) and "pleasing to God" (2:26; 7:26) are to be understood in terms of his own outlook. (2) His use of *proverbial quotations.* These apothegms are cited for various reasons, either because he agrees with them, particularly on practical matters, or because he wishes to modify or oppose them. His divergence is expressed either by an oblique comment (e.g., 2:13 f.; 7:1 ff., 8:10 ff.) or by juxtaposing a proverb of opposite intent (cf. 4:5, 6). (3) The existence of *collections of practical Wisdom proverbs,* with no unity among them (e.g. ch. 10) as in *Proverbs,* or bound together by a formal link, like the sevenfold use of *tōbh,* "good" (ch. 7). These conventional utterances are commented upon by the author from his own viewpoint.

When the stylistic traits of *Ecclesiastes* are recognized, it becomes clear that the entire book, aside from the Epilogue (12:9–14), which speaks of Koheleth in third person and contains valuable information about the author's life and work from a contemporary, is authentically the work of a single author. It was written, probably in old age, by a Wisdom teacher in a *cahier* or notebook, containing some eighteen sections or essays. Prose predominates, but the opening and the closing sections (1:2–11; 12:1–8) as well as other impassioned passages (e.g., 9:7 ff.) are rhythmic in character. This poetic framework, which is enclosed in the basic theme of "vanity of vanities, all is vanity" (1:2; 12:8), implies that the work was consciously prepared for a reading public.

II. Literary Relationships: The book reflects a familiarity with the Pentateuch and the Historical Books (for Gen. 3:19 see Ecc. 12:7; for Deut. 4:2; 13:1 see Ecc. 3:14; for Deut. 23:22 f. see Ecc. 5:3 f.; for I Sam. 15:22 see Ecc. 4:17b; for I Kings 8:46, see Ecc. 7:20). However, the author utilizes these earlier passages in a thoroughly original manner, in accordance with his own ideas. The same independent approach marks his use of such familiar Greek ideas as the theory of the "four elements" (1:1 ff.) or the "golden mean" (7:14 ff.). These ideas had permeated the atmosphere of Western Asia, particularly after Alexander the Great. Efforts to prove Ecclesiastes an Aristotelian, a Stoic, an Epicurean, a Cynic or a Cyrenaic have not been successful. The alleged Grecisms in style have also been shown to be authentically Hebrew or Semitic.

III. Language: The book is written in a late Hebrew, which falls midway between the classical biblical idiom and the Mishnic stages of the language (note, e.g., the use of *ḥēfeṣ* in 3:1, 17; 5:7; 8:6). It, therefore, contains Aramaisms and other late Hebrew constructions, as well as the word *pardes* (2:5), which is borrowed from the Persian. There are accordingly no convincing grounds for the theory that our book is a translation from the Aramaic. The book has reached us in its original form.

IV. Date: The degree to which Ecclesiastes is thought to have been influenced by Greek ideas brings, in the mind of many, the *terminus a quo* down until at least several decades after the death of Alexander the Greek in 323 B.C. The *terminus ad quem* is fixed by the absence of any echo of the Antiochian persecutions or the Maccabean revolt (168 B.C.) and by the use that *Ben Sira* made of *Ecclesiastes* in his book (190 B.C.). The book is accordingly to be dated 275–250 B.C. The countless efforts to identify the incident of "the lad of poor birth" (4:13 f.) and that of "the poor wise man" (9:14 f.) have not been successful. These two passages are not references to actual historical events at all. They exhibit a characteristic Oriental literary device, when an incident, typical rather than actual, is introduced, in order to drive a point home.

V. World View: *Ecclesiastes* can scarcely be described as "the most moving Messianic prophecy in the Old Testament" (Hertzberg) or as "the greatest triumph of Old Testament piety!" (Cornill). Basically, it is the work of a sensitive and clear-eyed observer of life, who is deeply troubled by man's inability to penetrate to the ultimate truth about man's place and purpose in the world and the destiny of the universe. Hence he sets up the attainment of happiness as the goal of human striving, not merely because he loves life, but because he cannot have justice and wisdom. Joy is the only purpose that he can find in a monotonous and meaningless world, in which all human values, such as wealth, piety, and ability, are vanity, where all men encounter the same fate and no progress is possible.

Koheleth's theology postulates the existence of God, coupled with his creative power and limitless sovereignty. God has revealed his will to his creatures by implanting in man an ineradicable desire for happiness. Koheleth's morality accordingly recognizes the pursuit of true and ultimate happiness as man's goal. His religion is the combination of his theology and his ethics. For *Ecclesiastes,* nothing really counts if truth and righteousness cannot be attained. Yet man lives and God rules, and God's manifest will is man's happiness.

The significance of the book, unlike that of the Prophets, lies not in its social implications, but in the guidance it offers the individual in enjoying life's blessings and in meeting those ills that must be transcended because they cannot be transformed.

Different readers will draw varying implications from Koheleth's frustrations and his doubts, but for all, it is a religious book in the deepest sense, because it seeks to grapple with reality in honesty and courage.

BIBLIOGRAPHY: In addition to the general works cited in the Bibliography of WISDOM LITERATURE, see the commentaries of G. A. Barton, 1909; V. Zapletal, 1911; E. Podechard, 1912; Ludwig Levy, 1912; M. Jastrow, *A Gentle Cynic*, 1919; K. Budde, 1923; H. Odeberg, 1929; H. W. Hertzberg, 1932; K. Galling, 1940; J. J. Weber, 1947; I. Bettan, 1950; R. Gordis, *Koheleth—the Man and His World*, 1951. The unity of the book is maintained, from somewhat varying points of view by the five last-named commentators, as well as by D. B. Macdonald, *The Hebrew Philosophical Genius*, 1936.

[Sup.] ROBERT GORDIS.

ECK, JOHANN: Not without reason has he been called the most dangerous opponent of Martin Luther (*q.v.*), as well as his most capable adversary in debate. He was easily the most readily equipped person for the battles fought with pen and spoken word, being very learned and sure of himself in tight spots. Like many of his contemporaries who had attracted wide attention, he was made the object of scurrilous attacks. Luther called him Dr. Geck (Dr. Crazy) and the Bavarian pig. He was accused of all manner of evil: avarice, vanity, loose living, drunkenness, bribery, etc. When viewed in the light of his time and environment he wielded a rather moderate and cautious pen. Among all the accusations made against him by contemporaries only that of being too willing to enter upon polemics can be proved correct, although naturally he, like all other human beings, was subject to various minor intellectual and physical ailments. It is to be regretted that in later times the charges made against him were repeated.

His *Encheiridion* was one of the first polemical textbooks and in this capacity it enjoyed a phenomenal success. In his method of presenting evidence for his claims he used the traditional scholastic approach. His knowledge of the church fathers was inadequate; he did not use them in the proper critical manner. Characteristic is his treatment of Dionysius the Areopagite. The works ascribed to this writer he defended against the great humanists, especially against the criticisms of Valla (*q.v.*) and Erasmus (*q.v.*). Wherever he cited these works he acted as if they had equal weight with the leading sources of the first century. He wrote excellent Latin, but his German was not in line with the popular diction until about 1540. His translation of the Old and New Testaments (1537), intended as a rival of Luther's famous accomplishment, was variously appraised and evaluated. It is certainly not to be considered as an outstanding piece of work.

BIBLIOGRAPHY: New editions of Eck's works have appeared in *Corpus Catholicorum: Werke katholischer Schriftsteller im Zeitalter der Glaubensspaltung*, initiated by J. Greving, Vols. I, II, VI, XIII, XIV, XVI, 1919 ff. (in the latest volume of 1930, J. Metzeler presents an extensive bibliography); W. Gussmann, ed. of Eck's 404 Articles, 1930; *Lexikon fuer Theologie und Kirche* III (1931), 523–526; P. Polman, *L'Elément historique dans la controverse religieuse du XVIe siècle*, 1932; K. Schottenloher, *Bibl. zur deutschen Geschichte im Zeitalter der Glaubensspaltung*, Vol. I, 1933; E. Iserloh, *Die Eucharistie in der Darstellung des Joh. Eck*, 1950.

[Sup.] MATHIAS GOOSSENS.

ECUADOR: Because of an unsettled boundary dispute with Peru, estimates of the area of the country vary widely. A United Nations Statistical Office estimate gives it as 106,178 square miles. A military estimate shows 175,-851 square miles. The population was estimated in 1949 as 3,404,000. Of these it is estimated that 8% are whites, 27% Indians, 54% mestizos, 6% mulattoes, 2% Negroes, and 3% others.

Primary education is free and compulsory. In 1947 there were 284,182 pupils in primary schools and 15,526 in secondary schools. There are six universities.

The state does not recognize any particular religion; freedom of worship is granted to all religions. Relations between the Ecuadorean government and the Holy See are regulated by a modus vivendi which was agreed upon in 1937. Divorce is permitted. The Roman Catholic Church has one archbishop and six suffragan bishops.

Eight Protestant missionary societies have work in Ecuador. Two outstanding projects are "The Voice of the Andes" Radio Station, broadcast in eighteen languages, and the United Andean Indian Mission, an agriculturally-based project in which four Protestant mission boards co-operate.

BIBLIOGRAPHY: W. Stanley Rycroft, ed., *Indians of the High Andes*, 1946; John Collier and Anibal Buitron, *The Awakening Valley*, 1949; Kenneth G. Grubb, *Northern Republics of South America*, 1931.

[Sup.] W. STANLEY RYCROFT.

ECUMENICAL INSTITUTE: Located at the Château de Bossey, Céligny, near Geneva (Switzerland), the institute was founded by the World Council of Churches (*q.v.*) in 1946. The initial gift was given by John D. Rockefeller, Jr. Through its courses and conferences the Institute seeks to accomplish two things: to enable members of churches to acquire ecumenical knowledge and become interpreters of the ecumenical idea, and to help laymen to live and think as Christians in the secular environment of their daily occupations. The institute has become a center for inspiration and the coordination of lay movements in many countries. In 1951 the Central Committee of the World Council decided to set up, under the auspices of the Ecumenical Institute and in co-operation with the faculty of theology of the University of Geneva, a Graduate Institute for Ecumenical Studies, which will provide longer courses on ecumenical subjects for advanced students. The director of the institute is Hendrik Kraemer, former professor of the University of Leiden, Holland.

W. A. VISSER 'T HOOFT

ECUMENICAL INSTITUTE, SCANDINAVIAN. See SIGTUNA.

ECUMENICAL MOVEMENT: The word ecumenical is derived from the Greek *oikoumene,* which had two meanings, "the inhabited world" and "the whole world." Insofar as the first was stressed, the emphasis was on unity. Thus *oikoumene* could mean the integrated culture of the Roman empire (as in Luke 2:1). Insofar as the second meaning was stressed, the emphasis was on universality. The *oikoumene* was then conceived of as embracing the human race (as in Matt. 24:14). In Christian usage these two meanings persisted, for the "ecumenical" councils were at once councils which safeguarded the religious unity of the empire and councils which claimed to have universal validity.

It is probably due to this double connotation that the word has been resuscitated in the twentieth century to designate the movement in and of the churches which seeks to manifest both the unity and the universality (in the dynamic, missionary sense) which are inherent in the Christian Church. Among those who introduced the term in its modern meaning the most influential, though not the first, was Nathan Soederblom (*q.v.*), of Sweden. In 1919 he proposed the creation of a permanent "ecumenical council" of the churches, and the word appears in the Greek and Latin titles of the Universal Conference on Life and Work, held in Stockholm (1925), of which he was the main pioneer. According to the report of the Oxford Conference, Life and Work (1937), "It is important to bear in mind the fundamental distinction between 'ecumenical' and 'international.' The term 'international' necessarily accepts the division of mankind into separate nations as a natural if not a final state of affairs. The term 'ecumenical' refers to the expression within history of the given unity of the church. The one starts from the fact of division and the other from the fact of unity in Christ."

The ecumenical movement therefore embraces all such bodies as, on an international, national, or local plane, seek to give expression to the solidarity and the fundamental unity of Christians of different confessions and denominations. In modern times the way was prepared by co-operative undertakings in the field of foreign missions, home missions, and social service, by international youth movements—Y.M.C.A. (*q.v.*), Y.W.C.A. (*q.v.*), Student Christian Federation (*q.v.*)—by the Evangelical Alliance (*q.v.*) and national federations of churches. A new chapter began in 1910 when the World Missionary Conference met in Edinburgh under the chairmanship of John R. Mott (*q.v.*). The continuation committee of this meeting later became the International Missionary Council (*q.v.*), which held its most significant world meetings in Jerusalem (1928) and Madras (1938). And the Edinburgh Confer-

ence inspired Bishop Brent (*q.v.*) to lay the foundations of the Faith and Order movement, which at its world meetings in Lausanne (1927) and Edinburgh (1937) gathered the churches to discuss problems of faith and order about which the churches are divided. Meanwhile, the World Alliance for International Friendship through the Churches (*q.v.*) was formed (1914) in order to mobilize the churches for common action in the realm of international relations. Late in 1919 and early in 1920 Nathan Soederblom and the Ecumenical Patriarchate issued almost simultaneous appeals to the churches to enter into co-operation in the field of "life and work," that is, of social and moral action. These appeals led to the Stockholm Conference on Life and Work (1925), which was followed by the Oxford Conference (1937) on Church, Community, and State. World Christian Youth Conferences were held in Amsterdam (1939) and Oslo (1947). Mention should also be made of the World Council for Christian Education and the United Bible Societies (*q.v.*).

During recent years these movements have learned to co-operate. Thus the movement for Life and Work and the movement for Faith and Order have joined in forming the World Council of Churches (*q.v.*), and the World Council and the International Missionary Council are "in association with" each other. William Temple (*q.v.*) has called the ecumenical movement "the great new fact of our time." Although the movement is still young, it has created a new spirit in the relationships of the member churches with one another and enabled them to render a common witness to the world.

BIBLIOGRAPHY: In addition to official reports of conferences mentioned above, see: William Adams Brown, *Toward a United Church,* 1946, with ecumenical bibliography; G. K. A. Bell (ed.), *Documents on Christian Unity,* 1st, 2nd, and 3rd series; Henry P. Van Dusen, *World Christianity,* 1948; Oliver S. Tomkins, *The Wholeness of the Church,* 1949; Leonard Hodgson, *The Ecumenical Movement,* 1951; Robert S. Bilheimer, *The Quest for Christian Unity,* 1952. Much of the best material on the ecumenical movement is in magazines: *Review of the Churches, Constructive Quarterly, Christian Union Quarterly, Christendom, The Ecumenical Review.* Detailed bibliographies on ecumenical literature by Auguste Senaud, 1937, and Henry R. T. Brandreth, 2nd edition, 1948.

W. A. VISSER 'T HOOFT.

ECUMENICAL STUDENT CONFERENCE. See STUDENT CHRISTIAN COUNCIL, UNITED.

EDDY, MARY BAKER: D. Dec. 3, 1910. Since her death Christian Science (*q.v.*) has grown to something over a quarter million members (Christian Scientists are loathe to disclose statistics). Her latter years were filled with bickerings with the Board of Directors of her movement; yet, despite this internal difficulty and the fact that no single person was ever to assume her position of leader, the impetus of her earlier leadership kept the movement going during the crucial years immediately following her death. Her publications include:

Historical Sketch of Christian Science Mind Healing (1888, 3rd ed., 1890); *Christian Science Series* (Vol. I, 1889; Vol. II, 1890—treatises partly by Mrs. Eddy and partly by her students); *Retrospection and Introspection* (1891); *No and Yes* (1891); *Rudimental Divine Science* (1891); *Christ and Christmas* (1893; a poem); *Poems; Personal Contagion* (1909); *The First Church of Christ, Scientist, and Miscellany* (1913); and *The Christian Science Hymnal* (with five hymns by Mrs. Eddy).

BIBLIOGRAPHY: Arthur Brisbane, *Mary Baker G. Eddy*, 1908; Edwin F. Dakin, *Mrs. Eddy, The Biography of a Virginal Mind*, 1929; Adam Dickey, *Memoirs of Mary Baker Eddy*, 1927; H. W. Dresser, *The Quimby Manuscripts*, 1921; Georgine Milmine, *Life of Mary Baker G. Eddy*, 1909; E. M. Ramsay, *Christian Science and its Discoverer*, 1923; Henry Robinson, *A Biographical Sketch of Reverend Mary Baker G. Eddy*; Hugh A. Studdert Kennedy, *Mrs. Eddy*, 1910; reissued 1947; S. Wilbur, *The Life of Mary Baker Eddy*, 1907; and see periodical index in E. F. Dakin (above), pp. 545–549.

[Sup.] RAYMOND W. ALBRIGHT.

EDDY, SHERWOOD: B. Leavenworth, Kansas; he studied at Yale (1891); and Union Seminary. In 1896 he went to India for fifteen years in student work, then fifteen years secretary for Asia of Y.M.C.A. For twenty years he has conducted Sherwood Eddy seminars to meet leaders of Europe. His books include: *India Awakening* (1911); *The New Era in Asia* (1913); *The New World of Labor* (1923); *New Challenges to Faith* (1926); *Religion and Social Justice* (1928); *The Challenge of Russia* (1930); *The Challenge of the East* (1931); *The Challenge of Europe* (1933); *Russia Today* (1934); *A Pilgrimage of Ideas* (1935); *Europe Today* (1938); *Revolutionary Christianity* (1939); *The Kingdom of God and The American Dream* (1941); *Man Discovers God* (1934); *A Portrait of Jesus: A Twentieth Century Life of Christ* (1943); *Pathfinders of the World Missionary Crusade* (1945); *God in History* (1947); *You Will Survive After Death* (1950).

EDEN: From biblical Eden a river "went out" and parted into four "heads" (Gen. 2:10). The obvious meaning of the Genesis passage—however out of line it may appear to be with present geography—is that Eden was located at the common source of the four rivers involved. Since the sources of the Tigris and Euphrates are in Armenia, many take that as the site of Eden. No locality in our present world answers to all the requirements of the biblical picture, and the original location of Eden must thus continue to remain unknown.

BIBLIOGRAPHY: W. F. Albright, "The Location of the Garden of Eden," *AJSL*, XXXIX (1922), 15–31; Paul Heinisch, *Das Buch Genesis* (1930), pp. 111–143.

[Sup.] EDWIN R. THIELE.

EDITAE SAEPE DEI: Encyclical of Pope Pius X issued on May 26, 1910, on the centenary of the canonization of Cardinal Borro-

meo (*q.v.*, Vol. II), who had been active in fighting the Reformation. The pope refers derogatively to the reformers, describing them as rebels, full of arrogance and immorality, "enemies of the cross of Christ." The evangelical princes of the Reformation era and their subjects are equally charged with moral corruption. Energetic protests from evangelical church circles in Germany, as well as from the royal government of Prussia, prevented the encyclical from being promulgated in the dioceses of the *Reich*, after the Vatican had declared unofficially that the pope's intentions were misunderstood, no offense being meant to German Protestantism as such.

Original text in *Acta Apostolicae Sedis*, Vol. II (1910), pp. 357–380. English translation in *American Catholic Quarterly Review*, XXXV (1910), 394–412.   GEORGES A. BARROIS.

EDMUND, SAINT, MARTYR:
BIBLIOGRAPHY: D. C. Douglas in *English Historical Review*, Vol. 43 (1928); F. Hervey, *The History of King Edmund the Martyr*, 1929; *Analecta Bollandiana*, Vol. 48 (1930), pp. 420–422.   [Sup.]

EDMUND, SAINT, OF CANTERBURY (EDMUND RICH): B. Nov. 20, about 1180 at Abingdon; d. Nov. 16, 1240; the name Edmund Rich stems from a later period. Older and more accurate is the name Edmund of Abingdon. His *Constitutiones provinciales* contain thirty-six canons for reformation which give evidence of his zeal for the maintenance of ecclesiastical discipline among clergy, people, and monasteries. The medieval popularity of his *Speculum ecclesiae* appears in the fifty-eight manuscripts (Latin, English, and French), besides the fourteen printed editions mentioned by Robbins.

BIBLIOGRAPHY: H. W. Robbins, *Le Merure de Sainte Église by Saint Edmund*, 1939; M. R. Newbolt, *Edmund Rich, Archbishop and Saint*, 1928; A. B. Emden, *An Oxford Hall in Medieval Times; Being the Early History of St. Edmund Hall*, 1927.

[Sup.] MATHIAS GOOSSENS.

EDOM, EDOMITES: The territory of the ancient biblical kingdom of Edom occupied the southernmost part of the high, narrow, broken, wooded, comparatively well-watered, and fertile plateau of Transjordan. Extending approximately fifty miles from its northern boundary formed by the canyon of the River Zered (Wadi Hesa) to the edge of the Jebel Shera, at the very southern edge of the plateau, and about twenty miles wide, it is bounded on the west by the deep and wide rift of the Arabah (Wadi el-Arabah) and on the east by the desert. At the height of its power, the Edomites controlled the desert the Jebel Shera overlooks to the south of it, which reaches into Arabia and to the seaport of Ezion-geber, Elath on the eastern arm of the Red Sea.

An advanced Bronze Age civilization had

flourished in this fertile highland territory until about the eighteenth century B.C., followed by an extended period of lack of sedentary civilization. This period of urban emptiness gave way then to the appearance and development of the Edomite kingdom, which flourished between the thirteenth and the eighth centuries B.C. Its civilization was based on agriculture, commerce, animal husbandry, and to a limited degree on mining. Its Semitic inhabitants, dwelling in numerous cities, towns, and villages, which were protected by many border fortifications, produced also excellent and distinctive types of pottery. Many of the Edomites were literate, as may be gleaned from references in Jeremiah, Obadiah, Job, and elsewhere. One of the chief deities was named Qos. The strongest and most striking city was known in the Bible as Sela and in later times as Petra. By the end of the sixth century B.C. the Edomite kingdom had succumbed to inner weaknesses and foreign aggression. Subsequently, some of its inhabitants found refuge in southern Palestine, where in the Hellenistic period they became known as Idumaeans.

The early strength of the Edomite kingdom is correctly indicated by the fact that it was impossible for the Israelites to win permission from the Edomites to traverse their territory on the way to the Promised Land (Num. 20:14 ff.). Genesis 36 lists eight Edomite "kings" who reigned in Edom before the Israelites had a king.

BIBLIOGRAPHY: Nelson Glueck, *Explorations in Eastern Palestine, ASOR, XIV, I, 1934; idem, XV, II, 1935; The Other Side of the Jordan, 1940; The River Jordan, 1946;* G. Ernest Wright and Floyd V. Filson, *The Westminster Historical Atlas to the Bible,* 1946.

[Sup.] NELSON GLUECK.

EDUCATIONAL MISSIONS. See EXPANSION OF CHRISTIANITY.

EDUCATION, CHRISTIAN: A ministry by which the Christian Church nurtures its constituency into mature discipleship. The term "religious education" was formerly employed to designate the training of children, youths, and adults by the local church, but since "religion" has become indefinite, many now prefer the definitive term, "Christian education." It is as old as the Christian community, which from the beginning sought in various ways to introduce its constituents to the Christian faith and all its implications. The Christian Church is rooted in the Old Testament community, which by schools and in other ways transmitted its great heritage from generation to generation. Christ did not come to destroy that covenant community but to fulfill its ideals. He served as Teacher, or Rabbi, teaching and preaching the Kingdom, of which he was the Originator and the Center. Through the early church, after Pentecost, he came alive in a new, dynamic, and abiding way, so that the church continued to be a nurturing fellowship, using the Old Testament with Christian interpretations, and centering everything in Christ, his ministry, death, resurrection, and living lordship.

During early centuries, when the church lived in a hostile world, Christian education consisted mainly in the services of worship, and the teaching of converts, with the moral instruction and discipline of believers. New members had to undergo two or three years of probation and instruction. After the Constantinian acceptance of Christianity as the imperial religion the church practically controlled education for a thousand years. Militant nurture declined as the church gained a monopoly of education and the state protected the church from heretical influences. During the medieval period examinations of candidates for full membership became shorter and less rigid. Laymen received little formal instruction, but absorbed much through ritual, pageantry, festivals, etc. For the chosen few there were schools of various grades, culminating in universities. With the Renaissance came a new concern about affairs in this world, affecting education in both content and method, so that modern secular education was born.

The Reformation brought new emphases: popular religious education, the vernacular Bible, biblical preaching, congregational singing, individual judgment, democratic congregational life, family religion, the concept of a Christian ministry in vocations other than church work, and the idea that Christian education is preparation for life. Romanism reacted educationally by establishing the Jesuit order, refurbishing its theological faith, and founding colleges. Subsequently great national systems of education developed in Europe, all of them making room for Christian education, until the American, French, and Russian revolutions. England has a mixed pattern of church and state-provided schools; with the consent of parents religious instruction may be given to elementary and secondary pupils. In the early American colonies all education was Christian. After the Revolution public schools developed, which have been increasingly denatured religiously because of the constitutional provision that church and state must remain separate. The churches have carried on their own Christian education, evolving a varied and complex set of agencies. The Sunday school, now called the Sunday church school, was primary, followed by the daily vacation church school, week day school, youth fellowship, summer conferences and camps, and denominational publications, together with theological seminaries, and many church-related colleges. Denominations have developed boards of Christian education with staffs expert in all phases of Christian work. Christian education is one of the major ministries in all the churches. Its importance has become increasingly apparent in view of appalling religious illiteracy among Protestants.

Christian education was a pioneer in ecumenical relations. From the beginning, the Sunday school was largely interdenominational in character and lay in personnel. In 1889 it held the first world convention, which developed into the World Council of Churches (1948). In the United States the Sunday School Union (1824) has through various stages become (1950) the Division of Christian Education of the National Council. Many new trends have emerged, some to strengthen and others to weaken Christian education. After the Reformation extreme doctrinal emphases in certain groups made Christian education largely a matter of rational (catechetical) instruction. Then the Pietists, stressing subjective experience, brought about a reaction. With the rise of liberalism (Schleiermacher) this subjective emphasis tended to prevail in progressive Christian education, not always closely identified with official churches, and much influenced by current psychology and philosophy. The stress often fell on educational process and method rather than theological content. L. J. Sherrill suggests that this trend was beneficial, as a corrective to static and irrelevant Christianity, but that religious education should now "return" to the church.

Since the 1930's, largely because of new theology, and the tragic human situation, there has been lively concern about Christian doctrine, Christocentricity, biblical content, church relatedness, common worship, evangelism, and home-centeredness, with new curricula to further these ends; also a new emphasis on group work, youth fellowship, young adult life, and ministry to the aged. New schools prepare leaders for work in the field, and churches work together in Christian education on a community and a national scale.

Two names stand out: Horace Bushnell and G. A. Coe. The former's *Christian Nurture* (1847) has become a classic. Over against the extreme individualistic revivalism of his day, Bushnell sought to establish a biblical basis for nurture in home and church. His successors have not always maintained his biblical and evangelistic basis; rather they have tended to separate Christian nurture from its historic moorings. Coe's vigorous thinking in *What is Christian Education?* (1929) placed it in the setting of contemporary social life rather than in the church. More recently two books have set in contrast the contemporary theological crisis: *Can Religious Education Be Christian?* (1940), by H. S. Elliott; *Faith and Nurture* (1941), by H. S. Smith. A partially constructive answer appears in *The Clue to Christian Education* (1950), by R. C. Miller.

BIBLIOGRAPHY: *Reports of the Ecumenical Institute of Christian Education*, 1950; *Religious Education*, Vol. II of *Jerusalem Conferences*, 1928; P. H. Vieth, *The Church* *and Religious Education*, 1947; W. E. Powell, *Education for Life with God*, 1934; T. Heckel, *How to Teach Evangelical Christianity*; L. A. Weigle, *Jesus and the Educational Method*, 1939; P. Lotz, ed., *Orientation in Religious Education*, 1950; articles in *Religion in Life, Religious Education*, and *Theology Today*.

ELMER G. HOMRIGHAUSEN.

EDUCATION, COUNCIL OF CHURCH BOARDS OF: Secretaries of denominational boards of education, who began meeting in 1911 to discuss common problems and united action, organized the Council in 1912. Its name was changed in 1947 to National Protestant Council on Higher Education, and in 1950 it became a commission in the Division of Christian Education, National Council of the Churches of Christ, U. S. A. Believing that religion is essential to a complete education, the Council undertook to strengthen church-related colleges and the ministry to students in tax-supported schools. Executive secretaries were Robert L. Kelly (1917–35); Gould Wickey (1935–47); E. Fay Campbell (1947–50).   GOULD WICKEY.

EDUCATION, THEOLOGICAL. See THEOLOGICAL EDUCATION, RECENT TRENDS IN; THEOLOGICAL ENCYCLOPEDIA; THEOLOGICAL LIBRARIES; THEOLOGICAL SCHOOLS, AMERICAN ASSOCIATION OF; THEOLOGICAL SEMINARIES IN NORTH AMERICA.

EDWARD VI, KING OF ENGLAND: He was the son of Henry VIII (*q.v.*) and Jane Seymour; ascended the English throne at the age of ten, and died six years later (1553). Calvinism for the first time had a chance to flourish in England, as Archbishop Cranmer invited the following scholars to lecture or preach in his country: Bucer (*q.v.*), A. Lasco (see LASCO), Ochino (*q.v.*), and Vermigli (*q.v.*, Vol. XII). Even more favorable to the Calvinists was the Protector, who was the chief regent of the boy king. For this reason the statute of 1552 was passed in which all interest on loans was prohibited. This was a great contrast to conditions under Henry VIII, who permitted 10% loans. It shows clearly that it was not the Calvinists who introduced capitalism into England. The Book of Common Prayer issued in 1549 was a compromise between Lutheranism and Calvinism, while the Forty-Two Articles were definitely Calvinistic. One of the chief religious leaders in the country was John Hooper. He spent two years at Zürich, and in 1551 was appointed bishop of Gloucester. He even went so far as to dispense with clerical vestments, which induced John Calvin to write: "While, therefore, I admire his firmness in refusing the anointing, I had rather he had not carried his opposition so far with respect to the cap and the linen vestment, even though I approve of these: I recently recommended this." Hooper was strongly opposed to interest given on loans. Another Calvinist was Robert Crowley, who did the most for getting the statute of 1552 passed. Thomas Lever was also a fervent Calvinist who was opposed to lending money on interest. See also CRANMER; MARY TUDOR; ELIZABETH; POLE, REGINALD.

BIBLIOGRAPHY: W. Turnbull, *Calendar of State Papers, Foreign Series, of the Reign of Edward VI*, 1861; F. Gasquet, *Edward VI and the Book of Common Prayer*, 2nd ed., 1928; G. Constant, *L'introduction de la Réforme en Angleterre sous Edouard VI*, 1939; J. Couturier, *Le "Book of Common Prayer" et l'Eglise Anglicane*, 1928; A. Hyma, *Renaissance to Reformation* (1951), pp. 540–563.
                                        ALBERT HYMA.

EDWARD (EADWARD), SAINT, THE CONFESSOR: He was not adequately prepared for his royal tasks. The favors which he bestowed upon the monasteries resulted in much good will among the monks of his time and also later on, for in their writings they idealized him to a great extent. This tendency was enhanced by the conquest of England by the Normans, who did not meet with immediate favor on the part of the Anglo-Saxons in England. The latter thought of their last Anglo-Saxon king with increased reverence, some of which he did not deserve.

BIBLIOGRAPHY: *La vie de S. Eduard le Confesseur par Osbert de Clare*, in *Analecta Bollandiana*, 41 (1923), 5–131.
               [Sup.] MATHIAS GOOSSENS.

EDWARDS, JONATHAN: Distrust of human reason, which was increasing in America in the 1930's and later, tended to emphasize the significance of Edwards, who opposed the rationalism of his day—as represented, for example, by Charles Chauncy—with frank and vigorous emphasis on the feelings ("affections") and will, not only in religious experience and in ethics, but in intellectual and cultural life as well. He emphasized the direct confrontation of the individual by God, and the immediate awareness of ultimate reality. This extra-rational element in Edwards' thinking was the more notable in view of his heavy indebtedness to John Locke and Isaac Newton.

BIBLIOGRAPHY: Perry Miller, *Jonathan Edwards* (1949) is a brilliant interpretation of Edwards' philosophic and cultural significance. Important biographies are O. E. Winslow, *Jonathan Edwards, 1703–1758*, 1940; A. C. McGiffert, Jr., *Jonathan Edwards*, 1932.
               [Sup.] LEFFERTS A. LOETSCHER.

EEKHOF, ALBERT: Reformed; b. at Steenwijk, the Netherlands, July 26, 1884; d. at Oegstgeest, March 23, 1933. At an early age he accompanied his father to the United States, but returned in 1895 to study theology at the University of Leiden. After completing his work there he did thorough research work in the United States, investigating church history. In 1910 became Reformed pastor at Diemen, and in 1924 professor of church history at Leiden. He was deeply interested in the first Protestants who emigrated to America. As a leading editor of the *Nederlandsche archief voor kerkgeschied-*

enis he performed very useful services. He wrote: *Bastiaen Jansz. Krol* (1910); *De Hervormde Kerk in Noord-Amerika* (1913); *De Avondmaalsbrief van Cornelius Hoen* (1917); *De Theologische Faculteit te Leiden in de 17e eeuw* (1921).   ALBERT HYMA.

EFFECTUAL CALLING. See SOTERIOLOGY.

EGEDE, INSTITUTE. See MISSION RESEARCH.

EGMOND, ABBEY OF ST. ADELBERT, O.S.B.: Founded by Dirk II, Count of Holland, in 950. Received many donations from his successors, ten of whom were buried there. The first monks came from Ghent, the Abbey of St. Bavo. Egbert, bishop of Trier, and son of Dirk II, presented the first books to the new abbey, which formed the nucleus of the famous library. The catalogue of this library was written by Boudewijn of The Hague (1520). Some of the manuscripts are preserved in Leiden, Alkmaar, Glasgow, the Vatican, and Wolfenbüttel. Documents of the abbey are in the Rijksarchief in The Hague. The tympanon of the church, the first piece of sculpture known in Holland, is in the Rijksmuseum in Amsterdam. At Egmond the oldest history of the County of Holland was written. The abbey had charge of twenty-five parishes and forty-five chapels. Its monks did much for the poor and the sick, offering also to leading scholars and authors opportunities for research. Among them were Cardinal Cusa, Melis Stoke, Alardus of Amsterdam, Jan van Leiden, Beka, Heda, and Emperor Maximilian. In 1573 the abbey was destroyed by soldiers in the employ of Dirk Sonoy, a Calvinist leader. A few years later a part of the income of the abbey was used to defray the expenses involved in employing professors at the newly founded University of Leiden. Restoration of the abbey was not begun until 1934, and not until 1950 was it recognized again as an abbey, namely, that of St. Adelbert.

BIBLIOGRAPHY: O. Oppermann, *Fontes Egmundensis*, 1933; P. A. Meilink, *De Egmondsche geschiedbronnen*, 1939; V. J. Roefs, *De Egmondsche abtenkroniek van Johannes a Leidis*, 1942; A. J. Vis, *Wilhelmus Procurator en zijn Chronicon*, 1950.
                          WILLIBRORD LAMPEN.

EGO AND EGOISM: What is the ego or "I" that is the experiencing or acting subject, and never merely an object, always in a sense at the centre and never at the circumference? On our answer depends our attitude to many of the problems of metaphysics and of ethics. Common sense usually relates the ego to the limits of the body (the ego is "first and foremost a body-ego," Freud); but this overlooks the fact that only self-conscious beings can be said to have an ego, and that, though in childhood self-consciousness develops through the discovery that the body "belongs" to the self in a way in which the external world does not, self-consciousness refuses to identify itself absolutely with the bodily organism.

Psychologically, the self-reference involved in all the thinking, feeling, and acting of a self-conscious being must somehow involve the possibility of the contents of consciousness becoming an object of knowledge. Many elements of our experience which may never be conscious also help to build the structure of the world in which we live, and the corresponding structure of the character which we acquire as we live in it. This necessary distinction is expressed by Freud (following Nietzsche) in his ego, id, and superego phraseology, and by Buber in a different sense in his equally famous I-thou-it distinction. To Freud, the ego is concerned with perception and therefore has direct relations with reality ("the ego is the representative of the outer world to the id"), while the id is concerned with instinct, and therefore is "subjective." But instinct affects the ego also. The ego is "subject to the influence of the instincts, too, like the id, of which it is in fact only a specially modified part." The id is a kind of precipitate or storehouse of the experiences of the ego, and is the "great storehouse of libido." The pleasure-principle "reigns supreme in the id." The ego represents what we call reason and sanity, in contrast to the id which contains the passions. So "the ego's position is like that of a constitutional monarch," striving to be moral, while the id is non-moral, and the superego may be hyper-moral, though Freud is not very clear as to the relations of the ego and the id to the super-ego.

Buber (whose relation to Kierkegaard in this is very similar to that of Freud to Nietzsche) starts from the difference between our relations as persons to things on the one hand, and to other persons on the other. The ego can never be an object of knowledge to itself; in fact, it can never be such an object to anyone. But the ego only acquires personality by recognizing the "thouness" of other individuals, i.e., by treating them with respect as persons, never as things. "As I say thou, I become I. All real life is meeting." Buber tries to find an antidote for isolationism in psychology, which will also be the cure for "egoism" in ethics. This has been the recurring danger of all modern philosophy, since Descartes's *cogito ergo sum* apparently gave the primacy to thinking as the constitutive principle of reality. If that be so, the ego acquires a magisterial authority; for, as Berkeley showed, even the external world could only be established as an inference from the primal reality of the thinking subject. To Buber, the source of all social sin is to treat the thou as it. The source of neighborliness is to rejoice in the otherness of the thou, not to

desire to possess or dominate, but to enrich the soul by respect for the personality of others.

One of the main problems of ethics is to escape from the ego-centric predicament, caused by psychological presuppositions and necessities. Egoism tends ethically to be identified with systematic selfishness, as the belief (and resultant behavior) that nothing counts except my own good, construed in terms of the satisfaction of self-interest. Although modern psychology has probably disposed of the theory at the basis of hedonism (*q.v.*)—namely, that the only effective motives in human affairs are the pursuit of pleasure and the avoidance of pain—hedonism in some form will probably persist. As feeling is always the most individualistic of our experiences, the hedonist is invariably confronted with the difficulty of reconciling the "good" of the individual, construed as pleasure or the satisfaction of self-interest, with the "common good," similarly construed, though in the process it becomes apparent that the "greatest happiness of the greatest number" is a psychological monstrosity.

In economics, the same theory of human nature led to the development of "enlightened self-interest" as the only possible motive in industry and commerce, on the assumption that "economic man" must be led to see that unenlightened self-interest means the suicide of a war of all against all. If unrestrained egoism is man's natural way of life, all government, all rules, and even all scruples are artificial restraints upon his "natural" activities. Thus an imperfect view of human nature leads to an impossible view of social structures, in which nature "red in tooth and claw" is disciplined into "moral" ways of behavior, which are artificial and conventional rules imposed upon man's true nature. Bishop Butler has a sounder psychology and a better ethic when he says: "there are as real and the same kind of indications in human nature, that we were made for society and to do good to our fellow-creatures; as that we were intended to take care of our own life and health and private good" (Sermon I). Not only does his treatment of the balance of human nature (self-love and benevolence) under the sway of conscience give a truer and less cynical reading of the facts of human nature than Hobbes and his followers did; it preserves us against the opposite extreme of the idealist view of human nature, which refuses any legitimate place to self-interest, attempts to banish the profit-motive from industry and commerce, and builds "castles in Spain" that contribute nothing to the housing of humanity.

The Freudian analysis of human nature, which begins and ends in crass materialism, gives little help in the integration of character or in devising patterns for social institutions. On the other hand, Buber's distinctions are of real value in showing how, from the religious point of view, the otherwise irreconcilable conflict between egoism and altruism need not arise. True personality, in the religious sense, is not a development of the libido—the lust for pleasure, power, wealth or any "thing"—but it is in essence capacity for fellowship; and in true religion the relation of faith as a fellowship-experience determines the character of all our relations to other persons and to things. This is the conversion by which human nature is redeemed from a process of more and more enlightenment of a primitive selfishness, and becomes in very truth, though not in immediate perfection, the child of God.

BIBLIOGRAPHY: Sigmund Freud, *The Ego and the Id,* Eng. tr., 1949; Martin Buber, *I and Thou,* Eng. trans., 1937; idem, *Between Man and Man,* Eng. tr., 1947.

WILLIAM ROXBURGH FORRESTER.

EGYPT, ANCIENT: I. Sources of Knowledge: Until recently, the principal sources of knowledge of ancient Egypt were the Bible and the classical writers, especially Herodotus and Diodorus. As excavation and publication of previously known and newly discovered monuments have progressed the situation has changed radically. Native sources now provide a constantly broadening vista of Egyptian culture and history. Nevertheless, they still fail to present a fully complete or satisfactory picture, owing to the fact that the Egyptians left virtually no purely historical records.

II. Neighbors: Isolated, though Egypt was, by the desert on east and west, the sea on the north, and the Nile cataracts on the south, yet the early inhabitants did not live in a vacuum. Other cultures existed round about her, especially in Mesopotamia, and scholars tend toward agreement that stimulus from one or more of these neighbors played an important role in the beginnings of Egyptian civilization. The problem can only be suggested here, but the accompanying table, adapted from Alexander Scharff's *Die Fruehkulturen Aegyptens und Mesopotamiens* (1941), presents current views both on Egyptian chronology and on Egypt's place in the ancient Near East. (See table.)

III. Beginnings of Egyptian Civilization: The much debated question whether Egyptian civilization began in the south (Upper Egypt) or the Delta (Lower Egypt) must now probably be answered in favor of the former. When Old Stone Age man began to manufacture his crude flint implements on the plateaus east and west of the Nile Valley, the latter for most of its length and all of the Delta consisted of uninhabitable marshes. By 5000 B.C., when the Late Stone Age began, the valley above the south apex of the Delta had developed into a region comparable in climate with the present, and it was in this elongated area that we can trace the beginnings of Egyptian culture. The Delta re-

mained, however, for several millennia an area of impenetrable, crocodile- and hippopotamus-infested marshes unfit for human habitation. Nevertheless, on the edge of the Delta where the desert begins, a small number of Lower Egyptian sites, such as Merimde, Beni Salami, and Omari, have been located in which a Late Stone Age culture flourished which consisted of farmers with abundant pottery but ignorant of copper.

IV. Amratian Culture: In Upper Egypt the Late Stone Age left numerous cemeteries; the modern names of several of these are now familiar as designations of the several stages of culture in later prehistoric Egypt. The first was discovered sixty years ago by Petrie. Its phases are known as Negada I and II. Thirty years later Brunton uncovered a culture at Badari which proved to be roughly contemporary with Negada I. A third, discovered at el-Amrah, of approximately the same age as the other two, has given its name—Amratian—to all the Negada I group. The Amratians were probably seminomadic shepherds of east Hamitic race. They buried their dead in cemeteries away from their settlements, in contrast to the Lower Egyptian farmers of Merimde and Omari (who were northwest Hamites), whose graves were placed within the inhabited area.

V. Gerzean Culture: The Negada II culture was much more widely distributed than any of the earlier ones, numerous cemeteries having been discovered from Lower Nubia in the south to Gerza (whence the term Gerzean for this culture), Abusir el-Meleq, and Ma'adi, the last on the edge of the Delta south of Cairo.

VI. Connections with Western Asia: While the Negada (= Gerzean) culture was purely African-Hamitic in character, the excavated graves yield numerous pottery types similar in form and decoration to Palestinian ware and a few with distinctive affinities with Syrian pottery. Much of the material in question comes from sites on the eastern edge of the Delta where contacts with western Asia may be indicated. Connections with Mesopotamia are corroborated likewise, slightly later, in the earliest dynastic tomb architecture, where elaborately niched brick walls have close parallels in Mesopotamian sites of the contemporary Jemdet-Naser period. The Gerzean period carries Egyptian culture down to the beginning of the dynastic era.

VII. Language and Writing: It now appears certain that the mingling of the three strata of primitive men described above produced the historical Egyptian race. Recent researches in the language confirm this view, for analysis of the vocabulary and syntax of Egyptian prove it to be mainly Hamitic in character, with both northwest Hamitic and east Hamitic strains, while an admixture of Semitic characteristics,

COMPARATIVE TABLE: EARLY CULTURES OF EGYPT AND MESOPOTAMIA

	Uppe Egypt	Lower Egypt	Mesopotamia	Iran
Before and ca. 4000	Tâsa Badari	Merimde Fayyum	Painted pottery of Tell Halaf, Samarra, etc. El-Obêd period to ca. 3700	Persepolis Susa I
ca. 3800	Negada I (Amratian)	?	Uruk period Warka VI, V, IV to ca. 3300	Susa "Inter-mediate period"
ca. 3400	Negada II (Gerzean)	Ma'adi		
	Prehistoric united kingdom		Jemdet-Naser period Warka III, II	Susa II
ca. 3200	Late Negada II Kingdom of Hierakon-polis	? Kingdom of Buto		
ca. 3000	Naga ed-Dêr First Dynasty Royal tombs of Abydos	Tura (Menes) Archaic tombs at Sakkara	to shortly after 3000 Early dynastic periods I/II (Mesilim of Kish, Warka I, Tell Asmar, Khafaje, Tell Agrab, Fara) to ca. 2900	
ca. 2800	Third Dynasty (Djoser)		Early dynastic period IIIa (Mari, Assur H-G)	
ca. 2600	Fourth Dynasty (Khufu, Khafre)		Early dynastic period IIIb (Urnanshe of Lagash, Royal tombs of Ur)	
ca. 2500	Fifth Dynasty (Sahurê)		Sargon of Akkad	

including important elements of vocabulary, suggests contact in the later stages of its development with Semitic-speaking peoples, such as might have inhabited the country to the east of the Nile Delta. The earliest written Egyptian clearly reflects its Gerzean origin, for a considerable number of the signs are pictures of objects of a type used only in the Gerzean period. Furthermore, a few essential characteristics of the Egyptian script are strikingly similar to those of the somewhat older Sumerian (*q.v.*) (though the actual signs used in writing the two languages have absolutely nothing in common), as if the Egyptians had derived from contact with writers of Sumerian at least the *idea* of writing but without taking over their

methods or their materials. Thus Egyptian civilization may be considered indigenous in the Nile Valley but to some degree stimulated and inspired by foreign contacts in the Gerzean period.

VIII. Results of Recent Excavations: Excavations undertaken since 1900 have greatly enriched our knowledge of the dynastic period likewise. At Sakkara, the vast funerary monument including the step pyramid of Djoser (founder of the Third Dynasty), the first great structure of stone, has been completely excavated and extensively restored. In the chambers under the pyramid not less than twenty thousand alabaster vessels have been recovered. Many of these bear inscriptions in the earliest known hieratic writing. During World War II the roofed causeway leading from the valley temple to the pyramid of Unis (last king of the Fifth Dynasty) was disclosed, yielding for the first time an actual example of this type of building. Among its remarkable representations, carved in low relief, is a unique scene showing the emaciated bodies of ancient Egyptian famine victims.

At Giza, the region about the great pyramids has been carefully explored and hundreds of new monuments discovered, including the secret tomb and personal possessions, many of gold and silver, of Queen Hetep-heres, mother of Khufu, who built the Great Pyramid, and, in 1954, two gigantic solar barques of wood which were provided for the celestial journeys after death of Khufu himself. Across the Nile at Helouan, vast cemeteries from the First and Second Dynasties have been excavated. Literally thousands of tombs have been found, many with important architectural features hitherto unknown. The countless objects found in these tombs will eventually give us a more detailed picture of the time than could have been considered possible ten years ago.

In Upper Egypt, much light has been thrown on the once obscure First Intermediate Period (2200–2000 B.C.), principally through excavations by New York's Metropolitan Museum. The discovery of a great variety of perfectly preserved tomb equipment and funerary models has provided us with wide knowledge of the daily life of this time. The political history of the Eleventh Dynasty has likewise been much clarified by the work of the Museum. Continued publication of the tombs of officials and nobles of the Egyptian Empire at Thebes has provided the best record of the manners and customs of Egypt's age of glory, and its incredible wealth and splendor, even after the Amarna revolution and the beginning of the decline, was sensationally revealed by the discovery in 1922 in his intact tomb of the magnificent funerary equipment of King Tutankhamun, the nature of which seems fully to justify the insistence of Amenhotep III's correspondents in the Amarna letters that "gold was as common as dust in Egypt."

French excavations at Tanis in the eastern Delta have brought to light a splendid royal cemetery of the Twenty-first and Twenty-second Dynasties with rich burial furnishings and even the mummies of members of the royal family. This was the family of Sheshonk I (= Shishak) who captured Jerusalem (I Kings 14:25–26). These unfinished excavations may yet yield historical records which will amplify the information about Palestinian-Egyptian relations during this era which we find in the pages of the Old Testament.

BIBLIOGRAPHY: The best up-to-date bibliography of Ancient Egypt is contained in *Aegypten und Vorderasien*

im Altertum, by Alexander Scharff and Anton Moortgat, 1950. For a very good one in English consult the footnotes in John A. Wilson, *The Burden of Egypt*, 1951.

[Sup.] KEITH C. SEELE.

EGYPT, MODERN. See AFRICA.

EICHRODT, WALTHER: Reformed; b. at Gernsbach (Baden) Aug. 1, 1890. He studied at the Theological School, Bethel-Bielefeld, and the universities of Greifswald and Heidelberg (Lic. Theol., 1914). He was privatdozent at the University of Erlangen (1918–22), professor of Old Testament and history of religion, Basel (1922–). His books include: *Die Quellen der Genesis* (1916), *Die Hoffnung des ewigen Friedens* (1920), *Theologie des Alten Testaments* (3 vols., 1933–39), *Das Menschenverstaendnis des Alten Testaments* (1944, *Man in Old Testament*, 1951), *Israel in der Weissagung des Alten Testaments* (1951), and *Gottes Ruf im Alten Testament* (1951).

EINHARD (EGINHARD): In his capacity of statesman he was more active as an advisor than as a politician. In the field of building, either structures of stone or institutions, he did more as inspirer than as technician. He is best known for his historical work, in which he excelled, having developed a sound critical spirit. Kleinclauss indicates that he was also a theologian of some significance, which fact has seldom been discussed. In the iconoclastic controversy he played an important part, while he also made contributions to hagiography.

BIBLIOGRAPHY: *Vita Caroli*, *Mon. Germ. Hist. in usu scholarum*, 6th ed., 1926; M. Buchner, *Einhards Kuenstler- und Gelehrtenleben*, 1922; A. Kleinclauss, *Eginhard*, 1942.

[Sup.] MATHIAS GOOSSENS.

EIRE: A treaty of separation was signed in 1921 by the British government and the leaders of the Irish independence movement. Under this treaty, which became effective in 1922, all of Ireland except the six northern counties (see IRELAND, NORTHERN) became an independent state, known as the Irish Free State, and later as Eire. It consists of twenty-six counties with four county boroughs; it has an area of 26,600 square miles and a population of about 3,000,000. Its capital city is Dublin.

Under the Constitution of Eire complete freedom of religion is allowed: "Freedom of conscience and the free profession and practice of religion are inviolable rights of every citizen." No church is established; but Roman Catholicism, being the professed faith of 90% of the population, is the religion of the state.

Protestant denominations are still represented in Eire. The largest Protestant denomination is the Church of Ireland (Episcopal). In 1926, at the first census after the partition treaty of 1921, its members in Eire numbered 164,000. By 1936 this number had declined to 145,000, and by 1946 to 124,000. Presbyterianism, never large in the area now covered by Eire, is likewise on the decline. In 1926 it claimed 32,000 members; in 1936, 28,000; and in 1946, 24,000. The Irish Methodist Church, unified in 1878 through a merger of the Wesleyan and Primitive Methodist groups, had 10,000 members in Eire in 1926, 9,000 in 1936, and 8,000 in 1946. Other non-Roman bodies totalled 13,400 in 1926, 11,750 in 1936, and 12,000 in 1946. From these statistics it appears that Protestantism in Eire is steadily dwindling in numbers.

The position of the Roman Catholic Church, both relatively and absolutely, appears to be growing stronger. In 1926 its adherents in Eire numbered 2,750,000; in 1936, 2,773,000; and in 1946, 2,786,000. Its organization covers not merely Eire, but all of Ireland. There are four archiepiscopal provinces and twenty-three episcopal dioceses.

BIBLIOGRAPHY: D. Macardle, *The Irish Republic*, 1937; "Ireland," in *The Catholic Encyclopedia*, Supplement II, Vol. XVIII, 1951.

[Sup. to IRELAND.] NORMAN V. HOPE.

EISELEN, FREDERICK CARL: Methodist; b. Mundelsheim, Germany, on Nov. 25, 1872; d. May 5, 1937. His preparatory education was taken in Germany and later he studied at New York University (A.M., 1899), Drew Theological Seminary (1900), University of Pennsylvania (1901–2), Columbia University (Ph.D., 1907), and at Berlin (1908). He was professor of Semitic languages at Garrett Biblical Institute (1902–32), dean (1919–24), and president (1924–32). He also served as professor of biblical literature in Northwestern University (1918–24). He wrote: *Sidon—A Study in Oriental History* (1907); *A Commentary on the Minor Prophets* (1907); *Prophecy and the Prophets* (1909); (with W. C. Barclay), *The Worker and His Bible* (1909); *The Christian View of the Old Testament* (1912); *Books of the Pentateuch* (1916); *The Psalms and Other Sacred Writings* (1918); *The Prophetic Books of the Old Testament* (2 vols., 1923); and he was also coeditor of *The Abingdon Bible Commentary*.

RAYMOND W. ALBRIGHT.

EISLER, ROBERT I.: B. at Vienna, April 27, 1882. In 1950 he was Wilde Lecturer at the University of Oxford, England. Among other works he wrote: *Yahwes Hochzeit mit der Sonne* (1919); *Orpheus—The Fisher: Comparative studies in Orphic and early Christian cult symbolism* (1921); *The Messiah Jesus and John the Baptist according to Flavius Josephus' Recently Rediscovered 'Capture of Jerusalem'* (1931); *La Monnaie, Cause et Remède de la Crise Economique Mondiale* (1932); *Das Raetsel d. Johannes-Evangeliums* (1935); *Zur Kritik d. psycholog. Konjunkturtheorie* (1935); *Flavius Josephus—*

Studien. Antwort a. Walter Bienert (1936); *The Royal Art of Astrology* (1947); *Winning the Peace* (1949); and *Plato, his Personality and Politic* (1949).

BIBLIOGRAPHY: *Kuerschners Deutsche Gelehrten- Kalender* (1950), col. 403.

RAYMOND W. ALBRIGHT.

EISSFELDT, OTTO HERMANN WILHELM LEONHARD: Lutheran; b. at Northeim, Hannover, Sept. 1, 1887. He studied theology and Oriental languages at the universities of Goettingen and Berlin (1905–8; Lic. Theol., Berlin, 1912; Dr. Phil., Goettingen, 1916). He was associate pastor at the Jerusalems und Neuen Kirche, Berlin (1912–22); taught Old Testament at Berlin (1913–22); and has been professor of Old Testament and Semitic religious history at Halle (1922–); rector of the University of Halle (1929–30, 1945–48). His major works include: *Die Maschal im Alten Testament* (1913); *Israels Geschichte* (1915); *Krieg und Bibel* (1915); *Die Heilige Schrift des Alten Testaments*, 4. Aufl. (1921); *Hexateuch Synopse* (1922); *Baal Zaphon* (1932); *Gottesknecht bei Deuterojesaja* (1933); *Einleitung in das Alte Testament* (1933); *Ras Schamra und Sanchunjaton* (1939); *Geschichtliches und Uebergeschichtliches im Alten Testament* (1947); *Geschichtsschreibung im Alten Testament* (1948).

BIBLIOGRAPHY: *Festschrift Otto Eissfeldt zum 60. Geburtstage 1. Sept., 1947* (1947), pp. 213–31.

RAYMOND W. ALBRIGHT.

EKID OR E.K.D. See GERMANY, I.

ELECTION: Election refers to the decree of God whereby from eternity he chose unto everlasting life a certain number of angels (I Tim. 5:21) and men (Rom. 8:28, 29; Eph. 1:4; II Tim. 1:9; I Pet. 1:1, 2). It is with the election of men that the revelation in Scripture is mainly concerned. The discrimination which election implies appears in the Old Testament most conspicuously in the choice of Jacob as over against Esau (Gen. 25:23; Mal. 1:2, 3; cf. Rom. 9:11–13), and the choice of the children of Israel as God's peculiar people is the typical example which sets the points for our understanding of what election involves—sovereign election in love unto redemption and the adoption of sons (Deut. 4:37; 7:7, 8; 10:15; 14:2; 33:3). Election guarantees all the means and provisions necessary for the achievement of its purpose. The choice in Christ before the foundation of the world is the source from which all saving grace as bestowed and as in exercise in the believer proceeds (Eph. 1:4–14). Foreknowledge (Rom. 8:29; I Pet. 1:2) cannot be construed as the mere foresight of believing and persevering grace but must be understood in the pregnant sense of distinguishing and purposive love (cf. Amos 3:2; Rom. 11:2). The reason of

God's election lies hid in the unsearchable riches of his own sovereign good pleasure. It is not ours to comprehend but to bow in holy amazement.   JOHN MURRAY.

ELEPHANTINE PAPYRI. See PAPYRI, BIBLICAL AND EARLY CHRISTIAN.

ELERT, WERNER: Lutheran; b. at Helddrungen, Germany, Aug. 19, 1885. He studied at the universities of Breslau, Leipzig, and Erlangen; (Dr. Phil.; Lic. Theol.). He was Direktor of the Breslau Lutheran Theological Seminary (1919–23) and is professor of systematic and historical theology at Erlangen (1923–). His most important works: *Der Kampf um das Christentum seit Schleiermacher und Hegel* (1921); *Morphologie des Luthertums* (2 vol., 1931–32); *Der christliche Glaube* (2nd ed., 1941); *Das christliche Ethos* (1949).

    J. ELERT.

ELIZABETH, QUEEN OF ENGLAND: B. 1533; d. 1603. Daughter of Henry VIII by Anne Boleyne. Elizabeth's dangerous position during the rule of her Catholic half sister Mary taught her the virtues of prudence and moderation, much needed upon her accession to the throne (1558). In foreign affairs she faced the attempt of her Catholic brother-in-law, Philip II of Spain, to keep England under Hapsburg influence. At home she had to find a stable basis for her rule. The moderation and gradualness of her religious settlement reflected both these problems. The Act of Supremacy (1559) forbade allegiance to any foreign prelate or prince, making Elizabeth "governor" of the church. Ecclesiastical commissioners were provided to enforce obedience, forming the Court of High Commission. The Act of Uniformity (1559) decreed external conformity to a liturgy using the Second Prayer Book of Edward VI, while the Thirty-nine Articles (1563) purged Edward VI's Forty-two Articles of their extreme Protestantism.

The liturgy was purposely kept vague and inclusive in order to undercut religious discontent. Thus Holy Communion could be interpreted either as transubstantiation or as a ceremony of remembrance. Clerical vestments, church music and ornaments were retained, together with bishops. While preserving the historic framework of the church, the crown's control over church government was enforced by the bishops against Puritan and Catholic dissatisfaction.

Catholic opposition was expressed internally through missionaries (e.g., Edward Campion, Robert Parsons) sent from the seminary established at Douai (1568) as well as through uprisings (rebellion of the northern earls, 1569) and plots in favor of Mary Queen of Scots, Catholic candidate to the throne. Abroad, the pope, excommunicating Elizabeth (1570), acknowledged her Protestantism, while Philip II, unable to win his sister-in-law through marriage, supported plots against her life. Elizabeth's aid to the Dutch rebels, as well as the execution of Mary (1587), her prisoner since 1576, determined Philip on war. The defeat of the Armada (1588), dashing Catholic hopes, crowned Elizabeth's policy of disentangling England from Hapsburg influence.

The Puritans attempted to reform the church from within, using pamphlet warfare and Parliaments, already opposed to Elizabeth's paternalistic economic policies. Archbishop Whitgift (1583–1604) began the active suppression of the Puritans. In spite of his efforts, a strong Puritan party remained within the church, resisting appeals by controversialists like Richard Hooker. Continual opposition to Elizabeth's religious and economic policies undermined the harmony and order which she had sought to obtain by putting national unity above religious dogmatism or private economic interests.

See also PURITANISM.

BIBLIOGRAPHY: J. B. Black, *Queen Elizabeth*, 1936; E. P. Cheyney, *History of England from the defeat of the Armada to the death of Queen Elizabeth*, 1914–26; J. Clapham, *Elizabeth of England*, 1951; E. T. Davis, *Episcopacy and Royal Supremacy in the Church of England in the 16th Century*, 1951; W. H. Frere, *The English Church in the Reign of Queen Elizabeth and James I*, 1904; W. P. M. Kennedy, *Elizabethan Episcopal Administration*, 1924; A. O. Meyer, *England and the Catholic Church under Queen Elizabeth*, 1916; J. E. Neale, *Queen Elizabeth*, 1934; J. E. Neale, *The Elizabethan House of Commons*, 1950; R. G. Usher, *Rise and Fall of the High Commission*, 1913; R. G. Usher, *The Reconstruction of the English Church*, 1910.

    GEORGE L. MOSSE.

ELKESAITES: I. The Founder: W. Brandt (*ERE*, V, 262 ff.) appears to be the first to have attempted a reconstruction of the several versions of the Book of Elxai and a connected history of the Elkesaite community from the fragments of the Scripture preserved in the Church Fathers together with the scant reference to the sect in other Christian, pagan, and Moslem sources. While the identification of the name "Elxai" (Aramaic formation signifies "hidden power" possibly with reference to the founder as a man slight in stature but possessing great charismata; Arabic form may mean "hidden God" possibly referring either to the revelation recorded in the Sacred Book or to the founder) either with the prophet or his recorded pronouncements remains uncertain, the outline of a dynamic personality characterized by spiritual and moral integrity can be perceived behind the book and in the devotional experience of the sect. He may be compared with John the Baptist in his preaching of a baptism of repentance, and more closely with Muhammed in his sense of vocation, emphasis upon a final judgment, relationship to his early companions, and in the diverse nature of the oracles he received.

II. The Book: This latter comparison does,

Brandt believes, throw considerable light upon the nature and formation of the Elkesaite scriptures. Diverse in content, these utterances and oracles may, like those of the Qur'an, have been collected into a volume by the piecing together of the several leaves each of which contained a revelation or commandment that had been delivered upon a particular occasion.

III. Ritual and Doctrine: A more definite distinction must be made between the two sacraments observed among the Elkesaites. Central not only in the cultic but also in the doctrinal expression of the sect was the baptismal rite of immersion in flowing water during which the candidate retained his clothes and committed himself to a vow of repentance and moral purity. Through this sacramental bath was obtained remission of all previous sin. A similar but probably not identical rite appears to have followed for medicinal and remedial benefits. What the Eucharist has meant in terms of all the claims concerning it, both material and spiritual, together with the articulation of doctrine written into its canon in Catholic Christianity, the baptismal ritual must have afforded the Elkesaite brotherhood. The other sacrament was a communion in bread and salt which Ritschl and Uhlhorn have described as the Elkesaite celebration of the Lord's Supper. It seems, however, hardly probable that any closer connection than certain ceremonial similarities between the two communions can be claimed. The tradition here is more certainly Jewish than Christian and the significance of the communion may well have been simply the seal of covenanted fellowship or the sign of the solidarity of life in the community such as was the case in the similar rite described in the Old Testament (Lev. 2:13; Num. 18:19).

IV. Life, Development, and Expansion of the Community: There is no evidence of organizational growth in the Elkesaite community beyond the stages of circle and brotherhood to an ecclesiastical institution. During the life of the founder authority was centered in him and in his recorded words which Hippolytus tells us were entrusted to certain Sobiai, i.e., baptized ones. As in the case of early Islam new pronouncements were made to meet the exigencies of life in the new society. One final word to the faithful, similar in its tone of accommodation to the Medinese Suras of the Qur'an, permits verbal apostasy in times of persecution. The circle around Elkesai formed first in Trans-Jordan exhibiting in the beginning marks of a reform movement in Judaism comparable to that of the Essenes who, indeed, accepted the founder and approved of his teaching, numbered in its fellowship many non-Jewish God-fearers. These accepted the Jewish seal of circumcision, observance of the Sabbath, and the qibla toward Jerusalem. Later appeal was made

to the Aramaic speaking Christians. This mission, according to Brandt's regrouping of the fragments, was supported by a document, supplied by Elkesai himself, which attributed his oracles to revelations received from two huge figures, male and female, in a valley measured against the mountains on either side. The male he identified as the Son of God, and the female as the Holy Spirit. Some time after the death of the founder members of the Elkesaite brotherhood extended their mission into Syria, directing their message largely to Greek speaking Jewish Christians. For this venture a Greek translation with one significant addition had been prepared. A new enumeration of the seven witnesses to the sacramental oath, included along with the older form, substituted "holy spirits" for "winds" and "angels of prayer" for "the aether." A conflation of the two lists was then the source of the list of eight witnesses invoked in a similar Ebionite ritual known to Epiphanius (*Haer.* 30:2, 17).

From Syria the sect sought to extend its fellowship westward in the first quarter of the third century. It was in preparation for this mission, Brandt believes, that the Christological notions of the fragments preserved in Epiphanius and Hippolytus were formulated. Also at this time the emendation in the baptismal formula of the words "and in the name of His Son, the Great King" was probably made. Upon reaching Rome Alcibiades, it may be inferred, was prepared to take advantage of the Christian dispute over the question of a second remission of carnal sins then raging between Callistus and Hippolytus. Probably to his hand may be traced the interpolation in the formula for the baptism of healing which changed the rite into a second baptism for the remission of carnal sins.

V. Relation of the Elkesaites to Other Religious Groups: With the failure of the Western mission and the defeat in Syrian cities at the hands of Catholic Christianity the sect was reduced to small groups of adherents among the Aramaic speaking peoples in the Syrian hinterland and to its foothold in Trans-Jordan. In this latter area it received support in the fourth century from the Sampsites (Sampaesans), a high born clan of non-Jewish God-fearers, and as a consequence de-emphasized or discarded its earlier adherence to elements of the Jewish ceremonial. Since the later Essenes (Ossaeans) had also liberated themselves from the regulations of legal purity, their fellowship with the Elkesaites continued (Epiphanius, *Haer.* liii).

In Islamic times the name of Elkesai appears (in the Kitab al Fihirist of Ibn Abi Ja'qub al-Nadim) in reference to a religious group (the Mughtasila—the washers) identified with the Sabeans of the Qur'an (ii. 59; v. 73; xxii. 17), "a people of the book" who thereby enjoyed toleration under Moslem rule. Brandt points out, however, that this reference tells us nothing more than that the Mughtasila knew of the Elkesaites and in claiming their scriptures could be accorded in Moslem lands the special rights of monotheists possessing a sacred book. It is of interest to note in this same source the statement that the father of Mani was a member of the Mughtasila.

The question of Elkesaite influence upon Muhammed. While there is no conclusive evidence to oppose Brandt's caution against the thesis of Elkesaite influence upon Muhammed some significance may be seen as Bell (*The Origin of Islam in Its Christian Environment*) points out the Jewish tendency and the geographic proximity of those Christian groups closest to Arabian caravan ways. The stronghold of the Elkesaites was also the seat of the heresiologists Beryll of Bostra, Paul of Samosata, and the Collyridians. Further, the parallels between Elkesai, his book, and his message; and Muhammed and the Qur'an are striking. Both were monotheists, both accorded the highest veneration to a revelation delivered from heaven, both emphasized the doctrine of the last judgment, both enjoined upon their followers the qibla towards Jerusalem. Indeed the Elkesaite watchword "I am a witness over you on the day of judgment" appears in the Qur'an. As already noted, the Sab'in mentioned in the Qur'an may be identified with the Elkesaites. Now, according to Wellhausen (*Reste arabischen Heidentums*) this was the very name by which in the beginning Muhammed and his companions were called. At most these parallels would lead to the possibility of including the Elkesaites with other Jewish and Christian groups which may have contributed to the shaping of Muhammed's mind. We must of course take into account that similar emphases upon a scripture, forgiveness, vows, and the last judgment characterized early Eastern Christianity.

BIBLIOGRAPHY: D. Chwolsohn, *Die Ssabier und der Ssabismus*, Vol. I (1865), pp. 100-138; W. Brandt, "Die jued. Baptismen," ZATW, XVIII, 1910; *Elchasai: ein Religionsstifter und sein Werk*, 1912 (a survey of former studies of Elkesaism); art. "Elkesaites" in ERE, V, (1916) 262 ff.; J. Chapman, "La date du livre d'Elchasai" in *Revue Bénédictine* (1909), 221 ff.; R. Bell, *Origin in Islam in its Christian Environment*, 1926; Burkitt, *Early Eastern Christianity*, 1904.

[Sup.] NOAH EDWARD FEHL.

ELLER, PAUL H.: Evangelical United Brethren; b. at Chadwick, Ill., Jan. 27, 1905. He studied at North Central College (B.A., 1926); Evangelical Theological Seminary (B.D., 1928); University of Chicago (M.A., 1930; Ph.D., 1933). He taught Church History in Evangelical Theological Seminary (1930-) and at Garrett Biblical Institute during summer sessions (1944 and 1945). He published: *History of Evangelical Missions* (1942) and *These Evangelical United Brethren* (1950).

ELLIGER, KARL: Lutheran; b. Wilhelmshaven, March 7, 1901; studied at the universities of Marburg, Halle, Tuebingen, Muenster (1919-23, Lic. Theol., 1927); was pastor und Religionslehrer in Muenster (1926-34), *Privatdozent* in Muenster (1929-34) and Leipzig (1934-37); professor of theology (Old Testament) at Tuebingen (1937-). His books include: *Die Einheit des Tritojesaja* (1928); *Deuterojesaja in seinem Verhaeltnis zu Tritojesaja* (1933); *Das Buch der zwoelf Kleinen Propheten, II: Nahum, Habakuk, Zephanja, Haggai, Sacharja, Maleachi uebersetzt und erklaert* (1950, 2nd ed. 1951); and he was coeditor of *Festschrift Alfred Bertholet* (1950).

ELLIOTT, GRACE LOUCKS (MRS. HARRISON S.): Methodist; b. at Alverton, Pa., Feb. 19, 1891. She studied at Findley College, (A.B., 1910), Teachers College and Union Theological Seminary (M.A., 1924), and Columbia University (Ph.D., 1936). She was on the staff of the National Board of the YWCA, visiting colleges and universities (1917-25); lectured in colleges, conferences, social and religious agencies on religious education and family relations (1925-43); was general secretary of the YWCA (1943-53). She has contributed to education, social and religious journals. She wrote: (with Harry Bone), *The Sex Life of Youth* (1929); *Understanding the Adolescent Girl* (1930); (with Harrison S. Elliott), *Solving Personal Problems* (1936); *Women After Forty* (1936).

ELLIOTT, HARRISON S.: Methodist; b. at St. Clairsville, Ohio, Dec. 13, 1882; d. at New York City, June 27, 1951. He studied at Antioch College (1898-1900), Valparaiso University (1900-1901), Ohio Wesleyan University (A.B., 1905); Drew Theological Seminary (B.D., 1911); Teachers College, Columbia University (M.A., 1922); Yale University (Ph.D., 1940). He was secretary to Bishop James W. Bashford of the Methodist Church in China (1905-8); assistant secretary of the African Diamond Jubilee of the Methodist Church (1909-10); secretary of the International Committee, YMCA (1910-22); instructor in religious psychology, Drew Theological Seminary (1921-23); Skinner and McAlpin professor of practical theology and head of the Department of Religious Education and Psychology, Union Theological Seminary (1925-50); ordained to the ministry of the Methodist Church (1944); chairman of the National Boys Work Committee of the YMCA (1927-46); president of the Religious Education Association (1939-42); general secretary of the Religious Education Association (1950-51). He was one of the outstanding leaders in the field of religious education and in the field of group process and group discussion. He directed the first large-scale use of group discussion in conferences at the International Conference of the YMCA, the first postwar assembly for boys' work sponsored by the International Committee of the YMCA, at Poertschach, Austria (1923); at the Student Volunteer conference of the United States in Indianapolis (1924); and the World Conference of the World Alliance of the YMCA in Helsingfors, Finland (1926). He was greatly interested in mental hygiene and helped to introduce courses in mental hygiene into the curriculum of theological seminaries. He wrote: (with Ethel Cutler), *Student Standards of Action* (1914); *How Jesus Met Life Questions* (1920); *The Bearing of Psychology upon Religion* (1927); *The Process of Group Thinking* (1928); *Group Discussion in Religious Education* (1930); (with Grace Loucks Elliott), *Solving Personal Problems* (1936); *Can Religious Education be Christian?* (1940).

ELLIS, JOHN TRACY: Catholic; b. at Seneca, Ill., July 30, 1905. He studied at St. Viator College (A.B., 1927); the Catholic University of America (A.M., 1928; Ph.D., 1930). He taught history at St. Viator College (1930–32); College of Saint Teresa (1932–34); and was director of the Southern Branch Summer Session, the Catholic University of America, at San Antonio, Texas (1935–37). He taught history at the Catholic University of America (1938–41); he has been professor of American church history (1947–); managing editor, *Catholic Historical Review* (1941–); secretary, American Catholic Historical Association (1941–); censor of books, Archdiocese of Washington (1948–). He wrote *Anti-Papal Legislation in Medieval England 1066–1377* (1930); *Cardinal Consalvi and Anglo-Papal Relations, 1814–1824* (1942); *The Formative Years of the Catholic University of America* (1946); *A Select Bibliography of the History of the Catholic Church in the United States* (1947); *The Life of James Cardinal Gibbons, Archbishop of Baltimore, 1834–1921* (2 vols., 1952).

ELOHIM: New evidence for the explanation of this term has been found in the Amarna (*q.v.*) letters, Amorite personal names, and in biblical theology and thought patterns, but the acceptance of such an explanation is far from unanimous among reputable scholars.

The term "elohim" is taken to be the plural of "eloah," itself derived from early northwest Semitic "ila," which must be supposed to contain a final *he,* and which is ultimately the origin of Arabic *allah* (*al-ilah*). This form *ila* is known in such names as *Ila-kabkabu* (God is a star), as well as attested in the Ras Shamra (*q.v.*) texts. Thus the singular form of this word for god is known from much earlier times than is the plural.

The reason for the use of the plural as the designation of one god is still under dispute. In the Amarna letters, various city-kings of Palestine and Syria address the Pharaoh as *ilaniia*: "my gods," in spite of the obvious fact that there was only one Pharaoh, and the presumption is that they were flattering the king of Egypt by ascribing to him the *totality* of divinity. Similarly, it is held, in early Israel the equivalent in Hebrew was used to ascribe to Yahweh *totality* of divinity.

The use of plural verbs does not imply a plurality of gods. For example, in Psalm 82, Job 1, and Deuteronomy 32:8 ff., it expresses the idea of the "council of the gods" as a poetic device.

BIBLIOGRAPHY: L. Koehler, *Lexicon in Veteris Testamenti Libros* (1948), pp. 50 f.
[Sup.] GEORGE E. MENDENHALL.

ELTESTER, WALTHER: Lutheran; b. in Hohenlandin/Uckermark, Germany, April 18, 1899. He studied at Jena and Berlin After serving as a university assistant in Berlin (1925–31) he was professor in the Prussian Academy in Berlin (1931–45) and also worked on the Commission on the Church Fathers. After four years as professor of church history in Humboldt University, Berlin (1945–49), he became professor of New Testament and ancient church history in Marburg (1949–). He has also served in an editorial capacity on the *Zeitschrift fuer neutestamentliche Wissenschaft* (1931–) and on the *Texte und Untersuchungen zur Geschichte der altchristlichen Literatur* (1938–).
RAYMOND W. ALBRIGHT.

ELY LECTURES: The Elias P. Ely Lectureship was founded at Union Theological Seminary, New York, by Zebulon Stiles Ely on May 8, 1865, in order that a course of ten public lectures might be given and published every two or three years on "the evidences of Christianity." In 1879 Mr. Ely broadened the scope of the lectures by permitting whatever subjects the faculty and directors deemed "for the good of man." Among those who have given the Ely Lectures are James McCosh, James Moffatt, Ernest Findlay Scott, and Rufus Jones.
ROBERT T. HANDY.

EMERSON, RALPH WALDO: New England Transcendentalism was a connecting link between America's early theological and its later secular culture; between American provincial thought and world literature of the mid nineteenth century. Arising amid national optimism and expansion in the years following the War of 1812, Transcendentalism used the thought forms of romanticism and philosophical idealism, together with insights borrowed from Oriental literature, to explore human nature and destiny and sought thus, on a consistently naturalistic basis, to inspire the individual and fortify his self-reliance. Nature as a whole, it was said, corresponds to the individual, so the knowledge of self is the foundation of all knowledge. Thus the intuitive and introspective study of self is placed above natural science, history, and all material values. The strong individualism of the movement was a democratizing influence, but its emphasis on culture was antiequalitarian. Transcendentalism stimulated, broadened, and did much to secularize American culture, causing observers at home and abroad to see American life in quite altered perspective.

Ralph Waldo Emerson (1803–82) was the most prominent of the New England Transcendentalists. After teaching school and serving as a Unitarian minister, he traveled abroad, meeting some of the European leaders of the romantic movement. Seeking to think through his ideas for himself, he became the great apostle of "self-reliance." He followed Coleridge in distinguishing between "reason" (intuition) and "understanding" (analytic reason), preferring the former as an organ of knowledge. Emphasizing moral values, he lent influence to contemporary reform movements, but was too individualistic to identify himself completely with any. He was a courageous and idealistic critic of thought and life, a secular prophet flashing fire against materialism and hypocrisy.

BIBLIOGRAPHY: For a brief treatment and a critical bibliography, see R. E. Spiller, *et al.* (eds.), *Literary History of the United States* (3 vols., 1946), Vol. I, pp. 345–387; Vol. III, pp. 346–348, 492–501.

LEFFERTS A. LOETSCHER.

EMERTON, EPHRAIM: D. Mar. 3, 1935. He was Winn professor of ecclesiastical history at Harvard (1882–1918). His later books include: *Unitarian Thought* (1911); *Beginnings of Modern Europe* (1917); *The Defensor Pacis of Marsiglio of Padua* (1920); *Learning and Living* (1921); and *Humanism and Tyranny—Studies in the Italian Trecento* (1925). He also translated *Correspondence of Pope Gregory VII* (1931) and *Correspondence of St. Boniface* (1934).   [Sup.] RAYMOND W. ALBRIGHT.

EMIGRANTS AND IMMIGRANTS, MISSION WORK AMONG: The immigration of foreign peoples to the United States, although a perennial factor in American history, has fluctuated in character and intensity so as to modify the response of religious organizations to its challenge. The decline of foreign immigration since 1914—occasioned by restrictive immigration acts, notably those of 1917, 1921 (Quota Act), and 1924, by the economic depression (*q.v.*) of the 1930's, and by World War II—led to abandonment or radical modification of the "meet-at-port" methods in vogue earlier.

The old-line work of the thirty-one homes and agencies operating in New York City in 1909 was largely supplanted by "The General Committee of Immigrant Aid at Ellis Island and New York Harbor," comprised in 1950 of the following constituent societies: American Baptist Home Mission Society; American Federation of International Institutes; Board of Home Missions of the Congregational and Christian Churches; Board of American Missions of the United Lutheran Church in America; Danish Evangelical Lutheran Church of America; Division of Home Missions and Church Extension of the Methodist Church; Hebrew Sheltering and Immigrant Aid Society; Italian Welfare League; Metropolitan Lutheran Inner Mission Society; National Catholic Welfare Conference (*q.v.*); New York Bible Society; New York Protestant Episcopal City Mission Society; Salvation Army (Immigration Bureau); Lutheran Seaman's Center of the Augustana Evangelical Lutheran Church; Travelers Aid Society (Port Department); United Service for New Americans.

With the decline of immigration, religious organizations became increasingly aware of the necessity to meet the continuing needs of minority language groups in their new home. *The Preliminary Report of 1950 Census of Population* (Series PC-7, No. 1) places the total foreign-born white population in the United States at 10,147,000—a decline of 11.1% since the 1940 tabulation of 11,419,138. The "non-white" (Indians, Japanese, Chinese, etc., not including Negroes) population of 588,887 remained about the same in 1950.

The follow-up care of this varied group, of which the Chinese, Japanese (mainly in western concentrations), French, Italians, Cubans, Filipinos, etc. represent an inherited task, was assumed by the home mission boards of American denominations. The recent heavy influx of Spanish-speaking people, Mexicans in the south and southwest and Puerto Ricans in the east—the former admitted either as temporary laborers or for permanent residence and the latter as United States citizens rating as migrants rather than as immigrants—presents problems reminiscent of the situation before 1914.

The ministry to the first and second generation of minority groups is characterized, in its first stage, by the exclusive use of their native language, by the establishment of wholly dependent foreign congregations sometimes organized into conferences and associations. The adoption of American mores by the rising younger generation raises the problem of bilingual services and churches. The third stage in the Americanization (*q.v.*) process is reached when churches which may already have become self-supporting either continue their existence as English-speaking communities or unite with and become absorbed in American denominations. The work of most denominations among immigrant groups is carried on in some form of transition between these stages.

To meet the varied needs, mission stations were established at strategic points, some under the care of local or regional organizations, others under national denominational supervision. These agencies, variously known as Christian, Goodwill, or International Centers, etc., after the manner of neighborhood houses (*q.v.*), seek to provide for physical, social, educational, and religious needs by means of clubs, kindergartens, nurseries, clinics, libraries, church services, and visitation. Where necessary, specialized training is offered for missionaries and ministers serving particular language groups.

Whereas the Catholic Committee for Refugees (New York) handles only refugees, the Bureau of Immigration of the National Catholic Welfare Conference (*q.v.*) concerns itself for so-called "voluntary or non-refugee immigrants." The American St. Boniface Society (see BONIFATIUS-VEREIN, Vol. II), the Bavarian *Ludwig-Missionsverein*, the Austrian St. Leopold's *Missionsverein*, and the Catholic Kolping Societies are particularly concerned with the integration of German immigrants into the parish and church life in midwestern United States.

European Protestants have also continued their ministry to emigrants which began early in the nineteenth century; Hamburg and Bremen, especially, became ports of embarkation for emigrants from eastern and southern as well as central Europe, and there, except for the interruption caused by two world wars, missionaries provided a pastoral ministry and offered numerous practical services to emigrants and, later, to refugees (*q.v.*).

BIBLIOGRAPHY: Reports and literature published by boards of home or national missions, by Protestant, Catholic, and Jewish co-operative national organizations, and by service agencies. *Reports of Bureau of the Census*, U. S. Department of Commerce; publications of *Interpreter Releases*, Common Council for American Unity, New York; W. S. Bernard, *American Immigrant Policy*, 1950; *Evangelische Kirche und Auswanderung*, 1932.

[Sup.] CARL E. SCHNEIDER.

EMMIUS, UBBO (UBBE EMMEN): Historian; b. at Greetsiel in East Friesland on Dec. 5, 1547; d. Dec. 9, 1625, at Groningen. His father, Emme Dijken, was a Lutheran pastor. Of his youth little is known; in May, 1570, he matriculated at the University of Rostock and studied under David Chytaeus, dogmatician but also author of the well-known historical work, *Chronicon Saxoniae*. From 1575 to 1578 he traveled widely and studied at Geneva under Beza. In July, 1576, he was at Strassburg. He returned to East Friesland in 1578, and to the surprise of the Calvinist leader Menso Alting, he was appointed rector of the Latin school in the Lutheran town of Norden, where he had relatives. But in 1587 he was forced to leave because of his Calvinistic convictions. In 1588

he became rector at Leer. Refugees from the city of Groningen, which was under Spanish control till 1594, met him from time to time, with the result that in 1595 he was appointed rector of the Latin school in that thriving city. He reorganized the schools there and helped to found the University of Groningen in 1614, of which he was the first rector magnificus. He remained a professor there till his death in 1625, and was always consulted when new members of the faculty were appointed. He exerted great influence in the northern provinces of the Dutch Republic. His most important published work was *Historiarum Frisicarum decades* (1596–1615), of which Elzevier at Leiden in 1616 published a new edition under the title of *Rerum Frisicarum historia*. He presented highly useful criticisms of the original sources in the field of Frisian history. Much unpublished work of his remains in the University of Groningen and in government archives at Aurich in East Friesland.

BIBLIOGRAPHY: Gomarus, *Programma funebre Ubbonis Emmii*, 1625; H. Brugmans and F. Wachter, eds., *Briefwechsel des U. Emmius* Vol. I, 1911, Vol. II, 1923; J. J. Boer, *Ubbo Emmius en Oost-Friesland*, 1936; J. J. Boer and J. Lindeboom, "Redevoeringen over Emmius (1547–1947)," in *Jaarboek der Rijksuniversiteit te Groningen* (1948), 39–57.

D. NAUTA.

EMPIRICAL THEOLOGY: An empirical or pragmatic element has characterized Christian thought since the time of Christ (Acts 4:20). The Christian experience of salvation has affected its apparently most metaphysical affirmations, as in St. Athanasius' battle, on soteriological grounds, for the deity of Christ. In modern times the pioneer of empirical theology as such was Friedrich Schleiermacher (*q.v.*, Vol. X), who instead of beginning with general principles or "revealed truths" proposed to "elucidate the contents of the Christianly pious soul" (so H. R. Mackintosh, *Types of Modern Theology*, p. 61). Since then there have been many exponents of this point of view, beginning with the data of experience, proceeding chiefly by the inductive method and validating doctrine thereby. The examples below illustrate various forms of empiricism. Albrecht Ritschl while repudiating Schleiermacher's subjectivism, laid the foundations of his system empirically in the historic Jesus, and found religion's validity in the support it offers to empirically observed values. Ernst Troeltsch (*q.v.*) found Christianity not absolute, but best (for us) not because more true but only because more fitting. "*Varieties of Religious Experience*" by Wm. James (1902) is a classic of sympathetic case-studies, for the most part waiving ontological questions. F. R. Tennant's (*q.v.*) *Philosophical Theology* (1928–30) excluding specifically religious experience, builds strictly on sensory (and therefore universal) experience. D. C. Macintosh (*q.v.*) (*Theology an Empirical Science*, 1919; *The Reasonableness of Christianity*, 1926), a critical realist, builds on the (admittedly optimistic) standpoint that the "highest Christian ideals are practicable, progressively realizable, and the values thus produced will be ultimately conserved" (*Reasonableness*, p. 47).

The claims of empirical theology are summarized in the statement by Macintosh, that "genuine knowledge of a divine Reality has been gained through religious experience at its best"; also that "this knowledge may be formulated and further developed by means of inductive procedure" (*Theol. an Emp. Sci.*, p. ix). Empirical theology is a protest against theology exclusively based on or concerned with metaphysical assumptions; or on general "truths of reason"; or on the bare authority of church, religious literature, or individual. That theology is focally concerned with experience is widely admitted. Empirical theology insists that theological propositions contrary to observable fact must be rejected.

Some criticisms of empirical theology are beside the mark. It is not purely individualistic and subjective; it has always tended to stress the universal rather than the particular. It is not pure psychologism or positivism, though sometimes tending in that direction. Its constant question is always: to what objective reality do the observed data point?

The following summarizes the criticism of the weaknesses or dangers inherent in empirical theology. Empiricists may claim too much, as when H. N. Wieman (*q.v.*) claims that the evidence for God is of the same order and cogency as for any physical fact. Again, empirical theologies have by no means reached identical conclusions; pure and indisputable fact can never be the sole basis of construction. Further, empiricists themselves do not agree as to what can be called basic data. Are sense perceptions alone admissible (Tennant), or is religious experience a primary datum as well (Schleiermacher, Macintosh and most others)? Is faith founded on history (Ritschl) thereby empirical? Are not all historical events irrecoverable, in the strict sense, so that for succeeding generations even their existence is inferential? Even assuming that all religious experience were uniform, might not the inferences drawn therefrom be colored by the wishes or the training of the experient? Further, in the Christian religion, the most decisive elements go beyond direct experience and observation and are not susceptible of empirical demonstration. The "leap of faith" is essential. The theology of revelation and the theology of experience are not exclusive opposites; each needs the other. Trustworthy revelation is supported by experience; on the other hand the most poignant questions of man can-

not be answered from within but require answer from Beyond.

See also THEOLOGICAL SCIENCE, AMERICAN CONTRIBUTIONS TO.

KENNETH J. FOREMAN.

EMPIRICISM: The doctrine that knowledge comes by way of experience is known as empiricism. In the course of the development of philosophical theories concerning the basis of human knowledge there have been those thinkers who have emphasized the innate qualities of mind as basic (rationalism, intuitionism, *a priorism*) and those who have maintained that without the stimuli of the senses (i.e., experience) knowledge would be barren.

In modern philosophy it was John Locke (1632–1704) who initiated a subsequent and prolonged debate on the issue between empiricism and rationalism, taking the view that a child begins his course with a mental clean slate (*tabula rasa*) upon which experience records impressions. There is no innate knowledge but knowledge is acquired by contact. His view is known as *passive empiricism*. Bishop George Berkeley (1685–1753) followed Locke's thesis in his earlier writings and with piercing logic showed that the ideas which represent the world-out-there are altogether mental: to be is to be perceived (*esse est percipi*). With mind taking over the role of chief actor in the scene Berkeley moved from empiricism to rationalism. It was David Hume (1711–76) who became the real spokesman for a *radical empiricism* holding that ideas are grounded in sensations (impressions conspicuously so, ideas being feeble perceptions). If one is consistent with a real empiricism, so said Hume, one must resort in the testing of ideas to some sense-experience for their validity (*sensationalistic empiricism*). Thus mind itself has no validity since we cannot trace any sense-experience to which it may point. The most we can say is that "there are impressions and ideas." Thus, with Hume, empiricism ran into the ground of scepticism (*q.v.*): for how can there be knowledge without a mind?

The founder of the Scottish school of *common sense realism*, Thomas Reid (1710–96), argued for empiricism of common sense on the basis of man's inherent trust in the presentation of empirical data as well as in the empirical reality of a mind that entertains such data. Immanuel Kant (1724–1804), troubled by the issues, tied the two views together by his famous dictum: percepts without concepts are blind, concepts without percepts are empty. Both empiricism and rationalism are right in their assertions but wrong in their minimization of the role of the other.

Modern pragmatism has reasserted empiricism by disavowing the cross dualism of mind and its external world, affirming that mind is less a spectator and more an actor in a world in which the senses stimulate the organism to respond. In experience, says John Dewey (1859–1952), the world and the organism are together ideas the tools for action and the senses the stimuli. See INSTRUMENTALISM.

In theological thought empiricism emerges wherever personal religious experience is stressed as basic. Religious empiricism holds that religious ideas issue from experience. The commandments of God are the result of tested human experience. God is not a conclusion of an argument; God is a Factor which responds empirically to right attitudes. *Religious empiricism* stresses a witness theology rather than a speculative theology or the mere affirmation of creeds. Friedrich D. E. Schleiermacher (1768–1834) (*q.v.*, Vol. X) is sometimes referred to as the "father of modern religious empiricism" in theological thought.

See also CONVERSION; EPISTEMOLOGY; THEOLOGICAL SCIENCE, AMERICAN CONTRIBUTIONS TO.

VERGILIUS FERM.

EMSER, HIERONYMUS: B. March 28, 1478, at Weidenstetter near Ulm. His translation of the Bible was incorporated by Eck (*q.v.*) in his own Bible. It is worth noting in particular that for the Apocalypse the illustration of Cranach was used, with the result that Rome was depicted as the modern Babylon, even in a Catholic Bible. In 1530 the Brethren of the Common Life (*q.v.*) at Rostock published Emser's Bible in the Low German version. At the urgent request of Martin Luther (*q.v.*) this work was suppressed by the Archduke of Mecklenburg. The National Library in Stuttgart possesses apparently the only copy still extant.

BIBLIOGRAPHY: His letters were published by O. Clemen, Muenster, 1908; Emser, *De disputatione Lipsicensi, and A venenatione Lutheriana Aegocerotis assertio*, ed. F. Thurnhofer, 1921; F. Thurnhofer, *H. Emser und die Eidgenossen*, 1922; K. Schottenloher, *Bibl. der deutschen Geschichte im Zeitalter der Glaubensspaltung*, Vol I, 1933.

[Sup.] MATHIAS GOOSSENS.

ENCYCLICAL LETTERS: Letters addressed by the pope to the hierarchy. in communion with Rome throughout the world, or, less often, to the hierarchy of a particular country, on matters of common interest in the church. Like other pontifical documents, they are indexed by their opening words. The following list includes the encyclicals of the popes since Leo XIII, with the exception of those issued for the promotion of such devotions as the Rosary, for the proclamation of jubilees or other anniversaries, or with regard to matters of local concern.

Encyclicals of Leo XIII: *Inscrutabili Dei consilio*, 1878 (evils of society); *Quod apostolici muneris*, 1878 (socialism); *Aeterni Patris*, 1879 (doctrine of Aquinas); *Arcanum*, 1880 (Christian marriage); *Sancta Dei civitas*, 1880

(societies for the propagation of the faith); *Diuturnum*, 1881 (civil power); *Humanum genus*, 1884 (Freemasonry); *Immortale Dei*, 1885 (Christian constitution of states); *Libertas*, 1888 (human liberty); *Exeunte iam anno*, 1888 (Christian life); *Sapientiae christianae*, 1890 (duties of Christian citizens); *Catholicae ecclesiae*, 1890 (abolition of slavery); *Rerum novarum*, 1891 (condition of working men); *Providentissimus Deus*, 1893 (Holy Scripture); *Christi nomen*, 1894 (propagation of the faith); *Satis cognitum*, 1896 (unity of the Church); *Divinum illud munus*, 1897 (Holy Ghost); *Tametsi futura prospicientibus*, 1900 (Jesus Christ our Redeemer); *Graves de communi re*, 1901 (Christian democracy); *Mirae caritatis*, 1902 (Eucharist).

Encyclicals of Pius X: *E supremi*, 1903 (restoration of all things in Christ); *Acerbo nimis*, 1905 (catechetical instruction); *Pascendi*, 1907 (modernism).

Encyclicals of Benedict XV: *Ad beatissimi Apostolorum*, 1914 (for peace); *Humani generis redemptionem*, 1917 (preaching office); *Quod iam diu*, 1918 (prayers for peace); *Paterno iam diu*, 1919 (child war victims); *Pacem, Dei munus pulcherrimum*, 1920 (reconciliation of nations); *Spiritus Paraclitus*, 1920 (Holy Scripture); *Annus iam plenus*, 1920 (child war victims).

Encyclicals of Pius XI: *Ubi arcano Dei consilio*, 1922 (peace through reign of Christ); *Studiorum ducem*, 1923 (doctrine of Aquinas); *Quas primas*, 1925 (kingship of Christ); *Rerum ecclesiae*, 1926 (missions); *Mortalium animos*, 1928 (religious unity); *Rerum Orientalium*, 1928 (Eastern Churches); *Divini illius magistri*, 1929 (Christian education); *Casti connubii*, 1930 (Christian marriage); *Quadragesimo anno*, 1931, (social order); *Non abbiamo bisogno*, 1931 (Catholic action); *Nova impendet*, 1931 (economic crisis); *Ad catholici sacerdotii*, 1935 (Catholic priesthood); *Mit brennender Sorge*, 1937 (persecution of the Church in Nazi Germany); *Divini Redemptoris*, 1937 (atheistic communism).

Encyclicals of Pius XII: *Summi pontificatus*, 1939 (Christian idea of the state); *Divino afflante spiritu*, 1943 (biblical studies); *Humani generis*, 1950 (subversive doctrines); *Evangelii praecones*, 1950 (missions); *Ad caeli Reginam*, 1954 (queenship of Mary).

Some encyclicals are of particular interest to Americans, such as, under Leo XIII: *In plurimis*, 1888 (slavery in Brazil); *Quam aerumnosa*, 1888 (Italian immigrants); *Magni nobis*, 1889 (foundation of the Catholic University of America); *Quarto abeunte saeculo*, 1892 (fourth Columbus centenary); *Longinqua*, 1895 (Roman Catholicism in the U. S.); *Affari vos*, 1897 (Manitoba school question); *Quum diuturnum*, 1898 (plenary council in Latin America); *In amplissimo,* 1902 (Roman Catholicism in the U. S.). Under Pius X: *Lamentabili statu,* 1912 (condition of Indians in Latin America). Under Pius XI: *Vigilanti cura,* 1936 (motion pictures). See also the separate articles treating most of these encyclicals.

BIBLIOGRAPHY: Original texts in *Leonis XIII Pontificis Maximi Acta,* 1881–1905; *Pii X Pontificis Maximi Acta,* 1905–14; *Acta Apostolicae Sedis,* since 1909. There is no wholesale collection in English. Bibliographical information in M. Claudia Carlen, *A Guide to the Encyclicals of the Roman Pontiffs from Leo XIII to the present day, 1878–1937,* 1939, and *Guide to the Documents of Pius XII, 1939–1949,* 1951.

GEORGES A. BARROIS.

ENCYCLOPAEDIA OF ISLAM, THE: The publication of this incomparable work on the civilization of all Muslim lands began in 1908 at Leiden, Holland, under the patronage of the International Association of Academies. It was edited by Drs. M. Th. Houtsma and A. J. Wensinck and eight other Orientalists, with distinguished Islamic scholars as contributors. It appeared in English, French and German editions simultaneously. The articles had Arabic rubrics in European transliteration and alphabetical order, thus requiring some knowledge of Arabic for its efficient use. The four main and fifth supplementary volumes were completed in 1938.

An Arabic edition has been appearing in Cairo, faithfully translating the articles and adding new material. A Turkish edition revises and expands the material. In 1941 a single volume of author revisions of the theological and historical articles was published, in German only, at Leiden, under different auspices and called *Handwoerterbuch des Islam.* A new Encyclopaedia of Islam, with entirely new articles, has been started, again under international auspices, with Prof. H. A. R. Gibb, of Oxford, as editor.   EDWIN E. CALVERLEY.

ENELOW, HERMAN GERSON: Rabbi; b. in Russia on Oct. 26, 1877; d. Feb. 6, 1934. He studied at the University of Chicago (1894–95); Cincinnati (B.A., 1897); and Hebrew Union College (rabbi, 1898; D.D., 1900; D.H.L., 1925). He served as rabbi of Temple Israel, Paducah, Ky. (1898–1901); Temple Adath Israel, Louisville, Ky. (1901–12); and Temple Emanu-El, New York (1912–34). He was president of the Central Conference of American Rabbis (1927–29). His books include: *Aspects of the Bible* (1911); *The Effects of Religion* (1917); *The Varied Beauty of the Psalms* (1917); *The Faith of Israel* (1917); *The Allied Countries and the Jews* (1918); *A Jewish View of Jesus* (1920); *The Adequacy of Judaism* (1920); *The Jew and the World* (1921); *The Diverse Elements of Religion* (1924); and he also edited *Yahwism* (1903); *Origins of Synagogue and Church* (1929); and Al-Nakawa's *Menorat Ha-Maor* (1929–31).   RAYMOND W. ALBRIGHT.

ENGLAND AND WALES: Work of the Churches in England and Wales since 1910 was greatly affected by two world wars. These, added to the secular and sceptical spirit of the age, contributed to apparent decline in church influence with diminished congregations and lessened membership, a loss of young manhood after World War I, and material loss of church buildings in World War II. Statistics, however, show that a substantial minority of the population is still directly or indirectly associated with the churches, and there are indications of a returning tide of interest in religion. One mark of resilience in the churches is seen in their youth work. Both wars affected it, the second being particularly disruptive owing to evacuation. But after each, the churches set out to win the new generation—and in a measure succeeded. Sunday schools report increases, and there has been a notable development of church youth clubs and fellowships, a response partly to a Government Service of Youth Circular of 1942.

The whole period should be seen in the context of the Ecumenical Movement (*q.v.*) which, ever since the Edinburgh Missionary Conference of 1910, has steadily influenced thought and life in the churches in Britain. The World Alliance for Promoting International Friendship through the Churches (*q.v.*), creation of two English Christian laymen (Willoughby Dickinson and J. Allen Baker, Anglican and Quaker, respectively) in 1914, for a generation proved an instrument of Christian action for world peace. The 1924 Conference on Christian Politics, Economics and Citizenship (*q.v.*) revealed deepening social concern among the churches. British churches have been active supporters of both the Life and Work and Faith and Order Movements, and the momentous conferences of the two movements at Oxford and Edinburgh in 1937 foreshadowed the establishment of the British Council of Churches (*q.v.*) in 1942 and the World Council of Churches (*q.v.*) in 1948.

The Church of England (*q.v.*) was led in this period by a trio of great ecclesiastical statesmen, Archbishops Davidson, Lang, and William Temple (*q.v.*), and their successor, Archbishop Fisher, carries on the tradition. Three Lambeth Conferences (*q.v.*) within the period (1920, 1930, and 1948) revealed a deepening sense within the Anglican Communion of being a world-wide community. An outstanding issue in each conference was church reunion. The particular interest of the Church of England, looking both East and West, declaring itself both Catholic and Protestant, and confronting strong Free Churches in England and Wales, was apparent throughout. The 1920 Conference led to an era of friendlier co-operation with the Free Churches, and in the famous Quadrilateral (q.v.)—Scriptures, Creed, Sacraments, and Ministry—laid down the basis of any possible reunion. The 1930 Conference did not make any substantial advance, while that of 1948, with the newly united Church of South India before it, made clear its attitude to further approaches to reunion. It is perhaps fair to say that there has been some hardening of the position, due to clarification of the issues, especially in insistence on episcopacy (q.v.) as an essential, and to inner tensions within the Church of England itself.

In the two decades prior to 1910 the Free Churches in England and Wales drew closer together by the creation, in 1896, of the National Free Church Council. Co-operation was not easy by reason of divergent traditions, history, and theological outlook. Independency and Presbyterian church government, Calvinistic and Arminian theologies, and conflicting views on baptism were substantial barriers. The National Free Church Council had no strictly denominational character or authority, being comprised of personal members and representatives of local Free Church Councils, constituted by free decision of local congregations. Nevertheless, its annual meetings constituted a platform for exchange and expression of Free Church opinion on matters of common interest in church and state. In 1919 a more authoritative body, the Federal Council of Evangelical Free Churches, was set up, to draw the denominations as such into closer official relations, and to assist the movement toward closer union. This Council was authorized by the constituent churches to take charge of conversations with the Church of England, following the Lambeth Conference of 1920. A further obvious step was taken in 1940 in the fusion of the Federal Council of Evangelical Free Churches with the National Free Church Council to constitute the existing Free Church Federal Council (q.v.).

A noteworthy ecclesiastical event occurred in 1932 in the union of the three major branches of Methodism in Great Britain—the Wesleyan, Primitive, and United Methodist Churches—to form the Methodist Church of Great Britain. The event was not only significant as healing the divisions of Methodism, but because it made the new Methodist Church the strongest single Free Church in the country. Other efforts looking toward union have followed, notably conversations between the Congregational Union of England and Wales and the Presbyterian Church of England. These, however, produced no tangible result except an increase of good will and the decision to co-operate in all possible ways. A tentative proposal for a United Free Church found little acceptance.

In a larger field, conversations continued between representative groups of Anglicans and Free Churchmen, convened by the Archbishop of Canterbury on the basis of a sermon at Cambridge in November, 1946, and on invitations addressed by him to the Free Churches and to groups within his own communion. The chief point of his enquiry was to elicit how far the Free Churches could include the principle of episcopacy into their ecclesiastical structure.

Church Statistics, 1951:

	Members	Ministers	Sunday School Pupils
Church of England (on Electoral Rolls)	2,989,702	12,000 (approx.)	1,420,106
Baptists (England & Wales)	357,741	1,953	323,111
Congregationalists (England & Wales)	350,369	2,417	277,216
Methodist Church of Great Britain (including 8,479 Probationer Members)	753,294	4,658	799,873
Presbyterian Church of England	69,676	291	33,699

The Roman Catholic "population" is estimated at 2,808,596.

BIBLIOGRAPHY: C. A. Alington, Christianity in England, 1942; E. A. Payne, Free Church Tradition in the Life of England, 1944; H. Townsend, Claims of the Free Churches, 1949; D. Mathew, Catholicism in England, 1937; M. B. Reckitt, Maurice to Temple: A Century of the Social Movement in the Church of England, 1947; S. C. Carpenter, Church and People, 1789–1889, 1933; W. K. Jordan, The Development of Religious Toleration in England, 4 vols., 1932–40; D. W. Brogan, The English People, 1943.

EVELYN CLIFFORD URWIN

ENGLAND, CHURCH OF (SEVENTH AND EIGHTH CENTURIES): The Synod of Whitby (664) must be looked upon as one of the great turning points in the history of the Church of England. It meant the parting of the ways as regards the forsaking of old Celtic customs and observances, which many people accepted with regret. But far more important was the fact that by the decisions taken at that conference, England was no longer "one remote corner of the most remote island," but henceforth was brought into the main stream of Western Christendom. An almost immediate and significant event was the pope's appointment of a Greek monk, Theodore of Tarsus as archbishop of Canterbury in 669. Together with his African friend Hadrian, who became abbot of St. Peter's at Canterbury, Theodore carried a complete reorganization of the church. Having first made a thorough visitation of the whole island, he increased the number of existing dioceses as he saw fit, he summoned the councils of Hertford (672) and Hatfield (679), and drew up a reasonably framed Penitential. By no means the least important of the labors of these two men was the establishment of a school at Canterbury, that became renowned for its learning, and produced scholars like Aldhelm, Bishop of Sherborne, noted on account of his florid and affected style, and later, through its influence spreading to other monasteries, the great missionary St. Boniface. Thus was the English Church enabled to make its magnificent contribution to Europe of the eighth century, and instead of being, as it had been in the preceding century, the recipient of religious and cultural influences, it became itself the donor. Indeed, for a brief period after the rise of Northumbria, England had a remarkable place in the world of art and letters.

Here we see the unusual instance of a people who, having received the Roman mission only a century before, undertook the task of carrying the gospel overseas, with Wilfrid founding, and his pupil Willibrord (q.v.) building up, the church in Frisia; and Boniface (q.v.) of Devon leading the mission to Germany, and later supervising the reform of the Frankish Church. From the libraries which Benedict Biscop had founded at Wearmouth and Jarrow, the Anglo-Saxon missionaries took books over to the Continent, and once there, they were constantly writing to England for further copies to assist them in their labors. Later Alcuin (q.v.), at the court of Charlemagne (q.v.), asked permission to borrow works from his library at home, and even Rome sought help from England in this connection.

The arrival of Theodore and Hadrian witnessed a new era in the history of Anglo-Saxon art (q.v.) and architecture. Survivals of this remain in the precious illuminated manuscripts, like the Lindisfarne Gospels, and in a number of churches, the most imposing of them being that of Brixworth in Northamptonshire, perhaps the work of the monks of Peterborough (ca. 670). The finely decorated crosses of Bewcastle and Ruthwell, both of which probably date from the late seventh or early eighth century, are but two examples of a series of stone memorials which are peculiar to this country alone. The latter cross bears upon its shaft several lines of that beautiful sample of Anglo-Saxon religious poetry, the "Dream of the Rood." Finally, modern scholarship has emphasized, even more than formerly, the vast and unrivalled learning of the Venerable Bede (q.v.), and the debt owed to him for his "Ecclesiastical History." No longer then, is it true to speak of "here and there a solitary form" standing out in the Church of England of the seventh and eighth centuries.

BIBLIOGRAPHY: S. J. Crawford, Anglo-Saxon Influences on Western Christendom 600–800, 1933; W. Levison, England and the Continent in the Eighth Century, 1946; F. M. Stenton, Anglo-Saxon England (1947), pp. 123–199; R. H. Hodgkin, A History of the Anglo-Saxons, Vol. I (1935), pp. 294–366; M. L. W. Laistner, Thought and Letters in Western Europe, A.D. 500–900 (1931), pp. 104–146; A. W. Clapham, English Romanesque Architecture before the Conquest, 1930; H. St. L. B. Moss, The Birth of the Middle Ages (1935), pp. 175–182, 209–210, 236.
[Sup.] GORDON HUELIN.

ENGLAND, CHURCH OF (TWENTIETH CENTURY): From 1903 to 1928 the wise diplomacy of Archbishop Randall Davidson led the Church of England through a series of critical situations, beginning with the integration of church elementary schools into the national school system under the Education Act of 1902. Davidson successfully resisted demands for sweeping condemnations of Modernists (q.v.) and also of "Ritualists"; and the church succeeding in reaffirming its historic faith without discouraging the intellectual efforts of individuals, and the proceedings of the Commission on Ecclesiastical Discipline (1904–6) led to the beginning of revision of the antiquated law of worship. From World War I came the Life and Liberty Movement, expressing a demand among army chaplains and younger leaders at home for greater freedom to allow the church to meet modern needs. The main result was the establishment in 1919 of the Church Assembly, composed of the Convocations and House of Laity, authorized to propose church legislation on which Parliament retained only a right of veto. The climax of Davidson's career was the Lambeth Conference (q.v.) of 1920, organized around the theme of "Fellowship," at which, by its "Appeal to All Christian People," the Anglican Communion took its place in the Ecumenical Movement (q.v.). In the 1920's a progressive orthodoxy came to the fore in the writings of Liberal Evangelicals (see EVANGELICALISM, ANGLICAN) and Liberal Anglo-Catholics (see ANGLO-CATHOLICISM), which offered hope of better understanding within the Church (see ESSAYS CATHOLIC AND CRITICAL). But the Prayer Book revision (see COMMON PRAYER, BOOK OF), though containing many generally acceptable features, developed on compromise lines at critical points (such as the Prayer of Consecration and the provisions for regulating Reservation of the Blessed Sacrament for the sick) which offended both Catholic and Protestant sentiments. Its rejection by the House of Commons in 1927–28 was carried by non-English votes, but was not unwelcome to many English churchmen. Subsequently the English episcopate affirmed the inherent right of the Church to establish its own standards of faith and worship, thus underlining the growing distinction, though not separation, of church and state.

William Temple (q.v.), philosopher, reformer, statesman, and pastor, was archbishop of York under Davidson's successor, Cosmo Gordon Lang (1928–42), and of Canterbury (1942–44). In either position he was the leading figure in Anglicanism; before his death, in non-Roman Christendom generally. His interest in church unity and social reform found signal expression in his leadership in the ecumenical conferences of 1937, his position as president of the World Council of Churches (q.v.) from 1938, his personal organization of the Malvern (q.v.) Conference (1941), and his intellectual distinction shone in his own writing and in the report on *Doctrine in the Church of England* (1938) prepared under his chairmanship. In theology a swing from mere liberalism made many Anglicans sympathetic to revivals of orthodox thought (neo-Protestant and neo-scholastic), and disposed to stress increasingly the biblical and liturgical roots of theology. Many new church societies and religious communities (see COMMUNITIES AND ORDERS, PROTESTANT) have taken a large part in Anglican life, and three monastic theologians have made outstanding contributions—Hebert of Kelham, Thornton of Mirfield, and Gregory Dix of Nashdom.

World War II called attention to the need of the world for the gospel, and to the relative weakness of religion in a professedly Christian nation, throwing the problems of the previous generation into better perspective. The report *Towards the Conversion of England* (1945), though somewhat superficial, is an important sign of interest. Meanwhile the Education Act of 1944 sounded the doom of many small church schools, but offered the prospect of worship and religious instruction (on the basis of "Agreed Syllabi") in all schools, an opportunity which the Church of England generally accepted, and in which Anglicans and Nonconformists have been able to co-operate. Under Geoffrey Fisher (q.v.), archbishop of Canterbury since 1945, the church met serious problems with sober confidence. The decline of ancient endowments threw it more on voluntary support, and candidates for the ministry were more systematically selected. A revision of canon law was under consideration, and the further development of relations with the state under discussion. As president of the British Council of Churches (q.v.), as a copresident of the World Council, and as a frequent visitor to other Anglican Churches, the archbishop advanced the broader contacts of the Church of England. A question still unsettled was that of relations with former Anglicans in the South India United Church, a Church of whose principles Anglicans cannot wholly approve.

BIBLIOGRAPHY: Cyril Garbett, *The Claims of the Church of England*, 1947; Roger Lloyd, *The Church of England in the Twentieth Century*, 2 vols., 1946–50; also biographies of men referred to, and of Charles Gore and Herbert Hensley Henson; for current affairs see *Official Year Book of the Church of England* (annual), periodicals such as *Theology* (monthly), and *Church Times* (weekly).

[Sup.] EDWARD ROCHIE HARDY.

ENGLISH LECTURER: Under an arrangement inaugurated by Dean W. P. Ladd in 1918, each year a distinguished English clergyman joins the teaching staff of Berkeley Divinity School, New Haven, Conn., for a term, and in addition to his courses at Berkeley is available for sermons, lectures, and conferences elsewhere; among notable English lecturers have been Percy Dearmer, G. A. Studdert-Kennedy, C. E. Hudson, C. F. Rogers, V. A. Demant, and A. G. Hebert.   EDWARD ROCHIE HARDY.

ENGLISH LECTURESHIP, THE JOHN M.: Established at Andover Newton Theological School by the alumni in honor of John Mahan English, professor from 1882 to 1927. The purpose is to strengthen interest in homiletics by bringing to the school eminent preachers and successful ministers. The lecturers on the foundation are expected, in addition to their public addresses, to be available for consultation with the students.   HERBERT GEZORK.

ENGNELL, KARL IVAN ALEXANDER: B. in Linkoeping, Sweden, Dec. 12, 1906. He was educated at Uppsala (Cand.Th., 1934; Lic.-Th., 1940; Th.D., 1943). He became instructor in Old Testament exegesis at Uppsala (1943); professor (1947). Among his works are: *Studies in Divine Kingship in the Ancient Near East* (1943); *Gamla Testamentet I* (1945); *The Call of Isaiah* (1949). He was editor and contributor to *Svenskt Bibliskt Uppslagsverk I-II* (1948–52).   ELMER E. FLACK.

ENLIGHTENMENT, THE, IN AMERICA: The development of urban life and the growth of commerce provided fertile soil for the spread of Enlightenment ideas in eighteenth century America. In the religious tradition were elements favorable to an emphasis on reason and humanity, evident in the drift toward Unitarianism in New England Congregationalism and the spread of latitudinarianism in Southern Anglicanism. The works of British and French rationalist and deist leaders such as Tillotson, Locke, Voltaire, Volney, and Paine became well known. Political, social, and economic theory was profoundly influenced by the idea of progress and like Enlightenment influences. The natural rights philosophy, forged earlier in Puritan circles, was further popularized and applied to the struggle with England. Many American Revolutionary leaders and framers of the Constitution were men of the Enlightenment, which had its greatest vogue in the last quarter of the century. At the close of the century came a conservative reaction, stimulated by aversion to the horrors of the French Revolution, the rise of currents of romanticism, and the crusades of the churches against militant deism as "French infidelity."

BIBLIOGRAPHY: Herbert M. Morais, *Deism in Eighteenth Century America*, 1932; Merle Curti, *The Growth of American Thought*, 1943.

[Sup.] ROBERT T. HANDY.

ENOCH. See PATRIARCHS, OLD TESTAMENT.

ENSLIN, MORTON SCOTT: Baptist; b. at Somerville, Mass., March 8, 1897. Following graduation from Harvard College and Newton Theological Institution he returned to Harvard for a doctorate in theology. In 1924 he became professor of New Testament at Crozer Theological Seminary. While at Crozer he has also been lecturer in patristics in the Graduate School of the University of Pennsylvania. In 1941 he became editor of *Crozer Quarterly*. In addition to many articles in professional and ecclesiastical journals he has written: *The Ethics of Paul* (1930); (with K. Lake), *Six Collations of New Testament Manuscripts* (1933); *Christian Beginnings* (1938); translated *God, the Eternal Torment of Man* (from the French of Marc Boegner, 1931).

EPHESIANS, EPISTLE TO THE. See PAUL THE APOSTLE.

EPHOD: Two recent developments in the study of the ephod require special mention: (1) At Ras Shamra on the Syrian coast there has been excavated a Ugaritic hymn (*ca.* 1400 B.C.) in which references is made to an ephod, probably a garment of the goddess Anath (cf. *Syria* XV [1934], 305 ff.). Whether this corresponds to the Hebrew priestly garment, or whether indeed the word is correctly translated by ephod, is a matter for further study. (2) H. G. May connects the Old Testament ephod with the sacred ark as a species of miniature temple. Similarly, J. Morgenstern likens it to the tentlike shrine brought into battle on camel back by certain Arabian tribes. The prevailing view, however, is that the ephod was a garment of some kind. At the same time the possibility must be held open that in certain cases it was an image or the metal coating of an image.

BIBLIOGRAPHY: W. F. Albright, in *BASOR*, 83 (1941), 39 ff.; M. Burrows, *What Mean These Stones?* (1941), p. 216; H. G. May, "Ephod and Ariel," *AJSL* (1939), 44–69; J. Morgenstern, *The Ark, the Ephod, and the Tent of Meeting*, 1945; H. Thiersch, *Ependytes und Ephod*, 1936.
[Sup.] GEORGE DAHL.

EPISCOPACY: During the later nineteenth century the conclusion of research was that monarchical episcopacy did not become the standard pattern of church government till about the end of the second century. Investigation has continued during the present century, and it has substantially confirmed the above position.

This conclusion has been challenged only by certain High Church Episcopalians who have sought to prove that episcopacy is the sole authentic form of church government sanctioned by the New Testament. The most ambitious attempt in recent years to establish this position is found in a volume edited by K. E. Kirk, bishop of Oxford. The argument of this book is that in the New Testament a clear distinction

is made between the essential ministry and the dependent ministry. The former is represented by the apostles, New Testament counterpart of the Old Testament *shaliach,* and as such the divinely-commissioned church leaders. The second century bishop exercised functions identical with those of the first century apostle, whose spiritual successor he therefore must have been. So, as Kirk puts it, "episcopacy . . . alone can permanently carry on in the church the essential ministry derived from the apostles of our Lord" (p. 14). It follows, of course, that however worthy and edifying non-episcopal ministries may be, they cannot be regarded as valid.

This point of view has not found widespread acceptance. Its advocates have been accused of "special pleading" in their handling of the evidence, particularly in their interpretation of the (to them) pivotal conception of *shaliach.* The overwhelming bulk of the evidence (so the objectors contend) shows that *shaliach* was simply a legal representative or proxy. "In the mission and commission of the apostles the emphasis is on the function of the disciples as eye-witnesses of the Resurrection and not on the persons of the Apostles. The whole New Testament doctrine of *shaliach* is one in which the person of the *shaliach* retreats into the background, so that the living person of the risen Christ comes to the fore" (Torrance, p. 193). The evidence seems to prove that the most that may reasonably be claimed for episcopacy is that it is of the *bene esse* (well-being) of the church, but not of its *esse* (being).

BIBLIOGRAPHY: Kenneth E. Kirk, ed., *The Apostolic Ministry*, 1946; T. F. Torrance, in *Scottish Journal of Theology*, I, 2, Sep., 1948; Arthur C. Headlam, *The Doctrine of the Church and Reunion*, 1920; Thomas W. Manson, *The Church's Ministry*, 1948; A. E. J. Rawlinson, *Problems of Reunion*, 1950.
[Sup.] NORMAN VICTOR HOPE.

EPISCOPALIANS. See PROTESTANT EPISCOPALIANS.

EPISCOPALIANS, REFORMED. See REFORMED EPISCOPALIANS.

EPISTEMOLOGY: This term is from the Greek, *episteme,* meaning "knowledge." What is the source of human knowledge? What are its limitations? How do we come by our knowledge of the external world, of ourselves, of others? How can we trust our ideas as valid?

Philosophers have long wrestled with such questions. Among the ancients, in Western thought, Socrates is famous for his long quest of their solution and Plato, his disciple, carried the problems raised by them forward. The question of human knowledge was basic with him as it is with anyone who thinks critically upon himself and his world. Plato made famous his discussion of the degrees of knowledge —from mere opinion to that of intuitive insight.

At the beginning of the modern period of Western thought epistemological questions came to the front in debates, with John Locke (1632–1704), Bishop George Berkeley (1685–1753) and David Hume (1711–76) building their theories of the source of knowledge on the basis of empiricism (q.v.), while René Descartes (1596–1650), Benedict Spinoza (1632–77) and Gottfried Wilhelm Leibniz (1646–1716) emphasized rationalism. The issue was: Are our ideas basically grounded in experiences which are garnered as we grow and develop or are our ideas very much dependent upon the innate structure of the mind itself? Empiricism stressed the former; rationalism the latter. Immanuel Kant (1724–1804) held both to be true but true only of the world which appears to us (phenomenalism, q.v.), not the world as it is in itself (noumenalism). Pragmatists believed the issues raised by their philosophical predecessors to be false in that both schools (empiricism and rationalism) rested upon an outdated concept of both mind and the world. Mind is not something apart from the world, nor the world apart from mind. We who think are nature which thinks. We are not apart from nature. Nature itself, wherever there is an appropriate organism, is operating at the mental level: having right ideas when such work, having wrong ideas when there is failure to meet situations. The whole problem of epistemology is thus reorientated by the pragmatist whose world is not two (mental and material) but one, that is, both.

Many terms have come into philosophical coinage by the debates on the issues. Such terms point to positions maintained. The following constitute some of the major terms in epistemology.

Epistemological realism affirms that the object is independent of the perceiving subject or mind. *Epistemological monism* (*presentative realism*) affirms that the object is immediately perceived by the perceiving subject, i.e., presented, without the help of any intervening entities. *Epistemological dualism* affirms that the object and the subject are two separate entities in the knowledge relation. *Subjectivism* (*subjective* or *epistemological idealism,* see IDEALISM) affirms that the object exists only for a subject, that its existence depends upon the perceiving subject. *Representative realism* affirms that ideas are representatives or copies of the external object. *Naive* (or *uncritical common sense*) *realism* affirms that a non-mental world exists apart from mind and that the mind is able to grasp it. *Critical realism* holds that there is an independent world which the mind may grasp and tries to show how this is possible (hence, critical).

There are two forms of *critical realism:* the school known as the *critical realists* and that of the *new realists.* The latter school was a protest movement against modern idealists who had emphasized the role of mind and the philosophy of spirit as the most fundamental characteristic of the world. The new realists took nature as the fundamental term and mind as a part of that nature. There is thus no hard and fast dualism between mind and the external object. Some form of epistemological monism was asserted: no ideas, images or representations are needed to stand between the object and the perceiving subject. The external world is literally given to the knowing mind, a direct awareness, presentation, awareness, a compresence, a disclosure. The *English school* of new realists (e.g., G. F. Stout, G. E. Moore, Bertrand Russell, S. Alexander, and others) asserted that consciousness is a transparent relation in a world including both mind and matter. The *American school* of new realists (e.g., F. J. E. Woodbridge, E. B. Holt, W. P. Montague, R. B. Perry, and others) asserted that the conscious mind is only that part of nature which responds with awareness. Both groups sought to overcome the dualism between mind and matter and thus make for the possibility of critically affirming real knowledge.

The critical realists (D. Drake, A. Lovejoy, J. B. Pratt, A. K. Rogers, G. Santayana, R. W. Sellars, C. A. Strong) thought that the new realists were affirming too much, that such epistemological monism did not account for error, for illusions and for hallucinations and therefore reasserted dualism. Mind has a more definite role to play in the knowledge relation. The position maintained was to the effect that the object is presented to the subject but through media, *i.e.,* not directly. Between the mind and the object is a medium through which knowledge is conveyed. This medium is itself not an object but a means of communication with the external world. Some critical realists (Santayana) thought this medium to be essences which refer to existence. Sellars held that such essences were unnecessary to explain the knowledge relation; rather, the mind, he said, becomes one epistemologically with its object although the two are existentially separate, for mind has the capacity to transcend itself into this unity of relationship. Against both schools was the position known as *critical monism* which was the view held by the late D. C. Macintosh. He argued that the object directly presents to the percipient subject its primary qualities (breadth, length, weight, number, etc.) but that the secondary qualities (color, taste, sound, etc.) are furnished by the subject. Unless, he said, we affirm some form of acknowledged epistemological monism we are never free from the charge of agnosticism inherent in any form of dualism.

Other terms in the epistemological field occur in philosophical literature. Kant's *phenomenalism* asserted that objects impinge upon sensations and the mind responds with its a priori categories projecting them as the world of appearance. The noumenal world (the real world apart from the categories) is never known (according to Kant). *Pragmatic realism* is the view held by the late John Dewey who asserted that any epistemological view must rest upon the assertion that there is a world to which the mind must make adjustment, the mind being a part of that world. A reconstruction of the traditional view of mind over against matter must be effected. Reality is a stern and practical thing. Mind is a tool of the organism to guide action (*instrumentalism*). From this premise all epistemological views must take their stand. It is futile to speculate further since such speculation vitiates the world as it is. The world is real (*realism*) and so is the mind. The whole picture of biological evolution is that of an interplay of these two facets of nature. Pragmatism emphasizes action with guiding results of adjustment. Pragmatism means work and getting on with the business of life-situations. Among other things, pragmatism was a reaction against a pan-objective idealism in which view the world was taken to be Idea and subjectivism was circumvented by the view that one's ideas can be trusted essentially because they are a part of a universal Idea (*objective idealism*).

Bound up with the question of knowledge is the question of truth. How does one know that one's knowledge, however acquired, is the truth? Two issues are involved in this query. The one relates to the *criteria* of truth and the other to its *nature*. The two queries are separate although interrelated. There are those criteria of truth which may be called the non-philosophical and those which are philosophical. Those who measure the yardstick of truth non-philosophically appeal to intuition, to a peculiar feeling for truth, to majority opinion (*consensus gentium*), to axioms, to authority, or to the a priori nature of reason. The chief difficulty encountered with any such criteria is the dogmatism of mere assertion or unverifiability since to appeal to reason (philosophy) would be inconsistent. An authoritarian, for example, holds up some name as guarantor of truth and thus reason cannot be a court of appeal—without appeal to reason (inconsistency). Among the philosophical criteria there are three: coherence, correspondence and pragmatism. According to the coherence view that is truth which harmonizes with a large body of ideas in an inner consistency. According to the correspondence view that is true which corresponds with what is presented. An idea is true if it matches what is given. The

pragmatic theory holds that truth is a judgment which in the long run satisfies or justifies itself by its workability. Most philosophers grant virtues in all three such criteria, one school giving emphasis to one or the other. The nature of truth presents the question of its independent existence, its place in the philosophy of reality. A pragmatist on this question may assert his disinterestedness in the problem of what truth is apart from any verification in function or he may say that there is no truth as such except as a statistical average of behavior or known data. Those who assert coherence generally are of the philosophical school of idealism, holding that the universe being spirit is a self-consistent whole which is the absolute and synoptic truth independent of anyone's judgment of it. Those who emphasize the correspondence theory are realists in the sense that there is an existential nature to which ideas must submit as a negative receives the imprint of light and shadows. All these theories have their difficulties taken apart from each other.

When philosophers discuss the origin of knowledge they divide into camps of *rationalists, intuitionists* (see INTUITIONISM), *empiricists,* and *pragmatists.* A rationalist emphasizes the role of reason in knowledge and minimizes the role of sense-perception. The empiricist holds experience to be basic. If the sensations are taken to be the origin of knowledge then we have the view known as *sensationalistic empiricism* (David Hume). An intuitionist looks to immediate awareness as the source of basic knowledge, a source which is non-rational and non-empirical. Life, according to Henri Bergson (1859–1941), can only be intuited, never rationalized in itself. A pragmatist reorientates the whole question in terms of nature and mind adjusting itself to situations resolving difficulties. Beyond that, the pragmatist recognizes no further fruitful issue of truth.

See also PHILOSOPHY; PSYCHOLOGISM.

BIBLIOGRAPHY: For an introductory survey of the various views and exponents of the epistemological positions see Vergilius Ferm, *First Adventures in Philosophy* (1936), Chaps. XX–XXII. For a detailed exposition see W. P. Montague, *The Ways of Knowing,* 1925; D. C. Macintosh, *The Problem of Knowledge,* 1915, and *The Problem of Religious Knowledge,* 1940. See also "Recent Epistemological Schools" by Ledger Wood in *A History of Philosophical Systems,* ed. by Vergilius Ferm, 1950.
VERGILIUS FERM.

EPISTLES. See HEBREWS, EPISTLE TO THE; JAMES, EPISTLE OF; JOHANNINE EPISTLES; JUDE, EPISTLE OF; PAUL THE APOSTLE; PETER THE APOSTLE.

EPISTLES OF JOHN. See JOHANNINE EPISTLES.

EPISTLES OF PAUL. See PAUL THE APOSTLE.

EPISTLES OF PAUL AND SENECA: See APOCRYPHA.

EPISTLES OF PETER. See PETER THE APOSTLE.

EPISTOLA APOSTOLORUM. See APOCRYPHA.

EPISTOLAE OBSCURORUM VIRORUM: Nearly all the letters were fictitiously addressed to "Ortwin Gratius of Deventer." This fact is seldom noted by experts in the history of the Northern Renaissance and the Reformation. Gratius is almost always referred to as a professor at the University of Cologne, which he was, but the name applied to him by a number of anonymous German humanists requires explanation. In following the Latin and English versions presented by F. G. Stokes in 1925, we may observe that in the title of Part II, No. LXIII, Gratius is said to be teaching Greek and Latin at Deventer, and in No. XXXII the writer reminds him of their companionship at Deventer, where Gratius used to write proverbs on a wall. The writer of No. V said that he used to live with Gratius at Deventer, and he who composed No. XL in Part I claimed that two years before he had parted company with Gratius at Zwolle. It is obvious that these writers had known Gratius in Deventer, and for this reason the title of the whole work calls him Gratius of Deventer. The fact that Zwolle is also mentioned is significant, for Deventer and Zwolle were the two chief centers of the Devotio Moderna in the Netherlands, and at the end of the fifteenth century the two schools in these towns attracted thousands of promising young scholars. It was no coincidence that Erasmus also went there with his mother.

Stokes in his illuminating introduction has shown how important the Brethren of the Common Life at Deventer were. These pious men caused a tremendous demand for reformation and enlightenment, which is reflected in the book under review here. The letters must be studied in the light of recent discoveries in western Germany and the Netherlands. Gratius was selected as a target in the letters, because he was so well known to the young humanists of northern Germany. They contain numerous references to Jacob van Hoogstraten and Arnold van Tongeren, two scholars from the region known as Belgium. Nearly all the letters state that Gratius was the teacher of the writers, and this was probably true. For example, one humanist says: "It behoves you to eat hard-boiled eggs and roasted chestnuts, and cooked beans sprinkled with poppy-seed, as is the custom in your country of Westphalia." That was truthfully said, for Gratius was brought up in Westphalia. It was in Muenster, the capital of West-phalia, that the Brethren of the Common Life had their most important house in Germany and did the most for the revival of classical learning.

In the second letter of Part II we read that the writer had learned much from Gratius at Cologne and Deventer, notably a poem criticizing Reuchlin. Now he was sending Gratius a poem of his own, very amusing to read, ridiculing the highest authorities in the papal curia as well as in the University of Cologne. The three men who always attract attention are Van Hoogstraten, Reuchlin, and Van Tongern. Pfefferkorn gets his share also, for he indirectly caused the great scandal in Germany and the notorious lawsuit in Rome. The problem was: What shall be done about Hebrew literature outside of the Old Testament? And what were the church leaders going to say about classical Greek and Latin? Should humanism prevail, or should the "barbarians" in the universities and the monasteries have their way? Erasmus had introduced the subject to some extent in his brilliant work, *Book Against the Barbarians*. But Reuchlin was the scholar who had emphasized the need of studying ancient Hebrew literature. Soon it was discovered, however, that the Hebrew writings did not contain much material that could be compared with the works of the Greeks and the Romans. For this reason the controversy between Reuchlin and Pfefferkorn soon lost its attraction, and the epistles in question did not retain their value as popular literature. If they had first appeared some ten or twenty years later than the year in which Luther issued his Ninety-five Theses, they would have had little historical value.

BIBLIOGRAPHY: Francis G. Stokes, *Epistolae Obscurorum Virorum: The Latin Text with an English rendering, and an Historical Introduction*, 1925.

[Sup.] ALBERT HYMA.

EPWORTH LEAGUE. See YOUNG PEOPLE'S SOCIETIES.

EQUAL RIGHTS AMENDMENT. See WOMAN, EMANCIPATION OF.

ERASMUS: I. Early Life: He was probably born in the year 1469, on Oct. 27. His father was a priest and his mother the priest's housekeeper. They were living in the town of Gouda, not far from Rotterdam, which is probably the birthplace of Erasmus, since the parents of his mother lived there. He attended the local school at Gouda, where Peter Winkel was his teacher. In the year 1475 his mother took him to Deventer, where he studied with some teachers belonging to the Brethren of the Common Life. In 1483 he was still there when he met Alexander Hegius, the new principal of the school attached to St. Lebwin's Church. He also met Rudolph Agricola, who was to him a great source of inspiration. From 1483 to 1486 he lived in a dormitory belonging to the Brethren of the Common Life at 's-Hertogenbosch, whose school in that town he also attended. For about ten years he was powerfully affected by the religious and pedagogical principles of the Devotio Moderna. In 1486 he was induced by his guardians to enter a monastery named Steyn, near Gouda, where he remained until 1492 or 1493. He was ordained a priest just before he entered the service of Henry of Bergen, Bishop of Cambray. After about one year of secretarial labor he became a student of theology in the University of Paris, remaining an Augustinian monk but free to travel abroad and study.

II. Humanistic Compositions: In the rionastery he composed several Latin poems, besides the original draft of his admirable treatise, *Book Against the Barbarians*. In this work he attacked the so-called barbarians, in imitation of Lorenzo Valla, the Italian humanist whom he always greatly admired. The men who seemed to be too reactionary in his opinion were those who taught scholastic philosophy, frowned upon the production of amorous poetry, failed to write classical Latin, and refused to reform methods of teaching and textbooks then in use. This book exerted considerable influence on Thomas More, whose *Utopia* shows evidence of this. Contrary to the opinion of many European scholars, Erasmus was little affected by his first trip to England, where he spent only six months (1499–1500), and did not learn to despise scholasticism, monasticism, and asceticism. Neither did he go there to study Greek, while he also refused to devour there the mystical works of Ficino and Pico della Mirandola. Upon his return to the Low Countries he published the first edition of his famous book, *Adages,* besides an edition of *De Officiis* by Cicero. He remained, as before, a real humanist, eager to read the works of the Greek and Roman scholars who flourished in the classical period of antiquity. He differed profoundly from his friend John Colet, who with great care distinguished between salutary books and those by immoral authors. He refused to teach theology at the University of Cambridge, but a few years later accepted a chair to teach classical learning. In the year 1506 he and Thomas More published in Paris numerous short works by the Greek satirist Lucian, thus indicating his interest in pagan literature. The *Adages* grew in size, until more than 4,000 proverbs were discussed in it, revealing his predilection for Greek and Roman authors of the pre-Christian era.

III. Attitude Toward the Reformation: Steeped as Erasmus was in the teachings of the Devotio Moderna, he involuntarily returned to those teachings after he had spent some twenty years imbibing classical learning (1490–1510). In his first book, *On the Contempt of the World,* composed about the year 1490, he repeated sentiments to be found in the world-famous book, *The Imitation of Christ.* But when an acquaintance of his was ready to publish the book in its original form, Erasmus quickly added a new chapter in which he attacked monasticism. This happened shortly before he finally obtained from Pope Leo X a permit to give up his monastic vows and vocation (1517). He remarked then that he would have been wiser in his youth to join the Brethren of the Common Life, for they did not demand irrevocable vows, nor were they members of monastic orders. Their piety, however, he admired, and he paid tribute to them in his literary labors. He issued a magnificent edition of the works of St. Jerome, whom he preferred to St. Augustine, since he disliked the latter's contempt of human nature and enjoyed the philological work of the former. He was at first pleased with Luther's work as a reformer, since both men wanted to expose the abuses in the Church. But in 1516 he began to see the tremendous difference between his own viewpoint and that of the German professor of theology. He chose to follow the humanistic point of view, following Valla, as contrasted with Luther. He believed in the dignity of man, not in the total depravity of man. His aim was peaceful reform, not revolt.

Luther's respect for Erasmus was much less than has often been assumed. He immediately recognized in his opponent the mentality of the humanists. Even before 1517 he could no longer approve of the humanistic approach to the problem of reform. Although he had spent only one year with the Brethren of the Common Life (at Magdeburg, 1497–98), he appreciated their deep search after personal piety much more than did the facetious Hollander. In 1500 Erasmus had stated that from the little book by Cicero on offices flowed the waters of salvation, but Luther held firmly to the medieval concept of salvation through Christ's atonement. Luther claimed that the author of the supposedly devotional work entitled, *Manual of the Christian Knight* (1503) showed more interest in classical learning than religious fervor. Luther also was very suspicious about the amusing tales in the *Colloquies,* begun in Paris about the year 1497, and enlarged from time to time, as were the *Adages.* Erasmus was the man of reason, who hoped to derive much from human resources. He was not greatly disturbed about heretical doctrines, for he assumed that each member of the Church was entitled to his own opinions, though they might not coincide with those of the higher clergy. When Luther and Melanchthon began to rely upon the support of their elector to suppress heresy in Saxony, Erasmus frowned on such measures. He wanted above all things tolerance and individual freedom. Luther shuddered when he first read the "big seller" of the time, *Praise of Folly,* in which

Erasmus ridiculed sacred practices and beliefs. On many occasions Erasmus felt amused, while Luther was profoundly grieved. Amusement does not in itself produce a reformation, but sorrow has the power to achieve results. What Erasmus lacked was not so much courage as sincere conviction of sin and depravity, both in himself and in his neighbors. Nevertheless, he contributed immensely to the negative element in the Reformation, as has been indicated in our new article on the Renaissance.

BIBLIOGRAPHY: The first comprehensive account of the early life was presented in Albert Hyma, *The Youth of Erasmus*, 1930. It contains a bibliography and the first edition of the *Antibarbarorum Liber*. See also Paul Mestwerdt, *Die Anfaenge des Erasmus: Humanismus und "Devotio Moderna,"* 1917. The first satisfactory biography in English is Preserved Smith, *Erasmus: A Study of His Life, Ideals and Place in History*, 1923. Very useful, but biased in favor of Catholicism is J. J. Mangan, *The Life, Character, and Influence of Desiderius Erasmus of Rotterdam*, 2 vols., 1927. From 1930 to 1951 no biography worthy of the great humanist was published. An excellent supplement to the *Opera Omnia* was published by Wallace K. Ferguson, *Erasmi Opuscula: A Supplement to the Opera Omnia*, 1933. Other publications of works by Erasmus are: Craig R. Thompson, *The Translations of Lucian by Erasmus and St. Thomas More*, 1940, mostly a discussion rather than a publication; Hoyt Hopewell, *The Praise of Folly by Desiderius Erasmus*, 1941; Lester K. Born, *The Education of a Christian Prince*, 1936; William J. Hirten, *Complaint of Peace*, 1946; P. S. Allen, *Opus Epistolarum Des. Erasmi Roterdami*, 11 vols., of which the last three were edited by Mrs. H. M. Allen and H. W. Garrod, 1906–47. Biographical studies: Augustin Renaudet, *Études érasmiennes*, 1939; Margaret Mann, *Erasme et les débuts de la Réforme française*, 1934; J. B. Pineau, *Erasme: Sa pensée religieuse*, 1924; Marcel Bataillon, *Erasme et l'Espagne*, 1937; Marie Delcourt, *Erasme*, 1945; Stefan Zweig, *Triumph und Tragik des Erasmus von Rotterdam*, 1935; Karl Schlechta, *Erasmus von Rotterdam*, 1940; Christian Dolfen, *Die Stellung des Erasmus von Rotterdam zur Scholastischen Methode*, 1936; Henry de Vocht, *The Earliest English Translations of Erasmus' Colloquia*, 1928; Maurice Wilkinson, *Erasmus of Rotterdam*, 1921; P. S. Allen, *Erasmus: Lectures and Wayfaring Sketches*, 1934; William E. Campbell, *Erasmus, Tyndale and More*, 1949; José Chapiro, *Erasmus and Our Struggle for Peace*, 1950; J. Huizinga, *Erasmus*, 1924, Dutch original, 3rd Ed., 1928; Margaret Mann Phillips, *Erasmus and the Northern Renaissance*, 1950; Robert H. Murray, *Erasmus and Luther*, 1920; Théodore Quoniam, *Érasme*, 1935; Karl A. Meissinger, *Erasmus von Rotterdam*, 1948; Walter Rueegg, *Cicero und der Humanismus: Formale Untersuchungen ueber Petrarca und Erasmus*, 1946; O. Schottenloher, *Erasmus im Ringen um die humanistische Bildungsform*, 1933; Albert Hyma, *Erasmus and the Humanists*, 1930.

[Sup.] ALBERT HYMA.

ERASTUS, THOMAS; ERASTIANISM: After the treatment by J. N. Figgis in the Appendix of the second edition of his work, *The Theory of the Divine Right of Kings* (1914), interest in Erastus declined, with the result that nothing is said about him in Volume VI of the monumental work by R. W. and A. J. Carlyle, *A History of Mediaeval Political Theory in the West* (2nd ed., 1950), whereas Luther is treated at great length. The same is true of two books by J. W. Allen on the history of political thought in England and Europe, notably *A History of Political Thought in the Sixteenth Century* (1928). In 1950, C. Garbett, Archbishop of York, published an illuminating study entitled, *Church and State in England*. He discussed Erastus on pp. 20–21, where he said that according to Figgis the Swiss theologian was ap-

parently not Erastian. Figgis had written an article on the question, "Was Erastus an Erastian?" If he was not, then why all this fuss about Erastianism? Figgis in his other book, *Studies of Political Thought from Gerson to Grotius 1414–1625* (2nd ed. reprint, 1923) says on pp. 65–66 that Erastus was only "considering the case of a State where but one religion is permitted." The name of Erastus does not appear in the huge catalogue at the British Museum in London under recent titles, and so it seems as if the whole matter might as well be dropped. In Paris, Amsterdam, Brussels and The Hague it was also very difficult to find material on Erastus.

Nevertheless, the name Erastianism was so widely used in early modern times, particularly in England, that historians must find a suitable answer to the knotty problem. Erastus as a physician in the Calvinistic city of Heidelberg when the Heidelberg Catechism was written there, reflected the political thought of his environment. His book on the question of excommunication brought up the issue of the power of the state versus that of the church. Erastus believed that a Christian who had committed a grievous sin should not be excluded from the Sacraments but be punished by the civil magistrate. Neither Christ nor the early apostles excluded a sinner from the communion service. Judas was permitted to attend and participate in the Last Supper. Moreover, the Christians in Corinth who had been guilty of gross sin were nevertheless granted permission to partake of the sacred elements. Sinners were to be rebuked, first in private and then in public. Since the civil magistrates were all members of the one and only true church, they were best qualified to take charge of this function. It must be remembered that in the Holy Roman Empire around 1580 the civil rulers had the right to determine what the religion of their subjects was to be. Figgis did not resolve the fundamental problem raised by the contemporaries of Erastus. Erastus did have a point which they fully understood, but which today is rarely appreciated. His contemporaries in England in particular were greatly interested in his proposition. Their king was head of the Church of England.

One of the few scholars to do justice to Erastus in our century was the Rev. Robert Henry Murray, author of an admirable work on the relation between Erasmus and Luther. In his more recent book, *The Political Consequences of the Reformation* (1926), he quoted from Erastus but repeated the argument used by Figgis. Here is the most important quotation: "For, as in managing secular affairs, the magistrate may not transgress the bounds of equity, justice and honour laid down in the laws of the State; so, much less, in disposing of and arranging religious matters and those which relate to the worship of God, is it permitted him to depart, in any particular, from what God has prescribed in His Word. This Word he should follow as his rule in all things, without departing from it any time in the smallest particular." Murray correctly concludes that "this terrible Heidelberg doctor maintains the Headship of Christ." At the end of the discussion on p. 263 he admits that according to Erastus there cannot be two supreme magistracies in the state, "just as there cannot be two supreme legislatures." He also points out that the celebrated British scholar, F. W. Maitland, in one of his best essays referred to Sir Thomas Smith, Secretary of State to Queen Elizabeth, who wrote an Erastian book entitled, *De Republica Anglorum,* published in 1583. He and Sir John Fortescue had great respect for their monarch; they agreed with Erastus in placing the king above the church. In their time the idea of a state church became very popular, not owing to Luther's influence, for Fortescue lived in the fifteenth century. Sir Thomas Smith also paid very little attention to Luther, and it is to be hoped that experts in the field of political science will look elsewhere than to the works of Martin Luther when searching for the sources of those ideas that have often been called Erastian. [Sup.] ALBERT HYMA.

ERDMAN, CHARLES ROSENBURY: Presbyterian; b. in Fayetteville, N. Y., July 20, 1866. A graduate of Princeton University and Princeton Theological Seminary, he was pastor of the Overbrook (Pa.) Church (1891–97); First Church, Germantown (1897–1906); First Church, Princeton, N. J. (1924–34); and professor of practical theology, Princeton Seminary (1906–36). He was moderator of the General Assembly of the Presbyterian Church in the U. S. A. (1925); president of its Board of Foreign Missions (1926–41); and the author of more than twenty volumes, mainly expositions of New Testament books.

FREDERICK WILLIAM LOETSCHER.

ERITREA. See AFRICA.

ERLANGEN THEOLOGY: A dynamic revival of Lutheran theology at the University of Erlangen (1830 ff.), given the original impetus by J. W. F. Hoefling (*q.v.,* Vol. V) and G. C. A. Harless (*q.v.,* Vol. V), and its most characteristic expression by J. C. K. Hofmann (*q.v.,* Vol. V) and F. H. R. Frank (*q.v.,* Vol. IV). It was extended by a series of distinguished scholars: G. Thomasius (*q.v.,* Vol. XI), K. A. G. Zezschwitz (*q.v.,* Vol. XII), Heinrich Schmid (*q.v.,* Vol. X), Theodosius Harnack (*q.v.,* Vol. V), Theodor Zahn (*q.v.,* Vol. XII), C. E. Luthardt (*q.v.,* Vol. VII), Ludwig Ihmels (*q.v.,* Vol. V). Its

influence has been far-reaching. Among American Lutherans profoundly influenced were J. Michael Reu (*q.v.*) and Charles M. Jacobs (*q.v.*). It reveals a positive as well as negative reaction to Pietism, the Enlightenment, Schleiermacher, and the philosophies of Hegel and Schelling. The main emphases are: (1) Faithfulness to the Lutheran Confessions, not as mere repristination but as a dynamic moving forward in the direction indicated by the Confessions. (2) The subjective starting point: From the experience of what it means to be a Christian (communion between God and man in Jesus Christ) the entire theological system is developed, both as to presuppositions and implications. This has often been misinterpreted as a false subjectivism, whereas, in truth, the objective basis in the events of revelation and the means of grace are from the beginning recognized. The certainty of the believer is not based upon his own subjective state, but there is no certainty except that of faith derived from God's objective acts; revelation and faith are corollary and the subject-object antithesis is overcome only in the right personal relationship. (3) The Bible is treated not as a compendium of proof texts, but as the witness to God's redemptive acts in history (*Heilsgeschichte,* history of salvation). (4) Faith and the Bible are viewed as an organic whole with its center in justification by grace alone (the re-establishment of communion between God and man and between man and man); there is no gap between dogmatics and ethics; true evangelical freedom is preserved; paradoxes are recognized but there are no irrational cleavages. (5) In the same spirit the connection between Christian faith and culture is preserved; God is active in all creation; there is no false "spiritualism."

BIBLIOGRAPHY: R. Seeberg, *Die Kirche Deutschlands im neunzehnten Jahrhundert,* 1904; Ferdinand Kattenbusch, *Die deutsche evangelische Theologie seit Schleiermacher,* 1926.

MARTIN J. HEINECKEN.

EROS: The word *eros* does not occur in the New Testament. It is, however, native to human nature. It is the love (*q.v.*) of desire, growing out of a sense of lack. It seeks to control, to dominate, to use the person or thing loved for the enhancement of the happiness of the lover. *Agape* (*q.v.*) seeks to liberate, to develop, and to enhance the happiness of the one loved. *Eros* is characteristic of Hellenism, *agape* of Christianity. Plato used *eros* of the upward striving of the individual; Aristotle used it of the upward striving of all creation from becoming to being. The *eros* idea invaded the Christian concept of love, and for more than a thousand years dominated it. With Martin Luther, Christian theology began to free itself from this Hellenistic concept and to recover the New Testament idea of love.

BIBLIOGRAPHY: Gerhard Kittel, *Theologische Woerterbuch zum Neuen Testament*, 1933; Moulton and Geden, *Concordance to Greek Testament*, 1897; Anders Nygren, *Agape and Eros*, 1932; Robert Young, *Analytical Concordance to the Bible*, 1919.

WILLIAM DOUGLAS CHAMBERLAIN.

ESBJORN, LARS PAUL: Swedish-American Lutheran pioneer pastor of the Augustana Lutheran Church in the U. S.; b. at Delsbo, province of Helsingland, Sweden, Oct. 16, 1808; d. at Ostervala, Sweden, July 2, 1870; studied at University of Upsala; ordained by church of Sweden (June 11, 1832); became known as an advocate of the temperance and revival movements; was the first Swedish Lutheran pastor to come to America in connection with the great immigration of the nineteenth century; settled in Andover, Ill.; organized congregations in Andover, Moline, and Galesburg, Ill. His American ministry culminated in the organization of the Augustana Synod and founding of Augustana College and Theological Seminary in 1860; served as president of the school until his return to Sweden in 1863.

BIBLIOGRAPHY: S. Ronnegard, *Lars Paul Esbjörn*, 1949; G. Stephenson, *The Founding of the Augustana Synod*, 1927.

G. EVERETT ARDEN.

ESCHATOLOGY: I. Personal Eschatology: In the past fifty years two ideas have become more widely spread: (1) There is a growing tendency to disbelieve in death as final, in the sense that it puts an end to further hope of salvation. P. T. Forsyth (*q.v.*) (*This Life and the Next*, reissued, 1948) writes: "There are more conversions on the other side than on this." C. S. Lewis (*q.v.*) (*The Great Divorce*, 1946) supports the same possibility. Teunis E. Gouwens, a Presbyterian (U. S.) minister, wrote without censure (*Can We Repeat the Creed?* 1936) his belief that God never finally shuts a sinner from his presence without any opportunity to accept Christ. (2) Beyond this, there is some tendency to universalism. N. F. S. Ferre (*q.v.*) (*The Christian Doctrine of God*, 1951, p. 219) calls God the "perfect parent who has no permanent problem children." H. H. Farmer (*q.v.*) (*God and Men*, Chap. VI) gives reasons why, in spite of himself, he leans to universalism. E. Brunner (*q.v.*) in *The Christian Doctrine of God*, Chapter 23, gives biblical and logical reasons to the contrary. See ETERNAL LIFE.

II. Cosmic Eschatology: Lines of thought have been diverse: (1) Dispensationalism (*q.v.*) views the race as meeting three destinies, not two as in the orthodox scheme. The saints will be in heaven, the unrepentant sinners in hell, the Jews (sacrificing at Jerusalem as of old) on this earth. (2) The premillennial view persists. The Seventh-day Adventist (*q.v.*) view, only one of many unfolded by contemporary literalists, affirms that the Second Coming will positively be in this generation; that then the righteous will rise, and for 1000 years reign with Christ in heaven while Satan inhabits an empty earth; after which the wicked dead will rise, be judged and annihilated, and this earth restored in the endless Kingdom. (3) Less stringently literalistic is the "Christological Eschatology" of W. C. Robinson (*Christ the Hope of Glory*, 1945) which maintains in general the position of historic Protestantism, is much more restrained than premillennialists in programming the future, and calls the millennium a "hieroglyph" (p. 313). (4) With the publication of Albert Schweitzer's (*q.v.*) *Von Reimarus zu Wrede* (*Quest of the Historical Jesus*, 1910) all New Testament scholarship was once more made aware of the undeniable centrality of eschatology in the Gospels as in the rest of the New Testament. There is among Christian scholars today a widespread tendency to agree with Reinhold Niebuhr (*q.v.*) (*Nature and Destiny of Man*, II. X) that "the symbol of the second coming of Christ can neither be taken literally nor dismissed as unimportant." Ways of interpreting vary. Schweitzer himself sees it thus: "Whereas He, Jesus, expected the Kingdom of God to come at the end of the world, we must endeavor, under the spirit of His ethical religion, to make the Kingdom a reality in this world by works of love" ("Religion in Modern Civilization," *Christian Century*, 1934). C. H. Dodd's (*q.v.*) theory of "realized eschatology" (*The Apostolic Preaching*, 1937, and other works) has been influential. The resultant view is that the "eschaton," the final age, is here. These are the last days, this is the final phase of God's dealing with men. (5) One form of eschatological concern is the active interest in the meaning of history (see HISTORY, THE CHRISTIAN INTERPRETATION OF). For John Baillie (*q.v.*) (*The Belief in Progress*, 1950) these are the "years of Grace." The Second Coming, the Last Judgment and the Resurrection are "symbols of a reality unimaginable by us except in symbolic form," indispensable as barriers against "secular progressivism." Reinhold Niebuhr (*op. cit.*) also, rejecting all literalism, finds the essence of eschatology in the dialectic: the final consummation of history lies beyond the temporal process, the consummation fulfils, not negates, the historical process. (6) Oscar Cullmann (*q.v.*) (*Christ and Time*, 1950) proposes to take literally the Hebrew idea of eternity as a simple extension of time and to abandon the Greek idea of qualitative difference between time and eternity. Karl Barth's (*q.v.*) earlier writings viewed eschatology as a continuous dialectic between time and eternity; but in his *Dogmatik* he admits the Consummation as a real future event. Nicholas Berdyaev (*q.v.*) (more philosopher than theologian) however, maintains the incommensurability of time and eternity, and sees "eternal life" not in the future, but as a deliverance from time (*Destiny of Man,* 1937).

See also ANNIHILATIONISM; ETERNAL LIFE; KINGDOM OF GOD; MILLENNIUM; RESTORATION OF ALL; SOTERIOLOGY.

BIBLIOGRAPHY: Besides the books mentioned above see: Lewis S. Chafer, *Systematic Theology,* Vol. IV (1948), pp. 401, 416 f. (dispensationalist); Harris F. Rall, *Modern Premillennialism and the Christian Hope,* 1920; Ernst von Dobschuetz, *Eschatology of the Gospels,* 1910; H. A. Guy, *The New Testament Doctrine of the Last Things,* 1948; Karl Barth, *Christliche Dogmatik* (1947-51), III. 2.47.5, III.3.51; Carlyle B. Haynes, *The Return of Jesus,* 1943 (Seventh-day Adventist).

[Sup.] KENNETH J. FOREMAN.

ESCHATOLOGY, MUSLIM: The fifth article in the orthodox Muslim creed proclaims belief in the Last Day, and all credal statements (*'aqā'id*) from the time of Abū Ḥanifah (d. 767) onwards contain some elaboration of this article. Muḥammad had shown himself much concerned with matters of judgment and the hereafter, so that the doctrine of "Last Things" bulks largely in the Qur'ān (Koran) and consequently in the traditions. It was details mentioned in the Quranic descriptions of the last things, viz., the coming day, the resurrection, the torment of the tomb, the balance, the bridge, the grand assizes, paradise and hell, which exercised the exegetes and the theologians. For the most part the theologians are uncomfortable about these matters, stating that they are to be believed in because mentioned in the Qur'ān and tradition, but taken without question of why or how. Rationalistic Mu'tazilites denied their literal reality; philosophic theologians attempted to spiritualize or allegorize them, while the orthodox labored to systematize the material in the sources. In the devotional literature, however, this doctrine lent itself to elaborate development for purposes of edification. The favorite topics of this treatment are: (1) death and the grave; (2) the intermediate state; (3) the signs of the hour; (4) resurrection; (5) assembling for judgment; (6) the search for an intercessor; (7) the weighing at the balances; (8) the bridge crossing; (9) the life of the blessed in paradise and of the damned in hell. There are some early tractates dealing with individual matters of eschatology, but for long the treatment of this subject formed part of larger works of edification. From the tenth century onwards, however, there is a growing number of independent treatises devoted solely to these matters, such as the pseudo-Ghazalian *al-Durra al-Fākhira,* the *Tadhkira* of al-Qurṭubī, Ibn Makhlūf's *al-'Ulūm al-Fākhira,* 'Abd al-Raḥmān's *Daqā'iq al-Akhbār,* and the many little eschatological treatises of al-Suyūṭī.

ARTHUR JEFFERY.

ESHER, JOHN JACOB: Evangelical United Brethren; b. Dec. 11, 1823, in Baldenheim, Germany; d. Apr. 16, 1901. Entering the ministry of the Evangelical Association in the Illinois Conference in 1845, he represented that body in general conference sessions from 1851 to 1863, when he was elected bishop. He organized the first annual conferences in Europe and Asia and was the first bishop of the church to visit the missions in the Orient and travel around the world. He wrote the first comprehensive theology of his denomination. At the time of the division of the Evangelical Association (1891–94) and the formation of the United Evangelical Church (*q.v.*) he was the senior bishop of the church and leader of the group which continued the original church.

He wrote *Katechismus der Evangelischen Gemeinschaft* (1882; 2nd ed. 1901; Eng. tr., 1883); *Ueber Laender und Meere* (1886); *Die Evangelische Gemeinschaft und Zwei Predigten* (1894); and *Christliche Theologie* (Vol. I, 1899; Vol. II, 1901). RAYMOND W. ALBRIGHT.

ESSAYS AND REVIEWS: Seven authors marked the battle for liberalism within the Church of England by publishing a volume of essays under this title early in 1860. The only common ground of the seven was the demand for freedom of discussion, and the articles were of such diverse titles as *The Mosaic Cosmogony, The Interpretation of Scripture, Bunsen's Biblical Researches, The Education of the World,* and *The National Church.* Although reaction was slow in coming, it was violent when it appeared. Petitions with thousands of names protested to the bishops, and in Feb., 1861, a remonstrance appeared as an encyclical of the archbishop of Canterbury with signatures of twenty-four bishops. The Lower House of Canterbury and the courts took cognizance of the volume, and several of the authors were prosecuted and condemned, only to have the sentence reversed on appeal to the Privy Council. On June 21, the Upper House of the Convocation of Canterbury condemned the book, but the action of the bishops was questioned in the House of Lords. Excitement gradually died down, the conservatives believing themselves vindicated by the action of the bishops. Nevertheless, many of the writers subsequently obtained prominent positions in the church—one, Frederick Temple, becoming archbishop of Canterbury.

BIBLIOGRAPHY: F. W. Cornish, *History of the English Church in the Nineteenth Century,* 1910.

[Sup.] NELSON RIGHTMYER.

ESSAYS CATHOLIC AND CRITICAL: In 1926 appeared a volume of essays under this title written by thirteen British scholars, members of the Anglican Church. Among them were A. E. Taylor, Kenneth E. Kirk, and A. E. J. Rawlinson. Often classed as "Liberal Catholics," the authors proposed to restate and synthesize the catholic faith with the methods of modern theological study in the tradition of the

Lux Mundi (*q.v.*) essays of 1888. Their emphasis was that the church is the living Body of Christ. "For the Catholic Christian *'Quid vobis videtur de Ecclesia?'* What think ye of the Church? is not merely as pertinent a question as *Quid vobis videtur de Christo?* What think ye of Christ? it is the same question differently formulated." The volume has had a wide and deep influence within the Anglican communion and has affected the Anglican approach to church unity.   NELSON RIGHTMYER.

ESTHER, BOOK OF: While conservative scholarship holds to its historicity, Esther is regarded as fiction by most modern scholars. Some see in it a reflection of events of the Hellenistic era. The study of the literary technique of the writer and of the folk-tale materials supposedly used by him has largely replaced earlier interest in mythological explanations. Gunkel's viewpoints have been most influential here. The ancient author linked his story with the Purim festival, for which he gives an explanation. It must have arisen among the eastern Jews—perhaps in adaptation of a pagan festival. Its name is derived from a word of Assyro-Babylonian derivation (*puru*, "lot"). The festival was introduced into Palestine by *ca.* 50 B.C. Yahuda explains Esther's name as Iranian translation of Hadassah, "myrtle" (*astra* in Medic).

BIBLIOGRAPHY: See Introductions by Pfeiffer, Eissfeldt, etc. Commentaries: H. Gunkel, 1916; M. Haller, 1940. Other literature: J. Hoschander, *The Book of Esther in the Light of History*, 1923; A. E. Morris, "The Purpose of the Book of Esther," *ET*, XLII (1930), 124 ff.; H. Striedl, "Untersuchung zur Syntax und Stilistik des hebraeischen Buches Esther," *ZATW*, N.F. XIV (1937), 73–108; H. Lewy, "The Feast of the 14th Day of Adar," *HUCA*, XIV (1939), 127 ff.; A. S. Yahuda, "The Meaning of the Name Esther," *JRAS* (1946), 174 ff.

[Sup.] EMIL G. KRAELING.

ESTONIA: A republic on the Baltic Sea with nearly 1,140,000 inhabitants in 1940 and an area of 47,549 square kilometers.

After many unsuccessful attempts to regain the freedom they had lost to the Russians, Estonians took advantage of the opportunity offered by the outbreak of the Russian Revolution. On Feb. 24, 1918, the Estonian National Council proclaimed Estonia a sovereign state, and some months later it received *de facto* recognition from Great Britain, Italy, and France. The young state was put to a hard test during the War of Liberation (1918–20). Three generations participated in desperate efforts to free the country from invaders: first to resist the Russians; then to throw back the German (*Landeswehr*) attack from the south; and finally to fight until Soviet Russia was ready to sign the peace treaty in which Soviet Russia renounced all sovereign rights to the territory "forever."

During the War of Liberation social and economic independence was established in the devastated country by the radical Agrarian Reform of 1919, whereby 65% of the population became independent. This reform, coupled with the rise of co-operative societies and the creation of industry, particularly the shale oil industry, raised the economy of the country so that it could soon develop foreign trade. In the field of social legislation progress was made, particularly in social insurance. A bill was in preparation to provide general insurance against old age and infirmity.

Freedom fostered spiritual life. Compulsory education was introduced in 1919. An important impetus was given by new educational institutions. In 1934 there was one university student for every 332 inhabitants.

The largest churches were the Lutheran (about 800,000 members) and the Greek Orthodox (about 200,000 members). Church and state were separated in 1925. But since the referendum in 1923 religious instruction was given in all public schools at the state's expense.

Although the population was extremely homogeneous, with nine tenths of the population genuine Estonians, full cultural autonomy was granted to minority groups.

In World War II Estonia, having been abandoned, fought to the point of exhaustion and was then overrun by Soviet Russia. All the achievements of the period of independence were destroyed. The theological faculty at the University of Tartu became the first victim, and its liquidation inaugurated the destruction of values, whether spiritual, religious, cultural, or material.

Owing to genocide on a large scale, the physical existence of the nation was seriously endangered. The period since 1941 was the saddest in the history of a country which, during the last seven centuries, fought about forty wars with its eastern neighbor.

BIBLIOGRAPHY: A. Pullerits, *Estonia: Population, Culture, and Economic Life*, 1937; I. H. Jackson, *Estonia*, 1948; K. R. Pusta, *The Soviet Union and the Baltic States*, 1943; E. Kareda, E. Blumfeldt, A. Rei, E. Poom, *Estonia*, 1948; K. Aun, *Der voelkerrechtliche Schutz nationaler Minderheiten in Estland*, 1951; H. Kruus, *Histoire de l'Estonie*, 1935; E. Uustalu, *The History of the Estonian Nation*, 1952.

[Sup. to RUSSIA.] ARTHUR VÖÖBUS.

ETERNAL LIFE: The origins of this phrase, eternal life, are to be found in the ancient Jewish rabbinical writings which are throughout deeply eschatological in outlook. The primary meaning is "life in the age that is eternal," eternal from the standpoint of its quality rather than its quantity. Eternal life signified "life in the eschotological age that is to be realized." Hence, to Jesus' hearers, his use of this phrase would have an eschatological implication.

The key to an understanding of the meaning of eternal life in the Gospels may lie in the fact that in St. John's Gospel this phrase "eternal life" has taken the place of the term "kingdom of God"(*q.v.*) or "kingdom of heaven" so frequently found in the three Synoptic Gospels. "Kingdom of God" is to be understood eschatologically in Jesus' teaching. The kingdom of God is the new age breaking into history in the Person of Jesus Christ, the age and realm in which God the Father reigns as sovereign Lord in majesty. Life in that kingdom, or in the age to come, is eternal in quality, free from the limitations of time, decay, evil, and sin. Thus "eternal life" is life in the kingdom of God. Eternal life signifies this basic eschatological idea of life in the inaugurated divine kingdom, where evil is at an end.

The accent in this biblical phrase "eternal life" is on "life" rather than "eternal": examples are found in the Synoptic Gospels of the use of "life" in exactly the same sense as "eternal life" is used (Matthew 7:14, 19:17; Mark 9:43). Jesus Christ's offer to men is life, not the frustrating, sin-corroded life of this age, but life that is in harmony with man's destiny as the child of God, life that belongs to the coming age. This use of the term "life" is virtually equivalent to the "kingdom of God" in Jesus' thought, for the two expressions seem interchangeable on his lips (Mark 9:43, 45 and 47).

The phrase "eternal life" occurs explicitly as well as implicitly in the Synoptic Gospels, most notably in the question put to Jesus by the inquiring ruler: "what shall I do to inherit eternal life?" (Matthew 19:16; Mark 10:17; Luke 18:18). The phrase was evidently current in thoughtful Jewish religious circles, and summed up what the coming Messiah would have to offer. Jesus answered the rich young ruler with a call to more perfect obedience to God's rule and law. The expected kingdom or realm of God offered men "eternal life."

"Eternal life" is the chief topic in the record of Jesus' teaching found in the Fourth Gospel, just as the kingdom of God is the emphasis in the Synoptic account of his teaching. The phrase, "eternal life," occurs seventeen times in St. John's Gospel and six times in the First Epistle of John, while the equivalent use of the term "life" is found many times as well. Here the eschatological idea, still fundamental to the right understanding of the term, has become more inward and spiritualized. There appears to be even less interest in duration in regard to eternal life which is presented as a potential present inward possession. The age to come has already broken into history with the coming of Jesus Christ; and those who believe in him, who are "in Christ," can already enjoy the life of the new age. Christian life is in this sense "realized eschatology."

Jesus teaches that his supreme gift to men is "eternal life" (John 17:2). Everlasting life is the form in which that offer is made in our Lord's great summary of what God's saving visitation means (John 3:16). It might almost be said that we have a precise definition of "eternal life" in this Fourth Gospel: "And this is life eternal, that they might know thee the only true God, and Jesus Christ whom thou hast sent" (John 17:3). As one of God's own children, to know the Father through saving faith in the Lord Jesus Christ is man's entry into the life of the world to come, and it is an inward possession here and now, as well as the pledge of fully realized "life" hereafter.

A believer then enters upon "eternal life" through the appropriation of the saving benefits offered in Jesus Christ. This emphasis on faith, faith in the sense of personal trust in and commitment to Jesus, is underlined in the dominical word: "Whoso eateth my flesh, and drinketh my blood, hath eternal life" (John 6:54). Whosoever receives Christ by faith is the possessor of eternal life; the life of the age to come is his here and now. Nevertheless a "not yet" still remains: "and I will raise him up at the last day" (John 6:54).

The Synoptic account of the promises made to these who accept Christ tells of blessings here and now, "and in the world to come eternal life" (Mark 10:30). After the final judgment, the righteous enter into "life eternal" (Matthew 25:46). Still, in regard to eternal life, the main emphasis of the Gospels remains on a realized spiritual possession rather than on immortality in any detached philosophical sense. The weary burden of hope deferred is not a New Testament conception, and the Christian hope is closely linked to the life of the kingdom, "eternal life," discoverable within the here and now. Even judgment is withdrawn from futurity: "we know that we have passed from death unto life" (I John 3:14). The new age is present in Jesus: "God hath given to us eternal life and this life is in his Son" (I John 5:11).

The present and future aspects of "eternal life" are drawn together in the Person of Jesus Christ, who can himself claim to be the Resurrection and the Life, both the future realization and the present possession of "eternal life" in one living Saviour (John 11:25-26). The essential eschatology of Jesus' teaching, which has continually to be recognized is "realized eschatology."

The life of the age to come, "eternal life," has broken into history with Jesus Christ's coming as Saviour. "Eternal life" is life in contrast to death; it is the full realization of our redemption in Jesus Christ. "The gift of God is eternal life through Jesus Christ our Lord" (Romans 6:23).

See also ESCHATOLOGY; ETERNITY; HISTORY, THE CHRISTIAN INTERPRETATION OF.

                                        R. STUART LOUDEN.

ETERNITY: Wherever this concept is involved, whether in the foreground or in the background of thought, we need to be peculiarly wary of the fallacy of equivocation of terms. For, though it is used in at least four different senses, it always expresses a certain superiority to the limitedness and relativity of the temporal, and thus it tends to evoke an emotion which, in proportion to its strength, threatens clarity of thought and causes the various senses to be confused.

We speak of "the eternal hills," knowing full well that they are not strictly eternal, but, while the poetic mood prevails, feeling pity or resentment for the philistine soul who would dare to mention that prosaic fact.

We identify eternity with time (*q.v.*), unreconstructed except by projecting it to infinity— either towards the past (e.g., "the eternity before time was"), or towards the future (e.g., "he now dwells in eternity"), or in both directions but on the same level as experienced time, or as "located" somehow "above" our finite time.

Eternity is regarded as infinite time, somehow "transcended." In this sense, eternity is not "when time shall be no more." Time remains real in eternity. It is infinite in dimension, but it is somehow reconstructed, or seen from a higher point of view. It is perhaps impossible for finite minds fully to specify the reconstructions necessary to transform the concept of infinite time into that of eternity; but at least some things can be said about it. Eternity must have a degree and kind of *unity* which is not suggested by the term infinite time. It must have at least the unity experienced by an Infinite Mind which, though it can move freely through infinite time, can also see it as a single "now." It is suggested, in popular terms, by such Scriptural passages as "before Abraham was, I am" (John 8:38); "For a thousand years in thy sight are but as yesterday when it is past, and as a watch in the night" (Ps. 90:4); "one day is with the Lord as a thousand years, and a thousand years as one day" (II Peter 3:8). We find analogies to such experience in our own ability, in memory and in anticipation, to transcend our involvement in the succession of finite moments. Perhaps a better analogy may be found in the experience of "the specious present" (see TIME), which can hold both something of the "no longer" and something of the "not yet" in the unity of a single "now." The fact that the length of the specious present, as measured by clock time, is variable suggests the possibility that a mind of infinite capacity might be able to treat infinite time as his specious present. This would be a first approach to the kind of unity which must distinguish eternity from infinite time; but certainly it must have more of unity in it than that.

In stark opposition to all these senses in which the term eternity is used, we also employ the term to signify that which negates time entirely, either in the sense that, when eternity is present, time has ceased to be (i.e., the eternity "when time shall be no more"), or in the sense that considerations of time are wholly irrelevant to it. In the latter category fall such experiences as logical validity ("once true, always true"), aesthetic values (e.g., "a thing of beauty is a joy for ever"), and moral values (e.g., "kind words can never die").

See also ETERNAL LIFE.

BIBLIOGRAPHY: A. Seth Pringle-Pattison, *The Idea of God* (1920), pp. 342 ff., and references there cited; Karl Heim, *The New Divine Order* (1930), pp. 51 ff.

ANDREW K. RULE.

ETHICAL CULTURE. See ETHICAL SOCIETIES.

ETHICAL SOCIETIES: Ethical Societies were formed since 1910 in Baltimore, Md., Hempstead, Long Island, Westchester, N. Y., Los Angeles, Calif., Washington, D. C., and elsewhere. Many societies now omit the word "Culture" from their official titles. A scattered "membership-at-large" brings the total of adherents in the American Ethical Union to about 5,000. Several English societies survived the two world wars, and the society in Vienna, Austria, suppressed by Hitler, was re-established.

Ideologically the main trends have been from transcendentalism toward humanism and from the "lecture platform" technique toward a warmer fellowship and more definitely religious emphasis. Practical activities included the first Universal Races Congress (1911), the development of the Fieldston Ethical Culture Schools, work on behalf of European refugees (*q.v.*), and an annual leadership-training Encampment for Citizenship.

BIBLIOGRAPHY: David S. Muzzey, *Ethics as a Religion*, 1951; Henry Neumann, *Spokesmen for Ethical Religion*, 1951.

[Sup. to ETHICAL CULTURE, SOCIETIES FOR.]

W. EDWIN COLLIER.

ETHICAL UNION, AMERICAN. See ETHICAL SOCIETIES.

ETHICS. See AGAPE (LOVE); ALTRUISM; CHARITY, CHRISTIAN; EGO AND EGOISM; HEDONISM; KINGDOM OF GOD; MORALITY, MORAL LAW; PHILOSOPHY; PHILOSOPHY OF VALUE; RESTITUTION, DUTY OF; RETALIATION; SELF-REALIZATION; SEX, ETHICS OF; SOCIAL GOSPEL; SOTERIOLOGY.

ETHIOPIA, CHURCH OF: The twentieth century has brought Ethiopia into closer contact with the rest of the world than ever before, and showed the continuing importance in its life of the national church. Under the Emperor Menelik (1889–1913), founder of the present dynasty, the new capital of Addis Abbaba also became the ecclesiastical center; some efforts were made at securing independence from the Coptic Church by negotiation with Syrian Jacobites or Russian Orthodox. The Moslem sympathies of Menelik's grandson, Lij Yasu, were a considerable factor in the movement that led to his deposition in 1916. Menelik's daughter Yaoditu (Judith) succeeded under the regency of her cousin Ras Tafari; in 1930 he assended the throne, taking the significant name of Haile Selassie ("Might of the Trinity"). Some native bishops had been consecrated to assist the Coptic abuna (archbishop); after the Italian conquest of 1935 one of these, Abraham, was persuaded to assume the office of abuna, and Abuna Kurillos was exiled to Egypt. When Haile Selassie was restored in 1941 Kurillos returned; but it was agreed that his successor should be elected locally. Accordingly in 1950 the first native abuna, Basileos, was chosen and installed. Foreign contacts of the Ethiopian Church include membership in the World Council of Churches, and increased intercourse with other churches of the Monophysite Communion.

Foreigners are naturally most interested in the unusual features of the Ethiopian Church—its exuberant liturgy (of Coptic and other traditions, locally added to), its ritual dances and other African customs, its extensive if sometimes disorganized monasticism. One must remember that basically it preserves the pattern of historic Christianity (in its monophysite form)—the Nicene faith (as expounded by the first three General Councils), the sacraments, the orders of bishop, priest, and deacon (assisted by lay cantors, *debteras,* who are often the real liturgical experts), and the Scriptures (including Enoch and other apocryphal works). Recent reforms include the publication of the Bible and liturgical books in modern Amharic vernacular translations as well as the ancient Ge'ez, the issue of catechisms and encouragement of preaching, and the transfer of some authority from abuna or emperor to a Spiritual Council headed by the ichege (Abbot-General of Debra Libanos). A modern school for clergy training is projected. Some 4,000,000 of a total population of 7,000,000 to 8,000,000 adhere to the Ethiopian Church; others are mainly pagan or Moslem. Numerous Protestant missions (especially Scandinavian) have done useful work, especially educational and medical, but are forbidden to engage in evangelistic activities in predominantly Ethiopian Church areas. The Ethiopian Catholic Church (about 50,000 adherents), formed by nineteenth century Roman Catholic missionaries, exists mainly in the former Italian colony of Eritrea, now federated with Ethiopia.

BIBLIOGRAPHY: Donald Attwater, *The Christian Churches of the East,* 1946-47; H. M. Hyatt, *The Church of Abyssinia,* 1928; David Mathew, *Ethiopia,* 1947; S. A. B. Mercer, *The Ethiopic Liturgy,* 1913; Douglas O'Hanlon, *Features of the Abyssinian Church,* 1946; J. Spencer Trimingham, *The Christian Church and Missions in Ethiopia,* 1950.

[Sup. to ABYSSINIA AND THE ABYSSINIAN CHURCH.]   EDWARD ROCHIE HARDY.

EUCHARIST: In Roman Catholic usage, this term applies to the Lord's Supper (*q.v.,* Vol. VII), considered either as a sacrament to be received, or as the sacrifice of the Mass (*q.v.,* Vol. VII). Canon law makes it an obligation for all persons in age of discretion to partake of the Eucharist at least once a year at Easter (see EASTER COMMUNION), and when they are in danger of death (see VIATICUM). They are encouraged, however, to partake of the Eucharist frequently, and even daily.

[Sup.] GEORGES A. BARROIS.

EUCHARISTIC CONGRESS: Since the twentieth international Eucharistic Congress held in Montreal, Canada, in 1910, Roman Catholics held the following international Congresses to glorify the Eucharist: Madrid, 1911; Vienna, 1912; Malta, 1913; Lourdes, France, 1914; Rome, 1922; Amsterdam, 1924; Chicago, 1926; Sydney, Australia, 1928; Carthage, 1930; Dublin, 1932; Buenos Aires, 1934; Manila, Philippine Islands, 1937; Budapest, 1938. World War II interrupted plans for a Congress in Nice, France, in 1940; it was finally held in Barcelona, Spain, in 1952. In addition to these international Congresses, there have been many national Congresses. Nine were held in the U. S. A. between 1895 and 1941. [Sup. to ROMAN CATHOLIC EUCHARISTIC CONGRESSES.]

THEODORE G. TAPPERT.

EUCKEN, CHRISTIAN RUDOLPH: Lutheran; b. at Aurich, East Friesland, Jan. 5, 1846; d. at Jena, Sept. 15, 1926. After studying at Goettingen and Berlin, he taught at the Frankfurt Gymnasium (1869–71), and was then called to a professorship in philosophy at the University of Basel (1871–74), and finally served as professor of philosophy at Jena (1874–1920). In 1908 he was awarded the Nobel Prize for Literature. In 1912 he visited the United States. Against the naturalistic positivism (*q.v.*) of his time he developed a neo-idealist metaphysics, and advocated the concept of spiritual activity as the source of the unity and evolution of the universe. The principal works of religious significance were: *Die Einheit des Geisteslebens* (1888); *The Problem of Human Life* (1890, Eng. tr., 1909); *The Truth of Religion* (1901, Eng. tr., 1913); *Life's Basis and Life's Ideal* (1907, Eng. tr., 1911); *The Life of the Spirit* (1908, Eng. tr., 1909); *Present-Day Ethics and their Relation to the Spiritual Life* (1909, Eng. tr., 1912); *Can We Still Be Christians?* (1911, Eng. tr., 1914).

BIBLIOGRAPHY: W. R. B. Gibson, *Rudolf Eucken's Philosophy of Life,* 1906; W. S. Morgan, *The Religious*

Philosophy of Rudolf Eucken, 1914; P. Kalweit, *Euckens Religionsphilosophie*, 1927.

EDWIN E. AUBREY.

EUDAEMONISM. See HEDONISM.

EUGENICS. See HEREDITY.

EUGENIUS: Eugenius I: Only the attacks by the Saracens on Constantinople saved him from the fate of his predecessors, who were unable to withstand the opposition of the Byzantines.

BIBLIOGRAPHY: L. Duchesne, *Les premiers temps de l'état pontifical*, 1904.

Eugenius II: Was of Roman birth. The Frankish emperor used the monk Wala to weaken him, thus strengthening the nobility which opposed his tactics.

Eugenius III:

BIBLIOGRAPHY: E. Caspar, *Die Kreuzzugsbullen Eugens III*, in *Neues Archiv fuer Geschichtskunde*, 1924; W. Reichert, *Das Verhaeltnis Eugens III zu den Kloestern*, 1912; B. Kugler, *Analekten zur Geschichte des zweiten Kreuzzugs*, 1878, 1883.

Eugenius IV: B. 1383; he was a nephew of Gregory XII. In 1407 became bishop of Siena, in 1408 cardinal. Emperor Sigismund persuaded him to deal amicably with the church council which he had considered annulled by his own bull. He admitted that it was ecumenical (1433). In 1434 a revolution broke out in Rome, whereupon he fled to Florence. Vitelleschi occupied Rome but did not thereby end the pope's rule. In 1438 Eugenius convoked the Council of Ferrara and excommunicated the prelates who were still holding the Council of Basel. The latter chose Amadeus, duke of Savoy anti-pope as Felix V. In 1445 he recognized Emperor Frederick III, thus insuring German support for him. He did all in his power to help the Christian princes who were trying in vain to hold back the Turkish armies. By promising one tenth of the papal income for this purpose he gave new impetus to the crusade of 1443, which nevertheless was a failure. In 1442 the antipope through his adviser brought about a reconciliation with him. Eugenius recognized the claims of Alfonso of Aragon to Naples, thereby inducing the latter to oppose the Council of Basel. Moreover, he now was able to return from Florence to Rome (1443). He was noted for his religious fervor and his support of the monastic orders that were introducing reforms. He was the first pope who put the Brethren of the Common Life upon a firm basis, thus ending some fifty years of attacks upon the new brotherhood by the mendicant monks.

See also POPES.

BIBLIOGRAPHY: W. Pueckert, *Die kurfuerstl. Neutralitaet waehrend des Basler Konzils*, 1858; F. Ph. Abert, *Papst Eugen IV*, 1884; G. Voight, *Aus den Annatenregistern der Paepste Eugen IV, Pius II, Paul II und Sixtus IV*, ed. K. Hayn, 1896; F. Gregorovius, *Rome in the Middle Ages*, Vol. VII, 1902; N. Valois, *Le pape et le concile*, Vol. II, 1904.

[Sup.] ALBERT HYMA.

EUROPE IN THE TWENTIETH CENTURY, CHRISTIANITY IN: The beginning of World War I in 1914 may be said to have marked the opening of a new era in European history. During its first forty years this era was one of wars and revolutions. Boundaries were altered, royal houses collapsed, vast property was destroyed, many people were killed or uprooted, and economic and social disturbances added to widespread suffering. The effect on the church appeared to be disastrous. Many church buildings were destroyed, large numbers of people who before had retained nominal connection with the church withdrew (see KIRCHENAUSTRITT), the influence of the church in molding social and political life waned, and the inner vitality of the church was sapped by the inroads of secularism (*q.v.*). The rise of communism (*q.v.*), fascism (see ITALY, SPAIN), and national socialism (see GERMANY) introduced sharp conflicts between church and state (*q.v.*), and wherever communism triumphed there were not only heavy losses in church membership but also persecutions of Christians (see BULGARIA, CZECHOSLOVAKIA, ESTONIA, HUNGARY, LATVIA, LITHUANIA, POLAND, RUMANIA, RUSSIA, YUGOSLAVIA).

Outwardly, therefore, the first half of the twentieth century was a period of decline in European church life. Yet the very forces which seemed to be undermining the church were bringing out hidden sources of strength. There are especially four areas in which this was manifest.

I. Theological Revival: Conditions in Europe were no longer hospitable to the optimistic liberalism (*q.v.*) which had been characteristic of the late nineteenth and early twentieth centuries. Its place was taken within Protestantism by dialectic theology (*q.v.*) and by a conscious return to the theology of the Reformation (see NEO-ORTHODOXY), accompanied by a somewhat more conservative use of the Scriptures. To be sure, the influence of liberalism was still felt (e.g., in F. R. Tennant, *q.v.*), and there were also streams of influence of a mystical or romanticist nature. But theologians like Peter T. Forsyth (*q.v.*), John Baillie (*q.v.*), Karl Barth (*q.v.*), Emil Brunner (*q.v.*), Karl Heim (*q.v.*), Paul Althaus (*q.v.*), Joseph L. Hromadka (*q.v.*), Gustaf Aulen (*q.v.*), Anders Nygren (*q.v.*), and Regin Prenter (*q.v.*) represented the dominant tendency. Parallel to the revived interest in the Reformation among Protestants was a revival of the theology and philosophy of Thomas Aquinas (*q.v.*, Vol. XI) in Roman Catholicism, and the chief exponents of this Neo-Thomism (*q.v.*) were men like Jacques Maritain and Etienne Gilson (*q.v.*). Leading representatives of Eastern Orthodoxy in Europe were Nicholas Berdyaev (*q.v.*) and Sergius Bulgakov (*q.v.*).

II. Social Concern: In the face of the deterioration which characterized so much of

European social life during the first half of the twentieth century, the concern expressed earlier in the Social Service Unions, in Christian Socialism (q.v.), in the Inner Mission (q.v.), and in the Evangelical Social Congress (q.v.) was sharpened and extended. Social problems of many kinds were discussed in the Conference on Christian Politics, Economics, and Citizenship (q.v.), and later in Malvern (q.v.) and the Sword of the Spirit (q.v.) movement in Great Britain. The ecumenical conferences on life and work (see ECUMENICAL MOVEMENT; NATHAN SÖDERBLOM) also devoted serious attention to social problems. Churches co-operated with governmental agencies in giving assistance to the 12,000,000 refugees (q.v.) who wandered about Europe. The destruction caused by war was alleviated by programs of relief and reconstruction (q.v.) engaged in by many church agencies, including Evangelisches Hilfswerk (q.v.) and the Roman Catholic Caritas (q.v.) on the Continent.

III. Evangelism: Often closely associated with the theological revival and expressions of social concern were new forms of evangelism which were intended to win back to the church as many as possible of the people who had been alienated. In addition to the use of older evangelistic techniques, the Iona Community (q.v.) in Scotland, the Evangelical Academies (q.v.) in Germany, Sigtuna (q.v.) in Sweden, the Kerk en Wereld Institute in Holland, and the Roman Catholic Mission de France (q.v.) were representative of new methods which achieved significant results. Special attempts were made to reclaim young people (see YOUTH MOVEMENTS; CATHOLIC ACTION). A tremendous impetus was given to church extension and the erection of new churches (see, e.g., DENMARK), and support of the foreign missionary enterprise continued despite the interruption of activity caused by two world wars (see ORPHANED MISSIONS; EXPANSION OF CHRISTIANITY, MODERN).

IV. Interchurch Co-operation: A variety of impulses led to co-operative movements among the churches in Europe during the twentieth century, and among these were the conditions in Europe itself. The International Missionary Council (q.v.) and the World Council of Churches (q.v.) included others than Europeans. Meanwhile national federations of Protestant churches were formed in countries with a diversity of confessions: the Protestant Federation of France (q.v., 1905), the Federation of Protestant Churches in Switzerland (1920), the Federation of German Evangelical Churches (q.v., 1922; reorganized in 1948 as the Evangelical Church in Germany), the Ecumenical Council of Evangelical Churches in the Netherlands (1935), and the British Council of Churches (q.v., 1942). The Eastern Orthodox (see EASTERN ORTHODOX CHURCHES) did not participate in such federations although they were active in the ecumenical movement. Some attempts were made to heal the four-centuries-old breach between Protestantism and Roman Catholicism (see MALINES, CONVERSATIONS AT; INTERFAITH RELATIONS), but no observable progress was made. Meanwhile Roman Catholicism (see ROMAN CATHOLIC CHURCH) made some gains in membership, nominally at the expense of Protestantism, in countries like England and Holland, while Protestant churches won converts in such Catholic strongholds as Austria (see LOS VON ROM).

See also UNITED STATES IN THE TWENTIETH CENTURY, CHRISTIANITY IN THE.

BIBLIOGRAPHY: A. Keller and G. Stewart, Protestant Europe, 1927; H. S. Leiper, ed., Christianity Today, 1947; Stewart W. Herman, Report from Christian Europe, 1953; Adolf Keller, Church and State on the European Continent, 1936; Cyril Garbett, In an Age of Revolution, 1953; Wilhelm Kuetemeyer, Die Krankheit Europas, 1951; George N. Shuster, Religion Behind the Iron Curtain, 1954; Kenneth S. Latourette, Advance through Storm, A.D. 1914 and After, Vol. VII of A History of the Expansion of Christianity, 1945; E. J. Bingle and K. G. Grubb, eds., World Christian Handbook, 1952; Walter M. Horton, Contemporary Continental Theology, 1936; idem, Contemporary English Theology, 1936; Ruth Rouse and Stephen C. Neill, eds., A History of the Ecumenical Movement, 1954. See also bibliographies under the several countries.

THEODORE G. TAPPERT.

EUROPEAN CENTRAL OFFICE FOR INTER-CHURCH AID: The first Protestant agency for relief work on an ecumenical basis, the Office was established in Geneva in 1922 with Adolphe Keller (q.v.) and later H. Hellstern as general secretary. In 1945 the Office was merged into the Department of Relief and Reconstruction of the World Council of Churches (q.v.), then in process of formation. ADOLPHE KELLER.

EUSEBIUS OF CAESAREA: It might be more correct to say that Hegesippus was the father of Church History.

It seems unlikely that Eusebius was once a slave of Pamphilus.

August Moehle claims the discovery of an almost complete text of his commentary on Isaiah in the margins of Ms. Florenz Bibl. Laur. Plut. XI. 4 ("Der Jesaiaskommentar des Eusebios von Kaisareia fast vollstaendig wieder aufgefunden," Zeitschrift fuer neutestamentliche Wissenschaft, 33 [1934], 87–89). Here too Eusebius depends largely on Origen.

Eusebius' role in the Council of Nicaea poses several problems: (1) What was the origin of the creed which he presented to the council? Ferdinand Kattenbusch (Das apostolische Symbol, 2 vols., 1894, 1900) and Matthias Weis (Die Stellung des Eusebius von Caesarea im arianischen Streit, 1919) thought that he had composed it himself. Hendrikus Berkhof (Die Theologie des Eusebius von Caesarea, 1939) maintained its relationship to an older, unknown creed. For a summary of those who regard it as the Caesarean Creed, cf., Francis Joseph Bacchus (*Catholic Encyclopedia*, V, 1909), who falls in the same category. (2) What was Eusebius' position in relation to Arianism? For a summary of opinions, cf., Weis, *op. cit.*, pp. 1–19, who thinks he was closer to Arianism than to the Nicene Creed. (3) What then motivated his signing of the creed? Some think he did so to prove his orthodoxy after the setback by the Synod of Antioch (Kattenbusch, *op. cit.*,; James Stevenson, *Studies in Eusebius*, 1924; Berkhof, *op. cit.*). Others think he did it for the sake of peace and harmony in the church at the wish of Constantine the Great, whom he greatly admired (cf., Frederick John Foakes-Jackson, *Eusebius Pamphili*, 1933; Berkhof). To this Foakes-Jackson added that he likely feared banishment.

Eusebius does not seem to leave much doubt in the formulation of his pastoral letter (Theodoretus, *Ecclesiastica historia,* I. 11; Socrates *Historia ecclesiastica*, I. 8; Athanasius, *De decrete synodi Nicaenae, passim*) that he gave the Caesarean Creed. His writings indicate clearly that he held opinions different from the Nicene Creed, and thus his subscription to it was likely for ulterior motives.

BIBLIOGRAPHY: For editions cf. *Der grosse Brockhaus,* 15th edition, V (1930), *s.v.;* G. Bardy, *Histoire ecclesiastique*, 1952. For translations cf. *Encyclopædia Britannica,* 14th edition, VIII (1929). *s.v.; Loeb Classical Library; Fathers of the Church.* H. Gressmann, *Studien zu Eusebs Theolphani*, 1903; A. Bauer, *Beitraege zu Eusebios und den byzantinischen Chronographen,* 1909; H. J. Lawlor, *Eusebiana,* 1912; H. Doergens, *Eusebius von Caesarea als Darsteller der griechischen Religion,* 1922; E. Caspar, *Die aelteste roemische Bischofsliste,* 1926; R. W. O. Helm, *Die neuesten Hypothesen zu Eusebius' (Hieronymus') Chronik,* 1929; R. Laqueur, *Eusebius als Historiker seiner Zeit,* 1929.

[Sup.] DANIEL JOHANNES THERON.

EUTHALIUS: Before significant progress can be made in the study of the Euthalian problem, many more data must be collected from New Testament manuscripts and from the ancient versions of the Acts and Epistles. Euthalian material is found in many New Testament codices (e.g., Hp, 1424, 82, 1175, 1874, 1880, 1895, 1898, 1891, 181, 1162, 1244, 1888, 1, 421, and 1894). Those which are mentioned here range from the sixth to the twelfth century in date. See also H. von Soden, *Die Schriften des Neuen Testaments* (1902–13), I. 1, pp. 674 ff.; and C. H. Turner in Hastings's *Dictionary of the Bible* (1899–1904), Extra Volume, p. 529.

Another primary desideratum in this field of research is a new and critical edition of the Euthalian apparatus. It should be based upon many more manuscripts than were used by L. A. Zacagni in preparing his edition, which was published in Rome in the year 1698. Furthermore, since the Euthalian material increased greatly in volume with the passage of time, the various strata of which it is composed should be clearly distinguished.

The following considerations prove conclusively that the earliest stratum of the Euthalian apparatus was in existence in the first half of the fourth century. In Codex Vaticanus there are two sets of chapters in the Book of Acts— one of thirty-six chapters and the other of sixty-nine; and both of these systems were derived ultimately from the work of "Euthalius." The division of the Acts into thirty-six chapters is closely connected with the division of the book into forty chapters, which is an essential part of the Euthalian tradition. Many of the forty chapters of the Acts were subdivided into smaller sections or subdivisions, and of these there were forty-eight. Sometimes the distinction between the chapters and the subdivisions was ignored, and the forty chapters and the forty-eight subdivisions were numbered continuously throughout the book. Thus there were in all eighty-eight sections in the Acts ($40 + 48 = 88$). In Codex Vaticanus, as was said above, the Acts is divided into sixty-nine sections or chapters. This system undoubtedly resulted from a shortening or condensation of the system of eighty-eight sections or chapters. In any case it is clear from their agreements that the two systems did not arise independently of one another. Codex Vaticanus was apparently written in Upper Egypt about the middle of the fourth century. The chapter numbers according to the system of thirty-six chapters were inserted in the margin of the manuscript by a very early hand—perhaps by the *diorthotes* or possibly by the scribe himself; and the chapter numbers according to the system of sixty-nine chapters were added by a somewhat later hand.

In Codex Sinaiticus the system of sixty-nine chapters was employed in the first fifteen chapters of the Acts, but for some unknown reason it was not continued to the end of the book. These chapter numbers were certainly introduced by a very early hand, and Kirsopp Lake was inclined to think that they were inserted before the manuscript was taken from the scriptorium. Neither of the earlier systems, i.e., that of thirty-six or that of forty chapters, appears in the manuscript. Codex Sinaiticus was apparently copied somewhere in Egypt at about the same time as Codex Vaticanus.

The conclusion to be drawn from the use of the two systems of chapter numbering mentioned above, in both of which the work of "Euthalius" is presupposed, is that the Euthalian editions of the Pauline Epistles and of the Acts and Catholic Epistles were produced before the middle of the fourth century. On the other hand the author used the *Chronological Canons* of Eusebius, and he quotes a passage *verbatim* from the same writer's *Ecclesiastical History*. Therefore "Euthalius" must have written after A.D. 323 or 324, for the *Ecclesiastical History* was finished either at the end of the year 323 or in 324. In other words the earliest stratum of the Euthalian material dates from the second quarter of the fourth century.

The Euthalian problem may be solved tentatively in this way: The earliest stratum of the Euthalian apparatus is the work of a biblical scholar who flourished in the second quarter of the fourth century. His name is now lost, but it may have been Evagrius or possibly Euthalius. Perhaps he was a deacon; and he may have lived in Alexandria, which was an important center of Christian learning. This substratum of the Euthalian material was revised, probably at Caesarea, in A.D. 396; and some new matter was added at this time. This revision may have been made by Evagrius, if he was not the author of the earliest stratum of the Euthalian apparatus. Finally, there was an ecclesiastical writer in the seventh century whose name was Euthalius; and he was bishop of Sulci, which was on the island of Plumbaria off the southwestern coast of Sardinia. He may be the "Euthalius" to whom the Euthalian material is traditionally ascribed. He may have published a revised edition of the apparatus, and he may have included some new matter in it. See also J. H. Ropes in F. J. Foakes-Jackson and K. Lake's *The Beginnings of Christianity* (1920–33), Part I, Vol. III, pp. xli–xliii, clii, cliv f., and clxxviii.   [Sup.] WILLIAM H. P. HATCH.

EUTHANASIA: The term is from the Greek *eu*, an adverb meaning "well," "happily," and *thanatos*, meaning "death." It thus means basically "a quiet and easy death," or "the action of inducing such a death." But that is not sufficient to define the term, as now employed, for that might possibly be predicated, in some cases at least, of suicide, homicide, or even murder. Euthanasia differs from suicide in that, in the case of the latter, the agent and the object of his action are the same person, whereas, in euthanasia, the agent is one person, or group of persons, and the object of the act is another. Whether or not euthanasia is really murder is a much debated question; but, as these terms are commonly understood, it differs, in the matter of its motivation and other subjective factors, from both homicide and murder. Homicide may or may not be committed with conscious intention; euthanasia and murder always are. In so far as homicide is done with conscious intention, it still differs from euthanasia and from murder in respect of the measure and kind of control which the agent is thought to have over his own action. Even when homicide is committed with conscious intention, the agent is still judged to have acted under a compulsion or limitation which rendered him not fully responsible; but murder and euthanasia are regarded as fully responsible actions. That which clearly differentiates euthanasia from both homicide and murder, as these terms are commonly employed, is the motivation. In the case of euthanasia, the motive, or at least the primary motive, is to be helpful to the object. For that reason, it is often popularly called "mercy killing." The object of the act is judged to be condemned to a life of intolerable suffering, ending in a proximate, and possibly horribly painful death, or, by reason of hopeless mental deficiency, to a life of deprivation and frustration. It is felt that, if the object himself were able to choose dispassionately, he would prefer a quick and easy death. Though the removal of an intolerable burden from his near relatives and from society is often advanced as a secondary motive and justification, euthanasia is primarily regarded as an act of mercy towards the sufferer. It is argued that the omission or refusal of such relief really betrays a cruelty which no sensitive person would for a moment permit himself or approve towards a horse or a dog. How much more, then, should a human person, infinitely more worthy of mercy than any mere animal, have his irremediable suffering or frustration mercifully ended?

Those who condemn euthanasia usually do so for one or both of two basic reasons. The first is that same high regard for the value of human life which is used by advocates of euthanasia to justify it. This objection of theirs may be naturalistically or supernaturalistically supported. It may be argued, with the naturalistic humanists, that a human person, as such, possesses infinite value, which confers on him "unalienable rights," among which is the right to life. This right, because it is by the very nature of things unalienable, may not properly be surrendered or infringed. Those who argue in this fashion may carry it through consistently and reject also, for example, the death penalty and the right to take up arms. Those who apply it to euthanasia and not to these other forms of killing usually do so because the second reason, coupled with the first, is for them determinative. The second reason may be called an argument from uncertainty. The uncertainty is twofold: (1) Who, it is asked, is capable of deciding that a case of mental or organic disease is really incurable, and who can decide that its real impact on the sufferer is necessarily deleterious? Cases are cited in which maladies, pronounced incurable by the best authorities available, have subsequently given place to health, and cases also in which the most excruciating and hopeless suffering have been transmuted into the spiritual blessing of the sufferer and of his friends and acquaintances. (2) The motives of men are uncertain and thus untrustworthy; and no machinery can be devised for detecting and frustrating such unworthy motives with the degree of reliability which would be absolutely essential where such an infinitely valuable thing as a human life is at stake. When it is replied that the judicial process, advised by a panel of doctors, would suffice, it is answered that, for one thing, reputable doctors are quite unwilling to assume such a responsibility and that, since the whole motivation of the medical profession is and must be the alleviation of suffering and the saving of life, their unwillingness is justified and will be permanent. To this the reply is made that doctors do find themselves occasionally confronted by situations in which, by omission at least but quite deliberately, they really, but without open acknowledgment, practice euthanasia. In such cases, so it is urged, their action is surreptitious and the whole responsibility rests upon the individual doctor. Would it not be better, for the medical profession and for society, that this practice be regularized and brought out into the open? Whatever one may decide as to such theoretical considerations, the fact is that in America medical men who have taken upon themselves openly to practice euthanasia have almost always, if not invariably, been disciplined by their own medical societies, and that the courts regard euthanasia as a crime.

But the opposition to euthanasia is also based on religious grounds. Here the Roman Catholic Church, though it stands by no means alone, is perhaps the best known and the most inflexible protagonist. It is argued that a human life is sacred to God, and that he alone has the right to preserve or to dispose of it. It is also feared that euthanasia may deprive the person, at the very time when he should be most intelligently engaged in the supremely important task of preparing to meet his Judge, of the capacity and opportunity of doing so. "The most that may be granted to those charged with responsibility in the case is to take up a passively permissive demeanour whenever it is certain that the departing soul has abundantly made ready for the great summons" ("Euthanasia," in *The Catholic Encyclopedia*).　Andrew K. Rule.

EUTIN: In 1920 the Evangelical Lutheran Church of Eutin was separated from the Evangelical Church of Oldenburg (*q.v.*), to which it had previously been attached. It occupies part of the German province of Schleswig-Holstein (*q.v.*). Its territory included 110,000 Lutherans and 8,000 Roman Catholics in 1950. The confessional complexion remained proportionately the same despite the influx of refugees (*q.v.*). There are fourteen congregations. These elect lay delegates to sit with the clergy in a synod. The government of the church between synods is in the hands of a provost or dean, who heads a superior church council of three members.

See also Germany; Lutheran Church in Germany, United Evangelical.

Wilhelm Kieckbusch.

EVANGELICAL ACADEMIES. See Academies, Evangelical.

EVANGELICAL AND REFORMED CHURCH: Formed by the union of the Evangelical Synod of North America (*q.v.*) and the Reformed Church in the United States (*q.v.*). Informal conversations preceded discussions between official commissions which in 1932 adopted a basic Plan of Union. This document, comprising a preamble and twelve short articles dealing with name, doctrine, supreme judicatory, General Synod and its functions, rights of property, members, worship, etc., having been approved by the supreme judicatory of both bodies, became the basis on which the union was effected at the first General Synod of the united church in June, 1934.

Statistics at the time showed: 2,648 pastors; 2,929 congregations; 631,271 communicant members; Sunday school enrollment, 538,308; value of church property, $73,449,782; congregational expenses, $7,005,534; benevolence, $1,315,286; thirty educational institutions (including those on foreign fields); nine hospitals; ten orphanages; eleven homes for the aged and two homes for epileptics and feeble-minded.

Pending the acceptance of a constitution (1940), the congregations, regional conferences, classes, districts, synods, boards, committees, commissions, and the governmental and administrative bodies of both churches, continued to be governed by the Plan of Union and by their own constitutions and by-laws. The respective boards and agencies had accomplished an effective merger prior to the adoption of the constitution. The union process had been hastened by the redivision, in 1938, of the fifty-six classes (Reformed) and twenty districts (Evangelical) into twenty-four synods.

In 1934 Central Theological Seminary, Dayton, O. (Reformed), merged with Eden Theological Seminary, Webster Groves, Mo. (Evangelical). Two years later periodicals of the two bodies merged into *The Messenger* and *Friedensbote*. In 1940 the boards for home and foreign missions were transformed respectively into the Board for National and the Board for International Missions (foreign mission stations in Africa, China, Honduras, India, Iraq, Japan, and South America). Similar mergers formed the Women's Guild and the Churchmen's Brotherhood.

The new constitution, approved at the second General Synod (1936), having been accepted by the respective classes (Reformed) and districts (Evangelical), was adopted by the third General Synod (1938), not becoming effective, however, until the convening of the fourth General Synod in 1940. The doctrinal position is: "The doctrinal standards of the Evangelical and Reformed Church are the Heidelberg Catechism,

Luther's Catechism, and the Augsburg Confession. They are accepted as an authoritative interpretation of the essential truth taught in the Holy Scriptures. Wherever these doctrinal standards differ, ministers, members, and congregations, in accordance with the liberty of conscience inherent in the gospel, are allowed to adhere to the interpretation of one of these confessions. However, in each case the final norm is the Word of God. In its relation to other Christian communions the Evangelical and Reformed Church shall constantly endeavor to promote the unity of the Spirit in the bond of peace."

The year 1940 marked the beginning not only of internal consolidations but also of informal union conversations with the Congregational-Christian Churches (*q.v.*). The first draft of a Basis of Union (1943), after various revisions, was adopted by the General Synod of 1948. Certain questions remained in abeyance, and further steps awaited the outcome of legal deliberations engaging the Congregational-Christian Churches. The Evangelical and Reformed Church retains membership in the Alliance of Reformed Churches. Statistics for 1950 show: 2,494 pastors; 2,746 congregations; 735,941 communicant members; Sunday school enrollment, 468,149; value of church property, $13,081,796; congregational expenses, $21,084,451; benevolence, $3,963,241.

BIBLIOGRAPHY: *Minutes* of General Conferences and files of *Messenger* and *Yearbook*, 1934– ; J. H. Horstmann and H. H. Wernecke, *Through Four Centuries*, 1938.

CARL E. SCHNEIDER.

EVANGELICAL ASSOCIATION. See EVANGELICAL CHURCH.

EVANGELICAL CHURCH: After the division of the Evangelical Association (1891–94) (*q.v.*, Vol. IV) and the formation of the United Evangelical Church (*q.v.*), the bishops and general officers of the Evangelical Association led the denomination in aggressive programs of advance. The Young People's Alliance grew rapidly and became a part of the general structure of the church (1907); the Deaconess Society (1903–38) served largely as a medium for the Christian service of nurses in denominational hospitals at Chicago, Ill., Freeport, Ill., Monroe, Wisc., and Waterloo, Iowa; the Board of Church Extension was developed (1899) to provide means for church buildings and was later united with the Missionary Society. The Evangelical Correspondence College gave way to the Evangelical School of Theology (1905) at Reading, Pa. A new mission in the Orient was begun in Hunan Province, China (1903).

The Forward Movement (1919) with co-operation of lay and clerical leadership resulted in new emphases on evangelism, devotion, missionary expansion, and church-related education; it

brought many new candidates for the ministry and provided $2,500,000 for the general agencies of the church. The Superannuation Fund (1911) was organized to provide proper pensions for the ministry.

During the first two decades of the twentieth century constant negotiations between the Evangelical Association and the United Evangelical Church ultimately resulted in the union of these bodies to form the Evangelical Church, in Detroit, Mich., Oct. 14, 1922. The reunited denomination now had a membership of approximately 260,000 with 420,000 enrolled in the Sunday schools and more than 1,850 full-time ministers. A small group, mostly in the East Pennsylvania Conference of the United Evangelical Church, did not unite but formed the new Evangelical Congregational Church (*q.v.*).

See also EVANGELICAL UNITED BRETHREN CHURCH.

BIBLIOGRAPHY: Raymond W. Albright, *A History of the Evangelical Church*, 1942, 2nd ed., 1945.

[Sup.] RAYMOND W. ALBRIGHT.

EVANGELICAL CHURCH IN GERMANY: See GERMANY, I.

EVANGELICAL CONGREGATIONAL CHURCH: After the reunion of the Evangelical Association (*q.v.*, Vol. IV) and the United Evangelical Church (*q.v.*) to form the Evangelical Church (*q.v.*) in 1922, a small group of approximately 20,000 persons of the former United Evangelical Church, largely under the leadership of William F. Heil, formed the Evangelical Congregational Church. This body is located almost exclusively in eastern Pennsylvania, with a few scattered congregations in the Midwest.

Headquarters are on the former Albright College campus in Myerstown, Pa., where the weekly, *The United Evangelical*, is published and where a school of theology is located. The polity of the denomination is patterned after the parent body. The term of office of bishops and presiding elders is limited to eight years. In 1952 the total membership was approximately 25,000, with about 150 ministers.

RAYMOND W. ALBRIGHT.

EVANGELICAL FREE CHURCH OF AMERICA: A kind of American parallel to the free church movement in Norway (*q.v.*) and Denmark (*q.v.*), and also a parallel to the Evangelical Mission Covenant Church of America (*q.v.*), the Free Church was organized in Boone, Iowa, in 1884. In June, 1950, it merged with the Evangelical Free Church Association, of similar origin.

The merged body is an association and fellowship of independent congregations of like faith and practice for the purpose of saving souls, edifying believers, organizing churches and Sunday schools, engaging in missionary work at home and abroad, maintaining schools, theological seminaries, and charitable institutions, and publishing and distributing Christian literature. Its official organ is *The Evangelical Beacon and Evangelist*. Headquarters are in Minneapolis, Minn.

Membership is about 30,000. Missions, engaging 125 missionaries and 270 native workers, are conducted in China, Hong Kong, Japan, South America, and the Belgian Congo.

E. A. HALLEEN.

EVANGELICALISM, ANGLICAN: The Evangelical revival was an outbreak of Christian vitality in eighteenth century England. The earliest leaders were Anglican clergymen who, after conversion, discovered one another and collaborated. Best known are John Wesley (*q.v.*, Vol. XII) and George Whitefield (*q.v.*, Vol. XII). The opposition of bishops, vicars, and gentry made them feel obliged to license their meeting-places as dissenting chapels. Other Anglican clergy refused to break from the Establishment, and from them Anglican Evangelicalism stems.

Some early leaders were Calvinists, like William Romaine (*q.v.*, Vol. X), others Arminians, like Grimshaw, but all proclaimed the traditional Evangelical convictions.

They differed from Wesley and Whitefield in regarding the Establishment as the divinely appointed means for England's conversion, and schism as sin. Later leaders, like John Newton (*q.v.*, Vol. VIII) and Charles Simeon (*q.v.*, Vol. X), besides stressing God's love proportionately more than his wrath, evoked the toil and wealth of able laity (as in the Clapham Sect, [*q.v.*]) to finance and direct great missionary organizations like the Church Missionary Society and philanthropic enterprises like the elimination of slavery, prison reform, ragged schools.

By 1800 the Evangelicals, though a minority movement, were the greatest spiritual force in England. They became the Evangelical Party about 1785. In the nineteenth century the movement grew numerically, fought Tractarianism over doctrinal and ritual points, attacked advanced scholarship over Biblical criticism and evolution (*q.v.*), and opposed Christian socialism (*q.v.*). It lost vitality. After World War I its spiritual descendants began to reorient the party so as to preserve its Reformation stress and appropriate some values of high churchmen and liberals. It published *Liberal Evangelicalism* (1924), and a later generation published *The Fulness of Christ* (1951), attempting statements about the gospel, the Bible, the sacraments, evangelization, and church union in forms relevant to modern questions.

Anglican Evangelicalism has gone through similar developments in the United States.

BIBLIOGRAPHY: Leonard E. Binns, *The Evangelical Movement in the English Church*, 1928; A. C. Zabriskie, ed., *Anglican Evangelicalism*, 1943; J. H. Overton, *History of the Evangelical Movement*, 1907; G. R. Ballein, *History of the Evangelical Party*, 1908; G. W. E. Russell, *Short History of the Evangelical Movement*, 1915; E. C. Chorley, *Men and Movements in the American Episcopal Church*, 1946.

ALEXANDER C. ZABRISKIE.

EVANGELICAL MISSION COVENANT CHURCH OF AMERICA. See MISSION COVENANT CHURCH OF AMERICA, EVANGELICAL.

EVANGELICAL PROTESTANT CHURCH OF NORTH AMERICA: Formed by consolidation of two associations in 1911. The continuing decline, due in large part to the independent spirit of pastors and congregations, the lack of centralized administration, and the loss of the youth because of adherence to the German language, led (about 1922) to union discussions with the German Evangelical Synod of North America (*q.v.*), the Unitarians, and the Congregationalists (*q.v.*). In union with the latter (1924–25), the church was constituted as the Evangelical Protestant Conference of Congregational Churches—the districts (now called associations) and congregations retaining autonomous status. This arrangement continued until the further dissolution in 1935, when local churches and pastors individually joined the Congregational Christian Associations in their respective areas.

BIBLIOGRAPHY: *Protestantische Zeitblaetter*, 1847–75, later merged with the *Union* and called *Protestantisches Familienblatt*, 1875–85; *Kirchenbote*, 1885–99; *Kirchenzeitung*, 1900– ; U. S. Census of Religious Bodies.

[Sup. to GERMAN EVANGELICAL PROTESTANT CHURCH.] CARL E. SCHNEIDER.

EVANGELICAL SYNOD OF NORTH AMERICA: The development of the Synod, prior to the merger with the Reformed Church in the United States (*q.v.*) into the Evangelical and Reformed Church (*q.v.*), was characterized largely by its continued Americanization (*q.v.*). The word "German" in the title of the body was dropped in 1925, and Americanization led toward basic revision and expansion of interests and activities.

The external expansion toward the west and north—the rise of new home mission projects at Biloxi, Miss.; in the Ozarks, Mo.; on Madeline Island, Wis.; and among the Germans and Russians in the northwest—was accompanied by an increase of religious service-functions and agencies. The need for more centralized integration of these varied activities led to the adoption of a new constitution (1927) which embodied a blending of congregational and presbyterian elements with a touch of the episcopal.

The ecumenical interests of the Synod led to participation in current national and international interdenominational movements and to church union conversations with the Moravians,

United Brethren, the Evangelical Church, and the Reformed Church in the United States.

Organic union with the latter was effected in 1934, at which time statistics showed: 1,254 congregations, 1,227 pastors serving in 21 districts; 281,598 individual members; 1,067 Sunday schools with enrollment of 193,447; value of church property, $34,698,749; congregational expenses, $3,310,817; benevolence, $477,358.

BIBLIOGRAPHY: H. Kamphausen, *Geschichte des religioesen Lebens in der Deutschen Evangelischen Synode von Nord Amerika*, 1924; A. Muecke, *Geschichte der Deutschen Evangelischen Synode von Nord Amerika*, 1915; Carl E. Schneider, *The German Church on the American Frontier*, 1939.

[Sup. to GERMAN EVANGELICAL SYNOD OF NORTH AMERICA.]   CARL E. SCHNEIDER.

EVANGELICAL UNION FOR THE PRESERVATION OF GERMAN PROTESTANT INTERESTS. See BUND, EVANGELISCHER.

EVANGELICAL UNION OF BOHEMIAN AND MORAVIAN BRETHREN. See CZECH-MORAVIAN BRETHREN OF NORTH AMERICA, EVANGELICAL UNITY OF.

EVANGELICAL UNITED BRETHREN CHURCH: Formed Nov. 16, 1946, by the union of the Church of the United Brethren in Christ (*q.v.*) and the Evangelical Church (*q.v.*). Since the polity and doctrines of the two churches were very similar, the *Discipline* of the new church perpetuates the two sets of Articles of Faith and the new polity reflects largely the traditions and customs of the former churches. A major change in the *Discipline* of 1951, adopted by the General Conference of 1950, is the new and enlarged section of rituals for the church.

The denomination has over 730,000 members in the United States and Canada with an additional 50,000 in Europe, Africa, South Africa, the West Indies, the Philippines, Japan, and China. Since 1950 the conferences in North America have been divided into seven episcopal areas with episcopal residences at Harrisburg, Pa., Pittsburgh, Pa., Indianapolis, Ind., Dayton, Ohio, St. Paul, Minn., Kansas City, Mo., and Peunte, Calif.

The major publications of the denomination are *The Telescope-Messenger, Builders,* and *Evangelischer Botschafter* (Stuttgart, Germany). In the interim between sessions of the General Conference the denomination operates through general boards of trustees, publications, missions, pensions, Christian education, evangelism, and the general council of administration which serves as a representative body for the other boards. The church provides for orphans and the aged in nine homes and three orphanages in the United States. Seven additional homes and orphanages are located in Germany, France, and Switzerland.

Colleges supported by the denomination are Albright, Reading, Pa.; Indiana Central, Indianapolis, Ind.; Lebanon Valley, Annville, Pa.; North Central, Naperville, Ill.; Otterbein, Westerville, Ohio; Shenandoah, Dayton, Va.; and Westmar, Le Mars, Ia. Three theological seminaries are located in Dayton, Ohio; Naperville, Ill.; and Reutlingen, Germany.

The historical society of the denomination has an official depository located at Dayton, Ohio. The publishing houses are located at Harrisburg, Pa.; Dayton, Ohio; Stuttgart, Germany; and Berne, Switzerland. The denomination has a standing commission on church federation and union.

There are 4,952 organized congregations in 3,024 charges, with a total of 3,767 ministers and approximately 500 men preparing for the ministry. In the church schools there is an enrollment of 708,121 pupils, and 106,000 women are enrolled in the Women's Society of World Service. In 1953 the total contributions of the denomination exceeded $34,000,000 with more than $6,000,000 used for missions and benevolence.

RAYMOND W. ALBRIGHT.

EVANGELISCHE KIRCHE IN DEUTSCHLAND. See EVANGELICAL CHURCH IN GERMANY.

EVANGELISCHE PEERLE AND VAN DEN TEMPEL ONSER SIELEN, THE UNKNOWN AUTHOR OF DIE: About this author very little is known, except the data to be found in the introduction to the edition of 1542 by Nicholas van Esch, a noted leader of beguines. The first work, *The Evangelical Pearl,* was written by a lady of noble birth, whose childhood was spent in or near Oisterwijk in Dutch Brabant. She led a deeply religious life in the home of her parents, and spent much time in the beguinage of Oisterwijk. She died on January 28, 1540, at the age of seventy-seven. Both of her mystic works exhibit remarkable talents. Of the second only one edition was published, in 1543. But the first had a different fate, as Dirc Loer van Hoogstraten, a Carthusian in Cologne, published four editions, of which the first two, in 1535 and 1536, were incomplete, while those of 1538 and 1539 contained the whole work. In 1542 Nicholas van Esch produced the fifth edition with an introduction; from 1543 to 1629 eight more editions followed. The treatise appeared also in Latin, German, and French editions. It reflects the influence of Ruysbroeck and Herp, but also of the German school. Characteristic of the writer are the teachings about the mystic union with Christ and the birth of the Word in the soul.

BIBLIOGRAPHY: L. Reypens, S.J., "Nog een vergeten mystieke grootheid, De schrijfster der Evangelische peerle," in *Ons Geest. Erf*, II (1928) 52–76, 189–213, 305–341; Dom J. Huyben O.S.B., "Nog een vergeten mystieke grootheid," in *Ons Geest. Erf*, II (1928), 361-392; *idem*, III (1929), 60-70, 144-164; *idem*, IV (1930), 5-26, 428-473;

A. de Wilt S.J., "De Duitsche vertaling der 'Evangelische Peerle' van Heribertus Hobusch O.M. Conv. (Keulen 1698) met een bibliographie van het boekje in de verschillende talen," in *Het Boek,* XXVIII (1944), 209–225.
M. M. J. SMITS VAN WAESBERGHE.

EVANGELISCHER BUND. See BUND, EVANGELISCHER.

EVANGELISCHES HILFSWERK. See HILFSWERK, EVANGELISCHES.

EVANGELISM: The effort made by Christians to win converts. Evangelism roots back to the very beginnings of Christianity, to the evangel or gospel which Jesus came to proclaim. The word evangelism does not appear in the New Testament; but the spirit of evangelism is dominant with Jesus and the disciples. He said, "I am come to seek and to save that which was lost." By preaching and personal interviews, he constantly attempted to lead people into the abundant life. He commanded his followers, "Go make disciples of all nations."

In the New Testament there are three references to evangelists. In Ephesians 4:11, they appear as a class bestowed by Christ upon the church. In Acts 21:8, Philip is spoken of as an "evangelist." In II Timothy 4:5, Timothy is enjoined, "Do the work of an evangelist." The writers of the four Gospels are spoken of as evangelists. An evangelist was not only a preacher of the gospel, but also a bearer of good news by personal witness. (See EVANGELISM, PERSONAL; and EVANGELISM, VISITATION.)

The word evangelist was seldom used prior to the Reformation. During the Reformation the term "evangelist" came into general usage again, laying stress upon the preaching of the gospel. In certain areas it meant "non-Catholic." Evangelism at times has been used as a synonym for revivalism. Many clergymen have given full time to the conduct of evangelistic meetings. Some churches conduct one or more evangelistic preaching endeavors each year. Jonathan Edwards and Dwight L. Moody were among the great evangelists. An evangelistic campaign has often meant a protracted meeting.

But evangelism has a far broader meaning. Evangelism attempts to bring all men into living, active fellowship with God through Jesus Christ as divine Saviour and through the regenerating power of the Holy Spirit, and to gather them into the fellowship of the church. It endeavors also to lead them to express their Christian discipleship in every area of human life, that the Kingdom of God may be realized.

There have been many methods of evangelism across the centuries. Modern evangelism has developed and uses various methods. Successful evangelistic movements and experiences in the Orient as well as in the Occident suggest wide usage of various emphases and practices. The preaching of the gospel in churches and in out-of-door meetings is paramount. Individual work for individuals is the most fruitful of all methods. Closely attached to it is what is known as visitation evangelism, the training of laymen who call in the homes of non-church people for private interviews. The training of personal workers is widely practiced. Religious education, ably planned and conducted, is a normal and natural way to secure Christian commitments from church-related families.

Programs of publicity calculated to arrest and hold attention on the subject of religion and its importance in present-day affairs is effective. The recognition of certain times or seasons for evangelistic effort is widely observed. Special emphasis is placed upon the Lenten season, particularly Holy Week, along with the urgency of the Nativity Season. Efforts centered on youth, especially of the adolescent age, are fostered in public meetings and private interviews. The concentration of all the Christian forces of a given area or class or interest in campaigns that may be city-wide or nation-wide, has been projected. Religious literature is widely distributed with the purpose of interesting people in the faith. Improved methods of assimilation and follow-up are being used to integrate the new disciples into the faith.

The motive and goal of evangelism is the conversion of the world and the advancement of the Kingdom of God.

See also REVIVALS OF RELIGION.

BIBLIOGRAPHY: A. M. Bailey, *Evangelism in a Changing World,* 1936; A. W. Blackwood, *Evangelism in the Home Church,* 1942; D. C. Bryan, *Building Church Membership through Evangelism,* 1952; *A Workable Plan of Evangelism,* 1945; *A Handbook of Evangelism for Laymen,* 1948; E. G. Homrighausen, *Choose Ye This Day,* 1943; A. E. Kernahan, *Visitation Evangelism,* 1928; C. G. Trumbull, *Taking Men Alive,* 1938.
DAWSON C. BRYAN.

EVANGELISM, PERSONAL: The endeavor of a Christian to bring another person to faith in Christ, and to a commitment of self to the Christian life. In the Gospels Jesus sets the example, both in his life and in his conversations with individuals. St. John contains thirteen such examples, such as the woman at the well, etc. Also, our Lord said to Peter and Andrew: "Follow me, and I will make you fishers of men." Andrew led Peter to Christ. Philip brought Nathaniel. To the apostolic band the Lord said: "Ye shall be witnesses unto me . . . unto the uttermost part of the earth." Examples of such personal evangelism appear also in the Acts. Philip won the Ethiopian eunuch and sent him as a light to Africa. Ananias ushered Paul into the full light of the gospel. Beyond these records in the Gospels and the Acts, there are many other evidences of such personal soul-winning. Indeed, the apostolic church seems to have been built up largely by personal witnessing.

There are two ways of personal evangelism.

The first consists in the conduct and example of Christians, who thus attract those outside the faith. The second calls for direct conversation, inviting the other to accept Christ and then confess him before men. Obviously, the two methods go hand in hand. Today more people are won to the Christian way of life through such personal contacts than by all other means together. While never spectacular, this method of showing personal concern for others is the most effective means that the church can employ to reach and win the unsaved and the unchurched.

The church of late has witnessed a revival of such concern. Whenever a person becomes imbued with the ideals of Christ, and feels grateful for all that he has done, that person must tell others, one by one. This is the way of the parent with the child, of friend with friend, and of a Christian with a stranger.

DAWSON C. BRYAN.

EVANGELISM, VISITATION: Is the name given to a widely-used method of evangelism in which men and women in teams of two visit the homes of the unchurched to secure commitments on confession of faith or by transfer of church membership. This is a rediscovery and adaptation to the modern way of life of the pattern of Jesus found in Luke 10:1-20. The local church uses various methods of finding prospects. The pastor selects capable lay workers, and trains them, usually in four nights of instruction. Following the instruction each evening, the laymen in teams of two visit the homes of those assigned to them and attempt to lead the prospects to Christian profession and church membership. Each team visits from three to four homes each evening.

Many churches carry on a permanent program with the lay teams visiting on one or two evenings each month. The permanent organization is sometimes called "The Fishermen's Club," taking its name from Jesus' invitation to the disciples, "Follow me, and I will make you fishers of men."

The results of this method are variable, depending upon the fidelity of the church in preparation and in determination to follow the plan. Often from one-third to one-half of the prospects make favorable decisions. Some churches following this procedure have doubled, trebled, and quadrupled their membership. It is equally effective in city, town and open country situations.

The permanence of the commitment depends upon the sincerity and determination of the convert, coupled with, and almost invariably in proportion to, the assimilation effort and program of the church receiving the new members. Visitation evangelism is probably responsible for more new members for the Christian churches of America than any other method of evangelism.

DAWSON C. BRYAN.

EVANGELISTIC PREACHING: Such a sermon brings the unsaved hearer face to face with Christ and moves for acceptance of him as Saviour and Lord. According to C. H. Dodd in *The Apostolic Preaching and Its Developments* (1944), the New Testament word "preaching" always refers to evangelism, with other terms for messages to believers. In church history evangelism has flourished in times of spirituality, and vice versa. (See *Revivals, Their Laws and Leaders*, by James Burns, 1909.) Among famous professional evangelists, with no settled abode, have been George Whitefield, D. L. Moody, William A. Sunday, and Gipsy Smith. Among pastors excelling in such work, C. H. Spurgeon and George W. Truett might be mentioned. After trying substitutes, most churches are returning to this emphasis. The National Council of Churches has extensive plans for mass evangelism. W. A. Maier and Charles E. Fuller have been radio evangelists. This work is usually done best by the pastor at home. Evangelistic preaching is biblical in substance (not usually expository), doctrinal in quality, popular in form, and moving in effect. Through appeals to intellectual and emotional powers, the sermon moves the will, which here means the entire person in action Godward. When freed from excrescences, such preaching accords with the spirit and ideals of the Scriptures, and meets the needs of many souls. A pulpit without evangelism would be like a sun without warmth. Gospel preaching should go hand in hand with Christian nurture. In the published sermons of Spurgeon and Phillips Brooks about half are evangelistic and half are pastoral.

ANDREW W. BLACKWOOD.

EVENING SERVICE: The "second service" once formed an important part of the church program. In the United States the hour was often eight o'clock; in Great Britain, an hour earlier. The pastor stressed evangelism, and strove to attract young people. Many churches now look on this service as a problem. Many have given it up, partly because of motion pictures, radio, and television. An occasional church succeeds on a different basis. Making morning worship inspirational, those in charge look on the evening hour as informative. After songs and prayers the minister delivers a biographical sermon, perhaps from the Old Testament, a doctrinal message, or an ethical. Occasionally he has a series. Such a program appeals to persons who do not attend in the morning. In a residential community conditions may call for "Vespers," a late afternoon service including beautiful music and meditative preaching, full of beauty. The "tone color" of the second service depends upon the setting and the time of day. One principle always obtains: during the week each service ought to differ from every other, in purpose and character. Often the second service dwindles through lack of careful preparation and through likeness to morning worship. The work of the leader calls for strategy and tactics.

ANDREW W. BLACKWOOD.

EVERARD, WILLIAM. See DIGGERS.

EVERLASTING LIFE. See ETERNAL LIFE.

EVOLUTION: Today, as in Darwin's time, biological evolution must be distinguished from the metaphysical doctrine of evolution. In biology the central evolutionary tenet, that all forms of life are organically related and have differentiated by natural means, is considered to have received additional confirmation since Darwin. Darwin's explanation of "natural means," however, has been extensively revised.

Darwin proposed as the major factors governing evolution: (1) chance variations, (2) natural selection by elimination of the unfit in competitive struggle, (3) inherited effects of use and disuse and (4) inherited effects of action of environment on organisms. First, Weissmann and others showed that hereditary characters transmitted by germ cells are not affected by acquired bodily alterations or by ordinary forms of environmental influence (see HEREDITY). The major advances, however, have come through the development of genetics since the rediscovery of Mendel's work in 1900.

Mendel's demonstration that inheritance is transmitted by particular, interacting, self-reproducing units (genes) which assort independently in subsequent generations, explained the distribution of variations within a population, but when combined with Weissmann's principle seemed to preclude introduction of novel characteristics necessary for major evolutionary changes. De Vries answered the difficulty by showing that occasional spontaneous changes (mutations) occur in which a newly emergent gene continues in place of its predecessor. How or why genes mutate is not known. Mutations, when not lethal, increase the genetic potential of species and may become essential in case of environmental change or in making accessible to life new areas of the environment. In the light of genetic structure and variation, natural selection is not primarily elimination through competitive struggle but differential reproduction in which interaction of genetic structure with environment in individual development, integration of individuals in ecological structure, utilization of food supply, care of young, elimination of intragroup discord, and exploitation of environmental possibilities are all regarded as factors.

Metaphysically, recognition of the complexity of biological evolutionary factors has generally led to abandonment of attempts both to reduce life to mere mechanism or automatism and to introduce a separate vitalistic substance. Most critical naturalists, recognizing that life has its own principles and functions, grant the existence of non-reductive dependent levels of organization of reality and account for their origin in terms of emergence, a concept analogous to mutation in biology. In some cases additional principles to explain emergence are offered (e.g., S. Alexander's nisus; R. W. Sellar's integrative causality). Non-naturalistic thinkers, while recognizing the descriptive validity of evolutionary emergence and integration of levels of reality, contend that this states rather than solves the problem and calls for further teleological interpretation.

See also SCIENCE, NATURAL.

BIBLIOGRAPHY: H. F. Osborn, *The Origin and Evolution of Life*, 1918; S. Alexander, *Space, Time and Deity*, 1920; R. W. Sellars, *Evolutionary Naturalism*, 1922; C. L. Morgan, *Emergent Evolution*, 1923; A. N. Whitehead, *Process and Reality*, 1929; R. A. Fisher, *The Genetical Theory of Natural Selection*, 1930; J. B. S. Holdane, *The Causes of Evolution*, 1932; T. H. Morgan, "Modern Views of the Evolution Theory," *American Scholar*, 4 (1936), 14–22; E. S. Brightman, *A Philosophy of Religion*, 1940; Th. Dobzhansky, *Genetics and the Origin of the Species*, 2nd. ed., 1941; George G. Simpson, *The Meaning of Evolution*, 1950.

[Sup.] RICHARD MARION MILLARD.

EXALTATION OF CHRIST: The word occurs rarely in the New Testament with reference to Christ; but the idea is prominent. In contrast to his "state of humiliation," i.e., his incarnate state as the Jesus of Nazareth who suffered under Pontius Pilate, Christ's state of exaltation begins with the Resurrection and continues for ever, a state of majesty no longer at the mercy of men or nature. The Apostles' Creed denotes the exaltation by the phrases "rose again . . . ascended . . . sitteth at the right hand . . . shall come to judge. . . ." The word can refer to the act of God the Father or to the "state" of Christ. The *locus classicus* is in Phil. 2:9, the verb used here not occurring elsewhere in the New Testament. Acts 2:33 and 5:31 use a less emphatic word which elsewhere refers to Christians (II Cor. 11:7) or to men in general (as in Matt. 23:12). The church doctrine uses Paul's word but with John's meaning. The impression a first reader would derive from Paul is that of an assumption of glory, whereas the impression gained from John (e.g., John 17) is that of a resumption of former glory. Hebrews stands closer to Paul than to John, though in harmony with both. The Father is always represented to be the source and agent of exaltation. Even in the exalted state Christ is still the Son. (Have we here on the loftiest level the principle which Jesus enunciated—"He that exalteth himself shall be abased"?) Concrete definiteness is lent to the concept by such words as "glory," "power," "authority," as well as by "he sat down at the right hand of the Majesty on high" (Heb. 1:3). Eph. 1:19–23 unites the cosmic exaltations of Christ with his headship of the church. The title of Christ by which the church most succinctly confesses his exaltation is "Lord." There is both a present and a future aspect of the exaltation, both being expressed in Christian hymns and liturgy. Christ's exaltation now is seen with the eye of faith. Not everywhere is he acknowledged to be Lord. But it is the church's belief that "every eye shall see him" (Rev. 1:7) and "every tongue confess that Jesus Christ is Lord" (Phil. 2:11; cf. I Cor. 15:24). The difference between present and future is not in the exaltation itself but in the degree and extent to which it is acknowledged on earth.   KENNETH J. FOREMAN.

EX CATHEDRA: Latin, "from the chair." A term which applied originally to all manner of authoritative pronouncements, but which is now reserved for infallible utterances of the pope. The Vatican Council (1870) proclaimed as an article of faith that the pope, whenever he speaks *ex cathedra,* that is, in his capacity as the pastor and doctor of the Church Universal, by virtue of his supreme apostolic authority, and in order to define a doctrine regarding faith and morals to make it binding for all Christians, is personally infallible. These stipulations were shaped after the terms used in conclusion of the Bull *Ineffabilis Deus,* by which Pope Pius IX had defined the dogma of the Immaculate Conception (1854). Since the proclamation of the papal infallibility in 1870, the only *ex cathedra* definition actually delivered is that of the Assumption (*q.v.*), by Pope Pius XII (1950).   GEORGES A. BARROIS.

EXCAVATIONS IN BIBLE LANDS. See ARCHAEOLOGY, BIBLICAL.

EXCOMMUNICATION. See CENSURES.

EXEGESIS. See HERMENEUTICS.

EXERCITIA SPIRITUALIA: Loyola's debt to Gerard Zerbolt (*q.v.*) of Zutphen was established by P. H. Watrigant. Mombaer, who copied from Zerbolt, supplied Garcia of Cisneros with helpful suggestion. But the latter copied the general outline of his course of spiritual exercises directly from Zerbolt. Chapters 49–52 of his work are almost verbally reproduced from Chapters 27–30 of the *Spiritual Ascensions* by Zerbolt. Garcia also borrowed heavily from Mombaer. As Watrigant showed: "Almost all the practical hints, and nearly everything relating to the general method simply are extracts

of the *Rosary.*" The latter was written by Mombaer.

BIBLIOGRAPHY: P. H. Watrigant, *La genèse des Exercitia Spiritualia,* 1897; A. Hyma, *Renaissance to Reformation* (1951), pp. 357–370; L. J. Puhl, S.J., *The Spiritual Exercises of St. Ignatius,* 1951; *Monumenta historica Societatis Jesu, Monumenta Ignatiana, Series Secunda: Exercitia Spiritualia,* 1919; Benedictines of Stanbrook, *The Spiritual Exercises of St. Ignatius Literally Translated,* 1928; R. P. Victoriano Larrañaga, S.J., ed., *Obras de San Ignacio de Loyola,* Vol. I, 1947.

[Sup.] ALBERT HYMA.

EXISTENTIALISM: A philosophical movement whose first exponent was the Dane, Sören Kierkegaard (1813–55, *q.v.*). Kierkegaard, whose thinking was bound up with his own inwardly troubled life, broke away from the tradition of Western philosophy by ranking speculative thinking lower than existential. The latter is the kind of thinking we carry on when we are making up our mind whether to marry a particular person, or whether we ought to emigrate, or when we are working out our proper vocation in life, or when we are facing the imminent prospect of death. Utterly removed from the dispassionate, spectator-like attitude of the normal philosopher or scientist, it is characterized by decision, isolation, and an absence of demonstrative certainty. His insistence that this, and not abstract reasoning, was the highest type of mental activity for us, led Kierkegaard sharply to criticise Hegelianism and also ultimately to break with the Danish church of his day. The latter was a church coextensive with the community and the young man who became a member of it did so as a matter of course along with all his acquaintances of the same age and without the inward searching of heart which he would have to go through if subsequently he contemplated marriage or emigration. It was from this standpoint that Kierkegaard was led to make his most drastic charge against the church, that it had abolished faith.

Kierkegaard's influence on Christianity is not merely negative. His insistence that discipleship involves voluntarily accepted suffering is a salutary challenge to all lukewarm Christianity and his stress on the doctrines of the divine incognito and the stumbling block give depth to his portrait of Christ. Equally important is his treatment of original sin. He links the latter with the state of dread or *Angst* in which the individual is faced with the choice between a number of possibilities, which, being free, he can realise but which, being finite, he cannot properly know. Instead of overcoming this state through faith, he seeks to escape from it by flying either from his freedom or his finitude. Those who abandon themselves to the slavery of sensual desires (cf. the well-known fact that alcoholics suffer from mental insecurity) and those who answer a tyrant's call for unconditional obedience are examples of the first kind of flight from the state of dread; those who, like our first parents, seek to be as God, illustrate the second. In either case the flight is vain and only precipitates the individual into sin. It will be seen that Kierkegaard has traced back to a common origin what are loosely called sins of the body and sins of the spirit.

Kierkegaard's work remained virtually unknown outside Denmark for many years after his death—it was only in the nineteen-thirties that such American scholars as Lowrie made it accessible to English readers. Modern existentialist thinkers, though influenced by Kierkegaard's thought, have developed it in several different directions, besides producing much original work. Thus Heidegger (b. 1889, q.v.) while paying tribute to Kierkegaard's work on dread, points out that his own concern is with *existential* rather than *existentiell* questions. He is dealing, that is, not with the concrete decisions which the individual must make for himself but with the abstract analysis of being. He maintains that such an analysis has hitherto been prevented by the way in which orthodox philosophy has applied to human existence categories such as substance, which are strictly only valid for inanimate objects. He is thus led to define the true categories or existentalia of human existence. Of these perhaps the most significant is *Erschlossenheit*, being open to oneself. The human being is aware of himself and according to the adequacy or otherwise of his concept of himself, so is his life authentic or unauthentic. Heidegger has influenced Christian theology through his impact on Bultmann (q.v.). By attempting to interpret the New Testament in terms of man's understanding of himself, though not, he contends, leaving out God's action in Jesus Christ, Bultmann has exposed himself to the charge of reading the New Testament through the eyes of Heidegger and has initiated the *Entmythologisierung* controversy (see MYTH IN THE NEW TESTAMENT).

Other existentialist philosophers include Jaspers (b. 1883) who contends that in the boundary situations of sin, death, and guilt, the individual is in touch with the Transcendent or God. Jaspers's position, while sympathetic to religion, is not that of Christianity, whose claim to exclusiveness he cannot accept. In his study of history, indeed, he finds the axial era not in the birth of Jesus but in the period around 500 B.C., when simultaneously in Greece, Palestine, India, and China, man for the first time learned to stand outside his life and criticise it from without. Yet he refuses to dismiss as merely accidental the fact that modern science arose in Europe, the adopted home of Christianity.

Of the two most noted French existentialists, one, Sartre (b. 1905), is an atheist and the other, Marcel (b. 1889), became a Roman Catholic in 1929. The idea of God, a necessary being, is unacceptable to Sartre for whom all existence is contingent. Yet he distinguishes his position from that of the nineteenth century atheists who were convinced that abandonment of belief in God left them still with the certainty of moral standards. Sartre has no such illusions; indeed like all existentialists, he is distrustful of moral codes. They are attempts to make man in accordance with a pattern whereas man makes himself by his own choice. Sartre's divergence from the Christian standpoint is perhaps seen most clearly in his identification of fallenness with being together. Love he reduces to the vain attempt of the individual to escape from the meaninglessness of his own existence. Marcel, on the other hand, like the Jewish thinker Buber (q.v.), whose thinking touches that of the existentialists, finds the high point of the individual's life in the I-thou relations which he can enter into with other men and with God.

In spite of some extravagances, existentialism does show that there is another approach to the universe than the scientific one and maintains the importance of the individual in a civilisation where he has seemed to count for little.

See also CRISIS, THE THEOLOGY OF; DIALECTICAL THEOLOGY; PHILOSOPHY.

BIBLIOGRAPHY: Kierkegaard, *Works*, especially *Training in Christianity* and *The Concept of Dread*; Lowrie, *Kierkegaard*; Heidegger, *Sein und Zeit, Existence and Being*; Bartsch, *Kerygma und Mythos*; Henderson, *Myth in the New Testament*; Jaspers, *The Perennial Scope of Philosophy, The European Spirit, Vom Ursprung und Ziel der Geschichte, Einfuehrung in die Philosophie, Philosophie, Von der Wahrheit*; Sartre, *Existentialism and Humanism, L'Être et le Néant*; Marcel, *Being and Having, The Mystery of Being*; Blackham, *Six Existentialist Thinkers*; Foulquié *Existentialism*.

IAN HENDERSON.

EXODUS, BOOK OF. See PENTATEUCH.

EXODUS OF ISRAEL. See ISRAEL, HISTORY OF.

EX OPERE OPERANTIS, OPERATO. See OPUS OPERANTIS, OPUS OPERATUM, in Volume VIII.

EXORCIST. See ORDERS, MINOR.

EXPANSION OF CHRISTIANITY (ANCIENT): The miracle of the triumphant rise of Christianity within five centuries from a despised sect of the lowly Nazarene to a church of temporal and spiritual power has been the cause of wonderment among Christians and non-Christians alike. The gospel spread from the very outset by means of lay witnessing. Its success was not dependent upon a priesthood at first, but upon house-to-house, person-to-person sharing of the "good news" in a fashion which took hold in the grass-roots where the rank and file of men and women lived. When, within a few years, it reached out beyond the Jews to include the great gentile world, it gradually de-

veloped along the line so familiar in modern
missions. Missionaries, of whom the great apostle Paul was the foremost, were sent out, first
from Antioch, and then from other cities of the
Mediterranean world. Following a strategy of
contacting the teeming populaces of the major
urban centers, the envoys of the way established
communities of disciples who came to be called
Christians.

There was a certain fluidity about the Christian movement, which had no single organizational pattern, no uniform system of beliefs, and
few universally established practices. It was a
witnessing movement of informal fellowships of
believers who met in homes for the breaking of
bread together and for prayer and instruction
under the guidance of those whom Jesus had
taught. Religion was intensely personal among
them. They attributed their experiences to the
Holy Spirit whom Jesus had sent as the authoritative guide for his disciples. It is not surprising, therefore, that tension arose very early between the ideal of an inclusive community and
the individualism which stemmed from the leading of the Holy Spirit. Moreover, the early
Christian communities were not particularly
concerned to transform the life of the Graeco-
Roman society of their day. Yet the amazing
fact is that the early Christians nevertheless
made such a marked influence upon the society
of their times that they were accused of fo-
menting social revolution (cf. Acts 17:6).

Thus the witnessing movement of the first
two generations, whether Jewish or Hellenistic,
made its influence felt through the example of
transformed lives, first among the humble in
the social scale, and later among the well-born
and ruling classes. To one man may rightly be
attributed the emergence of Christianity as essentially a Gentile movement which became
strong enough within three and a half centuries
to conquer the Roman Empire. That man was
the apostle Paul. He was a Jew, to be sure, but
first and foremost a man with a universal vision
of the spread of his gospel. Through his vigorous leadership, churches were planted from
Syria to Spain which became centers of missionary expansion for centuries after his death.

Christianity spread in the Roman world without official sanction and with considerable opposition prior to the reign of Constantine (A.D.
306–37). However, the very hindrances to the
spread of the gospel in the first three centuries
"became in the hands of Providence, means of
promotion." Persecution, first by the general
populace and then by emperors bent on saving
the tottering Roman society, led to martyrdom
for many Christians; martyrdom in turn led to
the most unselfish forms of ambition on the
part of men of all classes. Thus, in a very true
sense, "the blood of the martyrs became the
seed of the church."

Most rapid expansion of the new faith took
place in Asia Minor where Paul's missionary
work to a strongly Hellenistic populace was pre-
eminently successful. The native cultures with
their religious cults were disintegrating and were
adopting Graeco-Roman patterns. Moreover,
there were many Gentile proselytes to Judaism there. The work, therefore, begun by Paul
and his associates was carried on with growing
success in the next two centuries. Among the
more notable missionaries of the third century
was Gregory Thaumaturgos, a native of Pontus
and son of a wealthy pagan family, who was
greatly influenced by Origen whom he had met
at Caesarea in Palestine. His own winsome-
ness and appreciation of Greek philosophy
learned from the great Origen aided his work.
From A.D. 240–70, he was bishop of his native
city in Pontus. His remarkable success in winning the masses to Christianity was due partly
to his policy of opposing the fraudulent practices of pagan priests and, at the same time, of
encouraging the people to substitute Christian
practices for the pagan. (See the Life of Gregory by Gregory of Nyssa in Migne, *Patrologiae
Graecae*, Vol. XLVI, pp. 893–958.) This method
of making an easy transition from paganism to
Christianity was not without its shortcomings,
for it led here and elsewhere to a degree of corruption of Christian teaching which weakened
the spiritual vigor of the Faith.

Although Christianity was in Crete and some
of the islands in the Aegean, its strength is not
known. By A.D. 306, it was still a minority in
Greece proper. In Egypt, however, and in and
around Carthage (the present Tunis and Al-
geria), it was strong by the end of the second
century. Christianity was at Rome before the
arrival of Paul sometime between A.D. 58 and
62. By the middle of the third century, Italy
seems to have had about one hundred bishoprics. Early in the third century, Christianity
was fairly firmly established in Southern Spain.
Its presence in the Rhone Valley is indicated
by the fact that Christians were persecuted in
Lyons and Vienne in A.D. 177. Through merchants, the gospel was carried to Gaul and possibly also to Britain by the end of the second
century or earlier.

Christianity enjoyed an eastward expansion as
well. By A.D. 225 twenty Christian bishoprics
are known to have existed in the Tigris-Eu-
phrates Valley and on the borders of Persia.
In spite of this auspicious beginning, however,
Christians always remained a minority in Persia
because the Sassanids endorsed Zoroastrianism
and regarded Rome, which protected Christianity, as a rival. By the beginning of the third
century, Christianity penetrated Armenia, coming from Caesarea in Cappadocia and from Antioch and Edessa. The Goths, to the north and
west of the Black Sea, received the Faith from

captives taken in A.D. 258 from Cappadocian Christians. The most notable missionary to the Goths north of the Danube was Ulfilas (q.v.) who labored from about 341 to 380. The gospel may have arrived in India before the end of the third century by way of Alexandria and merchants to the East. (See Latourette, *The First Five Centuries,* Chap. 3.)

Estimates of the proportion of Christians in the Roman world by the reign of Constantine range all the way from one-twentieth to one-eighth of the population. Gibbon and Friedlaender, who are responsible for the lowest figure, are regarded by Schaff and more recent historians as too low. On the other hand, Matter and Robertson, who estimate one-fifth, are very likely too high. Harnack's generalizations are perhaps more accurate. According to him, one half of the population in Asia Minor, Thrace, and Armenia were Christians by A.D. 325. In Syria, Egypt, Greece, Macedonia, Central North Africa, Spain, Rome, and Southern Italy, there were more Christians than worshippers of any other religion. Christians were sparsely scattered in Palestine, along the Danube, Northern Italy, and Southern Gaul. There were few Christians in central and northern Gaul and along the German frontier. (See Harnack, *Mission and Expansion of Christianity,* Vol. II, pp. 327 ff.).

Early references of the church fathers to the social and cultural spread of the gospel indicate that within three centuries the Christian faith had spread into nearly every stratum of society. At the beginning of the second century, Pliny, governor of Bythinia, complained to the Emperor Trajan (q.v.) that people of every age, rank, and sex had forsaken the temples to follow the Christian teaching (*Ep. ad Trajan,* xcvi). About the middle of the same century, Justin Martyr reported that there were not people, Greek or barbarian, or of any other race, among whom there were not practicing Christians (*Dialogue with Trypho,* 117). Tertullian, just half a century later, boasted to the heathen: "We are but of yesterday, and yet we already fill your cities, islands, camps, your palace, senate and forum; we have left to you only your temples" (*Apol. ca.* 37).

After the recognition of Christianity by the state, it spread for a period of the next two centuries by "a kind of mass conversion," which was the work of the church itself through such active missionary bishops as Martin of Tours, Ambrose of Milan, Vigilius of Trent, Augustine of Hippo, and Chrysostom of Constantinople. As so much of society underwent collapse in these latter days of the empire, especially in the West, the church became increasingly the protector and guardian of society through its extensive humanitarian program. By its canon of Scriptures, its sacraments, and its organization

and discipline, it provided a steadying influence not only during the earlier centuries of persecution, but during the later period of social disintegration and barbarian invasion of the empire.

By A.D. 500, Christianity had introduced its influence into northern Europe chiefly through the labors of the Celtic monks; it had won over almost *en masse* Armenia under Gregory the Illuminator; it had moved beyond the Near East into the Orient and had penetrated Abyssinia, probably as early as the first half of the fourth century. Although it never manifested the same vigor in the East as in the West, largely because its missionaries never quite threw off the Syrian wrappings of the gospel and adapted themselves to the languages and cultural patterns of the Orient, it did pave the way for the more vigorous penetration of that area of the world in much later centuries. In the West which lay in the path of the advancing civilization of the times, it became one of the richly formative factors in the development of our modern age.

BIBLIOGRAPHY: J. C. Ayer, *A Source Book for Ancient Church History,* 1913; S. J. Case, *The Evolution of Early Christianity,* 1914; E. R. Goodenough, *The Church in the Roman Empire,* 1931; H. M. Gwatkin, *Early Church History to A.D. 313,* 2 vols., 1913; A. von Harnack, *The Mission and Expansion of Christianity in the First Three Centuries,* 2 vols., 1908; B. J. Kidd, *A History of the Church to A.D. 461,* 1922; K. S. Latourette, *The First Five Centuries,* Vol. I of *A History of the Expansion of Christianity,* 7 vols., 1937-45; J. Lebreton and J. Zeiller, *The History of the Primitive Church,* 2 vols., 1942, 1946; J. Moffatt, *The First Five Centuries of the Church,* 1938; W. M. Ramsay, *The Church in the Roman Empire before A.D. 170,* 1893; C. H. Robinson, *The Conversion of Europe,* 1917; P. Schaff, *History of the Christian Church,* Vols. I, II, 1889, 1891.

ROBERT J. TORBET.

EXPANSION OF CHRISTIANITY (MODERN): The continued expansion of Christianity in the period from 1910 to 1953 was intimately affected by world events. The only comparable period would be the time of the Mohammedan conquest, when Europe was effectively cut off from the rest of the world until the discovery of the sea routes to the Orient and the New World.

I. World Events: From 1814 to 1914 there was comparative peace. The wars which occurred were local and of short duration. In this era of peace the expansion of Christianity made great strides. But the two world wars (1914–18, 1939–45) involved the whole world, even those nations which were not actual belligerents. Many Christian missionaries were removed from the fields and interned, the funds of the continental societies were cut off, the transportation of missionaries to their fields became very hazardous, and even the transmission of funds from one country to another was made difficult (see ORPHANED MISSIONS). Between the wars the depression in the 1930's added to the difficulties of the missionary agencies. Many societies were forced to retrench and to curtail their activities and personnel (see DEPRESSION, ECONOMIC, THE CHURCHES AND THE).

The wars weakened the western nations and intensified the demand for self-determination on the part of the colonial peoples. The close of World War II was followed quickly by the liberation of India (q.v.), Pakistan (q.v.), the Philippines (q.v.), Indonesia (see MALAY ARCHIPELAGO), Israel (q.v.), etc., and their establishment as independent and sovereign states. Although in each of these new nations the constitution provides for religious liberty, the relation of the missions and the foreign missionaries to the new governments entered a new and uncertain situation. Intense nationalism tended to put the emphasis on "native" religions and to treat Christianity as a vestige of foreign domination. It is to be noted, however, that in general the missionary work in these new states continued relatively unhindered, and that in some respects the fact that the missionaries are no longer identified with a foreign colonial power tended to improve the relationship between the foreigners and the people among whom they work.

The churches which suffered most from the political events in this period were the Eastern Orthodox Churches (q.v.). During World War I the Armenian, the Nestorian, and the Greek Orthodox churches in the Near East were impoverished and greatly reduced in number by persecutions and deportations. Immediately after the war the Russian Revolution practically eliminated the church in that country as a factor in the Soviet social order. After World War II and the extension of Soviet power over the satellite countries of eastern Europe (see BULGARIA; CZECHOSLOVAKIA; ESTONIA; HUNGARY; LATVIA; LITHUANIA; POLAND; RUMANIA; YUGOSLAVIA), the churches in these areas, both Eastern and Roman, were shorn of their power and functions. Much church property was confiscated, schools were taken over by the government, and the church was advised to concern itself only with the spiritual life of those who asked for its ministration. Later the guarantee of religious freedom in the Soviet constitution seemed to have become more of a reality; but the government as such maintained its attitude of hostility and encouraged the preaching of atheism and materialism. As a result of these political developments the Eastern Orthodox Churches, which in the past manifested a fair power of expansion, were practically eliminated as factors in the present expansion of Christianity.

The churches in Central Europe met with almost the same fate at the hands of the Nazi powers. Both in Germany (q.v.) and in the occupied countries (see BELGIUM; DENMARK; FRANCE; HOLLAND; NORWAY) the churches were persecuted, the leaders imprisoned, and the work curtailed. In the other western countries the churches remained free, but even so the demands of total war made the work of the churches on distant fields difficult and hazardous.

The most disastrous blow to the expansion of Christianity was the rise of the communists to power in China (q.v.) and the consequent closing of that country to missionary work. Under the communists, China returned to the policy of isolation which characterized that country under the Mings and the Manchus. The entry of China into the war in Korea (q.v.) made the separation from the West even more effective and eliminated China for the present as a mission field of the church.

II. The Response of the Churches: Christianity has proved its character as a universal religion by its ability to adjust itself to new environments and changing situations. In this period of rapid and fundamental changes the church manifested its vitality by being able to adopt new methods and enter into new relationships. It has been proved again that persecution and tribulation serve to strengthen the church and increase its resourcefulness. The response of the churches to the demands of this period added a new and glorious chapter to the history of the church.

One of the effects of the wars has been to drive the churches closer together in co-operative efforts. When German missionaries were interned during World War I and the supply of funds was cut off, the other churches carried on the work. In their sense of essential unity the churches refused to let the battle lines set the limits for their work. The International Missionary Council (1921; q.v.) and its predecessor, the Edinburgh Continuation Committee, succeeded in having a clause inserted in the Treaty of Versailles which averted the confiscation of German mission property. Societies in Britain, France, Sweden, and America took over the leadership of German missions until the missionaries were permitted to return. The contribution from the U. S. A. for German missions from 1917 to 1926 amounted to $1,700,000, the greater part of this sum being contributed by the Lutherans, whose codenominationalists were most directly involved.

World War II caused much greater havoc and dislocation. By this time, however, the churches were better prepared. The International Missionary Council and the Lutheran World Federation (q.v.), working in close co-operation, took charge of the "orphaned" fields. When continental Europe had been conquered completely by the Nazis, the responsibility fell upon the churches in the United States. Total contributions to the care for orphaned missions (q.v.) from 1939 to 1947 was $6,393,092.81, as reported by IMC. Of this sum Lutherans in the United States contributed $2,619,449.31. The beneficiaries were primarily the German missions, but some help was given also to other continental and to British societies. Although these sums seem large, they were only a fraction of the annual budgets which these missions had required in the past. The help would have been entirely inadequate had it not been supplemented by the sacrifices of the missionaries and the contributions of the younger churches.

The younger churches proved their faithfulness and strength in these times of tribulation. When missionaries found themselves cut off from support, the members of their churches shared their meager supplies with them. Before the missionaries left, steps were taken to transfer responsibility to the native leaders and to organize the churches on an independent basis. The spirit of nationalism and concern for the church worked together. Native pastors proved themselves capable of guiding the churches in evangelism, education, and social welfare.

Thus two great gains may be noted as we survey the cataclysmic events of the decades since 1914. Christians throughout the world moved closer together. Ways of co-operation and mutual help were found which had been undreamed of in an earlier period. The Christian church became a world church, and Christians recognized one another, even though they came from different countries and races. The younger churches took their place in the life and work of Christendom. Christianity cannot any longer be designated as a Western religion. The church is firmly established in almost all parts of the world. It is recognized more and more that henceforth missionary work will have to be conducted through the younger churches. The evangelizing of the world is the task of the whole church, both the older and the younger churches.

Since the close of World War II the churches expanded their efforts. The Japanese people welcomed missionaries back again after the war. Several new agencies entered through the open door. Many American soldiers learned by actual contact what the missionaries had accomplished among the people of the Pacific Islands and in other parts of the world. Some decided to go back as missionaries, and others were awakened to a new interest in the mission of the church. Even the China missionaries remained among the Chinese in Hongkong, Formosa, and other Pacific islands to establish the church and train pastors for a time when they might be permitted to return to the mainland. In Indonesia, India, and Pakistan missionaries remained and worked to strengthen the church against the day when they may have to leave their post. In Africa (q.v.) the work was extended to tribes

which had not been reached before, and native leadership was trained for the church.

In ecumenical relations the younger churches began to take an active and significant part. At the meetings of the International Missionary Council in Jerusalem (1928) and Madras (1938), as well as in the ecumenical conferences in Oxford and Edinburgh (1937) and Lund (1952), the younger churches were ably represented (see ECUMENICAL MOVEMENT). Many of their leaders are impatient with divisions which have their historical roots in the development of Western Christianity. They feel more closely related to all Christians of their own national origins than to their British, German, or American brethren in their denomination. A most significant event was the formation of the United Church of South India in which Anglicans, Methodists, Congregationalists, and Presbyterians participated. National Christian councils were organized in nearly all missionary countries, and plans for union of churches were being discussed in Burma, North India, Ceylon, Indonesia, Japan, and in some parts of Africa. While these movements are significant of a trend, it is too early to say just what course the independent younger churches will follow when the pressure of the revolutionary changes of the present is lessened.

III. Organization: The agencies which assumed the task of world mission during the nineteenth century continued the work with intensified energy. In most European countries leadership remained in the hands of independent societies (Basel, Leipzig, Church Missionary Society, etc.), while in the United States the various denominations elected boards of foreign missions which were directly responsible to the churches. A number of so-called faith missions arose, but with the exception of the China Inland Mission and the Africa Inland Mission these societies were relatively small.

The Roman Catholic Church strengthened and expanded its work by adding new agencies. The Missionary Union of the Clergy was organized in 1917 in Italy. The Society of St. Patrick was founded in Ireland in 1930. In France several new organizations were formed. The greatest development was perhaps the organization in 1911 of the Catholic Foreign Missionary Society of America, better known from the name of its headquarters as Maryknoll. The Foreign Mission Sisters of St. Dominic is associated with Maryknoll. In 1942 the total number of missionaries, priests, and sisters was 2,739. All these societies work under the supervision of the Society for the Propaganda of the Faith in Rome.

In the Protestant world the most significant event was the formation of the International Missionary Council (q.v.) in 1921. It had its inception in the Missionary Conference in

Edinburgh (1910), followed by the Continuation Committee and the Emergency Committee of Co-operating Missions. This agency has headquarters both in London and New York. It has been of inestimable value to the missionary agencies. It was able to safeguard missionary property and personnel during the wars, provided support for orphaned missions, and in many ways succeeded in coordinating the work of the churches. With the organization of the World Council of Churches (q.v.) the American branch of IMC became a department in the National Council of Churches in the U. S. A. (q.v.) while the IMC as such co-operates as an independent agency with the World Council.

IV. Methods: During the nineteenth century earlier methods of mass conversion and baptism had been abandoned in favor of thorough instruction of candidates for baptism. In Protestantism in general the theological emphasis was on individual experience and conversion. Due to the pressure of external events and a shifting of theological emphasis the accent was placed, in the twentieth century, on the building and strengthening of the church. Naturally the individual must be brought to faith in Christ and prepared for baptism, but it was now realized that this is the beginning of his Christian life rather than the goal. He is incorporated into the fellowship of the church, and within this fellowship he is to grow into the full stature of the man in Christ. The church became a place of nurture for the Christian and an agency for reaching out into the community. The missionary task was thought of in terms of planting a church which would be the instrument in the hands of God for winning the whole people for Christ.

The Roman Catholic Church made great advances in admitting native Christians to responsible position in the mission churches. In Japan, China, Indo-China, India, and Africa the church consecrated many nationals as bishops. In 1939 the pope consecrated twelve missionary bishops, including one African, one Malagasy, one Chinese, and one Indian. The use of indigenous art and architecture in the building of churches was encouraged. Social customs not incompatible with Christianity were allowed to continue, or were adapted to new uses and given new significance.

New emphasis on the church was due, at least in part, to a realization that the winning of mission countries for Christ must be the task of native Christians rather than of foreign missionaries. The training of pastors and lay leaders therefore became of greatest importance. The situation in orphaned fields provided sufficient illustrations of this need. Native pastors proved their ability to assume leadership. When the Rhenish missionaries in Sumatra were interned, and later all missionaries were removed

during the Japanese occupation, the Batak church proved its ability to handle its own affairs and to maintain its work. It soon joined the Lutheran World Federation as an independent church. While it may still need and welcomes assistance from the West, it insists that foreigners must work under the jurisdiction of the Batak church. What happened there was duplicated in many other instances.

The new emphasis calls not only for a trained clergy, but also for an educated constituency. Education received greater attention, and the removal of illiteracy throughout the world was set as a goal. The campaign against illiteracy started with the work of Y. C. James Yen among Chinese coolies in France during World War I. After his return to China he became the head of the National Association of the Mass Education Movement. Later this idea was taken up and developed by F. C. Laubach (q.v.) in his work in the Philippines. The resulting literacy movement was introduced into many parts of the world and proved tremendously successful. For the church, with its emphasis on the Scriptures, this movement is of special importance.

The greater part of the people in the Orient are agricultural. Except for Japan and some parts of India and South Africa the population employed in industry is relatively small. Here again the emphasis on the church had certain implications. If the church was to grow and become self-propagating and self-sustaining, the standard of living of the people had to be raised. The church could not support itself while its people lived on a subsistence level. It was therefore a part of the missionary program to co-operate with other agencies and with governments in providing leadership in agricultural production, new methods, better seed, better care for domestic animals, new products on farms, etc. Agricultural missions assumed a larger place and a greater significance in the program of the church.

The first half of the twentieth century was characterized by world-wide turmoil and strife. It might be assumed, therefore, that Christianity must have lost ground and that its influence must have declined. Quite the opposite is true, however. At the mid-century Christianity was more of a world religion than ever before. It had become indigenous in most Oriental countries. The church was established as a permanent part of the life in all the principal countries. Subsidies from older churches, which kept the church going in these countries in the past, may have to continue for some time, but the younger churches no longer depend on them for their existence. No other religion, and no ideology, ever achieved such world-embracing dimensions. In spite of this great extension the churches became more conscious of their essential unity in Christ. The younger churches, un-inhibited by traditional divisions, pioneered in realizing this unity in actual union. Finally, in those parts of the world where governments carried on systematic persecution and suppression of the church, it showed itself capable of resisting pressure and even grew stronger. Under the cross the church realized new strength and saw new visions of the Lord and his mission.

See also titles beginning with the words, FOREIGN MISSIONS; MISSIONARY; MISSION(s).

BIBLIOGRAPHY: Kenneth Scott Latourette, *A History of the Expansion of Christianity*, 7 vols., 1937-45; W. O. Carver, *The Course of Christian Missions*, 1939; Robert H. Glover, *The Progress of Worldwide Missions*, 1939; *The Madras Series, Meeting of the IMC at Tambaram, Madras, India*, 1939; W. K. Anderson, ed., *Christian World Mission*, 1946. Each of these works is equipped with extensive bibliographies.
[Sup. to Missions to the Heathen.]

ERIC H. WAHLSTROM.

EXPERIENCE, RELIGIOUS. See CONTEMPLATION; CONVICTION OF SIN; EMPIRICAL THEOLOGY; REVIVALS OF RELIGION.

EXPOSITION OF THE BLESSED SACRAMENT: In the Roman Church, this expression refers to the practice of publicly displaying the Eucharistic bread, usually by means of a monstrance or ostensorium (*q.v.*), in order that it may be adored by the people, outside of the liturgical celebration of the Mass. The exposition of the Host, during which hymns, litanies, and other prayers are sung or recited by the people, is concluded with the Benediction of the Blessed Sacrament (*q.v.*).

GEORGES A. BARROIS.

EXPOSITORY PREACHING: A term variously employed. Here an expository sermon means one growing out of a Bible passage of more than two consecutive verses. The unit may be a paragraph, such as a parable, or a chapter, as with "The Greatest Thing in the World," by Henry Drummond (I Cor. 13). In "lecturing" a man works through a Bible book, passage after passage. At the "second service" in Brighton, F. W. Robertson "lectured" for six years from Genesis, Samuel, the Acts, and Corinthians. Expository preaching flourished in the early church (Augustine of Hippo) and at the Reformation (Luther and Calvin). Such sermons often have suffered from allegorizing or from mechanical analysis. When an expositor knows the Bible and the hearts of men, and has a mastery of his craft, he meets with a hearty response. Such men are often self-taught after leaving the divinity school (William M. Taylor, George A. Smith, G. C. Morgan, and Alexander Maclaren). Maclaren, "prince of expositors," began expository work after years of textual preaching. Expository preaching has been more common in Britain than in the United States. Among Lutherans "pericope"

sermons have long been customary, but not always with reference to the needs of the hour.

Often the stress falls on exposition, not preaching. Many laymen would enjoy interesting, practical interpretations of a Bible passage, with reference to personal and collective needs. With two services on the Lord's day, one may be expository. Some pastors are too busy to prepare this way. Others say they do not know how, since the seminary did not teach them. Seminary professors find that expository work calls for a knowledge of the Bible, insight into human lives, and depth of understanding, such as comes through pastoral experience. The available literature proves disappointing. The way to learn is to prepare such a message occasionally, while the hearers cultivate a taste for such biblical fare. In each case the sermon ought to accord with the spirit of the passage.

ANDREW W. BLACKWOOD.

EXTREME UNCTION: According to Roman canon law, the administration of extreme unction belongs normally to the rector of the parish or his delegates, although any priest can substitute validly in case of emergency. When there is doubt whether the patient is still alive, extreme unction is administered with the condition "if thou art living," but it is administered unconditionally when it seems probable that the patient, though actually unconscious, would have wished to receive this sacrament.

[Sup.] GEORGES A. BARROIS.

EZEKIEL, BOOK OF: Until recent years almost all scholars upheld the genuineness and unity of this book. Ezekiel stood as a criterion for dating events and documents. But the rigorous criticism to which the book has been subjected during the past quarter of a century has precipitated numerous conflicting theories regarding its origin. Exponents of radical views include: Hoelscher, who holds that only a poetic kernel of the prophecy is genuine; Irwin, that the dates given in the book are largely spurious; Torrey, that the book is a pseudepigraphon of the third century B.C., with a Palestinian setting in the days of Manasseh; James Smith, that Ezekiel was a prophet of Northern Israel in the eighth century B.C. serving Assyrian rather than Babylonian exiles; and Messel, that the exiles were those who had returned to Palestine after the time of Nehemiah.

Particularly complex has been the problem of Ezekiel's residence. How could he in distant Babylonia describe conditions in Judah and Jerusalem? Herntrich and Matthews claim that his residence was exclusively Palestinian; Bertholet, that his prophetic activity involved as many as three different residences, two in Palestine and one in Babylonia; O. R. Fisher, that he was deported in 598 B.C., returned to Jerusalem, witnessed its fall in 587 B.C., then later went back to Babylonia; Pfeiffer, that he returned to Babylonia before the fall of Jerusalem. Not a few scholars, Albright, Cooke, Eissfeldt, and others, support the traditional view that Ezekiel prophesied at Tel-Abib in Babylonia.

Since Ezekiel's ministry extended from 593 B.C. to at least 571 B.C., he had ample time to record his messages. That he prepared an edition of his book, made up of both oral addresses and written compositions, seems clear. But it is not certain when, by whom, and to what extent editorial changes were made. Probably some disciple or contemporary in Babylonia revised his materials, which appear, with rare exceptions (cf. 29:17 and 40:1) in a chronological sequence of fourteen dates. The three major sections are: (1) judgments on Judah and Jerusalem (1–24); (2) oracles against the nations (25–32); and (3) future restoration of Israel (33–48). The vision of the new temple and its setting (40–48) forms a distinct part of the last section. Regardless of the extent of later alterations in the text, the judgment prevails that the priest and prophet Ezekiel is the man who produced the book. A mystic of rare endowments, he has left a message which has had a profound influence on subsequent religious thought.

BIBLIOGRAPHY: J. Hermann, *Ezekiel* (KAT), 1924; G. Hoelscher, *Hezekiel: Der Dichter und das Buch*, 1924; C. C. Torrey, *Pseudo-Ezekiel and the Original Prophecy*, 1930; James Smith, *The Book of the Prophet Ezekiel*, 1931; V. Herntrich, *Ezekielfragen*, 1932; A. Bertholet, *Hezekiel*, 1936; G. A. Cooke, *Ezekiel* (ICC), 2 vols., 1937; I. G. Matthews, *Ezekiel*, 1939; William A. Irwin, *The Problem of Ezekiel*, 1943; Nils Messel, *Ezekielfragen*, 1945; Elmer E. Flack, *The Book of Ezekiel* (OTC) (1948), pp. 739–777; C. G. Howie, *The Date and Composition of Ezekiel*, 1950. See also works on Old Testament Introduction.

[Sup.] ELMER E. FLACK.

EZRA AND NEHEMIAH, BOOKS OF: Most scholars today hold that the present form of Ezra-Nehemiah is the work of the Chronicler whose date may be conservatively set at 400 B.C. (see *Chronicles, Books of*). Since it has been shown that the style and point of view of the Ezra Memoirs are identical with those of the Chronicler (Torrey), it is held by some, in accordance with Jewish tradition, that Ezra and the Chronicler are one and the same person (e.g., Albright).

The authenticity of the Nehemiah Memoirs found in the book bearing his name has never been questioned, although there is disagreement as to their exact extent. A few scholars, doubting the historical value of the Ezra Memoirs (Ezra 7–10; Neh. 8–10), consider the story of Ezra to be a purely fictitious legend of the Chronicler (Torrey, Pfeiffer, etc.), but this view has now been rejected by most scholars.

The question of the date of Ezra's arrival in Jerusalem and its bearing on the chronological order of Ezra and Nehemiah has aroused much discussion since A. Van Hoonacker presented his view in 1890 that Nehemiah belonged to the reign of Artaxerxes I and Ezra to that of Artaxerxes II. This theory, which dates Ezra's arrival in 397 B.C., although challenged by scholars of eminence who claim the traditional date of 457 B.C. for Ezra, is probably the most likely solution to the problem.

BIBLIOGRAPHY: C. C. Torrey, *Ezra Studies*, 1910; L. W. Batten, *The Books of Ezra and Nehemiah*, 1913; R. H. Pfeiffer, *Introduction to the Old Testament*, 1941; H. H. Rowley, "The Chronological Order of Ezra and Nehemiah," in *Ignace Goldziher Memorial Volume*, Part I (ed. by S. Loewinger and J. Somoqyi) (1948), 117–149; W. F. Albright, "The Biblical Period," in *The Jews: Their History, Culture and Religion* (ed. by L. Finkelstein) (1949), 3–69.

[Sup.] CHARLES T. FRITSCH.

F

FABER (FABRI), STAPULENSIS, JACOBUS (JACQUES LEFÈVRE D'ÉTAPLES): Precursor of the Reformation in France and promoter of classical studies at the University of Paris; b. at Étaples *ca.* 1450; d. at Nérac, 1536. He was probably reared in a home of comfortable circumstances since his parents were able to send him to the University of Paris and leave him a small fortune. As scholar and teacher at the university he displayed a love for the classics, the church fathers, and Christian mystics. In 1491 after reading Lull's *Contemplationes* he frequented the company of "holy men," such as Mombaer and Standonck, and debated entering a monastery. Visits to Italy in 1492 and 1500 deepened his appreciation for Aristotle and stimulated his interest in the

Christian mystics, for he returned to France, not only with translations of Aristotle, but with a work of Nicholas of Cusa (*q.v.*), whose teachings were to have a decided influence upon his thought. In 1507 Faber was invited to reside at St. Germain-des-Prés where his friend, Briçonnet, was abbot. Here appeared in 1509 his critical edition of the Psalter, the *Psalterium Quintuplex*. The year 1510 was spent in Germany collecting manuscripts of Cusa and other mystics. At Cologne Faber visited the house of the Brethren of the Common Life, with whose teachings he was already familiar through his friendship with Standonck, Mombaer, and Badius Ascensius, and through his knowledge of the *Imitation of Christ* and the philosophy of Cusa. After his return to France his task as

Biblical scholar and reformer began in earnest. He published commentaries on the Epistles (1512) and on the Gospels (1523) and translated the Bible into French (completed 1530). In 1517 and 1518 he attacked traditional dogmas in his essays on Mary Magdalene, and instigated a reform in the diocese of Meaux, where Briçonnet was now bishop. In 1525 Faber was forced, in face of persecution, to flee to Strasbourg, but was soon recalled at the order of Francis I, appointed tutor of the king's children and later librarian at Blois (1526). His last days were spent at the court of Marguerite d'Angoulême.

Faber's teachings revealed in his *Commentaries* contained basic Protestant doctrines as justification by faith and the supreme authority of the Bible, but he by no means subscribed to all the tenets of Protestantism. He accepted the doctrines of purgatory, the Real Presence, the Immaculate Conception, countenanced celibacy of the clergy, and deplored schisms in the church. Nevertheless, he prepared the way for Farel (his pupil) and Calvin. His translation of the Bible served as a basis for the later translation made by the Protestant, Olivétan, and his Psalter was used by Luther as a guide to his lectures on the Psalms.

BIBLIOGRAPHY: Sources for a life are G. Farel, *Du vray usage de la Croix de Jesus-Christ*, 1865; A. L. Herminjard, *Correspondance des Réformateurs*, Vol. I, 1878; *Journal d'un Bourgeois de Paris*, 1854; F. de Raemond, *L'Histoire . . . de l'hérésie de ce siècle*, 1610. Later sources are J. Barnaud, *J. Lefèvre d'Etaples*, 1936; L. Delaruelle, *G. Budé*, 1907; E. Doumergue, *J. Calvin*, Vol. I, 1899. P. Imbart de la Tour, *Les Origines de la Réforme*, Vol. III, 1914; G. V. Jourdan, *The Movement towards Catholic Reform*, 1914; M. Mann, *Erasme et les Débuts de la Réforme française*, 1934; A. Renaudet, *Préréforme et Humanisme à Paris*, 1916; C. L. Salley, Univ. of Michigan dissertation on Lefèvre and the Devotio Moderna, 1952.

[Sup.] CLAUDIA LOUISE SALLEY.

FABIAN SOCIETY: A society of English socialists, founded 1884, aimed "at the reorganization of society by the emancipation of land and industrial capital from individual and class ownership, and the vesting of them in the community for the general benefit." Its influential *Essays* appeared in 1889. Its membership has included George Bernard Shaw, Sidney Webb, H. G. Wells, J. Ramsay MacDonald, R. H. Tawney, G. D. H. Cole, and other notables. Rejecting doctrinaire Marxism (see COMMUNISM) in favor of gradual, democratic social reconstruction, the members studied, spoke, and published to bring all classes to see socialism (*q.v.*) as an inevitable stage in the evolution of democracy. The society maintains the ethical-religious elements of its predecessor, the Fellowship of the New Life. Joined to powerful social forces, it influenced the forming of the Independent Labor and Labor Parties, as well as the entire socialist movement in England.

BIBLIOGRAPHY: G. D. H. Cole, *The Fabian Society, Past and Present*, 1942.

WILLIAM ANTHONY CLEBSCH.

FAHS, SOPHIA LYON (Mrs. Charles H. Fahs): Unitarian; b. in Hangchow, China, Aug. 2, 1876. She studied at the College of Wooster (B.A., 1897), Columbia University (M.A., 1904), Union Theological Seminary, (B.D., 1926). She was traveling secretary for the Student Volunteer Movement in American Colleges (1899–1901); Y.W.C.A. Student Secretary at the University of Chicago (1901–2); lecturer in Religious Education, Union Theological Seminary (1926–44); and editor of Children's Materials for the American Unitarian Association (1936–51). She has edited the New Beacon Series in Religious Education, including thirty-five titles. She is author of *Uganda's White Man of Work* (1907); *Red, Yellow and Black* (1918); *Beginnings of Earth and Sky* (1937); *Teacher's Guide to Beginnings of Life and Death* (1939); *Leading Children in Worship* (1943); *Jesus: the Carpenter's Son* (1945, Teacher's Guide, 1945); *From Long Ago and Many Lands* (1948); and *Today's Children and Yesterday's Heritage* (1951); and is coauthor of *Martin and Judy* (Vols. I, II, and III, 1939–43); *Exploring Religion with Eight-Year-Olds* (1930); *Consider the Children: How They Grow* (1940, rev. ed., 1950).

FAIRBANKS, ROLLIN JONATHAN: Episcopalian; b. at Watertown, N. Y., Oct. 29, 1908. He studied at the University of Michigan (A.B., 1933); the Episcopal Theological School, Cambridge, Mass. (B.D., 1936); Worcester State Hospital, Worcester, Mass. (1934); and the Massachusetts General Hospital, Boston, Mass. (1936). He was rector of St. John's Church, St. Johns, Mich. (1936–39) and of St. James' Church, Grosse Ile, Mich. (1939–42). He served as special labor mediator for the state of Michigan (1941); Protestant chaplain at the Massachusetts General Hospital (1943–50); lecturer (1943–50); assistant professor of pastoral theology (1950–53); professor of pastoral theology (1953–) at the Episcopal Theological School, Cambridge; lecturer in pastoral theology at Harvard Divinity School (1941–), instructor at Boston University School of Theology (1946–48). He founded (1944) the Institute of Pastoral Care, an educational foundation which provides clinical pastoral training for seminarians and clergy, and served as its executive director (1944–50), field secretary (1951), and member of its board of governors (1944–). He started *The Journal of Pastoral Care* (1947), was editor-in-chief (1947–50) and is associate editor (1951–). He was director of the Pastoral Counseling Center, Boston, Mass. (1949–53). He has contributed to the following books: *And Ye Visited Me* (Russell L. Dicks, 1938); *Education for Professional Responsibility* (Elliott Dunlop Smith, 1948); *Clinical Pastoral Training* (Seward Hiltner, 1945) and *Pastoral Care* (J. Richard Spann, 1951).

FAITH AND ORDER. See ECUMENICAL MOVEMENT.

FAITH MISSIONS. See EXPANSION OF CHRISTIANITY (MODERN).

FALL. See MAN, DOCTRINE OF; RIGHTEOUSNESS, ORIGINAL.

FALLAW, WESNER: B. Woodruff, S. C., Jan. 4, 1907. He was a student at Furman University (B.A., 1927), Union Theological Seminary, Columbia University (M.A., 1936; Ed.D., 1944, Teachers College). From 1927–33 he was a Y.M.C.A. secretary. He taught at Furman (1934, 1937–39). He developed church-family education at the Community (Congregational) Church, Winnetka, Ill. (1940–46). Since 1946 he has been professor of religious education at Andover Newton Theological School. He is the author of *The Modern Parent and the Teaching Church* (1946), and *Toward Spiritual Security* (1952).

FAMILISTS: Elizabeth I's attempt to end the Familist sect in England was not wholly successful. Many survived, particularly around Ely, where they were still in existence more than a century later. The confession of two Familists made before a justice of the peace in 1561, indicates the procedure of their meetings and their tenets. The latter may have influenced Gerrard Winstanley (*q.v.*) founder of the "Diggers" (*q.v.*). In 1645, one Randall preached Familist doctrines in London, attracting many followers. Charges of false teaching and immorality were frequently brought against the sect. Evelyn's reference to the Familists as a "sort of refined Quakers," describes them fairly accurately.

BIBLIOGRAPHY: R. M. Jones, *Studies in Mystical Religion* (1909), pp. 428–448; E. Belfort Bax, *Rise and Fall of the Anabaptists* (1903), pp. 338–368; C. E. Whiting, *Studies in English Puritanism 1660–1688* (1931), pp. 283–288; R. A. Knox, *Enthusiasm* (1950), pp. 140, 171–172; *Notes and Queries*, Vol. 175; R. Barclay, *The Inner Life of the Religious Societies of the Commonwealth* (1876), pp. 25–32; C. Burrage, *The Early English Dissenters*, Vol. I (1912), pp. 209–214; L. H. Berens, *The Digger Movement* (1906), pp. 15–18.

[Sup.] GORDON HUELIN.

FAMILY WORSHIP: Ever since the days of the patriarchs religion has centered in the home (Gen. 18:19), with the father as leader of household devotions (Job 1:5). In *The Cotter's Saturday Night* the family sang a psalm, the father read a chapter, and then he prayed, with everyone kneeling. Of late, family prayers have largely been discontinued. Some households listen to devotions over the radio. Families that take religion seriously have prayers after the morning or the evening meal, preferably after both. Usually there is no singing. The lesson consists of a single Bible unit, perhaps a parable, with a brief prayer and the Lord's Prayer, this

in unison. A wise leader prepares in advance, to insure variety, interest, and helpfulness, especially for little ones. He may have them read the lesson in concert, or recite together a favorite psalm. From such homes come ministers, missionaries, and lay church leaders. How can a pastor help to stem secularism more surely than by encouraging each household in the parish to set up a family altar? The best time is immediately after a marriage. According to Augustine, when two gather for prayer, that means husband and wife; three includes the first-born child.   ANDREW W. BLACKWOOD.

FANATICISM: Fanaticism has been described as "the condition of being, or supposing oneself to be, inspired"; and the use of the word in English is due to the same circumstances that perverted the word "enthusiasm" into a term of reproach, as connoting the aberrations and extravagances of sectarianism. The Latin root of the word is *fanum,* meaning a temple, the place where the gods dwelt. A great deal depends on the source of the inspiration. To the rationalist or deist, of course, any claim to direct inspiration is presumptuous; but to the evangelical inspiration may come from the deity, in which case it will bring revelation and power, or from the devil, when it will issue in eccentricity, perversity, and downright sin. The weakness of the fanatic is that, as a man of one idea, he is not in a position to "try the spirits" and to discriminate between divine and diabolical inspiration. To the rationalist even Pentecost is a presumptuous and fanatical phenomenon; but to those who are aware of the true spiritual value of prophetical religion even pathological accompaniments do not invalidate the spiritual insight, the access of power, and the ethical consequences of true inspiration in high moments of vision and revelation. Fanaticism is the shadow that dogs the footsteps of true prophetical religion.

WILLIAM ROXBURGH FORRESTER.

FAREL, GUILLAUME: It seems strange that a man who exerted a powerful influence upon Calvin should have suffered neglect on the part of scholars during the past forty years. At the Bibliothèque Nationale in Paris only one recent work is listed, namely, a facsimile edition of Farel's *Sommaire et briefve Declaration* (ed. by A. Piaget, 1935), with a brief historical introduction. There is also the admirable work by a group of Swiss scholars who in 1930 published their composite biography. This is the only satisfactory and comprehensive study in any language up to 1952. It contains a full bibliography (pp. 77–89). Jean Barnaud covered Farel's life to 1521, and the deceased scholar, N. Weiss, and Jean Meyhoffer took the next three years, which were very important, for in 1523 Farel became interested in the work of Hinne Rode (*q.v.*), rector of the Brethren of the Common Life (*q.v.*) at Utrecht, who carried with him to Basel the well-known treatise by Cornelius Hoen on the Eucharist. The latter, partly through Farel's work, became the basis of the new view held by Zwingli, Bucer, Oecolampadius, Calvin, and Farel himself. In 1523 a French translation of Hoen's treatise was published in Basel, and the two authors of the chapter just mentioned have correctly concluded that Farel made this translation. The title was *La Summe de l'Escripture saincte et l'ordinaire des chrestiens enseignant la vraye foi chrestienne. . . .* In 1524 Farel wrote his first work, *Summaire et briefve déclaration,* which probably was inspired to some extent by the work of Hinne Rode. In the same year he was expelled from Basel. The third chapter was written by J. Meyhoffer and J. Pétremand, while sixteen others complete the work. Among the authors only Henri-Ph. Meylan has recently written noteworthy pages on Farel, and these only in one of his books on a more general subject.

[Sup.] ALBERT HYMA.

FARMER, HERBERT HENRY: Presbyterian Church of England; b. London, Nov. 27, 1892; he was educated at Cambridge University (M.A., 1918) and Westminster (Theological) College, Cambridge. He has been minister of Stafford Presbyterian Church (1919–22); of St. Augustine's Presbyterian Church, New Barnet, London (1922–31); Riley Professor of Christian Doctrine, Hartford Seminary Foundation (1931–35); Barbour Professor of Systematic Theology at Westminster College, Cambridge (1935); Stanton Lecturer in the Philosophy of Religion, Cambridge University (1937–40); Norris-Hulse Professor of Divinity in the University of Cambridge (1949–   ). He has written: *Things Not Seen* (1927); *Experience of God* (1929); *The World and God* (1935); *The Healing Cross* (1938); *The Servant of the Word* (1941); *Towards Belief in God* (1942); *God and Men* (1948).

FATHER DIVINE'S PEACE MISSION MOVEMENT: Founded about 1930, the movement is unique in believing that its founder is not a prophet, not a Messiah, but God himself. That he appears in human flesh as a short, stocky Negro, nattily dressed and well groomed, comes as a shock to many orthodox white Christians who regard it as nothing short of blasphemous that a mere man, and a Negro at that, should claim to be God. But a careful study reveals that his movement is one of the most remarkable religio-socio-economic movements of the contemporary world. And the cohesive force that binds the movement together and makes it function is the confident belief of his

followers in Father Divine, and their willingness to carry into practice what he teaches as the veritable will of God. When pressed for the reason for their belief in Father Divine, his adherents almost invariably say, "No one but God could do the things he does."

What is it he does? Specifically, they mean such things as providing abundant, nourishing meals in his restaurants for as little as 25 cents (this in 1952 in New York, Newark, Philadelphia, etc.), and the most sumptuous banquets, for which no one is required to pay more than that sum. They mean providing clean, sanitary, comfortable lodging for as little as $1.50 per week—never more than $2.00. They mean providing security for the individual in a day of great insecurity They refer to what appear to be remarkable healings of disease—all this and much more.

The origin of the movement is difficult to trace. There is no complete certainty as to Father Divine's past. He first attracted wide public attention in the twenties, when crowds flocked to his home in Sayville, Long Island. Later he moved into Harlem, in New York City, and his movement grew rapidly. He was brought into court and a judgment for $3,000 was secured against him. Although besought by his followers to be allowed to pay the amount, he steadfastly refused to do so, insisting that it was an unjust judgment, and moved his headquarters to Philadelphia.

The central features of the movement are the banquets, which are a kind of communion service, where prayer, song, testimony, and talks by Father Divine and others are a constant accompaniment of the meal; and his strong insistence upon the social implications of religion. He equates Americanism, democracy, and Christianity, is a rigid foe of racial segregation, and believes thoroughly in co-operation as over against competition in business. His movement is, to a considerable degree, a co-operative movement, bound together by a common allegiance to himself. *The New Day,* a weekly paper, publishes everything Father Divine says. Thus a new scripture is in the making.

Membership statistics are not available. The movement is strongest in and about New York and Philadelphia, but branches are found in many states and in several foreign countries.

Contrary to popular belief the movement attracts white people as well as colored. On the west coast those "of dark complexion," as Father Divine calls Negroes, unwilling even to use the term Negro or Colored, outnumber white members. The inner circle of followers live celibate lives, husband and wife being separated and living apart in separate hostels, or "heavens." Moral demands upon members are exceedingly strict. Heaven is here and now.

BIBLIOGRAPHY: John Hoshor, *God in a Rolls-Royce*, 1936; R. W. Parker, *Incredible Messiah*, 1937. Both exploit the more spectacular phases of the movement but contain valuable factual material. Sympathetic studies are: Marcus Bach, *They Have Found a Faith*, 1946, and Charles S. Braden, *These Also Believe*, 1949; Sara Harris, *Father Divine*, 1953.

CHARLES S. BRADEN.

FATHERHOOD OF GOD: The name of Father is infrequently applied to God in the Old Testament, and mostly in a figurative sense. God is the Father of Israel because he is the Creator of Israel's existence as a people, not by physical generation (as the relation of god to people was conceived in some heathen religions), but by sovereign divine election (Hos. 11:1). Israel was a foundling child on whom God took pity (Deut. 32:10; Ezek. 16:6), and God's fatherly love towards Israel as his adopted son constituted a claim upon Israel's obedient service. The Fatherhood of God in the Old Testament has its meaning in the context of the covenant and it relates primarily to Israel as a people. Rarely is it extended to individuals (Ps. 68:5). The invocation of God in prayer by the name of Father, which became current in post-canonical Judaism, is found in the Old Testament only in Jer. 3:4, 19.

Fatherhood is ascribed to God with so great frequency in the New Testament, especially in the teaching of Jesus, that it has been regarded as the distinctive mark of the Christian conception of God. Its Old Testament connotation is enriched with the thought of God's fatherly readiness to forgive (Matt. 6:14; Luke 15:11–32). The question has been much debated whether the Fatherhood of God, proclaimed by Jesus, is to be understood as extending to all men, or only to believers. Since both views can be supported by passages in the Gospels, it is evident that the alternative is false. The Fatherhood of God is indeed universal in so far as his providential care extends to all men indiscriminately (Matt. 5:45), but it is not effectively realized as a personal relationship except where it is correlated with sonship (Matt. 11:27). Jesus' proclamation of the Fatherhood of God is thus at the same time the benediction (Matt. 5:9), the challenge (Matt. 5:48) and the authorization (John 1:12) of divine sonship to men; for Jesus himself is *the* son who alone can properly speak of God as *my* Father (Matt. 11:27) and who by sharing his sonship with men can direct them to *your* Father (Matt. 6:8) and authorize them to say together *our* Father (Matt. 6:9). The name of Father is applied to God with great frequency in the Fourth Gospel and also in the Pauline Epistles, where it is expressly signified that God is primarily the Father of our Lord Jesus Christ (II Cor. 1:3), through whom we receive the adoption of sons (Gal. 4:5; Eph. 1:5), and by whose indwelling Spirit we are enabled to *be* the sons of God (Rom. 8:14–16; Gal. 4:6).

The Fatherhood of God in no wise precludes his holy wrath against sin and his disciplinary treatment of sinners (Deut. 8:5; Heb. 12:5–8). It was a sentimentalized conception of the Fatherhood of God that was used by some liberals in the Ritschlian tradition in an attempt to turn the flank of the historic doctrine of the atonement.

The gospel of the Fatherhood of God not only brings men into a relation of sonship to him, but unites them together as a family which is animated by brotherly love (I Thess. 4:9; Rom. 12:10), reconciliation (Matt. 18:21–35) and mutual submission (Eph. 5:21; Phil. 2:3). It is the ground of the catholicity and the ecumenical mission of the church.

BIBLIOGRAPHY: Standard works on biblical theology; P. T. Forsyth, *The Holy Father and the Living Christ*, 1897; J. S. Lidgett, *The Fatherhood of God*, 1902; A. Harnack, *What is Christianity?* 1904; T. W. Manson, *The Teaching of Jesus*, 1931; W. B. Selbie, *The Fatherhood of God*, 1936.

GEORGE S. HENDRY.

FATIMA, OUR LADY OF: Popular title given to Mary, the Mother of God, in honor of the apparitions at Cova da Iria, near Fatima, Portugal, in 1917.

On May 13, 1917, three shepherd children related that the Blessed Virgin had appeared to them and recounted how she would reappear to them at that spot on the thirteenth of every month until October. The children later related that in her July 13th appearance the Lady declared that the Lord desired devotion to her Immaculate Heart to be established throughout the world and that the faithful should offer a Communion of reparation on the first Saturday of each month.

Seventy thousand people gathered at the appointed place on October 13 to behold a predicted miracle. The vision was not apparent to the assembled throng but the three children testified that the Lady appeared and announced that she was the Lady of the Rosary, warned the people that they must not continue to offend God, and urged them to recite the rosary. Suddenly a heavy downpour of rain, which had been drenching the assembled thousands, abruptly ceased and the sun appeared, swiftly revolving, and throwing out shafts of varicolored light in all directions. Coming to rest, the sun then wheeled a second time and a third time. Thousands of spectators witnessed the celestial phenomenon.

In October, 1930, Roman Catholic ecclesiastical authority declared the apparitions worthy of belief, and devotion to Our Lady of Fatima was authorized under the title of Our Lady of the Rosary. Millions of pilgrims have since visited the site of the visions which is regarded as a religious and national shrine.

See also PILGRIMAGES.

BIBLIOGRAPHY: William Thomas Walsh, *Our Lady of Fatima*, 1950; C. C. Martindale, *The Meaning of Fatima*, 1950.

THOMAS J. MCCARTHY.

FAUNCE, WILLIAM HERBERT PERRY: D. Jan. 31, 1930. He was president of Brown University (1899–1930) and was widely interested in ecumenical and international affairs. He was once president of the World Peace Foundation. His later books include: *The Educational Ideal in the Ministry* (1908); *What Does Christianity Mean?* (1912); *Social Aspects of Foreign Missions* (1914); *Religion and War* (1918); and *The New Horizon of State and Church* (1918).

[Sup.] RAYMOND W. ALBRIGHT.

FEAR: Is a subject of common interest in psychology and religion. It is one of the points at which the two fields converge. As a motivating factor in religious behavior and a component part of religious experience, it has caused much discussion among psychologists and theologians.

Rudolph Otto, in *The Idea of the Holy* (*q.v.*), has given the clearest explanation of fear as a religiously significant emotion. In the presence of the numinous, the individual feels a sense of *mysterium tremendum*, which is composed of awe and fascination. Elements of fear are present in religious experience both because we tend to become religious in the presence of the mysterious and because our sense of guilt causes us to fear that we are about to be revealed as we really are.

Psychologists of every variety have paid attention to fear. John B. Watson, in *Behaviorism* (1924), reduced the fears of the newborn to two that are basic and inherited—the fears of "a loud sound and the loss of support." These, however, are neurologically complicated experiences which contemporary psychologists regard as arising out of maturation and learning, rather than from heredity. The impulse toward survival quite often is reversed into a fear of death, and one may wisely ask if such experiences as Watson mentions, and countless others, are not derivatives of this parent fear with which each individual has to deal, creatively or destructively, from very early in life.

Among depth psychologists, the difference between *fear* and *anxiety* has occasioned much discussion. Among Freudians, fear is defined as directed toward an externally real object, while anxiety arises from a psychic condition which tends "to ignore the object." Fear, for Freud, is a necessary and normal part of the individual's self-preservative impulse as he responds to external, reality-based danger; anxiety is an internally structured and derived psychic reality which is much more serious and which merits medical attention. In one way or another,

psychoanalysts make distinctions of this kind. See Sigmund Freud, *General Introduction to Psychoanalysis*, p. 343.

Otto Rank draws attention to the "fear of life," where the individual is reluctant to enter into responsible living situations because he basically fears responsibility, preferring to be passive, dependent and irresponsible; but he also makes much of the opposite kind of fear—that of "having to live as an isolated individual." See Rank, *Will Therapy* (1936), p. 175. The death fear, then, is the fear of going back into nonbeing, of losing individuality, or never having achieved a sustained place in the human community.

This latter opinion is closely akin to the thought of Soren Kierkegaard, in *The Sickness Unto Death*. He relates fear, or "despair," to the experience of becoming a self. The achievement of selfhood, of individuality, of personhood, he regards as the core of intentionality in personality. To do this without at the same time losing the approval of one's community is the dilemma of human existence. In the matrix of this dilemma fear is born.

Clinical psychiatrists call attention to another type of fear—that of the phobic and deluded neurotic and psychotic person. Usually these fears take a persecutory bent; the individual projects his inner fears upon the outer environment and reads them back as persecutions. Such persons are often completely incapacitated for effective family living and vocational pursuits; they are most often candidates for hospital care. They are thought of medically as psychotic.

An individual's fear may be organized into compulsive thoughts and acts which are extremely annoying to him, which he may keep secret, but which do not keep him from a minimum degree of function at home and at work. These compulsive feelings may issue into obsessive thoughts, such as thinking something extremely vulgar and fearing that he will say it. Or they may crystallize into compulsive phobias or manias. The person with a compulsive phobia will fear entering closed places, leaving the house, or handling certain things. It is a procedure of abstinence. The person with a compulsive mania cannot keep from doing certain things. He *must* touch every hand rail; or he *must* go through the elaborate ritual of arranging his shoes, evening his trouser legs, and tying a string across the back door before he can go to bed.

These fears are clearly irrational, compulsive, involuntary, and arise from distorted psychic processes in the individual. They painfully hamper his creative expression of life. Modern medical psychologists have made great progress in treating these disorders, and pastoral psychologists in interpreting their religious significance. The biblical concept of fear as opposed

to *agape* (see AGAPE [LOVE]) is the most rewarding interpretation. Paul repeats the theme that
God has not given a spirit of fear again unto
bondage, but of power and love and self-control. John insists that perfect love casts out
fear, and that the demonic is exorcised by the
power of love. This is the theme of the monumental work of Oskar Pfister, *Christianity and
Fear,* which is the most exhaustive study of the
subject of fear in its religious and psychological meanings in existence today.

BIBLIOGRAPHY: Rollo May, *The Meaning of Anxiety,*
1950; Bonaro W. Overstreet, *Understanding Fear in Ourselves and Others,* 1951.

WAYNE E. OATES.

**FEDERAL COUNCIL OF EVANGELICAL
FREE CHURCHES.** See ENGLAND AND WALES;
FREE CHURCH FEDERAL COUNCIL.

**FEDERAL COUNCIL OF THE CHURCHES
OF CHRIST IN AMERICA:** During the forty-
two years of its existence—1908 to 1950—the
Federal Council grew to be the largest church
federation in the world in terms of organization.
In 1950 it was merged, along with seven interdenominational functional agencies, into the National Council of the Churches of Christ in the
U. S. A. (*q.v.*).

I. Program and Organization: Bishop E. R.
Hendrix, the first president of the Council,
stated at the first meeting of its Executive Committee in December, 1909, that the Council "aspires less to be an organization than an influence, less to create a corporation than a climate." For several years Elias B. Sanford, as
corresponding secretary, directed the office of
the Council. It had no executive secretary.

The Commission on the Church and Social
Service was conspicuous for its work from the
beginning, especially in the field of industrial
strife. A statement on the "Social Ideals of the
Churches" was adopted in 1908. The Commission employed Charles S. Macfarland as secretary, beginning May 1, 1911. Later that year
he was designated also as acting executive secretary of the Council.

During 1911 the Commission on Peace and
Arbitration was organized. At the same time
the Council was encouraging the development
of state and local federations. There soon followed commissions on Evangelism, Country
Life, Education, and Foreign Missions. An
office was opened in Washington with a part-
time secretary. World War I called for a rapid
expansion of federated activities. War relief
funds were secured for stricken churches of Europe. The most important in terms of added
leadership for the Council was the General War-
Time Commission of the Churches (1917)—
Robert E. Speer, chairman; William Adams
Brown, secretary; and Samuel McCrea Cavert,
assistant secretary. The Commission on Army

and Navy Chaplains was initiated by the Council in the same year.

During the decade following the war various
new commissions or departments were constituted, each with its own supervisory group,
budget, and staff. At its quadrennial meeting
in 1932 the Council reorganized its structure.
Many commissions and committees were consolidated in eight major departments: Field,
Evangelism, Research and Education, Social
Service, Race Relations, International Justice
and Goodwill, Relations with Churches Abroad,
and Radio. There was also constituted a Committee on Worship.

At the same time all departments and committees were brought under the direction of the
Executive Committee of the Council, which was
a body composed of delegates designated directly by the constituent churches. Thus all
activities of the Council were brought more directly under the control of the member churches
themselves than had been the case during the
early years. The statement, "The Social Ideals
of the Churches," was revised.

During the period from 1932 to 1940 the
Council expanded gradually, consolidating its
position in the life of the constituent churches,
becoming increasingly representative of their interests and positions and responsive to their
needs for services.

World War II brought increased responsibilities. Its major new enterprises were for overseas relief, aliens and prisoners of war, and camp
and defense communities. The Department of
International Justice and Goodwill established
a special Commission on a Just and Durable
Peace, under the chairmanship of John Foster
Dulles, which was influential in the development of national public opinion.

II. Organizational Growth: The expansion of
the Council's organization and program is reflected in its annual receipts. A few reports are
cited: 1909—$9,000; 1912—$36,500; 1914—$67,-
000; 1917—$240,000; 1918 (including the Gen-
eral War-Time Commission)—$303,149; 1932—
$301,306; 1940—$302,342; 1948—$649,644.

In 1948 there was an executive staff of twenty-
eight.

In addition to the funds for its own operation,
the Council handled large sums for relief and
for special extra-budgetary services: e.g., between 1915 and 1924, $1,500,000 for the churches
of Belgium and France. During World War II
and the years following, Church World Service
(*q.v.*) handled nearly $50,000,000 of overseas aid
in money or in clothing, food, and medical supplies.

The scope and variety of the Council's work
expanded during the last twenty years of its
life. In 1948, the year of its fortieth anniversary, the Council's report included the following illustrative items: the Department of Na-

tional Religious Radio directed sixteen network programs each week and received over a thousand letters a day expressing appreciation and asking for copies of messages; Visitation Evangelism Campaigns were held in thirty-one cities; University Christian Missions were held on forty campuses (during the biennium); study conferences on the churches and world order and on the churches and economic life were held; chaplains were nominated to federal prisons; there were 227 state, city, and county councils of churches with employed executive leadership and 485 with voluntary leadership; the Department of Christian Social Relations conducted a National Conference on Protestant Homes for the Aged (see AGED, CARE OF THE), with representatives from twenty-six states; the Commission on Marriage and the Home reported sales of 700,000 for its pamphlet "If I Marry A Roman Catholic"; the Department of Race Relations distributed 140,000 pieces of literature; the Department of International Justice and Goodwill issued statements on "The Churches and the United Nations," "The Churches and the European Recovery Program," and "Cross-Roads of American Foreign Policy"; the Commission on Worship published "Hymns of the Rural Spirit"; and the Department of Pastoral Services reported a study of the religious ministry to older people; the Commission on the Ministry reported the publication of eleven pamphlets to aid the churches in recruiting youth for church vocations; the Washington office had made reports to denominational leaders on sixty subjects on which they had requested information.

BIBLIOGRAPHY: The development of the Federal Council may best be studied in its reports and its monthly publication, *The Federal Council Bulletin*; Samuel McCrea Cavert, ed., *Twenty Years of Church Federation*, 1929; E. B. Sanford, *Origin and History of the Federal Council*, 1916; Charles S. Macfarland, *Christian Unity in Practice and Prophecy*, 1933; John A. Hutchinson, *We Are Not Divided*, 1941; William Adams Brown, *Toward a United Church*, 1946.

[Sup. to CHURCH FEDERATION.]

ROSWELL P. BARNES.

FEDERATED CHURCHES: The term is applied to two or more local churches of different denominations which unite to carry on a common program under one minister. Largely rural, federated churches originated in part to solve the problem of providing religious service in population areas too thin to allow the maintenance of several denominational churches. Through 1916 they were listed by the U. S. Census as "independent churches," but since 1926 the term "federated churches" was substituted. Federated churches have sometimes become community churches (*q.v.*) when they have given up denominational affiliation. Because the terms are used differently in different places, federated churches are sometimes called union churches (*q.v.*).

BIBLIOGRAPHY: Ralph A. Felton, *Cooperative Churches*, 1947.

A. T. DEGROOT.

FEDERATION, GERMAN EVANGELICAL CHURCH. See GERMANY.

FEDERATION OF FRANCE, PROTESTANT. See FRANCE.

FEDOROV, NICOLAS: Eastern Orthodox; b. in 1828 (as it seems, he was an illegitimate son of Prince Paul Gagarine); d. at Moscow, Dec. 15, 1903. He studied at Odessa Richelieu-Lycaeum, but did not complete the course. In 1854–68 he was a schoolmaster in various small cities of central Russia. After 1868 he was a library clerk at the Rumjanzev Museum in Moscow, and later in the Moscow Archives of the Foreign Office. He was a close friend of Dostojevsky (*q.v.*), Vladimir Soloviev (*q.v.*), Leo Tolstoy and other prominent people in Moscow. He was a man of peculiar habits and convictions, a solitary thinker, or rather a dreamer. The initial inspiration came probably from the French positivism (*q.v.*) (late Auguste Comte) and French utopian socialism (especially Fourier). But Fedorov attempted a striking synthesis of Christianity and a religion of humanity, centered around the idea of Resurrection, which he interpreted as a task committed to men in history: they must resurrect the dead, the ancestors, and for that purpose erotic energy of man must be diverted from the procreation of children to the raising up of the fathers. As strange as this conception may seem, it exercised a considerable influence, even on such philosophers as Vladimir Soloviev, who was himself developing ideas to the same effect. The alleged influence of Fedorov on Dostojevsky is not to be exaggerated. After the Russian Revolution Fedorov's ideas were reinterpreted in a secular manner by a group of followers in the Soviet Union and outside Russia (mainly Kharbin in Mandjouria). Fedorov's papers were published (in Russian) in two volumes (not for sale). It seems that nothing has ever been written about him in Western languages.

GEORGES FLOROVSKY.

FEDOTOV, GEORGE P.: Eastern Orthodox; b. in Saratov, Russia, in 1886; d. Sept. 1, 1951. He graduated from the University of Petrograd and studied history at Berlin and Jena. He taught the history of Middle Ages as privatdocent in Petrograd and as professor in Saratov. He left Russia in 1925 for France where he taught church history at the Paris Orthodox Theological Institute (1925–40). He came to America in 1941 and taught as lay-professor of church history at the St. Vladimir Russian Orthodox Seminary in New York (1941–51). He was coeditor in Paris of the review *New City*

(1930–39). He has published the following books in English: *The Russian Church since the Revolution* (1927); *Russian Religious Mind* (1947); *Treasury of Russian Spirituality* (1949, 2nd ed., 1950). Some of his Russian books are *Saints of Ancient Russia; St. Philip, Metropolitan of Moscow; Russian religious Songs*.

FEEBLE-MINDED, CARE OF THE. See MENTALLY ILL, CARE OF THE.

FEES, MINISTERIAL: The Scriptures teach that a pastor should look to local brethren for support (I Cor. 9:11, 14; Gal. 6:6; etc.), and that the receiving of money from any person for special services is perilous (II Kings 5:26 and related passages). The custom of charging for such services as baptism or the burial of the dead grew up in the Roman Church before the Reformation, and still flourishes. Among Protestants customs vary widely. One pastor receives money for no such service except marriage, when the fee goes to his wife. Another accepts money as he would a gift of flowers. We need a uniform code of ethics. Such a code might discourage all such payments, except to defray expenses, as in a church wedding ceremony preceded by a rehearsal. Both pastor and church belong to the community. "Non ministrari, sed ministrare."

ANDREW W. BLACKWOOD.

FELLOWSHIP OF RECONCILIATION: Founded in Cambridge, England, in December, 1914, and in the United States in November, 1915. At a conference in Holland in 1919 the International Fellowship of Reconciliation was established to serve as a bond between national groups and determine their right to be affiliated with the international body, but it does not control or supervise their activities. The Fellowship now has groups in twenty-five countries, including Germany, Italy, Japan, several Latin American countries, South Africa, Australia, and New Zealand. There were small groups in several Iron Curtain countries, but if they still exist contact with them has been broken. There are about 14,000 active members in the United States, including nearly 3,000 clergymen and 500 teachers. Membership in Great Britain is about the same. Membership in other countries is much smaller, the over-all total being about 5,000.

According to its statement of purpose the Fellowship is composed of men and women of many nations and races who recognize the unity of the world-wide human family and "believe that love, such as that seen pre-eminently in Jesus," must serve as the guide for personal conduct and is "the effective force for overcoming evil and transforming society into a creative fellowship." Members specifically refuse to participate in any war or to sanction war preparations. The principal activity is, therefore, that of spreading the ideas of Christian pacifism (*q.v.*), especially in churches. There is also, however, strong interest in spreading the philosophy and method of non-violence in race and other conflict situations. The chief means employed are study groups, personal witness, and widespread literature distribution.

A. J. MUSTE.

FELLOWSHIP OF THE NEW LIFE. See FABIAN SOCIETY.

FERM, VERGILIUS TURE ANSELM: Lutheran; b. Jan. 6, 1896, Sioux City, Iowa. He was educated at Augustana College (A.B., 1916); Augustana Theological Seminary (B.D., 1919); Yale (M.A., 1923; Ph.D., 1925). He was ordained (1919); and is an affiliate member of the Wooster Presbytery. He was professor of philosophy, Albright College, Reading, Pa. (1927–28); Compton Professor of Philosophy, The College of Wooster (1928–); visiting professor, Auburn (N. Y.) Theological Seminary (summer, 1937).

He is author of: *The Crisis in American Lutheran Theology* (1927); *First Adventures in Philosophy* (1936); *First Chapters in Religious Philosophy* (1937); *What Can We Believe?* (1948); *A Protestant Dictionary* (1951). He is coauthor of: *The Nature of Religious Experience* (1937); (with Hugo Bieber), *Polarity* (1951). He is editor of: *What is Lutheranism?* (1930); *Contemporary American Theology* (Vol. I, 1932; Vol. II, 1933); *Religion in Transition* (1937); *An Encyclopedia of Religion* (1945); *Religion in the Twentieth Century* (1948); *Forgotten Religions* (1950); *A History of Philosophical Systems* (1950).

FERRARA-FLORENCE, COUNCIL OF. See BASEL, COUNCIL OF.

FERRÉ, NELS F. S.: Congregational Minister, Methodist layman; B. at Luleia, Sweden, June 8, 1908. He studied at Boston University (A.B., 1931), Andover Newton Theological School (B.D., 1934), and Harvard (A.M., 1936; Ph.D., 1938). He was Sheldon travelling Fellow to Universities of Uppsala and Lund (1936–37). He taught philosophy and Christian Theology at Andover Newton Theological School (1937–50), and Philosophical Theology at Vanderbilt University (1950–). His books include: *Swedish Contributions to Modern Theology* (1939); *The Christian Fellowship* (1940); *The Christian Faith* (1942); *Return to Christianity* (1943); *Faith and Reason* (1945); *Evil and the Christian Faith* (1946); *Pillars of Faith* (1948); *Christianity and Society* (1950); *Strengthening the Spiritual Life* (1951); *The Christian Understanding of God* (1951).

FERTILITY CULTS: This is a convenient designation of certain aspects of the nature religions of the ancient Near East. The productivity of the ground, flocks, and herds was associated with the gods and goddesses, often the storm, vegetation, or sun god and his consort. Expressed in mythology, the result was stories of the death and resurrection of the god, the marriage of the god and goddess, etc. The myth of the gods was dramatized in the ritual at the sanctuaries, and there might be professional cult prostitutes who participated in sacred marriage rites.

There were many manifestations of the myth of the dying and resurrecting deity. In Egypt it was Osiris. Among the Akkadians it was Tammuz, known to the earlier Sumerians as Dumu-zi. Among the Hittites it was Telepinus; and the Canaanite storm god Baal, the son of the grain god Dagon, played this role among the Canaanites. The worship of Tammuz at the time of Ezekiel existed in the Jerusalem temple (Ezek. 8:14), and Zech. 12:11 refers to the wailing for Hadad-rimmon, a form of Baal (see also Hos. 7:14). At the high places, beneath the sacred trees, the rites of sacred prostitution were carried on, bitterly denounced by the prophets (Jer. 3:2, 3, 6; Ezek. 16:30–34; Hos. 4:10, 14 ff.). The shrines profited from the income of such women (Mic. 1:7), and the law forbade bringing the offerings of a male or female cult prostitute to the temple (Deut. 23:17). The female cult prostitute was sometimes called a *qedeshah* or sacred woman (see Gen. 38), corresponding to the Babylonian *qadishtu*. Male prostitutes appear in I Kings 14:23, 24; 15:12; II Kings 23:7.

The bull, snake, fish, dove, tree, river, and stone symbolism of the fertility cults has many archaeological illustrations.

See also MYSTERY RELIGIONS, RELATION OF, TO EARLY CHRISTIANITY.

BIBLIOGRAPHY: W. W. Baudissin, *Adonis und Esmun*, 1911; T. H. Gaster, *Thespis: Myth, Ritual and Drama in the Ancient Near East*, 1950; S. H. Hooke, "Ritual Pattern in Canaan," in *Myth and Ritual* (1933), 40–67; H. G. May, "The Fertility Cult in Hosea," *AJSL*, XLVIII (1933), 73 ff.

HERBERT G. MAY.

FEY, HAROLD EDWARD: Minister, Disciples of Christ; managing editor of *The Christian Century;* b. at Elwood, Ind., Oct. 10, 1898. He was educated at Cotner College, Lincoln, Neb. (A.B., 1922); Yale Divinity School (B.D., 1927). He was ordained to the ministry (1923), and was pastor, First Christian Church, Hastings, Neb. (1927–29); professor, Union Theological Seminary, Manila, P.I. (1929–31); editor, *World Call*, Indianapolis, Ind. (1932–35); editor, *Fellowship*, and secretary, Fellowship of Reconciliation, New York (1935–40); he joined the staff of *The Christian Century* in 1940. He is author of: *Can Catholicism Win America*,

pamphlet (1945); *The Lord's Supper: Seven Meanings* (1948).

FIDELIS, SAINT (MARKUS ROY): He obtained his doctor's degree in theology and in both law faculties at Freiburg. In his practice at Ensisheim he earned the reputation of "advocate of the poor." In his capacity of Capuchin he became very famous for his eloquent sermons, and for his participation in the Catholic Reformation (Counter Reformation). He was the first martyr among the Capuchins.

BIBLIOGRAPHY: *Nel terzo centenario di San Fedele a Sigmaringa*, 1922; B. Gossens, *Der heilige Fidelis von Sigmaringen*, 1933.

[Sup.] MATHIAS GOOSSENS.

FIELD WORK: Part-time religious service rendered by a student while taking regular courses in a theological school. It differs from a full-time internship (*q.v.*). The most obvious need is economic, to help finance his education. Most faculties look on field work as valuable educationally, and assign a faculty supervisor, preferably full time. Professors of practical theology are relating their instruction to field work, which affords clinical opportunities. There are obvious hazards: the student has momentary, superficial contacts that he cannot "follow through"; he may also develop slovenly habits of sermon preparation; and he may rationalize his failures in school on the ground of overactivity in his field work.

WAYNE E. OATES.

FIFTH MONARCHY MEN: They based their teaching on Daniel 6: the fourth monarchy would be followed by the rule of the saints with Christ at its head. Some said this would first become visible on earth in 1666. Not all Fifth Monarchy Men at first opposed Cromwell, but when he disappointed them by establishing the Protectorate, they attempted to establish the true kingdom by force. After Venner's capture, the movement ceased to be militant, and its ideas spread to other religious bodies, including even Anglicanism. The resort to violence was not an essential feature of Fifth Monarchism, and largely arose out of the extraordinary political circumstances of the time.

BIBLIOGRAPHY: L. F. Brown, *The Political Activities of the Baptists and Fifth Monarchy Men in England during the Interregnum*, 1912; C. E. Whiting, *Studies in English Puritanism 1660–1688* (1931), pp. 234–241; G. Nuttall, *The Holy Spirit in Puritan Thought and Experience*, 1946; G. P. Gooch, *Political Thought in England from Bacon to Halifax* (1946), pp. 114–117; *Notes and Queries*, Vols. 191 and 192; C. Burrage, *The Fifth Monarchy Insurrections* (reprinted from the *English Historical Review*), 1910.

[Sup.] GORDON HUELIN.

FILIPPOV, DANIEL. See MESSIAHS, FALSE.

FILM ASSOCIATION, RELIGIOUS: A nonprofit service agency whose membership comprises twenty-five boards and agencies of major

Protestant denominations. Founded in 1942 for the stated purpose of helping churches make their educational programs more effective through the use of visual aids, the RFA operates nine film libraries and also acts as releasing agency for films produced by denominations, independent producers, and such interdenominational agencies as the Protestant Film Commission. A unique feature is the publication of a comprehensive catalog in which the film descriptions consist of critical evaluations rather than sales blurbs. The educational rather than the entertainment use of films is emphasized.

WILLIAM L. ROGERS.

FILSON, FLOYD VIVIAN: Presbyterian, U. S. A.; b. Hamilton, Missouri, November 15, 1896. He graduated from Park College (A.B., 1918); McCormick Theological Seminary (B.D., 1922; Nettie F. McCormick Fellow, 1922–24); University of Basel (Th.D., 1930). He has taught New Testament Greek at McCormick Theological Seminary (1923–30); New Testament literature and exegesis (1930–34); New Testament literature and history 1934–). He wrote: *St. Paul's Conception of Recompense* (1931); *Origins of The Gospels* (1938); *Pioneers of the Primitive Church* (1940); *One Lord, One Faith* (1943); *The New Testament Against Its Environment* (1950); and is coauthor with G. Ernest Wright of: *The Westminster Historical Atlas to the Bible* (1945); coeditor of: *The Westminster Study Bible* (1948); cotranslator of: Rudolph Otto, *The Kingdom of God and the Son of Man* (1938); translator of: Oscar Cullmann, *Christ and Time* (1950).

FINALISM. See TELEOLOGY.

FINEGAN, JACK: Disciples of Christ; b. Des Moines, Iowa, July 11, 1908. He was graduated from Drake University (B.A., 1928; M. A., 1929; B.D., 1930); Colgate-Rochester Divinity School (B.D., 1931; M.Th., 1932); Friedrich-Wilhelms-Universitaet, Berlin (Lic. theol., 1934). He was minister, First Christian Church, Ames, Iowa (1934–39); professor of religious education, Iowa State College (1939–46); professor of New Testament literature and interpretation, Pacific School of Religion (1946–). He has also been minister, University Christian Church, Berkeley, Calif., since 1949. He is author of: *Die Ueberlieferung der Leidens und Auferstehungsgeschichte Jesu* (1934); *Light from the Ancient Past, The Archeological Background of the Hebrew-Christian Religion* (1946); *Book of Student Prayers* (1946); *A Highway Shall Be There* (1946); *Youth Asks about Religion* (1949); *Like the Great Mountains* (1949); and *The Archeology of World Religions* (1952).

FINITE GOD. See GOD.

FINKELSTEIN, LOUIS: Jewish; b. Cincinnati, Ohio, June 14, 1895. He studied at the College of the City of New York (A.B., 1915); Columbia University (Ph.D., 1918); and the Jewish Theological Seminary of America (rabbi, 1919). He was rabbi of Congregation Kehillath Israel, New York City (1919–31). He taught at the Jewish Theological Seminary (instructor, 1920–24; lecturer, 1924–30; associate professor, 1930–31; and Solomon Schechter, Professor of Theology, 1931– ; assistant to the president, 1934–37; provost, 1937–40; president, 1940–51; chancellor and president of the faculties of the seminary, 1951–). In 1939 he founded the Institute for Religious Studies at the seminary, a graduate school conducted with the co-operation of Jewish, Catholic, and Protestant scholars. In 1940 at the invitation of President Roosevelt he served as the representative of Judaism in the United States to advise the president with regard to steps for world peace. In the field of scholarship, his contributions deal generally with the origin and development of Pharisaism.

Among his writings are: *Jewish Self-Government in the Middle Ages* (1924); *The Pharisees, Their Origin and Their Philosophy* (1925); *Akiba—Scholar, Saint, Martyr* (1936); *The Pharisees: The Sociological Background of Their Faith* (1938); *Beliefs and Practices of Judaism* (1952); *Pro-Maccabean Documents in the Passover Haggadah* (1943); he is coauthor of *Religions of Democracy* (1941) and *Faith for Today* (1941); he edited *The Jews: Their History, Culture, and Religion* (1950); *Saadia Gaon* (1943). He has published scientific editions of *Kimchi's Commentary on Isaiah* (1926); *Sifre on Deuteronomy* (1935 and 1936), and is coeditor of the Science, Philosophy and Religion annual symposia (1942 ff.).

FINLAND (SUOMI): Having secured independence from Russia on Dec. 6, 1917, Finland became a republic in 1919. Before the peace treaty with Russia in 1944, when the republic lost part of its territory in the southeast and along the Arctic Ocean, Finland's boundaries were about the same as when it was a grand duchy of Russia. With an area of 130,000 square miles, Finland has (1950) a population of 4,033,-000. About 95% of the population is Lutheran, and there were 71,700 Eastern Orthodox and 1,189 Roman Catholics in 1949.

The Ural-Altaic theory concerning the origin of the Finns has now been abandoned. People of the same racial family live to this day in the territory from the Baltic Sea to the Volga River. In prehistoric times the Finns lived south of the Gulf of Finland, where they had contacts with Germans and then with Swedes. Since the beginning of the twentieth century church schools have been supplanted by public schools. Before 1923 congregational registers provided the only official records of vital statistics, but in that year civil lists were introduced as permissive. By 1952 less than 3% of the population had availed itself of the right to be recorded on civil lists. A further step was taken in the separation of church and state in 1944, when powers previously exercised by the republic's minister of education were transferred to the church government.

There are 560 parishes in the Lutheran Church of Finland, and some of them, especially in the cities, are very large. Fourteen churches were destroyed during World War II. There are 1,450 clergymen, and about thirty are ordained every year. The theological faculty of the University of Helsinki has six professors, two assistant professors, four lecturers, and other instructors; in 1952 there were 300 theological students there. Since 1924 there has also been a Swedish theological faculty in Turku with four professors, two lecturers, and about fifty students; this school trains clergymen for Swedish-speaking inhabitants of Finland. A new Finnish hymnal appeared in 1938, a new Swedish hymnal in 1943, and a revision of the Finnish Bible in 1938.

BIBLIOGRAPHY: Jalmari Jaakkola, *Die Geschichte des finnischen Volkes*, 1942; idem, *Le problème orientale de la Finlande*, 1942; Aleksi Lehtonen, "The Church of Finland," in *Church Quarterly Review*, 1928; Ilmari Salomies, *Suomen kirkon historia*, 2 vols., 1944, 1949; "Die Kirche in Finnland," in *Ekklesia*, ed. by Friedrich Siegmund-Schultze, Vol. VIII, 1938.

LENNART PINOMAA.

FIRE BAPTIZED HOLINESS CHURCH OF GOD OF THE AMERICAS. See CHURCH (CHURCHES) OF GOD.

FISHER, DOUGLASS. See YOUTH FOR CHRIST.

FISHER, GEOFFREY FRANCIS: Anglican; b. May 5, 1887 at Higham, Nuneaton, Eng. He studied at Marlborough College (1901–6) and Exeter College, Oxford (1906–11; B.A., 1910; M.A., 1913). He served as assistant master, Marlborough College (1911–14) and as headmaster, Repton School (1914–32). After nineteen years in the priesthood of the Church of England he was elevated to the episcopate in 1932. He was bishop of Chester (1932–39); bishop of London (1939–45) and in 1945 was elected archbishop of Canterbury. The following year he was named one of the presidents of the World Council of Churches.

RAYMOND W. ALBRIGHT.

FISHER, JOHN, SAINT: Although he should not be classified with the actual humanists (see BENIANS), he did express great admiration for the work of the leading promotors of the Northern Renaissance, and he aided their cause at Cambridge University, notably the labors of Erasmus, who taught at Cambridge for five years. He also had contact with Reuchlin (*q.v.*, Vol. IX). His polemical works against Luther were rather vehement. In 1866 he was declared Blessed, together with Sir Thomas More (*q.v.*). On May 19, 1935, he was canonized.

BIBLIOGRAPHY: John Fisher, *Sacri sacerdotii defensio*, ed. by H. Klein-Schmeinkin, in *Corpus Catholicorum*, Vol. 9, Muenster, 1925; in 1935 there appeared an English ed. of his sermon against Luther and his defense of the Priesthood; P. Hughes, *Saint John Fisher, The Earliest English Life*, 1935; M. E. A. Benians, *John Fisher*, 1935; V. McNabb, *Saint John Fisher*, 1935; R. L. Smith, *John Fisher and Thomas More*, 1935; R. Chambers, *Thomas More*, 1935.

[Sup.] MATHIAS GOOSSENS.

FISHER, JONATHAN: Congregational minister; b. New Braintree, Mass., Oct. 7, 1768; d. Bluehill, Me., Sept. 22, 1847. Fitted for college with his uncle, the Rev. Joseph Avery, of Holden, Mass.; graduated from Harvard College, 1792, and continued as resident graduate in divinity, 1792–95; settled in Congregational Church in Bluehill, Me., 1795–1836. Artist of considerable merit; published a volume of woodcuts entitled *Scripture Animals* (1834); one of founders of the Maine Missionary Society (1807), Society for Theological Education (1811) and Bangor Theological Seminary (1814).

BIBLIOGRAPHY: Mary Ellen Chase, *Jonathan Fisher*, 1948.

RICHARD D. PIERCE.

FITZRALPH, RICHARD (RICARDUS Filius RADULPHI): Theologian and Preacher; Church of Ireland; b. probably at Dundalk towards the end of the thirteenth century, though his family may have belonged to Devonshire. He was educated at Oxford where he became a Fellow of Balliol College, and about 1333 obtained the Chancellorship of the University. In the following year he was promoted to Chancellor in Lincoln Cathedral and, in 1337, the pope provided him to the Deanery of Lichfield. In 1347 the Pope presented him to the Archbishopric of Armagh. He has left an account of conferences between Armenian ecclesiastics and the papacy in a book entitled *Richardi Radulphi Summa in Quaestionibus Armenorum*, wherein the erroneous doctrines of the Armenians are discussed and refuted. This treatise is one of the early books printed at Paris by Jean Petit in 1511. Fitzralph's reputation at this time stood at its highest. As a preacher he was extremely popular.

His conflict with the mendicant friars overshadowed the remaining years of his life. In his treatise *De Pauperie Salvatoris* he declared that our Lord never voluntarily begged and did not enjoin on any of his disciples to become mendicants; that no one can, with prudence and piety, devote himself to a life of perpetual begging. The secular clergy looked upon him as the champion of their cause, but the friars felt themselves aggrieved, became actively hostile, and were successful in having him cited to appear before Pope Innocent VI at Avignon. There, at the close of 1357, he defended his opinions in a sermon which many years later was printed under the title *Defensio Curatorum,* etc. The tendencies of many of the archbishop's utterances were, even from the first, regarded with apprehension, and not without some justification, as it appeared later. For Wyclif made it clear (in *Trialogus,* and still more in *De Dominio Divino*) how much he owed to the ideas of Fitzralph. As R. L. Poole notices, undoubtedly Wyclif, in the general view of human relations towards God, adopted Fitzralph's conceptions, but made them "the basis of a doctrinal theory which was soon discovered to be, if not heretical, at least dangerous." But no effective condemnation of the archbishop seems to have taken place. The Pope, indeed, wrote to the Archbishops and Bishops of England, enjoining on them to see that nothing to the prejudice of the Mendicants should be done in respect of the matters alleged by Fitzralph (Wadding, *Ann. Min.*). Wadding also states that silence was imposed on the great champion of the English clergy. Beyond these injunctions there is no certain evidence of any action against Fitzralph. It was hardly necessary that there should have been. The Friars had been confirmed fully in the rights and privileges which they had hitherto possessed. In any case, their bold adversary died at Avignon in November, 1360.

BIBLIOGRAPHY: In addition to Fitzralph's three principal works already mentioned Sir James Ware names some smaller treatises and collections of sermons, most of which are among the Bodleian MSS. at Oxford. A list of them may also be found in Thomas Tanner's *Bibliotheca Britannico-Hibernica,* 1748. *Defensiones Curatorum contra cos qui se dicunt privilegiatos,* Treschel, Lyons, 1496; R. L. Poole, *De Pauperie Salvatoris,* appended to Wyclif's *De Dominio Divino* (Wyclif Soc. Publ.); Sir James Ware, *Writers of Ireland,* Harris's ed., 1739; W. A. Phillips, *History of the Church of Ireland,* Vol. II (1934), pp. 106 ff.

GEORGE V. JOURDAN.

FJELLBU, ARNE: Lutheran; b. Decorah, Iowa, Dec. 19, 1890. He studied at Oslo. He has been bishop of Nidaros (1946–). Dean at the cathedral of Nidaros, he was discharged by Quisling (1942), owing to struggle against Nazism. His books are *Christian Student-Life in Norway; Pastoral Care; Christian Ethics; Christian Faith; The Distress of the Soul; The Meaning of Suffering;* and *Memories from the War Years.*

FLABELLUM: In the early church, a fan by means of which the deacon drove the flies away from the cup during the celebration of the Eucharist. Similar instruments are still used today in Eastern liturgies. Two ceremonial *flabella* of white feathers are born on either side of the *sedia gestatoria* (*q.v.*) when the Pope is carried in state. GEORGES A. BARROIS.

FLACIUS, MATTHIAS: In 1549 he left Wittenberg, because his bitter fight against the Augsburg and Leipzig interims (*q.v.*) had caused his break with Melanchthon. In 1551 he went to Magdeburg, where he supported the struggle by this Lutheran city against the Interim and Elector Maurice (Moritz) of Saxony. In Regensburg he attempted in vain to found an academy. There were two reasons why he frequently was forced to leave the different cities in which he was laboring: (1) his unyielding attitude in objecting to all attempts to meet the desires of the emperor and the Catholic forces in general, and (2) his unpleasant personality. He refused in particular to make a reconciliation with Melanchthon, even after the latter had admitted his own mistakes, thus arousing the antagonism of Elector August of Saxony.

The contributions made by Flacius to theology, historiography and the spread of Lutheranism may be divided into three categories: (1) He was the outstanding representative of the real orthodox dogmatism. After Luther's (*q.v.*) death, during the fierce contest over the questions of faith versus works, free will, original sin and Christology he stood for Luther's most pronounced and sharpest ideas, often with a scholastic tendency to be one-sided. (2) In his *Clavis scripturae sacrae* (1567) he set forth the basic exegesis and hermeneutics of Luther and Melanchthon in a highly capable manner, thus systematizing and organizing a body of teachings that needed this method, since Calvin (*q.v.*) had done a similar task for his churches and followers, while Luther and Melanchthon had failed to equal Calvin and the Catholics in this important field. Unfortunately his glosses on the Old Testament remained fragmentary and were never published. (3) He wrote the first comprehensive church history among the Protestants: *Ecclesiastica historia . . . secundum singulas centurias* (the "Magdeburg Centuries," 1559–74). The thirteen volumes of this great work (Vols. 14–16 were not completed nor published) are arranged in a chronological order, one part for each century. This history was based upon a large mass of manuscripts and printed books which he had collected on his journeys, while a staff of clerical assistants enabled him to turn out so huge an undertaking. His purpose was to show that the Reformation was a true revival of the early Christian church. In spite of the arbitrary division into centuries, this composition is the most noteworthy church history since that by Eusebius, being the first which actually and scientifically followed the original sources. Moreover, Flacius also published the first edition of the gospel poetry in German by Otfried von Weiszenburg, dating from the ninth century. He was not only one of the most significant figures in the second generation of Reformation times in Germany

but also honored in his native Yugoslavia as an
outstanding compatriot.

BIBLIOGRAPHY: K. Schottenloher, *Bibl. zur deutschen
Geschichte im Zeitalter der Glaubensspaltung*, Vol. I
(1933), Nr. 6353–6372, Vol. V (1939), Nr. 46285–46300;
G. Wolf, *Quellenkunde der deutschen Reformationsge-
schichte*, Vol. II, Part II (1922), pp. 54–65; J. Hausleiter,
"Matthias Flacius als Herausgeber von Luthers Koburger
Briefen und Trostspruechen (1536)," in *Neue kirchl.
Zeitschr.*, XXVIII (1917), 149–187; G. Bossert, "Ein un-
bekanntes Stueck aus dem Leben des Flacius," in *Archiv
fuer Ref.*, XX (1923), 49 ff.; H. Buschbeck, "Des M. F.
Illyricus Religionsgespraeche auf Burg Lehnhaus und
Schlosz Langenau im Jahre 1574," in *Jahrbuch d. Vereins
f. schlesische Kirchengesch.*, XXIV (1934), 3–23; O.
Ritschl, *Dogmengesch. d. Prot.* especially Vol. II, 1912;
R. Seeberg, *Lehrbuch der Dogmengesch.*, Vol. IV, Part
II (1920), pp. 480 ff.; H. E. Weber, *Reformation, Ortho-
doxie und Rationalismus*, Vol. I, Part I, 1937, Vol. I, Part
II, 1940; H. C. von Hase, *Die Gestalt der Kirche Luthers:
Der casus confessionis im Kampf des M. F. gegen das
Interim*, 1940; L. Haikola, *Gesetz und Evangelium bei
M. F. Illyricus*, 1952.
On his hermeneutics: W. Dilthey, *Gesammelte Schriften*,
Vol. II (1921), pp. 110 ff.; K. Holl, *Gesammelte Aufsaetze
zur Kirchengeschichte*, Vol. I (3rd ed., 1923), pp. 578 ff.;
K. A. von Schwartz, *Die theologische Hermeneutik des
M. F. Illyricus*, 1933; idem, *Luther-Jahrbuch* (1933), pp.
139–175; G. Moldaenke, *Schriftverstaendnis im Zeitalter
der Reformation*, Vol. I: *M. F. Illyricus*, 1936.
On his church history: F. C. Baur, *Die Epochen der
kirchl. Geschichtschreibung* (1852), pp. 39–71; K. Heussi,
"Centuriae," in *Harnack-Ehrung* (1852), 328 ff.; E. Seeberg, *Gottfried Arnold, Die Wissenschaft und Mystik
seiner Zeit*, 1923; W. Nigg, *Die Kirchengeschichtsschreib-
ung*, 1924.

[Sup.] D. HEINRICH BORNKAMM.

FLACK, ELMER ELLSWORTH: Lutheran;
b. at Mendon, Ill., Oct. 3, 1894. He studied at
Wittenberg (A.B., 1916); Hamma Divinity
School (1918; S.T.M., 1924); University of Chicago (A.M., 1923); Augustana (Th.D., 1926);
Berlin (1937). Ordained in 1918, he was pastor,
Chicago (1918–23); professor, Old Testament,
Hamma (1923–36); exegetical theology (1936–
); dean (1940–); delegate, Edinburgh Conference (1937); lecturer, German universities
(1937); Holman Foundation, Gettysburg (1949);
author, *The Revelation of John* (*New Testament Commentary*, 1936); coeditor, *Old Testament Commentary* (1948).

FLEMING, DANIEL J.: Presbyterian; b.
Xenia, O., Jan. 30, 1877. He studied at Wooster
College (B.A., 1898); Columbia (M.A., 1903;
Ph.D., 1914). He taught at Forman Christian
College, India (1904–12); was professor of missions, Union Theological Seminary, N. Y. (1915–
44). He was a member of the International
Commission on Village Education in India
(1919–20); member of the India Staff of Laymen's Foreign Missions Inquiry (1930–31), and
a consultant on India, Department of State
(1945–46). He is the author of: *The World at
One in Prayer; Christian Symbols in a World
Community; Each With His Own Brush; Bringing Our World Together;* and *Living as Comrades.*

FLEMING, SANDFORD: Baptist; b. at Ade-
laide, Australia, May 2, 1888. He studied at
South Australian Baptist College (1912); Yale
(B.D., 1917; M.A., 1926; Ph.D., 1929) and

Berkeley Baptist Divinity School (Th.M., 1924).
Son of an American citizen, he moved to the
United States for permanent residence in 1922.
He was ordained to the Baptist ministry (1913);
and was pastor, Port Pirie, South Australia
(1913–14); New Haven, Conn. (1914–17); superintendent, Baptist Home Missions, South Aus-
tralia (1918–20); pastor, Adelaide, (1920–22) and
San Francisco (1922–25). He became professor
of church history and religious education, Berke-
ley Baptist Divinity School (1926–); president
(1937–). He is the author of: *Children and
Puritanism* (1933); *Living Portraits of Jesus*
(1939); *Ninety-five Years Beside the Golden
Gate: a History of the First Baptist Church of
San Francisco* (1944); *God's Gold: The Story of
Baptist Beginnings in California* (1949); and
Where Jesus Walked (1952).

KENNETH G. HOBART.

FLETCHER, JOSEPH: Episcopalian; b.
Newark, N. J., April 10, 1905; studied at West
Virginia University (B.A.); Yale; University of
London, School of Economics; Berkeley Divinity School (B.D., S.T.B.); Kenyon (S.T.D.,
1938). He was curate at St. Peter's, Regent
Square, London, England (1930–32); chaplain
and lecturer, St. Mary's School and Junior
College, Raleigh, N. C. (1932–35); dean, St.
Paul's Cathedral (1936–38) and dean of Graduate School of Applied Religion (1936–44), Cincinnati, O.; since 1944, professor of Christian
ethics and pastoral theology, Episcopal Theological School, Cambridge, Mass. He is the
author of: *The Church and Industry* (1930);
(ed.), *Christianity and Property* (1948); *Morals
and Medicine* (1954).

FLEW, ROBERT NEWTON: Methodist; b.
at Holsworthy, Devonshire, May 25, 1886. He
studied at the Universities of Oxford (B.A.,
1909; B.D., 1925); Marburg; and Fribourg
(Switzerland). He was assistant tutor at Handsworth College, Birmingham (1910–13); minister
of Winchmore Hill Wesleyan Methodist Church
(1913–18); chaplain to the forces in Mesopo-
tamia-Persia (1918–20); acting professor of New
Testament language and literature at Bangalore,
United Theological College (1920–21); Wesleyan Methodist Minister at Clapham (1921–
24) and Muswell Hill (1924–27); first professor
of New Testament in Wesley House, Cambridge (1927–37); principal and professor of
systematic and pastoral theology (1937–). He
was vice chairman of the Faith and Order Continuation Committee (1947–52) and chairman of
the Theological Commission on the Church
(1938–52). He was moderator of the National
Free Church Federal Council of England and
Wales (1945–46), and president of the Methodist Conference of Great Britain and Ireland
(1946–47). He wrote: *The Teaching of the*

Apostles (1915); *The Forgiveness of Sins* (1916); *The Idea of Perfection in Christian Theology* (1934); *Jesus and His Church* (1938); and was editor and part author of *The Catholicity of Protestantism* (1950); *The Church* (1951); *The Nature of the Church* (1952).

FLICHE, AUGUSTIN: Roman Catholic; b. at Montpellier (France), Nov. 19, 1884; d. at Montpellier, Nov. 19, 1951. He studied at the University of Paris (Sorbonne; docteur des lettres, 1912) with his "thèse" on *Philippe I, roi de France.* He lectured at the University of Bordeaux (1913); he was maître de conférences at Montpellier (1919), professeur (1923); dean of the Faculté de Lettres (1934–46). He was vice-president of the National Committee of Historical Sciences; membre de l'Institut de France (1941). He exerted a very wide and deep influence by his lectures on medieval church history. He is most widely known both for his works on the period of Gregory VII and for the collections which he directed: *Bibliothèque de l'enseignement ecclésiastique* and, in collaboration with V. Martin and E. Jarry, *Histoire de l'Eglise depuis les origines jusqu'à nos jours,* in which he wrote Vol. VIII. *La Réforme grégorienne et la reconquête chrétienne* (1940); *Du premier concile de Latran à l'avènement d'Innocent III (1123–1198)* (1944–46); *La chrétienté romaine (1198–1274)* (1950). He published also: *La réforme grégorienne* (3 vols., 1925); *La querelle des investitures* (1946); in the collection Glotz, *L'Europe occidentale de 888 à 1125* (1930).

BIBLIOGRAPHY: F. L. Ganshof, *Revue belge; de philologie et d'histoire,* XXX (1952), 649.

LEOPOLD WILLAERT.

FLIGHT, JOHN WILLIAM: Congregationalist; b. at Cleveland, O., Dec. 12, 1890. He was educated at Hope College (B.A., 1914), Hartford Theological Seminary (B.D., 1917; Ph.D., 1921), William Thompson Fellow at universities of Strasbourg and Paris (1920–21), Yale University (A.M., 1929). He served pastorates at Waterbury, Winsted, Georgetown, Conn. (1918–19, 1921–29). He was instructor in Hebrew, Yale University (1927–29); professor of Biblical Literature at Haverford College (1929–   ). He is associate editor of the *Journal of Bible and Religion.* He has written: *The Nomadic Ideal in the Old Testament* (1923); *The Book of the Bible* (1929); *Moses, Egyptian Prince, Nomad Sheikh, Lawgiver* (1942); *The Drama of Ancient Israel* (1949).

FLOOD, THE: The common designation of the deluge, which, according to the biblical account, inundated the earth in the tenth generation after Creation. The narrative is recorded in Genesis 6–9 in two original recensions, J and P, eventually fused, however, by a P editor

into the present biblical account. Some divergences between the two recensions are thought to be discernible. The narrative implies the end of the first age or cycle in the life of the world and the beginning of the second, the age of Noah and his posterity, a new human race. This new age, like the first, was ushered in by a covenant between God and man.

Plainly the story of the flood could not be based on events and experiences in Palestine or any immediately adjacent land, where floods are absolutely unknown. Only in a country like Mesopotamia, where annually the Euphrates and Tigris inundate the land, could this narrative have an historical background. And indeed the biblical Flood account was antedated by an ancient Babylonian myth, inscribed upon Tablet XI of the famous Gilgamesh Epic, but the origins of which can be traced back to the third millennium B.C. The biblical J version seems somewhat closer to the Babylonian account than does P. The biblical record, however, has a lofty moral note, totally lacking in the antecedent. References to the Flood are frequent in the Bible (cf. Isa. 54:9 ff.).

BIBLIOGRAPHY: John Skinner, *Genesis,* 1910; Hugo Gressmann, *Altorientalische Texte zum Alten Testament* (1926), pp. 175–183, 198–201; S. H. Langdon, *Mythology of All Races,* Vol. V, *Semitic* (1931), pp. 203–269; Jack Finegan, *Light From the Ancient Past,* 1946.

JULIAN MORGENSTERN.

FLORENSKY, PAUL: Eastern Orthodox; b. in Tiflis, 1881. He studied at the University of Moscow and the Moscow Theological Academy. Since 1908 he was lecturer and then professor of the history of philosophy at this academy (till it was closed in 1918). He was editor of *Theological Messenger* (*Bogoslovsky Viestnik*), published by the academy faculty. In 1910 he took holy orders, and after the closing of the academy continued for some time his pastoral activities as a chaplain of a convent at Sergievsky Posad (now Zagorsk). Later on he was working for a period as engineer and scientific consultant, and was even chairman of the Technical Commission of the Sovnarkom. He was arrested (probably in 1929 or 1930) and confined first at Solovki, and then exiled to far eastern Siberia. Nothing definite is known of his fate. Florensky is a man of one book, although he published a number of articles and was engaged in writing more. But his fame and his place in the history of the Russian thought and literature has been determined by his *The Pillar and Foundation of Truth* (1914), with a subtitle: *An Essay Towards an Orthodox Theodicy.* It is a sketch of a religio-philosophical system, based on the doctrine of St. Sophia, which Florensky developed much further than it had been done by Vladimir Soloviev in his early writings. The whole approach to theology is deeply aesthetical. The book was in Russian, and never translated into English; a good selection of fragments is given in German in the anthology, edited by Dr. Hans Ehrenberg, *Das Oestliches Christenthum* (Vol. II, 1925).

BIBLIOGRAPHY: D. S. Mirsky, *A History of Russian Literature*, edited and abridged by Francis J. Whitfield (1949), pp. 427–428.

GEORGES FLOROVSKY.

FLOROVSKY, GEORGES: Greek-Orthodox; b. in Odessa, Russia, Aug. 28, 1893. He was graduated from the University of Odessa (1916); Prague (Phil. Mag., 1923). He was lecturer in philosophy, Odessa University (1919–20); professor of the Orthodox Theological Institute, Paris (1926–48); professor of divinity, St. Vladimir's Theological Seminary (1948–); adjunct professor of history and doctrine of the Eastern Orthodox Church, Union Theological Seminary (1951–). His main field of interest and research is historic theology, especially Greek patristics and Russian religious and philosophical thought. His ultimate purpose is to reinterpret tradition in modern terms and achieve a kind of a "neo-patristic synthesis." Florovsky is very active in the *rapprochement* between the Orthodox and Anglican Churches, chiefly in the Fellowship of St. Sergius and St. Albans. His main publications are in Russian: *Eastern Fathers of the Fourth Century* (Paris, 1931); *Byzantine Fathers, V–VIII Centuries* (Paris, 1933); *The Ways of Russian Theology* (Paris, 1937). See also RUSSIAN ORTHODOX CHURCH.

FOAKES-JACKSON, F. J. See JACKSON, FREDERICK JOHN FOAKES.

FOLEY, GEORGE CADWALADER: Episcopalian; b. June 29, 1851, at Philadelphia, Pa.; d. May 8, 1935. He studied at Griswold College (A.B., 1872) and the Philadelphia Divinity School of the Protestant Episcopal Church (B.D., 1875; D.D. in course, 1899). Ordained to the priesthood in 1875, he served as rector of St. James Church, Pittston, Pa. (1875–79); Trinity Church, Williamsport, Pa. (1879–1905). In 1905 he became professor of homiletics and pastoral care in the Philadelphia Divinity School and ten years later became professor of systematic theology there (1915–35). He edited *The Church Standard* (1907–8) and wrote *Anselm's Theory of the Atonement* (1909).

RAYMOND W. ALBRIGHT.

FOLK CHURCH: The conception of the church which makes the geographical boundaries of church and community coextensive, developed especially in countries where established Lutheran churches were conterminous with the state. The folk church is not dependent upon the state, however, for it is the totality of territorial parishes; the entire population shares the experience of being encircled alike by the geographical boundaries of the community and by

God's universal will to save. Historically, the folk church idea emerged where Christianity developed in conjunction with a people's national life, but the concept received fresh emphasis during the ecclesiastical revivals of the nineteenth and twentieth centuries. In Sweden "The Young Church Movement" advocated the ideal of a folk church, "The Swedish people, a people of God." In Denmark the Lutheran Church is known as "Den Danske Folkekirke."

BIBLIOGRAPHY: Theodosius Harnack, *Die freie lutherische Volkskirche*, 1870; Franz Rendtorff, *Kirche, Landeskirche, Volkskirche*, 1911; Nathan Söderblom, *Sveriges Kyrka*, 1908; Gustav Wingren, "The Theology of Einar Billing," *The Lutheran Quarterly*, Vols. II, III.

G. EVERETT ARDEN.

FOLKLORE: All the beliefs, traditional customs, tales, songs, sayings, superstitions and legendary materials created and preserved by a people or a nation constitute its folklore. Almost all folklore has its beginning in religion, and is part of it. Every religion has produced its own myths, beliefs, concepts, proverbs, customs, songs, superstitions and precepts, all of which came into being to serve the basic purposes of that religion. Religious lore developed certain literary forms as best suited for its purposes, just as the religion developed certain rituals and rites best suited for its purposes. These literary folklore forms comprise: the myth, the fable, the allegory, the legend, the parable, and the proverb. But however different a folklore may be in its *forms* from others, it is very similar to all others in two basic respects: (1) The probing toward an understanding of truth; and (2) The concern with "good" and "evil."

Folklore, in all its varied forms, came into being because people wanted to know the truth about the origin and meaning of the universe, in general, and of human destiny, in particular. They were concerned with the problem of how man ought to live so as to shun "evil" and attain the "good." Though it is often difficult to see any obvious affinity between these objectives and the extreme manifestations of given superstitions, yet, if carefully traced to their origins, it would be found that their mainspring is to resolve doubt or to ward off some evil.

Folklore concerns itself with every conceivable human experience, from birth to death—from before birth to the life hereafter. We therefore find that folklore reflects every conceivable human emotion, and every conceivable relationship between man and man, between man and his God, between man and his own inner self. Since the basic human needs are the same, and the quest for certainty is the same the world over, great similarities or parallels are to be found in practically all folklore customs, beliefs, superstitions; as well as in the legends or extraordinary events of Creation, the Flood, miraculous births, and in strange beliefs about the hereafter.

Every religion has inspired its own folklore, revolving around, mainly, its sacred scriptures. The lore represents the interpretation of the scriptures as conceived by the folk imagination, which often differs greatly from its conception in the mind of the prophet or apostle. By far the largest volume of such religious folklore was inspired by the Bible, and more particularly the Old Testament. The Bible is held in reverence, though in differing degrees, by three great living religions, Judaism, Christianity and Mohammedanism. And the adherents of each of these had continually used the Bible as the source of its folk inspiration. Even outside these faiths, the Bible is known and read by more people, and in more languages, and in a greater variation of versions, than any other religious scriptures. And as long as the Bible continues to hold the folk attention, the folk mind will continue to create lore, in all its forms, which will present the folk interpretation of the ethics and the precepts contained in the Bible.

Folklore is vast and complex; and it ranges from the simple precept and readily acceptable proverb, to the most abstruse symbolism and weird incantation. For the unknown has the greatest fascination over the folk mind; and, in the lore, it has developed an almost endless scheme of divination by oracles, by the stars, by sacrificed animals, by the behavior of birds, by mirrors and reflections, by writing in ashes, by walking in circles, by dropping molten wax into cold water, and by a vast variety of other methods. And for each kind of evil, feared and anticipated, the lore produced the proper remedy in the form of a talisman, a magic wand, an amulet, or one of the many other shields conjured up by the magician. Yet even at the lowest level of voodoo and superstition, religious lore reflects the folk concern with truth; and the determined struggle for "good" and against "evil." Folklore, more than any other branch of man's creativity, reflects more completely what the people really know, what they really fear, and to what they really aspire.

BIBLIOGRAPHY: Stith Thompson, *Motif-Index of Folk-Literature*, Indiana University Studies, Nos. 96, 97, released in 1932; A. Krappe, *The Science of Folklore*, 1930; J. G. Frazer, *The Golden Bough*, 1922; Andrew Lang, *The Origins of Religion*, 1908; L. H. Gray (ed.), *Mythology of All Races*, 1916; Smith-Marindin, *A Classical Dictionary of Greek and Roman Mythology*, 1899; Joseph Gaer, *The Lore of the Old Testament*, 1951, idem, *The Folklore of the New Testament*, 1952. John Fiske, *Myths and Myth-Makers*, 1886; see topical Index for various papers on this topic published by the American Folklore Society.

JOSEPH GAER.

FOLKLORE IN THE OLD TESTAMENT:

Until there is a generally accepted definition of folklore there can be no dogmatic statement about the amount of folklore in the Old Testament. According to some scholars a document

when written ceases to be folklore and becomes literature. No distinct line has been drawn between folklore and mythology. The Webster definition is: "traditional customs, beliefs, fables, or sayings, esp. those of a superstitious or legendary nature, preserved unreflectively among a people." If we accept this definition we can find evidences of folklore in the Old Testament from the first chapter of Genesis.

At present there is a tendency among theologians to discount the thesis that Israel developed from animism through polytheism through henotheism to monotheism. It can be pointed out that, when the Israelites arrived on the scene, the cultures from which they came, Babylonian and Egyptian, had long since emerged from any primitive animism. This does not mean, however, that there is not a great deal of folklore preserved in the Old Testament. No matter how sophisticated a people becomes, it preserves many attitudes which are folklore. Sir James G. Frazer in his monumental work has shown a host of similarities and parallels to the Old Testament stories and customs among primitive peoples. It does not follow that there is always diffusion from a single source; for under like stimuli identical sayings or customs may appear in cultures having no connection with each other. Consequently it is hazardous to attempt to trace a bit of folklore to its source without concrete evidence. For instance, it has been customary to explain the injunction against seething a kid in his mother's milk to belief in magical properties of milk. Now it seems that this command was prompted by hostility to the Canaanite ritual; for the Ugaritic texts have shown that such seething was a pagan religious rite.

We can say without fear of contradiction that the folk element is prominent in the Old Testament. The Song of Deborah (Judg. 5) and Jotham's fable (Judg. 9:7–15) are folk literature. Proverbs are folk sayings. Many of the psalms may be classed as folk ballads.

Recognition of folklore in the Old Testament in no way detracts from the lofty ethical and religious motives of those who incorporated it in their teachings. While the Hebrew writer enjoyed a good story and a clever saying, he used his material for the glory of God.

BIBLIOGRAPHY: Andrew Lang, *Custom and Myth*, 1885; James G. Frazer, *Folk-Lore in the Old Testament*, 3 vols., 1918, abridged 1 vol. edition, 1923; H. J. D. Astley, *Biblical Anthropology*, 1929.

OVID R. SELLERS.

FONDREN LECTURESHIP:

Established at Southern Methodist University in 1919 by Mr. and Mrs. W. W. Fondren, of Houston, Texas. For many years Mr. Fondren served as a member of the Board of Trustees of the University, and after his death Mrs. Fondren carried forward his work as a trustee. The lectureship brings to the campus each year a series of addresses on Christian missions. The lectures are published in book form.   EUGENE B. HAWK.

FOOT WASHING: A ritual, based on the example of Christ (John 13:1-17), was observed in the early church (I Tim. 5:10) and lingers among certain heads of state and high officials of the Roman Catholic Church. It is not observed in large Protestant bodies but is regarded as a sacrament or solemn ordinance in several small American churches. It is part of the worship in Primitive Baptist and allied groups and is prominent among small Negro sects. The River Brethren experienced a split over the principle, the "one mode" school holding that the same individual should both wash and dry the feet of others while the "two mode" school insisted that the two acts should be performed by different persons.

Among the bodies which practice foot washing are the following: New Congregational Methodist Church, Pentecostal Church of God of America, Pentecostal Fire-Baptized Holiness Church, House of God, Church of God and Saints of Christ, Mennonite Brethren in Christ, Primitive Baptists, and River Brethren. See PENTECOSTAL CHURCHES; CHURCH (CHURCHES) OF GOD.

BIBLIOGRAPHY: E. T. Clark, *The Small Sects in America*, rev. ed., 1949; see the periodicals and tracts issued by the groups mentioned.

ELMER T. CLARK.

F.O.R. See FELLOWSHIP OF RECONCILIATION.

FOREIGN MISSIONS. See EXPANSION OF CHRISTIANITY; and titles beginning with the words MISSIONARY or MISSION(s).

FOREIGN MISSIONS CONFERENCE OF NORTH AMERICA: When, in November, 1950, it became the Division of Foreign Missions of the National Council of the Churches of Christ, U. S. A. (*q.v.*), the Conference was the widest and one of the very oldest of interdenominational fellowships. It was organized January 12, 1893, by some seventy-five men, representing twenty-one mission boards, among them John R. Mott (*q.v.*), J. Campbell White, and Robert E. Speer. An unbroken line of annual meetings followed. By 1917 there were 287 delegates, 92 of them women, representing nearly 100 boards.

At first the Conference was an annual meeting for exchange of experience and counsel. The Edinburgh Conference (1910; see INTERNATIONAL MISSIONARY COUNCIL) gave an impetus to co-operative planning and action, and in 1917 the organization was incorporated as the Committee of Reference and Counsel of the Foreign Missions Conference. During the next two decades there were gradually developed, outside of the Conference, a number of localized pieces of administration. In 1939 the principle of repre-

sentative committees was incorporated into the constitution. These committees were authorized to do anything in the way of joint planning and administration which the boards desired. The first comprehensive formulation of tasks confronting North American boards was undertaken in 1947 under the slogan, "One World in Christ—an Advance in Foreign Missions."

The Conference went into the National Council with eighty-seven member boards and fourteen consultant agencies. The same strong program of fellowship and co-operation is being maintained.   SUE WEDDELL.

FOREIGN MISSIONS INQUIRY, LAYMEN'S: A survey of Christian mission fields in Asia made by a commission sponsored by laymen of seven Protestant churches in America. The areas studied were India, Burma, China, and Japan. The commission consisted of fifteen eminent persons, the chairman being William Ernest Hocking, professor of philosophy at Harvard University. The laymen were of northern Baptist, Congregational, Dutch Reformed, Protestant Episcopal, Methodist Episcopal, northern Presbyterian, and United Presbyterian churches.

Impelled by an apparent decline of missionary interest in the churches, the Inquiry made an unofficial examination of the principles, aspects, and administration of the missionary enterprise. The Institute of Social and Religious Research assembled a mass of data. The commission studied the data and visited the mission fields. In 1932 it published its findings in a volume, *Re-thinking Missions*. In 1933 appeared the *Regional Reports of the Commission of Appraisal* in three volumes, and the *Fact-finders' Reports* in four volumes.

Though the findings were partly commendatory, their adverse criticisms received greater publicity. The report was sharply criticized, especially for defining the missionary task as one of making common cause with other religions in the search for truth. Hocking's defense was made in the volume, *Living Religions and a World Faith*, 1940.

WILLARD D. ALLBECK.

FOREIGN RELATIONS, CHURCH OF ENGLAND COUNCIL ON: A body of clergy and laymen constituted by the English archbishops in 1933, in response to resolutions of the Church Assembly, to survey, assist in, and advise on the relations of the Church of England with non-Anglican Churches overseas (Eastern, Roman Catholic, Old Catholic, and Protestant). Under its first secretary, Canon J. A. Douglas (1933-45), long a leading figure in Anglican-Eastern rapprochement, and his successor, H. M. Waddams, the Council has been active in encouraging both official and unofficial contacts, but it does not itself initiate negotiations.

BIBLIOGRAPHY: *Official Yearbook of the Church of England,* annual.

EDWARD ROCHIE HARDY.

FOREST, JOHN: English martyr, declared Blessed. B. 1471 at Oxford; d. May 22, 1538. In 1491 he joined the Franciscans at Greenwich, whose monastery was very near the rural residence of King Henry VIII, and so it naturally happened that the royal princess Elizabeth was baptized in the church of this monastery at Greenwich. Forest was confessor of Catherine of Aragon, and he was very strongly opposed to her husband's plan for a divorce and for his elevation to the position of head of the Anglican Church. The treatise which Forest wrote against the king's anti-Catholic actions was lost. He probably was imprisoned as early as 1534, and in the same year condemned by the court called together by Cranmer, who accused him of treason and heresy. In 1538 he was burned at the stake.

BIBLIOGRAPHY: B. Camm, *Lives of the English Martyrs,* Vol. I (1904), pp. 274–326; M. Bacheca, *I martiri Francescani d'Inghilterra,* 1930.

MATHIAS GOOSSENS.

FORGIVENESS: The possibility of the forgiveness of sins is grounded in the nature of God (*q.v.*), whose covenant with his people is unchangeable (see COVENANT THEOLOGY). God's will for men, as expressed in that covenant, includes devotion and obedient living. Where men transgress his will, the covenant God is at once wrathful and gracious. The Bible is the only book of religion that posits faith in the God who completely forgives sin. In the Old Testament sin (*q.v.*) was often immediately followed by its consequence—death, as in the case of Achan's lust for gold (Josh., Chap. 7) or Saul's disobedience (I Sam. Chap. 31), or Uzzah's irreverence (II Sam. 6:1–11). Yet David could cry out in penitence for forgiveness of his great transgression (II Sam. 12:1–23). Leaders of the people often interceded with God for their people's forgiveness, as Moses after the making of the golden calf (Ex. Chap. 33), and in many instances of post-exilic times (Ezra, Chap. 9; Neh., Chap. 9; Dan., Chap. 9). The Psalms abound with the pleadings and the joyful release of men who have sought forgiveness. (See especially Ps. 6, 25, 32, 51, 107, 130.) The prophets proclaim the forgiving nature of the Lord, but insist that the experience of his grace must be attended by a change of heart and life (Isa. 1:18; Jer. 31:31–34; Hosea 14:1–2; Amos 5:24; etc.).

In the New Testament, the thought of forgiveness is not so common as that of salvation and its cognates, though Paul identifies redemption with the forgiveness of sins (Col. 1:14). Of the two most frequently occurring words for forgiveness, *aphesis* denotes the bearing away of sin, as in Zechariah's song (Luke 1:77), John

the baptizer's preaching (Luke 3:3), and Jesus' identification of himself with the Paschal lamb (Matt. 26:28). The other word, *charizesthai,* found oftener in Paul (II Cor. 12:13; Col. 2:13), means "to treat graciously." Thus both terms stress the initiative of God in forgiveness. Hence, forgiveness as viewed in the Bible is more than the remittance of a penalty; it is the establishment of a warm personal relationship with God. This note is sounded often in the Gospels, especially in the parable of the gracious father (Luke 15:11–32), who yearns for the prodigal while he is yet "at a distance" and entreats the cold-hearted elder son who is proud of his uprightness.

Yet, like the prophets, the New Testament emphasizes also the need of change in men who are forgiven. According to the preaching of both John and Jesus, there must be repentance and faith (Mark 1:4, 14–15). The man forgiven by Christ's act must become "a new creation" (II Cor. 5:17). Especially strong is the urgency that relations with our fellows test the reality of our own forgiveness. The woman who "loved much" could be forgiven gross sins, while the unloving Pharisee could receive no forgiveness (Luke 7:36–50). We may know that we have passed from death unto life only if we love (I John 3:14). The debtor who had been forgiven an impossible debt had his forgiveness revoked when he refused remission to one who owed him (Matt. 18:23–35). We are taught to pray for forgiveness only in so far as we are willing to forgive (Matt. 6:12; Mark 11:25). The classic biblical examples of men who forgave those who wronged them, such as Joseph and his brothers (Gen., ch. 45), David and Saul (I Sam., ch. 24), Stephen and those who stoned him (Acts 7:54–60), must all be tested in the light of the spirit of Jesus' forgiveness of his enemies even on the cross (Luke 23:34).

There are in the Gospels three difficult passages on forgiveness. In one, Jesus declares that he who "blasphemes against the Holy Spirit (*q.v.*) never has forgiveness" (Mark 3:29). In its setting this seems to mean that the man who fails to sense that all good comes from the Spirit of God is so spiritually dull as to be past forgiveness. A second (Mark 4:12) declares the purpose of the parables (*q.v.*) to be a blinding of those who are spiritually pervert lest they be forgiven. The third (Matt. 18:15–18), which represents Jesus as giving to the church the right to "bind" or "loose" from Christian fellowship, is often interpreted to mean that there is vested in the church the right to refuse forgiveness of sin or to grant it. This would signify that to the fellowship of believers there comes the understanding that enables them to know when a sinner is truly repentant and should be forgiven. It is, of course, a misinterpretation and misuse of this scripture for a church to arrogate to itself the right of forgiveness as an ecclesiastical prerogative. This led the medieval church to impose penance as a means for obtaining forgiveness. Later it sold indulgences through which the temporal pains of purgatory were remitted. From the whole tendency of prescribed acts the Protestant Reformation revolted to a more dynamic doctrine of the forgiveness of sin.

See also REMISSION OF SINS; SOTERIOLOGY.

JULIAN PRICE LOVE.

FORM CRITICISM: The term translates the German word *Formgeschichte,* literally, "history of form." Form Criticism studies the literary form of documents that preserve earlier tradition. Its basic assumption is that the earlier, oral use of the tradition shaped the material and resulted in the variety of literary forms found in the final written record. Study of these forms, therefore, throws light on the life and thinking of the people who thus preserved tradition.

I. Types of Oral Tradition: Ancient writings reflect many special types of oral tradition. The Homeric poems can be regarded as the written record of the work of numerous ancient bards. The Greek diatribe reflects discussion methods of Greek philosophical circles. Surviving missionary discourses, as Norden argued, show a typical form. The Mishnah and later the Talmud preserve in writing the Rabbinic tradition which had been orally shaped and transmitted through many generations.

Particularly influential in biblical study, however, was Olrik's analysis of the thirteen laws or principles that govern the form of oral tradition in the folk tales of common people. He laid bare the simple, concrete, vivid, and effective patterns that prevail where many people share through many generations in handing on a tradition.

II. Old Testament Record of Oral Tradition: H. Gunkel led the way in applying this viewpoint to Old Testament study. Particularly in the third edition of his commentary on Genesis (1917), but also in other writings, he called attention to the various *Gattungen* or literary forms in which ancient oral tradition had taken shape. In narrative he finds fable, myth, saga, legend, brief tale, and historical narrative. Lyric compositions include funeral hymns, love songs, taunt songs, wedding songs, royal songs, hymns for public worship, thanksgiving hymns, and laments of individual or congregation. In prophetic writings he finds visions in narrative form and various forms of prophetic sayings, including threat, promise, and rebuke. Gunkel's concern is to understand the literary forms by reconstructing the life situation in which they arose and developed.

III. Form Criticism of the Synoptic Gospels:

In New Testament study, and especially in study of the Synoptic Gospels, Form Criticism has received vigorous development. It appeared as a clear-cut method in works by K. L. Schmidt (1919), M. Dibelius (1919), and R. Bultmann (1921), the three scholars whose work still dominates this field of study. It built upon many forerunners: Olrik's studies of folktales; Gunkel's identification of oral traditions embedded in the Old Testament; Wellhausen's critical attention to the individual items of the gospel tradition and to the early stages of that tradition; Norden's study of prose style and mission discourses; etc. It built upon the concept that identification of written sources could not fully bridge the gap between Jesus and the written Gospels. A period of oral tradition had intervened and called for study. The prevailing sociological interest encouraged scholars to ask what part the total group of early Christians had in handing down the gospel.

Form Criticism follows this sociological interest. It minimizes the role of the individuals who finally wrote down the tradition. It views the Synoptic Gospels as a collection of many separate units whose present order in the Gospels is the result of late editorial grouping and so does not reflect the actual sequence of events and teaching in Jesus' ministry. It holds that these units can be classified according to their form, and that the *Sitz im Leben,* the life situation in the early church, determined the form each unit took. Therefore from the form these scholars believe that they can deduce the situation in the church that shaped this unit of tradition. The gospel material thus becomes a source of information about the life and interests of the church, and is only to a limited degree of use in determining what Jesus did and said. (Form critics differ among themselves as to how far the tradition gives a true picture of the historical Jesus, but most of them agree that the Gospels are primarily witnesses to the life and teaching of the early church.) They are viewed as preserving this developed tradition as it had been selected and shaped by use in worship, instruction, counseling, and controversy. They see true parallels to our Gospels not in the cultured literature of great writers but in the popular writings of ancient times that preserve the traditions of common people.

IV. Types of Gospel Tradition: Attempts to classify the forms of the gospel material have not led to clear agreement. Form critics agree that the *Passion Story* took form first; Form Criticism here sees one exception to its claim that each event or teaching of the gospel account was originally a separate unit. This is essential to their principle of procedure. A connected story of the Passion was needed from the first to make clear the innocence of Jesus and the meaning of his death and resurrection. The *Pronouncement Story,* to use V. Taylor's term, is a prominent form of the gospel tradition. Starting with a problem, controversy, or miracle, it comes to a climax in a saying or pronouncement of Jesus. *Parables* and *Sayings* take form according to their purpose. *Miracle Stories* have a typical form; the great need, the word or action of Jesus, and the amazing result are regular features in such narratives. Various *Stories about Jesus,* including those that give clues to his origin, greatness, and destiny, naturally center attention upon him and his significance for faith. They remind us that the tradition was preserved in constant touch with the worship and teaching of the church, to which Jesus was "Lord and Christ."

V. Criticism and Evaluation: Criticism of Form Criticism has not been wanting. It includes the following points: Form Criticism has not been able to assign all the gospel material to clear forms; it forgets the role of eye witnesses in preserving the original tradition; it does not do justice to the historical sense, intelligence, and integrity of the early Christians; while it rightly recognizes the extensive topical grouping of material in the Gospels, it goes too far in discrediting their basic outline of Jesus' ministry; while it correctly sees the importance of the early oral period, it hardly gives adequate weight to the fact that within some twenty years the writing of written sources began, and so the process of oral tradition was not so long as in folk tales and in the earliest Old Testament stories; its tendency to assume radical distortion of the tradition in the Hellenistic church is refuted by the prevailingly Semitic character of the common Synoptic tradition; and its results are warped by unexamined assumptions, such as that miracle stories are largely late creations and that explicit Christology arose first in the church rather than in the mind of Jesus.

Such criticisms contain much truth. Yet Form Criticism has rightly focused attention upon the early oral period and upon the preservation, transmission, and shaping of the tradition in the life of the church.

VI. Other Oral Tradition of the Early Church: Form Criticism deals essentially with the Synoptic Gospels. The Fourth Gospel is too plainly the work of an outstanding personality to be regarded as the product of popular tradition. Attempts to apply the method in Acts have limited justification. The speeches, for example, present in summary fashion the main points of the basic gospel message, the kerygma. Most of them follow a typical pattern, as C. H. Dodd has shown; the speeches in Acts 7:2–53; 14:15–17; and 17:22–30 diverge most from this common pattern, whose content is well represented in Acts 10:34–43.

Contemporary religious and philosophical traditions throw light on New Testament letters. Hymns and liturgical beginnings appear in the letters, as also in the Book of Revelation. Lists of vices and virtues, and of duties of household members, parallel somewhat similar lists found elsewhere. The spirited question and answer method of certain passages in Paul's letters recalls the diatribe known in Hellenistic philosophical circles.

In the entire New Testament, however, similarities to pagan literary form and use of tradition are accompanied by originality of essential content and skill in employing available forms to present the Christian message. See also NEW TESTAMENT STUDIES, TWENTIETH CENTURY TRENDS IN.

BIBLIOGRAPHY: A. Olrik, "Die epischen Gesetze der Volksdichtung," in *Zeitschrift fuer deutsches Altertum und Litteratur,* LI (1909), 1–12; H. Gunkel, *Genesis,* 1901, 3rd ed., 1917; E. Norden, *Agnostos Theos,* 1913; P. Wendland, *Die urchristlichen Literaturformen,* 1912; K. L. Schmidt, *Der Rahmen der Geschichte Jesu,* 1919; M. Dibelius, *Formgeschichte des Evangeliums,* 1919, 2nd ed., 1933, Eng. Trans., *From Tradition to Gospel,* 1935; R. Bultmann, *Die Geschichte der synoptischen Tradition,* 1921, 2nd ed., 1931; M. Albertz, *Die synoptischen Streitgespraeche,* 1921; G. Bertram, *Die Leidensgeschichte Jesu und der Christuscult,* 1922; E. Fascher, *Die formgeschichtliche Methode,* 1924; *Eucharisterion: Studien zur Religion und Literatur des Alten und Neuen Testaments, Hermann Gunkel zum 60. Geburtstage dargebracht,* Part II, 1923; V. Taylor, *The Formation of the Gospel Tradition,* 1933; L. J. McGinley, *Form-Criticism of the Synoptic Healing Narratives,* 1944; C. F. Burney, *The Poetry of Our Lord,* 1925; P. Carrington, *The Primitive Christian Catechism,* 1940.

FLOYD V. FILSON.

FORMOSA. See CHINA.

FORMULA OF CONCORD: The *Formula concordiae* of the year 1580 gave rise to the name of numerous colleges operated by the Missouri Synod of the Lutheran Church in the United States. At its headquarters in St. Louis this powerful denomination administers an enormous publishing house also called Concordia. This formula was published at the end of the *Book of Concord,* which contains the three oldest creeds accepted by the Lutherans: Apostolic, Nicene, and Athanasian; and also the Augsburg Confession, Melanchthon's Apology, the Schmalkaldic Articles, Melanchthon's *De Potestate et primatu Papae,* and Luther's two catechisms. Since three of Melanchthon's works appeared in this book his influence has been very great wherever orthodox Lutheranism has spread. The rising power of Calvinism impelled the church leaders in Germany to take a united stand. One third of the Lutherans at the time refused to sign the formula, for they preferred to merge with the Calvinists or stand aloof from both parties.

BIBLIOGRAPHY: H. Leube, *Kalvinismus und Luthertum im Zeitalter der Orthodoxie,* Vol. I, 1928.

[Sup.] ALBERT HYMA.

FORMULARIES: Collections of models for the various acts of legal procedure. The use of *formulae* in Roman law was made mandatory under Augustus, and remained an essential feature of imperial court proceedings in Rome and Constantinople. A great number of formularies for civil actions were compiled from the sixth to the eleventh century in France and northern Italy. Similar formularies for canonical procedure were used extensively in papal and episcopal courts and chanceries. Among the most important ecclesiastical formularies are: the *Liber Diurnus,* issued under the pontificate of Gregory the Great; the *Provinciale,* compiled during the thirteenth century, and the *Quaternus Albus,* which was used until 1560. Diocesan courts used extensively the Curialis, popular in France, and the *Ordo Iudicialis* of Bologna, both compiled during the second half of the thirteenth century. Modern ecclesiastical procedure does not use any general formularies.

BIBLIOGRAPHY: E. Besta, *Fonti, legislazione e scienza giuridica,* I, 1923; A. Van Hove, *Prolegomena,* 2nd ed., 1945.

GEORGES A. BARROIS.

FORSYTH, PETER TAYLOR: D. Nov. 11, 1921. He was principal of Hackney Theological College, Hampstead, London (1901–21) and was sometime chairman of the Congregational Union of England and Wales. Coming under the influence of strong teachers like Ritschl and Fairbairn he turned his thought, and creative energies as well, into a happy combination of evangelical, constructively modern, positive and social outlooks which recently have been coming to be recognized for their true worth. In addition to earlier books and *Children's Sermons,* his later books are: *Positive Preaching and the Modern Mind* (1907, Yale Lectures); *Missions in State and Church; The Cruciality of the Cross; The Person and Place of Christ; The Work of Christ; Christ on Parnassus* (1911); *Faith, Freedom and the Future* (1912); *The Religion and Ethic of Marriage* (1912); *The Principle of Authority* (1913); *Theology in Church and State* (1915); *The Christian Ethic of War* (1916); *The Justification of God* (1916); *The Soul of Prayer* (1916); *The Church and the Sacraments* (1917); and *This Life and the Next* (1918). [Sup.] RAYMOND W. ALBRIGHT.

FORTESCUE, ADRIAN: English Roman Catholic scholar; b. 1874. He studied at Rome (Ph.D., 1894) and Innsbruck (D.D., 1905), was parish priest at Letchworth, Herts, from 1907–23. Devout, erudite, and sprightly, he was most widely known for his practical manual, *The Ceremonies of the Roman Rite Described* (1917), and was distinguished for scholarly work in Liturgics (*The Mass, a Study of the Roman Liturgy,* 1912), and Eastern Church History. After his tragic death in 1923 appeared *The Uniat Eastern Churches* (1923); edited by J. Maspero, *Histoire des Patriarches d'Alexandrie;*

and an edition of Boethius, *De Consolatione Philosophiae* (1924).

BIBLIOGRAPHY: J. G. Vance and J. W. Fortescue, *Adrian Fortescue, A Memoir,* 1924.

EDWARD ROCHIE HARDY.

FORTY HOURS: This non-liturgical devotion of the Roman Catholic Church seems to have originated in Milan during the sixteenth century as a public supplication for the peace of Christendom, then threatened by the Turks. In Rome, it was practised increasingly as an expiation for the sins and sacrileges committed during carnival (*q.v.*). It consists essentially in the solemn Exposition of the Blessed Sacrament (*q.v.*), during approximately forty hours, while relays of worshippers keep a continuous watch, perhaps with reference to the traditional time Jesus remained in the power of death.

The following variation of the forty hours devotion has now prevailed: each church in turn takes up the exercise, so that the exposition of the Sacrament is in a certain measure continuous throughout the diocese. The adoration usually lasts from an early Mass to the close of the day, when the Benediction of the Blessed Sacrament (*q.v.*) is given with special solemnity.

BIBLIOGRAPHY: F. Beringer, *Die Ablaesse,* I (1921), 659 ff.

GEORGES A. BARROIS.

FOSDICK, HARRY EMERSON: B. Buffalo, N.Y., May 24, 1878. After graduation from Colgate University and the Union Theological Seminary, he was minister of the First Baptist Church, Montclair, N.J. (1904–15); professor of practical theology at the Union Theological Seminary (1915–46). In World War I he served with the American troops in France under the Y.M.C.A. and with the British troops under the British Ministry of Information. In 1919, in conjunction with his professorship, he became stated preacher at the First Presbyterian Church, New York City. Attacked by the fundamentalists for his liberal theological views, he resigned this position in 1925 to become minister at the Park Avenue Baptist Church, and under his leadership this congregation became the interdenominational Riverside Church, where he was minister until his retirement in 1946.

For twenty years his radio ministry was carried by the nation-wide National Vespers. One of his major interests has been the development of personal counseling in the churches in cooperation with psychiatric help. His books are as follows: *The Second Mile; The Manhood of the Master; The Assurance of Immortality; The Meaning of Prayer; The Meaning of Faith; The Meaning of Service; Christianity and Progress; Twelve Tests of Character; The Modern Use of the Bible; Adventurous Religion; Spiritual Values and Eternal Life; A Pilgrimage to Palestine; As I See Religion; The Hope of the*

World; The Secret of Victorious Living; The Power to See it Through; Successful Christian Living; A Guide to Understanding the Bible; Living Under Tension; On Being Fit to Live With; On Being a Real Person; A Great Time to be Alive; The Man From Nazareth; Rufus Jones Speaks to our Times; Keynotes of the Protestant Reformation; Great Voices of the Reformation.

FOUNDLING HOMES. See CHILDREN'S IN-STITUTIONS.

FOURSQUARE GOSPEL, THE INTERNA-TIONAL CHURCH OF THE: A body founded in 1918 by Mrs. Aimee Semple McPherson in Los Angeles, California. The founder, known as "Sister Aimee," was born in Ontario in 1890. Thrice-married, she carried the names of her first and second husbands. With Robert Semple, a Baptist missionary who died in China, she traveled widely as a preacher before settling in Los Angeles and founding there the large Angelus Temple, Echo Park Evangelistic Association, and Lighthouse of International Foursquare Evangelism, a training school known as L.I.F.E.

She was a woman of striking appearance and dramatic ability and adept in the methods of crowd psychology. Her preaching attracted great crowds, and Angelus Temple became a much-publicized center of healing and charity. Her name was linked with numerous scandals, one of which involved an alleged kidnapping which her opponents regarded as an amorous adventure, but none of these shook the confidence of her army of followers.

Mrs. McPherson was the ruling power in the International Church of the Foursquare Gospel, which was incorporated as a denomination in 1927, and all its subsidiary organizations, and at her death the office of president passed to her son. The body has an annual general assembly and a five-member board of directors which manages business affairs and names the district supervisors of the church. The local congregations are governed by councils.

The church is fundamentalistic in nature and its theology is orthodoxy of the most conservative type. Among the distinctive elements emphasized are spirit guidance, divine healing, the gift of tongues, holiness, and the expected imminent second coming of Christ.

The Foursquare Gospel spread rather widely in western United States and has missions in several foreign lands. Its creed is contained in a Declaration of Faith to which ministers and members must subscribe. It has around 500 congregations and more than 65,000 members (1952).

BIBLIOGRAPHY: Aimee Semple McPherson, *The Story of My Life*, 1951; E. T. Clark, *Small Sects in America*, rev. ed., 1949.

ELMER T. CLARK.

FOWLER, HENRY THATCHER: University professor; b. at Fishkill, N. Y., March 4, 1867; d. Jan. 23, 1948. He studied at Yale (A.B., 1890; Ph.D., 1896). He taught biblical literature and philosophy at Yale (1895–97); at Knox College (1897–1901) and was professor of biblical literature and history at Brown University (1901–34). His major works of religious interest include: (with M. C. Hazard), *The Books of the Bible with Relation to Their Place in History* (1903); *The Prophets as Statesmen and Preachers* (1904); (with F. K. Sanders), *Outlines for Study of Biblical History and Literature* (1906); *Studies in the Wisdom Literature of the Old Testament* (1907); *History of the Literature of Ancient Israel* (1912); *The Origin and Growth of the Hebrew Religion* (1916); *Great Leaders of Hebrew History* (1920); and *The History and Literature of the New Testament* (1925).   RAYMOND W. ALBRIGHT.

FOX, GEORGE: William Penn in his Preface to Fox's *Journal* wrote as follows: "Many left them [the Puritans], and all visible churches and societies, and wandered up and down, as sheep without a shepherd, and as doves without their mates; seeking their beloved, but could not find Him (as their souls desired to know Him) whom their souls loved above their chiefest joy. These people were called seekers by some, and the Family of Love by others; . . . they waited together in silence, and as anything rose in any of their minds that they thought savoured of a divine spring, so they sometimes spoke." They did not derive much edification from the Prayer Book or from church discipline when carried out along hard and fast lines. They advocated extemporaneous prayers and sermons. For pomp and ceremony they had extremely little respect. George Fox arose among them and introduced a semblance of order. He said that the human soul must not rely upon outward sacraments and mediation through the clergy but establish direct contact with God. Fox's courage overcame all obstacles put in his way by more conventional churchmen and by political leaders. See also INDEPENDENTS; CROMWELL, OLIVER; LAUD, WILLIAM; CHARLES I.

BIBLIOGRAPHY: Fox, *Journal*, ed. by Norman Penney, 2 vols., 1911; Fox, *The Short Journal of George Fox*, 1925; W. C. Braithwaite, *The Beginnings of Quakerism*, 1912; R. M. Jones, *Mysticism and Democracy in the English Commonwealth*, 1932.

[Sup.] ALBERT HYMA.

FRAME, JAMES EVERETT: Presbyterian clergyman; b. at Boston, March 24, 1868. He studied at Harvard (A.B., 1891; A.M., 1892); Union Theological Seminary (graduated, 1895), and Berlin and Goettingen (1895–97). He became instructor in New Testament at Union Theological Seminary, N. Y. (1897–1901), assistant professor (1901–3), associate professor

(1903–5), Edward Robinson professor of Biblical Theology (1905–19), Baldwin professor of Sacred Literature (1919–38), professor emeritus since 1938. In methodology of serious study of the New Testament, he has insisted by precept and example upon a thorough knowledge of Hebrew and cognate languages as an aid to understanding the deepest thought of the New Testament authors. Howard Chandler Robbins aptly characterized him theologically as a representative of "liberal Presbyterianism in its scholarly aspect" (*Charles Lewis Slattery*, p. 120). He has excelled in effectiveness in leading public worship. He wrote: the articles on the Epistles to the Colossians and to the Thessalonians, *Encyclopaedia Britannica*, 11th ed., (1910–11); "Paul's Idea of Deliverance," *J.B.L.*, 49 (1930), 1–12 (being the annual Presidential Address to the Society of Biblical Literature); many book reviews for *The Nation* (while Paul Elmer More was editor); and *A Critical and Exegetical Commentary on the Epistles of St. Paul to the Thessalonians* (International Critical Commentary, 1912).   BRUCE M. METZGER.

FRANCE: It is not the separation of church and state that is responsible for the religious crisis which confronted France in the twentieth century. This separation simply clarified a condition which had existed before. Freed from all obligation to a church, the Voltairian bourgeoisie, together with Freemasons (*q.v.*) and Marxist workers, adopted an attitude which was rather anti-ecclesiastical than anti-Christian. But it had the effect of precipitating the dechristianization of the country. Pope Pius XI (*q.v.*), considering the heritage of the nineteenth century, could declare that its great scandal was that the church lost the laboring class. In 1950 statistics revealed that only 8,000,000 or 10,000,000 in France's total population of 41,000,000 could claim to be practicing Christians in the several communions. France has become a "mission field," for three Frenchmen out of four regard themselves as irreligious.

Roman Catholicism appeared to be alarmed by the rapidity of this change. After having been dependent on the nobility, it had relied on the bourgeoisie. The loss of a considerable part of the bourgeoisie after two world wars compelled the Roman Church to turn to the proletariat, and it is the reconquest of the proletariat that is the most characteristic mark of the internal life of French Catholicism. In its attempts to Christianize the country various methods have been employed: (1) On the one hand, traditional methods have been used: the development of Mariolatry, pilgrimages, the procession of the Virgin of Boulogne across France, Catholic Action (*q.v.*), the "propaganda for unity" which seeks to make the church the perfect city which will unite all classes and

social conditions, the "apostolate of prayer" which recommends the "access of infidels to the Faith by means of the disappearance of Protestant sects," etc. (2) On the other hand, innovations have been introduced: by applying the principle of the lay apostolate, young Catholic workers, students, farmers, and teams of the apostolate of the Mission of France (see MISSION DE FRANCE) have multiplied. The parallel movement in Catholic thought is illustrated by writers of great talent like Paul Claudel and François Mauriac and by the development of Neo-Thomism (*q.v.*). A number of attempts have been made to make Catholic cultus more accessible to the masses by employing French in place of Latin, by suppressing Mass fees, by circulating several translations of the Bible. Certain renowned Dominicans and Jesuits, while maintaining traditional Catholic positions, engaged in so many conversations with representatives of other confessions or gave evidence of such a spirit of inquiry in scientific matters that the Roman hierarchy expressed its disapproval by warnings and sometimes by condemnations.

The movement of population to the cities, where people became lost in the masses, seemed to affect Protestantism especially. When rural parishes were discontinued, the Société Centrale d'Evangélisation created new parishes. While, in 1856, only 144 of the 518 pastoral charges of the Reformed Churches were in towns, in 1952 as many as 323 of the 548 charges were urban.

Although the doctrinal controversies of the nineteenth century had had the effect of dividing Protestant Churches, under the influence of the ecumenical movement (*q.v.*) conferences were held in 1935 in which Reformed Churches, Free Churches, and Methodists participated. These conferences ended in 1938 with the adoption of a constitution for the Reformed Church of France. Some "orthodox" churches refused to join this union for fear of being lured into the ways of liberalism (*q.v.*) and nascent Barthianism, and they formed the Evangelical Reformed Churches.

The Lutheran Church, with its center in Paris, seemed to be becoming more and more of a minority church when the return of Alsace-Lorraine (*q.v.*) at the end of World War I completely reversed the picture. Lutheran theological positions were strengthened, there was a veritable renaissance of confessional spirit and liturgical interest, and the Lutherans regained numerical strength which placed them on a par with the Reformed.

World War II and, above all, the clandestine struggle of the Resistance had the effect of drawing Christians and communists together in the tragic experience of suffering and imprisonment. Although the churches were not officially engaged in this struggle, as was the Church of Norway (*q.v.*), the opposition of the proletariat was sometimes diminished, above all because Barthian clergymen professed what appeared to be Marxist tendencies in social questions. A clear tendency toward authoritarianism became manifest in all ecclesiastical domains and baffled the bourgeoisie, traditionally inclined toward liberalism. Meanwhile young people reproached religious leaders for ignoring the problems of the day.

The Protestant Federation of France, representative and co-ordinating organ of all French Protestantism since 1909, acquired increasing moral influence, especially under the presidency of Marc Boegner, whose election to a copresidency of the World Council of Churches (q.v.) attested to the high esteem in which he was held outside as well as inside of France. In the troubled times between two world wars and their aftermath, the Federation became an agency of equilibrium which made its voice virtually identical with that of French Protestantism.

BIBLIOGRAPHY: C. H. Bishop, *France Alive*, 1947; M. Watmough, *A Renascent Church*, 1951; C. Bost, *La carte du protestantisme français*, 1924; H. Godin, *La France, pays de mission?* 1943, summarized in English in *France Pagan?* 1949. For further bibliography see *Evangelism in France*, Ecumenical Studies brochure, 1951.

[Sup.] JEAN G. H. HOFFMANN.

FRANCIS, PAUL JAMES. See ATONEMENT, FRIARS OF THE.

FRANCIS, SAINT OF ASSISI, AND THE FRANCISCAN ORDER:

The exact date of his birth is still unknown, and it cannot be stated with certainty that his mother was from Provence. In the year 1206 he had his first important vision as he recalled these words: "If any man will come after me, let him deny himself, and take up his cross daily, and follow me." The second message from the Gospels struck home on Feb. 24, 1208, when he was at Mass and accepted the commandment expressed in Matthew 10:9–12: "Provide neither gold, nor silver, nor brass, in your purses. . . . And when you come into a house, salute it." The third experience occurred on April 16, 1209, as he meditated on Matthew 19:21. These three passages taken in a literal sense formed his first rule, so he told his first two followers and companions, Bernard of Quintavalle and Peter Cataneus. He had no intention then of founding a religious order, but merely wished to execute Christ's commandments. Unfortunately the rule he did frame in 1210 for the purpose of getting permission from Pope Innocent III to preach and succor the sick and needy is no longer extant. It is highly probable that he joined the three evangelical passages just mentioned with a few simple resolutions. His followers were to live in hospitals or monasteries already existing, or else reside with those whom they wished to serve. They were not to cling to a permanent residence but remember the words of the Master, who said that foxes had holes, birds had nests, but the Son of Man had no place of his own for a home. Not even the whole group might own any property, since he feared that attachment to worldly possessions would dilute religious fervor. Formal teaching in schools was also out of the question; everything was to be as it was in Palestine under the leadership of Jesus. Wiser and more experienced men than Francis realized that he would have to readjust his original program if he wanted to succeed and build a permanent system of Christian living and preaching. Under Honorius III Francis submitted to new regulations, but his original aim was never entirely forgotten. The Franciscans became the owners of Gethsemaneh.

BIBLIOGRAPHY: A. Little, *Guide to Franciscan Studies*, 1920; V. Facchinetti, *San Francesco d'Assisi*, 1928, bibl. guide; H. Boehmer, *Analekten zur Geschichte des Franziscus von Assisi*, 1929; *Analecta Franciscana*, Vol. X, Quaracchi 1926–1928; H. Boehmer (ed.), *Opuscula St. Francisci*, 2nd ed., Quaracchi, 1919; C. Cuthbert, *The Romanticism of St. Francis and Other Studies in the Genius of the Franciscans*, 1924. New biographies by P. Sabatier, 44th ed., Paris 1933; L. le Monnier, 8th ed., Paris 1931; J. Joergensen, Eng. tr. by C. Cuthbert, London 1933; G. K. Chesterton, London 1923; P. Sabatier, *Etudes inédites sur François d'Assise*, 1932; H. Thode, *Franz von Assisi und die Anfaenge der Kunst der Renaissance in Italien*, 1926 (presents a widely-discussed thesis claiming that Renaissance art was largely based on the story of the early Franciscans, which is a bit far-fetched); H. Lemaitre and A. Masseron, *S. Fr. d'Assise: Son oeuvre, son influence, 1226–1926*, 1927; A. Masseron, *Les Franciscains*, 1931; D. Dobbins, *Franciscan Mysticism*, 1927; A. Zawart, *History of Franciscan Preaching and Preachers*, 1927; A. Gemelli, *Il Franciscanesimo*, 4th ed., 1942; P. Gratien, *Histoire de la fondation et de l'évolution de l'ordre des Frères-Mineurs au XIIIe siècle*, 1928.

[Sup.] ALBERT HYMA.

FRANCIS, SAINT, OF SALES:

After the religious wars in France there occurred a great revival of personal faith and devotion. A principal leader in this development was St. Francis of Sales, who represented devout humanism, with the same optimistic idea of human nature that Erasmus (q.v.) taught, but with more religious fervor to go with it than the Christian humanists of the sixteenth century professed. He believed with Zerbolt of Zutphen (q.v.) that human beings can do a great deal in their own power to reach perfection upon earth.

BIBLIOGRAPHY: St. Francis of Sales, *Oeuvres*, ed. by the monks at the Visitation d'Annecy, 26 vols., 1892–1932; new biographies by Msgr. Julien, Paris 1929; R. Cioni, Florence 1942; F. Fucher, Vol. I, Paris 1942, F. Strowski, Paris 1930; J. Calvet, *De François de Sales à Fénelon*, 1938; J. Leclercq, *S. Fr. de Sales, directeur de perfection*, 1928; E. Thamiry, *Le méthode d'influence de St. Fr. de Sales*, 1922; M. Couannier, *S. Fr. d. S. et ses amitiés*, 1929.

[Sup.] ALBERT HYMA.

FRANCISCA ROMANA, SAINT:

B. at the beginning of 1384; d. March 9, 1440. She belonged to the noble family called de Bussi. As mother of six children she was a model Christian wife. In 1425 she founded a convent known as the Oblates of St. Benedict. After the death of her husband in 1436 she acted as the superior of the convent. Her whole life was devoted to the service of others, especially through her labors in the field of education and the care of the poor. She was endowed with great mystic gifts, and her life was characterized by an extraordinary association with supernatural beings (guardian angel in particular).

BIBLIOGRAPHY: The oldest biographies and visions in ASB Mart., Vol. II; Berthem-Bontoux, Sainte Françoise Romaine et son temps, 2 vols., 1931-32.

MATHIAS GOOSSENS.

FRANCISCUS SOLANUS, SAINT: B. Feb. 10, 1549, at Montilla in the Spanish region known as Andalusia; d. July 14, year unknown. In 1568 he joined the Order of St. Francis of Assisi. After his consecration as priest he devoted himself first to the duties required of him in his native land. In 1589 he left as missionary for South America. He is known as the "Franciscus Xaverius of South America," and "the Thaumaturg of the New World." He was particularly successful among the colonists and Indians of Peru and Paraguay. In 1726 he was canonized.

BIBLIOGRAPHY: ASB Julii, V; L. Wadding, Annales Minorum, Vols. 20, 21, 22, 24; O. Maas, Der heilige Franz Solano, 1938; Lexikon fuer Theologie und Kirche, IV (1932), 120.

MATHIAS GOOSSENS.

FRATERNAL ORDERS, THE CHURCHES AND: The interrelations between the churches and organized fraternalism have taken a number of forms.

Perhaps the most explicit position taken by a church is that of the Roman Catholic Church. During the nineteenth century, several Roman Catholic prelates in America were disposed to deal somewhat sympathetically with certain "secret societies." Leo XIII's encyclical Humanum genus of April 20, 1884, condemned the Masonic order; and ten years later, at the request of the American archbishops, the Holy See clarified its position with regard to other secret societies as well, forbidding membership in them to the faithful under pain of mortal sin. The establishment of the Knights of Columbus (q.v.) in 1882 was at least partly a countermeasure aimed at providing a Roman Catholic equivalent to the fraternal orders.

While the Roman communion was thus clarifying its attitude toward fraternal orders, a group of Protestants representing seventeen denominations met in Pittsburgh, Pa., in 1868 and organized the National Christian Association, whose purpose it was "to expose, withstand, and remove secret societies." Believing that the fraternal orders represent a rival religion, the Association's journal, the Christian Cynosure, has continued this conflict ever since. A similar position is characteristic of a number of Protestant churches.

Other churches and churchmen in America and England have identified themselves with fraternalism on the grounds that it represents ideals and goals compatible with the Gospel. The decline in the religious nature of many fraternal orders has tended to lessen the tension between them and the churches, while the tension has continued between the churches and groups like the Freemasons (q.v.).

BIBLIOGRAPHY: Randolph Crump Miller, ed., The Church and Organized Movements, Vol. II of Interseminary Series, 1946; Fergus Macdonald, The Catholic Church and the Secret Societies in the United States, 1946; Christian Cynosure, 1868 ff; Theodore Graebner, A Handbook of Organizations, 1948.

JAROSLAV PELIKAN.

FRAZER, JAMES GEORGE: Anthropologist and man of letters; b. in Glasgow, Jan. 1854; d. May 8, 1941. He was educated at Larchfield Academy, Helensburgh, Glasgow University and Trinity College, Cambridge, where he was a classical scholar and subsequently a Fellow. Having been called to the bar of the Middle Temple, he became an honorary Bencher in 1934. In 1914 he was created a knight, in 1920 a Fellow of the Royal Society, in 1925 he was awarded the Order of Merit and in 1934 made an Honorary Freeman of the City of Glasgow. From 1907 until 1919 he was professor of social anthropology in the University of Liverpool, a chair instituted for him. He was instrumental in founding The Cambridge Review (1879), and in 1911 he delivered the first of his Gifford Lectures at St. Andrews on "Belief in Immortality and the Worship of the Dead." He was an original Fellow of the British Academy and a Fellow of the Royal Society of Edinburgh. Between 1890 and 1912 he produced his monumental work, The Golden Bough, in twelve volumes and three editions, having also written during this period volumes on Totemism and Exogamy (1910), edited Cowper's Letters (1911); Lectures on the Early History of Kingship (1905); Pausanias and Other Greek Sketches (1900). In 1918 he published Folk-Lore in the Old Testament (3 vols.); Sir Roger de Coverley and Other Literary Pieces (1920); The Worship of Nature (1926); The Gorgon's Head (1927); The Fasti of Ovid (5 vols., 1929); Myths of the Origin of Fire (1930); The Fear of the Dead in Primitive Religion (1933-34); and Totemica (1939). The Golden Bough and Folk-Lore in the Old Testament were also issued in abridged form in 1922 and 1923, respectively.

EDWIN OLIVER JAMES.

FREDERICK II, EMPEROR OF THE HOLY ROMAN EMPIRE: Born Dec. 26, 1194, at Jesi in the county of Ancona; d. Dec. 13, 1250, in Sicily. He was the son of Emperor Henry VI and Constance, Queen of Sicily. Orphaned at the age of four, he passed his youth amidst intrigues in Sicily. His chief tutor was the archbishop of Taranto, but he was instructed by both Arab and Christian teachers. His court resembled more that of an Oriental monarch than that of a western Christian. Pope Innocent IV called him the predecessor of the Antichrist ("infelix prenuntius antechristi"). He pretended to be a Christian emperor, was often called Frederick the Saint, and considered himself a chosen vessel to reform the church and return the clergy to the simplicity of the first century. It seems that the tales of his immorality were somewhat exaggerated. But he maintained a harem and employed Saracens in his educational system. His interest in Saracenic philosophy also indicates a trend away from Christian thinking. At first he was a ward of Pope Innocent III, but soon lost the friendship and support of that ambitious prelate. He spoke Greek, Arabic, Latin, French, and German. Dante considered him the father of Italian poetry. It was not for nothing that he was widely called *stupor mundi*, or the wonder of the world. Pope Innocent III, unaware of latent danger, persuaded him to leave Sicily and become emperor in Germany. Thereupon the young monarch decided to revive the empire of the Romans and reduce the power of the papacy. In the field of high politics he was quite unscrupulous, and showed the pope no gratitude. He wanted the pope to be no more than the head of the Christian Church. The struggle between church and state from 1214 to 1250 has attracted much less attention than from 1073 to 1085, but no doubt it should have been treated with more care by historians. Frederick's refusal to join the crusade from 1217 to 1221 caused its failure, much to the sorrow and chagrin of Pope Honorius III. But the latter did not oppose the coronation ceremony in Rome on November 22, 1220, and even presented the imperial crown to Frederick with his own hands.

In 1227 began the pontificate of Gregory IX, who took steps to curtail the pretensions of his imperial rival in Sicily and Germany. He pressed hard for a crusade and insisted that Frederick contribute a proper share. Frederick started from Brindisi with some 60,000 horsemen, but suddenly claiming to be ill with a fever, returned to the mainland of Italy. On September 29, 1227 the pope excommunicated him and declared an interdict upon Sicily and Germany. But there followed no Canossa. On the contrary, the emperor flourished. In March, 1228, his supporters in Rome were so strong that the pope had to flee from the city. In Sicily he carried on his work as usual, and on June 28, 1228, started on a crusade of his own which had little or no religious significance. He entered Jerusalem on March 17, 1229, pronouncing himself king of the Holy Land and successor of King David. His coronation was a spectacular

show, but the Franciscans and Dominicans continually preached against him. He returned to Italy in May, 1229, and upon his arrival observed that the people of Sicily, who before his departure had generally sided with him against the pope, were now beginning to turn against him, as a result of his long absence from his kingdom. Being a consummate diplomat, he made a treaty with the pope on July 23, 1230, granting many concessions. On August 28 his excommunication came to an end.

Seven years of peace followed. During that time Frederick abrogated some of the terms of the treaty as stated in the Constitutions of Melfi (Aug., 1231). He forced the clergy to be tried before civil courts, and he usurped again the right to try heretics. In Lombardy he won a great victory over the cities and wrote to the inhabitants of Rome that he was their emperor. On March 24, 1239, the enraged pontiff once more excommunicated him. But in Germany the princes refused to aid the pope, and at a meeting in Eger on June 1, 1239, they pledged Frederick their support. During the winter of 1239–40 several leading German cities sent armed forces in his behalf. Civil war followed also in Italy, but the death of the pope in 1241 caused a temporary suspension of hostilities. Under Innocent IV the clergy were unable to overcome the power of Frederick, and four years of stalemate followed, indicating that the days of Gregory VII and Henry IV were gone forever. Although the Council of Lyons condemned the emperor, during the next five years (1245–50) he was able to hold his own, except at the end when he grew weak and lost Germany to his political rivals. He retreated to Sicily, where he died in 1250. He had never been a true German, but loved his native Sicily. The pope went back to Rome, and a weak son of Frederick ruled with shaky hands in Germany and Italy. Upon his death in 1254 nineteen years of interregnum ensued, during which time it became fully apparent that no emperor, whether German or Italian, could hold both Italy and Germany. The attempt would be made during the fourteenth and fifteenth centuries, but it always ended in failure. At the same time the pope could never again free Italy from political masters, either foreign or Italian.

BIBLIOGRAPHY: F. Kampers, *Kaiser Friedrich II. der Wegbereiter der Renaissance*, 1929; E. Kantorowicz, *Friedrich der Zweite*, 1931; M. Brion, *Frédéric de Hohenstaufen*, 1948; B. Suetterlin, *Die Politik Kaiser Friedrichs II. und der roemischen Kardinäle in den Jahren 1239 bis 1250*, 1929; A. Fliche and V. Martin, *Histoire de l'Eglise*, Vol. X (1950), pp. 217–247. The fact that in the last-named volume by A. Fliche, C. Thouzellier, and Y. Azais a whole section is devoted to the career of Emperor Frederick II is a clear indication of his importance in the history of the Christian Church. This importance was not yet fully appreciated at the opening of the twentieth century.

ALBERT HYMA.

FREDERICK THE WISE, ELECTOR OF SAXONY: He chose to save Luther (*q.v.*) and the Protestant Reformation, first in 1518 and again in 1521. Erasmus (q.v.) had taken pains to explain to him during a meeting in Cologne that Luther represented the aspirations of the German people, to be free from the yoke of Roman dominion and from papal abuses. The elector was the founder of the University of Wittenberg; that institution meant a great deal to him, more than the collection of relics he had accumulated and the indulgences he had sponsored. Nevertheless, the crafty prince did not intend to lose favor with the leading authorities in the empire merely for the sake of getting more fame for his beloved university. There were other factors at work also. He observed that Luther captivated a popular desire for national glory, freedom from foreign control. Charles V (q.v.) was not a real German. He owed his imperial election to forces beyond the control of the Germans. Frederick would have made an excellent emperor and during the election in 1519 he had a great deal of support. He sensed in his own career the friction between emperor and electors. Moreover, his secretary, Spalatin, knew Luther well since 1514. He recommended to the elector that the professor be protected against the papal supporters and the house of Hapsburg. Luther was close to the hearts of the German people and stood for German independence, besides church reform. In this manner the Protestant Reformation was not crushed before it could get a good start. The elector's share in the spreading of the Reformation needs more emphasis than it usually receives.

BIBLIOGRAPHY: For a good discussion of the background and the environment involved in the whole career of Frederick see G. Barraclough, The Origins of Modern Germany (1947), pp. 355-369; K. F. Reinhardt, Germany 2000 Years (1950), pp. 205-283; R. Bainton, Here I Stand: A Life of Martin Luther (1950), passim; E. F. Henderson, A Short History of Germany, Vol. I, 1916; H. S. Lucas, Renaissance and Reformation (1934), pp. 439-470. The account by Henderson remains one of the best in the English language; see Chaps. 11-15. Here the whole problem which Luther had caused for the German princes in general and Frederick in particular is properly and succinctly treated. P. Kirn, Friedrich der Weise und die Kirche. Seine Kirchenpolitik vor und nach Luthers Hervortreten im Jahre 1517, 1926; J. Lortz, Die Reformation in Deutschland, Vol. I (1939), pp. 264-292.
[Sup.] ALBERT HYMA.

FREDERICQ, PAUL: B. Aug. 12, 1850, at Ghent, Belgium; d. March 31, 1920, at Ghent. In 1882 he became professor at the University of Liége and in 1883 at the University of Ghent. He taught principally history and Flemish literature. In 1876 he became a Protestant. He played an important role in the Flemish movement. His works are: Geschiedenis der Inquisitie in de Nederlanden (2 vols., 1892, 1897); Religieuze twisten in de Nederlanden (1894); Corpus documentorum inquisitiones haereticae Neerlandicae (3 vols., 1900–06).

ALBERT HYMA.

FREE CHRISTIANITY, GERMAN ALLIANCE FOR: With the rise of Neo-orthodoxy (q.v.) after World War I, the influence of liberal theology and of the free-church ideal waned in Germany (see PROTESTANT UNION, Vol. IX). But after World War II liberal forces (see LIBERALISM) regrouped, and in 1948 the first congress of the newly formed Deutscher Bund fuer Freies Christentum was held in Frankfurt am Main. Remnants of older free-church movements (Protestantenverein, Freunde der Christlichen Welt, and Freunde Evangelischer Freiheit) joined the Alliance. It rejects piety controlled by dogmas, advocates freedom for theological inquiry and liberty of conscience in the church, and demands the formation of a folk church (q.v.) independent of the state.

BIBLIOGRAPHY: Kurt Leese, Der Protestantismus im Wandel der neuen Zeit, 1941; Christliche Welt, periodical edited by Martin Rade, 42 vols., 1886-; Protokoll des 1. Kongresses fuer Freies Christentum, 1949.
ERICH MEYER.

FREE CHRISTIAN ZION CHURCH OF CHRIST: Founded July 10, 1905, in Redemption, Ark., by E. D. Brown and several other Negro ministers in protest against the levy of financial apportionments by the Methodist Churches to which they belonged. The new body remained Methodist in doctrine and polity, except that it has chiefs and superintendents instead of bishops. In 1950 there were 52 congregations in Arkansas and Texas with 4,798 members.
[Sup. to Vol. VII, p. 391.]
THEODORE G. TAPPERT.

FREE CHURCH ASSOCIATION, THE EVANGELICAL. See EVANGELICAL FREE CHURCH OF AMERICA.

FREE CHURCH FEDERAL COUNCIL: The Free Church Federal Council of England and Wales was constituted in 1940 by the fusion of two existing bodies: the National Free Church Council, dating from 1896, established on a basis of personal membership and representation of local Councils of Free Churches established throughout the country, and the Federal Council of the Evangelical Free Churches, set up in 1919 on a more official basis representative of the Free Churches as such. The new Council is thus representative of the 7,000,000 members and adherents of the Free Churches and provides a platform on which can be set forth the reasoned views of Free Churchmen on matters affecting religion, education, moral standards, and the common good. It does this by Annual Conferences, publications, and Departments. These latter deal with the appointment of Free Church chaplains in hospitals, co-ordination of youth work among the constituent denominations, supply and distribution of religious books, hymnals, Wayside Pulpit Posters, visual aids, projectors, and films. The Council also serves as an instrument for bringing together the views of the Free Churches on issues affecting reunion, especially with the Church of England. [Sup. to FREE CHURCH FEDERATION.]

EVELYN CLIFFORD URWIN.

FREE CHURCH FEDERATION. See FREE CHURCH FEDERAL COUNCIL.

FREE CHURCH OF AMERICA, THE EVANGELICAL. See EVANGELICAL FREE CHURCH OF AMERICA.

FREE CHURCH OF GOD IN CHRIST. See CHURCH (CHURCHES) OF GOD.

FREEDOM. See WILL, FREEDOM OF THE.

FREEMASONS: Since the last decade of the nineteenth century, the history of Freemasonry has been marked by struggle and growth. One of the areas of struggle was its continuing conflict with the Roman Catholic Church, which continued the program of opposition set down in the encyclical *Humanum genus* by holding the Anti-Freemasonic Congress in Trent in 1896. Despite occasional attempts at rapprochement, this program of opposition has continued. Another source of opposition to the Freemasons came from German National Socialism and Italian Fascism, which regarded its emphasis upon secrecy and certain other of its policies and principles as dangerous to the state.

In America, Freemasonry has developed a distinct "American Rite," as Albert Mackey terms the "York Rite," which exists alongside the Scottish Rite. This latter includes the higher degrees of Masonry, from the fourth to the thirty-third. There are, in addition, supplementary groups like the "Concordant Orders." It has continued to seek support and membership on the grounds of the social and economic advantages available to members. It continues to employ the symbols, rites, and terms of religion, and makes its appeal to some on these grounds; but its principal strength among most of its members seems to come from social and economic advantages and from its many charitable endeavors rather than from its specifically religious tenets.

The total membership of the various orders and rites numbers somewhat more than 3,000,-000.

See also FRATERNAL ORDERS, THE CHURCHES AND.

BIBLIOGRAPHY: Eugen Lennhoff, *The Freemasons*, 1934, especially helpful for a study of European Masonry; *Gould's History of Freemasonry throughout the World*, revised by Dudley Wright, 6 vols., 1936—the last two volumes contain a history of Masonry in the United States, state by state; A. G. Mackey, *Encyclopedia of Freemasonry*, new edition, 3 vols., 1946.

[Sup.] JAROSLAV PELIKAN.

FREE METHODIST CHURCH. See HOLINESS CHURCHES.

FREE PROTESTANTISM, UNION OF. See FREE CHRISTIANITY, GERMAN ALLIANCE FOR.

FREE SPIRIT, BROTHERS AND SISTERS OF: Also called Homines intelligentiae or Adamites. They were extremely pantheistic, teaching that man can freely unite himself with God and in that condition is no longer subject to sin. They had little respect for the sacraments and taught numerous heresies. Gerard Groote openly preached against some of them and condemned them in his constitution for the Sisters of the Common Life in Deventer (1379). The archbishops of Cologne, Trier and Mainz (1310) warned against them and so did the synod of Utrecht in 1303, 1318, and 1353.

BIBLIOGRAPHY: J. Lindeboom, *Stiefkinderen van het Christendom* (1929), pp. 140–163.

[Sup.] ALBERT HYMA.

FREE WORSHIP: People worship publicly in three ways: (1) The liturgical, which is well known; (2) The non-liturgical, as with the Friends, or the Salvation Army; (3) free worship. Those who employ free worship feel free to use historic forms or not to use them, except that they have stated ways of administering the sacraments. Such a group usually has for optional use a book of worship, including collects, litanies, and other historic ways of corporate worship. In the past these groups have been less formal in the United States than in Britain and on the Continent, but at present the trend is towards increased use of "an optional liturgy." In churches with two services on the Lord's day one may be formal and the other informal.   ANDREW W. BLACKWOOD.

FRELINGHUYSEN, THEODORUS JACOBUS: B. 1691 in Lingen, near the border between Germany and the Netherlands; d. 1748. As pastor of Dutch Reformed congregations at Raritan, New Jersey, he became the pioneer of the Great Awakening in the American Middle Colonies. He emphasized conversion and holiness, strict standards of admission to the Lord's Supper, and lay activity. Sharp opposition arose within his congregations, but Frelinghuysen's revivalism prevailed. His Presbyterian neighbor, Gilbert Tennent, was much influenced by him, and presently became a prominent Awakening leader. Later descendants of Frelinghuysen were prominent in American national life.

BIBLIOGRAPHY: P. H. B. Frelinghuysen, *Theodorus Jacobus Frelinghuysen*, 1938; L. J. Trinterud, *The Forming of an American Tradition* (1949), pp. 54–56.

LEFFERTS A. LOETSCHER.

FREUD, SIGMUND: Jew; b. Freiberg, Moravia, May 6, 1856; d. London, Sept. 23, 1939.

He studied both medicine and psychology at Allgemeines Krankenhaus under Ernst Bruecke, receiving an M.D. (1881) from Vienna University where he became a lecturer (1885), extraordinary professor (1902), and ordinary professor (1919). He was the first to discover the anesthetic properties of cocaine (1884). He studied under Charcot at Salpetriere Hospital, Paris (1885–86), and in Vienna with Joseph Breuer with whom he wrote *Studies in Hysteria* (1893) which explained that physical symptoms of hysteria are rooted in highly emotional experiences in early life, which have been "forgotten," i.e., repressed into the unconscious part of the mind and therefore normally inaccessible to the conscious mind (see SUBCONSCIOUS).

Freud developed a therapeutic process called *catharsis* which was produced through use of hypnosis; later he substituted free association for hypnosis and, adding the interpretation of dreams, he produced the psychological therapy called psychoanalysis which is based upon an original theory of personality. This theory, now widely accepted, states that there are three parts to the mind: the *id* (which is the amoral, primeval, instinctive self composed of needs, desires, passions, etc.); the *ego* (which is that part of the mind which implements the *id* in terms of reality); and the *super-ego* (which roughly is the conscience, the standards and conventions inherited from and imposed by society). The *ego* is caught in the cross fire between the incessant demands of the *id* and the stern voice of the *super-ego*. Emotional maturity is achieved only when a healthy and harmonious compromise is achieved by the *ego* between the impossible demands of the *id* and the *super-ego*. Until there is honest recognition of the demands of the *id*, self-deception and rationalization dominate. Variations of this theory were developed by two well known students of Freud, Alfred Adler (*q.v.*) and Carl Gustave Jung (*q.v.*).

Freud's insistence that the *libido* or sex drive constituted the primary factor in all emotional life set off an avalanche of criticism and misunderstanding. His theory of "infantile sexuality" (that the sex instinct begins with birth, subsides at about the age of five, and reappears at puberty) proved equally unacceptable at the time.

Further hostility was engendered by his attack on religion as an illusion concocted by man to explain the unknown. As the frontiers of ignorance shrank, man would become emancipated from his dependence upon the supernatural (*The Future of an Illusion*, 1927). Many of his most ardent disciples now deplore this book as "regrettable" and "unscientific." In *Moses and Monotheism* (1939) he examined the nature of religion, argued that monotheism was a distinctly Jewish contribution, offered a theory on recurring anti-Semitism, and maintained that

Moses was an Egyptian. Despite all attacks and criticism, Freud is gratefully acknowledged today as the father of "depth psychology" or dynamic psychiatry (*q.v.*), and a monumental contributor to contemporary culture. His studies continue to shed new light on sociology, anthropology, biography, literature, history, ethics, and religion.

Included among his many publications are the following: *The Interpretation of Dreams* (1900); *The Psychopathology of Everyday Life*; *Three Contributions to the Theory of Sex*; *Wit and Its Relation to the Unconscious* (1905); *Leonardo Da Vinci* (1910); *Totem and Tabu* (1913); *The Ego and the Id* (1923); *Repression, Symptoms and Anxiety* (1926); *The Discontents of Civilization* (1930).

ROLLIN JONATHAN FAIRBANKS.

FREUDIANISM. See SUBCONSCIOUS.

FRIDRICHSEN, ANTON JOHNSON: Lutheran: b. at Meråker, Norway, Jan. 4, 1888; d. Nov. 16, 1953. He studied at the University of Oslo (Cand. Theol., 1911). He served in the pastoral office (1913–14). He was assistant professor at the University of Oslo (1915–28); and has been professor of New Testament at the University of Upsala, Sweden (1928–). He founded several scientific societies (e.g., Uppsala exegetiska sällskap) and publications (e.g., Svensk exegetisk årsbok, Acta Seminarii Neotestamentici Upsaliensis, Coniectanea Neotestamentica, Symbolae Biblicae Upsalienses) for the furtherance of biblical studies. He has especially been working on the fields of New Testament philology and biblical theology. He has written: *Hagios-Qados. Ein Beitrag zu den Voruntersuchungen zur christlichen Begriffsgeschichte* (1916); *Le problème du miracle dans le christianisme primitif* (1925); (in co-operation with I. Heikel), *Grekisk-svensk ordbok till Nya Testamentet och de apostoliska fäderna* (Greek-Swedish Dictionary to the New Testament and the Apotolic Fathers, 1934); *The Apostle and his Message* (1947); (in co-operation with I. Engnell and others), *Svenskt-Bibliskt Uppslagsverk* (Swedish Biblical Encyclopaedia, 1948–52).

BIBLIOGRAPHY: "Zur Erinnerung an Anton Fridrichsen," *ZNTW*, XLV (1954), 123–129.

FRIEDRICH, GERHARD: Lutheran; b. at Jodszen, Kreis Pillkallen, East Prussia, on Aug. 20, 1908. He studied at the universities of Koenigsberg, Marburg and Tuebingen (Dr. theol., 1939). He assisted Professor Gerhard Kittel at Tuebingen (1933–35) and Professor H. J. Iwand in the theological seminary in Bloestau (1935–36). After military service he became lecturer in New Testament in Bethel b. Bielefeld (1947–) and since 1948 has been editor of the *Theologisches Woerterbuch zum Neuen Testament*.

RAYMOND W. ALBRIGHT.

FRIENDS OF GOD (GOTTESFREUNDE):

Was not an institution or even an organization but loosely knit association of mystics, devout clergymen, and pious laymen who wanted to reform the church along orthodox lines. One of them wrote the book known as *The German Theology*, which was wrongly ascribed to Tauler but probably composed in Sachsenhausen near Frankfort. This work contains pantheistic teachings, was highly praised by Luther, but bitterly condemned by Calvin.

BIBLIOGRAPHY: H. von Redern, *Der Gottesfreund Johann Tauler und die Freunde Gottes im 14ten Jahrhundert*, 4th ed., 1923; A. Chiquot, *Jean Tauler et le "Meisterbuch,"* 1922; M. Windstosser, *Etudes sur la "Théologie germanique,"* 1912; J. Paquier, *Un mystique allemand du XIVe siècle: L'Orthodoxie de la "Théologie germanique,"* 1922; Paquier reasons that the book is really safe and orthodox, but this is not the opinion of Galvano della Volpe, *Eckhart: O della filosofia mistica* (1952), pp. 253–264. W. Uhl, *Der Franckforter (Eyn Deutsch Theologia)*, 1930; K. Mueller, "Zum Text der deutschen Theologie," in *Zeitschrift fuer Kirchengeschichte* (1930), 307 ff.; F. Pfeiffer, *Theologia Deutsch*, 5th ed., 1923.

[Sup.] ALBERT HYMA.

FRIENDS SERVICE COMMITTEE, AMERICAN:

Organized in 1917 by American and Canadian Friends deeply concerned for the spiritual values endangered by World War I. Its first undertaking was the arrangement for youth of the Society of Friends (*q.v.*) and for other conscientious objectors (*q.v.*) to military service to carry on relief work in devastated areas of France in cooperation with English Quakers. The relief and reconstruction work was subsequently extended to other European countries, including Russia, Germany, Austria, Poland, and Serbia.

During its first three decades, the work of the AFSC can be characterized as follows: 1917–27, work for conscientious objectors to military service, foreign relief, and efforts in the interest of international peace; 1927–37, relief among unemployed miners in America during the depression (*q.v.*), resettlement of refugees (*q.v.*) from Fascist countries, especially Germany, and active endeavors through international centers in more than a dozen cities around the world to counteract the trend toward war; 1937–47, participation in relief in China, largely medical, through the Friends' Ambulance Unit's China Convoy, continuance of international and relief efforts in India and Europe, and the administration of Civilian Public Service for religious objectors to participation in war.

Work in the international field also includes publications, radio broadcasts, visits to tension areas, an international Quaker team at the UN General Assembly, and, in connection with the United Nations' New York offices, studies in methods of mediation and the reduction of armaments.

Peace education at various age levels is carried on through Institutes for adults, Seminars, Work Camps, Institutional Service Units for Students of college and university age, camps for high school students, and a children's department which supplies project materials for the elementary school age.

Relief and individual services are carried on for displaced persons and refugees, particularly in Germany and India. Neighborhood centers in Japan, Germany, and France offer a combination of self-help facilities and intellectual resources. Housing, health, and economic services among American Indians (*q.v.*) are being developed in two areas. Hundreds of young people volunteer their services every summer in behalf of peace in areas of economic and racial tension.

The annual expenditure, including gifts in kind, has increased from approximately $1,000,-000 in 1940 to $4,000,000 in 1950. During World War II it rose to a peak of $8,000,000. The headquarters of the Committee are located in Philadelphia.

BIBLIOGRAPHY: Rufus M. Jones, *A Service of Love in Wartime*, 1920; M. H. Jones, *Swords into Ploughshares*, 1937; Howard E. Kershner, *Quaker Service in Modern War*, 1950.

HOWARD H. BRINTON.

FRIENDS, SOCIETY OF:

In the twentieth century there exists in America a wide variety of faith and practice under the name of "Friends." The organizational structure resulting from the separations which occurred during the nineteenth century remains about the same as formerly and is as follows:

(1) The Friends General Conference (Hicksite) holds a general conference every two years without legislative authority and maintains a central office in Philadelphia. It is made up of six Yearly Meetings with a total membership of 18,668 (1950). Its chief organ is *The Friends Intelligencer*.

(2) The Philadelphia Yearly Meeting (Orthodox) has a membership of 5,515 (1950), and headquarters in Philadelphia. Its periodical is *The Friend*.

(3) The Conservative (Wilburite) group has no headquarters, though its chief center is the Friends Boarding School at Barnesville, Ohio. It is made up of five Yearly Meetings with a membership of 2,372 (1950).

(4) The most important recent event in American Quakerism has been the spontaneous growth of about 150 Independent Meetings in all parts of the country whose members are drawn from several branches of the Society of Friends or from none. Many of these meetings have given up their independent status and have joined one or more of the regularly constituted bodies. Some are united in Associations, and others in a new Yearly Meeting on the Pacific Coast.

(5) The Five Years Meeting comprises eleven Yearly Meetings in the United States and Canada with a total membership of 68,448

(1950). With it are associated Mission Yearly Meetings in Cuba, Jamaica, and Africa. These fourteen Yearly Meetings send delegates to the superior meeting held every five years. The headquarters of the Five Years Meeting are located in Richmond, Ind., where its organ, *The American Friend,* is published.

(6) A group of four independent Yearly Meetings (Ohio, Kansas, Oregon and Central in Indiana) holds a pronounced evangelical theology and makes much use of revivalistic methods. They have a total membership of 20,323 (1950). Foreign missions are a primary interest of this group.

In general, and cutting across these branches, there are today three main types of Friends: those who adhere to the historic unprogrammed Quaker meeting for worship based on silence; those who have adopted a programmed service conducted by a professional pastor and who lean toward modernism (*q.v.*); and those who have adopted a similar worship service with a strong fundamentalist (see FUNDAMENTALISM) emphasis. These three types are about equal in number. Groups (1), (2), (3), and (4) mentioned above are of the first type; (5) contains all three with the second in a considerable majority; and (6) is of the third type; (5) and (6) often call themselves "The Friends Church."

Movements toward unity of all branches are strong in the eastern yearly meetings which share most of their enterprises. In 1920 in London, in 1937 at Swarthmore College, Pennsylvania, and in 1952 in Oxford, England, conferences were held at which all Quaker bodies in the world were represented. All bodies, in varying degrees, support the American Friends Service Committee (*q.v.*) and Pendle Hill (*q.v.*). The American Friends Fellowship Council and the World Committee for Consultation are two agencies which represent all branches of Friends.

The Wider Quaker Fellowship consists of about 4,000 members who wish some affiliation with the Society of Friends but who do not wish to join it.

The Society of Friends in England has a membership of 21,969 (1950). Its chief organ is *The Friend* and its headquarters are in London. Friends in Ireland number about 2,000. Groups of Friends exist in Australia, China, Denmark, France, Germany, Holland, India, Japan, New Zealand, Norway, Palestine, South Africa, Sweden, and Switzerland. Some of these are organized into Yearly Meetings. All adhere to characteristic Quaker methods. Though small in numbers, they exert a wide influence. Friends Centers for the promotion of peace and international understanding exist in about a dozen cities throughout the world.

BIBLIOGRAPHY: W. C. Braithwaite, *The Beginnings of Quakerism,* 1912; idem, *The Second Period of Quakerism,* 1919; Rufus M. Jones, *The Quakers in the American Colonies,* 1911; idem, *The Later Periods of Quakerism,* 2 vols., 1921; A. Jorns, *The Quakers as Pioneers in Social Work,* 1931; W. W. Comfort, *The Quaker Way of Life,* 1941; A. Lloyd, *Quaker Social History,* 1948.
[Sup.] HOWARD H. BRINTON.

FRITH, JOHN: As a lad of fifteen, Frith frequented the meetings of those interested in reform, at the White Horse Inn, Cambridge. He fled most probably, not to Marburg, but to Antwerp, where he may have assisted in revising Tyndale's (*q.v.*) translation of the New Testament. In addition to his other works, he wrote a treatise on "The Supper of the Lord." Frith was a thinker, and a considerable scholar, who, in spite of his comparative youth, stood up in argument to Thomas More (*q.v.*). The latter always referred to him contemptuously as "this young man." It was for freedom of thought that Frith suffered.

BIBLIOGRAPHY: H. Maynard Smith, *Henry VIII and the Reformation* (1948), pp. 424-431; E. G. Rupp, *The English Protestant Tradition,* 1947; D. Alcock, *Six Heroic Men,* 1906.
[Sup.] GORDON HUELIN.

FRITSCH, CHARLES THEODORE: B. at Allentown, Pa., April 5, 1912. He studied at Muhlenberg College (A.B., 1932), Princeton Theological Seminary (Th.B., 1935) and Princeton University (Ph.D., 1940). He has taught Hebrew and Old Testament at Princeton Theological Seminary (1937–). His published works include *The Anti-Anthropomorphisms of the Greek Pentateuch* (1943); "Introduction and Commentary on Proverbs," in *The Interpreter's Bible;* "Commentary on Lamentations" in *The Lutheran Old Testament Commentary.*

FRITSCHEL BROTHERS: Conrad Sigmund and Gottfried Leonhard Wilhelm Fritschel were born in Nuernberg, Germany, on Dec. 2, 1833, and Dec. 19, 1836, respectively. They were educated under Wihelm Loehe (*q.v.*, Vol. VII) in Neuendettelsau, Bavaria, for foreign missions, but he induced them to go to America to work among recent German immigrants. Sigmund arrived in 1854 and participated in the formation of the Lutheran Synod of Iowa. In 1857 Gottfried followed his brother to America, and from 1858 until his death on July 13, 1889, they labored side by side as professors of Wartburg Theological Seminary, the training school of the new church body. The seminary shifted from Dubuque to St. Sebald in Iowa, to Mendota in Illinois, and eventually back to Dubuque, where Sigmund died April 26, 1900.

The brothers were vigorous in founding congregations and cultivating theology on a frontier. They set the theological pattern of their church body and stoutly defended its position, which was a confessional Lutheranism, without narrowness and with an eye to liturgical beauty and devout congregational life. They were prolific writers and editors, and Gottfried's works included a history of missions among the American Indians. His son George John Fritschel (1867–1941) published works on American Lutheranism, on the doctrine of election, and on the Formula of Concord.

BIBLIOGRAPHY: Gerhard S. Ottersberg,"The Evangelical Lutheran Synod of Iowa," doctoral dissertation, University of Nebraska, 1949; Herman L. Fritschel, *Biography of Drs. Sigmund and Gottfried Fritschel*, 1951.

                                    BERNARD HOLM.

FRONTIER, RELIGION AND THE AMERICAN: The greatest accomplishment of the American people has been the cultural conquest of the great vacant continent, the transplanting of Christian culture from the Atlantic seaboard to the Pacific slope. Here a vast struggle was going on between Christian civilization and the barbarizing influences which always attend the settlement of new areas. Upon the outcome of that struggle depended the fate of the new nation. The most effective agencies in combatting the incipient barbarism of the American frontier were the churches, and the most important task which the American churches faced to the year 1850 was that of saving the trans-Allegheny west for Christian civilization.

The two religious bodies which had been the established churches in the colonial period, the Congregationalists in New England and the Episcopalians in the southern colonies, were the least effective of the larger churches in dealing with the early frontier. The very fact that both had occupied a privileged position created an attitude ill-suited to deal with an equalitarian society. The non-English speaking churches— Lutheran and German and Dutch Reformed— were concerned with people of their own linguistic background, which practically eliminated them as effective agencies in dealing with the early trans-Allegheny west. The churches which made the largest impact on the early west were those bodies which developed the best way of following population westward, and thus they became not only the most evenly distributed religious bodies in the nation but also the largest in point of membership. These churches were the Presbyterian, the Baptist, and the Methodist, each of which developed its own method of performing its frontier task.

At the beginning of the national period a great proportion of the Presbyterians was made up of the Scotch-Irish who had swarmed across the Atlantic from North Ireland (*q.v.*) in the eighteenth century, most of whom settled in the back country since they were the last of the colonial immigrations from the Old World. Thus at the beginning of the national period the Presbyterians were already located farther west and in greater numbers than any other religious body. They have been termed by Theodore Roosevelt "America's first frontiersmen." In the process of following their own people west, the Presbyterians became a civiliz-

ing factor of large significance. It is true that their Calvinism, well-defined theology, and the Presbyterian method of congregations calling their ministers, retarded their effectiveness; for congregations were slow in forming and Calvinism was not a popular doctrine in the West. Because they had always maintained relatively high educational standards, Presbyterian ministers were often impelled to become school teachers as well as ministers. As a consequence the Presbyterian preacher-schoolmaster was a familiar figure on the frontier, and Presbyterian schools were numerously established, not a few of them developing into colleges. The large impact on education in the early West is indicated by the fact that by 1860 the Presbyterians had founded forty-nine permanent colleges in the nation.

The Baptist method of meeting frontier needs was quite in contrast to that of the Presbyterians. The frontier Baptist preacher was almost invariably a farmer who supported himself and his family on a farm and preached in a nearby meetinghouse on Sundays. He went west like other western pioneers, looking for better land and a freer air than he had found east of the mountains. He lived and worked exactly as other members of his flock. He cleared the ground, split rails, planted corn, and raised hogs on the same terms with his parishioners. Until well along in the nineteenth century Baptist preachers generally received no regular compensation, nor was it thought necessary for them to have any special educational training to preach the "simple gospel." Each Baptist congregation was completely autonomous, electing and ordaining its own minister. Thus the Baptists moved west with the people and were generally the first organized religious body on the advancing frontier.

The Methodist system of dealing with frontier religious needs was built around the circuit-rider. Devised by John Wesley (*q.v.*, Vol. XII) to follow people moving into the great industrial cities of England, the system was brought to America, primarily by Francis Asbury (*q.v.*, Vol. I), and it was found to be ideally suited to following people moving west. The preacher on horseback ministered to people living in scattered communities. Often, in the early west, the circuit was several hundred miles in circumference and required four to six weeks to get around once. In each community the circuit rider made it his object to form a class (see CLASS MEETING) and appoint a class leader, whose duty it was to look after the spiritual welfare of members week by week. So closely did the Methodist system enable the circuit preacher to follow moving population that not infrequently he called at a cabin before the mud in the stick chimney was dry or before the weight-poles were on the roof. Methodism was so organized as to follow, step by step, a moving population and to carry the gospel to the most distant cabin. Stressing free grace and free will, the democratic gospel of the Methodists made a large appeal to frontier society, the most democratic society in the world.

The relative effectiveness of the several Protestant bodies working in the west is shown by the statistics of church membership in the United States in 1850. The Methodists, the smallest and humblest religious body in the new nation at the time of independence, was now the largest Protestant body with a membership of 1,324,000. The Baptists came next with a membership of 815,000; the Presbyterians ranked third in point of size with 487,000 communicants. The Congregationalists, the largest religious body at the end of the colonial period, was now fourth with a membership of 197,000. The Lutherans ranked fifth with 163,000; the Disciples of Christ, a new religious body born of the American frontier, were 118,000 strong; and the Episcopalians, who had given little attention to the frontier previous to 1835, were in seventh place.

BIBLIOGRAPHY: P. G. Mode, Frontier Spirit in American Christianity, 1923; W. W. Sweet, Religion on the American Frontier, Vol. I, Baptists, 1931; idem, Vol. II, Presbyterians, 1936; idem, Vol. III, Congregationalists, 1939; idem, Vol. IV, Methodists, 1946; W. W. Sweet, Religion in the Development of American Culture, 1765–1840, 1952.
WILLIAM WARREN SWEET.

FROOM, LEROY EDWIN: Seventh-day Adventist; b. Belvedere, Ill., Oct. 16, 1890; educated at Walla Walla and Pacific Union Colleges, Washington Seminary, and University of Nanking; pastor at Baltimore and Wilmington (1913–15); editor, Signs of the Times Magazine (Calif.) (1915–18); Chinese Signs of the Times (Shanghai) (1918–21); Watchman Magazine (Tenn.) (1922–26); editor of The Ministry (1928–50). He has been professor of history of prophetic interpretation, S.D.A. Theological Seminary (Wash., D.C.) (1939–). His most widely known writing is: The Prophetic Faith of Our Fathers (4 vols., 1946–54).

FRY, FRANKLIN CLARK: American Lutheran; b. Aug. 30, 1900, at Bethlehem, Penna. He has served as second president of the United Lutheran Church in America since 1945. He is vice-chairman of the Central Committee of World Council of Churches; presided at the Constituting Session of the National Council of Churches of Christ, U.S.A.; treasurer, Lutheran World Federation; president, Lutheran World Relief; vice chairman, American Relief for Korea.

FUELOEP-MILLER, RENE: Lutheran; born at Caransebes, Hungary, March 17, 1891. He studied at the universities of Cluj (Hungary), Vienna, Lausanne, and Paris. He lectured on philosophical, psychological, historical, cultural,

religious, and sociological problems at the universities of Marburg and Zurich, and at the Kulturbund in Bern, Vienna, Prague, and Berlin. He came to the United States in 1939, became an American citizen and is teaching in the department of Russian civilization at Dartmouth College, Hanover, N. H., where he is a staff member of the Institute for Associated Research.

Among his best known works are: Mind and Face of Bolshevism (1927); Lenin and Gandhi (1927); Rasputin, the Holy Devil (1928); The Russian Theater (1928); Secret and Power of the Jesuits (1930); Machinery of Imagination (1930); Ochrana (A study of oppression) (1931); Under Three Tsars (1932); Cultural History of Medicine (1932); Leaders, Dreamers and Rebels (1935); Leo XIII (1937); Triumph Over Pain (History of anaesthesia) (1938); The Saints that Moved the World (1945); Dostoevsky (1950); The Web (Autobiographical novel) (1950); and Science and Faith in the Crisis of our Time (1952). He also edited nine volumes of posthumous works by Dostoevsky, the diary of Dostoevsky's wife, two posthumous works by Tolstoy, and a posthumous play by Tchechov.

FUERBRINGER, LUDWIG E.: Lutheran; b. at Frankenmuth, Mich., March 29, 1864; d. at St. Louis, Mo., May 6, 1947. He was graduated from Concordia Seminary, St. Louis, Mo. (1885), and was pastor of Lutheran church at Frankenmuth, Mich. (1885–93). He was professor of biblical interpretation and liturgics at Concordia Seminary (1893–1947), president (1931–43). He was president of the Evangelical Lutheran Synodical Conference (1920–47). For more than forty-five years he was editor of the German biweekly religious periodical Der Lutheraner. His publications include: Letters of C. F. W. Walther, Vol. I (1915), Vol. II (1916); The Book of Job (1927); The Eternal Why (1947); Persons and Events (1947). He was editor of M. Guenther Populaere Symbolik (3rd ed., 1898, 4th ed., 1913); Men and Missions Series (1924–33); Concordia Cyclopedia (with others) (1927); Die evangelischen Perikopen des Kirchenjahrs in Predigtstudien ausgelegt (1932); Thomasius Gospel Selections (1937); Eighty Eventful Years (autobiography) (1944).
FREDERICK E. MAYER.

FULCHER (FOUCHER) OF CHARTRES:
BIBLIOGRAPHY: Latest ed. of the Gesta Francorum by H. Hagemeyer, 1913; with description of the manuscripts and bibliography.

FULLONIUS, GULIELMUS: Willem de Volder (the Fuller), called himself in the humanistic style of his day Fullonius; usually, however, named Gnapheus, which is the Greek equivalent. He served from 1520 as rector of the Latin school in The Hague, and joined the so-called Sacramentarians, who were noted for their endeavors to use symbolism in explaining the origins of the sacraments, at least of the eucharist. He befriended Jan de Bakker (Pistorius), whose biography he composed and published (1546). Because of numerous difficulties with the inquisitors (Spanish Inquisition in the Netherlands) he removed to Germany.

BIBLIOGRAPHY: J. Lindeboom, *Het Bijbelsch humanisme in Nederland*, 1913; L. Knappert, *Het ontstaan en de vestiging van het Protestantisme in de Nederlanden*, 1924.

[Sup.] MATHIAS GOOSSENS.

FUNDAMENTAL CHURCHES OF AMERICA, INDEPENDENT:

Organized in June, 1930, at Cicero, Illinois, to succeed the American Conference of Undenominational Churches. It is a fellowship of churches that have no denominational affiliation. Its individual membership includes ministers, Bible teachers, evangelists, missionaries, editors of Christian periodicals, and men training for full-time service.

Membership is conditioned upon assurance of desire to co-operate with the fellowship's purpose and to oppose and counteract religious apostasy from Bible truth. Members are required to maintain the fellowship's standard of Christian ethics, morals, and conduct. A chief requirement is written assurance of belief, without reservation, in the doctrinal platform, which is ultraorthodox in its adherence to every foundational phase of the historic Christian faith. Annual renewal of membership is required.

Each congregational and individual member is assured full liberty of conscience regarding methods of operation and service. The constitution forbids organization as a denomination. The fellowship does not own property. It cannot own or administer any church, mission, missionary society, or school. Ordination is conducted and controlled by local churches.

In 1951 there were 365 churches and institutions, including 20 missionary agencies, and 1,100 ministers, evangelists, Bible teachers, Christian editors, and full-time workers in membership.

The fellowship functions through trustees, elected on a rotary system by an annual national convention. Auxiliary regional organizations function in portions of certain states; in greater areas, in an entire state. The national executive secretary and office headquarters are in Chicago, Illinois. An annual directory and an official monthly magazine, *The Voice*, are published. WILLIAM McCARRELL.

FUNDAMENTALISM.

See BIBLICISM; LIBERALISM.

FUNDAMENTALS ASSOCIATION, WORLD CHRISTIAN:

An organization originating in large interdenominational conventions held by Evangelicals in the United States during and immediately after World War I. The World Conference on Christian Fundamentals, which convened in Philadelphia in May, 1919, was the immediate stimulus. The Association requires its members to subscribe to a nine-point doctrinal statement affirming belief in the inspiration and inerrancy of the Scriptures; the Trinity; the deity and virgin birth of Christ; the creation and fall of man; the substitutionary atonement; the bodily resurrection and ascension of Christ; the personal, premillennial, and imminent return of Christ; the regeneration of believers; the bodily resurrection of men to everlasting blessedness or everlasting conscious punishment.

The president of the Association from its founding until 1930 was William B. Riley. Under his leadership mass meetings were held throughout the United States to promote antimodernism, premillennialism, and opposition to the teaching of organic evolution. Interest lessened after the first decade. From 1930 to 1952 Paul W. Rood was president, with headquarters in Glendale, Calif., where the quarterly organ, *The Christian Fundamentalist*, was issued. A merger with the Slavic Gospel Association in 1952 brought an end to the separate existence of the organization.

BIBLIOGRAPHY: *God Hath Spoken*, Conference Report, 1919; Stewart G. Cole, *The History of Fundamentalism*, 1931.

PAUL WOOLLEY.

FUNERAL:

Funeral customs vary widely, and present many problems. Roman Catholics still hold services only for deceased persons in good church standing locally. Many Protestant clergymen conduct services for unbelievers and evildoers, with no biblical warrant, but striving to help living persons in distress. Occasionally one tries to convert unsaved persons present. Most pastors prefer to present the claims of Christ afterwards, privately. The aim is to bring comfort and hope. If that is not possible, the service may become a matter of form, or a farce. Even at the funeral of a saint, local customs often seem pagan. The funeral director, or mortician, makes the arrangements, usually without consulting the minister. The plans may involve display that the bereaved cannot afford. The services may be held at the home, in funeral parlors, or occasionally at the church. Morticians have led to the discontinuance of Sunday funerals. Except in some rural communities the services tend to be formal and short, sometimes professional and cold, without music, eulogy, or sermon. If a fraternal order takes part, its ritual precedes the minister's services. At the grave, especially in bad weather, he does not tarry long. No part of Protestant worship stands more in need of improvement, to secure spirituality, with Christian consolation and hope. On the contrary, a man with a sense of God's presence and a shepherd heart seldom fails at a funeral service. For practical counsels see *The Funeral*, by A. W. Blackwood, 1942.

ANDREW W. BLACKWOOD.

G

GALATIANS, EPISTLE TO THE. See PAUL THE APOSTLE.

GALESBURG RULE. See UNIONISM.

GALILEO: His view that the Bible does not contain factual errors but must not be looked upon as the last word on any of the sciences was supported by numerous scholars in Italy. Leading Protestants had already rejected the heliocentric theory of Copernicus, and the Roman Inquisition condemned it. The Inquisition treated Galileo with some consideration but requested that he maintain silence on the subject. He promised to do so, but before long broke his promise. Urban VIII who came to the papacy in 1624 was very cordial to him. This emboldened the astronomer to publish his work, *Dialogue on the Two World Systems* in 1632. Having received official permission for this publication, he assumed that his breach of promise was not a serious offense. He was threatened with torture, but was too old (70) to be subjected to it. A decree called for his imprisonment but was not taken seriously. It has often been alleged that Galileo exclaimed: "But the earth does move around the sun" but there is no proof for this.

BIBLIOGRAPHY: E. Wholwill, *Galileo Galilei und sein Kampf fuer die kopernikanische Lehre*, Vol. I, 1909, Vol. II, 1926; L. Olschki, *Galilei und seine Zeit*, 1927; P. Aubanel, *Urbain VIII et Galilei*, 1929; W. Moock, "Neues zum Galileiprozess," in *Hochland*, XXVI (1929), 312–321.

[Sup.] ALBERT HYMA.

GALLAGHER, BUELL G.: Congregational; b. at Rankin, Illinois, Feb. 4, 1904. He studied at Carleton College, Northfield, Minn. (A.B., 1925); at Union Theological Seminary (B.D., 1929); at London School of Economics, England (1929–30); and at Columbia University (Ph.D., 1939). He was national secretary of the Interseminary Movement (1930–31); minister of the First Congregational Church at Passaic, N. J. (1931–33); president of Talladega (Ala.) College (1933–43); professor of Christian ethics, Pacific School of Religion (1944–49); consultant to the federal security administrator (1950–51); and a member of the Office of Education staff (1951–52), the last position being assistant commissioner for higher education; president of the College of the City of New York (1952–). His writings include: *American Caste and the Negro College* (1938); *Color and Conscience: The Irrepressible Conflict* (1946); *Portrait of a Pilgrim: A Search for the Christian Way in Race Relations* (1946).

GALLICANISM: The tense relation between church and state in France has been treated to some extent in the article on "Investiture" (*q.v.*). In the time of Charlemagne both Roman law and Germanic custom favored the emperor, while the age in which Pope Innocent III ruled was very different. On the one hand there arose the problem as to the relation between the church in France and the papacy in Rome; on the other hand stood the question about the contest between the civil government and the clergy. The Gallican party always wanted power and independence for the church in France; sometimes the king was thought too arrogant and at other times the pope was attacked for his ambitious program.

BIBLIOGRAPHY: L. O'Brien, *Innocent XI and the Revocation of the Edict of Nantes*, 1930; V. Martin, *Les origines du gallicanisme*, 1942; A. Fliche and V. Martin, *Histoire de l'Eglise*, Vol. X (1950), pp. 156–180, 435–445, Vol. XVII (1948), pp. 357–422; V. Martin, *Le Gallicanisme politique et le de France*, 1929; M. Dubruel, "Gallicanisme," in *Dict. de Théol. Cath.*, VI, cols. 1096–1137; F. Vigener, *Gallikanismus und episkopalistische Stroemungen im deutschen Katholizismus zwischen Tridentinum und Vaticanum*, 1913.

[Sup.] ALBERT HYMA.

GALLICAN LITURGIES: This term applies generically to the various rites and orders of prayer used in the Latin churches of the West prior to the Carolingian era, in contradistinction to the Roman liturgy, especially after its reformation by Gregory the Great. It includes the early liturgies of Gaul proper, and such liturgies as were in use in Great Britain, Ireland, Northern Italy, and Spain. The Ambrosian and Mozarabic liturgies (*qq.v.*), have been, often incorrectly, regarded as varieties of the Gallican rite.

The origin of the Gallican liturgies remains obscure. Numerous elements point toward an oriental derivation, or at least toward infiltration from Greek and Syriac liturgies. As a whole, Gallican liturgies are less sober than the Roman. The style is dramatic and redundant. Prayers are addressed directly to Christ, and not to God through Christ. The ceremonial of the Mass has borrowed typical elements of the Byzantine rite.

The introduction of the Roman liturgy in the Western churches under the reign of Charlemagne brought about the gradual abandonment of the Gallican rite, with the exception of such Gallican features as were retained in the Ambrosian and Mozarabic liturgies, as well as in the liturgy of Lyons and the local usages of a few French churches.

BIBLIOGRAPHY: "Gallicane, Liturgie" in *Dictionnaire d'Archéologie Chrétienne et de Liturgie*; B. Beck, *Adnotationes ad textus quosdam liturgicos e vitis Sanctorum aevi Merovingici selectos*, 1939.

GEORGES A. BARROIS.

GALLING, KURT: Lutheran; b. Aug. 1, 1900, at Wilhelmshaven, Germany. He received a classical education at Berlin and studied at Bern (D. Theol.); and Jena (Dr. Phil.). He was docent at Berlin (1925–30); extraordinary professor at Halle (1930–46) and since 1946 he has been professor of Old Testament and biblical archaeology at Mainz. His chief works include: *Der Altar in den Kulturen des Alten Orients* (1925); *Die Erwaehlungstraditionen Israels* (1928); *Hesekiel 40–44* (HAT., I, 13, 1936); *Biblisches Real-Lexikon* (HAT., I, 1, 1937); *Exodus 25–40* (HAT., I, 3, 1939); *Der Prediger Salomo* (HAT., I, 18, 1940); *Das Bild vom Menschen in biblischer Sicht* (1947); *Textbuch zur Geschichte Israels* (1950); and *The Sceptre of Wisdom* (BASOR 119, 1950).

GALLOWAY, GEORGE: Presbyterian; b. at Stenton, Fifeshire; d. March 1, 1933. He studied at the universities of St. Andrews, Edinburgh, Goettingen and Berlin. He was minister of Kelton Parish Church (1891–1915), when he became principal and primarius professor of theology, St. Mary's College, St. Andrews. He published *Studies in the Philosophy of Religion* (1904); *The Principles of Religious Development* (2 vols., 1909); *The Philosophy of Religion* (1914, 1935); *The Idea of Immortality* (1919); *Religion and Modern Thought* (1922); *Faith and Reason in Religion* (1929); and *Religion and the Transcendent* (1930).

ANDREW K. RULE.

GAMBLING: Gambling is a perversion of an apparently ineradicable tendency in human nature. All living involves an element of risk or "chance," and such an element associated with skill increases interest and excitement. It becomes evil when it is exploited to redistribute wealth without relation either to merit or to responsibility. Some forms of sport exist only or mainly as a basis for this sort of gambling; and the temptation to "rig" results tends both to destroy the sport in question and to create a corruption which spreads through society.

In the psychology of the gambler, his gambling is often an "escape," like its twin vices of intemperance and lust. Human nature requires to be taken out of itself. Gambling serves to do this, and to put possibilities of greatness into lives otherwise (in the absence of religion) condemned to insignificance. In the face of this motivation, prudential arguments, setting out the infinitesimal chances of success, are seldom effective.

Gambling is, and generates, a spirit and an attitude to life which, from a religious point of view, is peculiarly wicked because it makes true religion impossible. One cannot, at the same time, believe in luck and in God.

WILLIAM ROXBURGH FORRESTER.

GAMERTSFELDER, SOLOMON J.: Evangelical Association (*q.v.*); b. near Warsaw, O., Oct. 10, 1851; d. at Dearborn, Mich., Aug. 5, 1925. He received his education at North Central College (B.A., 1878); Evangelical Theological Seminary (B.D., 1878); Wooster College (Ph.D., 1893); and Harvard University and the University of Chicago. After serving five pastorates of his denomination in Ohio, he became assistant editor of the denominational weekly, *The Evangelical Messenger* (1887–95). He was professor of systematic theology at Evangelical Theological Seminary (1895) and president (1908–20). He edited: *The Baccalaureate Sermons and Addresses of President A. A. Smith* (1895), and wrote: *Systematic Theology* (1921).

BIBLIOGRAPHY: Family papers and records in the Library of Evangelical Theological Seminary.

PAUL H. ELLER.

GAMMA DELTA SOCIETIES. See STUDENT ORGANIZATIONS, RELIGIOUS.

GANDHI, MOHANDAS KARAMCHAND (MAHATMA): Vaishnavite Hindu; a true *karmayogin* (devotee of pathway of selfless action) in the tradition of the *Bhagavadgita;* profoundly influenced by Thoreau, Tolstoy and Sermon on the Mount; b. at Porbander, India, Oct. 2, 1869; m. at age of 13 to Kasturbai; assassinated at New Delhi by Hindu zealot, Jan. 30, 1948. He was a London matriculate, studied law at Inner Temple, called to bar June 10, 1891; in 1893 he went to Durban, Natal, took leadership of twenty-year nonviolent struggle for civil rights of Indians in South Africa and in 1915 returned to India. He was engaged until 1947 in nonviolent *Satyagraha* campaign of civil resistance to attain Indian independence. He spent 249 days in South African prisons, 2089 days in Indian jails, and fasted twelve times as vicarious penance. He was the architect of India's freedom through nonviolence and an unusual combination of saint, lawyer and politician. He sought to apply the principles of *Satyagraha* (truth-force), *Ahimsa* (nonviolence), *Brahmacharya* (chastity), nonattachment to possessions and renunciation, all for the attainment of complete self-rule for India through *Swadeshi* (indigenous self-sufficiency), the removal of untouchability for *Harijans* (God's children, his name for outcastes), Hindu-Muslim unity and village uplift. He aimed to free India through the moral emancipation of her people and the awakening of the soul. Regarding religion he wrote: "All faiths constitute a revelation of Truth; but all are imperfect and liable to error. . . . We would think it our duty to blend into our faith every acceptable feature of other faiths."

BIBLIOGRAPHY: M. K. Gandhi, *An Autobiography: or the Story of My Experiments with Truth*, 1927, 1929, and 1945; *Satyagraha in South Africa*, 1928; *Speeches and Writings of Mahatma Gandhi*, 1933; Louis Fischer, *The*

Life of Mahatma Gandhi, 1950; H. S. L. Polak, H. N. Brailsford and Lord Pethick-Lawrence, *Mahatma Gandhi,* 1949; Vincent Sheean, *Lead Kindly Light,* 1949; E. Stanley Jones, *Mahatma Gandhi: an Interpretation,* 1948; Romain Rolland, *Mahatma Gandhi,* 1924; S. Radhakrishnan, editor, *Mahatma Gandhi: Essays and Reflections on His Life and Work,* 1939.

WILSON M. HUME.

GANDZM, SOLOMON: Jewish; b. at Tarnoberzeg, Austria, Feb. 2, 1884; d. March 30, 1954. He studied at the University of Vienna (Ph.D., 1911) and at the Jewish Theological Seminary, Vienna (rabbi, 1914). He taught Jewish history and religion at the Junior Colleges of Vienna (1915–19). Since 1923 he lived in New York City, becoming a naturalized citizen in 1929. He was librarian and research professor at Yeshiva College (1924–34); research professor in the history of Semitic civilization, Dropsie College, Philadelphia (1942–54); Guggenheim Fellow (1936–37); and an Associate Editor of *Isis.* He wrote about 50 articles on the history of mathematics and civilization of the Semitic peoples and *Die Muallaqa des Imrulgais* (on pre-Islamic Arabic poetry, 1913); *Monumenta Talmudica II, Recht* (on public law and institutions of the Hebrews, 1913–14); and *The Dawn of Literature, Prolegomena to a History of Unwritten Literature. Osiris VII* (1939).

GANSFORT, WESSEL: Son of Herman Gansfort, and thus not named Wessel Harmenes, nor called Johann by the Brethren of the Common Life (*q.v.*) at Zwolle. To say that he was a member of the brotherhood would be misleading. He spent some seventeen years with the Brethren at Zwolle, but he merely studied and then taught at the "Parva domus." He certainly did not represent all the doctrines of the Devotio Moderna. It was not for nothing that Martin Luther made this testimony in 1522: "If I had read his works earlier, my enemies might think that Luther had absorbed everything from Wessel: his spirit is so in accord with mine. . . . He . . . is so consistently in accord with me in all things, not only as to substance, but in the use of almost the same words." Other Protestants have often made similar declarations, but the latest Dutch biographer and his teacher, Professor J. Lindeboom of the University of Groningen, agree with the writer of our original article on Gansfort that the latter was misunderstood by Luther, while C. Ullmann in his admirable work, *Reformers before the Reformation,* sided with Luther.

Gansfort, like Rudolph Agricola, belonged to a small group of humanists who prepared the way for the Reformation and the Counter Reformation. As W. F. Schirmer has shown in his admirable book, *Der englische Fruehhumanismus,* "Wessel Gansfort, Rudolph Agricola, and Alexander Hegius produced a firmly rooted humanism," while "the English had to wait for

another generation." Moreover, the Dutch scholars and their neighbors in western Germany expressed theological views so similar to those pronounced half a century later by Luther that one becomes very much impressed by Luther's own testimony. To argue that Gansfort was orthodox is merely to beg the question. Gansfort was not a man of heroic and dramatic action. He could have died a martyr's death or struck a mortal blow at the Roman Catholic authorities, but such was not to his liking. What he wanted was peaceful reformation. That is why Erasmus wrote: "Doctor Wessel has much in common with Luther, but how much more modestly and like Christ did he propagate his ideas than most of those [Lutherans] at Strasbourg!" Luther said himself that he had studied with the Brethren of the Common Life at Magdeburg, and he also admitted that nowhere else had he read such a good analysis of human depravity as that by Gerard Zerbolt, the librarian at the house of the Brethren at Deventer. One must not hastily jump at the conclusion that Luther did not know what he was saying when he referred to Gansfort and Zerbolt. Erasmus and Melanchthon made similar testimonies. It would seem incredible that all three of these keen thinkers were confused in this matter.

Gansfort developed ideas which powerfully affected Erasmus, Melanchthon, Zwingli, and Luther. He derived these ideas from his contact with the Brethren of the Common Life. But whereas his teachers at Zwolle were content to remain orthodox, Gansfort definitely broke with the theology of the chief leaders in the Roman Catholic Church. At the same time he did also cling to some doctrines which Luther and Zwingli rejected.

BIBLIOGRAPHY: E. Miller and J. W. Scudder, *Wessel Gansfort: His Life and Writings,* 2 vols., 1917; M. van Rhijn, *Wessel Gansfort,* 1917; Albert Hyma, *The Christian Renaissance: A History of the "Devotio Moderna,"* 1924.

[Sup. to WESSEL, JOHANN.] ALBERT HYMA.

GARBETT, CYRIL FORSTER: Archbishop of York; b. Feb. 6, 1875. He studied at Keble College, Oxford (B.A., 1898; M.A., 1902). Ordained a deacon in 1899 and a priest in 1901, he served in the church at Portsea (1899–1919); Portsmouth (1915–19); and as dean of Southwark (1919–32). He was consecrated bishop of Southwark, Oct. 18, 1919, where he served until translated to Winchester in 1932. Ten years later he became archbishop of York (1942–). With all of his administrative duties he has written widely such books as: *The Church and Modern Problems* (1911); *The Challenge of the King* (1915); *The Work of a Great Parish* (1919); *After the War* (1924); *Authority, Obedience and Reservation* (1925); *Secularism and Christian Unity* (1929); *In the Heart of South London* (1931); *The Challenge of the Slums*

(1933); *A Call to Christians* (1935); *The Church and Social Problems in Peace and War* (1940); *We Would See Jesus* (1941); *Physician, Heal Thyself* (1945); *The Christian Churches and International Peace* (1945); *The Claims of the Church of England* (1947); *Watchman, What of the Night?* (1948) and *Church and State in England* (1950).

RAYMOND W. ALBRIGHT.

GARDINER, STEPHEN: Like many other members of the higher clergy in his day, he received a humanistic education, which as a rule was accompanied by an irenic temperament. He had much respect for the civil government, but in his opinion the laws of the spiritual world and conscience were of a higher order. Nevertheless, he was willing to co-operate very fully with the civil authorities. He resembled his colleagues Tunstall and Bonner in his desire to acquiesce in the policies of King Henry VIII (*q.v.*) and to recognize the primacy of the latter in the church. He argued that the pope enjoyed merely the *primatus honoris,* while the king had the *primatus iurisdictionis.* In this manner he supported the king in his divorce proceedings. He and his colleagues reasoned that by giving up the papal supremacy in the Church of England they could withstand the onslaughts of Lutheranism from Germany and thus protect the purity of the Roman Catholic faith in their country. Three other well-known bishops, Cranmer, Barlow, and Latimer (*q.v.*), were ready to make a more common cause with the Lutherans. They got their chance in the reign of Edward VI (*q.v.*) (1547–53), but they then turned toward Calvinism, which was more radical. The contrast between the two large parties: Henricians and Cranmerians, can be seen in the polemical treatises by Gardiner, in which he opposed Cranmer. The contradictory passages in the First Prayer Book (1549) he explained in the orthodox Roman Catholic sense. In the version of 1552 those passages were eliminated. As Lord Chancellor under Mary Tudor (*q.v.*) he tried to heal the breach with Rome, for the events of the past few years had shown him that this breach could not be squared with orthodox Catholicism, which he favored above all things.

BIBLIOGRAPHY: S. Gardiner, *Letters,* ed. by J. A. Muller, 1933; idem, *Obedience in Church and State,* ed. by P. Janelle, 1936; J. A. Muller, *Stephen Gardiner and the Tudor Reaction,* 1926; G. Constant, *La Réforme en Angleterre,* Vol. II, 1939; L. B. Smith, *Tudor Prelates and Politics 1536–1558,* 1953.

[Sup.] MATHIAS GOOSSENS.

GARRARD, LANCELOT AUSTIN: Unitarian; b. at Skelbrooke, Yorks., May 31, 1904. Studied at the universities of Oxford (B.A., 1927; M.A., 1930; B.D., 1935) and Marburg. He was minister at the Unitarian Church, Dover (1932–33); Lewin's Mead, Bristol (1941–43);

Ancient Chapel of Toxteth, Liverpool (since 1943); Tutor at Manchester College, Oxford (1933–43); Unitarian College, Manchester (1945–51); editor of *The Hibbert Journal* since 1951. He wrote: *Duty and the Will of God* (1938); and *The Interpreted Bible* (1948).

GARRISON, WILLIAM LLOYD: Editor of *The Liberator* and the most important leader of the abolition crusade; b. in Newburyport, Mass., Dec. 10, 1805, the son of an intemperate sea captain who with his wife had emigrated from Nova Scotia to the United States; d. May 24, 1879. When his father deserted the family, William was placed in the home of a Deacon Bartlett who apprenticed him to the editor of the Newburyport *Herald,* where he learned the printer's trade and began to write anonymously for the paper. In 1826 he started a paper of his own, *The Free Press,* in which appeared the earliest poems of John Greenleaf Whittier, who became a lifelong friend. When the paper failed Garrison became a journeyman printer and eventually came into contact with a Quaker, Benjamin Lundy, who turned his attention to the evils of slavery, and they became associated in the publication in Baltimore of a weekly, *Genius of Universal Emancipation.* This marked the beginning of Garrison's advocacy of the immediate emancipation of slaves, which he made the central theme of *The Liberator,* established in Boston in 1831, and which he continued to edit until 1865. He was the founder of the American Anti-slavery Society and served as its president for twenty-two years. He represented the most radical of the antislavery advocates, but was an instigator rather than a leader.

BIBLIOGRAPHY: Lindsay Swift, *William Lloyd Garrison,* 1911, is the best brief biography. *William Lloyd Garrison, 1805–1879: The Story of his Life told by his Children,* 4 vols., 1885–90, is extremely laudatory.

WILLIAM WARREN SWEET.

GARRISON, WINFRED ERNEST: Disciples of Christ; b. St. Louis, Mo., Oct. 1, 1874. He studied at Eureka College (A.B., 1892); Yale (A.B., 1894); Chicago (B.D., and Ph.D., 1897). He was associate in history, Chicago (1897–98); professor of church history and Hebrew, Butler College (1898-1900; president 1904-6); president, New Mexico Normal University, Las Vegas (1907–8); president, New Mexico State College, Las Cruces (1908–13); headmaster and proprietor, Claremont School for Boys, Claremont, Calif. (1913–21); associate professor, then professor of church history, University of Chicago and Disciples Divinity House (1921–43; emeritus 1943–); literary editor of *The Christian Century* (1923–); president, New Mexico Educational Association, 1909–10; president, American Society of Church History, 1927–28; president, Disciples of Christ Historical Society, 1946–50; associate at Life and Work Conference, Oxford, 1937; delegate to Faith and Order Conference, Edinburgh, 1937; consultant at World Council of Churches Assembly, Amsterdam, 1948. Member of Faith and Order Commission, Theological Commission on the Church, and American Theological Committee. Member of New Mexico Constitutional Convention, 1910. He is the author of: *Wheeling Through Europe* (1900); *Alexander Campbell's Theology* (1900); *Catholicism and the American Mind* (1928); *Affirmative Religion* (1928); *Religion Follows the Frontier* (1931); *The March of Faith, Religion in America since 1865* (1933); *Intolerance* (1934); *An American Religious Movement* (1945); *Religion and Civil Liberty* (1946); *Disciples of Christ, Whence and Whither* (1948); (with A. T. DeGroot), *Disciples of Christ, A History* (1948); ed. (with T. C. Clark), *100 Poems of Peace* (1934); (with T. C. Clark), *100 Poems of Immortality* (1935); *Faith of the Free* (1940).

GARSTANG, JOHN: B. 1876. He was a mathematical scholar at Jesus College, Oxford (1895–99; also M.A., D.Sc.; C.B.E.). After serving as an honorary reader in Egyptian archaeology at Liverpool (1902), he taught the methods and practice of archeology (1907–41). Since 1897 he has also been engaged in archeological research, conducting excavations on Roman sites in Britain, in Egypt, Nubia, Asia Minor, and North Syria (1900–08); in the Sudan at Meroë (1909–14); and in Palestine at Askalon (1920–21) and Jericho (1930–36). He served as the director of the British School of Archeology in Jerusalem (1919–26) and directed the department of antiquities for the government of Palestine (1920–26). His publications include: *Roman Ribchester; El Arâbeh; Mahâsna and Bêt Khallâf; The 3rd Egyptian Dynasty; Burial Customs of Ancient Egypt; The Land of the Hittites; Meroë* (1911); *The Hittite Empire* (1929); *The Foundations of Bible History; Joshua, Judges* (1931); *The Heritage of Solomon* (1934); and *Reports on the Excavations of Abydos, Meroë, Jericho and Mersin* in the Liverpool *Annals of Archeology* (1908–40).

RAYMOND W. ALBRIGHT.

GASPARRI, PIETRO: Cardinal; b. at Capovallazza, prov. Macerata, Italy, May 5, 1852; d. at Rome, Nov. 18, 1934. He studied at the *Seminario Romano*, and was ordained in 1877. He taught canon law at Rome and Paris, and held various charges in the Vatican diplomacy. A cardinal (since 1907), he headed the Commission for the Codification of Canon Law. Secretary of State under Benedict XV and Pius XI, he prepared the accords of the Lateran between the Vatican and Italy (1929). In 1930, he published the *Catechismus Romanus,* as a model for the reduction of diocesan catechisms.

BIBLIOGRAPHY: F. M. Taliani, *Vita del cardinale Gasparri, segretario di Stato e povero prete,* 1938.
GEORGES A. BARROIS.

GAVIN, FRANK STANTON BURNS: Episcopalian; b. Cincinnati, Ohio, Oct. 31, 1890; d. New York, March 20, 1938. He was trained at University of Cincinnati, Hebrew Union College, General Theological Seminary, Columbia University (Ph.D., 1923), and Harvard University (Th.D., 1919). Gavin was a novice in the Society of St. John the Evangelist (1916–21); taught New Testament at Nashotah House, Wisc. (1921–23); and church history at General Seminary (1923–38). From a year in Athens came *Some Aspects of Contemporary Greek Orthodox Thought* (1923). He published *Aphraates and the Jews* (1923); *Jewish Antecedents of the Christian Sacraments* (1928); *Seven Centuries of the Problem of Church and State* (1938); edited *Liberal Catholicism and the Modern World* (1934).

BIBLIOGRAPHY: *American Church Monthly,* May 1938.
EDWARD ROCHIE HARDY.

GAY LECTURES: Established at the Southern Baptist Theological Seminary, Louisville, Ky., by the Rev. W. D. Gay in memory of his father, Julius Brown Gay. No subject is specified by the endowment.

GEHMAN, HENRY SNYDER: Presbyterian, U. S. A.; b. June 1, 1888, Ephrata Twp., Lancaster Co., Pa. He studied at Franklin and Marshall College (A.B., 1909; A.M., 1910); University of Pennsylvania (Ph.D., 1913); and the Philadelphia Divinity School (S.T.B., 1926; S.T.D., 1927). He was founder and pastor of Tabor Reformed Church, Philadelphia (1917–21). He is professor of Old Testament literature in Princeton Theological Seminary and lecturer in Semitic languages, Princeton University. He has written: *The Interpreters of Foreign Languages among the Ancients* (1914); *The Sahidic and the Bohairic Versions of the Book of Daniel* (1927); *Some Present-Day Values of Old Testament Studies* (1934); *Translation of the Peta-Vatthu from Pali into English* (1942); and was editor-in-chief of Old Testament section of Westminster Study Edition of the *Holy Bible* (1948); editor of Commentary on *Books of Kings* (J. A. Montgomery), International Critical Commentary (1951); joint editor, *Scheide Biblical Papyri—Ezekiel* (1938).

GEILER, JOHANN, OF KAISERSBERG: As a child of his time he shared in the witch hunt and the hatred of the Jews. His sermons were more moralizing than dogmatic. His greatest fault consisted in his extreme and merciless sarcasm, with the accompanying lack of real love and charity. Because of this unsympathetic approach to human frailities and folly his success was only moderate. For posterity his significance lies mostly in the wealth of data which he presented in his sermons. These facts provide much source material for cultural history.

BIBLIOGRAPHY: *Lexikon fuer Theologie und Kirche*, IV (1932), 340–341.

[Sup.] MATHIAS GOOSSENS.

GELASIUS I: cf. article by J. F. X. Murphy "Gelasius I" in *The Catholic Encyclopedia*, 1909; article by W. H. V. Reade in *The Cambridge Medieval History*, Vol. VI, 1929; Philip V. Bagan, *The Syntax of the Letters of Pope Gelasius I*, 1945. See also CANON OF SCRIPTURE, Vol. II, A (6).

[Sup.] JAMES M. BULMAN.

GEMEINSCHAFTSBEWEGUNG: A pietistic movement among German Protestants which has two roots. One goes back to small circles of awakened believers who gathered around the Bible in Wuerttemberg, the lower Rhine, parts of Westphalia, and elsewhere. The other root extends to England. German theologians like Theodor Christlieb (*q.v.*, Vol. III) visited the holiness conferences in Brighton and Oxford and on their return introduced ideas of evangelism into the small circles of the awakened. In 1888 an initiating conference was held in Gnadau to discuss questions of felowship, evangelism, lay activity, and holiness. Such conferences were then held biennially, later annually. Gradually the circles of the awakened in various provinces formed councils, and in 1898 these merged to form the German Alliance for the Cultivation of Fellowship and Evangelism, often called the *Gnadauer Verband*. In 1952 there were 6,000 circles of the awakened, 700 seminary-trained preachers, and 5,000 lay preachers. The movement regards itself as functioning independently within Protestant Churches. It attempts to gather church members who are in earnest about being Christians, deepen their knowledge and experience of the Bible, and help them to express their faith in activity. In addition to their own meeting houses, private homes and church buildings are sometimes used for assemblies.

BIBLIOGRAPHY: Andrew L. Drummond, *German Protestantism since Luther*, 1951.

THEOPHIL BARTELS.

GENESIS, BOOK OF. See PENTATEUCH.

GENETICS. See HEREDITY.

GERARD APPELMANS: About his life little is known. From the only extant manuscript concerning him we gather that he lived between 1250 and 1350, and that he was a hermit. He received a sound theological training and before he became a hermit he probably belonged to a religious order. With his *Glose op den*

Pater noster (*Glossary on the Lord's Prayer*) he reached one of the highest levels of mystic literature. He wrote from his own experiences, establishing a perfect synthesis of speculation and personal living experience. His method of turning inward reminds the reader of St. Augustine, while his emphasis upon the intellectual element in the mystical process points to the influence of the pseudo-Dionysius. His theology is Trinitarian and Christocentric. Striking is the admirable expression and formulation of thought in this very ancient Germanic work. See also MYSTICISM AND ASCETICISM IN THE NETHERLANDS.

BIBLIOGRAPHY: L. Reypens, S.J., "Gheraert Appelmans' Glose op het Vaderons," in *Ons Geestelijk Erf*, I (1927), 81–107; *idem*, "Een nieuw merkwaardig Duitsch mystiek," OGE, I, 113–141.

M. M. J. SMITS VAN WAESBERGHE.

GERHARDT, MARTIN: Lutheran; b. at Berlin, Germany, Dec. 1, 1894; d. at Cologne, Germany, May 27, 1952. He studied at the universities of Berlin (Lic. Theol., 1922), Tuebingen and Erlangen (Dr. Phil., 1924). He was lecturer at Erlangen University (1922); archivist of the "Rauhes Haus" at Hamburg (1923–31); established the Wichern archives and edited the youth diaries of Wichern (*Der junge Wichern*) and *The Inner Mission* (*Die Innere Mission*), a memorandum to the German Evangelical Church by J. Hinrich Wichern. From 1931 to 1937 he was archivist of the Kaiserswerth Deaconess-Institution and established the Fliedner archives and the special library on deaconess service. In 1937 he was appointed professor of church history at Goettingen University with an interruption (1940–45) for army service in Norway. He wrote: *Johann Hinrich Wichern* (3 vols., 1926–31); *Theodor Fliedner* (2 vols., 1933–37); *Norwegische Geschichte* (1942); *Ein Jahrhundert Innere Mission* (1948); (with Prof. Hubatsch) *Deutschland und Skandinavien im Wandel der Jahrhunderte* (1950); *Friedrich von Bodelschwingh* (1st vol., 1950; 2nd vol., 1952).

GERLEMAN, JOHN GILLIS HARRY: B. in Rogberga, Småland, Mar. 27, 1912. He was educated at Lund University (Lic. Th., 1941; Th.D., 1943). Ordained in 1943, he became instructor in biblical exegesis at Lund University that same year; professor (1949). Among his works are: *Zephanja textkritisch und literarisch untersucht* (1942); *Studies in the Septuagint I-II* (1946); *Synoptic Studies in the Old Testament* (1948).

ELMER E. FLACK.

GERMAN ALLIANCE FOR THE CULTIVATION OF FELLOWSHIP AND EVANGELISM. See GEMEINSCHAFTSBEWEGUNG.

GERMAN CHRISTIANS, FAITH MOVEMENT OF. See GERMANY, I.

GERMAN EVANGELICAL PROTESTANT CHURCH. See EVANGELICAL PROTESTANT CHURCH OF NORTH AMERICA.

GERMAN EVANGELICAL SYNOD OF NORTH AMERICA. See EVANGELICAL SYNOD OF NORTH AMERICA.

GERMANY THEOLOGY. See FRIENDS OF GOD.

GERMANY: Church and state were separated (1919) under the Weimar Republic, and accordingly the churches in Germany adopted new constitutions (1919–24) which provided for self-government. Since 1919 there have been no state churches in Germany.

I. Evangelical Churches: In 1922 the German Evangelical Church Federation, representing 62.7% of the total population, was formed by the territorial churches for the discussion of common interests. Although it had little authority, the federation encouraged co-operation among the churches.

Even before Adolf Hitler assumed power in 1933 the so-called "German Christians" made their appearance. Never a unified movement, these extremists arose in Prussia and Thuringia, and from there spread. With theological liberalism (q.v.) they combined anti-Semitism (q.v.) and extreme nationalism (q.v.), and they soon claimed to be representatives of National Socialism in the churches. A committee of the Church Federation, appointed to negotiate with the state and with the German Christians, proposed the formation of a national Evangelical Church and nominated Friedrich von Bodelschwingh as the first imperial bishop. Although acceptable to the territorial churches, he was not acceptable to the German Christians, whose candidate, Ludwig Mueller, was elected with the help of National Socialist propaganda when the German Evangelical Church was created in September, 1933. As a result German Christians gained control of some churches, especially in Prussia, Mecklenburg, Thuringia, and Hesse.

By 1934 it had become more evident that the German Christians were distorting the gospel and were intent on making the church a political instrument. Church youth was alienated by the Hitler Youth organization. Faithful pastors were suspended from office but had to be reinstated when their congregations supported them. Resistance began with the formation of the Pastors' Emergency Federation under the leadership of Martin Niemoeller (q.v.) and the meeting of the first Synod of the Confessing Church in Barmen in May, 1934. In the face of threats from National Socialism and from the German Christians, a theological declaration was adopted in Barmen according to which Jesus Christ is the only Word of God that men

are to hear, trust, and obey; the suggestion that there might be any source for the church's proclamation other than revelation was condemned. Although, as later became apparent, the declaration allowed of various interpretations by Lutherans and Reformed, it was a timely and effective utterance. The Barmen Synod also rejected the leadership of Ludwig Mueller in the church.

The attempt was now made to bring the territorial churches into subjection to the German Evangelical Church and to make the territorial bishops submit to the imperial bishop. Bishop Marahrens, of Hanover (q.v.), protested, and soon afterward Bishop Theophil Wurm, of Wuerttemberg (q.v.), and Bishop Hans Meiser, of Bavaria (q.v.), also protested and suffered temporary arrest. In October, 1934, the second Confessing Synod met in Dahlem and declared the Confessing Church to be the legal church administration in the emergency. The following month the leaders of three "intact churches" —so-called because their leadership remained unaffected by National Socialist and German Christian infiltration—united with councils of the Confessing Church in other provinces to establish a "provisional church administration" for the German Evangelical Church. Although acknowledged by the clergy and congregations, this *Vorlaeufige Kirchenleitung* did not secure state recognition.

In 1935, before the third synod of the Confessing Church met in Augsburg, the National Socialist state intervened more directly in church affairs. It assumed greater financial control. It also transferred legal cases which involved the churches from civil courts to the government's Ministry of Cultus, which henceforth made objective judgments impossible. With the establishment of a Ministry for Church Affairs the government attempted to pacify the churches. There was no agreement in the Confessing Church concerning co-operation with the new ministry, and at its synod in Oeynhausen in February, 1936, the Confessing Church established another *Vorlaeufige Kirchenleitung*. The Lutherans now formed a Council of the Evangelical Lutheran Church in Germany (*Lutherrat*) and, as a consequence, the earlier unity in the Confessing Church ceased (see LUTHERAN CHURCH IN GERMANY, UNITED EVANGELICAL).

Relations between the state and the Evangelical churches became increasingly difficult when, in 1936, anti-ecclesiastical propaganda was sharpened. Leading churchmen were prevented by the Gestapo from preaching. The sending of delegates to the ecumenical conferences in Edinburgh and Oxford (see ECUMENICAL MOVEMENT) was forbidden. Measures were introduced to curtail the jurisdiction of the churches over their own finances. After Niemoeller's arrest (July, 1937) another attempt was made to reconcile differences with the state (the *Gremium* of Cassel), but it proved fruitless. There was now no doubt that the National Socialist state was interested, not in protecting the church, but in harassing and ultimately destroying it. New arrests, deportations, and attacks followed in 1938 and 1939. The training of theological students and the gathering of offerings became difficult. Every fresh attempt to reach a settlement failed.

With the beginning of World War II a Confidential Council of the Clergy (*Vertrauensrat*), headed by Bishop Marahrens, was formed (1939) to provide leadership for the churches during the war. Although its utterances, under pressure of circumstances, were not always blameless, it had the courage to present grievances to the state: against euthanasia (*q.v.*) (1940), against reducing the church in Poland (*q.v.*) to the status of a secular society (1941), against the hostility of National Socialism to the churches (1942), against the expropriation of church funds and the persecution of Jews (1943). Meanwhile the work of the churches was made to suffer. Approximately 45% of the clergy were called to military service, leaving parish work to the old and weak. State and party observances were arranged to interfere with church services. After 1940 no paper was permitted for printing Bibles, and after 1941 most other religious publication was stopped. The work of chaplains in the armed forces was systematically sabotaged, and inner mission activity was impeded.

At the close of the war Bishop Wurm summoned leaders of the territorial churches to a meeting in Treysa in August, 1945. There the German Evangelical Church and its constitution were abandoned. In preparation for the formation of a new Evangelical Church in Germany (EKD), a council of twelve members, headed by Wurm, was appointed. This council created *Evangelisches Hilfswerk* (*q.v.*) as a relief agency and, at its second meeting, adopted the Stuttgart Declaration on war guilt. This declaration not only helped to restore relations between German churches and Protestant churches outside of Germany; it also sharpened the conscience of the German people, summoned them to repentance, and showed them the way to inner reconstruction.

It was not until July, 1948, that the constitution for EKD was adopted in Eisenach. The constitution declared EKD a federation of Lutheran, Reformed, and Union territorial churches. Its powers are limited to ecumenical relations, works of mercy, and such other activities as the member churches may commit to it. It has a Council of twelve members, a Conference in which each member church has one vote, and a Synod of 120 members which normally meets annually. The executive offices (*Kirchenkanzlei*) are in Hanover. Bishop Otto Dibelius, of Berlin, was elected first president of the Council. The formation of EKD brought the emergency government of the Confessing Church to an end and was accompanied, between 1945 and 1948, by the reorganization of the territorial churches (see BADEN; BAVARIA; BREMEN; BRUNSWICK; EUTIN; HAMBURG; HANOVER; HESSE; LIPPE; MECKLENBURG; OLDENBURG; POMERANIA; PRUSSIA; RHINELAND; SAXONY; SCHLESWIG-HOLSTEIN; SILESIA; THURINGIA; WESTPHALIA; WUERTTEMBERG).

The postwar period was marked by new activity within the churches. Besides the establishment of *Evangelisches Hilfswerk* (*q.v.*) and the reactivation of inner mission agencies, Evangelical Academies (*q.v.*) were founded to reach the churched and unchurched. Reinold von Thadden developed lay activity through the German Evangelical Church Diet (*Kirchentag*), youth movements (*q.v.*) and women's organizations resumed their work, and missionaries (see ORPHANED MISSIONS) began to depart for service in foreign fields.

In 1950 the Evangelical Churches embraced 51% of the population in western Germany, 80% in eastern Germany. In relation to Roman Catholics, two-thirds of the Germans were Protestants.

II. Free Churches: There are independent churches in Germany which represent, all together, about half of 1% of the total population. Some are made up of people who withdrew from territorial churches without changing their confession: Lutheran Free Churches, 70,000 members; Reformed Free Churches, 8,000 members. There are about 10,000 Moravians (*q.v.*) and 17,000 Mennonites (*q.v.*). In addition, religious bodies were formed as a result of evangelization, especially from America: 62,000 Baptists (*q.v.*); 60,000 Methodists (*q.v.*); 12,000 Evangelical United Brethren (*q.v.*); 32,000 Adventists (*q.v.*). Christian Scientists (*q.v.*) and Jehovah's Witnesses (*q.v.*) have engaged in active propaganda, but their numbers are not known. There are 24,000 Old Catholics (*q.v.*), 48,000 Eastern Orthodox, 17,000 adherents of Judaism (*q.v.*).

III. Roman Catholics: In 1933 Roman Catholics represented 32.5% of the population of Germany. They sustained losses to Protestantism and to the world (see KIRCHENAUSTRITT; LOS VON ROM), but they were in some respects better prepared than Protestants to meet National Socialism; they had an authoritative head outside of Germany in the pope, and they had long experience in a Catholic political party (see CENTER PARTY), which, however, was disbanded in 1933. A concordat of 1933 seemed to secure Catholic liberty within the new totalitarian state, but friction quickly arose over schools, financial practices, monasteries, and youth organizations. Some churchmen, like Cardinal Theodor Innitzer, of Austria, seemed to support National Socialism at first, while others, like Cardinal Michael Faulhaber, became strong resistance leaders. The common peril which Protestants and Catholics faced drew them closer together, and inter-faith conversations as well as co-operation continued after World War II.

In 1950 Catholics represented 45% of the population in western Germany, 17% in eastern Germany, or about one-third of the total German population.

Despite the open hostility to Christianity in the preceding decades, 96.3% of all Germans counted themselves Christians in 1950, according to the census of that year.

BIBLIOGRAPHY: Johannes Schneider and Joachim Beckmann, eds., *Kirchliches Jahrbuch*, annually except for interruptions caused by war, 1910–1951; Andrew L. Drummond, *German Protestantism since Luther*, 1951, an anecdotal survey, not always trustworthy; Stewart Herman, *It's Your Souls We Want*, 1943; idem, *The Rebirth of the German Church*, 1946; T. S. K. Scott-Craig, tr., *Germany's New Religion: the German Faith Movement*, 1937; Heinrich Hermelink, *Kirche im Kampf: Dokumente des Widerstands*, 1950; Walter Kuenneth, *Der grosse Abfall*, 1947; Johannes Neuheusler, *Kreuz und Hakenkreuz: der Kampf des Nationalsozialismus gegen die katholische Kirche*, 2 vols., 1946; Nathaniel Micklem, *National Socialism and the Roman Catholic Church*, 1939.

[Sup.] HEINZ BRUNOTTE.

GERONTOLOGY. See AGED, CARE OF THE.

GERSON, JOHN (JEAN): His importance in the history of the medieval church and of Western civilization is now considered so great that in the sixth volume of the encyclopedia issued by the Vatican staff in 1951 the article devoted to him was signed by three distinguished scholars: A. Combes, L. Mourin, and F. Simone (see cols. 185–191). Gerson is eulogized as one of the leading mystics in European history, besides a great educator, a prominent diplomat, an eloquent preacher, and a profound philosopher. That is the reason why he was often called the author of *The Imitation of Christ* (*q.v.*), as numerous fifteenth-century manuscripts and printed editions indicate. One recent book is devoted solely to the pedagogical work performed by Gerson in helping educate the dauphins of France, and another to his mysticism (*q.v.*). Combes in 1948 published an imposing volume on Gerson's reaction to Ruysbroeck's (*q.v.*) celebrated work, *On the Spiritual Marriage* (*De ornatu spiritualium nuptiarum*), and C. Schaeffer in 1935 devoted an admirable monograph to Gerson's political ideas. When in 1928 J. L. Connolly's biography of Gerson appeared (*John Gerson: Reformer and Mystic*), it seemed quite adequate. But André Combes indicated that Connolly had overlooked some significant Latin sources. Particularly useful is the recent study by P. Glorieux, published in 1951.

BIBLIOGRAPHY: D. G. Barron, *Jean Charlier de Gerson, the Author of the De Imitatione Christi*, 1936; G. U. Yule, *The Statistical Study of Literary Vocabulary*, Part III, 1944 (deals with the vocabulary of the *De Imitatione*

Christi and the works of Gerson); A. Hyma, *Renaissance to Reformation* (1951), pp. 79, 95–98, 135–136; idem, *Christianity and Politics* (1938), Chap. II; J. N. Figgis, *Studies of Political Thought from Gerson to Grotius 1414–1625*, 2nd ed., 1916; D. H. Carnahan, *The Ad Deum Vadit of Jean Gerson*, 1917; H. Dacremont, *Gerson*, 1929; P. Glorieux, "La vie et les oeuvres de Gerson," in *Archives d'histoire et littéraraire du Moyen Age*, XVIII (1950–51); J. Stelzenberger, *Die Mystik des Johannes Gerson*, 1928; W. Dress, *Die Theologie Gersons*, 1931.

[Sup.] ALBERT HYMA.

GERSTENMAIER, EUGEN: Lutheran; b. at Kirchheim Teck, Wuerttemberg, Aug. 25, 1906. He studied at the universities of Tuebingen, Rostock, and Zurich. He wrote: *Kirche, Volk und Staat* (1936) and *Die Kirche und die Schoepfung* (1938). On July 20, 1944, he was arrested by the Gestapo for participation in a plot against Hitler. He was founder (1945) and director (1945–) of Das Hilfswerk der Evangelischen Kirchen in Deutschland, Stuttgart; from 1948 CDU (Christian Democratic Union) member of the Bonn parliament (Bundestag); German delegate to the Council of Europe (1950–).

GERTRUDE OF NIVELLES: Saint, virgin, abbess O.S.B.; b. in 631; d. on March 17, 659. She was a daughter of Pippin of Landen and St. Iduberga, and a sister of St. Begga, abbess of Andenna. She refused a rich marriage and entered the convent of Nivelles in Brabant, founded by St. Amand and by her mother. In 652 she became the abbess of this convent. She excelled in charity and other virtues, especially by her knowledge of the Holy Scripture. In the Netherlands, England, and a part of Germany, she had an intense cult. Many churches took her name (Nijmegen, Geertruidenberg). She was invoked against vexation of mice and rats, and therefore she is represented in art with some of these animals.

BIBLIOGRAPHY: *Acta SS.Martii*, II, 594–596; 3rd ed., 592–594; Jos. Rijckel, *Vita S. Gertrudis*, 1632.

WILLIBRORD LAMPEN.

GEZER. See ARCHAEOLOGY, BIBLICAL.

GEZORK, HERBERT: Baptist; b. at Insterburg, Germany, June 15, 1900. He studied at University of Berlin; Divinity School in Hamburg; Southern Baptist Theological Seminary, Louisville (Ph.D., 1930). He was associate minister, First Baptist Church, Berlin (1925–28); general secretary, German Baptist Youth Movement (1930–34); professor of religion, Furman University, Greenville, S. C. (1937–38); professor of social ethics, Andover Newton Theological School (1939–50); lecturer, Wellesley College, (1939–50); Chief of Evangelical Affairs, U. S. Military Government in Germany (1946–48); president, Andover Newton Theological School since 1950. He wrote: *Die Gottlosenbewegung* (1932); *So Sah Ich die Welt* (in German, Dutch, Finnish, 1933).

GHÉON, HENRI: Pseudonym of Vangeon, Leon; Roman Catholic; b. at Bray-sur-Marne, France, March 15, 1875; d. 1944. He promoted a revival of the Christian theater in the spirit of the medieval scenic plays, through the following manifestos: *Nos directions* (1911); *L'homme né de la guerre* (1919); *Parti pris* (1924). His religious dramas usually borrow their theme from the legends of the saints, as, for instance, *Le comédien et la grâce; Les trois miracles de Sainte Cécile; Saint Maurice ou l'obéissance.* He wrote also hagiographic fragments and a few poems of mystical inspiration.

GEORGES A. BARROIS.

GIBBONS, JAMES: D. Mar. 24, 1921. For more than thirty-three years Cardinal Gibbons headed the Roman Catholic Diocese of Baltimore and was ranking head of the church in America. His last published work was *A Retrospect of Fifty Years* (1917).

BIBLIOGRAPHY: Tracy Ellis, *Cardinal James Gibbons,* 2 vols., 1952.

[Sup.] RAYMOND W. ALBRIGHT.

GIBRALTAR: Fortress town on the Spanish side of the Straits of Gibraltar, British possession since 1713. Gibraltar has a unique ecclesiastical as well as political status. The local population (about 17,000) is largely of Italian origin and Roman Catholic; in 1806 Gibraltar was made a Vicariate Apostolic, and in 1910 a diocese directly subject to the Holy See. The Church of the Holy Trinity, built in Moorish style in 1825, is the cathedral of the Anglican diocese of Gibraltar, established in 1842, with jurisdiction over the English churches and chaplaincies in southern Europe. The first bishop, George Tomlinson, was active in reopening communications between the Church of England and the Eastern Churches, and several other distinguished scholars and missionaries have occupied the see.

BIBLIOGRAPHY: E. B. Buckle, *Especially William* [Collins] *Bishop of Gibraltar and Mary his Wife,* 1911.

EDWARD ROCHIE HARDY.

GIDEONS INTERNATIONAL, THE: A society founded in 1899 for the purpose of placing Bibles, without cost, in such public places as hotels, hospitals, prisons, and schools. There were about 16,000 members in 1953.

THEODORE G. TAPPERT.

GIFFORD, WILLIAM ALVA: United Church of Canada; b. at Ottawa, Ontario, Oct. 31, 1877. He studied at University of Toronto (B.A., 1904); Victoria College, Toronto (B.D., 1907); Harvard University (S.T.M., 1913; Th.D., 1915). He was professor of ecclesiastical history, United Theological College, Montreal (1915–49). He wrote: *John Wesley, Patriot and Statesman*

(1922); *The Eternal Quest* (1939); and *The Story of the Faith* (1946).

GILBERT DE LA PORREE: The new monograph by Williams indicates that he probably made no clear distinction (*distinctio realis*) between the divine nature and the divine persons, although many contemporaries of his claimed that he had made such a distinction. Until 1951 it had been generally assumed that the real distinction formed an essential part of his teachings.

BIBLIOGRAPHY: M. E. Williams, *The Teaching of Gilbert Porreta on the Trinity,* 1951.

[Sup.] MATHIAS GOOSSENS.

GILKEY, CHARLES W(HITNEY): Baptist; b. July 3, 1882, at Watertown, Mass. He was educated at Harvard (A.B., 1903; A.M., 1904); Union Theological Seminary (B.D., 1908); Berlin and Marburg (1908–9); and at United Free Church College, Glasgow; New College, Edinburgh; and Oxford (1909–10). He was the student secretary of the International Committee of the Y.M.C.A. (1903–5). After ordination to the Baptist ministry in 1910 he became pastor of the Hyde Park Church, Chicago (1910–28). After teaching homiletics at the Divinity School of the University of Chicago (1926–47), he became the dean of the chapel at that University (1928–47), and was associate dean of the Divinity School (1938–47). After 1948 he became lecturer on homiletics at the Andover-Newton Theological School. He has been preacher to many colleges and universities and in 1924–25 was Barrows Lecturer (*q.v.*) to university centers in India. He has written: *Jesus and Our Generation* (1925); *New Frontiers for Faith* (1926); *Present Day Dilemmas in Religion* (1927); and *Perspectives* (1933).

RAYMOND W. ALBRIGHT.

GILMORE, GEORGE WILLIAM: D. Aug. 22, 1933. He compiled the valuable index volume of the *New Schaff-Herzog Encyclopaedia;* was the associate editor of *The Homiletical Review* (1911 ff.); and wrote the following books: *Animism—Thought Currents of Primitive Peoples* (1919); *Tax Talks* (1925); edited (with Robert Scott) *The Church, the People and the Age* (1913); *Selections from the Classics of Devotion* (1916); *Cobern's Archaeological Discoveries* (1922, 1924, and archaeological supplement, 1929); and he also translated from the German *Jesus as Problem, Teacher, Personality and Force* by Bornemann, Veit, Schuster, and Foerster (1910); and *The Apostles' Creed and the New Testament* by Johannes Kunze (1912).

[Sup.] RAYMOND W. ALBRIGHT.

GILSON, ETIENNE: Roman Catholic; b. at Paris, France, June 13, 1884. He studied at the University of Paris and at the Collège de

France. He taught philosophy in various French colleges (1908–12); was professor at the University of Lille (1913–14); army officer, war cross (1914–18); professor at the University of Strasbourg (1919–22); at the University of Paris (1922–32); at the Collège de France (1932–50); at the Pontifical Institute of Mediaeval Studies in Toronto since 1951. He is primarily an historian of mediaeval philosophies and theologies and has written *Le Thomisme; La philosophie de saint Bonaventure; Jean Duns Scot; La Philosophie au moyen âge; L'esprit de la philosophie médiévale; Dante et la philosophie; Héloise et Abélard; God and Philosophy; The Unity of Philosophical Experience.* He is cofounder and coeditor of *Archives d'histoire doctrinale et littéraires du moyen âge.*

GINGERICH, MELVIN: Mennonite; b. at Kalona, Iowa, Jan. 29, 1902. He studied at Hesston College, Goshen College, University of Iowa (Ph.D., 1938) and the University of Southern California. He taught in rural schools in Iowa and Indiana; in Washington High School and Junior College, Washington, Ia. (1927–41); Bethel College (1941–47); and in Goshen College (1949–); director of research, Mennonite Research Foundation (1947–). He is the author of *The Mennonites in Iowa* (1939); *Service for Peace* (1949); *Youth and Christian Citizenship* (1949), and coeditor of *Who's Who Among the Mennonites* (1943), managing editor of *The Mennonite Quarterly Review;* managing editor of *The Mennonite Encyclopedia;* coeditor *Mennonite Historical Bulletin;* and associate editor *Mennonite Life.*

GINGRICH, FELIX WILBUR: Evangelical United Brethren Church; b. Annville, Pa., Sept. 27, 1901. He studied at Lafayette College (A.B., 1923; A.M., 1927); University of Chicago (Ph.D., 1932). He has been professor of Greek and religion at Albright College (1923– ; on leave of absence 1949–). He is associate editor, *A Greek-English Lexicon of the New Testament* (University of Chicago Press).

GINSBERG, HAROLD LOUIS: Jewish Bible scholar; b. Dec. 6, 1903, in Montreal, Can. He studied at Jews' College, University of London (B.A., 1927; Ph.D., 1930). He has taught Bible at the Jewish Theological Seminary of America since 1936, as professor since 1941. He has published *Kitbe Ugarit* (Hebrew, 1936); *The Legend of King Keret* (1946); *Studies in Daniel* (1948); *Studies in Koheleth* (1950); and collaborated in *Ancient Near Eastern Texts Relating to the Old Testament* (1950).

GIRGENSOHN, KARL: Lutheran; b. Oesel, Latvia, 1875; d. Leipzig, 1925. He taught theology at Dorpat, Estonia (1903–18), Greifswald,

Germany (1919–22), Leipzig (1922–25). He was a conservative theologian, and a leader in experimental psychology of religion. His principal works are: *Die Religion, ihre psychischen Formen und ihre Zentralidee* (1903); *Der seelische Aufbau des religiösen Erlebens* (1921).

BIBLIOGRAPHY: Autobiography in *Die Religionswissenschaft in Selbstdarstellungen,* Vol. II, 1926.
                                        OTTO A. PIPER.

GIRL SCOUTS. See SCOUTS, BOY AND GIRL.

GLADDEN, WASHINGTON: D. July 2, 1918. He served as pastor of the First Congregational Church, Columbus, O. (1882–1914; emeritus 1914–18), leading it in his later years more and more in the direction of a community church. His latest books were: *Recollections* (1909); *Present Day Theology* (1913); and *Live and Learn* (1914).
                        [Sup.] RAYMOND W. ALBRIGHT.

GLIDE FOUNDATION LECTURES: In 1942 the Glide Foundation of San Francisco, Cal., designated a sum of money for a lectureship on Christian thought and life in Asbury Theological Seminary in Wilmore, Ky. The first lecturer was E. Stanley Jones (*q.v.*) in 1943.

GLOSSOLALIA. See TONGUES, MODERN SPEAKING WITH.

GLOUBOKOVSKY, NICHOLAS: Russian Orthodox; b. at Kitchmensky Gorodok, Vologda district, Dec. 6, 1863; d. at Sofia, Bulgaria, in 1937. He studied at the Theological Seminary of Vologda and the Theological Academy of Moscow (S.T.M., 1891). He has been lecturer, and professor of the New Testament at St. Petersburg Theological Academy (1893–1918), at the University of Belgrade (1923–24) and Sofia (from 1924). The main field of his research was theology of St. Paul. In 1918 he delivered Olaus Petri lectures at the University of Uppsala. He took interest in the Ecumenical Movement (*q.v.*) and was present at the Lausanne Conference (1927). In Russia he was an active member of the commission revising the Slavonic text and translation of the New Testament. His major works are in Russian, of which two must be mentioned: *St. Theodoret of Cyrus: his life and his writings* (2 vols., 1890); *The Gospel of St. Paul* (3 vols., 1905, 1910, 1912). He was a prolific writer; in English see "Orthodoxy in its Essence," in *The Constructive Quarterly,* June, 1913. His Olaus Petri lectures are published in Swedish and Bulgarian: *Den ortodoksa kyrkan och frogan on sammanslutning mellan den kristna kyrkorna* (1921). He was editor of the *Orthodox Theological Encyclopaedia* (14 volumes to date; publication interrupted by the revolution in Russia).
                                    GEORGES FLOROVSKY.

GLOVER, TERROT REAVELEY: Baptist; b. Bristol, England, July 23, 1869; d. Cambridge, May 26, 1943. Educated at St. John's College, Cambridge, he was professor of Latin, Queen's University, Kingston, Canada (1896–1901); classical lecturer, St. John's College, Cambridge (1901–39); and public orator, University of Cambridge (1920–39). He also served as Sather Professor, University of California. He was president of the Baptist Union of Great Britain and Ireland in 1924. He wrote: *Studies in Vergil* (1904); *The Conflict of Religions in the Early Roman Empire* (1909); *The Jesus of History* (1917); *Jesus in the Experience of Men* (1921); *The Pilgrim* (1921); *Paul of Tarsus* (1925); *The Influence of Christ in the Ancient World* (1929); *The World of the New Testament* (1931); *Greek Byways* (1932); *Horace* (1932); *The Disciple* (1941); *The Challenge of the Greek* (1942); and *Cambridge Retrospect* (1943).

BIBLIOGRAPHY: H. G. Wood, *Terrot Reaveley Glover; A Biography*, 1953.

                              F. W. DILLISTONE.

GLUECK, NELSON: Jewish; b. in Cincinnati, O., June 4, 1900. He studied at the University of Cincinnati (B.A., 1920); Hebrew Union College (ordained, 1923); University of Jena (Ph.D., 1926). At the American School of Oriental Research in Jerusalem he was a graduate fellow (1927–28) and the director (1932–33; 1936–40; 1942–47). While there, he explored archaeologically all of Trans-Jordan, examining and dating more than one thousand ancient sites there. In addition he discovered King Solomon's copper mines in the Wadi Arabah, excavated King Solomon's port city of Ezion-Geber on the Red Sea and the unique Nabataean Temple of Khirbet Tannur in the central Trans-Jordan. He became professor (1928) of the Hebrew Union College, president (1947) and president of the Jewish Institute of Religion, New York City (1949), with both institutions now merged under his direction as the Hebrew Union College-Jewish Institute of Religion. His main archaeological publications are contained in the four volumes of *Explorations in Eastern Palestine* and in the more popular books, *The Other Side of the Jordan* and *The River Jordan*.

GNOSTICISM. See BASILIDES AND THE BASILIDIANS; VALENTINUS AND HIS SCHOOL.

GOCH, JOHANN VON: Was not one of the "Reformers before the Reformation." Although the titles of his books were placed on the Index promulgated by the Council of Trent, this was done largely because *De libertate Christiana* had been published in 1521 with a Preface by Cornelius Grapheus, and the first part of the *Fragmenta* was published separately under the title of *Epistola apologetica* with a letter pre-sumably composed by Martin Luther. But it is by no means certain that Luther wrote that letter, although Professor F. Pijper, the editor of the above-mentioned works in 1910, accepted Clemen's verdict. Johann von Goch probably was a leading member of the house established by the Brethren of the Common Life (*q.v.*) at Harderwijk and the rector of the house in Gouda (1452–64). On Dec. 19, 1454, he matriculated at the University of Cologne. In 1459 he arrived at Mechlin with thirteen nuns and sisters from a convent in the German town of Cleves. Since he remained in their new house until his death, it cannot be proved that he opposed monasticism, although this is generally assumed by Protestant scholars in Europe. His own writings, composed near the end of his life, do indicate adverse criticism of strict vows and too much dependence being placed upon them, but such an attitude had often been displayed before by orthodox clergymen.

BIBLIOGRAPHY: An excellent edition of his most important works, mentioned above, appeared in *Bibliotheca Reformatoria Neerlandica*, ed. by S. Cramer and F. Pijper, Vol. VI, 1910.

                     [Sup.] ALBERT HYMA.

GOD: At the close of the nineteenth century the emphasis in the doctrine of God was upon the divine immanence. This emphasis harmonized with the prevailing interest in evolution as the key to the understanding of human life. The progressive revelation of God in Scripture and in history was accepted. The kingdom of God was interpreted as being progressively realized in history by men working with God to the building of a better society. The doctrine of the universal Fatherhood of God was generally accepted, sometimes in terms that obscured the divine wrath and the necessity for the new birth.

World War I and the difficult situation in postwar Europe gave a severe shock to this easy idealism with which the twentieth century had opened. The great depression, World War II, and the world conflict with communism have deepened the sense of tension and the understanding of the seriousness of the human dilemma. The history of the concept of God in this period reflects and interprets these tensions.

About the middle of the nineteenth century Sören Kierkegaard had pointed out the chasm between the Christianity of the New Testament and the Christianity of Europe in general and of Denmark in particular. The translation of his works into German prepared the way for his influence on the men who were to found the theology of crisis. The latter first attracted world-wide attention with the publication of a commentary on Romans in 1918 by Karl Barth, in which he developed the doctrine of the unknown God, particularly against the teaching of

Schleiermacher that the task of theology is the explication of the religious consciousness. Barth asserts that there is no way to God from man, but there is a way from God to man. God is known as he makes himself known in his word. We have here the recovery of the concept of the word of God as the starting point of our knowledge of God. The Scripture is accepted as the written witness to the word of God. But the word of God is conceived in dynamic rather than in static terms. The word of God is God's manifestation of himself in history, given to a chosen people and culminating in the life, death and resurrection of Jesus Christ. The word of the Lord, given in history and witnessed to in the Scripture, becomes the word of God to us as the Holy Spirit brings the message of Scripture home to those who are willing to hear it. This doctrine of the word of the Lord is directed against the idea of a knowledge of God that is general, timeless, and non-historical, and against mysticism in the sense that the great mystics claim a direct and unmediated knowledge of God.

The theology of crisis has also been called the theology of paradox. At times, our knowledge of truth must be stated in seemingly contradictory statements. We must affirm both that God is sovereign and that man, as a responsible being, is given a limited amount of freedom. He has the freedom to hear or not to hear the word of the Lord. We say that in Jesus, God was manifest in the flesh; but we must also say that in Jesus, God was veiled in the flesh.

Barth insists that the image of God in man has been completely destroyed by sin and must be recreated by a gracious act of God before man can hear the word of God. Brunner, however, who, as against the teaching of Schleiermacher and Ritschl, has much in common with Barth, holds that the image of God in man has been marred, but not utterly destroyed. Barth proclaims a knowledge of God based on revelation alone. With Brunner there is an effort to build a bridge between the message we receive in the word of the Lord and the truth that has come to us from other sources.

Theologians of this school insist that man receives his knowledge of God as God confronts him in his word. This prepares the way for the note of crisis or decision. When God speaks man must hear or refuse to hear the word that comes to him. This means that obedience to the Word of God is the road to spiritual knowledge.

The impact of the theology of crisis has profoundly influenced the concept of God in contemporary America. Religious forces in this country are divided roughly into three groups which may be called liberals, conservatives, and fundamentalists. Liberals still hold to the doctrines of divine immanence and the Fatherhood

of God which dominated the field of theological thought at the beginning of the century. Conservative or neo-orthodox groups have accepted many of the ideas which were emphasized in the theology of crisis. Fundamentalist groups continue to perpetuate the orthodoxy of the seventeenth century.

The general result of the movement of theological thinking in the last fifty years has been to call Christian thought back from vague generalities to the revelation of God which comes to us through the Bible as the only valid source of our knowledge of God. God has revealed himself in Jesus Christ. In him we have the light of the knowledge of the glory of God. The written witness to this revelation has been preserved for us in the Bible. The Spirit who spoke through prophet and apostle bears witness in our hearts to the truth of the word of God. This word of the Lord is the only basis upon which man can build an abiding civilization.

See also APOTHEOSIS; CHRISTOLOGY; HOLY SPIRIT; IMMANENCE AND TRANSCENDENCE; INFINITE; OMNIPOTENCE; PHILOSOPHY; PROOFS OF GOD'S EXISTENCE.

[Sup.] HOLMES ROLSTON.

GODS AND GODDESSES MENTIONED IN THE OLD TESTAMENT, PAGAN: The Old Testament contains many references to pagan deities, but we know even more about them from the archaeological records. Pagan temples have been excavated at such places as Bethshan, Lachish, Megiddo, and Shechem. Occasionally images of these gods or pictures of them on stone reliefs have been recovered. But it is from the alphabetic cuneiform records of the North Canaanite temple library at ancient Ugarit, modern Ras Shamra, on the north Phoenician coast, that we learn most about them.

The chief deity of the Canaanite pantheon was Baal, the storm-god and rider on the clouds, the dying and resurrecting god, who was killed by Mot, the god of death, and bewailed by his sister consort, Anath. He lived in the recesses of the north on the sacred mountain, and under his title Baal-zephon (meaning "Lord of the North") he gave his name to the city of that name in Ex. 14:2. Such places as Baal-hazor (II Sam. 13:23), Baal-hermon (Judg. 3:3), etc., were named in his honor, and in Transjordan the Hebrews encountered him as Baal of Peor (Num. 25:1-9). He was known at Shechem as Baal-berith ("Lord of the Covenant") or El-berith ("God of the Covenant"). See Judg. 8:33; 9:4, 46. At Ekron he appears as Baal-zebul ("Lord-Prince"), reported in II Kings 1:2, 6 as Baal-zebub ("Lord of Flies"). Baal was associated with the bull, and the golden calves at Dan and Bethel reflect influence of the worship of Baal.

The father of Baal was Dagon, the grain-god and inventor of the plow. He gave his name to Beth-dagon, and the Old Testament reports temples of him at Gaza (Judg. 16:23), Ashdod (I Sam. 5:1–5), and Beth-shan (I Chron. 10:10), and his temple has been excavated at Ugarit and possibly at Beth-shan. The father of the gods and the head of the Canaanite pantheon was El, and there may be a reference to him in Isa. 14:13. In the same verse are mentioned two other gods, Helel and Sharar, the former the god of the morning star; the latter, the god of the dawn. In Ugaritic mythology Shahar has a twin named Shalem, perhaps the god of the sunset and later of prosperity and welfare. He may have been the patron deity of Shalem or Jerusalem (Gen. 14:18), the name Jerusalem meaning "Creation of Shalem." The Canaanite sun-god was Shemesh, the Babylonian Shamash, and he gave his name to Beth-shemesh. The names of other pagan gods may be reflected in the place names, as Horon, the god of the underworld, in Beth-horon or Yarikh, the moon-god, in Jericho.

Among the more important goddesses mentioned in the Old Testament are Asherah and Ashtoreth. The former at Ugarit was known as "Asherah, Lady of the Sea," and was the wife of El and mother of the gods. In the Old Testament the word "Asherah" is used sometimes as the name of the goddess, and sometimes as her symbol. It is uncertain what the Asherahs (or Asherim) were, but they certainly are not groves (KJ). The Asherah may have been a sacred pole, simulating the sacred tree, or it may have been the image of the goddess (see Ex. 34:13; Judg. 6:25–28; I Kings 15:13; II Kings 23:6, 7). For the goddess see Judg. 3:7; I Kings 18:19; II Kings 21:7. The passage I Kings 18:19 ff. refers to four hundred and fifty prophets of Baal and four hundred prophets of Asherah, in the familiar story of the ordeal on Mt. Carmel. Ashtoreth, originally Ashtareth, appears in the plural as Ashtaroth, perhaps an honorific form of her name. She gave her name to the city of Ashtaroth in northern Transjordan, in Bashan (Deut. 1:4; Josh. 9:10; etc.). She is, of course, Astarte, and the name is related to Ishtar, the wife of Tammuz. Her temple at Beth-shan, which has been excavated, appears in the story of Saul's death (I Sam. 31:10). She is called the abomination of the Sidonians (I Kings 11:5). See also Judg. 2:13, 10:6. She was the goddess of the evening star. In the Egyptian records she is coupled with Anath, another important Canaanite goddess, the wife of Baal at Ugarit. Another goddess, Ashimah, worshiped by the people of Hamath (II Kings 17:30), may be mentioned in Amos 8:14 (RSV).

We should also mention Chemosh, the chief deity of the Moabites (I Kings 11:7; Num. 21:29; Jer. 48:46). There was Molech or Mil-com (i.e., "Melek," meaning "King"), the god of the Ammonites (I Kings 11:5, 33; Jer. 49:1; Zeph. 1:5), probably like Hadad-rimmon of Palestine and Damascus (Zech. 12:11); II Kings 5:18), a form of Baal. There were also the teraphim or household gods (Gen. 31:19 ff., 35:2–4; Judg. 17:4 ff.; Ezek. 21:21). The bronze serpent Nehushtan seems to have been worshiped as a god (II Kings 18:4).

A number of deities, like Tammuz, were imported. Amos 5:26 refers to Kaiwan and Sakkuth (Chiun and Sikkuth), known to us from the cuneiform sources, and associated with the planet Saturn. So also Nergal, the Babylonian god who ruled the underworld in II Kings 17:30, while Bel (= Marduk), the great god of Babylonia, the sun-god, and his son, the scribe of the gods, Nebo (Nabu) are found in Isa. 46:1. For Bel see also Dan. 4:8. Among the gods worshiped by aliens imported into Israel at the fall of Samaria were Succothbenoth, Nibhaz, Tartak, Adrammelech, and Anammelech.

Finally, there was the worship of the heavenly bodies mentioned in a number of passages in the Old Testament, as in II Kings 17:16; 21:3, 5; 23:4, 5; Jer. 8:2; 19:13; Zeph. 1:5. Deuteronomy forbids the worship of the sun, moon, and stars (4:19, 17:3). See also the reference to the queen of heaven in Jer. 44:17, 19, perhaps Anath or Astarte.

BIBLIOGRAPHY: W. C. Graham and H. G. May, *Culture and Conscience* (1936), pp. 100–139; W. F. Albright, *Archaeology and the Religion of Israel* (1942), pp. 68–94; C. Gordon, *Ugaritic Literature*, 1949; T. H. Gaster, *Thespis*, 1950.

HERBERT G. MAY.

GOEBEL, LOUIS WILLIAM: Evangelical and Reformed; b. Carlinville, Ill., June 8, 1884. Educated at Elmhurst College and Eden Seminary. Ordained April 7, 1907. Chairman of Committee on Union of former Evangelical Synod of North America during negotiations which led to union with Reformed Church in the United States, June 26, 1934. Vice-president of Evangelical and Reformed Church (1934–38), and president (1938). Delegate to World Conferences, Oxford and Edinburgh, and Amsterdam Assembly. Member Central Committee, World Council. Ecumenical in spirit and conviction. Author of *I Believe*.

GOEHRE, PAUL: German Lutheran; Socialist; b. Wurzen, Saxony, 1864; d. Buchholz, Germany, 1928. He established personal contact with the labor movement by working in a factory. He was pastor in Frankfort-Oder (1894–1907), particularly active in social work and cooperatives. Attacked by ecclesiastical circles, he left the church in 1901. He joined the Social Democratic Party and represented it in Reichstag (1903–18); and was a member of the Prussian Cabinet (1918–23). He advocated close co-operation of socialism and undogmatic Christianity. His books are: *Drei Monate Fabrik-arbeiter* (1891); *Der Unbekannte Gott* (1919).

OTTO A. PIPER.

GOGARTEN, FRIEDRICH: B. at Dortmund, Germany, 1887, he studied under Troeltsch and at the age of 40 became privatdozent at Jena. Three years later he was called to become professor of systematic theology at Breslau (1930-35) and later taught theology at Goettingen (1935-). His theological positions have shifted more radically than most. Even at the beginning, and in contrast to Troeltsch, he sought idealistically for a faith to support reason. Though enamored of Luther and Kierkegaard, and even after he had supported Barth enthusiastically, he later turned against their supernaturalism, coming more recently to hold a position similar to that of Buber (*q.v.*). During the period of National Socialism he gave his theological support to the socialistically minded "German Christians," in contrast to the "Confessional Church." His major works include: *Die religioese Entscheidung* (1921; 2nd ed., 1924); *Von Glauben und Offenbarung* (1923); *Ich glaube an den dreieinigen Gott* (1926); *Politische Ethik* (1932); *Gericht oder Skepsis: eine Streitschrift gegen Karl Barth* (1937); *Weltanschauung und Glaube* (1937); and *Das Bekenntnis der Kirche* (1939).

RAYMOND W. ALBRIGHT.

GOGUEL, (HENRY) MAURICE: B. at Paris, March 20, 1880. He received his education at the University of Paris (Docteur en théologie, 1905); Diplomé de l'Ecole des Hautes Etudes (1906). He has been on the Faculty of Protestant Theology at Paris (1906-); director of studies at l'Ecole des Hautes Etudes (1927-) and also dean of the Faculty of Letters at Paris (1937-). He wrote: *L'apôtre Paul et Jésus Christ* (1904); *Wilhelm Hermann et le problème religieux actuel* (1905); *L'Evangile de Marc* (1910); *L'Eucharistie des origines jusqu'à Justin Martyr* (1910); *Introduction au Nouveau Testament* (1922-26); *Jésus de Nazareth, mythe ou histoire* (1925, also in English); *Jean-Baptiste* (1928); *Vie de Jésus* (1932, also in English and German); *La naissance du christianisme* (1946); and *L'Eglise primitive* (1947).

RAYMOND W. ALBRIGHT.

GOLD COAST COLONY. See AFRICA.

GOLDEN RULE: The saying of Jesus in Matt. 7:12 and Luke 6:31 has been called "the golden rule" at least since the eighteenth century. In Matthew's Sermon on the Mount it is a summary and climax which comes just before the final series of warnings. In Luke's Sermon it fits gracefully between commands of non-resistance and generosity. Matthew adds the clause, "for this is the law and the prophets," thus making it a summary of the whole will of God, similar to Mark 12:29-31. The saying, in negative form, is frequently found in Jewish literature, its earliest appearance being in Tobit 4:15, where it occurs with counsels of prudence and generosity. The most famous Jewish form is that of Hillel, "What is hateful to you, do not do to your neighbor; this is the whole Torah, all the rest is interpretation" (Shabbath 31a). Other forms are found in a quotation from Philo (Eusebius, *Preparation for the Gospel*, VIII. 7. 6); in Testament of Naphtali, 1 (Hebrew text); and in Letter of Aristeas, 207, which connects the principle with the example of God, "who draws all men by forbearance." From Jewish tradition the negative form comes into Christian literature in the "Western" variant of Acts 15:29, and in Didache 1:2 (coupled with the commandments to love God and neighbor). The positive form appears in the church fathers only as a quotation from the gospels. Sayings similar to the golden rule, usually in negative form, are found in the sayings of Confucius and in Hindu scriptures, and in both forms in Greek philosophy from Thales on, and in Moslem tradition. Jesus' positive statement of the principle accords with his presentation of righteousness as the active doing of good rather than the avoidance of evil. Christians generally regard it as superior to the negative form, while Jewish teachers have contended that the latter is more realistic and profound. Taken out of its context, the golden rule need be no more than a prudential maxim which often proves practically advantageous. Jesus' teaching is, however, set against the background of God's goodness and constant activity. The good that his followers do to others, and that they wish may be done to them, is the outgoing love which exists among children of a heavenly Father.

BIBLIOGRAPHY: L. J. Philippidis, *Die "Goldene Regel" religionsgeschichtlich untersucht*, 1929; Israel Abrahams, *Studies in Pharisaism and the Gospels*, First Series (1917), pp. 21-25; for other bibliography see R. H. Pfeiffer, *History of New Testament Times* (1949), p. 384.

SHERMAN E. JOHNSON.

GOLDEN RULE FOUNDATION: Chartered by New York State in March, 1929, this "People's Foundation" offers to the American public services similar to those rendered by private foundations. It serves the donor, and the cause in which the donor is interested, rather than any one treasury or institution. It also offers a philanthropic service through stewardship education designed to increase systematic giving, in proportion to income, to religious, educational, and welfare institutions. Since 1935 the Foundation has selected the American Mother of the Year. This now includes annual selections of State Mothers, and recently National Mothers within the United Nations. Memberships, personal and organizational, and other contributions maintain this service.

ROBERT M. HOPKINS.

GOLDIN, JUDAH: Jewish; b. in N. Y., Sept. 14, 1914. He was educated at Columbia University and the Jewish Theological Seminary of America. He served (1943–45) as lecturer and visiting associate professor in Jewish literature and history at Duke University, and as associate professor of religion at the University of Iowa (1945–52), until his appointment as Dean and Associate Professor of Agada at the College of the Jewish Theological Seminary (1952). Among his publications are: *The Two Versions of Abot de Rabbi Nathan* (1945); *Hillel the Elder* (1946); *The Period of the Talmud* (1949).

GOLDMAN, SOLOMON: Jewish; b. at Kozin, Russia, August 18, 1893; d. May 14, 1953. He studied at New York University (B.A., 1917); Columbia University and University of Chicago, Yeshiva Rabbi Isaac Elchanan, New York, Jewish Theological Seminary of America (Rabbi, 1918; D.H.L., 1936). He served Congregation B'nai Israel, Brooklyn (1917–19); Cleveland Jewish Center (1921–29); Chicago, Anshe Emet (1929–). He belongs with the Reconstructionists in American Judaism. He is the author of: *A Rabbi Takes Stock* (1931); *The Jew and the Universe* (Philosophy of Maimonides) (1936); *The Golden Chain* (1937); *Crisis and Decision* (1938); *Undefeated* (1940); *The Book of Books* (1948); *In the Beginning* (1949).

GOMARUS, FRANCISCUS: From 1582 to 1584 he studied at Oxford and Cambridge, obtaining his M.A. at Cambridge on June 20, 1584. He did not enjoy his stay at Cambridge, however, as appears from some remarks in a letter he addressed to G. J. Vossius, who was thinking of going also to Cambridge to study. On Nov. 13, 1586, he became a pastor at Frankfort a. M., where in 1592 he published a new edition of the *Defensor Pacis* by Marsilius of Padua, which he dedicated to Frederick IV of the Palatinate. Early in 1594 he removed to Hanau. On January 25, 1594, he was appointed professor at Leiden, on March 14, 1594, he received his doctorate at Heidelberg, and in April he arrived at Leiden, where he was received with much festivity. In his inaugural lecture, *De foedere Dei,* he attacked Socinianism. From 1594 to 1598 he was also a pastor at Leiden, being partly relieved of his pastoral duties in 1598, and entirely in 1606. Upon the death of Arminius at Leiden Vorstius was appointed as his successor, and now Gomarus, because he objected to the teachings of Vorstius, left the university. He was not a quarrelsome person, although some authorities thought he was, but he did exhibit at times bad manners and temper. He was

rather weak and easily influenced by others. On May 28, 1611, he delivered his inaugural speech at the Illustre School at Middleburg. Here he did not get along well with Rev. Walaeus, as he later admitted to this pastor with some regret and apology. He had only a few students, and in 1614 he became professor at Saumur in France, shortly before he received an offer from the University of Groningen. At Saumur he disagreed with Capellus, who sided with Piscator. At the Synod of Dordrecht he took the same position over against Bogerman, the president. April 2, 1618, he left Saumur for Groningen.

He had a peculiar idea of the origin of the Sabbath, dating it from the time of Moses, rather than the creation. He also claimed that the institution of the Lord's Day was not derived from an apostolic dictum. His view of predestination was supralapsarian. When in 1640 he wanted to defend his position in a debate he was prohibited by the provincial government which felt that he opposed the official doctrine promulgated by the Synod of Dordrecht. But he was able to prove his ground in a different manner later on. His pupils did the same in their opposition to Maresius (1650). The prohibition in 1640 annoyed him so much that he wished to leave Groningen, but Voetsius, who had been one of his students, persuaded him to stay, while other friends did the same.

BIBLIOGRAPHY: A. W. Harrison, *The Beginnings of Arminianism,* 1926; K. Dijk, *De strijd over Infra- en Supralapsarisme in de Gereformeerde Kerken van Nederland,* 1912; G. P. van Itterzon, *Franciscus Gomarus,* 1929; D. Nauta, *Samuel Maresius,* 1935.

[Sup.] D. NAUTA.

GOOD, JAMES I(SAAC): D. Jan. 22, 1924. His later years were spent at the Central Theological Seminary, Tiffin, O., later at Dayton, O., where he taught church history and liturgics (1907–24). He was the president of the general Synod of the Reformed Church in the United States (1911–14). His later books include: *Famous Places of the Reformed Churches* (1910); *History of the Reformed Church in the United States in the Nineteenth Century* (1911); *History of the Swiss Reformed Church Since the Reformation* (1913); *The Heidelberg Catechism in Its Newest Light* (1914); *Famous Reformers of the Reformed and Presbyterian Churches* (1916); and *The Reformed Reformation* (1917).

[Sup.] RAYMOND W. ALBRIGHT.

GOODMAN, CHRISTOPHER: English Calvinist clergyman; b. *ca.* 1520; d. 1603; studied at Oxford (B.A., 1541; M.A., 1544; B.D., 1551); became divinity professor (*ca.* 1548). With the Marian exiles Goodman fled in 1554 to Strasbourg, Frankfort, and finally to Geneva. At Geneva he served as copastor of the English church, helped prepare the 1562 *Geneva Bible,* and wrote *How superior Powers oght to be obeyd* . . . (Geneva, 1558), one of the first pamphlets to urge overthrow of government for religious reasons. In it he approved of Wyatt's Rebellion, and argued that female government was never legitimate. This naturally angered Queen Elizabeth. He was among the first reformed ministers in Scotland (1559–64). He finally won permission to return to England (1565); to serve as a chaplain in Ireland (1566); and to occupy a living (*ca.* 1570). But his unorthodox political and religious ideas lost him the living (1571), and got him into further trouble (1584).

BIBLIOGRAPHY: *Dictionary of National Biography*, Vol. VIII (1921–1922), 128–130; Charles Martin, *Les Protestants Anglais, réfugiés à Genève au temps de Calvin, 1555–1560* . . . , 1915; C. H. Garrett, *The Marian Exiles*, 1938.
ROBERT M. KINGDON.

GOODSPEED, EDGAR J.: Baptist; b. at Quincy, Ill., Oct. 23, 1871. He studied at Denison University (A.B., 1890), University of Chicago (B.D., 1897; Ph.D., 1898); further study at Berlin and Oxford, travel in Europe, Egypt, and Palestine (1898–1900). He was associate in biblical and patristic Greek, University of Chicago (1900–2); instructor (1902–5); assistant professor (1905–10); associate professor (1910–15); professor (1915–37); secretary to the president (1920–24); chairman New Testament department (1923–37); distinguished service professor (1933–37). He lectured widely in the United States in defense of modern-speech translation of the New Testament. He was active in beginning to collate the N.T. Greek manuscripts in America (1898–1907), and in introducing study of Greek papyri in America, collaborating with Grenfell and Hunt in the Tebtunis Papyri, Vol. II (1907). He is best known for his American translation of the *New Testament* (1923). It was republished in 1931 as part of *The Bible, an American Translation,* and again with his *The Apocrypha, an American Translation* (the first such translation made throughout from the Greek) as part of *The Complete Bible, an American Translation* (1939). He collaborated with Prof. Ernest D. Burton in a *Harmony of the Synoptic Gospels* (1915) and *A Greek Harmony of the Synoptic Gospels* (1920). In the field of introduction he wrote *The Story of the New Testament* (1916); *The Story of the Old Testament* (1934); *The Story of the Bible* (1936), and *The Story of the Apocrypha* (1939). A fuller *Introduction to the New Testament,* appeared in 1937 and was dedicated to the forty-six men and women who had taken their Ph.D.'s while he was chairman, in the New Testament department. He explored particularly the first making of the Pauline letter collection, holding that Ephesians was written to introduce it to Christians of the tenth decade, *The Meaning of Ephesians* (1933). On

retiring to California (Los Angeles) in 1938, he lectured in history for one year in Scripps College, and at U.C.L.A. (1938–51). Other books of his are *Index Patristicus* (1907); *Index Apologeticus* (1912); *Die aeltesten Apologeten* (1914); *Making of the English New Testament* (1925); *Formation of the New Testament* (1926); *Strange New Gospels* (1931); *Ethiopic Martyrdom* (1931); *New Chapters in New Testament Study* (1937); *Christianity Goes to Press* (1940); *The Curse in the Colophon* (1935); *The Junior Bible* (1936); *The Four Pillars of Democracy* (1940); *How Came the Bible* (1940); *History of Early Christian Literature* (1942); *Goodspeed Parallel New Testament* (1943); *Problems of New Testament Translation* (1945); *How to Read the Bible* (1946); *Paul* (1947); *The Apostolic Fathers, an American Translation* (1950); *A Life of Jesus* (1950). Also (with J. M. P. Smith), *The Short Bible* (1933); and (with D. W. Riddle and H. R. Willoughby), *The Rockefeller McCormick New Testament* (3 vols., 1932). Between 1917 and 1941 he published a number of essays chiefly in the *Atlantic Monthly,* two volumes of which have been collected, *Things Seen and Heard* (1925); *Buying Happiness* (1932). He has been active in the Society of Biblical Literature (president 1929), in the Society of Midland Authors (president, 1929). He has been a member of the Revised Standard Bible Committee since its organization in 1930.

GOODWILL INDUSTRIES: Founded 1902 in Boston, Mass., by Edgar J. Helms, Methodist minister, to give employment to handicapped workers; 17,545 men and women were employed in 1952 in 101 factories in the U. S. A., 7 in Canada, and 7 in other countries. Castoff clothing, furniture, and other articles were gathered, repaired, and sold at reduced prices to slum dwellers and others. About 30% of the rehabilitated workers later found employment in private industry. The Industries, without attachment to any church body, are 90% self-supporting. THEODORE G. TAPPERT.

GORDIS, ROBERT: Hebrew; b. at Brooklyn, N. Y., Feb. 6, 1908. He studied at the College of the City of New York (B.A., 1926), at the Jewish Theological Seminary of America (M.H.L., 1932) and at the Dropsie College (Ph.D., 1929). He is rabbi of Rockaway Park Hebrew Congregation, Rockaway Park, N. Y. (1931–); associate professor of Bible at the Jewish Theological Seminary and lecturer in religion at Columbia University. His works include: *The Biblical Text in the Making—A Study of the Kethib-Qere; The Jew Faces A New World; Conservative Judaism—An American Philosophy; The Wisdom of Ecclesiastes; Koheleth—The Man and His World;* and a detailed study and scientific commentary on the book of Ecclesiastes. He is chairman of the Board of Editors of *Judaism,* a quarterly journal of Jewish life and thought. He was president of the Synagogue Council of America.

GORDON, ALEXANDER REID: Presbyterian; b. at Inverurie, Aberdeenshire, Feb. 11, 1872; d. Dec. 19, 1930. He studied at Aberdeen (M.A.), Edinburgh, Freiburg, Goettingen, and Berlin. Ordained in 1898, he was minister, Monikie, Forfarshire (1898–1907); professor, Old Testament, Presbyterian (now United Theological) College, Montreal (1907–30); McGill University (1914–30). His works include: *The Poets of the Old Testament* (1912); *The Prophets of the Old Testament* (1917); *The Faith of Isaiah* (1919); *The Prophetical Literature of the Old Testament* (1919). ELMER E. FLACK.

GORDON, CYRUS H.: Jewish; b. June 29, 1908, Philadelphia, Pa. He was educated at University of Pennsylvania (A.B., 1927; M.A., 1928; Ph.D., 1930). He was instructor of Hebrew at the University of Pennsylvania (1930–31); field archaeologist in Bible lands, American Schools of Oriental Research (1931–35); and teaching scholar in Semitics, John Hopkins University (1936–38). He was lecturer in Bible and religion at Smith College (1938–39, 1940–41). He was a member of the Institute for Advanced Study, Princeton (1939–40, 1941–42). He is professor of Assyriology and Egyptology, Dropsie College, Philadelphia, Pa. (1946–). His major books are: *Ugaritic Handbook* (1947) and *The Living Past* (1941).

GORDON, GEORGE A(NGIER): D. Oct. 25, 1929. His last and lengthy pastorate was at the Old South Church, Boston, Mass. (1884–1927). In addition to wide service beyond his congregation and denomination he was preacher to many colleges and universities and an overseer at Harvard (1897–1916). His later books included: *Ultimate Conceptions of Faith* (1903); *Religion and Miracle* (1909, rev. ed., 1910); *Revelation and the Ideal* (1913); *Aspects of the Infinite Mystery* (1916); *Humanism in New England Theology* (1920); and *My Education and Religion* (1925).
[Sup.] RAYMOND W. ALBRIGHT.

GORE, CHARLES: D. Jan. 17, 1932. He was bishop of Worcester (1902–05); Birmingham (1905–11); and Oxford (1911–19), from which responsibility he resigned to devote the remainder of his life to study and writing as well as travel and preaching. No man since Newman had influenced Oxford religiously as much as Gore, especially during his days at Pusey House (1884–93); and few, if any, have influenced the church in England more widely in the twentieth century than Gore. With him was begun a liberal Catholicism from which were to be born the social emphases of F. D. Maurice and others. The titles of his later books especially indicate the wide interests and influences of this prolific writer whose magnitude was first felt with the appearance of *Lux Mundi* which he edited in 1889. His later publications include: *Orders and Unity* (1909); *The Question of Divorce* (1911); *Son of Man* (1913); *Property, Its Duties and Rights* (1913); *A Prayer Book Revised* (1913); *The Basis of Anglican Fellowship* (1914); *The League of Nations, the Opportunity of the Church* (1916); *Reservation* (1917); *Religion of the Church as Presented in the Church of England* (1917); *Dominant Ideas and Corrective Principles* (1918); *Christianity Applied to the Life of Men and Nations* (1920); *Epistles of St. John* (1921); *The Proposed Scheme of Union in South India* (1921); *Belief in God* (1921); *Belief in Christ* (1922); *God in Christ* (1922); *Deity of Christ* (1922); *Catholicism and Roman Catholicism* (1923); *Holy Spirit and the Church* (1924); *The Anglo-Catholic Movement Today* (1925); *Can We Then Believe?* (1926); *Reconstruction and Belief* (1926); *Strikes and Lock-Outs* (1926); *The Prevention of Conception* (1927); *Christ and Society* (1928); *Jesus of Nazareth* (1929); *Philosophy and the Good Life* (1930); *Doctor Streeter and the Primitive Church* (1930); *Reflections on the Litany* (1932); and he edited *The New Commentary on the Holy Scripture* (1928).

BIBLIOGRAPHY: G. Crosse, *Charles Gore,* 1932; G. L. Prestige, *Life of Charles Gore,* 1935.
[Sup.] RAYMOND W. ALBRIGHT.

GOSPEL AND GOSPELS: I. Introduction: The world's literature offers no real parallel to the Gospels. Nothing like them had appeared earlier, and later times produced nothing but several pale imitations in Christian circles. It is important to see what they are not. They are not romances or folk tales; they tell actual events. They are not biographies; they concentrate on the public career of Jesus, with little study of inheritance, environment, training, and character development. They are not simply memoirs of a teacher, philosopher, or wise man; the ministry of Jesus included not merely word and example but action. They are not primarily literary products; not even Luke is dominated by literary aspiration; rather, they come from a much used tradition in whose preservation and shaping many persons had had a hand (see FORM CRITICISM). They do not give a neutral descriptive account of what happened; rather, they tell of the work of God in the career of Jesus, and they present their story as an offer of salvation to men.

The Gospel as a unique literary form was developed to present this unique message. It grows out of the witness and teaching of the church concerning what God has done in Christ for all who will believe. It is a document of the church, set down for the use of the church, and putting in permanent form the church's memory and testimony about Jesus. Each of the four gospel writers has his special point of view, which guides his selection, arrangement, and reshaping of what he tells on behalf of the church. Each author's wording and style appears in his reports of what Jesus said and even more in the narrative passages. But all four Gospels show the same basic character: in the tone of faith, and to further the church's Christian worship, witness, and teaching, each Gospel presents the story of God's redemptive work for men through Jesus Christ, the living Lord of the church.

II. Aramaic Originals? The mother tongue and usual teaching medium of Jesus and the Twelve was Aramaic. Yet our Gospels are in Greek. How did the transfer from Aramaic to Greek take place? Did it occur before the tradition was written down? Or were the earliest records of what Jesus did and said written in Aramaic? In the first half of the second century Papias said that Matthew composed the "Logia" in the "Hebrew" (or, as the word may mean, "Aramaic") language. Jerome later knew of a Gospel in the language of the Jews. Are these trustworthy clues?

Passing references of ancient church fathers help little. But the character of the Greek of the Gospels has led some recent scholars to conclude that one or more of our Gospels was first written in Aramaic. Already in the nineteenth century Marshall and Wellhausen, for example, had argued that one or more of our Greek Gospels is the translation of an original Aramaic work. In 1922, Burney declared that the Gospel of John was written in Aramaic at Syrian Antioch about A.D. 75. Even before this, however, Torrey had claimed that our Gospels were originally in Aramaic, and he later developed this argument in a series of books and essays. Since no Aramaic originals exist, the argument is that the style is Semitic, that the Greek overuses idioms that parallel Aramaic idioms, and especially that passages which make no good sense in Greek may be understood as mistranslations of an Aramaic original. Inability to agree on what passages contain mistranslations has weakened the case. Montgomery inclined to agree with Burney and Torrey. Olmstead did not claim that our Greek Gospels are translations of Aramaic originals, but insisted that a comprehensive Aramaic Gospel lay behind our present Gospels. More recently, Black has cautiously and carefully stated the linguistic evidence of Aramaic background.

Colwell, Riddle, and Goodspeed led the attack on Torrey and his allies. Their main points are: no Aramaic gospels survive; Greek literature offers parallels to many idioms supposed to be purely Semitic; the alleged mistranslations are intelligible Greek; while oral tradition was the form in which the Jewish Palestinian world preserved material, written Gospels appeared only when the Church entered the Greek-speaking world.

The case for written Aramaic originals of entire Gospels has not been proved. Possibly one or more Aramaic sources lie behind our present Gospels. In any event, their linguistic character shows that they preserve an early, Palestinian, Semitic tradition.

III. Sources of the Synoptic Gospels: Forty years ago there was widespread agreement that behind Matthew and Luke lay two written sources, the Gospel of Mark (in some form) and a document, usually called "Q," containing mainly sayings of Jesus. This Two-Document Theory still prevails, except among those who completely deny the use of sources, and in Roman Catholic circles, where scholars must maintain the priority of Matthew in some form. But since both Matthew and Luke have material found nowhere else, attempts to identify its source have been made. The suggestion that each Christian center possessed a different form of "Q," and that the writer of Matthew had one form and the writer of Luke another, has not won support. Streeter and V. Taylor proposed the Proto-Luke Theory: someone, perhaps Luke, gathered into one document ("L") previously unwritten stories and teachings, especially parables; Luke then combined "L" with "Q" to form Proto-Luke; later, Luke inserted large sections of Mark into Proto-Luke to form our Third Gospel. Streeter later suggested that a Jewish-Christian document "M" lies back of our Matthew, whose sources are thus Mark, "Q," and "M." This completed his Four-Document Theory, that back of Matthew and Luke, in addition to minor oral and written sources, were four documents: Mark, "Q," "M," and "L," which respectively embody the tradition of Rome, Antioch, Jerusalem, and Caesarea.

The Four-Document Theory, though widely accepted, has been vigorously challenged. Enslin rejects even the existence of "Q" and holds that the writer of Luke used Matthew as one source. Bacon, Bussmann, and Otto have held that some comprehensive Primitive Gospel or *Grundschrift* lay back of our Gospels. Some echo Grant's "multiple source" theory, which somewhat resembles Streeter's views.

The problem of sources does not yield to final solution, but the following statements seem warranted: the writers of Matthew and Luke used Mark; they used at least one other written source; we cannot determine conclusively the exact number and extent of such written sources; each writer, in using his sources, felt free to conform their style and wording somewhat to his own literary habits; possibly short written sources lay behind Mark.

IV. The Date of the Gospels: Exact dating of the Gospels is impossible. Few approve Torrey's views; he dates Mark about A.D. 40, Matthew almost immediately thereafter, and Luke and John not later than A.D. 60. More share Harnack's later view, that Acts was completed before Paul's trial at Rome; this dates Luke shortly before A.D. 60, and Mark even earlier. Others see reflected in one or more Gospels knowledge of the fall of Jerusalem in A.D. 70, and necessarily date them after that event. The waning view that Luke-Acts shows traces of the use of the Josephus' *Antiquities* dates these works after A.D. 95. Various factors, especially the finding of the Rylands Papyrus fragment (ca. A.D. 130?) of the Gospel of John, exclude former theories of a middle second century date for that Gospel. And the view of Knox, that Luke-Acts reflects the controversy with Marcion and therefore in final form dates about A.D. 150, is extremely improbable, to say the least. While no exact dating is possible, widespread scholarly opinion suggests a date A.D. 65–75 for Mark, in the eighties for Luke, in the eighties or nineties for Matthew, and in the nineties for John. The alternative, much less likely, would be to date Mark in the fifties, Luke-Acts about A.D. 60, Matthew some years later, and John toward the end of the first century.

V. Recent Study of the Individual Gospels: Recent study of Matthew debates and often rejects Streeter's theory of a written "M" source in addition to Mark and "Q." It is often suggested that the author used a document containing "Testimonies," i.e., Old Testament passages seen to be fulfilled in Christ. Scholars recognize a strongly Jewish-Christian strain in Matthew. By no means all accept Bacon's view that the five great discourses (chs. 5–7; 10; 13; 18; 24, 25) consciously imitate the five books of Moses and mean to say that Jesus' teaching replaces the Pentateuch as the supreme law for the Christian, but it is clear that interest in the codification of that teaching for use in the church guided the arrangement of the material. The Gospel reflects strong eschatological hopes, and also ecclesiastical interest. The supposed liturgical interest (Kilpatrick) must not be overstressed; topical arrangement rather than liturgically effective order and wording interested the writer, who was not Matthew, though he may well have used a source written by that apostle.

The Gospel of Mark has received renewed attention in recent study. It was the first written Gospel. Possibly written sources preceded it, but they have not survived. If they existed, they were not complete Gospels. So Mark originated the gospel form of writing.

It has long been held that Mark 16:9–20 was a much later addition; it is usually thought that the original ending was lost at an early date. Recently some have asserted that Mark 16:8 was the original ending. This is hardly convincing. Lohmeyer has found theological significance in the geography of this Gospel: Galilee, home of the Son of Man Christology, was the land of promise, the expected scene of the Parousia; the later Gospels give more theological importance to Jerusalem. No solid evidence supports this view. Many formerly thought and a few still claim that Mark represents partisan Paulinism. It is increasingly seen that it reflects rather the scope and outline of the *Kerygma,* the essential message of salvation, which announced the fulfillment of the Old Testament promises, began the narrative with the ministry of John the Baptist, presented the career of Jesus from his baptism through his ministry to his death and resurrection, and looked forward to his final appearance to complete God's purpose and act as judge of all. Just these points are covered in Mark; it reflects the scope of the basic gospel story of the early evangelists and teachers.

Recent study of Luke tends to stress its close connection with Acts, and often speaks of them as one work, Luke-Acts. It notes that the preface shows literary interest. Former claims of second century date and largely tendential character play little role today; the essential trustworthiness of Luke is widely recognized. This issue depends largely on the view of Acts. Since this Gospel begins with a literary preface, shows consciousness of authorship, and so must have been published under the name of its author, the unvarying tradition that Luke wrote it commands added respect.

Attempts have been made to find in John single units of oral tradition, such as Form Criticism discovers in the Synoptic Gospels, or to identify written sources, for example, a document containing miracle stories, or one of discourses (Bultmann). Such theories must reckon with the stubborn fact that the Gospel manifests a single style and way of thought (Chap. 21 is an appendix, perhaps added by a pupil of the author). The Gospel is the work of one great personality, who blends theological interpretation with historical facts but considers the historicity of his narrative essential to his argument. The increasing realization in recent years that all four Gospels look at Jesus with the eyes of faith, and that all historical study involves an element of interpretation, has modified the former tendency to disregard this Gospel in the search for the historical Jesus, although it remains true that John, with its eye for dramatic effect and its interpretive witness, is secondary to the Synoptic Gospels as a source for literal facts and sequence of events.

The theory of an Aramaic original, the evidence of Semitic mind, and the observed parallels with Jewish thought have checked former tendencies to regard this Gospel as a purely Hellenistic rewriting of the gospel tradition. While the author shows signs of Hellenistic (rather than purely Greek) influences and something like Gnostic strains of thought (as Bultmann and others strongly urge), his basic Jewish ties are unmistakable. Hence one may maintain, as many still do, that the Apostle John either wrote the Gospel or is the witness behind it. However, scholarship of the last half century has moved away from the insistence that to accept the witness of the Gospel requires acceptance of apostolic authorship. It is now widely held that a disciple of the apostle John, a Jerusalem disciple, or an unidentified disciple (the "Elder"? "Lazarus"?) may have been the writer. A satisfactory position must recognize in the Gospel a good independent source of information about Jesus, the strong theological interpretation of that information by the writer, and the basic agreement of his interpretation with the faith of the apostolic church.

See also JESUS CHRIST; MYTH IN THE NEW TESTAMENT.

BIBLIOGRAPHY: On the Gospel as a literary form: P. Wendland, *Die urchristlichen Literaturformen*, 1912; K. L. Schmidt, "Die Stellung der Evangelien in der allgemeinen Literaturgeschichte," in *EUCHARISTERION*, 1923; C. H. Dodd, *The Apostolic Preaching and its Developments*, 1937.
On possible Aramaic originals: C. F. Burney, *The Aramaic Origin of the Fourth Gospel*, 1922; E. C. Colwell, *The Greek of the Fourth Gospel*, 1931; C. C. Torrey, *The Four Gospels*, New York, 1933, second ed., 1947; *Our Translated Gospels*, 1936; *Documents of the Primitive Church*, 1941; E. J. Goodspeed, *New Chapters in New Testament Study* (1937), chap. 6; A. T. Olmstead, "Could an Aramaic Gospel Be Written?" *JNES*, I (1942), 41–75; M. Black, *An Aramaic Approach to the Gospels and Acts*, 1946, 2d edition, 1952.
On the Synoptic Gospels: A. Harnack, *The Sayings of Jesus*, 1908; *The Date of the Acts and of the Synoptic Gospels*, 1911; C. G. Montefiore, *The Synoptic Gospels*, 2 Vols., 1909, second ed., 1927; W. Sanday (ed.), *Oxford Studies in the Synoptic Problem*, 1911; R. Bultmann, *Die Geschichte der synoptischen Tradition*, 1921, second ed., 1931; B. H. Streeter, *The Four Gospels*, 1924, fourth ed., revised, 1930; V. Taylor, *Behind the Third Gospel*, 1926; W. Bussmann, *Synoptische Studien*, 3 vols., 1925–31; F. C. Grant, *The Growth of the Gospels*, 1933; M. S. Enslin, *Christian Beginnings* (1938), chap. 43; F. V. Filson, *Origins of the Gospels*, 1938; D. W. Riddle, *The Gospels: Their Origin and Growth*, 1939.
On Mark: M. Werner, *Der Einfluss paulinischer Theologie im Markusevangelium*, 1923; B. W. Bacon, *The Gospel of Mark: Its Composition and Date*, 1925; A. E. J. Rawlinson, *St. Mark*, 1925; E. Lohmeyer, *Das Evangelium des Markus*, 1937; F. C. Grant, *The Earliest Gospel*, 1943. On Matthew: A. Plummer, *The Gospel According to St. Matthew*, 1910; B. W. Bacon, *Studies in Matthew*, 1930; G. D. Kilpatrick, *The Origins of the Gospel According to St. Matthew*, 1946. On Luke: F. J. Foakes Jackson and K. Lake (eds.), *The Beginnings of Christianity*. Part I. *The Acts of the Apostles*, Vol. II, *Criticism*, 1922; B. S. Easton, *The Gospel According to St. Luke*, 1926; H. J. Cadbury, *The Making of Luke-Acts*, 1927; J. M. Creed, *The Gospel According to St. Luke*, 1930. On John: R. H. Strachan, *The Fourth Gospel: Its Significance and Environment*, 1917, third ed., revised, 1941; J. H. Bernard, *The Gospel According to St. John*, 2 vols., 1929; G. H. C. Macgregor, *The Gospel of John*, 1929; W. F. Howard, *The Fourth Gospel in Recent Criticism and Interpretation*, 1931; *Christianity According to St. John*, 1946; B. W. Bacon, *The Gospel of the Hellenists*, 1933; E. Schweizer, *Ego Eimi*, 1939; E. C. Hoskyns and F. N. Davey, *The Fourth Gospel*, 1940; R. Bultmann, *Das Evangelium des Johannes*, 1941, revised ed., 1950; P. Menoud, *L'évangile de Jean d'après les recherches récentes*, 1947.

[Sup.] FLOYD V. FILSON.

GOSPEL SONGS: In the latter part of the eighteenth century there appeared in the southeastern portion of the United States a type of religio-folk song that evolved into what is commonly called the gospel song. While not based upon the true folk song, it was akin in that the form had a folklike text and tune. Each dealt with a single theme, or thought, which was repeated and emphasized in a chorus or refrain. This song was taken over by leaders of camp meetings, which began about 1800, and later found its way into Sunday school song books in the middle of the century. Its success in the Sunday schools caused it to become immensely popular for use in prayer meetings, revivals, and social gatherings. Under magnetic leadership in revival meetings, which reached their climax about the turn of the century, its appeal became almost universal. Its significance as a cultural factor in American life seems not to have been appreciated by reputable historians. While the form was known in Britain it did not find favor in England, Scotland, and Ireland until introduced by Moody and Sankey in evangelistic campaigns, beginning in 1873. Thereafter it received the same general acclaim it had attained in America, and it has since gone round the world. The gospel song has been severely criticized by lovers of poetry and music but its appeal is by no means confined to the uncultured. It has been the means of bringing multitudes to the Christian way of life even though it has not proved effective as a means of fostering spiritual growth. Gospel songs have found their way into our "standard" hymnals, through individual merit. Because of early associations, rather than intrinsic worth, the gospel song is not likely to be discarded quickly. While other hymns more in keeping with religious emphases of the age will win their way, it is to the credit of gospel hymns that congregations have learned to sing them wholeheartedly.

ROBERT G. McCUTCHAN.

GOTTHEIL, RICHARD JAMES HORATIO: D. May 22, 1936. He was in charge of the American School of Archeology in Jerusalem (1909–10), and exchange professor at the University of Strasbourg (1920–21). He edited *The Syriac-Arabic Glosses of Isha bar Ali* (1910–27); and *Fragments from the Cairo Genizah in the Freer Collection* (1927). Among other works he wrote *Zionism* (1914); *The Belmont-Belmonte Family* (1917); and *The Life of Gustav Gottheil; memoir of a priest in Israel* (1936).

[Sup.] RAYMOND W. ALBRIGHT.

GOUDIMEL CLAUDE: B. at Besançon *ca.* 1514; d. at Lyon Aug. 28, 1572. He was not the teacher of Palestrina. He was living in Paris in 1554 and remained there until 1557, when he went on to Metz and then to Lyon. His contribution to the formation of Huguenot Melody is trifling; he was chiefly a genial commentator on it in his Psalms in counterpoint and in the form of motets. See BOURGEOIS (BOURGEOYS), LOYS.

BIBLIOGRAPHY: Auguste Castan, *Revue des sociétés savantes des départements* 5th series, VIII (1875), pp. 480–485; H. Expert, *Réédition en notation moderne des 150 psaumes de 1580,* 1896; Michel Brenet, *Annales Franc-Comtoises,* 1898; Grove's *Dictionary of Music and Musicians* (1908), pp. 205–208; H. Expert, *Réédition en notation moderne des messes de Goudimel,* 1928; H. Riemann, *Dictionnaire de Musique, éd. française* (1931), pp. 491–492; P. Pidoux and K. Ameln, *Fac-similé de l'éd. de Jaqui 1565,* 1935; P. André Gaillard, *Loys Bourgeoys,* 1948; F. Lesure, *Musica Disciplina,* Vol. II (1948), Fasc. 3 and 4, pp. 225–230; P. André Gaillard, *Kongressbericht der internationalen Gesellschaft fuer Musikwissenschaft* (1949), pp. 115–117; E. Trillat, *Claude Goudimel et la St. Barthélemy lyonnaise,* 1949; P. André Gaillard, *Revue musicale suisse* (1950), pp. 96–100; P. André Gaillard, *Revue internationale de Musique* No. 10 (1951), pp. 428–434; *idem,* No. 11, pp. 537–538.
[Sup.] P. ANDRÉ GAILLARD.

GOULART, SIMON: Goulart may have been a student at the Lausanne Academy, 1557–59. The Geneva Company of Pastors, with the grudging approval of the municipal council, did allow Goulart to serve briefly the French churches of Feurs in Forez (Loire) (1576), Tremilly in Champagne (1583), and Grenoble (1605). He also made several business trips to France without the approval of either body. In 1589 Goulart served as chaplain to Geneva troops campaigning in the nearby Pays de Gex. In 1600 he was named chaplain to Catherine of Navarre, but he never actually filled the position. Goulart followed Calvin and Beza as the third and last long-term moderator of the Geneva Company of Pastors in 1607 and from 1609–1612; weekly moderatorship became firmly established thereafter. He was also dean of the Company of Pastors (1605–1628). Goulart is best known as one of the most prolific of the Calvinist publicists. A stream of more than eighty-two revised editions, histories and books of sermons, meditations and pious verse poured from his study. Perhaps the best known is the *Histoire ecclésiastique des églises réformées au Royaume de France* (1580), the richest single source on the history of the beginnings of French Calvinism, published anonymously but actually co-authored by Goulart and other Geneva pastors. He also published nine volumes of songs set to the music of Orlando Lassus, *et al.* Though he never taught in Lausanne himself, Goulart helped du Buc organize a new course in systematic theology at the academy there.

BIBLIOGRAPHY: The basic study of Goulart is Leonard Chester Jones, *Simon Goulart, sa vie et son oeuvre, 1543–1628,* 1916. See also E. Droz, "Simon Goulart, éditeur de musique," *Bibliothèque d'humanisme et renaissance, Mélanges Augustin Renaudet,* XIV, 266–276; Albert Choisy, ed., "Journal de la guerre faite autour de Genève l'an 1590 par Simon Goulart," *Mémoires et Documents publiés par la Société d'histoire et d'archéologie de Genève,* XXXVI (1938), 1–189. For briefer mentions see

Charles Borgeau, *Histoire de l'Université de Genève . . .* Vol. I (1900), Henri Heyer, *L'Église de Genève . . . .* 1909; Henri Vuilleumier, *Histoire de l'église réformée du pays de Vaud sous le régime bernois,* 4 vols., 1927–33.
[Sup.] ROBERT M. KINGDON.

GRACE BRETHREN. See DUNKERS.

GRADED LESSONS: Were first launched at the 1908 meeting of the International Sunday School Association, held in Louisville. Some of the promoters had felt the influence of Pestalozzi, Herbart, and Froebel, all highly sensitive to stages of child growth and development. The Graded Lessons were designed to correct defects of the Uniform Lessons, by giving more attention to special interests and capacities of various age levels, and by dealing with parts of the Bible neglected by the Uniform Lessons. Many leaders called for more use of biblical narratives suitable for younger pupils, with extra-biblical materials, such as the study of nature, the history of the church and of Christian thought.

The first Graded Lessons were closely graded so as to be fully adaptable to each age or grade level. In preparation, careful thought was given to the interests and capabilities of the respective ages from four through eleven. Care was taken to choose subjects and biblical backgrounds consonant with the respective interests and abilities. The literature was so composed and the methodology was so planned that the lessons would specifically meet the needs of the particular groups for which they were prepared.

The Group Graded, or Departmental Graded, Lessons, were later designed to modify the apparent overgrading of the earlier Graded Lessons. The earlier plan was more adaptable in large schools, but small schools could not have separate classes for all ages, and found difficulty in administering the closely graded lessons. Under the Group Plan the same lesson is studied by all the pupils in a given department, and within the department the lessons follow a sequence with a three-year cycle, except that the kindergarten age-group has a two-year cycle. In 1932 the *International Curriculum Guide* became the basis for the preparation of the lessons. In 1945 the Cycle Graded Lessons superseded the Group Graded. See also UNIFORM LESSONS.

J. DONALD BUTLER.

GRAEBNER, THEODORE: Lutheran; b. at Watertown, Wis., Nov. 23, 1876; d. at St. Louis, Mo., Nov. 14, 1950. He was a graduate of Concordia Seminary, St. Louis, Mo. (1897); taught in Lutheran secondary schools (1897–1906); and was pastor of Lutheran parishes in Chicago (1906–13). He taught homiletics and also New Testament interpretation, dogmatics, and philosophy at Concordia Seminary (1913–49). He championed such causes as Christian elementary education, a program of youth activities, Lutheran unity, a realistic approach to the problem of separation of church and state. Among his many writings the following deserve special mention: *Dark Ages* (1917); *Spiritism* (1920); *Bible Student Quarterly* (1921–47); *Essays on Evolution* (1925); *God and the Cosmos* (1932); *Borderland of Right and Wrong* (1938); *Toward Lutheran Union* (1943); and *A Handbook of Organizations* (1948). He edited *Lehre und Wehre* and *The Lutheran Witness* (1914–49).

FREDERICK E. MAYER.

GRAHAM, WILLIAM FRANKLIN: Baptist; b. at Charlotte, N. C., Nov. 7, 1918. He studied at Florida Bible Institute, Bob Jones University, and Wheaton College (B.A., 1943) with graduate studies at Northwestern University. He was pastor First Baptist Church, Western Springs, Ill. (1943–46); first vice-president Youth for Christ, International (1944–   ). He was named president Northwestern Schools, Minneapolis (1947–52). He founded Billy Graham Evangelistic Association (1950), is sponsor of a nation-wide broadcast, Hour of Decision. He is now engaged in full-time evangelistic work, city-wide evangelistic campaigns (1947–   ). His campaigns in major cities of America attracted large crowds, e.g., Houston, Texas, 60,000; Washington, D. C., 40,000; Boston, Mass., 50,-000, at one time. Total attendance for an average four week campaign is often 500,000. He is author of *Calling Youth to Christ* (1947); *Revival in Our Time* (1950); *America's Hour of Decision* (1951); and a newspaper syndicated column, "This is my answer."

GRANGE, NATIONAL: Formed in 1867 by Oliver Hudson Kelley, the National Grange of the Patrons of Husbandry was the first American attempt to organize farmers for their own social and economic interests. It included in its membership both men and women, and later also young people, who were engaged in agriculture. Local, county, and state granges were represented in the National Grange, with headquarters in Washington. Kelley, who was a Freemason (*q.v.*), organized the Grange as a fraternal order (*q.v.*) with its own ritual and degrees.

The Grange engaged in political action to reduce railroad rates, secure more favorable farm loans, establish governmental agricultural bureaus, introduce rural mail delivery. It supported co-operatives (*q.v.*) for marketing produce and purchasing machinery, and it engaged in an educational program to improve agricultural methods and living conditions. After an early period of rapid growth, the Grange declined, but after World War I it recovered strength. In 1950 it included 8,000 local granges in a majority of the states of the U. S. A.

Other organizations formed for similar purposes were the Farmers' Alliance Movement (1880), the Farmers' Educational and Co-operative Union (1902), and the American Farm Bureau Federation (1919).

See also RURAL FELLOWSHIP.

BIBLIOGRAPHY: Solon J. Buck, *Granger Movement*, 1913; Wesley McCune, *The Farm Bloc*, 1943; Arthur L. Moore, *The Farmer and the Rest of Us*, 1945.

THEODORE G. TAPPERT.

GRANT, FREDERICK CLIFTON: Anglican biblical scholar and theologian; b. in Beloit, Wisc., Feb. 2, 1891. He was educated at Lawrence College; Nashotah House, General Theological Seminary; Western Theological Seminary, Chicago (Th.D., 1922). He served five parishes, including Trinity Church, Chicago (1920–24). He was dean of Bexley Hall (1924–26), and president of Western Theological Seminary during the years the new seminary was built in Evanston, Ill. and Seabury Divinity School was combined with it (1927–38). He is professor of biblical theology, Union Theological Seminary, New York (1938–   ); a member by appointment of the Standard Bible Committee since 1937; and also editor of the *Anglican Theological Review* since 1924. His viewpoint is that of liberal Anglicanism, with strong emphasis upon the historical study of religion. His chief works are *The Economic Background of the Gospels* (1926); *The Growth of the Gospels* (1933); *The Earliest Gospel* (1943); and *An Introduction to New Testament Thought* (1950).

BIBLIOGRAPHY: *Festschrift* published in his honor (Sherman E. Johnson, ed.), *The Joy of Study*, 1951.

GRANT, ROBERT McQUEEN: Episcopalian; b. at Evanston, Ill., on Nov. 25, 1917. He was educated at Northwestern University (A.B., 1938); Union Theological Seminary (B.D., 1941), and Harvard University (Th.D., 1944). He has taught New Testament language and interpretation in the School of Theology, University of the South (1944–53), acting dean (1947). He was research associate in New Testament at the University of Chicago (1952–53), and associate professor of New Testament there (1953–   ). He was a Guggenheim Fellow (1954). He is the author of: *Second-Century Christianity* (1946); *The Bible in the Church* (1948); *Natural Law and Miracle in Graeco-Roman and Early Christian Thought* (1951).

GRAY, JAMES M.: B. 1851; d. Sept. 21, 1935. He was, for many years, president of Moody Bible Institute, Chicago, Ill. He wrote: *Antidote to Christian Science* (1907); *How to Master the English Bible* (1909); *Great Epochs of Sacred History* (1910); *Progress in Life to Come* (1910); *Bible Problems Explained* (1913); *Christian Workers' Commentary on the Old and New Testaments* (1915); *Picture of the Resurrection* (1917); *Prophecy and the Lord's Return*

(1917); *Textbook on Prophecy* (1918); *Primer of Faith* (1920); *Synthetic Bible Studies* (1920); *Spiritism and the Fallen Angels* (1920); *My Faith in Jesus Christ* (1928); and *Steps on the Ladder of Faith* (1930).

RAYMOND W. ALBRIGHT.

GREBEL, CONRAD: Chief founder of the Anabaptist movement (see ANABAPTIST). B. in Zurich *ca.* 1498 as son of Junker Jacob Grebel into one of the leading patrician families of Zurich; d. 1526 at Maienfeld, Grisons. Educated at the universities of Basel, Vienna, and Paris, the young humanist returned in 1520 to his native city after six years of study, where he spent the rest of his life except for two months in Basel (fall of 1521) as proofreader in Cratander's shop, and except for his itinerant labors as an Anabaptist evangelist 1525–26.

Having experienced a profound religious renewal in 1522 under Zwingli's (*q.v.*) preaching, Grebel soon became one of the reformer's closest friends and most devoted supporters. But when Zwingli finally decided for a state church type of reformation, Grebel parted with him (1523–25) and became the leader of a small separating group, chiefly of Zurich and the nearby village of Zollikon. The Grebel party, believing that the New Testament called for a church of believers only, separate from the state, rejected infant baptism and inaugurated a new church through adult baptism in Zurich in January 21, 1525. Grebel performed the first baptism, that of George Blaurock. With great vigor the group spread its beliefs and rapidly built up a following throughout Zurich and the surrounding cantons. Grebel was a leader in this promotion, active in Schaffhausen and St. Gall, as well as in the Zurich territory of Grueningen. He was imprisoned in Zurich in October, 1525, as a propagator of a proscribed faith, escaped prison in April, wandered as an itinerant evangelist, and died of the plague as a harried fugitive at Maienfeld near Chur *ca.* August, 1526.

Grebel's significance lies wholly in the continuing Swiss Brethren movement, commonly called Anabaptism, and the vision of Christianity which it carried, which it derived initially largely from him. His controlling ideas were three: Christianity as essentially discipleship (*Nachfolge Christi*), with the new birth requiring an actual transformation of life after the pattern of Christ and his teaching; the church as a free church, a brotherhood of adult believers, voluntarily committed to follow Christ in full obedience, separated from the world and living in true holiness; and an ethic of love, in which war and violence are done away completely. (Modern Christian pacifism has its beginnings here.) He died before these principles could be fully developed and applied, and before his followers could be organized, but the Anabaptist-Mennonite movement carried the principles forward with considerable influence and geographic spread through Germany and Holland as far as England. These ideals can be traced particularly in English nonconformism. Grebel is thus seen as the forerunner of the modern free church movement in England and America. Grebel left no printed writings, although some seventy letters have survived, the most important of which, that to Thomas Muenzer of Sept. 4, 1524, is of great value as in effect the first Anabaptist manifesto.

BIBLIOGRAPHY: Harold Bender, *Conrad Grebel c. 1498–1526, The Founder of the Swiss Brethren Sometimes Called Anabaptists*, 1950, a definitive biography with an appendix of extracts from his writings and an exhaustive bibliography.

HAROLD S. BENDER.

GREEK RITE. See BYZANTINE RITE.

GREENBERG, SIMON: Jewish; b. Jan. 8, 1901 in Hareshon, Russia. He studied at Teachers Institute of the Jewish Theological Seminary of America (1919); University of Minnesota; the College of the City of New York (B.A., 1922); Hebrew University and the American School of Oriental Research in Jerusalem (1924–25); Dropsie College (Ph.D., 1932). Spiritual leader of Har Zion Temple in Philadelphia (1925–46). He taught education and homiletics at Rabbinical School of Seminary (1932– ; provost of the Seminary 1946–). He is the author of *Living as a Jew Today* and *Ideals and Values of the Jewish Prayer Book*.

GREENE, THEODORE MEYER: Episcopalian; b. in Constantinople, Turkey, Jan. 25, 1897. He studied at Amherst College (B.A., 1918); and the University of Edinburgh, Scotland (Ph.D., 1924). He was instructor in the Forman Christian College, Lahore, India (1919–21); instructor at Princeton University (1923–25); assistant professor (1925–28); associate professor (1928–39); professor (1938–45); McCosh Professor of Philosophy (1941–45). From 1941–45 he was chairman of the Divisional Program in the Humanities. He was visiting professor in the humanities at Leland Stanford (1945–46) and has been professor of philosophy at Yale since 1946 and Master of Silliman College, Yale, since 1947. He was for a while trustee of Lignam University, China, and is now a trustee of the Berkeley Divinity School, New Haven, Conn., and the Choate School, Wallingford, Conn. His chief publications are: (tr., with Hoyt H. Hudson, with intro.), *Kant's Religion Within the Limits of Reason Alone* (1934); (ed., with intro.), *Kant-Selections* (1929); (ed., with intro.), *The Meaning of the Humanities* (1938); (ed., with three other authors), *Liberal Education Re-examined: Its Role in a Democracy* (1943); *The Arts and the Art of Criticism* (1940); essays in *Christianity and Reason* (Edward D. Myers, ed.,

1951), *The Theology of Paul Tillich* (C. W. Kegley and Robert Bretall, eds., 1952), *Religious Perspectives of College Teaching* (Hoxie Fairchild, ed., 1952), and *The Christian Answer* (Henry P. Van Dusen, ed., 1945).

GREENE LECTURESHIP: Established at Andover Newton Theological School in 1917 by Mrs. Natalia L. Greene and her sons, Edwin, Harold, Everett, and Hartwell Greene, in memory of Stephen Greene. The income of the fund is to be used "to secure from time to time the services of scholars prepared to deliver lectures on important subjects related to Christianity in recent history."   HERBERT GEZORK.

GREENLAND: Missionary work conducted by Hans Egede (*q.v.*, Vol. IV) united with trade interests in the Danish colonization of the southwestern coast of this vast island. Missionary and trade stations were founded by the Danes in Godthaab (1728), Christianshaab (1734), Jakobshavn (1741), Frederikshaab (1742), Julianehaab (1775).

Danish missionary work was carried on during the following century, but only on the western coast of Greenland. Not until 1894 were missionaries sent to the eastern coast and was a station founded in Angmagssalik. In 1906 "The Greenland Church Cause" (*Den gronlandske Kirkesag*) was founded in Copenhagen. In co-operation with the Danish Society for Foreign Missions, this foundation sent out missionaries among the Greenlanders on the northeastern coast of the island. In 1937 the missionary work was brought to an end with the conversion of the last Eskimos in Greenland.

In 1951 there were in Greenland one dean, one vice-dean, and twenty-three pastors. Seven of the pastors were Danes and the rest native Greenlanders. There are eighteen pastors' districts; these are very extensive, from forty to ninety miles in each direction. Travel is undertaken in the summer by means of motorboats, in the winter by dogsleds. Wind and ice often impede pastoral work. The Lutheran bishop of Copenhagen has supervision over Greenland. In Godthaab there is a seminary. Since 1907 great awakenings swept over the country. The people used to be very fond of going to church and singing hymns, but World War II introduced changes for the worse. Most church buildings in Greenland are of wood, the largest of them in Jakobshavn.

BIBLIOGRAPHY: Vilhjalmur Stefansson, *Greenland*, 1942; E. N. Rolfsrud, *White Angakok: Hans Egede and the Greenlanders*, 1952.

K. E. JORDT JORGENSEN.

GREGORY: Gregory II: Saint, feast day Feb. 13. A letter of recommendation for St. Boniface to Charles Martel signified the beginning of a closer contact between Rome and the Frankish kings with reference to missionaries. Gregory also rendered useful services by restoring the ruined monastery of Monte Cassino.

Gregory III: Saint, feast day Nov. 28. Like Gregory II, he objected to the decision of Emperor Leo III in the iconoclast controversy (his action occurred in 731), and as a result Leo took away from him the possessions of the papal chair in southern Italy and Sicily. These he put at the disposal of the patriarch of Constantinople, thereby greatly weakening the Roman Church.

Gregory IV: The institution of the feast of All Saints is usually attributed to him. To Ansgar (Anscharius) he granted the pallium and appointed him legate of the North and East. As protection against the Saracens he rebuilt Ostia (Gregoriopolis).

Gregory V: The first German pope in the Middle Ages. He was noted for his high moral standards and admirable character. Emperor Otto III had him elected pope as successor to John XV, at the request of the German legation, and he was readily accepted by the clergy and the people of Rome. He crowned Emperor Otto IV. The cause of his death was malaria, not poison. The superscription on his tomb eulogizes his charity and his ability to preach eloquently in three languages.

Gregory VII: His excommunication of Henry IV was renewed in 1726 by Benedict XIII, and it was memorialized in the prescribed *officio* dated May 25, 1728, by the Congregation of Rites. This excommunication, because of its bold language, was condemned by the great majority of European governments who saw in it the proclamation of papal power above secular authorities. It was not permitted to be put into the breviarium by the rulers of Naples, Portugal, and France. Before long other Catholic states took the same measure. In the Austrian Netherlands (later named Belgium) it was Emperor Charles III (April 29, 1730) who took the same step, while Maria Theresia did the same on July 9, 1750, and Joseph II did it again in 1782. On Dec. 19, 1729, Benedict XIII declared all such secular decrees null and void.

Gregory VIII: He was at first an Augustinian Canon in Laon, then became cardinal deacon in 1155 or 1156. He served under Alexander III as legate or nuncio. From 1178 on he was chancellor of the Roman church. In Benevento he founded a congregation of Augustinian Canons, whose constitution was composed by him and indicates his strongly ascetic type of mind. His election to the papal chair came as the result of a recommendation by Cardinal Henry of Albano. He favored a policy of friendly relations with the Staufen emperors and family.

Gregory VIII: Antipope, with the nickname of "Burdinus is a donkey." Was born in southern France and became a Cluniac monk. Through the influence of Archbishop Bernard of Toledo he became in 1099 the bishop of Coimbra. He was suspended in 1114 by Paschal II on account of a dispute with the Spanish primate and papal legate, the archbishop of Toledo. Then he went to Rome and gained such favor that he was employed by the pope on important legations. He opposed the extreme Hildebrandine policy.

Gregory XI: The last pope to reside in Avignon. In central Italy the dissatisfied populace, complaining about the numerous French officials employed by the pope, took up arms under the leadership of Florence. It was a plain case of resurgent nationalism. But Gregory XI laid an interdict upon Florence. He engaged the warrior, Cardinal Legate Robert of Ghent, who served later as Pope Clement VII. The latter successfully put down the revolt.

Gregory XII: Successively bishop of Castello, Latin patriarch of Constantinople, cardinal priest of San Marco, and papal secretary. He was elected to succeed Innocent VII on condition that, if the anti-pope Benedict XIII at Avignon would give up his claim, he also would renounce his, in order that the long schism might be ended. As pope he concluded a treaty with Benedict XIII, stating that a general council was to be held at Savona in Sept. 1408, but King Ladislaus of Naples broke up the negotiations. Gregory had promised not to create more cardinals, but when he did add some, his former cardinals deserted him and, with the Avignon cardinals, convoked the Council of Pisa, which in July, 1409, decreed the deposition of both popes and the election of Alexander V. Gregory was opposed by Naples, Hungary, Bavaria, and by Rupert, king of the Romans in Germany. He had to seek protection with Ladislaus, and in a synod at Cividale del Friuli he proclaimed the deposition of Benedict and Alexander. John XXIII in 1410 replaced Alexander V. Being strongly supported by the leading statesmen and clergymen of Italy and Germany, he concluded a treaty with Ladislaus by which Gregory was banished from Naples and forced to give up his claim to the papal chair. See also Popes.

[Sup.] ALBERT HYMA.

GREGORY OF TOURS: His writings reveal that moral, social, and political corruption prevailed in his day. Consequently he was in frequent conflict with the rulers. In sincerity, with a firm belief in the supernatural—which was sometimes pure superstition—and in the teachings of the church he expanded her influence. He was canonized by acclamation shortly after his death.

BIBLIOGRAPHY: U. Chevalier, *Répertoire des sources historiques du moyen âge*, nouvelle éd., Vol. I (1905), pp. 1887–1889; *The History of the Franks*, translated by O. M. Dalton, 2 vols., 1927; S. H. MacGonagle, *The Poor in Gregory of Tours* . . . , 1936; W. C. McDermott, *Gregory of Tours, Selections from Minor Works*, 1949,
Bibliography pp. 101–106; M. Manitius, *Geschichte der lateinischen Literatur des Mittelalters*, 1931, cf. Index; R.-M. Meunier, *Grégoire de Tours et l' histoire morale du centre-ouest de la France*, 1946; A. Potthast, *Bibliotheca historica medii aevi* . . . 2. Auflage, Vol. I (1896), pp. 542–545.

[Sup.] DANIEL JOHANNES THERON.

GRENFELL, WILFRED THOMASTON: Labrador missionary doctor; b. Feb. 28, 1865, at Parkgate, near Chester, Eng.; d. Oct. 10, 1940. He studied at Marlborough College, Oxford University and London Hospital. In 1889 he joined the Royal National Mission to Fishermen and in 1892 went to Labrador. During forty years he established hospitals, nursing stations, orphanages, schools and other enterprises and operated medical ships. He wrote twenty-four books, of which *A Labrador Doctor* (1922) and *Forty Years for Labrador* (1932) are autobiographies.

EDWIN E. CALVERLEY.

GRENSTED, LAURENCE WILLIAM: Anglican; b. at Blundellsands, near Liverpool, Dec. 6, 1884. He studied at Oxford and Manchester. He was principal of Egerton Hall Theological College, Manchester (1919–24); fellow and chaplain of University College, Oxford (1924–30); professor of philosophy of the Christian religion, Oxford (1930–50). He is known for work in psychology of religion, and for writings on doctrine; also as an entomologist. Among his books are *Psychology and God* (1930); *The Person of Christ* (1933); *This Business of Living* (1939); *The Psychology of Religion* (1952).

GRIBALDI, MATTEO: Corresponded vigorously with John Calvin and objected strenuously to the death warrant against Servetus. He lived contentedly at Padua from 1548 to 1555, but civil war forced him to leave Italy. He composed an influential work, *De methodo ac ratione studendi in iure civili* (1541).

[Sup.] ALBERT HYMA.

GRIMM, HAROLD JOHN: Professor of history; Lutheran; b. at Saginaw, Michigan, August 16, 1901. He studied at Capital University (B.A., 1924); Evangelical Lutheran Theological Seminary, Columbus, Ohio (diploma, 1927); the universities of Leipzig and Hamburg (1929–30); and Ohio State University (M.A., 1928; Ph.D., 1932). He taught history at Capital University (1925–37); Ohio State University (1937–54); and Indiana University (1954–). He is one of the two American editors of the *Archiv fuer Reformationsgeschichte* (since 1949). He wrote: *Martin Luther as a Preacher* (1929); (with Tschan and Squires), *Western Civilization* (2 vols., 1942); *The Reformation Era* (1954).

GROOTE, GEERT (GERARD): His work as a reformer and educator is much more important than was generally understood before 1940. J. van Ginneken has shown that he studied law at Paris for eight years. Contrary to J. H. Gerretsen and E. Barnikol, he not only founded the first house of the Sisters of the Common Life but also the first house of the brothers, namely, in 1384 at Zwolle. The account by John Busch was not inaccurate (see COMMON LIFE, BRETHREN OF THE, in Vol. III, p. 182). Groote did not write *Sermo de septem verbis Domini*. The monastery he lived in was at Monnikhuizen, one of his friends was Jan Cele, another Johannes Vos (see GROOTE, in Vol. V, p. 82). His philosophical treatise, *De quatuor generibus meditabilium*, has been published by A. Hyma in *Arch. v. de gesch. van het Aartsb. Utrecht*, LI, 1925; and twenty-three letters by the same, Vol. LIII, 1928; Vol. LIV, 1929. The whole correspondence: W. Mulder (ed.), *Gerardi Magni epistolae*, 1933. He did not write *De imitatione Christi*.

BIBLIOGRAPHY: Jan van Ginneken, *Geert Groote's levensbeeld*, Amsterdam, 1942; J. G. J. Tieck, *De werken van Geert Groote*, Utrecht, 1941; K. de Beer, *Studie over de spiritualiteit van Geert Groote*, Nijmegen, 1938.

[Sup.] ALBERT HYMA.

GROPPER, JOHANN: No satisfactory biography of this important figure was published until 1951, when the significant work by Walter Lipgens appeared, *Kardinal Johannes Gropper 1503–1559*. Few experts in Germany were fully aware of Gropper's share in the Counter Reformation as a whole or even in the Holy Roman Empire. It was often alleged that Gropper refused the cardinal's hat because he was not satisfied with the program of church reform envisioned by his colleagues. His early education and his connection with the Devotio Moderna were as a rule ignored or misunderstood.

Gropper deserves the place accorded to him by Lipgens, who in his subtitle indicates what the learned and devout prelate accomplished: *Und die Anfaenge der katholischen Reform in Deutschland*. Gropper labored in a strategic spot, forcing the clergy in the Archbishopric of Cologne to withdraw from the Protestant standpoint and return to the doctrines and church discipline of the Roman Church. The manner in which he worked and the ideal of primitive Christianity which he derived from the Devotio Moderna have been ably presented by Lipgens. Young Gropper, as hitherto unused documents and manuscripts show, entered the University of Cologne on June 17, 1516, and a year later received an A.B. degree; then he spent two years studying in the Cornelianer Burse, where he was powerfully influenced by devout humanists. Cologne was at that time the largest city in Germany, and its university the greatest in German-speaking lands. The Low Countries, Westphalia, and the region around Cologne formed the center of the Northern Renaissance. Cologne was closely related to the lands which

nurtured Rudolph Agricola (*q.v.*), Wessel Gansfort (*q.v.*), Ortwin Gratius, and Desiderius Erasmus (*q.v.*). Although Gropper devoted six years to the study of law (1519–25) and was a distinguished jurist, his main interest, as was the case with Luther and Calvin, turned back to the field of religion and the social sciences. From 1526 to 1536 he acted as chancellor of the Archdiocese of Cologne, wielding tremendous power over both lower and higher clergy.

Hermann von Wied, archbishop of Cologne, contrary to numerous reports issued from time to time, was not at first inclined to favor Luther, but strongly withstood Lutheran teachings. As late as 1524 Von Wied and the three other Rhenish electors determined to check "the Lutheran and other heretical doctrines." Von Wied knew very little Latin, cared little about religion, and hunted with reckless abandon. He was true to his age and environment, not to the ideals of the church fathers. Only after Gropper urged him to become a real Christian did he show interest in his duties as archbishop and priest. Then for a time both he and his chancellor took the Christian religion so seriously that they offended their colleagues in Rome.

It was unfortunate for the University of Cologne that Ortwin Gratius, who was teaching there in the years when the *Epistolae obscurorum virorum* (*q.v.*) were published (three parts, 1515–1517), received a bad reputation at the hands of young and inexperienced humanists. The university suffered a drastic loss in enrollment as a result, while Wittenberg attracted large numbers of students. Gropper was unable to find professors who could rival Luther and Melanchthon. His friend and guide, Erasmus, refused an appointment. It seemed as if the old glory was gone forever. Gropper became professor of law in January, 1529, but soon left his post, though the sources do not tell when. Theological controversies must have intrigued him so much that he could no longer enjoy teaching law. In 1532 Gropper and his archbishop were so deeply engaged in church reform that Cologne was generally thought to be on the verge of Lutheran innovations in state and church. Gropper was at least as much involved as was Von Wied. Nevertheless, for reasons not clearly indicated in the sources, Gropper in 1532 or 1533 chose the Catholic position, while Von Wied in 1534 and 1535 became frightened by the Anabaptists in Muenster. Both men were now convinced that Protestantism was not good for them. Moreover, the political maneuvers of Philip of Hesse (*q.v.*) and Maurice of Saxony (*q.v.*), as has been indicated in the articles devoted to them, severely hurt the Protestant cause in Cleves and the Rhineland.

The astonishing thing about Gropper is that he was able to defeat his own archbishop when the latter in 1539 became a Protestant. The

Elector of Saxony had persuaded him to join the Lutheran cause, but during the next three years Von Wied moved with great caution and considerable secrecy, being fully aware of Gropper's sentiments and influence. The struggle between the two men lasted from 1539 to 1547. During that time the Duchy of Cleves to the northwest of Cologne had a Lutheran ruler, and Henry VIII of England married Anne of Cleves, while the archbishop of Cologne made Bucer a highly favored preacher in Bonn. Throughout the Low Countries Protestantism was advancing rapidly, even in the south.

That Catholicism was successful in Westphalia and in Cleves must not be ascribed merely to geographical or climatic factors. The region directly to the west of them is today dominated by Protestantism, except in the vicinity of Nijmegen, which used to be Protestant and is now nearly all Roman Catholic, owing to the upsurge of Catholic power in Limburg and the German Rhineland. At the same time Deventer and Zwolle remain flourishing strongholds of Protestantism. Why should they be Protestant and Muenster, not far to the east and at one time the other of the three chief centers of the Devotio Moderna, be overwhelmingly Catholic? Why is the Lower Rhine region in Germany so strongly Catholic and the valley to the west, especially near the North Sea, so very different?

Gropper's influence upon these remarkable developments is not easily evaluated. That he performed great tasks in behalf of the Roman Catholic cause is apparent, not only in Cologne and Soest but also at the Reichstag at Regensburg in 1541 and at the Council of Trent.

BIBLIOGRAPHY: W. van Gulik, *Der Scholaster Johannes Gropper und seine Taetigkeit im Kurfuerstentum Koeln bis zum Jahre 1540*, Muenster Dissertation, 1902; H. Schwartz, *Geschichte der Reformation in Soest*, 1932; W. Lipgens, *Kardinal Johannes Gropper: 1503–1559 und die Anfaenge der katholischen Reform in Deutschland*, 1951, see especially his admirable bibliography, pp. 241–252.

[Sup.] ALBERT HYMA.

GROS, ERWIN: Evangelical National Church of Germany; b. at Niederems, 1865; d. at Gonzenheim, 1927. A teacher's son, he was pastor of Hartenrod, Hoechstenbach, Esch and Gonzenheim, parishes of the Hessian National Church. He was a popular author. He published his sermons in eight small volumes, *Auf der Dorfkanzel*, and in two books of sermons, *Im Frieden Gottes*, and *Mit Gott zu Gott*. He wrote many rural romances, the most famous being, *Der Bauernpfarrer*. Also he was author of thrilling historical stories; the most famous are: *Die letzte Nonne von Walsdorf, Elsbeth von Helkhoven*, and *Es geht eine dunkle Wolke herein*. REINHOLD KUECKLICH.

GROS, JOHN DANIEL: B. in Webenheim in the Rhenish Palatinate, June 22, 1738, Gros studied at Heidelberg and Marburg Universities and offered himself to the Amsterdam Synod for service in Pennsylvania, where he arrived in 1764. He was ordained by the coetus of the German Reformed Church in 1765 and assigned to churches in the Lehigh Valley. After serving German Reformed churches in Baltimore and in Kingston, N. Y., he was called to the German Reformed Church in New York City. While in New York he taught geography and ethics at Columbia College and wrote *Natural Principles of Rectitude, a Systematic Treatise on Moral Philosophy* (1795), the first orderly treatment of ethical problems published in America. This work is an interesting mixture of rationalism (*q.v.*, Vol. IX) and pietism (*q.v.*, Vol. IX), stressing freedom of will and formulating the pietistic emphasis on the "awakened" conscience in rational terms. Gros died on May 25, 1812, after having trained several ministers for the German Reformed Church.

JOHN JOSEPH STOUDT.

GROSSETESTE, ROBERT: Philosopher, scientist, theologian, first chancellor of Oxford, Bishop of Lincoln (whence known as *lincolniensis* to the Middle Ages); Grosseteste was b. in Suffolk, perhaps at Stradbrooke, ca. 1175; d. at Buckden, Huntingdonshire Oct. 9, 1253. Of humble origin, he was well known for his learning by 1199, when Giraldus Cambrensis recommended him highly to the bishop of Hereford for his learning in the liberal arts and his proficiency in law and medicine. We are not clearly informed of his activities for the next decade, but it is reasonable to assume that he left Oxford with all the clerics at the university in 1209, when the university was closed consequent upon the hanging of two scholars by King John, and went to Paris with the majority of Oxford masters and students. Returning in 1214, when the interdict laid on England was lifted, he was soon named *magister scholarum*, a title which is essentially equivalent to that of chancellor. He held a number of minor livings in England from 1214 until 1229 including the archdeaconry of Leicester. In 1229 he became Archdeacon of Wilts. The years between had been busy with reading and teaching; his reputation was high and the newly arrived Franciscans were fortunate to get him, probably in 1229, to lecture to them in theology. In 1232, for reasons of health, he resigned all his preferments save a prebend at Lincoln, but continued to lecture to the Franciscans until his election to the bishopric of Lincoln (Mar. 27, 1235), then the largest see in England, including within its jurisdiction the University of Oxford.

The years of his episcopate from 1235 to his death in 1253 were prodigiously occupied. His work and influence, his prestige at home and abroad, were of perhaps more significance than that of any other Englishman of his century.

We may consider his activities under three headings: (1) his episcopal administration; (2) his participation in national and papal politics; (3) his scholarly and scientific work.

(1) From the very beginning of his episcopate Grosseteste showed his determination to raise the morals of both clergy and laity in his vast diocese, first by specific instructions to archdeacons and the regular clergy, then by arduous personal visitation. The latter raised a storm of protest, and appeals against his severity were lodged with the papal curia. The concise Constitutions he issued in 1238, based on the Lateran decrees of 1215, were taken over in greater or less degree by the synodal statutes of five other English dioceses. He refused to install clergy inadequately prepared, withstanding pressures of all sorts, and insisted that the *cura animarum* be taken seriously, both by the secular and beneficed clergy and by the monastic orders. These latter he specifically accused of laxity in the observance of their own rules, with especial emphasis on incontinence. Of the orders, the Austin canons gave him the most concern, though the Benedictines had occasion to complain of the severity with which he treated them. In 1236 he deposed eleven heads of religious houses in his diocese for various irregularities. Grosseteste's most bitter disputes within his own diocese were with the abbot of Bardney, whom he deposed, the prior and monks of Christ Church, Canterbury, who, *sede vacante*, excommunicated Grosseteste, and with his own dean and chapter at Lincoln over his rights of visitation. This last dispute dragged on for seven years. There were others of less severe proportions. It may be said that, through the maze of polemic and appeal and conflict of jurisdictions, Grosseteste, though sometimes arbitrary, comes out with much the better of the argument. Pope Innocent IV, to whom both sides of the controversy between Grosseteste and his own chapter appealed, decided in the bishop's favor by a bull of Aug. 25, 1245. The remainder of his episcopate was not affected by any unusual disturbance within the bounds of his diocese.

(2) The importance of his diocese and his own tremendous personal prestige brought Grosseteste into crucial prominence in national and international politics from the beginning of his episcopate. He took a firm position in opposition to the misrule of Peter des Roches, the king's favorite, and from 1236 on he opposed the king's interference with the rights of the church in selecting ecclesiastical persons to perform duties as royal servants. Several of his letters in the years 1236–40 are reasoned defenses of the church against royal encroachment. In other letters he states his clear belief that obedience is due the king so long as his actions are proper and just, and to the pope so long as he acts in accord with the teaching of the Scriptures. Grosseteste's own relations with king and pope were in line with these beliefs. From 1240 and during the vacancy of the see of Canterbury he was virtual head of the church in England. Having adopted a firm stand on royal interference in church matters, Grosseteste became naturally the leader of the opposition to Henry III. In 1243 he rebuked the king to his face for his tyrannous conduct and, directly or indirectly, forced the monarch to modify his policy. In November, 1244, he led the committee of twelve that demanded that the king agree to control over his expenditures and the appointment of his ministers, a landmark in English constitutional history. He attended the general council at Lyons called by Innocent IV in 1245 and obtained from the pope the final and favorable settlement of his long standing dispute with the dean and chapter of Lincoln. The next year brought increased demands from the pope for contributions from England. Though quite aware, from his stay at Lyons, of the parlous financial state of the papacy, he offered crisp opposition to the high handed way in which papal officials attempted to collect procurations in England. On the other hand, he took an active part over a period of several years in obtaining contributions of two thousand pounds toward the costs of the projected crusade. Again in 1248 he joined with other bishops and magnates in taking King Henry to task for his exactions and misrule. But Grosseteste himself was, on several occasions, guilty of overzealous pressure upon secular officials, at one point (1249) excommunicating the sheriff of Rutland for declining to act against a clerk whom Grosseteste had deprived. His friendship with Simon de Montfort was of long standing, and though they did not always agree, there was always mutual respect and affection. The influence of Grosseteste upon the thought and action of the earl may be assumed to have been great. The earl entrusted two of his sons to Grosseteste for their education.

In the spring of 1250 Grosseteste made a second trip to Lyons where Innocent IV and the curia were temporarily installed. Grosseteste had at this time three aims in mind: to nullify the resistance of the monastic orders to his establishment of vicarages, to inform the pope of the difficult situation in which the English church found itself, harassed by the king's aggressions and the irregular demands of Archbishop Boniface of Canterbury, and to obtain some modification of the excessive papal provisions which had confused and constricted the work of the church in England. On May 13, 1250, he presented to the pope and three cardinals a reasoned bill of particulars, and asked for careful consideration of his grievances. His success was only partial. Three years later the pope provided his nephew, Frederick of Lavagna, to a canonry in Lincoln. Grosseteste refused to accept the mandate, in a famous letter doubtless intended for the pope, but sent expressly to a certain Innocent, a *scriptor* of the pope, on the ground that the provisions of the pope destroyed the effectiveness of the cure of souls, and thus he had to refuse to obey the pope's mandate in the interests of the papacy. The pope was extremely angered by the report, but his advisers persuaded him not to attack a popular English prelate who was indubitably in the right.

(3) It now appears probable that, significant as Grosseteste was in the ecclesiastical and political world of his time, his greatest contribution to Western civilization lay in the area of culture and science. His philosophical, theological, literary and scientific production was prodigious. He learned Greek and translated into Latin the whole *corpus* of the Pseudo-Dionysius, then wrote a commentary upon it, translated the whole *corpus* of John of Damascus, the *Ethica Nicomachea* of Aristotle and the Greek commentators, the so-called *Testamenta XII Patriarcharum* (with the help of Nicholas the Greek to whom a benefice had been given on presentation by the monastery of St. Albans), and other lesser Greek works. His commentaries on Aristotle's *Posterior Analytics* and *Physics* were widely copied and quoted in the Middle Ages. He wrote some biblical commentaries and a number of *pastoralia* intended to help the clergy of his diocese in their work. He was interested in and conversant with Arabic science, and himself composed a calendar and many opuscula upon scientific subjects, light, motion, colors, tides, the sphere, the rainbow, geometry, comets and agriculture. He was the leader of the school of "Lichtmetaphysik" which was to predominate in Oxford for generations after his death. In theology he was a convinced Augustinian, finding Augustine's thought on illumination congenial to his own emphasis on *lux*. He wrote a number of works in Anglo-French, showing complete familiarity with the temper of contemporary folk-thought. His extant sermons, numbering at least seventy-five, show him an effective and powerful preacher to both learned and common folk. We have his collected letters, 143 in all, to friend and foe, king, queen, and pope, as well as to intimate friends, full of fervor, wit, and wisdom; and his widely used *Dicta*, collected sayings, in school and out, which were to be avidly copied and quoted well into the fifteenth century as far away as Bohemia by Hus (*q.v.*) and his followers. He shared the distinction of many great personalities of being plagiarized and of having at least sixty-five works ascribed to him

during the Middle Ages of which he was not or could not have been the author.

BIBLIOGRAPHY: For a complete bibliography of his works, manuscripts, and editions see S. H. Thomson, *The Writings of Robert Grosseteste*, 1940. Sources for his life: H. R. Luard (ed.), *Epistolae R. Grosseteste* (Rolls Series, No. 24), 1861; F. N. Davis (ed.), *Rotuli Roberti Grosseteste* (Lincoln Record Soc.), 1914; H. R. Luard (ed.), Matthew of Paris, *Chronica Majora*, Vols. III-V (Rolls Series, No. 57), pp. 1876 ff.; H. R. Luard (ed.), *Annales monastici* (Rolls Series, No. 36), 3 vols., pp. 1864 ff. Biographies: by S. Pegge, London, 1793; R. Pauli, Tuebingen, 1864; G. V. Lechler, Leipzig, 1884; G. G. Felton, Freiburg, 1887; F. S. Stevenson, London, 1899. The article in *D.N.B.*, Vol. XXIII, pp. 275-78 is still useful. Consult also: A. A. Gasquet, *Henry the Third and the Church*, 1910; D. E. Sharp, *Franciscan Philosophy at Oxford in the Thirteenth Century*, 1930; Marion Gibbs and Jane Lang, *Bishops and Reform 1215-1272*, 1934; C. R. Cheney, *English Synodalia of the Thirteenth Century*, 1941; D. A. Callus, *The Introduction of Aristotelian Learning in Oxford*, 1944; J. R. H. Moorman, *Church Life in England in the Thirteenth Century*, 1945; F. M. Powicke, *King Henry III and the Lord Edward*, 2 vols., 1947; A. C. Crombie, *Robert Grosseteste and the Origins of Experimental Science*, 1953.

[Sup.] S. HARRISON THOMSON.

GROTIUS, HUGO: Known in his day as the oracle of Holland, more learned than Erasmus, for he knew not only classical Latin and Greek as well as did Erasmus, but also Hebrew and Arabic. He wrote extensively in the Dutch language, which Erasmus despised, and he was also one of the greatest theologians of the modern world. Before the age of twelve he went to the University of Leyden, where his learning was such that in the first official book published about the university his name was that of the only student deemed worthy to rank with the professors. His uncle, Cornelis de Groot, was rector of the university; Justus Lipsius, the world-famous professor of classical languages, was there, soon to be followed by the still more famous Joseph Scaliger; while Franciscus Junius ranked with the best in the field of theology. At the home of the latter Grotius learned much about the relation between state and church and the need of religious toleration. Both subjects engrossed his mind until his death. In the year 1598 he took a short trip to France, where he was presented to King Henry IV, and then went to Orléans for a brief visit. After a thorough examination given him by "the ordinary professors in both laws," he received there the LL.D. In 1599, at the age of sixteen, he published an edition of the old textbook, *On the Marriage of Philology and Mercury*, a sort of encyclopedia in the seven liberal arts. In the same year he also published a mathematical treatise by Simon Stevin. In December he became attorney in The Hague, where at first he resided with Rev. Jan Uytenbogaert (*q.v.*). The latter taught him to become a liberal Calvinist. He disliked his profession, but remained a member for many years.

In 1600 he published *Syntagma Arateorum*, composed in the third century B.C. by the Greek writer Aratus. Grotius added learned commentaries, which won him great praise from experts.

Three years later he composed a monumental work entitled, *De jure praedae* (*On the Law of Prizes*), in which he defended the right of the Dutch East India Co. to seize cargoes belonging to Spain, which was at war with the Dutch Republic. The book was unknown to posterity until 1868, and only one of its chapters, *De mare libero,* was published by Grotius. It was long regarded as a separate composition, and was treated as such in the original Schaff-Herzog article on Grotius (*q.v.*). In 1613 Grotius was sent on a mission to London, where he represented the Dutch East India Company in an official capacity, but spent much time and energy promoting the cause of liberal Calvinism. In 1615 Grotius attended another conference of great importance, this time in The Hague. His patriotism had led him to write and publish a scholarly history of the Dutch people to 1566. It first appeared in Latin form (1610), but a few months later arrived the Dutch edition. The title was, *Treatise on the Antiquity of the Batavian Republic.* In 1612 Grotius completed a large work, *Annals and Histories,* describing the history of the Dutch revolt against Spain. It was first published in 1657. From 1613 to 1618 he became involved in a religious struggle, affected by his relations with King James I of England, whom he had warned against the Puritans. In 1618 he was arrested and the next year condemned to lifelong imprisonment at Loevestein. His dramatic escape, engineered by his brave wife, Maria van Reigersbergh, is as famous in Holland as is Luther's stand at Worms in Germany. Although Grotius was free, he could never again be a respected citizen in his native land. He wandered from place to place, settled down in Paris, but still could find no peace. At the end the young and capricious Christina, queen of Sweden, tried to use him at her court as a scholarly attraction, but he refused her offer, remembering only too well that upon her accession she had discharged him as the Swedish ambassador in Paris.

BIBLIOGRAPHY: A. Hallema, *Hugo de Groot: Het Delftsch orakel,* 1942; W. J. M. Eysinga, *Huigh de Groot,* 1945; O. Damsté, *Huigh de Groot: Verhandeling over het recht op buit,* 1934; Hugo Grotius, *Correspondence* (ed. P. C. Molhuysen, *Briefwisseling*), 2 vols., 1928, 1936; H. G. Hamaker (ed.), *De jure praedae commentarius,* 1868; G. N. Clark and W. J. M. Eysinga (eds.), *Reports of the Anglo-Dutch Conference in London* (1613) and *Reports of the Anglo-Dutch Conference in The Hague* (1615), 1940; A. H. Haentjes, *Hugo de Groot als godsdienstig denker,* 1946; Hans Klee, *Hugo Grotius und Johannes Selden,* 1946; W. S. M. Knight, *The Life and Work of Hugo Grotius,* 1925; J. Schlüter, *Die Theologie des Hugo Grotius,* 1919; Jacob ter Meulen, *Concise Bibliography of Hugo Grotius,* 1925; H. Vreeland, *Hugo Grotius: The Father of the Modern Science of International Law,* 1917; P. H. Winkelman, *Remonstranten en Katholieken in de eeuw van Hugo de Groot,* 1945. The correct English title of Grotius' masterpiece is, *On the Law of War and Peace.* By far the best bibliography is J. ter Meulen and P. J. Diermanse, *Bibliographie des écrits imprimés de Hugo Grotius,* 1950.

[Sup.] ALBERT HYMA.

GRUBER, JOHN ADAM: B. in Schaffhausen in 1694, came to Pennsylvania in 1726; d. in Germantown in 1763. He was the son of Eberhard Ludwig Gruber who, with Frederick Rock, was one of the leaders of the Congregation of the True Inspiration, a revival movement of prophetic spirit which, springing from the French Camisards of the Cevanese desert, spread over the Rhineland from 1700 to 1715. J. A. Gruber was the most important unattached religious individualist in the fermenting earlier years of Pennsylvania's history. While connected with no sect, his pen was busily engaged in controversy. Writing as *Ein Geringer,* he produced at least seven major tracts and a body of religious verse. His account of religious conditions in Pennsylvania, which appeared in *Die Geistliche Fama* in 1730, was one of the earliest surveys of Pennsylvania sectarianism. More than any other person, Gruber was responsible for Count Nicholas Zinzendorf's failure to unite Pennsylvania's sects into a Congregation of God in the Spirit. During the earlier years of his American period he was liaison between Pennsylvania sectarians and the radical pietists in Berleberg-Wittgenstein and corresponded with Dr. Carl, the separatist leader there.

JOHN JOSEPH STOUDT.

GRUNDEMANN, REINHOLD: Evangelical National Church of Germany; b. at Baerwalde, Neumark, 1836; d. at Belzig, 1924. He was pastor in Bitterfeld (1861); in Frankfurt/Oder (1862–64); cartographer at Perthes in Gotha (1865–69); and pastor in Moerz near Belzig (1869–1912). He was author of mission books and has been well known as coeditor of *Allgemeine Missionszeitschrift,* and through the pioneer drawing of a large and a small mission atlas: *Allgemeiner Missions-Atlas* (1868–71); *Neuer Missions-Atlas* (1895–1903); *Kleiner Missions-Atlas* (1883 and 1905). He was the founder of the Brandenburgische Missions-Konferenz and its president for twenty-five years.

REINHOLD KUECKLICH.

GUADALUPE. See PILGRIMAGES.

GUARINO OF VERONA: B. in 1374 in Verona; d. Dec. 4, 1460, in Ferrara. He went to Constantinople to study Greek, and upon his return to Italy taught classical letters at Florence, Venice, and Verona. Objecting to the humanistic contention that before 1375 Italian civilization was steeped in darkness, he sought to harmonize the best elements of classical literature with the Christian faith, and inculcated religious fervor in the minds of numerous distinguished young men. He wrote three volumes of illuminating letters (published 1915–19).

BIBLIOGRAPHY: R. Sabbadini, *Vita di Guarino Veronese,* 1891; idem, *La scuola e gli studi di Guarino Veronese,* 1896; G. Bertoni, *Guarino Veronese fra letterati e cortigiani a Ferrara,* 1921.

ALBERT HYMA.

GUATEMALA. See CENTRAL AMERICA.

GUIANA: I. British Guiana: The area of British Guiana is 83,000 square miles, and the population is estimated at 414,887 (1949). The bulk of the population lives in a strip 270 miles along the coast and from twenty to thirty miles inland. Much of this area is below sea level, and the houses are raised on piles above the ground. The capital, Georgetown, has 107,264 inhabitants.

The aboriginal Indians number less than 10,000 and most of them live in the interior. The East Indians, brought originally as indentured labor from India when slavery was abolished, are the largest element in the population, 184,773 (1949). Next come the Africans or Negroes The official language is English.

There are 195 schools supported by government grant, and they have 71,249 pupils.

The first church was founded by Dutch Lutherans at New Amsterdam in 1743. In 1807 the London Missionary Society began work among the slave population, and in 1810 the Church of England became the established church. In 1819 the Church of Scotland started work.

Present religious groups include: Anglicans, Lutherans, Presbyterians, Methodists, Roman Catholics, Moslems, and Hindus. There are eight North American missionary societies, four British, one international, and two national church organizations. There is a Protestant community of 123,508 (1948), and a Christian Council in which Roman Catholics and Protestants co-operate.

Roman Catholic work is under the Jesuits, and there are a vicariate apostolic, twelve parishes, three missions, ten stations with four secular priests and seventeen regular, ten convents, one high school, thirty-two elementary schools, two orphanages.

About 5% of the East Indians are Christian; the rest follow Hindu and Moslem practices and worship.

II. Netherlands Guiana: Area, 55,060 square miles; population estimated at 216,000 (1949). This figure includes the Bush Negroes and Indians living in the forests.

There is complete religious freedom. Religious bodies in 1949 were: Reformed and Lutherans (14,200), Moravian Brethren (36,000), Roman Catholics (35,500), Jews (500), Moslems (50,000), Hindus (47,000), Confucians (4,000), and others (3,200).

III. French Guiana: Area, 90,000 square miles; population, 28,537. Primary education is free and there are several church schools with 1,000 pupils.   [Sup.] W. STANLEY RYCROFT.

GUIBERT OF NOGENT: Died in 1124. His autobiography is now generally considered the most original of the Middle Ages.

BIBLIOGRAPHY: B. Monod, *Le moine Guibert et son temps* (1905), contains a translation of his autobiography; G. Bourgin, *Guibert de Nogent*, 1907; I. Grise'mann, "Die Stellung des Guibert von Nogent in der eucharistielehre fruehscholastik," in *Theologische Quartalschrift*, 110 (1929), 66–84, 279–305.

[Sup.] MATHIAS GOOSSENS.

GUIDO OF AREZZO:

BIBLIOGRAPHY: K. Kornmuller, *Guido von Arezzo*, 1870; G. Ristori, *Biografia di Guido monaco*, 3rd ed., 1880; M. Balchi, *Studii su Guido monaco*, 1882; A. Brandi, *Il beato Guido d' Arezzo*, 1882.

[Sup.] MATHIAS GOOSSENS.

GUIGNEBERT, CHARLES: B. in Villeneuve Saint Georges near Paris, June 18, 1867; baptized a Roman Catholic; d. August 27, 1939 at Clamency, Nièvre. He studied at the Lycée de Versailles and at the Sorbonne, Paris. His teaching career began in the Lycées of Evreux, Pau, Toulouse, and Paris. His doctoral dissertation on Tertullian was so outstanding that in 1906 he was appointed by the minister of National Education to the newly created chair of history of Christianity at the Sorbonne, which he occupied until retirement at seventy. His religious outlook was liberal. He was primarily an historian, but his presentation of Christianity was so profound that many regarded him a specialist in New Testament. His lectures combining learning and excellent speech drew many hearers. His main works are: *Tertullien. Étude sur ses sentiments à l'égard de l'empire et de la société civile* (dissertation) (1901); *Manuel d'histoire ancienne du Christianisme. Les origines* (1906); *Modernisme et tradition catholique en France* (1908); *Le primauté de Pierre et la venue de Pierre à Rome* (1909); *L'evolution des dogmes* (2me edition, 1929); *Le problème de Jésus* (1914); *Le Christianisme antique* (1921); *La vie cachée de Jésus* (1921); *Le Christianisme médiéval et moderne* (1922); *Le problème religieux dans la France d'aujourd'hui* (1922); *Christianity; Past and Present* (1927); (translator), *A Short History of the French People* (1930); *Jésus* (1933, English transl., 1935); *Le monde juif vers le temps de Jésus* (1935, English transl., 1939); and *Le Christ* (1944).

BIBLIOGRAPHY: Marguerite Brunot, *Les Annales de l'Université de Paris*, 4 and 5, 1939; Alfred Loisy, Marcel Simon, *Revue Historique*, 188, 1940.

[Sup.] DANIEL JOHANNES THERON.

GUILDAY, PETER: Catholic; b. at Chester, Pa., Mar. 25, 1884; d. at Washington, D. C., July 31, 1947. He studied at St. Charles Borromeo Seminary, Philadelphia, and the Catholic University of Louvain (D.Sc.Hist., 1914); taught American church history in the Catholic University of America, Washington (1914–47); ordained to the priesthood July 11, 1909, at Louvain; founded the *Catholic Historical Review*, April, 1915, of which he remained editor to his death; founded the American Catholic Historical Association, December 30, 1919, of which he was secretary to 1941 and thereafter honorary president to his death. He was a distinguished orator, a stimulating teacher, and a very productive scholar. He wrote: *The English Colleges and Convents in the Low Countries, 1558–1795* (1914); *An Introduction to Church History* (1925); *The Life and Times of John Carroll, First Archbishop of Baltimore, 1735–1815* (2 vols., 1922); *The Life and Times of John England, First Bishop of Charleston, 1786–1842* (2 vols., 1927); *A History of the Councils of Baltimore, 1791–1884* (1932). In addition Monsignor Guilday edited three volumes of the papers from the annual meetings of the A.C.H.A., and wrote several other monographs.

BIBLIOGRAPHY: J. J. Kortendick, "Contemporary Catholic Authors: Monsignor Peter Guilday, Historian of the American Catholic Church," in *Catholic Library World* (May, 1941); J. T. Ellis, "Peter Guilday," in *Catholic Historical Review*, XXXIII (October, 1947), 257-268.

JOHN TRACY ELLIS.

GUILD OF ST. MATTHEW: Founded by Stewart D. Handlam, priest of the Church of England, in 1877, when curate in London. The Guild was established to oppose secularism (*q.v.*), the object being "to get rid, by every possible means, of the existing prejudices, especially on the part of secularists, against the church, her sacraments, and her doctrines, and to endeavor to justify God to the people." Passionate concern for social justice inherited from the Christian Socialists accompanied the religious purpose. The Guild, though notable, never exceeded 400 in numbers.

BIBLIOGRAPHY: Maurice B. Reckitt, *Maurice to Temple: A Century of the Social Movement in the Church of England,* 1947.

EVELYN C. URWIN.

GUINEA. See AFRICA.

GUMMEY, HENRY RILEY, JR.: Protestant Episcopal; b. at Philadelphia, Pa., January 12, 1870; d. at Philadelphia, Pa., May 30, 1941. He studied at the University of Pennsylvania (B.A., 1890); Divinity School of the Protestant Episcopal Church, Philadelphia, Pa., (D.D., in course 1905). He was professor of liturgics and canon law at the Divinity School of the Protestant Episcopal Church, Philadelphia, Pa. (1929–41). His chief literary contribution is: *The Consecration of the Eucharist—A Study of the Prayer of Consecration in the Communion Office from the Point of View of the Alterations and Amendments Established Therein by the Revisers of 1789* (1908).

SCOTT FRANCIS BRENNER.

GUNKEL, JOHANN FRIEDRICH HERMANN: D. 1932. After teaching Old Testament exegesis at Berlin he later taught in this field at Giessen and Halle. From 1903 to 1920 he was associated in study and publication with J. F. W. Bousset (*q.v.*) and with him developed the religious-historical approach to biblical literature. From this approach developed the form-historical method also known as form criticism (*q.v.*). His *Die Wirkung des Heiligen Geistes nach den populaeren Anschauungen der apostolischen Zeit und nach der Lehre des Paulus* (1888) was reissued in a third edition in 1909. His other major works include: *Zum religionsgeschichtlichen Verstaendnis des Neuen Testaments* (2nd ed., 1910); *Schoepfung und Chaos in Urzeit und Endzeit* (2nd ed., 1921); *Die Propheten* (1917); *Das Maerchen im Alten Testament* (1917); and *Einleitung in die Psalmen* (1928–33).

[Sup.] RAYMOND W. ALBRIGHT.

GUNPOWDER PLOT:

BIBLIOGRAPHY: J. Gerard, *What was the Gunpowder Plot?* 1897, Gerard concludes that the plot was merely a fiction, to which S. R. Gardiner replied in his work of the same year; L. Pastor, *The History of the Popes from the Close of the Middle Ages*, Vol. XXVI (1937), pp. 131-161; C. Williams, *James I* (1952), pp. 181, 194-196.

[Sup.] ALBERT HYMA.

GUNSAULUS, FRANK W(AKELEY): D. Mar. 19, 1921. He served simultaneously as the minister of Central Congregational Church, Chicago (1889–1919) and president of the Armour Institute of Technology (1893–1921). He also lectured regularly at the University of Chicago. He wrote: *Life of William Ewart Gladstone* (1898); and *The Minister and the Spiritual Life* (1911).

[Sup.] RAYMOND W. ALBRIGHT.

GUSTAV ADOLF-VEREIN: Renamed in 1946 the *Gustav Adolf-Werk der Evangelischen Kirche in Deutschland,* the tasks confronting the society were altered by World War I, and especially by World War II. Almost all the Protestants in eastern Europe were driven out, and once solidly Protestant areas of eastern Germany were dispersed. Among the refugees (*q.v.*) who fled to western Germany, about 2,000,000 Protestants settled in Roman Catholic areas. To provide a ministry for them chapels, catechists, and deaconesses (*q.v.*) became a pressing need. Literature and pastoral care were likewise a desideratum. From 1946 to 1951 a total of *DM*106,000,000 were expended in aid to 7,000 congregations. Relations with sister societies in Sweden, Switzerland, Austria, and Holland have been kept alive. Central headquarters are in Kassel.

[Sup.] ERNST WAGNER.

GUSTAVUS ADOLPHUS: B. in Stockholm on Dec. 9, 1594, the eldest son of King Charles' second marriage with Christina of Holstein; d. at the Battle of Lützen, November 16, 1632. He was the greatest monarch in the history of Sweden and raised his country to a first-class nation. But it was not until the year 1953 that a satisfactory account of his career appeared in the English language. Such is the biography by Professor Michael Roberts, *Gustavus Adolphus: A History of Sweden 1611–1632*. The author shows that in 1611 Sweden was "a beaten, impoverished and insignificant" country that "lay almost unregarded on the periphery of the Protestant world," while in 1632 she "gave the law to Germany, bullied Richelieu, dominated the Baltic, and stood unchallenged at the head of evangelical Europe." (The term "evangelical" is identical here with "Lutheran.") This valuable work contains a lengthy bibliography on pp. 528–564.   [Sup.] ALBERT HYMA.

H

HAAG, HENRI: B. at Aubange, Belgium, Dec. 4, 1917. He studied at the University of Louvain (Docteur en Philosophie et Lettres, 1944; Agrégé de l'enseignement superieur, 1950). He was maître de conferences at the same university (1951). He wrote: *Les Droits de la Cité* (1946); *Les Origines du Catholicisme libéral en Belgique* (1950).

HAAS, JOHN A(UGUSTUS) W(ILLIAM): D. July 22, 1937. For a generation he was the president of Muhlenberg College, Allentown, Pa. (1904–37), where during the earlier years of this service he also taught religion and philosophy. His major writings came late in his life: *In the Light of Faith* (1922); *Freedom and Christian Conduct* (1923); *The Unity of Faith and Knowledge* (1926); *The Truth of Faith* (1927); *What Ought I to Believe?* (1929); *The Christian Way of Liberty* (1930); and *Christianity and Its Contrasts* (1932).
          [Sup.] RAYMOND W. ALBRIGHT.

HABAKKUK, BOOK OF: The discovery of a commentary on Habakkuk among the Dead Sea Scrolls (*q.v.*) (1947) has awakened fresh interest in this prophecy. Nothing definite is known about the author. The book has suffered greatly at the hands of critics. Some (Mowinckel, Horst) date it before the fall of Nineveh in 612 B.C. Others (Duhm, Sellin, Torrey) refer it to the time of Alexander the Great (331 B.C.). The majority still support the traditional date (*ca.* 605–597 B.C.). While the book embraces two distinct parts, oracles of judgment (chs. 1 and 2) and an appended psalm (ch. 3), it is probably the work of a single author, who was both a cultic prophet and a poet or musician (Albright, Leslie).

BIBLIOGRAPHY: P. Humbert, *Problèmes du livre d'Habacuc*, 1944; W. F. Albright, "The Psalm of Habakkuk," in *Studies in Old Testament Prophecy* (H. H. Rowley, ed.) (1950), 1–18. See also commentaries and works on Introduction.
          [Sup.] ELMER E. FLACK.

HABAKKUK SCROLL. See DEAD SEA SCROLLS.

GWATKIN, HENRY M(ELVILL): D. Nov. 14, 1916. He served with marked distinction as Dixie Professor of Ecclesiastical History in Cambridge University and was fellow of Emmanuel College (1891–1916). The culmination of his scholarly writing came in his *Early Church History to A.D. 313* (2 vols., 1909; 2nd ed., 1912; 1927) and he also served as joint editor of the *Cambridge Medieval History* after 1911.
          [Sup.] RAYMOND W. ALBRIGHT.

HABIRU: The Habiru are well known from numerous references in Mesopotamian, Canaanite, and Egyptian sources during the third and second millennia B.C. The possible relationship between these Habiru and the Hebrews of the Old Testament is a chief unresolved problem of scholarship. Formerly the equivalence, Habiru = Hebrew, was generally accepted. It is now known, however, that the correct form of this word is *'apiru*, as Ugaritic *'prm* (pl.) and Egyptian *'a-pi-ru* show. The familiar form *ḥa-bi-ru* represents the Akkadian transcription of the original West Semitic word: thus *ḥ* regularly stands for Canaanite *ayin*, and the sign BI may indicate the pronunciation *pi* as well as *bi*. Biblical *'ibrî*, "a Hebrew" (from *'ēber*) may be a dialectal form of *'iprî;* the phonetic shift *p-b* can be demonstrated in a number of cases. Then *'apiru* would be an adjectival formation from *'iprî*. The equation therefore is quite possible, even probable, but as yet not proven.

Aside from the linguistic material, the traditions about the Hebrews and the data on the *'apiru* have striking similarities. There is a strong note of disparagement and contempt in the use of the terms. The *'apiru* everywhere have inferior status. In some cases they are mercenary soldiers, or bandit raiders; on the other hand, they are often captives and slaves. In Old Testament usage "Hebrew" is frequently a term of reproach: the Israelites in the days of bondage are so designated by the Egyptians; and again by the Philistines during the oppression in the promised land. As its wide usage indicates, the word *'apiru* cannot be limited to the Israelites; but this is true also of *'ibrî* in the Old Testament. The genealogical tables as well as other references show: (1) that the Hebrews were an important element in the population of Israel, but also (2) that the Israelites were only one of many groups to whom that term applied.

BIBLIOGRAPHY: H. W. Rowley, *From Joseph to Joshua: Biblical Traditions in the Light of Archaeology* (1950), pp. 38–56.
          DAVID NOEL FREEDMAN.

HACKETT, WILLIAM: See Messiahs, False.

HADEWYCH: The great artist and mystic known under the name of Hadewych lived about the middle of the thirteenth century. According to a tradition, not well established as yet, she belonged to a noble family in Antwerp. At any rate, she received an exceptionally good education; she knew not only her native tongue, Flemish, but also French and Latin. She witnessed the early development of the beguinages (see Beghards and Beguines). Although she did not join one of these, she lived for a time with some women who were closely associated with the beguines. This friendship of hers caused her much disappointment and grief, as her writings indicate.

Hadewych's literary work comprises forty-five strophic poems, fourteen visions, thirty-one letters, and sixteen didactic poems. In this work she reveals a consummate art, her language being enriched with beautiful rhyme and artistic sound. She was the troubadour of the courtly, divine love. Sometimes this is the love which the soul enjoys in God; sometimes Christ is the love which she depicts. The reading of her works requires thoughtful study and application. According to some experts Hadewych is one of the greatest mystic poets of all time.

See also Mysticism and Asceticism in the Netherlands.

Bibliography: Hadewych, *Visioenen* (J. van Mierlo, ed.), 1924; Hadewych, *Strophische gedichten* (J. van Mierlo, ed.), 1942; Hadewych, *Brieven* (J. van Mierlo, ed.), 1947; Hadewych, *Mengeldichten* (J. van Mierlo, ed.), 1952.

M. M. J. Smits van Waesberghe.

HAEMSTEDE, ADRIAAN (CORNELIS) VAN: B. *ca.* 1525; d. 1562 at Oldersum in East Friesland. He studied at Louvain. In 1552 he published his work, *Tabulae totius Sacrosancti Juris Canonici*. In 1556 he was a pastor in Emden, and in the same year went to Antwerp, remaining there until August, 1557, and laboring with great success. Many monks and priests were persuaded by him to leave for Emden, where Calvinism was predominant and life more simple than in the great commercial city. He was not always pleased with developments among the Protestants in Antwerp, complaining about differences of opinion among members of local churches. The elders in the Walloon Church argued that preaching should not be done in public, but he felt that the congregation had become so large as to make preaching in secret no longer feasible. On Dec. 1, 1557, he wrote a letter to King Henry II of France, exhorting the monarch to restrict the persecution of the French Calvinists. About this time he held a debate at Oudenaarde with a certain Jan Daelman, who had previously been a member of the local Calvinist church but had out-wardly conformed to Catholicism. He fought hard against such neo-Nicodemites. In Antwerp difficulties arose over his practice of holding meetings in homes of persons who did not belong to the Calvinist congregations, but the authorities at Emden decreed that he was correct. The sermon preached by him at Antwerp on June 9, 1558, which was Sacrament Day, resulted in vehement persecution of the local Calvinists. A price of 300 Caroline guilders was put on his head.

In February, 1559, he and some Flemish families removed to Aachen, where he founded a pilgrim church. For this church he sent a request to the Diet at Augsburg for religious toleration. He also prepared a confession of faith, written in Latin, a copy of which was sent on Sept. 12, 1559, to the Elector of the Palatinate. It was very practical in nature, based very largely on the Bible, not definitely Protestant, in order to obtain recognition at the Diet of Augsburg. But he kept up contacts with the Calvinists, resembling Melanchthon in his efforts to promote peace and harmony among orthodox Christians. Some sections agree almost verbally with those in the Confession of the Martyrs published in the Martyr Book by Haemstede. Haemstede's confession was directed against Roman Catholics and Anabaptists (*q.v.*).

In May, 1559, he was in London, where he served the Calvinist congregation for a few months as preacher. He experienced considerable opposition from the authorities, both English and Dutch, because he adopted a conciliatory attitude toward the Baptists, and on Nov. 16, 1560, he was excommunicated by Bishop Grindall. Returning from London in December, 1560, he settled at Oldersum in East Friesland. In the summer of 1562 he was back in London, but on Aug. 21, 1562, it was decreed that he must leave England within fifteen days or suffer the death penalty. He returned to Oldersum where he died the same year. His lack of success in London and to some extent elsewhere was due partly to his disagreeable temperament and his refusal on occasion to make concessions to opponents. But he was a very able scholar and preacher.

In 1559 appeared the first edition of his Martyr Book in Antwerp. It covered the history of martyrdom from the time of Christ to the year 1559, as the lengthy title indicated. The second edition followed in 1565, and was probably published at Vianen, and sponsored by Hendrik van Brederode. Between this year and 1657 his name did not appear on the title page of his popular book, because he was considered too liberal in his theology.

Bibliography: J. Lindeboom, *Austin Friars* (1950), pp. 41–45; *Biogra. Woordenboek van Prot. Godgeleerden in Ned.*, III, 439–446, with extensive bibliography; T. S. Jansma, "De boeken van Van Haemstede," in *Huldeboek-*

Kruitwagen (1949), 196–203; J. H. Wessels, *De leerstellige strijd tusschen Nederlandsche Gereformeerden en Doopsgezinden in de zestiende eeuw* (1945), *passim.*

D. NAUTA.

HAERING, THEODOR: B. at Stuttgart, Germany, April 22, 1848; d. at Tuebingen, March 10, 1928. Influenced much by Wuerttemberg's Pietism and the teaching of Albrecht Ritschl he developed, nevertheless, an individual theological system and influenced an entire generation of pastors. His chief later works are: commentaries on Romans, Hebrews, and the Pastoral Epistles; collections of sermons; and *Von Ewigen Dingen* (1922).

BIBLIOGRAPHY: *Festschriften zum 70. Geburtstag* (1918); F. Traub, *Deutscher Nekrolog.*

[Sup.] RAYMOND W. ALBRIGHT.

HAERING, THEODOR L.: B. April 22, 1884, at Stuttgart, Germany. He studied theology and philosophy at Tuebingen, Halle, Berlin, and Bonn. He taught at Tuebingen (1912–51; emeritus, 1951–) and devoted himself primarily to the history of philosophy and related fields. His chief works are: *Der Duisburgische Kantnachlass um 1775* (1910); *Untersuchungen zur Psychologie der Wertung* (1913); *Die Materialisierung des Geistes* (1919); *Die Struktur der Weltgeschichte* (criticism of Spengler) (1921); *Philosophie der Naturwissenschaft* (1923); *Hegel, sein Wollen und sein Werk* (Vol. I, 1928; Vol. II, 1938); *Individualitaet in Natur- und Geisteswelt* (1925); *Grundprobleme der Geschichtsphilosophie* (1924); and *Schwabenspiegel* (1950).

RAYMOND W. ALBRIGHT.

HAGGAI, BOOK OF: Archaeological investigation has given reality to that period of Jewish history following the edict of Cyrus. Haggai may have been one of the exiles who returned from Babylon, or perhaps an old man who had seen the first temple, but had remained behind during the captivity. Marti and Klostermann suggest that his name is not a proper name at all, and that the book is therefore anonymous. Rothstein believes the apparent "revolt" against Zerubbabel may reflect itself in the Samaritan schism. In part he is followed by Finkelstein and Morgenstern. Recent study in the minor prophets and in this book primarily concerns the metrical and cultic background. Mitchell suggested the poetic form and is followed by Engnell and Bentzen. Mowinckel, Haldar and Johnson, following Gunkel, are interested in the cultic prophet, of whom Haggai is taken as a typical example. The prophetic torah in 2:10 ff. is no longer considered antithetical to a priestly torah, but complementary to it. The versions also emphasize the priestly descent of Haggai and their attribution to him of several psalms reinforces this newer approach.

BIBLIOGRAPHY: J. Rothstein, *Juden und Samaritaner,* 1908; P. F. Bloomhardt, *The Poems of Haggai,* 1928; J. Morgenstern, *Amos Studies,* 1940. See also works on Introduction and commentaries on the Minor Prophets.

[Sup.] C. UMHAU WOLF.

HAGUE ASSOCIATION, THE: After 1900 the society clung to its liberal maxim that it is better to maintain Christianity by impartial research than by adhering to old notions and refuting different opinions. International prizes were offered at regular times for the advancement of the scientific study of Christianity. In 1910 the purely scientific sphere was abandoned and a seminary was established to impress upon teachers the significance of religion in human life. In 1924 the society founded two private chairs at the University of Utrecht to counterbalance a one-sided orthodoxy. Thus its aims have completely changed and it has become liberal. [Sup.] WILLEM JAN KOOIMAN.

HAIN, FRIEDRICH AUGUST. See MESSIAHS, FALSE.

HAITI. See WEST INDIES.

HALDANE, J(OHN) B(URDON) S(ANDERSON): B. Nov. 5, 1892. He was educated at Eton and New College, Oxford. He taught biochemistry at Cambridge (1922–32); genetics at London University (1933–37); and since then has been professor of biometry at University College, London. His books of interest to readers of religious background include: *Science and Ethics* (1928); *The Inequality of Man* (1932); *The Causes of Evolution* (1933); *Fact and Faith* (1934); *The Marxist Philosophy and the Sciences* (1938); and *Science Advances* (1947). RAYMOND W. ALBRIGHT.

HALDAR, ALFRED OSSIAN: B. in Vedby, Skane, March 31, 1907. He studied at Lund University (Cand.Phil., 1930; Cand.Th., 1932) and at Uppsala (Lic.Th., 1940; Ph.D., 1945). He became instructor in comparative religion at Uppsala in 1945; professor of Assyriology, 1951. Among his works are: *Associations of Cult Prophets Among the Ancient Semites* (1945); *Studies in the Book of Nahum* (1946–47); *The Notion of the Desert in Sumero-Accadian and West-Semitic Religions* (1950).

ELMER E. FLACK.

HALE LECTURES: According to terms of the will of Charles Reuben Hale, bishop coadjutor of Springfield (1892–1900), a lectureship was established at Western Theological Seminary, Chicago (now Seabury-Western Theological Seminary, Evanston, Ill.) for the general purpose of promoting the catholic faith, the lectures to deal with one of the following fields: liturgics, church music, the history of the Eastern or national churches, and general church history since 1833. Sixteen volumes of lectures have been published between 1910 and 1951. Lecturers included Peter C. Lutkin, John Wordsworth, Anthony Mitchell, S. A. B. Mercer, Frank Gavin, Frederick C. Grant, Burton Scott Easton, John Rathbone Oliver, William G. Peck, Winfred Douglas, Henry St. George Tucker, Fleming James, E. Clowes Chorley, Frank A. McElwain, Alec Vidler, Leonard Hodgson.

ALDEN DREW KELLEY.

HALL, GRANVILLE STANLEY: Protestant; psychologist and educator; b. at Ashfield, Mass., Feb. 1, 1846; d. 1924. He studied at Williams College (A.B., 1867; A.M., 1870); Union Theological Seminary (1867–68); Berlin and Bonn (1868–71); Berlin and Heidelberg (1871–72); and Harvard (Ph.D., 1878). He taught psychology at Antioch College (1872–76), English at Harvard (1876–77), psychology at Harvard and Williams (1880–81), and psychology at Johns Hopkins (1881–88), where he founded one of the first psychology laboratories in the country and included among his students John Dewey (q.v.) and Joseph Jastrow. When Clark University was opened in 1889 in Worcester, Mass., he was appointed president and professor of psychology. During his administration considerable educational research was carried out. He resigned in 1920 but continued to write until his death. While his methods often lacked the precision of other social scientists in his day, he, nevertheless, precipitated active interest and research in the fields of psychology and education. He perhaps was best known as an advocate of the culture-epoch theory which was set forth in his most influential book, *Adolescence.*

He was the founder and editor of the *American Journal of Psychology* (1887–1921); *American Journal of Religious Psychology and Education* (1904–15); and the *Journal of Applied Psychology.* His publications include: *Aspects of German Culture* (1881); *Contents of Children's Minds on Entering School* (1884); *Hints Towards a Select and Descriptive Bibliography of Education* (1886); *Adolescence* (1904); *Youth— Its Education, Regimen and Hygiene* (1907); *Educational Problems* (1911); *Founders of Modern Psychology* (1912); *Jesus Christ in the Light of Psychology* (1917); *Morale: The Supreme Standard of Life and Conduct* (1920); *Senescence* (1922); *Life and Confessions of a Psychologist* (1923).

ROLLIN JONATHAN FAIRBANKS.

HALLER, WILLIAM: B. in New York, N. Y., May 12, 1885. He studied at Amherst College (A.B., 1908) and Columbia University (Ph.D., 1916). He was instructor and professor of English in Barnard College and faculty of philosophy, Columbia University (1909–50); honorary fellow, Folger Shakespeare Library

(1950–   ). He was editor with others of Columbia edition, *Works of John Milton;* edited *Tracts on Liberty in the Puritan Revolution* (1944); author of *The Rise of Puritanism* (1938). His studies in the history of Puritanism and related topics are the outgrowth of studies in English literature and English and American history.

HALLUCINATION: Defined technically as "an abnormal sensory experience that has no real and external stimulus" (Maslow and Mittelman, *Principles of Abnormal Psychology* [1951], p. 578). In American culture, particularly of strata of society above the middle class, hallucinations are taken as *prima facia* evidence of mental illness and an indication for psychiatric hospitalization. Usually these symptoms consist of "hearing voices" or "seeing things" of a bizarre nature. In some instances, hallucinations of touch, such as crawling vermin, and hallucinations of smell may appear.

The pastor or persons working in other religious roles occasionally discover these symptoms in persons whom they counsel. Several things need to be noted here.

First, the pastor who works with people of lower social classes or persons who live on a much more primitive level of reality needs to be very careful not to interpret *culturally expected* religious "visions" and "voices" as *necessarily* being signs of mental illness. Like trances, these experiences, according to Ruth Benedict in her book, *Patterns of Culture,* are considered "abnormality in our society. Even a very mild mystic is aberrant in Western Civilization." Even Benedict's statement needs qualification by saying: "at certain levels of Western civilization and in certain areas of the Western Hemisphere." Anyone who has worked among industrial and rural people in the United States can tell of people who relate auditory and visual mystical experiences and yet who function smoothly in their homes and at their work. The provincialism of upper class and middle class Americans can be surpassed only by the provincialism of the submerged tenth!

Second, the pastor needs to pay attention to the symbolic meaning and qualitative structure of the hallucinations. Anton Boisen likes to say that *what* the voices say is extremely important. Some voices are accusing, condemning and destructive voices. Others are reassuring, instructive, and positive in their message. Boisen suggests wisely that the pastor's task, and particularly that of the mental hospital chaplain, is to help the patient make sense out of the nonsense by seeking to discern what the real communication means.

Finally, hallucinations can be understood psychologically by reference to the nature and function of the unconscious. The forces of repression can become so effective in sealing off one part of the self of an individual from the rest (these are symbolic terms in themselves) that the unconscious needs are totally alienated. Any communication, therefore, that gets through to consciousness literally bursts through and is perceived as being from the outside of the self, or even as being from another world. The perceptive result is an auditory or even visual hallucination.

See also PSYCHOLOGY.

BIBLIOGRAPHY: A. H. Maslow and B. Mittleman, *Principles of Abnormal Psychology*, rev. ed., 1951; Anton Boisen, *The Exploration of the Inner World*, 1951; Karl Menninger, *The Human Mind*, 3rd ed., 1947.

WAYNE E. OATES.

HAMBURG: After 1937, when the old territory of the Hanseatic city of Hamburg was enlarged by the annexation of adjacent sections of the provinces of Schleswig-Holstein (*q.v.*) and Lower Saxony, the city limits and the church boundaries were no longer the same. The Evangelical Lutheran Church in the State of Hamburg now extended only over the historical territory of the original free city. Its membership was about 850,000 in 1953, approximately 80,000 below the membership of 1939. This decrease was due to high losses during the bombings of World War II which damaged Hamburg considerably, and also to the general shift of population in Germany. The so-called "movement away from the church" (see KIRCHENAUSTRITT) of the years from 1935 to 1939 did little harm. The Roman Catholic Church gained considerably through the influx of refugees (*q.v.*) from eastern Germany who made up about 10% of the population in 1953. Hamburg is a part of the Roman Catholic diocese of Osnabrueck. All free churches in Hamburg are represented by smaller congregations of the different denominations.

The Lutheran Church of Hamburg consists of 55 congregations with 153 pastors. The constitution in force was adopted on May 30, 1923, and amended July 4, 1946, when provision was made for a bishop. This constitution represents a happy mixture of traditional elements inherited from the time of the Reformation and modern democratic tendencies. The highest and final administrative body is the synod, consisting of pastors and lay representatives of the congregations. In addition to the synod there is a time-honored institution of the so-called *Hauptpastoren*, or chief pastors, five in number, who are supposed to represent the spiritual and intellectual elite of the clergy. These five men, who are at the same time chairmen of the five conferences which make up the synod, have the additional title of *Oberkirchenrat*. Together with the bishop, they form the executive body of the church which acts in the name of the synod. In 1948 the church became a member

church of the United Lutheran Church in Germany (*q.v.*).

In many respects Hamburg is a leader in the work of the church at large. It is the seat of the German Evangelical Mission Assembly (*Missionstag*) under the presidency of Professor Walter Freytag. The Preachers' Seminary of the Federation of Evangelical Free Churches in Germany is located there. In 1948, because there was then no theological faculty in the state university, the Evangelical Lutheran Church founded a seminary with an excellent teaching staff under Professor Kurt-Dietrich Schmidt. With an enrollment of over 100, this seminary became the theological faculty of the University of Hamburg in 1953. Immediately after World War II an Evangelical Academy (*q.v.*) came into existence under the direction of Hermann Junge.

Hamburg is also a center for the work of the Inner Mission (*q.v.*). Amalie Sieveking (*q.v.*, Vol. X) founded the Women's Organization for the Care of the Poor and the Sick, and thus began the first such organized work of deaconesses in the church. John William Rautenberg (*q.v.*, Vol. IX), under English sponsorship and with English financial help, organized the first Sunday school. John Henry Wichern (*q.v.*, Vol. XII) in 1833 opened the gates of the *Rauhes Haus*, a noted educational institution for boys and educators of boys. In the year 1848 the Rev. Mr. Sengelmann began his work for the mentally ill which finally grew into the Alsterdorf Institutions.

BIBLIOGRAPHY: Simon Schoeffel, *Kirchengeschichte Hamburgs*, Vol. I, 1929; Hermann Reincke, *Hamburg, Ein Abriss der Stadtgeschichte von den Anfaengen bis zur Gegenwart*, 1925; *Das Lutherische Hamburg. Aufsaetze zu Geschichte und Gegenwart des Luthertums in Hamburg*, 1929.

[Sup.] HAGEN STAACK.

HAMILTON, JOHN TAYLOR: Retired 1928; d. at Bethlehem, Pa., Jan. 29, 1951. He wrote the following additional book: *Twenty Years of Pioneer Missions in Nyasaland* (1912); and the following monographs: *The Recognition of the Episcopate of the Moravian Church by Act of Parliament in 1749* (1925); *The Contacts of the Moravian Church with the Iroquois League* (1931). [Sup.] KENNETH G. HAMILTON.

HAMILTON, KENNETH GARDINER: Moravian bishop; b. at Bethlehem, Pa., Feb. 20, 1893. He was educated in Moravian schools in Germany and America, taking postgraduate work at Columbia University. He served successively as pastor, Y.M.C.A. secretary among prisoners of war, missionary in Nicaragua, professor and dean at Moravian Theological Seminary, vice-president of his denominational executive board and executive officer of its interprovincial mission board. He is author of: *Meet Nicaragua* (1939); and *John Ettwein and* *the Moravian Church during the Revolutionary Period* (1941).

HAMMURABI: No unanimity has been reached in explaining the name, though "great as to kin" seems to have preference. It is now known to be fairly common among Amorites of the time. The identification of Hammurabi of Babylon with Amraphel (Gen. 14:1) has been given up for linguistic and historical reasons. The date has been lowered considerably in the past forty years, preference now given to 1728–1686 B.C. for his rule, though several scholars believe this must be raised to some extent. See also BABYLONIA.

BIBLIOGRAPHY: F. M. Boehl. *King Hammurabi of Babylon in the Setting of His Time*, 1946; W. F. Albright, *BASOR*, Vol. 88, pp. 28–33.
                                                     [Sup.] GEORGE E. MENDENHALL.

HAMPTON COURT CONFERENCE:
BIBLIOGRAPHY: E. Cardwell, *A History of Conferences* (1840), pp. 198–203; C. Williams, *James I* (1952), pp. 188–191; G. Davies, *The Early Stuarts 1603–1660* (1937), pp. 68–71.   [Sup.] ALBERT HYMA.

HANDY, ROBERT THEODORE: Church historian; b. Connecticut, June 30, 1918. He was educated at Brown University (A.B., 1940), Colgate Rochester Divinity School (B.D., 1943), and the University of Chicago (Ph.D., 1949). Ordained to the Baptist ministry in 1943, he served two years as pastor of the South Church (Community-Baptist) of Mount Prospect, Illinois. After a two-year period as an army transport chaplain, he became instructor in the history of religions at the Baptist Missionary Training School in Chicago (1948–49), and chairman of the division of humanities at Frances Shimer College at Mount Carroll, Ill. (1949–50). He has taught church history at Union Theological Seminary, New York (1950– ; associate professor, 1954–).

HANOVER: After World War I a new constitution was drafted for the Lutheran Church of Hanover and went into effect in 1924. August Marahrens was elected the first bishop (1925–47) and was a vigorous opponent of the "German Christians" (see GERMANY, I). The church suffered from the hostility of National Socialism and the effects of World War II; in the spring of 1945, 450 clergymen were in the army and 782 churches had been destroyed or rendered unusable. At the close of the war the constitutional order of the church was restored and Johannes Lilje was elected bishop.

Congregations, each with pastors and church councils, are divided among eighty-six districts, each with its district council and synod. There are nine dioceses under the oversight of superintendents. The bishop is the spiritual head of the whole church and presides over a senate (with legislative powers) and a *Landeskirchen-*

amt (with executive powers). The ultimate source of authority is the territorial synod, which has a standing committee. Auxiliaries for work among men, women, and young people and for inner mission activity are loosely related to the ecclesiastical organization.

Except for a few congregations outside, the territory of the church is identical with that of the province of Lower Saxony (*Niedersachsen*), 74% of whose population is Lutheran. In 1950 there were 3,900,000 members, about 30% of them refugees (*q.v.*). The church is a member of the United Evangelical Lutheran Church in Germany (*q.v.*), of the Lutheran World Federation (*q.v.*), and of the Evangelical Church in Germany (see GERMANY, I).

BIBLIOGRAPHY: Johannes Meyer, *Kirchengeschichte Niedersachens*, 1939.
                                                     [Sup.] PHILIPP MEYER.

HARD-SHELL BAPTISTS: The remnant of hyper-Calvinists among Baptists who opposed all agencies not strictly authorized by Scripture, including missionary societies, Bible societies, Sunday schools, temperance societies, and secret societies. Some practiced foot-washing. They undoubtedly reflected not only the influence of their biblicism, but the general hostility and suspicion with which the East was held by most frontier settlers. Called by such names as Old School, Regular, Antimission, or Primitive Baptists, Hard-Shell Baptists enjoyed a rapid growth at first, increasing from over 1,600 churches with 61,000 members in 1844 to well over 121,000 members in nearly 3,000 churches in 1890. They were strongest in Southern states, Illinois, and Indiana. By 1951 their number had decreased to about 69,000.

BIBLIOGRAPHY: Frank S. Mead, *Handbook of Denominations in the United States*, 1951; Robert G. Torbet, *A History of the Baptists*, 1950.
                                                     ROBERT G. TORBET.

HARDY, EDWARD ROCHIE, JR.: Episcopalian; b. New York, June 17, 1908; Byzantinist and church historian; trained at Columbia University, and General and Union Theological Seminaries, New York. He was a fellow, tutor, and instructor at General Seminary (1929–44), and taught church history at Berkeley Divinity School, New Haven, Conn. (1945–). He is the author of: *The Large Estates of Byzantine Egypt* (1931); *Militant in Earth: Twenty Centuries of the Spread of Christianity* (1940); *Christian Egypt: Church and People* (1952); and editor of *Orthodox Statements on Anglican Orders* (1946).

HARKNESS, GEORGIA ELMA: Methodist; b. at Harkness, N. Y., April 21, 1891. She was educated at Cornell University (A.B., 1912), Boston University (Ph.D., 1923), and at Harvard, Yale, and Union Theological Seminary.

After teaching at Elmira College (1922–37), Mount Holyoke College (1937–39), and Garrett Biblical Institute (1939–50), she became professor of applied theology at the Pacific School of Religion, Berkeley, Calif. (1950–). Major interests are world peace, the devotional life, and interpretation of theology to laymen. She has written: *The Church and the Immigrant* (1921); *Conflicts in Religious Thought* (1929); *John Calvin: the Man and His Ethics* (1931); *Holy Flame* (verse) (1935); *The Resources of Religion* (1936); *The Recovery of Ideals* (1937); *Religious Living* (1937); *The Faith by Which the Church Lives* (1940); *The Glory of God* (1943); *The Dark Night of the Soul* (1945); *Understanding the Christian Faith* (1947); *Prayer and the Common Life* (1948); *The Gospel and Our World* (1949); *Through Christ our Lord* (1950).

HARKNESS, REUBEN ELMORE ERNEST: Baptist; b. at Sarnia, Ontario, Canada, Oct. 27, 1884. He studied at McMaster University, Toronto (B.A., 1907), University of Chicago (M.A., 1915; B.D., 1917; Ph.D., 1927). He was pastor First Baptist Church, Belvidere, Ill. (1915–19); Union Congregational, Waupun, Wisc. (1919–24); Woodstock, Ill. (1924–27); professor history of Christianity, Crozer Theological Seminary, Chester, Pa. (1927–50; professor emeritus, 1950–). He was editor, *The Crozer Quarterly* (1937–40), *The Chronicle* (since founding, 1938).

HARMON, NOLAN BAILEY, JR.: Methodist; b. Meridian, Miss., July 14, 1892. He was educated at Millsaps College, Emory, and Princeton. He was a chaplain, pastor, and editor of church organ of Baltimore Conference (M. E. Church South) successively; elected book editor of the (United) Methodist Church (1940), and of *Religion in Life*. His books include: *The Rites and Ritual of Episcopal Methodism; The Organization of The Methodist Church;* and *Ministerial Ethics and Etiquette.*

HARMONY OF THE GOSPELS (TATIAN'S): In 1935 there was published a tiny parchment fragment of Tatian's Diatessaron in Greek, thus putting to an end the long debate whether or not Tatian's Harmony ever existed in Greek. The following translation of this fragment, discovered among the debris used in fortifying the Roman garrison city, Dura, on the Euphrates, just prior to its fall to the Persians under King Shapur I in A.D. 256–257, will give an idea of Tatian's painstaking attention to details in making a cento of all the distinctive elements of the four Gospels. (The restorations are enclosed within square brackets, and Scripture references—which are not, of course, in the fragment—are enclosed within parentheses.)

"[. . . the mother of the sons of Zebed]ee (Matt. 27:56) and Salome (Mark 15:40) and the wives [of those who] had followed him from [Galile]e to see the crucified (Luke 23:49b–c). And [the da]y was Preparation; the Sabbath was daw[ning] (Luke 23:54). And when it was evening (Matt. 27:57), on the Prep[aration], that is, the day before the Sabbath (Mark 15:42), [there came] up a man (Matt. 27:57), be[ing] a member of the Council (Luke 23:50), from Aramathea (Matt. 27:57), a city of Judea (Luke 23:51), by name Jo[seph] (Matt. 27:57), good and ri[ghteous] (Luke 23:50), being a disciple of Jesus, but se[cret]ly, for fear of the [Jew]s (John 19:38). And he (Matt. 27:57) was looking for [the] kingdom of God (Luke 23:51b). This man [had] not [con]sented to [their] p[urpose . . .] (Luke 23:51a)" (translated from C. H. Kraeling's edition in *Studies and Documents*, III, 1935).

Perhaps the most interesting variant reading preserved only in this fragment is the reference (based, it is true, partly on a restoration) to "the wives [of those who] had followed" Jesus from Galilee.

Secondary and tertiary witnesses to Tatian's Diatessaron are the following:

I. Eastern Witnesses: (1) The Syriac commentary on the Diatessaron by Ephraem (fourth century), preserved in an Armenian translation extant in two manuscripts (re-edited and translated by Louis Leloir [1954]); (2) an Arabic Diatessaron made from the Syriac and extant in two forms (A. S. Marmardji, ed.; see also A. J. B. Higgins, in *JTS*, Vol. XLX [1944], pp. 187–199; Georg Graf, *Geschichte der christlichen arabischen Literatur*, Vol. I [*Studi e Testi*, 118 (1944)], pp. 152–154; Paul Kahle, *The Cairo Geniza* [1947], pp. 197 ff.); (3) a Syriac Diatessaric lectionary for Passiontide extant in about twenty-five manuscripts (see appendix in Marmardji, *op. cit.*, pp. 1*–75*; also D. Willy in *Expository Times*, Vol. XXV [1913–14], pp. 31–35); (4) a medieval Persian Harmony of the Gospels made from a Syriac base (Giuseppe Messina, ed., *Diatessaron Persiano*, 1951), which contains also certain influence from the Protoevangelium of James; (5) evidence in various Syriac and Armenian Church Fathers, e.g., Aphraates, the *Liber Graduum*, Agathangelos, Eznik, etc., as well as the Armenian Breviary and Ritual (see St. Lyonnet, *Les origines de la version arménienne et le Diatessaron*, 1950), and Coptic Manichaean fragments (Polotsky and Allberry, eds.).

II. Western Witnesses: (6) the Codex Fuldensis (sixth century); (7) various medieval German Harmonies; (8) Middle Dutch (Flemish) Harmonies, the best known of which is the Liège Manuscript (Daniel Plooij, C. A. Phillips, and A. H. A. Bakker, eds., parts I–V, 1929–38); (9) two Old Italian Harmonies, one in the Tuscan dialect preserved in twenty-four manuscripts, the other in the Venetian dialect preserved in one manuscript (V. Todesco, A. Vaccari, and M. Vattasso, eds., *Il Diatessaron in volgare italiano*, 1938); (10) a Middle English Harmony which once belonged to Samuel Pepys (Margery Goates, ed., *The Pepysian Gospel Harmony*, 1927); (11) the harmonized Gospel text on which Zacharias Chrysopolitanus (Zachary of Besançon) wrote a commentary, early twelfth century (Migne, *PL*, CLXXXVI, cols. 11–620).

Not long after the Dura fragment was published another leaf (to be dated from the fifth or sixth century), believed to be from the Greek Diatessaron, was edited by Otto Stegmueller (*ZNTW*, Vol. XXXVII [1938], pp. 223–229). Further research, however, has not supported the original editor's belief, and Curt Peters has argued convincingly that at most this fragment reveals the influence of Tatian's Diatessaron in its variant readings (*Biblica*, Vol. XXI, [1940], pp. 51–55). The selections from Matthew and John which Agnes Smith Lewis published as "Fragments of a Greek Harmony of the Gospels" (in *Codex Climaci Rescriptus* [1909], xxvii–xxx) were drawn up in accord with a different plan from that of Tatian's Diatessaron.

A critical comparison of the sources mentioned above reveals the following characteristic details which scholars believe were present in the original Diatessaron. Several of these are noticeably colored by Tatian's Encratite leanings. (1) The account of light or fire seen at the baptism of Jesus; (2) the Davidic descent of Mary; (3) avoidance of reference to Joseph as the husband of Mary; (4) avoidance of reference to Joseph as Jesus' father; (5) the reduction of the married life of Hannah the prophetess to seven days; (6) the modification of the diet of John the Baptist to milk and honey; (7) transfer from God to Adam of the statement that a man and his wife shall be one flesh; (8) the addition of "with a rope" to the account of Judas' having hanged himself.

BIBLIOGRAPHY: The literature is very extensive. The best recent monograph is: Curt Peters, *Das Diatessaron Tatians; seine Ueberlieferung und sein Nachwirken im Morgen- und Abendland, sowie der heutige Stand seiner Erforschung*, 1939. Subsequent studies include: C. C. Torrey, *Documents of the Primitive Church*, (1941), pp. 271–295; C. Peters, "Die Entstehung der griechischen Diatessaron-uebersetzung und ihr Nachhall in byzantinischen Kirchen-poesie," in *Orientalia christiana periodica*, VIII (1942), 468–476; A. J. B. Higgins, "Tatian's Arabic Diatessaron" (summary, Ph.D. dissertation), in *Journal of the Manchester University Egyptian and Oriental Society*, XXIV (1942–45), 28–32; Matthew Black, *An Aramaic Approach to the Gospels and Acts* (1946), pp. 220–230; A. F. J. Klijn, *A Survey of the Researches into the Western Text of the Gospels and Acts* (dissertation, Utrecht, 1949), pp. 87–110; B. M. Metzger, "Tatian's Diatessaron and a Persian Harmony of the Gospels," in *JBL*, LXIX (1950), 261–280; Johannes Quasten, *Patrology*, Vol. I (1950), pp. 224–228; C. S. C. Williams, *Alterations to the Text of the Synoptic Gospels and Acts* (1951), pp. 19–24; B. M. Metzger, *Annotated Bibliography of the Textual Criticism of the New Testament, 1914–1939* (1955), pp. 73–81.

[Sup.] BRUCE M. METZGER.

HARNACK, (KARL GUSTAV) ADOLF: D. 1930. He was professor of church history at Berlin (1888–1921) where he also served as the librarian of the Prussian State Library. He was the founder and president (1903–12) of the Evangelical Social Congress. Recognized as the outstanding church historian of his generation, his most famous writings were: *History of Dogma; Apostles' Creed; What is Christianity? Expansion of Christianity in the First Three Centuries;* and *Marcion: das Evangelium vom fremden Gott* (1921). His other later works include: *Bible Reading in the Early Church* (1912; tr. by J. R. Wilkinson); *Ein juedisch-christliches Psalmbuch aus dem ersten Jahrhundert* (1910); *Der Scholien Kommentar des Origenes zur Apokolypse Johannis* (1911); *Constitution and Law of the Church in the First Two Centuries* (1910; tr. by F. L. Pogson); *Date of the Acts and the Synoptic Gospels* (1911; tr. by J. R. Wilkinson); *Die Entstehung des Neuen Testaments und die wichtigsten Folgen der Neuen Schoepfung* (1914; tr. by J. R. Wilkinson, 1925); (with Wilhelm Hermann), *Essays on the Social Gospel* (1917); *Des heiligen Irenaeus Schrift zum Erweise der apostolischen Verkuendigung* (1907); *Ist die Rede des Paulus in Athen ein urspruenglicher Bestandteil der Apostelgeschichte?* (1913); *Der kirchengeschichtliche Ertrag der exegetischen Arbeiten des Origenes* (1918–19); *Kritik des Neuen Testaments von einem griechischen Philosophen des 3. Jahrhunderts* (1911); *Neue Studien zu Marcion* (1923); *Neue Untersuchungen zur Apostelgeschichte und zur Abfassungszeit der synoptischen Evangelien* (1911); *New Testament Studies* (1907–12); *Das Leben Cyprians von Pontius* (1913); *Sayings of Jesus* (tr. J. R. Wilkinson, 1908); *Ueber den privaten Gebrauch der Heiligen Schriften in der alten Kirche* (1912); and *Zur Revision der Prinzipien der neuentestamentlichen Textkritik* (1916).

BIBLIOGRAPHY: W. W. Baudissin, and others, *Festgabe von Fachgenossen und Freunden A. von Harnack zum siebzigsten Geburtstag dargebracht*, 1921.

[Sup.] RAYMOND W. ALBRIGHT.

HARNER, NEVIN COWGER: Evangelical and Reformed; b. Feb. 5, 1901, near Berlin, Pa.; d. July 24, 1951. He studied at Franklin and Marshall College, Theological Seminary of the Reformed Church in the U.S., Union Theological Seminary, and Columbia University. He was professor of Christian Education, Theological Seminary of the Evangelical and Reformed Church (1929–45; 1947–51). He was president, Heidelberg College (1945–47); visiting professor, Union Theological Seminary, Princeton Theological Seminary, Garrett Biblical Institute; vice-chairman of the Division of Christian Education, National Council of the Churches of Christ in the U.S.A.; and executive secretary, American Association of Theological Schools. Author: *The Educational Work of the Church; Youth Work in the Church;* (with David D. Baker), *Missionary Education in Your Church; Religion's Place in General Education; I Believe; About Myself.*

HARRIS, GEORGE K.: Baptist; b. at Winona, Minn., Feb. 17, 1887. He studied at the Moody Bible Institute, Chicago. He went to China as a missionary of the China Inland Mission in November, 1916. His main evangelistic efforts have been among the Chinese Muslims, mostly in Sining, Tsinghai, the political capital of Chinese Islam. He has translated a series of seven booklets for them, called *The Sevenfold Secrets,* by Miss Lilias Trotter; and prepared three Christian posters in Arabic and Chinese, writing the Arabic script himself. He has written: *How to Lead Moslems to Christ* (1946); and some seven articles on Chinese Islam for the *Muslim World.*

CLAUDE L. PICKENS, JR.

HARRIS, JAMES RENDEL: D. March 1, 1941. In 1910 he was Haskel lecturer at Oberlin College, and until 1918 director of studies at the Friends' Woodbrooke Settlement near Birmingham. From then until 1925 he was curator of manuscripts at the John Rylands Library at Manchester, whence he traveled extensively in the East. Among other works he wrote or edited the following: *New Testament Autographs* (1882); *Double Text of Tobit* (1899); *Verse Division of the New Testament* (1900); *Aaron's Breastplate* (1908); *Side-Lights on New Testament Research* (1909); *An Early Christian Psalter* (1909); *Some Woodbrooke Liturgies* (1909); *The Odes and Psalms of Solomon* (1st ed., 1910; 2nd ed., 1916–20); *Boanerges* (1913); *The Suffering and the Glory* (1916); (ed., with Vachar Burch), *Testimonies* (1917); *Picus who is also Zeus* (1917); *The Origin of the Prologue to St. John's Gospel* (1917); *The Origin of the Doctrine of the Trinity* (1919); *The Return of the "Mayflower"* (1919); *The Masque of the Apple* (1920); *The Finding of the "Mayflower"* (1920); *The Last of the "Mayflower"* (1920); *Souvenirs of the "Mayflower" Tercentenary* (1920); *Leyden Documents relating to the Pilgrim Fathers* (1920); *The Mayflower Song Book* (1920); (ed., with Stephen K. Jones and Dr. Plooij), *The Pilgrim Press* (1922); *Eucharistic Origins* (1927); *The Twelve Apostles* (1927); *Dionysius bar Salibi* (1927); and *The Migration of Culture* (1936). From 1914 to 1929 he contributed regularly to the *Bulletin* of the John Rylands Library at Manchester on a variety of religious, literary, and historical questions. A wide range of in-

terests, biblical, literary, and archaeological, is revealed by five series of essays written between 1927 and 1935, and given successively the titles, *Woodbrooke, Caravan, Sunset, Evergreen,* and *After-Glow.*

BIBLIOGRAPHY: *Amicitiae Corolla,* 1932; *The Rendel Harris Papyri of Woodbrooke College,* 1936; *The Bulletin* of the John Rylands Library, Manchester, Vol. 26 (Oct.-Nov., 1941), pp. 10–14; Wilbert F. Howard, *The Romance of New Testament Scholarship* (1949), pp. 92–104.

[Sup.] RAYMOND W. ALBRIGHT.

HART, HORNELL: Friend; b. St. Paul, Minn., Aug. 2, 1888. He was educated at Oberlin College (A.B., 1910); University of Wisconsin (M.A., 1914), and State University of Iowa (Ph.D., 1921). He was professor of social economy, Bryn Mawr College (1924–33); professor of social ethics, Hartford Theological Seminary (1933–38); professor of sociology, Duke University (1938–). He wrote: *Living Religion* (1937); *Sceptic's Quest* (1938); *New Gateways to Creative Living* (1941); *Toward Consensus for World Law and Order* (editor, 1950); "Religion and Psychical Research," in *Religion Today* (Arthur L. Swift, ed.) (1933); and "Psychical Research and the Life Beyond Death," in *Man's Destiny in Eternity* (Garvin Lectures, 1949).

HARTSHORNE, HUGH: Congregationalist; b. in Lawrence, Mass., Nov. 13, 1885. He attended Amherst College (B.A., 1907), Yale University (M.A., 1910; B.D., 1911), Teachers College, Columbia University (Ph.D., 1913), and Union Theological Seminary (1911–13). He was ordained in 1913. From 1912 to 1922 he was principal of the Union School of Religion, and instructor and assistant professor of religious education at Union Seminary from 1913 to 1922. In 1922 he went to the University of Southern California as professor of religious education and in 1924 to Teachers College, Columbia University, as codirector with Mark A. May of the Character Education Inquiry. In 1929 he became research associate in religion at Yale and since 1950 has been professor of the psychology of religion there. For many years he was connected with various national youth organizations, and continues as president of the Friends of Boys, Inc., and as a director of the Religious Education Association. He has written: *Worship in the Sunday School* (1913); *Childhood and Character* (1919); (with Mark A. May) *Studies in Deceit* (1928), *Studies in Service and Self-Control* (1929), and *Studies in the Organization of Character* (1930); *Character in Human Relations* (1932); *Friendship Triumphant* (1937); and six books with other authors.

HARTWICK, JOHN CHRISTOPHER: Lutheran; b. Jan. 6, 1714, in Thuringia, Germany; d. July 17, 1796, in Clermont, N. Y. Educated in Halle, Germany, Hartwick (or Hartwig) arrived in America in 1746 and served congregations in New York, New Jersey, Pennsylvania, Maryland, and Virginia. In 1754 the eccentric bachelor bought thirty-six square miles of land from the Indians and in his will provided that a school be erected thereon. After many difficulties Hartwick Seminary (a combination academy and theological seminary) was opened in 1815 near Cooperstown, N. Y. In 1940 the theological department was discontinued. The rest of the school had moved to Oneonta, N. Y., in 1928 as a coeducational college.

BIBLIOGRAPHY: Henry H. Heins, *Throughout All the Years: Bicentennial Story of Hartwick*, 1946.

THEODORE G. TAPPERT.

HASIDISM. See CHASIDISM.

HASKELL LECTURES: Established by Mrs. Caroline E. Haskell, of Chicago, in the Graduate School of Theology of Oberlin College, Oberlin, Ohio, annual lectures are provided on "some phase of the relationship of Christianity with the life of the Near and Middle East."

HASSELQUIST, TUFVE NILSSON: Swedish-American Lutheran pastor, journalist, and educator; b. at Ousby, province of Scania, Sweden, March 2, 1816; d. at Rock Island, Ill., Feb. 4, 1891; studied at Lund University; ordained by the Church of Sweden, 1839. He emigrated to America in 1852, having been called to become pastor of First Lutheran Church of Galesburg, Ill. He carried on an extensive missionary program, and in 1855 launched a newspaper, *Hemlandet, det Gamla och det Nya* (The Homeland, Old and New), in which he discussed the religious and political issues of the day. At the organization of the Augustana Lutheran Synod in 1860, he became its first president, and in 1863 was chosen president of Augustana College and Theological Seminary.

BIBLIOGRAPHY: O. F. Ander, *T. N. Hasselquist*, 1931.

G. EVERETT ARDEN.

HASTINGS, JAMES: D. Oct. 15, 1922. He served as pastor of St. Cyrus church, Montrose, Kincardineshire (1901–11), after which he moved to Aberdeen where he continued his literary career. He was also editor of *The Expository Times* (Vols. 1–32; 1890–1921). His *Encyclopaedia of Religion and Ethics* was completed by 1922 (12 vols., 1908–22); he also edited: *The Dictionary of the Apostolic Church* (Vol. I, 1915; Vol. II, 1918); *Great Texts of the Bible* (1910 ff.); *The Greater Men and Women of the Bible* (1913 ff.); *The Scholar as Preacher* series; and another series on *Great Christian Doctrines*: Vol. I, *Prayer* (1915), Vol. II, *Faith* (1919), and Vol. III, *Peace* (1921).

[Sup.] RAYMOND W. ALBRIGHT.

HATCH, WILLIAM H. P.: Episcopal clergyman; b. at Camden, N. J., Aug. 2, 1875. He studied at Harvard (A.B., 1898; A.M., 1899; Ph.D., 1904; S.T.B., 1906), the Episcopal Theological School, Cambridge, Mass. (B.D., 1902), Union Theological Seminary, N. Y. (D.D., in course, 1915), and University of Strasbourg (D. Théol., 1925). He taught New Testament at General Theological Seminary, N. Y. (1908–17); at Episcopal Theological School (1917–46). In theology he is a liberal. He wrote: *The Pauline Idea of Faith* (1917); (with C. C. Edmonds), *The Gospel Manuscripts of the General Theological Seminary* (1918); *The Idea of Faith in Christian Literature from the Death of St. Paul to the Close of the Second Century* (1925); *Greek and Syrian Miniatures in Jerusalem* (1931); *The Greek Manuscripts of the New Testament at Mount Sinai* (1932); *The Greek Manuscripts of the New Testament in Jerusalem* (1934); *The "Western" Text of the Gospels* (1937); *The Principal Uncial Manuscripts of the New Testament* (1939); *An Album of Dated Syriac Manuscripts* (1946); and *Facsimiles and Descriptions of Minuscule Manuscripts of the New Testament* (1951).

BRUCE M. METZGER.

HAUGEANISM: Haugeanism grew out of the activity of the Norwegian lay preacher, Hans Nielsen Hauge (*q.v.*, Vol. V). Characteristic of the movement was the stress on a thorough conversion and genuine sanctification. On the subject of worldliness, amusements and adiaphora (*q.v.*, Vol. I), its attitude was stern. It continued to be a movement of loosely connected brotherhoods for over half a century. Those who felt called and were encouraged by brethren traveled about as lay preachers. Haugeanism thus gave lay preaching a prominent place in the Norwegian Church. It was out of this soil that, later, many societies for home and foreign missions grew.

Haugeanism clashed with the Grundtvigian movement (see GRUNDTVIG, N. F. S., Vol. V) and triumphed under the leadership of Gisle Johnsen, who united the revival movement with the older orthodoxy. In the course of time Haugeanism became rather stern. By stressing the right "order" of salvation, it could make salvation conditional. In 1870 Rosenianism, with its stress on the free, unconditional gospel, entered Norway from Sweden (see BORNHOLMERS, Vol. II). After a clash the two united and inaugurated the most fruitful period in the religious life of Norway. Haugeans led the struggle for full religious freedom (see CONVENTICLE ACT), freedom of preaching, and church reforms. They also took a prominent part in the growing political liberalism of the nineteenth century.

BIBLIOGRAPHY: M. O. Wee, *Haugeanism*, 1919; Ivar Welle, *Norges Kirkehistorie*, 1948; S. S. Gjerde and P. Ljostveit, *The Haugean Movement in America*, 1941.

IVER IVERSEN.

HAWAIIAN ISLANDS: The population of the Islands (425,000 in 1950) more than quadrupled since 1900. In that population are racial strains from the Pacific Islands, the Occident, and the Orient. Yet this U. S. Territory is a thoroughly American community. The process of Americanization (*q.v.*) has been very rapid, though it has not completely wiped out traditions from other nations.

Churches and other religious institutions have continued in the changing situation. Protestant denominations existing at the beginning of the century have expanded their operations, and the Congregationalists are now supported wholly within the Territory; other denominations— Lutherans, Southern Baptists, Pentecostals (*q.v.*), Assemblies of God (*q.v.*), the Door of Faith—have entered the field. Councils of Churches have been organized, but they neither include all groups nor have their functions been defined. Protestantism exhibits divisions and competitive animosities. The number of Protestant churches has increased, but the number of adherents (70,000 in 1952) has failed to keep pace with the growing population.

The Roman Catholic Church has grown in the number of churches and communicants. Parochial schools have enrolled nearly 25% of the child population; hospitals, charity societies, and other community organizations have been established. The Hawaiian Islands are now a diocese with their own bishop.

Mormons (*q.v.*) continue their mission program. A number of houses of worship have been built, among which is a tabernacle of noteworthy architecture in the city of Honolulu.

The religions which the Oriental people brought with them are still practiced by a decreasing number of people. The one exception is Japanese Buddhism (*q.v.*). During World War II open observance of this faith was banned; since the war it has shown new and increasing vitality. It has borrowed from American Protestantism, so that there are formal services of worship and Sunday schools in the temples. It has developed a Young Buddhist Association with branches throughout the Territory and carries on a well planned program of activity. Buddhism claims the allegiance of a large section of the population of Japanese ancestry.

BIBLIOGRAPHY: Henry S. Leiper, *Christianity Today,* 1947.

J. LESLIE DUNSTAN.

HAZELTON, ROGER: Congregationalist; b. at Chicago, Illinois, November 11, 1909. He studied at Amherst College (B.A., 1931), Chicago Theological Seminary (B.D., 1934), the University of Chicago (A.M., 1934), and Yale University (Ph.D., 1937). He served as pastor in Oak Park, Ill., and Chester, Conn.; was tutor in religion at Olivet College, Michigan (1936–39); dean of the Shove Memorial Chapel at Colorado College (1939–45); professor of philosophy of religion and Christian ethics at Andover Newton Theological School (1945–). He has written: *The Root and Flower of Prayer* (1943); *The God We Worship* (1946); *Renewing the Mind* (1949); and *On Proving God* (1952).

HAZEN FOUNDATION: Established in 1925 by Edward W. Hazen in Haddam, Conn., the purpose of the foundation is "to promote the public welfare either by supporting existing agencies or through independent activities, . . . such agencies and activities to be exclusively religious, charitable, scientific, literary, or educational in character." The religious and moral development of young people has especially been emphasized by conducting conferences and theological discussion groups and by subsidizing the publication of religious books and pamphlets.

HAZOR. See ARCHAEOLOGY, BIBLICAL.

HEADLAM, ARTHUR CAYLEY: D. 1945. He was principal of King's College, London (1903–12); professor of dogmatic theology (1903–17); Regius professor of divinity and canon of Christ Church, Oxford (1918–23), and chaplain to the king (1922–23). On Jan. 25, 1923 he was consecrated Bishop of Gloucester (1923–45). His additional books include: *Authority and Archeology* (1899); *History, Authority and Theology* (1911); *Christian Miracles* (1911); *St. Paul and Christianity* (1913); *Miracles of the New Testament* (1914); *The Revenue of the Church of England* (1917); *The Study of Theology* (1918); *The Doctrine of the Church and Christian Reunion* (1920; 2nd ed., 1923); *Life and Teaching of Jesus Christ* (1923); *The Church of England* (1924); *Jesus Christ in History and Faith* (1925); *Economics and Christianity* (1926); *The New Prayer Book* (1927); *The Building of the Church of Christ* (1928); *The New Prayer Book, Directions for Its Use* (1929); *Christian Unity* (1930); *What It Means to Be a Christian* (1933); *Christian Theology* (1934); *The Doctrine of God* (1934); *The Task of the Christian Church* (1942); *The Holy Catholic Church* (1945); *The Fourth Gospel as History* (1948); he was coauthor of *The Ministry and Sacraments* (1937); and for Hastings' *Encyclopaedia of Religion and Ethics* wrote the articles "Acts," "Herod," "Simon Magus" and others.

[Sup.] RAYMOND W. ALBRIGHT.

HEARD, HENRY FITZGERALD: Church of England; b. Oct. 6, 1889, London. He was educated at Sherborne and Cambridge University. He was lecturer for Guild Church, Ethical Church and Ethical Society, London. He wrote: *Ascent of Humanity; Social Substance of Religion; Source of Civilization; Pain, Sex and Time; Creed of Christ; Code of Christ; Preface to Prayer; Man the Master; Training for Life of Spirit; Is God Evident? Is God in History?* and *Morals 1900–1950.*

HEARING AIDS: No scientific invention can equal the mechanism of the human ear, with its ability to distinguish sounds and interpret meanings. A normal ear can detect almost half a million sound impressions. Impaired hearing may come from disease, or from changes in later years, with stiffening of lever bones in the outer ear, or loss of sensitivity in tiny nerve endings of the inner ear. By counteracting this condition, hearing aids greatly benefit multitudes suffering from partial deafness. A small instrument picks up sound and by electrical energy magnifies it, sometimes as much as 3,-000,000 times. One or more highly sensitized microphones may be installed in the chancel, and in the pews hearing aid receivers, with individual volume controls for personal adjustment. In the average church six or more receivers are desirable, in various places, for convenience of family groups, and to avoid embarrassment through centralized equipment. A church with poor acoustics can install a loudspeaker system to amplify the chancel program, especially reinforcing sounds in all dead spots.

ROBERT CASHMAN.

HEART OF MARY, THE IMMACULATE: A Roman Catholic devotion, paralleling the devotion to the Sacred Heart of Jesus, the object of which is to recognize and honor Mary's love for God and mankind. It was promoted chiefly by a French priest, (Saint) Jean Eudes, 1601–80, in spite of the opposition of the Jansenists, and obtained a limited liturgical status. It was approved officially by Popes Leo XIII and Pius X. Pius XII consecrated the church and the human race to the Immaculate Heart of Mary on Dec. 8, 1942, and ordered that the feast in its honor be observed in the entire church on August 22.

BIBLIOGRAPHY: C. Lebrun, *La dévotion au Coeur de Marie,* 1918; E. Puyolras, *Cultus purissimi Cordis B. M. Virginis,* 1942; *Conferenze della Settimana di Studi Mariani,* 1946.

GEORGES A. BARROIS.

HEBREW CHRISTIAN ALLIANCE, INTERNATIONAL. See JEWS, MISSIONS TO.

HEBREW CULTURAL AND SOCIAL CONDITIONS. See CULTURAL AND SOCIAL CONDITIONS, HEBREW.

HEBREW LANGUAGE AND LITERATURE: Hebrew, the language in which almost the whole of the Old Testament was written, is a branch of the Semitic linguistic family (see SEMITIC LANGUAGES). Until forty years ago there were, to all intents and purposes, but few ancient Hebrew manuscripts, few documents in Hebrew outside the Bible. Today we can list some hundreds of early Hebrew inscriptions belonging to the first half of the first millenium B.C.

A significant find was made at Samaria in 1908. This comprised some eighty ostraca, or inscribed potsherds, belonging to the eighth century B.C. These proved to be invoices of oil and wine, the writing being in ink in a beautiful cursive style of the early Hebrew script. Here, indeed, were samples of the dialect and current hand of the Northern Kingdom of Israel.

During the last fifteen years there have become available two new sources of paramount importance for our knowledge of biblical Hebrew. The first were the twenty-one letters and other documents from Lachish (Southern Palestine), which were discovered in 1935 and 1938. They are written in ink in a bold current hand in perfect biblical Hebrew, with interesting idiomatic and orthographic features. They date to the early sixth century B.C., i.e., the period of Jeremiah. Together with the Siloam inscription they reflect the southern Judaean dialect of Hebrew, the classical language of the Old Testament. The philological importance of this and other new material has been considerable in several directions, e.g., in textual criticism, in the knowledge of Hebrew personal names, in historical-religious problems, etc. Perhaps of highest importance is the fact that the scholar of today has at his disposal a much broader and more detailed conspectus of the linguistic milieu of the biblical records.

The second, and more recent, source is furnished by the remarkable discovery in 1947 of the Dead Sea Scrolls (*q.v.*). In a cave near the northwestern end of the Dead Sea were discovered eleven leather manuscripts including hitherto unknown books, a scroll and a fragmentary scroll containing the text of Isaiah, and other items. As yet, there is no unanimity of opinion as to the exact date of these documents. The writer prefers the theory, held by many eminent scholars, that they belong to the second or first century B.C. The debate will no doubt continue for some considerable time. Nevertheless, it could in the meantime be said that the importance of these documents for our knowledge of Hebrew language and literature is paramount.

Hebrew was spoken and written in Palestine for more than a thousand years. After the fifth century B.C. it was gradually supplanted by Aramaic, but it is erroneous to think that it ever died out. Actually, it continued to be employed in "national" circles, and as the language of religious literature and poetry. In time a new form was developed, known as Mishnaic Hebrew. Even in later times, in the Middle and Modern Ages, Hebrew has never ceased to be current among Jews. This is evidenced by the vast Talmudic literature of the early Christian centuries, the *piyyutim*, or liturgical poems, composed in the sixth to the eleventh centuries, many of which survived in the Jewish prayer books, also by the numerous works of medieval Jewish scholars, poets, and philosophers, particularly of Spain, France, Italy, and Germany. Hebrew has, of course, remained the language of the synagogues, of the Jewish prayers, and of the Jewish religious schools. It was also the lingua franca and the language of correspondence of Jewish scholars of all ages and all countries. Since the late nineteenth century there has developed a flourishing modern Hebrew literature. The rebirth of Hebrew as a living language is one striking result of the development of Zionism. Its re-establishment as the language of the country in the new State of Israel is a striking fact. Indeed, spiritual and practical considerations have combined to associate the return of the Jews to Palestine with the return to Hebrew as their mother tongue.

BIBLIOGRAPHY: H. Bauer and P. Leander, *Historische Grammatik der hebraeischen Sprache*, 1918–22; G. Bergstraesser, *Hebraeische Grammatik*, 29th ed., W. Gesenius, 2 vols., 1918–29; H. Torczyner, *The Lachish Letters*, 1938; L. Koehler and W. Baumgartner, *Lexicon in Veteris Testamenti Libros*, 1948– ; M. Burrows, J. C. Trever and W. H. Brownlee (eds.), *The Dead Sea Scrolls of St. Mark's Monastery*, 1950.

[Sup.] DAVID DIRINGER.

HEBREWS, EPISTLE TO THE: Several additional theories regarding the identity of the author of the Epistle have been proposed: Priscilla (suggested by Harnack, in *ZNTW*, Vol. I [1900], pp. 16–41), Peter (A. Welch, *The Authorship of the Epistle to the Hebrews*, 1898), Aristion (John Chapman, in *Rev. Bén.*, Vol. XXII [1905], pp. 50–62; and Richard Perdelwitz, in *ZNTW*, Vol. XI [1910], pp. 105–110), Philip the Deacon (Wm. M. Ramsay, *Luke the Physician*, pp. 301–308), Stephen (J. V. Brown, in *Bibliotheca Sacra*, Vol. LXXX [1923], pp. 505–538), and Jude, who used notes provided by Paul (A. M. Dubarle, in *Rev. Biblique*, Vol. XLVIII [1939], pp. 506–521). On June 24, 1914, the Pontifical Biblical Commission decreed that Paul was the author of the Epistle, but that another may have been responsible for its present literary form (see also William Leonard, *The Authorship of the Epistle to the Hebrews*, 1939).

In P[46], which is a third century papyrus codex of the Pauline Epistles, Hebrews stands immediately after Romans and before I Corinthians (Wm. H. P. Hatch, "The Position of Hebrews in the Canon of the New Testament," in *HTR*,

Vol. XXIX [1936], pp. 133–151). This order of Epistles may have been dictated by considerations of the length of the respective letters, and need not have any bearing upon the opinion of authorship.

The date of the Epistle is generally held to be in the 80's, but a strong case can be made out for a date prior to 70; so, e.g., Geo. A. Barton, in *JBL*, Vol. LVII (1938), pp. 195–207; see also Richard Heard, *Introduction to the New Testament* (1950), p. 211.

Regarding the identity of the recipients of the Epistle, the prevailing view that they were Jewish Christians in danger of relapsing, under stress of persecution, into Judaism was challenged by Juelicher, McGiffert, Moffatt, E. F. Scott, Knopf, and others, who maintained that they were Gentiles in danger of drifting into paganism. In a fresh treatment, William Manson recently proposed that Stephen was the true spiritual precursor of the author of the Epistle, which was written to Jewish-Christians (in Rome about A.D. 60) who were not spiritually different from the men who resisted Stephen.

BIBLIOGRAPHY: Some of the more important commentaries and studies include those by Marcus Dods, in *Expositor's Greek Testament*, 1910; A. S. Peake, in *New Century Bible*, 1902; E. Riggenbach, in Zahn's *Kom.*, Vol. XIV, 1913, 3te Aufl., 1922; A. Naine, *The Epistle of Priesthood*, 1913; H. L. MacNeill, *The Christology of the Epistle to the Hebrews*, 1914; E. C. Wickham, in *Westminster Com.*, ca. 1914; E. F. Scott, 1922; James Moffatt, in *I.C.C.*, 1924; Hans Windisch, in Lietzmann's *Handbuch*, Vol. XIV, 1913, 2te Aufl., 1931; T. H. Robinson, in *Moffatt Com.*, 1933; O. Michel, in Meyer's *Kom.*, 7te Aufl., 1936; Léon Vaganay, "Le plan de l'Épître aux Hébreux," in *Mémorial Lagrange* (1940), 269–277; William Manson, *The Epistle to the Hebrews, an Historical and Theological Reconsideration*, 1951; C. Spicq, *L'épître aux Hébreux*, 1953.

[Sup.] BRUCE M. METZGER.

HEBREW UNIVERSITY OF JERUSALEM: Inaugurated in Jerusalem, April 1, 1925, after preparations begun at the Eleventh Zionist Congress (Vienna, 1913). Judah Leib Magnes (1877–1948), leading American Jewish scholar, was the first chancellor and president. By 1950 the university comprised faculties of humanities, science, agriculture, medicine, law and education. During the Arab-Israeli war (1947–48), the university was immobilized and subsequent demarcation of the city of Jerusalem made the university site on Mt. Scopus inaccessible. Since April, 1949, the university was temporarily established in a single building of Terra Sancta College, Jerusalem. During the 1949–50 academic year about 1,400 students were enrolled. The university library contains the world's largest collection of Hebraica and Judaica.

BIBLIOGRAPHY: *The Hebrew University, Jerusalem: Its History and Development*, 1948.

MORRIS FINE.

HEDONISM: We may distinguish psychological hedonism, which is the theory that human behavior is always motivated by the quest for pleasure and the avoidance of pain, from ethical hedonism, which teaches that pleasure ought to be the sole end of human conduct. Some thinkers have inconsistently maintained both types of hedonism at the same time.

Aristippus of Cyrene, a disciple of Socrates, and the founder of the Cyrenaic school, maintained that pleasure is the sole ultimate good and pain the sole evil. Since pleasure is transient, and can only be realized in successive experiences, the true art of life is to crowd as much enjoyment as possible into every moment. Physical pleasures and pains are keener than those of the mind, and are therefore to be preferred.

Epicurus reversed this order of preference, and regarded the pleasures of the mind and of friendship as greater and of more value than those of the body. He emphasized the need for self-control and for the guidance of reason, and believed that the perfection of pleasure consisted in freedom from pain and from anxiety (*ataraxia*). In its more austere Epicurean form hedonism had a widespread influence upon Hellenistic and Roman thought, and one of its most attractive exponents was Lucretius.

Hedonism was revived in the seventeenth century by Thomas Hobbes, who combined the view that there is no good other than pleasure with the psychological theory that men do in fact always seek it. He maintained that such emotions as pity and sympathy were in reality motivated simply by concern for the self. Only an unlimited despotism could curb men's antisocial tendencies and protect society from disruption into a state of war.

There was a strong reaction against the teaching of Hobbes, and in the next century, Shaftesbury, Hutcheson, and Hume rejected hedonism in its psychological form, maintaining the naturalness of unselfish tendencies and emotions. Good conduct consisted not in the pursuit of pleasure, but in following the directions of the moral sense (Shaftesbury) or in obedience to conscience (Butler).

In the writings of Jeremy Bentham and of John Stuart Mill, hedonism took on a more social form in the doctrine known as utilitarianism, of which Mill writes: "The creed which accepts, as the foundation of morals, Utility, or the Greatest Happiness Principle, holds that actions are right in proportion as they tend to promote happiness, wrong as they tend to produce the reverse of happiness. By happiness is intended pleasure and the absence of pain; by unhappiness, pain and the privation of pleasure" (*Utilitarianism*, Chap. II). Bentham popularized the principle of "the greatest happiness of the greatest number," set up a calculus for determining when an action would be conducive to the greatest pleasure, working on the basis that everybody should count for one and no-

body for more than one. Mill derived ethical from psychological hedonism, but maintained that the agent should be strictly impartial as between his own happiness and that of others. He made a distinction between "higher" and "lower" pleasures, thus introducing, according to his critics, another criterion than that of "pleasure" as the ultimate standard of ethical conduct.

See also ETHICS.

BIBLIOGRAPHY: J. S. Mackenzie, *Manual of Ethics*, 1929; Henry Sidgwick, *Outlines of the History of Ethics*, 1939; C. D. Broad, *Five Types of Ethical Theory*, 1930.

ANTHONY S. CHADWICK.

HEGEL, G. W. FRIEDRICH. See IDEALISM.

HEGESIPPUS: His *Memoirs* likely survived until the sixteenth and seventeenth centuries. Eusebius might have employed them more than he indicates, and Epiphanius evidently relied on them too but without acknowledgment. A fragment from Gobarus is also attributed to Hegesippus.

It is still a question whether *diadochén epoiésamen* (Eusebius, *H. E.*, IV.22.3) means a list of bishops. Harnack suggested *diatribén*—a stay—for *diadochén* (*Chronologie*, I, 312). Schwartz regarded *epoiésamen* as an insertion to fill a lacuna and assumed total text corruption. Caspar followed him partly and retained *diadochén*. On the basis of the context he interpreted it as the correct teaching. But there is no direct evidence to substantiate text corruption, and the context seems to sustain the opinion that Hegesippus did make a "succession-list." If so, it is doubtful whether it was part of the *Memoirs*.

BIBLIOGRAPHY: O. Bardenhewer, *Geschichte der altkirchlichen Literatur*, 2. Auflage, Vol. I (1913), pp. 385–392; E. Caspar, *Die aelteste Roemische Bischofsliste* . . . , 1926, pp. 447–451; Eusebius, *Church History*, tr. by H. J. Lawlor and J. E. Oulton, 2 vols., 1927–28, cf. Index; H. J. Lawlor, *Eusebiana* . . . (1912), pp. 1–107; Th. Zahn, . . . *Kanon* . . . , Vol. IV (1900), pp. 228–273.

[Sup.] DANIEL JOHANNES THERON.

HEIDEGGER, MARTIN: In a highly idiosyncratic style with poetic and religious overtones Heidegger (b. 1889) attempts to revitalize the problem of Being (*q.v.*) neglected in Western philosophy (he contends) since pre-Socratic times. Though his objective is a comprehensive ontology (*q.v.*), his fragmentary major work, *Sein und Zeit*, and his later essays are largely existential (see EXISTENTIALISM) in execution. Starting with the Kierkegaardian antithesis of the authentic vs. the unauthentic life, he analyzes standard existential themes—care, dread, nothingness, estrangement, being-in-the-world, being-toward-death—with a view to providing ontological insights. A more definitive sequel to *Sein und Zeit* is still awaited.

BIBLIOGRAPHY: *Sein und Zeit*, 1927, 6th ed., 1949; *Existence and Being*, with an Introduction by Werner Brock, 1949 (a summary of *Sein und Zeit*, with translations of four of Heidegger's essays); *Was ist Meta-physik?* 5th ed., 1949; *Plato's Lehre von der Wahrheit, mit einem Brief ueber den "Humanismus,"* 1947; A. de Waehlens, *La Philosophie de Martin Heidegger,* 1942.

GEORGE K. STRODACH.

HEILER, FRIEDRICH: B. Jan. 30, 1892, at Munich, Germany. He studied at Munich (Dr. Phil., 1917). He taught history of religions at Munich (1918–20); at Marburg (1920–　). He was a Roman Catholic; became a Lutheran in 1919, and in 1930 was consecrated by a Gallican bishop. He is a champion for Christian unity. His works include: *Das Gebet* (1918; 5th ed., 1923; Eng. tr., 1932); *Buddhistische Versenkung* (1918; 2nd ed., 1922); *Katholizismus* (1923); *Sadhu Sundar Singh* (1923; 4th ed., 1925; Eng. tr., 1927); *Mystik in den Upanishaden* (1925); *Christlicher Glaube und indisches Geistesleben* (1926); *Evangelische Katholizitaet* (1926); *Spirit of Worship* (1926); *Mission des Christentums in Indien* (1931); *Im Ringen um die Kirche* (1931); *Urkirche und Ostkirche* (1937); *Altkirchliche Autonomie und paepstlicher Zentralismus* (1941); *Alfred Loisy* (1947); *Mysterium caritatis, Predigten* (1949); and was editor of *Hochkirche* (1930–33), *Eine heilige Kirche* (1934–42), and *Oekumenische Einheit* (1948–　).

HEIM, KARL: Lutheran; b. Jan. 20, 1874, in Kreis Heilbronn, Wuerttemberg. After studying at Tuebingen (Dr. Phil., 1899), he became general secretary of the German Christian Student Association (1900–1903). He taught theology at Halle (1903–14), at Muenster (1914–20), and at Tuebingen (1920–39), where he was also morning preacher (1920–48). In the German church crisis his sympathies were with the Confessional Church. His life's ambition was to build a bridge between theology and the natural sciences. He has written: *Psychologismus oder Antipsychologismus?* (1902); *Das Weltbild der Zukunft* (1904); *Das Wesen der Gnade bei Alexander Halesius* (1907); *Das Gewissheitsproblem in der Systematischen Theologie bis zu Schleiermacher* (1911); *Leitfaden der Dogmatik zum Gebrauch bei akademischen Vorlesungen* (1912); *Glaubensgewissheit* (1916); *Glaube und Leben* (1926); *Der evangelische Glaube und das Denken der Gegenwart:* Band I: *Glaube und Denken* (1931), Band II: *Jesus der Herr* (1935), Band III: *Jesus der Weltvollender* (1937), Band IV: *Der christliche Gottesglaube und die Naturwissenschaft* (1949), and Band V: *Die Wandlung im naturwissenschaftlichen Weltbild* (1951).

RAYMOND W. ALBRIGHT.

HEIN MEMORIAL LECTURES: Inaugurated in 1942 by the American Lutheran Church to honor its first president (1931–37), Carl Christian Hein. The lectures are given at both Capital Theological Seminary, Columbus, Ohio, and Wartburg Theological Seminary, Dubuque, Iowa. The list of past lecturers includes names like Ralph H. Long, O. P. Kretzmann, Roland H. Bainton, and H. Richard Niebuhr.

BERNARD HOLM.

HELLENISM: In antiquity "Hellenism" meant the correct use of Greek and, in II Maccabees 4:13, the adoption of Greek manners. But since J. G. Droysen's *Geschichte des Hellenismus* (1836, 1843) "Hellenism" means the culture of the Hellenistic Period, from Alexander's rule (336–323 B.C.) to that of Augustus (27 B.C.-A.D. 14). The classical Athenian culture of the Periclean age was lowered to the level of the masses: popularized in Europe by Rome, it became a pillar of Western civilization; but in Egypt and Western Asia it only flourished among the upper classes in the new cities (Alexandria, Seleucia, Antioch, etc.)—despite the opposition of Jews and Parthians—until the spread of Christianity in the second and third centuries.

The absorption of the independent Greek *poleis* (city states) in Philip's and Alexander's empires substituted cosmopolitan and individualistic trends for local patriotism. With the world empire came the feeling of the unity of mankind, in which there is "neither Greek nor Jew . . . barbarian, Scythian" (Col. 3:11), but only *kosmopolitai* (citizens of the world). The *koine* (common) form of Greek replaced local dialects and became international, just as customs and manners, laws, art, literature, and religion tended to become uniform in the Mediterranean world. Citizens were deprived of their vote in the assembly, and devoted more time to private matters and to their wives. This new individualism is apparent in life, literature, philosophy, and religion. Great leaders now determine the course of history: not only men like Ptolemy I, Seleucus I, Antiochus III, Herod the Great, but also such women as Berenice, Cleopatra VII the Great, Herodias. Two new types of historical writing now become popular: universal histories (Diodorus Siculus, Nicholas of Damascus, Pompeius Trogus, all in the days of Augustus) and biographies (romanticized lives of Alexander, the *Parallel Lives* of Plutarch, etc.). The New Comedy of Menander (342–291 B.C.), a precursor of Plautus and of Molière, and the novel, a typical product of Hellenism, deal with personal adventures—and misadventures. The greatest Hellenistic poets, Theocritus and Callimachus, devote some attention to the individual; similarly the Stoic, Epicurian, Cynic, and Skeptic schools of philosophy, which arose after Alexander, are concerned with the morals and happiness of the individual, while the Hellenistic mystery cults promise personal salvation to the initiated.

The outstanding achievements of Hellenism

are however in science and scholarship, notably in geography, mathematics, astronomy, botany, medicine, and humanistic studies (historical investigation, literary criticism, and philological research).

BIBLIOGRAPHY: P. Wendland, *Die hellenistisch-roemische Kultur in ihren Beziehungen zu Judentum und Christentum,* 2nd and 3rd eds., 1912; W. W. Tarn, *Hellenistic Civilization,* 2nd ed., 1930; A. J. Fustigière and P. Fabre, *Le monde greco-romain au temps de nôtre Seigneur,* 2 vols., 1935; M. I. Rostovtzeff, *The Social and Economic History of the Hellenistic World,* 3 vols., 1941; R. H. Pfeiffer, *History of New Testament Times* (1949), pp. 93–165.

[Sup.] ROBERT H. PFEIFFER.

HELLENISTIC GREEK: The extensive discoveries of new materials within the last half century have greatly increased our knowledge of Hellenistic Greek. Most important have continued to be the non-literary papyri (*q.v.*), ostraca, inscriptions, etc., publications of which have been legion. An important resource has also been the literary *koine* of such prose writers as Polybius, Diodorus, and Arrian; and modern Greek, in its spoken form a lineal descendant of the *koine,* has been exploited with valuable results. The findings of research have been helpfully integrated into new treatments of the history of the Greek language such as those of Norden (4th ed., 1923), Meillet (3rd ed., 1930) and Costas (1936), as well as into grammatical works. The important modern Greek studies initiated at the turn of the century have been carried forward in significant fashion by Pernot and others.

In lexicography (see LEXICONS OF THE GREEK NEW TESTAMENT) the new Liddell and Scott (completed 1940) includes the usage of papyri and early Christian "non-theological" literature. The new data have also been incorporated in several New Testament lexicons, from the brief works of Souter and Ebeling to the more extensive of Abbott-Smith, Zorell, Bauer, and Kittel. Special contributions have come from Moulton and Milligan and from Preisigke in papyrology, from Goodspeed in early Christian literature (*Index Patristicus* and *Index Apologeticus*). An important lexicon of Patristic Greek being prepared at Oxford is nearing completion.

Among grammatical studies Mayser completed (1934) his excellent grammar of the papyri of the Ptolemaic period, and some beginnings were made by L. R. Palmer in the later documents. Of New Testament grammars revised to take account of the new knowledge the best is Debrunner's revision of Blass (7th ed., 1943; reprinted 1949; Anhang, 1950). Significant new treatments have come also in German from Radermacher (2nd ed., 1925), in French from Abel (1927), in English from Robertson (5th ed., 1931) and Moulton and Howard (see Bibliography). The Septuagint is increasingly recognized as an important monument of Hel-

lenistic Greek in spite of its patent Semitisms, but as yet no comprehensive grammar has been produced. Likewise no over-all grammar of Hellenistic Greek has been attempted, though tentative suggestions have been made toward that end and special studies have appeared in countless monographs and articles.

This research has confirmed the view that biblical Greek cannot be isolated from the Greek language as a whole. Hellenistic Greek, of which it is a part, was a language of great variety and vigor, whose influence was dominant even in Palestine in the first century (see Saul Lieberman, *Greek in Jewish Palestine,* 1942). Attempts to account for the Semitic quality in certain New Testament writings by supposing them to be translations from Semitic documents have not been fully convincing, partly on philological and partly on historical grounds.

BIBLIOGRAPHY: Félix Marie Abel, *Grammaire du Grec Biblique,* 1907; Adolf Deissmann, *Light from the Ancient East,* tr. from the 4th German ed. by L. R. M. Strachan, 1927; Albert Debrunner, *Friedrich Blass' Grammatik des neutestamentlichen Griechisch,* 8th ed., 1949; Camden McCormack Cobern, *The New Archaeological Discoveries and Their Bearing upon the New Testament,* 5th ed., 1921; Robert Helbing, *Die Kasussyntax der Verba bei der Septuaginta,* 1928; James Hope Moulton and Wilbert Francis Howard, *A Grammar of New Testament Greek:* Vol. I, *Prolegomena,* 3rd ed., 1908, revised German edition, 1911; Vol. II, *Accidence and Word Formation,* 1929; Ludwig Radermacher, *Neutestamentliche Grammatik,* 2nd ed., 1925; Archibald Thomas Robertson, *A Grammar of the Greek New Testament in the Light of Historical Research,* 5th ed., 1931; Henry St. John Thackeray, *A Grammar of the Old Testament in Greek:* Vol. I, *Introduction, Orthography and Accidence,* 1909.

[Sup.] ALLEN WIKGREN.

HELVETIC CONFESSION (SECOND):

BIBLIOGRAPHY: Abram Ruchat, *Histoire de la Reformation de la Suisse* (Vulliemin, ed.), 7 vols., 1838; H. Vuilleumier, *Histoire de l'Eglise réformée du pays de Vaud . . . ,* 1927–33; A. Bouvier, *Henri Bullinger,* 1940; W. Hildebrandt and R. Zimmermann, *Bedeutung und Geschichte des Zweiten Helvet. Bekenntnisses,* 1936; idem, *Das Zweite Helv. Bekenntniss,* 1936, the German text; W. Herrenbrueck, "Confession helvétique postérieure," in *Bekenntnisschriften und Kirchenordnungen der nach Gottes Wort reform. Kirche,* 1938, the Latin text. One finds in these last three works all the bibliography on the subject. See also *La Confession helvétique postérieure,* 1944, Introduction and notes by Jaques Courvoisier.

[Sup.] JAQUES COURVOISIER.

HEMPEL, JOHANNES: Lutheran; b. July 30, 1891, at Baerenstein, Saxony. He studied at Leipzig (Dr. Phil.) and Halle (1921). He was privatdozent at Halle (1925–28); and has taught Old Testament at Greifswald (1928–37), Goettingen (1937–49), Berlin (1949–). His works include: *Die Schichten des Deuteronomiums* (1914); *Untersuchungen zur Ueberlieferung von Apollonius von Tyana* (1922); *Gebet und Froemmigkeit im Alten Testament* (1923); *Die Altisraelitischen Vorstellungen von Segen und Fluch* (1925); *Gott und Mensch im Alten Testament* (1926; 2nd ed., 1936); *Altes Testament und Geschichte* (1930); *Die althebraeische Literatur* (1934); *Das Ethos des Alten Testaments* (1938); *Politische Absicht und politische Wirkung im biblischen Schrifttum* (1939); *Worte* *der Propheten neu uebertragen* (1949). He was also the editor of *Zeitschrift fuer die alttestamentliche Wissenschaft* (1927–   ).

RAYMOND W. ALBRIGHT.

HENOTHEISM. See MONOLATRY AND HENOTHEISM.

HENRY II: Saint, king of Germany and Roman emperor; b. May 6, 973, Abbach Castle, Bavaria; d. July 13, 1024, at Grona, Germany. He was the last German king of the Saxon house. Destined for priesthood, he was acquainted with ecclesiastical sciences. In 1002 he was elected emperor. He insisted on the reform of monasteries. He favored the bishops, restored the see of Merseburg (1004), and founded that of Bamberg (1007). Several churches were built by him. He married St. Kunigunda but had no children. Pope Benedict VIII gave him the Roman crown. Henry confirmed this pope in the possession of the Patrimony of St. Peter. He was pious, charitable and merciful, but just. He was canonized March 12, 1152. Feast, July 15. His tomb is in the cathedral of Bamberg.

BIBLIOGRAPHY: "Vita S. Henrici," author (probably) Adalboldo ep. Ultraiectensi, in *Acta S. Julii*, III, 744–755; H. Mueller, *Das heilige Kaiserpaar Heinrich und Kunigunde*, 1903; H. Guenter, *Kaiser Heinrich II, der Heilige*, 1904; H. Lesêtre, *Saint Henri*, 1926; Feind, *Die Persoenlichkeit Heinrichs II*, 1914; H. Mikoletski, *Kaiser Heinrich und die Kirche*, 1920.

WILLIBRORD LAMPEN.

HENRY VIII: King of England. B. June 28, 1491, at the royal palace of Greenwich, the second son of King Henry VII of England and Elizabeth of York. His elder brother Arthur died before his father. Henry, who loved sports and was boisterous and energetic, soon became the most popular figure at the royal court. Arthur had married Catherine of Aragon and Castile, but had died six months after the wedding. The widow, only eighteen years old, remained in England and became engaged to Henry, who had reached the age of twelve (1503). In the same year Henry's elder sister, Margaret, married King James IV of Scotland. On April 22, 1509, King Henry VII died, bequeathing to his only surviving son the throne of England. Although the young man was not yet eighteen he determined to marry at once, and chose Catherine. The engagement had been only an empty ceremony, but he liked her and was favorably impressed by her saintly character. On June 11th they were married, and soon thereafter they were both crowned at Westminster Abbey.

There is no need of recounting the numerous flirtations in which Henry indulged, both before and after his marriage. They have been partly reported in an astonishing tale by Michael Glenne entitled *Henry VIII's Fifth Wife* (1948). This monarch and his friend Cardinal Wolsey (*q.v.*) were very free with money and with some other things, whence came much criticism. For example, Dr. H. M. Smith in his admirable study, *Henry VIII and the Reformation* ([1948], p. 13), makes this significant remark: "Like so many reformers, Wolsey did not see that reformation should begin with himself." Henry VIII soon grew tired of his Spanish wife, but the main reason why he sought to divorce her was that she did not present him with a male heir. Emperor Charles V (*q.v.*), not willing to let his aunt suffer ignominy in England, informed Pope Clement VII that the divorce must never be granted. The pope, not wishing to alienate the English farther than was necessary, withheld a decision as long as possible, while Wolsey had to bear the brunt of the king's ire. In the midst of all the fuss and fury Wolsey died.

The Reformation Parliament (1529–36) passed a number of acts that had momentous consequences. England was lost to the papacy, and Henry became the head of the Church of England. Henry dissolved abbeys and monasteries, and sought to ally himself with Lutheran princes in Germany and to employ Melanchthon as one of his professors. One of the least creditable episodes in the reign of Henry VIII was his treatment of Thomas Cromwell, the new chancellor. The latter had recommended a Lutheran princess named Anne of Cleves. He had just received a letter from Christopher Mount who wrote: "The lady Anne excels her sister, the Duchess of Saxony, as the golden sun does the silver moon." Poor Cromwell passed on these words to the king, but to his amazement learned later that Henry, after having seen the young woman, found her wanting. As a result England did not get a Lutheran queen and Cromwell lost his head. But Anne remained in England and was treated as the king's sister, enjoying her many new dresses and the devotion of well-paid maids of honor. In the meantime the king took his fifth wife, Catherine Howard, amidst general rejoicing and felicitations. Archbishop Cranmer, through the use of torture, was able to extort a confession from Catherine Howard's friend Francis Dereham, and the fourth divorce soon followed, and not long after that the beheading of Catherine for having loved another man. But the king lived on till illness claimed him, on January 28, 1547.

H. M. Smith has concluded that Henry VIII "founded a secularised state and may be called the Maker of Modern England." He goes on to show that Henry was directly responsible "for all the developments which have since taken place." His place in English history and in the Church of England is such that the relation between church and state in England after 1530 bears the indelible imprints of his career.

See also CROMWELL, THOMAS and MORE, THOMAS.

BIBLIOGRAPHY: Henry VIII, Letters (S. Byrne, ed.) 1936; R. B. Merriman, Life and Letters of Thomas Cromwell, 1902; J. A. Gee, Life and Works of Thomas Lupset, 1928; Thomas Cranmer, Remains (H. Jenkyns, ed.), 1843; N. Pocock, Records of the Reformation, 2 vols., 1870; G. Baskerville, English Monks and the Suppression of the Monasteries, 1937; R. W. Chambers, Thomas More, 1935; G. Mattingly, Katherine of Aragon, 1941; M. Glenne, Henry VIII's Fifth Wife, 1948; H. M. Smith, Henry VIII and the English Reformation, 1948; P. Hughes, The Reformation in England, 1951.

ALBERT HYMA.

HENRY, CARL F. H.: Baptist; b. at New York City, Jan. 22, 1913. He studied at Wheaton College (B.A., M.A.), Northern Baptist Seminary (B.D., Th.D.), Boston University (Ph.D.). Professor of theology and philosophy of religion at Northern Baptist Theological Seminary, Chicago (1942–47), he joined in 1947 in the founding of Fuller Theological Seminary, Pasadena, as professor of theology and Christian philosophy. His writings include: *Successful Church Publicity* (1942); *Remaking the Modern Mind* (1946); *The Uneasy Conscience of Modern Fundamentalism* (1947); *The Protestant Dilemma* (1948); *Notes on the Doctrine of God* (1948); *Fifty Years of Protestant Theology* (1950); *The Drift of Western Thought* (1951); and *Personal Idealism and Strong's Theology* (1951).

HENRY OF BOZEN: Blessed; b. at Bozen (Bolsano, Tyrol); d. June 10, 1315. He was born of poor parents and found work as a "facchino," a porter, at Treviso. In his old age he lived from charity. He led an austere life, continuously praying and helping others. His relics are in the cathedral of Treviso since 1712. Pope Benedict XIV approved his cult. Feast June 10.

BIBLIOGRAPHY: Acta SS Junii II, pp. 371–375, 3rd. ed., pp. 365–369. Rambaldus degli Azzoni Avogari, De beato Henrico qui Tarvisii decessit anno Christi 1315, 1760.

WILLIBRORD LAMPEN.

HENRY OF GOUDA: B. at Gouda, Holland, in 1469; d. unknown. He was canon regular of the congregation of Windesheim and lived in the monastery Thabor at Tirns near Sneek, Friesland. He wrote: *A Chronicle of Holland, West-Frisia and Zeeland,* important for the history of the Netherlands. His source is the so-called *Divisiekroniek.* Henry's work has not been edited. There is an autograph in the Library of the University of Groningen and a copy in the Royal Library in the Hague.

WILLIBRORD LAMPEN.

HENRY OF UPSALA: The "Apostle of Finland," saint, bishop and martyr; b. in England; d. on Jan. 20, 1156, at Kjulo. In 1152 he became bishop of Upsala, Sweden. Together with Eric, king of Sweden, he went to Finland in order to convert and baptize the Finns. After the return of Eric, Henry remained in Finland and worked from 1155 to 1156 at the extension of the church. He was killed by a peasant, named Lalli, who had already been punished for murder. The death of Henry has been glorified by songs and tales till today. His body was transported to Nousiainen. He was canonized in 1158. His feast is on Jan. 20.

BIBLIOGRAPHY: Acta SS. Jan., II, 249; A. Malin, Der Heiligenkalender Finlands, 1925; H. Holma, Sant 'Enrico, vescovo-apostolo martire di Finlandia, 1944.

WILLIBRORD LAMPEN.

HEPHZIBAH FAITH MISSIONARY ASSOCIATION. See HOLINESS CHURCHES.

HERALDRY: Originally, the science of the distinguishing marks which fighting men wore on their banners, shields, etc. Ecclesiastical heraldry originates in the miscellaneous emblems engraved on the seals of the bishops, abbots, and higher dignitaries of the Western Church during the middle ages. Its further developments are due to the fact that prelates having territorial jurisdiction were regarded as or assimilated to feudal landlords. The use of coats of arms by Roman Catholic dignitaries has been maintained by archaism, and their design and symbolism are most degenerate and seldom in accordance with proper heraldic usage. Ecclesiastical coats of arms are usually oval-shaped and surmounted, in place of a crest, by a mitre and crozier if the bearer is a bishop, and by a flat hat adorned on either side with rows of tassels, the number and color of which vary according to the rank of the prelate. In the United Kingdom, the arms of Roman Catholic sees are not recognized by the Heralds' College, which has charge of the arms of the Anglican sees, on account of the establishment.

BIBLIOGRAPHY: Woodward, Ecclesiastical Heraldry, 1894; idem., Treatise on Heraldry, British and Foreign, 1896; D. L. Galbreath, Papal Heraldry, 1930.

GEORGES A. BARROIS.

HERBERGEN ZUR HEIMAT: Christian hospices (q.v.) which existed in Germany since 1854. These were transformed into old people's homes when, before and during World War II, workingmen ceased to itinerate. But the earlier purpose was restored after 1945 to provide lodging, food, and help for multitudes uprooted and rendered homeless by the war.

[Sup.] FRIEDRICH M. MUENCHMEYER.

HEREDITY: Is transmission, through biological reproduction of the potentialities for development, of physical and psychological characteristics. While the recognition of a difference between "nature" and "nurture" has long found expression in prejudices and blood myths, scientific concern with the problem of the nature of heredity has been relatively recent. The modern science of heredity (genetics) dates from the rediscovery in 1900 by deVries, Correns, and von Tschermak of the work of Gregor Johann Mendel.

Mendel, a contemporary of Darwin, working with seven characteristics of peas, demonstrated that inheritance is transmitted not through a general fusion of parental characteristics but by particular, interacting, usually exactly self-reproducing units (since called genes) which maintain their integrity by separating (assorting) independently in subsequent generations. Each inherited character of an individual is controlled by two interacting genes, one from each parent. Every individual is a new combination of the many segregating gene pairs of its parents. Because in any differing pair one character is often dominant over the other (recessive), an offspring receiving two recessive genes may not resemble either parent. The Mendelian ratio (¼, ½, ¼) indicates probable distribution of genes in the third generation after hybridization.

While genes usually reproduce themselves exactly, de Vries was able to account for novel inheritable characteristics in terms of mutations, occasional spontaneous changes in which a newly emergent gene continues in the place of its predecessor. Even though mutations can be experimentally induced (X-ray, etc.) their causes, under ordinary circumstances, are not known.

T. H. Morgan and others showed that genes are carried in linearly arranged groups by thread-like paired structures (chromosomes) in all nuclei. In the formation of reproductive cells (gametes) each pair of chromosomes splits so that every gamete contains one of the pair. Human cells contain 48 chromosomes (24 pairs) yielding 2^{24} possible combinations. The chance that any human being will repeat either parental combination is about one in 8,388,608. Recent work shows the existence of further complicating plasmagenes in the cytoplasm of cells.

Gene structures (genotypes) are not to be confused with the manifest traits of individuals (phenotypes). The genes determine patterns of potential development, but the outcome of development results from interaction of genetic structure and environment. While certain gene groups may be statistically more prominent in some populations than others, geneticists find no evidence of "pure" or superior races. Because of the wide genetic potentialities, the non-appearance of carried recessive traits in hybrids, and the lethal character of many pure recessives, eugenics through sterilization and genocide is not genetically feasible.

Present Soviet rejection (Lysenko) of Mendelian laws seems to rest on the nonconformity of the relative stability of genes to Marxist doctrines of social control rather than on evidence.

See also EVOLUTION.

BIBLIOGRAPHY: G. J. Mendel, Experiments in Plant Hybridization, 1948; T. H. Morgan, The Theory of the Gene, 1926; A. W. Lindsey, A Textbook of Genetics, 1935; Th. Dobzhansky, Genetics and the Origin of Species, 1941; J. B. S. Haldane, New Paths in Genetics, 1942; L. C. Dunn and Th. Dobzhansky, Heredity, Race, and Society, 1946; T. Lysenko, The Science of Biology Today, 1948; H. Kalmos, Genetics, 1948; W. C. Boyd, Genetics and the Race of Man, 1950.

RICHARD MARION MILLARD.

HERETIC BAPTISM: The Roman Church recognizes the validity of baptism as practiced in schismatic or heretic churches, as well as of private baptism administered by non-Catholics, provided that the essential ritual is observed, namely, the use of water together with the words "I baptize thee in the name of the Father, and of the Son, and of the Holy Ghost," and the intention of doing "what the church does." In practice, converts from Protestantism are often rebaptized, since there may be some doubt as to the proper intention and the use of the correct formula. [Sup.] GEORGES A. BARROIS.

HERETICS IN EARLY CHRISTIANITY: The heretical perversions of what is known as the ancient church may be divided into four groups: (1) those which arose almost at the outset of the Christian movement; (2) those which developed during the second and third centuries concerning the doctrine of the church; (3) those which centered in the discussion of the Person of Christ and his relation to the Trinity; (4) those which concerned the doctrine of man's nature and grace.

Among the first group were the Judaizing Christians, the Christian Gnostics, the Marcionites, and the Montanists. Judaistic Christianity was confined to territory east of the Jordan and to Syria. It did not play any significant role in the formulation of Christian doctrine, largely because of the wedge which Paul drove between Jewish and Gentile Christianity and because of the destruction of Jerusalem in A.D. 70, which weakened the influence of that church. There were two types of Jewish Christians: (1) the Nazarenes who accepted the concept of redemptive Christianity and acknowledged Paul, but remained faithful to their Jewish law; and (2) the Ebionites who rejected Paul as an apostate from the law, denied the divinity and virgin birth of Jesus, and taught that the messianic work of Christ was only that of a prophet and teacher.

Also within the first group were the Christian Gnostics, most of whom were Gentiles in Asia Minor and Antioch. Under the influence of pagan Gnosticism, they engaged in theosophic speculations and developed a strong asceticism. Theirs was essentially an esoteric Christianity which rejected the Incarnation and taught that Christ only seemed to suffer, while it was only the man Jesus who was the real sufferer. Because of their exaltation of knowledge above faith and their conception of Christianity as doctrine, they forced the church to determine positively its own doctrine.

Closely related to Gnostic teaching was the anti-Judaistic emphasis of Marcion, a man of prominence in the church at Rome about A.D. 140. His reform efforts were in the direction of eliminating the Old Testament from Christian consideration. When he was excommunicated about 144, he founded his own sect and established the first canon of the New Testament. His movement spread for a few centuries as far east as Mesopotamia. It was, for a time, a threat to the church because it cut away, as did Gnosticism, the historical backgrounds of Christianity.

The reform movement led by Montanus, a native of Phrygia and a converted priest of Cybele, was based upon his claim to be the passive instrument through whom the dispensation of the Holy Spirit had arrived. He gained a following because of the fading of the consciousness of the constant inspiration of the Holy Spirit in the church by the middle of the second century. Moreover, the hope of Christ's imminent return was dimming. It is not surprising, therefore, that he should seek to restore the pristine vigor of the first disciples who had manifested in their lives the gifts of the Spirit. But the church rejected his extreme teaching, and sought to offset it by a greater emphasis upon the authority of biblical revelation and of the bishops of the church to interpret the will of God for believers.

The two heresies which concerned the nature of the church and its discipline developed during the persecutions under Decius and Diocletian. In the middle of the third century, there were many who lapsed from the faith under Decius' persecution, only to seek re-entrance later. Novatian led a movement of protest against their readmission. The church generally, however, was more lenient. Synods in Rome and Carthage in 251 and 253 permitted restoration of the lapsed, so long as they met conditions of penance. The issue divided Christians, nevertheless, till the seventh century. The church in North Africa was divided again, fifty years later, over a similar issue because of a charge by the strict party that the new bishop of Carthage, Caecilian, had received ordination from one who had been guilty of surrendering the sacred Scriptures during the recent persecution under Diocletian. Donatus the Great, who became Caecilian's successor in 316, led the rigorists in their insistence that ordination was invalid at the hands of an unworthy cleric. This position the church generally refused to recognize on the grounds that the validity of the sacraments was determined by the Holy Spirit, not by the personal worthiness of the administrant.

The third group of heresies included the Sabellians, the Samosatenes, Arians, Nestorians, and the Eutychians or Monophysites. All had their source within the church as various theologians sought to determine the nature of Christ's Person and his relationship to the Trinity. Sabellius (ca. A.D. 215) taught in Rome that Father, Son, and Holy Spirit were all manifestations at different times of the one divine person. Paul of Samosata, Metropolitan of Antioch in Syria, insisted that Jesus was a man upon whom God exercised his Logos-influence. Arius endeavored to solve the problem of the Trinity by explaining that Jesus Christ was created by the Father, divine but not coequal and coeternal with God. Nestorius, Patriarch of Constantinople (428-31), taught that the man Jesus was the bearer of the Logos from his inception. Yet it was Jesus, not the Logos, who suffered and died on the cross. Eutyches taught, on the other hand, that Christ had one nature after the Incarnation, a fusion of the human and divine; therefore God actually suffered and died on the cross. This was the monophysite position, which was rejected by the church because it did not give room enough to the union of two distinct natures in Jesus Christ, the God-Man.

The fourth classification of heretics involved Augustine, bishop of Hippo and Pelagius, a British monk. The issue concerned the nature of man after Adam. Augustine insisted that man, through the fall, became irretrievably vile and could be saved only by an act of irresistible grace. Pelagius taught that Adam's original sin did not pass on to his descendants, that man did not become totally depraved in the fall, and that God's grace only assists him to do good, but never compels him. The church officially condemned Pelagius' teachings in A.D. 431; but Pope Gregory the Great's interpretation of Augustine's theology (590-604) modified it considerably, so that medieval doctrine became semi-Augustinian rather than Augustinian.

BIBLIOGRAPHY: For a guide to the chief primary sources, see Joseph C. Ayer, A Source Book for Ancient Church History, 1913; A. von Harnack, History of Dogma, 7 vols., 1900; A. C. McGiffert, A History of Christian Thought, Vol. I, 1932; J. T. McNeill et al. (eds.), Environmental Factors in Christian History (1939), pp. 114-30; J. L. Neve, A History of Christian Thought, Vol. I, 1946; P. Schaff, History of the Christian Church, Vol. II, 5th ed. rev., 1891; H. B. Workman, Christian Thought to the Reformation, 1911.

ROBERT G. TORBET.

HERMAN, STEWART WINFIELD: Director, Service to Refugees of The Lutheran World Federation, Geneva, Switzerland; b. Aug. 4, 1909, Harrisburg, Pa. He studied at Gettysburg College (A.B., 1930), Gettysburg Seminary (B.D., 1934), University of Strasbourg (B.Th., 1935) and also at Goettingen and Berlin. He was pastor of the American Church, Berlin (1936-41); interned in Germany (Dec. 1941-

June 1942); lectured on ecumenical subjects, Hamma Divinity School (1943); served in the Office of Strategic Services (1943–44); World Council of Churches, Geneva (deputy director Reconstruction Department, 1945–47). He wrote: *It's Your Souls We Want* (1943); *The Rebirth of the German Church* (1946); and *The Church and the World* (1950).

HERMANN, RUDOLF: Lutheran; b. Oct. 3, 1887, at Barmen, Germany. After studying at Marburg, Halle and Greifswald he lectured at Goettingen (1916–19); taught at Breslau (1919–26); and has been professor of theology at Greifswald (1926–   ). In addition to many articles on systematic theology he has written: *Christentum und Geschichte bei Wilhelm Hermann* (1914); *Zur Frage des religionspsychologischen Experiments* (1922); *Das Verhaeltnis von Rechtfertigung und Gebet* (1926); *Luthers These: Gerecht und Suender zugleich* (1930); *Die Bedeutung der Bibel in Goethes Briefen an Zelter* (1948).   RAYMOND W. ALBRIGHT.

HERMANSSON, OSKAR HERMAN: Swedish State Church and Svenska Missionsförbundet; b. in Östergötland, Sweden, Sept. 17, 1889; d. June 11, 1951. He studied at Missionsförbundets Training College (1914–18), and, after ordination, ancient languages and Arabic. He served in Sinkiang, East Turkestan (1920–38) and in India (1939–45). On April 17, 1933, Muslim rebel rulers at Yarkand condemned to death Hermansson and four other leading Christians, one Turki being martyred, the others reprieved. During 1934–46 he translated the Bible into Turki, mostly singlehanded. Elected an honorary member of the British and Foreign Bible Society, he saw the Turki translation through the press (1946–51).
     EDWIN E. CALVERLEY.

HERMENEUTICS: Five problems are found in the foreground of the recent discussion of hermeneutics, viz., the significance of history for biblical interpretation, the authority of the interpreter, the problem of understanding, the oneness of the Bible, and the purpose of the Bible.

I. Interpretation and History: The application of historical criticism to the Bible seemed to drag its contents into the relativity of history. Wide agreement has been reached, however, to the effect that biblical history has to be interpreted as being divinely controlled, e.g., as progressive stages of revelation (Ramm), as *Heilsgeschichte,* i.e., holy history or history of redemption (e.g., Piper, Rust, Wendland), as a succession of dispensations (e.g., Burridge, Chafer), or as supra-history reflected in the earthly events (Kaehler, Oepke, Brunner). Accordingly the emphasis in exegesis is to be placed upon the divine plan and goal of history rather than upon the single event as such.

II. Authority and Relevancy: Except for the Roman Catholic Church, the dogmatic method which subordinates the interpretation of the Bible to a preconceived theological system has been repudiated, as also the opposite view that the Bible is but the record of first century Christianity. But why then should the exegete's work have any bearing upon theology? Various are the answers. Many continue to adhere to the divine inspiration of Scripture, preferring however some theory of plenary inspiration to verbal dictation. The idealistic school differentiates between the eternal values in the Bible, on the one hand, and the historically conditioned materials on the other (e.g., Harnack, Weinel, Bacon, Dibelius, Dodd). A few advocate "pneumatic exegesis," teaching that wherever the Bible overwhelms the exegete, the Holy Spirit has spoken (e.g., W. Herrmann, Oman, Bultmann). Relatively widespread is the view of those who consider the historical Jesus as the firm basis of their faith, assigning lesser degrees of authority to the other portions of the Bible. Others again establish the exegete's authority on his acting as a member of the church as the Body of Christ (e.g., Grosheide, Reu, Piper). Thereby the rigidity of an objective standard is tempered by subjective faith, both being the work of the same Spirit.

III. Understanding: The controversies between the above mentioned groups have vindicated Schleiermacher's insistence on the problem of understanding. Recognition of a proposition or of a fact is not tantamount to comprehension. The idealistic schools, and more recently existentialism (*q.v.*) (Bultmann), contend that the individual has an innate or acquired comprehension of the universe and life, and that biblical interpretation consists in assimilating the content of the Bible to the individual's comprehension. Over against this view, Dilthey and his followers (e.g., Torm, Wach) have objected that by doing so our knowledge would never increase, and that even in purely historical research the understanding demands a serious effort on the part of the interpreter to identify himself with the author's mind and intention and, in general, with the "life situation" in which the document originated. A similar conclusion has been reached from a new discussion of the nature of inspiration. Some (e.g., Barth in his commentary on Romans) hold that the Holy Spirit uses the biblical text merely as an instrument to create in the reader or hearer a divine conviction of the saving truth, and thus deny that the critical approach has any bearing upon the spiritual understanding of the text. Others (e.g., von Dobschuetz, Grosheide, Schlatter, the editors of *The Interpreter's Bible*) think in various ways that historical and spiritual comprehension will supplement each other in the student's mind.

IV. The Oneness of the Bible: Those who consider the Bible as a more or less incidental collection of religious documents must admit that so understood the Bible serves only as a stimulus to religious life. Those who accept the authority of the Bible are constrained to posit its oneness despite the apparent disparity of its parts. Some circles still think of an intrinsic system of doctrine underlying the whole Bible (e.g., Dana, Greijdanus, Grosheide, Berkhof, Ramm). Against this some contend that such a view not only neglects the difference of the covenants but also fails to explain the presence of historical records in the Bible. Another school sees the two Testaments connected by their common reference to Christ (e.g., W. Vischer, Barth, Hebert), thereby reviving a "typological" interpretation. Some New Testament scholars (e.g., Dodd, Stauffer) discover the oneness of the New Testament in its *kerygma*, treating the Old Testament more or less as a preface to the New. Finally we have the view of those who interpret the two Testaments as the record of a progressing and integrated process (e.g., Bleeker, Rowley, Fosdick, Eichrodt).

V. Purpose of the Bible: The modern emphasis placed upon a scholarly method of exegesis has raised the question, What is the use of such interpretation for the life of the church? In answer to this question the correlation between the Bible and faith has been freshly discussed and the practical character of exegesis has been stressed. Biblical interpretation is to nurture the life of faith and is not complete until the "challenge" of the text, i.e., the specific significance it has for the life of faith, has been discovered (the exegetical "circle" or "spiral" moving from incipient to mature faith). Several recent sets of commentaries (e.g., *Torch Commentaries, Das Neue Testament Deutsch, Die Prophezei, Interpreter's Bible*) proceed from this viewpoint.

BIBLIOGRAPHY: General Works: Louis Berkhof, *Principles of Biblical Interpretation*, 1950; R. T. Chafer, *The Science of Biblical Hermeneutics*, 1940; S. Greijdanus, *Schriftbeginselen ter Schriftverklaring*, 1946; Bernard Ramm, *Protestant Biblical Interpretation*, 1950. Old Testament: L. H. K. Bleeker, *Hermeneutik von het Oude Testament*, 1948. New Testament: Harvey E. Dana, *Searching the Scriptures: A Handbook of New Testament Hermeneutics*, 1936; F. W. Grosheide, *Hermeneutik ten Dienste van de Bestudeering van het Nieuwe Testament*, 1929; Frederik Torm, *Hermeneutik des Neuen Testaments*, 1930. Particular Problems: Karl Barth, *Lehre von Worte Gottes*, 1927, Eng. tr., *The Doctrine of the Word of God*, 1936; Rudolf Bultmann, *Glauben und Verstehen*, 1933; Martin Dibelius, *Gospel Criticism and Christology*, 1935; Ernst von Dobschuetz, *Vom Auslegen insonderheit des Neuen Testaments*, 1922, 2nd ed., 1927; C. H. Dodd, *The Authority of the Bible*, 1928; C. W. Dugmore (ed.), *Interpretation of the Bible*, 1944; Harry E. Fosdick, *A Guide to Understanding the Bible; the Development of Ideas within the Old and New Testaments*, 1938; Kemper Fullerton, *Prophecy and Authority; A Study in the History of the Doctrine and Interpretation of Scripture*, 1919; Otto Piper, *Gottes Wahrheit und die Wahrheit der Kirche*, 1933; J. Wach, *Das Verstehen:*

Bd. 2, *Die theologische Hermeneutik von Schleiermacher bis Hofmann*, 1929.

[Sup.] OTTO A. PIPER.

HERMENIGILD: Saint and martyr; d. April, 585, at Tarragona. He was the son of king Leovigild of Spain. He married in 579 Ingundis, daughter of King Sigibert of Neustria. Through her influence and that of St. Leander, he became a Catholic and was opposed to the persecution of Catholics by his father, who considered him a traitor. He was imprisoned at Valencia and beheaded at Tarragona. St. Gregory the Great says (*Dial.* 3, 31) that Hermenigild refused to receive Holy Communion from an Arian priest. So he considered him a martyr. His feast in Roman Catholic liturgy is on April 13.

BIBLIOGRAPHY: *Acta SS. Aprilis*, II, 136–137; H. Leclerc, *L'Espagne chrétienne*, 1906.

WILLIBRORD LAMPEN.

HERMES TRISMEGISTUS: "Thrice-greatest Hermes," i.e., the Egyptian liturgical title, "Thoth the very great [god]." Thoth-Hermes, scribe of the gods and himself god of wisdom, was supposedly the author, i.e., source, of the revelation contained in the eighteen Greek Hermetic tractates beginning with the *Poimandres* and supplemented by the Latin *Asclepius* (translated from a fourth century Greek "Logos teleios"). The earliest may date from the second century; they belong with the growing astrological literature of that period. The later tractates are more markedly Gnostic in content. Only the astrological elements belong to Egyptian religious tradition; other elements belong to the world of Hellenistic syncretism, and reflect an enthusiasm for ancient secret religious lore derived (presumably) from the Orient and Egypt. There is little evidence of any cultus or organization; Hermetism had no rites of purification like Orphism, no theurgy or magic. It was a private, individual, literary and intellectual practice of personal religion, and formed at most a school of mystical religious thought.

BIBLIOGRAPHY: W. Scott, A. S. Ferguson, *Hermetica*, 4 vols., 1924–26; A. D. Nock, A. J. Festugière, *Corpus Hermeticum*, 2 vols., 1945; A. J. Festugière, *La révélation d'Hermès Trismégiste*, 2 vols. thus far, 1944, 1949; *L'Hermétisme*, 1948; C. H. Dodd, *The Bible and the Greeks*, Pt. II, 1935.

FREDERICK C. GRANT.

HERP, HENRIK: Probably born in Erp in Dutch Brabant, about 1400. He joined the Brethren of the Common Life (*q.v.*), and in 1445 became rector of their house in Delft. In the same year he received the offer to found the new house in Gouda, which offer he accepted, notwithstanding the disapproval of his colleagues in Delft. In 1450 he joined the Franciscan Observants in Rome; in 1453 he was appointed guardian in Mechlin; in 1477 he died there while still holding that position. The period of his greatest literary activity lies between 1450 and 1470.

In addition to two large volumes of sermons he wrote five important ascetic-mystic works: *Eden contemplativorum; Scala amoris; Spiegel der volcomenheit (Mirror of Perfection); Soliloquia super Cantica;* and *De processu humani profectus.* Of these the work in Flemish is by far the most significant. It was translated into Latin by Petrus Blommevenna, a Carthusian in Cologne, under the title of *Directorium aureum contemplativorum;* in 1509 the first edition was published in Cologne. The work was also issued in Italian, Spanish, Portuguese, French, and German translations. These five works by Herp were worked over into a new volume by Bruno Loer, a Carthusian in Cologne. The title was *Theologia mystica,* first ed. in 1538, followed by six others by 1611. Herp has been called the "Herald of Ruysbroeck" (*q.v.*). It is true that he did incorporate Ruysbroeck's ideas in his own works and spread them, but he remained to a large extent original. He was more practical than his Flemish predecessor, and also more concrete and more objective. His influence was very great, especially in Spain and France, but unfortunately it was not until about 1940 that this was noted, even in the Netherlands.

See also MYSTICISM AND ASCETICISM IN THE NETHERLANDS.

BIBLIOGRAPHY: L. Verschueren, "Leven en werken van Hendrik Herp," in *Collectanea Franciscana Neerlandica,* II (1931), 345–393; H. Herp, *Spiegel der volkomenheit* (L. Verschueren, ed.), 1931.

M. M. J. SMITS VAN WAESBERGHE.

HERRIOTT, FRANK W.: Baptist; b. at Winfield, Kansas, June 27, 1893. He studied at Ottawa University (A.B., 1915), Union Theological Seminary (B.D., 1926), and Columbia University (Ph.D., 1933). He has served as pastor of the First Baptist Church, Winfield, Kan. (1920–22), as minister of religious education at the Central Presbyterian Church of Montclair, N. J. (1926–29) and as a member of the staff of the Religious Education Department of Union Theological Seminary (1929–). He has written: *A Community Serves Its Youth* (1933); and *Christian Youth in Action* (1935).

HERRIOTT, GEORGE FREDERICK: D. Oct. 28, 1926. He served as a missionary of the Congregational Churches in Turkey (1859–1911) and in addition to his other achievements he was the joint superintendent of publications (1893–1911). His last publication was: *Christian and Mohammedan* (1912).

[Sup.] RAYMOND W. ALBRIGHT.

HERRMANN, WILHELM: Theologian; b. 1846; d. 1922. He studied at Halle; became privatdozent there in 1875, and professor ordinarius at Marburg in 1879. He followed Ritschl in freeing theology from the shackles of philosophical systems by means of the Kantian separation of the practical from the theoretical reason, and in concentrating his attention on the historical Jesus. But, since he regarded the New Testament records as historically unreliable, he sought to discover the "inner life of Jesus" in its ethico-religious significance, assuring men that, as they unite their imperfect moral lives with the universal ethical ideal there revealed, they will receive the ability to do good. The effect of Christ's work thus terminates, for him, on men, and does not, nor does it need to, produce any change in God's attitude towards sinners. Like Ritschl, and for the same reason, he would not attribute metaphysical deity to Jesus, but his intense ethical devotion to the Person of Jesus lent an attractive warmth to his personality and to his thought.

His best known book, first published in 1886, was translated into English with the title: *The Communion of the Christian with God.* His lectures on dogmatics were posthumously published in 1925 by Martin Rade, and were translated into English in 1927, with the title: *Systematic Theology.* ANDREW K. RULE.

HERRON, GEORGE D.: B. 1862; d. 1925. He sprang into national prominence as a social prophet in the early 1890's. A midwestern Congregational minister, he lectured and wrote extensively on social Christian themes. Called in 1893 to be professor of applied Christianity at Iowa (now Grinnell) College, he became the central figure in the influential "Kingdom Movement." But as he moved steadily in a radical direction, both socially and theologically, he was rejected by the churches and found his support in certain religio-social reform movements of the late 1890's. He resigned his chair in 1900 and became a leading figure in the organization of the American Socialist Party in 1901. That same year he was divorced by his wife, speedily remarried, and was deposed from the ministry. Living abroad, he was conspicuous as a socialist leader until 1914; through the Wilson administration he served as a diplomatic agent in Europe. See also SOCIAL GOSPEL.

BIBLIOGRAPHY: Mitchell P. Briggs, *George D. Herron and the European Settlement,* 1932; Robert T. Handy, *George D. Herron and the Social Gospel in American Protestantism, 1890–1901,* 1949.

ROBERT T. HANDY.

HERSHBERGER, GUY FRANKLIN: Mennonite; b. at Kalona, Iowa, Dec. 3, 1896. He studied at Hesston College (B.A., 1923) and the universities of Chicago, Michigan, and Iowa (M.A., 1925; Ph.D., 1935); he taught history and sociology at Goshen College (1925–). His published works are: *Can Christians Fight?*

(1940); *Christian Relationships to State and Community* (1942); *War, Peace, and Nonresistance* (1944); *The Mennonite Church in the Second World War* (1951).

HESCHEL, ABRAHAM JOSHUA: B. in Warsaw, 1907; studied at University of Berlin (Ph.D., 1933); graduate Hochschule fuer die Wissenschaft des Judentums, Berlin (1934). He was instructor, Talmud, Hochschule f. d. Wiss. d. Jud., Berlin (1932–33); lecturer, Mittelstelle fuer Juedische Erwachsenenbildung, Frankfurt a. M. (1937–38); docent, philosophy, Institute for Judaistic Studies, Warsaw (1937–38); founder, Institute for Jewish Learning, London (1940). He taught Jewish philosophy and rabbinics, Hebrew Union College, Cincinnati (1940–45), and has been assistant professor of Jewish ethics and mysticism, Jewish Theological Seminary of America, New York, since 1945. He is the author of: *Maimonides* (1935; Fr. tr., 1936); *Die Prophetie* (1936); *Abravanel* (1937; Polish tr., 1938); *Der Begriff des Seins* (1937); *Der Begriff der Einheit* (1938); *Das Wesen der Dinge nach der Lehre Gabirols* (1939); *An Analysis of Piety* (1942); *The Holy Dimension* (1943); *The Quest for Certainty in Saadia's Philosophy* (1944); *Faith* (1944); *Prayer* (1945); *Did Maimonides Strive for Prophetic Inspiration?* (1946); *Inspiration in the Middle Ages* (1950); *The Earth Is the Lord's, The Inner Life of the Jew in East Europe* (1950); *Man Is not Alone, A Philosophy of Religion* (1951); *The Sabbath* (1951).

HESSE AND NASSAU: The territory of the state of Hesse in the Federal Republic of Germany is divided among three Evangelical churches: (1) The Evangelical Church in Hesse and Nassau, embracing the largest part of the state in the west and south; (2) The Evangelical Church of Waldeck-Pyrmont (*q.v.*) in the north; and (3) The Evangelical Church in the Rhineland (*q.v.*), embracing the district of Wetzlar.

The first and largest of these churches has 2,850,000 members and 720 congregations. The Roman Catholic Church in the same territory has 1,500,000 members attached to the bishoprics of Mainz and Limburg. As a consequence of the introduction of about 550,000 refugees (*q.v.*) after 1945, the confessional complexion of the state has become mixed.

Before the Church of Hesse and Nassau was formed in 1947, there were three independent churches—Hesse, Nassau, and Frankfurt. When, in 1918, the former relation of state and church was dissolved, each of these three churches was compelled to develop a new form of church organization. This was completed in Hesse-Darmstadt and in Nassau in 1922, and in Frankfurt am Main in 1923. In every case ultimate authority was vested in a synod, but there were

differences in church offices. The former consistory was replaced in Hesse and in Nassau by a *Kirchenregierung*, in Frankfurt by a *Landeskirchenrat*. Moreover, the superintendents of Rhine-Hesse, Starkenburg, and Upper Hesse were retained, together with the title of prelate for the heads of the church government in Hesse, while the episcopal office was reintroduced into Nassau, and two theologians took places beside the former jurist as ecclesiastical councilors in Frankfurt.

The confessional position of the churches remained unchanged; all three were, administratively, union churches (*q.v.*). Lutheran congregations in Hesse-Darmstadt and parts of Nassau acknowledged the Augsburg Confession and its Apology (*q.v.*, Vol. I), the Concord of Wittenberg, the Schmalkald Articles (*q.v.*), and Luther's Small Catechism (see CATECHISMS, II, 2 in Vol. II). The same was true in Lutheran congregations in Frankfurt, except that the Wittenberg Concord was omitted. The Reformed congregations had no common confessional basis, but the Heidelberg Catechism (*q.v.* in Vol. V) was generally adhered to. Union congregations sometimes acknowledged the Apostles' Creed (*q.v.*) and the Augsburg Confession, sometimes (in Rhine-Hesse) also a union formula for the administration of Holy Communion. These confessional differences survived all subsequent changes in the churches.

During the church struggle under National Socialism the so-called German Christians were opposed by the Confessing Church (see GERMANY, I), which had its Hessian center of influence in Frankfurt. In 1947 the three churches of Hesse, Nassau, and Frankfurt were united in the Evangelical Church of Hesse and Nassau, and Martin Niemoeller (*q.v.*) was elected president. Two years later a new constitution was adopted according to which the Barmen Declaration (see GERMANY, I) was recognized alongside the ancient creeds and the Augsburg Confession. The territory of the church is divided into six visitation districts, each headed by a provost. Two preachers' seminaries in Friedberg and Herborn were continued, but the closing of Giessen University by the state in 1946 deprived the church of its only theological faculty. Inner mission work is carried on by three societies, supplemented by the activity of *Evangelisches Hilfswerk* (*q.v.*). There are four deaconess (*q.v.*) motherhouses, and there is an Evangelical Academy in Assenheim. Since World War II the Jehovah's Witnesses (*q.v.*), Adventists (*q.v.*), and other sects and cults (*q.v.*) have been active.

BIBLIOGRAPHY: W. Diehl, *Die Vereinigung der beiden protestantischen Konfessionen in Rheinhessen*, 1922; J. Kuebel, *Ev. Kirchenrecht fuer Frankfurt a. M.*, 1932; A. Adam, *Die Nassauische Union von 1817*, 1949.

[Sup. to HESSE.] ALFRED ADAM.

HEWETT LECTURESHIP: Established in 1921 by Professor Waterman T. Hewett, of Cornell University, the terms of this trust provide that lectures shall dicuss: (1) the truths of Christianity as shown in revelation, reason, and history; (2) the value and authority of the Holy Scriptures and the influence of the church in the world, especially through Christian missions; and (3) the results of fresh discoveries as bearing upon Christian truths. The lectures are delivered annually, biennially, or triennially, as the trustees of the fund may appoint, at Andover Newton Theological School, the Episcopal Theological School in Cambridge, Mass., and Union Theological Seminary, New York City. There is no provision for publication, but many of the lectures have been published as books, pamphlets, or in various religious journals.   HERBERT GEZORK.

HEXATEUCH. See PENTATEUCH; JOSHUA, BOOK OF.

HEYDEN, GASPAR VAN DER (HEYDANUS): B. 1530 at Mechlin; d. May 7, 1586, at Bacherach. His parents belonged to the upper classes. At the age of sixteen or seventeen he became a Protestant, which necessitated his leaving home. In Antwerp he earned his living repairing shoes, and joined what was called the Church under the Cross, a name given to Calvinist congregations in the Low Countries at the time. When in 1551 the local pastor, Jan van Ostende, was martyred, Van der Heyden became his successor, first in a subordinate capacity, then as regular pastor. In 1557 he spent some time in Emden for more training, and it was then that he became a fullfledged minister. In July he was back in Antwerp, where he had to act as mediator between the congregation and Haemstede (q.v.). In 1558 he left the city to find safer quarters in Frankfurt am Main. There a dispute arose between him and Dathenus over the desirability of having children of Calvinist parents baptized in Lutheran churches. In 1562 Calvin was consulted, and he ruled that this was permissible, thus supporting Dathenus. A little later Van der Heyden labored at Frankenthal in the Palatinate, again with Dathenus. In April, 1566, he was in Antwerp, which he used as a focal center for his preaching in Flanders, e.g., at Axel, Hulst, etc. His preaching was often followed by iconoclasm. In November he was summoned with others to Amsterdam, because several preachers among the Calvinists had concluded that art. 10a and 13 of the Augsburg Confession were acceptable to them.

In April, 1567, he removed once more to Frankenthal, where Arnoldus Cornelii (q.v.), became his colleague. Here he became a leading figure, with the result that in 1571 at the

Synod of Emden he acted as President. In 1574 he was presiding pastor at the provincial synod at Dordrecht, while at the national synod at Dordrecht in 1578 he was assessor. For a short time he was itinerary preacher in the service of the Elector of the Palatinate, but in May or June, 1574, he became a pastor in the church at Middelburg, which he left on Oct. 2, 1579. He preached in Antwerp until in 1585 the city fell into the hands of the Spaniards. After a short visit to Holland he left for Frankenthal, where he resumed his preaching and became inspector at Bacherach.

He was a prominent leader among the Dutch Calvinists, winning the respect of Prince William of Orange and Marnix of St. Aldegonde. He contributed much to the making of the liturgical writings of the Dutch Reformed Church. His son, Gaspar van der Heyden Jr., was a pastor in Amsterdam, and another son, Abraham, became a well-known professor at Leiden.

BIBLIOGRAPHY: *Biogr. Woordenboek van Prot. Godgeleerden in Ned.*, Vol. III, pp. 807-816, with bibliography; T. Ruys, *Petrus Dathenus*, 1919; H. J. Jaanus, *Hervormd Delft ten tijde van Arent Cornelisz (1573-1605)*, 1950.
                                                D. NAUTA.

HEYER, JOHN CHRISTIAN FREDERICK: Lutheran missionary; b. in Helmstedt, Germany, July 10, 1793; emigrated to Philadelphia in 1807; d. there Nov. 7, 1873. Licensed (1817) and ordained by the Pennsylvania Ministerium, he served congregations in Pennsylvania and Maryland. Surveying home mission areas as far west as Missouri, he also introduced Sunday schools in eastern parishes. As the first American Lutheran foreign missionary (1842), he served in South India (Guntur, Rajahmundry) intermittently for seventeen years. He helped to organize the first Lutheran synod in Minnesota. Contemporaries affectionately called him "Father" Heyer.

BIBLIOGRAPHY: E. Theodore Bachmann, *They Called Him Father*, 1942; George Drach and C. F. Kuder, *The Telugu Mission*, 1914.
                                    E. THEODORE BACHMANN.

HIBBATH ZION. See ZIONISM.

HIGGER, MICHAEL: Talmudic author; b. Rogovo, Lithuania, Jan. 6, 1898; d. New York City, Nov. 22, 1952. He studied at New York University (B.A., 1922), at Columbia University (Ph.D., 1926), and at the Jewish Theological Seminary of America (rabbi, 1926).

Higger published critical editions and English translations of the minor tractates of the Talmud (1929–37), and wrote *Intention in Talmudic Law* (1927), and *The Jewish Utopia* (1932), a reconstruction of the rabbinic concept of the ideal social life on earth. He also published ten volumes, *Ozar Ha-Beraitot* (1938–

48), classifying and listing the Baraitot, statutes not found in the Mishnah but cited in the discussions of the Amoraim, and found scattered through the Babylonian and Palestinian Talmuds.

HIGGINBOTTOM, SAM: Presbyterian; b. in Manchester, England, on Oct. 27, 1874. On arrival in the United States he studied at Mt. Hermon School (1894–99), Amherst College, Princeton University (A.B., 1903; A.M., 1911), and Ohio State University (B.Sc. in Agr., 1911). He was a Presbyterian missionary in India from 1903 to his retirement. He organized the Agricultural Institute to provide a means for disseminating information for the improvement of crop production in India. He also worked incessantly to improve the status of lepers and the blind. He is president emeritus of Allahabad Christian College and was moderator of the General Assembly of the Presbyterian Church, U.S.A., in 1939. Since his retirement he founded and directed the Christian Service Training Center, Inc., at Babson Park, Fla., for the preparation of foreign missionaries in the customs and conditions of the foreign lands of their choice. He wrote: *The Gospel and the Plow* (1921); *What Does Jesus Expect of His Church?* (1940); and *Sam Higginbottom, Farmer* (1949).   RAYMOND W. ALBRIGHT.

HIGH PLACES: (Heb. *bâmâh, bâmôth;* cf. Akkadian *bâmtu, bamâti,* "height") Heights or tops of mountains (see Deut. 33:29; II Sam. 1:19; Ps. 18:33; Isa. 58:14); more particularly, the cultic "high places," especially those local sanctuaries where pagan gods were worshiped. Solomon built a high place for Chemosh, the chief god of the Moabites and also for Milcom, the god of the Ammonites (I Kings 11:7). Jeremiah refers to the high places of Baal and that in the Valley of Ben-hinnom where human sacrifices were made to Molech (Baal; Jer. 7:31; 19:5; 32:35). There was a place Bamoth-baal in Moab (Num. 22:41; Josh. 13:17). The word "high place" occurs on the Moabite Stone. There were the high places of the satyrs by the entrance of a city gate of Jerusalem (II Kings 23:8). At the high places the hosts of the heavens were also worshiped and idolatrous priests functioned there (II Kings 23:5; Hos. 10:5; Zeph. 1:4).

These sanctuaries were doubtless mostly on elevated sites, although a "high place" might be in a valley, city, or even in the temple. The idea of the deity dwelling on a mountain was common in the ancient Near East. In one sense Mt. Sinai, Mt. Nebo, and Mt. Zion might be thought of as high places (cf. the Babylonian *ziqquratu,* "mountain peak").

At the Canaanite high places there were sacred trees, pillars, and the Asherah (I Kings

14:23; Jer. 2:27). The sacrifice of incense at the high places, which was strongly although not exclusively associated with paganism, was condemned (II Kings 16:4; Jer. 32:29). Idols were worshiped there (Deut. 12:3). These high places were largely outdoor sanctuaries, although some had buildings associated with them, and we hear of houses of the high places (I Kings 13:33; II Kings 23:19). There were many of these high places. Each locality probably had at least one. At such sanctuaries pagan influences were strong and the rites of sacred prostitution were carried on (I Kings 14:23, 24; Hos. 4:14).

When the Hebrews first took over the high places from the Canaanites, many of these sanctuaries were doubtless devoted to the worship of Yahweh. The high place at Gibeon was known as "the great high place." There Solomon made sacrifices to Yahweh (I Kings 3:4). The prophets of Yahweh functioned at a high place (I Sam. 10:5, 10). The increasing importance of the temple at Jerusalem and the growing opposition of the prophets to the paganism of these local shrines decreased their significance (I Kings 12:29–33; Jer. 2:28; 9:13, 14; Hos. 4:11–14). The reform of Josiah in 621 B.C. proscribed completely their existence and many were destroyed by him (II Kings 23; cf. Deut. 12:4–17; 17:6, 7).

Archaeological researches have revealed sanctuaries with sacred pillars, as at Ader and Bab edh-Dhra in Moab and Lejjun in Transjordan. There are also well-known illustrations of high places at Petra, with rock altar, water reservoir, and court for sacrificial feasts.

BIBLIOGRAPHY: W. F. Albright, *Archaeology and the Religion of Israel,* 1942; G. L. Robinson, *The Sarcophagus of an Ancient Civilization,* 1930; M. Burrows, *What Mean These Stones?* 1941; W. C. Graham and H. G. May, *Culture and Conscience,* 1936.
          [Sup.] HERBERT G. MAY.

HILARION (TROITZKY): Eastern Orthodox. He pursued his studies at the Theological Academy of Moscow, where he was later professor of the New Testament and provost (up to the Revolution). Later he was consecrated bishop, and was archbishop of Krytitzy (a ruling bishop of the Moscow diocese). After a confinement at Solovky he died from consumption. His main scholarly work was: *History of the Dogma of the Church* (in Russian, 1912). He was a fervent opponent of Western influence in Orthodox theology and advocate of a return to the patristic tradition.
          GEORGES FLOROVSKY.

HILFSWERK, EVANGELISCHES: The Evangelical Church in Germany (*q.v.*) organized the "Relief Agency [*Hilfswerk*] of the Evangelical Church in Germany" in Aug., 1945, immediately after the close of World War II. Shortly afterwards "Church" in the title was changed to "Churches" to indicate that the organization represented the small free churches (see GERMANY, II) as well as the larger territorial churches (Lutheran, Reformed, Union). Thus it was a united Protestant agency, parallel to the Roman Catholic *Caritas* (*q.v.*).

On the collapse of Germany Hilfswerk was confronted by widespread destruction, hunger, and disease, accompanied by dislocation, demoralization, and despair. Eugene Gerstenmaier, Lutheran theologian with experience in business and politics, established headquarters in Stuttgart, branch offices in each territorial church, and made every parish clergyman a volunteer worker. A staff of 5,000 was employed. The immediately pressing problem was to provide food, clothing, medicine, and housing for bombed-out and impoverished natives and 12,000,000 refugees (*q.v.*), expellees, and displaced persons. Material aid from Churches abroad (see RELIEF, RECONSTRUCTION, AND INTER-CHURCH AID), supplemented by money and goods gathered in Germany, was distributed without distinction of race or creed where need was greatest.

Between 1945 and 1950 more than 68,000 tons of food and clothing from outside Germany and 100,000 tons from within Germany were given out. In addition, $8,700,000, almost two-thirds of it from outside Germany, were applied to the alleviation of want. A total of 3,500,000 children and 16,000 students were fed in emergency stations, 75 institutions of mercy equipped, 9,802 houses built, 49 rehabilitation schools established, 48 rubble churches and 35 barracks churches erected, 11,000,000 Bibles and other religious books provided. When material aid became less urgent in western Germany (it continued in eastern Germany), Hilfswerk made long-range provision for refugees, displaced persons, uprooted youth, disabled soldiers, and prisoners of war.

Gerstenmaier was elected a member of Parliament in 1950 and was succeeded as head of Hilfswerk by Herbert Krimm.

See also INNER MISSION.

BIBLIOGRAPHY: *Jahrbuch: Das Hilfswerk, 1945–1950*, 1950. For biography of Gerstenmaier see Eric H. Boehm, *We Survived*, 1949.

THEODORE G. TAPPERT.

HILLEL FOUNDATION. See STUDENT ORGANIZATIONS, RELIGIOUS.

HILLIS, NEWELL DWIGHT: D. Feb. 25, 1929. With distinction he served the Plymouth Congregational church in Brooklyn, N. Y. (1899–1924), was a popular preacher in this country and Great Britain and was also the president of Plymouth Institute (1914–29). His later publications include: *Contagion of Character* (1911); *Anti-Slavery Epoch* (1911); *Prophets of a New Era* (1912); *All the Year Round*

(1912); *Battle of Principles* (1912); *Misfortunes of a World Without Pain* (1912); *Noble Thoughts* (1912); *Story of Phaedrus* (1913); *Message of David Swing* (1913); *Studies of the Great War* (1915); *German Atrocities* (1918); *The Blot on the Kaiser's 'Scutcheon* (1918); *Rebuilding the Ruined Lands of Europe* (1919); *The Better American Lectures* (1921); and he compiled *Lectures of Henry Ward Beecher* (1913). [Sup.] RAYMOND W. ALBRIGHT.

HILPRECHT, HERMAN VOLRATH: B. July 28, 1859, at Hohenerxleben, Germany; d. Mar. 20, 1925. He studied theology, philology, and law at Leipzig (1880–85; Ph.D., 1883). He taught Old Testament theology in Erlangen (1885–86); was Clark research professor of Assyrian and professor of comparative Semitic philology at the University of Pennsylvania (1886–1911). During this time he was also curator of the Semitic section of the University Museum (1887–1911), containing over 50,000 original Babylonian antiquities largely presented by him. From 1895 he was the scientific director of the University of Pennsylvania's four expeditions to Nippur, Babylonia, and editor-in-chief of its publications, *The Babylonian Expedition of the University of Pennsylvania*, 4 series. He reorganized the Babylonian section of the Imperial Ottoman Museum in Constantinople (1893–1909) and made frequent scientific researches in Asia Minor and Syria as well as India, China, Ceylon, Korea and Japan. He was a leading authority on cuneiform research. His works include: (with A. T. Clay), *Business Documents of Murashû Sons of Nippur; Mathematical, Metrological and Chronological Texts from the Temple Library of Nippur* (Part 1, 1906); and *Assyriaca, Eine Nachlese auf dem Gebreite der Assyriologie*.

RAYMOND W. ALBRIGHT.

HILTNER, SEWARD: Presbyterian (U.S.A.); b. Nov. 26, 1909, Tyrone, Pa. He studied at Lafayette College (A.B., 1931); Divinity School, University of Chicago (1931–35). He was secretary, Westminster Foundation, University of Chicago (1933–35); Executive Secretary, Council for Clinical Training (1935–38); and Executive Secretary, Department of Pastoral Services, Commission on Religion and Health, Commission on Ministry in Institutions, Federal Council of the Churches of Christ in America (1938–50). He is associate professor of pastoral theology, Federated Theological Faculty, The University of Chicago (1950–). He has written: (ed.), *Christianity and Mental Hygiene* (1939); *Religion and Health* (1943); (ed.), *Clinical Pastoral Training* (1945); *Pastoral Counseling* (1949); *Self-Understanding* (1951).

HINCMAR OF REIMS: His first treatise on predestination was not published until 1889, and for this reason little has been written on it. In this work Hincmar indicated that Christ's atonement was sufficient for all human beings, and that the latter have a certain amount of personal responsibility for their misdemeanors, as well as a limited amount of inherent goodness left with which to do some good. But his opponent Gottschalk was equally resourceful, as has been admirably indicated in Freystedt's article.

BIBLIOGRAPHY: The treatise on predestination mentioned above was published in *Zeitschrift fuer Kirchengeschichte*, Vol. X (1889), pp. 258-309; see also A. Fliche and V. Martin, *Histoire de l'Eglise*, Vol. VI (1937) (this volume is by Emile Amann), pp. 324-338, 383-393.

[Sup.] ALBERT HYMA.

HINDUISM: New forces from without and within have produced a new vigor in Hinduism, a new synthesis, the parallel in modern terms of the syntheses which represent the creative periods of Hindu history.

The forces from without have been the introduction of Western methodology in science and history and the opening up of the knowledge of the Western world in its history and philosophy, its religion and ethics; the passion of the Western world for improvement in the ways of living, for material advance, for the good life as expressed in social development, in the usefulness of industry to living patterns. All these have profoundly influenced the history of Hinduism in the first half of the twentieth century.

The influences from within have been a rediscovery of India's past, the interpretation of creative minds of the religious history of the Hindu in social terms, recognizing the twin streams of social and religious history as not necessarily or inevitably joined; the movements for theological and social reform undertaken by Ram Mohan Roy and others; the "back to the Vedas" of Swami Dayananda Sarasvati and the Arya Samaj; the exotic Hinduism of the Theosophical Society, particularly under Mrs. Annie Besant; and, finally, the religious genius of Sri Ramakrishna with his philosopher-interpreter and disciple, Swami Vivekananda. These have all been precursors of the new intellectual life and social conscience influencing Hindu thinkers and reformers. In the words of Sri Aurobindo Ghose, one of the apostles of this Renaissance, it sets itself the following tasks: "The recovery of the old spiritual knowledge and experience in all its splendor, depth, and fullness is its most essential work; the flowing of this spirituality into new forms of philosophy, literature, art, science and critical knowledge is the second; an original dealing with modern problems in the light of the Indian spirit and the endeavor to formulate a greater synthesis of a spiritualized society is the third and most difficult. Its success on these three lines will be the measure of its help to the future of humanity."

The new interpretations of Hinduism have "rescued Indians from a philosophy of listless inaction" and have been responsible for the paying of much more attention to the wellbeing of society and life on earth. The culmination of social reform within Hindu society may be seen in The Constitution of the Republic of India which was put into effect Jan. 26, 1950. This constitution has outlawed untouchability and many of its declarations strike at the fundamental caste traditions of Hindu society. No one can be restricted in access to shops, restaurants, hotels, places of entertainment, or in his use of wells, tanks, bathing places, roads or meeting places maintained wholly or partly by the state on the grounds of religion, race, caste, sex or place of birth. The discrimination against women has largely been abolished even to the extent that one objective of economic life relating to the employment of women puts women on exactly the same basis as men with equal pay for equal work. Such reforms are in the main opposed by the orthodox Hindu political parties.

The Constitution of the Republic of India mentioned above does not recognize the peculiar rights of any religious community. This has not always been accepted by the majority community of Hindus whose orthodoxy has been represented by the Akhil Bharat Hindu Mahasabha which was founded in 1915. This more orthodox element is pledged to attempt to reunite India, for it has never recognized partition. It is very inimical to the interests of Pakistan (*q.v.*). It is against India as a secular state and stands for the establishment of Hindu rule with a form of government "in accordance with the Hindu conception of polity and economy." The party has an orthodox approach to agriculture, industry and social legislation and wants to make military education compulsory. It also favors the severance of commonwealth relationships. This position follows normally on that of the Arya Samaj whose declaration that to be an Indian is to be a Hindu makes the idea of a secular state difficult. For the Mahasabha the policies of the Indian National Congress, of Mahatma Gandhi and Jawaharlal Nehru, are far too liberal and give too much play to the power of other communities. The Mahasabha contended against these more liberal forces in the elections of 1951-52.

Hinduism is now being viewed apart from its old mythological and ritualistic forms. (For a fuller report of the new Brahmanism, see BRAHMANISM.)

The India of the mid-twentieth century is one which finds Hinduism fluid, active in reform and uncertain of its own future except that it must change if it is to survive all of the impacts of the twentieth century including that of communism which is making very real inroads on the older conservative type of religion. The future of India depends largely upon whether or not Hinduism can adjust itself to the problems of the mid-century. She is making efforts so to do.

See also BRAHMO SAMAJ; JAINISM; INDIA.

[Sup.] MALCOLM S. PITT.

HINKE, WILLIAM JOHN: Reformed; b. Mar. 24, 1871, at Giershofen, Rhein Province, Germany; d. Jan. 1, 1947. After early training in Germany he studied at Calvin College, Cleveland; Ursinus School of Theology, Collegeville, Pa. (1892–94); Princeton Seminary (1894–85), and the University of Pennsylvania (1900–1906; Ph.D., 1906). He taught Latin and Greek at Calvin College (1890–92); taught at Ursinus College (German, 1892–94; Hebrew, 1895–1907) and in the School of Theology where he taught Old Testament (1907–09). He was professor of Semitic languages and religions at Auburn (N. Y.) Theological Seminary (1909–39; also librarian, 1923–39). He wrote: *Bibliography of the Reformed Church in the United States* (1901); *A New Boundary Stone of Nebuchadnezzar I, from Nippur* (1907); *Selected Babylonian Kudurru Inscriptions* (1911); *Life and Letters of the Rev. John Philip Boehm* (1916); *History of Goshenhoppen Reformed Charge, 1727–1833* (1920); *History of the Tohickon Union Church, 1745–1854* (1925); and he also edited and translated: *The Minutes and Letters of the Coetus of Pennsylvania 1747–1792* (1903); *General Biographical Catalog of Auburn Theological Seminary, 1818–1918* (1918); *The Latin Works of Huldreich Zwingli,* Vol II (1922); and *Pennsylvania German Pioneers* (3 vols., 1934).   RAYMOND W. ALBRIGHT.

HINSLEY, ARTHUR: Roman Catholic; b. Carlton, Yorkshire, 1865; d. Buntingford, Hertfordshire, March 17, 1943. He was educated at Ushaw; the English College, Rome; and the Gregorian University. He was professor at Ushaw (1893–97); headmaster of St. Bede's Grammar School, Bradford (1899–1904); in pastorates (1904–17); rector of English College, Rome (1917–28); visitor apostolic to the Catholic missions in Africa (1927); titular archbishop of Sardis (1930); apostolic delegate to Africa (1930–34); archbishop of Westminster (1935–43); and cardinal (1937–43).

F. W. DILLISTONE.

HIPPOLYTUS: The importance of Hippolytus has been recognized more fully in the last forty years. Working independently, E. Schwartz and R. H. Connolly proved that what was formerly known as the Egyptian Church Order is actually the *Apostolic Tradition* of Hippolytus. This treatise, available to English readers in the editions of Easton and Dix, deals with the liturgical practice of the Roman church as recorded either in 215 (Dix) or perhaps in 197 (Richardson). In either case, the liturgical material is traditional and reflects usage at least as early as the last decade of the second century.

In 1936 C. Martin noted the striking resemblances between a homily on the Passover ascribed to Chrysostom and what little is known of Hippolytus' treatise *On the Passover;* he ascribed the homily directly to Hippolytus. More recent studies, especially by Nautin, prove that it is a fourth-century homily based on Hippolytus.

In the last few years a controversy has been aroused by Nautin. He has argued that a certain Josephus, otherwise unknown, wrote the *Refutation,* the *Chronicon,* and the lost treatise *On the Universe;* Photius ascribes the last work to "Josephus." According to Nautin, Hippolytus wrote *On Antichrist;* the fragment called *Against Noëtus;* commentaries on Daniel, Canticles, and the benedictions of Jacob and Moses; the *Apostolic Tradition;* and some prologues to the Psalms. The famous Roman statue with its list of treatises is a statue of Josephus. Nautin's arguments have been refuted in detail by Bardy, Capelle, and Richard. The controversy is significant, however, for the stimulus provided for further study and the proof it provides that not enough detailed work had been done in Hippolytus.

Hippolytus was not only a bishop of the Roman church but also a philosophical and literary teacher of the community; it is as such a teacher that his statue represents him. His work in the *Refutation* and the *Chronicon* marks an important advance in the cultural life of the Christian church. His philosophical analyses of various heresies reflect a fairly adequate understanding of the history of philosophy. He uses a good doxographical source (cf. H. Diels, *Doxographi graeci* [1879], pp. 144–156, 551–576), as well as some other secular works which he rather ostentatiously reproduces. His information about Gnostic systems is generally accurate. In his *Chronicon* he uses various historical and geographical sources, especially a *periplus* (coastal pilot's list) of the Mediterranean. We possess excellent modern editions of the *Refutation* by Wendland and of the *Chronicon* by A. Bauer-R. Helm.

BIBLIOGRAPHY: B. S. Easton, *The Apostolic Tradition of Hippolytus,* 1934; G. Dix, *The Treatise on the Apostolic Tradition of St. Hippolytus of Rome,* 1937; C. C. Richardson in *Anglican Theological Review,* Vol. XXX (1948), pp. 38–44; P. Nautin, *Une homélie inspirée du traité sur la Pâque d'Hippolyte,* 1950; *Hippolyte et Josipe,* 1947; *Hippolyte Contre les hérésies,* 1949; B. Capelle in *Rech. de théol. anc. et méd.,* Vol. XVII (1950), pp. 145–174; M. Richard in *Mélanges de science religieuse,* Vol. VII (1950), pp. 237–268; Vol. VIII (1951), pp. 19–50.

[Sup.] ROBERT M. GRANT.

HIRSCH, EMANUEL: Lutheran; b. at Bentwisch, Brandenburg, June 14, 1888. He studied at the University of Berlin (B.D., 1911); was assistant at Goettingen (1912–14; Lic.Theol., 1913); dozent at Bonn a.Rh. (1914–21; D.Theol., 1921); professor at Goettingen (1921–45). His literary work may be divided into four sections. The *first* section comprises his studies of the history of modern philosophy and theology: *Fichte's Religionsphilosophie* (1914); *Luthers Gottesanschauung* (1918); *Die Theologie des Andreas Osiander* (1919); *Christentum und Geschichte in Fichte's Philosophie* (1920); *Die idealistische Philosophie und das Christentum* (1926); *Kierkegaard-Studien* (2 vols., 1930–33); *Geschichte der neuern evangelischen Theologie im Zusammenhang mit den allgemeinen Bewegungen des europaeischen Denkens* (5 vols., 1949 ff.). The *second* section concerns biblical research: *Jesus Christus der Herr* (1926); *Das vierte Evangelium verdeutscht und erklaert* (1936); *Studien zum vierten Evangelium* (1936); *Die Auferstehungsgeschichten und der christliche Glaube* (1940); *Fruehgeschichte des Evangeliums* (2 vols., 1941). The *third* section concerns the problems of present Christian doctrine: *Deutschlands Schicksal,* outlines of an ethical view of history (1920); *Der Sinn des Gebets* (1921, 1928); *Staat und Kirche im 19. und 20. Jahrhundert* (1929); *Schoepfung und Suende* (1931); *Die gegenwaertige geistige Lage* (1934); *Das Alte Testament und die Predigt des Evangeliums* (1936); *Zweifel und Glaube* (1937); *Der Weg der Theologie* (1937); *Leitfaden zur christlichen Lehre* (1938); *Das Wesen des Christentums* (1939). The *fourth* section embraces practical books: *Luthers deutsche Bibel* (1928); *Der Wille des Herrn* (Sermons, 1925); *Das Evangelium* (Sermons, 1929); *Hilfsbuch zum Studium der Dogmatik* (1937); *Die Umformung des christlichen Denkens* (1938). He was editor of *Theologische Literaturzeitung* (1921–30).

HIRSCH, EMIL GUSTAV: D. Jan. 7, 1923. A leader in radical liberal and Jewish religious movements he served as rabbi of the Sinai Congregation in Chicago (1880–1923) and as professor of rabbinical literature and philosophy in the University of Chicago (1892–1923). In addition to his other editorial duties he translated and edited Einhorn's *Ritual for Jewish Reform Congregations.*

[Sup.] RAYMOND W. ALBRIGHT.

HISTORICAL ASSOCIATIONS: Closely allied with the American Historical Association are three groups interested in religious history:

1. The American Society of Church History was founded by Philip Schaff (*q.v.,* Vol. X) in 1888 and eight years later merged with the American Historical Association. In 1906 the body was activated once more as an independent group and was incorporated in the State of New York in 1916. Beginning in 1888 this society began to publish volumes of *papers* which ran through two series until 1932, when the quarterly, *Church History,* made its first appearance. The membership is approximately 600.

2. The American Catholic Historical Association was organized in Cleveland, Ohio, on Dec. 30, 1919. It publishes *The Catholic Historical Review,* official quarterly magazine published at the Catholic University of America, Washington, D. C., where the business office of the society is also located.

3. The American Society for Reformation Research, organized in 1946, was designed as a medium for mutual exchange among scholars interested in the Reformation and also to facilitate the revival and continued publication of *Archiv fuer Reformationsgeschichte,* originally published by the Verein fuer Reformationsgeschichte in Germany. The first issues since the formation of this society appeared as Volume 42 in 1951 under the sponsorship of the German and the American societies.

Most of the major denominations in North America also sponsor their own historical societies. Among these are the Presbyterian (Philadelphia, Pa.), Moravian (Bethlehem, Pa.), Schwenkfelder (East Greenville, Pa.), Protestant Episcopal (Philadelphia, Pa.), Methodist (New York City), Friends (Swarthmore, Pa.), Evangelical United Brethren (Naperville, Ill. and Dayton, Ohio), Lutheran (Gettysburg, Pa.), Concordia [Missouri Lutheran] (St. Louis, Mo.), Mennonite (Goshen, Ind.), Evangelical and Reformed (Lancaster, Pa.), Congregational (Boston, Mass.), Baptist (Chester, Pa.), Disciples of Christ (Nashville, Tenn.).

See also ARCHIVES, ECCLESIASTICAL.

RAYMOND W. ALBRIGHT.

Outside of North America, national and regional historical societies sometimes pay considerable attention to ecclesiastical history, but in addition to these there are societies devoted exclusively to church history. The most important are the following.

Argentina: *Junta de la Historia Eclesiástica Argentina* (Society of Argentine Church History), founded 1938, publishes *Revista Archivum.*

Austria: *Gesellschaft fuer die Geschichte des Protestantismus,* founded 1879, publishes *Jahrbuch.*

Belgium: *Société des Bollandistes,* founded 1630 (see BOLLANDISTS). The Catholic University of Louvain also publishes, since 1900, the *Revue d'Histoire Ecclésiastique.*

Finland: *Suomen Kirkkohistoriallinen Seura* (Finnish Society of Ecclesiastical History), founded 1891, publishes *Vuosikirja Årsbok.*

France: *La Société de l'Histoire du Protes-*

tantisme Français, founded 1852, publishes *Bulletin Historique et Litteraire du Protestantisme Français;* also the Roman Catholic *Société de l'Histoire Ecclésiastique de la France* publishes the *Revue de l'Histoire de l'Eglise de France.*

Germany: *Kirchengeschichtliche Gesellschaft* publishes the *Zeitschrift fuer Kirchengeschichte;* the *Verein fuer Reformationsgeschichte,* founded 1883, publishes *Schriften des Vereins* and the *Archiv fuer Reformationsgeschichte.*

Great Britain: The Scottish Church History Society, founded 1926, publishes *Records;* the Historical Society of the Church in Wales was founded 1946; and in England are the Wesleyan Historical Society (1893), the Friends Historical Society (1903), and the Presbyterian Historical Society (1913).

Sweden: *Kyrkohistoriska Föreningen* (Society for Church History), founded 1899, publishes *Kyrkohistorisk Årsskrift.*

Switzerland: *Zwingli-Verein* publishes *Zwingliana; Arbeitsgemeinschaft katholischer Historiker der Schweiz* publishes the *Zeitschrift fuer schweizerische Kirchengeschichte.*

THEODORE G. TAPPERT.

HISTORICITY OF JESUS. See JESUS CHRIST; MYTHOLOGY IN THE NEW TESTAMENT.

HISTORY, THE CHRISTIAN INTERPRETATION OF: The "interpretation" of history, when it is fully recognized as a legitimate and necessary aspect of the historian's task, calls for a philosophy of history, and this, in turn, calls for a more ultimate philosophical point of view. But historians, either through oversight or through such positive pressures upon them as the "scientific" ideal, with its anti-philosophical and anti-religious implications, have not always been willing to acknowledge this fact or to face it resolutely. But, since interpretation is inescapable, if only to guide the selection of the facts deemed significant, a failure or refusal to acknowledge and deal explicitly with its philosophical implications really means that a philosophy functions surreptitiously and that it is likely to be only by a happy accident adequate and relevant to the facts of history. Even when some sort of philosophy is acknowledged, it is likely to be brought to the facts from some alien source and to disturb, rather than to assist, the historian's labors. Instances may be Harnack's attempt to determine the historical facts of the teaching of Jesus by appeal to the sense of permanent validity entertained by nineteenth century Europeans (cf. *What is Christianity?* p. 15); and perhaps the common employment of the concept of the "superhistorical" as understood in the light of the Barthian philosophical conception of "the absolute qualitative difference between time and eternity."

Among those who now more or less frankly acknowledge that a philosophy is involved in the necessary interpretative aspect of the historian's task, perhaps the most widely employed is some kind of evolutionary naturalism. Such a philosophy is taken for granted or defended by the anthropologists; it is passionately asserted by the Marxians; it appears to be basic to the work even of such religiously-minded interpreters of history and of modern society as Toynbee and Sorokin.

It is, however, coming to be recognized more and more widely and openly both that the Hebrew-Christian tradition is ineradically historical and that the distinctive characteristic of it is a religious reference. For Christianity, all history represents an unfolding purpose of God. in judgment and redemption. This purpose, in general and in some details, has been authoritatively revealed by God himself, chiefly if not exclusively, through certain "mighty acts" of his in the history of "the chosen people," as reported and interpreted by certain divinely prepared witnesses, culminating in God's own entering into history in the Person of his Son. But, though his purpose was thus revealed exclusively, it is a universal purpose; and, though interpretations of history, or of some part of it, based on some other philosophy or point of view, may have a relative validity and usefulness, history can be finally understood only as seen in the light of this divinely revealed divine purpose.

See also HISTORY, THE INTERPRETATION OF.

ANDREW K. RULE.

HISTORY, THE INTERPRETATION OF: I. Fact and Interpretation: History, as a discipline, would seem to represent a highly unstable equilibrium between hard fact and facile interpretation. Histories of historiography display a bewildering variety of viewpoints as to what the facts mean: this variance of interpretation is revealed most markedly not in the lesser, but in the greatest, historians of the past. The serious student of history, when he is first confronted by this irremediable situation, is likely to be considerably shaken, and indeed seriously alarmed at the fog of uncertainty which threatens to becloud his labors.

Such doubts are new. Up to the mid-point of the last century historians, we may say, took the facts as they found them. But that interpretation was primary in importance was something so obvious that it required no special statement of intent, much less explanation.

II. The Concept of the Scientific Fact: Suddenly the nineteenth century invested facts with a character they had never hitherto possessed. Three centuries of advance in the natural sciences—an advance as uninterrupted as it was astounding—had spawned at length the concept of the *scientific* fact: a fact that was something more than the "event" of history or the "datum" of philosophy, for now it was clothed with a certainty and a precision rooted in the laws of nature. It was incumbent on the other disciplines to follow the lead of the natural scientists.

If historians, therefore, adopted the "scientific method," this should occasion no surprise. Inevitably they sought to refashion history as a science. Their facts henceforth must be as reliable as those of the natural scientists, for the latter based the most prodigious conclusions upon myriads of immutable facts. So, for the first time, historians sought for facts almost as ends in themselves. Their major task was cast into a slogan by Leopold von Ranke: to find out "how it actually happened." This was the historian's way of saying, "Get the facts!"

III. The Historiography of Fact-Finding, 1850–1950: The resources of human beings, in the mass as in individuals, are not inexhaustible. For over two millennia historians, with rare exceptions, had taken their facts as they found them. Their nineteenth century successors felt obliged, within a single generation, to subject the accumulated data of the past to searching and scientific scrutiny. A task so enormous obsorbed, in the main, the entire energy and ingenuity of historians. Interpretation seemed to fade into the background, or to be confined to limited areas, or segments of time. And the labor of sifting the facts of the past had to be bequeathed to a second, a third, and even a fourth generation of chroniclers.

How soon would the underpinnings of historic fact be adjudged so scientifically firm that the *laws* of history could be promulgated? The decision was postponed, decade by decade. The American, Edward Cheyney, caused a sensation when in 1923 he presented certain "laws of history" before the American Historical Association; judging from the adverse reception, the attempt was premature. As the year 1950 approached, however, the Englishman Arnold Toynbee was evoking not merely controversy, but also widespread applause; and there was even some acceptance of his views as to the laws and patterns that operate in history.

We stand at the end of an epoch of historical fact-finding. The reign of scientific fact is over. It was a necessary reign. It taught scholars in every field what things may be measured with a precise exactitude. It was a reign of honest men, for it is the natural scientists themselves who have now confessed that certain data cannot be measured at all, including many that lie within their own special realm. Within that realm, few will still cavil at the relativity theory of Einstein, or even at Heisenberg's law of *uncertainty*. The physicist Eddington calmly surveys the logical wreckage of his discipline: at

the heart of the atom "something unknown is doing we don't know what." That historians have subjected themselves for a century to the rigors of scientific analysis has been a necessary and salutary experience. If that fact-finding age be over, as historians we may perhaps fix its chronological limits at *ca.* 1850–1950.

Such fact-finding periods had occurred before in the history of Western European society. In the century which extended from *ca.* 1150–1250, most of Europe's best minds were occupied with the task of translating into Latin many works of the Greek writers of antiquity. Again, in the hundred years from *ca.* 1350–1450 the greatest scholars of Western Europe spent lavishly of their time and effort simply in order to unearth the physical remains of still other ancient books. Without the labors of the medieval translators, Thomas Aquinas could not have replied to the trenchant questions raised by Peter Abelard. The treasure hunt of the humanists was indispensable to the Renaissance. When a whole age must go to school, there is little surplus energy for *independent* interpretation. The men of the High Middle Age and the Renaissance took their interpretations, as they took their facts, from the ancients. Historians of the last century were unusual only in that they went to school to their contemporaries—the natural scientists.

Students of history have never willingly abandoned interpretation. Even the Hebrew and Greek writers faced mountains of antecedent data, meaningless unless judged by the mind, and sifted and arranged by the art, of the chronicler. The stupendous character of scientific fact, to be sure, gave pause to several generations of historians. They were warned by the scientific method to "suspend judgment," and they resolved to "let the facts speak for themselves." *But such a dedication to the facts was itself an interpretation of history.*

IV. Historical Objectivity: Thus was produced, during the past hundred years, the objectivist school of historians. Its practitioners have preferred to be known by the subschools into which they have arranged themselves. But "objectivity" and "suspended judgment" have characterized them all. The majority, however, deceived themselves. The historians of institutions may have hewed close to the line of scientific fact; but even the sober nationalist followed the mad pipings of romanticism. Some flirted with, or espoused, the economic determinism of Karl Marx, convinced by his plea that *his* analysis was truly scientific. It is now becoming clear that Marx's "science" was at least a faith, and mayhap a frantic religion.

The objectivist school of history was not objective in the total sense because it could not be. The natural scientist, in his cloistered laboratory, could well afford to let a fact—just one

—speak for itself. The result might well be a machine, a cure, or a gadget. For the historian there are no such facts.

The long apprenticeship of historians to natural scientists threatened to produce an unnatural dichotomy between fact and interpretation. This peril should no longer exist. Many of the most sacred scientific "facts" of the nineteenth century have been disavowed by the natural scientists of the twentieth. Above all, it is now clear that many of the facts (or events) of history are not susceptible of determination by the precision methods of the laboratory. Nor should the historian's conclusions be always subjected to the contracting yardstick of that scientific method.

See also HISTORY, THE CHRISTIAN INTERPRETATION OF.

BIBLIOGRAPHY: Karl G. Lamprecht, *What is History? Five lectures on the Modern Science of History*, tr. by E. A. Andrews of *Moderne Geschichtswissenschaft*, 1905; James H. Robinson, *New History, Essays Illustrating the Modern Historical Outlook*, 1913; Frederick J. Teggart, *Theory of History*, 1925; Edward P. Cheyney, *Law in History and Other Essays*, 1927; Karl Marx, *Contribution to the Critique of Political Economy*, tr. by N. I. Stone of *Zur Kritik der politischen Oekonomie*, 1911; George M. Trevelyan, *Clio, a Muse and Other Essays, Literary and Pedestrian*, 1913; Shailer Mathews, *Spiritual Interpretation of History*, 1916; Robert McLaughlin, *Spiritual Element in History*, 1926. Benedetto Croce, *History: its Theory and Practice*, tr. by D. Ainslie from Vol. IV *Teoria e storia della storiografia*, of *Filosofia dello spirito*, 1921; E. Bernheim, *Lehrbuch der historischen Methode und der Geschichtsphilosophie*, 1908; Leopold von Ranke, *Zur Kritik neuerer Geschichtschreiber*, 1824; Charles V. Langlois and Charles Seignobos, *Introduction to the Study of History*, tr. by G. B. Berry from *Introduction aux études historiques*, 1912; Allen Johnson, *The Historian and Historical Evidence*, 1926; Alfred North Whitehead, *Science and the Modern World*, 1926; B. Adams, *The Law of Civilization and Decay; an Essay on History*, 1943; Carl Becker, *Everyman his Own Historian*, 1932; M. Mandelbaum, *The Problem of Historical Knowledge; an Answer to Relativism*, 1938; James C. Malin, *Essays on Historiography*, 1948.

SHERWOOD WARWICK.

HITTITES: Hugo Winckler's discovery of cuneiform archives at Boghazköy (1906–7, 1911–12) and Professor Hrozny's decipherment of the Hittite language (1915) made the original sources available and thus led to an entirely new understanding.

I. Language and Writing: Most of the cuneiform documents from Boghazköy are written in a language commonly called Hittite. Its ancient name was "Nesian" (*nesili*, from a city-name Nesa). Hittite morphology is clear now; of the vocabulary, enough is known to render most texts intelligible, although the meaning of many words remains to be established. The language may be called Indo-European on the ground of general structure, morphology, and a considerable stock of Indo-European words of basic meaning. Certain peculiarities led Sturtevant to consider Hittite as part of a special "Anatolian" group, only related to Indo-European.

Cuneiform Hittite is, however, not the only language used in the Hittite Empire. Cunei-

form writing requires some knowledge of Sumerian and Akkadian. Literary texts in these languages were copied by the Hittite scribes, and Akkadian was used for diplomatic correspondence and treaties. In religious texts, gods of different ethnic groups are sometimes addressed in their own idiom. Of such languages, Luwian (*luili*) and Palaic (*palaumnili*) are Indo-European or "Anatolian" like Hittite. The countries Hatti (with its capital Hattusa, now Boghazköy), Pala (to the north) and Luia (south and southwest) apparently were the three areas first settled by Indo-European-speaking immigrants. In Hatti, however, these immigrants found an older population who spoke *hattili*, "in the language of Hatti." This language, named "Hattic" or "Proto-Hattic" in distinction from "Hittite," is not related to any known language. The addition of Hittite translations to some Hattic texts shows that it was no longer generally understood when the texts were written down. The use of Hurrian (*q.v.*) (*hurlili*), a language spoken in North Mesopotamia and North Syria, in Boghazköy texts is due to the adoption of Hurrian gods into the state cult. Hurrian, too, does not belong to any known linguistic group.

Besides cuneiform, the Hittites also had a hieroglyphic system of writing, the decipherment of which has recently made considerable progress and is now being further advanced by the discovery of a bilingual in Hittite hieroglyphs and Phoenician at Karatepe in Cilicia. The oldest hieroglyphic inscriptions date from the New Empire (1400–1200 B.C.); single signs used as mere symbols even occur around 1900 B.C. When the knowledge of cuneiform became lost at the downfall of the Empire (*ca.* 1200 B.C.), the hieroglyphs survived in the Late Hittite states down to *ca.* 700 B.C. The language is Indo-European or "Anatolian" in the above sense. It is different from cuneiform Hittite and Palaic, more closely related to Luwin but—at least in the late inscriptions—not identical with it. Unfortunately, the imperial hieroglyphic inscriptions are hardly intelligible. Whether they represent a dialect of Luwian—the term *luili* seems to cover various dialects—or a different language is not yet clear. In any case, cuneiform script and hieroglyphic writing were used side by side during the Empire, both for official purposes, apparently by different scribal schools.

II. History: Proper names of Hittite type first occur in documents of Assyrian merchant colonies of the nineteenth century B.C. An inscription of king Anitta who reigned in Kussar and Nesa at that time is preserved in a later copy. Hittite tradition, however, begins with Labarna, whose second successor, Mursili I, raided Babylon, thus putting an end to the Hammurabi (*q.v.*) dynasty. So Labarna, the founder of the Old Kingdom, is dated to the seventeenth century B.C. Among Mursili's successors, Telipinu is known for his regulation of the succession to the throne. The Hittite laws may, on inner evidence, be attributed to the same period.

The New Kingdom or Empire was created by Suppiluliuma (ca. 1380–50 B.C.), who overthrew the Mitanni Empire and extended Hittite rule into Armenia and Syria. Under him, Hatti became one of the great powers of the Amarna (q.v.) age. The widow of Tutankhamen even wanted to marry one of his sons, but the plan failed. Suppiluliuma's son Mursili II had to regain his father's empire. He was the first to write detailed annals. His son Muwatalli fought at Qadesh against Ramses II in the latter's sixth year. Muwatalli's brother Hattusili III concluded the famous treaty in Ramses' twenty-first year and later gave his daughter to the same Pharaoh. His son Tutkhaliya IV reorganized the cult. Toward 1200 B.C. the sources become silent; at Boghazköy and elsewhere the Hittite buildings were destroyed by fire. This catastrophe is attributed to the invasion of the "Peoples of the Sea" mentioned in Egyptian records. The Empire was a feudal state in which vassals were bound to the Great King by treaties.

After a dark age, we find the Phrygians in central Asia Minor. In the southeast new states emerge, such as Tabal (around Kayseri), Milit (Malatya), Gurgum (Marash), Carchemish on the Euphrates, Hattina and Hamath on the Orontes. The Assyrians (q.v.), who fought many wars in this region, called it Hatti, and Hittite hieroglyphic writing was in use there. After 950 B.C., Aramaeans (q.v.) infiltrated the Late Hittite states of Syria, Sam'al (Zenjirli) being the best-known example of Aramaean domination. Around 715 B.C. Sargon II completed the incorporation of these states into the Assyrian Empire, thus ending a millennium of Hittite history.

III. Religion: The polytheism of the Hittite Empire preserved the multitude of local cults. A certain amount of systematization was achieved by writing the names of deities of similar character with the same Sumero-Akkadian word-sign, such as "Weather-god" for the most common type of local gods, or Ishtar for a number of goddesses, by the conception of divine families and of the supremacy of the central deities: divine couples were worshiped in many towns, but the Weather-god of Hatti and his consort, the Sun-goddess of Arinna, were king and queen of the gods, and some deities were considered their children or grandchildren. It seems that the Indo-Europeans added little to the pantheon but rather adopted the gods of the earlier population. Hurrian gods entered the state cult after the conquest of the southeastern provinces. An attempt toward syncret-

ism can be seen in the occasional equation of the Hittite main couple with the Hurrian Teshub and Hebat, but generally the Hurrian gods kept their own personality. Among the "Thousand Gods"—as the texts call them—we can only mention a few types: sun- and moongods, warrior-gods, other individual gods and goddesses, and minor deities such as mountains, rivers and springs, winds and clouds.

All gods had their festivals. The king himself celebrated the great festivals, elaborate rituals for which are preserved. He was not a god during his lifetime; only when he died he "became god." The will of the gods was investigated by oracles, of which detailed records were kept. The only prayers preserved are royal prayers; among them, the "Plague Prayers" of Mursili II are outstanding for their deep conception of sin and confession.

Myths concerning Anatolian gods are contained in magic texts. The only mythological texts of a strictly literary form are Hittite versions of Hurrian epics. By their striking similarity to Hesiod's Theogony they are important for the history of mythology and literature, but they have little to do with Hittite religion proper.

BIBLIOGRAPHY: F. Hrozný, Die Sprache der Hethiter, 1917; A. Goetze, Das Hethiterreich, 1928; idem, Kleinasien, 1933; idem, Die Annalen des Mursilis, 1933; idem, (with E. H. Sturtevant), The Hittite Ritual of Tunnawi, 1938; "Hittite Texts" in Ancient Near Eastern Texts Relating to the Old Testament (J. B. Pritchard, ed.), 1950; I. J. Gelb, Hittite Hieroglyphs, Vols. I-III, 1931–42; H. Th. Bossert, Altanatolien, 1932; E. H. Sturtevant, A Comparative Grammar of the Hittite Language, 1933, rev. ed., Vol. I, 1951; idem, A Hittite Glossary, 2nd ed., 1936, Supplement, 1939; idem (with G. Bechtel), A Hittite Chrestomathy, 1935; E. A. Speiser, Introduction to Hurrian, 1941; B. Landsberger, Sam'al, 1948; K. Bittel, Grundzuege der Vor- und Fruehgeschichte Kleinasiens, 2nd ed., 1950; H. G. Gueterbock, "Hittite Religion" in Forgotten Religions (V. Ferm, ed.), 1949; O. R. Gurney, The Hittites, 1952; J. Friedrich, Hethitisches Woerterbuch, 1952.

[Sup.] HANS GUSTAV GUETERBOCK.

HIYANE, ANTEI: Methodist (Church of Christ in Japan); b. in Tokyo, Oct. 3, 1892. He was graduated from the Aoyama Gakuin Seminary in 1917. He is professor of comparative religion and history of Christianity in Japan in Union Theological Seminary and Aoyama Gakuin. Among his more than twenty publications are: tr. into Japanese of William James, Varieties of Religious Experience (1922); History of the Religions of the World (1926); History of Christianity in Japan (5 vols., 1938–40); and History of Religions in Japan (5 vols., 1941–43).   RAYMOND W. ALBRIGHT.

HOCEDEZ, EDGAR: Catholic Priest, Jesuit; b. at Genth, Belgium, July 1, 1877; d. at Faytlez-Manage, Sept. 5, 1948. He studied at the Philosophical and Theological College of the Society of Jesus, at Louvain; he taught theology at Kurseong, India (1908–12); at Louvain (1912–14); at Hastings (1914–19); at Louvain (1919–28); at the Gregorian University,

Rome (1928–40). He was editor of the *Nouvelle Revue Théologique* from 1920 to 1926. He is most widely known by his studies in the history of philosophy and theology in the Middle Ages, published mainly in *Gregorianum*. He wrote: *Richard de Middleton* (1925); *Aegidii Romani Theoremata de esse et essentia* (1925); *Histoire de la théologie au XIXe siècle* (3 vols., 1947, 1949, 1952).

BIBLIOGRAPHY: J. Levie, "Le P. Edgar Hocedez, S.I. In memoriam," in *Nouvelle Revue Théologique*, Vol. LXX (1948), pp. 786–793.

HOCKING, WILLIAM ERNEST: B. Cleveland, Ohio, Aug. 10, 1873. He was educated in physical sciences at Ames, Iowa; in philosophy at Harvard (Ph.D., 1904) and Germany. He taught in California, Yale, and Harvard (1914–43); lectured in England, Scotland, Holland, Germany, Syria, India, China, and other places. He visited the Near East in 1938, to study the working of the mandates; the Far East in 1931–32, to study the working of certain Protestant Missions. The result of the former journey is embodied in *Spirit of World Politics* (1932); of the second in *Re-thinking Missions* (1932). His major works bearing directly on religion are *The Meaning of God in Human Experience* (1912); *Human Nature and its Remaking* (1918); and *Living Religions and a World Faith* (1940). The first of these contained two theses which have influenced religious and metaphysical thinking, especially in France and Germany: that in experience the "I" and the "Thou" are inseparable—a fundamental revision of Descartes; and that God is to be experienced not alone in the universal, but also in the particular, in sensation. Both of these concepts have played a part in the existentialist movements. Hocking has written eighteen books and some two hundred articles.

HODGES, GEORGE: D. May 27, 1919. He was the dean of the Episcopal Theological School, Cambridge, Mass. (1894–1919). He also gave time to community interests and served as president of The South End House Association. His later publications include: *A Child's Guide to the Bible* (1911); *Saints and Heroes* (1911); *Class Book of Old Testament History* (1914); *The Early Church* (1914); *Henry Codman Potter, Seventh Bishop of New York* (1915); and *Religion in a World at War* (1917).

[Sup.] RAYMOND W. ALBRIGHT.

HODGSON, LEONARD: Church of England; b. London, England, Oct. 24, 1889. He studied at St. Paul's School and Hertford College, Oxford; and St. Michael's College, Llandaff. He was curate, St. Mark's Church, Portsmouth (1913–14); vice-principal, St. Edmund Hall, Oxford (1914–19); official fellow and dean of divinity, Magdalen College, Oxford (1919–25);

professor of Christian apologetics, General Theological Seminary, New York City (1925–31); residentiary canon, Winchester Cathedral (1931–38); canon of Christ Church, Oxford (1938–); regius professor of moral and pastoral theology, Oxford (1938–44); regius professor of divinity and Honorary Fellow of St. Edmund Hall, Oxford (1944–). His publications include: *The Place of Reason in Christian Apologetic* (1925); *And Was Made Man* (1928); *Eugenics* (1933); *The Lord's Prayer* (1934); *Democracy and Dictatorship in the Light of Christian Faith* (1935); *The Grace of God in Faith and Philosophy* (1936); *This War and the Christian* (1939); *The Christian Idea of Liberty* (1941); *Towards a Christian Philosophy* (1942); *The Doctrine of the Trinity* (1943); *Theology in an Age of Science* (1944); *Biblical Theology and the Sovereignty of God* (1946); *Christian Faith and Practice* (1950); *The Doctrine of the Atonement* (1951); *The Ecumenical Movement* (1951); he was joint editor with G. R. Driver of Nestorius: *The Bazaar of Heracleides* (1925).

HOEFFDING, HARALD: D. 1931. A Danish philosopher who under the influence of Kierkegaard showed interest in ethical and religious values and with his "conservation of values" concept influenced the later Chicago idea of religion (see CHICAGO SCHOOL OF THEOLOGY). His later and major works were translated as follows: *History of Modern Philosophy* (1900); *Problems of Philosophy* (1905); and *Philosophy of Religion* (1906).

BIBLIOGRAPHY: J. de la Herpe, *Le religion comme conservation de la valeur dans ses rapports avec philosophie general de Harald Hoeffding*, 1920.

[Sup.] RAYMOND W. ALBRIGHT.

HOEN, CORNELIUS. See HONIUS, CORNELIUS.

HOEY AWARD: Two medals presented annually by the Catholic Interracial Council to two members of the Roman Catholic laity, white and Negro, who have done the most significant work throughout the year to promote the spirit of justice between the races. The award is dedicated to the memory of James M. Hoey, one of the Council founders. The 1950 medals went to J. Howard McGrath, U. S. attorney general, and Lou Montgomery, president of the Catholic Interracial Council, of Hartford, Conn.   THOMAS J. McCARTHY.

HOFFMANN, CONRAD: Presbyterian; b. Chicago, Ill., Sept. 16, 1884. He studied at the universities of Wisconsin, Halle, and Goettingen (1909–10). He served as a student Y.M.C.A. secretary at the University of Kansas (1913–15); senior secretary for prisoner of war work in Germany (1915–19); director of European student relief under the World Student Christian

Federation (1921–27); director of the Committee on the Christian Approach to the Jews of the International Missionary Council (1930–36). In 1936 he became Secretary of the Christian Approach to the Jews, Board of National Missions, Presbyterian Church, U. S. A. He became Director again of the I.M.C.'s Committee on the Christian Approach to the Jews (1945–51). He wrote: *In the Prison Camps of Germany* (1920); *The Rebuilding of Europe; The Jews Today, A Call to Christian Action* (1941); and *What Now for the Jews* (1948).

HOFFMANN, MELCHIOR: After his preaching in Strassburg and East Friesland he arrived in the Netherlands about the year 1530. There he obtained a tremendous following, with the spectacular result that until 1566 the Anabaptists (*q.v.*) in that country outnumbered all the other Protestants put together. Furthermore, the English Baptists owe their origin largely to the labors of Hoffmann and his satellites. He issued a new translation of the Apocalypse, in the notes of which he declared that Luther (*q.v.*) was the modern Judas, while Hoffmann turned out to be the apostle of the last days. He was the Elias who in 1533 was to introduce the Last Judgment. The elect must unite; their sign of election was their adult baptism. Strassburg would be the final Zion, the center of the world empire announced in the last chapter of the Apocalypse. In his writings appeared revolutionary ideas which were developed further and disseminated by Jan Matthijsz, the new Enoch, and the tailor Jan Breukelsz of Leiden. Through their efforts the peaceful Melchiorites became the revolutionary fanatics in the Kingdom of Jerusalem, that is, Muenster in Westphalia. The two last-named Anabaptists went to Muenster and soon had the city in their power. Thirty ships with some 3,000 Anabaptists came from Amsterdam alone, but they were detained at Genemuiden; the leaders were killed (March 24, 1534) and the rest sent back to their homes. On Feb. 10, 1535, five fanatics ran through the streets of Amsterdam, stark naked, shouting, "Woe, woe! Do penance and go to Muenster, which has been given to the children of God." Jan Breukelsz became King of Zion, and there he introduced communism and polygamy. These disorders enabled Cardinal Gropper and other Roman Catholic leaders to restore Catholicism in the whole of Westphalia.

BIBLIOGRAPHY: L. Knappert, *Het ontstaan en de vestiging van het Protestantisme in de Nederlanden* (1924), pp. 180–236, with extensive bibliography; K. Loeffler, *Die Wiedertaeufer zu Muenster 1534–35: Berichte, Aussagen und Aktenstuecke von Augenzeugen und Zeitgenossen*, 1923; F. H. Littell, *The Anabaptist View of the Church: An Introduction to Sectarian Protestantism*, 1952; S. H. Smith, *The Story of the Mennonites*, 1950.

[Sup.] ALBERT HYMA.

HOGAN'S SCHISM. See TRUSTEEISM.

HOH, PAUL J(ACOB): Lutheran; b. at Reading, Pa., Sept. 20, 1893; d. at Philadelphia, Jan. 20, 1952. He studied at the University of Pennsylvania (A.B., 1914) and at the Lutheran Theological Seminary at Philadelphia (B.D., 1924; S.T.M., 1930); was pastor at St. Mark's Church, Bethlehem, Pa. (1918–20); Holy Trinity Church, Wildwood, N. J. (1920–21); Ascension Church, Philadelphia, Pa. (1921–30); was editor of the Parish and Church School Board of the United Lutheran Church in America (1930–37); professor of practical theology at Lutheran Seminary at Philadelphia (1937–52), and president of same (1945–52). He has written: *Little Children Come unto Me* (1927); *The Gospel according to St. Luke, A Study* (1936); *Studies in First Corinthians* (1937); and *Parish Practice* (1944).

HOLINESS CHURCHES: There are probably 200 or more religious bodies in the United States that lay heavy emphasis on perfectionism. Many, perhaps most, of these arose from Methodist sources and broke from the main stem because it was felt that the large bodies were departing, as indeed they were, from John Wesley's (*q.v.*, Vol. XII) doctrine of Christian perfection or perfect love as set forth in his *A Plain Account of Christian Perfection* and *Brief Thoughts on Christian Perfection*.

There are, of course, shades or degrees of perfectionism which are held by nearly all churches, but those that take the doctrine seriously enough to be classed as Holiness bodies stress the following points: (1) Holiness or sanctification is a work of grace which purges the heart of inbred or original sin. (2) It is a distinct experience separate from and subsequent to justification or forgiveness, hence the term "second blessing." (3) It is an instantaneous blessing, though there may be growth previous and subsequent thereto.

Within the total Holiness camp there are two schools, or what may be called right wing or moderate and left wing or radical branches, though at the border line it is not always possible to separate them into definite categories. The moderates stress "second blessing" sanctification as the crown of Christian experience. The radicals add certain superior outpourings of the Spirit, usually the gift of tongues (*q.v.*); sometimes the *charismata* take extreme forms and devotees handle venomous reptiles, see visions, receive divine revelations, or enjoy other forms of Spirit baptism. These are the so-called Pentecostal Churches (*q.v.*) and are excluded from the present discussion. See also CHURCHES OF GOD; HOLY ROLLERS.

In modern times the Holiness movement has been stimulated by two revivals. The first was the Wesleyan Revival in Great Britain. John Wesley explicitly taught the "second blessing" doctrine, although with some contradictions and obscurities; though neither he nor any of his prominent fellow-workers ever claimed the experience for themselves, Methodist preachers to this day are exhorted to "go on to perfection." Later departure from holiness as a vital principle caused fifty or more defections from Methodism, directly or indirectly, and nearly all the departing groups espoused sanctification. Typical of these is the Free Methodist Church.

The second was the National Holiness Movement which swept the U.S.A. after the latter half of the nineteenth century. This was part of the protest against the decline of vital holiness in Methodism, and most of its adherents and members of the numerous independent bodies which arose from it came out of Methodist churches. The largest denomination emerging from this movement is the Church of the Nazarene (q.v.), formerly the Pentecostal Church of the Nazarene.

It would hardly be possible to compile a complete and accurate list of Holiness churches. The tenet is only one of many held by the various bodies, and the vitality of the principle tends to fade with the second or third generation and as the churches grow in size, wealth, and administrative complexity. Most of the small Methodist sects began as holiness groups, but in some of them the doctrine is no longer vital. Some churches magnify the sanctification experience, or something very like it, without definitely espousing the "second blessing" doctrine; this is true of many small Negro sects. The following may be regarded as typical Holiness churches of the moderate type. Statistics in all cases are approximate only. Numerous other groups have Holiness traditions or leanings.

Body	Churches	Members
Church of the Nazarene (q.v.)..	3,315	210,000
Free Methodist Church	1,200	50,000
Wesleyan Methodist Church...	900	34,000
Primitive Methodist Church..	88	12,000
Holiness Methodist Church....	8	800
Reformed Methodist Church..	13	300
Apostolic Christian Church of America	55	7,000
Apostolic Christian Church (Nazarean) (q.v.)	30	1,700
Church of Daniel's Band (q.v.)	3	130
Church of God (Apostolic)...	45	3,000
Church of God (Anderson, Ind.)	1,665	93,000
Apostolic Methodist Church...	2	40
Mennonite Brethren in Christ	38	4,000
Pilgrim Holiness Church		
Missionary Bands of the World	6	200
Metropolitan Church Association (q.v.)	21	1,300
Hephzibah Faith Missionary Association	20	700

(see Vol. VII, p. 392)

Body	Churches	Members
Christian Congregation (q.v.)	38	4,300
Pillar of Fire (q.v.)	60	5,000
Peniel Missions		
Church of the Gospel	2	40
Christian Nation Church	5	115
Kodesh Church of Immanuel (q.v.)	9	560
Churches of Christ in Christian Union	113	4,000
Apostolic Faith Mission	17	2,300
Missionary Church Association (q.v.)	60	5,000

BIBLIOGRAPHY: Elmer T. Clark, *The Small Sects in America*, rev. ed., 1949; Alma White, *Looking Back from Beulah*, 1929; J. B. Chapman, *A History of the Church of the Nazarene*, 1926; C. B. Jernigan, *Pioneer Days of the Holiness Movement in the Southwest*, 1928.

ELMER T. CLARK.

HOLINESS CODE. See PENTATEUCH; LAW CODES, ANCIENT.

HOLINESS OF THE CHURCH. See MARKS OF THE CHURCH.

HOLL, KARL: D. 1926. A contemporary of Adolf Harnack (q.v.) at the University of Berlin, he was professor of church history there (1906–26). He taught and wrote most extensively in the early and reformation periods of Christianity. In addition to his earlier works he produced in the former area the critical edition of *Epiphanius* in the Berlin edition of the Greek Fathers (Vol. I, 1915; Vol. II, 1922); and in the latter area his great late achievement is *Gesammelte Aufsaetze zur Kirchengeschichte* (1922–28), of which Vol. I deals with *Luther*, Vol. II, with *Der Osten*, and Vol. III with *Der Westen*. In many ways Holl was responsible for the renewed interest in studies about Luther. [Sup.] RAYMOND W. ALBRIGHT.

HOLLAND: In a population (1950) of 10,-026,773, 45% are Protestant, 38% Roman Catholic, and 17% unchurched. Since the middle of the nineteenth century there has been a steady decrease in the number of Protestants and a corresponding increase in the number of unchurched. All except the Reformed free churches (*Gereformeerde Kerken, Christelijke Gereformeerde Kerken, Gereformeerde Gemeenten*, etc.), which refuse aid, are subsidized by the state.

1. The *Nederlandse Hervormde Kerk* was weakened during the nineteenth century by the separations of 1837 (de Cock) and 1886 (Abraham Kuyper, q.v.) and by a bitter party spirit. Since 1900 the Church has recovered its strength and self-consciousness. There is a general synod made up of ministers and of elders and deacons. Delegates are elected by the fifty-four classes (presbyteries) which are distributed among ten

synods. Local congregations are governed by consistories made up of at least one minister and a number of elders and deacons elected by the adult membership. In 1950 the Church had 1,426 churches, 1,900 ministers. A new constitution was adopted in 1951 according to which all ecclesiastical activities, including missions, are brought under the control of the Church. Religion is no longer taught in public schools, but there is provision for instruction by churches, and many Roman Catholic as well as Protestant private schools have been established. There are about 1,600,000 members in the foreign fields in which the Dutch Reformed Church has missionaries.

2. The *Gereformeerde Kerken,* formed by a merger in 1892, represent the largest body of Reformed free churches. With 792 churches and 1,061 ministers in 1950, they represent 8.5% of the entire population. Clergymen are trained in a seminary in Kampen and in the theological faculty of the Free Reformed University at Amsterdam. They have considerable influence on the public as a result of political activities, education, and publication. The *Christelijke Gereformeerde Kerk* is a small free church that did not participate in the union of 1892; it has a theological school in Apeldoorn.

3. In 1944 a new schism occurred in the *Gereformeerde Kerken* as a result of a controversy over federal theology (see COCCEIUS, JOHANNES, AND HIS SCHOOL, Vol. III). Under the leadership of Professor K. Schilder the *Gereformeerde Kerk Art. 31* (i.e., the Reformed Church Adhering to Article XXXI of the decrees of Dort, *q.v.,* Vol. III) was formed. In 1950 it had 293 churches, 296 ministers. This body is exclusive in its relations with others.

4. Since 1853, when they were freed from disabilities, the Roman Catholics have gained in influence in the Netherlands. Hundreds of churches were built, thousands of schools, monasteries, and charitable institutions. Their influence on public and political life is increasing.

5. Since 1791 two Lutheran Churches existed side by side in the Netherlands: the Evangelical Lutheran Church with fifty congregations, and the Restored Evangelical Lutheran Church with eight congregations. These bodies were reunited in 1952 as a result of an impetus given by the Lutheran World Federation (*q.v.*). World War II caused many German Lutherans to leave the country. In 1952 the total number of Lutherans remaining was 60,000.

6. Jews are concentrated in the cities. About 100,000 of them lost their lives during the Nazi occupation of Holland. Only 28,000 remain, half of whom are members of synagogues in Rotterdam, Amsterdam, The Hague, and Enschede.

BIBLIOGRAPHY: T. Delleman, *Kerken in Nederland,* 2nd ed., 1949; W. F. Golterman, *De kerkelijke situatie,* 1951; J. Reitsma, *Geschiedenis van de Hervorming en de Her-*

vormde Kerk der Nederlanden; L. Knappert, *Geschiedenis van de Ned. Herv. Kerk,* 2 vols, 1911, 1912; J. Loosjes, *Geschiedenis der Luthersche Kerk in de Nederlanden,* 1921; L. J. Rogier, *Geschiedenis van het Katholicisme in Noord Nederland,* 2 vols., 1947; H. Brugmans and A. Frank, *Geschiedenis der Joden in Nederland,* 1940.

[Sup.] WILLEM JAN KOOIMAN

HOLLAND LECTURES: 1. Annual lectures are delivered at Southwestern Baptist Theological Seminary, Fort Worth, Texas, on some doctrinal, denominational, missionary, or practical subject "helpful to the life of the seminary." A gift of the Rev. Lewis Holland, of San Antonio, Texas, led to the founding of the lectureship in 1914. E. D. HEAD.

2. A trust fund was established at Oxford University, England, to commemorate the life and work of Henry Scott Holland. It was provided that courses of lectures be given triennially on "the religion of the incarnation in its bearing on the social and economic life of man." The lectureship was inaugurated in 1922 with R. H. Tawney's *Religion and the Rise of Capitalism.* Other lecturers were C. E. Osborne (1925), William Temple (1928), A. D. Lindsay (1930), Walter Moberly (1933), S. C. Carpenter (1936), L. S. Thornton (1943), M. B. Reckitt (1946), V. A. Demant (1949).

THEODORE G. TAPPERT.

HOLMAN, CHARLES T.: Baptist; b. Cheltenham, England, Feb. 6, 1882. He studied at McMaster University (B.A., 1909; M.A., 1910); University of Chicago (B.D., 1915); Indiana University (1915–18). He was pastor of Baptist churches in Canada (1907–13), and churches in Bloomington, Indiana and Chicago, Ill. (1914–23). He taught pastoral duties, Federated Theological Faculties, University of Chicago (1923–47), and was dean of Baptist Divinity House, University of Chicago (1942–47). He has been pastor of Union Church of Guatemala (1947–52). He has been a pioneer in utilizing insights from psychological and social sciences in pastoral counseling. He is the author of: *The Cure of Souls; The Religion of a Healthy Mind; Getting Down to Cases; Psychology and Religion for Everyday Living.*

HOLMAN LECTURES: A lectureship on the Augsburg Confession was established at the Lutheran Theological Seminary, Gettysburg, Pa., in 1865 by the Rev. S. A. Holman. This provides for the delivery of a lecture every two years on one of the articles of the Confession. The lecturer is nominated by the faculty and elected by the board of directors.

HARRY F. BAUGHMAN.

HOLMES, JOHN HAYNES: Clergyman and author; b. at Philadelphia, Pa., Nov. 29, 1879. He studied at Harvard College (A.B., 1902), and Harvard Divinity School (S.T.B., 1904). He received the annual Gottheil medal for outstanding service of Jews (1933). He was ordained and installed as minister of Third Religious Society (Unitarian), Dorchester, Mass. (March 2, 1904); minister of Church of the Messiah (now Community Church), New York (1907–49; emeritus, 1949–). He has been vice-president of the National Association for the Advancement of Colored People (1909–); and director of the American Civil Liberties Union (1917– ; chairman, 1939–49). He is the author of: *The Revolutionary Function of the Modern Church* (1912); *Marriage and Divorce* (1913); *Is Death the End?* (1915); *New Wars for Old* (1916); *Religion for Today* (1917); *Life and Letters of Robert Collyer* (1917); *Readings from Great Authors* (1918); *The Grail of Life* (1919); *Is Violence the Way Out?* (1920); *New Churches for Old* (1922); *Patriotism Is not Enough* (1925); *Palestine Today and Tomorrow* (1929); *The Heart of Scott's Poetry* (1932); *The Sensible Man's View of Religion* (1933); (with Reginald Lawrence), *If This Be Treason* (a play, produced by the Theatre Guild, 1935); *Through Gentile Eyes* (1938); *Rethinking Religion* (1938); *Out of Darkness* (1942); *The Second Christmas* (1943); and *The Affirmation of Immortality* (Ingersoll Lecture at Harvard) (1947).

HOLY CHURCH OF AMERICA, INC., THE UNITED. See UNITED HOLY CHURCH OF AMERICA.

HOLY GRAIL, MOVEMENT OF THE. See MESSIAHS, FALSE.

HOLY LAND: Name commonly given to Palestine on account of the many places sanctified by the presence of Jesus, and identified on the grounds of Scriptural documents, history, or legend. During the Turkish domination over Palestine, which ended in 1918, the rights of the various Christian confessions established in Palestine over the Holy Places were recognized and regulated by the authority of the Sultans. The supervision of the Greek Orthodox shrines and sanctuaries is exercised by the autocephalous patriarch of Jerusalem, who is at the same time the head of the congregation of the Holy Sepulcher. The shrines and sanctuaries of the Latin, i.e., of the Roman Catholic Church, are administered and staffed by the Custody of the Holy Land, an international congregation within the Franciscan Order. Its superior, the *Custos Terrae Sanctae,* is independent from the Latin patriarch of Jerusalem.

The status of the Holy Places remained practically unchanged under the British administration of Palestine by mandate from the League of Nations, and since the *de facto* partition of the country following the war between Jews and Arabs.

Here is the list of the major sanctuaries enjoying the official status of Holy Places: Bethlehem, Jordan, Church of the Nativity—rights shared by the Greek, Latin, and Armenian communities; Jerusalem, Jordan, Church of the Holy Sepulcher (and Calvary)—rights shared by the Greek, Latin, Armenian, Syrian, and Coptic communities; Garden of Gethsemane with the basilica of the Agony—Latin; Church of the Tomb of Mary—rights shared by the Greek and Armenian communities; Nazareth, Israel, Church of the Annunciation—Latin.

Negotiations are conducted by the parties concerned and their representatives at the United Nations (*q.v.*), for the drafting of a new status of the sanctuaries listed above, as well as of minor shrines controlled by the religious bodies in charge of the Holy Places in the technical sense, and eventually of other religious foundations in Palestine. Two alternate schemes were proposed, namely a trusteeship of the U.N. over the Holy Places, or a system of international guaranties. No decision has been reached thus far. See also PALESTINE.

BIBLIOGRAPHY: G. Golubovich, *Biblioteca bio-bibliografica della Terra Santa,* since 1906; D. Baldi, *La Custodia francescana di Terra Santa,* 1918; G. Zanella, *Memoriale sui Luoghi Santi,* 1945; ESCO Foundation for Palestine, *Palestine, a Study of Jewish, Arab, and British Policies,* 1947.

GEORGES A. BARROIS.

HOLY NAME, SOCIETY OF THE: A Roman Catholic society of laymen whose object is to promote reverence for the Holy Name of God and Jesus Christ, and to suppress blasphemy, profanity, and the taking of unlawful oaths. It originated in Dominican circles following the Council of Lyons, 1274, and it was repeatedly approved by the popes. Local branches of the society extant in various American churches have been organized into diocesan unions since 1882, under the authority of a director general appointed by the hierarchy. The society, which has its headquarters in New York, counts over 2,500,000 members.

GEORGES A. BARROIS.

HOLY PLACES. See HOLY LAND.

HOLY ROLLERS: Designation of ridicule applied to adherents of the small sects which cultivate highly emotional experiences and exhibit motor automata in their services. There is no sect that bears or accepts the name officially. The title is usually applied to small Pentecostal groups (*q.v.*) or some of the Churches of God (*q.v.*) and the reference is to such manifestations as trances and shouting.

ELMER T. CLARK.

HOLY ROMAN EMPIRE: It is no longer fashionable to apply the name "Holy Roman

Empire" to the group of states which were somewhat loosely held together from 962 to 1806, except for the period after 1250, when Emperor Frederick II died. The best name for the early period is Germanic-Roman Empire. As a result of Voltaire's ridicule historians have been rather apt to conclude with him that the state governed by such capable potentates as Maximilian I and Charles V (q.v.) was merely an ideal, not an actual fact. It certainly was a state under Henry III and Frederick III, while Charles IV and Sigismund also knew how to keep their nobles in check. But during the sixteenth and seventeenth centuries it became the custom for each new emperor to sign away a great many powers in the *Wahlkapitulation*. If a candidate, even the mighty king Charles of Spain and ruler of the Low Countries in his own right, chose to object, he was politely informed that other princes could be readily found who would not refuse to sign.

During the Reformation era emperors were chosen by seven electors. In addition to them there were other princes, notably the duke of Bavaria, who possessed relatively extensive powers. They were in a position to make a contract with each new emperor, and if he broke his contract he could be deposed. The reason why Luther was not treated as Hus had been was the change in the political situation between 1415 and 1520. Although Luther was excommunicated by the pope and outlawed by the Diet (Reichstag) of the empire, his friend, the elector of Saxony, merely laughed at both authorities and did what he pleased with his professor as the latter was returning home from the Diet of Worms in 1521. No amount of threatening in Rome or Vienna made him swerve from the path he had chosen for himself. In this way Protestantism was made politically possible. Calvin also labored in the Holy Roman Empire, and he, like Luther, was protected by local authorities who defied both pope and emperor.

Luther and Calvin, as well as Zwingli and Farel, were favored by political fortune. There were other capable theologians who could not found new churches largely because the political conditions in their respective states were not suitable for the creation of independent denominations. It must not be imagined that the four men just named deliberately set out upon a career of denomination building. They received somewhat unwittingly a whole collection of fortunate circumstances which they utilized to the best of their ability. In Spain and France there were able theologians and religious leaders, but there these men had to comply with certain rules and regulations. If their books and doctrines did not suit the inquisitors, they would receive severe punishment as well as loss of

prestige. That had already happened to Wycliff (q.v.) and Hus (q.v.).

The actions of the elector of Saxony were of such importance that two thirds of Germany, of the Netherlands, of Great Britain, and of the United States were lost to the Roman Catholic Church. In subsequent times a little change was made here and there, sometimes in favor of the Protestants, and sometimes going the other way. But upon the whole, the situation has remained the same as it was three hundred years ago. The Lutheran, Calvinist, and Anabaptist movements owed their strength on the physical side to certain political conditions in the Holy Roman Empire. Spain had lost its hold on the northern Netherlands, and Geneva lay beyond the reach of papal or imperial authority when English refugees consorted with so-called heretics in such places.

In 1555 the Peace of Augsburg was signed, creating a temporary status quo and a queer arrangement with regard to the two established churches in the Holy Roman Empire. Each prince had the power to enforce his particular religion upon his subjects. Calvinism was not recognized as a legitimate religion. A tug of war ensued between the Lutherans and the Roman Catholics. The emperor was always a Catholic and about two thirds of his subjects were Protestants. But the real battle was in each local state. Gradually the Catholics regained some power. In the three great archbishoprics of Cologne, Mainz and Trier the Protestants never had much chance to win many converts, and on the other hand, in the northern states the Catholics were always at a disadvantage.

BIBLIOGRAPHY: E. H. Zeydel, *The Holy Roman Empire in German Literature*, 1918; G. Barraclough, *The Origins of Modern Germany*, 1947; V. Valentin, *The German People*, 1949; G. P. Gooch, *Studies in German History*, 1948; F. Schevill, *The Making of Modern Germany*, 1916; B. Jarrett, *The Emperor Charles IV*, 1935; B. Chudoba, *Spain and the Empire 1519–1643*, 1952; D. B. W. Lewis, *Charles of Europe*, 1931; W. Friedensburg, *Kaiser Karl V. und Papst Paul III*, 1932; idem, *Johannes Sleidanus und die Schicksalsmaechte der Reformationszeit*, 1935; H. von Schubert, *Der Reichstag von Augsburg*, 1930; R. Stupperich, *Der Humanismus und die Wiedervereinigung der Konfessionen*, 1936; P. Rassow, *Die Kaiseridee Karls V., dargestellt an der Politik der Jahre 1528–1540*, 1932.

[Sup.] ALBERT HYMA.

HOLY SPIRIT: Although the literature on the subject is extensive, it is frequently said that the doctrine of the Holy Spirit is much neglected in modern theology. Biblical studies have disclosed the pivotal place of the Spirit in both testaments; historically there has been virtual unanimity as to the centrality of the doctrine in theological and creedal statements; since the *filioque* controversy, there has been no radical dispute among the various churches on the person and work of the Holy Spirit.

The history of the doctrine, however, reveals

some interesting emphases. The Spirit forms part of the earliest apostolic preaching or *kerygma* (C. H. Dodd, *The Apostolic Preaching*, pp. 42 f., 51 f.), and it has traditionally been assumed that a trinitarian structure (God, Christ, Holy Spirit) of the faith was consciously elaborated by the disciples (Matt. 28:19). Oscar Cullmann (*The Earliest Christian Confessions,* 1949) insists that the basic and primary Christian affirmations in both apostolic and post-apostolic ages were Christological, and that the bi- and tri-partite confessions were later and more formal developments. (For a somewhat different view, consult J. N. D. Kelly, *Early Christian Creeds,* 1950.) By the fifth century the ecumenical creeds of the undivided church incorporated the doctrine of the Holy Spirit into a trinitarian formula which has been reaffirmed by subsequent creeds, confessions, and catechisms of the Orthodox Churches, the Roman Catholic Church, and most Protestant denominations (P. Schaff, *Creeds of Christendom,* 3 vols., 1931).

Running parallel with this trinitarian development, and sometimes in opposition to it, there has been a long and controversial history of various kinds of Christian groups which laid special stress on the direct illumination of the Spirit on the minds and lives of the individual believer. Consult in this connection: Montanism, Donatism, Manicheanism in the early church; the medieval mystics, the Albigenses, the Cathari in the middle ages; the Anabaptists and other "left-wing" Protestants in the sixteenth century; the Quakers, John Wesley, the "pentecostal" and "holiness" sects in the post-Reformation and modern periods (Ronald Knox, *Enthusiasm,* 1950; C. W. Ferguson, *The Confusion of Tongues,* 1940).

The positive contribution of these groups was to relate the doctrine of the Holy Spirit to the doctrine of salvation and the Christian life; the Holy Spirit in this sense is a soteriological as well as a trinitarian doctrine. Roman Catholic theology (cf. T. Aquinas, *Summa Theologica*) tends to restrict the Holy Spirit to the doctrine of the Trinity, and, while Luther and Calvin emphasized both the trinitarian and soteriological aspects, post-Reformation Protestantism tended to follow the Roman pattern (cf. H. Heppe, *Reformed Dogmatics,* 1950). Lacking in both these parallel developments is any serious concern for the relation of the Holy Spirit to the church. Either this relationship has been obscured or undue emphasis has been placed upon individual illumination and sanctification. The Apostles' Creed, however, "clearly indicates that the Holy Spirit should not be separated from the church, nor the church from the Holy Spirit" (R. Prenter, *Le Saint-Esprit et le renouveau de l'Eglise,* 1949).

See also Advocate.

Bibliography: F. W. Dillistone, *The Holy Spirit in the Life of Today,* 1947; George Johnston, "Spirit," in *A Theological Word Book of the Bible,* 1951; Abraham Kuyper, *The Work of the Holy Spirit,* 1900; H. Wheeler Robinson, *The Christian Experience of the Holy Spirit,* 1928; E. F. Scott, *The Spirit in the New Testament,* 1923; N. H. Snaith, *The Doctrine of the Holy Spirit,* 1937; Regin Prenter, *Spiritus Creator,* 1952.
[Sup.] Hugh Thomson Kerr, Jr.

HOLY, THE IDEA OF THE: In modern theology, is associated with Rudolf Otto's book *Das Heilige,* first published in 1917 and thereafter in more than fourteen German editions; the English translation is entitled *The Idea of the Holy,* with the sub-title, "An Inquiry into the non-rational factor in the idea of the divine and its relation to the rational," translated by John W. Harvey, Oxford University Press, 1923, second edition, 1950.

Rudolf Otto (b. 1869; d. 1937) was professor of theology at Goettingen, Breslau, and Marburg. He travelled extensively, especially in the Far East where he became interested in the study of comparative religions. Shortly before his death he was invited to deliver the Gifford Lectures in Scotland. *The Idea of the Holy* was his most important book; it made an immediate impression on theological thinking and introduced the word "numinous" (Latin *numen*) into the modern theological vocabulary.

The word "holy," according to Otto, is a distinctively religious term, suggesting the ineffable, that which is nonconceptual, and, as such, akin to the word "beautiful." It contains an "overplus of meaning" beyond the rational or the ethical. "There is no religion in which it does not live as the real innermost core" (p. 6). It is not, as in Schleiermacher, a mere *self-consciousness* of "absolute dependence on God," nor a perception of "something there," as in William James; it involves something "objective and outside the self" (p. 11). It cannot be defined or taught, it must be evoked or awakened and can only be described in analogy and metaphor. To designate this sense of the holy, Otto coined the word "numinous." The object to which the numinous consciousness is directed he called the "mysterium tremendum."

The "tremendum" involves such aspects as: (1) awefulness and overpoweringness, (2) "majestas," (3) urgency and energy. The "mysterium" implies: (1) the "wholly other" (*das ganz Andere*), (2) the element of fascination ("fascinans"). Thus the "mysterium tremendum" is a "harmony of contrasts" suggesting "boundless awe and boundless wonder, quelling and yet entrancing the soul" (p. 41).

Sin, therefore, is something more than unlawfulness or iniquity, it is a sense of "self-disvaluation" (p. 50), and the need for atonement arises out of man's sense of "profaneness." Referring to non-Christian religions, Otto nevertheless concentrates on the specifically Christian character of the "numinous" which he finds in both the Old Testament and the New Testament, in the history of the church, the mystics, in Roman Catholic piety, and in Luther. Protestantism, however, tends to "schematize" the "numinous" with the result that religion is identified with rational and ethical concepts. What is needed, Otto maintains, is the recognition of the nonrational element in religion, not to exclude or supersede the rational but to "deepen the rational meaning of the Christian conception of God by permeating it with its nonrational elements" (p. 108). This means that religion has a unique a priori character, underived from rational postulates, with its own "independent roots in the hidden depths of the spirit" (p. 136). The final chapters (XVIII-XXI) deal with the implication of this for revelation ("divination") and the question of the uniqueness or essence of the Christian religion.

BIBLIOGRAPHY: R. F. Davidson, *Rudolf Otto's Interpretation of Religion*, 1947 (bibliography); H. E. Eisenhuth, *Der Begriff des Irrationalen als philosophisches Problem*, 1931; F. K. Feigel, *"Das Heilige"; Kritische Abhandlung . . .* , 1948 (bibliography); J. M. Moore, *Theories of Religious Experience with special reference to James, Otto, and Bergson*, 1938; T. Siegfried, *Grundfragen der Theologie bei Rudolf Otto*, 1931.

HUGH THOMSON KERR, JR.

HOLY WEEK: For the background see HOLY WEEK, Vol. V. Practically all denominations now observe the week as the high drama of Christian faith, when worshipers relive the tremendous events of the final days before triumph on Easter. The themes: Palm Sunday, Triumphal Entry; Monday, Cleansing the Temple; Tuesday, Conflicts and Colloquies; Wednesday, Day of Silence, with Christ and the twelve in Bethany; Maundy Thursday, Last Supper; Good Friday, Crucifixion; Saturday, In the Tomb. Days of greatest emphasis: Palm Sunday, with confirmation of the young; Maundy Thursday, a time of special communion for the entire congregation; and Good Friday, observed in community-wide noon services, or the traditional three-hour service, the hours of darkness around the Cross, the worship centering round the Seven Last Words. Brief addresses may deal devotionally with The Forgiveness of Wrongs (Luke 23:34); The Forgiveness of Sins (Luke 23:43); The Sympathy of Our Saviour (John 19:27a); The Mystery of the Cross (Matt. 27:46b); The Humanity of Our Lord (John 19:28b); The Finished Work of Redemption (John 19:30a); and The Triumph of the Cross (Luke 23:46a). Thus Holy Week prepares for the coming of Easter, as the most glorious day of the Christian Year.

[Sup.] GEORGE MILES GIBSON.

HOLY YEAR. See JUBILEE.

HOME MISSIONS: The outstanding feature of American home missions in the nineteenth century was the need and opportunity to establish the organized church throughout the United States. This basic fact did not change with the beginning of the present century, but American Protestantism did find itself in a changing climate. A new spirit—the spirit of co-operation—began to inspire and influence the church and its missionary enterprise.

I. New Emphasis: Immediately after the Spanish-American War in 1898, the West Indies became a home mission responsibility. As Protestant denominations launched their work in Puerto Rico, their representatives agreed upon an allocation of territory, which procedure was destined later to become a significant policy in the first decades of the new century.

In 1908 the Home Missions Council (*q.v.*) and the Council of Women for Home Missions, national and interdenominational agencies, came into being. The formation of these organizations, bringing together representatives of many Protestant communions for fellowship, conference, and co-operation, gradually came to influence the total home missions enterprise. The long-range objective of the movement remained the same—to proclaim the Gospel in all its fullness, establish the church in new communities, and invigorate it in communities where it needed help.

II. Work Among Immigrants: The coming of immigrants from Europe to the shores of America continued—indeed, was accelerated—during the first two decades of the century. America was looked upon as a melting pot where people from many lands needed to be integrated into a common life. The foreign-born, who entered the country between 1900 and 1920 from southern and eastern Europe, numbered about 9,700,000. This influx of population introduced many new and difficult problems for church as well as state. Three-fifths of them settled in New England and the Middle Atlantic states, very largely in the cities, thus creating both city and industrial problems which challenged the home mission efforts of the Church. By 1916 thirty-nine different societies, with an accredited force of fifty-six missionaries, were maintaining representatives at Ellis Island, in New York, where three-fourths of all incoming immigrants were received. Other ports of importance where work was done were Boston and Philadelphia. See also EMIGRANTS AND IMMIGRANTS.

III. Women's Boards: The women of the Church became increasingly aware of the opportunity and need for service. As time went on, women's home mission boards were organized in many denominations. These boards were interested particularly in specialized types of work (schools, hospitals, social centers) and for special groups of neglected and underprivileged people. They, too, assisted in the holding and promoting of summer conferences and the preparation and publication of mission study books. The Council of Women for Home Missions continued to function with increasing collaboration and co-operation with the Home Missions Council until December, 1940, when the two agencies were merged to form the Home Missions Council of North America. For this Council since 1950 see NATIONAL COUNCIL OF CHURCHES OF CHRIST, U.S.A.

IV. Comity and Co-operation: During the first two decades of the century much was accomplished in the line of interdenominational comity and co-operation. Intensive surveys were made of home mission fields, a number of states organized home mission councils, territories were allocated to different denominations, specific mission enterprises were undertaken jointly, important conferences (such as the joint meeting of the Home Missions Council and the Council of Women for Home Missions in Washington, D.C., in 1911) were held, and new lines of co-operative missions were introduced. The Young People's Missionary Movement began to function unitedly in 1902 in the publication and promotion of mission study books and materials and the holding of summer conferences. Its scope and activities expanded so effectively that in 1911 the name of the organization was changed to the Missionary Education Movement of the United States and Canada.

While these co-operative efforts were becoming more prevalent and receiving greater recognition, there was no special committee on comity and co-operation until 1913. This committee made its first report in 1914, in which it submitted a "Proposed Plan for Comity and Co-operation." This was the first attempt to set up an actual plan of co-operation, including definite comity principles. Although it was a negative approach to a difficult problem, it was a decided step in advance, and continued to be used as a controlling policy until a more positive approach to church planning and strategy became necessary during and after World War II.

V. Town and Country Church: An interdenominational Committee on Rural Fields was set up in 1912. Several boards organized departments of town and country work and appointed specialists in the work of the rural church. In-service training and graduate courses for country pastors came to be considered important. A number of church colleges and state universities introduced courses in their summer schools for country ministers. Three outstanding needs were recognized by the denominations—a trained country ministry, an adequate country church program, and appropriate buildings and equipment. Great progress was made, during these years, in rural life work

through conferences, surveys, schools, institutes, and other types of work. See also RURAL FELLOWSHIP, CHRISTIAN.

VI. City Churches: Similarly there was an awakened interest in the importance of the city church. This, too, became the concern of home mission boards. Church life in the cities was studied. Policies and methods of city evangelization were worked out. Several things affecting the home missions task in the city were discovered, resulting in some fundamental and constructive work in connection with the city church. More scientific church planning and more effective city mission programs were developed from this emphasis on the city church. City mission departments, headed by specialists, were set up by several of the major denominations.

VII. Indian, Spanish, Negro Work: About the same time, between 1908 and 1918, there developed a renewed interest in mission work among American Indians (q.v.), numbering some 330,000 in the United States and Alaska, one-half not connected with any church. This resulted in definite ventures of co-operation in mission work among the Indians, and with the Indian Bureau of the U.S. Government. A new concern for Spanish-speaking people, especially in the Southwest, expressed itself in 1911 in the organization of "The Interdenominational Council of Spanish-speaking Work in the Southwest." With the large influx of Spanish-speaking people into the United States from Cuba and Mexico during World War I, the work of this committee became increasingly important. Another minority group, the Negro, was looked upon as a problem, but not much work was developed among Negroes interdenominationally. Some home boards did carry on work among them, especially along educational lines. Able papers on this phase of home missions were read. Resolutions were adopted. Few constructive forward steps were taken.

VIII. Church Building: Increasingly more attention was given by some home mission boards to church building. By 1915 twenty-six denominations had set up church building departments, nearly half of which had separate boards. The function of these departments and boards was to assist in the building of churches with both grants and loans. While limited by resources, ground had been prepared for a tremendous outburst in the construction of churches during the lush years of the 1920's.

IX. Reconstruction and Extension: Following World War I staggering tasks of reconstruction and reclamation faced the church as well as the nation. Home missions suffered through sheer neglect. No new work had been undertaken. The cost of maintaining ongoing work was doubled. Missionary workers had been taken away from their fields for war work, both at home and "over there." Recruits for home mission work were few. At the end of the war the needs of the home mission fields were great. Denominational leaders joined hands in setting up the Interchurch World Movement (q.v.), and for a time it appeared as if the millennium was about to dawn.

The aroused sense of need and opportunity gave rise to a forward movement among the home mission forces of the church. Denominationally and interdenominationally, great plans were launched for church extension by denominational boards. Indeed, some boards overextended themselves in making grants and loans —much to their regret when the lean years of the economic depression (q.v.) set in. The building of new highways, improved means of transportation, the use of new media for communication—these and other factors were bound to affect, for good or for ill, the home missions enterprise during the years ahead.

X. Co-operative Projects: Great progress was made. Co-operative projects of great significance were launched. The ministry to migratory laborers began in 1920 and expanded until, at the mid-century mark, it had gained national recognition. A staff of more than two hundred workers was engaged in this interdenominational ministry in twenty-five states in 1950. In 1919 a joint central committee on Indian Work was created "to co-ordinate as far as possible all Christian agencies working for the Indians." Religious work directors were placed in a number of government schools, working closely with school administrators, providing religious counsel and education, and assisting in relating students to the churches of the vicinity or providing services of worship for them. Projects like these, including (after 1940) a special program intended to improve the status of the sharecroppers who for various reasons were being crowded off the plantations, were sponsored jointly through the Home Missions Council of North America. Through the years these programs were undergirded by support from denominational boards, the women's organizations of the churches, and the offerings of the World Day of Prayer, sponsored by the United Council of Church Women.

XI. Church Comity Conference, 1928: Of historic importance was the Church Comity Conference held in Cleveland, Ohio, in January, 1928. This conference was the first serious attempt, on a large scale, to study the question of comity and church planning in a comprehensive way. Two significant projects emerged: (1) The Five-year Program of Survey and Adjustment; and (2) the "North American Home Missions Congress" held in Washington, D. C., in December, 1930. The former was projected in the field of comity. The latter was set up to deal with changing conditions and increased demands upon

the home mission forces of the church. As a result of these projects, the church came to see more clearly that home missions is "not merely an aggregate of local enterprises, but is a vital aspect of the whole life of the church and a process in which the whole church must participate."

XII. The Depression of the 1930's: Hardly had this renewed and enlarged interest in home missions been created when the church, with the nation, was plunged into the greatest economic depression (q.v.) experienced in American history. It appeared as if the need for church extension and further expansion of home mission efforts had reached an end. Then the nation was plunged into the throes of World War II. People began to migrate to new communities until, by the end of the fifth decade, one-half of the population of the country had moved to a different geographic area. So it was that the impact of world events upon American life created new and critical problems of tremendous importance for home missions.

XIII. National Congress, 1950: It seemed not only desirable, but absolutely necessary, for representatives of home mission agencies to reappraise their task and redefine their objectives in order to develop a comprehensive strategy of home missions. For this purpose a National Congress on Home Missions was called and held at Columbus, Ohio, in Jan., 1950. Nearly one thousand church leaders, representing thirty-four denominations, gathered to participate in this congress.

BIBLIOGRAPHY: Hermann N. Morse, *Home Missions Today and Tomorrow*, 1934; Truman B. Douglass, *Mission to America*, 1951; William P. Shriver, *Missions at the Grass Roots*, 1949; Samuel Kincheloe, *The American City and its Church*, 1938; Rockwell C. Smith, *The Church in our Town*, 1943.

I. GEORGE NACE.

HOME MISSIONS, COUNCIL OF WOMEN FOR. See HOME MISSIONS.

HOMILETICAL COMMENTARIES: Sets of books consisting of sermon outlines and other materials ready for use in preaching. Such works, as a rule, are compiled in wooden fashion. Even if expertly edited, they deprive a minister of joy in using his intellectual muscles. For speedy reference every pastor needs a one-volume commentary (not homiletical) on the whole Bible; also a standard exegetical commentary or two on every major book of the Bible. In scholarly fashion such a work deals with meanings and values, but leaves the reader free to use the materials in his own way. A suggestive list of works suitable for a pastor appears in the appendix of *Preaching from the Bible*, by Andrew W. Blackwood, 1941.

ANDREW W. BLACKWOOD.

HOMILETICS: "The science of which preaching is the art and the sermon is the finished product." This definition suggests three ways of study, all in use: (1) Many come to homiletics as a science, applying rules of rhetoric, which go back to Greece and Rome (see Edwin Hatch, *The Influence of Greek Ideas and Usages on the Christian Church* [1888]). (2) Deans C. R. Brown of Yale and W. L. Sperry of Harvard, with others, have dealt with preaching as an art. This approach has led to increased appreciation of master preachers, and more study of history. (3) Another group stresses the study of master sermons, past and present. Each approach has merits and limitations. If the curriculum affords time, the student may follow the three methods in successive years. Then he will probably learn how to preach after he is ordained. Many have become master preachers out on the field: H. W. Beecher, Phillips Brooks, J. H. Jowett, and Alexander Maclaren. Hence a graduate may serve an apprenticeship under a mature pastor, or enter a field that affords time to master this art.

Many observers feel the need of changes in the teaching of homiletics. The professor should know the history of preaching, beginning with the prophets. He should have had pastoral experience, to understand human needs. Then he should coach each student, as in G. P. Baker's "workshop" at Harvard. Such a plan calls for small classes; in a large seminary, a large staff. As for "practice preaching" before students, it has an air of unreality. With a recording machine a student can secure the reproduction of an actual service he has conducted elsewhere, and then go over it with the instructor, perhaps in the presence of other students, but not in a place of worship. Gradually a student should develop the art of self-criticism, so that he will never rest content with second-rate performances of his own. Fortunately, most professors of homiletics have also developed the art of self-criticism. Hence the teaching of tomorrow ought to be less wooden and more rewarding.

BIBLIOGRAPHY: The literature is boundless and much of it strong. Augustine's *De Doctrina Christiana, Liber IV*, and Brooks's Lyman Beecher *Lectures on Preaching* still lead the field. See also E. D. Jones, *The Royalty of the Pulpit*, an account of the Yale Lectures, 1951. Recent guidebooks include: J. A. Broadus, *The Preparation and Delivery of Sermons*, rev. by J. B. Weatherspoon, 1944; A. W. Blackwood, *The Preparation of Sermons*, 1948.

[Sup.] ANDREW W. BLACKWOOD.

HOMMIUS, FESTUS: Dutch Reformed theologian, secretary of the Synod of Dordrecht (1618–19); b. Feb. 10, 1576, at Jelsum in Friesland; d. July 5, 1642, at Leiden. He attended the Latin school at Leeuwarden, and on Nov. 6, 1593, matriculated at the University of Franeker, but left for France in 1595 to learn the French language at La Rochelle and other places. He matriculated at Leiden Nov. 20, 1596, where he studied under Junius, Gomarus, and Treleatius, and took active part in disputations, defending his own views with marked ability. In 1599 he became preacher at Dokkum, and at the end of 1602 at Leiden. In the summer of that year he preached in the armed camp of the Dutch forces, and attended the siege of Grave.

At Leiden he observed with keen attention the rising tide of the Remonstrant or Arminian movement. Arminius, during the public defense of his theses to get the degree of D.D., was attacked by Hommius (July 10, 1603). Hommius was also present at disputations which Arminius later held, and at the meeting of the church board in Leiden he actively participated in the attack on Arminius. Hommius bitterly complained about the excessive powers assumed by the civil authorities in the field of religion, attacking the theories of Utenbogaert.

He seems to have composed the Counter Remonstrance which during the written conference at The Hague in 1611 was presented to the provincial estates of Holland, replying to the Remonstrance of 1610 by Utenbogaert and his colleagues. He also was present at the conference of Delft in Feb., 1613, stating here and elsewhere that only a lawfully convoked synod could settle the disputes. But he was willing that those who did not object to the teachings of the Dutch Reformed Church any farther than the Five Articles by the Remonstrants be permitted to remain in the church on condition that they would not make propaganda for their opposition. He attended the meetings in Amsterdam where delegates from various provinces considered action against the Remonstrants, and at the first of these, in Sept., 1615, he was secretary. As soon as it had been decided that a national synod would be held he prepared instructions published in his book, *Specimen controversiarum Belgicarum* (October, 1618), which soon appeared also in Dutch translation, addressed to the States-General of the Dutch Republic. Through correspondence with the pastor of the Dutch church in London, S. Ruytinck, he tried to persuade the Archbishop of Canterbury to send orthodox delegates to the synod. At the particular synod of South Holland held at Delft in October, 1618, he was appointed delegate to the national synod, which made him the first secretary. He took personal charge of the drafting of the acts of the synod, while he also took care of many other tasks. He urged that the Remonstrants be treated with consideration and respect; if they would be equally courteous they should not be kept from the communion service. He also objected to the measures which deprived the Remonstrants of freedom of worship.

From the beginning he gave private homiletic lessons to university students. After the death of Arminius he devoted two lecture periods a week to dogmatics, based upon the Heidelberg Catechism. He also covered the same material in disputations, paying particular attention to the current attack upon Bellarmine (*LXX dis-putationes theologiae adversus Pontificios*, 1614). It is not surprising that in 1619 he was elected regent of the State College, which under the leadership of Bertius, a close friend of Hugo Grotius and Utenbogaert, had been inclined to favor the Remonstrants (1607-15). Later, under Gerard Vossius it had continued its liberal attitude. He was expected to make the learned body conform to the ideals current in the days of his father-in-law, Johannes Cuchlinus, who was regent from 1595 to 1606. He succeeded in making this institution highly respectable and influential. He served as regent till July 1641, when old age caused his retirement.

Although he was not named one of the translators of the Bible by the Synod of Dordrecht, but only a revisor, he took an active part in the actual translation, particularly after the death of the ranking translator. In the translation of the New Testament he played a leading part, and also in that of the Apocryphal Books. Moreover, he prepared the elaborate Index.

He was a capable leader of the orthodox Calvinists. His views on predestination were supralapsarian, but he was not so intolerant as he used to be regarded. Among his works must be listed particularly his translation of the explanation of the Heidelberg Catechism by Ursinus, which he completed at Dokkum in 1602. Later he added an independent commentary in a popular work which was first published in 1617: *Het Schatboek der verclaringhen over de Catechismus der Chr. religie*, etc. It exerted a powerful influence upon the Dutch nation.

BIBLIOGRAPHY: J. Lindeboom, *Austin Friars* (1950), pp. 93-95; P. J. Wyminga, *Festus Hommius*, 1899; *Biogr. woordenboek van Prot. Godgel. in Nederland*, Vol. IV (1931), pp. 198-218, with extensive bibliography; G. P. van Itterzon, *Franciscus Gomarus*, 1929; C. C. de Bruin, *De Statenbijbel en zijn voorgangers*, 1937.

D. NAUTA.

HOMRIGHAUSEN, ELMER GEORGE: Presbyterian U. S. A.; b. Wheatland, Iowa, April 11, 1900. He studied at Mission House College (A.B.), Princeton Theological Seminary (Th.B.), and at Dubuque, Butler, Rutgers, Chicago, and Geneva universities. He was minister of the English Reformed Church at Freeport, Ill. (1924-29) and of Carrollton Avenue Evangelical and Reformed Church, Indianapolis, Ind. (1929-37). He occupied the Thomas W. Synnott chair of Christian education at Princeton Theological Seminary since 1938. He taught in the University of Dubuque, Occidental College, and Butler University. He is the author of: *Current Theological Trends* (1938); *Christianity in America—A Crisis* (1937); *Let the Church Be the Church* (1940); *Choose Ye This Day* (1943); *I Believe in the Church* (1951); and co-translator of Barth-Thurneysen, *Come Holy Spirit; idem, God's Search for Man;* and Barth, *God in Action.*

HONDURAS. See CENTRAL AMERICA.

HONESTY: Honesty is closely related to honor, which has been described as "a certain system of reciprocal rights and obligations belonging to a social station or relation, and also the individual's recognition of these" (*Dict. Phil. and Psych.*, Vol. I, p. 485). Such a system develops its own code of "honor" which may be almost identical with properly ethical standards, but may also be supplementary, indifferent, or even hostile to them; e.g., every craft and profession develops its own "honor," but "honor among thieves" bears little relation to honesty, commonly understood. "Honor" here means fidelity to those associated with us and observance of their accepted code. In Christian ethics, the conception of "honor" is governed by the belief in a moral Judge, who is also Redeemer, in what is due to Him as such, and is in consequence due from one person to another, regarded as made in the image of God, standing under His judgment, and claiming His forgiveness.

The wide variety of meanings attached to "honesty" is due to the fact that it is the characteristic excellence of the just man in different surroundings. Honesty can mean conformity to codes of varying adequacy. At its best it involves integrity in thought, word, and deed, with motives higher than mere respect for a properly constituted social order or desire for esteem, namely devotion to an ideal of righteousness and truth. This explains Whately's meaning when he says, "Honesty is the best policy, but he who acts on that principle is not an honest man." Honesty is here regarded in its highest sense as no longer mere refined and enlightened self-interest, but as sincere devotion to principle.

As civilized society has become more commercialized, honesty has tended to become identified less with respect for moral rights in general, and more with the rights and laws of property in particular. The honest man is trustworthy and conscientious in work and business relationships; he "will not lie or cheat or steal." Honesty, so regarded, becomes the supreme virtue of a commercialized society. But even here professional and other standards may claim a relative autonomy. What is perfectly justifiable and even meritorious in a business man may be unprofessional conduct in a lawyer. The general principle of honesty must be articulated in each sphere. It is probable that only a strict sense of individual and corporate responsibility to God can enable adjustments to be made. The honest man is one who retains his integrity and fidelity to principle amid the compromises of policies, programs and practical necessities; his sense of duty is strong; he is a man of honor

and cannot but be honest as he stands before
God.

WILLIAM ROXBURGH FORRESTER.

**HONIUS, CORNELIUS (CORNELIS
HOEN):** His treatise on the eucharist, published
in 1525 by Zwingli, was discovered by Professor
A. Eekhof of the University of Leyden and
published by him in photostatic reproduction.
Its influence upon Bucer and Zwingli was epoch-
making. See also FAREL, GUILLAUME; RODE,
HINNE.

BIBLIOGRAPHY: A. Eekhof, *De avondmaalsbrief van Cornelis Hoen*, 1917, 1925; Albert Hyma, *The Christian
Renaissance*, 1924; Walther Koehler, *Zwingli und Luther*,
1924.

[Sup.] ALBERT HYMA.

HOOKER, RICHARD: Deserves all the praise
given by D. S. Schaff. He was fully aware of
the theory which permitted Henry VIII and his
daughter Elizabeth to act as head of the Anglican Church. Perhaps for personal reasons,
such as seeking favors from the powers in the
civil government, he did not support the rigid
Calvinists in their political views. The latter
did not like the idea of having a king or queen
rule a church.

BIBLIOGRAPHY: *The Cambridge Bibliography of English
Literature*, Vol. I (1940), pp. 685-688—here many titles
are given; C. J. Sisson, *The Judicious Marriage of Mr.
Hooker and the Birth of "The Laws of Ecclesiastical
Polity,"* 1940; G. Michaelin, *Richard Hooker als politi-
scher Denker*, 1933; A. Hyma, *Christianity and Politics*
(1938), Chaps. 5 and 6; F. J. Shirley, *Richard Hooker
and Contemporary Political Ideas*, 1949.

[Sup.] ALBERT HYMA.

HOOVER, HARVEY DANIEL: Lutheran;
b. at New Oxford, Pa., June 17, 1880. He was
educated at Gettysburg College, Susquehanna
University (A.B., 1899; A.M., 1900; B.D., 1902),
and at Illinois Wesleyan University (Ph.D.,
1907). He also studied at Union Theological
Seminary. He was pastor of the Friedens, Pa.
Church (1902-4), and of Hebron Church, East
Pittsburgh (1904-7). He was professor of theology and sociology at Susquehanna University
(1907-9); and president of Carthage College
(1909-26). Since that date he has been professor of practical theology in the Lutheran Theological Seminary, Gettysburg, Pa. He was editor of *Light for Today* (1935-47); associate editor of *The Lutheran Church Quarterly* (1938-
48); editor of 5 vols., National Lutheran Education Association (1920-25); editor of The
Bible Reading Fellowship since 1930. He is
the author of *History of Carthage College;* and
Living the Liturgy.

HOOVER LECTURES: The William Henry
Hoover Lectureship on Christian Unity was established by the Disciples Divinity House of
the University of Chicago in 1945 with funds
which had been donated by W. H. Hoover,
North Canton, Ohio. The lectures are delivered

at the University of Chicago and are normally
given annually. It is a provision of the lectureship that the lectures must be published.
Lecturers have been Angus Dun, Walter M.
Horton, G. B. Oxnam, and Clayton C. Morrison.

W. BARNETTE BLAKEMORE.

HOPE, NORMAN VICTOR: Presbyterian
Church, U. S. A.; b. Edinburgh, Scotland, April
7, 1908. He studied at Edinburgh University
(M.A., 1930; B.D., 1933; Ph.D., 1944). He was
minister of Busby West Church of Scotland
(1935-38). He taught theology at New Brunswick Theological Seminary, New Brunswick,
N. J. (1938-46); he is Alexander Professor of
Church History, Princeton Theological Seminary, Princeton, N. J. He translated Karl Holl's
Urchristentum und Religionsgeschichte, under
the title, *The Distinctive Elements in Christianity* (1937). He is the author of *One Christ,
One World, One Church: A Short Introduction
to the Ecumenical Movement* (1953).

HORITES. See HURRIANS.

HORN, WILLIAM: D. April 27, 1917. He
served the Evangelical Association (*q.v.*) for
many years as an editor and then as a bishop
(1891-1915). In addition to his episcopal duties
here and in Germany, where he often supervised the work of his church, Bishop Horn
added several books in his later years: *Gold-
koerner; Lust und Lehre, ein Blumenstrausz von
Erzaehlungen; Der Goldene Wegweiser* (1881);
Illustrierte Reisebilder (1890); *Erfuellte Prophe-
zeiungen* (1907); *Illustrationen oder Bilder und
Beispiele zum Gebrauch fuer Prediger, Eltern
und Lehrer* (1900); he wrote an introduction to
*Lebens-Spiegel oder Ein Fuehrer zur Ewigen
Jugend;* and translated *Unser Land* from the
English of Josiah Strong.

[Sup.] RAYMOND W. ALBRIGHT.

HORTON, DOUGLAS: Congregational Christian; b. in Brooklyn, N. Y., July 27, 1891. He
was educated at Princeton University; New
College, Edinburgh; Mansfield College, Oxford;
University of Tuebingen, Germany; and Hartford Theological Seminary. He was minister
and executive secretary of the General Council
of Congregational-Christian Churches in America and was appointed moderator of the International Congregational Council in 1949. Before taking his national post with the General
Council, he served pastorates at Middletown,
Conn., Brookline, Mass., and Chicago, Ill., and
was a chaplain in the United States Navy. He
was a board member of a number of ecclesiastical and educational institutions, among them
the American University, Cairo, Egypt, of which
he was chairman of the board; Union Theological Seminary; and Princeton University.

Active in the councils of the ecumenical movement, he took a prominent part in the First Assembly of the World Council of Churches at Amsterdam in 1948, being chairman of the American Committee for the World Council (1945–48). Among his books are: *Out into Life; A Legend of the Grail; Taking a City;* and *The Art of Living Today.* He translated from the German, K. Barth, *The Word of God and the Word of Man;* and was the editor of *The Basic Formula for Church Union.*

HORTON, WALTER MARSHALL: Congregational Christian; b. at Somerville, Mass., April 7, 1895; studied at Harvard (A.B., 1917), Columbia (M.A., 1920; Ph.D., 1926), Union Theological Seminary (B.D., 1920; S.T.M., 1923), and also at Paris, Strasbourg, and Marburg. He was instructor at Union Theological Seminary (1922–25); since 1925, he taught systematic theology at the Oberlin Graduate School of Theology. A "realist" in theology, he tried to purge liberal theology of idealistic illusions while retaining its sound elements. His principal writings: *The Philosophy of the Abbé Bautain* (1926); *Theism and the Modern Mood* (1930); *A Psychological Approach to Theology* (1931); *Theism and the Scientific Spirit* (1933); *Realistic Theology* (1934); *Contemporary English Theology* (1936); *Contemporary Continental Theology* (1938); (with H. N. Wieman), *The Growth of Religion* (1938); *Can Christianity Save Civilization?* (1940); *Our Eternal Contemporary* (1942); *Our Christian Faith* (1945); and *Toward a Reborn Church* (1949).

BIBLIOGRAPHY: (V. Ferm, ed.), *Contemporary American Theology,* First Series (1932), pp. 161 ff.; George Hammar, *Christian Realism in Contemporary American Theology* (1940), pp. 254–316.

HOSEA, BOOK OF: Like Amos, Hosea began his career before 752 B.C. (cf. 1:1, 4; and Amos 1:1, 7:10 ff.). His allusions not only to the fall of the house of Jehu then (7:7; 8:4), but also to the Assyrian aggression begun by Tiglath-pileser III in 745 B.C. (8:8 ff.; 10:6) and possibly to Menahem's payment of tribute *ca.* 743–741 B.C. (5:13) indicate activity later than Amos.

Hosea's marriage to Gomer has been variously interpreted. An old view (Luther) has been revived (Hoelscher, Pfeiffer, and others) that Gomer and her children are innocently designated as wife and children "of whoredoms" simply because of Israel's religious apostasy (cf. 1:2). But this does not agree with Hosea's story of marrying a harlot (3:1 f.). The classic modern view represents the call of Hosea arising from his domestic tragedy (ch. 1). Of this he made a parable of Israel's faithlessness to the Lord (ch. 2). In this view (W. R. Smith and others) Gomer's infidelity became only gradually apparent. Her defaming by the

terms of 1:2 is then editorial. This interpretation also suggests that Gomer was redeemed from slavery, into which her sinful course had brought her (ch. 3). This somewhat sentimentalizes the relations of Hosea and Gomer. Moreover, the unusual word translated "bought" at 3:2 appears from Ugaritic usage to mean "to pay the marriage price for." This is actually the first mention of marriage in the story. In 2:2 ff. the Lord's situation is exactly parallel to Hosea's.

A more recent view (Robinson and others) holds that Gomer was a sacred prostitute. The woman the prophet was led of God first to love (ch. 1) and ultimately to marry (ch. 3) is clearly described as an adulteress (3:1). This fact and the terms by which she and her offspring are introduced (1:2) are also descriptive of Israel throughout the book (1:2; 2:2, 5 ff.; 4:2, 10, 18; 5:4; 6:10; 8:9; 9:1). Gomer was indeed a harlot whom the prophet was initially called to redeem and discipline through marriage as a sign of God's inestimable love for an unworthy people. Amidst his denunciations of the many recurring manifestations of Israel's political, social, moral, and religious degeneracy, Hosea reveals the Lord's readiness to forgive and his yearning desire to save his people (2:18–23; 10:9–15; 11:8–11; 14:1–9).

See also AMOS.

BIBLIOGRAPHY: J. Lindblom, *Hosea literarisch untersucht,* 1927; S. L. Brown, *The Book of Hosea,* 1932; H. S. Nyberg, *Studien zum Hoseabuche,* 1935; T. H. Robinson, *Die zwoelf kleinen Propheten, Hosea bis Micha,* 1936.

[Sup.] CHARLES M. COOPER.

HOSKIER, HERMAN CHARLES: Episcopalian; b. London, Nov. 12, 1864; d. Sept. 8, 1939. He studied at Eton College; in France and Germany; and at Amsterdam (Th.D.). He entered banking and brokerage in New York and retired to devote himself to New Testament textual criticism. He served in the French army (1914–19). He was particularly interested in the interrelations of the Syriac, Coptic, Ethiopic, Latin, and Greek texts of the New Testament. His main writings were . . . *Account and Collation of the Greek Codex Evangelium 604* (1890); *The Golden Latin Gospels JP in the Library of J. Pierpont Morgan* (1910); *Concerning the Genesis of the Versions of the New Testament* (2 vols., 1910–11); *Concerning the Date of the Bohairic Version* (1911); *Codex B and its Allies* (2 vols., 1913–14); *Immortality* (1925); *Concerning the Text of the Apocalypse* (2 vols., 1929); *The Complete Commentary of Oecumenius on the Apocalypse* (1928); *Bernard of Cluny's De contemptu mundi* (1929); *In Tune with the Universe* (1931); *The Back of Beyond* (1934).

DANIEL JOHANNES THERON.

HOSKYNS, EDWIN: Anglican; b. May 22, 1851, at Aston-Tirrold, Berkshire; d. at Southwell, Dec. 2, 1925. He studied at Jesus College, Cambridge, where he became a fellow; ordained a deacon (1874), and a priest (1875); curate, Welwyn, Herts; Quebec Chapel, London (1879–81); vicar, St. Clements, North Kensington (1881–86); rector, St. Dunstan, Stepney (1886–95); vicar of Balton (1895–1901); honorary canon of Manchester from 1899; rector of Burnley (1901–4); bishop of Burnley (1901–5); bishop of Southwell (1905–25). He devoted himself to the improvement of the workers' conditions.

BIBLIOGRAPHY: *Alumni Cantabrigienses*, Vol. II, 1752–1900; *The New International Year Book*, 1925.

DANIEL JOHANNES THERON.

HOSPICE: As early as the reign of Constantine hospices appeared as shelters for the sick, the poor, orphans, the old, and travelers. Through the centuries, as hospitals (*q.v.*), orphanages (see CHILDREN, CARE OF), and other specialized agencies arose to meet the needs of specific groups, the term "hospice" came to apply only to shelters for travelers. Established in uninhabited areas, at difficult mountain passes, and in other places of extreme need, hospices served thousands of the faithful who in the Middle Ages undertook pilgrimages.

In modern times the hospice of the Great St. Bernard Pass in the Swiss Alps has been the best known. It was founded by St. Bernard of Menthon in 962 and has sheltered as many as 25,000 travelers a year. From the hospice and small huts on adjacent mountains the monks of St. Bernard with their famous dogs have gone out to search for travelers lost in the snow. Once hospitality was free to all. Because of abuse by tourists the Great St. Bernard Hospice today receives, between July and September, only pedestrians and travelers definitely in need. Others are referred to a standard hotel on the grounds.

Among Protestants the name "hospice" has been applied to guest houses in which people are offered a substitute for the atmosphere of a Christian home while traveling or during temporary residence in a town. Since 1860 more than 125 such hospices were established in Germany, Austria, Switzerland, and Sweden to supplement the *Herbergen zur Heimat* (*q.v.*), and in 1904 they formed an Association of Christian Hospices.

In Great Britain and America the Y.M.C.A. (*q.v.*) and Y.W.C.A. (*q.v.*) performed a similar function. However, some church bodies and the Salvation Army (*q.v.*) also established what were variously called hospices, hostels, shelters, residence houses, and residence clubs to provide accommodation and a Christian environment for students, young men or women employed in business or industry, and others who were temporarily away from home.

GROVER L. HARTMAN.

HOSPITALERS, OR KNIGHTS OF ST. JOHN: Were founded in 1048 at a hospital in Jerusalem built by merchants from the Italian port of Amalfi. The hospital was intended for the care of sick pilgrims and was dedicated to John the Baptist. St. Gerard (d. 1120) provided a new and better organization. The next chief officer was Raymond de Puy (1120–1160), who supplied the first definitive rule for the order, confirmed in 1130 by Pope Innocent II. After 1137, secular knights were also permitted to join and then become religious knights. They were called upon to protect the pilgrims who went unarmed. The order was modeled after the Templars (*q.v.*). After 1113 it possessed other hospitals and homes for pilgrims, particularly in France. After the loss of Jerusalem to the Seljuk Turks in 1187, Acre became the center of the order, and later Rhodes. In 1522 the knights were driven out of Rhodes, whereupon Charles V gave them the island of Malta. Napoleon deprived them of this haven of refuge, and upon his overthrow it became a possession of the British.

BIBLIOGRAPHY: R. G. Kingsley, *The Order of St. John of Jerusalem*, 1918; R. Cohen, *Knights of Malta 1523–1798*, 1920; F. W. Ryan, *The House of the Temple*, 1930; E. W. Schermerhorn, *Malta of the Knights*, 1930; E. J. King, *The Knights Hospitalers in the Holy Land*, 1931; E. E. Hume, *Medical Works of the Knights Hospitalers of Saint John of Jerusalem*, 1940; E. W. S. Schermerhorn, *On the Trail of the Eight-pointed Cross: A Study of the Heritage of the Knights Hospitalers in Feudal Europe*, 1940; H. von Huelsen, *Tragoedie der Ritterorden: Templer, Deutsche Herren, Malteser*, 1948.

[Sup.] ALBERT HYMA.

HOSPITALS, CHURCH-RELATED: The interrelationship between religion and healing antedates the Christian era, but Christ's concern for the sick gave it not only a new but a more intense impetus. Through his influence his disciples cultivated an attitude of compassion, and after his ascension his Spirit continued to motivate his followers with concern for the welfare of others down through the centuries until the present time.

The pattern was set in the ancient church, where there were three dominant beliefs concerning the health of the human body: (1) Some denied the needs of the flesh. They withdrew from the world and made no constructive contribution in the field of Christian healing. (2) Many maintained that God created the body and could miraculously heal any of its diseases if he so desired. However, it was believed that God healed through those whom he endowed with special powers for that purpose, and some saints became better known than others for their healing powers. It was also believed that since they were endowed with miraculous forces while they were alive, their remains as well as their possessions continued to have such power after death. (3) The majority believed that God could use the healing arts, both medicine and surgery, to restore health or to heal when it would benefit the patient spiritually. Motivated by compassion, many of them devoted their lives and their wealth in a ministry to the sick, to orphans (*q.v.*), widows, and the aged (*q.v.*).

During the first four centuries of the Christian era, xenodochia were built and serviced in which medication, surgery, and Christian nursing care were offered to the sick. Pioneers in the field of Christian healing were wealthy Roman matrons who became deaconesses (*q.v.*), such as Paula, Macrina, Fabiola, and others. The xenodochia, ancestors of modern church-related hospitals, were built and maintained through the generosity of Christians who devoted their wealth to this expression of compassion.

Hospitals were constructed by the church throughout the Middle Ages, and nursing service was given by male and female orders, such as the Knights Hospitalers, Alexians, Brothers of Charity, Benedictines, Sisters of Mercy. Beghards (*q.v.*), Beguines, and others.

For more than two hundred years after the Reformation, Protestants defaulted in the healing of the sick, as far as institutions are involved in it, although some leaders realized the importance of religion in health and sickness. From 1820 to 1845 at least four different Protestant religious leaders of Germany succeeded in reviving the ancient diaconate. Theodor Fliedner (*q.v.*, Vol. IV), the founder of the Kaiserswerth Institutions where Florence Nightingale trained, did more than any other to revive interest in Christian healing among the Protestants of Europe and North America.

In 1848 a Lutheran clergyman of Pittsburgh, Pa., W. A. Passavant (*q.v.*, Vol. VIII), rented a house and started what is believed to be the first Protestant hospital in the United States. Members of other Protestant denominations watched the experiment closely and soon other denominations were doing the same thing. Various Lutheran bodies, as well as Methodist, Evangelical and Reformed, Presbyterian, Baptist, Salvation Army, Mennonite, Episcopal, Seventh-day Adventist, and other bodies, established hospitals in the United States.

In almost every instance the motivation in founding the institutions of healing was compassion for the sick and the suffering. The movement gained momentum around the turn of the century, and in the years between 1900 and 1920 many Protestant hospitals were founded. The movement has waned since then, due in part, perhaps, to a decline in the number of women entering the office of deaconess in the various denominations. But the movement still has considerable impetus, and new hospitals are being founded each year under Protestant aus-

pices. The same may be said of Roman Catholic orders and of the Jews.

At the present time Protestant church-related hospitals are organized in the American Protestant Hospital Association, and representatives of the institutions meet in convention annually. There are 520 church-related hospitals affiliated with the Association. These institutions serve approximately 2,300,000 patients annually and have a daily occupancy of a little over 60,000. It should also be said that there may be many other Protestant sponsored hospitals of which the writer has no knowledge because they are not known in the records of the Association.

In 1908 Elwood Worcester, rector of Emmanuel Episcopal Church of Boston, his associate Samuel McComb, and the physician Isador Coriot became the authors of a book entitled *Religion and Health*. It grew out of their clinics, which were held in Boston, and was widely read as well as discussed. It served the purpose of reviving an interest in the interrelationship of religion and health.

The next important step was sponsored by the Federal Council of the Churches of Christ in America (*q.v.*) when the Commission on Religion and Health was organized in 1926, although considerable groundwork was done in this field by a small group of leaders in medicine and religion for a number of years prior to the formal organization of the department.

Leaders in the field soon became aware of the need for more spiritual care in Protestant hospitals. *The Art of Ministering to the Sick* (1936), by Richard C. Cabot and Russell L. Dicks, became and still is considered to be a classic in this field. The movement grew, and the American Protestant Hospital Association made surveys to ascertain how much spiritual work was actually being done in hospitals. In 1946 the Chaplains Association was organized at the annual meeting in Philadelphia. This organization has grown constantly and indicates that the spiritual care of patients is considered important in church-related hospitals. See also Chaplains.

In 1947 the Catholic Hospital Association of the United States and Canada reported 1038 hospitals with 160,058 beds. Catholic hospitals usually have resident clergymen who are designated as chaplains of the institutions. In 1951 there were also fifty-seven hospitals in the United States under Jewish auspices in twenty-seven different communities. These have a bed capacity of 15,837 and they served 419,809 patients during that year.

Bibliography: *Yearbook of Jewish Social Services*, 1952; Carl J. Scherzer, *The Church and Healing*, 1950; Albert G. Hahn (ed.), American Protestant Hospital Association *Bulletin*; G. Uhlhorn, *Die christliche Liebestaetigkeit*, 1895.

CARL J. SCHERZER.

HOSTEL. See HOSPICE.

HOTMAN, FRANCIS: French jurist and Calvinist layman; b. Aug. 23, 1524; d. Feb. 12, 1590. Hotman studied civil law in Orleans and began lecturing on it in Paris, 1546. He fled to Lyons, ca. 1548, and got in touch with Calvin. From then on he was in constant contact with the leaders of Reformed Protestantism. Through Calvin he got a job teaching Latin in Lausanne (1549–55). Thereafter he taught law in Strasbourg (1555–63); Valence (1563–66); Bourges (1567–72); Geneva (1573–78); Basle (1578–84); Geneva (1584–89); Basle (1589–90). Religious persecution often forced him to stop teaching, notably in 1567–70 and 1572. Political activity also interrupted his scholarly work. He was active in the planning of the Conspiracy of Amboise (1560). He often served as diplomatic representative of the Huguenot leaders at the courts of the German Protestant princes and in the Swiss cantons. He was Historiographer of the King of France for a short time in 1567. Alchemy seems to have fascinated him.

In some fifty legal works and political pamphlets Hotman attacked Roman and canonical legal concepts (see especially ANTI-TRIBONIAN), and defended the French Protestant cause. He bitterly attacked Catholic ecclesiastical authorities in such works as *Le Tigre* and *Brutum fulmen.* He is especially famous for his *Franco-Gallia,* an eloquent attempt to prove the historic right of lesser French magistrates to overthrow a royal tyrant. It was written in 1573, soon after the St. Bartholomew's Massacre. Many years later, when Protestant Henry of Navarre became heir to the French throne, Hotman turned to a defence of royal legitimacy in his *De jure successionis.*

BIBLIOGRAPHY: *Franc. Hotmani Iuriconsulti Operum,* 3 vols., 1599–1600; . . . *Epistolae* . . . , 1700; Eug. and Em. Haag, *La France Protestante* . . . , Vol. V (1846–58), pp. 525–540; R. Dareste, "François Hotman, sa vie et sa correspondence," in *Revue historique,* II (1876), 1–59, 367–435, and supplement in *ibid.,* XCVII (1908), 297–315; Beatrice Reynolds, *Proponents of limited monarchy in sixteenth century France: Francis Hotman and Jean Bodin,* 1931; Pierre Mesnard, *L'Essor de la philosophie politique au XVIe siècle* (1936), pp. 327–336.
ROBERT M. KINGDON.

HOUGH, LYNN HAROLD: B. Sept. 10, 1877. He studied at Scio College (A.B., 1898); and Drew Theological Seminary (B.D., 1905; Th.D., 1919). He was pastor, among other churches, of Central Methodist, Detroit, and American Presbyterian Church, Montreal. He was professor of historical theology at Garrett Biblical Institute (1914–19), and dean of Drew Theological Seminary (1934–47). Among his books are: *Athanasius the Hero* (1906); *The Theology of a Preacher* (1912); *The Man of Power* (1916); *A Living Book in a Living Age* (1918); *The Significance of the Protestant Reformation* (1918); *The Productive Beliefs* (1919); *The Opinions of John Clearfield* (1921); *Life and History* (1922); *The Strategy of the Devo-*

tional Life (1922); *The Inevitable Book* (1922); *Synthetic Christianity* (1923); *Evangelical Humanism* (1925); *Adventures in the Minds of Men* (1927); *Imperishable Dreams* (1929); *The Artist and the Critic* (1930); *Personality and Science* (1930); *The University of Experience* (1932); *Vital Control* (1934); *The Church and Civilization* (1934); *The Great Evangel* (1935); *The Civilized Mind* (1937); *Free Men* (1939); *The Christian Criticism of Life* (1941); *Adventures in Understanding* (1941); *Patterns of the Mind* (1942); *Living Democracy* (1943); *The Meaning of Human Experience* (1945); *Christian Humanism and the Modern World* (1947); and *The Dignity of Man* (1950).

HOUSE OF DAVID: A communal religious sect and colony founded at Benton Harbor, Mich., in 1903 by "King Benjamin" Purnell, who styled himself the "seventh messenger" of Rev. 8:6, 11–15. The members surrendered their property to the leader and carried on certain agricultural and industrial pursuits.

In 1923 Purnell became involved in one of the worst scandals in the history of American religious movements; financial and sexual irregularities were charged, and he died while these matters were in the courts.

The adherents of the House of David number around 350 persons. They are vegetarians, the men do not shave or cut their hair, and ardent millennial hopes are entertained.

BIBLIOGRAPHY: E. T. Clark, *The Small Sects in America,* rev. ed., 1949; and the literature cited there.
ELMER T. CLARK.

HOUSE OF FAITH. See HOUSE OF PRAYER FOR ALL THE PEOPLE.

HOUSE OF GOD. See CHURCH (CHURCHES) OF GOD.

HOUSE OF PRAYER FOR ALL THE PEOPLE: An extreme pentecostal (*q.v.*) Negro sect founded by a "Bishop" Grace in the 1930's. Its services are characterized by highly emotional experiences and such motor automata as trances, dances, shouting, and speaking with tongues (*q.v.*). The leader is regarded as a messiah or near-divinity. He has headquarters in Philadelphia and the Harlem section of New York City, and has several churches elsewhere. No statistics were ever available.

A small group broke away and took the name House of Faith. A similar body is the "Latter House of the Lord for All People and the Church on the Mountain, Apostolic Faith," founded at Cincinnati, Ohio, in 1936 by L. W. Williams; it has half a dozen churches and claims 4,000 members. Still another bears the long name of the "House of God, the Holy Church of the Living God, the Pillar and Ground of the Truth, House of Prayer for All

People." It was founded at Washington, D. C., in 1914, by R. A. R. Johnson and has four or five churches and about two hundred members.

BIBLIOGRAPHY: E. T. Clark, *The Small Sects in America*, rev. ed., 1949.

ELMER T. CLARK.

HOUSE OF THE LORD. See CHURCH (CHURCHES) OF GOD.

HOUTIN, ALBERT: Roman Catholic modernist, priest, and historian; b. 1867; d. 1926. His *Question biblique*, written at Loisy's suggestion, was placed on the Index (1903). He left the church in 1912, shortly before publishing his *Histoire du modernisme catholique*. Complete bibliography in *Mon Expérience*, Vol. II (1928), pp. 405–465. WALTER MARSHALL HORTON.

HOWARD, WILBERT FRANCIS: Methodist; b. at Gloucester, England, Dec. 30, 1880; d. at Cambridge, England, July 12, 1952. He studied at Manchester and London. After several pastorates (1905–19), he became professor of New Testament language and literature at Handsworth College, Birmingham (1919–51; principal, 1943–51). He was editor and joint author of J. H. Moulton's *Grammar of N. T. Greek*, Vol. II (1929); I & II Corinthians in *Abingdon Commentary* (1929); Acts in *Study Bible* (1929), John in *Interpreter's Bible* (1952); *The Fourth Gospel in Recent Criticism and Interpretation* (1931); *Christianity according to St. John* (1943); *The Romance of N. T. Scholarship* (1949).

HOWISON, GEORGE HOLMES: B. Nov. 29, 1834, in Montgomery Co., Md.; d. 1916. He studied at Marietta College (A.B., 1852; A.M., 1855); Lane Theological Seminary (grad., 1855); and at Berlin (1881–82). He taught at Washington University, St. Louis, Mo. (mathematics, 1864–66; political economy, 1866–69); was professor of logic and philosophy of science at Massachusetts Institute of Technology (1871–79); lectured on ethics at Harvard (1879–80); on philosophy at Michigan (1883–84); and was Mills professor of philosophy at the University of California (1884–1909). A very inspiring and successful teacher of philosophy, Howison stressed a theistic personalism in which he defined God as Perfect Person, Final Cause and Center of the republic of persons with emphasis on the freedom and dignity of the soul. Among his books are: (coauthor), *The Conception of God* (1897); *Limits of Evolution, and Other Essays in Philosophy* (1901; 2nd ed., 1904); *Philosophy—Its Fundamental Conceptions and Methods* (in Vol. I, Congress of Arts and Sciences, 1904); and (coauthor), *The Conception of God* (1907).

BIBLIOGRAPHY: J. W. Buckham and G. M. Stratton, *George Holmes Howison, Philosopher and Teacher* (1933): contains biography and *The Limits of Evolution* and

other writings; C. M. Bakewell, "The Personal Idealism of George Holmes Howison," in *Philosophical Review*, XLIX (1940); and J. W. Buckham, "The Contribution of Professor Howison to Christian Thought," in *Harvard Theological Review*, IX (1916).

RAYMOND W. ALBRIGHT.

HOYT MEMORIAL FOUNDATION: Established at Auburn Theological Seminary in 1927 as a memorial by his friends to Arthur S. Hoyt, who had been professor of Homiletics at Auburn for many years until his death in 1924. Its purpose was to bring to Auburn distinguished teachers and preachers. From 1939, when Auburn Seminary became associated with Union Theological Seminary, the lectures were given in New York. Among lecturers on the Foundation have been John Baillie, Douglas V. Steere, James S. Stewart, Theodore O. Wedel, and Halford E. Luccock. ROBERT T. HANDY.

HROMÁDKA, JOSEF L.: Evangelical Church of Czech Brethren; b. at Hodslavice, Moravia, Czechoslovakia, June 8, 1889. He studied theology at the universities of Vienna, Basel, Heidelberg, United Free Church College, Aberdeen (1907–12); philosophy at the University of Prague (Ph.D., 1920). He was minister of Evangelical Church (1912–20); professor of systematic theology, John Hus Theological Faculty, Prague (1920–39); and guest professor of apologetics and Christian ethics, Princeton Theological Seminary, Princeton, N. J. (1939–47). After returning to Czechoslovakia, he became professor of systematic theology, John Hus Theological Faculty (1947–50), dean (head) of John Amos Comenius Faculty, Prague (1950–). He wrote among others: *Catholicism and the Struggle for Christianity* (1925); *Principles of the Evangelical Church of Czech Brethren* (1927); *The Ways of a Protestant Theologian* (1927); *Masaryk* (1930); *Christianity in Thought and Life* (1931); *Luther* (1935); *Calvin* (1936); *Theology and Church* (1949); *Doom and Resurrection* (1945; tr. into Japanese); and is editor of *Křeslanksk á Revue* (Christian Review).

HUDSON, WINTHROP S.: Baptist; b. at Schoolcraft, Mich., Aug. 28, 1911. He studied at Kalamazoo College (B.A., 1933), Colgate-Rochester Divinity School (B.D., 1937), and University of Chicago (Ph.D., 1940); was minister of the Normal Park Baptist Church, Chicago (1937–42); instructor in the Colgate-Rochester Divinity School (1942–44); assistant professor in the University of Chicago (1944–47); and professor of the history of Christianity in the Colgate-Rochester Divinity School (1947–). He was president of the American Society of Church History (1948), vice-president of the American Baptist Historical Society (1950–), and editor of *Church History* (1950). He wrote: *John Ponet: Advocate of Limited Monarchy* (1942); and *The Great Tradition of the American*

Churches (1953); he edited: Henry Scougal, *Life of God in the Soul of Man* (1948); and Roger Williams, *Experiments of Spiritual Life and Health* (1951); and was coeditor of *Christian Leadership in a World Society* (1945).

HUEGEL, FRIEDRICH VON: B. 1852; d. 1925. A Roman Catholic interpreter of religion who warned against the impoverishment that inevitably came to any form of the Christian religion that neglected to hold the three principal elements of religion: the mystical, the institutional, and the intellectual together in a dynamic tension. As the "theologian's theologian" his influence on Protestant thought in England where he resided during his adult life was immense. His *Mystical Element of Religion* (2 vols., 1908; 2nd ed., 1923) is a classic study of the phenomena of the mystical life and of their psychological and philosophical interpretation. His emphasis upon the givenness of God and upon the transcendent quality of the reality of God antedated by a decade the Barthian accent in this direction and prevented Barthianism from sweeping England with its novelty. This placing of the interpretation of the essential religious experience in a realist frame appears with increasing clarity in the volumes that follow: *Eternal Life* (1912); *Essays and Addresses in the Philosophy of Religion* (First Series, 1921; Second Series, 1926); *Selected Letters* (1927); and *The Reality of God* (1931). The best biography is Bedoyere, *Baron Friedrich von Huegel;* and the best interpretation of his thought is Nedoncelle, *Baron Friedrich von Huegel.*   Douglas V. Steere.

HUGHES, EDWIN HOLT: D. Feb. 12, 1950. A most distinguished representative of the Methodist church of his generation as a scholar, educator and preacher, he served as a bishop (1908–40), being the senior bishop of his church during the last four years. He began his episcopal service in California and after his retirement served again in the Washington, D.C. area (1943–47), and in Wisconsin (1947–48). He was the acting president of Boston University (1923) and acting chancellor of American University (1933). He was the chairman of the joint commission on the union of the American Methodist Churches. His later books are: *Thanksgiving Sermons* (1909); *The Teaching of Citizenship* (1909); *A Boy's Religion* (1914); *The Bible and Life* (1914); *God's Family* (1926); *Christianity and Success* (1928); (coauthor), *Worship in Music* (1929); *Are You an Evangelist?* (1937); *Evangelism and Change* (1938); and *I Was Made a Minister* (autobiography, 1943). [Sup.] Raymond W. Albright.

HUGHES, PHILIP: Roman Catholic; b. in Manchester, England, 1895. He graduated from the seminary at Leeds (1920). After his ordination he went to the University of Louvain, became a member of the Seminar Historique, and received the Lic. en sciences hist. (1921). He did research work in Rome (1921–23) under the direction of Cardinal Gasquet, O.S.B. He worked in the parishes of Manchester, England (1924–31) and he was archivist of Westminster (1934–39). After a period as secretary to Bishop Casartelli he came to the College of St. Thomas at St. Paul, Minnesota, and took up a professorship then vacated by the leave of absence of Rev. Nicholas M. Moelter. Father Hughes' works include: *The Catholic Question, 1688–1829; A Study in Political History; History of the Church* (3 vols., 1934 ff.); *St. John Fisher; Pope Pius XI* (1937); *The Faith in Practice* (1938); *A Popular History of the Church;* and *Pope's New Order* (1943).

HUGO OF ST. VICTOR: Although some Dutch writers have recently declared that he was born at Ypres in Flanders in 1096 (as in J. de Jong, *Handboek der kerkgeschiedenis,* Vol. II [4th ed., 1947], p. 197: error by R. R. Post), he is correctly called Hugo of Blankenburg in A. Fliche and V. Martin, *Histoire de l'Eglise,* Vol. VIII (1946), p. 459.

Bibliography: C. Buttimer, *Hugonis de S. V. Didascalion. De studio legendi,* 1939; P. Wolff, *Die Viktoriner. Mystische Schriften, ausgewaehlt,* 1936; H. Koester, *Die Heilslehre des Hugo von St. Viktor,* 1940; E. Poppenberg, *Die christologie des Hugo von St. Viktor,* 1937; H. Weisweiler, *Die Wirksamkeit der Sakramente nach Hugo von St. Viktor,* 1932; W. Schneider, *Geschichte und Geschichtsphilosophie bei Hugo von St. Viktor,* 1933.

[Sup.] Albert Hyma.

HUGUENOTS: Study of the Huguenot movement has developed along two lines.

First, there has been expansion of knowledge about French Protestantism. This work has been promoted by the Society for the History of French Protestantism with headquarters in Paris. Beginning about the middle of the nineteenth century monographs have appeared describing all aspects of Huguenot history. The journal, *Bulletin de la Société de l'histoire du Protestantisme français,* has presented much valuable material. Other works, especially documents and memoirs, have appeared dealing with the people concerned in the Huguenot movement. J. W. Thompson, *The Wars of Religion (1559–1576)* (1909), is sound though biased. Special attention has been given Huguenot political theory, as Guy H. Dodge, *The Political Thought of the Huguenots with special reference to the thought and influence of Pierre Jurien* (1947). In addition to the usual bibliographical sources the following may be valuable: E. E. Strude, *A Bibliography of works relating to the huguenot refugees* (1886); Eugène Arnaud, *Bibliographie huguenot du Dauphiné pendant les trois derniers siècles*

(1894); *Catalogue or Bibliography of the Huguenot Society of America* (1920).

Secondly, Huguenot research has been directed towards the emigrant families in the lands beyond France. Because of the social conditions and political pressures the refugees were at pains to hide their French origins and many changed or translated their family names: Tonnellier became Kieffer and Cooper, Garrigues became Garrick, etc. In Leyden the *Commission Wallone* has created a Huguenot-Walloon Card Index listing Protestants who fled France and Belgium between 1566 and 1800. More than a million and a half names are listed, alphabetically by family names, lexicographically by given names, and chronologically by families. The section covering the period 1566–1700 contains more than half a million cards. Both church and civil records have been searched and almost all Huguenot refugees now are known.

This special interest in the Huguenots of the Dispersion, as they are called, and their integration into European and American culture has led to the founding of Huguenot societies on three continents. The foremost of these is the Huguenot Society of London. There also are Huguenot societies in Berlin, in the Union of South Africa, and in North America. The Huguenot Society of America, located in New York, maintains an excellent library, and the Huguenot Society of South Carolina is associated with the oldest French-speaking Protestant congregation in America. The Huguenot Society of Pennsylvania has led in the celebration of significant Huguenot anniversaries. Other societies have been organized in New Jersey, Michigan, California, West Virginia, Virginia, Ohio, North Carolina, and other states. In 1950 the National Huguenot Society was formed, supplanting a looser federation.

The London Society has led in publishing records of the refugees, especially of Huguenots in Great Britain. Their first volume appeared in 1885 and the forty-second in 1950. Gilbert Chinard has written *Les Refugées huguenots en Amérique* (1925); other works about the migrations are: G. L. Lee, *The Huguenot Settlements in Ireland* (1936); Arthur H. Hirsch, *The Huguenots in Colonial South Carolina* (1928); A. Stapelton, *Memorials of the Huguenots in America with Special Reference to their Emigration to Pennsylvania* (1901); L. J. Fosdick, *The French Blood in America* (1906).

A short survey with bibliography is found in Otto Zoff, *The Huguenots Fighters for God and Human Freedom* (1942).

In 1924 the Federal Council of Churches, through its Huguenot-Walloon Commission directed by John Baer Stoudt, caused Huguenot anniversaries to be celebrated in America and Europe. Monuments were dedicated. The United States government issued a set of stamps commemorating the Huguenots and a memorial half-dollar was minted.

[Sup.] JOHN JOSEPH STOUDT.

HUMANI GENERIS: An encyclical issued by Pope Pius XII on August 12, 1950. It denounces "historicism," which tends to reinterpret Christian doctrines on the basis of an evolutionistic philosophy, and "existentialism," a system which, according to the Pope, "neglects the immutable nature of things, while being concerned exclusively with the 'existence' of individual realities." Both ideologies are held responsible for introducing elements of relativity into dogmatics, and for tying essential Christian beliefs with the passing conditions of history, thus threatening faith itself. A strict adherence to the philosophy of Aquinas is considered as the best way to secure a foundation for theology. Catholics are urged to observe an extreme caution in meeting non-Roman scholars, lest they may be tempted to harmonize their differences of belief at the expense of the official teaching of the church. The encyclical concludes with urging Roman Catholic exegetes to follow scrupulously the decree of the Pontifical Biblical Commission (June 30, 1909), on the interpretation of the first eleven chapters of Genesis as history, not myth. The original text is in *Acta Apostolicae Sedis,* Vol. XXXII (1950), pp. 561–578.

GEORGES A. BARROIS.

HUMANISM, CONTEMPORARY: Humanism as an intellectual conception sprang from a spacious etymology and developed along broad avenues. That which is characteristically human, not supernatural, that which belongs peculiarly to man and not to nature at large, that which elevates man or at least satisfies him, is likely to be called humanism. Even as classical humanism was sometimes a form, sometimes a subject and at other times a spirit, later humanism may mean many things. It may be the even balance of life rediscovered in Hellenism, it may be the responsiveness to all the human passions as described by a romantic poet or it may be a philosophy of which man is the core. It is in this last sense that humanism has had its greatest significance since the sixteenth century.

The term humanism has been readily applied to several philosophical movements whose views of the world would make humanity the primary object of interest. Their fundamental formula is found in the statement of Protagoras that "man is the measure of all things." This critical proposition stresses the relativity of all knowledge to human capacity and questions any attempt to elevate human knowledge to some superhuman level (see RELATIVISM).

F. C. S. Schiller used humanism as a technical term in philosophy, making the word describe his own variety of pragmatism (*q.v.*). Schiller followed the philosophic movement of William James and in 1903 he proposed to James that he change the name of his movement from pragmatism to humanism. As Schiller uses the word he opposes it to the two attitudes which dominated the philosophical world, absolutism and naturalism. Absolutism was the attempt to describe reality by assuming the standpoint of the ultimate whole; humanism was critical of this as it asserted that the hypothesis of absolute knowledge by absolute reality in no way proved or assisted human knowing (see ABSOLUTE; IDEALISM). Naturalism tried to describe reality in terms of a nature wherein man was reduced to a mere natural phenomenon; again humanism criticized that this view overlooked human activity and could not truly interpret nature with man excluded. Thus humanism is essentially a protest against the dehumanizing and depersonalizing aspects of both the natural sciences (*q.v.*) and metaphysics. Its chief interest is in epistemology (*q.v.*) and its critique is directed against those logics which ignore the volitions, desires, emotions and purposes of the human personality.

The same term, humanism, also applies to the American movement led by Irving Babbitt and Paul Elmer More. This form protests against excessive vocationalism in education and advocates the revival of liberal education in classical literature. This philosophy maintains that man is capable of self-direction and that his character may grow in clarity and strength of purpose. The humanist contends that we are free agents accountable for our errors and that self-complacency is the deadliest foe to human excellence.

Another self-styled humanism is the Continental movement led by Jean Paul Sartre. Under influence from Kierkegaard and Heidegger, being is for Sartre the final reality and nothingness is its content (see EXISTENTIALISM). This nothingness is an objective metaphysical entity to which we subjectively respond in anxiety or dread. Man is utterly alone. He is condemned to be free and no help can come to him from the outside. He aspires always striving for the impossible which cannot be. Free and alone, he is doomed to frustration and eternal incompleteness.

See also POSITIVISM.

BIBLIOGRAPHY: Norman Foerster (ed.), *Humanism and America*, 1930; Erich Kahler, *Man the Measure*, 1943; J. S. Mackenzie, *Lectures on Humanism*, 1907; Paul E. More, *On Being Human*, 1936; J. P. Sartre (tr. by Bernard Fretchman), *What is Literature?* 1949; F. C. S. Schiller, *Humanism: Philosophical Essays*, 1912; *idem*, *Studies in Humanism*, 1912.

EUGENE LIGGITT.

HUME, DAVID. See EMPIRICISM.

HUNGARY: After World War I, Hungary, which had fought on the side of the Central Powers, was for a short time seized by the Communists. But Admiral Horthy overthrew this regime and himself became regent (presumably in behalf of the Habsburg dynasty). By the Treaty of Trianon, the territory of the country was reduced to about one third of its former size. The Magyars refused to accept this postwar settlement. Consequently, when World War II started, Hungary soon gravitated into the German orbit. In 1944 Nazis occupied the country and deposed Horthy. Hungary was invaded by the Russian Army late in 1944. But despite the support given to the Hungarian Communist party, the latter was too small to take over the regime immediately. In 1946 a republic was set up, and the power was in the hands of the Small Landowners Party. But two years later the Communists, with the support of the Soviet regime and the use of force and chicanery, succeeded in seizing the government.

The Roman Catholic population of the land amounted to 66%; the primate of the Church since 1945 was Cardinal Mindszenty. He had been imprisoned by the Nazis, and opposed the Communists as well, particularly the confiscation of church lands and the secularization of the educational system. In 1946 all religious associations were dissolved; this was particularly aimed at Catholic youth. The most serious danger came from the determined policy of the state to bring up the young generation in its radically secularist view of life: textbooks in use were completely rewritten from the Communist point of view; teaching of religion was forbidden; and finally the parochial schools (5,500 of them, of which 3,000 were Catholic) were nationalized. Cardinal Mindszenty and the episcopate vigorously protested and the cardinal was arrested (1948).

All Catholic publications were banned in 1949 and the presses were confiscated. Leaders of Catholic Action (*q.v.*) were jailed. The cardinal, broken by torture, confessed to the "crimes" imputed to him and was sentenced to life imprisonment. The formula in use in the Soviet Union, granting "freedom of religious worship and antireligious propaganda," was incorporated into the constitution. Bishops and clergy were called upon to take an oath of loyalty. Bishops refused, but allowed the priests to take the oath with reservations. Many monasteries were confiscated, and some monastic orders expelled.

Protestants (1,935,000 of whom were Calvinists, 557,000 Lutherans) yielded to the pressure without great struggle. The Reformed bishop, Ladislas Ravasz, was deposed, and his place of leadership was taken by a subservient ecclesiastic, Bereczky. The submission of the Hungarian Church to the Communists is said to have been counseled by Karl Barth (*q.v.*). Lutheran Bishop Lajos Ordass was falsely charged with transgression of the currency laws and likewise deposed.

The Jews suffered persecution and many fled abroad. All Zionist organizations were dissolved (see ZIONISM). Many were deported to labor camps in Siberia. All Jewish wealth was confiscated.

BIBLIOGRAPHY: Kenneth G. Grubb and E. J. Bingle (eds.), *World Christian Handbook*, 1949; Gary MacEoin, *The Communist War on Religion*, 1951.

[Sup.] MATTHEW SPINKA.

HUNT, WILLIAM HOLMAN: B. London, April 2, 1827; d. London, Sept. 7, 1910. He was educated in private schools and entered the Royal Academy Schools in 1843. At the Academy his great friendship with Millais began. In 1840 with Millais and Rossetti, Hunt laid the foundation of the Pre-Raphaelite Brotherhood. His painting, "The Light of the World," was exhibited in the Academy in 1854. Hunt benefited much through the friendly support of John Ruskin. Hunt travelled in Europe and made several visits to Palestine. He developed a profound religious passion. He desired to illuminate the scenes of Scripture by his work as a painter. He liked to think of himself as an artistic priest interpreting the beauty of the work of God. His great pictures were all the products of long periods of work. He received the Order of Merit in 1905 and the D.C.L. from Oxford in the same year. His body rests in Saint Paul's Cathedral. He wrote *Pre-Raphaelitism and the Pre-Raphaelite Brotherhood* (2 vols., 1905). LYNN HAROLD HOUGH.

HUNZINGER, AUGUST WILHELM: B. 1871; d. 1920. After teaching theology at Leipzig and Erlangen he became the chief pastor in Hamburg yet continuing his major theological interest, seeking especially a possible resolution of the differences between the critically liberal and the conservative theology which was a real issue in his generation. His major works include: *Lutherstudien* (1906); *Der Glaube und das religionsgeschichtliche Christentum der Gegenwart* (1907); *Zur apologetischen Aufgabe der evangelischen Kirche in der Gegenwart* (1907); *Probleme und Aufgaben der gegenwaertigen systematischen Theologie* (1909); *Theologie und Kirche* (1912); *Das Wunder* (1912); *Hauptfragen der Lebensgestaltung* (1916); and *Das Christentum im Weltanschauungskampf der Gegenwart* (3rd ed., 1919).

RAYMOND W. ALBRIGHT.

HURLBUT, JESSE L(YMAN): D. Aug. 2, 1930. After a varied ministry in his earlier years he resumed his active pastoral work and served Methodist churches at South Orange (1904–5) and Bloomfield (1906–9), and was named district superintendent of the Newark district (1909–14). In his later years he became a counsellor for the Chautauqua Literary and Scientific Circle. His later books include: *Handy Bible Encyclopedia* (1906); *Teacher Training Lessons* (1908); *Organizing and Building Up the Sunday School* (1909); *Traveling in the Holy Land Through the Stereoscope* (1913); *Story of Jesus* (1915); *Story of the Christian Church* (1918); and *The Story of Chautauqua* (1921). [Sup.] RAYMOND W. ALBRIGHT.

HURRIANS: Modern scholarship has been aware of the Hurrians only since the third decade of the present century. Yet the Hurrians are now known to have played a major part in the history of the ancient Near East. Their impact was felt from Asia Minor to Southern Babylonia and from Northern Syria to Egypt. In the Old Testament they appear as the Horites.

One reason for the late rediscovery of the Hurrians is their language. Hurrian has no family ties whatsoever with Semitic, Indo-European, or Sumerian. Among the ancient languages of the region the only established relative of Hurrian was Urartian, the speech of ancient Armenia. Distant modern relatives may be found among the dialects of the Caucasic family.

Prior to the discovery of the Hittite archives at Boghazkoy the sole extant record in Hurrian was a long letter from the Mitannian king Tushratta to Amenophis III of Egypt, which was part of the cuneiform archive from Tell el-Amarna. The Boghazköy documents include numerous Hurrian texts, mostly fragmentary. Other Hurrian documents have turned up at Ugarit, Mari, and in Northern Babylonia. With the aid of these widely scattered sources, which cover a span of a thousand years, Hurrian is gradually becoming intelligible. Hurrian personal names are now easily recognized and can readily be separated from other linguistic contexts such as Hittite, Akkadian, Ugaritic, and Canaanite proper. These names are our primary evidence for the geographic expansion of the Hurrians.

Another reason for the prolonged obscurity of the Hurrians was their rare ability to blend with other and more familiar groups. They did so most notably with the Hittites, but they were on intimate terms also with the Akkadians, the Ugaritians, and the Israelites. The Hittites owed much to the Hurrians in religion, art, script, and vocabulary. Some of these items the Hurrians had borrowed in turn from Babylonia. In the case of Israel the Hurrians left their imprint on various social customs, among them the provisions for inheritance by daughters where male heirs were lacking. See also NUZI TABLETS.

The link between the Hurrians and the biblical Horites is based on more than the linguistic identity of the two terms. Hurrian names occur on the Taanach tablets from Central Palestine. Moreover, the term *ḥorî*, "Horite," appears to have been more prominent originally than the present text of the Old Testament would lead us to expect. Thus Gen. 36:2 reads "Hiwwite," as against "Horite" in v. 20, although the same principals are involved in both passages. The Greek version reads "Horite" for "Hiwwite" not only in Gen. 36:2 but also in Josh. 9:7(13 in the Greek text). In Josh. 11:3, moreover, the Greek reads "Hittite" for the Hebrew "Hiwwite." It follows that mention of the Horites was intended in several instances which now feature Hiwwites or Hittites, the three terms being very close graphically in the Hebrew scripts.

The most independent political creation of the Hurrians was the Kingdom of Mitanni, which flourished in the third quarter of the second millennium B.C.

BIBLIOGRAPHY: E. A. Speiser, *Ethnic Movements in the Near East in the Second Millennium B. C.*, 1933; idem, *Introduction to Hurrian*, 1941; Albrecht Goetze, *Hethiter, Churriter und Assyrer*, 1936; Arthur Ungnad, *Subartu*, 1936; Ignace J. Gelb, *Hurrians and Subarians*, 1944.

EPHRAIM AVIGDOR SPEISER.

HUS, JOHN (1371–1415): The date of his birth has recently been definitely determined. He has been commonly regarded as a mere echo of Wyclif; but such is not the case. He was the product of the native Czech reform dating back to the middle of the fourteenth century. The English and Czech movements merged in Bohemia after the opening of the fifteenth century.

Hus was at first an adherent of Wyclif's philosophical realism, for the latter's theological works were not then known in Bohemia. When Hus became acquainted with Wyclif's theological views, he never accepted them fully: thus, for instance, he continued to hold the doctrine of transubstantiation. But along with Wyclif and the native reform, Hus held to the supreme authority of the Scriptures. Hence, he was not the most advanced of the Czech Wyclifites—men like Stanislav of Znojmo, Stephen of Páleč, and Jakoubek of Stříbro, were far more radical than Hus (until the defection of the two first-named).

Hus' involvement in a conflict with the ecclesiastical authorities is well known and need not be restated. It had its origin not so much in Hus' views as in the contemporaneous ecclesiastical politics. Thus the conflict with Archbishop Zbyněk arose over the latter's adherence to Pope Gregory XII, as against King Wenceslas' acknowledgments of Alexander V. The Czech university masters supported the king. When the latter forced Zbyněk to abandon Gregory, the archbishop's ire turned against

Hus' reform movements. Zbyněk's untimely death (in 1411, at the age of thirty-six) might have terminated the struggle with Hus, but by this time the case had been appealed to John XXIII. Moreover, another cause complicated the struggle. Hus lost King Wenceslas' support because he opposed the preaching of indulgences decreed by the pope. This led to his excommunication. He retired from Prague, and during this period of exile wrote some of his most radical works. Among them were *On Church* and *On Simony*. In both he advocated reform views shared generally by men like Marsiglio of Padua, William of Ockham, Henry of Langenstein, John Gerson, Peter d'Ailly, and Dietrich of Niem. Cardinal d'Ailly was among his chief accusers and judges at the Council of Constance. He was condemned as a Wyclifite heretic and burned at the stake on July 6, 1415.

BIBLIOGRAPHY: Matthew Spinka, *John Hus and the Czech Reform*, 1941; F. M. Bartoš, *Co víme nového o Husovi*, 1946; idem, *Čechy v době Husově*, 1947; David Schaff, *John Hus*, 1915. John Hus, *The Church* (David Schaff, tr.), 1915; idem, "On Simony" (M. Spinka, tr.), in *The Library of Christian Classics*, XIV (1953).

[Sup.] MATTHEW SPINKA.

HUSSERL, EDMUND. See PHENOMENALISM.

HUTCHINSON, PAUL: Methodist; b. at Madison, N. J., Aug. 10, 1890. He graduated from Lafayette College (Ph.B., 1911), and Garrett Biblical Institute (B.D., 1915). He began his career as a church journalist on the *Epworth Herald*, Methodist youth weekly published in Chicago, and in 1916 went to China, where he edited the *China Christian Advocate* and *Tsing Hua Pao*, and had general supervision of Methodist publications. In 1942, after returning to the United States, he became managing editor of *The Christian Century*, an undenominational weekly with editorial offices in Chicago and an international circulation. In 1947 be became editor. He wrote for many magazines and newspapers, and was the author of: *The Next Step* (1921); *The Spread of Christianity* (1922); *China's Real Revolution* (1924); (with H. E. Luccock), *The Story of Methodism* (1926; rev. ed., 1951); *What and Why in China* (1927); *The United States of Europe* (1929); *Men Who Made the Churches* (1930); *World Revolution and Religion* (1931); *Storm over Asia* (1932); *The Ordeal of Western Religion* (1933); *From Victory to Peace* (1943); and *The New Leviathan* (1946).

HUTTEN, KURT: Lutheran; b. at Langenburg, Germany, March 6, 1901. He studied at the universities of Tuebingen, Marburg, and Berlin (1919–23), was assistant at some churches in Wuerttemberg (1923–27), teacher at the theological seminary, Urach (1927–29; Dr. Phil., 1928). Then he worked as assistant and, since 1933, as leader of the Evangelische Presseverband for Wuerttemberg in Stuttgart. During the Nazi period he fought as a member of the Confessing Church against the philosophy of the National Socialists, was temporarily removed from his office and in 1941 his presswork was forbidden. Then he became a secretary of the Council of the Evangelical Lutheran Church in Germany in Berlin; he was called out as soldier (1943), wounded in Russia (1944), and captured by the Americans (1945). Discharged, he rebuilt his presswork in Stuttgart as representative of the Wuerttemberg Landeskirche. He wrote: *Die Bhakti-Religion in Indien und der christliche Glaube im Neuen Testament* (1928); *Kulturbolschewismus* (1932); *Um Blut und Glauben —Evangelium und voelkische Religion* (1934); *Ein neues Evangelium?* (1936); *Christus oder Deutschglaube?* (1936); *Seher, Gruebler, Enthusiasten—Sekten und religioese Sondergemeinschaften der Gegenwart* (1950).

HUTTEN, ULRICH VON:

BIBLIOGRAPHY: H. Holborn, *Ulrich von Hutten and the German Reformation*, 1937; R. Bainton, *Here I Stand: A Life of Martin Luther*, 1950; H. S. Lucas, *Renaissance and Reformation*, 1934; E. G. Schwiebert, *Life and Times of Martin Luther*, 1950—Schwiebert has made a signal contribution to our knowledge of this controversial figure; P. Kalkoff, *Ulrich von Hutten und die Reformation*, 1940; idem, *Huttens Vagantenzeit und Untergang*, 1925; D. F. Strauss, *Ulrich von Hutten*, new ed. with commentary by O. Clemen, 1927; P. Held, *Ulrich von Hutten*, 1928; F. Walser, *Die politische Entwicklung Ulrichs von Hutten waehrend der Entscheidungsjahre der Reformation*, 1928; O. Flake, *Ulrich von Hutten: Die tragische Historie des ersten politischen Deutschen*, 1929; H. Holborn, *Ulrich von Hutten*, 1929; H. Grimm, *Huttens Lehrjahre*, 1938.   [Sup.] ALBERT HYMA.

HUTTERIAN BRETHREN. See MENNONITES; COMMUNISTIC SOCIETIES.

HUTTON, JOHN ALEXANDER: Presbyterian; b. Coatbridge, Scotland, April 21, 1868; d. Jan. 13, 1947. He studied at Glasgow University, was ordained in Alyth, Perthshire (1892). He served as minister in Newcastle-on-Tyne, (1900–1906); Glasgow (1906–23), and Westminster Chapel, London (1923–25). From 1925–46 he was editor of *The British Weekly*. He often preached and lectured in the United States. He published many volumes of sermons and essays including: *Ancestral Voices; The Dark Mile; Finally; Guidance from Robert Browning in Matters of Faith.*   F. W. DILLISTONE.

HYATT, JAMES PHILIP: Disciples of Christ; b. Monticello, Ark., Feb. 16, 1909. He was educated at Baylor, Brown, and Yale Universities (Ph.D., 1938), and American School of Oriental Research in Jerusalem. He taught biblical history at Wellesley College (1935–41). In 1941 he went to Vanderbilt University; professor of Old Testament and head of the Department of Religion (1944–). He has been a member of the Revised Standard Bible Committee since 1945. He has published: *The Treatment of Final Vowels in Early Neo-Babylonian* (1941); and *Prophetic Religion* (1947).

HYDE, WILLIAM DeWITT: D. June 29, 1917. He was the president of Bowdoin College and also taught mental and moral philosophy (1885–1917). His later books are: *The College Man and the College Woman* (1906); *Self-Measurement* (1908); *The Teacher's Philosophy in and out of School* (1910); and his greatest book which ran through many editions, *The Five Great Philosophies of Life* (1911).

[Sup.] RAYMOND W. ALBRIGHT.

HYDE LECTURESHIP ON FOREIGN MISSIONS: Founded at Andover Newton Theological School in January, 1867, by Henry Hazen Hyde, of Boston, Mass., for the purpose of instructing and stimulating the interest of young men, who are preparing to be preachers of the gospel, in the nature and importance of foreign missionary work and the best methods of supporting it, whether they are to be foreign missionaries or pastors of churches. Lectures are given each year on this foundation, and lecturers are appointed by the board of trustees.

HERBERT GEZORK.

HYMA, ALBERT: Presbyterian; b. at Groningen, The Netherlands, March 18, 1893. He studied at Calvin College and the University of Michigan (Ph.D., 1922). He taught at Knox College (1916–17), University of North Dakota (1922–24), University of Redlands (1944–45), and University of Michigan (1924–44, 1945–). He lectured at the universities of Heidelberg and Marburg in 1952. He is most widely known for his works on the Devotio Moderna, Erasmus, and the Reformation. His most important books are: *The Christian Renaissance* (1924); *The Youth of Erasmus* (1930); *Europe From the Renaissance to 1815* (1930); *The Dutch in the Far East* (1942); *The Life of John Calvin* (1943); *Albertus C. Van Raalte and His Dutch Settlements in the Far East* (1947); *The Brethren of the Common Life* (1950); and *Renaissance to Reformation* (1951).

HYMNOLOGY: Social forces dominant early in the twentieth century led to a change of emphasis on the Kingdom of God here on earth and on the brotherhood of man, with comparatively few new hymns about doctrine, and almost none with denominational leanings. The idea of worship has been accentuated, so that the older didactic and homiletical hymns have almost entirely disappeared from standard hymnals. These books with "aids to devotion" are rich manuals of worship and may be used as such in private devotion. On the other hand, newer hymns do not excel in the expression of deep personal experience. The editors wisely include a large number of songs from other times. There has been a corresponding change in the quality of church music. No longer do clergymen alone serve as editors of hymnals.

Competent lay masters of music have introduced a rich variety of hymn tunes, both modern and ancient. A modern hymnal affords a wide variety of musical offerings, such as: (1) ancient plainsong melodies and carols; (2) ecclesiastical melodies recently discovered in old service books of France; (3) German chorales and traditional melodies; (4) tunes from the Genevan, English, and Scottish psalters of the sixteenth and seventeenth centuries; (5) tunes by such English masters as Tallis, Gibbons, Clark, and Croft; (6) later tunes and folk songs up to the middle of the nineteenth century; (7) Victorian tunes of the part-song variety; (8) comparatively recent Scottish, Welsh, and Irish tunes, some of them going back to earlier periods; (9) gospel songs; (10) modern tunes, many of them by contemporary composers.

Both in words and in music the compilers of recent hymnals have striven, successfully, to represent various tastes, and to provide for special needs. A hymnal cannot be an anthology of fine poetry or fine music, for it must serve a wide variety of purposes and occasions, with all sorts and conditions of men. Instead of the older "Annotated Hymnals," such as the Irish Church Hymnal (1876), the various denominations now supply Handbooks, with illuminating comments about the author of each hymn and the composer of the music. These handbooks, as well as many other volumes dealing with the whole field of hymnology, have made twentieth century Christians more hymn-conscious than ever before. Hymn societies have done much to cultivate a wider knowledge of hymns and hymn tunes, as well as to encourage the writing and publication of hymns that express the spirit and needs of Christian life and thought in modern society. Hymn societies hold public meetings, hymn festivals, and anniversary celebrations; promote new hymn and tune projects; and publish pertinent literature. Such societies in England and the United States have conferred about revising and amplifying Julian's monumental Dictionary of Hymnology (second and last edition, 1907; reprinted in 1925), but the international situation has prevented such action.

No clear line can be drawn between the hymnody of the various English-speaking countries, which have a common tradition. The Church of England has had no official hymnal. Ever since 1861 Hymns Ancient and Modern has had a dominant influence. Since 1906 The English Hymnal, with Anglo-Catholic leanings, has been influential. Songs of Praise (1925; revised and enlarged in 1931), has had even more influence on hymnals recently published in the United States. Presbyterians of the British Empire have united in issuing (1927) a revision of The Church Hymnary (1898). The United Church of Canada issued in 1930 The Hymnary,

one of the ablest compilations. In the United States most denominational hymnals have had at least two revisions since 1900. Both in the United States and in Britain hymnals issued by individuals and by self-appointed groups have been much fewer than in the latter half of the nineteenth century.

Among the newer churches in mission lands abroad, there is a tendency to co-operate in making hymnals. In 1936 the Christian Literature Society of China issued Hymns of Universal Praise. This United Hymnal Committee of twenty-three represented six branches of the Protestant Church. The format of the book resembles that in Western Christendom. Both in text and in music the work is carefully edited. Most of the hymns are translations, but there are others by Chinese authors. The greater portion of the music has been taken from western sources, but there are enough native melodies, traditional and new, to give the work a distinct flavor. The book has supplanted a number of other hymnals previously used in China, and seems well adapted for general use. How the recent political upheavals will affect the use of the hymnal only time can tell. In Japan a committee representing six Protestant denominations published in 1901 Uniform Hymns (Kyōtsū Sambika), which was enlarged and issued in 1903 as The Hymnal (Sambika). In 1931 appeared the Revised Sambika. This well-edited work with texts and tunes from various sources consists of hymns, gospel songs, chants, and responses, to the number of 604, together with anthems and scriptural texts. It compares favorably with hymnals in Western countries, and has proved highly satisfactory in use, another evidence of the general trend towards ecumenicity.

Bibliography: J. M. Ashton, Music in Worship, 1943; L. F. Benson, The Hymnody of the Christian Church, 1927; Benjamin Brawley, History of the English Hymn, 1932; B. F. Crawford, Religious Trends in a Century of Hymns, 1938; Percy Dearmer, Preface to The Oxford Book of Carols, 1931; Winfred Douglas, Church Music in History and Practice, 1937; J. B. Ewens, Let Us Sing, 1935; H. W. Foote, Three Centuries of American Hymnody, 1940; F. J. Gillman, The Evolution of the English Hymn, 1927; A. S. Gregory, Praises with Understanding, 1936; C. W. Laufer, Hymn Lore, 1932; E. S. Lorenz, The Singing Church, 1938; R. G. McCutchan, Hymns in the Lives of Men, 1945; E. S. Ninde, The Story of the American Hymn, 1921; Millar Patrick, The Story of the Church's Song, 1947; C. S. Phillips, Hymnody Past and Present, 1937; John B. Pratt, Present Day Hymns and How They Were Written, 1940; W. S. Pratt, Musical Ministries in the Church, 1915.

[Sup.] Robert G. McCutchan.

HYMNS IN THE EARLY (GREEK) CHURCH:

These were of two main varieties: prose hymns which achieved a certain rhythm by using parallelism of members, and hymns involving quantitative meters imitating ancient Greek poetry.

I. Prose Hymns: That the primitive Christian Church used the Book of Psalms is well known. It is less well known that this Psalter was supplemented for Greek-speaking Christians by an appendix containing other biblical passages. The number and selection of these Odes, as they were called, varied somewhat in different countries and at different times. In the famous Codex Alexandrinus (fifth century), the following fourteen Odes appear after the Psalter: two songs of Moses (Ex. 15:1–19; Deut. 32:1–43), that of Hannah (I Sam. 2:1–10), Isaiah (Isa. 26:9-20), Jonah (Jonah 2:3–10), Habakkuk (Hab. 3:2–19), Ezekiel (Ezek. 38:1–20), Manassah (Prayer of Manassah, Septuagint), Azariah (Dan. 3:26–45, Septuagint), the Three Young Men (Dan. 3:52–88, Septuagint), Mary (Luke 1:46–55), Simeon (Luke 2:29–32), Zachariah (Luke 1:68–79), and the angelic hymn (Luke 2:14). (See Walter Till and Peter Sanz, *Eine griechisch-koptische Odenhandschrift*, 1939; H. Schneider, "Die biblischen Oden im christlichen Altertum," in *Biblica*, XXX [1949], 28–65).

Already in the first Christian century other "psalms and hymns and spiritual songs" (Eph. 5:19) were composed. Echoes of such productions seem to be found in Rom. 11:36; Eph. 3:21; 5:14; I Tim. 1:17; 3:16; 6:15; II Tim. 2:11–13; Rev. 4:8; 5:9 f., 12, 13; 15:3 f. (on the last mentioned passages, see Otto A. Piper, "The Apocalypse of John and the Liturgy of the Ancient Church," in *Church History*, XX [1951], 3–15).

From the second century there have been preserved several orthodox hymn-like compositions (e.g., Didache, 9 and 10; Epistle to Diognetus, 7, 8, 11, and 12), as well as two Gnostic hymns (Acts of John, 94 f.; Acts of Thomas, 6 f.). See also ODES OF SOLOMON.

II. Hymns in Meter: The earliest Christian hymns employing the ancient poetic meters appear to have been composed by Gnostics. From the second century come the hymn of the Naasenes and a specimen of the psalms of Valentinus (preserved by Hippolytus, *Philosophoumena*, V, 10; VI, 37), both of which exhibit logaoedic anapaests. Clement of Alexandria, who attempted to reconcile Christianity and Hellenistic culture, composed a metrical hymn in anapaests in honor of Christ (*Paidagogos*, end):

> Bridle of colts untamed,
> Over our wills presiding;
> Wing of unwandering birds,
> Our flight securely guiding.
>
> . . . .
>
> King of saints, almighty Word
> Of the Father highest Lord;
> Wisdom's head and chief;
> Assuagement of all grief,
> Lord of all time and space,
> Jesus, Saviour of our race;
>
> . . . .
>
> (*ANF*, II, 295).

During the past half century three fragments of Christian hymns were discovered among the Greek papyri preserved in Egypt: P. Amh 2, B. P. Grenfell and A. S. Hunt (eds.), *The Amherst Papyri*, Vol. I (1900), pp. 23–28; Berlin 8299, C. Schmidt and W. Schubart (eds.), *Altchristliche Texte* (*Berliner Klassikertexte*, Vol. VI, 1910), pp. 125–126; P. Oxy 1786, Grenfell and Hunt (eds.), *The Oxyrhynchus Papyri*, Vol. XV (1922), pp. 21–25. The Amherst fragment (fourth century) is arranged in triple acrostic form. Each of its twenty-five lines (with the exception of the last) is divided into three parts, which are metrically equivalent and are marked off by colons. Each of the first twenty-four lines begins successively with the twenty-four letters of the Greek alphabet. Furthermore, each of the three parts of a line begins with the same letter. The meter is somewhat elastic, being sometimes anapaestic, sometimes dactylic. Moreover, the metrical value of words is sometimes made to depend on quantity, sometimes on accent (as in mediaeval and modern poetry). The contents are of a hortatory character, dwelling on the life and precepts of our Lord, and the joys of heaven as contrasted with the terrors of hell. On the basis of its Christology, E. Preuschen dated the original composition of the hymn in the second century (*ZNTW*, Vol. II [1901], pp. 73–80).

The Berlin fragment (fourth century), which also involves an acrostic, appears to speak of the Good Shepherd who takes the lamb on his shoulders and brings it back to the flock. The final strophe closes with a doxology to Christ: "O Word [Logos] of the Father ineffable, to thee be glory [and] power for ever."

The rhythm of the Oxyrhynchus fragment (third century), which is purely quantitative and uninfluenced by accent, is apparently anapaestic. It is remarkable as being by far the most ancient piece of church music extant. Written on the reverse side of a papyrus strip which had previously been used for an account of corn, the musical notation includes at least eight notes, all of which occur in the diatonic Hypolydian key of Alypius (see Th. Reinach, *La musique grécque* [1926], pp. 207 f.). The mode appears to be the Hypophrygian or Iastian. In addition to the notes, various signs are used also; two of these denote long and short syllables, another denotes the rest; the function of the other two is not clear. As regards the words which have been preserved, all creation is called upon to join in a chorus of praise to Father, Son, and Holy Spirit.

BIBLIOGRAPHY: W. Christ and M. Paranikas, *Anthologia graeca carminum christianorum*, 1871; J. Mearns, *The Canticles of the Christian Church, Eastern and Western in Early and Medieval Times*, 1914; J. Kroll, *Die christliche Hymnodik bis zu Klemens von Alexandreia: Programm der Akademie von Braunsberg*, 1921–22; H. Leclercq, "Hymnes," in *DACL*, VI, 2 (1925), cols. 2826–2928; E. R. Smothers, "Phos hilaron," in *RSR*, XIX (1929), 266–283; J. Quasten, *Musik und Gesang in den Kulten* der heidnischen Antike und christlichen Fruehzeit, 1930; C. Blume, Unsere liturg. Lieder. Das Hymnar der altchristl. Kirche, 1932; C. del Grande, Liturgiae, preces et hymni Christianorum e papyris collecti, 1928, 2nd ed., 1933; J. Quasten, "The Liturgical Singing of Women in Christian Antiquity," in CHR, XXVII (1941), 149–165; E. J. Wellesz, "Melito's Homily on the Passion: An Investigation into the Sources of Byzantine Hymnography," in JTS, XLIV (1943), 41–52; Eric Werner, "The Doxology in Synagogue and Church, a Liturgico-Musical Study," in Hebrew Union College Annual, XIX (1945–46), 275–351; idem, "The Conflict between Hellenism and Judaism in the Music of the Early Christian Church," in ibid., XX (1947), 407–470; idem, "Hebrew and Oriental Christian Metrical Hymns, a Comparison," in ibid., XXIII, 2 (1950–51), 397–432; Jefim Schirmann, "Hebrew Liturgical Poetry and Christian Hymnology," in JQR, XLIV (1953), 123–161.

BRUCE M. METZGER.

HYPERDULIA: A technical expression of Roman Catholic theology to define the special homage due to the Virgin Mary on account of her unique dignity as the mother of Christ, and of her holiness and nearness to God. As such, hyperdulia differs essentially from dulia (q.v., Vol. IV), which is the common homage or service paid to angels or saints in glory. It is essentially distinct from latria, viz., the worship rendered to God alone. There is, therefore, a clear and sharp distinction between these three terms: hyperdulia, latria, and dulia.

GEORGES A. BARROIS.

I

"I AM" MOVEMENT: Founded in 1930 by Mr. and Mrs. Guy Ballard in Chicago, Ill., this movement claimed, at the time of Mr. Ballard's death in 1939, as many as three million followers. Guy Ballard, a mining engineer, while visiting Mt. Shasta in Northern California, had a remarkable set of experiences, related in the book which has become one of the basic Scriptures of the movement, Unveiled Mysteries. An Ascended Master, St. Germain, appeared to him and, giving him a magic potion, then and later took him on extended journeys in space, as well as backward in time, and revealed to him truths, recorded in this and subsequent books, now regarded as basic in the new movement which grew out of them.

The teachings are a blend of Theosophy (q.v.), New Thought (q.v.), Spiritualism (q.v.), and Christianity, dramatically presented. In essence the belief is that the Mighty I Am is the source of all power and abundance, and that this is available to man through the Ascended Masters, of whom St. Germain and Jesus are the ones chiefly called upon, though since Mr. Ballard's death, he is also regarded as an Ascended Master. The Ascended Masters speak to the present age through the Accredited Messengers who were Guy Ballard, Edna his wife, and their son Donald. The central New Thought values—health, prosperity, and happiness—are made available to man through decrees to the various Ascended Masters. These, given in concert, constitute the major feature of the meetings of the I Am groups. The decrees correspond to prayer, but are in no sense mere petition. They are commands given to the Masters.

The movement started slowly but had, by the middle thirties, become quite influential. From then until 1939 the growth was unprecedented. The death of Mr. Ballard, in 1939, and certain charges of fraud brought against the movement in the courts, adversely affected it. Convicted

on several counts, the Ballards were enjoined against further use of the mails for their propaganda. Though a superior court set aside the judgment on a technicality, the ban on the mails had not been lifted in 1951. The movement flourishes still in a number of cities, and Edna Ballard continues to receive messages from the Ascended Masters. Mr. Ballard's books and the magazine, The Voice of I Am, are still circulated. Headquarters are in Chicago.

BIBLIOGRAPHY: Unveiled Mysteries and other writings of Mr. and Mrs. Ballard; Gerald B. Bryan, Psychic Dictatorship in America, 1940; Charles S. Braden, These Also Believe, 1949.

CHARLES S. BRADEN.

ICELAND: Since 1944 Iceland has been an independent republic (see DENMARK). The population (1951) totals 127,000, of whom about 99% are Lutherans. The Lutheran Church has been the established church of Iceland since 1874, but according to a law of 1920 religious freedom is guaranteed. Head of the Icelandic Church is the bishop of Reykjavik (the capital city), who until 1909 was ordained by the primate of the Danish Church; after that time he has been ordained by two officials in Iceland. The entire country forms only one bishopric. There are 112 pastors, 273 churches, and the country is divided into twenty-one deaneries.

In 1931 a Church Council was elected which has the right to counsel in all "internal church affairs" (i.e., concerning liturgy, etc.). In several places a highly developed Christian social work is carried on, and in Reykjavik there is a large home for aged people.

Two currents are discernible in the spiritual life of the church. On the one hand there is a moderate, conservative wing, and on the other hand a liberal wing represented by members of the theological faculty of the University of Reykjavik (three professors), the bishop, and some pastors. Large influence was exerted in the liberal camp by Bishop Jon Helgason (d. 1939), famous church historian, as well as by the present bishop, Sigurgeir Sigurdsson.

BIBLIOGRAPHY: Vilhjalmur Stefansson, *Iceland*, 1945; Knut Gjerset, *History of Iceland*, 1924.

K. E. JORDT JORGENSEN.

IDEA OF THE HOLY, THE. See HOLY, THE IDEA OF THE.

IDEALISM: I. The Decline of Idealism: Prior to about 1910, idealism was the accepted background of much philosophy of religion and theology. The Scottish and English neo-Hegelians, Berkeleians like A. C. Fraser, Americans like Josiah Royce (*q.v.*), Mary W. Calkins, James E. Creighton, and G. Watts Cunningham, and also Rudolph Herrmann Lotze and personalists influenced by him, exemplified the sway of idealism. Maine de Biran, Victor Cousin, and Charles Renouvier had developed spiritualistic idealism in France. But G. E. Moore wrote his "Refutation of Idealism" in 1903 (*Mind*). In 1910 Bowne died; American neo-realists and Bertrand Russell were developing analytic philosophy, Santayana attacked "the genteel tradition," positivism (*q.v.*) was emerging anew, John Dewey's (*q.v.*) naturalistic instrumentalism (*q.v.*) was anti-idealistic and anti-theistic, although ethical and democratic; and the non-Hegelian and non-rationalistic Sören Kierkegaard (and Karl Barth [*q.v.*]) influenced theological circles.

II. Revival of Hegelian Influence: In honor of the centenary (1931) of Hegel's death, Hermann Glockner edited (1927–30) a reprint of the original edition of Hegel's works in twenty volumes (the *Jubilaeumsausgabe*), a two-volume work on Hegel's life and thought (1929, 1940) and an invaluable Hegel lexicon (1935–39). Meanwhile there had been appearing Georg Lasson's revised critical text of Hegel's works (1905–), continued by Johannes Hoffmeister. The *Hegelbund* (Hegel Alliance) held International Congresses (1930–33), its proceedings being edited by B. Wigersma (1931 ff.). Hegel's historical importance was recognized by Benedetto Croce in *What is Living and What is Dead of the Philosophy of Hegel* (Eng. tr., 1915), by Nicolai Hartmann in his great two-volume work, *Die Philosophie des deutschen Idealismus* (1923), and by the standard work of Theodor Haering, *Hegel: sein Wollen und sein Werk* (Vol. I, 1929; Vol. II, 1938). Also noteworthy is Richard Kroner, *Von Kant bis Hegel* (Vol. I, 1921; Vol. II, 1924). Other writers on Hegel can barely be mentioned. In German, there were Franz Rosenzweig (1920), Wilhelm Dilthey (1921), Karl Loewith (1941), and Ivan Iljin (1948). In French, Henri Niel (1945) and Jean Hyppolite (1946) are notable. Important in English are Hugh A. Reyburn (1921), and

W. T. Stace (1924), while T. M. Knox (1942) and Knox and Kroner (1948) contributed new Hegel translations. This literature, although appreciative of many of Hegel's special insights, is rarely committed to his absolutism.

An indirect contribution to interest in Hegel has been made by students of Marxism. Lenin's notes on Hegel's dialectic have been translated from Russian into French by Henri Lefebvre and N. Guterman (1935). Sidney Hook, *From Hegel to Marx* (1936), is instructive.

III. Other Idealistic Movements: Rudolf Eucken and Andrew Seth Pringle-Pattison (*q.v.*) developed original types of idealism. Reference should be made to panpsychism (*q.v.*) and personalism (*q.v.*). The influence of idealism on education, secular and religious, in the United States and the counter-influence of John Dewey's naturalism (*q.v.*) can only be mentioned.

See also EPISTEMOLOGY.

BIBLIOGRAPHY: E. S. Brightman, *A Philosophy of Ideals*, 1928; Clifford Barrett (ed.), *Contemporary Idealism in America*, 1932; G. Watts Cunningham, *The Idealistic Argument in Recent British and American Philosophy*, 1933; and A. C. Ewing, *Idealism*, 1934.

EDGAR SHEFFIELD BRIGHTMAN.

IDENTICAL SERVICES: To relieve congestion at the "eleven o'clock hour," and to meet the desires of those who cannot be present then, the pastor and other leaders of worship hold practically the same service at an earlier time, perhaps eight-thirty. This dual plan may operate only during Lent, and on other special days; between October first and the end of May; or in an exceptional case, throughout the year. A few object to the plan as patterning after the Roman Catholics. Many who have tried it a number of years endorse it heartily. The pastor may have difficulty in making the service live twice in one morning. Brooks and Beecher, or Spurgeon and Maclaren, would have welcomed the idea, but would have brought each time a new message, with different songs and prayers. Most observers agree that few congregations can thrive spiritually with only one hour of public worship each Lord's Day. See also EVENING SERVICE.

ANDREW W. BLACKWOOD.

IGNATIUS OF ANTIOCH: Today the controversy over the manuscript tradition of the Ignatian letters has ended with universal acceptance of the authenticity of the shorter Greek version; the longer version contains interpolations from the fourth century, while the short Syriac collection was abbreviated from the original Greek version. A fifth-century papyrus fragment (P. Berol. 10581) contains *Smyrn.* iii. 3—xii. 1.

The date of Ignatius' martyrdom is difficult to determine. In his *Chronicon* Eusebius seems to associate it with Pliny's investigation of the

Bithynian Christians (which took place in 112), but there is no reason to believe that such investigations were universal or that they were connected with a "persecution." Ignatius addresses Polycarp as a young man, and if with Grégoire we place Polycarp's martyrdom (at the age of eighty-six) in 177, he would have been fairly young in the early years of Hadrian's reign. All that can be said is that Ignatius probably died early in the reign of Hadrian.

The language of Ignatius is florid, with a good many allusions to New Testament phrases. He clearly knows the gospels of Matthew and John, and probably that of Luke. Some of his opponents know astrological terminology, but Ignatius himself is better acquainted with contemporary religious language, including "gnostic" phraseology. His style is intensely personal and formless. To say, however, with Streeter that this style reflects "the egoism of a noble mind unstrung" is to exaggerate—primarily in order to prove that "to Ignatius the importance of the bishop had become a real obsession."

Some recent studies have endeavored to show that Ignatius' point of departure is not the Christian tradition but a kind of *gnosis* current in Syria in his time; his Christ is the "gnostic redeemer" supposedly fashionable in the first century. Such theories are not closely related to the facts of the history of religions. What Ignatius actually does is to interpret the Christ of the gospels in the light of some (relatively few) gnostic ideas, especially in *Eph.* xix-xx. C. Maurer has shown how he takes Johannine ideas and develops them in the direction of "gnosis," without regard for their possible origin in the Old Testament and Judaism. He makes very little use of the Old Testament.

Ignatius is deeply concerned with two groups of opponents. On the one hand, he is fighting the docetists, those who believed on semi-philosophical grounds that Jesus merely "seemed" (*dokein*) to live and die as a real man (especially *Trall.* x; *Smyrn.* ii-vii); such persons have no Christian love and they "abstain from Eucharist and prayer." On the other hand, he condemns the Judaizers, who apparently observed the Sabbath and followed other Jewish customs, and insisted on the primacy of the Old Testament revelation (*Magn.* viii-x; *Philad.* vi-ix). Against all his opponents he upholds obedience to the monarchical episcopate with its subordinate college of presbyters and the deacons. He is in anguish over the episcopal succession at Antioch. When he writes the Romans, Jesus Christ is bishop at Antioch (*Rom.* 9:1); when he writes the Philadelphians, however, the Antiochene church is "at peace," and emissaries from neighboring churches are gathering there to rejoice with it (*Philad.* x. 1; cf. *Smyrn.* xi. 2–3; *Polyc.* vii. 1–2). It seems unlikely that this "peace" lasted very long, for from Ignatius

to Theophilus (*ca.* 170–180) we know only "gnostic" Christians at Antioch.

In Ignatius' time there is a great conflict over the monarchical episcopate at Antioch. Does opposition come from those who desire other forms of ministry, or from those who desire no form at all? From what evidence we have, it appears that Ignatius' struggle is not with alternative orders of ministers, but simply with heretics who create schisms. At least at Antioch and in Asia, no alternative seems to exist, although Ignatius apparently does not know whether Rome has a bishop or not.

BIBLIOGRAPHY: W. Bauer, *Die Briefe des Ignatius*, 1920; H. Schlier, *Religionsgeschichtliche Untersuchungen zu den Ignatiusbriefen*, 1929; A. D. Nock in *JTS*, Vol. XXXI (1929–30), pp. 310–313; B. H. Streeter, *The Primitive Church* (1929), pp. 168–183; F. Loofs, *Theophilus von Antiochien und die anderen theologischen Quellen bei Irenaeus* (1930), pp. 194–205; W. Bauer, *Rechtglaeubigkeit und Ketzerei im aeltesten Christentum* (1934), pp. 65–71; C. C. Richardson, *The Christianity of Ignatius of Antioch*, 1935; J. Moffatt in *Harvard Theological Review*, Vol. XXIX (1936), pp. 1–38; C. Maurer, *Ignatius von Antiochien und das Johannesevangelium*, 1949.

[Sup.] ROBERT M. GRANT.

IGNATIUS OF LOYOLA: Many historians have discussed his *Spiritual Exercises,* which stimulating work deserves proper attention, but often his equally powerful production, *Constitutiones,* is overlooked. In the latter he appears as the great lawgiver, telling his followers how they must organize the Society of Jesus. More than 250 times he uses the famous phrase, "ad maiorem Dei gloriam," or, "for the greater glory of God." His order reflects the tremendous urge he felt for reform, not only institutional but also personal.

BIBLIOGRAPHY: H. Böhmer, *Studien zur Geschichte der Gesellschaft Jesu:* Vol. I, *Loyola*, 1914; H. Watrigant, *La genèse des Exercitia spiritualia*, 1897; F. Thompson, *The Life of St. Ignatius*, 1910; H. D. Sedgwick, *Ignatius Loyola: An Attempt at an Impartial Biography*, 1923; I. Loyola, *Spiritual Exercises*, 1928; A. Brou, *La spiritualité de S. Ignace*, 1928; idem, *S. Ignace, maître d'oraison*, 1925.

[Sup.] ALBERT HYMA.

IHMELS, LUDWIG HEINRICH: D. 1933. He spent his later years as professor of theology at Leipzig (1903–) and as bishop of Saxony. His later important works were: *Centralfragen der Dogmatik in der Gegenwart* (1911); and *Das Christentum Luthers in seiner Eigenart* (1917). [Sup.] RAYMOND W. ALBRIGHT.

IKONASTASIS. See BYZANTINE RITE.

ILLUMINATION, THE CHURCH OF THE: A religious body organized in 1908 to meet the demand of those who once professed membership in one of the various denominations but discontinued their activity because they were no longer satisfied with the biblical interpretations offered by these churches. It was not the intent to establish formal churches in the usual sense. The entire effort has been to offer a spiritual, esoteric, philosophic interpretation of vital biblical teachings, thereby satisfying the inner spiritual needs of seekers after spiritual truth, yet permitting them to return to their former church membership if inclined to do so.

The specific foundation of the Church of the Illumination is based on an interpretation of Gen. 2:7 and John 3:3. It is claimed that if man actually became a living soul when he first breathed in the breath of life, it would not be necessary to be born again. The church teaches that man is born with the ability to bring the embryonic soul into a living entity. When he has accomplished this, man is reborn of the spirit, as he was of the body from his mother's womb.

Although there are a few churches for those who desire formality, it is the purpose of this movement to instruct rather than to gather people. Men are trained by directed study and attendance at conferences, whereupon they are ordained as ministers-at-large. Headquarters are in Quakertown, Pa., where there is an Academy and Temple of Illuminati.

BIBLIOGRAPHY: R. Swinburne Clymer, *The Interpretation of St. Matthew*, 2 vols., 1945.

R. SWINBURNE CLYMER.

ILLUSTRATIONS IN SERMONS: This word, derived from the Latin, means that which throws light upon the truth or duty in hand. The illustration ought to be secondary to the truth in view. An example may make the truth clear, add to interest, impart a touch of beauty, or otherwise make the truth memorable. Illustrations come mainly from the Bible, from other writings, and from life today. Phillips Brooks insisted that the best illustrations of New Testament truths come from the Old. Our Lord drew examples from the common things of life. So did Paul. In *The Metaphors of St. Paul*, J. S. Howson showed that they came chiefly from four fields, all masculine: agriculture, architecture, army life, and athletics. In preparing sermons a man with imagination sends out a decree that the whole world should be taxed. He values illustrations by their worth, not their number. Young men tend to employ too many; older men, too few. The sermon, or paragraph, ought to seek the illustration. If that part of the structure needs a window, very well. If not, let the time be given to something important. In preparing sermons the preacher should avoid the use of "canned goods," from other men's compilations, and also keep from anecdotes, especially with the preacher as hero. On the other hand, Bunyan and Guthrie, Spurgeon and Moody, W. W. Watkinson and William M. Taylor prove that no homiletical ability grows by use more quickly than knack of using illustrations. One learns best by study of masters, and by using illustrations all one's own. Among the manu-

als, these two stand out in different ways: Dawson C. Bryan, *The Art of Illustrating Sermons* (1937); and W. E. Sangster, *The Craft of Sermon Illustration* (1950).

ANDREW W. BLACKWOOD.

IMAGE OF GOD. See MAN, DOCTRINE OF.

IMAGINATION IN PREACHING: Modern writers use the term in various ways. Here it means ability to see what lies hidden from other eyes (II Kings 6:17), and then to use words in helping others see. "Fancy" means seeing what is not "there," as in allegorical treatments of a Bible passage not allegorical. This view of imagination goes back to Wordsworth and Coleridge, who accounted for what preachers have always done. In the Bible, the word "imagination" occurs infrequently, and usually in an unfavorable sense, but the writings of Isaiah and the psalmists, with many others, embody the products of inspired imagination. According to Horace Bushnell, the gospel itself is "the gift of God to the imagination." This matter concerns preaching today because most hearers born in our century have been educated imaginatively, and not logically. If the minister would appeal to them "where they are," mentally, he must help them see. This holds true especially in preaching to boys and girls. On the lowest level, imagination works descriptively; on a higher plane, structurally (it also means "the synthesizing power"); on the highest level, creatively, as with John Bunyan. When a minister begins reverently to employ this gift for the glory of God from whom it comes, he is using a power that preachers in all ages have employed in addressing common people. For examples turn to John Chrysostom's *Sermons on the Statues*.

ANDREW W. BLACKWOOD.

IMITATION OF CHRIST: The most widely read book ever composed in Europe. It was originally written by Gerard Zerbolt of Zutphen, the teacher of Thomas à Kempis. His version, however, did not appeal to the monastic leaders, who greatly preferred that by the pious monk just mentioned. The latter had never attended institutions of higher learning, and he was afraid of science. He was ascetic in his interpretation of the powers of man, but Zerbolt urged his followers to imitate Jesus Christ literally, not the man of sorrows only but also the Word, through whom and by whom the universe was created. See also MYSTICISM; GROOTE; ZERBOLT.

BIBLIOGRAPHY: Albert Hyma, *The Original Version of the Imitation of Christ by Gerard Zerbolt of Zutphen*, 1950; idem, *The Brethren of the Common Life*, 1950.

[Sup. to KEMPIS, THOMAS À, II.] ALBERT HYMA.

IMMANENCE AND TRANSCENDENCE (Latin, *in manere*, "dwell in"; *trans scandare*, "climb across"): **I. Meanings and Problem:** The generic meaning of "immanence" is "being within"; of "transcendence," "being apart or independent." Although these terms have been used in many disciplines, only their theological use, referring to God's immanence in or transcendence of the world, will be considered here.

The problem of divine immanence and transcendence is posed by the very existence of both philosophical theology (*q.v.*) and religion, for they are based on the thesis that God causes (philosophical) (see CAUSALITY) or cares for (religious) (see CREATION AND PRESERVATION) the world. Since this implies that God must be distinct from, yet at work in, the world, extreme immanence and extreme transcendence operate both logically and chronologically primarily as limiting positions (though each has been very closely approximated) to define a scale of relative immanence and transcendence. Thus God (*q.v.*) may be regarded as almost completely transcendent, related to the world solely by an original creative act (deism); or as a being whose *substance* is apart from the world but whose *activity* or handiwork the world is ("effective" immanence, or theism in a narrow sense); or finally as a being whose substance and activity are almost identical with the world ("substantial" immanence), either wholly (pantheism) or partially (panentheism: the world is in God). Such substantial immanence may consist either of an identification of the world with God, which deifies the world (e.g., Neo-Platonism and medieval mysticism [*q.v.*]), or of an identification of God with the world, which naturalizes God (e.g., renaissance mysticism and modern romanticism). Thus each of the extreme positions tends to be incompatible with its philosophical and religious *raison d'etre*: extreme transcendence tends to destroy God's efficacy and hence man's religiosity, while extreme immanence tends to destroy either man's humanity—his individual freedom (see WILL, FREEDOM OF THE) and ethical categories—or God's divinity—his perfection and power.

II. History: The history of the problem of divine immanence and transcendence consists largely, therefore, in a constant swinging of the theological pendulum from one extreme to the other, seeking constantly for a "vital center" with swings which may shorten for a time only to lengthen their arc once more. The swing of the pendulum started with the hylozoism of the pre-Socratic Greeks (*ca.* 600–450 B.C.), when the divine was conceived immanently either as reality itself (e.g., Anaximander and the Eleatics) or as the governing law of reality in Heraclitus. From Socrates through Plato to Aristotle (450–322 B.C.) the transcendence of God was increasingly stressed to the point that, in Aristotle, God, as "self-thinking thought," is unaware of the world. This was followed by a rapid return toward substantial immanence in Stoicism (*ca.* 322 B.C.-A.D. 200), where God was conceived as the indwelling semipersonal logos of nature.

The archetypal cycle having been set by the swing from Aristotelian transcendence to Stoic immanence, the rhythm continued, unevenly but steadily, through the theologians of the Christian era. Stoic pantheism was transformed into a panentheism where God's being and activity were understood as identical with the world, though transcending it: the divine "One" of Neo-Platonism (*ca.* A.D. 1–458, e.g., Philo, Plotinus, and Proclus) "emanates" the world which yearns through "epistrophé" for reunion with it; and for the Christian Scotus Eriugena (*ca.* 800–877), God as Father "unfolds" the Son and through him the world which then returns again to its source. Since, however, a more moderate position of substantial transcendence and effective immanence had already been maintained, in the midst of Neo-Platonism, by Augustine and some of the early church fathers, the swing was increasingly away from immanence toward the extreme transcendence of thirteenth and fourteenth century nominalism (e.g., William of Occam and Nicholas of Autrecourt). But there again arose, this time almost simultaneously, a return to substantial immanence in the pantheism and panentheism of the thirteenth and fourteenth century Christian mystics (e.g., Meister Eckhart) and the modern, more rationalistic, mysticism (*q.v.*) of Bruno (1548–1600) and Spinoza (1632–77), for whom God is the sole substance and "*natura naturans*" in contradistinction to "*natura naturata*" which is the world.

With the development of the physical sciences in the seventeenth and eighteenth centuries and the consequent picture of the world as a machine, there was again a swing toward transcendence, beginning with Descartes and Hobbes and culminating in eighteenth century deism, where God was needed only to start a world machine whose internal laws of motion were adequate for its continuance (see SCIENCE, NATURAL). Meanwhile, however, German Pietism and English Evangelicalism were stressing God's role in the human heart; and with the rise of the biological sciences in the nineteenth century and the resulting view of the world as an organism, there occurred again a return toward substantial immanence, with God conceived as the inner meaning and life of the world—a position whose emotional expression in romanticism and rational expression in Hegelianism Schleiermacher attempted to synthesize (see IDEALISM). Beginning in the last half of the nineteenth century, finally, and continuing on down to the present time, the pendulum's swing has been back toward substantial transcendence with effective immanence, in both

Protestantism and Catholicism, on the basis, this time, of ethical and religious, rather than scientific, considerations. The two most active agents in this swing have perhaps been the existentialism (*q.v.*) of Kierkegaard and his followers (e.g., K. Barth and P. Tillich in Protestantism and G. Marcel and J. Maritain in Catholicism) and a general revival of orthodoxy (e.g., the Protestant "Neo-orthodoxy" [*q.v.*] exemplified by K. Barth and E. Brunner in Europe and Reinhold Niebuhr in America, and in Catholicism the papal condemnation of the "modernists" in 1907 and the development [from 1879] of Neo-Thomism [*q.v.*], as in E. Gilson).

BIBLIOGRAPHY: H. R. Mackintosh, *Types of Modern Theology*, 1939; F. J. Tennant, *Philosophical Theology*, Vol. II, 1930; W. Temple, *Nature, Man, and God*, 1934; K. Barth, *The Doctrine of the Word of God*, 1936; E. Gilson, *The Spirit of Medieval Philosophy*, 1936; G. Marcel, *The Mystery of Being*, especially Vol. I, 1950; P. Tillich, *Systematic Theology*, 1951.

FRANCIS HOWARD PARKER.

IMMIGRANTS. See EMIGRANTS AND IMMIGRANTS, MISSION WORK AMONG; HOME MISSIONS, II.

IMPLICIT FAITH: Roman Catholic theology refers to Christian faith as being implicit whenever the church, and individual believers, are not fully aware of all the particulars or consequences of the revealed truth to which they actually give their wholehearted assent. Such particulars or consequences are believed implicitly, inasmuch as they are assumed to be implied in a given article of faith. For instance, it is alleged that the early church implicitly believed in the Immaculate Conception (*q.v.*, Vol. V) and in the Assumption of Mary (*q.v.*), which are deemed to be organically related to her election as the mother of Christ, although the former two articles of faith were defined respectively in 1854 and 1950.

The notion of implicit faith has a direct bearing on the problem of the salvation of Christians and eventually of unbaptized persons who, through no fault of their own, are unable actually to give a specific assent to all the revealed truths explicitly defined by the church. Thus the minimum faith requirements unto salvation, as held by most Roman Catholic theologians, are the belief and trust in God as Lord and Judge of all men, and in Jesus Christ as Saviour, or in such provisions as were made by God for the salvation of men from sin and death.

It may be assumed that the faith of many church members remains, to a certain extent, implicit, inasmuch as they give their assent to "all truths that are taught by the church" generally, even though they are not always in a position of giving a satisfactory account of the specific objects of their belief. The term "implicit faith" is often used by Protestant polemists with reference to these blanket endorsements of ecclesiastical tenets by uninformed Roman Catholics.

BIBLIOGRAPHY: H. Davis, *Moral and Pastoral Theology*, Vol. I, 1938; F. Tillmann, *Die katholische Sittenlehre*, IV, 1, 1935.

GEORGES A. BARROIS.

IMPUTATION. See SOTERIOLOGY.

INABILITY. See WILL, FREEDOM OF THE.

INCARNATION. See CHRISTOLOGY; SOTERIOLOGY.

INDEFECTIBILITY. See PERSEVERANCE OF THE SAINTS, in Vol. VIII.

INDEPENDENTS: The name has sometimes been used broadly to include not only Congregationalists, but also Baptists, Quakers, and tens of thousands of others who did not yet belong to a large denomination. The term "Independents" is often thought to be synonymous with "Separatists," but that is not the case. What the Independents had in mind was independence of each congregation and not of a whole denomination. They wanted no authority above a congregation, just as they wanted no coercion in the matter of individual beliefs and practices. Among the first in England to suggest this idea was Tyndale (*q.v.*). His treatises and his translation of the Bible had tremendous influence. The average English citizen became delighted with the notion that he could understand the Bible just as readily as did the theologians and the ministers and elders or deacons. In large meetings it often happened that an untrained speaker swayed the emotions of auditors who enjoyed the feeling that the Holy Spirit was interested in the lowly and ignorant. During the fourteenth and fifteenth centuries the great mystics (*q.v.*) had popularized the thought of direct contact between the sinner and God the Creator.

Unfortunately the masses of the people have always been inarticulate in the matter of composing literary records of their own experiences. They do not organize great institutions, they do not attend the general assemblies in which divines set the standard of moral conduct and draw up confessions. Large quantities of Bibles were circulated in England during the regime of Oliver Cromwell (*q.v.*). To whom did those Bibles go and what was their effect upon all the pious souls who could read in their own tongue what the experts had in former times thought was only for them to study? Many thousands of these people were Independents, unorganized, not well disciplined, not well taught, not well supplied with creeds.

Godfrey Davies has told a sound tale about those Independents in his admirable volume on the early Stuarts, the seventh in the Oxford History of England. In discussing the Westminster Assembly he speaks of the conflict between the Presbyterians and the Independents: "Throughout 1644 the independents were in steady opposition to the presbyterians, and their stubbornness delayed until autumn the resolution to adopt the presbyterian form of church government, and, a little later, the directory for public worship." It was only a delay that they caused in 1644, but in 1648 they forced all the Presbyterians out of the House of Commons. It was they who got control of the army, although it had been dominated for years by the Scotch and English Presbyterians. It was they also who were responsible for the execution of Charles I (*q.v.*) and the introduction of a republican form of government, with a Council of State. In 1651 Cromwell suggested to the Dutch that the two Protestant republics be united into one. If the Dutch had accepted his proposal the whole course of English history would have been altered, and so would that of other countries. Godfrey Davies wonders how a handful of persons in 1640 could have found so many recruits within the space of only ten years. He reasons that in the sixty years preceding 1640 an "enormous output of devotional literature" had taken place. He mentions Arthur Dent's *Plaine Mans Path-Way to Heaven,* which went through twenty-five editions in the period from 1601 to 1640. There was also Thomas Egerton's *Briefe Method of Catechizing,* which in 1631 reached its thirty-ninth edition, while John Norden's *Pensive Mans Practise* had enjoyed forty editions by 1627. In reading these books the average English citizen believed that now he was truly independent of priests and bishops. Davies refers to the Independents as sectaries, for they represented numerous sects. Many of them resorted to adult baptism through immersion, which proved offensive to other Christians. But the chief reason why they could not maintain control of the army and the parliament after 1659 is that they tried to impose upon their fellowmen too much discipline and were too much opposed to proper training of their clergymen. There was also no need of going to such an extreme as having their king executed. This crude course of action antagonized millions of good Protestants in all European countries. It made Charles I look like a martyr, and it hastened the Restoration.

Among the Independents in the broad sense of the term was the Quaker, George Fox (*q.v.*), who has been called "the greatest religious leader the Puritan Revolution produced." He and his fellow-Quakers made much of the work of the Holy Spirit. Outsiders called them Quakers because they thought that they were being moved to quake by the Holy Spirit, but

their proper name is Friends. Early Baptists and Congregationalists also showed some tendencies in the same direction. Their influence upon the United States has been such that no historian can depict the development of American civilization without a careful study of the Independents.

The widespread misunderstanding of the Independents would have been less if the following work had been more widely known: Robert Baylie (Baillie), *A Dissuasive from the Errours of the Time: Wherein the Tenets of the Principall Sects, especially of the Independents, are drawn together in one Map* (1645). The author on p. 198 makes the following observation: "Independencie is the full liberty of such a Church to discharge all the parts of Religion, Doctrine, Sacraments, Discipline, and all within it selfe without all dependence, all subordination to any other on earth." He also indicates that not only the Congregationalists but also the Baptists, whom he calls Anabaptists, belonged to the Independents, besides "many sects." He suspected that John Milton also belonged, and on p. 63 he says that Roger Williams told him about his purchase of land from the Indians, in order that the exiles from the English colony might set up one of their own. They were disarmed by the governor, lest "the Tragedy of *Munster* should be acted over again in New-England." He referred to the notorious Kingdom of Jerusalem set up by the Anabaptists in Westphalia. He also said on p. 90 that the Independents tried to prevent the meeting of the Westminster Assembly, and when this proved impossible, their delegates caused so much trouble "that to this day, after two yeares time and above, in more frequent and longer Sessions then wee ever reade of in any Assembly since the world began, there is nothing at all set up for the comfort of the afflicted Kingdome." Baillie was afterward the principal of Glasgow University. His book was vehemently attacked by Thomas Hooker and John Cotton in a work of 1648, *A Survey of the Summe of Church-Discipline.*

BIBLIOGRAPHY: G. M. Trevelyan, *England Under the Stuarts,* numerous eds.; G. Davies, *The Early Stuarts 1603–1660* (1937), pp. 188–196; Ph. Hughes, *The Reformation in England,* Vol. I (1951), pp. 90–155; C. H. Smyth, *Cranmer and the Reformation under Edward VI,* 1926; W. K. Jordan, *The Development of Religious Toleration in England,* 4 vols., 1932–40.

                                              ALBERT HYMA.

INDIA: Since the separation of Pakistan, the name India has become ambiguous. Here it will be used for the entire subcontinent up to 1947, and for the Indian Union alone thereafter.

Great advances have been made in the knowledge of Indian history and religion since the writing of the article on India in the former edition of this encyclopedia. This supplement can only refer to a few points of additional information and add a statement on recent religious movements. The appended bibliography should be consulted.

I. **The Indus Valley Civilization:** The archaeological discoveries made since 1922 at Mohenjo-daro, Harappa, and other sites in the Indus valley have radically altered our view of pre-Vedic times. The highly developed city civilization there brought to light can be approximately dated through its connections with Mesopotamian remains. It is certainly preVedic, and is assigned by Sir John Marshall to a period between 3250 and 2750 B.C. Seals containing pictographic signs have been found, but thus far attempts to read their language have not met with general acceptance. Certain of the objects discovered appear to have a religious character, and suggest relationships with the Hindu cults of Siva and the mother-goddess. These finds are significant in correcting the impression derived from the Vedas that the coming of the Aryans marks the beginning of Indian civilization.

II. **Non-Vedantic and theistic trends in Hinduism:** Although the *Advaita Vedanta* of Sankara continues to be considered a very important element in Indian thought, new knowledge enables us to see it as one of many competing systems rather than as completely dominating the rest. The studies of Indian scholars have not only greatly increased our knowledge of the six *darśanas,* including the many schools of the Vedanta itself, but have shown their close interrelationships with unorthodox schools. We have also become acquainted with a wealth of theistic and devotional literature, some in Sanskrit and even more in the regional languages. In the Tamil speaking South we have the poems of Appar, Sambandhar, Manikkavasagar, Tayumanavar, and many others in praise of Siva, and of the Alvars whose *bhakti* is directed toward Vishnu. The former movement finds its theological expression in the Saiva Siddhanta, the latter in the work of Ramanuja. A somewhat later movement in Western India was due to the poet saints who wrote in the Marathi language among whom Tukaram is outstanding. Still later Tulsi Das in his version of the Ramayana performed a similar service in the Hindi tongue. Once again, it is realized today that a religion is to be known not only through its theological formulations but also in its rites and practices. Some work has been done in investigating this aspect of Hinduism.

III. **Recent Religious Movements:** Most of the movements here listed had their origin before 1900, but they have developed significantly since that date. The Brahma Samaj and the Arya Samaj are dealt with elsewhere.

A. **Theosophy:** The Theosophical Society is an international movement which originated in New York in 1875 through the initiative of a Russian, Madame Helena Blavatsky (1831–91), and an American, Colonel Olcott. However it has become thoroughly acclimatized in India, and its headquarters since 1882 have been at Adyar, a suburb of Madras. In its beginnings the Society was specially interested in the phenomena of spiritualism and in occult knowledge derived from many non-Indian sources. After their arrival in India, however, its leaders enthusiastically endorsed such teachings of Hinduism and Buddhism as karma and transmigration, as well as many practices which were being rejected by Western-educated Indians. The Society maintains that followers of any religious faith can share also in its membership. Madame Blavatsky taught that her work was inspired by a hierarchy of Adepts in Tibet with whom she had mysterious means of communication.

A notable convert was Mrs. Annie Besant (1847–1932), an English woman who came from Free Thought (*q.v.*) to Theosophy, became a member of the Society in 1889, and reached India in 1893. During her long career she extended the educational and social work of the Society, developed the Hindu University in Benares (no longer under Theosophist auspices), made a widely used translation of the Gita, and lectured and wrote widely. She identified herself with Indian national aspirations and was at one time president of the Indian National Congress, although later she opposed Mahatma Gandhi (*q.v.*). There has been much controversy about certain events in the life of the society, details of which can be read in the accounts of Farquhar and Sarma. The Adyar headquarters has a valuable library of Sanskrit and other manuscripts, and some valuable scholarly work has been done in editing and translating ancient texts. A more recent president of the Society is Śri Jinarajadasa. See also THEOSOPHY.

B. **The Ramakrishna Mission:** This organization, which has spread not only within India but into the West, had its inspiration in the life of a Hindu ascetic, generally known as Ramakrishna Paramahansa (1834–86). This man, although uneducated in any formal sense, produced a powerful impression upon those who knew him, both because of his personal history of intense religious striving, and because of remarkable ability to express Hindu teachings through vivid analogies. He believed that he had demonstrated through his own experience that spiritual realization can be achieved not only through the various disciplines of Hinduism but through Islam and Christianity. He therefore testified that the religions of the world were but different paths to the same goal. Although he wrote nothing, his sayings have been extensively preserved by his hearers.

His most distinguished follower was a student from Calcutta later known as Swami Vivekananda (1863–1902). Fascinated by Ramakrishna's teaching, after his master's death he undertook to spread it throughout the world. He spoke as the representative of India at the World's Parliament of Religions at Chicago in 1893, and on his return to India he was received with great enthusiasm. He adopted certain Western methods of organization and created a well disciplined body of workers. The headquarters of the mission is at Belur near Calcutta, but there are centers in many Indian cities. In some of these a considerable degree of Christian influence is evident. An extension of the mission's work is the Vedanta Society in the United States.

C. **Aurobindo Ghose:** The son of Bengali parents, Aurobindo Ghose (1872–1950) received his education entirely in England. On his return to India he entered the service of the state of Baroda. There he learned Sanskrit and other Indian languages. He then entered political life in Bengal in 1906 as an extreme nationalist. During an imprisonment he experienced a religious conversion, renounced political activity, and spent his remaining life as a voluntary exile in the French state of Pondicherry, where he established an ashram (q.v.) for his Indian and Western disciples. Like Dayananda he maintained that the source of true philosophy is to be found in the Vedas, the Upanishads and the Gita. He interpreted these texts distinctively, extracting from them teachings of the importance of intuition and the course of cosmic evolution which suggest Bergson. Among the most important of his many writings are *The Life Divine* and *Essays on the Gita*.

D. **Indian nationalism:** As the preceding paragraphs indicate, religious movements in India have been closely connected with nationalism. Outstanding leaders in the political struggles which eventually led to Indian independence in 1947 are M. G. Ranade (1842–1900), one of the founders of the Indian National Congress (1885); B. G. Tilak (1856–1920), who gave a militant turn to the interpretation of the Gita; and G. K. Gokhale (1866–1915), founder of the Servants of India Society (1905). By far the most significant figure among religious nationalists is Mohandas Karamchand Gandhi (1869–1948) (q.v.). While helping the Indians in South Africa to overcome their political disabilities he devised a method which he called *satyāgraha*, or firmness in the cause of truth. Those using this method renounced all violence in thought, word and deed, and sought to overcome untruth with truth, hatred with love. Closely related concepts are *ahimsā* (non-violence), civil disobedience, and non-cooperation. Under Gandhi's leadership these methods proved remarkably effective in the

immediate issues in South Africa. Returning to India in 1914, he introduced them into the Indian struggle for independence, training workers at the Sabarmati Ashram near Ahmedabad, and later at Wardha and Sevagram in Madhya Pradesh. Despite some failures, *satyāgraha* under Gandhi's leadership undoubtedly had much to do with the eventual achievement of Indian independence. Although in his younger days Gandhi was influenced by other religions and especially by Christianity, he remained in his own thought a faithful member of the Hindu community, deducing his own characteristic teachings largely from the Gita. These include, beside non-violence, a theistic belief along the lines of the Gita, a strong opposition to discrimination against the outcastes (although he believed that the caste system in its original form was good), reverence for the cow, and the conviction that all religions are good for those born in them, so that conversion from one religion to another is unnecessary. Gandhi's writing was mostly done for the periodicals he edited. His most important books are *Hind Swaraj*, written in South Africa, and *The Story of My Experiments with Truth*.

E. **Other Movements:** A more complete account of religious tendencies in modern India would have to take account of the influence of Marxian communism; the *Dravida Kalagam* (an anti-Brahman movement in Southern India); the Hindu Mahasabha; the Radha Saomi Satsang; Maher Babha, a Parsi Messiah; Ramana Rishi; as well as recent movements in Islam, Jainism and other religions.

See also BRAHMANISM; BRAHMO SAMAJ; HINDUISM; JAINISM; PAKISTAN.

BIBLIOGRAPHY: (1) General: W. Norman Brown (ed.), *India, Pakistan, Ceylon*, 1951; Vincent A. Smith, *Oxford History of India*, 1923; *Cambridge History of India*, Vol. I, 1922—6 vols. projected; A. A. Macdonell, *India's Past*, 1927; *The Cultural Heritage of India*, 3 vols., 1936. (2) Literature: J. N. Farquhar, *An Outline of the Religious Literature of India*, 1920; M. Winternitz, *History of Indian Literature*, Eng. tr., 2 vols., 1927, 1933—a third volume of the original German has not yet been translated. (3) Philosophy: M. Hiriyanna, *Outlines of Indian Philosophy*, 1932; M. H. Harrison, *Hindu Monism and Pluralism*, 1932; S. Radhakrishnan, *Indian Philosophy*, 2 vols. 1923, 1927; S. N. Das Gupta, *History of Indian Philosophy*, 4 vols., 1922 seq. (4) Religions: D. S. Sarma, *A Primer of Hinduism*; Nicol Macnicol, *The Living Religions of India*, 1934; J. B. Pratt, *India and its Faiths*, 1915; Mrs. Sinclair Stevenson, *The Rites of the Twice-Born*, 1920; W. T. Elmore, *Dravidian Gods in Modern Hinduism*; Nicol Macnicol, *Indian Theism*, 1913; Estlin Carpenter, *Theism in Medieval India*, 1921; R. G. Bhandarkar, *Vaisnavism, Saivism and Minor Religious Systems*, 1913; F. Kingsbury and G. Phillips, *Hymns of the Tamil Saivite Saints*, 1921; Nicol Macniol, *Psalms of the Maratha Saints*, 1919; V. Paranjothi, *The Saiva Siddhanta*; Mrs. Sinclair Stevenson, *The Heart of Jainism*, 1915; Murray T. Titus, *Indian Islam*, 1930. (5) Indus Valley Civilization: Sir John H. Marshall, *Mohenjodaro and the Indus Civilization*, 3 vols., 1931; E. J. H. Mackay, *Early Indus Civilizations*, 1948. (6) Modern Movements: J. N. Farquhar, *Modern Religious Movements in India*, 1915; D. S. Sarma, *The Renaissance of Hinduism*, 1944—at present the best general account from a liberal Hindu viewpoint; Paul Brunton, *A Search in Secret India*, 1935—a journalistic account containing information not readily accessible elsewhere. (a) Theosophy: See Farquhar and Sarma above: the latter is the best guide to the voluminous literature in India; Mrs. A. Besant, "Theosophy," in

The Encyclopedia of Religion and Ethics. (b) Ramakrishna mission: Max Mueller, *Ramakrishna, his Life and Sayings*, 1898; *The Gospel of Sri Ramakrishna*, 1942; *The Complete Works of Swami Vivekananda*, 7 vols.; Romain Rolland, *Prophets of the New India*, 1931. (c) Aurobindo Ghose: Aurobindo Ghose, *The Life Divine*, 2 vols., 1939–40; Aurobindo Ghose, *Essays on the Gita*, 1st and 2nd series, 1921, 1928. (d) Indian Nationalism and Mahatma Gandhi: B. Pattabhi Sitaramayya, *The History of the Indian National Congress.* 2 vols., 1946–47; M. K. Gandhi, *The Story of my Experiments with Truth*, 1948; L. Fischer, *The Life of Mahatma Gandhi*, 1950; Romain Rolland, *Mahatma Gandhi*, 1924; C. F. Andrews, *Mahatma Gandhi's Ideas*, 1939.

[Sup.] MAX HUNTER HARRISON.

INDIANS OF NORTH AMERICA, MISSIONS TO THE: In 1951 there were almost 400,000 Indians in the United States, most of them west of the Mississippi River. Thirty-six Protestant denominations were then doing mission work among the Indians. In addition, there were some nondenominational and independent organizations engaged in mission work in some form. But with all this effort there were still Indians who had no opportunity to hear the gospel. This is particularly true in some of the remote areas of the Indian country in the southwest, where lack of roads and language handicaps make it difficult or impossible to reach the people.

There are no complete data on mission work among the Indians. Hence, the exact number of Indians professing Christianity is not known. But the number of Protestant Christians in the United States has been variously estimated from 39,000 to 100,000. The former estimate appears to be too low, while the latter appears to be too high. A more conservative estimate is between 65,000 and 70,000. The Roman Catholic Church estimates that it has a membership of 100,000 Eskimos and Indians, over 95,000 of them Indians on eighty-one reservations in the United States. This estimate also appears to be too high.

Both Catholics and Protestants have mission work among the Indians in Canada and Alaska. The work once done by Presbyterians and Methodists in Canada has come largely under the control of the United Church of Canada (q.v.). In Alaska there are probably 25,000 Indians and 15,000 Eskimos. Presbyterians, Protestant Episcopalians, Methodists, and others are doing mission work among them.

The mission work is carried on through a number of mediums, such as mission stations, mission schools, Christian centers, hospitals, and established churches.

There are over three hundred Indian ministers in the United States, many of them in Oklahoma. Few of these had opportunity to do special study in preparation for the ministry. Less than 6% have had both college and seminary training. The churches have generally failed adequately to train an indigenous leadership. Indeed, more than half of the denominations now doing mission work have not so much

as one Indian minister. Among the leading denominations, both in the number of Indian ministers and in the number of members, are the Baptist, Presbyterian, and Methodist.

See also HOME MISSIONS, VII.

BIBLIOGRAPHY: B. Frank Belvin, *The Status of the American Indian Ministry*, 1949; G. E. E. Lindquist, *Indians in Transition; National Catholic Almanac*, 1950; William David Schermerhorn, *The Christian Mission in a Modern World*, 1933.

B. FRANK BELVIN.

INDIGENOUS CHURCHES. See EXPANSION OF CHRISTIANITY.

INDIVIDUALISM: The primary meaning of individualism defines a state of mind or attitude which is produced by a certain type of society. This social milieu is one which pays little respect to tradition or authority. Tribal custom and convention have little control, there exists no overpowering social unity and individual initiative is unconfined. Such an individualistic society is one where people "think for themselves" and persons are not simply absorbed into the social organism as nonentities comprising a larger entity. There are evidences of such a spirit among the philosophers of Greek society. The ideal of self-sufficiency is an element in the Socratic character and the political theory of individualism is proposed by Plato in the *Republic*.

Modern individualism rests upon two concepts: the idea of the worth of the individual from a religious view and the commercial practice of free exchange. This former derived from the early Christian period and was strongly revived in the time of the Reformation. Individualism in economics simply asserted that if the processes of free exchange were allowed to operate without check, then the greatest good to the greatest number would automatically result.

Religious individualism did not originate in the Christian religion nor is it characteristic of earlier Judaism. The main strain of Hebrew literature makes Israel, the people or nation, the primary concern of God, but with the collapse of national hopes there emerges through the prophets a new sense of God's dealings directly with the individual. The Gospels take for granted the direct relation of the individual with God which is a particular implication of the Christian doctrine of the Fatherhood (q.v.) of God. The supreme value of the individual and the idea of human equality are complementary concerns of the New Testament. A central doctrine of the Reformation was the universal priesthood of believers and this in its didactic expression is individualistic and democratic.

The rise of individualism in commercial enterprise appears in the spirited mercantile cities of the Renaissance. The broad horizons opened by discovery and the stimulation of trade with the East, called for resourcefulness and activity. While medieval man had been organized and unified, this new European was incited to inventiveness, diversity and enterprise. The theory of economics devolved that exchanging parties in commercial dealings have a common interest. Free exchange and the division of labor lead to an increase in human satisfactions and happiness. Indeed the good of the community is served when man may trade without restraint. Under the philosophical school named Utilitarianism, the view sought the simplification of antiquated laws. The proposed theory was that law was not to make people do what was right but that law simply maintained a system of equal rights and provided men with the liberty essential to living the good life. A magnificent presentation of the principle of individualism was made by the last great utilitarian, John Stuart Mill writing *On Liberty* in 1859.

In the absolute sense, consistent individualism is not reasonable in a society. There is an interdependence and interaction between the individual and the group. Even the most pronounced individualists must recognize the role played by institutions and society at large in the development of individuality. When individualism is considered a tradition or "modus operandi" which must be defended to the bitter end, then it loses its force and dwindles to mere egoism.

See also DEMOCRACY; MAN, DOCTRINE OF; SOCIALISM.

BIBLIOGRAPHY: C. H. Cooley, "Personal Competition" in *Economic Studies*, IV, 1899; John Dewey, *Individualism, Old and New*, 1930; J. S. Mill, *On Liberty*, 1859; R. H. Tawney, *Religion and the Rise of Capitalism*, 1926; Max Weber, (Talcott Parsons, tr.), *The Protestant Ethic and the Spirit of Capitalism*, 1930.

EUGENE LIGGITT.

INDO-CHINA, FRENCH: Consists politically of three associated states within the French union of Vietnam, Cambodia, and Laos. Excluded from inland regions in each of these states is an extensive tribal area, part of which has been organized as a separate tribal territory under the Vietnam government. There are three main language groups—Vietnamese, Cambodian, and Laotian—as well as several score or more of dialects used by the mountain tribes' people.

The Christian and Missionary Alliance (*q.v.*) is the largest evangelical missionary agency in Indo-China, having commenced work in that country in 1911. The present missionary staff numbers 106. National church groups functioning on a completely indigenous basis comprise 124 church centers with 150 outstations. During 1951 there were 1,840 baptized converts and more than 7,000 inquirers. In 7 Bible Training Institutes there was an enrollment of 264 students. The dean of the oldest and largest Bible

Seminary was a Vietnamese, Ong van Huyen. Sunday school and young people's work was increasing. Alliance and Swiss Brethren missionaries, with national helpers, were engaged for many years in Bible translation, the preparation of hymnals, and other literature. Of Indo-China's 27,000,000 people, more than 90% soon will have the whole Bible in their own language (see BIBLE SOCIETIES).

In the Vietnamese Church self-government is complete. Administration and Christian fellowship is local, regional, and national. Financial independence, nearly complete before Japanese occupation during World War II and effective during that occupation, was interrupted by wide-scale fighting after that war. It became necessary to give some financial assistance, but the church maintained a steadfast effort to build up its financial independence. More than half a dozen Vietnamese couples, including one Laotian family, were engaged in missionary work among the tribes' people. Another couple from Cambodia was serving Cambodian-speaking groups in East Siam. Three Chinese churches were in operation, one of them outstanding in its influence.

BIBLIOGRAPHY: E. F. Irwin, *With Christ in Indo-China*, 1937.

A. C. SNEAD.

INDONESIA. See MALAY ARCHIPELAGO.

INDUSTRIAL CHRISTIAN FELLOWSHIP: A home mission of the Church of England, founded in 1919 by the fusion of the Navy Mission with the Christian Social Union. It stood and stands for Christ as Lord of *all* life, and for the redemption and renewal of both individual and society. Its lay missioners at factories, mines, and docks seek to reach those outside or on the fringe of the church. Area directors (mostly priests) seek to bring home to church people their obligation to social witness and action. Study and discussion groups are encouraged, for which literature is published.   PHILIP SAVILLE WATSON.

INDUSTRY, THE CHURCHES AND: The origin of modern industry is traceable to the industrial revolution of the eighteenth century when far-reaching economic and technological developments eventually substituted the factory system for the domestic economy then extant.

Such a radical sociocultural change was bound to bring in its wake both desirable and undesirable consequences. The beneficial effects have been, indeed, many and varied: man's capacities have been heightened; health has been improved and the span of human life has been lengthened; endless novel avenues to cultural growth have been opened; fabulous wealth has been produced, and a very much higher standard of living has been achieved; new forms of association, co-operation, and community have emerged. To ignore these and the many other benefits of modern industrialism is to distort the facts, which most certainly do not warrant the conclusion that this period has been "an orgy of soulless cupidity" (Tawney).

Captivated by the tremendous advances of industry, the churches of Europe and America generally supported the status quo up to about 1860. The greed of the successful was excused as being a necessary factor for progress. The misery of the exploited was theoretically explained on theological or economic grounds and practically alleviated somewhat through various charitable measures. Dissenters there were, but, for the most part, they were outside the main influential stream of Christian thought and practice.

The development of modern industry also involved the emergence of a number of problems: industrial strife, centralization of economic power in small groups, monopolistic and impersonal character of industrial organization, monotonous and repetitive operations, production not for use but for profit, and violent fluctuations in industrial activity. By the second half of the nineteenth century, some of these had become so severe as to induce Washington Gladden (q.v.), Joseph Cook (q.v., Vol. III), and others to speak and write repeatedly of the Christian law of love as a check upon the undesirable tendencies in economic theory and practice.

Under the impact of violent economic dislocations in the eighties and the nineties, the claim of moral supervision, formerly used for the preservation of the status quo and in opposition to radicalism, was transformed into the social gospel (q.v.). It acquired much prestige and influence throughout large sections of American Protestantism. It was also, until about 1925, a most powerful force in the development of the social policies of the Federal Council of the Churches of Christ in America (q.v.).

A turn toward a more "realistic" theology in Europe and in America in the period just before World War II tended to undermine some of the religious basis of the social gospel. And in the last decade, religious progressivism appeared to be losing some of its prestige and self-confidence along with other varieties of optimistic liberalism (q.v.). See also NEO-ORTHODOXY.

Nevertheless, Protestantism is still vitally concerned over current industrial problems, as attested by the pronouncements made at the First Assembly of the World Council of Churches (q.v.) at Amsterdam in 1948 and at the sessions of the National Council of the Churches of Christ in the U.S.A. (q.v.) at Denver in 1952.

Another outstanding current development in Protestant circles is the three-year research study of ethics in relation to modern economic life which was initiated in 1949 by the Federal Council of Churches, now part of the National Council of Churches, through its Department of the Church and Economic Life. With the support of a substantial grant from the Rockefeller Foundation, the study was undertaken in recognition of the urgent need for careful and realistic investigation of economic life and a reappraisal of its relation to spiritual and moral values. The findings in six volumes, published in late 1952 and during 1953, should provide a solid basis for responsible Christian individual and social action.

The Roman Catholic Church has likewise concerned itself with industrial maladjustments. During the nineteenth century, Cardinals H. E. Manning (q.v., Vol. VII) of England, Mermillod of Switzerland, James Gibbons (q.v.) of the United States, Archbishop W. E. Ketteler (q.v., Vol. VI) of Germany, and Bishop C. E. Freppel (q.v., Vol. IV) of France, all provided able leadership. Leo XIII (q.v., Vol. VI), first as bishop of Perugia and later as pope, did much, especially through his memorable encyclical, Rerum Novarum (1891) (q.v.), to define the relationship of Roman Catholic teaching to industrial problems. More recently, the encyclical Quadragesimo Anno (q.v.) of Pius XI (1931), the broadcast La Sollenita Della Pentecoste of Pius XII (1941), and the latter's numerous other acts and pronouncements have constituted notable attempts to relate Christian ethical principles to modern industry.

See also LABOR, THE CHURCHES AND.

BIBLIOGRAPHY: C. H. Hopkins, The Rise of the Social Gospel in American Protestantism, 1940; P. Hughes, The Pope's New Order, 1944; E. Mayo, The Social Problems of an Industrial Civilization, 1945; M. J. Williams, Catholic Social Thought, 1950; World Council of Churches, The Church and the Disorder of Society, Amsterdam Assembly Series, Vol. III, 1948.

CHARLES GARABED CHAKERIAN.

INEFFABILIS DEUS. The bull by which Pope Pius defined the dogma of the Immaculate Conception on December 8, 1854. It lists testimonies from the ecclesiastical tradition prior to the definition, and endeavors to show how the Fathers bear witness to the dogma formally, though implicitly. It appropriates the arguments of convenience formulated by Duns Scotus, and quotes Gen. 3:15 and Luke 1:28,42, as indirectly supporting the doctrine of the Immaculate Conception, the proclamation of which as an essential article of faith concludes the document.

Original text in Acta Pii IX, 1854–78.

GEORGES A. BARROIS.

INFANTICIDE. See ABANDONMENT AND EXPOSURE.

INFERIORITY COMPLEX. See ADLER, ALFRED.

INFINITE, INFINITY (Latin, *infinitus, -as,* "not limited"): Although "infinite" has had many meanings in many disciplines, they seem reducible to two: (1) the indeterminate, either extrinsically (the endless, e.g., number series) or intrinsically (the indefinite, e.g., spatial or temporal continua); (2) the complete or perfect (not necessarily the all-inclusive), that which lacks limitation either in one respect (e.g., man's will for Descartes) or in all respects (e.g., the medieval God). Though these meanings are contrary, they are logically and chronologically connected. The infinite as the indeterminate is what lacks determinate being, and which is therefore limited by a determinate being which in turn is not limited by anything else and is therefore infinite in the sense of being complete or perfect. Thus the infinite in the first sense is a negation which, seen as thus limited or finite, is negated by the infinite in the second sense, which is therefore a double negation or affirmation.

Historically, so long as there was little conception of a complete or perfect being, "infinity" was used primarily in the negative sense of indeterminacy. Thus infinity for the Greeks was the indeterminacy of reality, either intrinsically (e.g., Zeno's paradoxical continua), or extrinsically (e.g., the unboundedness of Melissus' "One" and the infinite number of atoms of Democritus), or both (e.g., Anaximander, "the Unlimited" of the Pythagoreans, and the infinitely various and divisible "seeds" of Anaxagoras). For Plato it was the material "Receptacle," his craftsman-god and eternal Forms being finite; for Aristotle matter (potentiality) is the only infinite, though his "Unmoved Mover," being pure actuality, anticipated the positive infinity of later thought.

With the entrance of Judaeo-Christian religious thought into the Greco-Roman philosophical tradition and the consequent theological conception of God (*q.v.*) as complete or perfect, "infinity" came to be used primarily in the second sense. Since the infinite of the Greeks was seen to be finite (limited in determinate being), a positive infinity in all respects was ascribed to God by medieval thought in general, though the interpretation of positive infinity as all-inclusiveness to produce a pantheism (*q.v.*) or panentheism in such thinkers as Plotinus, Scotus Eriugena, and Meister Eckhart and also in such modern philosophers as Bruno, Spinoza, and Hegel implied an ultimate identity of the two meanings of "infinity." Recent thought is characterized by the controversy as to whether God is positively infinite (especially conservative Protestantism and Catholicism), or finite in one or more respects (liberal Protestantism [see LIBERALISM] and naturalism [*q.v.*], e.g., J. S. Mill, William James, H. Rashdall, and E. S. Brightman), or both (e.g., A. N. Whitehead and C. Hartshorne).

BIBLIOGRAPHY (principally of the theological use of "infinity"): There is a good general account in F. J. Tennant, *Philosophical Theology,* Vol. II, 1930. Other especially noteworthy works of varying viewpoints are: S. Alexander, *Space, Time, and Deity,* Vol. II. A. N. Whitehead, *Process and Reality,* 1929; E. S. Brightman, *Philosophy of Religion,* 1940; E. L. Mascall, *He Who Is,* 1945; E. Brunner, *The Christian Doctrine of God,* 1950; and P. Tillich, *Systematic Theology,* 1951.

FRANCIS HOWARD PARKER.

INFUSION OF GRACE. Protestant theology, usually meaning by "grace" the undeserved favor of God, does not speak of infusion of grace. Roman Catholic theology, following Tertullian and Augustine, uses "grace" to mean also divine power. The classic expression of the doctrine of infusion of grace is in St. Thomas Aquinas. Grace is poured into the soul not as water into the pitcher but as light into a lens; it is a quality in the essence of the soul, not innate but imparted to the justified by divine action and without previous necessary disposition of the heart "save what God himself hath made"; not in itself virtue, but the principle and root of infused supernatural virtues. It is the first necessity of justification; by it guilt is remitted and the will moved to turn from evil toward eternal good. See also SOTERIOLOGY.

BIBLIOGRAPHY: Besides discussions in textbooks of theology, see St. Thomas Aquinas. *Summa Theol.* Part II (1st part) Q. 110.2,3,4; Q. 113.2,3,6,7,8.

KENNETH J. FOREMAN.

INGE, WILLIAM RALPH: d. Feb. 26, 1954. He was vicar of All Saints' Church, Ennismore Gardens (1905–7); Lady Margaret professor of divinity and fellow of Jesus College, Cambridge (1907–11) and Dean of St. Paul's, London (1911–34). Known as the "gloomy dean," he has realistically faced the problems of the church and his times, been a progressive leader in the Church of England, occupied major theological lectureships in Great Britain and America, and has most especially championed the cause of Christian devotion. His many interests are reflected in his prolific writings. Among his books of the last forty years are: *Faith* (1909); *Speculum Animae* (1911); *The Church and the Age* (1912); *Types of Christian Saintliness* (1915); *The Philosophy of Plotinus* (1918); *Outspoken Essays* (1919; second series, 1922); *The Idea of Progress* (1920); *The Victorian Age* (1922); *Personal Religion and the Life of Devotion* (1924); *The Platonic Tradition* (1926); *England* (1926); *Lay Thoughts of a Dean* (1926); *The Church in the World* (1927); *Assessments and Anticipations* (1929); *Christian Ethics and Modern Problems* (1930); *Everyman's Bible* (1930); *More Lay Thoughts of a Dean* (1931); *Things New and Old* (1933); *God and the Astronomers* (1933); *Vale* (1934); *The*

Gate of Life (1935); *Freedom, Love and Truth* (1936); *A Rustic Moralist* (1937); *Our Present Discontents* (1938); *A Pacifist in Trouble* (1939); *The Fall of Idols* (1940); *Talks in a Free Country* (1943); and *Diary of a Dean* (1949). [Sup.] RAYMOND W. ALBRIGHT.

INGERSOLL LECTURE: At her death in 1894 Miss Caroline Haskell Ingersoll bequeathed a sum to Harvard University for the establishment of the Ingersoll Lecture on the Immortality of Man, in memory of her father, George Goldthwait Ingersoll. The lecturer may be a clergyman or a layman of any profession and of any religious denomination. The lectures are published in the *Harvard Divinity School Bulletin.*
　　　　　　　　　　　　　　　　G. WHITE.

INGLIS, CHARLES: The son of the Rev. Archibald Inglis was born in Ireland in 1734 and after studying privately became S.P.G. catechist at Lancaster, Pa., in 1755, returning to England for orders in 1758. The following year he was appointed missionary at Dover, Del., where he remained until Feb., 1764, when he went to Trinity Parish in New York. At the evacuation of that city by the British he resigned as rector and returned to England. In 1787 he was consecrated, as the first British bishop outside the British Isles, bishop of Nova Scotia; d. Halifax, N.S., Feb. 24, 1816.

BIBLIOGRAPHY: Rightmyer, *Anglican Church in Delaware*, 1947; Dix, *History of Trinity Parish*, 1910; Lydekker, *Life and Letters of Charles Inglis*, 1946.
　　　　　　　　　　　　　　NELSON RIGHTMYER.

INGMAN, ANTERO WILHELM. Lutheran; b. at Lohtaja, Finland, July 7, 1819; d. at Helsinki, Sept. 5, 1877. He grew up amid a religious and national awakening in the Finnish student world. He was pastor in South Ostrobothnia, where he wrote a booklet in defense of the awakening. Together with a friend he translated into Finnish Luther's Church Postil (1848–50). As pastor in southern Finland he studied J. T. Beck's (*q.v.*, Vol. II) theology and was for the rest of his life an adherent of Beck. He was made professor of exegetical theology at the University of Helsinki in 1864. His most important work was a new translation of the Bible (1859). Ingman's life reflects a turning point in the spiritual life of Finland. Since 1840 the leading clergymen had belonged to the revival movement, but from now on they were also adherents of Beck's Biblical theology.
　　　　　　　　　　　　　LENNART PINOMAA.

INIQUITY: The English word "iniquity" is ultimately derived from the Latin *in*, "not," plus *aequus*, "even" or "equal," and therefore suggests a deviation from that which is just. It is used to translate a variety of Hebrew and Greek words. The word most frequently trans-

lated "iniquity" in the Bible is *'āwôn*, which occurs about 232 times. It is derived by some from a root meaning "bend" or "twist" and by others from a root meaning "err." It is used in such a way that it tends to combine the ideas of sin (*q.v.*) (Jer. 11:10; Isa. 43:24), guilt (Ex. 34:7; Ps. 32:2,5), and punishment (Gen. 4:13; II Kings 7:9; Ezek. 14:10). Sometimes the guilty persons are said to bear their own iniquity (Lev. 5:17; Num. 5:31), but at other times their iniquity is vicariously borne (Lev. 10:17; 16:22). In this connection special attention should be given to Isa. 53:11 (cf. 53:6,12).

The word *'āwĕn* is often translated "iniquity" and is to be associated with such ideas as worthlessness, trouble, sorrow, idolatry, and wickedness. Often it is used in the expression "workers of iniquity." Such persons are trouble makers who treat others unjustly (Pss. 59:2; 94:4–7; Hos. 6:8). The words *'āwĕl* and *'awlāh* usually denote "injustice" and "unrighteousness" (Deut. 32:4; Hab. 2:12).

In the New Testament the words most frequently translated "iniquity" are *anomia*, "lawlessness" (Matt. 7:23), and *adikia*, "unrighteousness" (Luke 13:27). All of the Hebrew words mentioned above are sometimes translated by *anomia* and *adikia* in the Septuagint.
　　　　　　　　　　　ARNOLD BLACK RHODES.

INNER LIGHT: This term characterizes a doctrine characteristic of the Quakers, and perhaps most fully developed by Robert Barclay in his *Apology for the True Christian Divinity*, though he uses the term "saving light" instead. As he expounds the doctrine, this light is in all, but it is not natural but a supernatural gift. Thus, it is not to be identified with the conscience, nor is it a relic of the light remaining in Adam after the Fall. It is not an accident but a real, spiritual substance. If it were an accident, when a man has it he would be holy since "no accident can be in a subject without it give the subject its own denomination"; but this light "subsists in the hearts of wicked men," since it is universal.

More positively, Barclay describes this light as "the gospel which the apostle saith expressly is preached 'in every creature under heaven.'" He distinguishes it from the "outward gospel" which apparently he identifies with the declaration of the history of Christ. He strenuously maintains that man can be, and is, saved apart from the outward gospel, but none can be saved apart from the saving light. "For to speak properly, the gospel is this inward power and life which preacheth glad tidings in the hearts of all men, offering salvation unto them, and seeking to redeem them from their iniquities, and therefore it is said to be preached 'in every creature under heaven': whereas there are many thousands of men and women to whom the outward gospel was never preached." This saving light is sufficient for salvation, but it can be resisted. Therefore, though none of those to whom the outward gospel is preached are saved, but by the inward operation of this light, and though this light which is sufficient is in all men, not all men are saved.

ANDREW K. RULE.

INNER MISSION (INNERE MISSION):

I. Germany: During World War I inner mission societies and agencies in Germany provided courses of instruction for chaplains in the armed services and supplied Bibles and other religious literature to soldiers and sailors. After the war endowments were lost by inflation. As a result of financial stringency and opposition from political groups, but also as a result of the development of German welfare work in general, inner mission activity was more sharply concentrated on: (1) evangelization, comprehended since 1918 under the term *Volksmission,* (2) relief, and (3) social action, or influence on public life, especially with reference to social problems.

The period of National Socialism introduced serious conflicts. Large institutions—many nurseries and training schools—were confiscated and turned over to National Socialist welfare organizations. Attempts to introduce euthanasia in inner mission institutions were energetically, and successfully, resisted. A leader in this resistance was the younger Friedrich von Bodelschwingh (*q.v.*). One-third of the institutions were severely damaged and many of them totally destroyed by air-raids during World War II.

With the end of the war in 1945 earlier activities were resumed or reinaugurated. In dealing with urgent postwar needs *Evangelisches Hilfswerk* (*q.v.*), whose branches were usually closely connected with inner mission agencies, made important contributions. Inner Mission work was seriously affected by the currency reform of 1948, for endowments were lost again and some activities had to be curtailed. The postwar occupation of eastern Germany by Russians and Poles resulted in the closing of many flourishing institutions.

Despite these difficulties thirty territorial societies were associated with the Central Committee of the Inner Mission in 1952. Workers included 47,000 deaconesses (*q.v.*), 4,200 deacons, 2,100 clergymen, physicians, and similarly trained personnel, 5,500 nurses, teachers, and youth leaders, and about 25,000 employees. There were 378 hospitals (*q.v.*), 123 homes for the physically and mentally handicapped, 403 convalescent homes, 1,005 homes for the aged (*q.v.*), 3,805 day nurseries, 81 hospices (*q.v.*), and many other homes for seamen (*q.v.*), mothers, the homeless, transients, etc.

BIBLIOGRAPHY: Wilhelm Engelmann, *Unser Werk: ein ABC der Inneren Mission,* 1939; Martin Gerhardt, *Ein Jahrhundert Innere Mission: die Geschichte des Central-Ausschusses,* 1948.

[Sup.] FRIEDRICH M. MUENCHMEYER.

II. Scandinavia: In Scandinavia, more than in Germany, the inner mission kept its original aim, the evangelization of the masses within the church. In Norway it grew out of the Haugean revival (see HAUGEANISM), in Sweden out of the revival led by C. O. Rosenius (see BORNHOLMERS, Vol. II), and in Denmark in connection with the evangelical awakening early in the nineteenth century. In all three countries evangelistic work was carried on by lay groups before the appearance of organizations.

Interest in inner and foreign missions usually went together in these groups. In Norway the first general organization (1842) was for foreign missions. In Sweden the first general organization was the *Evangeleska Fosterlandsstiftelse* (Evangelical Fatherland Foundation), organized in 1856 under impulses from Scotland by followers of Rosenius. Its original scope included only the publication and distribution of Christian literature through colporteurs. But soon the program was broadened. The colporteurs became evangelists. By 1861 the society included foreign and seamen's missions. In 1876 a dispute over the doctrine of the atonement (see PAUL P. WALDENSTROEM, Vol. XII) brought about the organization of the Swedish Mission Covenant (*q.v.*).

In Norway the first attempt to combine the many groups and societies engaged in inner mission work resulted (1868) in *Lutherstiftelse* (Luther Foundation), led by Gisle Johnsen. The emphasis was on publication and distribution of Christian literature, but the colporteurs conducted devotional meetings in close co-operation with clergymen. It did not succeed in uniting the lay forces to any large extent, for lay preaching was accepted only as an emergency measure. But it did good work in evangelization and publication until 1891, when *Det Norsk Lutherske Indremissionsselskap* (Norwegian Lutheran Inner Mission Association) was formed on a broader basis. Lay preaching was recognized as a normal rather than as an abnormal function in the church. This organization, representing conservative churchmen, covers most of the country, but evangelization is directed by local societies.

The more progressive and aggressive laymen, especially in western Norway, are associated in the Norwegian Evangelical Lutheran Mission Association, organized in 1891 and formerly known as the China Mission Association, which combined both inner and foreign missions, and in the Western Inner Mission Association, organized in 1898 by societies in and around Bergen. The latter emphasizes the independence of local societies and sometimes entertains a free-church tendency.

In Denmark organization began in 1853. In 1861 *Kirkelig Forening for Indre Mission* (Churchly Society for Inner Mission) was organized and was led for many years by Vilhelm Beck. The clergy play a greater part in the government of this association than elsewhere in Scandinavia. It also puts a greater emphasis on the sacraments. In Denmark, as in the other countries, there are several smaller organizations.

In contrast to Germany, the Scandinavian movement still puts the main emphasis on evangelism. However, various social and charitable institutions are more or less directly connected with it. Each of the larger societies maintains a Bible school for the training of workers. In Norway these workers are more than twice as numerous as the pastors. Mission houses built by the societies are found almost everywhere.

BIBLIOGRAPHY: P. G. Lindhardt, *Den Nordiske Kirkes Historie*, 1945; Ivar Welle, *Norges Kirkehistorie*, Vol. III, 1948; Edvard Sverdrup, *Fra Norges Kristenliv*, 1918.

IVER IVERSEN.

III. America: The inner mission movement, transplanted to America, found root especially among Lutherans. Many institutions were established for orphans (see CHILDREN, CARE OF), the aged (*q.v.*), seamen (*q.v.*), and immigrants (*q.v.*). Hospitals (*q.v.*) and hospices (*q.v.*), were established, and deaconesses (*q.v.*) were trained to minister in the various institutions. The German pattern was followed to a large extent by men like William A. Passavant (*q.v.*, Vol. VIII) and Jeremiah F. Ohl, while the Scandinavian pattern was also introduced, especially in the Midwest, where several societies united (1920) to form the Hauge Lutheran Inner Mission Federation.

There is a tendency to substitute Social Work (*q.v.*), Welfare Work, or Social Missions for the older term.

BIBLIOGRAPHY: J. F. Ohl, *The Inner Mission*, 1911; M. S. Greth, *Inner Mission Services on the Territory of the Ministerium of Pennsylvania*, 1951; S. S. Gjerde and P. Ljostveit, *The Haugean Movement in America*, 1941.

THEODORE G. TAPPERT.

INNITZER, THEODORE: Cardinal; b. Dec. 25, 1875, at Neugeschrei, Erzgebirge. Educated at the University of Vienna and its theological school, he was ordained there in 1902 and served in the parish at Pressbaum, Niederoesterreich. After serving several years as Studienpraefekt and Subregens at the theological seminary in Vienna he taught New Testament in the theological faculty at the University of Vienna and served three terms as dean of the theological faculty. During 1928–29 he was minister of social administration and on Sept. 19, 1932, Pope Pius XI named him archbishop of Vienna. He was named cardinal, with the titular church San Crisogono, on March 13, 1933.

RAYMOND W. ALBRIGHT.

INNOCENT: Innocent II: Rendered valuable services to the church as a whole and to the local clergy in Rome. Rebuilt Sta. Maria Trastevere, where he was buried. Contributed much to the maintenance of peace with the Germanic-Roman Empire. Originally was a Benedictine monk.

Innocent IV: Became professor of canon law at Bologna in 1226; auditor at the papal Curia in 1227; Cardinal of St. Lorenzo in Lucino, 1228; Vice-chancellor, 1235–40; also served as rector of the Mark of Ancona and legate in northern Italy.

See also POPES.

[Sup.] ALBERT HYMA.

IN PARTIBUS INFIDELIUM: Latin, "in the regions of the infidels." This name was given formerly to Roman Catholic non-residential bishops consecrated to the title of dioceses abandoned because of Moslem or heathen invasions. The official terminology of the canon law is now "titular bishop" (*q.v.*, Vol. II).

INQUISITION: The "Holy Roman and Universal Inquisition," organized as a Congregation by Paul III in 1542, is officially designated since 1908 as "Congregation of the Holy Office." It has exclusive competence in matters concerning the Catholic faith and the validity of the sacraments. It has charge of the *Index of forbidden books* since 1917, and is competent in several matters previously of the jurisdiction of the Congregation of Indulgences, now suppressed. Cf. "Congregazioni Romane," in *Enciclopedia Cattolica*.

[Sup.] GEORGES A. BARROIS.

INQUISITION, SPANISH. See TORQUEMADA, TOMAS DE.

INSCRIPTIONS, ANCIENT HEBREW AND RELATED SYRO-PALESTINIAN: The earliest known examples of alphabetic inscriptions appear in Syria-Palestine in the early second millennium B.C. For the most part, those dating earlier than 1000 B.C. are fragmentary and only partly deciphered. There are, however, notable exceptions. The great cache of Canaanite (Ugaritic, *q.v.*) mythological tablets from the 14th century B.C., discovered beginning in 1929 on the North Syrian coast, have yielded readily to decipherment and interpretation. They are written in a cuneiform alphabet (also represented in Palestine proper), and have proved of immense value for biblical studies. An even earlier corpus of inscriptions from about 1500 B.C., the Proto-Sinaitic inscriptions discovered at Serabit el-Khadem in the Sinai Peninsula in 1905, has yielded slowly to decipherment. The inscriptions now appear to be funerary inscriptions of Canaanite slave (or hired) laborers in Egyptian turquoise mines.

Byblus has produced a series of inscriptions written in the old Canaanite alphabet. The majority of these are royal inscriptions, the most famous being the Sarcophagus Inscription of Ahiram (early tenth century B.C.). A large corpus of standard Phoenician inscriptions follows upon the Byblian inscriptions. Of the earlier exemplars, the most important are the Kilamuwa inscriptions from Zinčirli (ninth century B.C.), and the newly-discovered monumental inscriptions from Karatepe (eighth century B.C.), the longest of old Phoenician texts.

Old Aramaic inscriptions from Syria begin to appear in the tenth—ninth century B.C. Of particular interest are the votive stele to Melqart set up by Ben Hadad (ca. 850 B.C.), the contemporary of Ahab of Israel; the stele of Zakir king of Hamath (early eighth century B.C.), the Panamu Inscriptions of Zinčirli (eighth century B.C.), and the lengthy, though poorly preserved Sujin Stele recording a treaty between Aramaean kings in the period of Assyrian weakness before the rise of Tiglath-pileser III to power (745 B.C.). About the middle of the eighth century, inscriptions in "Empire Aramaic," the language of the late Assyrian, Neo-Babylonian, and Persian empires begin to appear.

The Moabite Inscription of King Mesha (ca. 840 B.C.) has been known since 1868. It remains of decisive importance by reason of its intimate relation in language and script to Hebrew epigraphic materials, not to mention its direct value for Israelite political history. The inscription records the events of Moab's war of independence against Israel begun in the days of Ahab and completed, to judge from the biblical account (II Kings 3:4 ff.), in the days of Joram.

The earliest extant Hebrew inscription is the Gezer Plaque from the tenth century B.C. It is a school boy's practice tablet containing an ancient jingle about the seasons of the year. It is written in a script virtually identical with that of contemporary Phoenician inscriptions.

In the excavations of Samaria in 1910, G. A. Reisner discovered some sixty-three business notations inscribed in ink on ostraca. They date from the years 778–770 B.C. in the reign of Jeroboam II of Israel. The ostraca record payments (in oil and wine) to the crown. The ostraca provide rich sources for the study of personal names and place names in eighth century Israel, and provide a basis for distinguishing the dialectical peculiarities of (North) Israel. The script of the ostraca is the forerunner of the smooth Hebrew cursive of the seventh and early sixth centuries; the spelling of the ostraca follows "Aramaic" practice as opposed to the Phoenician system in use in early Israel.

One of the most important of all Hebrew inscriptions is the Siloam Inscription from the age of Hezekiah (ca. 700 B.C.). The inscription was found in the entrance to Hezekiah's tunnel in Jerusalem. It records in good, classical Hebrew details concerning the completion of the conduit (cf. II Kings 20:20; II Chron. 32:30).

The most extensive and interesting of the pre-exilic Hebrew inscriptions are the Lachish Letters (q.v.). The main corpus, some eighteen ostraca, were found in 1935 by the Starkey excavation at Tell ed-Duweir (ancient Lachish). The letters can be dated accurately to the last months of 589 B.C. Of the eighteen letters, some six are clearly legible. These contain a military correspondence between one Hoshaiah, an army officer, and Yaosh, military governor of Lachish. Careful philological and epigraphic study of the ostraca has slowly chipped away early sensational theories regarding them; there yet remains, however, an impressive amount of linguistic and historical data throwing light on the last days of Judah and the book of Jeremiah.

From the period of the kings come some hundreds of short inscriptions on seals, seal impressions, and stamped jar-handles. Notable in this classification are the royal stamped handles from late pre-exilic Judah (late eighth to early sixth centuries B.C.). These carry the legend, "to the king," and a place-name, presumably a royal store-city or administrative center.

Jewish inscriptions in the native Hebrew script dwindle in number and importance in the postexilic period, but do not completely die out until the second century A.D. A series of stamped jar-handles, and coins bearing the legend, yĕhûd (Judah) come from Persian and early Greek times. Hasmonean coins inscribed in an archaizing Hebrew script (from which the Samaritan script evolves) first appear in the time of John Hyrcanus (135–104 B.C.), and continue into the first century B.C. There is a brief revival, finally, of the use of the old script on the coins of the First Revolt (A.D. 66–70), and the Second Revolt (A.D. 132–135).

At the same time, Jewish documents and inscriptions in Aramaic are abundant in Palestine and the Dispersion from the Persian period onwards. By the Maccabean period literary texts and inscriptions in Hebrew are regularly written in the Aramaic script. By the Herodian period, this script has evolved into the so-called "square character," the script of the tomb and ossuary inscriptions from Jerusalem and its environs in the last decades before the fall of Jerusalem in A.D. 70, and the antecedent of the "Hebrew" script of the inscriptions of Late Roman and Byzantine synagogues.

BIBLIOGRAPHY: D. Diringer, *Le iscrizioni antico-ebraiche palestinesi*, 1934; idem, *The Alphabet, A Key to the History of Mankind*, 1948; G. R. Driver, *Semitic Writing, From Pictograph to Alphabet*, 1948; J. B. Pritchard (ed.), *Ancient Near Eastern Texts Relating to the Old Testament*, 1950; T. C. Vriezen and J. H. Hospers, *Palestine Inscriptions*, 1951; K. Galling, "Ostrakon,"

"Muenze," "Ossuar," "Siegel," "Krugstempel," "Stele," "Synagoge," and "Schreibmaterial (and Schrift)," in *Biblisches Reallexikon*, 1937.

[Sup.] FRANK M. CROSS, JR.

INSTITUTE FOR ECUMENICAL STUD-IES, GRADUATE. See ECUMENICAL INSTITUTE.

INSTITUTE FOR RELIGIOUS AND SO-CIAL STUDIES. Founded in 1938 by the Jewish Theological Seminary in New York through an initial gift of Lucius N. Littauer, the purpose of the institute has been to give clergymen and other religious teachers of all faiths and backgrounds the opportunity to discuss the common problems of all religious traditions. In 1944, a branch was founded in Chicago, which functions in co-operation with the University of Chicago; in 1945, another branch was opened in Boston, conducted in co-operation with the American Academy of Arts and Sciences. The three sections of the institute conduct series of courses annually. The institute has published several volumes in a Religion and Civilization Series. The institute's director is Louis Finkelstein (*q.v.*).

BIBLIOGRAPHY: Jewish Theological Seminary catalogues; Religion and Civilization series.

MORRIS FINE.

INSTITUTIONAL CHURCHES: The accelerated industrialization of the United States after the Civil War, with crowded living conditions, with the "newer," predominantly non-Nordic, non-Protestant immigration (see EMIGRANTS AND IMMIGRANTS), and with some alienation of labor (*q.v.*) from the churches, created for the churches the then widely discussed problem of "how to reach the masses." City evangelism and the institutional church were the two most frequently attempted solutions.

The institutional program was experimental and fluid—recreation for children, adult education, clubs, forums, even financial assistance—in a word, Christian friendliness. A well rounded institutional program often involved a special building, social, and even medical workers, as well as ministers, and a large budget. Neighborhood (*q.v.*) and settlement houses (see SETTLEMENT MOVEMENT) were closely akin, while denominational and non-denominational "missions" and church extension societies often supported "institutional" features. Such institutional work owed much to the social gospel (*q.v.*) ideology.

Institutional churches were not notably successful in bringing non-Protestants into Protestant church membership, but they fostered Christian good will and mutual understanding, and helped many needy people; they gave the churches new realization of social needs; and thus indirectly strengthened many reform movements such as those for free pews, temperance, better housing, suppression of vice, industrial justice, and adult education. In a somewhat less patronizing and more democratic form, social and "institutional" features are characteristic of many leading "downtown" churches today.

BIBLIOGRAPHY: T. Abel, *Protestant Home Missions to Catholic Immigrants*, 1933; A. I. Abell, *The Urban Impact on American Protestantism 1865–1900* (1943), pp. 137–193.

LEFFERTS A. LOETSCHER.

INSTITUTUM DIVI THOMAE: A graduate school of scientific research of the Athenaeum of Ohio, founded by the late Archbishop John T. McNicholas of Cincinnati in 1935. Under the direction of cofounder George S. Sperti the Institutum carries on basic research in the natural sciences while training a limited number of graduate students for a master's or doctor's degree. Located in Cincinnati, Ohio, the Institutum also operates marine biological laboratories in Palm Beach, Fla.

The major project of the school is the study of the cellular growth in cancer in an effort to find more effective therapeutic agents to combat the disease. During and following World War II various government agencies employed school facilities on restricted national defense work.   THOMAS J. McCARTHY.

INSTRUMENTALISM: This term is associated with the thought of John Dewey (1859–1952) (*q.v.*). It is a particular form of pragmatism sponsored by those functionalists in psychology and philosophy who hold that the mind is not something *sui generis* but rather the instrument or tool of the organism. All organisms to survive must make adaptation to their environment, otherwise they perish. The function of mind is just such a tool, much like the hands, the legs, the capacity to run, to ward off the enemy. Ideas are means of getting on in the world, true if successful and wrong if unsuccessful. Instrumentalism holds that the traditional view of mind as a spectator looking out at the world from some unique position, a soul-like substance having its origin in some special creation or in a world of spirit, is outmoded. We must see it as it is: an evolving tool in the medium of Nature, useful biologically and fundamentally functional.

The first manifesto of the theory of instrumentalism appeared in *Studies in Logical Theory* (1903). William James in his *Principles of Psychology* (1890) had toyed with the view as he did with many of his seminal ideas. In 1899 John Dewey in a famous address entitled "Psychology and Philosophic Method" banished the assumption of the soul or ego from psychological language and substituted the concept of behavior-experience in which mind had its setting and function. (Behaviorism in psychology had here its early protagonist.)

Thus mind became symbolized along with the body in psychological literature as S-R (stimulus-response) or as more conservative functionalists now say S-O-R (stimulus-organism-response)—suggesting the pragmatic theory of mind as part and parcel of nature (not something supernatural).

Instrumentalism has had a successful vogue in recent psychology and philosophy largely because of the importance given to the evolutionary viewpoint; it also enjoyed acclaim because of the hope that by its basic conception of mind more progress could be made in the understanding of behavior following scientific procedures. If, it was held, mind is something quite unique, supernaturally grounded, then no scientific psychology could be constructed since, patently, a scientific method presupposes a causal nexus in the warp and woof of nature. Furthermore, the old view of mind rested upon a psychology wed to philosophical premises (e.g., Plato's theory of the soul) and to a standardized theology in which the soul issued from God and returned to God. Such views made impossible the extension of scientific method and hindered full and proper investigation of behavior. Moreover, animal psychology had been preparing the way.

Instrumental logic (functional logic) looks upon thought as a means by which experience is deliberately organized and its function to be that of reconstructing experience effectively. Thinking is intelligent guidance to experience: facing facts, issues, solving problems (frustrations). Ideas are tools, platforms of response, tentative and uncertain until tested by their results. Knowledge is functional, instrumental and as such is both a science and an art. Logic is a practical discipline giving no entrance into the realm of any absolute truth. Truth is forged on the anvil of experience.

See also EPISTEMOLOGY. VERGILIUS FERM.

INTERCHURCH AID. See RELIEF, RECONSTRUCTION, AND INTERCHURCH AID.

INTERCHURCH WORLD MOVEMENT OF NORTH AMERICA: This movement grew out of a meeting of representatives of various Protestant home and foreign missionary boards meeting in New York City on Dec. 17, 1918. The national organization consisted of a General Committee of more than a hundred persons nominated by the co-operating boards, and an Executive Committee of which Dr. John R. Mott (q.v.) was chairman, and a Canadian Council to consider matters peculiar to Canada. There was a staff headed by a general secretary, Dr. S. Earl Taylor, and associate general secretaries. Full organization of interdenominational forces was also contemplated for each state and local community.

The Interchurch World Movement was not, like an unsuccessful attempt made in these same years (1918–20), an effort to achieve organic unity among the churches; nor was it intended to be, like the Federal Council of Churches (q.v.), a federation of church bodies limited in its powers and authority by the constituting churches. It was patterned more after the co-operative financial "drives" of the recent World War I days, and was an effort of numerous interdenominational and denominational agencies to co-ordinate their various enterprises in home and foreign missions, Christian education, and social services in the interests of greater efficiency.

The Movement contemplated two types of activity: (1) There was to be an extensive program of fact finding by national and community surveys, both at home and abroad, which would examine large areas of modern society, such as the city and rural life, and analyze the church's efficiency in these areas. The social horizons were to be broad, and the viewpoint super-denominational. (2) The second type of activity dealt with "means"—the united raising of funds and greater co-ordination of all services rendered. The Movement was not to dictate to the denominations and was to have actual control over only its own administrative budget.

In spite of its high hopes, the Movement collapsed in less than two years. It had presupposed a greater unity of ideas and objectives than yet existed among the American churches. It had counted on large financial support from unchurched friendly citizens which did not materialize. Its sociological far overshadowed its theological emphasis. Its bold stand on the steel strike alienated some potential supporters, and it suffered from postwar weariness and disillusionment.

Part of the research program of the Interchurch Movement was later carried out in distinguished surveys by the Institute of Social and Religious Research. Most notable perhaps of the achievements of the Movement was its courageous report on the steel strike of 1919, which informed and powerfully influenced public opinion, and produced direct effects on industrial conditions.

BIBLIOGRAPHY: See *The Handbook* (1919) and *Report on the Steel Strike of 1919* (1920) and other writings by the Interchurch World Movement. For opinions about the Movement, see the *Christian Century* and various denominational newspapers.

LEFFERTS A. LOETSCHER.

INTERCOMMUNION: The problem of intercommunion is a by-product of the denominational development of Protestantism, in which differences regarding the Lord's Supper have been prominent since the Reformation. It was in the period of the Reformation, too, that the issue of intercommunion arose in those areas of

Germany and Switzerland where the Reformed and Lutheran groups were in close contact. Generally speaking, the Reformed were inclined to favor the practice, while the Lutherans were opposed to it; but there were many exceptions on both sides.

It was in America, however, that the issue of intercommunion assumed major proportions. During the intense denominational rivalries of the nineteenth century, a number of Protestant groups observed what came to be termed "close communion." With the decline of those rivalries in the twentieth century the ecumenical movement (q.v.) served to raise the question of the propriety of forbidding intercommunion as a means for demonstrating the unity of the church and achieving greater unity. The European churches participating in ecumenical activity were also compelled to re-examine their positions in the matter. Out of this discussion several answers to the problem have arisen.

Those who favor the practice of intercommunion maintain that the Lord's Supper was instituted as a means for unity rather than division. Unity of a doctrinal or confessional nature, therefore, follows logically and chronologically from joint communion, not vice versa. The ultimate responsibility for worthy participation lies with the conscience of the communicant himself rather than with that of the officiant. This viewpoint has been instrumental in the arrangement of community communion services, in which congregations of various denominations have participated.

At the other extreme are those who hold that joint participation in the sacrament is a confession of a common faith, and that therefore only those who share a common doctrinal faith ought to commune together. They regard it as the duty of the church to deny the privilege of the Lord's table to those who are not thus qualified, and many require registration prior to communion as a means for carrying out this duty. Between these two viewpoints lie many varieties and combinations, for only rarely has either of these positions been maintained with complete consistency.

A special problem has been posed by the contention of Roman Catholic, Eastern Orthodox, and some Anglican theologians that only legitimate ordination in the apostolic succession can validate the administration of the Eucharist, and that therefore communion at the hands of a priest lacking such ordination is a mutilated sacrament, or none at all. They have consequently discouraged or prohibited their faithful from communing at alien altars.

Particular instances of the problem have been the communion services held in connection with various ecumenical conferences, where churches of several different denominations celebrated simultaneously, each at its own altar; the ad-ministration of the sacrament to the armed forces, where chaplains of the various denominations have not always been available; and the situation of German Protestantism during and since the era of National Socialism, when circumstances seemed to make intercommunion expedient (see GERMANY, I).

BIBLIOGRAPHY: Donald Baillie and John Marsh (eds.), *Intercommunion* (1952), and the proceedings and reports of various ecumenical conferences; Hans Asmussen (ed.), *Abendmahlsgemeinschaft?* (1937), a discussion growing out of the German situation; John T. Christian, *Close Communion*, a study by an American Baptist; E. S. Freemen, *The Lord's Supper in Protestantism*, 1945.

JAROSLAV PELIKAN.

INTERDENOMINATIONAL FOREIGN MISSION ASSOCIATION OF NORTH AMERICA: Founded in 1917 by a group of "faith missions" desirous of banding together for fellowship and prayer. It is a fellowship of foreign missionary societies without denominational affiliation and has set up a standard for missionary procedure and practice to which each member society must adhere.

The basis of fellowship is a common adherence to the historic Christian faith as expressed in its doctrinal statement. The societies unite in reliance upon God through faith and prayer for the provision of their needs. The aim of the I.F.M.A. is to present a strong united testimony to the need for a complete and speedy evangelization of the world.

Its (December, 1951) membership of twenty-eight societies with about 4,500 missionaries gives the I.F.M.A. a world coverage. A series of pamphlets presenting many phases of missionary work is published by the I.F.M.A. for distribution.   J. O. PERCY.

INTERDICT. See CENSURES.

INTERFAITH RELATIONS: As distinguished from the term "interdenominational," which in common usage is applied to relations among Protestant church bodies, the term "interfaith" is generally applied in the Western world to relations between Protestants and Roman Catholics, Protestants and the Eastern Orthodox, and Christians and Jews.

I. Protestants and Roman Catholics: Relations between Protestants (see PROTESTANTISM) and Catholics (see ROMAN CATHOLIC CHURCH) were sometimes more and sometimes less friendly, depending partly on shifting climates of opinion (e.g., Romanticism, q.v., Vol. X), partly on political and social conditions (e.g., the Thirty Years' War, q.v.), and partly on movements in the life of the church (e.g., Tractarianism). Generally speaking, unfriendliness toward Rome was more marked in free churches than in established churches, and more deep-seated in American than in European Protestantism. On the other hand, hostility toward Protestantism was usually greater in predominantly Roman Catholic countries (e.g., see LATIN AMERICA; SPAIN) than in predominantly Protestant countries, and sharper among Jesuits than among Benedictines.

Protestantism and Roman Catholicism represent divergent interpretations of Christianity. Besides notable areas of agreement, important differences in the conceptions of authority color the doctrines of God and man, grace and works, church and sacraments. Accordingly even the most irenic advocates of reunion (see MELANCHTHON, PHILIP; GROTIUS, HUGO; DURIE, JOHN; LAUD, WILLIAM; PUSEY, EDWARD B., Vol. IX) recognized the need for prior reform. Actual but unofficial negotiations looking toward union were conducted by the Anglican William Wake (q.v., Vol. XII) and the Roman Catholic Louis E. Du Pin (q.v., Vol. IV) early in the eighteenth century, and again between Anglicans and Roman Catholics in the Conversations at Malines (q.v.) in the present century. Such negotiations seemed to be rendered futile by papal denials of the validity of Anglican orders, and also by the later (1950) papal definition of the dogma of the assumption of the Virgin Mary. Nevertheless, a few Protestants, influenced by the liturgical movement and such societies as the Confraternity of Unity (q.v.), continued to advocate rapprochement with Rome.

In addition to doctrinal differences, a variety of practical issues repeatedly introduced friction. Roman Catholic policies with regard to intermarriage, education, censorship, and political activity alarmed Protestants and others in Europe and America. This was especially so in the United States, where the Know-Nothing movement (organized in 1852 with a nativist program), the American Protective Association (organized in 1887 and later claiming 1,000,000 members), and the Ku Klux Klan (q.v.) adopted anti-Catholic platforms. Still later, agitation for diplomatic representation at the Vatican (q.v.) was opposed by many and was a factor in the formation of the organization called Protestants and Other Americans United for Separation of Church and State (q.v.).

Since 1848 successive popes invited Protestants and the Eastern Orthodox to unite with the Roman Church, but it was made clear that full submission to Rome was the condition. On the other hand, the pope was invited to send official representatives to the first assembly (1948) of the World Council of Churches (q.v.) and to similar meetings which preceded and followed. The pope refused in every case on the ground that representatives of the Roman Church could not participate as equals with heretics. However, unofficial observers were often present. On the whole, like the ecumenical movement (q.v.), the effects of two world wars also softened more than they sharpened

the conflict between Protestants and Roman Catholics (see GERMANY, III; HILFSWERK, EVANGELISCHES; NATIONAL CONFERENCE OF CHRISTIANS AND JEWS; SWORD OF THE SPIRIT).

II. Protestants and Eastern Orthodox: Cultural and geographical distance and linguistic difficulties made Protestant contacts with the Eastern Orthodox (q.v.) less close in the centuries immediately following the Reformation. In addition, there were striking religious differences, among them the Eastern rejection of the filioque (q.v., Vol. IV), emphasis on tradition, invocation of saints and angels, and a different conception of the sacraments. However, a few conversations with the Orthodox began during the Reformation, when a number of Easterners studied in Wittenberg. Philip Melanchthon (q.v) corresponded with men from the East and prepared a Greek translation of the Augsburg Confession (q.v.) in the hope of preparing the ground for mutual understanding. Later the Lutheran Hans von Ungnad arranged conversations (1576–81) with the patriarch of Constantinople. There were also relations between Geneva and the Orthodox, and Patriarch Cyril Lukaris (1572–1637) returned from the West to propose a reform of the Greek Church on Calvinistic lines.

Anglican relations with the East developed later, although William Wake, who had correspondence with Roman Catholics (see I above), was also drawn into negotiations with the Orthodox. Interest in Eastern Churches was awakened by the Oxford Movement (see TRACTARIANISM, Vol. XI) in the nineteenth century. Especially after 1870, when Anglo-Roman enthusiasm waned as a result of the decree of the infallibility of the pope (q.v., Vol. V), private negotiations were opened with Russian, Greek, and Serbian churches. Lambeth Conferences (q.v.) then occupied themselves with the question officially, and after 1923 the patriarchates of Cyprus, Jerusalem, Constantinople, and Alexandria recognized the validity of Anglican orders, and the Church of Rumania granted limited intercommunion (q.v.).

Congregationalists, Baptists, Presbyterians, Methodists, and others established missions in Orthodox countries during the nineteenth century and engaged especially in educational and medical work. The political and social effects of two world wars and the rise of communism (q.v.) in the twentieth century made some of the Orthodox more sympathetic toward the West. Unlike the Roman Church, Eastern Churches participated in the ecumenical movement (q.v.), and a few Orthodox Churches, organized in the New World as a result of immigration, joined the National Council of the Churches of Christ in the U. S. A. (q.v.). Meanwhile relations between Roman Catholics and the Eastern Orthodox were marked by friction resulting from secular and ecclesiastical politics (see RUMANIA; YUGOSLAVIA).

III. Christians and Jews: Relations between Christians and Jews (see JUDAISM, RECENT) were of a different order from those between Christian communions. Despite common roots, Judaism was quite uniformly regarded as a different religion rather than as a different interpretation of the same religion. Basic in the cleavage was the Jewish rejection of Jesus as Messiah (q.v.). Religious differences were heightened by what appeared to many to be an identification of religion with race, which set Jews farther apart from Christian neighbors. This isolation was partly a cause and partly a result of the deplorable persecutions which Jews suffered again and again in nominally Christian countries—persecutions in which political, social, and economic factors played a part (see ANTISEMITISM; KU KLUX KLAN; PROTOCOLS OF THE ELDERS OF ZION; REFUGEES; ZIONISM).

Friendlier attitudes, although strongly resisted, were reflected in Christian attempts to convert Jews to Christianity (see JEWS, MISSIONS TO THE). Efforts were also made to dissipate prejudices and establish cordial social and civic relationships, as a rule without glossing over religious differences which actually existed (see NATIONAL CONFERENCE OF CHRISTIANS AND JEWS).

BIBLIOGRAPHY: C. E. Silcox and G. M. Fisher, *Catholics, Jews, and Protestants*, 1934; E. R. Clinchy, *All in the Name of God*, 1934; J. T. McNeill, *Unitive Protestantism*, 1930.

On Catholicism: Ludwig Pastor, *Die kirchlichen Reunionsbestrebungen waehrend der Regierung Karls V.*, 1879; E. S. Middleton, *Unity and Rome*, 1922; W. H. van de Pol, *The Christian Dilemma*, 1952; Karl Adam, *One and Holy*, 1951; Ludwig Lambinet, *Das Wesen des katholisch-protestantischen Gegensatzes*, 1946; R. A. Billington, *The Protestant Crusade*, 1938; Friedrich Heiler, *Im Ringen um die Kirche*, 1931; W. E. Garrison, *Catholicism and the American Mind*, 1928; Paul Blanshard, *American Freedom and Catholic Power*, 1949.

On Eastern Orthodoxy: Ernst Benz, *Wittenberg und Byzanz*, 1949; G. E. Zachariadis, *Tuebingen und Konstantinopel*, 1941; P. E. Shaw, *American Contacts with the Eastern Churches, 1820-70*, 1937; idem, *The Early Tractarians and the Eastern Church*, 1930; J. A. Douglas, *The Relations of the Anglican Churches with the Eastern Orthodox*, 1921.

On Judaism: James W. Parkes, *The Conflict of the Church and the Synagogue*, 1934; C. H. Moehlman, *The Christian-Jewish Tragedy*, 1933; A. R. Eckhardt, *Christianity and the Children of Israel*, 1948.

THEODORE G. TAPPERT.

INTERIM:

BIBLIOGRAPHY: J. Lortz. *Die Reformation in Deutschland*, Vol. II (1939), pp. 270-281; H. Bornkamm, "Moritz von Sachsen," in *Zeitschr. fuer deutsche Geisteswissenschaft* (1938), 398 ff.; K. Brandi, *Karl V*, 1937.   [Sup.]

INTERNATIONAL APOSTOLIC HOLINESS UNION. See HOLINESS CHURCHES.

INTERNATIONAL ASSOCIATION FOR LIBERAL CHRISTIANITY AND RELIGIOUS FREEDOM: Founded May 25, 1900, upon the initiation of the American Unitarian Association, which called a conference of liberal religious thinkers and workers, the Association changed its name several times without affecting the continuity of its organization. In 1949, for the first time since World War II, an International Congress of Religious Liberals was held in Amsterdam, and in 1952 the second postwar Congress was held in Oxford, England.

The purposes of the Association are to bring into closer union the historic liberal churches, the liberal elements in all churches, and isolated congregations and workers for religious freedom; to draw into the same fellowship free religious groups throughout the world which are in essential agreement with the Association's ways of thinking; and to open and maintain communications with free Christian groups in all lands which are striving to unite religion and liberty.

The I.A.R.F. is not an exclusively Christian organization, although the bulk of its membership is from the liberal wing of Christian denominations. Its member groups include the American Unitarian Association, U.S.A.; Universalist Church of America; Le Foyer de l'Ame, Belgium; General Assembly of Unitarian and Free Christian Churches, England; Czechoslovak Church; Unitarian Church in Czechoslovakia; the Free Church Union, Denmark; Eglise reformée du Foyer de l'Ame, France; Centrale Commissie voor het Vrijzinnig Protestantisme in Nederland, Holland; Unitarian Church in Hungary; the Brahmo Samaj Movement (q.v.), India; the Independent Church of the Philippines; Unitarian Churches in Transylvania, Rumania; Sveriges Religiosa Reformforbund, Sweden; Schweizerischer Verein fuer freies Christentum, Switzerland; Deutscher Bund fuer freies Christentum, Germany; Bund Deutscher Unitarier, Germany; Japan Free Religious Association; Non-Subscribing Presbyterian Church of Ireland. EDWARD A. CAHILL.

INTERNATIONAL BIBLE STUDENTS. See JEHOVAH'S WITNESSES.

INTERNATIONAL CHURCH CONGRESS FOR INVESTIGATING THE SITUATION OF PROTESTANTISM IN EUROPE. See EUROPEAN CENTRAL OFFICE FOR INTERCHURCH AID.

INTERNATIONAL CONGREGATIONAL COUNCIL: During the years following the American Civil War it became customary for Congregationalists in Britain and the United States to exchange delegates and observers at their international conventions, but no serious attempt was made to assemble a joint conference of Congregationalists from the two countries and other lands until about 1890. The Rev. Alexander Hanny, secretary of the Congregational Union of England and Wales, was instrumental in bringing together the first Inter-

national Congregational Council at London in July, 1891, at a cost to the Union of £1,059. Representatives from Congregational churches throughout the world were assembled, and a constitution was adopted, fixing the size of the Council at 450 members—150 from Great Britain and Ireland, 150 from the United States, and 150 from the rest of the world. Subsequent meetings of the Council have been held as follows: 1899 at Boston, Mass.; 1908 at Edinburgh; 1920 at Boston; 1930 at Bournemouth, England; and 1949 at Wellesley, Mass. The Councils ordinarily confine themselves to the discussion of broad Christian issues relating to Congregationalism and attempt, by sharing mutual experience and ideals, to cement international understanding and goodwill among the Congregationalists of all lands. Large numbers of persons not officially appointed as delegates ordinarily attend the sessions. In 1930 more than 500 Americans journeyed to Bournemouth on a Good Will Tour in connection with the Council. The constituent Congregational bodies of the Council represent Africa, Argentina, Australia and New Zealand, Brazil, British Guiana, British Isles, Finland, Holland, Jamaica, and the United States, together with church groups from eighteen other areas.

BIBLIOGRAPHY: Albert Peele, *These Hundred Years*, 1931; G. G. Atkins and F. L. Fagley, *History of American Congregationalism*, 1942.

RICHARD D. PIERCE.

INTERNATIONAL CONSTITUTIONAL CHURCH. See SPIRITUALISM.

INTERNATIONAL COUNCIL OF CHRISTIAN CHURCHES: An international organization to foster the co-operation of Bible-believing Churches in maintaining a pure testimony to historic Christianity, opposing Modernism (*q.v.*), resisting governmental restrictions upon religious and missionary activity, and promoting Christian education both in day and Sunday schools.

Organized at Amsterdam, Holland, in August, 1948, immediately before the constituting of the World Council of Churches (*q.v.*), it frankly opposes the latter organization, which it accuses of lack of loyalty to evangelical doctrine. Its voting membership in 1951 was composed of forty denominations, many quite small, in fourteen countries. There is a non-voting consultative and associate membership. Headquarters are in Amsterdam. Regional councils exist in Latin America and East Asia, and national councils in India and Japan. The president, first elected in 1948, is Carl McIntire, of Collingswood, N. J.

The Council has protested what it considers an attempt by the International Missionary Council (*q.v.*) and the World Council of Churches to restrict foreign missionary activity in certain countries to societies approved by the latter bodies, and has had some success in persuading governmental authorities not to require such approval. It has issued pronouncements against communism (*q.v.*) and Roman Catholicism.

BIBLIOGRAPHY: Carl McIntire, *Modern Tower of Babel*, 1949.

PAUL WOOLLEY.

INTERNATIONAL COUNCIL OF COMMUNITY CHURCHES. See COMMUNITY CHURCHES.

INTERNATIONAL COUNCIL OF RELIGIOUS LIBERALS. See INTERNATIONAL ASSOCIATION FOR LIBERAL CHRISTIANITY AND RELIGIOUS FREEDOM.

INTERNATIONAL FEDERATION OF SETTLEMENTS. See SETTLEMENT MOVEMENT.

INTERNATIONAL LEAGUE FOR THE DEFENSE AND FURTHERANCE OF PROTESTANTISM: Organized in Berlin on May 24, 1923, under the influence of the ecumenical movement (*q.v.*) and as a reaction against the threat of a new Roman Catholic Counter Reformation, the purpose of the League was to establish co-operation among those organizations in various countries which were already active in developing and defending Protestant consciousness. It included in its membership representatives of thirty-four national organizations, among them the Evg. Maatschappij of Holland, the Protestantischer Volksbund of Switzerland, the Gabriel Bethlen League of Hungary, and the Evangelical Union (see BUND, EVANGELISCHER) of Germany and Austria. Its counterpart in England was the United Protestant Council. Political disturbances preceding and during World War II interrupted the League's activities. See also EVANGELICAL ALLIANCE, Vol. IV.

BIBLIOGRAPHY: *The Protestant Review*, published quarterly in Berlin since 1923, also appeared in German and French editions.

THEODORE G. TAPPERT.

INTERNATIONAL LIAISON COMMITTEE OF PEACE ORGANIZATIONS. See PEACE MOVEMENTS.

INTERNATIONAL MINISTERIAL FEDERATION: Incorporated in California in 1937, the Federation was organized as an outgrowth of the movement represented by tabernacles, community, and undenominational churches in America (see COMMUNITY CHURCHES; FEDERATED CHURCHES). At the beginning of World War II, certain difficulties were experienced by pastors of such churches in matters of clergy certificates, draft boards, etc. The Federation grants credentials to pastors of independent churches. It is non-supervisory and is a fellowship of pastors, evangelists, and missionaries.

SIDNEY CORRELL.

INTERNATIONAL MISSIONARY COUNCIL: The chief organ of liaison in the growth of co-operation among Protestant missions and a major factor in the entire ecumenical movement (*q.v.*). The Council developed directly from the Continuation Committees and the War Emergency Committee which carried on the work of the World Missionary Conference held at Edinburgh in 1910. The Council was established at London in 1921, divided its work with a co-ordinate office in New York from 1924, and has provided for a Far Eastern Office as well.

The International Missionary Council links some fourteen interdenominational associations of sending societies—such as the Division of Foreign Missions of the National Council of Churches of Christ, U.S.A. (*q.v.*) (formerly the Foreign Missions Conference of North America, *q.v.*); the Conference of Missionary Societies in Great Britain and Ireland; and the Deutscher Evangelischer Missionstag—with some sixteen interdenominational field bodies, such as the National Christian Council of India, Pakistan, and Burma; the Near East Christian Council; and the Conseil Protestant du Congo. The Council derives from the thirty constituent bodies its mandate to promote consultation, investigation, publication, and co-operation in "the work of presenting the Gospel to non-Christian peoples, whether carried on by the younger or by the older churches." Obviously, variety of belief and practice is recognized as fact, and is subordinated to fellowship in the total task of missions.

The Council has rendered unique services in the protection, maintenance, and renewal of particular missions grievously affected by war. It has frequently proved to be the most effective agency for dealing with governments in matters of religious liberty or other public concerns of Christian interest in many lands. The great conferences of Jerusalem (1928) and Madras (1938), and the significant meeting at Whitby, Ontario (1947), were valuable foci of study, consultation, and publication. Scores of important books and pamphlets sponsored by the Council hold a high place in missionary literature, as does the excellent quarterly, *International Review of Missions*.

Though wide-based in the participation of thousands of Christian workers of many nationalities, the Council is deeply indebted to the formative leadership and services of J. H. Oldham (*q.v.*), John R. Mott (*q.v.*), William Paton, and A. L. Warnshuis. Three of these men have been prominent in other co-operative organizations moving directly into the forma-

tion of the World Council of Churches (*q.v.*). The two Councils explicitly operate in intimate association with each other, and much thought has been given to possible measures of more formal combination.

See also EXPANSION OF CHRISTIANITY (MODERN).

BIBLIOGRAPHY: W. R. Hogg, *Ecumenical Foundations, a History of the International Missionary Council and Its Nineteenth-Century Background*, 1952; *World Missionary Conference, 1910*, 9 vols., 1910; *The Jerusalem Meeting of the International Missionary Council*, 8 vols., 1928; *The Madras Series*, 7 vols., 1939; K. S. Latourette and W. R. Hogg, *Tomorrow Is Here*, *The Mission and Work of the Church As Seen From the Meeting of the International Missionary Council at Whitby, Ontario*, 1948; *The International Review of Missions*, quarterly, from 1912.

MINER SEARLE BATES.

INTERNATIONAL MOVEMENT OF CATHOLIC STUDENTS. See PAX ROMANA.

INTERNATIONAL REFUGEE ORGANIZATION. See REFUGEES.

INTERNATIONAL VOLUNTARY SERVICE FOR PEACE. See PEACE MOVEMENTS.

INTERNSHIP: Full-time service by a theological student under supervision while practicing his art. The term and the method come from medical education. Theologically, internship takes various forms: (1) service in a hospital, mental or general, or a correctional institution; (2) a "residency" where a student engages in a second year of such in-service, and receives a considerable stipend; (3) under faculty supervision at Duke Divinity School and elsewhere students during the summer serve in prearranged units of work done in various churches, and receive compensation; (4) on graduation inexperienced or immature men serve as assistants to experienced and mature pastors. This accomplishes four objectives: The student has limited responsibility; he does not inflict trial-and-error methods on a people dependent on him alone as leader; he is as financially secure as if he were in a small church as pastor; he has the opportunity to stabilize his concept of himself as minister by relating himself spiritually to an older pastor in whom he has confidence. (5) In certain branches of the Lutheran Church a student remains out of the seminary between the second and the third year, and out on the field enters into full-time service, under the supervision of a resident pastor. In any case the value of an internship depends largely on the ability and the spirit of the supervising minister.

WAYNE E. OATES.

INTERSEMINARY MOVEMENT: A fellowship among students and faculties of 125 theological seminaries in the United States, its purpose is to introduce theological students to the ecumenical movement (*q.v.*) by providing various types of ecumenical experiences, supplying information about the movement, and keeping before them its challenges. The Movement was organized in 1898. The Movement as such is not committed to any particular interpretation of Christian unity, nor concerned to propagate any one idea of it. It seeks rather, by bringing theological students of various backgrounds together, to acquaint them with the problems of unity among the churches and with the challenge of the mission of the church in the world.

The responsible national committee is the Interseminary Committee, made up of representatives of various student and ecumenical agencies, and sponsored by the National Council of the Churches of Christ (*q.v.*). Maintaining a full-time staff, the chief activities of the national committee are the stimulation of regional conferences each year, retreats, various projects on individual seminary campuses, and the holding of a large, national, triennial seminary student conference. ROBERT S. BILHEIMER.

INTERSTITIA: The actual discipline of the Roman Church concerning the *interstitia,* or intervals to be observed between the degrees of the sacrament of order, is as follows: intervals between the tonsure and the minor orders, or between each of the minor orders, are at the discretion of the bishop; between the minor orders and subdeaconate, one year; between each of the major orders, three months.

It is forbidden to confer the tonsure with the minor orders, or all minor orders together upon one subject during the same ceremony of ordination, all customs to the contrary being explicitly reproved. [Sup.] GEORGES A. BARROIS.

INTER-VARSITY FELLOWSHIP. See STUDENT ORGANIZATIONS, RELIGIOUS.

INTROIT: One of the variable parts in the worship of the Western Church. Originally an Introit consisted of verses of psalms sung while the ministers were entering the sanctuary. An antiphon (a short seasonal verse) was sung before the psalm, and repeated after the Gloria Patri, with which the psalm ended. In the time of Gregory the Great the Introit assumed the form it has today, as a highly formal and liturgical entrance hymn. This old Latin form is retained in the Lutheran Church, but in English. The service opens with the confession of sins. After that the minister goes to the altar for the beginning of the service proper. Then the Introit for the Day is sung, or else read by the minister, and the Gloria Patri is sung by the congregation. Musically the Introit may vary widely, with forms both archaic and modern. In churches less liturgical an Introit is sometimes sung by the choir at the beginning of a service. Such an Introit is usually a brief anthem or chant, of simple design and free text, to provide a devotional and aspirational introduction to the worship. In still other cases a suitable hymn is used as a sort of free Introit. [Sup.] GEORGE R. SELZER.

INTUITIONISM: This term refers to the position that there is a kind of knowledge that comes immediately to and within the mind itself. It is to be distinguished from mediated knowledge, from discursive reasoning. Mediate knowledge is acquired by sense-experience through ideas or by the process of thinking through to conclusions. Intuitionists affirm that under certain conditions there comes a flash of insight or (with Henri Bergson, *q.v.*), that certain areas of experience (such as motion, life itself) are not amenable to rational processes since the latter distort the very process of fluidity. Reason chops up experience into static and frozen items or entities; life itself is a process (like motion) which by its nature cannot thus be abstracted without vitiating its very character. A bird on the wing can only be intuited since intuition takes in the whole flash of motion; reason, on the other hand, goes dialectically from position to position which gives only a series of rests or points or positions.

Intuitionists generally believe that this form of knowing is altogether unlike other forms (such as sense-experience and reason) and the highest and most profound form. An intuition, it is regarded, is a special form of knowing. The critic may well suggest that the flash-form of knowledge itself has a history rooted in reason and sense-experience. He may hold, for instance, that an intuition is only the rearrangement of items already acquired in the ordinary way by both accumulated experience and thought. On this interpretation intuition is no special form of knowledge.

Intuitionism is most generally associated with the emotional life rather than with any a priori category of the mind. Feelings, it is said, furnish cognitive experience unlike any other. When used in this sense (cognition rooted in deep feeling) intuitionism goes under the name of mysticism. It is an insight that comes with power of conviction of its reality, its own self watermark, its own authenticity (needing no other corroboration), personally appropriated, and passively as though the subject had no hand in the matter.

Both in ethics and in religion intuitionists are found challenging the overclaims of the rationalists and empiricists. Religious history is full of testimonies and defenses of this form of knowledge (religious experience as the ground of belief in God, contact with the supernatural, special information or clue to religious ideas or action such as a "call" of God, etc.). Intuition and imagination are closely related: both imply a fertility of mind, a mellowness of mental patterns which does not resist impressions; the one more forcefully and conclusively presented to the mind while the other more tentative in character.

Some philosophers have regarded intuitive insight as the highest achievement of wisdom: Plato and Benedict Spinoza being the classical examples in Western thought, the Upanishads in the East.

See also EPISTEMOLOGY.

BIBLIOGRAPHY: W. P. Montague, *The Ways of Knowing*, 1925; D. C. Macintosh, *The Problem of Religious Knowledge*, 1940; Henri Bergson, *Creative Evolution*, 1913; idem, *The Two Sources of Morality and Religion*, 1935.

VERGILIUS FERM.

INVESTITURE: In England the conciliatory attitude of King Henry I enabled the papal representatives to obtain favorable terms in the concordat of 1107, which the next year was followed by the Council of London, in which practical application was given to the terms of the concordat. In France the situation was also much more pleasant than it had been in Germany. The decree of Pope Gregory VII had been applied with great moderation. No serious quarrel ensued until the year 1100, when a prelate had to be chosen by the local clergy at Beauvais. Since the candidate who won the election was not fit to exert the duties of his exalted office, the civil rulers issued a complaint. But King Philip I seems to have had a hand in the election and did not wish to express his own opinion about investiture. The French clergy was very favorable to the king, and in 1104 the case at Beauvais was settled in a friendly manner. Moreover, Pope Paschal II took a trip to France, where he was well received by the secular powers. A satisfactory compromise was arranged between him and King Louis VI. The original sources indicate that during the first quarter of the twelfth century the whole atmosphere was serene. In 1516 the Concordat of Bologna settled matters in about the same fashion as had been done by Louis VI and Paschal II. This gives the most important reason why the kings of France during the most crucial years of the sixteenth century did not wish to imitate the Lutheran princes in Germany nor King Henry VIII of England.

BIBLIOGRAPHY: A. Fliche, *La querelle des investitures*, 1946; E. Bernheim, *Quellen zur Geschichte des Investiturstreites*, 1930; F. Barry, *The Papal Monarchy, 590–1303*, 1923; A. Hyma, *Christianity and Politics* (1938), Chap. I; A. Fliche and V. Martin, *Histoire de l'Eglise*, Vol. VIII: *La Réforme grégorienne et la Reconquête chrétienne (1057–1123)*, by A. Fliche (1946), pp. 110–147; A. Cartellieri, *Der Aufstieg des Papsttums im Rahmen der Weltgeschichte (1047–1095)*, 1937; idem, *Der Vorrang des Papsttums zur Zeit der ersten Kreuzzuge (1095–1150)*, 1941; R. W. and A. J. Carlyle, *A History of Mediaeval Political Theory in the West*, Vols. II–IV, 1919–22.

[Sup.] ALBERT HYMA.

INVOCATION: God is everywhere, but often we do not sense his presence. At the opening of public worship this prayer calls on him to make himself known, and the people ready to receive his blessing. In liturgical churches a special Invocation is also given at the consecration of the Eucharist, the laying on of hands in baptism, and confirmation-rites that call for the blessing of the Spirit. Elsewhere the Invocation may assume many forms. At best it is objective. Following a Call to Prayer, which the pastor addresses to the people, the Invocation may include a few sentences of adoration. After a brief pause, it goes on to confession, by the pastor on behalf of the people, or in concert as he leads in some form of General Confession, after which he may voice the Declaration of Pardon. Since the Invocation comes early in the hour, before some people have caught the mood of worship, the pastor may find it the most difficult of all the prayers to make real and helpful. Since rules about plagiarism do not apply to prayers, he may borrow from some master in the art. Many ministers who employ words of their own in the more personal and local "pastoral prayer" feel free to borrow earlier in the hour. More than one leader makes it a rule always to read any prayer not his own, and never to read one he has composed. While the Call to Prayer and the Invocation need not anticipate the theme of the sermon, they ought to strike the motif for the hour of worship. If the leader has mastered this part of his work, few people willingly come late to worship.

ANDREW W. BLACKWOOD.

IONA COMMUNITY: A movement started in Scotland in 1938 by George F. Macleod. In 1930 he accepted a call to the densely populated industrial parish of Govan, in Glasgow. In the "hungry thirties" he became increasingly aware that the Church of Scotland was failing to bring the gospel effectively to bear upon the life of the people, over half of whom had no vital contact with organized religion. Convinced that a fresh and more imaginative approach must be made to this problem, Macleod resigned his parish in 1938 to build up the Iona Community.

The method by which this movement seeks to reclaim Scotland for Christianity is through dedicated men and women, lay and clerical, living under something like monastic discipline, but seeking to work out in ordinary human relationships and activities the personal and social implications of the Gospel. They live by a strict rule of stewardship—of time, talents, and money. During the summer they work at restoring the ruined abbey on the island of Iona, traditional birthplace of Scottish Christianity. The rest of the year they labor on the mainland, laymen pursuing their daily tasks in the spirit of Christian vocation, ministers serving in places of special need—in city slums, dockland areas, and new housing developments on the outskirts of great cities.

The Community is financed partly by its members themselves and partly by the Friends of Iona Community, drawn from all over the world.

For some time the Iona Community was suspect in certain circles. It was thought of as "Romanist"—particularly because it appeared to favor clerical celibacy—as pacifist, and as left wing in its social and economic views. Such suspicions have been largely dispelled. In 1951 the General Assembly of the Church of Scotland gave its official blessing to the movement.

BIBLIOGRAPHY: John Highet, *The Churches in Scotland Today*, 1950; George F. Macleod, *We Shall Rebuild*, 1945.

NORMAN V. HOPE.

IRAN (Persia): The name Persia came to the West through the Greeks who got it from Parsa, the name for the southern province of the country known to its own people from early times as Iran. The area of the present nation is about 628,000 square miles, or the size of the United States east of the Mississippi with the exception of the states touching the Gulf of Mexico.

On the north Iran borders Soviet Russia and the Caspian Sea, the latter being a source of revenue in fish, caviar and other products. On the east there are Afghanistan and Baluchistan, on the west Iraq and Turkey. There are three types of climate in Iran. On the Persian Gulf in the south it is extremely hot; on the central plateau, which embraces much of the country, the climate is arid and hot in summer with snow and cold weather in some sections during winter, because of the altitude; the Caspian littoral climate is very damp with forty to sixty inches of rainfall a year. This is a region of dense forests in contrast to the denuded mountains of the plateau. Southern Iran is very rich in oil.

The official religion of the country is Shi'a Islam, which recognizes twelve *Imams* or leaders, descended from Mohammed through his daughter Fatimeh and son-in-law Ali whom they count as the first legitimate Caliph, though he was actually the fourth to hold that office. There are less than a million followers of Sunni Islam in Iran; there remain about 10,000 Zoroastrians in the country, some 40,000 Jews, about 50,000 Armenians and 25,000 Nestorian Christians. There are some Roman Catholics among the Armenian and Assyrian Christians. Protestant congregations are in most of the important cities and some villages. These churches embrace converts from Islam and Judaism as well as members of the Eastern Christian races.

The southern half of the country is the terri-tory of the Church Missionary Society and the northern half that of the Presbyterian U.S.A. Mission. A Lutheran Mission has operated among the Kurds southwest of Lake Urumia, and there are Seventh Day Adventist Missions in several of the large cities.

All foreign educational institutions were taken over under Reza Shah Pahlavi (1935) and incorporated in the government school system which now embraces nearly 10,000 schools all the way from primary to the national university in Teheran.

The Shi'a religious leaders have lost much power in recent decades to the civil authority. There are a number of Shi'a shrines in Iran, the chief places of pilgrimage being Meshed and Qum, as well as Najaf and Kerbela in Iraq. These Shrines and most mosques have endowments (*waqf*), much of which is now used in Iran for charitable and educational purposes. There are two bishops of the Gregorian Armenian Church—one at Tabriz and the other at Julfa, across the river from Isfahan.

BIBLIOGRAPHY: Wilson, *A Bibliography of Persia*, 1930; Overseas Consultants, *Report of Seven Years Development Plan*, 5 vols., 1949; Sykes, *A History of Persia*, 1930; Groseclose, *Introduction to Iran*, 1947; Wilber, *Iran Past and Present*, 1948.

[Sup.] J. CHRISTY WILSON.

IRAQ: At the end of World War I the vilayats of Mosul, Baghdad, and Basrah, comprising eastern Mesopotamia, were separated from the Ottoman Empire to form the Kingdom of Iraq. King Hussein's second son Faisal, ousted by the French from Damascus as King of Syria, was proclaimed King of Iraq under a British mandate on August 23, 1921. He reigned over the country with increasing acceptance until his death in 1933. He secured Iraq's admission as a free nation to the League of Nations in 1932.

Faisal's youthful son Ghazi reigned until his death by automobile accident in 1939. Ghazi's infant son was proclaimed King Faisal II, with King Ghazi's cousin, Amir Abd al-Ilah, as Regent until 1953, when Faisal II attained his majority.

Iraq's population consists of Sunni and Shi'i Muslims, with a large minority of Christians of various sects and other groups, including Jews who are decreasing in number through immigration to the State of Israel.

The development of oil resources is giving the country great wealth which is being used to promote the permanent welfare of all sections and classes of the people. This wealth, the racial and religious differences and a certain anti-foreign nationalism, somewhat increased by Zionist activities, provide the nation with its problems. The difficulties are different from Iran's in that the population is more heterogeneous, and the oil agreement, which provides the most revenue, involves nationals of several countries. Nationalism there is not based on religious solidarity. Nevertheless, the country's legislators are making wise plans for the nation's progress in the near and more distant future.

BIBLIOGRAPHY: H. A. Foster, *The Making of Modern Iraq*, 1935; Majid Khadduri, *Independent Iraq, A Study in Iraqi Politics since 1932*, 1951.

EDWIN E. CALVERLEY.

IRELAND. See EIRE; IRELAND, NORTHERN.

IRELAND, NORTHERN: In 1921 Ireland was allowed to resume her political independence (see EIRE). The six northern counties of Ulster, however—Antrim, Armagh, Down, Fermanagh, Londonderry, and Tyrone, with the two county boroughs of Belfast and Londonderry—were, at their own insistence, partitioned off and allowed to retain their political affiliation with Great Britain. These counties of Northern Ireland have a population of over 1,250,000, and their capital is Belfast. The reason for the partition of Ireland was that the two areas are somewhat different in race—the Northern Irelanders are mainly descendants of Scots, settled in Ulster in the early seventeenth century—in culture, and in religion.

In Northern Ireland there is no established church, but the area is predominantly, and even self-consciously, Protestant in religion. The largest single Protestant Church is the Presbyterian, whose chief governing body is its General Assembly, meeting annually. It is organized under thirty-two presbyteries and numbers close to 500 local congregations. Though the Presbyterian Church extends into Eire, it draws its main strength from the northern counties. At the first census after partition in 1926, there were 393,000 professed Presbyterians in Ulster; in 1936, 390,000; and in 1951, 410,000. The Irish Presbyterian Church keeps up the Presbyterian tradition of high educational requirements for its ministers. Certain Irish students take one year of theological education abroad, but all must finish their training at the theological school of their Church in Belfast, which is well equipped, well staffed, and affiliated with Queen's University.

Evangelical and conservative in its theological outlook, the Presbyterian Church of Ireland has during the present century felt the impact of modern biblical criticism. This came out into the open in 1927 when J. Ernest Davey, professor of biblical literature at the Assembly's College, was accused of heresy. After due trial he was acquitted.

The next largest Protestant body in Northern Ireland is the Church of Ireland (Episcopal), which, like the Presbyterian, extends into Eire but draws its main strength from Ulster. In 1926 it numbered 338,000 in Northern Ireland; 345,000 in 1936; and 353,000 in 1951. It is organized in two archdioceses, that of Armagh (Northern Ireland) and Dublin (Eire), and

twelve dioceses. It is governed by two bodies, the General Synod and the so-called "Representative Body." The General Synod is its highest judicial court, and consists of the archbishops and bishops, together with lay and clerical representatives from each diocese, laymen outnumbering the clergy. The "Representative Body," which holds and administers the church's property, was incorporated in 1870. It consists of the archbishops and bishops, plus thirty-nine lay and clerical elected members and thirteen co-opted members. The Church of Ireland is usually regarded as the most strongly evangelical branch of the Anglican communion. It began the revision of its Prayer Book in 1908, completing it in 1926.

There are also several smaller Protestant churches, notably the Methodists, who number 66,000 members; other Protestant groups—e.g., the Plymouth Brethren—have an aggregate membership of 69,000.

The Roman Catholic Church, though a minority, is the largest single religious body in Northern Ireland. It numbered 420,000 in 1926; 428,000 in 1936; and 471,000 in 1951. The fact that it is relatively large and growing, and that in Eire it is predominant, has made for some tension between Roman Catholicism and Protestantism.

BIBLIOGRAPHY: R. P. McDermott and D. A. Webb, *Irish Protestantism: A Demographic Study*, n.d. but *ca.* 1945; W. A. Phillips (ed.), *History of the Church of Ireland*, 3 vols., 1933.

[Sup. to IRELAND.] NORMAN V. HOPE.

IRENAEUS: In the last forty years a great deal of work has been done on the sources of Irenaeus. C. Schmidt found the source of *Adversus haereses* i. 29–30 in a Coptic papyrus at Berlin containing the *Apocryphon of John*. Other versions of this document have recently been discovered in Egypt. Harnack isolated traditions of the Asiatic elders in *Adversus haereses* iv. 27–32; his investigations were continued by Bousset, and finally elaborated by Loofs, who separated Irenaeus Asiatic sources from those derived from Antioch and claimed that most of his distinctive theology was really due to the lost treatise *Against Marcion* by Theophilus of Antioch (*q.v.*). Loofs's claims were somewhat exaggerated, but it remains a fact that Irenaeus was influenced by Theophilus. Another important study has been made by Sagnard, who has examined Irenaeus treatment of Valentinian sources. Reynders has studied the methods Irenaeus used in his arguments against Gnosticism in general, and the present author has investigated some of his scientific and rhetorical arguments.

Since Zahn wrote, one fragment of Irenaeus on a potsherd has been found (W. E. Crum, *Coptic Ostraca* [1902], no. 23), as well as a lengthy fourth-century papyrus containing *Ad-*

versus haereses v. 3. 2–13. 1 (H. Lietzmann in *Nachrichten . . . Goettingen* [1912], 291–320).

The "balanced security" of Irenaeus, mentioned by Zahn (p. 30 b), has been ascribed by Audet to the fact that unlike many other Christian writers he was born a Christian (compare Polycarp). Certain recent students have tried to argue that he was a "biblical theologian," but biblical theology is a modern archaistic reconstruction; for Irenaeus the tradition of the church, guaranteed by episcopal succession from the apostles, was normative. "Tradition consists in the Holy Scriptures and the truths therein contained," as Molland says; but only those who stood within the succession had the right to say what the tradition meant. Irenaeus was defending a dynamic situation in relatively static terms. Against the Gnostics he could not admit that the tradition was being developed. Against them he holds that the Roman church has the "strongest origin" in the apostles Peter and Paul.

The problem of succession in Irenaeus is somewhat difficult. There is no trace whatever of an episcopal chain of ordainers and ordinands. The only interest Irenaeus has in the succession lies in its legitimacy. The bishop is not infallible; he can fall into heresy, schism, or hypocrisy. He is apparently ordained by his fellow-presbyters.

Irenaeus' theology is important because of its influence not only in his own day but also afterwards. It is essentially unphilosophical and represents a statement of the common faith of the church. Where churches differ in their emphases, Irenaeus simply places their ideas side by side. The primary belief of Christians is in God the Creator; at this point Irenaeus follows Hermas, without philosophical analysis. He uses Theophilus' idea of the two "hands" of God, his Word and his Wisdom. The Son of God is the Word or Logos, as in the apologists, though Irenaeus refuses to ask how the Logos was generated. With the Logos, the Spirit is the mediator of revelation in the prophets and at baptism. Man, whose soul and body were created by God, sinned by disobedience which resulted in death; hence he needed to be redeemed by the Son of God, who became Son of Man that we might become Sons of God and thus recover our lost immortality. He recapitulated (a very common expression in Irenaeus) the career of Adam, reversing Adam's disobedience and death. By his suffering he destroyed death. Christians practise perfection and are nourished by the Eucharist. Their life is not essentially ascetic, however; they will ultimately rise and enjoy the miraculous fertility of the earth in the millennial age (from Papias).

Irenaeus fuses the ideas of various writers before him (he seems to have had a good collection of books, including the Bible, most of the apostolic fathers and several of the apologists), and presents a mediating theology in a fairly lucid form. He is not at all speculative, primarily in reaction against the speculations of his opponents. He is a missionary bishop, not a schoolman.

Bibliography: C. Schmidt and A. Harnack, in *Philotesia Kleinert*, 1907; F. R. M. Hitchcock, *Irenaeus of Lugdunum*, 1914; W. Bousset, *Juedisch-christlicher Schulbetrieb in Alexandria und Rom* (1915), pp. 272–282; F. Vernet, in *Dictionnaire de théologie catholique*, Vol. VII (1923), pp. 2394–2533; N. Bonwetsch, *Die Theologie des Irenaeus*, 1925; F. Loofs, *Theophilus von Antiochien Adversus Marcionem und die anderen theologischen Quellen bei Irenaeus*, 1930; D. B. Reynders, in *Rech. de théol. anc. et méd.*, Vol. VII (1935), pp. 5–27; F. R. M. Hitchcock, in *JTS*, Vol. XXXVIII (1937), pp. 130–139, 255–266; T. A Audet, in *Traditio*, Vol. I (1943), pp. 15–54; F. Sagnard, *La gnose valentinienne et le témoignage de saint Irénée*, 1947; R. M. Grant, in *Harvard Theological Review*, Vol XLII (1949), pp. 41–51; E. Molland, in *Journal of Ecclesiastical History*, Vol. I (1950), pp. 12–28. Sagnard has prepared a new edition of the Latin Irenaeus.

[Sup.] Robert M. Grant.

I.R.O. See International Refugee Organization.

IRRATIONALISM: Two major types of irrationalism may be singled out in the development of Christianity.

I. Experiential: One type suggests that the knowledge of God is appropriated in an experience transcending man's rational capacity. It is noteworthy that the major creeds of both Catholicism and Protestantism have affirmed the incomprehensibility of God.

A. MYSTICISM: Early medieval thought, drawing as it did on a Platonized Stoicism, sometimes defined God in such a way as to make him an object for human reasoning (e.g., Anselm). Subsequently God's nature was believed to be reproduced in theological compendia (e.g., Peter Lombard), and his will became synonymous with ecclesiastical manuals of morals, civil law, and the dictates of man's moral reason (e.g., Thomas Aquinas). While the principle of analogical reasoning saved scholasticism from equating theological propositions with the speech of God, it rarely took the theologian beyond a rational method. In transcendence of strictly rational methods, the mystics (e.g., Bernard of Clairveau, Hugh of St. Victor) believed it possible to experience God through a religious discipline characterized more by affection than by reflection. "A God who is thought is no God" (Tersteegen).

B. PIETISM, MORALISM, ROMANTICISM: A similar clash of method is manifested in the reactions of the German pietists to the Protestant scholasticism of the seventeenth century, of Kant to the rationalism of the seventeenth and eighteenth centuries, and of the evangelicals (e.g., Wesley and Edwards) and romanticists (e.g., Schleiermacher) to the deism of the eighteenth and nineteenth centuries. God is known not in theological formulae but in meditation and prayer, Spener and Francke believed. God is known not by the methods of the natural sciences, nor even by the methods of rational metaphysics, Kant believed, but rather in moral experience, in the obedience of the practical reason to its inherent imperatives. God is known not through his lifeless traces upon the created world, but in the religious affections, the evangelicals and romanticists believed.

Albrecht Ritschl (*q.v.*) and Wilhelm Hermann represent modifications of this theological irrationalism, but Rudolf Otto's (*q.v.*) is the most competent of the modern efforts to perpetuate this line. Generally the term "irrationalism" has been a label tinctured by apologetics. Otto, however, avowed it in *The Idea of the Holy* (see HOLY, THE IDEA OF THE), associating the relation to God with "irrational" factors, with a sense of fascination in the presence of the tremendous mystery of God's holiness.

C. PHILOSOPHY: It is a temptation to suppose that in the warfare of irrationalism with rationalism, theology and philosophy are in opposite camps. Philosophy, however, has honored the irrational. Socrates relied on an inner voice when his reason failed him. Plato regarded the ultimately real, the "idea of the good," as transcending rational penetration. Aristotle conceded superior status to the "Alogoi," who were advised by functions that operated without, or even against the reason. Moreover, the most notorious philosophical rationalists (e.g., the Stoics, Spinoza, Hegel, F. H. Bradley) rejected any identification of truth with rational exactitude and found in the more aesthetic and supra-cognitive functions of love, art, and religion a more excellent truthgiving talent. Latterly, the process (Whitehead), life (Dilthey, Bergson), and existential (Heidegger, Sartre) philosophies, affirming an open and incremental universe, have been to that extent committed to irrationalism.

II. Revelational: A second type of irrationalism has developed, however, in such a way as to do justice to theological convictions which are not included in these concessions philosophers have allowed. This type is concerned less with transcendence of purely rational faculties and more with attacking the supposition that human faculties of any sort can become organs for the discernment of God. God manifests himself as he will, it is held. Whenever God reveals himself, he does so freely, by grace. The adversary of this type is not simply reason but autonomy in any form, not the rational process but any kind of righteousness by works, be these works moral, emotional, or intellectual.

A. IN HISTORY: This may be taken to be the force of Tertullian's fideism. To the apologists of the early church, who had blended revelation with Stoic forms of thought, Christian truth was synonymous with certifiable intellectual content. To Tertullian, however, Christian truth was given in the paradoxical Christ about whom one can only resolve in an act of faith. To the Averroists of the Middle Ages, man's reason had independent access to the divine mysteries. It was the force of Thomism to regard the most rational act of man as the act in which man's reason depends on God's truth revealed to the church. To Aquinas, however, a large area of truth about God, called "natural theology," was properly within the capacities of the independent reason. In the face of this autonomy, the voluntarists and nominalists at the end of the Middle Ages (Scotus and Occam) reduced this independence almost to the vanishing point and thus paved the way for Luther's Paulinism in which the knowledge of God is *sola gratia, sola fide.* In a similar spirit, Nicholas of Cusa and Jacob Boehme attributed to the very being of God characteristics so deep and so contradictory that God's nature outranged every human effort to know him.

At the beginning of modern thought in the West, Descartes equated the true with what was rationally clear and distinct; but Pascal equated the true with the mysterious Christ in whom faith from a rational standpoint is hazardous. At the summit of modern thought, Hegel equated the true with what is universal; but Kierkegaard equated the true with the particular reality of Christ. The Christian truth for these so-called irrationalists is not innate to the reason or to any other human capacity. It is incarnated by a gracious act of God in the person of Jesus Christ. To have the truth is to appropriate the Christ in the receptive act of gratitude, or faith.

B. IN THE PRESENT: It is this latter type of irrationalism which is suggested by the "neo-orthodox" (*q.v.*) theology of the twentieth century. There is an irrationality in God's free decision, in his gracious love in Christ, in the Godless nature of man, and in the cosmos itself as the battlefield between God and demonic powers.

Contemporary philosophers label this theological development "irrationalism" because its meanings cannot be translated into the language of the natural sciences (logical positivism) or because its meanings are humanly incommunicable (Karl Jaspers' existentialism, *q.v.*). The more philosophically oriented among contemporary theologians charge it with "irrationalism" because it is based on an epistemological agnosticism. "Neo-orthodox" theologians, however, decline the label. While they concede an epistemological silence which man is unable to overcome, they believe that silence is overcome in the speech which God empowers through revelation (*q.v.*) and its proclamation. The revelatory action of God, it is believed, far from destroying the reason, restores and orients the reason.

See also DIALECTICAL THEOLOGY; PARADOX.

BIBLIOGRAPHY: Emil Brunner, *Erlebnis, Erkenntnis, und Glaube*, 1921; idem, *The Philosophy of Religion*, 1937; Karl Jaspers, *Vernunft und Existenz*, 1935; Sören Kierkegaard, *Philosophical Fragments*, 1942; Edwin Lewis, *A Philosophy of the Christian Revelation*, 1940; D. C. Macintosh, *The Problem of Religious Knowledge*, 1940; Richard Niebuhr, *The Meaning of Revelation*, 1941; Paul Tillich, *Systematic Theology*, Vol. I, 1951.

CARL MICHALSON.

IRVINGITE. See CATHOLIC APOSTOLIC CHURCH.

IRWIN, WILLIAM ANDREW: Methodist; b. Ontario, Canada, 1884. He was educated at Toronto, Victoria, and Chicago universities. He taught in the department of Semitics, Toronto (1919–30); in Old Testament at Oriental Institute and Divinity School, Chicago (1930–50; Professor Emeritus, 1950–) Southern Methodist (1950–). He was a member, Oriental Institute Megiddo Expedition (1934); member, Standard Bible Committee, and secretary Old Testament Section (1937–). He was editor of: J. M. P. Smith, *The Prophets and their Times* (2nd ed., 1941); (with A. P. Wikgren), I. M. Price, *The Ancestry of our English Bible* (2nd ed., 1949); rev. ed. of the Old Testament in *The Bible, an American Translation* (1954). He is the author of: *The Problem of Ezekiel* (1943); (with Frankfort, Jacobsen, and Wilson), *The Intellectual Adventure of Ancient Man* (1947); and (with H. R. Willoughby and others), *The Study of the Bible Today and To-morrow* (1947).

ISAAC OF NINEVEH: Nestorian monk and author of celebrated treatises on ascetic-mystical discipline and doctrine, was born and lived as monk and teacher in the province of Qatar in northeast Arabia until the Patriarch George (661–80) visited Qatar around 676. George took Isaac back with him to Ctesiphon and ordained him bishop of Nineveh. But Isaac found the duties of a bishop incompatible with the contemplative life and soon surrendered his see and retired to the monastery of Rabban Shabur near Tustar, where he died, and in which he probably composed his treatises.

Isaac's mystical treatises depend largely, as do those of Nestorian and Monophysite mystics generally, on the works of Evagrius Ponticus, the pupil of Origen and Gregory of Nyssa. They were translated into Greek, Arabic, Ethiopic and Latin.

BIBLIOGRAPHY: A. J. Wensinck, *Mystic Treatises of Isaac of Nineveh*, 1923; J. Hausherr, "The 'Book of Hierothes' and Isaac of Nineveh," in *Orientalia Christiana* (1933); idem, "Les grands courants de la spiritualité orientale," in *Orientalia Christiana Periodica* (1935); idem, "Ignorance Infinie," in *ibid.* (1936); idem, "Aux origines de la mystique Syrienne," in *ibid.* (1938); idem, "Contemplation et Sainteté," in *Revue d'ascetique et de mystique*, (1933); M. Viller, *La Spiritualité des premiers siècles chrétiens*, 1930; William Thomson, *Isaac of Nineveh* (doctoral thesis

in Widener Library, Harvard University); J. Labourt, *Le Christianisme dans l'Empire Perse*, 1904; L. S. Marsh, *The Book of the Holy Hierotheos* (Text and Translation Society, Vol. X), 1927.

[Sup.] WILLIAM THOMSON.

ISABELLA OF CASTILE: Daughter of King John II of Castile and Isabella of Portugal, his second wife; b. April 22, 1451; d. Nov. 26, 1504, she passed her childhood under the clouds of insurrection and intrigues at the court, where two kings ruled simultaneously: Henry IV, son of John II and his first wife; and Alfonso, his half-brother and son of John II and his second wife. The father died in 1455, and Henry would have succeeded him if it had not been for the fact that the leading personages in the realm opposed him. They called him Henry the Impotent. In 1468, while Isabella was living in a convent at Avila, the crown of Castile was offered to her by the leaders in the nation. At first she refused to accept and wanted Alfonso to rule, but he was not wanted by the great men, and in 1468 Henry abdicated in her presence. The next year she married her cousin, Ferdinand, who in 1479 became king of Aragon. In this manner the kingdom of Spain was created out of several petty states.

Isabella's coronation occurred in 1474, while her husband was fighting against the French at Perpignan. Ferdinand was furious for having been treated thus, but Isabella had taken advantage of his desire to marry her as quickly as possible, and in the marriage contract, which he had failed to study carefully, her own rights were carefully protected. She remained until her death a queen in her own name and power. It was she who established the Spanish Inquisition and made it a state institution; and it was she who negotiated directly with Columbus, urging him above all things to win converts for the Roman Catholic Church.

BIBLIOGRAPHY: J. H. Mariéjol, *L'Espagne sous Ferdinand et Isabelle*, 1892; J. Dieulafoy: *Isabelle, la grande Reine de Castille*, 1920; H. Vignaud, *Histoire critique de la grande enterprise de Christophe Colomb*, 1911; J. Bouissounouse, *Isabelle la Catholique: Comment se fit l'Espagne*, 1949; César Silió Cortés, *Isabella la Católica: Fundadora de España: Su via, su tiempo, su reinado*, 1943.

ALBERT HYMA.

ISAIAH, BOOK OF: The Dead Sea Scroll (*q.v.*) (DSS) of the Book of Isaiah, dating from *ca.* the first century B.C., in general confirms the Masoretic Text (MT). The chief divergences are orthographical and morphological. Where the texts disagree, the MT is usually to be preferred, but there are not a few instances where DSS is clearly superior and often has the support of the versions. In 3:24 DSS improves a notably corrupt text by the addition of *shame* (*bosheth*): *instead of beauty, shame*; in 14:4 it reads with LXX and Syr. *insolent fury* (*marhebhah*) for the unlikely *golden* (city) (*madhhebhah*) of MT; in 21:8 it reads *hāro'eh* for MT *lion* ('*aryēh*): *the seer cried;* in 45:8 it reads *wᵉyiphraḥ* for MT *wᵉyiphrū: that salvation may blossom forth;* in 49:24 it reads with LXX, Syr., and Vulg. '*arîẓ* for MT *ẓaddiḳ: or the captives of the tyrant be rescued.* Recent studies of the LXX (Joseph Ziegler) have shown that the underlying Hebrew text is often close to MT. In other instances, however, LXX is paraphrastic and unreliable.

The prophetic oracles of Isaiah are usually brief. Invectives and threats are especially common (1:4–9; 2:6–21; 5:8–24; 29:9–15; 30:15–17; 3:1–9; 3:16–4:1; 30:27–33). Numerous other literary types occur, however, such as the dirge of 1:21–26 and the folksong of 5:1–8. In sharp contrast are the poems of jubilation of Second Isaiah (chs. 40–55). Here the hymn style is present (40:12–26; 42:10–13; 43:16; 44:23; 44:24–28), and the singing, lyrical mood expresses itself in other forms also. The oracles of salvation (41:8–13, 14–16, 17–20; 43:1–7; 44:1–5; 45:1–7; 54:4–6, 7–10, 11–12; 55:8–13) and the judicial proceedings (41:1–5, 21–29; 43:8–13; 48:1–11; 50:1–2a) express Yahweh's vindication of Israel and himself before the world. The literary units are much more extensive than in Isaiah and seldom appear as a single literary type. The poems follow one another in perceptible order and are to be understood in their general eschatological context.

While many critics continue to follow Duhm in his excision of the Servant Songs (42:1–4; 49:1–6; 50:4–9; 52:13–53:12), the difficulties involved in this operation are becoming increasingly clear. There is the greatest diversity of view as to the extent of the Songs, and the literary contexts have given rise to numerous difficulties. Moreover, the word "Israel" in 49:3 cannot be deleted on any defensible textual or literary grounds. The identification of the Servant has received the most diverse answers. In general they fall into individual or collective categories. Many names have been proposed for the former, among them Moses, Jehoiachin, Zerubbabel, Jeremiah, a contemporary of the prophet, or even the prophet himself. Identification with the Messiah, either the Son of David or some other figure, is upheld by many Roman Catholic scholars and others. Mythological influences in the portrait are seen by many. Some see features of the Tammuz-Adonis myth of the dying and rising god in the Servant, and many believe that the language of the fourth song has been influenced by the Tammuz liturgies. The collective view is still supported by a number of scholars, but not so much as the "ideal Israel" as Israel as a collective personality (Eissfeldt, Wheeler Robinson). It is becoming more clear that a sharp distinction between the two is impossible. The figure of the sufferer who gives his life in atoning and substitutionary sacrifice for the sins of the nations, standing at an eschatological point of time, allows Messianic interpretation.

BIBLIOGRAPHY: Commentaries: G. B. Gray, *A Critical and Exegetical Commentary on the Book of Isaiah* (chs. i–xxvii), 1912; J. Skinner, *The Book of the Prophet Isaiah* (*CB*), rev. ed., Vol. I, 1915, Vol. II, 1917; B. Duhm, *Das Buch Jesaja uebersetzt und erklaert*, 3rd ed., 1914, 4th ed., 1922; H. Guthe, *Das Buch Jesaja* (*HSAT*), 1922; K. Budde, *Das Buch Jesaja Kap. 40–66* (*HSAT*), 1922; Reuben Levy, *Deutero-Isaiah*, 1925; Franz Feldmann, *Das Buch Jesaja*, Vol. I, 1925, Vol. II, 1926; E. Koenig, *Das Buch Jesaja*, 1926; G. A. Smith, *The Book of Isaiah*, 2 vols., rev. ed., 1927; C. C. Torrey, *The Second Isaiah*, 1928; G. W. Wade, *The Book of the Prophet Isaiah*, 1929; Otto Procksch, *Jesaja I*, 1930; Paul Volz, *Jesaja II*, 1932; Johann Fischer, *Das Buch Isaias*, Vol. I, 1937, Vol. II, 1939; Edward J. Kissane, *The Book of Isaiah*, Vol. I, 1941, Vol. II, 1943.

The Servant of the Lord: S. Mowinckel, *Der Knecht Jahwes*, 1921; Otto Eissfeldt, "The Ebed-Jahwe in Isaiah xl–lv . . ." in *ET*, XLIV (1932–33), 261–268; J. S. Van der Ploeg, *Les Chants du Serviteur de Jahve dans la seconde partie du livre d'Isaie*, 1936; Christopher North, *The Suffering Servant in Deutero-Isaiah*, 1948; J. P. Hyatt, "The Sources of the Suffering Servant Idea," *JNES*, III (1944), 79–86; Ivan Engnell, "The Ebed Yahweh Songs and the Suffering Messiah in 'Deutero-Isaiah'," in *Bulletin of the John Rylands Library*, XXXI, No. 1 (1948); Curt Linghagen, *The Servant Motif in the Old Testament . . .*, 1950; J. Lindblom, *The Servant Songs in Deutero-Isaiah*, 1951; H. H. Rowley, *The Servant of the Lord and Other Old Testament Essays*, 1951.

Text: Joseph Ziegler, *Untersuchungen zur Septuaginta des Buches Isaias*, 1934; I. L. Seeligmann, *The Septuagint Version of Isaiah*, 1948.

[Sup.] JAMES MUILENBURG.

ISIDORE OF SEVILLE: Those who call him the last of the Church Fathers have this much in their favor that he was thoroughly orthodox. He wrote: "We are not permitted to form any belief of our own will, or to choose a belief that someone else has accepted as his own. We have God's apostles as authorities, who did not themselves choose anything of what they should believe, but they faithfully transmitted to the nations the teaching received from Christ." In praising monasticism (*q.v.*) he argued that it was advantageous for those who are well and strong to mortify the flesh, for otherwise "through the vigor of their health they be defiled by illicit passions and the desire for luxury." His encyclopedia, however, indicates a love of inquiry into all sorts of beliefs. This learned work for three centuries became an integral part of all good libraries in Western Europe.

BIBLIOGRAPHY: An excellent edition of his encyclopedia, the *Origines*, is that of W. Lindsay, 1911; see also: A. Schmekel, *Die positive Philosophie in ihrer geschichtlichen Entwicklung*, Vol. II: *Isidorus von Sevilla, sein System und seine Quellen*, 1914; P. Séjournée, *S. Isidore de Séville: Son rôle dans l'histoire du droit canonique*, 1929—ascribes the *Collectio Hispana*, or *Isidoriana* to Isidore of Seville; J. Geiselmann, *Die Abendmahlslehre an der Wende des christlichen Spaetantike zum Fruehmittelalter: Isidor von Sevilla und das Sakrament der Eucharistie*, 1933.

[Sup.] ALBERT HYMA.

ISLAM: For readers of the *New Schaff-Herzog Encyclopedia of Religious Knowledge* who are especially interested in Islam, it is a fortunate fact that since the *Encyclopedia's* previous edition of 1910 a journal specifically devoted to Islam has been published. The volumes of this journal could serve as continuing yearbooks of knowledge about Islam in the twentieth century. The quarterly issues of *The Moslem World,* founded by Samuel M. Zwemer, in 1911, and since 1948 entitled *The Muslim World* and published by the Hartford Seminary Foundation at Hartford, Conn., have noticed and described most, if not all, of the historical events, new religious movements, and changes in social life and attitudes in Islamdom. One of the foremost present day Orientalists, H. A. R. Gibb (now Sir Hamilton), Professor of Arabic in Oxford (England) University (beginning 1955, at Harvard), in his book on *Modern Trends in Islam* (1947), says ". . . the present religious attitudes and movements of the Muslim peoples is the least-studied of all" subjects connected with Islam. He adds, ". . . never before has the Muslim world been in such close contact with the Western nations and . . . never a year passes without the publication of several books, both in Europe and America, dealing with one or other of the Muslim countries and peoples. To the Western student of the specifically religious aspects of modern Islamic culture, however, most of them offer little satisfaction. The fullest documentation is to be found in the quarterly issues of the *Moslem World* since 1910." For subjects of Islamic interest not dealt with in this edition of *The Encyclopedia of Religious Knowledge,* readers may be referred to the more than forty volumes of *The Moslem World* and *The Muslim World.* This applies particularly to Islam in the last four decades. Beginning with 1947, students should refer to the volumes of *The Middle East Journal* (Washington, D. C.).

I. Islam as Religion: Dogmas: The first thing to be brought to the attention of students and others wishing to know about Islam is that the name covers not only the religion founded by Muhammad (*q.v.*) in Arabia in the seventh Christian century, but also the whole system of life developed in the later centuries by those who accepted and promoted that religion. The new article on Muhammad in this edition of the *Encyclopedia* discusses in sufficient detail the life of the Arabian prophet and the growth of his religious convictions. Here attention is called to the two brief statements of belief that Muslims are required to make in order to be accepted as members of that faith. These statements, both found in these precise forms, are: "There is no god at all but Allah" (37:34; 47:21), and "Muhammad is the Apostle of Allah" (48:19). These phrases form the Short Creed of Islam. The very first utterance of them, with intention, by any person, under any circumstances, even by an enemy on a battlefield, immediately makes that person a Muslim, whose life and property thereby become legally inviolable to all other Muslims. This creed be-

came the first of the six articles of the Muslim faith. It is recited in every call to Islam's formal worship, and also by Muslims upon any occasion of any possible religious significance.

Belief in the angels is the second article of faith in the longer or standard and official creed of both Sunni and Shi'i Islam.

Faith in Allah's revelation is the third belief required of all Muslims. This includes belief in the 100 lost "leaves," of which ten were given to Adam, fifty to Seth, whose name, however, does not occur in the Qur'an, thirty to Idris, who is the biblical Enoch and ten to Abraham, as well as belief in the four "books," which are the *Tawrah* of Moses, and the *Zabūr* of David, the *Injil* of Jesus Christ, and the Qur'an of Muhammad. These revelations are acknowledged to be permanently valid, since they all teach the same truth about the One God, who is Allah. Each book, however, presents new rules and regulations, which, although they do not abolish or even supersede those of the previous revelations, should, nevertheless, be adopted because they represent later and therefore better systems of life and worship. The Qur'an definitely confirms the teaching of the earlier Scriptures. Obvious differences between biblical and quranic doctrines are explained by later Muslim theologians as due to corruptions in the extant sacred texts of the previous religions. To that problem historical criticism has provided a solution satisfactory to Christians.

The fourth article of the Muslim creed requires belief in the prophets and apostles. The prophets number 124,000, or 224,000 or, better, an unspecified figure, lest others in excess of that number be deprived of their right to belief. The apostles, of whom twenty-eight are named in the Qur'an, including three not mentioned in the Bible, are the prophets who have received the messages which prophets teach. All apostles are prophets; some prophets are also apostles or messengers.

The fifth article of faith is the resurrection of all the dead to judgment and a rarified material but personal existence either in immediate and eternal bliss in the Garden because they are Muslim martyrs, or else in misery in the Fire, which is a temporary Purgatory for believers who are deficient in good works, or permanent for unbelievers.

All Muslims must also believe in the decree by Allah of both good and evil. There are permissible variations in their views about the degree of Allah's responsibility and man's freedom of action.

To this list of dogmas the Shi'i Muslims only add belief in the necessity of the imamate, or the sole legitimacy of the House of Muhammad, beginning with 'Alī, his cousin and son-in-law, to be the heirs of Muhammad's leadership (*imāmiyyah*) in Islam.

II. Religious Duties: In addition to the doctrines presented above, Islam prescribes five practical duties for all adherents. These include the recital of the short creed, which is also called the witness; the daily performance of the ritual worship, five times for Sunnis and three for Shi'is, in the state of ceremonial cleanliness; fasting during the month of Ramadan; the payment of the *zakāt,* or income tax; and the pilgrimage to Mecca. These duties are not rigid or strict, but may be modified by reasonable extenuating circumstances. Except for the payment of the *zakāt,* performance of the duties is left to social pressure and individual conscience.

Another requirement, that of *jihād,* or Muslim war, is a general public obligation, rather than a duty imposed upon all individuals. It also is subject to reasonable modification, for, while it is imperative for defense under attack, aggressive warfare is not obligatory unless success may be confidently expected. One further fact of political importance needs to be noticed. Any call to *jihād* applies only to the group whose acknowledged leader issues the call. Thus the Shi'ah of Iran would not participate in a Sunni *jihād,* but might even call a *jihād* against Sunnis. Sometimes a Muslim group will find occasion to proclaim on religious grounds a *jihād* against other Muslims of a different political allegiance.

III. Islam's Early Centuries: The first hundred years after Muhammad's death (A.D. 632) marked the period of the first great geographical expansion of Islam eastward to Central Asia and westward to Spain. After this political conquest Islam took several centuries more to consolidate its social and cultural domination of western and central Asia, and of all the southern Mediterranean countries as well as of Sicily and Spain. During this period innumerable individuals and whole communities of varying religious allegiances or none, found it proper and advisable to join the dominant political and religious society. These converts adopted the confessions and practices of Islam, but also as Muslims, continued many of their ethical, ascetic and spiritual exercises for the nurture of their religious life. The protected communities (millets, *q.v.*) of doctrinally-divided Christians professed and followed no single catholic faith. Islam tolerated the religious liberty of such communities, but also tolerated within Islam, after acceptance of its principal dogmas and duties, much freedom of belief and conduct. From the first both doctrinal heresies and differences of political allegiance were common among Muslims. Nevertheless, and notwithstanding all difficulties, it was during the first three and a half centuries after Muhammad's death that the Qur'an was edited, the innumerable traditions about Muhammad and the early believers were collected, appraised and recorded, the articles of

the new religion were formulated and the principles and codes of law were systematized. By the end of the fourth Muslim century, the political and legal implications of the duties of Islam, and the theological and philosophical interpretations of Islam's doctrines about God, man and the world had reached a measure of fixity for most Muslim religious leaders. Even the dissident sects, the Kharijiyyah and the two large sections of the Shi'ah, which had separated permanently from the Sunnis, chiefly for political reasons, had stabilized their doctrines and customs. Although the beliefs and practices of Muhammad remain valid to this day, it is really the religion of Islam's fourth century that is the dominant orthodoxy of the present Muslim fourteenth century.

During these first centuries of Islam's development and consolidation attention to the philosophical and spiritual aspects of religion was given by only comparatively few and exceptional individuals. Most Muslims accepted the naïve creationist theory of the universe and the slavish legalistic relation of Allah with man.

IV. Islam's Medieval Period: Islam changed greatly during its second or medieval age. This extended from about the middle of the fourth Muslim century to the beginning of the thirteenth (A.D. 900–1800). In the first place, Islamdom's political vicissitudes were many and various. The distressing crusades, the comparatively peaceful penetration into western Asia of the Seljuk Turks, the terrible invasions of the Mongols and the successful expansion of the Ottoman Turks cover in broad general terms what occurred during the rise of uncounted separate states, dynasties, and governments that ruled for a while over small or large regions and peoples and then passed away. The theory and goal of Pan-Islam has never been a political or geographical reality.

It was during this same period, however, that Islam produced and developed its finest contribution to the religious life of its adherents. The earlier era had given the Muslims a theology that was simple and straightforward enough to satisfy the religious requirements of millions of people. Also the social and civil needs of these millions were provided for by the definite rules and regulations of Islam. Any Muslim could learn from his religious leader all that he had to know and do to live a life acceptable to his God and his society. But many Muslims wanted more than a strictly orthodox Islam could provide. The philosophies and sciences of the Hellenic followers of Aristotle and Galen and the ethical and spiritual teachings of such Christian writers as Evagrius and Hunain bin Ishaq were now known to more than the few. Many devout and earnest Muslims flocked to teachers of their own communities who, accepting the Neo-Platonic emanationist philosophy, taught that man came from God, as the Qur'an also taught, but that he was created in the image of God and retained his affinity with God, and would return to God, as the Qur'an also taught, being united with and even absorbed in Him. Such Muslims wanted communion and fellowship with Allah. They felt the need of a more intimate and spiritual relationship with their Creator. They desired to cultivate the interior life of the spirit which the outward performances of rituals, fastings, payment of quarter-tithes and pilgrimages did not satisfy. By this time the religious and ethical doctrines of the teachers and adherents of the religions that Islam had supplanted had been translated from Greek, Syriac, and other languages into Arabic for educated Muslims to read. Just as the Arabs had retained much of their pre-Islamic ideas and customs, so also the Syrians, Persians, Egyptians, Berbers, and other peoples who had accepted Islam brought with them into Islam religious convictions and practices that enriched their lives.

Teachers with these ideas began to form organizations. Indeed, such organizations began to flourish about the same time among both Christians and Muslims. The systems of doctrine, the types of organization, the methods of instruction and discipline varied with the teachers. In Christendom the orders were called Brotherhoods, for brotherly social service was their distinguishing characteristic. The Muslims called themselves Sufis, because their woolen garb was their distinguishing mark. Hundreds of such orders were formed. Some remained local; others became Islam-wide in their constituency, with branches named after their local founders or leaders. Only central Arabia kept itself free from these non-orthodox spiritual and mystical teachings and teachers, preferring the simple, primitive Islam of Muhammad and his companions of seventh-century Arabia. The greatest teacher of the spiritual possibilities of Islam was Abū Ḥāmid Muḥammad al-Ghazālī (d. A.D. 1111), who remained a Muslim Sufi. The greatest exponent of the Muslim brand of Neo-Platonic mysticism was Muḥyid-Dīn Ibn 'Arabī (d. A.D. 1240), whose writings are considered in part dangerous to orthodoxy. These and many other Muslim mystics are highly praised for their spiritual insight. They all taught and cultivated in themselves and others the God-related life. The emphasis is upon the individual's personal religious welfare. Sociologists and students of comparative religion will be interested in the striking fact that in Christendom the brotherhoods practiced service to the poor and needy, while in Islamdom each devotee appeared to be concerned with his own religious development. Sufi Islam has its numerous saints to whom and through whom prayers of petition are addressed.

V. Islam's Modern Period: The influences that have brought about Islam's modern age began in the nineteenth century and have become accelerated and productive of results in the twentieth. This period is Islam's thirteenth and fourteenth centuries. Although western Europe freed itself of Islam when Spain expelled its Muslim population in the year of the discovery of America, eastern Europe, particularly the Balkan peoples, felt the power of Turkey's Muslim caliphs for several more centuries. It was Napoleon's eastward ambitions that again brought all Europe's interest and influence to bear upon Muslim life and institutions, both political and social. Although Napoleon failed in Egypt and western Asia at the beginning of the nineteenth century, within three decades France controlled much of north Africa, which was until then important parts of Turkey's still extensive empire. Later, lest Russia replace Turkey at Constantinople, British power prevented the expulsion of political Islam from Europe. Elsewhere the Muslim peoples were coming to be increasingly under the direct or indirect authority of European powers. Islam appeared to be disintegrating as more of its political divisions became colonies under European governments. Books began to be published expressing that conviction. Islam and other Oriental religions seemed to have exhausted themselves theologically and spiritually, as well as politically and socially. Turkey, which had been so strong, was now shown to be politically weak, if not hopelessly sick, for the caliph's empire was still shrinking.

But, as the Western governments had been extending their control in Africa and the East, Western religious and benevolent organizations had been introducing Western cultures and religious ideals to Eastern peoples. And, of all the world of Islam, it was in Turkey that a new trend began to appear. It was a movement away from the absolute rule of the divinely authoritative caliph towards government according to a constitution that effectively recognized the rights of the people who were to be governed. The caliphate with its claim to the religious leadership of all Muslims was retained, but its power over the welfare of the Turkish people was greatly reduced. Persia followed Turkey's example in demanding an effective constitution and parliament to guide its shah.

World War I produced tremendous changes in Europe. But in the Near East its results were cataclysmic. Its most important effect upon Islam was to separate all Muslim peoples from their allegiance to Islam's caliph, the symbol of Islam's religious unity. Without consulting any other people, Turkey abolished the office of caliphate. Although most of the people remained Muslim, Turkey was the first nation of Muslims to become a republic, thus adopting a Western system of government, with a constitution that no longer declared Islam to be the state religion and with European codes of law to replace the sacred *sharī'ah* law. The great political, civil, and legal changes made during the last half century in Turkey and to a less extent in Iran are still accounted as innovations and are not yet (1953) approved by the majority of Muslim leaders in other lands. It is still a question whether or not the rest of the world of Islam will follow Turkey and Iran in abolishing the strictly Islamic *sharī 'ah* law in favor of modern Western codes of civil, commercial, and criminal law.

Another result of World War I was the establishment of former Turkish provinces as separate nations, although with more or less connection through the mandate system with European governments. It took World War II to give these and other countries, viz., Lebanon, Syria, Indonesia, Egypt, Iraq, Pakistan and Libya (*qq.v.*) the complete or almost complete independence that Saudi Arabia had already won for itself. The first four of the countries mentioned are now republics.

VI. Islam Today: Three new influences are now strongly affecting the Muslims of the world. The first is the establishment of the State of Israel (*q.v.*) in Palestine. The Arab League was organized to prevent that accomplishment but it failed because of dynastic and personal antagonisms and ambitions among the rulers of the seven (now eight) nations composing the league. But the early active assistance and continued support that several Western countries have been giving to the Israeli government and the desperate plight of the million Arab refugees deprived of their homeland and livelihood have produced strong disapproval, on the part of all Muslims, of all the governments concerned.

The second influence active among Muslims is organized communism (*q.v.*). Communism is not welcome among Muslims on religious or political grounds. Its apparent provision of social and cultural autocracy and its specious promises of economic betterment do not appeal to Muslims any more than its suppression of real religious liberty and its absolute dictatorship of political and civil conduct attract them. Only those Muslims in the Middle East who are dissatisfied and disheartened by their own governments so that any change would seem to be for the better, are attracted to Russian communism. There is nothing in Islamic principles, practices, or history that favors Russia or communism.

The third strong influence upon Islam today is the eager desire of young Muslims and their present governments for Western education in the modern sciences and technologies. Of the humanistic studies, constitutional and international law are greatly favored. Thousands of students from eastern, middle, and western Asia and Egypt, many of them from Muslim families, are studying in European and American universities and other educational institutions. The interchange of cultural and social training and the increase of personal friendships between people of the East and West, all conducted with good will and mutual benefit, may be expected to bear splendid fruit. The steady development of common objectives may be hoped for from such new contacts. Muslims and Christians both desire social, political, economic, cultural and spiritual progress toward righteousness and peace for the world, freedom of conscience for individuals and cordial obedience to the will of God. See also Arabia; Iran; Lebanon; Missions to Muslims; Muhammad; Muslims in the U. S. A.; Pakistan; Shi'ism; Sufism; Turkey; Wahhabis.

Bibliography: P. K. Hitti, *History of the Arabs*, 5th ed., rev., 1951; C. Brockelmann (C. Carmichael and M. Perlmann, trs.), *History of the Islamic Peoples*, 1947; H. A. R. Gibb, *Mohammedanism*, 1949; S. M. Zwemer, *The Disintegration of Islam*, 1916; P. W. Ireland (ed.), *The Near East, Problems and Prospects*, 1942; A. J. Arberry & R. Landau (eds.), *Islam Today*, 1943; H. A. R. Gibb, *Modern Trends in Islam*, 1947; L. E. Browne, *The Prospects of Islam*, 1944; G. E. von Grunebaum, *Medieval Islam*, 1944; *The Middle East*, 1953.

[Sup. to Mohammed; Mohammedanism.]

Edwin E. Calverley.

ISLAM, THE ENCYCLOPAEDIA OF. See Encyclopaedia of Islam, The.

ISRAEL, HISTORY OF BIBLICAL: Israel had its development within the large world of the ancient Orient. Through the investigation of that area the history of Israel has come into new and brighter light.

I. New Aspects: The scene of the history of Israel is between the old cultural areas on the Nile and Euphrates-Tigris on the one hand and those around the Mediterranean Sea on the other. In its culture and history Israel has been permanently influenced by both sides. The pre-Israelite history of Syria-Palestine, entered by Israel at the beginning of its history, is still dark in various details. But through the fund of archaeological discoveries (see Archaeology, Biblical) and literary remains it has become well enough known to provide an idea of the situation in which the history of Israel began in the land of culture. During the chalcolithic (fourth millennium B.C.) and the bronze age (*ca.* 3000–1200 B.C.) a town culture developed within Syria-Palestine, especially on the plains and above all along the Mediterranean shores, while the mountainous inner country was sparsely colonized by bronze-age villages.

One of the most important cultural improvements of the late bronze age in Syria-Palestine was the invention and development of an alphabetical system of writing, making possible a common spreading of the art of reading and writing (cf. Judg. 8:14). The religious history of the period is better known to us since 1929 through the alphabetical cuneiform texts (fourteenth century B.C.) of old Ugarit (Ras Shamra, q.v.). The ethnographical combination of the population of pre-Israelite Syria-Palestine is to be inferred from the numerous names of persons known from the Ras Shamra texts and the Egyptian "Execration Texts." Subsequently the main constituent of the population was formed by people speaking a Semitic dialect ("Canaanite"). In addition there were many people of Hurrian (q.v.) (Horite) and Asia Minor origin and of other elements. Of significance also is a group of people of Semitic tongue who by their names are directly related to immigrants who appeared during the nineteenth century B.C. on the Euphrates, well known since 1934 by cuneiform texts of Mari (on the Middle Euphrates). Since the Mari (q.v.) texts have striking connections with the Old Testament, it is probable that those relatives of the Mari people who apparently immigrated to Syria-Palestine during the nineteenth century B.C. also belong to the background of Israelite beginnings.

Archaeological researches in Syria-Palestine have brought to light, through many excavations and surface analyses, the remains of pre-Israelite and Israelite history (see PALESTINE). Through well-established techniques and methods the possibility of exact dating and interpreting has advanced more and more. Thus archaeology has contributed a great deal to our knowledge of the culture entered by Israel and of Israelite life itself, and has made the history of Israel more real and clear to us. Above all, it has given us a definite foundation of topography pointing out the settlements in Israelite times and enabling us very often to locate the events of Israelite history.

Finally, the steadily growing exploration of the Old Testament has led to a more precise distinction between the various elements and a clearer insight into its origin and development, so that we can now express a more positive judgment about the historical contents of the different units. That is above all an important fact relative to the investigation of the beginnings of Israel since from this time there are only national narratives in the Old Testament. Sources of documentary worth in the Old Testament were first written down for the time from the constitution of the state onwards.

II. The Beginnings of Israel: The oldest concept in the Old Testament denotes "Israel" as an association of twelve tribes bound together by a common faith in God. Such "twelve-tribe associations" with a worship center are known in the surrounding areas of Israel as well as in ancient Greece and Italy. In Greece they were called "Amphiktyonies." As an historical fact

the Israelite twelve-tribe association is to be seen clearly first within the borders of Palestine cultivation. Apart from the old bronze-age towns, the Israelite tribes settled down mainly in the mountains where only a few people had settled before them. Their invasion seems to have been completed about 1200 B.C. Most of them settled on the West-Jordan in mountains; only single groups occupied the East-Jordan mountains on the eastern edge of the Jordan Valley. Their worship center was formed by the holy "ark." This "ark" was found at an early time at the sanctuary at Shechem, thereafter for a short time at Bethel (cf. Judg. 20:26a), and later at Shiloh (I Sam. 3:3; 4:3 ff.).

It remained for the single tribes or groups to take care of themselves by defending the land of their occupation from attacks of the Canaanite towns and of other neighbors, especially the Moabites (q.v.) and the Ammonites (q.v.) (cf. Judg. 3:12–30; 10:6–12:6) from the East-Jordan cultivation and the nomadic Midianites (Judg. 6–8). Repeatedly some tribes succeeded in enlarging their territories at the expense of the Canaanite town districts.

The uniqueness of the Israelite twelve-tribe association was that it found itself in absolute obedience to its God Jahweh, excluding all other gods (Ex. 20:3). This close bond with Jahweh was evident in Israel's history. There was the central creed that God had chosen Israel as a special instrument to fulfill his will. At Sinai (q.v.) God had appeared in a theophany to their ancestors to declare himself "their God" and by concluding a "covenant" he established an enduring relation of obligation between himself and the nation. Furthermore, there was the miraculous help of God "at the sea" in the deliverance from Egypt, by which Israel, whose ancestors had gone down to Egypt because of famine and had served there as oppressed laborers, became free from bondage. By this miraculous help God had bound himself to them in a special way.

Next there was record of the helpless situation of Israel in the wilderness and how God took care of them and drew them unto himself. Finally, there was the history of the patriarchs (q.v.) as the forefathers of Israel to whom God promised numberless progeny and the possession of a homeland for their descendants, and about the fulfillment of these promises. It is apparent that the persons and events mentioned may not be put into a simple and plain historical connection, and that actually each time only some of the ancestors of later Israel had participated. In their own ways they had experienced God's coming to Israel and had added their experiences to the basis for the later united "Israel." Thus in a diversified way this "Israel" became conscious of itself as "the people of God."

III. The Constitution of the State: For a

time the sacred twelve-tribe association of Israel lived among the nations that had an established government. About 1000 B.C. the Israelites also established political entities. Under the pressure of attacks by the Philistines (q.v.) and kindred nations which had settled down during the twelfth century B.C. along the western maritime country where they established their rule, the twelve-tribe association called the Benjamite Saul as "king" (see KINGSHIP IN ISRAEL). But his kingdom was soon defeated by the power of the Philistines. In his stead David (q.v.) arose. As a Judean from Bethlehem he first asked the tribes of the southern West-Jordan country to make him "king of Judah" (II Sam. 2:1-4a). Shortly thereafter the other Israelites of the middle and north West-Jordan and of the East-Jordan country, where an insignificant son of Saul had reigned temporarily, made him "king of Israel" (II Sam. 5:1-5). Having now become "king of Judah and Israel," he defeated the Philistines in a decisive battle (II Sam. 5:17-25) and occupied the still Canaanite town of Jerusalem, situated neutrally between the two kingdoms of Judah and Israel, making it his residence (II Sam. 5:6-9). At the same time he transferred the ark to Jerusalem and then made that place the worship center of all Israelite tribes (II Sam. 6). Through the annexation of the other independent Canaanite town-state districts to the states of Israel and Judah and the subjugation of numerous neighboring nations (II Sam. 8), he created a mighty Palestine empire. After the death of his son Solomon, the kingdom of Israel separated from the dynasty of David and established its own kingship. Thus the empire of David fell into parts, only the small kingdom of Judah remaining with the dynasty of David (926 B.C.). These small kingdoms of Israel and Judah fell into the complex political and belligerent developments of the Syria-Palestine powers until finally the area was overthrown by the great Assyrian (q.v.) power. In 733 and 721 B.C. the kingdom of Israel was occupied by the Assyrians and divided into four Assyrian provinces. At the same time the kingdom of Judah became a vassal of Assyria. Then in 587 B.C. the Neo-Babylonian (see BABYLONIA) power, which replaced the Assyrian, swept out the kingdom of Judah also and made it a Neo-Babylonian province. The royal town Jerusalem was devastated and the temple was robbed and burned. In the overthrow of the two kingdoms the upper classes were deported to other provinces throughout the great empire while the lower primitive people remained at home as dependent political subjects.

IV. The Cultic Community of Jerusalem: After the Persian (see MEDO-PERSIA) king Cyrus had brought the Neo-Babylonian Empire under his rule in 539 B.C., he issued the order (538

B.C.) for the rebuilding of the temple of Jerusalem (Ezra 6:3-5), for it seemed wise to him to re-establish the ancient cults of the many conquered nations. Thus the temple was reconstructed and in 515 B.C. reconsecrated. Worship and leaders of worship at the former public sanctuary were granted numerous privileges by the Persian king (cf. Ezra 5:8b-10; 7:20-24). Around this newly-established worship at Jerusalem those descendants of the old Israel who desired to return to or maintain the pre-exhilic Israelite worship gathered together as a worshiping community. This parish consisted first of the large elements of the Israelite tribes that remained undeported in Palestine, together with those descendants of the people deported in 598 and 587 B.C. who had reached their old home again, having been repatriated by Persian license. Furthermore, many Israelites remaining in the Diaspora mainly in Babylon and Lower Egypt, belonged to this parish.

This cultic community acquired a new order, a "law," through Ezra, who apparently at the close of the reign of King Artaxerxes I (465-424 B.C.) was sent officially (cf. Ezra 7:12-26) from Babylon to Jerusalem to settle the inner affairs of the congregation at Jerusalem. Strained relations arose between the congregation at Jerusalem and the mixed populace in the province of Samaria. This tension continued until finally, perhaps at the time of Alexander the Great, there was established on Mt. Gerizim a peculiar Samaritan cult, with which the larger elements of the province became affiliated.

V. Political Conflicts and the End of Israel: After the fall of the Persian Empire the district of the cultic community at Jerusalem was brought under the reign of the Macedonian Diadochian dynasties, first the Ptolemies and then the Seleucidae. The tyrannical treatment of the Jerusalem congregation and its orders by the Seleucid king Antiochus IV led to a revolt against the Seleucid government guided by the priestly family of the Hasmonaeans (168 B.C.). Following a rapid restoration of the traditional order of worship, they finally aimed at political independence. In connection with the decline of the Seleucid rule an independent Hasmonaean kingship was established. Aristobulus I (104-103 B.C.) first took the title of "king." The swift degeneration of the Hasmonaean dynasty, however, allowed the Romans soon to intervene in Palestine (Pompey, 63 B.C.). Herod I, son of a high official and adviser of the last Hasmonaeans, through the favor of his Roman friends occupied the reign over Israel in Palestine (37-4 B.C.). But after his death his incapable sons one by one were deposed by the Romans, who brought the country under their own direct administration. In the bloody but futile revolutions against the Roman government in A.D. 66-70 and 132-135 the old Israel perished, leaving Judaism without a worship center and any real home.

BIBLIOGRAPHY: R. Kittel, *Geschichte des Volkes Israel,* 3 vols., 1923–29; W. O. E. Oesterley and T. H. Robinson, *A History of Israel,* 1932; M. Noth, *Geschichte Israels,* 1950. Old Oriental sources: J. B. Pritchard (ed.), *Ancient Near Eastern Texts Relating to the Old Testament,* 1950; A. Scharff und A. Moortgat, *Aegypten und Vorderasien im Altertum,* 1950; M. Noth, *Die syrisch-palaestinische Bevoelkerung des zweiten Jahrtausends vor Christum im Lichte neuer Quellen,* 1942. Archaeology: C. Watzinger, *Denkmaeler Palaestinas,* 2 vols. 1933–35; W. F. Albright, *Archaeology and the Religion of Israel,* 2nd ed., 1946; *The Archaeology of Palestine,* 1949. Topography: Numerous articles in *BASOR*; Nelson Glueck, *Explorations in Eastern Palestine, Annual ASOR,* Vols. XIV, XV, XVII–XIX, XXV–XXVIII, 1934–51. Monographs on the History of Israel: M. Noth, *Das System der zwoelf Staemme Israels,* 1930; A. Alt. *Die Landnahme der Israeliten in Palestina,* 1925; *Die Staatenbildung der Israeliten in Palaestina,* 1930; E. Bickermann, *Der Gott der Makkabaeer,* 1937.

[Sup.] MARTIN NOTH.

ISRAEL, HISTORY OF, POSTBIBLICAL: Since the time of Napoleon, competitive national sentiment has characterized European peoples, and persecution of the Jewish people, from which they have never had long respite, became increasingly sharpened by propaganda. The pogroms in Russia, especially in 1881 *seq.,* the Dreyfus Case in France in 1894, and the forged *Protocols of the Elders of Zion (q.v.)* necessitated some corporate action on the part of Judaism for its own spiritual and physical salvation. In the United States, emotional provincialism in relation to the Jewish people has sometimes seemed less dangerous than European anti-Semitism, though mental cruelty is tragically widespread. A desire on the part of certain Christians to convert Jewish people to Christianity is interpreted as a childish sense of superiority on the part of members of the majority faith. Also, the interpretation by a number of Christians of certain prophetic passages as predictive of the return of Israel to its former land has given opportunity for those who hold this view to find no occasion for America's sharing the burden of receiving and rehabilitating displaced Jews from other countries. Gentile Anglo-Saxon approval of the Zionist cause has therefore suffered from mixed motives.

The beginnings of the Zionist Organization were made in 1897; Theodore Herzl was the moving spirit. Attempts to enlist Abdul-Hamid, Sultan of Turkey, then Kaiser Wilhelm II, the Tsar, even the Pope, in the cause of Jewish escape to Palestine, failed, though in England it got a more sympathetic hearing. Herzl's diplomacy, however, touched world-wide imagination, both Jewish and Gentile. At the close of World War I the Balfour Declaration and the responsibility of Britain for the mandate of Palestine seemed to bring diplomatic victory to the Jewish hopes. The disappointment of the local Arab population of Palestine, who had hoped for eventual autonomy, was during the next thirty years expressed in varying degrees of violence, much of it under the leadership of

the Grand Mufti of Jerusalem. The moral injustice done to an indigenous population, which was not sufficiently consulted regarding the establishment of a "national home" for the Jewish people in its territory, has been seriously underestimated because inadequate presentation of the Arab cause has limited the effective western appreciation of their problem. On May 14, 1948, the Jewish Provisional Government proclaimed the State of Israel. Open war with the Arab states ensued for several months.

The conflict of the indigenous Arab population with the immigrants rests upon a wide disparity in culture, insufficiently described as primarily political or religious. Arab freedom is expressed in terms of family rather than of individual, in appreciation of open lands, sparsely inhabited, in poetic rather than practical discourse. To the pioneers of Israel, the Arab appears lazy; but to the Arab, the ambition of the pioneer is objectionably secular and slavish. In this conflict, Arab leadership has been unfortunately inferior; several of the Jewish leaders, notably the late Dr. Judah Magnes, of the Hebrew University, have had remarkable insight into the problems involved, though they have been unable fully to inspire the community of Israel with their own amicable spirit.

The effective colonization of Palestine by Jewish immigrants in modern times begins with the establishment of Zikron Ya'kob, on the southern shoulder of Mount Carmel, in 1880, and of Petach Tikvah nearer Jaffa in 1883. The Jewish population of the country at the beginning of World War II had risen to an estimated 100,000, with fifty-four agricultural communities, active in international trade. Since World War I there has been continuous immigration, though at times it was severely restricted by the Mandatory Power. In the years of the Nazi regime in Germany about 200,000 entered the country. After the new political State of Israel was proclaimed, immigration increased to many times its previous rate.

Geographically the State of Israel includes the Plain of Esdraelon and the hills to the north as far as the border of Lebanon, eastward to the Sea of Galilee; the coastal plain, eastward from the Mediterranean to the hills with a narrow wedge reaching to Jerusalem, whose New City outside the walls is Jewish; and the Negeb, in the south, with the exception of the narrow "Gaza Strip" along the coast, assigned to Egypt. With the exception of the Negeb and the land around Jerusalem, this territory is the most fertile part of Palestine. The destiny of population is far greater in Israel than in the Hashimite Kingdom of Jordan, and it is increasing rapidly.

Fundamental law of the State of Israel will be democratic, constitutional. Formulations of details require time for development, but the significant parts of the picture are already clear. Universal equal suffrage of persons over twenty-one is by proportional representation. The unicameral Keneseth or Chamber of Deputies, which is the legislative side of the government, has one representative for each 10,000 persons. Deputies may not be judges, civil servants, military personnel, or citizens of any other State than Israel. The executive power is vested in the President of the Republic and in the Executive Council. The president is elected by the Keneseth for a term of five years, and may be re-elected for a second term, but not more. Upon consultation he appoints the prime minister, also ambassadors, diplomatic ministers, and the commander-in-chief of the army. The Executive Council, not over fifteen persons, includes the prime minister and heads of departments of state, all members of the Keneseth. The judiciary courts are of five categories: magistrates' courts, district courts, high court, supreme court; also the religious courts, each serving its own sect. The law is "the basic principles of Jewish law." The fundamental and general expressions of constitutional guarantee are significant: "Ideals of peace and righteousness of the Prophets of Israel"; "no discrimination . . ."; "international disputes . . . by pacific means only"; no death penalty and "no moral or physical violence in police investigation." "The economic order of the State of Israel shall be based on the principles of social justice. Every citizen shall have an equitable share in the national income and a right to social security. The state shall encourage and aid every form of cooperative effort." "A decent standard of living and a fair and equal opportunity of earning a livelihood" are to be protected by the government.

Israel has become the present fulfilment of the Golden Age in the Land of Promise. The Zionism of poetic faith has culminated in a sovereign state. The faith has been both compromised and given practical expression. Though supposedly professing a religion of peace, the Jewish state has been established and defended by war. Within the state the forces of orthodoxy and of a secular pioneer spirit are in conflict. An intensely democratic spirit from the West is being considerably diluted by the immigration of great numbers of Jews from eastern countries; the culture of these orientals is quite as retarded as that of the peoples whom they leave. Freedom is the dominant spirit within the state, though its application to dispossessed Arabs and to religious minorities has not yet been worked out in practice. Probably there are few places in the world where the political, economic, social and religious problems of the twentieth century are more concentrated than in the State of Israel. If Zionistic Israel can resolve its inner tensions without destroy-

ing its own vitality, and can become genuinely friendly with the surrounding Arab communities and states, its ideal will win the world's approval.

See also ZIONISM.   MOSES BAILEY.

ITALY: Since World War II Italy comprised 116,224 square miles and had a population (in 1953) of 47,566,000. The majority of people were nominally Roman Catholic. No marked changes in religious adherence took place since the religious census of 1931 when there were 82,569 Protestants, 47,485 Jews, and 5896 Eastern Orthodox in Italy.

I. Roman Catholic Church: After 1870, when the temporal power of the pope ended in Italy, there was friction between the new kingdom and the Vatican. The pope refused to accept this limitation of his sovereignty and forbade Italian Catholics participation in political life. Before World War I this prohibition was relaxed, and in 1919 it was removed when Luigi Sturze organized the Popular Party. The Vatican lost interest in this party, however, when it opposed the Fascist State of Benito Mussolini, and it was disbanded. The reconciliation of Pope Pius XI (q.v.) and Mussolini brought the "Roman Question" to a close when the Lateran Pacts were adopted in 1929. These pacts comprised a treaty, a concordat, and a financial agreement. The treaty recognized Roman Catholicism as "the only religion of the state," acknowledged "the sovereignty of the Holy See in the international sphere," and created Vatican City as sovereign territory of the pope. The concordat guaranteed the Roman Church the free exercise of its functions in Italy, granted priests exemption from military service, and acknowledged that Catholic religious instruction was "the foundation and culmination of public education." Thus cordial relations were established with the Fascist government which resulted in collaboration during the Ethiopian War (1935–36) and the early stages of World War II. After World War II the provisions of the Lateran Pacts were reaffirmed by the new Italian Republic.

In 1873 all Roman Catholic theological faculties in state universities were abolished. Pope Leo XIII (q.v., Vol. VI) opened the secret Vatican archives to scholars in 1880 and also founded the Academy of St. Thomas to promote Thomism. In his struggle against Modernism Pius XI founded the Pontifical Biblical Institute in 1909, and among other new schools were the Catholic University of the Sacred Heart (1920), the Pontifical Institute of Christian Archaeology (1925), and the Pontifical Academy of Sciences (1936).

In 1953 there were 288 archbishoprics and bishoprics in Italy. In addition there were thirteen abbeys and prelatures without dioceses.

II. Protestant Churches: Italian Protestantism includes the Waldensian Church, the Evangelical Methodist Church of Italy, the Baptist Evangelical Church, the Evangelical Lutheran Church, and several smaller groups. In 1946 the first three of these formed the Federal Council of Evangelical Churches in Italy.

Since 1848, when the Waldensians (see WALDENSES) were granted religious liberty, they founded congregations in the major Italian cities and in some rural areas. In 1953 they counted 63 congregations and 26,297 members. Some Waldensians migrated to Uruguay between 1856 and 1860, and in 1893 a community was established by emigrants in North Carolina and named Valdese. In Italy the Waldensians conduct elementary schools, a high school, a theological seminary in Rome (with the only Protestant theological library in Italy), a publishing house, several hospitals, and other charitable institutions. The church has a presbyterian organization. It has an annual synod, and an administrative board elected by the synod and presided over by a moderator.

The Evangelical Methodist Church of Italy was formed in 1946 by a merger of Methodist bodies organized in 1861 from England and in 1873 from America. In 1953 it had 54 congregations, 35 mission stations, and about 7000 members. It also maintains several charitable institutions.

Baptist missionary work in Italy was begun from England in 1866 and from America in 1870. After 1923 all Baptist work in Italy was under the guidance and support of the Southern Baptist Convention in the U.S.A. In 1953 there were 71 congregations with about 9000 souls. Baptists conduct several orphans' homes, a Bible School for the training of missionaries, and a Women's Bible Institute in Rome.

The Lutheran congregations in Italy were established and supported from Germany, but during and immediately after World War II they suffered heavy losses in membership. They were then aided by the Lutheran World Federation (*q.v.*), and in 1948 they organized the Evangelical Lutheran Church in Italy and began a program of evangelization in the Italian language. In 1953 the Lutherans numbered about 6000. Their church is governed by a consistory headed by a dean.

The Salvation Army (*q.v.*) began its work in Italy in 1887, and the Y.M.C.A. (*q.v.*) was introduced during World War I. The Seventh-day Adventists (*q.v.*) entered Italy in 1874, the Pentecostals (*q.v.*) in 1900, the Church of Christ in 1947.

III. Religious Liberty: The relations between the Roman Church and the state were fixed by the Lateran Pacts, but the religious liberty (*q.v.*) of minority groups in Italy remained uncertain. Since 1930 governmental consent was

required for the erection of a Protestant church building, and since 1931 police permission was required for religious assemblies in private homes. A series of incidents and trials took place since World War II to test the laws, and magistrates generally recognized the rights of religious minorities without being able to guarantee their future status.

BIBLIOGRAPHY: On Roman Catholicism: S. W. Halperin, *The Separation of Church and State in Italian Thought from Cavour to Mussolini*, 1927; idem, *Italy and the Vatican at War*, 1939; S. Jacini, *La crisi religiosa del Risorgimento*, 1938; V. del Giudice, *La questione romana*, 1947; E. Buonaiuti, *Il modernismo cattolica*, 1943; F. Magri, *L'Azione cattolica in Italia*, 2 vols., 1953. On Protestantism: Giovanni Luzzi, *The Struggle for Christian Truth in Italy*, 1913; C. Crivelli, *I protestanti in Italia*, 2 vols., 1936–38; M. Piscentini, *I culti ammessi nello Stato Italiano*, 1934; *Die Lage der Protestanten in katholischen Laendern*, 1953; Giovanni Luzzi, *The Waldensian Church*, 1914; G. B. Watts, *The Waldenses in the New World*, 1941; G. Miegge, *L'Eglise sous le joug fasciste*, 1946; T. Elze and E. Lessing, *Geschichte der protestantischen Bewegungen in Venedig*, 1928; E. Schubert, *Geschichte der deutschen evangelischen Gemeinde in Rom*, 1930; E. Schubert, *Geschichte der evangelischen Gemeinde in Neapel*, 1926.

[Sup.] VALDO VINAY and ERICH DAHLGRUEN.

ITALY, THE REFORMATION IN: Theologians and historians are fairly well agreed on the nature of the Reformation in Spain, but it is still difficult to find a satisfactory account of the rise of Protestantism in Italy. Spain had its great cardinal Ximenes, who refused to introduce in his kingdoms the sale of indulgences. But in Italy lived the so-called Renaissance popes, and here was the seat of papal authority. Spain was being unified under autocratic kings who were in a position to throttle religious liberty. Italy, on the other hand, was ruled in the south by Spaniards, and in the north French and Spanish invaders often clashed with each other. Heretics fled from Spain to Italy, and in this way the Italian situation became very confused. Protestant theologians have often claimed that Italy was never Christian until Martin Luther forced the papal party to reform the whole church. Again, the popes were so irreligious that they gladly allied themselves with the Turks against the emperor of the Holy Roman Empire. On the other hand, well-known Roman Catholic authorities have claimed that Italy was exceptionally pious at the opening of the sixteenth century.

The learned work, *Histoire de l'Eglise depuis les origines jusqu'a nos jours*, Vol. XVII (1948), p. 245 says: "If the Council of Trent was able to become unified again and its decrees could finally be accepted, confirmed and put into practice, if a veritable religious and moral revival was produced at the heart of the Catholic Church, it was because reform movements had been manifest to some extent everywhere, and particularly in Italy, where they had become widely known and exerted considerable influence." This volume lists a number of saintly persons who flourished in Italy during the first half of the sixteenth century and whose lives

compare favorably with those of the most famous Protestants. On March 16, 1517, the
Lateran Council (see LEO X) closed its last
session. There had been much talk about reformation, and a number of decrees had been
passed which the Council of Trent nearly half
a century later adopted, although with revisions.
On the first day of the first session (May 3,
1512), the General of the Augustinians said:
"Men must be changed by religion, and religion must not be changed by men." But, so
continues the volume already mentioned, Pope
Leo X was not interested in reform. Italy in
the period of the Renaissance was led for the
most part by irreligious men: "The times were
not ready for a profound transformation of
morals in Italy of the Renaissance. The abuses
in the Curia were not touched. Pope Leo remained inert, in face of the needs of the Church,
immersed as he was in profane luxury and the
cult of the arts." How then did the overwhelming desire to reform the Church originate
in Italy? Did the Protestants provide the main
stimulant, or did others do so?

Before the death of Leo X a number of devout men came together and planned to do
what the pope refused to do. The group was
named "The Oratory of Divine Love." Its
patron saint was St. Jerome. Among these
men was the future Pope Paul IV, and one of
the presidents of the Council of Trent under
Julius III. Before long several diplomats attached to the Curia joined the circle. The German historian Leopold von Ranke, Protestant
though he was, said that this institution was
very similar to the first Protestant groups in
Italy. What he had in mind probably was that
these pious men were sincere in their desire to
remove the real abuses in the church, but not
to change doctrines. Another group of reformers was called the Theatins. Another influence for good was the shock with which the
Roman populace was struck when in 1527 an
army in the service of Emperor Charles V, the
political enemy of the pope, sacked Rome,
committing horrible crimes. It caused many to
do some serious thinking about the evil of
luxurious living. After this sacking in 1527,
Rome was not the same. In other cities of Italy
a similar change occurred, stimulated no doubt
by a variety of causes, some secular, others religious.

Without a doubt the Protestants played their
part, but many of those who have been designated as Protestants were merely followers of
Erasmus or other orthodox Catholics in the
northern countries. Juan de Valdés (q.v.), for
example, was not a Protestant, although it has
been said of him that "he wrought in an elect
circle at Naples, as the most strongly intellectual and original of the Italian Reformers."
Recent research has shown that Juan de Valdés

was not a real Protestant, and that his admirable treatise, Doctrina Christiana, was thoroughly
Erasmian. It was recognized as such by the
most devout prelates in Spain, until they saw
ideas in it that Luther sponsored, and for that
reason, so they argued, they must needs be of
the devil and thus heretical. Another source
of misunderstanding is the idea that to spread
copies of the Bible in the vernacular is an act
of anti-Catholic mentality. It is supposed that
the Roman Catholic authorities did not want
laymen to read the Scriptures in their own language. They must be kept in ignorance in
order to remain good Catholics. It was also a
sign of Protestantism to translate Luther's
purely political tract, To the Christian Nobility
of the German Nation. But, though certain
prelates in 1530 or 1540 considered this heresy
and delighted in burning those who dared to
sell it or read it, that did not make the book
heretical, and certainly not Protestant.

BIBLIOGRAPHY: J. E. Longhurst, Erasmus and the Spanish Inquisition: The Case of Juan de Valdés, 1950;
M. Bataillon, Erasme et l'Espagne, 1937; idem, Juan de
Valdés: Diálogo de Doctrina Christiana (1925): Bataillon
was the first to find this important treatise, which shows
that Valdés was not a Protestant; A. G. Bonet-Maury,
Early Sources of English Unitarian Christianity (1884):
see particularly p. 142, where the author indicates that
Valdés never left the Roman Catholic Church; G. K.
Brown, Italy and the Reformation to 1550 (1933): discusses on pp. 223-235 the so-called Valdesian Movement,
meaning that Valdés was a great organizer of Protestantism in Italy; actually he repeated the old legend and
failed to use the latest sources; D. Cantimori, Eretici
italiani del cinquecento (1939): the author believes incorrectly that Servetus agreed with Valdés on those points
for which he was condemned by the Catholic authorities
in France and burned by the Protestant powers in Switzerland; C. Cantù, Gli eretici d'Italia: Discorsi storici, 3
vols., (1865-66): the author considers Juan de Valdés a
"perfidious heretic." F. C. Church, The Italian Reformers, 1534-1564 (1932): a scholarly book; J. Hepe,
Juan de Valdés: Seine Religion—sein Werden—seine Bedeutung (1900): clearly indicates that Valdés was not a
Protestant and not a good Roman Catholic for his time;
A. Savelli, Storia d'Italia, 1940; L. Salvatorelli, Som-
mario della stroia d'Italia, 1928, 2nd ed., 1939; G. Tof-
fanin, Storia dell'Umanesimo, 1933, 2nd ed., 1940; A.
Fliche and V. Martin, Histoire de l'Eglise depuis; les
origines jusqu'a nos jours, Vol. XVII (1948), pp. 245-337.
The spread of Protestantism in the Italian section of
Switzerland was caused very largely by Italians, and their
work is a part of the Reformation in Italy. Important
books on the subject are: P. Dalbert, Die Reformation in
den Italienischen Talschaften Graubuendens nach dem
Briefwechsel Bullingers, 1948; E. Camenisch, Geschichte
der Reformation und Gegenreformation in den italienischen Suedtaelern Graubuendens und den ehemaligen
Untertanenlanden Chiavenna, Veltlin und Bormio, 1950.
[Sup.] ALBERT HYMA.

ITE MISSA EST: The Latin words with
which the deacon (or the priest) dismisses the
congregation at the end of the Mass in the
Western liturgies. The meaning is: "Depart ye,
now is the dismissal." This formula is used on
Sundays and on the feasts of the saints. Alle-
luias are added during the Easter season. On
ordinary weekdays and on Sundays in Advent
and Lent, the words Benedicamus Domino:
"Let us bless the Lord" are substituted for the
Ite Missa est.   GEORGES A. BARROIS.

IVORY COAST. See AFRICA.

J

JACKS, LAURENCE PEARSALL: Unitarian; b. Nottingham, 1860. Educated at the University of London (M.A., 1886), Manchester College, Nottingham, and Harvard, he entered the ministry as assistant to Stopford Brooke in 1887. He ministered in Liverpool and Birmingham. He became professor of philosophy, Manchester College (1903); principal of Manchester College (1915–31). He was the editor of the *Hibbert Journal* from its foundation in 1902 to his retirement in 1947. He has written: *Life and Letters of Stopford Brooke; The Legends of Smokeover; Constructive Citizenship* (1927); *The Education of the Whole Man* (1931); *Elemental Religion* (1934); *The Confessions of an Octogenarian* (1942); *A Living Universe; The Challenge of Life; Religious Perplexities;* and numerous other books, including translation of works by A. Loisy.   F. W. DILLISTONE.

JACKSON, FREDERICK JOHN FOAKES: D. Dec. 1, 1941. He was dean and tutor in Jesus College, Cambridge (1895–1916), after which he served with distinction as Briggs Graduate Professor of Christian Institutions at Union Theological Seminary in New York (1916–34). He also lectured in the Jewish Institute in New York and in the General Theological Seminary. After coming to America he published: *St. Luke and a Modern Writer* (1916); *English Society, 1750–1850* (Lowell Lectures) (1916); *Introduction to Church History, 590–1314* (1921); *Anglican Church Principles* (1924); *Studies in the Life of the Early Church* (1924); *Life of St. Paul* (1926); *Rise of Gentile Christianity* (1927); *Peter, Prince of Apostles* (1927); *Josephus and the Jews* (1930); *The Church in England* (1931); *Eusebius, Bishop of Caesarea and First Christian Historian* (1933); *The Church in the Middle Ages* (1934); *History of Church Historians* (1939); and in addition he edited: *Parting of the Roads* (1911); *Faith and War* (1916); and (with Kirsopp Lake), *The Beginnings of Christianity* (Vol. I, 1919; Vol. II, 1922; Vol. III, 1926; Vols. IV and V, 1932).

[Sup.] RAYMOND W. ALBRIGHT.

JACKSON, SAMUEL MACAULEY: Presbyterian; b. June 19, 1851, in New York City; d. at Washington, Conn., Aug. 2, 1912. He studied at the College of the City of New York (A.B., 1870; A.M., 1876); Princeton Theological Seminary (1870–71); Union Theological Seminary (B.D., 1873); and studied abroad (1873–75). Ordained in 1876 he served as pastor of the Presbyterian Church, Norwood, N. J., and was professor of church history in New York

University (1895–1912). He was president of the board of trustees of the Canton Christian College in China and an honorary fellow of the Huguenot Society of London, having edited the Papers and Proceedings of the Huguenot Society of America (*Tercentenary of the Edict of Nantes,* 1899, and additional volumes in 1902 and 1904). Much of his life was devoted to literary work. He was a member of the publication committee of the Ecumenical Missionary Conference held in New York (1900); and edited a *Missionary Bibliography* and the *Report of the Centenary Conference on the Protestant Missions of the World* (1888). His major publications include: *The Latin Works and the Correspondence of Huldreich Zwingli, together with Selections from his German Works, in English Translation* (Vol. I, 1912); *Zwingli Selections* (a preliminary study to the previous work) (1901); *Huldreich Zwingli* (Heroes of the Reformation Series) (1901); *The Source of Jerusalem the Golden and other pieces attributed to Bernard of Cluny* (1910). In addition to this he was: editor-in-chief of the *New Schaff-Herzog Encyclopedia of Religious Knowledge* (12 vols., 1907–11); and associate editor of the earlier edition of this set (1884); assistant editor *Schaff's Bible Dictionary* (1880); editor for religious literature in *Johnson's Universal Cyclopaedia* (1893–95; new ed. called *The Universal Cyclopaedia,* 1900); editor of the department of religion in *New International Encyclopaedia* (1902–4); joint editor of *Cyclopaedia of Living Divines* (1887); editor, *Concise Dictionary of Religious Knowledge* (1891); editor of *Heroes of the Reformation* (1898–1906); and editor of church terms in *Standard Dictionary* (1895), and *New International Dictionary* (1900).   RAYMOND W. ALBRIGHT.

JACKSON LECTURESHIP: A memorial at Southern Methodist University from the sons and daughters of Mr. and Mrs. Robert Malone Jackson, who were pioneers in eastern Texas and members of the Tennessee Colony. The general subject is the Bible. The lectures are given under the direction of the Perkins School of Theology and are given annually during the first full week of February. EUGENE B. HAWK.

JACOB. See PATRIARCHS, OLD TESTAMENT.

JACOB CHRISTOPH. See COUNTER REFORMATION IN SWITZERLAND.

JACOBINS: Nickname given to the Dominicans of the convent of St. James (*Conventus Sancti Jacobi*) in Paris, and, by extension, to Dominicans in general. During the French Revolution, a republican club assembled in the disaffected cloister of St. James and the name Jacobins subsequently applied to political extremists.

JACOBS, CHARLES MICHAEL: Lutheran; b. Dec. 5, 1875, at Gettysburg, Pa.; d. March 30, 1938. He studied at the University of Pennsylvania (A.B., 1895); the Lutheran Theological Seminary, Mt. Airy, Philadelphia (graduated, 1899); and did graduate study at Pennsylvania and Leipzig. Ordained in the Lutheran ministry in 1899, he served pastorates at St. Peter's Church, North Wales, Pa. (1899–1904) and Christ Church, Allentown, Pa. (1904–13). He became professor of church history and director of the graduate school at the Lutheran Seminary, Philadelphia (1913–38; president, 1927–38). He was coeditor of: *Luther's Works in English* (6 vols., 1915–32); and (with Preserved Smith), *Luther's Correspondence,* Vol. II (1916). He also wrote: *The Way—A Little Book of Christian Truth* (1922); *The Story of the Church—An Outline of Its History* (1925); and *An Outline of Christian Doctrine* (tr. from German of W. Elert, 1926).

RAYMOND W. ALBRIGHT.

JACOBS, HENRY EYSTER: D. July 7, 1932. He taught systematic theology at the Lutheran Theological Seminary, Philadelphia (1883–1932; dean, 1894–1920; president, 1920–27). In addition to his teaching he widely represented his denomination and often was named chairman of important boards of national and international Lutheran groups. He translated a number of German theological works into English, contributed to Hastings' *Encyclopaedia of Religion and Ethics, The International Standard Bible Encyclopedia,* and also published an additional volume, *Lincoln's Gettysburg World Message* (1920).

[Sup.] RAYMOND W. ALBRIGHT.

JACQUIER, EUGENE: Roman Catholic biblical scholar; b. 1847, Vienne, France; d. Feb. 7, 1932, Lyons; ordained (1871); Th.D., Lyons (1891); professor of biblical studies, Catholic Faculties, Lyons (1894–1927). His works include: *Histoire des livres du Nouveau Testament* (4 vols., 2nd ed., 1903; Eng. tr., *History of the Books of the New Testament,* Vol. I, 1907); *Le Nouveau Testament dans l'Eglise chrétienne* (2 vols., 1911–13); *Etudes de critique et de philologie du Nouveau Testament* (1920); *Les Actes des Apôtres* (Etudes Bibliques) (1926).

OTTO A. PIPER.

JAINISM: The strict adherence of the Jains to the principle of Ahimsa has limited them to occupations which have made the laity, paradoxically, a small but extremely wealthy community. They reside largely in Gujarat and Rajputana. They have survived revivals of orthodox Hinduism, but with only a remnant of numerical strength. In the 1941 census they numbered 1,433,286, an increase of 200,000 over 1931. Modern Jains are noted for contributions to temples, making of a once rich tradition of architecture and sculpture a monument of questionable taste, an abandonment of primitive simplicity. They are known for the endowment and maintenance of hospitals for animals—a modern implementation of Ahimsa.

The fact of their business preoccupation (largely finance and commerce) disposes them to an education to these ends. This has "protected" the community from the adjustments and reforms a more liberal contact with modern thought would necessitate.

The conservative nature of the Jain community is further supported by the Bharata Jaina Mahamandala (all India Jain association) founded in 1911. This association has a dual aim—the consolation of the community and the spread of its doctrine. The peculiar combination of business acumen with strict ethics and elements of sainthood is well illustrated by Raychandbhai of whom Mahatma Gandhi once said: "Raychandbhai's commercial transactions covered hundreds of thousands. He was a connoisseur of pearls and diamonds. No knotty business problem was too difficult for him. But all these things were not the center around which his life revolved. The center was the passion to see God face to face."

Many Jains have ceased to distinguish between their faith and that of Hinduism and the separate identity of the community has been often in jeopardy. The Hindu community in its warm catholicity would readily absorb it were it not for the determination of a few to maintain vitality and even "evangelize" under the banner of Ahimsa.

See also HINDUISM; INDIA.

BIBLIOGRAPHY: Mrs. Sinclair Stevenson, *Notes on Modern Jainism,* 1910; idem, *The Heart of Jainism,* 1915; Harisatya Bhattacharyya, *A Comparative Study of the Indian Science of Thought from the Jaina Standpoint,* 1925; Jahmanderlal Jaini, *Outlines of Jainism,* 1940.

[Sup.] MALCOLM S. PITT.

JAMES I: King of Scotland (as James VI) and England. He was b. June 19, 1566, at the Castle of Edinburgh, the son of Lord Henry Stuart, Earl of Darnley, and Mary Stuart (*q.v.*). Died March 25, 1625, at Hampton Court Palace, and was buried in Westminster Abbey. He was a learned theologian and took certain steps that proved of great significance in the history of England and Scotland. He and his son Charles I (*q.v.*), through their dynastic relations, often favored Roman Catholic statesmen, thereby alienating the majority of their subjects and indirectly paving the way for the Glorious Revolution of 1688. As the distinguished British historian, G. M. Trevelyan, said in the Introduction to his famous work, *England Under the Stuarts*, the great contribution by the English people to the making of Western civilization was the manner in which they disposed of two ruling members of the House of Stuart. The growth of Parliamentary institutions in England and the checking of royal absolutism were two outstanding English political developments. Together with these changes there occurred certain ecclesiastical alterations that make the reign of James highly significant.

Very soon after his birth the child was sent to Stirling Castle, where he remained for twelve years. In December following he was baptized with the Roman Catholic rites, his three sponsors being Elizabeth, the Protestant Queen of England; Charles IX, the Catholic King of France; and the Catholic Duke of Savoy. He received two names: Charles and James, the former from the King of France, the latter from his grandfather, James V of Scotland. His mother had been the wife of the late King Francis II of France, and she wished to honor the French nation in this manner.

Mary Stuart abdicated the throne of Scotland in 1567, and on July 29th her son was crowned king as James VI, this time under the auspices of Presbyterians rather than Roman Catholics. On the same day John Knox preached on the great event and quoted this text: "I was crowned young." So it was indeed. Soon after the ceremony his mother fled to England and sought shelter with her cousin and enemy, Queen Elizabeth (*q.v.*) of England. In the meantime the boy grew and was well educated under strict orders from the Estates of Scotland, who in 1569 appointed four preceptors. One of them was Peter Young, a minister, who had recently returned from Geneva, the bulwark of Calvinism. The chief tutor was George Buchanan, a famous humanist, who had taught in Paris and Bordeaux. In the latter place the elegant Montaigne had been his pupil. He had also tutored the sons of King James V of Scotland. In 1563 he had joined the Presbyterian Church and became principal of St. Andrews College, being appointed by the regent of the young king, the Earl of Murray. These preceptors taught him a great deal of Latin and theology; they told him that his mother had "once dwelt with the leopards of France," the Catholic lords and ladies who were in the service of the devil. He spent one year (1582–83) at the University of St. Andrews, and then returned to Edinburgh to enter the arena of active politics.

James was not only a politician but also a scholar. In 1585, at the age of nineteen he published a work of poetry and some translations: *The Eassayes of a Prentise, in the Divine Art of Poesie*. He was always proud of his Latin and his theological knowledge, but little is known about his poetical ability, or his romances. In 1588 he composed a religious meditation entitled *Apocalypse*, and in 1589 *Chronicles*. In 1597 there followed his *Demonology*, while in the next year appeared a political treatise of great significance: *The Trew Law of Free Monarchies; or The Reciprock and Mutuall Duetie betwixt a Free King and his Natural Subjects*. It contained only some ten thousand words, but Andrew Melville, leader of the scholars at the University of St. Andrews, found in it some terrible pestilence called "Anglopiscopapistical." He and another divine called Dykes showed the book to the General Assembly and warned the preachers against it, not saying who the author was, for the book had appeared anonymously. But everybody knew who had written it. Dykes had to flee the country, but Melville remained. James ignored Melville's actions and ordered the formal publication of his book. He remained favorable to the episcopal form of church government. In 1589 he had agreed to marry Anne, daughter of the King of Denmark; first came the marriage by proxy on August 20, then the real wedding in November. Anne was a Lutheran, but she later became a Catholic, and James was well aware of the fact that the Lutherans in Scandinavia were much less opposed to bishops than were those in Germany. He experienced many unpleasant arguments with the outstanding Presbyterian ministers of Scotland.

James felt that the Presbyterian pastors were too much inclined to favor democratic principles. In the year 1613 he had a long talk in London with Hugo Grotius (*q.v.*) on the subject. The Dutch scholar showed the king that he had never fully understood the English Puritans, who, like the Scotch Presbyterians, did not want any higher authorities in the churches than the ordinary ministers and the elders (*presbyters*). James was delighted with this information, and told Grotius that henceforth he would no longer be so kind to the Puritans as he had been before. In 1598 he had written that "the King is king in himself, and not by assent of his subjects." Kings were established before there were any laws. Subjects must render obedience to their king from the day of his coronation until that of his death. In another political treatise, the *Basilikon Doron*, James expressed similar opinions. This work ended with a quotation from Virgil. The last line appealed to him very much; and he published it in italics: "Parcere subjectis, et debellare superbos." That became the maxim of Cardinal Richelieu: "To spare the subjects and to smash the proud." What he had in mind was that those who rose against him must be subdued.

He could not understand why so kind a monarch as he considered himself to be should ever have to face such tribulations as he encountered and he claimed that he had been persecuted "not from my birth only, but even since four months before my birth."

When in March 1603 he became King of England also, as James I, his first care was to withdraw the recusancy laws against the Roman Catholics. Priests were permitted to enter England again. The queen, though not openly professing her preference for the Roman Catholic faith, refused to receive communion in a Protestant church. But the king heard rumors he did not like: he was going to join the Roman Catholic Church. That was too much for him, and in 1605 he renewed the laws against the Catholics. The notorious Gunpowder Plot (q.v.) followed. Nevertheless, in 1618 and 1619 he carried on secret negotiations with Gondomar, the Spanish Ambassador in London. He wanted the Spaniards to save Frederick, his son-in-law in Bohemia, from losing his throne. He almost fell into a Spanish trap. A few years later he negotiated once more with Spaniards. This time Charles, his son and heir, would marry a Spanish princess. The plan did not succeed, but something much worse for England happened: Charles married the sister of the King of France, and she took great pains to make the next two kings of England (Charles II and James II) Roman Catholic. Her plan worked well.

Much has been written about the King James Version of the Bible, but it need not be discussed at length here. The king had less to do with it than the title of the work might imply. But he did favor its promotion. Perhaps he was personally more interested in another task, the publication of his *Collected Works*. They appeared in 1616, and the editor, Bishop Montague, translated some of them into Latin. The conceited monarch was immensely proud of this.

BIBLIOGRAPHY: C. and H. Steeholm, *James I of England*, 1938; G. Davies, *The Early Stuarts 1603–1660*, 1937; C. Williams, *James I*, 1952; C. H. McIlwain, *The Political Works of James I*, 1938.

ALBERT HYMA.

JAMES, EDWIN OLIVER: University professor; b. March 30, 1888, in London. He was educated at University College School; Exeter College, Oxford; and University College, London (Ph.D.). Ordained in 1911, he beneficed in London, Reading, and Oxford (1911–33). He was professor of history and philosophy of religion in the University of Leeds (1935–45); in the University of London (1945–   ). He was president of the Folk-Lore Society (1930–32); editor of *Folk-Lore* since 1932; Fellow of University College, London, and King's College. He wrote: *Primitive Ritual and Belief* (1917); *Introduction to Anthropology* (1920); *Origins of Sacrifice* (1933); *Christian Myth* (1933); *So-*

cial Function of Religion (1940; French ed., 1950); *Concept of Deity* (1950).

JAMES, FLEMING: Old Testament scholar; Episcopalian; b. at Gambier, O., Jan. 11, 1877. He studied at the University of Pennsylvania (B.A., 1895; M.A., 1896; Ph.D., 1899); and at the Philadelphia Divinity School (graduated, 1901). He had charge of a small church in Philadelphia (1901–2, as deacon); the Church of Our Saviour in Shanghai, China (1902–6, as priest); St. Anna's Mission in Philadelphia (1906–12); and was rector of St. Paul's, Englewood, N. J. (1912–21). He was professor of Old Testament literature and interpretation at Berkeley Divinity School (1921–40), and taught Old Testament for nearly ten years in the Yale Divinity School also. He was dean of the School of Theology, University of the South, Sewanee, Tenn. (1940–47). Thereafter he served as executive director of the Old Testament section of the Revised Standard Bible Committee until its publication in 1952. He was a courageous leader in forward-looking social struggles, and a pacifist. He was coauthor of: *The Beginnings of Our Religion* (1935); and author of: *Thirty Psalmists* (1938); and *Personalities of the Old Testament* (1939).

JOSEPH FLETCHER.

JAMES, WILLIAM: D. Aug. 27, 1910. He was noted for his remarkable ability to popularize the classical philosophical issues, using the empirical rather than the dialectical approach. In his radical empiricism (q.v.) he accepted religious phenomena as real experience, making extensive use of analytical psychology. His method fostered psychological positivism. In his famous *The Will to Believe* he propounded the thesis that when we are faced with two undemonstrable alternatives, the course of wisdom is to choose tentatively the one which reflects our hopes rather than our fears, and to act as if it were true.

[Sup.] JOHN G. DEKRUYTER.

JAMES, EPISTLE OF: The author of this epistle uses Greek fluently and accurately, observing grammatical niceties (such as the classical distinction in the usage of the two negatives in Greek). His choice of vocabulary is wide; proportionate to its length the epistle contains more *hapax legomena* than any other New Testament document (Thayer lists seventy-three). Semitisms are rare, and those that occur may perhaps be explained by the author's familiarity with the Septuagint. He shows considerable skill in the use of rhetorical devices affected by the best koine authors, e.g., alliteration and paronomasia, or linking clauses by the repetition of the leading word or some of its cognates. As to literary genre, Ropes and others have argued that the epistle resembles closely the manner and the substance of Stoic popular moral addresses, or diatribes (i.e., brief sentences first spoken orally and compiled later in writing). On the other hand, the manifest affinity of the epistle to certain prophetic and sapiential elements in Jewish literature as well as the abundance of imperatives (60 in 108 verses) suggest that it belongs to the paraenetic or hortatory genre. In any case, the epistle breathes a Palestinian atmosphere which is redolent with hidden allusions to the teaching of Jesus, e.g., James 1:2 compared with Matthew 5:10–12; James 1:4 with Matt. 5:48; James 1:5, 17 with Matt. 7:7–11; James 1:22 with Matt. 7:21–27; James 2:10 with Matt. 5:19; James 3:18 with Matt. 5:9; James 4:4 with Matt. 6:24; James 4:12 with Matt. 7:1 and 10:28; James 5:1 ff. with Matt. 6:19 and Luke 6:24; James 5:10 with Matt. 5:12; James 5:12 with Matt. 5:34–37; James 1:6 with Mark 11:23 ff.

The theory of John Wordsworth (*Studia Biblica*, Vol. I, [1885], pp. 142–150), that James composed the epistle first in Aramaic, was revived by F. C. Burkitt (*Christian Beginnings* [1924], pp. 65–71) with the additional suggestion that it was perhaps Hegesippus of Rome (middle of second century) who freely translated it into excellent Greek and recast it into a general epistle for Gentile Christians. Most scholars, however, believe that the numerous examples of paronomasia and alliteration in the epistle preclude any possibility of its being a translation.

The theory of Arnold Meyer, that an unknown Christian produced the epistle by modifying an older Jewish allegory of Jacob and the twelve tribes, has failed to convince many other scholars. More probable is the ingenious suggestion of J. H. Moulton that James, writing to unconverted Jews, deliberately avoided mentioning the name of Jesus but introduced many of Jesus' sayings in order to win his readers by the intrinsic worth of these sayings. With the growth of knowledge regarding the use of Greek in Jewish Palestine (see Saul Lieberman's research) earlier objections to James's authorship on the score of the relatively high degree of excellence of his Greek have lost much of their cogency. Furthermore, it is quite within the realm of possibility that James may have secured the service of a Hellenist (perhaps of Stephen's circle, so Kittel conjectures) to draw up the epistle. Hence a growing number of scholars are disposed to accept the traditional authorship; e.g., Hauck, Chaine, Schlatter, Rendall, Kittel, Cadoux, and authors of recent Introductions to the New Testament, e.g., W. Michaelis (1946), P. Feine and J. Behm (9th ed., 1950), and R. Heard (1950).

It may well be that this epistle is the earliest book in the New Testament, composed *ca.* A.D. 45, not long after Paul had begun preaching at Antioch and when that apostle's earlier teaching on justification by faith was misunderstood and misrepresented.

BIBLIOGRAPHY: Commentaries: R. J. Knowling, 1904; F. J. A. Hort (1909): covers 1:1 to 4:7; W. E. Oesterley in *Expositor's Greek Testament*, 1911; H. Maynard Smith, 1914; J. H. Ropes, in the *International Critical Commentary*, 1916; Martin Dibelius, in Meyer's *Kom.*, 7th ed., Vol. XV, 1921; Friedrich Hauck, in Zahn's *Kom.*, Vol. XVI, 1926; Joseph Chaine, 1927; James Moffatt, in the Moffatt series, 1928; Hans Windisch, in Lietzmann's *Handbuch*, 2nd ed., Vol. XV, 1930; Eugene C. Caldwell, 1931; Adolf Schlatter, 1932; Jacques Marty, 1935; R. C. H. Lenski, 1938; Eduard Thurneysen, 1942. Studies: J. H. Moulton, "The Epistle of James and the Sayings of Jesus," in *Expositor*, 7th Series, IV (1907), 45–55; J. B. Mayor, "Reminiscences of the Parable of the Sower contained in the Epistle of St. James," in *Expositor*, 8th Series, IV (1912), 407–414; L. Gaugusch, *Der Lehrgehalt der Jakobusepistel*, 1914; A. Koehler, *Glaube und Werke in Jakobus*, 1914; A. T. Robertson, *Studies in the Epistle of James*, 1915; E. M. Wilson, "The Annointing of the Sick in the Epistle of James," in *Princeton Theological Review*, XIX (1921), 64–95; G. H. Rendall, *The Epistle of St. James and Judaistic Christianity*, 1927; Arnold Meyer, *Das Raetsel des Jakobusbriefes*, 1930; Gerhard Kittel, "Der geschichtliche Ort des Jakobusbriefes," in *ZNTW*, XLI (1942), 71–105; A. T. Cadoux, *The Thought of St. James*, 1944; Kurt Aland, "Der Herrenbruder Jakobus und der Jakobusbrief," in *ThLZ*, LXIX (1944), cols. 97–104; C. H. Powell, "'Faith' in James and its Bearing on the Problem of the Date of the Epistle," in *Expository Times*, LXII (1951), 311–314.

[Sup.] BRUCE M. METZGER.

JAN VAN LEEUWEN: From Affligem in Belgian Brabant. At an advanced age he became the second lay brother in the monastery of Groenendaal near Brussels. For thirty-four years he managed the kitchen there and was for that reason known as "the cook of Groenendaal," or "the Good Cook." He died Feb. 5, 1378. He was a man of the common people, without a formal education. He became a devout pupil of Ruysbroeck (*q.v.*), whom he served with admiration. In spite of his busy life in the kitchen he wrote ten mystic treatises of which only one has been properly published thus far. They form a large body of very interesting literature, fresh and spontaneous, full of exuberance and true devotion. The combination of a high mystic flight with clear expression in words for the common people makes the long tracts most valuable for future study.

See also MYSTICISM AND ASCETICISM IN THE NETHERLANDS.

BIBLIOGRAPHY: Steph. Axters, *Jan van Leeuwen: Een bloemlezing uit zijn werken*, (1943): with extensive bibliography on pp. lxxviii–lxxxiii; J. W. N. Delteyk, *Jan van Leeuwen en zijn tractaat van vijf manieren broederliker minnen*, 1947.

M. M. J. SMITS VAN WAESBERGHE.

JANSEN, CORNELIUS; JANSENISM: The following corrections need to be made in the original article in Vol. VI: (1) The two propositions which formed the basis for the censure of Arnauld in the Sorbonne were taken from his *Seconde lettre á un duc et pair* and not from *Lettre á une personne de condition* (p. 97, col. 1). (2) Only sixty, not eighty, doctors left the Sorbonne when Arnauld was condemned (p. 97, col. 1). (3) The sentence beginning, "Those who refused," has had words left out and should read: "Those who refused were imprisoned, including De Sacy, one of the most excellent men of the Port Royal group, who was sent to the Bastile" (p. 97, col. 1).

The following is supplementary to the original article. The Jansenist controversy was the seventeenth-century phase of the age-old controversy on grace (q.v., Vol. V) and predestination (q.v., Vol. IX). The Jansenists, who were Augustinians and were opposed by the semi-Pelagian Jesuits, held that the divine grace necessary to turn man's corrupt will to good is bestowed by God to some men regardless of human merit. Being irresistible, grace inevitably inclines the will to acceptance of God's will, without, however, constraining it in any way. The sacraments, in the Jansenist view, were efficacious only when accompanied by interior conversion (q.v.) and were not the means for obtaining grace. All of the sacraments, but especially the Lord's Supper, were God's gifts to those to whom he gave grace. The Jansenists were opposing any efforts, such as that by the Jesuits, to make the sacraments the effective instruments for meriting the gift of grace. The Jansenist position exalted the power of God in human life at the expense of real human freedom. It was pessimistic in its denial of the possibility of salvation to all mankind, and in its expectation of evil in all men who lacked the gift of grace.

From the fact that not all men were recipients of divine grace, the Jansenists drew the conclusion that the church need not concern itself with all mankind. Also, since the church was divine it must be kept free of all contamination, which was the reason for the Jansenists' fervent attacks on everything which did not indisputably have divine sanction. This attitude was in conflict with the Jesuit belief that the mission of the church, dictated by the possibility that all men would be saved, was to bring all mankind into the church, administer the sacraments to them, and lead them on the path to salvation. The Jansenists would have made the church a restricted organization aimed at completing that which God had begun in the human soul. The Jesuit church would have been a universal organization aimed at beginning in the human soul that which God would complete. The Jansenists would have used the sacraments to limit the church to those upon whom grace had been bestowed by making access to them exceedingly difficult to most men. Since the hierarchical system of the church was based on the centrality of the sacraments in Christian life and their necessity for salvation, this Jansenist attitude was a threat to the organization of the Catholic Church and was recognized as such by the Jesuits and other opponents of the Jansenists. The Jansenist lack

of respect for the hierarchy extended even to the pope whose decree on the presence of the five propositions in Jansen's Augustinus (fait) they refused to accept, although they did recognize his right to declare the five propositions themselves heretical (droit). Antipapal sentiment is one of the distinguishing marks of Jansenist influence in the Catholic Church.

Since righteousness and moral purity were signs of faith and conditions for proper reception of the sacraments, the Jansenists upheld a severe moral code, and refused to make any concessions to weaknesses. Their ascetic lives and outstanding virtue in a period of growing moral laxity brought them contemporary renown, and made them attack the Jesuit moral system, which assumed that men would sin, but promised relief from the guilt of sin through the saving grace of Christ, given to man through the agency of the church and its sacraments. Pascal's Provincial Letters was only the most effective of a number of polemical works attacking the laxist tendencies of Jesuit morality.

The persistent opposition of the Jesuits was necessitated by the fact that Jansenism represented a threat to their authoritarian idea of church government and to their concept of the universal mission of the church. The two points of view were quite incompatible. According to the Jansenists, the true path lay in a return to the practices and beliefs of the early church. They refused to recognize a developing tradition, preferring the example of the primitive church and the teaching of the early fathers and Augustine as their sole guide in matters of doctrine and morals. They upheld the bishops' independence of papal authority; opposed encroachments of papacy and absolutionist state on clerical independence; and asserted the freedom of the individual's conscience on all matters except doctrine. The peace of Clement IX in 1668 represented a partial success for the Jansenists, as did the fact that Arnauld and all of his generation died in communion with the church in spite of numerous attempts to have them expelled as heretics. But by 1713 the condemnation of their ideas in the Bull Unigenitus (q.v., Vol. XII), and the destruction of their headquarters at Port Royal brought an end to their effective opposition within the church. Eighteenth century manifestations of Jansenism were far different in spirit and method from those of the days of Arnauld and Pascal (q.v.). The earlier Jansenist ideas continue to the present day to exercise an influence on the attitudes of the French Catholics toward theology, morality, the papacy, and the Jesuits which not even the excesses of the eighteenth century could obliterate. The influence even extended to England where word of the Jansenist ideas and their exemplary virtue was brought by various English visitors to Port Royal.

In addition to the four thousand volumes produced in the controversy after the Bull *Unigenitus,* there are over five thousand volumes in the Bibliotheque Mazarin in Paris written during the seventeenth century. The pamphlets were often sold in the streets. The controversy evoked wide popular interest, being the first theological dispute in which appeal was made to the wider public by use of the vernacular as well as Latin.

BIBLIOGRAPHY: Dominique de Colonia, *Bibliothèque janséniste,* 1731; idem, *Dictionnaire des livres jansénistes,* 4 vols., 1755; Godefroi Herman, *Mémoires sur l'histoire ecclésiastique du XVIIe siècle, 1640–63,* 6 vols., 1905–10; Nigel Abercrombie, *The Origins of Jansenism,* 1936; Wallace K. Ferguson, "The Place of Jansenism in French History," in *Journal of Religion,* VII (1927), 16–42; Augustin Gazier, *Histoire générale du mouvement janséniste depuis ses origines jusqu'à nos jours,* 2 vols., 1923–24; Jean La Porte, *La doctrine de Port-Royal,* 2 vols., 1923; Albert de Meyer, *Les premières controverses jansénistes en France, 1640–49,* 1919; Jean Orcibal, *Correspondence de Jansénius,* 1947; J. Paquier, *Le jansénisme. Etude doctrinale,* 1909; E. Préclin, *Les jansénistes du XVIIIe siècle et la constitution civile du clergé,* 1929; Paule Réguron, *Les origines du mouvement anti-janséniste et l'evolution de Pascal des "Provinciales" aux "Pensées,"* 1934; S. J. Willaert, *Les origines du jansénisme dans les Pays-Bas Catholiques,* 1948.

[Sup.] NORMAN D. KURLAND.

JANSENIST CHURCH IN HOLLAND: The Union of Utrecht, over which the Old Catholic bishop of Utrecht presides as *primatus amoris,* maintains connections with Old Catholics (*q.v.*) in various parts of the world by holding conferences of bishops and participating in mutual consecrations. The episcopal conferences are sometimes attended by Anglican, Orthodox, and even Lutheran bishops. Intercommunion (*q.v.*) between Old Catholics and Anglicans was established in 1931. The Old Catholic Church in Holland had 3 bishops (Utrecht, Haarlem, Deventer), 32 priests, 25,000 members in 1951. It has had a Dutch liturgy since 1910. Sacerdotal celibacy was abolished in 1922.

BIBLIOGRAPHY: C. Beaufort Moss, *The Old Catholic Movement and Reunion,* 1927; B. A. van Kleef, *Geschiedenis der Oud-Katholieke Kerk,* 1952; A. J. van der Ven, *Over de Oorsprong van het aartsbisschoppelijk Kapittel van Utrecht,* 1923.

[Sup.] WILLEM JAN KOOIMAN.

JAPAN: From 1910 to 1952 Japan swept through a whirlwind of crises and changes. The course was marked by the annexation of Korea (1910), participation in World War I (1915), naval expansion, recognition as one of the Four Powers, the Siberian expedition (1918), rapid industrialization, and enlarged overseas trade. During the 1920's there was a comparative lull, with trends toward democratization at home and attempts at international adjustment. But the Manchurian Incident (1931) was the introduction to continuous struggle on the mainland, and domestic unrest, assassinations (1932), and military insurrection (1936). Withdrawal from the League of Nations (1933), the Shanghai Incident (1935), the Peking outbreak (1937), and full-scale war with China leading to Pearl Harbor (1941), the Pacific War, defeat, surrender (1945), military occupation (1945–52), and reconstruction.

I. Period of Christian Growth (1910–30): Conditions were propitious and the churches grew: Roman Catholics from 64,118 to about 93,500; the Russian Orthodox from 31,538 to about 37,000; Protestants from 60,635 to 220,967. Sunday school work trebled, as did Christian school enrollments, from 13,322 to 36,857. Missionaries numbered 1,442, but the direction of churches and schools was steadily passing to capable Japanese leadership. The Christian movement, largely urban, middle-class, and entirely literate, closely paralleled the Protestant churches of the West. Women were active and youth work was advanced. Settlements in large cities and various rural projects expressed the social outreach. Christians took the lead in reform and peace movements, and to a degree in public life. The National Christian Council embraced over thirty denominations, as many foreign missions, and a dozen national agencies for Christian activities.

II. Period of Conflict and Recession (1930–45): These years of ardent nationalism and war were disadvantageous to the free growth of any voluntary religion. Only State Shinto flourished. The churches barely held their own in numbers, although they were almost continuously engaged in evangelistic campaigns, such as the Kingdom of God Movement (*q.v.*), spearheaded by Kagawa (*q.v.*) (1929–35), and its successor, the National Evangelistic Campaign (1936–41). None of the major Christian activities was abandoned, and the schools were filled to overflowing. But the national crisis occupied the minds of the public.

In August, 1940, the Christian churches felt the pressure, first to remove foreign personnel from places of influence and then to consolidate religious bodies and activities into a few centralized units. The Pan-Religions League, the All-Christian Federation, and the two "Kyodans," Roman Catholic and Protestant, followed by June, 1941. Thirty-four denominations united in the last-named, the Church of Christ in Japan (Nihon Kirisuto Kyodan). It included over 90% of all Protestants, reporting 233,463 members. Roman Catholics reported 119,224, and the Orthodox Church 41,000.

During the war years (1941–45) the churches in general co-operated heartily in required services at home and overseas, and suffered little or no official opposition, though the apocalyptic creeds of certain Holiness (*q.v.*) and Adventist (*q.v.*) groups led to police suspicion, some three hundred arrests, and several deaths in prison. In 1944 and 1945 increasing hardship and scarcity moved into actual bombing, ruin, and death. In the cities over five hundred churches and about one-half of the school plants were destroyed. Social work had to stop. Active church membership probably fell to one-half, though records are scanty.

III. Occupation and Reconstruction (1945–52): A benevolent military occupation was met by a Christian community desiring restored cooperation; so reconstruction began quickly. First came basic human rehabilitation (1946–47), then rebuilding of schools and a few central churches (1948–49). With the steady return to normal living (1950–52) and at least semi-permanent buildings replacing about 85% of the property losses, the churches got back on their feet. Virtually all prewar activities were resumed and most of the former institutions, agencies, and national organizations reconstituted. Public sentiment was marked by an unprecedented openness to Christian teaching, although no unusual influx of members occurred. Statistics for 1951: Members—Protestants, 193,606; Roman Catholics, 151,370; Orthodox, 8,911; total, 353,887. Schools—414 enroll 106,487 students, of which 47 universities and junior colleges have 33,625; 462 kindergartens enroll 25,354 pupils.

Significant postwar developments are: (1) Rapid growth of Roman Catholic strength in church constituency and schools. (2) Large numbers (over seven hundred) of foreign missionaries from newer denominations and groups hitherto without work in Japan, and the introduction of mass evangelism. (3) Survival of a vigorous, united Church of Christ in Japan, notwithstanding the withdrawal of the Lutheran, Anglican-Episcopal, and some Presbyterian Churches.

BIBLIOGRAPHY: G. B. Sansom, *Japan, A Short Cultural History*, 1931; D. C. Holtom, *The National Faith of Japan*, 1938; Charles Eliot, *Hinduism and Buddhism*, 1921; *Japan Christian Yearbook*, 1932–41, 1950 seq.; W. C. Kerr, *Japan Begins Again*, 1949.

[Sup.] CHARLES IGLEHART.

JARRELL LECTURES: Established in 1927 at Emory University, in Georgia, by the Rev. C. C. Jarrell in memory of his father, A. J. Jarrell. Among the lecturers were Halford E. Luccock, Paul E. Scherer, Joseph R. Sizoo, and Clovis G. Chappell.

JAVA. See MALAY ARCHIPELAGO.

JEDIN, HUBERT: Roman Catholic; b. at Grossbriesen, Silesia, on June 17, 1900. He studied at Breslau, Munich and Freiburg. He did research studies in history in the Vatican Library (1926–30, 1939–49), taught church history at Breslau (1930–33) until dismissed by the Nazis, was archivist of the archdiocese of Breslau (1936–39), and was professor of church history at Bonn (1949– ; dean, 1950–). In addition to more than fifty articles in theological journals he has written: *Des Johannes Cochlaeus Streitschrift De libero arbitrio hominis 1525*

(1927); *Studien ueber die Schriftstellertaetigkeit Albert Pigges* (1931); *Die Erforschung der kirchlichen Reformationsgeschichte seit 1876* (1931); *Girolamo Seripando* (2 vols., 1937; Amer. ed., 1947); *Concilium Tridentinum* (1938); *Der Quellenapparat der Konzilsgeschichte Pallavicinos* (1940); *Krisis und Wendepunkt des Trienter Konzils 1562/3* (1941); *Katholische Reformation oder Gegenreformation?* (1946); *Das Konzil von Trient* (1948); *Kardinal Contarini als Kontrovertstheologe* (1949); *Geschichte des Konzils von Trient* (1949); *Il tipo ideale di vescovo secondo la riforma cattolica* (1950); and *Die deutsche Romfahrt von Bonifatius bis Winckelmann* (1951).

RAYMOND W. ALBRIGHT.

JEFFERSON, CHARLES E(DWARD): D. Sept. 12, 1937. From 1898 he spent a long generation until his death as the pastor of the Broadway Tabernacle in New York City. He also served widely beyond his denomination and was known as one of the great preachers of his day. His later books include: *The Building of the Church* (1910); *Why We May Believe in Life After Death* (1911); *The Minister as Shepherd* (1912); *Forefather's Day Sermons* (1917); *Old Truths and New Facts* (1918); *Quiet Talks with the Family* (1922); *Under Twenty* (1922); *The Friendship Indispensable* (1923); *The Character of Paul* (1923); *Five Present-Day Controversies* (1924); *Cardinal Ideas of Isaiah* (1925); *Cardinal Ideas of Jeremiah* (1928); *Christianizing a Nation* (1929); *Other Nature Sermons* (1931); and *Like a Trumpet* (1934).

[Sup.] RAYMOND W. ALBRIGHT.

JEFFERY, (WILLIAM) ARTHUR: Methodist; b. Oct. 18, 1892. He studied at Queens College, Melbourne University (M.A. and B.D.), and Edinburgh (Ph.D.). He was on the staff of Madras Christian College, India (1916–20); professor of Semitic philology, School of Oriental Studies, American University, Cairo, Egypt (1921–37); and was professor of Semitic languages, Columbia University, and adjunct professor of Semitic languages, Union Theological Seminary (1937–). He is the author of: *The Foreign Vocabulary of the Qur'an* (1938); and *Materials for the History of the Text of the Qur'an* (1937).

JEHOVAH. See YAHWEH.

JEHOVAH'S WITNESSES: Charles Taze Russell had attracted a numerous and enthusiastic following long before his death in 1916. But under his successor, Judge J. F. Rutherford, the movement entered a new phase. During World War I, because of their attitude toward the war, Judge Rutherford and others of the movement were sent to prison and the movement as a whole suffered a marked reversal. But after his release, it took on new life and became more aggressive than ever. Judge Rutherford was an able controversialist who turned out pamphlets and books in rapid succession. Gradually his writings took the place of those by Pastor Russell and were circulated in incredible numbers by the growing body of workers. The name of the movement was changed in 1931 to Jehovah's Witnesses. Rutherford died in 1942 and was succeeded by N. K. Knorr, who has succeeded in greatly widening the outreach of the group. Thus far, Rutherford's writings have not been superseded, but the official presses continue to turn out new books and pamphlets, usually anonymously authored, and their circulation climbs steadily.

Though there are three legal corporations, the Watch Tower Bible and Tract Society of New York is really the main controlling body. Composed of about forty members, it elects a Board of Directors who are the chief power in directing the movement.

Under this Board are six "regional servants" in the United States who supervise the work of the "zone servants," who in turn exercise direction over more limited areas. Local groups limited to 200 members are called "companies," and their leaders "company servants." These are assisted by "literature servants," "accounts servants," etc. To carry on their propaganda work in new areas there are "pioneers" who give full time to the work, and "publishers" who give part time service. All of these work on essentially a subsistence basis, as do all employed workers, including the national leaders. At present work is carried on in more than 80 countries by more than 425,000 workers.

A great publishing plant in Brooklyn, N. Y., prints the periodicals *Watch Tower* and *Awaken* as well as books and pamphlets. A training school, known as Gilead, was founded in 1943. A chief feature of the year's activities is the great annual convention held each summer. In New York in 1950 the Witnesses claimed an attendance of over 100,000.

The burden of their teaching is the imminence of the end of the age, the great battle of Armageddon, and the ushering in of the Theocracy, the rule of God here on earth.

BIBLIOGRAPHY: H. H. Stroup, *Jehovah's Witnesses*, 1945; Charles S. Braden, *These Also Believe*, 1949; Marcus Bach, *They Have Found a Faith*, 1947; *The Annual Yearbook*, official source concerning activities.
[Sup. to MILLENNIAL DAWN.]

CHARLES S. BRADEN.

There have been several schisms in the movement. The most important led to the formation of the Church of the Kingdom of God under the leadership of F. L. Alexandre Freytag (1870–1947). In 1917 this Russelite leader in Switzerland began to criticize the movement's preoccu-

pation with calculations of the world's end and called for reform of life. Three years later a bitter separation occurred and the publications of Freytag (especially *Botschaft an die Menschheit*, 1922) soon attained canonical authority in the new organization. As among the Jehovah's Witnesses, much was made of the kingdom of God; it will be introduced, however, by the activity and holiness of men of good will rather than by divine intervention. From Switzerland the movement spread to other countries and claimed 50,000 adherents in 1948.

BIBLIOGRAPHY: Kurt Hutten, *Seher, Gruebler, Enthusiasten*, 1950.

THEODORE G. TAPPERT.

JENKINS, CLAUDE: Anglican; b. May 24, 1877. Educated at New College, Oxford, and ordained in 1903, he was lecturer, fellow, and later professor of King's College London, in the department of ecclesiastical history (1905–34); Canon of Christ Church and Regius Professor of Ecclesiastical History, Oxford University (1934–). He has written: *An Unpublished Visitation of Archbishop Parker* (1911); *The Monastic Chronicler* (1922); *Sir Thomas More* (1935); *F. D. Maurice and the New Reformation* (1938); and has translated Duchesne's *History of the Christian Church*, Vol. III. F. W. DILLISTONE.

JEREMIAH, BOOK OF: Much new light has been shed on Jeremiah in recent years through archaeological discoveries, textual criticism, research in prophecy, and fresh study of the relation of this book to Deuteronomy (see PENTATEUCH). Of particular interest have been the Lachish (*q.v.*) Ostraka (discovered in 1935 and 1938), which date from the times (589– B.C.) and which touch Jeremiah at various points, in language, historical allusions, and personal names. More is known about Jeremiah than about any other Old Testament prophet. Born *ca.* 645 B.C., he received his call to prophesy in the thirteenth year of Josiah (1:2; 25:3), or 626 B.C., and probably shared largely in the Deuteronomic reform instituted a few years later (621 B.C.). His ministry extended over more than half a century.

The prophecy falls roughly into three parts: (1) chaps. 1–25, embracing for the most part judgments on Judah; (2) chaps. 26–45, largely biographical materials; (3) chaps. 46–51, prophecies against foreign nations. Chap. 52 is an historical appendix (cf. II Kings 24:18 ff.). Chap. 36 provides the key to an understanding of the origin of parts of the book. Jeremiah dictated messages to Baruch, his amanuensis, who in turn recorded them (v. 4). Following the burning of the roll by King Jehoiakim, Jeremiah repeated his messages to his scribe, who prepared a second roll, to which numerous additions were made (v. 32). Thus the composition of the book involved several stages.

Critics are not in agreement as to the genuine parts. According to Oesterley and Robinson, a compiler, probably living in the fourth century B.C., brought together three types of materials: (1) oracles of Jeremiah in poetic form; (2) biographical prose materials; and (3) autobiographical prose selections, some of which are to be regarded as genuine. The biographical parts come largely from a contemporary of the prophet, probably Baruch. Some passages are exilic or post-exilic. In arranging the collections the compiler prefixed prose selections to the oracular utterances to suit his purpose, without due regard for chronological order. Pfeiffer recognizes in the work two books, Jeremiah's oracles and Baruch's biography of the prophet, supplemented by miscellaneous contributions from later authors and redactors.

While some critics (Duhm, Skinner, Volz, and others) have rejected the collection of ten oracles against the nations (chaps. 46–51) as non-Jeremianic, the majority of scholars (e.g., Eissfeldt, Pfeiffer, Rudolph) have regarded a nucleus as genuine. Jeremiah considered himself ordained "a prophet unto the nations" (1:5). The references in 25:15 ff. seem to infer that he uttered foreign prophecies. Rudolph accepts chap. 47 as Jeremianic and sees also some general material in chaps. 46, 48, and 49.

The problem of the relation of Jeremiah to Deuteronomy has been much discussed in recent years. Hyatt dates the prophet later than the reformation under Josiah. Schofield makes Deuteronomy dependent upon Jeremiah. Rowley, however, holds that Jeremiah at first advocated the Deuteronomic reform but later, recognizing its failure, acted independently.

In the study of the text it is observed that LXX is about 2700 words shorter than the Masoretic Text. Although some of the variations may be explained on the basis of textual criticism, the large number of displacements and lacunae reflects divergent originals.

Of special significance in the book are the so-called "Confessions" of Jeremiah (11:18–23; 12:1–6; 15:10–21; 17:12–18; 18:18–23; 20:7–18), which reveal deep inner struggles of soul. In devotional expression they match many of the Psalms. Doubtless Jeremiah had a profound influence on psalmody. Through personal struggles, conflicts with authorities, courageous preaching and teaching he turned attention from externals to personal religious experience. His messages center in the new covenant relation with God (31:31 ff.)

BIBLIOGRAPHY: S. Mowinckel, Zur Komposition des Buches Jeremia, 1914; P. Volz, Der Prophet Jeremia, 1918, 3rd ed., 1930; idem, Studium zum Text des Jeremia, 1920; idem, Jeremia (KAT), 2nd ed., 1928; J. Skinner, Prophecy and Religion: Studies in the Life of Jeremiah, 1922, 3rd ed., 1930; H. W. Hertzberg, Prophet und Gott, 1923; W. F. Lofthouse, Jeremiah and the New Covenant,
1925; A. C. Welch, Jeremiah: His Time and His Work, 1928; G. A. Smith, Jeremiah, 4th ed., 1929; R. Calkins, Jeremiah the Prophet, 1930; T. C. Gordon, The Rebel Prophet, 1932; G. R. Driver, "Linguistic and Textual Problems: Jeremiah," in JQR, XXVIII (1937–38), 97–129; V. Herntrich, Jeremia: der Prophet und sein Volk, 1938; J. P. Hyatt, "Jeremiah and Deuteronomy," in JNES, I (1942), 156–173; J. N. Schofield, "The Significance of the Prophets for Dating Deuteronomy," in Studies in History and Religion (E. A. Payne, ed.) (1942), 44–60; Wilhelm Rudolph, Jeremia (HZAT), 1947; H. H. Rowley, "The Prophet Jeremiah and the Book of Deuteronomy," in Studies in Old Testament Prophecy (1950), 157–174.

[Sup.] ELMER E. FLACK.

JEREMIAH, LAMENTATIONS OF: Authorship by Jeremiah or a single writer is widely rejected. The form-critical approach of Gunkel is in the foreground of interest. The lamentation type of poem has its origin in the dirge at the funeral of an individual. It is an extension of the use of the form when a nation or city is personified and made object of a dirge. Chaps. 1, 2, and 4 are such "political lamentations," while 3 and 5 are individual and collective lamentations respectively.

BIBLIOGRAPHY: Commentaries: W. Rudolph, 1939; M. Haller, 1940; F. Noetscher, 1947. Other literature: H. Gunkel, in RGG, Vol. III (1912), pp. 1499 f.; Hedwig Jahnow, Das Hebraeische Leichenlied, 1923. On the qinâ meter see further Budde, in ZATW, N.F., Vol. X (1933), pp. 306 f.

[Sup.] EMIL G. KRAELING.

JEREMIAS, JOACHIM: Lutheran; b. at Dresden, Germany, Sept. 20, 1900. He studied at the theological seminary of the Bruedergemeine in Herrnhut and at the University of Leipzig (Dr.Phil.). He taught in the University of Berlin and was director of the Institutum Judaicum (1928); was professor of New Testament at the University of Greifswald (1929–35), and at Goettingen (1935–). His works include: Jerusalem zur Zeit Jesu (2 vols., 1923–37); Golgotha (1926); Jesus als Weltvollender (1930); Passahfeier der Samaritaner (1932); Die Briefe an Timotheus und Titus (1933; 5th ed., 1947); Die Abendmahlsworte Jesu (1935; 2nd ed., 1949); Hat die Urchristenheit die Kindertaufe geuebt? (1938; 2nd ed., 1949); Die Gleichnisse Jesu (1947); Unbekannte Jesuworte (1948); Die Wiederentdeckung von Bethesda (1949).   RAYMOND W. ALBRIGHT.

JERICHO. See ARCHAEOLOGY, OLD TESTAMENT.

JERUSALEM. See ARCHAEOLOGY, OLD TESTAMENT.

JERUSALEM, ANGLICAN-GERMAN BISHOPRIC IN: Upon restoration of the see as a purely Anglican venture in 1886, Bishop Popham Blythe became "bishop of the Church of England in [not of] Jerusalem" and the proselytizing work among the Orthodox was discountenanced in favor of co-operation. For the same reason the cathedral was given the style

"St. George's Collegiate Church," recognizing the Church of the Holy Sepulcher as "the Cathedral of Jerusalem." Bishop Blythe was succeeded by R. MacInnes (1914), G. F. G. Brown (1932), and Weston Henry Stewart (1943–). Co-operating with the Orthodox in educational work, the jurisdiction comprises the Anglican congregations in Palestine, Trans-Jordan, Syria, Lebanon, Cyprus, Haytay, and, by special request of the archbishop of Canterbury, Iraq. One American priest, supported by the Good Friday Offering, is a canon on the cathedral staff.

BIBLIOGRAPHY: J. W. C. Wand, *The Anglican Communion*, 1948; *Bible Lands*, a quarterly published by the mission from London.

[Sup.] NELSON RIGHTMYER.

JESUITS: As Johannes Cardinal de Jong has indicated in Vol. III of his monumental church history (4th ed., 1948), the work of the men who produced the religious movement known as the Devotio Moderna was continued by the Jesuits. Not only was the famous treatise by Loyola, *Spiritual Exercises,* in part a result of the Devotio Moderna, but the schools of the Jesuits owed much to those of the Brethren of the Common Life, notably that at Liége, where John Sturm had taught. Sturm himself testified to the noble labors of the Brethren in Liége, and the learned Jesuit scholar in Belgium, E. de Moreau, has shown in Vol. IV of his work, *Histoire del' Eglise en Belgique,* that the school of the Brethren in Liége was indeed important. Much has been written about the moral standards of the Jesuits, especially the idea that "the end justifies the means." Many authors have stated that the Jesuits went very far in this direction, much to the surprise of the Jesuits themselves. Consequently, a Jesuit named Roh in 1852 and again in 1861 offered the equivalent of $400 as a reward to anybody who could prove that any Jesuit ever taught the idea so often attributed to Jesuits as a whole. Several scholars made an attempt to produce the proof, but they all failed to find it. Again, in 1903 a chaplain named Dasbach, a member of the Prussian Landtag, offered $800 for the same purpose. The Count Von Hoensbroech, a former Jesuit but now a convert to Protestantism, tried to collect the money, but the Oberlandesgericht of Cologne determined that he had failed to prove his point.

BIBLIOGRAPHY: Ignatius Loyola, *Constitutiones Societatis Jesu,* Rome, 1934; P. Rosa, *I Gesuiti dalle origini ai nostri giorni,* 1914; J. Brucker, *La Compagnie de Jésus: Esquisse de son institut et son histoire,* 1919; Th. Campbell, *The Jesuits,* 1921; L. de Jonge, *De orde der Jezuiten,* 3 vols., 1928–31; G. Bernoville, *Les Jésuites,* 1935; H. Boehmer, *Die Jesuiten,* 4th ed., 1921; P. de Chastonay, *Die Satzungen des Jesuitenordens,* 1938; R. Fuelop-Miller, *Macht und Geheimnis der Jesuiten,* 1929; A. Astrain, *Historia de la Compania de Jesus en la Asistencia de Espana,* 7 vols., 1902–25; H. Fouqueray, *Histoire de la Compagnie de Jésus en France des origines à la suppression,* 5 vols., 1910–25; J. Burnichon, *La Compagnie de Jésus en France 1814–1914,* 4 vols., 1919–22; B. Duhr, *Geschichte der Jesuiten in den Laendern deutscher Zunge,* 4 vols., 1907–28;

T. Hughes, *History of the Society of Jesus in North America,* 1907; A. Poncelet, *Histoire de la Compagnie de Jésus dans les anciens Pays-Bas,* 2 vols., 1927–28; A. Farrel, *The Jesuit Code of Liberal Education,* 1938; J. Schroeteler, *Die Erziehung in den Jesuiteninternaten des 16. Jahrhunderts,* 1940; W. McGucken, *The Jesuits and Education,* 1932; J. Brodrick, *The Economic Morals of the Jesuits,* 1934; H. Boehmer, *The Jesuits,* 1928; A. F. Pollard, *The Jesuits in Poland,* 1892; L. Koch, *Jesuiten-Lexicon,* 1934; M. Hay, *The Jesuits and the Popish Plot,* 1934; idem, *The Enigma of James II,* 1938; B. Duhr, *Jesuitenfabeln,* 1913.

[Sup.] ALBERT HYMA.

JESUS AS A PREACHER: Believers in Christ's deity find it difficult to discuss his preaching, but this aspect of his ministry bulks large in the Gospels. He did not deliver sermons, in our sense, but in a fashion all his own he served as the Supreme Interpreter of God's truth for sinful men. The Gospels show the following: (1) Usually he preached from the Bible. (See Luke 4:14–27, which A. B. Bruce calls the "frontispiece" of his gospel.) (2) Like John the Baptist, our Lord preached about the Kingdom, and called for repentance. (3) Unlike the Forerunner, Christ preached much about divine mercy and redeeming grace. (4) He spoke much about the "last days," an aspect of his preaching and teaching that has caused much debate and confusion. (5) He set an example of how to gain a hearing even for an unwelcome message. Frequently he began with a question of interest to everyone; often also with a problem, or a "life situation." He showed how to start with the hearers "where they are," mentally. (6) He constantly appealed to the imagination. According to Bushnell, his gospel is "the gift of God to the imagination." Especially in the parables he entered the City of Mansoul through Eye-gate. (7) He employed the language of the common people, who heard him gladly, as one of themselves. Even in English, the reports of his spoken words impress us with what Wendt terms "pregnant simplicity." (8) He preached with authority, like that of no other. In various ways as preachers, the prophets and apostles resembled him, but he towered above them as much in the spoken word as in character. (9) Much as he taught and preached by word of mouth, he preached and taught vastly more by what he did. Often he employed miracles as "signs" of truths he wished the hearers to see as well as hear. Thus he employed the "case method," which many of his followers today consider a modern invention. Supremely on the Cross and through the Resurrection he taught vastly more by what he did than by what he said. (10) Most of all, as the Divine Truth through the Divine Personality he taught and preached by what he was, as the sinless Son of God, Saviour of the world, and Lord of Glory. For this aspect of his work see the Book of Acts. Also study the Lord's Supper as a sermon in action. In I Cor. 11:26 the word translated "proclaim," or "show," is the term often rendered, correctly, as "preach." Herein lies much truth full of mystery, which has to do with the deity of our Lord. Perhaps for this reason few writers have dealt with his preaching, and those few not effectively.

See also JESUS AS A TEACHER; JESUS CHRIST.
ANDREW W. BLACKWOOD.

JESUS AS A TEACHER: The Gospels contain about two hundred references to Jesus as Teacher, or Rabbi. He taught "with authority," and not as the scribes; that is, with an inherent sense of firsthand knowledge. He was a preacher-teacher, always striving to bring about a decision in the lives of the hearers. They were amazed at what he taught and how he taught. At the age of twelve he was in the temple among the doctors (teachers), "hearing them and asking them questions." During his ministry he encountered persons and groups as a teacher, asking and answering questions, telling parables, performing signs and wonders, to reveal his character and power; also to confront them with vital truths. By his various acts (washing the disciples' feet, instituting the Lord's Supper, etc.), he taught truths unforgettably. His Crucifixion was his supreme act. Through it he has taught men finally and adequately his obedience to the Father's will, as well as the nature, extent, and power of divine love for sinful men.

Jesus as Teacher used effective methods. Often he introduced a subject by raising a question or posing a problem. "Whose superscription is this?" "Whosoever shall humble himself as this little child." He took advantage of every opportunity to help others learn. He used the principle of apperception, always approaching persons with an appreciation of what they already knew or had experienced. He used illustrations from ordinary life, and made his teaching vivid by putting truths in recognizable forms. Though the Son of God incarnate, Christ's teaching partook of naturalness. Occasionally he used humor. He was not only concerned about truth from God; by winsome grace he awakened latent possibilities and encouraged men to express their new-found selves. Recognizing the differences among individuals, he treated each one uniquely.

His supreme characteristic as teacher was a profound sense of mission to save men from false and ruinous ways. His divine consciousness gave him a unique love for persons, a passionate desire to help them know God and themselves, a sacrificial spirit by which he taught abstract truth and communicated the truth to those who "received" him and "followed" him. Although he is still our Supreme Example, as Teacher Christ is vastly more. He is the living, personal truth that he taught. As

the Teacher come from God he used the methods his love knew as necessary to teach men the truth. In his own Person he exemplified all the truths he taught. Today through the Holy Spirit Christ still serves as our Supreme Teacher.

See also JESUS AS A PREACHER; JESUS CHRIST.

BIBLIOGRAPHY: H. H. Horne, *Jesus the Master Teacher,* 1920; C. F. McKay, *The Art of Jesus as a Teacher,* 1930; L. A. Weigle, *Jesus and the Educational Method,* 1939; N. E. Richardson, *The Christ of the Classroom,* 1932; T. R. Glover, *The Jesus of History,* 1917; H. B. Sharman, *Jesus As Teacher,* 1934.
ELMER G. HOMRIGHAUSEN.

JESUS CHRIST: I. General Survey: In his *Quest of the Historical Jesus* (1910), Albert Schweitzer contended that the writing of a "Life of Jesus" would prove to be impossible in the future. It seems that his prediction rightly assessed the mood of Continental Protestant theology, for the number of "Lives" published after World War I in that part of the world is negligible. The reason for that dearth, however, lies probably in the theological outlook of the Continental Protestant churches rather than in methodological difficulties. For in the Anglo-Saxon world a few hundred works have been published in that same period, the Roman Catholics have entered the field with a considerable number of outstanding critical and devotional works, the Jews are obviously stirred to the depth of their souls by the question of how to interpret and evaluate the gospel story, theosophical and mystical groups claim the Jesus of the Gospels for themselves, and a host of writers have composed more or less fictional biographies of the Lord.

The modern Christian "Lives" can be divided into three groups, viz., harmonies of the Gospels, critical studies, and devotional-interpretative works. It was obviously the second group which Schweitzer had primarily in mind. The principal reason why modern scholars are reluctant to compose a critical "Life of Jesus" is to be found in the nature of the Gospels. Those books were never intended to present a purely historical biography of Jesus. Rather, they proclaim Jesus of Nazareth as the Lord and Saviour of mankind, i.e., they combine the record of facts with the Christian valuation. Those scholars, who consider this combination as a distortion of the records, must confine themselves to a discussion of the historical circumstances of Jesus' life, and to parallels and antecedents of his teaching, without being able to furnish a total picture of his personality or of his life work. Such a result is most unsatisfactory, however, because apart from the personality of Jesus the gospel proclamation makes no sense historically or theologically.

II. Harmonies: Compiling a harmony of the Gospels and annotating it is the simplest way to write a life of Jesus, but also the least satisfactory one. For unless the life of Jesus is reinterpreted by the modern writer, the narratives of the single Gospels are preferable to a harmony, in which their individual viewpoints are lost. Nor are matters improved by adding apocryphal material (e.g., Daniel-Rops, Séché). The majority of harmonies differ from each other only by the quantity and the nature of the explanatory material added. Most of them follow the tradition (Andrews, Dushaw, Langford, Lowrie, Mitchell, Montgomery, Morris, Ponsonby, Reynolds, A. W. Ross, J. J. Scott, B. S. Whitman, and Beaufays and Klein among the Roman Catholics. Critical elements are introduced by Gardiner-Smith, Lees, Moffatt, Wikings, A. R. Whitman, and the Roman Catholics Fahling and Lagrange.

III. Critical Works: The few works that in a strict sense continue the critical tradition (e.g., Goguel, Guiguebert, Heitmueller, Mackinnon, Quimby, Wernle) all bear witness to the almost unsurmountable difficulties presented by the methodological problem. Even when dealing primarily with the historical "background" they have to integrate their material in some way in order to show that it refers to the Jesus of history. Thus they try to give either a psychological portrait of Jesus or a systematized presentation of his teaching. The majority of the "critical" works, however, are hardly more than continuations of the older liberal "Lives." According to the different viewpoints, emphasis is placed upon Jesus the teacher or on his exemplary life and personality. Even so the positivistic scholar cannot deny that the portrayal of the personality of Jesus as given in the Gospels is rather perplexing with the contrast between his claims and the actual circumstances of his life. According to some, Jesus was mistaken in considering himself as the Messiah (e.g., C. J. Cadoux, Case, Schweitzer, Warschauer), and this interpretation was taken by others as an indication that Jesus was eccentric (Gronbech) or motivated by ecstatic experiences (Oscar Holtzmann). No wonder that some psychologists contended that Jesus belonged to the neurotic (Baumann, Van Delius, Rasmussen) or even paranoiac type (Binet-Sanglé, William Hirsch, de Loosten). These views were refuted, however, by A. Schweitzer and Bundy.

The attempt to prove the non-historicity of Jesus and to explain the Gospels as myths was continued (Drews, Dujardin, Mead, Niemojewski, J. M. Robertson, Sadler, W. B. Smith, G. A. van den Bergh van Eysinga, Thielscher). This view was modified by Couchoud and, in a different way, by the school of Form Criticism, especially Bultmann and M. Dibelius. The latter school, while not denying that Jesus actually lived, holds nevertheless that the original historical nucleus of the Gospels was soon so completely overgrown by legendary and mythical features that the historian must content himself with the portrait of Jesus as seen by the primitive church. Others hope to avoid the difficulties raised by critical scholarship by abandoning the idea of a biography of Jesus. They resign themselves to the presentation of Jesus as teacher. Opinions concerning his message are divided, however, in this group. Some consider him as the prophet of a new type of ethics (e.g., Cadman, Gilkey, Jenkinson, Shailer Mathews, McCown, C. C. Morrison, Poteat, K. S. Ross, Schell, Stamm, Bouck White) or of a deepened religion (D. E. Adams, Bundy, Cone, Paradise, Puritan-Costello, R. W. Stewart). Others, following W. Herrmann, hope to move on critically safe ground by focussing their attention upon the inner life or the character of Jesus (e.g., F. D. Adams, F. L. Anderson, Bowie, M. E. Lyman, A. W. Martin). A number of Roman Catholic scholars took up the cudgels to defend the historical reliability of the Gospels (e.g., Lebreton, Fillion, Grandmaison, Lagrange, Lepin, Prat, Ricciotti). They tried with remarkable success to beat the critics with their own weapons by showing that the "critical" approach was never as unbiased as it pretended to be. Less convincing are the Protestant apologetic works, in which a "Life of Christ" is established upon a "critically defendable residue" of Gospel material (e.g., Buechsel, Burkitt, Carpenter, Feine, Fiske, Glover, Hall, Hill, Headlam, Lemme, Nordsten, Rimmer, Sawyer), because they lack the firm position from which their Roman Catholic colleagues are able to set definite limits to critical research.

IV. Interpretations: The majority of modern writers have realized that in order to be relevant, any historical presentation of the gospel material requires an interpretation of the life of Jesus. In the "conservative" Lives of Jesus an attempt is made to weld the traditionally interpreted Gospel materials into a consecutive story (e.g., Campbell, Edwards, Garrett, Gore, Goudge, K. F. B. Mackay, Poling, R. E. Speer, Zahn). The purely pragmatic character of such a narrative does not do justice to the Gospels, however, because it fails to bring the personality of Jesus to life.

Various approaches to that goal are possible—there is, e.g., a tendency among certain writers to point out the naturalness of Jesus and the significance of his out-of-door life (e.g., Barton, Grist, Kagawa, Kirkland, McIntyre, Skinner, Quayle). Schweitzer advocated "consistent eschatology," according to which Jesus acted in his ministry as a fanatical believer in an apocalyptic program. That view was adopted with modifications by Cecil J. Cadoux, H. G. Hatch, Hartt, Hooke, Paisley, Peck, and Warschauer. Others (e.g., W. R. Bowie, C. R. Brown, Raven, B. W. Robinson, D. M. Ross, Shepherd, Sperry) describe Jesus as a person whose whole life was motivated by goodness and sympathy for men. Strength of character and spiritual power form the characteristics of Jesus according to Carey, Coates, Hodgkin, Russell, David Smith, Stead, Terhune, and Wendling. Such approaches tend, however, to bring Jesus down to the level of the average man, and in some Unitarian "Lives" this tendency assumes pathological features (e.g., Lenwood, Raupert, Rihbany). Yet it is obvious that the Gospels would never have been written unless Jesus had been an eminent personality. Hence, in order to do him full justice, writers will emphasize the uniqueness of his personality (Browne, Case, Filson, Ray O. Miller, Leonard, Puritan, Riley), of his character (Murry, Martin J. Scott), of his spiritual insight (F. W. Lewis, Tolson) or of his spiritual life (Frame, Irvine, Rittelmeyer, Sledd, Steer). All these presentations share the assumption that Jesus differed only by degree from other people, whereas in the Gospels he is pictured as God incarnate. No less violence is done to the Gospels, however, when their material is used merely as a collection of evidences for the truth of the Christological dogma (e.g., Boettner, Negley, W. C. Robinson, Schaller, Sibley, R. A. Torrey, Vine), because such procedure not only neglects considerable portions of the Gospels, but also treats their arrangement as irrelevant. On the whole, Roman Catholic scholars have done much better in blending the gospel story with the dogma (e.g., Beaufays, Dawson, Fahling, Fernessole, Lagrange, Morino, Reatz).

V. The Transcendence of Jesus: The real problem of the Life of Jesus consists in fully utilizing the Gospels and so presenting Jesus that to the people of our generation the divine purpose and power of his life become manifest. A number of remarkable solutions of this problem have been offered recently. Like the critics they take the human life of Jesus seriously, not his human nature only, while showing at the same time how in his very human life Jesus transcended all other people (e.g., Berger, Paisley). This element of transcendence is experienced in various ways. Some describe it as the irresistible challenge that emanates from the gospel portrait (e.g., Carnson, P. C. Simpson, Gogarten). Others consider his perfection as a revelation of God that overawes the reader (Bos, Douglas Edwards, John Knox, Macaulay, Mauriac, G. Campbell Morgan, A. W. Robinson, David Ross, C. A. Johnston Ross, Charles A. Anderson Scott). Again, witness is borne by others to the strange paradox that in all he is and does, Jesus shocks people, and yet they feel attracted by him (e.g., Borchert, Fiske, R. Mackintosh, Richard Roberts, Schilder, Schlatter, Spens, Wilkinson). Finally there are those who confess that it was the picture of Jesus' life that changed their lives completely, thereby disclos-

ing his divine dignity and power (T. H. Davies, Otto Dibelius, George S. Duncan, Ferguson, Horton, Pell, P. Whitwell Wilson).

VI. Non-Protestant Works: One of the most remarkable developments is the fact that the interest in the life of Christ, during the nineteenth century almost exclusively confined to Protestant circles, has reached out into many and very diverse circles. Some of the most accomplished books come from the pen of Roman Catholic writers. In addition to the above named we mention Karl Adam, Chesterton, Fulliquet, Guardini, Marmion, Papini, Pinard de la Boullaye. The wide circulation of their works reveals a profound change that is taking place in the spiritual life of the Church of Rome.

No less noteworthy is the rapidly growing interest Judaism takes in Jesus, some praising him as one of their greatest teachers (e.g., Sholem Asch, Enclow, Isaac, Merrifield, Montefiore, J. Norden), some granting him a condescending toleration (Friedlaender, Jacobs, Klausner, Trattner, Rollin), and some taking him severely to task (e.g., Paul Goldman). Christian Science and kindred groups see in Jesus the great teacher of the power of the Spirit (e.g., Gilmore, Sprague, Workman). The adherents of Psychic Research, Theosophy, and Spiritualism follow similar lines (e.g., Carrington, Clark, Haines, A. Boyd Scott, Steiner), whereas others cherish apocryphal stories and mystical obscurities (e.g., *Adept of Galilee, Aquarian Gospel, Gospel of Philip, Resurrectio Christi,* and the books by Akhilamanda, Franz, Hartmann, H. Spencer Lewis, Marriott, and Mereshkovski).

A new feature of our age is the treatment of Jesus as a subject for fiction. Most satisfactory, because in keeping with the nature of the subject, are the narratives which follow very closely the gospel story (e.g., A. K. Chalmers, Elizabeth Goudge, Dorothy Sayers). The remainder of that literature can be divided into two groups, one of them exploiting the Galilean as a cheap subject for literary success (e.g., Mary Austin, Cooke, Fleg, G. Hauptmann, Keable, Riegel), whereas the other group presents Jesus as the alleged proclaimer of their specific programs and ideals (e.g., Barbusse, Gibran, Lepsius, Sutphen, "An Unknown Disciple," Wittig).

See also BIBLICAL THEOLOGY, II; CHRISTOLOGY; GOSPEL AND GOSPELS; JESUS CHRIST, PICTURES AND IMAGES OF; MESSIANIC SECRET; MYTH IN THE NEW TESTAMENT.

BIBLIOGRAPHY: Survey Works: S. J. Case, *The Historicity of Jesus,* 1912; idem, *Jesus Through the Centuries,* 1932; N. Gorodetzky, *The Humiliated Christ in Modern Russian Thought,* 1938; A. M. Hunter, *Interpreting the New Testament 1900–1950,* 1952; J. Leipold, *Vom Jesusbild der Gegenwart,* 1925; Gösta Lindeskog, *Die Jesusfrage im neuzeitlichen Judentum,* 1938; C. P. Maus, *Christ and the Fine Arts, An Anthology,* 1938; C. C. McCown, *The Search for the Real Jesus,* 1940; A. Meyenberg, *Leben Jesu-Werk,* 1922; Albert Schweitzer, *The*

Quest of the Historical Jesus, 1910; *idem, The Psychiatric Study of Jesus*, 1948; Thomas Walker, *Jewish Views of Jesus*, 1931; H. Weinel and A. G. Widgery, *Jesus in the Nineteenth Century and After*, 1914; S. M. Zwemer, *The Moslem Christ*, 1912.

Critical Works: Rudolf Bultmann, *Jesus and the Word*, 1934; Martin Dibelius, *Jesus*, 1949; Robert Eisler, *The Messiah Jesus and John the Baptist*, 1931; P. Gardner-Smith, *The Christ of the Gospels*, 1938; Maurice Goguel, *Life of Jesus*, 1933; *idem, Jesus*, 1950; E. G. Goodspeed, *A Life of Jesus*, 1950; Charles Guignebert, *Jesus*, 1935; *Le Christ*, 1948; F. C. Grant, *Life and Times of Jesus*, 1921; Wilhelm Heitmueller, *Jesus*, 1913; Charles Stanley Lester, *The Historic Jesus; a Study of the Synoptic Gospels*, 1912; James Mackinnan, *The Historic Jesus*, 1931; Eduard Meyer, *Ursprung und Anfaenge des Christentums*, 3 vols., 1921–23; A. T. Olmstead, *Jesus in the Light of History*, 1942; Chester Warren Quimby, *Jesus as They Remembered Him*, 1951; Paul Wernle, *Jesus*, 1916.

Particular Aspects of the Life of Jesus: Chronology: Urban Holzmeister, *Chronologia Vitae Christi*, 1933; G. Ogg, *Chronology of the Public Ministry of Jesus*, 1940. Birth: Douglas Edwards, *Virgin Birth in History and Faith*, 1943; G. H. Box, *Virgin Birth of Jesus*, 1916; J. G. Machen, *The Virgin Birth of Christ*, 1930; Vincent Taylor, *Historical Evidence for the Virgin Birth*, 1920. Passion: Georg Bertram, *Leidensgeschichte Jesu und der Christuskult*, 1922; Karl Bornhaeuser, *Leidens- und Auferstehungsgeschichte Jesu*, 1947; Nathan Levison, *Passiontide*, 1927; Hans Lietzmann, *Prozess Jesu*, 1931; E. H. Phillips, *The Outcast Christ*, 1930; Klaas Schilder, *Christ in His Suffering; Christ on Trial; Christ Crucified*, 3 vols., 1938–40; George W. Thompson, *Trial of Jesus*, 1927. Resurrection: P. Gardner-Smith, *Narratives of the Resurrection*, 1926; D. A. Hayes, *The Resurrection Fact*, 1932; W. B. Hill, *The Resurrection of Jesus Christ*, 1930; Emanuel Hirsch, *Auferstehungsgeschichten und der Christliche Glaube*, 1940; W. Michaelis, *Erscheinungen des Auferstandenen*, 1944. Intention of Jesus: J. W. Bowman, *The Intention of Jesus*, 1943; H. G. Hatch, *Messianic Consciousness of Jesus*, 1939; Louis Howland, *Mind of Jesus*, 1926; John D. Rhoades, *Master Purpose of Jesus*, 1929. Mental Health: Walter E. Bundy, *Psychic Health of Jesus*, 1932; G. Stanley Hall, *Jesus the Christ in the Light of Psychology*, 2 vols., 1917.

Mythical Views: P. L. Couchoud, *Le Mystère de Jésus*, 1924; *idem, Creation of Christ*, 1939; A. Niemojewski, *Gott Jesus im Lichte fremder und eigener Forschungen*, 1910; J. M. Robertson, *The Historical Jesus*, 1916; G. T. Sadler, *Has Jesus Christ Lived on Earth?* 1914; *idem, Behind the New Testament*, 1921; Wm. B. Smith, *Ecce Deus*, 1912; Paul Thielscher, *Unser Wissen um Jesus*, 1930. See also T. J. Thorburn, *Jesus Christ, Historical or Mythical?* 1912.

Apologetic and Conservative "Lives": F. C. Burkitt, *Jesus Christ, an Historical Outline*, 1932; Douglas Edwards, *Jesus, the Gospel Portrait*, 1947; Alfred C. Garrett, *The Man from Heaven*, 1939; Charles Gore, *Jesus of Nazareth*, 1929; Arthur C. Headlam, *Jesus Christ in History and Faith*, 1925; William Bancroft Hill, *Life of Christ*, 1917; Theodor Zahn, *Grundriss der Geschichte des Lebens Jesu*, 1928.

Liberal Interpretations: Benjamin W. Bacon, *Jesus the Son of God*, 1930; W. R. Bowie, *The Master*, 1928; W. C. Bundy, *Our Recovery of Jesus*, 1929; H. J. Cadbury, *Jesus, What Manner of Man?* 1947; S. J. Case, *Jesus*, 1927; William F. Cooley, *Aim of Jesus Christ*, 1925; Sherwood Eddy, *A Portrait of Jesus*, 1943; Harry E. Fosdick, *The Manhood of the Master*, 1913; *idem, The Man from Nazareth*, 1950; George H. Gilbert, *Jesus*, 1912; T. R. Glover, *Jesus in the Experience of Men*, 1921; Mary Ely Lyman, *Jesus*, 1937; Robert Norwood, *The Man who Dared to be God*, 1929; Kirby Page, *The Personality of Jesus*, 1932; Ralph W. Sockman, *Paradoxes of Jesus*, 1936; Ernest F. Tittle, *Jesus after Nineteen Centuries*, 1932.

Naturalistic Interpretations: Bruce Barton, *The Man Nobody Knows*, 1924; William A. Grist, *The Historic Christ in the Faith of Today*, 1911; T. Kagawa, *Jesus Through Japanese Eyes*, 1934; Winifred Kirkland, *Portrait of a Carpenter*, 1931; John E. McIntyre, *Idealism of Jesus*, 1928; William A. Quayle, *Out-of-Doors with Jesus*, 1924.

Philosophical Interpretations: John Erskine, *Human Life of Jesus*, 1945; P. E. Moore, *Christ of the New Testament*, 1924; J. Middleton Murry, *Life of Jesus*, 1926; G. S. Painter, *Philosophy of Christ's Temptation*, 1914; Ricardo Rojas, *The Invisible Christ*, 1931; George Santayana, *The Idea of Christ in the Gospels*, 1946.

Transcendental Interpretations: Otto Borchert, *The Original Jesus*, 1933; Jacob Bos, *The Unique Aloofness of Jesus*, 1931; Colin and Maxwell Carnson, *The Christ of the Twentieth Century*, 1930; T. H. Davies, *Gospel of*

the Living Jesus, 1928; George S. Duncan, *Jesus, Son of Man*, 1947; Douglas Edwards, *Shining Mystery of Jesus*, 1928; Charles Fiske, *The Christ We Know*, 1927; Vilhelm Groenbech, *Zeitwende*, I: *Jesus der Menschensohn*, 1941; Friedrich Gogarten, *Die Verkuendigung Jesu Christi*, 1948; John Knox, *The Man Christ Jesus*, 1942; William Manson, *Jesus the Messiah*, 1946; G. Campbell Morgan, *The Great Physician*, 1937; A. G. Paisley, *Emotional Life of Jesus*, 1931; Adolf Schlatter, *Geschichte des Christus*, 2nd ed., 1923; P. Carnegie Simpson, *The Fact of Christ*, 1916; Maisie Spens, *Concerning Himself*, 1937; W. C. Wilkinson, *Concerning Jesus Christ the Son of God*, 1916; P. Whitwell Wilson, *The Christ We Forget*, 1917.

Roman Catholic Works: Karl Adam, *Jesus Christ*, 1934; G. K. Chesterton, *The Everlasting Man*, 1925; L. de Grandmaison, *Jesus Christ*, 1928; Romano Guardini, *Der Herr*, 1937, rev. ed., 1938; Jules Lebreton, *Life and Teaching of Jesus Christ Our Lord*, 1934; François Mauriac, *Life of Jesus*, 1937; Giovanni Papini, *Life of Christ*, 1923; F. Prat, *Jesus Christ, His Life, His Teaching and His Work*, 1950; August Reatz, *Jesus Christ*, 1933; G. Ricciotti, *Life of Christ*, 1947; Fulton J. Sheen, *The Eternal Galilean*, 1934.

Jewish Works: Morris Goldstein, *Jesus in the Jewish Tradition*, 1950; Samuel Krauss, *Das Leben Jesu nach juedischen Quellen*, 1912; Joseph Klausner, *Jesus of Nazareth*, 1925; Hugh J. Schonfield, *According to the Hebrews* (Tr. of the Toledoth Jeshu), 1937; Ernest F. Trattner, *As a Jew Sees Jesus*, 1931; Bernard Pick, *Jesus in the Talmud*, 1913; A. Lukyn Williams, *The Hebrew Christian Messiah*, 1916.

Novels: Sholem Asch, *The Nazarene*, 1939; Mary Austin, *A Small Town Man*, 1925; Henri Barbusse, *Jesus*, 1927; E. Fleg, *Jesus: Told by the Wandering Jew*, 1934; Dimitri Merejkowski, *Jesus the Unknown*, 1933; *idem, Jesus Manifest*, 1935; *By an Unknown Disciple*, 1910.

[Sup.] OTTO A. PIPER.

JESUS CHRIST, PICTURES AND IMAGES OF: I. The Chalice of Antioch:

According to one of several conflicting accounts of the discovery of this chalice, in 1910 some Arab workmen came upon it while they were digging a well in Antioch. The chalice consists of a plain inner cup of silver, about seven and one half inches high, with an original widest diameter of about six inches. The outer, heavily gilded, silver holder is fashioned so as to display twelve highly individualized figures set within a frame of vines, birds, and animals. The figures are divided into two groups, in each of which five figures believed to be apostles are placed about a central figure believed to be Jesus Christ. In the preliminary report on the chalice, G. A. Eisen expressed his conviction that the outer shell was made in the first century by someone who had known Christ and his apostles, and that the inner cup can be none other than that used at the Last Supper, the Holy Grail itself. Such momentous conclusions, expressed with great confidence in their reliability, soon aroused a large literature on the subject. Eisen's views were repeated in part by Strzygowski, Newbold, Cook, and various popularizers. On the other hand, many authorities (e.g., Stuhlfauth, Volbach, McDaniel, Morey, Jerphanion, Wilpert, Filson, Arnason), on the basis of convincing artistic and historical considerations, have assigned dates to the chalice which range from the second to the sixth centuries. Obviously its maker, therefore, could not have been acquainted with the personal appearance of Jesus and his apostles.

BIBLIOGRAPHY: H. H. Arnason, "The History of the Chalice of Antioch," in *BA*, IV (1941), 49–64, V (1942),

10–16; G. A. Eisen, "Preliminary Report on the Great Chalice of Antioch Containing the Earliest Portraits of Christ and the Apostles," in *AJA*, XX (1916), 426–437; F. V. Filson, "Who Are the Figures on the Chalice of Antioch?" in *BA*, V (1942), 1–10; G. A. Eisen, *The Great Chalice of Antioch*, 2 vols., 1923, also popular edition, 1933; W. B. McDaniel, "The Great Chalice of Antioch," in *CW*, XVIII (1925), 123–127; Josef Strzygowski, "The Authenticity of Early Christian Silver," in *Art Bulletin*, X (1927–28), 370–376; G. de Jerphanion, *Le calice d'Antioche (Orientalia christiana)*, VII, 27, 1926; G. A. Eisen, "The Great Chalice of Antioch," in *BR*, XI (1926), 40–75; W. R. Newbold, "The Eagle and Basket on the Chalice of Antioch," in *AJA*, XXIX (1925), 357–380; A. B. Cook, *Zeus*, II, 2 (1925), pp. 1197–1210; C. R. Morey, "The Chalice of Antioch," in *Art Studies*, III (1925), 73–80; G. Stuhlfauth, *Die "aeltesten Portraets" Christi und der Apostel*, 1918; J. Wilpert, "Early Christian Sculpture: Its Restoration and Modern Manufacture," in *Art Bulletin*, IX (1926), 89–141.

II. Paintings in the Christian Chapel at Dura-Europos:

In 1931–32 excavators found at Dura-Europos, the Roman frontier garrison on the Euphrates which fell to the Persians under Shapur I in A.D. 256, the remains of a house in which was a Christian chapel. This chapel had seven mural paintings (which are now in the Gallery of Fine Arts, Yale University), three of which contain representations of Christ. One of them is a majestic picture of Christ as the Good Shepherd, standing behind his flock and carrying on his shoulders a huge ram. The composition is free and full of movement. The symbolism of Christ as Saviour is enhanced by the juxtaposition of another picture representing the Fall of Adam and Eve. On another wall were two scenes depicting the miracle of Christ healing the paralytic and the miracle on the lake. In the latter Christ is walking on the water with outstretched right hand which Peter is about to grasp.

These seven paintings, which are the earliest known decorations of a Christian assembly hall, are of the greatest importance for our knowledge of the development of art by early Christians. The art tradition has nothing to do with Rome, but is apparently an indigenous Syrian style dating not more than two centuries after the birth of Christ.

BIBLIOGRAPHY: P. V. C. Bauer, "The Paintings in the Christian Chapel," in *The Excavations at Dura-Europos, Preliminary Report of Fifth Season of Work* (1934), 254–283; M. I. Rostovtzeff, *Dura-Europos and Its Art* (1938), pp. 130–134.

III. An early Caricature of Jesus:

According to several church fathers (e.g., Tertullian, *Adv. Nat.*, I, 14, *Apol.* 16; Minucius Felix, *Octavius*, 9), the early Christians were ridiculed for worshipping an ass's head. In 1856 excavators discovered in a house attached to the royal palace on the Palatine in Rome a graffito depicting the crucifixion of a human being with an ass's head. To the left and somewhat below is the figure of a man facing the crucifix with his left arm raised toward the crucifix. Beneath is an inscription in Greek which reads, "Alexander is worshipping [his] god." The date of this blasphemous graffito is difficult to ascertain, but many archaeologists assign it to the third cen-

tury. Since the mimes (the burlesque shows of the Roman world) made use of animal-headed actors to ridicule kings and deities, it may be that this graffito should be taken as evidence that the Passion of Jesus was the object of derision in the lower levels of drama.

BIBLIOGRAPHY: F. X. Kraus, *Das Spottcrucifix vom Palatin*, 1872; Hermann Reich, "Der Mann mit dem Eselkopf. Ein Mimodrama vom klassischen Altertum verfolgt bis auf Shakespeare," in *Jahrbuch der deutschen Shakespeare-Gesellschaft*, XL (1904), 108–128; J. Reil, *Fruehchristliche Darstellungen der Kreuzigung* (1904), 105–108; H. Leclercq, "Ane," in *DACL*, I, 2 (1907), cols. 2041 ff.; *idem*, "Caricature," in *DACL*, II, 2 (1910), cols. 2158–2164; F. de Mely, "Le Christ à tête d'âne du Palatin," in *Comptes rendus de l'Acad. des inscr. et belles-lettres* (1908), 82–92.

IV. A Papyrus Fragment:

A fragmentary leaf of papyrus measuring 22 by 9.5 cm. (said to be from Oxyrhynchus and now in the Royal Museum in Florence) preserves on the verso-side a rough drawing of what is probably intended to represent the incident on the Sea of Galilee recorded in Matt. 8:23–25 and Mark 4:38. A beardless man, adorned with a cruciform nimbus, is depicted sleeping at one end (the stern?) of a boat, resting his head on his right hand. Also in the boat, and looking toward the one sleeping, is a group of nine men. (The drawing, mutilated at this point, may have originally depicted twelve in the group.) It is thought that the fragment dates from the fifth or sixth century. Since the recto-side of the leaf contains in Greek a lease for a plot of ground, it is likely that the artist was a poverty-stricken Christian who made use of a discarded sheet of papyrus.

BIBLIOGRAPHY: A. Minto in *Bollettino d'Arte*, Vol. V (1925–26), pp. 190–192; G. Coppola in *Pubblicazioni della Società Italiana . . . Papiri greci e latini*, Vol. VIII (1927), pp. 87–88 and plate # 920; M. Salmi, "I dipinti paleocristiani di Antinoe," in *Scritti dedicati alla memoria di Ippolito Rosselini* (1945), p. 163; G. Bovini, *Monumenti figurati paleocristiani conservati a Firenze* (1950), pp. 51–52.

V. The Holy Shroud of Turin:

The most famous of the forty or more sheets supposed by some to be the cloth within which Joseph of Arimathea wrapped the body of Jesus (Matt. 27:59) is the one at Turin. This is about thirteen and a half feet long and four and a half feet wide and bears an almost invisible brownish stain which some have imagined to be the outline of Jesus' body. Although both Pope Sixtus IV and Pope Julius II declared the shroud to be authentic, the preponderance of opinion among scholarly Roman Catholics is adverse to its authenticity (see Baumgarten's statement regarding the approximately 3500 articles, books, etc. which had been written on the subject prior to 1903).

BIBLIOGRAPHY: Representative treatments during this century in favor of its authenticity: P. Vignon, *Le linceul du Christ*, 1902, Eng. tr., *The Shroud of Christ*, 1902; A. Loth, *Le photographie du saint-suaire de Turin, authenticité du suaire, documents nouveaux et concluants*, 1910; K. A. Meissinger [a Protestant], *Das Turiner Grablinen*, 1947; G. Caselli, in *Salesianum*, Vol. XV (1952), pp. 384–393. Representative treatments against its authenticity:

W. Chevalier, *Étude critique sur l'origine du saint suaire*, 1900; P. M. Baumgarten, *Historisches Jahrbuch* (1903), pp. 319-343; H. Thurston, "Shroud, the Holy," in *The Catholic Encyclopedia*, XIII (1913), 762-763; J. Blinzler, *Das Turiner Grablinen und die Wissenschaft*, 1952; Paul Gaecheter, "Zum Begraebnis Jesu," *Zeit. f. kath. Theol.*, LXXV (1953), 220 ff.; E. A. Wuenschal, "The Truth about the Holy Shroud," *Amer. Eccl. Rev.*, CXXIX (1953), 3-14, 100-114, 170-187; *idem, Self-Portrait of Christ*, 1954.

GENERAL BIBLIOGRAPHY: H. Graeven, "Ein Christustypus in Buddahfiguren," in *OC*, I (1901), 159-167; Johannes Reil, *Die fruehchristlichen Darstellungen der Kreuzigung Christi (Studien ueber christliche Denkmaeler*, II), 1904; *idem, Die altchristlichen Bildzyklen des Lebens Jesu (Studien ueber christliche Denkmaeler*, X), 1910; G. F. Hill, *The Medallic Portraits of Christ; The False Shekels, The Thirty Pieces of Silver*, 1920; G. E. Meille, *Christ's Likeness in History and Art*, 1924; J. Sauer. *Die aeltesten Christusbilder*, ca. 1924; R. Berger, *Die Darstellung des thronenden Christus in der romanischen Kunst*, 1926; H. Preuss, *Das Bild Christi im Wandel der Zeiten*, 1932; H. Schrade, *Ikonographie der christlichen Kunst, die Sinngehalte und Gestaltungsformen*, Vol. I: *Die Auferstehung Christi*, 1932; C. C. Dobson, *The Face of Christ; Earliest Likenesses from the Catacombs*, 1933; S. H. Gutberlet, *Die Himmelfahrt Christi in der bildenden Kunst von den Anfaengen bis ins hohe Mittelalter*, 1934; W. J. A. Visser, *Die Entwicklung des Christusbildes in Literatur und Kunst in der fruehchristlichen und fruehbyzantinischen Zeit*, Proefschrift. 1934; *Christ's Image*, Intro. by P. Mornand. with a foreword. "What Was the Beauty of Jesus?" by F. Mauriac. 1939; F. Gerke, *Christus in der spaetantiken Plastik*. 1940; B. Rowland. Jr.. "Gandhāra and Early Christian Art: Buddha Palliatus," in *AJA*, XLIX (1945). 445-448.

[Sup.] BRUCE M. METZGER.

JESUSISM. See LIBERALISM.

JEWISH AGENCY FOR PALESTINE: The Mandate for Palestine (1922) granted to Great Britain by the League of Nations provided for the establishment of "an appropriate Jewish agency" to co-operate with the administration of Palestine on matters affecting the Jewish population. These functions were fulfilled first by the Zionist Organization, but in 1929 an enlarged Jewish Agency for Palestine was established to include participation of non-Zionists (see ZIONISM), a practice later discontinued. With the establishment of Israel, the agency has been assigned specific tasks in Israel relating to immigration and settlement.

BIBLIOGRAPHY: Israel Cohen, *A Short History of Zionism*, 1951.

MORRIS FINE.

JEWISH COMMITTEE, AMERICAN: Founded Nov. 11, 1906, in the wake of Russian pogroms, with the object of preventing the infraction of the civil and religious rights of Jews in any part of the world and of securing for Jews equality of economic, social, and educational opportunity. During the first fifteen years of its existence, the committee was primarily concerned with improving the status of Jews abroad and liberalizing American immigration laws. With the rise of German Nazism and the spread of Nazi propaganda in the United States, the committee engaged in a program aimed to combat the influence of Nazi and racist propaganda in the United States and exposing the activities of Nazi agents who co-operated with domestic anti-Semites (see ANTI-SEMITISM).

The committee has undertaken a long-range educational program calling for a basic understanding of the roots of group prejudice and a concerted attack on it by all segments of American society. While supporting the State of Israel, the committee nevertheless rejects the Zionist nationalist concept of Jewish homelessness outside of Israel (see ZIONISM).

The Committee is organized in forty-three chapters in the United States, with a membership of over 21,000. Since 1907 the Committee has published the *American Jewish Year Book* and many other important publications, including the monthly magazine *Commentary*.

BIBLIOGRAPHY: Nathan Schachner, *The Price of Liberty*, 1948; American Jewish Committee, *Annual Reports*.

JOHN SLAWSON.

JEWISH CONGRESS, AMERICAN: Organized 1917, reorganized 1922, an association of American Jews and of affiliated national and local Jewish organizations, functioning through 400 chapters and councils throughout the United States. Purposes: to contribute to the preservation and extension of the democratic way of life; to eliminate all forms of racial and religious discrimination; to protect the rights of Jews in all lands; to promote the democratic organization of Jewish communal life; to foster the affirmation of Jewish religious, cultural, and historic identity; to strengthen the bonds between Israel and America; and to help the people of Israel to develop in freedom and security.

Major activities in which the American Jewish Congress played part have included the organization of a commission at the end of World War I to negotiate at the Paris Peace Conference on the rights and status of Jews in many lands; mobilization of American support for the Balfour Declaration for the establishment of a Jewish national home; organization of the anti-Nazi boycott movement after the rise of Hitlerism; creation of the World Jewish Congress (*q.v.*); development of legal and legislative techniques in combatting racial discrimination; application of modern social science to study of inter-group relations.

Presidents of the Congress have included Judge Julian Mack, Nathan Strauss, Bernard Deutsch, Stephen S. Wise (*q.v.*), Rabbi Irving Miller, and Israel Goldstein. Executive Director (1952) was David Petegorsky. Address: Stephen Wise Congress House, New York City.

MILTON R. KONVITZ.

JEWISH CONGRESS, WORLD: A voluntary association of the Jewish communities of sixty-five countries, organized in 1936, to secure and defend the rights, status, and interests of Jews and to represent its affiliated organizations before governmental, inter-governmental, and other international authorities on matters affecting the Jewish people as a whole. It is the successor to the Comite des Delegations Juives, established at the end of World War I to defend Jewish rights at the Versailles Peace Conference. It has helped to organize world-wide anti-Nazi action; engaged in extensive operations for the rescue and relief of Jewish communities threatened with extermination by the Nazis; secured the first authentic information of the Nazi plans for the extermination of European Jewry; has developed and pressed for the enactment of new concepts in international law with regard to crimes against humanity, human rights, statelessness and the protection of minorities, indemnification for the victims of persecution. It functions through an Executive Committee with branches in London, Tel-Aviv, and New York, a General Council which meets annually, and a Plenary Session convened triennially, and maintains offices in principal Jewish communities throughout the world. It has published many volumes and periodicals. Presidents: Stephen S. Wise (*q.v.*) (1936–49), Nahum Goldmann (1949–).

MILTON R. KONVITZ.

JEWISH INSTITUTE OF RELIGION: Founded in 1922 in New York by Stephen S. Wise (*q.v.*) and a group of associates, the institute had as its primary purpose the training of men for service to American Jewry through the rabbinate and of students fitted for Jewish research and Jewish education. January 25, 1950, the institute merged with Hebrew Union College to form the Hebrew Union College-Jewish Institute of Religion, thus consolidating the forces of liberal (reform) American Judaism. The combined schools, in New York and Cincinnati, maintain a Pre-Rabbinic Department, Graduate Department, Department of Human Relations, and the Hebrew Union School of Education and Sacred Music, offering degrees of bachelor, master, and doctor of Hebrew Letters, and teacher's certificates.

BIBLIOGRAPHY: *Hebrew Union College Bulletin-Jewish Institute of Religion.*

MORRIS FINE.

JEWISH WOMEN, NATIONAL COUNCIL OF. See WOMEN, NATIONAL COUNCIL OF JEWISH.

JEWS AND CHRISTIANS, NATIONAL CONFERENCE OF: Organized in 1928 by Charles Evans Hughes, Newton D. Baker, and S. Parkes Cadman, the Conference functions as an American civic organization of religiously motivated persons working together against prejudice, intolerance, and bigotry and for a brotherhood of man based on the Fatherhood of God. It sponsors a program that includes co-operation with religious and educational organizations in the field of human relations; improving intergroup relations among industrial personnel; obtaining the co-operation of fraternal, civic, labor, and other community groups in opposing intolerance; and enlisting the aid of all the media of communications and the arts. It prepares program materials and projects designed to promote understanding among Protestants, Catholics, and Jews. Everett R. Clinchy served as president (1928–).

In 1950 the Conference helped to organize world brotherhood to reduce hostilities created by religious, racial, national, and cultural differences.

STERLING W. BROWN.

JEWS, MISSIONS TO: The Christian Church has more direct contact with the Jews than with any other non-Christian group. Residing in virtually all countries of the world, the Jews now number approximately 11,500,000. The Nazi massacre of nearly 6,000,000 Jews in Central Europe shifted the center of Jewish population to the United States, where between 4,500,000 and 5,000,000 Jewish people reside. The first half of the twentieth century witnessed an increasing awareness of the part which the local congregation and the individual Christian must play if the widely-distributed Jewish population is to be reached with the gospel. Definite statistics concerning the work are lacking, as much of it is a normal part of the parish outreach. In his survey, *The Progress of World-wide Missions* (1939), Glover estimated 150 missionary agencies and 800 workers engaged in this field of evangelism. In North America there has been a growing tendency for this work to become a regular function of general church bodies, although there are still many independent agencies. Thus responsibility has been assumed by the Presbyterian Church in the U. S. A. in co-operation with the Presbyterian Church in the United States, by six Lutheran church bodies acting co-operatively through the National Lutheran Council, by the Southern Baptist Convention, and by the Church of England in Canada. Responsibility in this field has also received consideration on higher levels. An international "Committee on the Christian Approach to the Jews" was organized in 1930 under the International Missionary Council (*q.v.*). The World Council of Churches (*q.v.*), meeting in Amsterdam in 1948, recommended to member churches "that they seek to recover the universality of our Lord's commission by including the Jewish people in their evangelistic work" and that they join the struggle to overcome prejudice and misunderstanding.

The integration of Hebrew Christians into the life and fellowship of the church has always been particularly pressing in view of the ostracism which converts frequently experience in the Jewish community. Because of a felt need for fellowship and mutual strengthening there was organized in London (1925) the International Hebrew Christian Alliance, a universal fellowship of Christian men and women of the Hebrew race. This organization now has thirteen national Alliances affiliated with it.

It was inevitable that World War I should have disrupted missions among the Jews to some extent. Far more serious was the combination of the Nazi persecution of the Jews, World War II, and the creation of the "Iron Curtain" by Russia and her satellites—a combination which ended Jewish mission activity in most of central and eastern Europe. A number of mission societies in the Protestant countries of northern and western Europe had previously maintained missions in the affected areas. With former fields closed to them, these societies have been turning their attention to North Africa, the new state of Israel, and South America. The Nazi persecution confronted the church with a serious test of her concern for the Jews. Unfortunately, when the church did take a stand, its actions were generally feeble, considering the intensity of the sufferings of both Jews and Hebrew Christians. Quite a number of individual Christians, however, did act heroically to help victims. Of organized efforts, the work of the Presbyterian Church in Ireland (in Hamburg) and that of the Swedish Mission (in Vienna) were outstanding examples. The founding of the new state of Israel in May, 1948, also came as a test to the church, for it has challenged her to consider the centuries of opportunity Christians have had to witness by word and deed to a non-Christian people living in their midst and to evaluate how truly Christian has been the response to this opportunity. The future will soon reveal in what measure the shaking events in this generation have aroused the church to face seriously her responsibility to the Jewish people.

BIBLIOGRAPHY: International Missionary Council, *The Christian Approach to the Jew*, 1927; J. Jocz, *The Jewish People and Jesus Christ*, 1949; H. Einspruch, *When Jews Face Christ*, 1932.

[Sup.] HAROLD FLOREEN.

JIRKU, ANTON: Lutheran; b. April 27, 1885, at Birnbaum in Moravia. He studied at Vienna (Dr.Phil.), Berlin, and Rostock (Dr. Theol.). Specializing in the history of religions and the ancient history of Palestine and Syria, he taught at Kiel (1914–22), Breslau (1922–35), and Bonn (1935–49). He has written: *Die Daemonen und ihre Abwehr im Alten Testament* (1912); *Die magische Bedeutung der Kleidung in Israel* (1914); *Materialien zur Volksreligion Israels* (1914); *Die aelteste Geschichte Israels im Rahmen lehrhafter Darstellungen* (1917); *Altorientalischer Kommentar zum Alten Testament* (1923); *Die Wanderungen der Hebraeer im 3. und 2. Jahrtausend v. Chr.*

(1924); *Das Weltliche Recht im Alten Testament* (1928); *Geschichte des Volkes Israel* (1931); *Die aegyptischen Listen palaestinensischer und syrischer Ortsnamen* (1937); and *Die aeltere Kupfersteinzeit Palaestinas und der bandkeramische Kulturkreis* (1941).

RAYMOND W. ALBRIGHT.

JOAD, C(YRIL) E(DWIN) M(ITCHINSON): Anglican; b. Aug. 12, 1891; d. April 9, 1953. He was educated at Blundell's, Tiverton, and Balliol College, Oxford. He served in the civil service, board of trade (1914–30) and in his later years taught philosophy at the University of London (1930–53) and achieved fame for his participation in broadcasts. An agnostic until his later years, he was converted to Christianity and became a strong Anglican. His books of interest to students of religion include: *Matter, Life and Value; Guide to Philosophy; Guide to the Philosophy of Morals and Politics; Philosophy for Our Times; Philosophy; God and Evil; Common Sense Theology; Guide to Modern Thought; Return to Philosophy; Mind and Matter; The Future of Life; The Meaning of Life; Great Philosophies; Liberty Today; The Present and Future of Religion; The Future of Morals; Samuel Butler; The Story of Civilization;* (with Arnold Lunn), *Is Christianity True? About Education;* and *A Critique of Logical Positivism.*

RAYMOND W. ALBRIGHT.

JOB, BOOK OF: Much has been written on this book since the original Schaff-Herzog article, but there is still wide disagreement in results. The usual dating is 400–200 B.C. Edomite origin around 600 B.C. is claimed by Pfeiffer. Few defend absolute unity of book. It is widely held that the third cycle of speeches is damaged, and that chaps. 28 (praise of Wisdom), 32–37 (Elihu Speeches), and 40:15–41:26 (Behemoth Leviathan descriptions) are secondary, though Elihu Speeches are not disparaged as much as formerly. From the form-critical angle Gunkel defines the dialogue as "polemical discourses of wise men." Koehler would invoke the situation at the bar of justice rather than the mere debate. The great critical question is whether a single author wrote the book as a whole (conceding the possible deletions mentioned) or whether an original dialogue of a still more limited nature has been secondarily expanded. The question has two important subheads: (1) Did the author compose prologue and epilogue as they now stand? (2) Were the Speeches of God rebuking Job part of the original work? In the view of Hempel, Baumgaertel, Kraeling, the real scope of the original work is to be determined from the debate in its earlier portion. An afflicted wise man, who sees himself in the role of the ancient sage, Job rejects the inference which others would draw on the basis of the doctrine of retributive justice, namely, that he must be a great sinner, and maintains his belief in his own righteousness and vindication by God through chap. 19. The original intent of 19:25–27 is the hope of vindication before death. (These authorities hold that the "redeemer" is really the vindicator of the accused at the bar of justice. Allusion to Christ or the resurrection is rarely found in this passage, though a *post-mortem* vindication is favored by some, e.g., Hoelscher). To the aforementioned critics the rebuke to Job administered in the Speeches of God is an unwarranted sequel to the basic dialogue. Since the prologue of the book gives a solution for the problem of Job's sufferings of which the rest of the book takes no account, Alt, Kraeling, Eerdmans, Lindblom, Stevenson, hold that the author did not have the prologue in its present form. Varying reconstructions are attempted. Kraeling regards 2:11–13, 42:7–9 as surviving elements of the author's framework narrative; and 1:1–2:10, as torso of an older tale. Other scholars, Gunkel, Eissfeldt, Bentzen, Hoelscher, believe that the author either used a traditional story loosely, without following out its ideas or implications, or that he intentionally moved on two planes— with those on the terrestrial unaware of what was transpiring in the celestial.

BIBLIOGRAPHY: Commentaries: S. R. Driver and G. B. Gray, 1921; E. Koenig, 1929; P. Dhorme, 1926; G. Hoelscher, 1937. Other studies: J. Hempel, "Das theologische Problem des Hiob," in *ZST*, VI (1929), 621 f.; F. Baumgaertel, *Der Hiobdialog*, 1933; A. Alt, "Zur Vorgeschichte des Buches Hiob," in *ZATW*, N. F. XIV (1937), 265 ff; E. G. Kraeling, *The Book of the Ways of God*, 1939; J. Lindblom, *La Composition du livre de Job*, 1945; W. B. Stevenson, *The Poem of Job*, 1947; H. Hertzberg, *Der Aufbau des Buches Hiob, Festschrift fuer A. Bertholet*, 1950.

[Sup.] EMIL G. KRAELING.

JOEL, BOOK OF: The unity of the book is by no means as obvious as was asserted by Volck (unquestioned by McCurdy). Chaps. 1–2 and 3–4 are widely regarded as "heterogeneous" (Pfeiffer). Many scholars hold that in the first part a prophet interprets a real locust plague as "the beginning of the Day of Judgment" (Bentzen), whereas the second part is throughout a prediction dwelling on themes characteristic of late eschatological prophecy (cf. Isa. 4:5–6; 24: 3–23; 32:15–17; Zech. 12–14). Yet both parts are by many dated in the same period (fourth-third century B.C.), and even ascribed to the same author. Kapelrud (1948) believes that a prophet Joel was active *ca.* 600 B.C., but that the book took form two or three centuries later. Most recent writers agree that 3:1–3 can refer only to the period of the Dispersion; and the "Jewanim" (Ionians) of 4:6, to the Greeks of the age following Alexander. The evidence of the language and of apparent literary dependence on earlier works is inconclusive, but is in keeping with the arguments for a fourth century date cited by McCurdy.

BIBLIOGRAPHY: Commentaries: J. A. Bewer, *Obadiah and Joel*, 1911; G. W. Wade, *Micah, Obadiah, Joel, and Jonah*, 1925; E. Sellin, *Das Zwoelfprophetenbuch*, 1922; T. H. Robinson, *Die Zwoelf kleinen Propheten*, 1938; A. S. Kapelrud, *Joel Studies*, 1948. Introductions: O. Eissfeldt, *Einleitung in das Alte Testament*, 1934; R. H. Pfeiffer, *Introduction to the Old Testament*, 1941; A. Bentzen, *Introduction to the Old Testament*, 2 vols., 1948.

[Sup.] R. B. Y. SCOTT.

JOGUES, ISAAC: French Jesuit missionary; b. in Orleans, Jan. 10, 1607. He entered the Society of Jesus in 1624 and, after having been professor of Literature at Rouen, was sent to Canada to do missionary work. He was the first Catholic priest on Manhattan Island. He spent six years in hazardous Indian country with Jean de Brebeuf (*q.v.*) and other Jesuit missionaries. Though a daring missionary, Jogues' primary purpose was always to establish his Indian converts in permanent habitations. He proposed to convert not only the Indians of Lake Superior but also the Sioux tribe living at the head waters of the Mississippi. This plan was thwarted on Aug. 3, 1642, by his capture near Three Rivers in Canada. His captivity lasted thirteen months, during which he endured cruel torture. He was subsequently released but asked immediately to be sent back among the Indians. He was captured a second time, and this time his life was not spared. He was martyred near Ossernenon, New York, on Oct. 18, 1646. In 1930 the Catholic Church canonized him a saint, and his feast day is September 26.

BIBLIOGRAPHY: J. G. Shea, *The Life of Father Jogues*, 1885; Francis Talbot, *Saint Among Savages*, 1931.

GILBERT L. ODDO.

JOHANNEAN CHURCH, EVANGELICAL. See MESSIAHS, FALSE.

JOHANNINE EPISTLES: I. Authorship: One widely recognized church leader, who calls himself "the Elder" in II and III John, wrote all three Epistles. Evidence of language and thought indicates that he also wrote John but not Revelation. Dodd and others, appealing to differences of vocabulary, style, and thought, argue that the author of I John cannot have written the Gospel. But change in literary form and purpose may explain the differences (Howard). "We" in I John 1:1–3 probably identifies the writer as an eyewitness of Jesus' ministry or a spokesman for an eyewitness.

II. Date and Place of Writing: The place was probably Asia Minor, in or near Ephesus; the date, about A.D. 90–100. No decisive evidence determines whether these Epistles preceded, accompanied, or followed the Gospel of John.

III. Literary Character: II and III John are clearly real letters. II John went, not to a Christian lady, but to a local church (the "children" of the "elect lady" are the church members). III John 9 could refer to II John; this is uncertain. Roller argues that I John represents a special letter-form familiar in western Asia. So general a writing, lacking in specific references, is better called a tract or pamphlet, which deals probably with the situation in western Asia Minor.

IV. The Literary Structure of I John: Lohmeyer finds here, as in John and Revelation, seven skillfully constructed parts, individual parts containing a further sevenfold structure. Wendt and Bultmann think the writer used a source containing discourses of Jesus, but differ on what this material includes and how it is used. They show the kinship of I John with John, but demonstrate no clear or logical outline. I John 3:23 states the two main themes.

V. The False Teaching Combated: The writer combats an incipient dualistic Gnosticism, which thinks that incarnation would degrade deity and so denies the real physical life of Christ. They boast of superior knowledge, are arrogant towards other Christians, and think themselves free from sin and moral danger. The writer insists that all have sinned, that "Jesus Christ has come in the flesh," and that all must live in brotherly love (I John 1:8-10; 4:2, 7).

VI. Church Leadership: II and III John show that the Elder exercises leadership over a large area. Harnack sees in Diotrephes' revolt (III John 9) a movement toward the monarchical episcopate, to control traveling teachers and give continuity and strength to local leadership. In any event, the Elder writes before the monarchical episcopate has established itself in western Asia Minor.

BIBLIOGRAPHY: Commentaries: A. E. Brooke (ICC), 1912; A. Loisy (included in *Le Quatrième Évangile*, 2nd ed.), 1921; H. Windisch (HNT), 2nd ed., 1930; C. H. Dodd (MC), 1946. Special Studies: A. Harnack, *Ueber den dritten Johannesbrief*, in *Texte und Untersuchungen*, IV, 3, 1897; H. H. Wendt, *Die Johannesbriefe und das Johanneische Christentum*, 1925; R. Bultmann, "Analyse des ersten Johannesbriefes," in *Festgabe fuer Adolf Juelicher* (1927), 138-158; E. Lohmeyer, "Ueber Aufbau und Gliederung des ersten Johannesbriefes," in *ZNTW*, XXVII (1928), 225-263; O. Roller, *Das Formular der paulinischen Briefe*, 1933; C. H. Dodd, "The First Epistle of John and the Fourth Gospel," in *Bulletin of the John Rylands Library*, XXI (1937), 129-156; W. F. Howard, "The Common Authorship of the Johannine Gospel and Epistles," in *JTS*, XLVIII, (1947), 12-25.

[Sup. to JOHN THE APOSTLE, II, 2.]

FLOYD V. FILSON.

JOHANSSON, GUSTAF: B. 1844; d. 1930; archbishop of Finland. He became professor of systematics at Helsinki (1877); bishop of Kuopio (1885) and of Nyslott (1896); archbishop of Åbo (1899). Johansson was early influenced by the pietistic revival in Finland and was a disciple of Professor J. T. Beck at Tuebingen. He repudiated the new currents in theology and the ecumenical movement (*q.v.*). Through his powerful religious personality he exercised a great influence. He has been very much blamed for his passivity during the attempts at Russification of Finland.

CARL-GUSTAF ANDRÉN.

JOHN: John VIII: He ended the schism of Photius. In his immediate vicinity he experienced the opposition of noble families in Rome. The synod of 876 condemned some of these opponents, notably Formosus, bishop of Porto, who was deposed and excommunicated. John fostered the scholarly work of Anastasius Bibliothecarius. He defended the Roman state and the authority of the Holy See against the Saracens and the nascent feudalism which was represented by the dukes of Spoleto and the marquises of Tuscany. He adopted Boso, the duke of Provence, as his son. According to the analist of Fulda, he was murdered by members of his own household.

John IX: A native of Tivoli, where he was a Benedictine abbot. He recognized Lambert of Spoleto as emperor, but the latter soon died from an injury. He induced the Curia to decree that henceforth the consecration of popes should take place only in the presence of the imperial legates.

John X: He crowned Berengarius, king of Italy, as emperor. As pope he allied himself with Theophylast, the husband of Theodora, and Alberic, marquis of Camerino, then governor of the duchy of Spoleto. After the death of Theodora he tried to make himself independent of the Byzantines, being assisted by his brother, the influential Petrus, but he was imprisoned by Maronia, the daughter of Theodora, and suffocated there.

John XI: Was elected pope at the age of twenty-one. He was only the exponent of his mother's desires. He was probably the natural son of Alberic I, and not of Pope Sergius III. When his mother married Hugo of Provence, she and her son were imprisoned by Alberic II.

John XII: He was probably the first pope to change his name. The accounts about his scandalous behavior are undoubtedly exaggerated. He became pope at the age of eighteen.

John XIII: Was a member of the family of the Crescenzis, a noble house in Rome. The Roman citizens considered his subservience to the imperial power so objectionable that they imprisoned him. With the help of the emperor he afterwards took revenge upon his enemies. Shortly after holding a council with the emperor at Ravenna in 967, he gave the imperial crown to Otto II in Rome, in assurance of his succession to his father. In 972 he also crowned Theophano as empress. This occurred immediately before her marriage.

John XIV: Born at Pavia, he died in prison from hunger or poison. His own name was Petrus Campanova.

John XV: He was the son of Leo, a Roman presbyter. His authority was hampered by Crescentius, but the presence of the Empress Theophano in Rome from 989 to 991 restrained the ambition of Crescentius. At the end of his life he was sadly maltreated and ridiculed. He was the first pope who pronounced a beatification, namely that of Ulrich, bishop of Augsburg.

John XVI: His own name was John Philagatus. In 995 he was sent by Emperor Otto III on a mission to Constantinople, in order to negotiate a marriage with a Greek princess. On his way back he either accidentally or at the special request of Crescentius visited Rome. Then he took the papal tiara from the hands of Crescentius. Upon Otto's arrival in Rome in the spring of 998 John fled. He was discovered and brought back to Rome, where he was blinded in prison. He did not die until after 1001, which occurred in a Roman prison. He belonged to the Benedictine Order.

John XVIII: He abdicated in 1009 and retired to a monastery, where he died shortly afterwards. He earned the reputation of being a learned and pious man.

John XIX: Member of the house of Tusculum. After the death of Crescentius II (1012) the power of the Crescenzis, who frequently for a period of a century had dominated Rome and the papacy, was transferred to the counts of Tusculum. The first pope representing this house, Benedict VIII, who was well fitted for the papal chair, was succeeded by his brother, John XIX, a Roman senator with sufficient power to secure his own election. He was, however, little inclined to promote the cause of reform. He agreed, upon payment of a large bribe, to grant to the patriarch in Constantinople the title of an ecumenical bishop, but the general indignation in Italy compelled him almost immediately to cancel this agreement. Canute the Great, king of Denmark, made an arrangement with him regarding the appointments of bishops, tithes, and Peter's Pence.

John XX: Is missing in the lists of popes, probably because in former times it had been the custom to insert between Boniface VII and John XV another pope John. When this appeared erroneous, the popes of the tenth and eleventh centuries continued to receive the proper numbers but for John XXI and his successors the wrong numbers were retained.

John XXI: If he can be identified with Petrus Hispanus, he must be considered one of the most influential scholars of the Middle Ages. He is well known for his support of Charles I of Anjou, king of Sicily, against Rudolph of Habsburg. As pope he excommunicated Alfonso III of Portugal for interfering with episcopal elections. He sent legates to the Great Khan. His enemies accused him of dabbling in magic arts, and they considered his death by the fall of a ceiling a divine judgment.

John XXII: He condemned the teachings of the *Spirituales* (like Petrus Olivi) and the radical mystics (notably Master Eckhardt), though only in part. He strongly supported the mis-sions in central Asia, which during his rule offered much hope of success. In the Curia he introduced important reorganizations, such as in the chancery, the judiciary, and the treasury. He kindled keen animosity among those who advocated the independence of the laity and absolute religious poverty, notably the Franciscans named Exalted or Spiritual. In the Bull *Quorundam Exigit* (1317) he revealed a hostile attitude, and in that entitled *Gloriosam Ecclesiam* (1318) he objected to the protests that had come from seventy-four Spirituals delivered in Avignon by Bernard Délicieux. Very soon after this event four Spirituals were burned at Marseille; they were promptly proclaimed martyrs by the pope's enemies, who now called him the anti-Christ. He in turn excommunicated the Spiritual Franciscans in the Bull *Sancta Romana* (1318), and condemned their book, *Commentary on the Apocalypse* (1326). The Bull *Cum inter Nunnullos* (1323) stated that the propositions promulgated at the general chapter of the Franciscans at Perugia in 1322, to the effect that neither Christ nor the Apostles had owned any property, either personal or common, were false. Michael of Cesena, the minister general of the Franciscans, supported the Spirituals in their protest against the condemnation of evangelical poverty. Treatises on the ownership of property suddenly became very popular. The Occamists in particular demanded that the pope be officially condemned in a general church council. But the spiritual Franciscans fared badly, being confused with Beghards (*q.v.*), Fratricelli, and even heretical groups of all sorts. Nevertheless, they carried on their work in southern France, notwithstanding the activities of the Inquisition.

See also POPES.   [Sup.] ALBERT HYMA.

JOHN FREDERICK: Frederick the Wise was Elector of Saxony until his death in 1525. He supported Luther mainly for political and economic considerations, remaining aloof from the new religious doctrines and practices. During his reign the University of Wittenberg was, as before 1517, dominated by Roman Catholic scholars. From 1525 to 1532 his brother John ruled Electoral or Ernestine Saxony, while Albertine Saxony, ruled by a duke, witnessed the reign of George from 1500 to 1539, who was succeeded by Moritz or Maurice. Elector John took advantage of the decision made at the Diet of Speyer in 1526 which permitted a prince in the Holy Roman Empire to control the church in his dominions. Luther, who in 1523 had written that civil rulers had no right or power to determine what sort of religion their subjects should follow, changed his mind in 1528, suggesting to Elector John that he suppress heresy, meaning the Roman Catholic faith and radical Protestant sects. John Frederick was even more favorable to Lutheranism than his father had been. As a result of his active support of Luther as early as 1530, at the Diet of Augsburg, and until he was captured in 1547 in the Battle of Muehlberg in the Schmalkaldic War, losing thereby his Electoral title to Moritz, Saxony became solidly Lutheran, so solidly in fact that even today the other denominations remain insignificant.

BIBLIOGRAPHY: E. F. Henderson, *A Short History of Germany*, Vol. I (1926), chap. XVI; R. Suchenwirth, *Deutsche Geschichte* (1934), pp. 268–315; H. Rueckert, *Die Verfassung der evangelischen Landeskirchen Deutschlands*, 1929; E. G. Schwiebert, *Luther and His Times*, 1950.

[Sup.] ALBERT HYMA.

JOHN OF DAMASCUS: I. Biography: The withdrawal from office of John of Damascus (hereafter JD) occurred probably about 706. His first *Oration on Images* (726) was written after his retirement, for iconoclasm is not mentioned among the heresies abjured in his Confession of Faith, when he entered the monastic life (Migne, *Patrologia Graeca* 95: cols. 417–438). On the other hand, his father still held office after the accession of Abd al-Malik (685–705). He was in time succeeded by JD, who withdrew from office voluntarily, for the council which beatified him (Nicaea, 787) spoke of him as "forsaking all things, emulating the Evangelist Matthew." Government attitudes toward Christians began to deteriorate after 695. His withdrawal is placed, therefore, soon after the accession of al-Walid. (See M. Jugie, "Jean de Damas," in *Dict. de Théologie Catholique*, 1924.)

II. Writings. The *Tractate on Islam* of JD and the accompanying *Disputations* (the former found in JD's *Against Heresies*, Part II of his *Fountain of Knowledge;* translations of *Tractate* and *Disputations* by John W. Voorhis in *The Moslem World* [Oct. 1934, July 1935]; for critical work consult originals) contain the earliest extended Christian report about Muhammad and the Muslims, and have been regarded as displaying thorough knowledge of Islam. Later Christian writers made use of them.

The standard text of *Against Heresies* (Migne, *PG* 94: cols. 675–780) contains descriptions of 103 heresies, the *Tractate* being the 101st. Originally it was the last of one hundred (col. 777), and descriptions 100, 102 and 103 are glosses from another document. (See Stiefenhofer, *Des hlg. Johannes von Damaskus genaue Darlegung des orthodoxen Glaubens . . . mit Einleitung* [*Bibl. der Kirchenvaeter*, Bd. 44], 1923.)

The *Tractate* deals with six matters: historical orientation, the pseudo-prophet Mamed, his teachings (confined almost to Christological), Christian-Saracen discussions, samples from Mamed's Book, regulations he imposed. Christians repel Saracen charges that they are poly-

theists when they speak of Christ as God, and idolators when they reverence the Cross, and attack Mamed as without authenticating prophecies or signs, his Book as received in sleep, and his followers as having accepted it without proof. JD tells contemptuously how the Book sanctions shameful practices, and contains ridiculous stories. Many of his statements can be verified from the Koran (*Qur'ān*), but others prove inaccurate or definitely in error, showing he was unacquainted with the Koran textually, and had only oral reports of passages from a few suras. There are no details about the early history of Islam. The Koran contains many passages the Saracens might have adduced in rebuttal of Christian charges, but apparently they did not know of them, many also that would have modified statements made by JD. (See Merrill, "The Tractate of JD on Islam," in *The Muslim World* [April, 1951]).

The *Disputations* exist in two forms: the standard text of Lequiens (Migne, *PG* 94: cols. 1585–1598), a summary with numbered items, and the text of Galland, *Bibliotheca Patrum* xiii. 272 (cf. Migne, Addenda, *PG* 96: cols. 1335–1348), which is fuller, and judging from internal evidence earlier and in historical order. The standard text discusses in three sections: (1) mainly Christological problems, (2) mainly the cause of evil, (3) an historical argument. The Galland text lacks this last section, and reverses the order of the other two. In the discussions of the *Tractate,* Christians charged with being "associators" argued that the Saracens, "since you say that Christ is Word of God and Spirit," quoting the Koran, were themselves "mutilators," because they separated God's "Word" and "Spirit" from His Being. The *Disputations* report Christological discussions in which the Saracens, familiar with this reasoning which they cannot meet, fight shy of it. Christians are advised to compel them to confirm the statement, and then to ask whether the "Word of God" is created, or uncreated. Already arguing against the Christian claim of "uncreated," the Saracen must say "created." Then the Saracen will flee, "for according to the Saracens such persons (who say the "Word of God" is "created," meaning the Koran) are heretics, and everywhere accursed and outcast, and if you purpose to report him to the other Saracens, he will fear you greatly" (Galland text).

The historical argument is reported by Theodore, bishop of Harran in Mesopotamia (*ca.* 760–825), and is found among his writings. (See Graf, "Die arabischen Schriften des Theodor Abu Qurra," in *Forschungen zur christlichen Literatur u. Dogmengeschichte*, Bd. 10 [1910].) In brief, a Saracen says to a bishop, "If pagans who accepted Moses were pious, and Jews who accepted Jesus, have not Christians accepting Muhammad shown piety?" The bishop replies that signs are essential, and Jesus said prophecy ended with John the Baptist. Like the *Tractate,* this section is contemptuous in tone; the others are irenic, and constructive in intent.

Tractate and *Disputations* presuppose different historical backgrounds: (1) The *Tractate* belongs to a time when the Koran was transmitted orally, when Muslims knew little of the Koran, and when Koran and Tradition might be confused. (2) Mu'āwiya's seizure of the caliphate roused great misgivings in Iraq and the Hijaz, and started the long debate as to whether God can be the Cause of evil. The crude discussions of the *Disputations* show the Arabs at Damascus as aware of the Christian position, but unacquainted with Christian reasoning. They listen interestedly to an exposition of self-determination. Hishām (724–743) mutilated (724) and later executed Ghaylān al-Dimashqi for maintaining freedom of the will—evidently at a later date. (3) The Christological discussions presuppose that the Koran is commonly called "the Word of God," "created or uncreated" has become a matter of debate, and to say "created" is dangerous. Hisham executed Ja'd ibn Dirham for teaching the Koran was created. (4) The historical argument presents an independent Muslim apologetic, refers to conversions to Islam, and cites Christ's signs and teaching in reply.

BIBLIOGRAPHY: Graf, "Das arabische Original der Vita des hlg. Johannes von Damaskus," in *Der Katholik,* Bd. 12, (1918). Gueterbock, *Islam im Lichte des byz. Polemik,* 1912. C. H. Becker, "Christliche Polemik u. islamische Dogmenbildung," in *Zeitschrift fuer Assyriologie* (1912).

[Sup.] JOHN E. MERRILL.

JOHN OF DELFT: Known also as John Brants and Joannes Delpius. B. March 6, 1524, at Delft; d. July 14, 1582, at Strassburg. Studied at the University of Cologne, was sent by the archbishop of Trier to the Council of Trent to defend the doctrine of the Eucharist (September, 1551); also argued in favor of obligatory confession and against the use of sacramental wine by the laity. Was chosen auxiliary bishop of Strassburg in 1553. When the famous cathedral became a Protestant edifice he removed to the abbey of Eschau, where he wrote *De potestate Pontificis et notis Ecclesiae.*

BIBLIOGRAPHY: W. Lampen, "Joannes Delfius," in *Bijdragen . . . van Haarlem,* XLIV (1926), 463–469.

WILLIBRORD LAMPEN.

JOHN OF DIEST: B. at Diest in Brabant, was chaplain at the court of Count William II of Holland, who for a short time was Emperor of the Holy Roman Empire during the infamous Interregnum. Pope Innocent IV persuaded him to support William II in his struggle against the Hohenstaufens. *Ca.* 1252 he became bishop of Samland and auxiliary bishop of Utrecht; in 1254 bishop of Luebeck and *cooperator in spir-*

itualibus of the bishop of Utrecht. Died Sept. 21, 1260, at Essen, buried at Neuss.

BIBLIOGRAPHY: W. Lampen, "Joannes van Diest," in *Bijdragen . . . van Haarlem,* XLIV (1926), 299–312; J. Weyling, *Bijdrage tot de geschiedenis van de wijbisschoppen van Utrecht,* 1951.

WILLIBRORD LAMPEN.

JOHN THE APOSTLE. See GOSPEL AND GOSPELS; JOHANNINE EPISTLES; REVELATION, BOOK OF.

JOHN THE BAPTIST AS A PREACHER: John made a mighty impression as a preacher of revival, and influenced younger men to become evangelists. With a rugged personality like that of Elijah or Amos, John preached repentance, with warnings of judgment. He preached from his Bible (Luke 3:1–20), especially the prophetic books, but always in thought-forms of his time. His open-air sermons were doctrinal (about the Kingdom), Christ-centered, and practical (stressing the fruits of righteousness). He called on hearers to repent, confess, and be baptized. For the meaning of such terms see Alan Richardson (ed.), *A Theological Word Book of the Bible* (1951). John offered "remission," originally meaning freedom from disease, debt, or prison. The reports of his preaching show vivid imagination, mastery of "live words" like those of Amos, a spirit of urgency, and courage in addressing hearers directly. John's power lay in assurance of a call from God, and of a message about the Messiah.

BIBLIOGRAPHY: For some of the scant literature see the bibliography in A. T. Robertson, *John the Loyal,* 1911.

ANDREW W. BLACKWOOD.

JOHN, GOSPEL OF. See GOSPEL AND GOSPELS.

JOHN MILTON SOCIETY. See BLIND, RELIGIOUS LITERATURE FOR THE.

JOHNS LECTURES: Established in 1945 with proceeds of bequest of Mrs. S. B. (Geneva) Johns in memory of herself and her late husband, S. B. Johns, at Bethel College, McKenzie, Tenn., for the benefit of the Theological Department. These lectures are set up on a quadrennial basis. The first series was delivered by Andrew W. Blackwood in 1950.

THOMAS H. CAMPBELL.

JOHNSON, AMANDUS: B. in Sweden, Oct. 27, 1877. He studied at Gustavus Adolphus College (A.B., 1904); Colorado (M.A., 1905); Berlin (1907); and Pennsylvania (Ph.D., 1908). He taught at Pennsylvania (1910–22) and directed the West African Educational Exposition (1922–25). He was founder and director of American Swedish Historical Museum (1926–40). He has written: *Religious and Educational*

Contributions of the Swedes to American Culture (1922); *In The Land of the Marimba; Mbundu English-Portuguese Grammar and Dictionary* (1930); *The Swedish Settlements on the Delaware,* I-II; *The Biography and Journal of Nicholas Collin;* (tr. and ed.), *The Records of the Swedish Lutheran Churches of Raccoon and Penns Neck, New Jersey;* he is now writing the *Swedes in America* in sixteen volumes.

JOHNSON, ELMER ELLSWORTH SCHULTZ: Schwenkfelder; b. June 26, 1872. He studied at Princeton University (A.B., 1899); and the Hartford Theological Seminary (B.D., 1902; Ph.D., 1911). He was pastor of the First Schwenkfelder Church, Philadelphia (1902–4). From 1904 to 1919 he lived in Wolfenbuettel, Germany, as a member of the editorial staff of *Corpus Schwenkfeldianorum* (letters and treatises of Casper von Schwenkfeld [*q.v.*] [1490–1561], 15 vols. so far), and of which he became later and until 1950 the editor in chief. He was Waldo professor of medieval and modern church history at the Hartford Theological Seminary (1923–43) and also served during these years as pastor of the Hereford Mennonite Church, Bally, Pa. (1921–47). He has been a member of the editorial staff of *The Schwenkfeldian* (1903–53) and was the custodian of the Schwenkfelder Historical Library at Pennsburg, Pa.   RAYMOND W. ALBRIGHT.

JOHNSON, FREDERICK ERNEST: Methodist; b. at Ontario, Canada, Oct. 31, 1884. He was educated at Albion College; Union Theological Seminary (B.D., 1912); and Columbia University. He was executive secretary of the Dept. of Research and Education, Federal Council of Churches (1924–50), and was executive director, Central Department of Research and Survey, National Council of Churches, and editor of *Information Service* (1918–). He held a professorship in Teachers College, Columbia University (1931–50). He directed the International Survey of Y.M. and Y.W.C.A.'s (1929–31). He is the author of: *The New Spirit in Industry* (1919); *Economics and the Good Life* (1934); *The Church and Society* (1935); *The Social Gospel Re-Examined* (1940); (with Arthur E. Holt), *Christian Ideals in Industry* (1924); (with H. S. Warner), *Prohibition in Outline* (1927). He edited the volumes: *Social Work of the Churches* (1930); *Religion and the World Order* (1944); *World Order: Its Intellectual and Cultural Foundations* (1945); *Foundations of Democracy* (1947); *Wellsprings of the American Spirit* (1949).

JOHNSON, PAUL EMANUEL: Methodist; b. Niantic, Conn., Feb. 19, 1898. He was educated at Cornell College (A.B., 1920); University of Chicago (A.M., 1921); and Boston University (S.T.B., 1923; Ph.D., 1928). He was instructor in ethics, West China Union University (1925–27); associate professor of philosophy, Hamline University (1928–36); dean and professor of philosophy, Morningside College (1936–41); professor of psychology of religion, Boston University (1941–). Standing in the Personalistic tradition (see PERSONALISM), he has developed a Psychology of Interpersonalism, and contributed to the training of ministers in pastoral counseling and group therapy. His publications include: *Who Are You?* (1937); *Psychology of Religion* (1945); and *Christian Love* (1951).

JOHNSON, SAMUEL: B. 1709; d. 1784; English essayist, poet, critic, and lexicographer. Johnson's significance lies in the fact that, though he was the literary dictator of England and one of the most famous personalities of the eighteenth century, an age of skepticism, rationalism, and deism, he remained fiercely and vocally faithful to orthodoxy and the Church of England. All his works are informed by Christian faith, though this may not be overtly stated. In the literature of devotion he is best known for his meditations and prayers, which breathe a profound fear and love of God in Christ, expressed in the best tradition of the collect form. The latest edition is *Doctor Johnson's Prayers* (Elton Trueblood, ed., 1945). The introduction to this edition by Trueblood and *The Religion of Dr. Johnson and Other Essays,* by William T. Cairns (1946), are the best available discussions of Johnson's faith, which is little dealt with in the standard biographies, the most recent of which is Joseph Wood Krutch, *Samuel Johnson* (1944).
     JOHN W. DOBERSTEIN.

JOHNSON, SHERMAN ELBRIDGE: Episcopalian; b. at Hutchinson, Kan., March 7, 1908. After studying at Northwestern (A.B., 1933) and Chicago universities (Ph.D., 1936) and Seabury-Western Theological Seminary, he served as professor at Nashotah House (1936–40) and the Episcopal Theological School, Cambridge, Mass. (1940–51); was annual professor in the American School of Oriental Research, Jerusalem (1947–48); and in 1951 became dean of the Church Divinity School of the Pacific, Berkeley, Calif. Among his publications is a commentary on Matthew in *The Interpreter's Bible* (1951).

JOHNSON, TORREY. See YOUTH FOR CHRIST.

JOHNSON LECTURES: Established at Seabury-Western Theological Seminary, Evanston, Ill., in 1946, the M. Dwight Johnson Memorial Lectureship provides for biennial lectures in the field of church history and for their publication. Lecturers have been Joachim Wach, Cyril C. Richardson, John David Lee.

JONAH, BOOK OF: The allegorical interpretation, as previously the historical, has been discarded by most modern scholars. The book is now widely regarded as a prophetic parable, exhibiting the contrast between what is seen as a bigoted and selfish spirit manifested by Jonah and the outreach of God's mercy to all mankind, and even to animals. Nineveh is the typical city of this world, a heathen city and an enemy. The concluding rhetorical question (4:11), as in Luke 10:36, shows that the preceding story is intended to teach a lesson.

The story bears the characteristics of ancient Oriental fiction. The extreme size ascribed to Nineveh—the circuit of whose walls in the time of Sennacherib was about eight miles—is explained by Robinson as referring to the group of adjacent cities in the angle between the Tigris and the Upper Zab. Nineveh fell in 612, not in 606 B.C.

The unity of the book, except for the psalm in chap. 2, is generally admitted. The psalm is thought by many to have been inserted after completion of the parable, since it is primarily a liturgy of thanksgiving for deliverance from death by drowning. The book is to be dated 450–350 B.C.

BIBLIOGRAPHY: Commentaries: J. A. Bewer, *Jonah*, 1912; H. C. O. Lanchester, *Obadiah and Jonah*, 1918; G. W. Wade, *Micah, Obadiah, Joel, and Jonah*, 1925; E. Sellin, *Das Zwoelfprophetenbuch*, 1922; T. H. Robinson, *Die Zwoelf kleinen Propheten*, 1938. Introductions: O. Eissfeldt, *Einleitung in das Alte Testament*, 1934; R. H. Pfeiffer, *Introduction to the Old Testament*, 1941; A. Bentzen, *Introduction to the Old Testament*, 2 vols., 1948.

[Sup.] R. B. Y. SCOTT.

JONAS, JUSTUS: Studied from 1511 to 1515 at Wittenberg, and from 1515 to 1518 for the second time at Erfurt. In 1518 he obtained his doctorate at Erfurt. In 1521 he became Provost of the Allerheiligenstift at Wittenberg, which through his influence and that of Luther became Protestant. He translated Melanchthon's *Apology* into Latin and the following from Latin into German: the Preface of the Augsburg Confession, and the Brandenburg-Nuremberg Catechism (1539). As a result of this translation the catechism was translated into English by Archbishop Cranmer (1548), while afterward it was issued in Icelandic. In 1541 he became superintendent of Halle, which was the city of the archbishop of Mainz (the notorious Albrecht of Hohenzollern, who had caused a great scandal by becoming archbishop in two dioceses). Once a week he delivered a sermon on the catechism, attracting on numerous occasions as many as five thousand auditors. After the unfortunate ending of the Schmalkaldic War in 1547 he had to flee to Hildesheim, but in 1548 Maurice of Saxony enabled him to return.

This time, however, he was not permitted to resume his labors as preacher because he was opposed to the Augsburg Interim and Melanchthon's viewpoint of the *Adiaphora*. Until the present day his hymn, "Wo Gott der Herr nicht bei uns haelt" has been included in the Evangelical hymnal. It was published for the first time in 1524, in the Erfurt *Enchiridion*. Even during the worst years of the Schmalkaldic War he composed hymns.

BIBLIOGRAPHY: E. G. Schwiebert, *Luther and His Times* (1950), *passim*; R. Bainton, *Here I Stand: A Life of Martin Luther* (1950), *passim*; R. Jordan, "Die Familienbeziehungen des Propstes Justus Jonas zur Stadt Muehlhausen," in *Zeitschrift des Ver. fuer Kirchengeschichte der Provinz Sachsen*, VII (1910), 156 ff.; M. Schellbach, *Justus Jonas*, 1941; O. Clemen, "Zwei vergessene Uebersetzungen von Justus Jonas," in *Zeitschr. fuer Bibliothekswesen*, Beiheft 73, (1942), 45 ff.; Walter Delius, "Justus Jonas und Erasmus," in *Theologia Viatorum*, I (1948–49), 71 ff.; *idem*, "Ergaenzungen zum Briefwechsel des Justus Jonas," in *Arch. fuer Ref. Gesch.*, XLII (1951), 136 ff.; *idem*, *Justus Jonas* (1952): this is the best biography of Jonas thus far.

[Sup.] D. HEINRICH BORNKAMM.

JONES, E(LI) STANLEY: Methodist; b. at Clarksville, Howard Co., Md., on Jan. 3, 1884. He was educated at Asbury College (A.B., 1906; A.M., 1912). He went to India as a missionary in 1907 and still continues his missionary work, spending six months in India and the Far East each year and six months in America. He has been an evangelist to the educated classes of India. In 1928 the Methodist church elected him a bishop but he resigned to continue his missionary work. He founded two Christian ashrams (*q.v.*) at Sat Tal and Lucknow, India. In addition to his missionary work he conducts religious retreats (ashrams) in India and America and he has been active in a crusade for Christian unity on the basis of federal union. His publications include: *The Christ of the Indian Road* (1925), which has been translated into 20 languages and has sold over 700,000 copies; *Christ at the Round Table* (1928); *The Christ of Every Road* (1930); *The Christ on the Mount* (1931); *Christ and Human Suffering* (1933); *Christ's Alternative to Communism* (1934); *Victorious Living* (1936); *The Choice Before Us* (1937); *Along the Indian Road* (1939); *Is the Kingdom of God Realism?* (1940); *Abundant Living* (1942); *The Christ of the American Road* (1944); *The Way; The Way to Power and Poise; Mahatma Gandhi—An Interpretation*; and *How to be a Transformed Person* (1951).

RAYMOND W. ALBRIGHT.

JONES, RUFUS M.: B. Jan. 25, 1863, at South China, Me.; d. June 16, 1948. He studied at Haverford (A.B., 1885), Heidelberg, Pennsylvania, and Harvard. An American Quaker interpreter of mystical religion to his generation; a great teacher of philosophy in Haverford College for forty years; the founder and lifetime chairman of the American Friends Service

Committee (*q.v.*). He was the author of more than fifty books which ranged from his important: *Studies in Mystical Religion* (1908), and *Spiritual Reformers in the 16th and 17th Centuries*, through his: *Later Periods of Quakerism* (which went to make up the classic Rowntree series of Quaker history which he edited), and his philosophical contributions such as: *Fundamental Ends of Life*, and *Pathways to the Reality of God*, to his more popular and widely read: *New Eyes for Invisibles*, *The Luminous Trail*, and *A Call to What is Vital*, in which he sought to make the appeal of spiritual religion reach out to those of all persuasions. Within Quaker circles he was the acknowledged leader of Quaker thought who was largely responsible for a renewing of its outreach to the world. In religious and educational circles his contribution was to draw attention to the untapped resources in the souls of men, to teach them that they are "more than they know" and to point to an interior religion which transcends all boundaries and creeds and tests its authenticity by the life it produces. His autobiography is carried through his middle life in three little volumes: *Finding the Trail of Life; Finding the Trail of Life in College; and Finding the Trail of Life in the Middle Years.*

[Sup.] Douglass V. Steere.

JONES LECTURES, SAM P.: Founded at Emory University, in Georgia, by members of the family of the evangelist after whom the foundation is named. The lectures are on evangelism.

JORDAN: The Hashimite Kingdom of the Jordan. With the division of the Ottoman Empire after World War I, the Supreme Council of the Allies assigned to Great Britain the mandates for Palestine and Transjordania. Emir Abdullah bin Hussein was made Ruler in 1921. In 1923 the country was organized as an autonomous state, under the Emir. Abdullah became King of Trans-Jordan (*q.v.*) in 1946 and in 1949 King of the Hashimite Kingdom of the Jordan. Because of the Israeli tensions and possible intrigues with Syria and Iraq, he was assassinated on July 20, 1951, in the mosque area in Old (Arab) Jerusalem. Abdullah's son Talal was proclaimed king in September, but on account of his ill health, in October, 1952, the Parliament proclaimed his son Hussein as his successor, to begin reigning in 1953. Oil pipe lines across its territory now provide new but insufficient revenues for the kingdom, nearly a third of whose population of about 1,200,000 consists of Arab refugees from what is now Israeli Palestine. Nearly all the people are Arab Muslims, and the others Arab Christians.

Bibliography: *King Abdullah of Transjordan, Memoirs,* Tr. from the Arabic by G. Khuri, ed. with notes and a foreword by P. P. Graves, 1950.

Edwin E. Calverley.

JÖRGENSEN, K. E. JORDT: Lutheran; b. in Copenhagen, Denmark, Aug. 30, 1906. He studied at the university of Copenhagen (Cand. Th., 1930), at the seminaries of Gettysburg, Pa.; Philadelphia; and Northwestern, Minneapolis, Minn. (S.T.M., 1932); and also at the university of Erlangen, Germany; and in Warsaw and Krakow, Poland. He was second pastor at the Danish congregations in South Slesvig (1933–45) and at the cathedral of Roskilde (1945); and secretary of the Danish Bible Society (1951). His publications include *Oekumenische Bestrebungen unter den Polnischen Protestanten bis zum Jahre 1645* (1942); and *Tolv Aar i Sydslesvig* (Twelve Years in South Slesvig) (1949).

JORIS, DAVID: B. 1501–2; d. 1556. David Joris was the Messiah of the Davidists, one of the more extravagent groups of the Anabaptists. From a provocative Lutheran agitator, Joris became, through the sight of Anabaptist martyrdoms, an adherent of their group. He was ecstatic in predictions of the wonders of the coming new day of the Lord, but in the meantime only confusion reigned on earth and among the Anabaptists themselves. The Muensterites had recourse to revolution and introduced polygamy. The Battenbergers became violent outlaws ravaging the countryside. The Mennonites repudiated revolution, polygamy, and millenarianism and espoused the ideal of the gathered church, separated from the world and from all political life. Joris attempted mediation and in so doing, became himself the founder of a new sect. He called himself the third David. The first was David, the king; the second, Christ, the Son of David; and the third, David Joris. He was accused of making himself the greatest of the three. From this pretension he was saved by an increasing tendency to allegorize the three Davids into three stages of the spiritual life.

Declared an outlaw by the court at the Hague, for five years with a price upon his head, he flitted from hiding place to hiding place, visiting only occasionally at great risk his wife and children. Hearing that Basel, in Switzerland, would tolerate Anabaptists if they did not obtrude their faith, he sought here an exile under the name of Johann van Brugge, was received, and settled with a numerous colony. Here he enjoyed high public esteem. Two years after the deaths of Joris and his wife, strife broke out in the colony. Disquiet during his lifetime had been difficult to allay among those of his followers who felt acutely the impropriety of living in opulence in Basel on contributions from followers who stood in danger of death in the Netherlands, and he who had once inspired faith in his messiahship by his daring, now awakened doubts when he dressed in velvet, romped with the children, and spent his days writing interminable tracts or painting pictures. He was an accomplished artist. "The old gentleman" pacified the insurgents while he lived, but after his death the colony was split and dissension came to public notice. In consequence, Joris was exhumed and burned as a heretic while the colony was compelled to make public abjuration in the Basel Muenster.

David Joris was more than an eccentric; his defense of religious liberty moved in the area of mysticism. None of the externals, whether of the creed or of the Bible, was of any moment apart from the spirit, and the spirit cannot be constrained. "Consider," said he, "in what faith consists. If it is in earthly, temporal, outward things, you are right to drag men in or drive them out, but if faith consists in heavenly, eternal things, then the heart cannot be forced." While the trial of Servetus was in progress, Joris addressed to the town counselors at Geneva a plea for his life which went unheeded and since it was in the Dutch language, may not even have been read.

BIBLIOGRAPHY: Friedrich Nippold, "David Joris von Delft," in *Zeitschrift fuer historische Theologie* (1863, 1864); Roland H. Bainton, "David Joris, Wiedertaeufer und Kaempfer fuer Toleranz," in *Archiv fuer Reformationsgeschichte*, Ergaenzungsband VI (1937); Paul Burckhardt, "David Joris und seine Gemeinde zu Basel," in *Basler Zeitschrift fuer Geschichte und Altertumskunde* (1949): corrects errors in Bainton's readings in the documents and employs some new ones. Does not alter the essential picture.

[Sup.] ROLAND H. BAINTON.

JOSEPH. See PATRIARCHS, OLD TESTAMENT.

JOSEPHUS, FLAVIUS: Since 1910 the following significant additions to our knowledge of Josephus have been made: (1) Study of the Old Slavonic translation of the *Jewish War*, which contains a number of passages not found in the extant Greek text (the principal additions are given in an English translation from the Berendts-Grass German rendering of the Slavonic text in an appendix to Volume III of the Loeb Classical Library edition of Josephus), has led to considerable discussion of the authenticity of these additions and of the theory held by a few scholars that the Slavonic rendering is based on an earlier, non-extant Greek version of the Aramaic original of the *Jewish War*, called *Halōsis* or "Capture [of Jerusalem]." Most scholars who have studied these additions, some of which concern John the Baptist and Jesus, believe that they are interpolations, made by Byzantine writers. (2) There is some evidence that Josephus' paraphrase of the Greek Bible, which contains haggadic amplifications, includes material taken from written Aramaic Targums resembling the extant Targum of Onkelos on the Pentateuch and the Targum of Jonathan on the Prophets (*i.e.*, the historical writings), which would indicate Josephus' use

of an "Ur-Targum." (3) Thackeray has convincingly argued that in composing the last six books of the *Jewish Antiquities* Josephus relied heavily upon two assistants, one, the "Sophoclean" assistant being found in *Ant.*xv–xvi, and the other, the "Thucydidean" assistant being found in *Ant.*xvii–xix, although traces of both appear elsewhere in Josephus' works. (4) Thackeray has also shown that in his paraphrase of the Greek Bible covering I Samuel to I Maccabees (*Ant.*vi–xii), Josephus used a text closely related to that of Lucian of Antioch (*ca.* A.D. 300), which would indicate that there was an "Ur-Lucian" in use during the first century A.D.

BIBLIOGRAPHY: (1) Editions and translations: Henry St. J. Thackeray and Ralph Marcus, *Josephus with an English Translation* (Loeb Classical Library), 7 vols. to date, 1926–43; Théodore Reinach (ed.), *Oeuvres complètes de Flavius Josèphe traduites en français*, 8 vols., 1900–1929; Alexander Berendts and Konrad Grass, *Flavius Josephus vom juedischen Krieg, B. i-iv, nach der slavischen Uebersetzung*, 2 pts., 1924–27; V. Istrin, A. Vaillant, P. Paschal, *La Prise de Jérusalem de Josèphe le Juif, texte vieux russe avec notes et version française*, 2 vols., 1934–39; Giuseppe Ricciotti, *Flavio Giuseppe tradotto e commentato*, 4 vols. to date, (1937–39): Vol. I is Introduction; A. Schorr, *Qadmoniot ha-yehudim* (Hebrew tr. with notes), 2 vols. to date (*Ant.* i-viii), 1940–45; A. Schalit, *Qadmoniot ha-yehudim* (Hebrew tr. with notes), 1 vol. to date (*Ant.* i-x), 1944.
(2) Textual, lexical, and stylistic studies: Henry St. J. Thackeray and Ralph Marcus, *A Greek Lexicon to Josephus*, 3 parts to date (to *engōnios*), 1930–48; G. C. Richards and R. J. H. Shutt, "Critical Notes on Josephus' *Antiquities*," in *Classical Quarterly*, XXXI (1937) 170–177; Elchanan Stein, *De woordenkeuze in het Bellum Iudaicum van Flavius Josephus*, 1937.
(3) General works: Norman Bentwich, *Josephus*, 1914; H. St. J. Thackeray, *Josephus, the Man and the Historian*, 1929; Giuseppe Ricciotti, *Flavio Giuseppe, lo storico giudeo-romano*, 1937.
(4) Special works on religion, history, literary form, etc.: Erwin Nestle, *Judaea bei Josephus*, 1911; Leo Haefeli, *Samaria und Peraea bei Flavius Josephus*, 1913; Richard Laqueur, *Der juedische Historiker Flavius Josephus*, 1920; Wilhelm Weber, *Josephus und Vespasian*, 1921; H. Guttmann, *Die Darstellung der juedischen Religion bei Flavius Josephus*, 1928; Robert Eisler, *Iēsous basileus ou basileusas, die messianische Unabhaengigkeitsbewegung . . . aus der neuerschlossenen Eroberung von Jerusalem des Flavius Josephus . . .*, 2 vols., 1928–29, abridged Eng. tr. by A. H. Krappe, *The Messiah Jesus and John the Baptist*, 1931; Solomon Zeitlin, "The Slavonic Josephus," in *JQR*, N. S. XX (1929–30), 1–50, 281; Salomo Rappaport, *Agada und Exegese bei Flavius Josephus*, 1930; J. M. Creed, "The Slavonic Version of Josephus' History of the Jewish War," in *HTR*, XXV (1932), 277–319; Adolf Schlatter, *Die Theologie des Judentums nach dem Bericht des Josephus*, 1932; Giulia Marchiano, *Lo storico Fl. Giuseppe e i suoi giudizie sugl' imperatori del casa Giulia-Claudia*, 1934; G. C. Richards, "The Composition of Josephus' *Antiquities*," in *Classical Quarterly*, XXXIII (1939), 36–40.

[Sup.] RALPH MARCUS.

JOSHUA, BOOK OF: The source situation in Joshua is generally thought to reflect a continuation of that pertaining to the Pentateuch. The general framework of the latter, however, is ascribed to P, whereas that of Joshua and Judges was furnished by the Deuteronomist. More attention has been given recently to the underlying oral and written materials of Joshua, with a growing impression that the pre-literary and literary history of the book is far more complicated than would appear from the original article. The literary history, as set forth by Noth, may be outlined broadly as follows: (1)

chaps. 13:1–21:42, composed of two main parts, an early history of tribal boundaries, and a later list of places in the Judean Kingdom according to its twelve district divisions; (2) Chaps. 1–12, 24, composed of various stories and hero tales, and an account of the Shechemite ceremony brought together by a compiler. (3) The book was strongly influenced by Deuteronomic editors who thoroughly reworked the old stories (1–12, 24) and brought them into a coherent unity from their point of view. They greatly enriched the material at hand by adding an introduction (1:1–18), inserting a specific injunction demanding cult unity (8:30–35), and other materials, such as 21:43–22:6; 23; 24:31; and 14:6–15. (4) The P writer also had a hand in the book. He is responsible for the Levitical list (21:1–42), the story of the Transjordan tribes (22:9–34), and the outline of the cities of refuge (ch. 20), based on Num. 35:9 ff.

The historicity of Joshua, in broad outline, has been remarkably confirmed by recent study, although some modifications of details are considered necessary as a result of archaeological considerations.

BIBLIOGRAPHY: O. Eissfeldt, *Hexateuch Synopse*, 1922; J. Garstang, *The Foundations of Bible History: Joshua-Judges*, 1931; S. Mowinckel, *Zur Frage nach dokumentarischen Quellen in Joshua 13–19*, 1946; M. Noth, *Das Buch Josua (HAT)*, 1938; *Ueberlieferungsgeschichtliche Studien I*, 1943. See also works on Introduction
[Sup.] JACOB M. MYERS.

JOURDAN, GEORGE VIVILIERS: Church of Ireland; b. at Dublin, April 3, 1867. He was educated at Trinity College, University of Dublin (B.A., 1893; B.D., 1909). He held curacies in Cavan; Westmeath; and Cork; became incumbent of Rathbarry, Ross (1906); St. Mary Shandon, Cork (1915); and Dunboyne, Meath (1940); was elected canon of St. Patrick's Cathedral, Dublin (1931); appointed professor of ecclesiastical history in the University of Dublin (1933). His publications are: *The Movement towards Catholic Reform in the Early Sixteenth Century* (1914); *The Stress of Change* (1931); and seven chapters in *The History of the Church of Ireland* (W. A. Phillips, ed.) (1933–34).

JOURNALISM, RELIGIOUS: Vocationally, religious journalism manifests itself as: (1) gathering and writing religious news for secular and religious newspapers, magazines, radio, and other media of communication; (2) preparation of articles, editorials, columns, and departmental materials for such outlets; (3) editing and illustrating such materials.

In one sense Matthew, Mark, Luke, and John were religious journalists. They reported the meaning of Christ's life. Much of what appears in the Scriptures is journalistic because it is news. In a more literal sense, however, religious journalism began with printing. From the fifteenth century presses of Europe poured broadsides, tracts, and pamphlets, in effect separately printed religious editorials.

The first journalistic publication of religious sponsorship was a Jewish biweekly paper, the Amsterdam *Courant*, published in Holland (1686–87). The first religious periodical (about 1690) was the Roman Catholic *Mémoires sur l'histoire ecclésiastique* of France. Meantime, however, the gazettes of the century preceding carried discussions of religion.

A similar development took place in the United States. The early colonial printers issued pamphlets and tracts for the Puritans, who relied upon the Mathers and other New England clergymen to write sermons comparable to editorials. The first secular publications recognized the theological disputes of the day or made room for sermons.

Religious journalism had a chance to survive during the first half of the eighteenth century because there was almost none of the competition from secular activities now so common. It was in this fruitful time that the first American religious magazine was born; periodicals have remained dominant ever since. This pioneer was a weekly, *Christian History*, founded in Boston in 1743. It lasted two years. None other came forth until 1764, when Christopher Sower (*q.v.*, Vol. XI) published *Ein Geistliches Magazien*, a weekly printed in German at Germantown, Pa. He gave it away during its six years of life.

Every few years thereafter publications were founded, some by denominations and others by private individuals. Religious journalists were active, also, in the establishment and operation of secular publications that gave generous space to religion. Whether religious or secular, however, mortality was great and obstacles many: writers could be paid little or nothing and it was thus difficult to obtain suitable copy; printing equipment was poor as well as expensive; distribution difficult and circulation often profitless; trained or experienced journalists were scarce.

Doctrinal differences and religious controversies brought about by slavery and then the Civil War added new problems to religious journalism during the nineteenth century. The rise of denominationalism narrowed the wide reach of some portions of the religious press, but the subsidies and the appeals to denominational loyalty strengthened other parts. To the general religious publications were added papers and magazines that were to become the numerically most important publications: missions and Sunday school periodicals. For the most part all were unprepossessing in appearance, by present-day standards, and edited largely for the clergy and devout laity. The writing was conventional and didactic, illustrations were few and ill presented. Yet in some there was a spirit that made their reading exciting, if not altogether religious.

By the end of the nineteenth century secular newspapers and magazines of general circulation had been carried to positions of power by the spread of transportation, development of mass production of commodities, giant gains in circulation, and vast growth of advertising. The church press neither then nor since has been able to share even proportionately in this expansion. Unable to meet this competition, the religious press settled into the position of being either a denominational promotional organ or a unit in the world of educational literature on religion, with occasional exceptions.

By the middle of the twentieth century virtually all denominations in the United States issued one to one hundred publications, as did their counterparts in other countries except in a few areas where religious bodies have only slight access to presses. Among the most active were the several Baptist, Lutheran, and Presbyterian groups, the Methodists, the Seventh-Day Adventists, Roman Catholic, and Congregationalist-Christians. One-fourth of the secular dailies employed religious or church editors. Religious news had found a place, although small, on occasional radio and television programs. Religious news and feature syndicates and promotion offices were organized. Courses in religious journalism appeared in the curricula of more than a score of universities and seminaries. Interdenominational and nondenominational publications, while few, were among the more widely known, influential, and successful, such as *The Christian Herald* and *The Christian Century*. Circulations were rising. The approximately 1,100 religious papers and magazines in the United States had an estimated circulation of 15,000,000, but only a few exceeded 100,000. See also NEWS SERVICES, RELIGIOUS; PRESS AND INFORMATION SERVICES.

BIBLIOGRAPHY: A. W. Baumgartner, *Catholic Journalism*, 1931; Carl F. H. Henry, *Successful Church Publicity*, 1943; *The Jewish Chronicle*, 1941; F. L. Mott, *A History of American Magazines*, 1938; Ralph Stoody, *Religious Journalism: Whence and Whither?* 1939; Roland E. Wolseley, *Interpreting the Church Through Press and Radio*, 1951.

ROLAND E. WOLSELEY.

JOWETT, JOHN HENRY: D. Dec. 19, 1923. He was the minister of the Fifth Avenue Presbyterian Church, New York (1911–18); and returned to his native land to be the minister at Westminster Chapel, London (1918–23). Reputed widely as a preacher, he also wrote much. Among his later books are: *Our Blessed Dead; School of Calvary; The Transfigured Church; The Preacher, His Life and Work; Things That Matter Most;* and *My Daily Meditation.*
[Sup.] RAYMOND W. ALBRIGHT.

JUBILEE, YEAR OF: Also called "Holy Year." After the political disturbances of the nineteenth century, which caused the celebration of the jubilees to be omitted or simplified, the following years of jubilee were observed with the traditional ceremonial: 1900 (Leo XIII); 1925 (Pius XI); 1950 (Pius XII).

The essential ceremony of the jubilee consists in the solemn opening of the *Porta Santa*, the walled "Holy Door," in the Roman basilicas of St. Peter, St. John Lateran, St. Mary Major, and St. Paul. After the conclusion of the jubilee, the Holy Door is walled again. Considerable indulgences are granted to the pilgrims who visit the aforesaid basilicas and fulfill certain conditions, which usually are: the reception of the sacrament of penance, holy communion, and the offering of prayers to the pope's intentions. Persons physically unable to travel to Rome may earn similar indulgences in their home country, according to the provisions specified in the bull proclaiming the jubilee or in a similar document.

Extraordinary jubilees with special indulgences were proclaimed by Pius X on the fiftieth anniversary of the definition of the Immaculate Conception (1904), and on the sixteenth centennial of the Edict of Constantine (1913); by Pius XI on the fiftieth anniversary of his ordination (1929), and on the nineteenth centennial of "the redemption of mankind" (1923). In the latter instance, the *Porta Santa* was solemnly opened.

BIBLIOGRAPHY: See "Giubileo" in *Enciclopedia Cattolica*.
[Sup.] GEORGES A. BARROIS.

JUDAISM, LECTURES ON: Established in 1936 by Jewish friends of the institution in order to promote an understanding of Judaism in its relation to Christianity. Annual lectures are delivered in the Graduate School of Theology of Oberlin College, Oberlin, Ohio.

JUDAISM, RECENT: In the little more than a half-century since 1900, Judaism, i.e., the religion of the Jewish people, reflected the stresses and tragedies as well as the general history of that people.

I. Transplanting: This is the period of the great mass migrations of Jews. The century was ushered in by a series of government-promoted massacres—"pogroms" (*q.v.*)—in Tzarist Russia. The majority of Jews at the time lived in Tzarist lands, the only part of the civilized world where civil rights continued to be denied to Jews and where Jews were yet compelled to live under severely restricted legislation and in government-defined ghettos ("The Pale of Jewish Settlement").

With the outbreak of the pogroms in the first half-decade of the twentieth century, Jews despaired of any improvement in their status in the Russias. Accordingly, there began a mass migration to the West, largely to the United

States. This flight continued until the outbreak of World War I in 1914 and was arrested only by the war's contingencies. In this period, several million Jews came to the United States until, with only minor additions since 1914, the Jewish community in the United States is estimated, in 1953, to number some five million souls.

II. Effects: A. ECONOMIC: During the first period of such resettlement in new lands, there were economic adjustments to be made and many tragedies were witnessed. But with the passing of years, under America's free opportunities, the new settlers became rooted and integrated in the economic and social life of the United States.

B. EDUCATIONAL: Emerging out of the ghettos of eastern and southeastern Europe where their opportunities for secular education were rigorously limited, and finding themselves now in the free climate of the Western World, they avidly embraced every opportunity that was available and their young people and elders hungrily reached out for this education and acquitted themselves creditably.

C. RELIGIOUS: As they came out of the isolation of the ghettos of Russia, Poland, and Galicia, and were compelled of necessity to strike new economic roots in the new environment in which they found themselves and become oriented and adjusted to the new world, there was little time at first for religious development. However, as they became settled, the hunger, and not for bread, made its demands.

Most of them came out of an Orthodox religious milieu. The only religion they knew was the Orthodoxy of their ghetto communities. Some rebelled against it at first and wandered away completely. Some attempted heroically to re-establish, in the new environment, the religious forms and modes of their old-world religious experiences. Many neither rebelled nor clung. They drifted.

But, there existed in the United States, as developed by earlier Jewish settlers, three religious trends: (1) Traditional Orthodoxy; (2) Reform Judaism which stressed the progressive character of Judaism and placed its major emphasis upon the universalism of the prophets of Israel; (3) Conservative Judaism, occupying a middle ground between Orthodoxy and religious liberalism, making concessions to modernism whilst attempting to cling to most of the observances enjoined by the tradition.

As the newcomers became adjusted and the earlier pressures of resettlement were eased, they began to satisfy the spiritual hunger. There began a remarkable return to the Synagogue and, by 1953, the return had assumed the character of a mass movement. All three groupings were vigorous and growing, not only numerically, but in program development, in religious education for children and adults, in social programs motivated and sponsored by spiritual concerns and implemented by a greatly increased attendance at public worship and by greatly enriched religious observances in the homes.

The organizational forms which carry on this religious revival are largely: (1) For the Reform or Progressive group—the Union of American Hebrew Congregations (which is the federation of the organized Progressive Synagogues), the Hebrew Union College-Jewish Institute of Religion, located in Cincinnati and New York City (the training schools for rabbis), and the Central Conference of American Rabbis, the organization of the Liberal or Reform rabbis of the country. (2) For the Conservative group—the United Synagogue of America (the organized congregations), the Jewish Theological Seminary of America (the Rabbinical school), and the Rabbinical Assembly of America, the organization of the Conservative rabbis. (3) For the Orthodox group—the Union of Orthodox Jewish Congregations (the organized congregations), Yeshiva and several smaller institutions for the training of rabbis, and the Rabbinical Council of America, the organization of rabbis.

These three groups were working together on the national scene through the Synagogue Council of America, consisting of delegations of all three points of view. It is a council of organizations speaking for the Synagogue in the United States and promoting the common and overlapping interests of all religious Jewry.

III. Theological Views: A. THE GOD IDEA: All religious Jews stress the idea of the unity of God, his indivisibility and incorporeality. All alike teach that he is the Creator of all that is, transcending time and space yet immanent, the indwelling Presence in the world and in the hearts and souls of men. He is the Lord of all in the universe, altogether righteous, and because of his righteousness intolerant of evil which is the negation of righteousness. He is all-holy and holiness is conceived of as moral perfection. In his relation to men he is as a Father and in relation to him all men are his children.

B. REVELATION: All Jews believe that God makes himself known through nature and its majesty and orderliness; through the longing for him in human hearts; and through the minds, the words and the works of God-inspired men. Judaism teaches and all religious Jews accept the belief that this revelation of God was not only of and in the past but is a progressive, continuing process. God revealed himself not only to Moses and the prophets, but through all the subsequent ages. All religious Jews believe that the Jewish sages had a unique insight into religious truth as reflected not only in the "Old Testament," but in the later religious literature of the Jews. This revelation is not restricted to Israel or to anyone within Israel, but Judaism does teach that the Jew—"Israel is My first born"—has a deeper and more mature insight into godliness and this insight became enshrined in the sacred literature of Israel and in the unique religious idioms of observances, sanctions, norms, laws, precepts, all intended to keep alive the awareness of God, "that you may remember and do all my commandments and thus be holy unto your God." Of course, many laws and precepts changed in the course of the ages, but his spiritual ideals have continued to challenge the Jewish people with the imperative of "Holy shall ye be because I the Lord your God am Holy."

C. THE CONCEPT OF MAN: All religious Jews believe that man is created in the spiritual likeness of God, that man is God's tool and agent, God's partner and coworker in the ongoing process of creation. In this position of dignity man has been endowed with freedom of will and with the corollary of accountability and responsibility.

D. SIN AND RETRIBUTION: All religious Jews believe that the deviation from doing the will of God is sin. All Jews believe that there is retribution both in this life and beyond this life; both reward for merit and punishment for wilfulness. All Jews believe also, that in those sins which effect their fellow men one may not expect divine forgiveness except through an honest and sincere repentance and an effort to receive the forgiveness of the wronged fellow man. In sins against God not affecting human beings, one may, through repentance and atonement, hope to receive God's forgiveness.

E. IMMORTALITY: All religious Jews believe that man is immortal, that life is continuous "from everlasting to everlasting." But there are differences between the Orthodox and the Liberal schools in the matter of the specific speculations as to the hereafter. The Orthodox believe in a place of bliss, "The Garden of Eden" or Paradise, to which the souls of the righteous go. They believe also in "Gehenna," the place of punishment and purging for the misdeeds on this earth. The followers of the Liberal interpretation of Judaism do not accept the belief in Paradise or Gehenna as locales and do not speculate much on the geography and organization of the hereafter. But all religious Jews believe in deathlessness, in personal survival beyond what is termed "death."

F. THE UNIQUENESS OF ISRAEL: Most religious Jews believe that the Jewish people is unique in that it was the first to receive the revelation of the highest truth. Jews believe that the Jewish people constitutes indeed, "a kingdom of priests and a holy nation"; that it has been called from the very beginning of its history to bear witness to the reality of God;

called or chosen not as the pet or darling of deity but commissioned, covenanted, despite adversity, despite paganism, despite materialism, to be "priests of the Most High God." It is believed by all Jews that Israel is an eternal people, dedicated to the task of being the continuing servant of God and to help usher in God's kingdom on earth.

G. RELIGION AND ETHICS: All religious Jews believe that religion and ethics constitute an indissoluble unity. The emulation of God's righteousness in society is an inabrogable obligation. Without righteousness religion is dead. "It hath been told thee, O man, what is good and what the Lord doth require of thee, only to do justly, to love mercy, and to walk humbly with thy God." One worships God not only through uttered prayers but more especially through the doing of those ethical deeds which express righteousness. "Love of God" must be translated into love of one's fellow men or it is not genuine. One seeks God largely through righteousness and justice. Judaism teaches and all religious Jews accept the doctrine that there is no sphere of life that is exempt from religious imperatives which must be translated into, and made manifest through, ethical conduct. Nothing touching human well-being, whether in the economic order or national and international affairs is beyond the purview of religious obligation.

H. PRAYER: All religious Jews believe in and practice prayer. Prayer is the "voice of religion." It directs man's heart to God and all religious Jews believe that prayer needs no intermediary, because "the Lord is nigh unto all who call upon Him, to all who call upon Him in truth."

I. THE HOLY SCRIPTURES: All religious Jews accept the "Old Testament" as the Holy Scriptures of Judaism. The traditionalists or Orthodox Jews believe that the Pentateuch was written by Moses at the divine dictation, and that the rest of the "Old Testament" was written under divine but not necessarily verbal inspiration. The Liberals in Judaism, however, have accepted the historico-critical analysis of the "Old Testament" and whilst believing that it is all inspired, ascribe no verbal or literal inspiration to any part of that literature.

J. CEREMONIES AND PRACTICES: All Jews believe in the religious value and importance of religious ceremonies and practices. The Orthodox, however, believe that the ceremonies which have come down from and through the tradition are all part of the commandment of God and therefore, may not be modified or changed. The Liberals have rejected this concept of the value of ceremonies. They believe in their practice where they convey any inspiration and offer challenge. Where they are no longer meaningful in modern times, ceremonies are discarded, adapted, changed and new ones created. In general, all religious Jews believe in the importance of ceremonies as being the Jewish way, warm, intimate and familiar, of making real to each generation and individual the inspiration of the Jewish religion.

K. THE MESSIANIC IDEA: All religious Jews believe in the coming of a Messianic Age when God's will would be translated into social forms and social experiences on earth. There are differences, however, between the Orthodox and the Liberal interpretations of how the Messianic Age will come about. The Orthodox believe that the Messianic Age will be ushered in through a personal Messiah, someone of the household of Jewish faith who, in God's own time and in God's own way, will be revealed as the leader in the Messianic fulfillment. The Liberals and Progressives of modern Jewry have rejected the belief in a personal Messiah and stress only the obligation of Jews to function together as the servants of God and in cooperation with godly men and women of all peoples all over the earth to stand shoulder to shoulder to help usher in the age of fulfillment. But all religious Jews believe that neither Messiah nor Messianic Age has as yet appeared.

BIBLIOGRAPHY: K. Kohler, *Jewish Theology*, 1918; M. Joseph, *Judaism as Creed and Life*, 1910; M. Sternberg, *Basic Judaism*, 1947; S. S. Cohon, *What we Jews Believe*, 1931; Abraham J. Feldman, *The Faith of a Liberal Jew*, 1931; idem, *Reform Judaism—A Guide for Reform Jews*, 1953.

ABRAHAM J. FELDMAN.

JUDEA. See PALESTINE.

JUDE, EPISTLE OF: With the discovery (1886–87) and publication (1892) of the Greek versions of the Book of Enoch, it was noted that Jude's reference (in vss. 14–15) to Enoch's prophecy is an almost verbatim quotation (Enoch 1:9). Regarding this quotation, three different opinions were held in the early church. Tertullian, on the one hand, argued that Jude's testimony authenticates the entire Book of Enoch as inspired Scripture (Tert. *de cultu fem.* i.3) and referred to Enoch as the most ancient prophet through whom the Holy Spirit spoke (Tert. *Idol.* xv). On the other hand, according to Jerome many rejected the canonicity of Jude because he had dared to quote an apocryphal book (Jerome, *de Vir. Ill.* iv). Rejecting both of these views, Augustine held that the approval of the apostle need not be supposed to extend to the whole of the Book of Enoch, but only to the passage quoted by him (*Civ. Dei* XV. xxiii. 4).

Jude 9 is thought by many to allude to an account which was recorded in another apocryphal book, *The Assumption of Moses* (R. H. Charles, ed., 1897). Certain parallels in thought may also suggest an acquaintance with the Testament of Moses (*ibid.*).

As to the identity of the author, many re-

gard Jude as a pseudonym. B. H. Streeter (*The Primitive Church* [1929], pp. 185 ff.), suggested the Jude who, according to the *Apostolic Constitutions* (vii. 46), was the third bishop of Jerusalem early in the reign of Trajan (A.D. 98–117). On the other hand, Wohlenberg, Ward, Lenski, Chaine, Feine-Behm (*Einleitung in das N.T.*, 9te Aufl., 1950), and Richard Heard (*Introduction to the N.T.* [1950], pp. 215 f.), find no reason to abandon the traditional view that this Jude was the brother of Jesus.

BIBLIOGRAPHY: Some of the more important commentaries are: J. B. Mayor, in *Expositor's Greek Testament*, 1912; G. Wohlenberg, in Zahn's *Kom.*, Vol. XV, 3te Aufl., 1923; James Moffatt, in Moffatt series, 1928; Hans Windisch, in Lietzmann's *Handbuch*, Vol. XV, 2te Aufl., 1930; J. W. C. Wand, in *Westminster Commentary*, 1934; R. C. H. Lenski, *Interpretation of the Epistles of St. Peter and of St. Jude*, 1938; and Joseph Chaine, *Les épitres catholiques*, 2 éd., 1939.

[Sup.] BRUCE M. METZGER.

JUDGES, BOOK OF: The *shophet* in Israel was a charismatic, a spirit-possessed person rather than a dictator. He was a man of ability, a gifted person who was singularly blessed of the Lord. His special position may have been won by military or judicial proficiency. His leadership in one realm would naturally carry over into the other at appropriate times.

The literary history of Judges, according to modern scholarship may be sketched briefly. The stories were transmitted for a considerable period in oral tradition, most likely in poetic form. Sometime later they were reduced to writing, mostly in prose form, and were subsequently collected by a compiler. The hand of the Deuteronomist is clearly evident in the editing of materials found in 2:6–16:31, except for chap. 9 and the sections dealing with the minor judges. Still later the introduction was added (1:1–2:5), though from very early sources; also the appendices (17–21) and the exceptions noted above. Whether the same documentary sources carry over into Judges from the Pentateuch and Joshua is a matter of debate, though some of the stories doubtless belong to the same general cycle of traditions.

The minimum chronology of Judges covers a period of roughly 180 years, including that of Samuel's incumbency. Several of the oppressions took place simultaneously, e.g., the Samson and Gideon movements (*ca.* 1100 B.C.), and the Jephthah deliverance and the second stage of Philistine pressure culminating in the battle of Ebenezer (*ca.* 1050 B.C.). To harmonize with present archaeological data the time limit must be greatly compressed. Garstang's treatment is based on the early date for the Exodus (1447 B.C.).

BIBLIOGRAPHY: C. F. Burney, *The Book of Judges*, 1918; G. A. Cooke, *The Book of Judges*, 1913; O. Eissfeldt, *Die Quellen des Richterbuches*, 1925; John Garstang, *The Foundations of Bible History: Joshua-Judges*, 1931; M. Noth, "Das Amt des 'Richters Israels' " in *Festschrift fuer A. Bertholet* (1950), 404-417.

[Sup.] JACOB M. MYERS.

JUNG, CARL GUSTAV: Protestant; b. in Basle, Switzerland, July 26, 1875; son of a Swiss clergyman. He studied at Basle University where he received an M.D. He was a disciple of Freud (*q.v.*) until 1911 when, with Maeder, he founded a new school at Zurich. Preferring the term "analytical psychology" to psychoanalysis, Jung believes that everyone is both an introvert and an extrovert, and the physical make-up determines which predominates. The primary functions of the mind are thinking, feeling, sensation, and intuition. He acknowledges the conscious and the unconscious, but the latter is made up of undeveloped rather than repressed material. The unconscious also includes both personal and collective factors, the latter being inherited from ancestors (see SUBCONSCIOUS). He stresses "individuation" which is similar to religious conversion (*q.v.*). Less of a scientist than a philosopher, Jung has given a religious emphasis to many of his ideas. His use of religious symbols has attracted the favor of religious people. It is doubtful, however, whether such symbols have the same meaning for both. Publications are somewhat fewer than in the case of Freud and Adler, and include: *Psychology of the Unconscious* (1916); *Studies in Word Association* (1918); *Psychological Types* (1923); and *Modern Man in Search of a Soul* (1934). ROLLIN JONATHAN FAIRBANKS.

JUNIOR SERMON: From three to five minutes in length and designed to meet the needs of boys and girls who attend Sunday morning worship with their parents, or are dismissed from the church school to attend the first part of public worship as a group, sitting together. Normal ages are approximately from six to twelve. In some churches boys and girls, preponderantly from the fourth to the seventh grade, meet separately as a Junior Congregation, their worship including a junior sermon. While the literature of the subject is abundant, any that gives systematic guidance is scanty. So-called "object-lessons" and parable sermons, prevalent in the past, are being superseded. In a day with more general understanding of child psychology and educational principles, leaders prefer other types, notably stories, including those from the Bible. Through stories boys and girls identify themselves with people whose experience clarifies, heightens, or interprets their own. They also make their own applications, an opportunity denied them in sermons given to moralization.

BIBLIOGRAPHY: E. P. St. John, "Do Sermons to Children Educate?" (a symposium), in *Religious Education* (December, 1924); S. P. Franklin, *Measurement of the Comprehension Difficulty in the Precepts and Parables of Jesus*, Iowa City, University Studies in Character, III, 1 (1928).

HULDA NIEBUHR.

JUSTIFICATION. See SOTERIOLOGY.

JUSTIN MARTYR: The extent of Justin's acquaintance with philosophy can easily be exaggerated, since he is the most famous of the second-century apologists. In fact it does not amount to a great deal. His own description of his education, given in *Dial.* ii, is in part conventional, modeled after Plato's *Protagoras*, and in part a revelation of Justin's lack of acquaintance with any of the disciplines preparatory to the study of philosophy (except for grammar and rhetoric). He could not understand Stoic logic or physics. He had never studied music, astronomy, or geometry. The only philosophy in which he felt at home was a contemplative religious form of Middle Platonism in which he expected the vision of God. His inadequate understanding of Plato made him give the wrong answer to several Christian questions. His report of his conversion may well be intended for study by Christian apologists or catechists, but it could not convince any adequately instructed Platonist.

Significantly, Justin regards the shaping of the universe by the Platonic demiurge as the same as Moses' idea of creation (*Apol.* i. 59); as a Platonist he had already held that the universe had come into existence (*Dial.* v. 1). He is not a "thorough Hellene" (p. 283 b); he is one of the earliest Christian Platonists, though his Platonism is hardly profound and his Christianity has certain oddities about it. For example, he lists as the objects of Christian worship the Father, the Son who came from him, "the array of the other good angels who follow him and are like him," and the prophetic Spirit (*Apol.* i. 6). Do these angels come from Palestinian Judaism (so Goodenough) or from Platonic literature like the *Oracula Chaldaica*?

As Justin's theology is almost never original, so his dealing with the problems of Old Testament exegesis in his *Dialogue* is based primarily on previously collected materials. These have been examined by W. Bousset, who shows that much of the *Dialogue* consists of fragments of commentaries on books of the Old Testament. It is not a real dialogue but a compendium. It is probable that Justin often relies on "testimony books" of Old Testament quotations.

His New Testament quotations are interesting. The gospel of Matthew can almost be recovered entire from his works, while Mark, Luke, and John are much less highly favored. Justin apparently knows the traditional authorship of these books, for he refers to treatises "drawn up by the apostles and their followers" (*Dial.* ciii. 8). He also uses traditions which come either from oral tradition or from apocryphal gospels. He knows the Pauline epistles but never refers to them as Scripture or mentions their author. The reason for this is not hard to find; Justin had written against Marcion, to whom Paul was the only apostle, and while Marcion had left the Roman church a decade before Justin's *Apology* was written, no opening could be given him.

The climax of his *Apology* comes in the baptismal and eucharistic teaching at the end (this suggests that much of the work may be re-written catechetical material). Baptism means rebirth and "illumination"; it results in forgiveness of sins previously committed and in a new sinless life. Eucharist is explained as similar to incarnation. The bread and drink are no longer "ordinary," but just as they nourish our flesh and blood after being digested, so they are the flesh and blood of the incarnate Jesus. In the Sunday service there are lections from apostles *or* prophets, a sermon by the presiding officer (bishop?), common prayers for all men, the kiss of peace, prayers of thanksgiving over the bread and mixed wine, and administration of the bread and cup. The consecrated food is called "Eucharist" and it is "offered as a memorial of the Passion" (*Dial.* 41).

BIBLIOGRAPHY: J. M. Pfaettisch, *Der Einfluss Platos auf die Theologie Justins*, 1910; W. Bousset, *Juedisch-christlicher Schulbetrieb in Alexandria und Rom* (1915), pp. 282–308; E. R. Goodenough, *The Theology of Justin Martyr*, 1923; M. Pellegrino, *Gli apologeti greci del ii secolo* (1947), pp. 90–94; J. H. Srawley, *The Early History of the Liturgy* (1947), pp. 30–35; a commentary forthcoming in *Corpus Apologetarum* (Amsterdam).

[Sup.] ROBERT M. GRANT.

JUSTIN THE GNOSTIC: Justin's system really has nothing to do with the Ophites, to whose cardinal theories he is opposed. His three "first principles" resemble the late Marcionite teaching of three first principles (cf. Eusebius, *H. E.* v. 13. 4: the good God, the just Creator, and evil matter; cf. A. v. Harnack, *Marcion* [2d ed., 1924], pp. 164–171). Moreover, according to Eznik the Marcionites taught that the God of the Law created everything in co-operation with matter, as if matter were his bride. Later he ascended into heaven and left matter and her sons below (Harnack, p. 374).

It is an important feature of his system that the Good is identified with the cosmic Priapus; the first commandment is "Increase and multiply." Evil is essentially transgression of this commandment, and is brought about by Eve in her frustration after Elohim leaves her. Justin also identifies the twelve angels of Eden with the signs of the Zodiac, with which in turn ancient writers sometimes identified the labors of Hercules.

BIBLIOGRAPHY: H. Leisegang, *Die Gnosis* (1924), pp. 156–168; H. Herter, *De Priapo*, 1932; R. M. Grant, "Gnosis Revisited," in *Church History*, XXIII (1954), 36–45.

[Sup.] ROBERT M. GRANT.

JUVENILE DELINQUENCY. See CRIME.

K

KADUSHIN, MAX: Jewish; b. Dec. 6, 1895. He studied at New York University (B.A., 1916) and Jewish Theological Seminary of America (rabbi, 1920; D. H. L., 1932). He was rabbi of Temple B'nai Israel, New York (1921–26); of Humbolt Blvd. Temple, Chicago (1926–31); director of Hillel Foundation, University of Wisconsin (1931–42); and of the Hebrew High Schools of Greater New York (1942–52). He wrote: *The Theology of Seder Eliahu* (1932); *Organic Thinking* (1938); *The Rabbinic Mind* (1952).

KAFTAN, JULIUS WILHELM MARTIN: Lutheran; d. 1926. He was professor of apologetics and philosophy of religion in Berlin (1883–1926). A member of the religio-historical school, he wrote extensively on Kant and his influences on Protestant thought. His last major work was *The Philosophy of Protestantism* (1917).

BIBLIOGRAPHY: Erich Stange, *Die Religionswissenschaft in Selbstdarstellungen*, 1928.

[Sup.] RAYMOND W. ALBRIGHT.

KAFTAN, THEODOR: Lutheran; b. 1847; d. 1932. He was a church administrator and theologian, spending many years as the general superintendent of the church in Schleswig. Theologically he was opposed to Ernst Troeltsch (*q.v.*) and tried to develop a new support for the traditional faith by a use of modern developments in science and thought. His publications include: *Moderne Theologie des alten Glaubens* (1905); *Zur Verstaendigung ueber moderne Theologie des alten Glaubens* (1909); *Ernst Troeltsch* (1912).

RAYMOND W. ALBRIGHT.

KAGAWA, TOYOHIKO: B. July 10, 1888, in Kobe, Japan. At the age of fifteen, he became Christian, greatly influenced by American missionaries, Dr. C. A. Logan and Dr. H. W. Myers. He studied at Meiji Christian College in Tokyo and Kobe Seminary. He entered the slums of Kobe on Christmas Eve, 1909, to devote himself to Christian service among the poor, the helpless, and the fallen. Later he studied in Princeton Seminary (1914–16). He became an outstanding evangelist and Christian leader, distinguished social worker, leader of labor movements and co-operatives of various kinds. He is a Christian poet and author of 180 books on religious, social, scientific and other subjects; chairman of Mission to Lepers, of International Peace Association, of Moral

New Life Society, of Medical Co-operative, of Credit Co-operative, of Tree Crop Agricultural Research Institute; president of All Japan Farmers' Association, of Japan Co-operative Association, of Christian News Weekly. He established churches, missions, kindergartens, nurseries, and gospel schools in cities, in rural, mining, fishermen's districts. He received 225,-000 decision cards from Japanese audiences who want to follow Christ. He also travelled widely abroad on evangelistic tours to the United States, Canada, Australia, New Zealand, China, India, the Philippine Islands, England, Ireland, Germany, Denmark, Norway, and Sweden.

KAHLE, PAUL ERNST: B. Jan. 21, 1875, at Hohenstein, East Prussia, Germany. After studying at Marburg, Halle (Ph.D., 1898; Lic.Theol., 1902), and Berlin he was German pastor in Cairo, Egypt (1903–8). He taught Oriental languages at Halle (1909–14); at Giessen (1914–23); and at Bonn (1923–38). Since 1939 he has been at Oxford. His major works are: *Masoreten des Ostens* (1913); *Masoreten des Westens* (1927, 1930); *Biblia Hebraica, ed. Kittel: Textum masoreticum curavit* (1927); *The Cairo Geniza* (1947); *Die Hebraeischen Handschriften aus der Hoehle* (1951); *Piri Re'is, Bahrije (das tuerkische Segelhandbuch fuer das Mittelmeer)* (1926); *Leuchtturm von Alexandria* (1930); *Die verschollene Columbuskarte von 1498* (1933); and *Chronik des Ibn Ijas* (1931, 1932, 1935).

BIBLIOGRAPHY: *Studien zur Geschichte und Kultur des Nahen und Fernen Ostens*, 1935.

RAYMOND W. ALBRIGHT.

KAMERUN. See AFRICA.

KANT, IMMANUEL. See EPISTEMOLOGY; PHENOMENALISM; SCEPTICISM.

KANTONEN, TAITO ALMAR: Lutheran; b. at Karstula, Finland, April 24, 1900. He studied at Suomi College, and at the following universities: Minnesota (A.B., 1924), Harvard (A.M., 1926), and Boston (S.T.B., 1928; Ph.D., 1931). He was pastor in Brainerd, Minn. (1920–24) and Boston, Mass. (1924–32). Since 1932 he was professor of systematic theology in Hamma Divinity School, Springfield, O. He has written: *The Message of the Church to the World of Today* (1941); *Resurgence of the Gospel* (1948); *The Lutheran Church and American Culture* (1950); and *The Theology of Evangelism* (1954).

KARAITES: The main advances in knowledge of the Karaites have come through further publication of Karaite documents and attempts to elucidate the origins of the movement. Many such documents were published in Jacob Mann's *Texts and Studies*, Vol. II; *Karaitica* (1935). L. Nemoy has edited the

Karaite Law Book, al-Qirqisani's *Kitāb al-Anwār* (5 vols., 1939–43), and issued a *Karaite Anthology* (1952), with translations from Karaite authors down to the fifteenth century. Increase in knowledge of Karaite exegesis has come through further publication of their commentaries on the Bible. Zvi Cahn in *The Rise of the Karaite Sect* (1937), attempted to explain the movement as a reaction against Persian influences, and Raphael Mahler in *The Karaites, a Jewish Redemption Movement* (in Yiddish, 1947), has explained it bizarrely as a Marxist movement.

[Sup.] ARTHUR JEFFERY.

KARMIRIS, JOHN: Greek Orthodox; b. at Brallas, Parnassis, Nov. 5, 1904. He studied at the universities of Athens, Bonn, and Berlin and was professor for dogmatic and symbolical theology at the Theological Faculty in the University of Athens (1939–45). Since 1945 he was general director of religions and king's councillor at the Holy Synod of the Orthodox Church of Greece. His writings include: *Unpublished Dogmatic and Other Works of Rousanos* (1935–36); *Heterodox Christological Teaching of the 16th Century* (1935); *Thomas Aquinas' "Summa Theologica," Introduction and Translation*, Vol. I (1935); *Metrofhanes Kritopoulos and his Unpublished Correspondence* (1937); *The Confession of Kritopoulos, with replies to Goad, and his Dogmatic Teaching* (1948); *Dogma—Dogmatics—History of Dogma* (1937); *Orthodoxy and Protestantism*, Vol. I (1937); *External Influences upon the Confessions of the 17th Century* (1948); *The Lord's Descent into Hades* (1939); *The Dogmatic Teaching of John Damascene* (1940); *The Symbolical Texts of the Orthodox Catholic Church* (1946); *The Division of the Church and Unionist Efforts* (1946); *The Confession of Faith by Dositheus, Patriarch of Jerusalem* (1949); *The Latin Confession of Faith of 1274, Attributed to Michael VIII Palaeolologus* (1947); *The Orthodox Catholic Church and her Relations with the other Churches and the World Council of Churches* (1949); *The Schism of the Roman Church* (1950); *The Dogmatical and Symbolical Texts of the Orthodox Catholic Church*, Vols. I–II (1951).

KATTENBUSCH, (FRIEDRICH WILHELM) FERDINAND: Lutheran; d. 1936. He was professor of theology at Goettingen (1904–6) and at Halle (1906–23). Also trained in history, his major interests lay in historical theology and doctrine and especially comparative symbolics. His major additional works include: *Luthers Lehre vom unfreien Willen und von der Praedestination* (1875; 2nd ed., 1905); *Die deutsche evangelische Theologie seit Schleiermacher* (1892; 6th ed., 1934); *Deus absconditus* *bei Luther* (1920); *Der Quellort der Kirchenidee* (1921); and *Die Doppelschichtigkeit in Luthers Kirchenbegriff* (1928).

[Sup.] RAYMOND W. ALBRIGHT.

KELLER, ADOLPHE: B. Ruedlingen, Schaffh., Feb. 7, 1872. He studied theology at the universities of Basle, Berlin, and Geneva. He was pastor in Cairo, Egypt, Stein/Rh., Geneva, and Zurich; general secretary of the International Christian Social Institute founded by the Ecumenical Conference at Stockholm; secretary, Swiss Church Federation; assistant professor of ecumenism and descriptive ecclesiology at universities of Zurich and Geneva (1929); director European Central Office for Inter-Church Aid, Geneva (1922); and founder and director of Ecumenical Seminar, Geneva. His books include: *Eine Sinai-Fahrt* (1901); *A Philosophy of Life* (Henri Bergson) (1914); *Dynamis: Forms and Forces of American Protestantism* (1922); *Die Kirchen und der Friede* (1927); (with George Stewart), *Protestant Europe* (1927); *Der Schweizerische Evangelische Kirchenbund* (1928); *Auf der Schwelle* (1929); *Der Weg der dialektischen Theologie durch die christliche Welt* (1932); Eng. Tr., *Karl Barth and Christian Unity; Vom unbekannten Gott* (1933); *Von Geist und Liebe* (1934); *Religion and the European Mind* (1934); *Church and State on the European Continent* (1936); *Five Minutes to Twelve* (1938); *Am Fusse des Leuchtturms* (1940); *Christian Europe Today* (1942); *Amerikanisches Christentum Heute* (1943); *Unbekanntes Amerika* (1944); *Wiederaufbau der Welt* (1944); *Zeit-Wende* (1946).

KELSO, JAMES ANDERSON: Presbyterian; b. at Rawal Pindi, India, June 6, 1873; d. at Pittsburgh, Pa., Nov. 3, 1951. He studied at Washington and Jefferson (A.B., 1892); Western Theological Seminary (B.D., 1896); Berlin and Leipzig (Ph.D., 1900). He was professor of Hebrew and Old Testament (beginning 1901) and president Western Theological Seminary (1909–43). He wrote: *Die Klagelieder, Der Massorethische Text und die Versionen* (1901); *Hebrew-English Vocabulary to the Book of Genesis* (1917); *A History of the Hebrews in Outline* (1921); and *The Hebrew Prophet and His Message* (1922). ALEXANDER MACKIE.

KELSO, JAMES LEON: United Presbyterian; b. Duluth, Minn., Oct. 21, 1892; was educated at Monmouth College, Indiana University, and Xenia Theological Seminary. He has been professor of Semitics and biblical archaeology, Pittsburgh-Xenia Theological Seminary (since 1923). He has been archaeologist for three campaigns at Tell Beit Mirsim; president of the staff of Bethel excavation, and director of Herodian Jericho and Nitla excavations; annual

director of American School of Oriental Research (1949–50). He is author of: *Ceramic Vocabulary of the Old Testament;* and *Excavations at Herodian Jericho and Nitla.*

KEMPIS, THOMAS À: His fame rests almost entirely on the share he had in the authorship of *The Imitation of Christ* (q.v.). As his own personal friend Herman Rijd testified, he was merely a compiler and copyist, adding a number of passages that do not enhance the value of the immortal work, except in a few instances. See also MYSTICISM; GROOTE; ZERBOLT.

BIBLIOGRAPHY: Albert Hyma, *The Brethren of the Common Life,* 1950.

[Sup.] ALBERT HYMA.

KENNEDY, GEOFFREY ANKETELL STUDDERT: Anglican; d. Mar. 8, 1929. Ordained in 1908, he was vicar of St. Paul's, Worcester (1914–21). He became famous for his work as a chaplain during World War I; was awarded the military cross for bravery and became affectionally known as Woodbine Willie. Later he was rector of St. Edmund, Lombard St., London (1922–29) and chaplain to the king. He wrote: *Rough Rhymes of a Padre; Lies; Food for the Fed-up; The Wicket Gate; The Word and the Work.*

F. W. DILLISTONE.

KENNETT, ROBERT HATCH: Church of England; b. at Nether Court, St. Lawrence-in-Thanet, Sept. 9, 1864; d. at Cambridge, Feb. 15, 1932. He studied at Cambridge (1882–87), where he was lecturer in Hebrew, Syriac, and Aramaic (1887–1903); regius professor of Hebrew and canon of Ely (1903–32). His works include: *The Composition of Isaiah* (1910); *The Servant of the Lord* (1911); *Deuteronomy and the Decalogue* (1920); *Sacrifice* (1924); *Old Testament Essays* (1928); *Ancient Hebrew Social Life and Custom* (Schweich Lectures) (1931). ELMER E. FLACK.

KENT, CHARLES FOSTER: D. May 2, 1925. He founded the National Council on Religion in Higher Education to train men for positions in colleges in the field of religion. *The Historical Bible* (6 vols.) and *The Shorter Bible* (2 vols.) completed his writings. [Sup.]

KENYA. See AFRICA.

KENYON, FREDERIC GEORGE: B. in London, Jan. 15, 1863; d. Aug. 23, 1952. He was educated at Winchester and New College, Oxford (M.A.); and Halle (Ph.D.). He was director and principal librarian, British Museum (1909–30) and professor of ancient history, Royal Academy (1918). He wrote: *Aristotle on the Constitution of Athens* (1891, 1904, and 1920);

Classical Texts from Papyri in the British Museum (1891); *Catalogue of Greek Papyri in the British Museum* (3 vols., 1893–1907); *Our Bible and the Ancient Manuscripts* (1895, rev. ed., 1939); *Palaeography of the Greek Papyri* (1899); *Facsimiles of Biblical Mss. in the British Museum* (1900); *Handbook of Textual Criticism of the New Testament* (1901 and 1912); *Recent Developments in the Textual Criticism of the Greek Bible* (1933); *The Chester Beatty Biblical Papyri*, I-VIII (1933–41); *The Text of the Greek Bible* (1937, rev. ed., 1949); *The Story of the Bible* (1937); *The Bible and Archaeology* (1940); *Reading the Bible as History* (1944); *The Bible and Modern Scholarship* (1948).

DANIEL JOHANNES THERON.

KEPLER, THOMAS SAMUEL: Methodist; b. Mt. Vernon, Iowa, Sept. 20, 1897. He was educated at Cornell College (A.B., 1921); Boston University (S.T.B., 1927; Ph.D., 1931); Marburg University (1928–29); and Cambridge University (1929). He was professor of Bible and philosophy, Mt. Union College (1930–34); professor of Bible and religion, Lawrence College (1934–46); and is professor of New Testament, Graduate School of Theology, Oberlin College (1946–   ). His books include: *Why Was Jesus Crucified?*; *Contemporary Religious Thought*; *Credo: Fundamental Christian Beliefs*; *Contemporary Thinking About Jesus*; *A New Look at Old Doctrines*; *The Fellowship of the Saints*; *Contemporary Thinking About Paul*; *A Journey with the Saints*; *Concise Bible Dictionary*; and *Jesus' Spiritual Journey—and Ours*.

KERET. See RAS SHAMRA.

KERR, HUGH THOMSON: Presbyterian; b. Elora, Ont., Feb. 11, 1871; d. Pittsburgh, Pa., June 27, 1950. He was educated at University of Toronto (B.A., 1894; M.A., 1895); Western Theological Seminary (S.T.B., 1897). He held several pastorates, the last being Shadyside Presbyterian, Pittsburgh (1913–45). He was moderator of the General Assembly (1930), president Board of Christian Education (1923–40), secretary Pitcairn-Crabbe Foundation (1941–50). He was one of the first radio preachers in America (1922–42). He was the author of more than twenty books, e.g.: *Children's Story Sermons* (1911); *The Gospel in Modern Poetry* (1926); *A God-Centered Faith* (1935); *The Christian Sacraments* (1944).

HUGH THOMSON KERR, JR.

KERR, HUGH THOMSON, JR.: Presbyterian; theological professor; b. Chicago, July 1, 1909. He was educated at Princeton University (A.B., 1931); Western Theological Seminary (S.T.B., 1934); University of Pittsburgh (M.A.,

1934); and Edinburgh University (Ph.D., 1936). He taught doctrinal theology at Louisville Presbyterian Theological Seminary (1936–40) and at Princeton Theological Seminary (1940–   ). He was editor of the religious quarterly *Theology Today*; and author of: *Compend of Calvin's Institutes* (1939); *Compend of Luther's Theology* (1943); and *Positive Protestantism* (1950).

KESSLER LECTURES: A foundation at Hamma Divinity School, Springfield, Ohio, established in 1921 by Mrs. Emma Kessler of Louisville, Ky., who provided an endowment of $10,000, the interest accruing to be used periodically for "a series of lectures dealing with subjects related to the practical work of the ministry." These lectures, which at first were held annually, are now scheduled in alternate years in the interest of publication. Several volumes have appeared.

ELMER E. FLACK.

KHLYSTY. See MESSIAHS, FALSE.

KHOMYAKOV, ALEXEI S. See RUSSIAN ORTHODOX CHURCH.

KIDD, BERESFORD JAMES: Anglican; b. Birmingham, Jan. 1, 1864; d. May 15, 1948. Educated at Keble College, Oxford. Ordained in 1887, he was assistant curate of SS. Philip and James, Oxford (1887–1900); vicar of St. Paul's Oxford (1904–20); chaplain and lecturer in theology at Pembroke College, Oxford; warden of Keble College, Oxford (1920–39); prolocutor of the Convocation of Canterbury (1932–36); and honorary canon of Christ Church (1915). He taught and examined in the School of Theology, Oxford, and wrote: *The Thirty-Nine Articles* (1899); *The Continental Reformation* (1902); *Documents Illustrative of the Continental Reformation* (1911); *Documents Illustrative of the History of the Church to A.D. 461*; *A History of the Church to A.D. 461* (3 vols., 1922); *The Churches of Eastern Christendom from A.D. 451* (1927); *The Counter-Reformation* (1933); and *The Primacy of the Roman See* (1936).

F. W. DILLISTONE.

KIERKEGAARD, SÖREN AABYE. See CRISIS, THE THEOLOGY OF; DIALECTICAL THEOLOGY; EXISTENTIALISM.

KING, HENRY CHURCHILL: Congregationalist; d. Feb. 27, 1934. He was professor of theology at Oberlin College (1897–1925), dean (1901–12), and president (1912–27). He lectured widely, was director of religious work for the Y.M.C.A. in France (1918–19), and moderator of the National Council of Congregational Churches (1919–21). Among his later books are: *The Ethics of Jesus* (1910); *Religion as*

Life (1913); *Its All in the Day's Work* (1916); *Fundamental Questions* (1917); *The Way to Life* (1918); *For a New America in a New World* (1919); *A New Mind for the New Age* (1920); and *Seeing Life Whole* (1923).

[Sup.] RAYMOND W. ALBRIGHT.

KINGDOM MOVEMENT. See HERRON, GEORGE D.

KINGDOM OF GOD. See BROTHERHOOD OF MAN; DISPENSATIONALISM; ETERNAL LIFE; MILLENNIUM; SOCIAL GOSPEL.

KINGDOM OF GOD, LEAGUE OF THE: Founded in 1906 by P. T. R. Widdrington, priest of the Church of England prominently identified with the existing Christian Social Union of the same communion, the League carried on the tradition of Frederick Denison Maurice. Widdrington's concern was to find a theological basis for a Christian sociology. The League contributed powerfully to the growth of a school of Catholic sociology in the Church of England, based on the doctrines of the incarnation, the atonement, and the Trinity. It cooperated in the holding of the Anglo-Catholic Summer School of Sociology in 1925, out of which grew the Christendom Movement, in which the League is now merged.

BIBLIOGRAPHY: Maurice B. Reckitt, *Maurice to Temple: A Century of the Social Movement in the Church of England*, 1947.

EVELYN C. URWIN.

KINGDOM OF GOD MOVEMENT IN JAPAN. See JAPAN, II.

KINGS, BOOKS OF: The older literary-critical analysis of the Books of Kings in general is still considered correct. Meanwhile it is regarded that these books, combined and edited by the Deuteronomist, form the concluding part of a large Deuteronomic work of history embracing mainly the books of Deuteronomy, Joshua, Judges, Samuel, and Kings.

I. Deuteronomic Redaction: The *terminus a quo* for the definitive redaction of the Books of Kings is the death of the Judean king Jehoiachin (II Kings 25:29, 30), who was deported in 598 B.C. and who died sometime shortly after the accession to the throne of the Babylonian king Amil-Marduk (562 B.C.). Since the Deuteronomist seems to know nothing about the new beginning under Cyrus in 539 B.C., the final Deuteronomic redaction is to be placed about 550 B.C. A point of controversy is the question concerning the unity of the Deuteronomic redaction. Very often a first combination and redaction of the Books of Kings, concluding the history of the kings with the reign of King Josiah in II Kings 23:25a–28, is supposed to have been made about 600 B.C. then later revised and completed by a second Deuteronomist (so at last R. H. Pfeiffer). But the arguments for this assumption are insufficient. The details in this connection, assigned to an older Deuteronomist, probably do not belong to a Deuteronomic redaction at all but to the sources being used (so at last M. Noth). Hence only one composition of the whole Deuteronomic work of history and the Deuteronomic Books of Kings about 550 B.C. should be considered.

II. Sources: It is to be seen very clearly that the Deuteronomist has secured a variety of material of official documentary value from the "Annals of Solomon" (I Kings 11:41), the "Annals of the Kings of Judah," and ". . . of Israel" respectively. It was the source for the chronological statements, including the synchronizing of the accessions of kings in Judah and Israel and also, for example, of the list of the districts of the kingdom of Israel in I Kings 4:7–19. The statements about the two catastrophes of the kingdom of Judah (598 and 587 B.C.) the Deuteronomist has taken from the Book of Jeremiah (Jer. 29:2; 39–41). For the remainder the Deuteronomist introduced into the Books of Kings several stories of prophets. The hypothesis that the "Hexateuch" sources J and E are still to be found in the pre-Deuteronomic material (Benzinger, Hoelscher, and others) cannot be proved and is entirely improbable.

BIBLIOGRAPHY: A. Sanda, *Die Buecher der Koenige*, 1911–12; A. Alt, *Israels Gaue unter Salomo*, 1913; H. Gressmann, *Die aelteste Geschichtsschreibung und Prophetie Israels*, 2. Aufl., 1921; I. Benzinger, *Jahvist und Elohist in den Koenigsbuechern*, 1921; G. Hoelscher, *Das Buch der Koenige, seine Quellen und seine Redaktion*, 1923; J. Begrich, *Die Chronologie der Koenige von Israel und Juda*, 1929; M. Noth, *Ueberlieferungs-geschichtliche Studien*, Vol. I (1943), pp. 66–87; R. H. Pfeiffer, *Introduction to the Old Testament*, 2nd ed. (1948), pp. 379 ff.

[Sup.] MARTIN NOTH.

KINGSBURY LECTURESHIP: Established at Berkeley Divinity School, New Haven, Conn., by Miss Alice Kingsbury in 1929 for one or more lectures each year on "Christian social service" or related topics; usually held by the English Lecturer (*q.v.*).

KING'S DAUGHTERS AND SONS, INTERNATIONAL ORDER OF THE. See YOUNG PEOPLE'S SOCIETIES.

KINGSHIP IN ISRAEL: I. Origin: Monarchial government was instituted in Israel some two centuries after the nation had seized and occupied a sizable portion of Palestine (*q.v.*). The reorganization of the people by the first three kings (Saul, David [*q.v.*], and Solomon) was occasioned by what the people regarded as political necessity. Israel believed that it either had to have a king to fight its battles and to secure justice, or else lose its independence to the Philistines and suffer an internal collapse (I Sam. 4–10). Before this time Israel's political organization had been very different. It consisted of a confederation of tribes bound together by sacred compact (covenant) around a central sanctuary where the tabernacle and ark rested. The God of the covenant, Yahweh (q.v.), was acknowledged as the true King of the nation and its direct Ruler (cf. Judg. 8:22–23). It was he who had initiated the covenant, supplied its law, and directed the nation's wars. He did this through chosen agents, of whom the chief priest was confirmed in office by considerations of heredity and the holy rite of anointing with oil. The "secular" leaders who carried both political and judicial responsibility were all of a charismatic nature, i.e., they were believed to be directly empowered by a special gift (charisma) from God for their particular functions, but they held no institutional "office."

The confederacy broke down under the impact largely of Canaanite religion, which weakened the unifying ideology of the covenant theology. This weakening is represented in the Book of Judges as an interior decay which left the nation an easy prey to predatory neighbors, chief among whom were the Philistines (q.v.). In this situation the elders demanded of Samuel a new form of government; they desired a king "like all the nations" (I Sam. 8:5). Opposition appealed to the older divine order in which there had been no king but Yahweh. Hence Hebrew kingship, no matter how hard it tried, was never quite able to achieve the sanctity or absolutism encountered elsewhere. The nation had once existed without it and would do so again.

II. Theology of Kingship: Saul and David carried on the old charismatic tradition, as both were charismatic leaders. Thereafter, however, dynastic succession was instituted and the conception of an eternal covenant with the dynasty of David replaced the charismatic principle (cf. II Sam. 7:4 ff.). The latter survived in prophecy, and presumably also, at least in ideal, in the kingship of North Israel, when the latter broke with the Davidic dynasty after the death of Solomon. It was in the Davidic dynasty, however, that there existed an elaborate theology of kingship. The king was anointed with holy oil, hitherto reserved for the office of priest (cf. Ex. 30:22 ff.). His person was thus consecrated, separated, and hallowed for office. Divinely appointed, he was thus God's elected representative, and could be called a "son," "begotten" of God (II Sam. 7:14; Ps. 2:7). Several of the Psalms which the church has interpreted messianically were royal psalms in the sense that they were hymns composed for religious ceremonies in which the king played a prominent part (e.g., at a coronation, a royal marriage, and perhaps at a New Year's service in which Yahweh's enthronement as King of the world was celebrated). These Psalms were liturgical and

preserve considerable information concerning the theological ideal of kingship (cf. Pss. 2, 18, 20, 21, 45, 61, 72, 89, 101, 110, 132). A group of Scandinavian scholars believe that the central religious rite of Israel was a New Year's festival, patterned after that in Mesopotamia. But this is quite hypothetical and cannot be proved. Yet it is clear that the theology of the Davidic dynasty included within it the nation's eschatological hope. The Judean prophets, beginning with Isaiah, were thus able to see in it a depicting of the coming universal reign of Yahweh through the agency of the Anointed (Messiah) or Branch from the Davidic root. In so doing they shifted the focus of the royal theology from the reigning king to the eschatological king whom God was about to establish over his universal kingdom (cf. Isa. 9, 11; Zech. 3, 4, 8).

III. Sociological and Cultural Change: The radical nature of the shift in political organization from confederacy to monarchy cannot be exaggerated. The old tribal order was set aside, and the country was divided into provinces, each with its governor (I Kings 4). The tenth century organization of the royal administrative cabinet seems to have followed Egyptian precedents, the chief exception being the inclusion of the chief priest in the cabinet, so that the latter became dependent upon the throne and its supporter. The central sanctuary was brought under royal patronage and protection. The royal palace with its large entourage fostered and encouraged large international commercial enterprises previously unknown in Israel, and a wealthy class of traders and landowners came into being. This was in sharp contrast to the old simple agrarian order and a source of internal contention. Yet royal patronage of the arts and literature was very great, so that the tenth century is now emerging as one of the most productive eras of Israel's history. Yet kingship was no final solution to the problem of security and justice. When it failed to cope with Israel's political problems it fell and with it the divided nation. And its fall brought popular agreement with the prophetic censure of it.

BIBLIOGRAPHY: A. Alt, *Die Staatenbildung der Israeliten in Palaestina*, 1930; J. Pedersen, *Israel, Its Life and Culture*, Vols. III-IV, 1940; W. F. Albright, *Archaeology and the Religion of Israel*, 1942; A. Bentzen, *Messias—Moses redivivus—Menschensohn*, 1948; H. Frankfort, *Kingship and the Gods* . . . , 1948.

[Sup.] G. ERNEST WRIGHT.

KIRCHENAUSTRITT: Voluntary withdrawal of an individual from a state or folk church (q.v.). For Catholicism such withdrawal from a Roman Catholic Church is apostasy (q.v.), technically unallowable, and subject, in predominantly Catholic countries (see, e.g., SPAIN), to civil disabilities. Protestantism permits its adherents to change their confession, and countries with Protestant state or folk churches make legal provision for this.

In the twentieth century the term *Kirchen-austritt* was applied especially to periodic movements which involved severance from all religious affiliation rather than transfer from one confession to another. Secularism (*q.v.*) and anticlericalism (see CLERICALISM) were accompanied by unwillingness to pay church taxes and objection to religious instruction in public schools. In Germany, where the term was coined, as many as 8% withdrew from Protestant Churches (and a like percentage from the Roman Catholic Church and Jewish synagogues) to become "religionless" after World War I. Some of these later returned. Similar movements in other countries cannot be established with the same statistical accuracy.

See also Los von Rom.

BIBLIOGRAPHY: J. Schneider *et al.*, *Kirchliches Jahrbuch fuer die evangelischen Landeskirchen Deutschlands*, annually from 1900–1934, occasionally since.

THEODORE G. TAPPERT.

KIRJATH-SEPHER. See ARCHAEOLOGY, BIBLICAL.

KIRK, HARRIS ELLIOTT: Presbyterian; b. Pulaski, Tenn., Oct. 12, 1872; d. Nov. 6, 1953. He was a graduate of Southwestern College and Divinity School, Clarksville, Tenn. (1897). He was minister, Cottage Church, Nashville, Tenn. 1897–99); First Church, Florence, Ala. (1899–1901); Franklin Street Church, Baltimore, Md. (1901–53). He was special lecturer at Hartford Theological Seminary on homiletics and psychology of religion (1919–24); annual lecturer at Princeton University on historical Christianity (1924–30); professor of biblical literature, Goucher College (1928–40; emeritus, 1940). In theology Kirk was a liberal evangelical. He wrote: *The Religion of Power* (1916); *The Consuming Fire* (1919); *One Generation To Another* (1924); *The Spirit of Protestantism* (1930); *The Glory of Common Things* (1930); *Stars, Atoms and God* (1932); *A Man of Property* (1935); *A Design for Living* (1939).

KIRKRIDGE: Retreat-and-study center in the Pennsylvania Appalachians. Begun in 1942, the movement has its center at Bangor, Pennsylvania, in a 350-acre mountain tract with buildings for religious retreats. Original inspiration came from the Iona Community (*q.v.*) in Scotland, from work-camps, Pendle Hill (*q.v.*), etc. Since 1942 a group, numbering up to 150, has also reported quarterly on the Kirkridge Discipline, devotional and ethical rules and intentions for daily life. Object of the program is to sharpen the devotional and vocational relevance of Christianity by retreats (silence, manual work, worship, instruction), by colloquies on the arts and other areas of expression, and by maintaining fellowship among a widely scattered membership of ministers and laymen, men and women. Originally Presbyterian, Kirkridge is widely inclusive and has inspired six similar programs elsewhere. Dozens of Kirkridge-sponsored retreats and dozens of others are held at the center yearly.

JOHN OLIVER NELSON.

KISCH, GUIDO: Jewish (Jur. utr. D., Pol. S.D.). B. Prague, Czechoslovakia; studied at the University of Prague. He was professor of history of law at the universities of Koenigsberg, Prague, and Halle; dismissed by the Nazi government in 1933 he came to the United States in 1935 and became an American citizen. He was research associate, University of Notre Dame (1942–47); visiting professor, University of Lund, Sweden (1949). He lectured at Jewish Theological Seminary; New School for Social Research; and the universities of Leiden, Utrecht, and Amsterdam, Holland. He was research professor of Jewish History, Hebrew Union College (1937–). His more recent publications are: *Sachsenspiegel and Bible* (1941); *The Jews in Medieval Germany: A Study of Their Legal and Social Status* (1949); *Jewry-Law in Medieval Germany* (1949); as well as *Pseudo-Philo's Liber Antiquitatum Biblicarum* (1949).

KITTEL, GERHARD: Lutheran; b. Breslau, Germany, Sept. 23, 1888; d. Tuebingen, July 11, 1948. He was privatdozent at Kiel (1913) and Leipzig (1917); professor of New Testament, Greifswald (1921–26) and Tuebingen (1926–45). Kittel's work was mainly devoted to the study of the Jewish background of the New Testament. In his opinion the Jewish element prevailed over the Hellenistic element in the making of the New Testament books. Kittel became famous as the editor of the voluminous *Theologisches Woerterbuch zum Neuen Testament* (1933–). Following the example of Cremer and Koegel and the suggestions of Schlatter, he insisted that a lexicon of the New Testament must fully trace the semasiological history of each word. That meant a combination of its secular usage in classical Greek and *koine* (*q.v.*), on the one hand, with the religious connotations derived from the Septuagint and its Hebrew background, on the other. His pamphlet *Die Judenfrage* (1934) aroused a bitter controversy and landed him in prison, when the Allies occupied Germany in 1945. Other works: *Jesus und die Rabbinen* (1914); *Der Midrasch Sifre zum Deuteronomium* (1922); *Das Problem des spaetpalaestinensischen Judentums und des Urchristentums* (1926); *Urchristentum, Spaetjudentum, Hellenismus* (1926); and *Die Religionsgeschichte und das Urchristentum* (1932).   [Sup.] OTTO A. PIPER.

KITTEL, RUDOLF: D. at Leipzig, Oct. 20, 1929. He was professor of Old Testament exegesis at the University of Leipzig (1898–1929). His later works include: *The Scientific Study of the Old Testament* (1910); *Die Religion des Volkes Israel* (1921); *Geschichte des Volkes Israel* (3 vols.; completed, 1929); *Great Men and Movements in Israel* (1929).

[Sup.] ELMER E. FLACK.

KLEIN, HARRY MARTIN JOHN: Evangelical and Reformed; b. at Hazleton, Pa., Dec. 9, 1873. He studied at Muhlenberg College, (1889–91); Franklin and Marshall College (1891–93); Theological Seminary of the Reformed Church (1893–96); University of Berlin (1899). He was pastor, Grace Reformed Church, York, Pa. (1896–1905); Zion Reformed Church, Allentown, Pa. (1905–10); Audenried Professor of History and Archaeology, Franklin and Marshall College (1910–45). He wrote: *A Century of Education at Mercersburg* (1936); *History of the Eastern Synod of the Reformed Church in U. S.* (1943); *History of Cedar Crest College* (1948); *History of Franklin and Marshall College* (1952).

KLETT, GUY SOULLIARD: Presbyterian; b. at Rexmont, Lebanon Co., Pa., Nov. 8, 1897. He studied at Lafayette College (Ph.B., 1920); Gettysburg College (M.A., 1923); Pennsylvania State College; University of Michigan; and University of Pennsylvania (1923–24, 1929–31). He taught at Gettysburg College (1921–23); University of Pennsylvania (1923–24); Pennsylvania State College (1924–25); Heidelberg College (1925–29); research historian, Department of History, Presbyterian Church, U. S. A. (1936–   ). He is author of: *Presbyterians in Colonial Pennsylvania* (1937); *Scotch-Irish in Pennsylvania* (1948); and is associate editor of the *Journal* of the Presbyterian Historical Society.

KNAPP, FORREST LAMAR: Congregational-Christian; b. near Monte Vista, Colorado, Dec. 12, 1899. He studied at Colorado A. and M. (B.S., 1921) and Yale University (B.D., 1924; Ph.D., 1927). He was assistant pastor and director of religious education, the United Church, Bridgeport, Conn. (1924–27); superintendent of Christian education, Cleveland (Ohio) Federation of Churches (1927–28); director of leadership education, International Council of Religious Education (United States and Canada) (1929–39). In 1939 he became associate general secretary of the World's Sunday School Association (now the World Council of Christian Education) and general secretary (1940–   ). He was a member of the Division of Foreign Missions and the Division of Christian Education of the National Council of Churches of Christ in the U. S. A. He wrote: *Leadership*

Education in the Church (1933); and *Next Steps in Latin America* (1942). Since 1954 he has been executive secretary of the Massachusetts Council of Churches.

KNIGHTLY ORDERS. See HOSPITALERS; TEMPLARS; TEUTONIC KNIGHTS.

KNIGHTS OF COLUMBUS: A fraternal benefit society of Roman Catholic men established in the United States, March 29, 1882. The New Haven, Conn., headquarters places the membership rolls, as of 1940, at 784,437 Knights. The organization has spread throughout the United States, Canada, the Philippines, Alaska, Cuba, Mexico, and Puerto Rico.

The charter defines that the purposes of the society are: (1) to render pecuniary aid to its members and the beneficiaries of its members, (2) to render assistance to sick and disabled members, (3) to promote social and intellectual intercourse among its members, and (4) to promote and conduct educational, charitable, religious, social, and relief work. The society is devoted to the guiding ideals of charity, unity, fraternity, and patriotism.

The society has gained international attention for its work in the youth field. The Columbian Squires, a program for boys of high school age, is operated under the guidance of more than 2,892 individual councils.

Contributions and endowments by the local and national bodies of the Knights have been registered at many colleges and academies. Over $500,000 in scholarship funds is distributed by the Catholic University of America, where the Knights of Columbus have endowed a chair of American history. An educational trust fund insures the college education of sons and daughters of members killed in World War II.

In 1948 the Knights inaugurated an advertising campaign in secular periodicals explaining Catholic doctrine and practice. Free booklets describing the faith and a correspondence course of instruction have elicited thousands of requests.

BIBLIOGRAPHY: Theodore Roemer, *The Catholic Church in the United States*, 1950.

THOMAS J. MCCARTHY.

KNOWLES, MICHAEL CLIVE (in religion, David): Roman Catholic; b. at Studley, Warwickshire, 1896. He studied at Downside; Christ's College, Cambridge; and Collegio Sant Anselmo, Rome; was ordained priest (1922). He became fellow of Peterhouse, Cambridge (1944), professor of mediaeval history at Cambridge (1947). He has written: *The Monastic Order in England* (1940); *The Religious Houses of Mediaeval England* (1940); *The Religious Orders in England* (1948); *The Monastic Constitutions of Lanfranc* (1951).

F. W. DILLISTONE.

KNOW-NOTHING PARTY. See INTERFAITH RELATIONS; POLITICAL ACTION, THE CHURCHES AND.

KNOX, JOHN: I. Birth Date and Education: The interpretation of Knox's career was long colored by a mistaken birth-date (1505). In articles published in the *Athenaeum* (Nov. 5, and Dec. 3, 1904), and in the *Bookman* (September, 1905), D. Hay Fleming showed that there is far better evidence for a date between late 1513 and early 1515. Thus at the time of his first association with George Wishart, he was still under thirty. Hence the reformer is not to be identified with a namesake who matriculated at Glasgow in 1522. The probability is that his university was not Glasgow but St. Andrew's, and that he there became a student of John Major in 1531 or later. In political theory, Knox was apparently, like George Buchanan, a disciple of Major. We have no knowledge of the extent of Knox's formal education. His great interest in improving Scottish education is evident from the First Book of Discipline, 1560.

II. Knox's Liturgy: As minister (with John Goodman) of the church of the English exiles in Geneva, Knox used a form of worship which he published in 1556 under the title: *The Forme of Prayers and Ministration of the Sacraments etc., Used in the Englishe Congregation at Geneva, and Approved by the famous and Godly learned man, John Calvyn.* Not only was the book "approved by Calvin," it was essentially a rendering of Calvin's liturgy, which in turn was based on that of Strasbourg. W. D. Maxwell, whose research in this field has greatly clarified the whole subject of early Reformed Church worship, calls attention, however, to the verbal independence of Calvin's service that is shown in the English book, and its minor debt to the Book of Common Prayer. On Knox's communion service, he remarks: "This is the Eucharist reduced to its simplest elements, but . . . it is by no means an inadequate vehicle of devotion, and its composition is unmistakably catholic" (*An Outline of Worship*, pp. 123–124). In Knox's church in Geneva, communion was probably celebrated monthly; in Scotland however the service was quarterly; in country places it was less frequent. The communicants gathered about a communion table. The *Form of Prayers* was taken by Knox to Scotland, and reappeared with alterations and extensive additions as *The Book of Common Order*, adopted by the General Assembly of the Church of Scotland in 1564.

III. Presbyterianism of Knox: The Scottish Reformed Church under Knox's leadership took on organization without the episcopate. He had no respect for the Scottish bishops ("pestilent prelattis") before the Reformation, and was re-

pelled by Morton's reintroduction of episcopacy (1572) as a device for channelling the episcopal revenues to the government (*tulchan* bishops). The "superintendents" of the kirk were not designed to hold the rank of bishops, but were subject to synods of preaching presbyters. Thus presbyters constituted the one order of ministers of the Word and sacraments. Yet Knox's attitude to episcopacy as such was not (as it is represented by J. L. Ainslie) that of absolute repudiation. In England he did not condemn it: he gave other reasons for his refusal of the see of Rochester. In 1559 he wrote to English readers suggesting that, to overcome neglect resulting from the excessive size of dioceses, these be divided so that ordinarily one would become ten ("Brief Exhortation to England" in *Works of Knox*, [Laing, ed.], V, 518). He would thus have multiplied the number of English bishops, and reduced their flocks, in order to increase their usefulness.

BIBLIOGRAPHY: W. C. Dickinson has edited Knox's *History of the Reformation in Scotland* with an admirable introduction, notes, and appendices, 2 vols., 1949. The best biography since Hume Brown's is by Lord Eustace S. C. Percy, *John Knox*, 1937. H. Watt in *John Knox in Controversy* (1950) reviews informatively Knox's literary and personal controversies. See also: Ch. Borgeaud, "Le Vrai portrait de John Knox," in *Bulletin de la Société de l'histoire du Protestantisme Français*, (1935) 11–36; E. Muir, *John Knox: Portrait of a Calvinist*, 1929; A. R. MacEwan, *A History of the Church in Scotland*, Vol. II, 1918; D. H. Fleming, *The Scottish Reformation, Causes, Characteristics, Consequences*, 1910; J. A. Duke, *History of the Scottish Church to the Reformation*, 1937. For Knox's liturgy see especially: W. McMillan, *The Worship of the Scottish Reformed Church, 1550–1638*, 1931; W. D. Maxwell, *John Knox's Geneva Book, 1556*, 1931; and *Outline of Christian Worship*, 1936. The work by J. L. Ainslie referred to is *The Doctrines of Ministerial Order in the Reformed Churches of the Sixteenth and Seventeenth Centuries*, 1940.

JOHN T. MCNEILL.

KNOX, JOHN: Methodist: b. at Frankfort, Ky., Dec. 30, 1900. He studied at Randolph-Macon College (A.B., 1919); Emory University (B.D., 1925); and the University of Chicago (Ph.D., 1935). He taught at Emory University (1924–27), Hartford Theological Seminary (1938–39), and the University of Chicago (1939–43); director of studies and Baldwin Professor of Sacred Literature at Union Theological Seminary (1943–   ). He also served as the minister of Fisk University (1929–36); as Managing Editor of *Christendom* (1936–38). He is the author of the following books: *"He Whom a Dream Hath Possessed"* (1932); *Philemon Among the Letters of Paul* (1935); *The Man Christ Jesus* (1941); *Marcion and the New Testament* (1942); *Christ the Lord: The Meaning of Jesus in the Early Church* (1945); *The Fourth Gospel and the Later Epistles* (1945); *On the Meaning of Christ* (1947); *Chapters in a Life of Paul* (1950); exegesis of Romans, in *Interpreter's Bible;* and co-author of: (ed.), *Religion and the Present Crisis* (1942); *The Vitality of the Christian Tradition* (1944); *The Christian Answer* (1945); *The Gospel, The Church and the*

World (1946); exposition of Luke, in *Interpreter's Bible* (1952).

KNOX, RONALD ARBUTHNOT: Roman Catholic; b. Feb. 17, 1888. Educated at Eton and Balliol College, Oxford; he was a fellow and lecturer of Trinity College, Oxford (1910–17). Originally ordained into the Church of England, he was received into the Church of Rome in September, 1917. He has been Roman Catholic chaplain to the University of Oxford (1926–39); and a protonotary apostolic since 1951. Perhaps his greatest literary work has been the translation of the Bible (N.T., 1945; O.T., 1949). A notable historical study is *Enthusiasm, A Chapter in the History of Religion* (1950). In addition he has written many books of apologetic, satire, instruction, and mystery. They include: *Some Loose Stones* (1913); *Reunion all Round* (1914); *A Spiritual Aeneid* (1918); *The Belief of Catholics* (1927); *Let Dons Delight* (1939); *God and the Atom* (1945); *A Retreat for Priests* (1946); *The Mass in Slow Motion* (1948); *The Creed in Slow Motion* (1949), and *On Englishing the Bible* (1949).

F. W. DILLISTONE.

KNUBEL-MILLER LECTURES: Founded in 1943, this lectureship was established in the United Lutheran Church in America as a testimonial to Frederick H. Knubel and E. Clarence Miller, the church's first president and treasurer, respectively. Lectures are delivered at five points in North America each year. The purpose is to "furnish fresh, inspiring, and practical lectures to pastors of the church in active charge of congregations." All lectures are published in book form. F. EPPLING REINARTZ.

KNUDSEN, JOHANNES H. V.: Lutheran; b. at Nysted, Neb., Oct. 10, 1902. He studied at the University of Copenhagen (Cand.Mag., 1927); Hartford Seminary (S.T.M., 1941; Ph.D., 1943). He taught at Grand View College, Des Moines, Iowa (1927–35); and was minister at Askov, Minn. (1935–39), and Hartford, Conn. (1939–42); president of Grand View College and dean of Grand View Seminary (1942–). He wrote: *Introduction to the Danish Language* (1935); and (coauthor), *The Danish American Immigrant* (1950).

KNUDSON, ALBERT CORNELIUS: Methodist theologian; b. at Grandmeadow, Minn., Jan. 23, 1873; d. Aug. 28, 1953. He was educated at the University of Minnesota (B.A., 1893); Boston University (S.T.B., 1896; Ph.D., 1900); and the universities of Jena and Berlin (1897–98). After brief terms of service as professor in Denver and Baker universities and Allegheny College, he became professor at Boston University School of Theology (1906–43),

where he also served as dean (1926–38) and dean emeritus (1938–53). Early in his career he wrote three books on Old Testament subjects: *The Beacon Lights of Prophecy; The Religious Teaching of the Old Testament;* and *The Prophetic Movement in Israel.* But under the inspiration of Borden Parker Bowne (*q.v.*), the founder of American personalism (*q.v.*), he gradually transferred his literary activities to philosophical theology. In this field he has written eight books. Three of these have a more or less apologetic purpose: *The Philosophy of Personalism; The Validity of Religious Experience;* and *Present Tendencies in Religious Thought.* Three others are strictly theological, two of them systematic theology: *The Doctrine of God; The Doctrine of Redemption;* and *Basic Issues in Christian Thought.* The other two are: *The Principles of Christian Ethics;* and *The Philosophy of War and Peace.* These eight books are the product of a long sustained effort to rethink Christian theology as a whole in the light of modern personalism. The resulting personalistic system of theology belongs to the Arminian tradition, but it has its own distinctive character and may properly be called neo-Arminianism.

KOCH, HAL (HANS HARALD): Lutheran; b. in Hellerup at Copenhagen, May 6, 1904. He studied at the University of Copenhagen (Cand.Theol., 1926); and in Tuebingen and Paris. He taught theology and church history at Copenhagen (1937–). He was leader (1940–46) of "Dansk Ungdomssamvirke" (Danish Youth Cooperation), in which capacity he came to be one of the best known figures in Danish democratic life. From 1946, without giving up his professorship, he continued this work as leader of a peoples' high school (Krogerup). He was influenced by K. Barth and later by Grundtvig. His main works are: *Pronoia und Paideusis; Studien ueber Origenes und sein Verhaeltnis zum Platonismus* (1932); *Danmarks Kirke i den begyndende Höjmiddelalder* I-II (1941). He was coeditor of *Dansk teologisk Tidsskrift* (1938–); and of *Frie Ord* (1946–48).

NIELS SÖE.

KODESH CHURCH OF IMMANUEL: Organized 1929 in Philadelphia by Frank Russell Killingsworth, formerly minister in the African Methodist Episcopal Zion Church, as one of the so-called Holiness Churches (*q.v.*). The use of alcohol, tobacco, and extravagant dress is forbidden, as are dancing, theater attendance, and membership in secret societies (see FRATERNAL ORDERS). Churches are supported by tithes. In 1936 there were nine congregations in Pennsylvania, the District of Columbia, and Virginia with 562 members.

THEODORE G. TAPPERT.